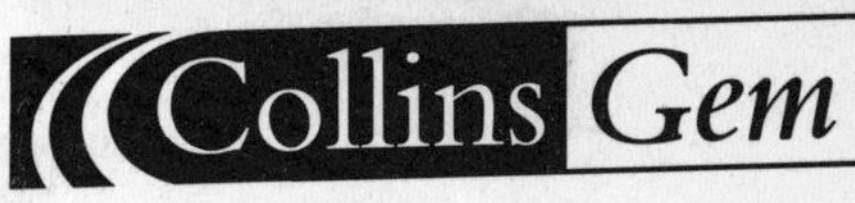

School FRENCH DICTIONARY

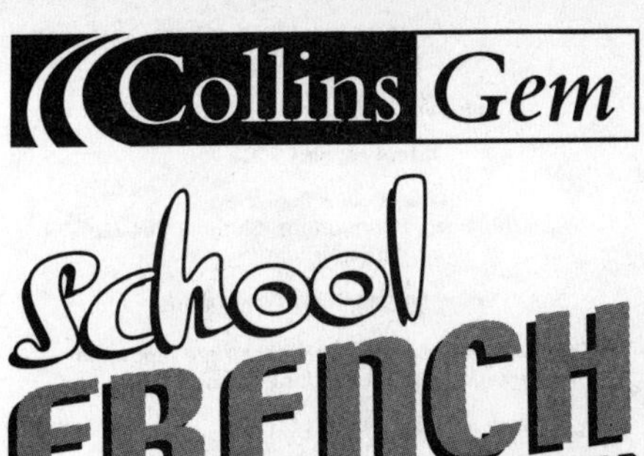

Collins Gem
An Imprint of HarperCollins*Publishers*

first edition 2003

latest reprint 2003

HarperCollins Publishers
Westerhill Road, Bishopbriggs, Glasgow G64 2QT
Great Britain

www.collinsdictionaries.com

ISBN 0-00-714871-2

Acknowledgements

We would like to thank those authors and publishers who kindly gave permission for copyright material to be used in the Bank of English. We would also like to thank Times Newspapers Ltd for providing valuable data.

Note

Entered words that we have reason to believe constitute trademarks have been designated as such. However, neither the presence nor absence of such designation should be regarded as affecting the legal status of any trademark.

A catalogue record for this book is available from the British Library

Dictionary text typeset by
Morton Word Processing Ltd, Scarborough
Supplement typeset by Wordcraft

Printed and bound in Great Britain by
The Bath Press, Bath

CONTENTS

Contributors
Jean-François Allain, Sabine Citron
Catherine Love, Joyce Littlejohn,
John Podbielski, Gaëlle Amiot-Cadey,
Marianne Davidson

Based on the first edition of the
Collins Gem French Dictionary by
Pierre-Henri Cousin
Renée Birks, Elizabeth Campbell, Hélène Lewis,
Claude Nimmo, Phillipe Patry
Lorna Sinclair Knight

USING THE COLLINS GEM SCHOOL FRENCH DICTIONARY

Using a dictionary is a skill you can improve with practice and by following some basic guidelines. This section gives you useful tips on how to use the Collins Gem School French Dictionary to ensure you get the most out of it.

▸MAKE SURE YOU LOOK IN THE RIGHT SIDE OF THE DICTIONARY

The **French-English** side comes first: you look there to find the meaning of a French word. The second part is **English-French**. That's the side you need for translating into French. (To remind yourself which side is which, you could remember the phrase *French first*.)

The middle pages of the book have a dark border so you can see where one side finishes and the other starts.

▸FINDING THE WORD YOU WANT

To help you find a word more quickly, look at the two words appearing at the top of each page: they indicate the first and last word on that page. For example, to find the word "vélo", flick through the dictionary until you find words starting with the same first few letters. In this case, "vélo" is on page 290, between "varice" and "vendredi".

▸MAKE SURE YOU CHOOSE THE RIGHT PART OF SPEECH

Some entries are split into several parts of speech. For example, "glue" can either be a noun ("Can I borrow your

glue?") or a verb ("**Glue** this picture onto your page."). Parts of speech within an entry are separated by a black lozenge ◆. They are given in their abbreviated form (*n* for noun; *adj* for adjective, etc). For the full list of abbreviations, look at pp xiv–xv.

glue [glu:] *n* colle *f* ◆ *vt* coller

Here the French noun for "glue" is "colle", and the verb is "coller".

▸CHOOSING THE RIGHT TRANSLATION

When an English word has more than one meaning, you will find bracketed words in italics before the translation. These help you to choose the correct translation because they give information about the meaning or the context in which it can be used. For example, which translation would you use to translate "I need to fix my bike."?

fix [fɪks] *vt* (*date, amount etc*) fixer; (*organize*) arranger; (*mend*) réparer; (*meal, drink*) préparer

Answer: you would use "**réparer**" because in this sense "fix" means "mend".

You will also find abbreviated words in brackets before and after translations ((*fam*), (*MUS*), (*AUT*) etc). To find out what they mean, look at pp xiv–xv.

▸SYMBOLS USED IN ENTRIES

The phonetic spelling of words is given in square brackets after the headword. For example, the phonetic spelling of the

USING THE DICTIONARY

French word "cher" is [ʃɛʀ]. These symbols tell you how to pronounce a word. You can find a guide to these symbols on pp xvi–xvii.

The symbol ~ within an entry represents the headword. For example, in the entry **news, ~paper** stands for **newspaper**, and **a piece of ~** stands for **a piece of news.**

▶KEYWORDS / MOTS-CLÉS

Certain English and French words are considered "key" words. These are very common words which can have several meanings and are difficult to translate. These entries (for example, **go**, **of**, **that** on the English side, or **faire**, **même**, **pas** on the French side) are given special treatment, using a combination of lozenges and numbers to help you identify different parts of speech and different meanings.

▶VERBS

Verbs have different endings, depending on whether you are talking about **je**, **tu**, **nous**, **ils** etc. They also have different forms for the present, future, past etc. **Je chante** (= I sing), **nous chantons** (= we sing), **j'ai chanté** (= I sang *past tense*). **Chanter** is the infinitive and this is the form that appears in the dictionary.

Most verbs are "regular", which means they follow certain patterns. To form regular verbs you add the appropriate ending to the appropriate tense stem. However, there are a certain number of verbs which are "irregular" and do not conform to these patterns. For example, *go* is **aller** but *I go* is

je vais. To help you with verb formation there is a section at the back of the dictionary giving the rules for regular verbs, followed by irregular verb tables. You will see in the verb tables that some parts of the verbs are highlighted in bold. This indicates that they behave irregularly.

▸REMEMBER!

Never take the first translation you see without looking at the others. Always look to see if there is more than one translation, or more than one part of speech.

NOUNS

▸ The Gender of Nouns

In French, all nouns are either masculine or feminine, whether denoting people, animals or things. Unlike in English, there is no neuter gender for inanimate objects and abstract nouns.

In the Collins Gem School French Dictionary, genders of nouns are indicated as follows: *nm* for a masculine noun and *nf* for a feminine noun on the French-English side, and *m* or *f* on the English-French side.

When nouns are either masculine OR feminine depending on the sex of the person they refer to, they will be indicated as *nm/f*, e.g.

camarade *nm/f* friend, pal

▸ The Formation of Feminines

As in English, male and female are sometimes differenciated by the use of two quite separate words, e.g.

mon oncle/ma tante *my uncle/my aunt*

There are, however, some words in French which show this distinction by the form of their ending.

Some nouns add an **e** to the masculine singular to form the feminine:

un ami	une ami**e**	in dictionary
a (male) friend	a (female) friend	**ami, e** *nm/f*

If the masculine singular form already ends in **e**, no further **e** is added in the feminine:

un élève	une élève	in dictionary
a (male) pupil	a (female) pupil	**élève** *nm/f*

Some nouns undergo a further change when **e** is added:

un danseur a dancer	une dans**euse** a dancer	in dictionary **danseur, -euse** *nm/f*
un inspecteur an inspector	une inspec**trice** an inspector	in dictionary **inspecteur, -trice** *nm/f*

▸ The Formation of Plurals

Most nouns add an **s** to the singular form.

When the singular form already ends in **-s**, **-x** or **-z**, no further **s** is added.

Most words ending in **-au**, **-eau** and **-eu** add an **x** in the plural. The plural ending is given in the dictionary:

un bateau boat	les bateau**x** boats	in dictionary **bateau, x**

Most words ending in **-al** and **-ail** change to **-aux** in the plural. The plural ending is given in the dictionary:

un cheval a horse	des chev**aux** (some) horses	in dictionary **cheval, -aux**

Some masculine nouns ending in **-ou** add **x** in the plural. These are given in the dictionary:

un genou a knee	les genou**x** knees	in dictionary **genou, x**

Finally, some plurals are totally unpredictable. You will find them next to the singular form in the dictionary:

un œil an eye	les yeux eyes	in dictionary **œil** (*pl* **yeux**)

ADJECTIVES

Most adjectives agree in number and in gender with the noun or pronoun they describe.

▸ The Formation of Feminines

Most adjectives add an **e** to the masculine singular form. On the French-English side, the feminine form is given after the masculine form. On the English-French side, it is given in brackets:

M		F	in dictionary:	
petit	→	petite	**petit, e** (FE side)	petit(e) (EF side)
noir	→	noire	**noir, e** (FE side)	noir(e) (EF side)
vert	→	verte	**vert, e** (FE side)	vert(e) (EF side)

If the masculine singular form already ends in **-e**, no further **e** is added. Because both the masculine and the feminine forms are identical, only the basic masculine form is given in the text:

M		F	in dictionary:
agréable	→	agréable	**agréable**

When the feminine form of an adjective is different, the ending is always given:

M		F	in dictionary:
sport**if**	→	sport**ive**	**sportif, -ive**
heur**eux**	→	heur**euse**	**heureux, -euse**
travaill**eur**	→	travaill**euse**	**travailleur, -euse**

When the feminine form of an adjective is irregular, the whole form is given:

M		F	in dictionary:
blanc	→	blanche	**blanc, blanche**

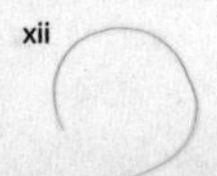

ADJECTIVES

▸ The Formation of Plurals

The plural of both regular and irregular adjectives is formed by adding an **s** to the masculine or feminine singular form, as appropriate:

M	F	MPL	FPL
grand	grande	grand**s**	grande**s**

When the masculine singular form already ends in **-s** or **-x**, no further **s** is added:

M	MPL
français	français
dangereux	dangereux

For masculine singulars ending in **-eau**, the masculine plural is **-eaux**. For most masculine singulars ending in **-al**, the masculine plural is **-aux**:

M	MPL	in dictionary
chapeau	chapeaux	**chapeau, x**
amical	amicaux	**amical, -aux**

▸ Invariable Adjectives

Finally, some adjectives remain the same whether they are masculine, feminine or plural. They are called invariable adjectives:

M, F, MPL, FPL	in dictionary
orange	**orange** *adj inv*
chic	**chic** *adj inv*

ABBREVIATIONS

abréviation	*ab(b)r*	abbreviation
adjectif, locution adjective	*adj*	adjective, adjectival phrase
administration	*ADMIN*	administration
adverbe, locution adverbiale	*adv*	adverb, adverbial phrase
agriculture	*AGR*	agriculture
anatomie	*ANAT*	anatomy
architecture	*ARCHIT*	architecture
article défini	*art déf*	definite article
article indéfini	*art indéf*	indefinite article
automobile	*AUT(O)*	the motor car and motoring
aviation, voyages aériens	*AVIAT*	flying, air travel
biologie	*BIO(L)*	biology
botanique	*BOT*	botany
anglais de Grande-Bretagne	*BRIT*	British English
chimie	*CHEM*	chemistry
commerce, finance, banque	*COMM*	commerce, finance, banking
comparatif	*compar*	comparative
informatique	*COMPUT*	computing
conjonction	*conj*	conjunction
construction	*CONSTR*	building
nom utilisé comme adjectif	*cpd*	compound element
cuisine, art culinaire	*CULIN*	cookery
article défini	*def art*	definite article
déterminant: article; adjectif démonstratif ou indéfini etc	*dét*	determiner: article, demonstrative etc
diminutif	*dimin*	diminutive
économie	*ÉCON, ECON*	economics
électricité, électronique	*ÉLEC, ELEC*	electricity, electronics
exclamation, interjection	*excl*	exclamation, interjection
féminin	*f*	feminine
langue familière (! emploi vulgaire)	*fam(!)*	colloquial usage (! particularly offensive)
emploi figuré	*fig*	figurative use
(verbe anglais) dont la particule est inséparable du verbe	*fus*	(phrasal verb) where the particle cannot be separated from the main verb
généralement	*gén, gen*	generally
géographie, géologie	*GÉO, GEO*	geography, geology
géométrie	*GÉOM, GEOM*	geometry
impersonnel	*impers*	impersonal
article indéfini	*indef art*	indefinite article
langue familière (! emploi vulgaire)	*inf(!)*	colloquial usage (! particularly offensive)
infinitif	*infin*	infinitive
informatique	*INFORM*	computing
invariable	*inv*	invariable
irrégulier	*irrég, irreg*	irregular

ABBREVIATIONS

domaine juridique	*JUR*	law
grammaire, linguistique	*LING*	grammar, linguistics
masculin	*m*	masculine
mathématiques, algèbre	*MATH*	mathematics, calculus
médecine	*MÉD, MED*	medical term, medicine
masculin ou féminin, suivant le sexe	*m/f*	either masculine or feminine depending on sex
domaine militaire, armée	*MIL*	military matters
musique	*MUS*	music
nom	*n*	noun
navigation, nautisme	*NAVIG, NAUT*	sailing, navigation
nom ou adjectif numéral	*num*	numeral noun or adjective
	o.s.	oneself
péjoratif	*péj, pej*	derogatory, pejorative
photographie	*PHOT(O)*	photography
physiologie	*PHYSIOL*	physiology
pluriel	*pl*	plural
politique	*POL*	politics
participe passé	*pp*	past participle
préposition	*prép, prep*	preposition
pronom	*pron*	pronoun
psychologie, psychiatrie	*PSYCH*	psychology, psychiatry
temps du passé	*pt*	past tense
quelque chose	*qch*	
quelqu'un	*qn*	
religions, domaine ecclésiastique	*REL*	religions, church service
	sb	somebody
enseignement, système scolaire et universitaire	*SCOL*	schooling, schools and universities
singulier	*sg*	singular
	sth	something
subjonctif	*sub*	subjunctive
sujet (grammatical)	*su(b)j*	(grammatical) subject
superlatif	*superl*	superlative
techniques, technologie	*TECH*	technical term, technology
télécommunications	*TÉL, TEL*	telecommunications
télévision	*TV*	television
typographie	*TYP(O)*	typography, printing
anglais des USA	*US*	American English
verbe (auxiliaire)	*vb (aux)*	(auxiliary) verb
verbe intransitif	*vi*	intransitive verb
verbe transitif	*vt*	transitive verb
zoologie	*ZOOL*	zoology
marque déposée	®	registered trademark
indique une équivalence culturelle	≈	introduces a cultural equivalent

PHONETIC SYMBOLS

▸Consonnes		▸Consonants
NB. p, b, t, d, k, g sont suivis d'une aspiration en anglais.		NB. p, b, t, d, k, g are not aspirated in French.
poupée	p	puppy
bombe	b	baby
tente thermal	t	tent
dinde	d	daddy
coq qui képi	k	cork kiss chord
gag bague	g	gag guess
sale ce nation	s	so rice kiss
zéro rose	z	cousin buzz
tache chat	ʃ	sheep sugar
gilet juge	ʒ	pleasure beige
	tʃ	church
	dʒ	judge general
fer phare	f	farm raffle
valve	v	very rev
	θ	thin maths
	ð	that other
lent salle	l	little ball
rare rentrer	ʀ	
	r	rat rare
maman femme	m	mummy comb
non nonne	n	no ran
agneau vigne	ɲ	
	ŋ	singing bank
hop!	h	hat reheat
yeux paille pied	j	yet
nouer oui	w	wall bewail
huile lui	ɥ	
	x	loch
Divers		**Miscellaneous**
pour l'anglais: le r final se prononce en liaison devant une voyelle	r	in French wordlist: no liaison
pour l'anglais: précède la syllabe accentuée	ˈ	in French transcription: no liaison before aspirate h

PHONETIC SYMBOLS

▸Voyelles		▸Vowels
NB. La mise en équivalence de certains sons n'indique qu'une ressemblance approximative.		NB. The pairing of some vowel sounds only indicates approximate equivalence.
ici vie lyre	i iː	heel bead
	ɪ	hit pity
jouer été	e	
lait jouet merci	ɛ	set tent
plat amour	a æ	bat apple
bas pâte	ɑ ɑː	after car calm
	ʌ	fun cousin
le premier	ə	over above
beurre peur	œ	
peu deux	ø əː	urn fern work
or homme	ɔ	wash pot
mot eau gauche	o ɔː	born cork
genou roue	u	full soot
	uː	boon lewd
rue urne	y	

▸Diphtongues		▸Diphthongs
	ɪə	beer tier
	ɛə	tear fair there
	eɪ	date plaice day
	aɪ	life buy cry
	au	owl foul now
	əu	low no
	ɔɪ	boil boy oily
	uə	poor tour

▸Nasales		▸Nasal Vowels
matin plein	ɛ̃	
brun	œ̃	
sang an dans	ɑ̃	
non pont	ɔ̃	

TIME

Quelle heure est-il? What time is it?
Il est... It's...

une heure

une heure dix

une heure et quart

une heure et demie

deux heures moins vingt

deux heures moins le quart

À quelle heure? At what time?

à minuit

à midi

à une heure (de l'après-midi)

à huit heures (du soir)

In France times are often given in the twenty-four hour clock.

à 11.15
or
onze heures quinze

à 20.45
or
vingt heures quarante-cinq

DATES

▸ Days of the Week

lundi	Monday
mardi	Tuesday
mercredi	Wednesday
jeudi	Thursday
vendredi	Friday
samedi	Saturday
dimanche	Sunday

▸ Months of the Year

janvier	January	**juillet**	July
février	February	**août**	August
mars	March	**septembre**	September
avril	April	**octobre**	October
mai	May	**novembre**	November
juin	June	**décembre**	December

▸ **Quand?**	▸ **When?**
en février	in February
le 1er décembre	on 1 December
le premier décembre	on the first of December
en 2002	in 2002
en deux mille deux	in two thousand and two

▸ **Quel jour sommes nous?**	▸ **What day is it?**
Nous sommes le...	**It's...**
dimanche 1er octobre *or* **dimanche premier octobre**	Sunday, 1 October *or* Sunday, the first of October
lundi 26 février *or* **lundi vingt-six février**	Monday, 26 February *or* Monday, the twenty-sixth of February

NUMBERS

▸ Cardinal Numbers

1	un(e)	21	vingt et un(e)
2	deux	22	vingt-deux
3	trois	30	trente
4	quatre	40	quarante
5	cinq	50	cinquante
6	six	60	soixante
7	sept	70	soixante-dix
8	huit	71	soixante et onze
9	neuf	72	soixante-douze
10	dix	80	quatre-vingts
11	onze	81	quatre-vingt-un(e)
12	douze	90	quatre-vingt-dix
13	treize	91	quatre-vingt-onze
14	quatorze	100	cent
15	quinze	101	cent un(e)
16	seize	200	deux cents
17	dix-sept	201	deux cent un(e)
18	dix-huit	300	trois cents
19	dix-neuf	1,000	mille
20	vingt	1,000,000	un million

▸ Fractions etc

½	un demi, une demie
⅓	un tiers
⅔	deux tiers
¼	un quart
¾	trois quarts
⅕	un cinquième
0.5	zéro virgule cinq (0,5)
3.4	trois virgule quatre (3,4)
10%	dix pour cent
100%	cent pour cent

NUMBERS

▸ Ordinal Numbers

1st **premier (1er), première (1re)**
2nd **deuxième, second(e) (2e)**
3rd **troisième (3e)**
4th **quatrième (4e)**
5th **cinquième (5e)**
6th **sixième (6e)**
7th **septième (7e)**
8th **huitième (8e)**
9th **neuvième (9e)**
10th **dixième (10e)**
11th **onzième (11e)**
12th **douzième (12e)**
13th **treizième (13e)**
14th **quatorzième (14e)**
15th **quinzième (15e)**
16th **seizième (16e)**
17th **dix-septième (17e)**
18th **dix-huitième (18e)**
19th **dix-neuvième (19e)**
20th **vingtième (20e)**
21st **vingt et unième (21e)**
22nd **vingt-deuxième (22e)**
30th **trentième (30e)**
100th **centième (100e)**
101st **cent unième (101e)**
1000th **millième (1000e)**

FRANÇAIS – ANGLAIS
FRENCH – ENGLISH

A, a

a [a] *vb voir* **avoir**

MOT-CLÉ

à [a] (*à* + *le* = **au**, *à* + *les* = **aux**) *prép* **1** (*endroit, situation*) at, in; **être à Paris/au Portugal** to be in Paris/Portugal; **être à la maison/à l'école** to be at home/at school; **à la campagne** in the country; **c'est à 10 km/à 20 minutes (d'ici)** it's 10 km/20 minutes away

2 (*direction*) to; **aller à Paris/au Portugal** to go to Paris/Portugal; **aller à la maison/à l'école** to go home/to school; **à la campagne** to the country

3 (*temps*): **à 3 heures/minuit** at 3 o'clock/midnight; **au printemps/mois de juin** in the spring/the month of June

4 (*attribution, appartenance*) to; **le livre est à Paul/à lui/à nous** this book is Paul's/his/ours; **donner qch à qn** to give sth to sb

5 (*moyen*) with; **se chauffer au gaz** to have gas heating; **à bicyclette** on a *ou* by bicycle; **à la main/machine** by hand/machine

6 (*provenance*) from; **boire à la bouteille** to drink from the bottle

7 (*caractérisation, manière*): **l'homme aux yeux bleus** the man with the blue eyes; **à la russe** the Russian way

8 (*but, destination*): **tasse à café** coffee cup; **maison à vendre** house for sale

9 (*rapport, évaluation, distribution*): **100 km/unités à l'heure** 100 km/units per *ou* an hour; **payé à l'heure** paid by the hour; **cinq à six** five to six

abaisser [abese] *vt* to lower, bring down; (*manette*) to pull down; **s'~** *vi* to go down; (*fig*) to demean o.s.

abandon [abɑ̃dɔ̃] *nm* abandoning; giving up; withdrawal; **être à l'~** to be in a state of neglect

abandonner [abɑ̃dɔne] *vt* (*personne*) to abandon; (*projet, activité*) to abandon, give up; (SPORT) to retire *ou* withdraw from; (*céder*) to surrender; **s'~ à** (*paresse, plaisirs*) to give o.s. up to

abasourdir [abazuʀdiʀ] *vt* to stun, stagger

abat-jour [abaʒuʀ] *nm inv* lampshade

abats [aba] *nmpl* (*de bœuf, porc*) offal *sg*; (*de volaille*) giblets

abattement [abatmɑ̃] *nm*: **~ fiscal** ≃ tax allowance

abattoir [abatwaʀ] *nm* slaughterhouse

abattre [abatʀ] *vt* (*arbre*) to cut down, fell; (*mur, maison*) to pull down; (*avion, personne*) to shoot down; (*animal*) to shoot, kill; (*fig*) to wear out, tire out; to demoralize; **s'~** *vi* to crash down; **ne pas se laisser ~** to keep one's spirits up, not to let things get one down; **s'~ sur** to beat down on; (*fig*) to rain down on

abbaye [abei] *nf* abbey

abbé [abe] *nm* priest; (*d'une abbaye*) abbot

abcès [apsɛ] *nm* abscess

abdiquer [abdike] *vi* to abdicate

abdominaux [abdɔmino] *nmpl*: **faire des ~** to do exercises for one's abdominals, do one's abdominals

abeille [abɛj] *nf* bee

aberrant, e [abeʀɑ̃, ɑ̃t] *adj* absurd

aberration [abeʀasjɔ̃] *nf* aberration

abêtir [abetiʀ] *vt* to make morons of (*ou* a moron of)

abîme [abim] *nm* abyss, gulf
abîmer [abime] *vt* to spoil, damage; **s'~** *vi* to get spoilt *ou* damaged
ablation [ablasjɔ̃] *nf* removal
aboiement [abwamɑ̃] *nm* bark, barking
abois [abwa] *nmpl*: **aux ~** at bay
abolir [abɔliʀ] *vt* to abolish
abominable [abɔminabl] *adj* abominable
abondance [abɔ̃dɑ̃s] *nf* abundance
abondant, e [abɔ̃dɑ̃, ɑ̃t] *adj* plentiful, abundant, copious; **abonder** *vi* to abound, be plentiful; **abonder dans le sens de qn** to concur with sb
abonné, e [abɔne] *nm/f* subscriber; season ticket holder
abonnement [abɔnmɑ̃] *nm* subscription; (*transports, concerts*) season ticket
abonner [abɔne] *vt*: **s'~ à** to subscribe to, take out a subscription to
abord [abɔʀ] *nm*: **au premier ~** at first sight, initially; **~s** *nmpl* (*environs*) surroundings; **d'~** first
abordable [abɔʀdabl] *adj* (*prix*) reasonable; (*personne*) approachable
aborder [abɔʀde] *vi* to land ♦ *vt* (*sujet, difficulté*) to tackle; (*personne*) to approach; (*rivage etc*) to reach
aboutir [abutiʀ] *vi* (*négociations etc*) to succeed; **~ à** to end up at; **n'~ à rien** to come to nothing
aboyer [abwaje] *vi* to bark
abréger [abʀeʒe] *vt* to shorten
abreuver [abʀœve]: **s'~** *vi* to drink; **abreuvoir** *nm* watering place
abréviation [abʀevjasjɔ̃] *nf* abbreviation
abri [abʀi] *nm* shelter; **être à l'~** to be under cover; **se mettre à l'~** to shelter
abricot [abʀiko] *nm* apricot
abriter [abʀite] *vt* to shelter; **s'~** *vt* to shelter, take cover
abrupt, e [abʀypt] *adj* sheer, steep; (*ton*) abrupt
abruti, e [abʀyti] *adj* stunned, dazed ♦ *nm/f* (*fam*) idiot, moron; **~ de travail** overworked
absence [apsɑ̃s] *nf* absence; (MÉD) blackout; **avoir des ~s** to have mental blanks
absent, e [apsɑ̃, ɑ̃t] *adj* absent ♦ *nm/f* absentee; **absenter: s'absenter** *vi* to take time off work; (*sortir*) to leave, go out
absolu, e [apsɔly] *adj* absolute; **absolument** *adv* absolutely
absorbant, e [apsɔʀbɑ̃, ɑ̃t] *adj* absorbent
absorber [apsɔʀbe] *vt* to absorb; (*gén* MÉD: *manger, boire*) to take
abstenir [apstəniʀ] *vb*: **s'~ de qch/de faire** to refrain from sth/from doing
abstraction [apstʀaksjɔ̃] *nf* abstraction
abstrait, e [apstʀɛ, ɛt] *adj* abstract
absurde [apsyʀd] *adj* absurd
abus [aby] *nm* abuse; **~ de confiance** breach of trust; **abuser** *vi* to go too far, overstep the mark; **abuser de** (*duper*) to take advantage of; **abusif, -ive** *adj* exorbitant; (*punition*) excessive
acabit [akabi] *nm*: **de cet ~** of that type
académie [akademi] *nf* academy; (SCOL: *circonscription*) ≃ regional education authority

Académie française

The **Académie française** *was founded by Cardinal Richelieu in 1635 during the reign of Louis XIII. It consists of forty elected scholars and writers who are known as "les Quarante" or "les Immortels". One of the Académie's functions is to regulate the development of the French language and its recommendations are frequently the subject of lively public debate. It has produced several editions of its famous dictionary and awards various literary prizes.*

acajou [akaʒu] *nm* mahogany

acariâtre [akaʀjɑtʀ] *adj* cantankerous
accablant, e [akɑblɑ̃, ɑ̃t] *adj* (*chaleur*) oppressive; (*témoignage, preuve*) overwhelming
accablement [akɑbləmɑ̃] *nm* despondency
accabler [akɑble] *vt* to overwhelm, overcome; **~ qn d'injures** to heap *ou* shower abuse on sb
accalmie [akalmi] *nf* lull
accaparer [akapaʀe] *vt* to monopolize; (*suj*: *travail etc*) to take up (all) the time *ou* attention of
accéder [aksede]: **~ à** *vt* (*lieu*) to reach; (*accorder*: *requête*) to grant, accede to
accélérateur [akseleʀatœʀ] *nm* accelerator
accélération [akseleʀasjɔ̃] *nf* acceleration
accélérer [akseleʀe] *vt* to speed up ♦ *vi* to accelerate
accent [aksɑ̃] *nm* accent; (PHONÉTIQUE, *fig*) stress; **mettre l'~ sur** (*fig*) to stress; **~ aigu/grave/circonflexe** acute/grave/circumflex accent; **accentuer** *vt* (LING) to accent; (*fig*) to accentuate, emphasize; **s'accentuer** *vi* to become more marked *ou* pronounced
acceptation [akseptasjɔ̃] *nf* acceptance
accepter [aksɛpte] *vt* to accept; **~ de faire** to agree to do
accès [aksɛ] *nm* (*à un lieu*) access; (MÉD: *de toux*) fit; (: *de fièvre*) bout; **d'~ facile** easily accessible; **facile d'~** easy to get to; **~ de colère** fit of anger; **accessible** *adj* accessible; (*livre, sujet*): **accessible à qn** within the reach of sb
accessoire [akseswaʀ] *adj* secondary; incidental ♦ *nm* accessory; (THÉÂTRE) prop
accident [aksidɑ̃] *nm* accident; **par ~** by chance; **~ de la route** road accident; **~ du travail** industrial injury *ou* accident; **accidenté, e** *adj* damaged; injured; (*relief, terrain*) uneven; hilly; **accidentel, le** *adj* accidental
acclamations [aklamasjɔ̃] *nfpl* cheers
acclamer [aklame] *vt* to cheer, acclaim
acclimater [aklimate]: **s'~** *vi* (*personne*) to adapt (o.s.)
accolade [akɔlad] *nf* (*amicale*) embrace; (*signe*) brace
accommodant, e [akɔmɔdɑ̃, ɑ̃t] *adj* accommodating, easy-going
accommoder [akɔmɔde] *vt* (CULIN) to prepare; **s'~ de** *vt* to put up with; (*se contenter de*) to make do with
accompagnateur, -trice [akɔ̃paɲatœʀ, tʀis] *nm/f* (MUS) accompanist; (*de voyage*: *guide*) guide; (*de voyage organisé*) courier
accompagner [akɔ̃paɲe] *vt* to accompany, be *ou* go *ou* come with; (MUS) to accompany
accompli, e [akɔ̃pli] *adj* accomplished
accomplir [akɔ̃pliʀ] *vt* (*tâche, projet*) to carry out; (*souhait*) to fulfil; **s'~** *vi* to be fulfilled
accord [akɔʀ] *nm* agreement; (*entre des styles, tons etc*) harmony; (MUS) chord; **d'~!** OK!; **se mettre d'~** to come to an agreement; **être d'~ (pour faire qch)** to agree (to do sth)
accordéon [akɔʀdeɔ̃] *nm* (MUS) accordion
accorder [akɔʀde] *vt* (*faveur, délai*) to grant; (*harmoniser*) to match; (MUS) to tune; **s'~** *vt* to get on together; to agree
accoster [akɔste] *vt* (NAVIG) to draw alongside ♦ *vi* to berth
accotement [akɔtmɑ̃] *nm* verge (BRIT), shoulder
accouchement [akuʃmɑ̃] *nm* delivery, (child)birth; labour
accoucher [akuʃe] *vi* to give birth, have a baby; **~ d'un garçon** to give birth to a boy; **accoucheur** *nm*: **(médecin) accoucheur** obstetrician
accouder [akude]: **s'~** *vi* to rest one's elbows on/against; **accoudoir** *nm* armrest
accoupler [akuple] *vt* to couple; (*pour*

la reproduction) to mate; **s'~** *vt* to mate
accourir [akuRiR] *vi* to rush *ou* run up
accoutrement [akutRəmɑ̃] (*péj*) *nm* (*tenue*) outfit
accoutumance [akutymɑ̃s] *nf* (*gén*) adaptation; (*MÉD*) addiction
accoutumé, e [akutyme] *adj* (*habituel*) customary, usual
accoutumer [akutyme] *vt*: **s'~ à** to get accustomed *ou* used to
accréditer [akRedite] *vt* (*nouvelle*) to substantiate
accroc [akRo] *nm* (*déchirure*) tear; (*fig*) hitch, snag
accrochage [akRɔʃaʒ] *nm* (*AUTO*) collision; (*dispute*) clash, brush
accrocher [akRɔʃe] *vt* (*fig*) to catch, attract; **s'~** (*se disputer*) to have a clash *ou* brush; **~ qch à** (*suspendre*) to hang sth (up) on; (*attacher*: *remorque*) to hitch sth (up) to; **~ qch (à)** (*déchirer*) to catch sth (on); **~ un passant** (*heurter*) to hit a pedestrian; **s'~ à** (*rester pris à*) to catch on; (*agripper*, *fig*) to hang on *ou* cling to
accroissement [akRwasmɑ̃] *nm* increase
accroître [akRwatR]: **s'~** *vi* to increase
accroupir [akRupiR]: **s'~** *vi* to squat, crouch (down)
accru, e [akRy] *pp de* **accroître**
accueil [akœj] *nm* welcome; **comité d'~** reception committee; **accueillir** *vt* to welcome; (*aller chercher*) to meet, collect
acculer [akyle] *vt*: **~ qn à** *ou* **contre** to drive sb back against
accumuler [akymyle] *vt* to accumulate, amass; **s'~** *vi* to accumulate; to pile up
accusation [akyzasjɔ̃] *nf* (*gén*) accusation; (*JUR*) charge; (*partie*): **l'~** the prosecution
accusé, e [akyze] *nm/f* accused; defendant; **~ de réception** acknowledgement of receipt
accuser [akyze] *vt* to accuse; (*fig*) to emphasize, bring out; to show; **~ qn de** to accuse sb of; (*JUR*) to charge sb with; **~ réception de** to acknowledge receipt of
acerbe [asɛRb] *adj* caustic, acid
acéré, e [aseRe] *adj* sharp
acharné, e [aʃaRne] *adj* (*efforts*) relentless; (*lutte*, *adversaire*) fierce, bitter
acharner [aʃaRne] *vb*: **s'~ contre** to set o.s. against; (*suj*: *malchance*) to dog; **s'~ à faire** to try doggedly to do; (*persister*) to persist in doing
achat [aʃa] *nm* purchase; **faire des ~s** to do some shopping; **faire l'~ de qch** to purchase sth
acheminer [aʃ(ə)mine] *vt* (*courrier*) to forward, dispatch; **s'~ vers** to head for
acheter [aʃ(ə)te] *vt* to buy, purchase; (*soudoyer*) to buy; **~ qch à** (*marchand*) to buy *ou* purchase sth from; (*ami etc*: *offrir*) to buy sth for; **acheteur, -euse** *nm/f* buyer; shopper; (*COMM*) buyer
achever [aʃ(ə)ve] *vt* to complete, finish; (*blessé*) to finish off; **s'~** *vi* to end
acide [asid] *adj* sour, sharp; (*CHIMIE*) acid(ic) ♦ *nm* (*CHIMIE*) acid; **acidulé, e** *adj* slightly acid
acier [asje] *nm* steel; **aciérie** *nf* steelworks *sg*
acné [akne] *nf* acne
acolyte [akɔlit] (*péj*) *nm* associate
acompte [akɔ̃t] *nm* deposit
à-côté [akote] *nm* side-issue, (*argent*) extra
à-coup [aku] *nm*: **par ~-~s** by fits and starts
acoustique [akustik] *nf* (*d'une salle*) acoustics *pl*
acquéreur [akeRœR] *nm* buyer, purchaser
acquérir [akeRiR] *vt* to acquire
acquis, e [aki, iz] *pp de* **acquérir** ♦ *nm* (accumulated) experience; **son aide nous est ~e** we can count on her help
acquit [aki] *vb voir* **acquérir** ♦ *nm* (*quittance*) receipt; **par ~ de conscience** to set one's mind at rest

acquitter [akite] *vt* (*JUR*) to acquit; (*facture*) to pay, settle; **s'~ de** *vt* (*devoir*) to discharge; (*promesse*) to fulfil

âcre [ɑkʀ] *adj* acrid, pungent

acrobate [akʀɔbat] *nm/f* acrobat; **acrobatie** *nf* acrobatics *sg*

acte [akt] *nm* act, action; (*THÉÂTRE*) act; **prendre ~ de** to note, take note of; **faire ~ de candidature** to apply; **faire ~ de présence** to put in an appearance; **~ de naissance** birth certificate

acteur [aktœʀ] *nm* actor

actif, -ive [aktif, iv] *adj* active ♦ *nm* (*COMM*) assets *pl*; (*fig*): **avoir à son ~** to have to one's credit; **population active** working population

action [aksjɔ̃] *nf* (*gén*) action; (*COMM*) share; **une bonne ~** a good deed; **actionnaire** *nm/f* shareholder; **actionner** *vt* (*mécanisme*) to activate; (*machine*) to operate

activer [aktive] *vt* to speed up; **s'~** *vi* to bustle about; to hurry up

activité [aktivite] *nf* activity; **en ~** (*volcan*) active; (*fonctionnaire*) in active life

actrice [aktʀis] *nf* actress

actualiser [aktɥalize] *vt* to bring up to date

actualité [aktɥalite] *nf* (*d'un problème*) topicality; (*événements*): **l'~** current events; **les ~s** *nfpl* (*CINÉMA, TV*) the news; **d'~** topical

actuel, le [aktɥɛl] *adj* (*présent*) present; (*d'actualité*) topical; **à l'heure ~le** at the present time; **actuellement** *adv* at present, at the present time

acuité [akɥite] *nf* acuteness

acuponcteur [akypɔ̃ktœʀ] *nm* acupuncturist

acuponcture [akypɔ̃ktyʀ] *nf* acupuncture

adaptateur [adaptatœʀ] *nm* (*ÉLEC*) adapter

adapter [adapte] *vt* to adapt; **s'~ (à)** (*suj: personne*) to adapt (to), **~ qch à** (*approprier*) to adapt sth to (fit); **~ qch sur/dans/à** (*fixer*) to fit sth on/into/to

additif [aditif] *nm* additive

addition [adisjɔ̃] *nf* addition; (*au café*) bill; **additionner** *vt* to add (up)

adepte [adɛpt] *nm/f* follower

adéquat, e [adekwa(t), at] *adj* appropriate, suitable

adhérent, e [adeʀɑ̃, ɑ̃t] *nm/f* member

adhérer [adeʀe]: **~ à** *vt* (*coller*) to adhere *ou* stick to; (*se rallier à*) to join; **adhésif, -ive** *adj* adhesive, sticky; **ruban adhésif** sticky *ou* adhesive tape; **adhésion** *nf* joining; (*fait d'être membre*) membership; (*accord*) support

adieu, x [adjø] *excl* goodbye ♦ *nm* farewell

adjectif [adʒɛktif] *nm* adjective

adjoindre [adʒwɛ̃dʀ] *vt*: **~ qch à** to attach sth to; (*ajouter*) to add sth to; **s'~** *vt* (*collaborateur etc*) to take on, appoint; **adjoint, e** *nm/f* assistant; **adjoint au maire** deputy mayor; **directeur adjoint** assistant manager

adjudant [adʒydɑ̃] *nm* (*MIL*) warrant officer

adjuger [adʒyʒe] *vt* (*prix, récompense*) to award; (*lors d'une vente*) to auction (off); **s'~** *vt* to take for o.s.

adjurer [adʒyʀe] *vt*: **~ qn de faire** to implore *ou* beg sb to do

admettre [admɛtʀ] *vt* (*laisser entrer*) to admit; (*candidat: SCOL*) to pass; (*tolérer*) to allow, accept; (*reconnaître*) to admit, acknowledge

administrateur, -trice [administʀatœʀ, tʀis] *nm/f* (*COMM*) director; (*ADMIN*) administrator

administration [administʀasjɔ̃] *nf* administration; **l'A~** ≃ the Civil Service

administrer [administʀe] *vt* (*firme*) to manage, run; (*biens, remède, sacrement etc*) to administer

admirable [admiʀabl] *adj* admirable, wonderful

admirateur, -trice [admiʀatœʀ, tʀis] *nm/f* admirer

admiration [admiʀasjɔ̃] *nf* admiration

admirer [admiʀe] *vt* to admire

admis, e [admi, iz] *pp de* **admettre**

admissible [admisibl] *adj* (*candidat*) eligible; (*comportement*) admissible, acceptable

admission [admisjɔ̃] *nf* admission; acknowledgement; **demande d'~** application for membership

ADN *sigle m* (= *acide désoxyribonucléique*) DNA

adolescence [adɔlesɑ̃s] *nf* adolescence

adolescent, e [adɔlesɑ̃, ɑ̃t] *nm/f* adolescent, teenager

adonner [adɔne]: **s'~ à** *vt* (*sport*) to devote o.s. to; (*boisson*) to give o.s. over to

adopter [adɔpte] *vt* to adopt; **adoptif, -ive** *adj* (*parents*) adoptive; (*fils, patrie*) adopted

adorable [adɔʀabl] *adj* delightful, adorable

adorer [adɔʀe] *vt* to adore; (REL) to worship

adosser [adose] *vt*: **~ qch à** *ou* **contre** to stand sth against; **s'~ à** *ou* **contre** to lean with one's back against

adoucir [adusiʀ] *vt* (*goût, température*) to make milder; (*avec du sucre*) to sweeten; (*peau, voix*) to soften; (*caractère*) to mellow

adresse [adʀɛs] *nf* (*domicile*) address; (*dextérité*) skill, dexterity

adresser [adʀese] *vt* (*lettre*: *expédier*) to send; (: *écrire l'adresse sur*) to address; (*injure, compliments*) to address; **s'~ à** (*parler à*) to speak to, address; (*s'informer auprès de*) to go and see; (: *bureau*) to enquire at; (*suj*: *livre, conseil*) to be aimed at; **~ la parole à** to speak to, address

adroit, e [adʀwa, wat] *adj* skilful, skilled

adulte [adylt] *nm/f* adult, grown-up ♦ *adj* (*chien, arbre*) fully-grown, mature; (*attitude*) adult, grown-up

adultère [adyltɛʀ] *nm* (*acte*) adultery

advenir [advəniʀ] *vi* to happen

adverbe [advɛʀb] *nm* adverb

adversaire [advɛʀsɛʀ] *nm/f* (SPORT, *gén*) opponent, adversary

adverse [advɛʀs] *adj* opposing

aération [aeʀasjɔ̃] *nf* airing; (*circulation de l'air*) ventilation

aérer [aeʀe] *vt* to air; (*fig*) to lighten; **s'~** *vi* to get some (fresh) air

aérien, ne [aeʀjɛ̃, jɛn] *adj* (AVIAT) air *cpd*, aerial; (*câble, métro*) overhead; (*fig*) light; **compagnie ~ne** airline

aéro... [aeʀɔ] *préfixe*: **aérobic** *nm* aerobics *sg*; **aérogare** *nf* airport (buildings); (*en ville*) air terminal; **aéroglisseur** *nm* hovercraft; **Aéronavale** *nf* ≃ Fleet Air Arm (BRIT), ≃ Naval Air Force (US); **aérophagie** *nf* (MÉD) wind, aerophagia (MÉD); **aéroport** *nm* airport; **aéroporté, e** *adj* airborne, airlifted; **aérosol** *nm* aerosol

affable [afabl] *adj* affable

affaiblir [afebliʀ]: **s'~** *vi* to weaken

affaire [afɛʀ] *nf* (*problème, question*) matter; (*criminelle, judiciaire*) case; (*scandaleuse etc*) affair; (*entreprise*) business; (*marché, transaction*) deal; business *no pl*; (*occasion intéressante*) bargain; **~s** *nfpl* (*intérêts publics et privés*) affairs; (*activité commerciale*) business *sg*; (*effets personnels*) things, belongings; **ce sont mes ~s** (*cela me concerne*) that's my business; **ça fera l'~** that will do (nicely); **se tirer d'~** to sort it *ou* things out for o.s.; **avoir ~ à** (*être en contact*) to be dealing with; **les A~s étrangères** Foreign Affairs; **affairer**: **s'affairer** *vi* to busy o.s., bustle about

affaisser [afese]: **s'~** *vi* (*terrain, immeuble*) to subside, sink; (*personne*) to collapse

affaler [afale] *vb*: **s'~ (dans/sur)** to collapse *ou* slump (into/onto)

affamé, e [afame] *adj* starving

affectation [afɛktasjɔ̃] *nf* (*nomination*) appointment; (*manque de naturel*) affectation

affecter [afɛkte] *vt* to affect; **~ qch à** to allocate *ou* allot sth to; **~ qn à** to

appoint sb to; (*diplomate*) to post sb to
affectif, -ive [afɛktif, iv] *adj* emotional
affection [afɛksjɔ̃] *nf* affection; (*mal*) ailment; **affectionner** *vt* to be fond of; **affectueux, -euse** *adj* affectionate
affermir [afɛʀmiʀ] *vt* to consolidate, strengthen; (*muscles*) to tone up
affichage [afiʃaʒ] *nm* billposting; (*électronique*) display
affiche [afiʃ] *nf* poster; (*officielle*) notice; (*THÉÂTRE*) bill
afficher [afiʃe] *vt* (*affiche*) to put up; (*réunion*) to put up a notice about; (*électroniquement*) to display; (*fig*) to exhibit, display; **"défense d'~"** "stick no bills"
affilée [afile]: **d'~** *adv* at a stretch
affiler [afile] *vt* to sharpen
affilier [afilje]: **s'~ à** *vt* (*club, société*) to join
affiner [afine] *vt* to refine
affirmatif, -ive [afiʀmatif, iv] *adj* affirmative
affirmation [afiʀmasjɔ̃] *nf* assertion
affirmer [afiʀme] *vt* to assert
affligé, e [afliʒe] *adj* distressed, grieved; **~ de** (*maladie, tare*) afflicted with
affliger [afliʒe] *vt* (*peiner*) to distress, grieve
affluence [aflyɑ̃s] *nf* crowds *pl*; **heures d'~** rush hours; **jours d'~** busiest days
affluent [aflyɑ̃] *nm* tributary
affluer [aflye] *vi* (*secours, biens*) to flood in, pour in; (*sang*) to rush, flow
affolant, e [afɔlɑ̃, ɑ̃t] *adj* frightening
affolement [afɔlmɑ̃] *nm* panic
affoler [afɔle] *vt* to throw into a panic; **s'~** *vi* to panic
affranchir [afʀɑ̃ʃiʀ] *vt* to put a stamp *ou* stamps on; (*à la machine*) to frank (*BRIT*), meter (*US*); (*fig*) to free, liberate; **affranchissement** *nm* postage
affréter [afʀete] *vt* to charter
affreux, -euse [afʀø, øz] *adj* dreadful, awful
affront [afʀɔ̃] *nm* affront; **affrontement** *nm* clash, confrontation
affronter [afʀɔ̃te] *vt* to confront, face
affubler [afyble] (*péj*) *vt*: **~ qn de** to rig *ou* deck sb out in
affût [afy] *nm*: **à l'~ (de)** (*gibier*) lying in wait (for); (*fig*) on the look-out (for)
affûter [afyte] *vt* to sharpen, grind
afin [afɛ̃]: **~ que** *conj* so that, in order that; **~ de faire** in order to do, so as to do
africain, e [afʀikɛ̃, ɛn] *adj, nm/f* African
Afrique [afʀik] *nf*: **l'~** Africa; **l'~ du Sud** South Africa
agacer [agase] *vt* to irritate
âge [ɑʒ] *nm* age; **quel ~ as-tu?** how old are you?; **prendre de l'~** to be getting on (in years); **âgé, e** *adj* old, elderly; **âgé de 10 ans** 10 years old
agence [aʒɑ̃s] *nf* agency, office; (*succursale*) branch; **~ de voyages** travel agency; **~ immobilière** estate (*BRIT*) *ou* real estate (*US*) agent's (office)
agencer [aʒɑ̃se] *vt* to put together; (*local*) to arrange, lay out
agenda [aʒɛ̃da] *nm* diary
agenouiller [aʒ(ə)nuje]: **s'~** *vi* to kneel (down)
agent, e [aʒɑ̃, ɑ̃t] *nm/f* (*aussi:* **~(e) de police**) policeman (policewoman); (*ADMIN*) official, officer; **~ d'assurances** insurance broker
agglomération [aglɔmeʀasjɔ̃] *nf* town; built-up area; **l'~ parisienne** the urban area of Paris
aggloméré [aglɔmeʀe] *nm* (*bois*) chipboard
aggraver [agʀave]: **s'~** *vi* to worsen
agile [aʒil] *adj* agile, nimble
agir [aʒiʀ] *vi* to act; **il s'agit de** (*ça traite de*) it is about; (*il est important de*) it's a matter *ou* question of
agitation [aʒitasjɔ̃] *nf* (hustle and) bustle; (*trouble*) agitation, excitement; (*politique*) unrest, agitation
agité, e [aʒite] *adj* fidgety, restless; (*troublé*) agitated, perturbed; (*mer*) rough
agiter [aʒite] *vt* (*bouteille, chiffon*) to

shake; (*bras*) to wave; (*préoccuper, exciter*) to perturb; **s'~** *vi* (*enfant*) to fidget

agneau, x [aɲo] *nm* lamb

agonie [agɔni] *nf* mortal agony, death pangs *pl*; (*fig*) death throes *pl*

agrafe [agʀaf] *nf* (*de vêtement*) hook, fastener; (*de bureau*) staple; **agrafer** *vt* to fasten; to staple; **agrafeuse** *nf* stapler

agrandir [agʀɑ̃diʀ] *vt* to enlarge; **s'~** *vi* (*ville, famille*) to grow, expand; (*trou, écart*) to get bigger; **agrandissement** *nm* (PHOTO) enlargement

agréable [agʀeabl] *adj* pleasant, nice

agréé, e [agʀee] *adj*: **concessionnaire ~** registered dealer

agréer [agʀee] *vt* (*requête*) to accept; **~ à** to please, suit; **veuillez ~ ...** (*formule épistolaire*) yours faithfully

agrégation [agʀegasjɔ̃] *nf highest teaching diploma in France*; **agrégé, e** *nm/f* holder of the *agrégation*

agrément [agʀemɑ̃] *nm* (*accord*) consent, approval; **agrémenter** *vt* to embellish, adorn

agresser [agʀese] *vt* to attack; **agresseur** *nm* aggressor, attacker; (POL, MIL) aggressor; **agressif, -ive** *adj* aggressive

agricole [agʀikɔl] *adj* agricultural; **agriculteur** *nm* farmer; **agriculture** *nf* agriculture, farming

agripper [agʀipe] *vt* to grab, clutch; **s'~ à** to cling (on) to, clutch, grip

agroalimentaire [agʀoalimɑ̃tɛʀ] *nm* farm-produce industry

agrumes [agʀym] *nmpl* citrus fruit(s)

aguerrir [ageʀiʀ] *vt* to harden

aguets [agɛ] *nmpl*: **être aux ~** to be on the look out

aguicher [agiʃe] *vt* to entice

ahuri, e [ayʀi] *adj* (*stupéfait*) flabbergasted

ai [ɛ] *vb voir* **avoir**

aide [ɛd] *nm/f* assistant; carer ♦ *nf* assistance, help; (*secours financier*) aid; **à l'~ de** (*avec*) with the help *ou* aid of; **appeler (qn) à l'~** to call for help (from sb); **~ familiale** home help, mother's help; **~ judiciaire** ♦ *nf* legal aid; **~ sociale** ♦ *nf* (*assistance*) state aid; **aide-éducateur, -trice** *nm/f* classroom assistant; **aide-mémoire** *nm inv* memoranda pages *pl*; (key facts) handbook; **aide-soignant, e** *nm/f* auxiliary nurse

aider [ede] *vt* to help; **s'~ de** (*se servir de*) to use, make use of

aie *etc* [ɛ] *vb voir* **avoir**

aïe [aj] *excl* ouch!

aïeul, e [ajœl] *nm/f* grandparent, grandfather(-mother)

aïeux [ajø] *nmpl* grandparents; (*ancêtres*) forebears, forefathers

aigle [ɛgl] *nm* eagle

aigre [ɛgʀ] *adj* sour, sharp; (*fig*) sharp, cutting; **aigre-doux, -ce** *adj* (*sauce*) sweet and sour; **aigreur** *nf* sourness; sharpness; **aigreurs d'estomac** heartburn *sg*; **aigrir** *vt* (*personne*) to embitter; (*caractère*) to sour

aigu, ë [egy] *adj* (*objet, douleur*) sharp; (*son, voix*) high-pitched, shrill; (*note*) high(-pitched)

aiguille [egɥij] *nf* needle; (*de montre*) hand; **~ à tricoter** knitting needle

aiguiller [egɥije] *vt* (*orienter*) to direct; **aiguilleur du ciel** *nm* air-traffic controller

aiguillon [egɥijɔ̃] *nm* (*d'abeille*) sting; **aiguillonner** *vt* to spur *ou* goad on

aiguiser [egize] *vt* to sharpen; (*fig*) to stimulate; (: *sens*) to excite

ail [aj, o] *nm* garlic

aile [ɛl] *nf* wing; **aileron** *nm* (*de requin*) fin; **ailier** *nm* winger

aille *etc* [aj] *vb voir* **aller**

ailleurs [ajœʀ] *adv* elsewhere, somewhere else; **partout/nulle part ~** everywhere/nowhere else; **d'~** (*du reste*) moreover, besides; **par ~** (*d'autre part*) moreover, furthermore

aimable [ɛmabl] *adj* kind, nice

aimant [ɛmɑ̃] *nm* magnet

aimer [eme] *vt* to love; (*d'amitié, affec-*

tion, par goût) to like; (*souhait*): **j'~ais ...** I would like ...; **bien ~ qn/qch** to like sb/sth; **j'~ais mieux faire** I'd much rather do

aine [ɛn] *nf* groin

aîné, e [ene] *adj* elder, older; (*le plus âgé*) eldest, oldest ♦ *nm/f* oldest child *ou* one, oldest boy *ou* son/girl *ou* daughter

ainsi [ɛ̃si] *adv* (*de cette façon*) like this, in this way, thus; (*ce faisant*) thus ♦ *conj* thus, so; **~ que** (*comme*) (just) as; (*et aussi*) as well as; **pour ~ dire** so to speak; **et ~ de suite** and so on

aïoli [ajɔli] *nm* garlic mayonnaise

air [ɛʀ] *nm* air; (*mélodie*) tune; (*expression*) look, air; **prendre l'~** to get some (fresh) air; **avoir l'~** (*sembler*) to look, appear; **avoir l'~ de** to look like; **avoir l'~ de faire** to look as though one is doing, appear to be doing; **en l'~** (*promesses*) empty

aisance [ɛzɑ̃s] *nf* ease; (*richesse*) affluence

aise [ɛz] *nf* comfort; **être à l'~** *ou* **à son ~** to be comfortable; (*pas embarrassé*) to be at ease; (*financièrement*) to be comfortably off; **se mettre à l'~** to make o.s. comfortable; **être mal à l'~** to be uncomfortable; (*gêné*) to be ill at ease; **en faire à son ~** to do as one likes; **aisé, e** *adj* easy; (*assez riche*) well-to-do, well-off

aisselle [ɛsɛl] *nf* armpit

ait [ɛ] *vb voir* **avoir**

ajonc [aʒɔ̃] *nm* gorse *no pl*

ajourner [aʒuʀne] *vt* (*réunion*) to adjourn; (*décision*) to defer, postpone

ajouter [aʒute] *vt* to add

ajusté, e [aʒyste] *adj*: **bien ~** (*robe etc*) close-fitting

ajuster [aʒyste] *vt* (*régler*) to adjust; (*vêtement*) to alter; (*coup de fusil*) to aim; (*cible*) to aim at; (*TECH, gén*: *adapter*): **~ qch à** to fit sth to

alarme [alaʀm] *nf* alarm; **donner l'~** to give *ou* raise the alarm; **alarmer** *vt* to alarm; **s'alarmer** *vi* to become alarmed; **alarmiste** *adj, nm/f* alarmist

album [albɔm] *nm* album

albumine [albymin] *nf* albumin; **avoir de l'~** to suffer from albuminuria

alcool [alkɔl] *nm*: **l'~** alcohol; **un ~** a spirit, a brandy; **bière sans ~** non-alcoholic *ou* alcohol-free beer; **~ à brûler** methylated spirits (*BRIT*), wood alcohol (*US*); **~ à 90°** surgical spirit; **alcoolique** *adj, nm/f* alcoholic; **alcoolisé, e** *adj* alcoholic; **une boisson non alcoolisée** a soft drink; **alcoolisme** *nm* alcoholism; **alcootest** ® *nm* Breathalyser ®; (*test*) breath-test

aléas [alea] *nmpl* hazards; **aléatoire** *adj* uncertain; (*INFORM*) random

alentour [alɑ̃tuʀ] *adv* around, round about; **~s** *nmpl* (*environs*) surroundings; **aux ~s de** in the vicinity *ou* neighbourhood of, round about; (*temps*) round about

alerte [alɛʀt] *adj* agile, nimble; brisk, lively ♦ *nf* alert; warning; **~ à la bombe** bomb scare; **alerter** *vt* to alert

algèbre [alʒɛbʀ] *nf* algebra

Alger [alʒe] *n* Algiers

Algérie [alʒeʀi] *nf*: **l'~** Algeria; **algérien, ne** *adj* Algerian ♦ *nm/f*: **Algérien, ne** Algerian

algue [alg] *nf* (*gén*) seaweed *no pl*; (*BOT*) alga

alibi [alibi] *nm* alibi

aliéné, e [aljene] *nm/f* insane person, lunatic (*péj*)

aligner [aliɲe] *vt* to align, line up; (*idées, chiffres*) to string together; (*adapter*): **~ qch sur** to bring sth into alignment with; **s'~** (*soldats etc*) to line up; **s'~ sur** (*POL*) to align o.s. on

aliment [alimɑ̃] *nm* food; **alimentaire** *adj*: **denrées alimentaires** foodstuffs; **alimentation** *nf* (*commerce*) food trade; (*magasin*) grocery store; (*régime*) diet; (*en eau etc, de moteur*) supplying; (*INFORM*) feed; **alimenter** *vt* to feed; (*TECH*): **alimenter (en)** to supply (with);

to feed (with); (*fig*) to sustain, keep going

alinéa [alinea] *nm* paragraph

aliter [alite]: **s'~** *vi* to take to one's bed

allaiter [alete] *vt* to (breast-)feed, nurse; (*suj*: *animal*) to suckle

allant [alɑ̃] *nm* drive, go

alléchant, e [aleʃɑ̃, ɑ̃t] *adj* (*odeur*) mouth-watering; (*offre*) enticing

allécher [aleʃe] *vt*: **~ qn** to make sb's mouth water; to tempt *ou* entice sb

allée [ale] *nf* (*de jardin*) path; (*en ville*) avenue, drive; **~s et venues** comings and goings

allégé, e [aleʒe] *adj* (*yaourt etc*) low-fat

alléger [aleʒe] *vt* (*voiture*) to make lighter; (*chargement*) to lighten; (*souffrance*) to alleviate, soothe

allègre [a(l)lɛgʀ] *adj* lively, cheerful

alléguer [a(l)lege] *vt* to put forward (as proof *ou* an excuse)

Allemagne [almaɲ] *nf*: **l'~** Germany; **allemand, e** *adj* German ♦ *nm/f*: **Allemand, e** German ♦ *nm* (LING) German

aller [ale] *nm* (*trajet*) outward journey; (*billet*: *aussi*: **~ simple**) single (BRIT) *ou* one-way (US) ticket ♦ *vi* (*gén*) to go; **~ à** (*convenir*) to suit; (*suj*: *forme, pointure etc*) to fit; **~ (bien) avec** (*couleurs, style etc*) to go (well) with; **je vais y ~/me fâcher** I'm going to go/to get angry; **~ voir** to go and see, go to see; **allez!** come on!; **allons!** come now!; **comment allez-vous?** how are you?; **comment ça va?** how are you?; (*affaires etc*) how are things?; **il va bien/mal** he's well/not well, he's fine/ill; **ça va bien/mal** (*affaires etc*) it's going well/not going well; **~ mieux** to be better; **s'en ~** (*partir*) to be off, go, leave; (*disparaître*) to go away; **~ retour** return journey (BRIT), round trip; (*billet*) return (ticket) (BRIT), round trip ticket (US)

allergique [alɛʀʒik] *adj*: **~ à** allergic to

alliage [aljaʒ] *nm* alloy

alliance [aljɑ̃s] *nf* (MIL, POL) alliance; (*bague*) wedding ring

allier [alje] *vt* (POL, *gén*) to ally; (*fig*) to combine; **s'~** to become allies; to combine

allô [alo] *excl* hullo, hallo

allocation [alɔkasjɔ̃] *nf* allowance; **~ (de) chômage** unemployment benefit; **~s familiales** ≃ child benefit

allocution [a(l)lɔkysjɔ̃] *nf* short speech

allonger [alɔ̃ʒe] *vt* to lengthen, make longer; (*étendre*: *bras, jambe*) to stretch (out); **s'~** *vi* to get longer; (*se coucher*) to lie down, stretch out; **~ le pas** to hasten one's step(s)

allouer [alwe] *vt* to allocate, allot

allumage [alymaʒ] *nm* (AUTO) ignition

allume-cigare [alymsigaʀ] *nm inv* cigar lighter

allumer [alyme] *vt* (*lampe, phare, radio*) to put *ou* switch on; (*pièce*) to put *ou* switch the light(s) on in; (*feu*) to light; **s'~** *vi* (*lumière, lampe*) to come *ou* go on

allumette [alymɛt] *nf* match

allure [alyʀ] *nf* (*vitesse*) speed, pace; (*démarche*) walk; (*aspect, air*) look; **avoir de l'~** to have style; **à toute ~** at top speed

allusion [a(l)lyzjɔ̃] *nf* allusion; (*sous-entendu*) hint; **faire ~ à** to allude *ou* refer to; to hint at

MOT-CLÉ

alors [alɔʀ] *adv* **1** (*à ce moment-là*) then, at that time; **il habitait alors à Paris** he lived in Paris at that time

2 (*par conséquent*) then; **tu as fini? alors je m'en vais** have you finished? I'm going then; **et alors?** so what?;

alors que *conj* **1** (*au moment où*) when, as; **il est arrivé alors que je partais** he arrived as I was leaving

2 (*pendant que*) while, when; **alors qu'il était à Paris, il a visité ...** while *ou* when he was in Paris, he visited ...

3 (*tandis que*) whereas, while; **alors**

que son frère travaillait dur, lui se reposait while his brother was working hard, HE would rest

alouette [alwɛt] *nf* (sky)lark
alourdir [aluʀdiʀ] *vt* to weigh down, make heavy
aloyau [alwajo] *nm* sirloin
Alpes [alp] *nfpl*: **les ~** the Alps
alphabet [alfabɛ] *nm* alphabet; (*livre*) ABC (book); **alphabétique** *adj* alphabetical; **alphabétiser** *vt* to teach to read and write; (*pays*) to eliminate illiteracy in
alpinisme [alpinism] *nm* mountaineering, climbing; **alpiniste** *nm/f* mountaineer, climber
Alsace [alzas] *nf* Alsace; **alsacien, ne** *adj* Alsatian ♦ *nm/f*: **Alsacien, ne** Alsatian
altérer [alteʀe] *vt* (*vérité*) to distort; **s'~** *vi* to deteriorate
alternateur [altɛʀnatœʀ] *nm* alternator
alternatif, -ive [altɛʀnatif, iv] *adj* alternating; **alternative** *nf* (*choix*) alternative; **alternativement** *adv* alternately; **alterner** *vi* to alternate
Altesse [altɛs] *nf* Highness
altitude [altityd] *nf* altitude, height
alto [alto] *nm* (*instrument*) viola
aluminium [alyminjɔm] *nm* aluminium (*BRIT*), aluminum (*US*)
amabilité [amabilite] *nf* kindness
amadouer [amadwe] *vt* to mollify, soothe
amaigrir [amegʀiʀ] *vt* to make thin(ner); **amaigrissant, e** *adj* (*régime*) slimming
amalgame [amalgam] (*péj*) *nm* (strange) mixture
amande [amɑ̃d] *nf* (*de l'amandier*) almond; **amandier** *nm* almond (tree)
amant [amɑ̃] *nm* lover
amarrer [amaʀe] *vt* (*NAVIG*) to moor; (*gén*) to make fast
amas [amɑ] *nm* heap, pile; **amasser** *vt* to amass; **s'amasser** *vi* (*foule*) to gather
amateur [amatœʀ] *nm* amateur; **en ~** (*péj*) amateurishly; **~ de musique/sport** *etc* music/sport *etc* lover
amazone [amazon] *nf*: **en ~** sidesaddle
ambassade [ɑ̃basad] *nf* embassy; **l'~ de France** the French Embassy; **ambassadeur, -drice** *nm/f* ambassador (-dress)
ambiance [ɑ̃bjɑ̃s] *nf* atmosphere
ambiant, e [ɑ̃bjɑ̃, jɑ̃t] *adj* (*air, milieu*) surrounding; (*température*) ambient
ambigu, ë [ɑ̃bigy] *adj* ambiguous
ambitieux, -euse [ɑ̃bisjø, jøz] *adj* ambitious
ambition [ɑ̃bisjɔ̃] *nf* ambition
ambulance [ɑ̃bylɑ̃s] *nf* ambulance; **ambulancier, -ière** *nm/f* ambulance man(-woman) (*BRIT*), paramedic (*US*)
ambulant, e [ɑ̃bylɑ̃, ɑ̃t] *adj* travelling, itinerant
âme [ɑm] *nf* soul
amélioration [ameljɔʀasjɔ̃] *nf* improvement
améliorer [ameljɔʀe] *vt* to improve; **s'~** *vi* to improve, get better
aménager [amenaʒe] *vt* (*agencer, transformer*) to fit out; to lay out; (: *quartier, territoire*) to develop; (*installer*) to fix up, put in; **ferme aménagée** converted farmhouse
amende [amɑ̃d] *nf* fine; **faire ~ honorable** to make amends
amener [am(ə)ne] *vt* to bring; (*causer*) to bring about; **s'~** *vi* to show up (*fam*), turn up
amenuiser [amənɥize]: **s'~** *vi* (*chances*) to grow slimmer, lessen
amer, amère [amɛʀ] *adj* bitter
américain, e [ameʀikɛ̃, ɛn] *adj* American ♦ *nm/f*: **A~, e** American
Amérique [ameʀik] *nf*: **l'~** America; **l'~ centrale/latine** Central/Latin America; **l'~ du Nord/du Sud** North/South America

amertume [amɛʀtym] *nf* bitterness
ameublement [amœbləmɑ̃] *nm* furnishing; (*meubles*) furniture
ameuter [amøte] *vt* (*peuple*) to rouse
ami, e [ami] *nm/f* friend; (*amant/maîtresse*) boyfriend/girlfriend ♦ *adj*: **pays/groupe ~** friendly country/group
amiable [amjabl]: **à l'~** *adv* (JUR) out of court; (*gén*) amicably
amiante [amjɑ̃t] *nm* asbestos
amical, e, -aux [amikal, o] *adj* friendly; **amicalement** *adv* in a friendly way; (*formule épistolaire*) regards
amidon [amidɔ̃] *nm* starch
amincir [amɛ̃siʀ] *vt*: **~ qn** to make sb thinner *ou* slimmer; (*suj*: *vêtement*) to make sb look slimmer
amincissant, e [amɛ̃sisɑ̃, ɑ̃t] *adj*: **régime ~** (slimming) diet; **crème ~e** slimming cream
amiral, -aux [amiʀal, o] *nm* admiral
amitié [amitje] *nf* friendship; **prendre en ~** to befriend; **~s, Christèle** best wishes, Christèle; **présenter ses ~s à qn** to send sb one's best wishes
ammoniaque [amɔnjak] *nf* ammonia (water)
amnistie [amnisti] *nf* amnesty
amoindrir [amwɛ̃dʀiʀ] *vt* to reduce
amollir [amɔliʀ] *vt* to soften
amonceler [amɔ̃s(ə)le] *vt* to pile *ou* heap up; **s'~** *vi* to pile *ou* heap up; (*fig*) to accumulate
amont [amɔ̃]: **en ~** *adv* upstream
amorce [amɔʀs] *nf* (*sur un hameçon*) bait; (*explosif*) cap; primer; priming; (*fig*: *début*) beginning(s), start; **amorcer** *vt* to start
amorphe [amɔʀf] *adj* passive, lifeless
amortir [amɔʀtiʀ] *vt* (*atténuer*: *choc*) to absorb, cushion; (*bruit, douleur*) to deaden; (COMM: *dette*) to pay off; **~ un achat** to make a purchase pay for itself; **amortisseur** *nm* shock absorber
amour [amuʀ] *nm* love; **faire l'~** to make love; **amouracher**: **s'amouracher de** (*péj*) *vt* to become infatuated with; **amoureux, -euse** *adj* (*regard, tempérament*) amorous; (*vie, problèmes*) love *cpd*; (*personne*): **amoureux (de qn)** in love (with sb) ♦ *nmpl* courting couple(s); **amour-propre** *nm* self-esteem, pride
amovible [amɔvibl] *adj* removable, detachable
ampère [ɑ̃pɛʀ] *nm* amp(ere)
amphithéâtre [ɑ̃fiteɑtʀ] *nm* amphitheatre; (*d'université*) lecture hall *ou* theatre
ample [ɑ̃pl] *adj* (*vêtement*) roomy, ample; (*gestes, mouvement*) broad; (*ressources*) ample; **amplement** *adv*: **c'est amplement suffisant** that's more than enough; **ampleur** *nf* (*de dégâts, problème*) extent
amplificateur [ɑ̃plifikatœʀ] *nm* amplifier
amplifier [ɑ̃plifje] *vt* (*fig*) to expand, increase
ampoule [ɑ̃pul] *nf* (*électrique*) bulb; (*de médicament*) phial; (*aux mains, pieds*) blister; **ampoulé, e** (*péj*) *adj* pompous, bombastic
amputer [ɑ̃pyte] *vt* (MÉD) to amputate; (*fig*) to cut *ou* reduce drastically
amusant, e [amyzɑ̃, ɑ̃t] *adj* (*divertissant, spirituel*) entertaining, amusing; (*comique*) funny, amusing
amuse-gueule [amyzgœl] *nm inv* appetizer, snack
amusement [amyzmɑ̃] *nm* (*divertissement*) amusement; (*jeu etc*) pastime, diversion
amuser [amyze] *vt* (*divertir*) to entertain, amuse; (*égayer, faire rire*) to amuse; **s'~** *vi* (*jouer*) to play; (*se divertir*) to enjoy o.s., have fun; (*fig*) to mess around
amygdale [amidal] *nf* tonsil
an [ɑ̃] *nm* year; **avoir quinze ~s** to be fifteen (years old); **le jour de l'~, le premier de l'~, le nouvel ~** New

Year's Day

analogique [analɔʒik] *adj* (*INFORM, montre*) analog

analogue [analɔg] *adj*: ~ **(à)** analogous (to), similar (to)

analphabète [analfabɛt] *nm/f* illiterate

analyse [analiz] *nf* analysis; (*MÉD*) test; **analyser** *vt* to analyse; to test

ananas [anana(s)] *nm* pineapple

anarchie [anaʀʃi] *nf* anarchy

anatomie [anatɔmi] *nf* anatomy

ancêtre [ɑ̃sɛtʀ] *nm/f* ancestor

anchois [ɑ̃ʃwa] *nm* anchovy

ancien, ne [ɑ̃sjɛ̃, jɛn] *adj* old; (*de jadis, de l'antiquité*) ancient; (*précédent, ex-*) former, old; (*par l'expérience*) senior ♦ *nm/f* (*dans une tribu*) elder; **~-combattant** ♦ *nm* war veteran; **anciennement** *adv* formerly; **ancienneté** *nf* (*ADMIN*) (length of) service; (*privilèges obtenus*) seniority

ancre [ɑ̃kʀ] *nf* anchor; **jeter/lever l'~** to cast/weigh anchor; **ancrer** *vt* (*CONSTR*: *câble etc*) to anchor; (*fig*) to fix firmly

Andorre [ɑ̃dɔʀ] *nf* Andorra

andouille [ɑ̃duj] *nf* (*CULIN*) *sausage made of chitterlings*; (*fam*) clot, nit

âne [ɑn] *nm* donkey, ass; (*péj*) dunce

anéantir [aneɑ̃tiʀ] *vt* to annihilate, wipe out; (*fig*) to obliterate, destroy

anémie [anemi] *nf* anaemia; **anémique** *adj* anaemic

ânerie [ɑnʀi] *nf* stupidity; (*parole etc*) stupid *ou* idiotic comment *etc*

anesthésie [anɛstezi] *nf* anaesthesia; **faire une ~ locale/générale à qn** to give sb a local/general anaesthetic

ange [ɑ̃ʒ] *nm* angel; **être aux ~s** to be over the moon

angélus [ɑ̃ʒelys] *nm* angelus; (*cloches*) evening bells *pl*

angine [ɑ̃ʒin] *nf* throat infection; **~ de poitrine** angina

anglais, e [ɑ̃glɛ, ɛz] *adj* English ♦ *nm/f*: **A~, e** Englishman(-woman) ♦ *nm* (*LING*) English; **les A~** the English; **filer à l'~e** to take French leave

angle [ɑ̃gl] *nm* angle; (*coin*) corner; **~ droit** right angle

Angleterre [ɑ̃glətɛʀ] *nf*: **l'~** England

anglo... [ɑ̃glɔ] *préfixe* Anglo-, anglo(-); **anglophone** *adj* English-speaking

angoisse [ɑ̃gwas] *nf* anguish, distress; **angoissé, e** *adj* (*personne*) distressed; **angoisser** *vt* to harrow, cause anguish to ♦ *vi* to worry, fret

anguille [ɑ̃gij] *nf* eel

anicroche [anikʀɔʃ] *nf* hitch, snag

animal, e, -aux [animal, o] *adj, nm* animal

animateur, -trice [animatœʀ, tʀis] *nm/f* (*de télévision*) host; (*de groupe*) leader, organizer

animation [animasjɔ̃] *nf* (*voir animé*) busyness; liveliness; (*CINÉMA*: *technique*) animation; **~s culturelles** cultural activities

animé, e [anime] *adj* (*lieu*) busy, lively; (*conversation, réunion*) lively, animated

animer [anime] *vt* (*ville, soirée*) to liven up; (*mener*) to lead; **s'~** *vi* to liven up

anis [ani(s)] *nm* (*CULIN*) aniseed; (*BOT*) anise

ankyloser [ɑ̃kiloze]: **s'~** *vi* to get stiff

anneau, x [ano] *nm* (*de rideau, bague*) ring; (*de chaîne*) link

année [ane] *nf* year

annexe [anɛks] *adj* (*problème*) related; (*document*) appended; (*salle*) adjoining ♦ *nf* (*bâtiment*) annex(e); (*jointe à une lettre*) enclosure

anniversaire [anivɛʀsɛʀ] *nm* birthday; (*d'un événement, bâtiment*) anniversary

annonce [anɔ̃s] *nf* announcement; (*signe, indice*) sign; (*aussi*: **~ publicitaire**) advertisement; **les petites ~s** the classified advertisements, the small ads

annoncer [anɔ̃se] *vt* to announce; (*être le signe de*) to herald; **s'~ bien/difficile** to look promising/difficult; **annonceur, -euse** *nm/f* (*publicitaire*) advertiser; (*TV, RADIO*: *speaker*) announcer

annuaire [anɥɛʀ] *nm* yearbook, annual; **~ téléphonique** (telephone) directory, phone book
annuel, le [anɥɛl] *adj* annual, yearly
annuité [anɥite] *nf* annual instalment
annulation [anylasjɔ̃] *nf* cancellation
annuler [anyle] *vt* (*rendez-vous, voyage*) to cancel, call off; (*jugement*) to quash (*BRIT*), repeal (*US*); (*MATH, PHYSIQUE*) to cancel out
anodin, e [anɔdɛ̃, in] *adj* (*blessure*) harmless; (*détail*) insignificant, trivial
anonymat [anɔnima] *nm* anonymity
anonyme [anɔnim] *adj* anonymous; (*fig*) impersonal
ANPE *sigle f* (= *Agence nationale pour l'emploi*) *national employment agency*
anorak [anɔʀak] *nm* anorak
anormal, e, -aux [anɔʀmal, o] *adj* abnormal
anse [ɑ̃s] *nf* (*de panier, tasse*) handle
antan [ɑ̃tɑ̃]: **d'~** *adj* of long ago
antarctique [ɑ̃taʀktik] *adj* Antarctic ♦ *nm*: **l'A~** the Antarctic
antécédents [ɑ̃tesedɑ̃] *nmpl* (*MÉD etc*) past history *sg*
antenne [ɑ̃tɛn] *nf* (*de radio*) aerial; (*d'insecte*) antenna, feeler; (*poste avancé*) outpost; (*succursale*) subbranch; **passer à l'~** to go on the air
antérieur, e [ɑ̃teʀjœʀ] *adj* (*d'avant*) previous, earlier; (*de devant*) front
anti... [ɑ̃ti] *préfixe* anti...; **antialcoolique** *adj* anti-alcohol; **antiatomique** *adj*: **abri antiatomique** fallout shelter; **antibiotique** *nm* antibiotic; **antibogue** *adj* debugging ♦ *nm* debugging device; **antibrouillard** *adj*: **phare antibrouillard** fog lamp (*BRIT*) *ou* light (*US*)
anticipation [ɑ̃tisipasjɔ̃] *nf*: **livre/film d'~** science fiction book/film
anticipé, e [ɑ̃tisipe] *adj*: **avec mes remerciements ~s** thanking you in advance *ou* anticipation
anticiper [ɑ̃tisipe] *vt* (*événement, coup*) to anticipate, foresee
anti...: anticonceptionnel, le *adj* contraceptive; **anticorps** *nm* antibody; **antidote** *nm* antidote; **antigel** *nm* antifreeze; **antihistaminique** *nm* antihistamine
antillais, e [ɑ̃tijɛ, ɛz] *adj* West Indian, Caribbean ♦ *nm/f*: **A~, e** West Indian, Caribbean
Antilles [ɑ̃tij] *nfpl*: **les ~** the West Indies
antilope [ɑ̃tilɔp] *nf* antelope
anti...: antimite(s) *adj, nm*: **(produit) antimite(s)** mothproofer; moth repellent; **antimondialisation** *nf* antiglobalization; **antipathique** *adj* unpleasant, disagreeable; **antipelliculaire** *adj* anti-dandruff
antipodes [ɑ̃tipɔd] *nmpl* (*fig*): **être aux ~ de** to be the opposite extreme of
antiquaire [ɑ̃tikɛʀ] *nm/f* antique dealer
antique [ɑ̃tik] *adj* antique; (*très vieux*) ancient, antiquated; **antiquité** *nf* (*objet*) antique; **l'Antiquité** Antiquity; **magasin d'antiquités** antique shop
anti...: antirabique *adj* rabies *cpd*; **antirouille** *adj inv* anti-rust *cpd*; **antisémite** *adj* anti-Semitic; **antiseptique** *adj, nm* antiseptic; **antivol** *adj, nm*: **(dispositif) antivol** anti-theft device
antre [ɑ̃tʀ] *nm* den, lair
anxiété [ɑ̃ksjete] *nf* anxiety
anxieux, -euse [ɑ̃ksjø, jøz] *adj* anxious, worried
AOC *sigle f* (= *appellation d'origine contrôlée*) *label guaranteeing the quality of wine*

AOC

AOC is the highest French wine classification. It indicates that the wine meets strict requirements concerning the vineyard of origin, the type of vine grown, the method of production, and the volume of alcohol present.

août [u(t)] *nm* August
apaiser [apeze] *vt* (*colère, douleur*) to soothe; (*personne*) to calm (down),

pacify; **s'~** *vi* (*tempête, bruit*) to die down, subside; (*personne*) to calm down

apanage [apanaʒ] *nm*: **être l'~ de** to be the privilege *ou* prerogative of

aparté [apaʀte] *nm* (*entretien*) private conversation; **en ~** in an aside

apathique [apatik] *adj* apathetic

apatride [apatʀid] *nm/f* stateless person

apercevoir [apɛʀsəvwaʀ] *vt* to see; **s'~ de** *vt* to notice; **s'~ que** to notice that

aperçu [apɛʀsy] *nm* (*vue d'ensemble*) general survey

apéritif [apeʀitif] *nm* (*boisson*) aperitif; (*réunion*) drinks *pl*

à-peu-près [apøpʀɛ] (*péj*) *nm inv* vague approximation

apeuré, e [apœʀe] *adj* frightened, scared

aphte [aft] *nm* mouth ulcer

apiculture [apikyltyʀ] *nf* beekeeping, apiculture

apitoyer [apitwaje] *vt* to move to pity; **s'~ (sur)** to feel pity (for)

aplanir [aplaniʀ] *vt* to level; (*fig*) to smooth away, iron out

aplatir [aplatiʀ] *vt* to flatten; **s'~** *vi* to become flatter; (*écrasé*) to be flattened; **s'~ devant qn** (*fig*: *s'humilier*) to crawl to sb

aplomb [aplɔ̃] *nm* (*équilibre*) balance, equilibrium; (*fig*) self-assurance; nerve; **d'~** steady

apogée [apɔʒe] *nm* (*fig*) peak, apogee

apologie [apɔlɔʒi] *nf* vindication, praise

a posteriori [apɔsteʀjɔʀi] *adv* after the event

apostrophe [apɔstʀɔf] *nf* (*signe*) apostrophe

apostropher [apɔstʀɔfe] *vt* (*interpeller*) to shout at, address sharply

apothéose [apɔteoz] *nf* pinnacle (of achievement), (MUS) grand finale

apôtre [apotʀ] *nm* apostle

apparaître [apaʀɛtʀ] *vi* to appear

apparat [apaʀa] *nm*: **tenue d'~** ceremonial dress

appareil [apaʀɛj] *nm* (*outil, machine*) piece of apparatus, device; (*électrique, ménager*) appliance; (*avion*) (aero)plane, aircraft *inv*; (*téléphonique*) phone; (*dentier*) brace (BRIT), braces (US); **"qui est à l'~?"** "who's speaking?"; **dans le plus simple ~** in one's birthday suit; **appareiller** *vi* (NAVIG) to cast off, get under way ♦ *vt* (*assortir*) to match up; **appareil(-photo)** *nm* camera

apparemment [apaʀamɑ̃] *adv* apparently

apparence [apaʀɑ̃s] *nf* appearance; **en ~** apparently

apparent, e [apaʀɑ̃, ɑ̃t] *adj* visible; (*évident*) obvious; (*superficiel*) apparent

apparenté, e [apaʀɑ̃te] *adj*: **~ à** related to; (*fig*) similar to

apparition [apaʀisjɔ̃] *nf* appearance; (*surnaturelle*) apparition

appartement [apaʀtəmɑ̃] *nm* flat (BRIT), apartment (US)

appartenir [apaʀtəniʀ]: **~ à** *vt* to belong to; **il lui appartient de** it is his duty to

apparu, e [apaʀy] *pp de* **apparaître**

appât [apɑ] *nm* (PÊCHE) bait; (*fig*) lure, bait; **appâter** *vt* to lure

appauvrir [apovʀiʀ] *vt* to impoverish

appel [apɛl] *nm* call; (*nominal*) roll call; (: SCOL) register; (*MIL*: *recrutement*) call-up; **faire ~ à** (*invoquer*) to appeal to; (*avoir recours à*) to call on; (*nécessiter*) to call for, require; **faire ~** (JUR) to appeal; **faire l'~** to call the roll; to call the register; **sans ~** (*fig*) final, irrevocable; **~ d'offres** (COMM) invitation to tender; **faire un ~ de phares** to flash one's headlights; **~ (téléphonique)** (tele)phone call

appelé [ap(ə)le] *nm* (MIL) conscript

appeler [ap(ə)le] *vt* to call; (*faire venir*: *médecin etc*) to call, send for; **s'~** *vi*: **elle s'appelle Gabrielle** her name is Gabrielle, she's called Gabrielle;

comment ça s'appelle? what is it called?; **être appelé à** (*fig*) to be destined to
appendice [apɛ̃dis] *nm* appendix; **appendicite** *nf* appendicitis
appentis [apɑ̃ti] *nm* lean-to
appesantir [apəzɑ̃tiʀ]: **s'~** *vi* to grow heavier; **s'~ sur** (*fig*) to dwell on
appétissant, e [apetisɑ̃, ɑ̃t] *adj* appetizing, mouth-watering
appétit [apeti] *nm* appetite; **bon ~!** enjoy your meal!
applaudir [aplodiʀ] *vt* to applaud ♦ *vi* to applaud, clap; **applaudissements** *nmpl* applause *sg*, clapping *sg*
application [aplikasjɔ̃] *nf* application
applique [aplik] *nf* wall lamp
appliquer [aplike] *vt* to apply; (*loi*) to enforce; **s'~** *vi* (*élève etc*) to apply o.s.; **s'~ à** to apply to
appoint [apwɛ̃] *nm* (extra) contribution *ou* help; **chauffage d'~** extra heating
appointements [apwɛ̃tmɑ̃] *nmpl* salary *sg*
apport [apɔʀ] *nm* (*approvisionnement*) supply; (*contribution*) contribution
apporter [apɔʀte] *vt* to bring
apposer [apoze] *vt* (*signature*) to affix
appréciable [apʀesjabl] *adj* appreciable
apprécier [apʀesje] *vt* to appreciate; (*évaluer*) to estimate, assess
appréhender [apʀeɑ̃de] *vt* (*craindre*) to dread; (*arrêter*) to apprehend; **appréhension** *nf* apprehension, anxiety
apprendre [apʀɑ̃dʀ] *vt* to learn; (*événement, résultats*) to learn of, hear of; **~ qch à qn** (*informer*) to tell sb (of) sth; (*enseigner*) to teach sb sth; **~ à faire qch** to learn to do sth; **~ à qn à faire qch** to teach sb to do sth; **apprenti, e** *nm/f* apprentice; **apprentissage** *nm* learning; (COMM, SCOL: *période*) apprenticeship
apprêté, e [apʀete] *adj* (*fig*) affected
apprêter [apʀete] *vt*: **s'~ à faire qch** to get ready to do sth
appris, e [apʀi, iz] *pp de* **apprendre**
apprivoiser [apʀivwaze] *vt* to tame
approbation [apʀɔbasjɔ̃] *nf* approval
approchant, e [apʀɔʃɑ̃, ɑ̃t] *adj* similar; **quelque chose d'~** something like that
approche [apʀɔʃ] *nf* approach
approcher [apʀɔʃe] *vi* to approach, come near ♦ *vt* to approach; (*rapprocher*): **~ qch (de qch)** to bring *ou* put sth near (to sth); **s'~ de** to approach, go *ou* come near to; **~ de** (*lieu, but*) to draw near to; (*quantité, moment*) to approach
approfondir [apʀɔfɔ̃diʀ] *vt* to deepen; (*question*) to go further into
approprié, e [apʀɔpʀije] *adj*: **~ (à)** appropriate (to), suited to
approprier [apʀɔpʀije]: **s'~** *vt* to appropriate, take over
approuver [apʀuve] *vt* to agree with; (*trouver louable*) to approve of
approvisionner [apʀɔvizjɔne] *vt* to supply; (*compte bancaire*) to pay funds into; **s'~ en** to stock up with
approximatif, -ive [apʀɔksimatif, iv] *adj* approximate, rough; (*termes*) vague
appt *abr* = **appartement**
appui [apɥi] *nm* support; **prendre ~ sur** to lean on; (*objet*) to rest on; **l'~ de la fenêtre** the windowsill, the window ledge; **appui(e)-tête** *nm inv* headrest
appuyer [apɥije] *vt* (*poser*): **~ qch sur/contre** to lean *ou* rest sth on/against; (*soutenir: personne, demande*) to support, back (up) ♦ *vi*: **~ sur** (*bouton, frein*) to press, push; (*mot, détail*) to stress, emphasize; **s'~ sur** to lean on; (*fig: compter sur*) to rely on
âpre [ɑpʀ] *adj* acrid, pungent; **~ au gain** grasping
après [apʀɛ] *prép* after ♦ *adv* afterwards; **2 heures ~** 2 hours later; **~ qu'il est** *ou* **soit parti** after he left; **~ avoir fait** after having done; **d'~** (*selon*) according to; **~ coup** after the event, after-

wards; **~ tout** (*au fond*) after all; **et (puis) ~?** so what?; **après-demain** *adv* the day after tomorrow; **après-guerre** *nm* post-war years *pl*; **après-midi** *nm ou nf inv* afternoon; **après-rasage** *nm inv* aftershave; **après-shampooing** *nm inv* conditioner; **après-ski** *nm inv* snow boot

à-propos [apʀɔpo] *nm* (*d'une remarque*) aptness; **faire preuve d'~-~** to show presence of mind

apte [apt] *adj* capable; (*MIL*) fit

aquarelle [akwaʀɛl] *nf* watercolour

aquarium [akwaʀjɔm] *nm* aquarium

arabe [aʀab] *adj* Arabic; (*désert, cheval*) Arabian; (*nation, peuple*) Arab ♦ *nm/f*: **A~** Arab ♦ *nm* (*LING*) Arabic

Arabie [aʀabi] *nf*: **l'~ (Saoudite)** Saudi Arabia

arachide [aʀaʃid] *nf* (*plante*) groundnut (plant); (*graine*) peanut, groundnut

araignée [aʀeɲe] *nf* spider

arbitraire [aʀbitʀɛʀ] *adj* arbitrary

arbitre [aʀbitʀ] *nm* (*SPORT*) referee; (*: TENNIS, CRICKET*) umpire; (*fig*) arbiter, judge; (*JUR*) arbitrator; **arbitrer** *vt* to referee; to umpire; to arbitrate

arborer [aʀbɔʀe] *vt* to bear, display

arbre [aʀbʀ] *nm* tree; (*TECH*) shaft; **~ généalogique** family tree

arbuste [aʀbyst] *nm* small shrub

arc [aʀk] *nm* (*arme*) bow; (*GÉOM*) arc; (*ARCHIT*) arch; **en ~ de cercle** semi-circular

arcade [aʀkad] *nf* arch(way); **~s** *nfpl* (*série*) arcade *sg*, arches

arcanes [aʀkan] *nmpl* mysteries

arc-boutant [aʀkbutɑ̃] *nm* flying buttress

arceau, x [aʀso] *nm* (*métallique etc*) hoop

arc-en-ciel [aʀkɑ̃sjɛl] *nm* rainbow

arche [aʀʃ] *nf* arch; **~ de Noé** Noah's Ark

archéologie [aʀkeɔlɔʒi] *nf* arch(a)eology; **archéologue** *nm/f* arch(a)eologist

archet [aʀʃɛ] *nm* bow

archevêque [aʀʃəvɛk] *nm* archbishop

archi... [aʀʃi] (*fam*) *préfixe* tremendously; **archicomble** (*fam*) *adj* chock-a-block; **archiconnu, e** (*fam*) *adj* enormously well-known

archipel [aʀʃipɛl] *nm* archipelago

architecte [aʀʃitɛkt] *nm* architect

architecture [aʀʃitɛktyʀ] *nf* architecture

archives [aʀʃiv] *nfpl* (*collection*) archives

arctique [aʀktik] *adj* Arctic ♦ *nm*: **l'A~** the Arctic

ardemment [aʀdamɑ̃] *adv* ardently, fervently

ardent, e [aʀdɑ̃, ɑ̃t] *adj* (*soleil*) blazing; (*amour*) ardent, passionate; (*prière*) fervent

ardeur [aʀdœʀ] *nf* ardour (*BRIT*), ardor (*US*); (*du soleil*) heat

ardoise [aʀdwaz] *nf* slate

ardu, e [aʀdy] *adj* (*travail*) arduous; (*problème*) difficult

arène [aʀɛn] *nf* arena; **~s** *nfpl* (*amphithéâtre*) bull-ring *sg*

arête [aʀɛt] *nf* (*de poisson*) bone; (*d'une montagne*) ridge

argent [aʀʒɑ̃] *nm* (*métal*) silver; (*monnaie*) money; **~ de poche** pocket money; **~ liquide** ready money, (ready) cash; **argenté, e** *adj* (*couleur*) silver, silvery; **en métal argenté** silver-plated; **argenterie** *nf* silverware

argentin, e [aʀʒɑ̃tɛ̃, in] *adj* Argentinian, Argentine

Argentine [aʀʒɑ̃tin] *nf*: **l'~** Argentina, the Argentine

argile [aʀʒil] *nf* clay

argot [aʀgo] *nm* slang; **argotique** *adj* slang *cpd*; (*très familier*) slangy

argument [aʀgymɑ̃] *nm* argument

argumentaire [aʀgymɑ̃tɛʀ] *nm* sales leaflet

argumenter [aʀgymɑ̃te] *vi* to argue

argus [aʀgys] *nm guide to second-hand car etc prices*

aride [arid] *adj* arid
aristocratie [aristɔkrasi] *nf* aristocracy; **aristocratique** *adj* aristocratic
arithmétique [aritmetik] *adj* arithmetic(al) ♦ *nf* arithmetic
armateur [armatœr] *nm* shipowner
armature [armatyr] *nf* framework; (*de tente etc*) frame; **soutien-gorge à/sans ~** underwired/unwired bra
arme [arm] *nf* weapon; **~s** *nfpl* (*~ment*) weapons, arms; (*blason*) (coat of) arms; **~ à feu** firearm
armée [arme] *nf* army; **~ de l'air** Air Force; **~ de terre** Army
armement [arməmɑ̃] *nm* (*matériel*) arms *pl*, weapons *pl*
armer [arme] *vt* to arm; (*arme à feu*) to cock; (*appareil-photo*) to wind on; **~ qch de** to reinforce sth with; **s'~ de** to arm o.s. with
armistice [armistis] *nm* armistice; **l'A~** ≃ Remembrance (*BRIT*) *ou* Veterans (*US*) Day
armoire [armwar] *nf* (tall) cupboard; (*penderie*) wardrobe (*BRIT*), closet (*US*)
armoiries [armwari] *nfpl* coat *sg* of arms
armure [armyr] *nf* armour *no pl*, suit of armour; **armurier** *nm* gunsmith
arnaque [arnak] (*fam*) *nf* swindling; **c'est de l'~** it's a rip-off; **arnaquer** (*fam*) *vt* to swindle
aromates [arɔmat] *nmpl* seasoning *sg*, herbs (and spices)
aromathérapie [arɔmaterapi] *nf* aromatherapy
aromatisé, e [arɔmatize] *adj* flavoured
arôme [arom] *nm* aroma
arpenter [arpɑ̃te] *vt* (*salle, couloir*) to pace up and down
arpenteur [arpɑ̃tœr] *nm* surveyor
arqué, e [arke] *adj* arched; (*jambes*) bandy
arrache-pied [araʃpje]: **d'~-~** *adv* relentlessly
arracher [araʃe] *vt* to pull out; (*page etc*) to tear off, tear out; (*légumes, herbe*) to pull up; (*bras etc*) to tear off; **s'~** *vt* (*article recherché*) to fight over; **~ qch à qn** to snatch sth from sb; (*fig*) to wring sth out of sb
arraisonner [arɛzɔne] *vt* (*bateau*) to board and search
arrangeant, e [arɑ̃ʒɑ̃, ɑ̃t] *adj* accommodating, obliging
arrangement [arɑ̃ʒmɑ̃] *nm* agreement, arrangement
arranger [arɑ̃ʒe] *vt* (*gén*) to arrange; (*réparer*) to fix, put right; (*régler: différend*) to settle, sort out; (*convenir à*) to suit, be convenient for; **s'~** *vi* (*se mettre d'accord*) to come to an agreement; **je vais m'~** I'll manage; **ça va s'~** it'll sort itself out
arrestation [arɛstasjɔ̃] *nf* arrest
arrêt [arɛ] *nm* stopping; (*de bus etc*) stop; (*JUR*) judgment, decision; **à l'~** stationary; **tomber en ~ devant** to stop short in front of; **sans ~** (*sans interruption*) non-stop; (*très fréquemment*) continually; **~ de travail** stoppage (of work); **~ maladie** sick leave
arrêté [arete] *nm* order, decree
arrêter [arete] *vt* to stop; (*chauffage etc*) to turn off, switch off; (*fixer: date etc*) to appoint, decide on; (*criminel, suspect*) to arrest; **s'~** *vi* to stop; **~ de faire** to stop doing
arrhes [ar] *nfpl* deposit *sg*
arrière [arjɛr] *nm* back; (*SPORT*) fullback ♦ *adj inv*: **siège/roue ~** back *ou* rear seat/wheel; **à l'~** behind, at the back; **en ~** behind; (*regarder*) back, behind; (*tomber, aller*) backwards; **arriéré, e** *adj* (*péj*) backward ♦ *nm* (*d'argent*) arrears *pl*; **arrière-goût** *nm* aftertaste; **arrière-grand-mère** *nf* great-grandmother; **arrière-grand-père** *nm* great-grandfather; **arrière-pays** *nm inv* hinterland; **arrière-pensée** *nf* ulterior motive; mental reservation; **arrière-plan** *nm* background; **arrière-saison** *nf* late autumn; **arrière-train** *nm* hindquarters *pl*

arrimer [aʀime] *vt* to secure; (*cargaison*) to stow
arrivage [aʀivaʒ] *nm* consignment
arrivée [aʀive] *nf* arrival; (*ligne d'~*) finish
arriver [aʀive] *vi* to arrive; (*survenir*) to happen, occur; **il arrive à Paris à 8h** he gets to *ou* arrives in Paris at 8; **~ à** (*atteindre*) to reach; **~ à faire qch** to succeed in doing sth; **en ~ à** (*finir par*) to come to; **il arrive que** it happens that; **il lui arrive de faire** he sometimes does; **arriviste** *nm/f* go-getter
arrobase [aʀɔbaz] *nf* (INFORM) @, 'at' sign
arrogance [aʀɔgɑ̃s] *nf* arrogance
arrogant, e [aʀɔgɑ̃, ɑ̃t] *adj* arrogant
arrondir [aʀɔ̃diʀ] *vt* (*forme, objet*) to round; (*somme*) to round off
arrondissement [aʀɔ̃dismɑ̃] *nm* (ADMIN) ≃ district
arroser [aʀoze] *vt* to water; (*victoire*) to celebrate (over a drink); (CULIN) to baste; **arrosoir** *nm* watering can
arsenal, -aux [aʀsənal, o] *nm* (NAVIG) naval dockyard; (MIL) arsenal; (*fig*) gear
art [aʀ] *nm* art
artère [aʀtɛʀ] *nf* (ANAT) artery; (*rue*) main road
arthrite [aʀtʀit] *nf* arthritis
artichaut [aʀtiʃo] *nm* artichoke
article [aʀtikl] *nm* article; (COMM) item, article; **à l'~ de la mort** at the point of death; **~s de luxe** luxury goods
articulation [aʀtikylasjɔ̃] *nf* articulation; (ANAT) joint
articuler [aʀtikyle] *vt* to articulate
artifice [aʀtifis] *nm* device, trick
artificiel, le [aʀtifisjɛl] *adj* artificial
artisan [aʀtizɑ̃] *nm* artisan, (self-employed) craftsman; **artisanal, e, -aux** *adj* of *ou* made by craftsmen; (*péj*) cottage industry *cpd*; **de fabrication artisanale** home-made; **artisanat** *nm* arts and crafts *pl*
artiste [aʀtist] *nm/f* artist; (*de variétés*) entertainer; (*musicien etc*) performer; **artistique** *adj* artistic
as¹ [a] *vb voir* **avoir**
as² [ɑs] *nm* ace
ascendance [asɑ̃dɑ̃s] *nf* (*origine*) ancestry
ascendant, e [asɑ̃dɑ̃, ɑ̃t] *adj* upward ♦ *nm* influence
ascenseur [asɑ̃sœʀ] *nm* lift (BRIT), elevator (US)
ascension [asɑ̃sjɔ̃] *nf* ascent; (*de montagne*) climb; **l'A~** (REL) the Ascension

Ascension

La fête de l'Ascension *is a French public holiday, usually in May. As it falls on a Thursday, many people take Friday off work and enjoy a long weekend; see also faire le* **pont**.

aseptisé, e (*péj*) *adj* sanitized
aseptiser [asɛptize] *vt* (*ustensile*) to sterilize; (*plaie*) to disinfect
asiatique [azjatik] *adj* Asiatic, Asian ♦ *nm/f*: **A~** Asian
Asie [azi] *nf*: **l'~** Asia
asile [azil] *nm* (*refuge*) refuge, sanctuary; (POL): **droit d'~** (political) asylum; **~ (de vieillards)** old people's home
aspect [aspɛ] *nm* appearance, look; (*fig*) aspect, side; **à l'~ de** at the sight of
asperge [aspɛʀʒ] *nf* asparagus *no pl*
asperger [aspɛʀʒe] *vt* to spray, sprinkle
aspérité [aspeʀite] *nf* bump, protruding bit (of rock *etc*)
asphalte [asfalt] *nm* asphalt
asphyxier [asfiksje] *vt* to suffocate, asphyxiate; (*fig*) to stifle
aspirateur [aspiʀatœʀ] *nm* vacuum cleaner; **passer l'~** to vacuum
aspirer [aspiʀe] *vt* (*air*) to inhale; (*liquide*) to suck (up); (*suj*: *appareil*) to suck up; **~ à** to aspire to
aspirine [aspiʀin] *nf* aspirin
assagir [asaʒiʀ]: **s'~** *vi* to quieten down, settle down
assaillir [asajiʀ] *vt* to assail, attack
assainir [asениʀ] *vt* (*logements*) to clean

up; (*eau, air*) to purify

assaisonnement [asɛzɔnmɑ̃] *nm* seasoning

assaisonner [asɛzɔne] *vt* to season

assassin [asasɛ̃] *nm* murderer; assassin; **assassiner** *vt* to murder; (*esp* POL) to assassinate

assaut [aso] *nm* assault, attack; **prendre d'~** to storm, assault; **donner l'~** to attack

assécher [aseʃe] *vt* to drain

assemblage [asɑ̃blaʒ] *nm* (*action*) assembling; (*de couleurs, choses*) collection

assemblée [asɑ̃ble] *nf* (*réunion*) meeting; (*assistance*) gathering; (POL) assembly

assembler [asɑ̃ble] *vt* (*joindre, monter*) to assemble, put together; (*amasser*) to gather (together), collect (together); **s'~** *vi* to gather

assener, asséner [asene] *vt*: **~ un coup à qn** to deal sb a blow

assentiment [asɑ̃timɑ̃] *nm* assent, consent

asseoir [aswaʀ] *vt* (*malade, bébé*) to sit up; (*personne debout*) to sit down; (*autorité, réputation*) to establish; **s'~** *vi* to sit (o.s.) down

assermenté, e [asɛʀmɑ̃te] *adj* sworn, on oath

asservir [asɛʀviʀ] *vt* to subjugate, enslave

assez [ase] *adv* (*suffisamment*) enough, sufficiently; (*passablement*) rather, quite, fairly; **~ de pain/livres** enough *ou* sufficient bread/books; **vous en avez ~?** have you got enough?; **j'en ai ~!** I've had enough!

assidu, e [asidy] *adj* (*appliqué*) assiduous, painstaking; (*ponctuel*) regular

assied *etc* [asje] *vb voir* **asseoir**

assiéger [asjeʒe] *vt* to besiege

assiérai *etc* [asjeʀe] *vb voir* **asseoir**

assiette [asjɛt] *nf* plate; (*contenu*) plate(ful); **il n'est pas dans son ~** he's not feeling quite himself; **~ à dessert** dessert plate; **~ anglaise** assorted cold meats; **~ creuse** (soup) dish, soup plate; **~ plate** (dinner) plate

assigner [asiɲe] *vt*: **~ qch à** (*poste, part, travail*) to assign sth to

assimiler [asimile] *vt* to assimilate, absorb; (*comparer*): **~ qch/qn à** to liken *ou* compare sth/sb to

assis, e [asi, iz] *pp de* **asseoir** ♦ *adj* sitting (down), seated; **assise** *nf* (*fig*) basis, foundation; **assises** *nfpl* (JUR) assizes

assistance [asistɑ̃s] *nf* (*public*) audience; (*aide*) assistance; **enfant de l'A~ publique** child in care

assistant, e [asistɑ̃, ɑ̃t] *nm/f* assistant; (*d'université*) probationary lecturer; **~(e) social(e)** social worker

assisté, e [asiste] *adj* (AUTO) power assisted; **~ par ordinateur** computer-assisted

assister [asiste] *vt* (*aider*) to assist; **~ à** (*scène, événement*) to witness; (*conférence, séminaire*) to attend, be at; (*spectacle, match*) to be at, see

association [asɔsjasjɔ̃] *nf* association

associé, e [asɔsje] *nm/f* associate; (COMM) partner

associer [asɔsje] *vt* to associate; **s'~** *vi* to join together; **s'~ à qn pour faire** to join (forces) with sb to do; **s'~ à** (*couleurs, qualités*) to be combined with; (*opinions, joie de qn*) to share in; **~ qn à** (*profits*) to give sb a share of; (*affaire*) to make sb a partner in; (*joie, triomphe*) to include sb in; **~ qch à** (*allier à*) to combine sth with

assoiffé, e [aswafe] *adj* thirsty

assombrir [asɔ̃bʀiʀ] *vt* to darken; (*fig*) to fill with gloom

assommer [asɔme] *vt* (*étourdir, abrutir*) to knock out, stun

Assomption [asɔ̃psjɔ̃] *nf*: **l'~** the Assumption

Assomption

La fête de l'Assomption *on August*

15 is a French national holiday. Traditionally, large numbers of holidaymakers set out on this date, frequently causing chaos on the roads; see also faire le **pont**.

assorti, e [asɔRti] *adj* matched, matching; (*varié*) assorted; **~ à** matching; **assortiment** *nm* assortment, selection
assortir [asɔRtiR] *vt* to match; **~ qch à** to match sth with; **~ qch de** to accompany sth with
assoupi, e [asupi] *adj* dozing, sleeping
assoupir [asupiR]: **s'~** *vi* to doze off
assouplir [asupliR] *vt* to make supple; (*fig*) to relax; **assouplissant** *nm* (fabric) softener
assourdir [asuRdiR] *vt* (*bruit*) to deaden, muffle; (*suj*: *bruit*) to deafen
assouvir [asuviR] *vt* to satisfy, appease
assujettir [asyʒetiR] *vt* to subject
assumer [asyme] *vt* (*fonction, emploi*) to assume, take on
assurance [asyRɑ̃s] *nf* (*certitude*) assurance; (*confiance en soi*) (self-) confidence; (*contrat*) insurance (policy); (*secteur commercial*) insurance; **~ maladie** health insurance; **~ tous risques** (*AUTO*) comprehensive insurance; **~s sociales** ≃ National Insurance (*BRIT*), ≃ Social Security (*US*); **assurance-vie** *nf* life assurance *ou* insurance
assuré, e [asyRe] *adj* (*certain*: *réussite, échec*) certain, sure; (*air*) assured; (*pas*) steady ♦ *nm/f* insured (person); **assurément** *adv* assuredly, most certainly
assurer [asyRe] *vt* (*FIN*) to insure; (*victoire etc*) to ensure; (*frontières, pouvoir*) to make secure; (*service*) to provide, operate; **s'~ (contre)** (*COMM*) to insure o.s. (against); **s'~ de/que** (*vérifier*) to make sure of/that; **s'~ (de)** (*aide de qn*) to secure; **~ à qn que** to assure sb that; **~ qn de** to assure sb of; **assureur** *nm* insurer
asthmatique [asmatik] *adj, nm/f* asthmatic
asthme [asm] *nm* asthma
asticot [astiko] *nm* maggot
astiquer [astike] *vt* to polish, shine
astre [astR] *nm* star
astreignant, e [astRɛɲɑ̃, ɑ̃t] *adj* demanding
astreindre [astRɛ̃dR] *vt*: **~ qn à faire** to compel *ou* force sb to do; **s'~** *vi*: **s'~ à faire** to force o.s. to do
astrologie [astRɔlɔʒi] *nf* astrology
astronaute [astRonot] *nm/f* astronaut
astronomie [astRɔnɔmi] *nf* astronomy
astuce [astys] *nf* shrewdness, astuteness; (*truc*) trick, clever way; **astucieux, -euse** *adj* clever
atelier [atəlje] *nm* workshop; (*de peintre*) studio
athée [ate] *adj* atheistic ♦ *nm/f* atheist
Athènes [atɛn] *n* Athens
athlète [atlɛt] *nm/f* (*SPORT*) athlete; **athlétisme** *nm* athletics *sg*
atlantique [atlɑ̃tik] *adj* Atlantic ♦ *nm*: **l'(océan) A~** the Atlantic (Ocean)
atlas [atlɑs] *nm* atlas
atmosphère [atmɔsfɛR] *nf* atmosphere
atome [atom] *nm* atom; **atomique** *adj* atomic, nuclear
atomiseur [atɔmizœR] *nm* atomizer
atout [atu] *nm* trump; (*fig*) asset
âtre [ɑtR] *nm* hearth
atroce [atRɔs] *adj* atrocious
attabler [atable]: **s'~** *vi* to sit down at (the) table
attachant, e [ataʃɑ̃, ɑ̃t] *adj* engaging, lovable, likeable
attache [ataʃ] *nf* clip, fastener; (*fig*) tie
attacher [ataʃe] *vt* to tie up; (*étiquette*) to attach, tie on; (*ceinture*) to fasten ♦ *vi* (*poêle, riz*) to stick; **s'~ à** (*par affection*) to become attached to; **s'~ à faire** to endeavour to do; **~ qch à** to tie *ou* attach sth to
attaque [atak] *nf* attack; (*cérébrale*) stroke; (*d'épilepsie*) fit; **~ à main armée** armed attack
attaquer [atake] *vt* to attack; (*en jus-*

tice) to bring an action against, sue ♦ *vi* to attack; **s'~ à** ♦ *vt* (*personne*) to attack; (*problème*) to tackle

attardé, e [ataʀde] *adj* (*enfant*) backward; (*passants*) late

attarder [ataʀde]: **s'~** *vi* to linger

atteindre [atɛ̃dʀ] *vt* to reach; (*blesser*) to hit; (*émouvoir*) to affect; **atteint, e** *adj* (MÉD): **être atteint de** to be suffering from; **atteinte** *nf*: **hors d'atteinte** out of reach; **porter atteinte à** to strike a blow at

atteler [at(ə)le] *vt* (*cheval, bœufs*) to hitch up; **s'~ à** (*travail*) to buckle down to

attelle [atɛl] *nf* splint

attenant, e [at(ə)nɑ̃, ɑ̃t] *adj*: **~ (à)** adjoining

attendant [atɑ̃dɑ̃] *adv*: **en ~** meanwhile, in the meantime

attendre [atɑ̃dʀ] *vt* (*gén*) to wait for; (*être destiné ou réservé à*) to await, be in store for ♦ *vi* to wait; **s'~ à (ce que)** to expect (that); **~ un enfant** to be expecting a baby; **~ de faire/d'être** to wait until one does/is; **attendez qu'il vienne** wait until he comes; **~ qch de** to expect sth of

attendrir [atɑ̃dʀiʀ] *vt* to move (to pity); (*viande*) to tenderize; **attendrissant, e** *adj* moving, touching

attendu, e [atɑ̃dy] *adj* (*visiteur*) expected; (*événement*) long-awaited; **~ que** considering that, since

attentat [atɑ̃ta] *nm* assassination attempt; **~ à la bombe** bomb attack; **~ à la pudeur** indecent assault *no pl*

attente [atɑ̃t] *nf* wait; (*espérance*) expectation

attenter [atɑ̃te]: **~ à** *vt* (*liberté*) to violate; **~ à la vie de qn** to make an attempt on sb's life

attentif, -ive [atɑ̃tif, iv] *adj* (*auditeur*) attentive; (*examen*) careful; **~ à** careful to

attention [atɑ̃sjɔ̃] *nf* attention; (*prévenance*) attention, thoughtfulness *no pl*; **à l'~ de** for the attention of; **faire ~ (à)** to be careful (of); **faire ~ (à ce) que** to be *ou* make sure that; **~!** careful!, watch out!; **attentionné, e** *adj* thoughtful, considerate

atténuer [atenɥe] *vt* (*douleur*) to alleviate, ease; (*couleurs*) to soften

atterrer [ateʀe] *vt* to dismay, appal

atterrir [ateʀiʀ] *vi* to land; **atterrissage** *nm* landing

attestation [atɛstasjɔ̃] *nf* certificate

attester [atɛste] *vt* to testify to

attirail [atiʀaj] (*fam*) *nm* gear; (*péj*) paraphernalia

attirant, e [atiʀɑ̃, ɑ̃t] *adj* attractive, appealing

attirer [atiʀe] *vt* to attract; (*appâter*) to lure, entice; **~ qn dans un coin** to draw sb into a corner; **~ l'attention de qn** to attract sb's attention; **~ l'attention de qn sur** to draw sb's attention to; **s'~ des ennuis** to bring trouble upon o.s., get into trouble

attiser [atize] *vt* (*feu*) to poke (up)

attitré, e [atitʀe] *adj* (*habituel*) regular, usual; (*agréé*) accredited

attitude [atityd] *nf* attitude; (*position du corps*) bearing

attouchements [atuʃmɑ̃] *nmpl* (*sexuels*) fondling *sg*

attraction [atʀaksjɔ̃] *nf* (*gén*) attraction; (*de cabaret, cirque*) number

attrait [atʀɛ] *nm* appeal, attraction

attrape-nigaud [atʀapnigo] (*fam*) *nm* con

attraper [atʀape] *vt* (*gén*) to catch; (*habitude, amende*) to get, pick up; (*fam: duper*) to con; **se faire ~** (*fam*) to be told off

attrayant, e [atʀɛjɑ̃, ɑ̃t] *adj* attractive

attribuer [atʀibɥe] *vt* (*prix*) to award; (*rôle, tâche*) to allocate, assign; (*imputer*): **~ qch à** to attribute sth to; **s'~** *vt* (*s'approprier*) to claim for o.s.; **attribut** *nm* attribute

attrister [atʀiste] *vt* to sadden

attroupement [atʀupmɑ̃] *nm* crowd

attrouper [atʀupe]: **s'~** *vi* to gather
au [o] *prép +dét* = **à +le**
aubaine [obɛn] *nf* godsend
aube [ob] *nf* dawn, daybreak; **à l'~** at dawn *ou* daybreak
aubépine [obepin] *nf* hawthorn
auberge [obɛʀʒ] *nf* inn; **~ de jeunesse** youth hostel
aubergine [obɛʀʒin] *nf* aubergine
aubergiste [obɛʀʒist] *nm/f* inn-keeper, hotel-keeper
aucun, e [okœ̃, yn] *dét* no, *tournure négative* +any; (*positif*) any ♦ *pron* none, *tournure négative* +any; any(one); **sans ~ doute** without any doubt; **plus qu'~ autre** more than any other; **~ des deux** neither of the two; **~ d'entre eux** none of them; **aucunement** *adv* in no way, not in the least
audace [odas] *nf* daring, boldness; (*péj*) audacity; **audacieux, -euse** *adj* daring, bold
au-delà [od(ə)la] *adv* beyond ♦ *nm*: **l'~-~** the hereafter; **~-~ de** beyond
au-dessous [odsu] *adv* underneath; below; **~-~ de** under(neath), below; (*limite, somme etc*) below, under; (*dignité, condition*) below
au-dessus [odsy] *adv* above; **~-~ de** above
au-devant [od(ə)vɑ̃]: **~-~ de** *prép*: **aller ~-~ de** (*personne, danger*) to go (out) and meet; (*souhaits de qn*) to anticipate
audience [odjɑ̃s] *nf* audience; (JUR: *séance*) hearing
audimat ® [odimat] *nm* (*taux d'écoute*) ratings *pl*
audio-visuel, le [odjovizɥɛl] *adj* audio-visual
auditeur, -trice [oditœʀ, tʀis] *nm/f* listener
audition [odisjɔ̃] *nf* (*ouïe, écoute*) hearing; (JUR: *de témoins*) examination; (MUS, THÉÂTRE: *épreuve*) audition
auditoire [oditwaʀ] *nm* audience
auge [oʒ] *nf* trough
augmentation [ɔgmɑ̃tasjɔ̃] *nf* increase; **~ (de salaire)** rise (in salary) (BRIT), (pay) raise (US)
augmenter [ɔgmɑ̃te] *vt* (*gén*) to increase; (*salaire, prix*) to increase, raise, put up; (*employé*) to increase the salary of ♦ *vi* to increase
augure [ogyʀ] *nm*: **de bon/mauvais ~** of good/ill omen; **augurer** *vt*: **augurer bien de** to augur well for
aujourd'hui [oʒuʀdɥi] *adv* today
aumône [omon] *nf inv* alms *sg*; **aumônier** *nm* chaplain
auparavant [opaʀavɑ̃] *adv* before(hand)
auprès [opʀɛ]: **~ de** *prép* next to, close to; (*recourir, s'adresser*) to; (*en comparaison de*) compared with
auquel [okɛl] *prép +pron* = **à +lequel**
aurai *etc* [ɔʀe] *vb voir* **avoir**
auréole [ɔʀeɔl] *nf* halo; (*tache*) ring
aurons *etc* [ɔʀɔ̃] *vb voir* **avoir**
aurore [ɔʀɔʀ] *nf* dawn, daybreak
ausculter [ɔskylte] *vt* to sound (the chest of)
aussi [osi] *adv* (*également*) also, too; (*de comparaison*) as ♦ *conj* therefore, consequently; **~ fort que** as strong as; **moi ~** me too
aussitôt [osito] *adv* straight away, immediately; **~ que** as soon as
austère [ostɛʀ] *adj* austere
austral, e [ɔstʀal] *adj* southern
Australie [ostʀali] *nf*: **l'~** Australia; **australien, ne** *adj* Australian ♦ *nm/f*: **Australien, ne** Australian
autant [otɑ̃] *adv* so much; (*comparatif*): **~ (que)** as much (as); (*nombre*) as many (as); **~ (de)** so much (*ou* many); as much (*ou* many); **~ partir** we (*ou* you *etc*) may as well leave; **~ dire que** ... one might as well say that ...; **pour ~** for all that; **d'~ plus/mieux (que)** all the more/the better (since)
autel [otɛl] *nm* altar
auteur [otœʀ] *nm* author
authenticité [otɑ̃tisite] *nf* authenticity
authentique [otɑ̃tik] *adj* authentic,

genuine
auto [oto] *nf* car
auto...: **autobiographie** *nf* autobiography; **autobronzant** *nm* self-tanning cream (*or* lotion *etc*); **autobus** *nm* bus; **autocar** *nm* coach
autochtone [ɔtɔktɔn] *nm/f* native
auto...: **autocollant, e** *adj* self-adhesive; (*enveloppe*) self-seal ♦ *nm* sticker; **auto-couchettes** *adj*: **train auto-couchettes** car sleeper train; **autocuiseur** *nm* pressure cooker; **autodéfense** *nf* self-defence; **autodidacte** *nm/f* self-taught person; **auto-école** *nf* driving school; **autographe** *nm* autograph
automate [ɔtɔmat] *nm* (*machine*) (automatic) machine
automatique [ɔtɔmatik] *adj* automatic ♦ *nm*: **l'~** direct dialling; **automatiquement** *adv* automatically; **automatiser** *vt* to automate
automne [ɔtɔn] *nm* autumn (BRIT), fall (US)
automobile [ɔtɔmɔbil] *adj* motor *cpd* ♦ *nf* (motor) car; **automobiliste** *nm/f* motorist
autonome [ɔtɔnɔm] *adj* autonomous; **autonomie** *nf* autonomy
autopsie [ɔtɔpsi] *nf* post-mortem (examination), autopsy
autoradio [otoʀadjo] *nm* car radio
autorisation [ɔtɔʀizasjɔ̃] *nf* permission, authorization; (*papiers*) permit
autorisé, e [ɔtɔʀize] *adj* (*opinion, sources*) authoritative
autoriser [ɔtɔʀize] *vt* to give permission for, authorize; (*fig*) to allow (of)
autoritaire [ɔtɔʀitɛʀ] *adj* authoritarian
autorité [ɔtɔʀite] *nf* authority; **faire ~** to be authoritative
autoroute [otoʀut] *nf* motorway (BRIT), highway (US)
auto-stop [otostɔp] *nm*: **faire de l'~-~** to hitch-hike; **prendre qn en ~-~** to give sb a lift; **auto-stoppeur, -euse** *nm/f* hitch-hiker

autour [otuʀ] *adv* around; **~ de** around; **tout ~** all around

MOT-CLÉ

autre [otʀ] *adj* **1** (*différent*) other, different; **je préférerais un autre verre** I'd prefer another *ou* a different glass
2 (*supplémentaire*) other; **je voudrais un autre verre d'eau** I'd like another glass of water
3: **autre chose** something else; **autre part** somewhere else; **d'autre part** on the other hand
♦ *pron*: **un autre** another (one); **nous/vous autres** us/you; **d'autres** others; **l'autre** the other (one); **les autres** the others; (*autrui*) others; **l'un et l'autre** both of them; **se détester l'un l'autre/les uns les autres** to hate each other *ou* one another; **d'une semaine à l'autre** from one week to the next; (*incessamment*) any week now; **entre autres** among other things

autrefois [otʀəfwa] *adv* in the past
autrement [otʀəmɑ̃] *adv* differently; (*d'une manière différente*) in another way; (*sinon*) otherwise; **~ dit** in other words
Autriche [otʀiʃ] *nf*: **l'~** Austria; **autrichien, ne** *adj* Austrian ♦ *nm/f*: **Autrichien, ne** Austrian
autruche [otʀyʃ] *nf* ostrich
autrui [otʀɥi] *pron* others
auvent [ovɑ̃] *nm* canopy
aux [o] *prép +dét* = **à +les**
auxiliaire [ɔksiljɛʀ] *adj, nm/f* auxiliary
auxquelles [okɛl] *prép +pron* = **à +lesquelles**
auxquels [okɛl] *prép +pron* = **à +lesquels**
avachi, e [avaʃi] *adj* limp, flabby
aval [aval] *nm*: **en ~** downstream, downriver
avalanche [avalɑ̃ʃ] *nf* avalanche
avaler [avale] *vt* to swallow

avance [avɑ̃s] *nf* (*de troupes etc*) advance; progress; (*d'argent*) advance; (*sur un concurrent*) lead; **~s** *nfpl* (*amoureuses*) advances; **(être) en ~** (to be) early; (*sur un programme*) (to be) ahead of schedule; **à l'~, d'~** in advance

avancé, e [avɑ̃se] *adj* advanced; (*travail*) well on, well under way

avancement [avɑ̃smɑ̃] *nm* (*professionnel*) promotion

avancer [avɑ̃se] *vi* to move forward, advance; (*projet, travail*) to make progress; (*montre, réveil*) to be fast; to gain ♦ *vt* to move forward, advance; (*argent*) to advance; (*montre, pendule*) to put forward; **s'~** *vi* to move forward, advance; (*fig*) to commit o.s.

avant [avɑ̃] *prép, adv* before ♦ *adj inv*: **siège/roue ~** front seat/wheel ♦ *nm* (*d'un véhicule, bâtiment*) front; (*SPORT*: *joueur*) forward; **~ qu'il (ne) fasse/de faire** before he does/doing; **~ tout** (*surtout*) above all; **à l'~** (*dans un véhicule*) in (the) front; **en ~** forward(s); **en ~ de** in front of

avantage [avɑ̃taʒ] *nm* advantage; **~s sociaux** fringe benefits; **avantager** *vt* (*favoriser*) to favour; (*embellir*) to flatter; **avantageux, -euse** *adj* (*prix*) attractive

avant...: **avant-bras** *nm inv* forearm; **avantcoureur** *adj inv*: **signe avant-coureur** advance indication *ou* sign; **avant-dernier, -ière** *adj, nm/f* next to last, last but one; **avant-goût** *nm* foretaste; **avant-guerre** *nm* pre-war years; **avant-hier** *adv* the day before yesterday; **avant-première** *nf* (*de film*) preview; **avant-projet** *nm* (preliminary) draft; **avant-propos** *nm* foreword; **avant-veille** *nf*: **l'avant-veille** two days before

avare [avaʀ] *adj* miserly, avaricious ♦ *nm/f* miser; **~ de** (*compliments etc*) sparing of

avarié, e [avaʀje] *adj* (*aliment*) rotting

avaries [avaʀi] *nfpl* (*NAVIG*) damage *sg*

avec [avɛk] *prép* with; (*à l'égard de*) to(wards), with; **et ~ ça?** (*dans magasin*) anything else?

avenant, e [av(ə)nɑ̃, ɑ̃t] *adj* pleasant; **à l'~** in keeping

avènement [avɛnmɑ̃] *nm* (*d'un changement*) advent, coming

avenir [avniʀ] *nm* future; **à l'~** in future; **politicien d'~** politician with prospects *ou* a future

aventure [avɑ̃tyʀ] *nf* adventure; (*amoureuse*) affair; **aventurer**: **s'aventurer** *vi* to venture; **aventureux, -euse** *adj* adventurous, venturesome; (*projet*) risky, chancy

avenue [avny] *nf* avenue

avérer [aveʀe]: **s'~** *vb +attrib* to prove (to be)

averse [avɛʀs] *nf* shower

averti, e [avɛʀti] *adj* (well-)informed

avertir [avɛʀtiʀ] *vt*: **~ qn (de qch/que)** to warn sb (of sth/that); (*renseigner*) to inform sb (of sth/that); **avertissement** *nm* warning; **avertisseur** *nm* horn, siren

aveu, x [avø] *nm* confession

aveugle [avœgl] *adj* blind ♦ *nm/f* blind man/woman; **aveuglément** *adv* blindly; **aveugler** *vt* to blind

aviateur, -trice [avjatœʀ, tʀis] *nm/f* aviator, pilot

aviation [avjasjɔ̃] *nf* aviation; (*sport*) flying; (*MIL*) air force

avide [avid] *adj* eager; (*péj*) greedy, grasping

avilir [aviliʀ] *vt* to debase

avion [avjɔ̃] *nm* (aero)plane (*BRIT*), (air)plane (*US*); **aller (quelque part) en ~** to go (somewhere) by plane, fly (somewhere); **par ~** by airmail; **~ à réaction** jet (plane)

aviron [aviʀɔ̃] *nm* oar; (*sport*): **l'~** rowing

avis [avi] *nm* opinion; (*notification*) notice; **à mon ~** in my opinion; **changer d'~** to change one's mind; **jusqu'à nouvel ~** until further notice

avisé, e [avize] *adj* sensible, wise; **bien/mal ~ de** well-/ill-advised to

aviser [avize] *vt* (*informer*): **~ qn de/que** to advise *ou* inform sb of/that ♦ *vi* to think about things, assess the situation; **nous ~ons sur place** we'll work something out once we're there; **s'~ de qch/que** to become suddenly aware of sth/that; **s'~ de faire** to take it into one's head to do

avocat, e [avɔka, at] *nm/f* (*JUR*) barrister (*BRIT*), lawyer ♦ *nm* (*CULIN*) avocado (pear); **~ de la défense** counsel for the defence; **~ général** assistant public prosecutor

avoine [avwan] *nf* oats *pl*

MOT-CLÉ

avoir [avwaʀ] *nm* assets *pl*, resources *pl*; (*COMM*) credit

♦ *vt* **1** (*posséder*) to have; **elle a 2 enfants/une belle maison** she has (got) 2 children/a lovely house; **il a les yeux bleus** he has (got) blue eyes

2 (*âge, dimensions*) to be; **il a 3 ans** he is 3 (years old); **le mur a 3 mètres de haut** the wall is 3 metres high; *voir aussi* **faim**; **peur** *etc*

3 (*fam*: *duper*) to do, have; **on vous a eu!** you've been done *ou* had!

4: **en avoir contre qn** to have a grudge against sb; **en avoir assez** to be fed up; **j'en ai pour une demi-heure** it'll take me half an hour

♦ *vb aux* **1** to have; **avoir mangé/dormi** to have eaten/slept

2 (*avoir +à +infinitif*): **avoir à faire qch** to have to do sth; **vous n'avez qu'à lui demander** you only have to ask him

♦ *vb impers* **1**: **il y a** (+ *singulier*) there is; (+ *pluriel*) there are; **qu'y-a-t-il?, qu'est-ce qu'il y a?** what's the matter?, what is it?; **il doit y avoir une explication** there must be an explanation; **il n'y a qu'à ...** we (*ou* you *etc*) will just have to ...

2 (*temporel*): **il y a 10 ans** 10 years ago; **il y a 10 ans/longtemps que je le sais** I've known it for 10 years/a long time; **il y a 10 ans qu'il est arrivé** it's 10 years since he arrived

avoisiner [avwazine] *vt* to be near *ou* close to; (*fig*) to border *ou* verge on

avortement [avɔʀtəmɑ̃] *nm* abortion

avorter [avɔʀte] *vi* (*MÉD*) to have an abortion; (*fig*) to fail

avoué, e [avwe] *adj* avowed ♦ *nm* (*JUR*) ≃ solicitor

avouer [avwe] *vt* (*crime, défaut*) to confess (to); **~ avoir fait/que** to admit *ou* confess to having done/that

avril [avʀil] *nm* April

poisson d'avril

The traditional prank on April 1 in France is to stick a cut-out paper fish, known as a **poisson d'avril**, *to someone's back without being caught.*

axe [aks] *nm* axis; (*de roue etc*) axle; (*fig*) main line; **axer** *vt*: **axer qch sur** to centre sth on

ayons *etc* [ɛjɔ̃] *vb voir* **avoir**

azote [azɔt] *nm* nitrogen

B, b

baba [baba] *nm*: **~ au rhum** rum baba

babines [babin] *nfpl* chops

babiole [babjɔl] *nf* (*bibelot*) trinket; (*vétille*) trifle

bâbord [bɑbɔʀ] *nm*: **à ~** to port, on the port side

baby-foot [babifut] *nm* table football

baby-sitting [babisitiŋ] *nm*: **faire du ~-~** to baby-sit

bac [bak] *abr m* = **baccalauréat** ♦ *nm* (*récipient*) tub

baccalauréat [bakalɔʀea] *nm* high school diploma

baccalauréat

In France the **baccalauréat** *or* **bac** *is the school-leaving certificate taken at a lycée at the age of seventeen or eighteen, enabling entry to university. Different subject combinations are available from the broad subject range studied.*

bâche [baʃ] *nf* tarpaulin
bachelier, -ière [baʃəlje, jɛʀ] *nm/f holder of the baccalauréat*
bâcler [bakle] *vt* to botch (up)
badaud, e [bado, od] *nm/f* idle onlooker, stroller
badigeonner [badiʒɔne] *vt* (*barbouiller*) to daub
badiner [badine] *vi*: **~ avec qch** to treat sth lightly
baffe [baf] (*fam*) *nf* slap, clout
baffle [bafl] *nm* speaker
bafouer [bafwe] *vt* to deride, ridicule
bafouiller [bafuje] *vi, vt* to stammer
bâfrer [bafʀe] (*fam*) *vi* to guzzle
bagages [bagaʒ] *nmpl* luggage *sg*; **~ à main** hand-luggage
bagarre [bagaʀ] *nf* fight, brawl; **bagarrer**: **se bagarrer** *vi* to have a fight *ou* scuffle, fight
bagatelle [bagatɛl] *nf* trifle
bagne [baɲ] *nm* penal colony
bagnole [baɲɔl] (*fam*) *nf* car
bagout [bagu] *nm*: **avoir du ~** to have the gift of the gab
bague [bag] *nf* ring; **~ de fiançailles** engagement ring
baguette [bagɛt] *nf* stick; (*cuisine chinoise*) chopstick; (*de chef d'orchestre*) baton; (*pain*) stick of (French) bread; **~ magique** magic wand
baie [bɛ] *nf* (GÉO) bay; (*fruit*) berry; **~ (vitrée)** picture window
baignade [bɛɲad] *nf* bathing; **"~ interdite"** "no bathing"
baigner [beɲe] *vt* (*bébé*) to bath; **se ~** *vi* to have a swim, go swimming *ou* bathing; **baignoire** *nf* bath(tub)
bail [baj, bo] (*pl* **baux**) *nm* lease
bâillement [bajmɑ̃] *nm* yawn
bâiller [baje] *vi* to yawn; (*être ouvert*) to gape; **bâillonner** *vt* to gag
bain [bɛ̃] *nm* bath; **prendre un ~** to have a bath; **se mettre dans le ~** (*fig*) to get into it *ou* things; **~ de soleil**: **prendre un ~ de soleil** to sunbathe; **~s de mer** sea bathing *sg*;
bain-marie *nm*: **faire chauffer au bain-marie** (*boîte etc*) to immerse in boiling water
baiser [beze] *nm* kiss ♦ *vt* (*main, front*) to kiss; (*fam!*) to screw (*!*)
baisse [bɛs] *nf* fall, drop; **être en ~** to be falling, be declining
baisser [bese] *vt* to lower; (*radio, chauffage*) to turn down ♦ *vi* to fall, drop, go down; (*vue, santé*) to fail, dwindle; **se ~** *vi* to bend down
bal [bal] *nm* dance; (*grande soirée*) ball; **~ costumé** fancy-dress ball
balade [balad] (*fam*) *nf* (*à pied*) walk, stroll; (*en voiture*) drive; **balader** (*fam*): **se balader** *vi* to go for a walk *ou* stroll; to go for a drive; **baladeur** *nm* personal stereo, Walkman ®
balafre [balafʀ] *nf* (*cicatrice*) scar
balai [balɛ] *nm* broom, brush; **balai-brosse** *nm* (long-handled) scrubbing brush
balance [balɑ̃s] *nf* scales *pl*; (*signe*): **la B~** Libra
balancer [balɑ̃se] *vt* to swing; (*fam: lancer*) to fling, chuck; (*: jeter*) to chuck out; **se ~** *vi* to swing, rock; **se ~ de** (*fam*) not to care about; **balançoire** *nf* swing; (*sur pivot*) seesaw
balayer [baleje] *vt* (*feuilles etc*) to sweep up, brush up; (*pièce*) to sweep; (*objections*) to sweep aside; (*suj: radar*) to scan; **balayeur, -euse** *nm/f* roadsweeper
balbutier [balbysje] *vi, vt* to stammer
balcon [balkɔ̃] *nm* balcony; (THÉÂTRE) dress circle

baleine [balɛn] *nf* whale
balise [baliz] *nf* (NAVIG) beacon; (marker) buoy; (AVIAT) runway light, beacon; (AUTO, SKI) sign, marker; **baliser** *vt* to mark out (with lights *etc*)
balivernes [balivɛʀn] *nfpl* nonsense *sg*
ballant, e [balɑ̃, ɑ̃t] *adj* dangling
balle [bal] *nf* (*de fusil*) bullet; (*de sport*) ball; (*fam: franc*) franc
ballerine [bal(ə)ʀin] *nf* (*danseuse*) ballet dancer; (*chaussure*) ballet shoe
ballet [balɛ] *nm* ballet
ballon [balɔ̃] *nm* (*de sport*) ball; (*jouet*, AVIAT) balloon; **~ de football** football
ballot [balo] *nm* bundle; (*péj*) nitwit
ballottage [balɔtaʒ] *nm* (POL) second ballot
ballotter [balɔte] *vt*: **être ballotté** to be thrown about
balnéaire [balneɛʀ] *adj* seaside *cpd*; **station ~** seaside resort
balourd, e [baluʀ, uʀd] *adj* clumsy
balustrade [balystʀad] *nf* railings *pl*, handrail
bambin [bɑ̃bɛ̃] *nm* little child
bambou [bɑ̃bu] *nm* bamboo
ban [bɑ̃] *nm*: **mettre au ~ de** to outlaw from; **~s** *nmpl* (*de mariage*) banns
banal, e [banal] *adj* banal, commonplace; (*péj*) trite; **banalité** *nf* banality
banane [banan] *nf* banana; (*sac*) waist-bag, bum-bag
banc [bɑ̃] *nm* seat, bench; (*de poissons*) shoal; **~ d'essai** (*fig*) testing ground
bancaire [bɑ̃kɛʀ] *adj* banking; (*chèque, carte*) bank *cpd*
bancal, e [bɑ̃kal] *adj* wobbly
bandage [bɑ̃daʒ] *nm* bandage
bande [bɑ̃d] *nf* (*de tissu etc*) strip; (MÉD) bandage; (*motif*) stripe; (*magnétique etc*) tape; (*groupe*) band; (: *péj*) bunch; **faire ~ à part** to keep to o.s.; **~ dessinée** comic strip; **~ sonore** sound track

bande dessinée

The **bande dessinée** *or* **BD** *enjoys a huge following in France amongst adults as well as children. An international show takes place at Angoulême in January every year. Astérix, Tintin, Lucky Luke and Gaston Lagaffe are among the most famous cartoon characters.*

bandeau, x [bɑ̃do] *nm* headband; (*sur les yeux*) blindfold
bander [bɑ̃de] *vt* (*blessure*) to bandage; **~ les yeux à qn** to blindfold sb
banderole [bɑ̃dʀɔl] *nf* banner, streamer
bandit [bɑ̃di] *nm* bandit; **banditisme** *nm* violent crime, armed robberies *pl*
bandoulière [bɑ̃duljɛʀ] *nf*: **en ~** (slung *ou* worn) across the shoulder
banlieue [bɑ̃ljø] *nf* suburbs *pl*; **lignes/quartiers de ~** suburban lines/areas; **trains de ~** commuter trains
banlieusard, e *nm/f* (suburban) commuter
bannière [banjɛʀ] *nf* banner
bannir [baniʀ] *vt* to banish
banque [bɑ̃k] *nf* bank; (*activités*) banking; **~ d'affaires** merchant bank; **banqueroute** *nf* bankruptcy
banquet [bɑ̃kɛ] *nm* dinner; (*d'apparat*) banquet
banquette [bɑ̃kɛt] *nf* seat
banquier [bɑ̃kje] *nm* banker
banquise [bɑ̃kiz] *nf* ice field
baptême [batɛm] *nm* christening; baptism; **~ de l'air** first flight
baptiser [batize] *vt* to baptize, christen
baquet [bakɛ] *nm* tub, bucket
bar [baʀ] *nm* bar
baraque [baʀak] *nf* shed; (*fam*) house; **baraqué, e** (*fam*) *adj* well-built, hefty; **baraquements** *nmpl* (*provisoires*) huts
baratin [baʀatɛ̃] (*fam*) *nm* smooth talk, patter; **baratiner** *vt* to chat up
barbare [baʀbaʀ] *adj* barbaric; **barbarie** *nf* barbarity
barbe [baʀb] *nf* beard; **la ~!** (*fam*)

damn it!; **quelle ~!** (*fam*) what a drag *ou* bore!; **à la ~ de qn** under sb's nose; **~ à papa** candy-floss (*BRIT*), cotton candy (*US*)
barbelé [baʀbəle] *adj, nm*: **(fil de fer) ~** barbed wire *no pl*
barber [baʀbe] (*fam*) *vt* to bore stiff
barbiturique [baʀbityʀik] *nm* barbiturate
barboter [baʀbɔte] *vi* (*enfant*) to paddle
barbouiller [baʀbuje] *vt* to daub; **avoir l'estomac barbouillé** to feel queasy
barbu, e [baʀby] *adj* bearded
barda [baʀda] (*fam*) *nm* kit, gear
barder [baʀde] (*fam*) *vi*: **ça va ~** sparks will fly, things are going to get hot
barème [baʀɛm] *nm* (*SCOL*) scale; (*table de référence*) table
baril [baʀi(l)] *nm* barrel; (*poudre*) keg
bariolé, e [baʀjɔle] *adj* gaudily-coloured
baromètre [baʀɔmɛtʀ] *nm* barometer
baron, ne [baʀɔ̃] *nm/f* baron(ess)
baroque [baʀɔk] *adj* (*ART*) baroque; (*fig*) weird
barque [baʀk] *nf* small boat
barquette [baʀkɛt] *nf* (*pour repas*) tray; (*pour fruits*) punnet
barrage [baʀaʒ] *nm* dam; (*sur route*) roadblock, barricade
barre [baʀ] *nf* bar; (*NAVIG*) helm; (*écrite*) line, stroke
barreau, x [baʀo] *nm* bar; (*JUR*): **le ~** the Bar
barrer [baʀe] *vt* (*route etc*) to block; (*mot*) to cross out; (*chèque*) to cross (*BRIT*); (*NAVIG*) to steer; **se ~** (*fam*) *vi* to clear off
barrette [baʀɛt] *nf* (*pour cheveux*) (hair) slide (*BRIT*) *ou* clip (*US*)
barricader [baʀikade]: **se ~** *vi* to barricade o.s.
barrière [baʀjɛʀ] *nf* fence; (*obstacle*) barrier; (*porte*) gate
barrique [baʀik] *nf* barrel, cask
bar-tabac [baʀtaba] *nm* bar (*which sells tobacco and stamps*)
bas, basse [bɑ, bɑs] *adj* low ♦ *nm* bottom, lower part; (*vêtement*) stocking ♦ *adv* low; (*parler*) softly; **au ~ mot** at the lowest estimate; **en ~** down below; (*d'une liste, d'un mur etc*) at/to the bottom; (*dans une maison*) downstairs; **en ~ de** at the bottom of; **un enfant en ~ âge** a young child; **à ~ ...!** down with ...!; **~ morceaux** *nmpl* (*viande*) cheap cuts
basané, e [bazane] *adj* tanned
bas-côté [bɑkote] *nm* (*de route*) verge (*BRIT*), shoulder (*US*)
bascule [baskyl] *nf*: **(jeu de) ~** seesaw; **(balance à) ~** scales *pl*; **fauteuil à ~** rocking chair
basculer [baskyle] *vi* to fall over, topple (over); (*benne*) to tip up ♦ *vt* (*contenu*) to tip out; (*benne*) to tip up
base [bɑz] *nf* base; (*POL*) rank and file; (*fondement, principe*) basis; **de ~** basic; **à ~ de café** *etc* coffee *etc* -based; **~ de données** database; **baser** *vt* to base; **se baser sur** *vt* (*preuves*) to base one's argument on
bas-fond [bɑfɔ̃] *nm* (*NAVIG*) shallow; **~-~s** *nmpl* (*fig*) dregs
basilic [bazilik] *nm* (*CULIN*) basil
basket [baskɛt] *nm* trainer (*BRIT*), sneaker (*US*); (*aussi*: **~-ball**) basketball
basque [bask] *adj, nm/f* Basque
basse [bɑs] *adj voir* **bas** ♦ *nf* (*MUS*) bass; **basse-cour** *nf* farmyard
bassin [basɛ̃] *nm* (*pièce d'eau*) pond, pool; (*de fontaine, GÉO*) basin; (*ANAT*) pelvis; (*portuaire*) dock
bassine [basin] *nf* (*ustensile*) basin; (*contenu*) bowl(ful)
basson [basɔ̃] *nm* bassoon
bas-ventre [bɑvɑ̃tʀ] *nm* (lower part of the) stomach
bat [ba] *vb voir* **battre**
bataille [bataj] *nf* (*MIL*) battle; (*rixe*) fight; **batailler** *vi* to fight

bâtard, e [bɑtaʀ, aʀd] *nm/f* illegitimate child, bastard (*pej*)
bateau, x [bato] *nm* boat, ship; **bateau-mouche** *nm* passenger pleasure boat (*on the Seine*)
bâti, e [bɑti] *adj*: **bien ~** well-built
batifoler [batifɔle] *vi* to frolic about
bâtiment [bɑtimɑ̃] *nm* building; (*NAVIG*) ship, vessel; (*industrie*) building trade
bâtir [bɑtiʀ] *vt* to build
bâtisse [bɑtis] *nf* building
bâton [bɑtɔ̃] *nm* stick; **à ~s rompus** informally
bats [ba] *vb voir* **battre**
battage [bataʒ] *nm* (*publicité*) (hard) plugging
battant [batɑ̃, ɑ̃t] *nm*: **porte à double ~** double door
battement [batmɑ̃] *nm* (*de cœur*) beat; (*intervalle*) interval; **10 minutes de ~** 10 minutes to spare
batterie [batʀi] *nf* (*MIL, ÉLEC*) battery; (*MUS*) drums *pl*, drum kit; **~ de cuisine** pots and pans *pl*, kitchen utensils *pl*
batteur [batœʀ] *nm* (*MUS*) drummer; (*appareil*) whisk
battre [batʀ] *vt* to beat; (*blé*) to thresh; (*passer au peigne fin*) to scour; (*cartes*) to shuffle ♦ *vi* (*cœur*) to beat; (*volets etc*) to bang, rattle; **se ~** *vi* to fight; **~ la mesure** to beat time; **~ son plein** to be at its height, be going full swing; **~ des mains** to clap one's hands
battue [baty] *nf* (*chasse*) beat; (*policière etc*) search, hunt
baume [bom] *nm* balm
baux [bo] *nmpl de* **bail**
bavard, e [bavaʀ, aʀd] *adj* (very) talkative; gossipy; **bavarder** *vi* to chatter; (*commérer*) to gossip; (*divulguer un secret*) to blab
bave [bav] *nf* dribble; (*de chien etc*) slobber; (*d'escargot*) slime; **baver** *vi* to dribble; (*chien*) to slobber; **en baver** (*fam*) to have a hard time (of it); **baveux, -euse** *adj* (*omelette*) runny; **bavoir** *nm* bib
bavure [bavyʀ] *nf* smudge; (*fig*) hitch; (*policière etc*) blunder
bayer [baje] *vi*: **~ aux corneilles** to stand gaping
bazar [bazaʀ] *nm* general store; (*fam*) jumble; **bazarder** (*fam*) *vt* to chuck out
BCBG *sigle adj* (= *bon chic bon genre*) preppy, smart and trendy
BCE *sigle f* (= *Banque centrale européenne*) ECB
BD *sigle f* = **bande dessinée**
bd *abr* = **boulevard**
béant, e [beɑ̃, ɑ̃t] *adj* gaping
béat, e [bea, at] *adj*: **~ d'admiration** struck dumb with admiration; **béatitude** *nf* bliss
beau (bel), belle [bo, bɛl] (*mpl* **beaux**) *adj* beautiful, lovely; (*homme*) handsome; (*femme*) beautiful ♦ *adv*: **il fait beau** the weather's fine; **un ~jour** one (fine) day; **de plus belle** more than ever, even more; **on a ~essayer** however hard we try; **bel et bien** well and truly

MOT-CLÉ

beaucoup [boku] *adv* **1** a lot; **il boit beaucoup** he drinks a lot; **il ne boit pas beaucoup** he doesn't drink much *ou* a lot
2 (*suivi de plus, trop etc*) much, a lot, far; **il est beaucoup plus grand** he is much *ou* a lot *ou* far taller
3: beaucoup de (*nombre*) many, a lot of; (*quantité*) a lot of; **beaucoup d'étudiants/de touristes** a lot of *ou* many students/tourists; **beaucoup de courage** a lot of courage; **il n'a pas beaucoup d'argent** he hasn't got much *ou* at lot of money
4: de beaucoup by far

beau...: beau-fils *nm* son-in-law; (*remariage*) stepson; **beau-frère** *nm* brother-in-law; **beau-père** *nm* father-

in-law; (*remariage*) stepfather
beauté [bote] *nf* beauty; **de toute ~** beautiful; **finir qch en ~** to complete sth brilliantly
beaux-arts [bozaʀ] *nmpl* fine arts
beaux-parents [boparɑ̃] *nmpl* wife's/husband's family, in-laws
bébé [bebe] *nm* baby
bec [bɛk] *nm* beak, bill; (*de théière*) spout; (*de casserole*) lip; (*fam*) mouth; **~ de gaz** (street) gaslamp
bécane [bekan] (*fam*) *nf* bike
bec-de-lièvre [bɛkdəljɛvʀ] *nm* harelip
bêche [bɛʃ] *nf* spade; **bêcher** *vt* to dig
bécoter [bekɔte]: **se ~** *vi* to smooch
becqueter [bekte] (*fam*) *vt* to eat
bedaine [bədɛn] *nf* paunch
bedonnant, e [bədɔnɑ̃, ɑ̃t] *adj* pot-bellied
bée [be] *adj*: **bouche ~** gaping
beffroi [befʀwa] *nm* belfry
bégayer [begeje] *vt, vi* to stammer
bègue [bɛg] *nm/f*: **être ~** to have a stammer
beige [bɛʒ] *adj* beige
beignet [beɲɛ] *nm* fritter
bel [bɛl] *adj voir* **beau**
bêler [bele] *vi* to bleat
belette [bəlɛt] *nf* weasel
belge [bɛlʒ] *adj* Belgian ♦ *nm/f*: **B~** Belgian
Belgique [bɛlʒik] *nf*: **la ~** Belgium
bélier [belje] *nm* ram; (*signe*): **le B~** Aries
belle [bɛl] *adj voir* **beau** ♦ *nf* (SPORT) decider; **belle-fille** *nf* daughter-in-law; (*remariage*) stepdaughter; **belle-mère** *nf* mother-in-law; stepmother; **belle-sœur** *nf* sister-in-law
belliqueux, -euse [belikø, øz] *adj* aggressive, warlike
belvédère [bɛlvedɛʀ] *nm* panoramic viewpoint (*or small building there*)
bémol [bemɔl] *nm* (MUS) flat
bénédiction [benediksjɔ̃] *nf* blessing
bénéfice [benefis] *nm* (COMM) profit; (*avantage*) benefit; **bénéficier**: **bénéficier de** *vt* to enjoy; (*situation*) to benefit by *ou* from; **bénéfique** *adj* beneficial
bénévole [benevɔl] *adj* voluntary, unpaid
bénin, -igne [benɛ̃, iɲ] *adj* minor, mild; (*tumeur*) benign
bénir [beniʀ] *vt* to bless; **bénit, e** *adj* consecrated; **eau bénite** holy water
benjamin, e [bɛ̃ʒamɛ̃, in] *nm/f* youngest child
benne [bɛn] *nf* skip; (*de téléphérique*) (cable) car; **~ basculante** tipper (BRIT), dump truck (US)
BEP *sigle m* (= *brevet d'études professionnelles*) *technical school certificate*
béquille [bekij] *nf* crutch; (*de bicyclette*) stand
berceau, x [bɛʀso] *nm* cradle, crib
bercer [bɛʀse] *vt* to rock, cradle; (*suj*: *musique etc*) to lull; **~ qn de** (*promesses etc*) to delude sb with; **berceuse** *nf* lullaby
béret (basque) [beʀɛ (bask(ə))] *nm* beret
berge [bɛʀʒ] *nf* bank
berger, -ère [bɛʀʒe, ɛʀ] *nm/f* shepherd(-ess); **~ allemand** alsatian (BRIT), German shepherd
berlingot [bɛʀlɛ̃go] *nm* (*bonbon*) boiled sweet, humbug (BRIT)
berlue [bɛʀly] *nf*: **j'ai la ~** I must be seeing things
berner [bɛʀne] *vt* to fool
besogne [bəzɔɲ] *nf* work *no pl*, job
besoin [bəzwɛ̃] *nm* need; **avoir ~ de qch/faire qch** to need sth/to do sth; **au ~** if need be; **le ~** (*pauvreté*) need, want; **être dans le ~** to be in need *ou* want; **faire ses ~s** to relieve o.s.
bestiaux [bɛstjo] *nmpl* cattle
bestiole [bɛstjɔl] *nf* (tiny) creature
bétail [betaj] *nm* livestock, cattle *pl*
bête [bɛt] *nf* animal; (*bestiole*) insect, creature ♦ *adj* stupid, silly; **il cherche la petite ~** he's being pernickety *ou* overfussy; **~ noire** pet hate

bêtement [bɛtmɑ̃] *adv* stupidly
bêtise [betiz] *nf* stupidity; (*action*) stupid thing (to say *ou* do)
béton [betɔ̃] *nm* concrete; **(en) ~** (*alibi, argument*) cast iron; **~ armé** reinforced concrete; **bétonnière** *nf* cement mixer
betterave [bɛtʀav] *nf* beetroot (*BRIT*), beet (*US*); **~ sucrière** sugar beet
beugler [bøgle] *vi* to low; (*radio etc*) to blare ♦ *vt* (*chanson*) to bawl out
Beur [bœʀ] *nm/f person of North African origin living in France*
beurre [bœʀ] *nm* butter; **beurrer** *vt* to butter; **beurrier** *nm* butter dish
beuverie [bøvʀi] *nf* drinking session
bévue [bevy] *nf* blunder
Beyrouth [beʀut] *n* Beirut
bi... [bi] *préfixe* bi..., two-
biais [bjɛ] *nm* (*moyen*) device, expedient; (*aspect*) angle; **en ~, de ~** (*obliquement*) at an angle; **par le ~ de** by means of; **biaiser** *vi* (*fig*) to sidestep the issue
bibelot [biblo] *nm* trinket, curio
biberon [bibʀɔ̃] *nm* (feeding) bottle; **nourrir au ~** to bottle-feed
bible [bibl] *nf* bible
biblio... [bibl] *préfixe*: **bibliobus** *nm* mobile library van; **bibliographie** *nf* bibliography; **bibliothécaire** *nm/f* librarian; **bibliothèque** *nf* library; (*meuble*) bookcase
bic ® [bik] *nm* Biro ®
bicarbonate [bikaʀbɔnat] *nm*: **~ (de soude)** bicarbonate of soda
biceps [bisɛps] *nm* biceps
biche [biʃ] *nf* doe
bichonner [biʃɔne] *vt* to pamper
bicolore [bikɔlɔʀ] *adj* two-coloured
bicoque [bikɔk] (*péj*) *nf* shack
bicyclette [bisiklɛt] *nf* bicycle
bide [bid] (*fam*) *nm* (*ventre*) belly; (*THÉÂTRE*) flop
bidet [bidɛ] *nm* bidet
bidon [bidɔ̃] *nm* can ♦ *adj inv* (*fam*) phoney
bidonville [bidɔ̃vil] *nm* shanty town
bidule [bidyl] (*fam*) *nm* thingumajig

MOT-CLÉ

bien [bjɛ̃] *nm* **1** (*avantage, profit*): **faire du bien à qn** to do sb good; **dire du bien de** to speak well of; **c'est pour son bien** it's for his own good
2 (*possession, patrimoine*) possession, property; **son bien le plus précieux** his most treasured possession; **avoir du bien** to have property; **biens (de consommation** *etc*) (consumer *etc*) goods
3 (*moral*): **le bien** good; **distinguer le bien du mal** to tell good from evil
♦ *adv* **1** (*de façon satisfaisante*) well; **elle travaille/mange bien** she works/eats well; **croyant bien faire, je/il ...** thinking I/he was doing the right thing, I/he ...; **c'est bien fait!** it serves him (*ou* her *etc*) right!
2 (*valeur intensive*) quite; **bien jeune** quite young; **bien assez** quite enough; **bien mieux** (very) much better; **j'espère bien y aller** I do hope to go; **je veux bien le faire** (*concession*) I'm quite willing to do it; **il faut bien le faire** it has to be done
3: bien du temps/des gens quite a time/a number of people
♦ *adj inv* **1** (*en bonne forme, à l'aise*): **je me sens bien** I feel fine; **je ne me sens pas bien** I don't feel well; **on est bien dans ce fauteuil** this chair is very comfortable
2 (*joli, beau*) good-looking; **tu es bien dans cette robe** you look good in that dress
3 (*satisfaisant*) good; **elle est bien, cette maison/secrétaire** it's a good house/she's a good secretary
4 (*moralement*) right; (: *personne*) good, nice; (*respectable*) respectable; **ce n'est pas bien de ...** it's not right to ...; **elle est bien, cette femme** she's a nice woman, she's a good sort; **des gens biens** respectable people

5 (*en bons termes*): **être bien avec qn** to be on good terms with sb

♦ *préfixe*: **bien-aimé** *adj, nm/f* beloved; **bien-être** *nm* well-being; **bienfaisance** *nf* charity; **bienfaisant, e** *adj* (*chose*) beneficial; **bienfait** *nm* act of generosity, benefaction; (*de la science etc*) benefit; **bienfaiteur, -trice** *nm/f* benefactor/benefactress; **bien-fondé** *nm* soundness; **bien-fonds** *nm* property; **bienheureux, -euse** *adj* happy; (REL) blessed, blest; **bien que** *conj* (al)though; **bien sûr** *adv* certainly

bienséant, e [bjɛ̃seɑ̃, ɑ̃t] *adj* seemly

bientôt [bjɛ̃to] *adv* soon; **à ~** see you soon

bienveillant, e [bjɛ̃vɛjɑ̃, ɑ̃t] *adj* kindly

bienvenu, e [bjɛ̃vny] *adj* welcome; **bienvenue** *nf*: **souhaiter la bienvenue à** to welcome; **bienvenue à** welcome to

bière [bjɛʀ] *nf* (*boisson*) beer; (*cercueil*) bier; **~ (à la) pression** draught beer; **~ blonde** lager; **~ brune** brown ale

biffer [bife] *vt* to cross out

bifteck [biftɛk] *nm* steak

bifurquer [bifyʀke] *vi* (*route*) to fork; (*véhicule*) to turn off

bigarré, e [bigaʀe] *adj* multicoloured; (*disparate*) motley

bigorneau, x [bigɔʀno] *nm* winkle

bigot, e [bigo, ɔt] (*péj*) *adj* bigoted

bigoudi [bigudi] *nm* curler

bijou, x [biʒu] *nm* jewel; **bijouterie** *nf* jeweller's (shop); **bijoutier, -ière** *nm/f* jeweller

bikini [bikini] *nm* bikini

bilan [bilɑ̃] *nm* (*fig*) (net) outcome; (*: de victimes*) toll; (COMM) balance sheet(s); **un ~ de santé** a (medical) checkup; **faire le ~ de** to assess, review; **déposer son ~** to file a bankruptcy statement

bile [bil] *nf* bile; **se faire de la ~** (*fam*) to worry o.s. sick

bilieux, -euse [biljø, øz] *adj* bilious; (*fig: colérique*) testy

bilingue [bilɛ̃g] *adj* bilingual

billard [bijaʀ] *nm* (*jeu*) billiards *sg*; (*table*) billiard table; **~ américain** pool

bille [bij] *nf* (*gén*) ball; (*du jeu de ~s*) marble

billet [bijɛ] *nm* (*aussi:* **~ de banque**) (bank)note; (*de cinéma, de bus etc*) ticket; (*courte lettre*) note; **~ Bige** *cheap rail ticket for under-26s*; **billetterie** *nf* ticket office; (*distributeur*) ticket machine; (BANQUE) cash dispenser

billion [biljɔ̃] *nm* billion (BRIT), trillion (US)

billot [bijo] *nm* block

bimensuel, le [bimɑ̃sɥɛl] *adj* bimonthly

binette [binɛt] *nf* hoe

bio... [bjɔ] *préfixe* bio...; **biochimie** *nf* biochemistry; **biodiversité** *nf* biodiversity; **bioéthique** *nf* bioethics *sg*; **biographie** *nf* biography; **biologie** *nf* biology; **biologique** *adj* biological; (*produits, aliments*) organic; **biologiste** *nm/f* biologist; **bioterroriste** *nm/f* bioterrorist

Birmanie [biʀmani] *nf* Burma

bis [bis] *adv*: **12 ~** 12a *ou* A ♦ *excl, nm* encore

bisannuel, le [bizanɥɛl] *adj* biennial

biscornu, e [biskɔʀny] *adj* twisted

biscotte [biskɔt] *nf* toasted bread (*sold in packets*)

biscuit [biskɥi] *nm* biscuit; **~ de savoie** sponge cake

bise [biz] *nf* (*fam: baiser*) kiss; (*vent*) North wind; **grosses ~s (de)** (*sur lettre*) love and kisses (from)

bisou [bizu] (*fam*) *nm* kiss

bissextile [bisɛkstil] *adj*: **année ~** leap year

bistro(t) [bistʀo] *nm* bistro, café

bitume [bitym] *nm* asphalt

bizarre [bizaʀ] *adj* strange, odd

blafard, e [blafaʀ, aʀd] *adj* wan

blague [blag] *nf* (*propos*) joke; (*farce*)

trick; **sans ~!** no kidding!; **blaguer** *vi* to joke

blaireau, x [blɛʀo] *nm* (ZOOL) badger; (*brosse*) shaving brush

blairer [bleʀe] (*fam*) *vt*: **je ne peux pas le ~** I can't bear *ou* stand him

blâme [blɑm] *nm* blame; (*sanction*) reprimand; **blâmer** *vt* to blame

blanc, blanche [blɑ̃, blɑ̃ʃ] *adj* white; (*non imprimé*) blank ♦ *nm/f* white, white man(-woman) ♦ *nm* (*couleur*) white; (*espace non écrit*) blank; (*aussi:* **~ d'œuf**) (egg-)white; (*aussi:* **~ de poulet**) breast, white meat; (*aussi:* **vin ~**) white wine; **~ cassé** off-white; **chèque en ~** blank cheque; **à ~** (*chauffer*) white-hot; (*tirer, charger*) with blanks; **blanche** *nf* (MUS) minim (BRIT), half-note (US); **blancheur** *nf* whiteness

blanchir [blɑ̃ʃiʀ] *vt* (*gén*) to whiten; (*linge*) to launder; (CULIN) to blanch; (*fig: disculper*) to clear ♦ *vi* to grow white; (*cheveux*) to go white; **blanchisserie** *nf* laundry

blason [blɑzɔ̃] *nm* coat of arms

blasphème [blasfɛm] *nm* blasphemy

blazer [blazɛʀ] *nm* blazer

blé [ble] *nm* wheat; **~ noir** buckwheat

bled [blɛd] (*pej*) *nm* hole

blême [blɛm] *adj* pale

blessant, e [blesɑ̃, ɑ̃t] *adj* (*offensant*) hurtful

blessé, e [blese] *adj* injured ♦ *nm/f* injured person, casualty

blesser [blese] *vt* to injure; (*délibérément*) to wound; (*offenser*) to hurt; **se ~** to injure o.s.; **se ~ au pied** to injure one's foot; **blessure** *nf* (*accidentelle*) injury; (*intentionnelle*) wound

bleu, e [blø] *adj* blue; (*bifteck*) very rare ♦ *nm* (*couleur*) blue; (*contusion*) bruise; (*vêtement: aussi:* **~s**) overalls *pl*; **~ marine** navy blue; **bleuet** *nm* cornflower; **bleuté, e** *adj* blue-shaded

blinder [blɛ̃de] *vt* to armour; (*fig*) to harden

bloc [blɔk] *nm* (*de pierre etc*) block; (*de papier à lettres*) pad; (*ensemble*) group, block; **serré à ~** tightened right down; **en ~** as a whole; **~ opératoire** operating *ou* theatre block; **~ sanitaire** toilet block; **blocage** *nm* (*des prix*) freezing; (PSYCH) hang-up; **bloc-notes** *nm* note pad

blocus [blɔkys] *nm* blockade

blond, e [blɔ̃, blɔ̃d] *adj* fair, blond; (*sable, blés*) golden; **~ cendré** ash blond; **blonde** *nf* (*femme*) blonde; (*bière*) lager; (*cigarette*) Virginia cigarette

bloquer [blɔke] *vt* (*passage*) to block; (*pièce mobile*) to jam; (*crédits, compte*) to freeze; **se ~** to jam; (PSYCH) to have a mental block

blottir [blɔtiʀ]: **se ~** *vi* to huddle up

blouse [bluz] *nf* overall

blouson [bluzɔ̃] *nm* blouson jacket; **~ noir** (*fig*) ≃ rocker

blue-jean [bludʒin] *nm* (pair of) jeans

bluff [blœf] *nm* bluff; **bluffer** *vi* to bluff

bobard [bɔbaʀ] (*fam*) *nm* tall story

bobine [bɔbin] *nf* reel; (ÉLEC) coil

bocal, -aux [bɔkal, o] *nm* jar

bock [bɔk] *nm* glass of beer

body [bɔdi] *nm* body(suit); (SPORT) leotard

bœuf [bœf] *nm* ox; (CULIN) beef

bof! [bɔf] (*fam*) *excl* don't care!; (*pas terrible*) nothing special

bogue [bɔg] *nm*: **le ~ de l'an 2000** the millennium bug

bohème [bɔɛm] *adj* happy-go-lucky, unconventional; **bohémien, ne** *nm/f* gipsy

boire [bwaʀ] *vt* to drink; (*s'imprégner de*) to soak up; **~ un coup** (*fam*) to have a drink

bois [bwɑ] *nm* wood; **de ~, en ~** wooden; **boisé, e** *adj* woody, wooded

boisson [bwasɔ̃] *nf* drink

boîte [bwat] *nf* box; (*fam: entreprise*) firm; **aliments en ~** canned *ou* tinned (BRIT) foods; **~ aux lettres** letter box; **~**

d'allumettes box of matches; (*vide*) matchbox; ~ **(de conserve)** can *ou* tin (*BRIT*) (of food); ~ **de nuit** night club; ~ **de vitesses** gear box; ~ **postale** PO Box; ~ **vocale** (*TEL*) voice mail

boiter [bwate] *vi* to limp; (*fig*: *raisonnement*) to be shaky

boîtier [bwatje] *nm* case

boive *etc* [bwav] *vb voir* **boire**

bol [bɔl] *nm* bowl; **un ~ d'air** a breath of fresh air; **j'en ai ras le ~** (*fam*) I'm fed up with this; **avoir du ~** (*fam*) to be lucky

bolide [bɔlid] *nm* racing car; **comme un ~** at top speed, like a rocket

bombardement [bɔ̃baʀdəmɑ̃] *nm* bombing

bombarder [bɔ̃baʀde] *vt* to bomb; ~ **qn de** (*cailloux, lettres*) to bombard sb with

bombe [bɔ̃b] *nf* bomb; (*atomiseur*) (aerosol) spray; **bombé, e** *adj* (*forme*) rounded; **bomber** *vt*: **bomber le torse** to swell out one's chest

MOT-CLÉ

bon, bonne [bɔ̃, bɔn] *adj* **1** (*agréable, satisfaisant*) good; **un bon repas/restaurant** a good meal/restaurant; **être bon en maths** to be good at maths

2 (*charitable*): **être bon (envers)** to be good (to)

3 (*correct*) right; **le bon numéro/moment** the right number/moment

4 (*souhaits*): **bon anniversaire** happy birthday; **bon voyage** have a good trip; **bonne chance** good luck; **bonne année** happy New Year; **bonne nuit** good night

5 (*approprié, apte*): **bon à/pour** fit to/for

6: bon enfant *adj inv* accommodating, easy-going; **bonne femme** (*péj*) woman; **de bonne heure** early; **bon marché** *adj inv* cheap ♦ *adv* cheap; **bon mot** witticism; **bon sens** common sense; **bon vivant** jovial chap; **bonnes œuvres** charitable works, charities

♦ *nm* **1** (*billet*) voucher; (*aussi*: **bon cadeau**) gift voucher; **bon d'essence** petrol coupon; **bon du Trésor** Treasury bond

2: avoir du bon to have its good points; **pour de bon** for good

♦ *adv*: **il fait bon** it's *ou* the weather is fine; **sentir bon** to smell good; **tenir bon** to stand firm

♦ *excl* good!; **ah bon?** really?; *voir aussi* **bonne**

bonbon [bɔ̃bɔ̃] *nm* (boiled) sweet

bonbonne [bɔ̃bɔn] *nf* demijohn

bond [bɔ̃] *nm* leap; **faire un ~** to leap in the air

bondé, e [bɔ̃de] *adj* packed (full)

bondir [bɔ̃diʀ] *vi* to leap

bonheur [bɔnœʀ] *nm* happiness; **porter ~ (à qn)** to bring (sb) luck; **au petit ~** haphazardly; **par ~** fortunately

bonhomie [bɔnɔmi] *nf* goodnaturedness

bonhomme [bɔnɔm] (*pl* **bonshommes**) *nm* fellow; ~ **de neige** snowman

bonifier [bɔnifje] *vt* to improve

boniment [bɔnimɑ̃] *nm* patter *no pl*

bonjour [bɔ̃ʒuʀ] *excl, nm* hello; (*selon l'heure*) good morning/afternoon; **c'est simple comme ~!** it's easy as pie!

bonne [bɔn] *adj voir* **bon** ♦ *nf* (*domestique*) maid; **bonnement** *adv*: **tout bonnement** quite simply

bonnet [bɔnɛ] *nm* hat; (*de soutien-gorge*) cup; ~ **de bain** bathing cap

bonshommes [bɔ̃zɔm] *nmpl de* **bonhomme**

bonsoir [bɔ̃swaʀ] *excl* good evening

bonté [bɔ̃te] *nf* kindness *no pl*

bonus [bɔnys] *nm* no-claims bonus

bord [bɔʀ] *nm* (*de table, verre, falaise*) edge; (*de rivière, lac*) bank; (*de route*) side; **(monter) à ~** (to go) on board;

jeter par-dessus ~ to throw overboard; **le commandant de/les hommes du ~** the ship's master/crew; **au ~ de la mer** at the seaside; **être au ~ des larmes** to be on the verge of tears
bordeaux [bɔʀdo] *nm* Bordeaux (wine) ♦ *adj inv* maroon
bordel [bɔʀdɛl] *nm* brothel; (*fam!*) bloody mess (*!*)
bordelais, e [bɔʀdəlɛ, ɛz] *adj* of *ou* from Bordeaux
border [bɔʀde] *vt* (*être le long de*) to line; (*qn dans son lit*) to tuck up; (*garnir*): **~ qch de** to edge sth with
bordereau, x [bɔʀdəʀo] *nm* (*formulaire*) slip
bordure [bɔʀdyʀ] *nf* border; **en ~ de** on the edge of
borgne [bɔʀɲ] *adj* one-eyed
borne [bɔʀn] *nf* boundary stone; (*aussi*: **~ kilométrique**) kilometre-marker; ≈ milestone; **~s** *nfpl* (*fig*) limits; **dépasser les ~s** to go too far
borné, e [bɔʀne] *adj* (*personne*) narrow-minded
borner [bɔʀne] *vt*: **se ~ à faire** (*se contenter de*) to content o.s. with doing; (*se limiter à*) to limit o.s. to doing
bosquet [bɔskɛ] *nm* grove
bosse [bɔs] *nf* (*de terrain etc*) bump; (*enflure*) lump; (*du bossu, du chameau*) hump; **avoir la ~ des maths** *etc* (*fam*) to have a gift for maths *etc*; **il a roulé sa ~** (*fam*) he's been around
bosser [bɔse] (*fam*) *vi* (*travailler*) to work; (*travailler dur*) to slave (away)
bossu, e [bɔsy] *nm/f* hunchback
botanique [bɔtanik] *nf* botany ♦ *adj* botanic(al)
botte [bɔt] *nf* (*soulier*) (high) boot; (*gerbe*): **~ de paille** bundle of straw; **~ de radis** bunch of radishes; **~s de caoutchouc** wellington boots; **botter** *vt*: **ça me botte** (*fam*) I fancy that
bottin [bɔtɛ̃] *nm* directory
bottine [bɔtin] *nf* ankle boot
bouc [buk] *nm* goat; (*barbe*) goatee; **~ émissaire** scapegoat
boucan [bukɑ̃] (*fam*) *nm* din, racket
bouche [buʃ] *nf* mouth; **rester ~ bée** to stand open-mouthed; **le ~ à ~** the kiss of life; **~ d'égout** manhole; **~ d'incendie** fire hydrant; **~ de métro** métro entrance
bouché, e [buʃe] *adj* (*temps, ciel*) overcast; **c'est ~** there's no future in it
bouchée [buʃe] *nf* mouthful; **~s à la reine** chicken vol-au-vents
boucher, -ère [buʃe] *nm/f* butcher ♦ *vt* (*trou*) to fill up; (*obstruer*) to block (up); **se ~** *vi* (*tuyau etc*) to block up, get blocked up; **j'ai le nez bouché** my nose is blocked; **se ~ le nez** to hold one's nose; **boucherie** *nf* butcher's (shop); (*fig*) slaughter
bouche-trou [buʃtʀu] *nm* (*fig*) stopgap
bouchon [buʃɔ̃] *nm* stopper; (*de tube*) top; (*en liège*) cork; (*fig*: *embouteillage*) holdup; (PÊCHE) float
boucle [bukl] *nf* (*forme, figure*) loop; (*objet*) buckle; **~ (de cheveux)** curl; **~ d'oreille** earring
bouclé, e [bukle] *adj* (*cheveux*) curly
boucler [bukle] *vt* (*fermer*: *ceinture etc*) to fasten; (*terminer*) to finish off; (*fam*: *enfermer*) to shut away; (*quartier*) to seal off ♦ *vi* to curl
bouclier [buklije] *nm* shield
bouddhiste [budist] *nm/f* Buddhist
bouder [bude] *vi* to sulk ♦ *vt* to stay away from
boudin [budɛ̃] *nm*: **~ (noir)** black pudding; **~ blanc** white pudding
boue [bu] *nf* mud
bouée [bwe] *nf* buoy; **~ (de sauvetage)** lifebuoy
boueux, -euse [bwø, øz] *adj* muddy
bouffe [buf] (*fam*) *nf* grub (*fam*), food
bouffée [bufe] *nf* (*de cigarette*) puff; **une ~ d'air pur** a breath of fresh air
bouffer [bufe] (*fam*) *vi* to eat
bouffi, e [bufi] *adj* swollen

bougeoir [buʒwaʀ] *nm* candlestick
bougeotte [buʒɔt] *nf*: **avoir la ~** (*fam*) to have the fidgets
bouger [buʒe] *vi* to move; (*dent etc*) to be loose; (*s'activer*) to get moving ♦ *vt* to move; **les prix/les couleurs n'ont pas bougé** prices/colours haven't changed
bougie [buʒi] *nf* candle; (AUTO) spark(ing) plug
bougon, ne [bugɔ̃, ɔn] *adj* grumpy
bougonner [bugɔne] *vi, vt* to grumble
bouillabaisse [bujabɛs] *nf type of fish soup*
bouillant, e [bujɑ̃, ɑ̃t] *adj* (*qui bout*) boiling; (*très chaud*) boiling (hot)
bouillie [buji] *nf* (*de bébé*) cereal; **en ~** (*fig*) crushed
bouillir [bujiʀ] *vi, vt* to boil; **~ d'impatience** to seethe with impatience
bouilloire [bujwaʀ] *nf* kettle
bouillon [bujɔ̃] *nm* (CULIN) stock *no pl*; **bouillonner** *vi* to bubble; (*fig: idées*) to bubble up
bouillotte [bujɔt] *nf* hot-water bottle
boulanger, -ère [bulɑ̃ʒe, ɛʀ] *nm/f* baker; **boulangerie** *nf* bakery; **boulangerie-pâtisserie** *nf* baker's and confectioner's (shop)
boule [bul] *nf* (*gén*) ball; **~s** *nfpl* (*jeu*) bowls; **se mettre en ~** (*fig: fam*) to fly off the handle, to blow one's top; **jouer aux ~s** to play bowls; **~ de neige** snowball
bouleau, x [bulo] *nm* (silver) birch
bouledogue [buldɔg] *nm* bulldog
boulet [bulɛ] *nm* (*aussi:* **~ de canon**) cannonball
boulette [bulɛt] *nf* (*de viande*) meatball
boulevard [bulvaʀ] *nm* boulevard
bouleversant, e [bulvɛʀsɑ̃, ɑ̃t] *adj* (*scène, récit*) deeply moving
bouleversement [bulvɛʀsəmɑ̃] *nm* upheaval
bouleverser [bulvɛʀse] *vt* (*émouvoir*) to overwhelm; (*causer du chagrin*) to distress; (*pays, vie*) to disrupt; (*papiers, objets*) to turn upside down
boulon [bulɔ̃] *nm* bolt
boulot, te [bulo, ɔt] *adj* plump, tubby ♦ *nm* (*fam: travail*) work
boum [bum] *nm* bang ♦ *nf* (*fam*) party
bouquet [bukɛ] *nm* (*de fleurs*) bunch (of flowers), bouquet; (*de persil etc*) bunch; **c'est le ~!** (*fam*) that takes the biscuit!
bouquin [bukɛ̃] (*fam*) *nm* book; **bouquiner** (*fam*) *vi* to read; **bouquiniste** *nm/f* bookseller
bourbeux, -euse [buʀbø, øz] *adj* muddy
bourbier [buʀbje] *nm* (quag)mire
bourde [buʀd] (*fam*) *nf* (*erreur*) howler; (*gaffe*) blunder
bourdon [buʀdɔ̃] *nm* bumblebee; **bourdonner** *vi* to buzz
bourg [buʀ] *nm* small market town
bourgeois, e [buʀʒwa, waz] (*péj*) *adj* ≃ (upper) middle class; **bourgeoisie** *nf* ≃ upper middle classes *pl*
bourgeon [buʀʒɔ̃] *nm* bud
Bourgogne [buʀgɔɲ] *nf*: **la ~** Burgundy ♦ *nm*: **b~** burgundy (wine)
bourguignon, ne [buʀgiɲɔ̃, ɔn] *adj* of *ou* from Burgundy, Burgundian
bourlinguer [buʀlɛ̃ge] (*fam*) *vi* to knock about a lot, get around a lot
bourrade [buʀad] *nf* shove, thump
bourrage [buʀaʒ] *nm*: **~ de crâne** brainwashing; (SCOL) cramming
bourrasque [buʀask] *nf* squall
bourratif, -ive [buʀatif, iv] (*fam*) *adj* filling, stodgy (*pej*)
bourré, e [buʀe] *adj* (*fam: ivre*) plastered, tanked up (BRIT); (*rempli*): **~ de** crammed full of
bourreau, x [buʀo] *nm* executioner; (*fig*) torturer; **~ de travail** workaholic
bourrelet [buʀlɛ] *nm* fold *ou* roll (of flesh)
bourrer [buʀe] *vt* (*pipe*) to fill; (*poêle*) to pack; (*valise*) to cram (full)
bourrique [buʀik] *nf* (*âne*) ass
bourru, e [buʀy] *adj* surly, gruff

bourse [buʀs] *nf* (*subvention*) grant; (*porte-monnaie*) purse; **la B~** the Stock Exchange

boursier, -ière [buʀsje, jɛʀ] *nm/f* (*étudiant*) grant holder

boursoufler [buʀsufle]: **se ~** *vi* to swell (up)

bous [bu] *vb voir* **bouillir**

bousculade [buskylad] *nf* (*hâte*) rush; (*cohue*) crush; **bousculer** *vt* (*heurter*) to knock into; (*fig*) to push, rush

bouse [buz] *nf* dung *no pl*

bousiller [buzije] (*fam*) *vt* (*appareil*) to wreck

boussole [busɔl] *nf* compass

bout [bu] *vb voir* **bouillir** ♦ *nm* bit; (*d'un bâton etc*) tip; (*d'une ficelle, table, rue, période*) end; **au ~ de** at the end of, after; **pousser qn à ~** to push sb to the limit; **venir à ~ de** to manage to finish

boutade [butad] *nf* quip, sally

boute-en-train [butɑ̃tʀɛ̃] *nm inv* (*fig*) live wire

bouteille [butɛj] *nf* bottle; (*de gaz butane*) cylinder

boutique [butik] *nf* shop

bouton [butɔ̃] *nm* button; (*sur la peau*) spot; (*BOT*) bud; **~ d'or** buttercup; **boutonner** *vt* to button up; **boutonnière** *nf* buttonhole; **bouton-pression** *nm* press stud

bouture [butyʀ] *nf* cutting

bovins [bɔvɛ̃] *nmpl* cattle *pl*

bowling [buliŋ] *nm* (tenpin) bowling; (*salle*) bowling alley

box [bɔks] *nm* (*d'écurie*) loose-box; (*JUR*): **~ des accusés** dock

boxe [bɔks] *nf* boxing; **boxeur** *nm* boxer

boyaux [bwajo] *nmpl* (*viscères*) entrails, guts

BP *abr* = **boîte postale**

bracelet [bʀaslɛ] *nm* bracelet

braconnier [bʀakɔnje] *nm* poacher

brader [bʀade] *vt* to sell off; **braderie** *nf* cut-price shop/stall

braguette [bʀagɛt] *nf* fly *ou* flies *pl* (*BRIT*), zipper (*US*)

brailler [bʀɑje] *vi* to bawl, yell

braire [bʀɛʀ] *vi* to bray

braise [bʀɛz] *nf* embers *pl*

brancard [bʀɑ̃kaʀ] *nm* (*civière*) stretcher; **brancardier** *nm* stretcher-bearer

branchages [bʀɑ̃ʃaʒ] *nmpl* boughs

branche [bʀɑ̃ʃ] *nf* branch

branché, e [bʀɑ̃ʃe] (*fam*) *adj* trendy

brancher [bʀɑ̃ʃe] *vt* to connect (up); (*en mettant la prise*) to plug in

brandir [bʀɑ̃diʀ] *vt* to brandish

branle [bʀɑ̃l] *nm*: **mettre en ~** to set in motion; **branle-bas** *nm inv* commotion

braquer [bʀake] *vi* (*AUTO*) to turn (the wheel) ♦ *vt* (*revolver etc*): **~ qch sur** to aim sth at, point sth at; (*mettre en colère*): **~ qn** to put sb's back up

bras [bʀɑ] *nm* arm; **~ dessus, ~ dessous** arm in arm; **se retrouver avec qch sur les ~** (*fam*) to be landed with sth; **~ droit** (*fig*) right hand man; **~ de fer** arm wrestling

brasier [bʀɑzje] *nm* blaze, inferno

bras-le-corps [bʀalkɔʀ] *adv*: **à ~-~-~** (a)round the waist

brassard [bʀasaʀ] *nm* armband

brasse [bʀas] *nf* (*nage*) breast-stroke

brassée [bʀase] *nf* armful

brasser [bʀase] *vt* to mix; **~ l'argent/les affaires** to handle a lot of money/business

brasserie [bʀasʀi] *nf* (*restaurant*) café-restaurant; (*usine*) brewery

brave [bʀav] *adj* (*courageux*) brave; (*bon, gentil*) good, kind

braver [bʀave] *vt* to defy

bravo [bʀavo] *excl* bravo ♦ *nm* cheer

bravoure [bʀavuʀ] *nf* bravery

break [bʀɛk] *nm* (*AUTO*) estate car

brebis [bʀəbi] *nf* ewe; **~ galeuse** black sheep

brèche [bʀɛʃ] *nf* breach, gap; **être toujours sur la ~** (*fig*) to be always on the go

bredouille [bʀəduj] *adj* empty-handed

bredouiller [bʀəduje] *vi, vt* to mumble, stammer

bref, brève [bʀɛf, ɛv] *adj* short, brief ♦ *adv* in short; **d'un ton ~** sharply, curtly; **en ~** in short, in brief

Brésil [bʀezil] *nm* Brazil; **brésilien, -ne** *adj* Brazilian ♦ *nm/f*: **Brésilien, ne** Brazilian

Bretagne [bʀətaɲ] *nf* Brittany

bretelle [bʀətɛl] *nf* (*de vêtement, de sac*) strap; (*d'autoroute*) slip road (*BRIT*), entrance/exit ramp (*US*); **~s** *nfpl* (*pour pantalon*) braces (*BRIT*), suspenders (*US*)

breton, ne [bʀətɔ̃, ɔn] *adj* Breton ♦ *nm/f*: **B~, ne** Breton

breuvage [bʀœvaʒ] *nm* beverage, drink

brève [bʀɛv] *adj voir* **bref**

brevet [bʀəvɛ] *nm* diploma, certificate; **~ (d'invention)** patent; **breveté, e** *adj* patented

bribes [bʀib] *nfpl* (*de conversation*) snatches; **par ~** piecemeal

bricolage [bʀikɔlaʒ] *nm*: **le ~** do-it-yourself

bricole [bʀikɔl] *nf* (*babiole*) trifle

bricoler [bʀikɔle] *vi* (*petits travaux*) to do DIY jobs; (*passe-temps*) to potter about ♦ *vt* (*réparer*) to fix up; **bricoleur, -euse** *nm/f* handyman(-woman), DIY enthusiast

bride [bʀid] *nf* bridle; **tenir qn en ~** to keep a tight rein on sb

bridé, e [bʀide] *adj*: **yeux ~s** slit eyes

bridge [bʀidʒ] *nm* (*CARTES*) bridge

brièvement [bʀijɛvmɑ̃] *adv* briefly

brigade [bʀigad] *nf* (*POLICE*) squad; (*MIL*) brigade; **brigadier** *nm* sergeant

brigandage [bʀigɑ̃daʒ] *nm* robbery

briguer [bʀige] *vt* to aspire to

brillamment [bʀijamɑ̃] *adv* brilliantly

brillant, e [bʀijɑ̃, ɑ̃t] *adj* (*remarquable*) bright; (*luisant*) shiny, shining

briller [bʀije] *vi* to shine

brimer [bʀime] *vt* to bully

brin [bʀɛ̃] *nm* (*de laine, ficelle etc*) strand; (*fig*): **un ~ de** a bit of; **~ d'herbe** blade of grass; **~ de muguet** sprig of lily of the valley

brindille [bʀɛ̃dij] *nf* twig

brio [bʀijo] *nm*: **avec ~** with panache

brioche [bʀijɔʃ] *nf* brioche (bun); (*fam*: *ventre*) paunch

brique [bʀik] *nf* brick; (*de lait*) carton

briquer [bʀike] *vt* to polish up

briquet [bʀikɛ] *nm* (cigarette) lighter

brise [bʀiz] *nf* breeze

briser [bʀize] *vt* to break; **se ~** *vi* to break

britannique [bʀitanik] *adj* British ♦ *nm/f*: **B~** British person, Briton; **les B~s** the British

brocante [bʀɔkɑ̃t] *nf* junk, second-hand goods *pl*; **brocanteur, -euse** *nm/f* junkshop owner; junk dealer

broche [bʀɔʃ] *nf* brooch; (*CULIN*) spit; (*MÉD*) pin; **à la ~** spit-roasted

broché, e [bʀɔʃe] *adj* (*livre*) paper-backed

brochet [bʀɔʃɛ] *nm* pike *inv*

brochette [bʀɔʃɛt] *nf* (*ustensile*) skewer; (*plat*) kebab

brochure [bʀɔʃyʀ] *nf* pamphlet, brochure, booklet

broder [bʀɔde] *vt* to embroider ♦ *vi* to embroider the facts; **broderie** *nf* embroidery

broncher [bʀɔ̃ʃe] *vi*: **sans ~** without flinching, without turning a hair

bronches [bʀɔ̃ʃ] *nfpl* bronchial tubes; **bronchite** *nf* bronchitis

bronze [bʀɔ̃z] *nm* bronze

bronzer [bʀɔ̃ze] *vi* to get a tan; **se ~** to sunbathe

brosse [bʀɔs] *nf* brush; **coiffé en ~** with a crewcut; **~ à cheveux** hairbrush; **~ à dents** toothbrush; **~ à habits** clothesbrush; **brosser** *vt* (*nettoyer*) to brush; (*fig*: *tableau etc*) to paint; **se brosser les dents** to brush one's teeth

brouette [bʀuɛt] *nf* wheelbarrow

brouhaha [bʀuaa] *nm* hubbub

brouillard [bRujaR] *nm* fog
brouille [bRuj] *nf* quarrel
brouiller [bRuje] *vt* (*œufs, message*) to scramble; (*idées*) to mix up; (*rendre trouble*) to cloud; (*désunir: amis*) to set at odds; **se ~** *vi* (*vue*) to cloud over; (*gens*) to fall out
brouillon, ne [bRujɔ̃, ɔn] *adj* (*sans soin*) untidy; (*qui manque d'organisation*) disorganized ♦ *nm* draft; **(papier) ~** rough paper
broussailles [bRusɑj] *nfpl* undergrowth *sg*; **broussailleux, -euse** *adj* bushy
brousse [bRus] *nf*: **la ~** the bush
brouter [bRute] *vi* to graze
broutille [bRutij] *nf* trifle
broyer [bRwaje] *vt* to crush; **~ du noir** to be down in the dumps
bru [bRy] *nf* daughter-in-law
brugnon [bRyɲɔ̃] *nm* (*BOT*) nectarine
bruiner [bRɥine] *vb impers*: **il bruine** it's drizzling, there's a drizzle
bruire [bRɥiR] *vi* (*feuilles*) to rustle
bruit [bRɥi] *nm*: **un ~** a noise, a sound; (*fig: rumeur*) a rumour; **le ~** noise; **sans ~** without a sound, noiselessly; **~ de fond** background noise; **bruitage** *nm* sound effects *pl*
brûlant, e [bRylɑ̃, ɑ̃t] *adj* burning; (*liquide*) boiling (hot)
brûlé, e [bRyle] *adj* (*fig: démasqué*) blown ♦ *nm*: **odeur de ~** smell of burning
brûle-pourpoint [bRylpuRpwɛ̃]: **à ~-~** *adv* point-blank
brûler [bRyle] *vt* to burn; (*suj: eau bouillante*) to scald; (*consommer: électricité, essence*) to use; (*feu rouge, signal*) to go through ♦ *vi* to burn; (*jeu*): **tu brûles!** you're getting hot!; **se ~** to burn o.s.; (*s'ébouillanter*) to scald o.s.
brûlure [bRylyR] *nf* (*lésion*) burn; **~s d'estomac** heartburn *sg*
brume [bRym] *nf* mist; **brumisateur** *nm* atomizer
brun, e [bRœ̃, bRyn] *adj* (*gén, bière*) brown; (*cheveux, tabac*) dark; **elle est ~e** she's got dark hair
brunch [brœntʃ] *nm* brunch
brunir [bRyniR] *vi* to get a tan
brushing [bRœʃiŋ] *nm* blow-dry
brusque [bRysk] *adj* abrupt; **brusquer** *vt* to rush
brut, e [bRyt] *adj* (*minerai, soie*) raw; (*diamant*) rough; (*COMM*) gross; **(pétrole) ~** crude (oil)
brutal, e, -aux [bRytal, o] *adj* brutal; **brutaliser** *vt* to handle roughly, manhandle
Bruxelles [bRysɛl] *n* Brussels
bruyamment [bRɥjamɑ̃] *adv* noisily
bruyant, e [bRɥjɑ̃, ɑ̃t] *adj* noisy
bruyère [bRyjɛR] *nf* heather
BTS *sigle m* (*= brevet de technicien supérieur*) *vocational training certificate taken at the end of a higher education course*
bu, e [by] *pp de* **boire**
buccal, e, -aux [bykal, o] *adj*: **par voie ~e** orally
bûche [byʃ] *nf* log; **prendre une ~** (*fig*) to come a cropper; **~ de Noël** Yule log
bûcher [byʃe] *nm* (*funéraire*) pyre; (*supplice*) stake ♦ *vi* (*fam*) to swot (*BRIT*), slave (away) ♦ *vt* (*fam*) to swot up (*BRIT*), slave away at; **bûcheron** *nm* woodcutter; **bûcheur, -euse** (*fam*) *adj* hard-working
budget [bydʒɛ] *nm* budget
buée [bɥe] *nf* (*sur une vitre*) mist
buffet [byfɛ] *nm* (*meuble*) sideboard; (*de réception*) buffet; **~ (de gare)** (station) buffet, snack bar
buffle [byfl] *nm* buffalo
buis [bɥi] *nm* box tree; (*bois*) box(wood)
buisson [bɥisɔ̃] *nm* bush
buissonnière [bɥisɔnjɛR] *adj*: **faire l'école ~** to skip school
bulbe [bylb] *nm* (*BOT, ANAT*) bulb
Bulgarie [bylgaRi] *nf* Bulgaria
bulle [byl] *nf* bubble
bulletin [byltɛ̃] *nm* (*communiqué, jour-*

nal) bulletin; (*SCOL*) report; **~ d'informations** news bulletin; **~ de salaire** pay-slip; **~ (de vote)** ballot paper; **~ météorologique** weather report

bureau, x [byʀo] *nm* (*meuble*) desk; (*pièce, service*) office; **~ de change** (foreign) exchange office *ou* bureau; **~ de poste** post office; **~ de tabac** tobacconist's (shop); **~ de vote** polling station; **bureaucratie** [byʀokʀasi] *nf* bureaucracy

burin [byʀɛ̃] *nm* cold chisel; (*ART*) burin

burlesque [byʀlɛsk] *adj* ridiculous; (*LITTÉRATURE*) burlesque

bus[1] [by] *vb voir* **boire**

bus[2] [bys] *nm* bus

busqué, e [byske] *adj* (*nez*) hook(ed)

buste [byst] *nm* (*torse*) chest; (*seins*) bust

but[1] [by] *vb voir* **boire**

but[2] [by(t)] *nm* (*cible*) target; (*fig*) goal, aim; (*FOOTBALL etc*) goal; **de ~ en blanc** point-blank; **avoir pour ~ de faire** to aim to do; **dans le ~ de** with the intention of

butane [bytan] *nm* (*camping*) butane; (*usage domestique*) Calor gas ®

buté, e [byte] *adj* stubborn, obstinate

buter [byte] *vi*: **~ contre** (*cogner*) to bump into; (*trébucher*) to stumble against; **se ~** *vi* to get obstinate, dig in one's heels; **~ contre une difficulté** (*fig*) to hit a snag

butin [bytɛ̃] *nm* booty, spoils *pl*; (*d'un vol*) loot

butiner [bytine] *vi* (*abeilles*) to gather nectar

butte [byt] *nf* mound, hillock; **être en ~ à** to be exposed to

buvais *etc* [byvɛ] *vb voir* **boire**

buvard [byvaʀ] *nm* blotter

buvette [byvɛt] *nf* bar

buveur, -euse [byvœʀ, øz] *nm/f* drinker

C, c

c' [s] *dét voir* **ce**

CA *sigle m* = **chiffre d'affaires**

ça [sa] *pron* (*pour désigner*) this; (: *plus loin*) that; (*comme sujet indéfini*) it; **comment ~ va?** how are you?; **~ va?** (*d'accord?*) OK?, all right?; **où ~?** where's that?; **pourquoi ~?** why's that?; **qui ~?** who's that?; **~ alors!** well really!; **~ fait 10 ans (que)** it's 10 years (since); **c'est ~** that's right; **~ y est** that's it

çà [sa] *adv*: **~ et là** here and there

cabane [kaban] *nf* hut, cabin

cabaret [kabaʀɛ] *nm* night club

cabas [kabɑ] *nm* shopping bag

cabillaud [kabijo] *nm* cod *inv*

cabine [kabin] *nf* (*de bateau*) cabin; (*de piscine etc*) cubicle; (*de camion, train*) cab; (*d'avion*) cockpit; **~ d'essayage** fitting room; **~ (téléphonique)** call *ou* (tele)phone box

cabinet [kabinɛ] *nm* (*petite pièce*) closet; (*de médecin*) surgery (*BRIT*), office (*US*); (*de notaire etc*) office; (: *clientèle*) practice; (*POL*) Cabinet; **~s** *nmpl* (*w.-c.*) toilet *sg*; **~ d'affaires** business consultancy; **~ de toilette** toilet

câble [kɑbl] *nm* cable

cabosser [kabɔse] *vt* to dent

cabrer [kɑbʀe]: **se ~** *vi* (*cheval*) to rear up

cabriole [kabʀijɔl] *nf*: **faire des ~s** to caper about

cacahuète [kakaɥɛt] *nf* peanut

cacao [kakao] *nm* cocoa

cache [kaʃ] *nm* mask, card (for masking)

cache-cache [kaʃkaʃ] *nm*: **jouer à ~-~** to play hide-and-seek

cachemire [kaʃmiʀ] *nm* cashmere

cache-nez [kaʃne] *nm inv* scarf, muffler

cacher [kaʃe] *vt* to hide, conceal; **se ~** *vi* (*volontairement*) to hide; (*être caché*)

to be hidden *ou* concealed; **~ qch à qn** to hide *ou* conceal sth from sb
cachet [kaʃɛ] *nm* (*comprimé*) tablet; (*de la poste*) postmark; (*rétribution*) fee; (*fig*) style, character; **cacheter** *vt* to seal
cachette [kaʃɛt] *nf* hiding place; **en ~** on the sly, secretly
cachot [kaʃo] *nm* dungeon
cachotterie [kaʃɔtʀi] *nf*: **faire des ~s** to be secretive
cactus [kaktys] *nm* cactus
cadavre [kadɑvʀ] *nm* corpse, (dead) body
Caddie ®**, caddy** [kadi] *nm* (supermarket) trolley
cadeau, x [kado] *nm* present, gift; **faire un ~ à qn** to give sb a present *ou* gift; **faire ~ de qch à qn** to make a present of sth to sb, give sb sth as a present
cadenas [kadnɑ] *nm* padlock
cadence [kadɑ̃s] *nf* (*tempo*) rhythm; (*de travail etc*) rate; **en ~** rhythmically
cadet, te [kadɛ, ɛt] *adj* younger; (*le plus jeune*) youngest ♦ *nm/f* youngest child *ou* one
cadran [kadʀɑ̃] *nm* dial; **~ solaire** sundial
cadre [kɑdʀ] *nm* frame; (*environnement*) surroundings *pl* ♦ *nm/f* (ADMIN) managerial employee, executive; **dans le ~ de** (*fig*) within the framework *ou* context of
cadrer [kɑdʀe] *vi*: **~ avec** to tally *ou* correspond with ♦ *vt* to centre
cafard [kafaʀ] *nm* cockroach; **avoir le ~** (*fam*) to be down in the dumps
café [kafe] *nm* coffee; (*bistro*) café ♦ *adj inv* coffee(-coloured); **~ au lait** white coffee; **~ noir** black coffee; **~ tabac** *tobacconist's or newsagent's serving coffee and spirits*; **cafetière** *nf* (*pot*) coffee-pot
cafouiller [kafuje] (*fam*) *vi* to get into a shambles
cage [kaʒ] *nf* cage; **~ d'escalier** (stair)well; **~ thoracique** rib cage
cageot [kaʒo] *nm* crate
cagibi [kaʒibi] (*fam*) *nm* (*débarass*) boxroom
cagnotte [kaɲɔt] *nf* kitty
cagoule [kagul] *nf* (*passe-montagne*) balaclava
cahier [kaje] *nm* notebook; **~ de brouillons** roughbook, jotter; **~ d'exercices** exercise book
cahot [kao] *nm* jolt, bump
caïd [kaid] *nm* big chief, boss
caille [kaj] *nf* quail
cailler [kaje] *vi* (*lait*) to curdle; **ça caille** (*fam*) it's freezing; **caillot** *nm* (blood) clot
caillou, x [kaju] *nm* (little) stone; **caillouteux, -euse** *adj* (*route*) stony
Caire [kɛʀ] *nm*: **le ~** Cairo
caisse [kɛs] *nf* box; (*tiroir où l'on met la recette*) till; (*où l'on paye*) cash desk (BRIT), check-out; (*de banque*) cashier's desk; **~ d'épargne** savings bank; **~ de retraite** pension fund; **~ enregistreuse** cash register; **caissier, -ière** *nm/f* cashier
cajoler [kaʒɔle] *vt* (*câliner*) to cuddle; (*amadouer*) to wheedle, coax
cake [kɛk] *nm* fruit cake
calandre [kalɑ̃dʀ] *nf* radiator grill
calanque [kalɑ̃k] *nf* rocky inlet
calcaire [kalkɛʀ] *nm* limestone ♦ *adj* (*eau*) hard; (GÉO) limestone *cpd*
calciné, e [kalsine] *adj* burnt to ashes
calcul [kalkyl] *nm* calculation; **le ~** (SCOL) arithmetic; **~ (biliaire)** (gall)stone; **calculatrice** *nf* calculator; **calculer** *vt* to calculate, work out; **calculette** *nf* pocket calculator
cale [kal] *nf* (*de bateau*) hold; (*en bois*) wedge; **~ sèche** dry dock
calé, e [kale] (*fam*) *adj* clever, bright
caleçon [kalsɔ̃] *nm* (*d'homme*) boxer shorts; (*de femme*) leggings
calembour [kalɑ̃buʀ] *nm* pun
calendrier [kalɑ̃dʀije] *nm* calendar; (*fig*) timetable
calepin [kalpɛ̃] *nm* notebook

caler [kale] *vt* to wedge ♦ *vi* (*moteur, véhicule*) to stall
calfeutrer [kalføtʀe] *vt* to (make) draughtproof; **se ~** *vi* to make o.s. snug and comfortable
calibre [kalibʀ] *nm* calibre
califourchon [kalifuʀʃɔ̃]: **à ~** *adv* astride
câlin, e [kɑlɛ̃, in] *adj* cuddly, cuddlesome; (*regard, voix*) tender; **câliner** *vt* to cuddle
calmant [kalmɑ̃] *nm* tranquillizer, sedative; (*pour la douleur*) painkiller
calme [kalm] *adj* calm, quiet ♦ *nm* calm(ness), quietness; **calmer** *vt* to calm (down); (*douleur, inquiétude*) to ease, soothe; **se calmer** *vi* to calm down
calomnie [kalɔmni] *nf* slander; (*écrite*) libel; **calomnier** *vt* to slander; to libel
calorie [kalɔʀi] *nf* calorie
calotte [kalɔt] *nf* (*coiffure*) skullcap; (*fam*: *gifle*) slap; **~ glaciaire** (*GÉO*) icecap
calquer [kalke] *vt* to trace; (*fig*) to copy exactly
calvaire [kalvɛʀ] *nm* (*croix*) wayside cross, calvary; (*souffrances*) suffering
calvitie [kalvisi] *nf* baldness
camarade [kamaʀad] *nm/f* friend, pal, (*POL*) comrade; **camaraderie** *nf* friendship
cambouis [kɑ̃bwi] *nm* dirty oil *ou* grease
cambrer [kɑ̃bʀe]: **se ~** *vi* to arch one's back
cambriolage [kɑ̃bʀijɔlaʒ] *nm* burglary; **cambrioler** *vt* to burgle (*BRIT*), burglarize (*US*); **cambrioleur, -euse** *nm/f* burglar
camelote [kamlɔt] (*fam*) *nf* rubbish, trash, junk
caméra [kameʀa] *nf* (*CINÉMA, TV*) camera; (*d'amateur*) cine-camera
caméscope ® [kameskɔp] *nm* camcorder ®
camion [kamjɔ̃] *nm* lorry (*BRIT*), truck; **~ de dépannage** breakdown (*BRIT*) *ou* tow (*US*) truck; **camion-citerne** *nm* tanker; **camionnette** *nf* (small) van; **camionneur** *nm* (*chauffeur*) lorry (*BRIT*) *ou* truck driver; (*entrepreneur*) haulage contractor (*BRIT*), trucker (*US*)
camisole [kamizɔl] *nf*: **~ (de force)** straitjacket
camomille [kamɔmij] *nf* camomile; (*boisson*) camomile tea
camoufler [kamufle] *vt* to camouflage; (*fig*) to conceal, cover up
camp [kɑ̃] *nm* camp; (*fig*) side; **~ de vacances** children's holiday camp (*BRIT*), summer camp (*US*)
campagnard, e [kɑ̃paɲaʀ, aʀd] *adj* country *cpd*
campagne [kɑ̃paɲ] *nf* country, countryside; (*MIL, POL, COMM*) campaign; **à la ~** in the country
camper [kɑ̃pe] *vi* to camp ♦ *vt* to sketch; **se ~ devant** to plant o.s. in front of; **campeur, -euse** *nm/f* camper
camping [kɑ̃piŋ] *nm* camping; **(terrain de) ~** campsite, camping site; **faire du ~** to go camping; **camping-car** *nm* camper, motorhome (*US*); **camping-gaz** ® *nm inv* camp(ing) stove
Canada [kanada] *nm*: **le ~** Canada; **canadien, ne** *adj* Canadian ♦ *nm/f*: **Canadien, ne** Canadian; **canadienne** *nf* (*veste*) fur-lined jacket
canaille [kanɑj] (*péj*) *nf* scoundrel
canal, -aux [kanal, o] *nm* canal; (*naturel*) channel; **canalisation** *nf* (*tuyau*) pipe; **canaliser** *vt* to canalize; (*fig*) to channel
canapé [kanape] *nm* settee, sofa
canard [kanaʀ] *nm* duck; (*fam*: *journal*) rag
canari [kanaʀi] *nm* canary
cancans [kɑ̃kɑ̃] *nmpl* (malicious) gossip *sg*
cancer [kɑ̃sɛʀ] *nm* cancer; (*signe*): **le C~** Cancer; **~ de la peau** skin cancer
cancre [kɑ̃kʀ] *nm* dunce
candeur [kɑ̃dœʀ] *nf* ingenuousness,

guilelessness
candidat, e [kɑ̃dida, at] *nm/f* candidate; (*à un poste*) applicant, candidate;
candidature *nf* (*POL*) candidature; (*à poste*) application; **poser sa candidature à un poste** to apply for a job
candide [kɑ̃did] *adj* ingenuous, guileless
cane [kan] *nf* (female) duck
caneton [kantɔ̃] *nm* duckling
canette [kanɛt] *nf* (*de bière*) (flip-top) bottle
canevas [kanvɑ] *nm* (*COUTURE*) canvas
caniche [kaniʃ] *nm* poodle
canicule [kanikyl] *nf* scorching heat
canif [kanif] *nm* penknife, pocket knife
canine [kanin] *nf* canine (tooth)
caniveau, x [kanivo] *nm* gutter
canne [kan] *nf* (walking) stick; **~ à pêche** fishing rod; **~ à sucre** sugar cane
cannelle [kanɛl] *nf* cinnamon
canoë [kanɔe] *nm* canoe; (*sport*) canoeing
canon [kanɔ̃] *nm* (*arme*) gun; (*HISTOIRE*) cannon; (*d'une arme*: *tube*) barrel; (*fig*: *norme*) model; (*MUS*) canon
canot [kano] *nm* ding(h)y; **~ de sauvetage** lifeboat; **~ pneumatique** inflatable ding(h)y; **canotier** *nm* boater
cantatrice [kɑ̃tatʀis] *nf* (opera) singer
cantine [kɑ̃tin] *nf* canteen
cantique [kɑ̃tik] *nm* hymn
canton [kɑ̃tɔ̃] *nm district consisting of several communes*; (*en Suisse*) canton
cantonade [kɑ̃tɔnad]: **à la ~** *adv* to everyone in general
cantonner [kɑ̃tɔne]: **se ~ à** *vt* to confine o.s. to
cantonnier [kɑ̃tɔnje] *nm* roadmender
canular [kanylaʀ] *nm* hoax
caoutchouc [kautʃu] *nm* rubber
cap [kap] *nm* (*GÉO*) cape; (*promontoire*) headland; (*fig*: *tournant*) watershed; (*NAVIG*): **changer de ~** to change course; **mettre le ~ sur** to head *ou* steer for
CAP *sigle m* (= *Certificat d'aptitude professionnelle*) *vocational training certificate taken at secondary school*
capable [kapabl] *adj* able, capable; **~ de qch/faire** capable of sth/doing
capacité [kapasite] *nf* (*compétence*) ability; (*JUR, contenance*) capacity
cape [kap] *nf* cape, cloak; **rire sous ~** to laugh up one's sleeve
CAPES [kapɛs] *sigle m* (= *Certificat d'aptitude pédagogique à l'enseignement secondaire*) *teaching diploma*
capillaire [kapilɛʀ] *adj* (*soins, lotion*) hair *cpd*; (*vaisseau etc*) capillary
capitaine [kapitɛn] *nm* captain
capital, e, -aux [kapital, o] *adj* (*œuvre*) major; (*question, rôle*) fundamental ♦ *nm* capital; (*fig*) stock; **d'une importance ~e** of capital importance; *voir aussi* **capitaux**; **~ (social)** authorized capital; **capitale** *nf* (*ville*) capital; (*lettre*) capital (letter); **capitalisme** *nm* capitalism; **capitaliste** *adj, nm/f* capitalist; **capitaux** *nmpl* (*fonds*) capital *sg*
capitonné, e [kapitɔne] *adj* padded
caporal, -aux [kapɔʀal, o] *nm* lance corporal
capot [kapo] *nm* (*AUTO*) bonnet (*BRIT*), hood (*US*)
capote [kapɔt] *nf* (*de voiture*) hood (*BRIT*), top (*US*); (*fam*) condom
capoter [kapɔte] *vi* (*négociations*) to founder
câpre [kɑpʀ] *nf* caper
caprice [kapʀis] *nm* whim, caprice; **faire des ~s** to make a fuss; **capricieux, -euse** *adj* (*fantasque*) capricious, whimsical; (*enfant*) awkward
Capricorne [kapʀikɔʀn] *nm*: **le ~** Capricorn
capsule [kapsyl] *nf* (*de bouteille*) cap; (*BOT etc, spatiale*) capsule
capter [kapte] *vt* (*ondes radio*) to pick up; (*fig*) to win, capture
captivant, e [kaptivɑ̃, ɑ̃t] *adj* captivating
captivité [kaptivite] *nf* captivity

capturer [kaptyʀe] *vt* to capture
capuche [kapyʃ] *nf* hood
capuchon [kapyʃɔ̃] *nm* hood; (*de stylo*) cap, top
capucine [kapysin] *nf* (BOT) nasturtium
caquet [kakɛ] *nm*: **rabattre le ~ à qn** (*fam*) to bring sb down a peg or two
caqueter [kakte] *vi* to cackle
car [kaʀ] *nm* coach ♦ *conj* because, for
carabine [kaʀabin] *nf* rifle
caractère [kaʀaktɛʀ] *nm* (*gén*) character; **avoir bon/mauvais ~** to be good-/ill-natured; **en ~s gras** in bold type; **en petits ~s** in small print; **~s d'imprimerie** (block) capitals; **caractériel, le** *adj* (*traits*) (of) character; (*enfant*) emotionally disturbed
caractérisé, e [kaʀakteʀize] *adj* sheer, downright
caractériser [kaʀakteʀize] *vt* to be characteristic of
caractéristique [kaʀakteʀistik] *adj, nf* characteristic
carafe [kaʀaf] *nf* (*pour eau, vin ordinaire*) carafe
caraïbe [kaʀaib] *adj* Caribbean ♦ *n*: **les C~s** the Caribbean (Islands)
carambolage [kaʀɑ̃bɔlaʒ] *nm* multiple crash, pileup
caramel [kaʀamɛl] *nm* (*bonbon*) caramel, toffee; (*substance*) caramel
carapace [kaʀapas] *nf* shell
caravane [kaʀavan] *nf* caravan; **caravaning** *nm* caravanning
carbone [kaʀbɔn] *nm* carbon; (*double*) carbon (copy); **carbonique** *adj*: **gaz carbonique** carbon dioxide; **neige carbonique** dry ice; **carbonisé, e** *adj* charred
carburant [kaʀbyʀɑ̃] *nm* (motor) fuel
carburateur [kaʀbyʀatœʀ] *nm* carburettor
carcan [kaʀkɑ̃] *nm* (*fig*) yoke, shackles *pl*
carcasse [kaʀkas] *nf* carcass; (*de véhicule etc*) shell
cardiaque [kaʀdjak] *adj* cardiac, heart *cpd* ♦ *nm/f* heart patient; **être ~** to have heart trouble
cardigan [kaʀdigɑ̃] *nm* cardigan
cardiologue [kaʀdjɔlɔg] *nm/f* cardiologist, heart specialist
carême [kaʀɛm] *nm*: **le C~** Lent
carence [kaʀɑ̃s] *nf* (*manque*) deficiency
caresse [kaʀɛs] *nf* caress
caresser [kaʀese] *vt* to caress; (*animal*) to stroke
cargaison [kaʀgɛzɔ̃] *nf* cargo, freight
cargo [kaʀgo] *nm* cargo boat, freighter
caricature [kaʀikatyʀ] *nf* caricature
carie [kaʀi] *nf*: **la ~ (dentaire)** tooth decay; **une ~** a bad tooth
carillon [kaʀijɔ̃] *nm* (*air, de pendule*) chimes *pl*
caritatif, -ive [kaʀitatif, iv] *adj*: **organisation caritative** charity
carnassier, -ière [kaʀnasje, jɛʀ] *adj* carnivorous
carnaval [kaʀnaval] *nm* carnival
carnet [kaʀnɛ] *nm* (*calepin*) notebook; (*de tickets, timbres etc*) book; **~ de chèques** cheque book; **~ de notes** school report
carotte [kaʀɔt] *nf* carrot
carpette [kaʀpɛt] *nf* rug
carré, e [kaʀe] *adj* square; (*fig*: *franc*) straightforward ♦ *nm* (MATH) square; **mètre/kilomètre ~** square metre/kilometre
carreau, x [kaʀo] *nm* (*par terre*) (floor) tile; (*au mur*) (wall) tile; (*de fenêtre*) (window) pane; (*motif*) check, square; (CARTES: *couleur*) diamonds *pl*; **tissu à ~x** checked fabric
carrefour [kaʀfuʀ] *nm* crossroads *sg*
carrelage [kaʀlaʒ] *nm* (*sol*) (tiled) floor
carrelet [kaʀlɛ] *nm* (*poisson*) plaice
carrément [kaʀemɑ̃] *adv* (*franchement*) straight out, bluntly; (*sans hésiter*) straight; (*intensif*) completely; **c'est ~ impossible** it's completely impossible
carrière [kaʀjɛʀ] *nf* (*métier*) career; (*de roches*) quarry; **militaire de ~** professional soldier

carrossable [kaʀɔsabl] *adj* suitable for (motor) vehicles

carrosse [kaʀɔs] *nm* (horse-drawn) coach

carrosserie [kaʀɔsʀi] *nf* body, coachwork *no pl*

carrure [kaʀyʀ] *nf* build; (*fig*) stature, calibre

cartable [kaʀtabl] *nm* satchel, (school)bag

carte [kaʀt] *nf* (*de géographie*) map; (*marine, du ciel*) chart; (*d'abonnement, à jouer*) card; (*au restaurant*) menu; (*aussi:* **~ de visite**) (visiting) card; **à la ~** (*au restaurant*) à la carte; **donner ~ blanche à qn** to give sb a free rein; **~ bancaire** cash card; **~ de crédit** credit card; **~ de fidélité** loyalty card; **~ d'identité** identity card; **~ de séjour** residence permit; **~ grise** (AUTO) ≃ (car) registration book, logbook; **~ postale** postcard; **~ routière** road map; **~ téléphonique** phonecard

carter [kaʀtɛʀ] *nm* sump

carton [kaʀtɔ̃] *nm* (*matériau*) cardboard; (*boîte*) (cardboard) box; **faire un ~** (*fam*) to score a hit; **~ (à dessin)** portfolio; **carton-pâte** *nm* pasteboard

cartouche [kaʀtuʃ] *nf* cartridge; (*de cigarettes*) carton

cas [kɑ] *nm* case; **ne faire aucun ~ de** to take no notice of; **en aucun ~** on no account; **au ~ où** in case; **en ~ de** in case of, in the event of; **en ~ de besoin** if need be; **en tout ~** in any case, at any rate

casanier, -ière [kazanje, jɛʀ] *adj* stay-at-home

cascade [kaskad] *nf* waterfall, cascade; (*fig*) stream, torrent; **cascadeur, -euse** *nm/f* stuntman(-girl)

case [kɑz] *nf* (*hutte*) hut; (*compartiment*) compartment; (*sur un formulaire, de mots croisés etc*) box

caser [kɑze] (*fam*) *vt* (*placer*) to put (away); (*loger*) to put up; **se ~** *vi* (*se marier*) to settle down; (*trouver un emploi*) to find a (steady) job

caserne [kazɛʀn] *nf* barracks *pl*

cash [kaʃ] *adv*: **payer ~** to pay cash down

casier [kɑzje] *nm* (*pour courrier*) pigeonhole; (*compartiment*) compartment; (*à clef*) locker; **~ judiciaire** police record

casino [kazino] *nm* casino

casque [kask] *nm* helmet; (*chez le coiffeur*) (hair-)drier; (*pour audition*) (head-)phones *pl*, headset

casquette [kaskɛt] *nf* cap

cassant, e [kɑsɑ̃, ɑ̃t] *adj* brittle; (*fig: ton*) curt, abrupt

cassation [kɑsasjɔ̃] *nf*: **cour de ~** final court of appeal

casse [kɑs] (*fam*) *nf* (*pour voitures*): **mettre à la ~** to scrap; (*dégâts*): **il y a eu de la ~** there were a lot of breakages; **casse-cou** *adj inv* daredevil, reckless; **casse-croûte** *nm inv* snack; **casse-noix** *nm inv* nutcrackers *pl*; **casse-pieds** (*fam*) *adj inv*: **il est casse-pieds** he's a pain in the neck

casser [kɑse] *vt* to break; (JUR) to quash; **se ~** *vi* to break; **~ les pieds à qn** (*fam: irriter*) to get on sb's nerves; **se ~ la tête** (*fam*) to go to a lot of trouble

casserole [kasʀɔl] *nf* saucepan

casse-tête [kɑstɛt] *nm inv* (*difficultés*) headache (*fig*)

cassette [kasɛt] *nf* (*bande magnétique*) cassette; (*coffret*) casket

casseur [kɑsœʀ] *nm* hooligan

cassis [kasis] *nm* blackcurrant

cassoulet [kasulɛ] *nm bean and sausage hot-pot*

cassure [kɑsyʀ] *nf* break, crack

castor [kastɔʀ] *nm* beaver

castrer [kastʀe] *vt* (*mâle*) to castrate; (*: cheval*) to geld; (*femelle*) to spay

catalogue [katalɔg] *nm* catalogue

cataloguer [katalɔge] *vt* to catalogue, to list; (*péj*) to put a label on

catalyseur [katalizœʀ] *nm* catalyst; **catalytique** *adj*: **pot catalytique** catalytic convertor

catastrophe [katastʀɔf] *nf* catastrophe, disaster; **catastrophé, e** (*fam*) *adj* stunned

catch [katʃ] *nm* (all-in) wrestling

catéchisme [kateʃism] *nm* catechism

catégorie [kategɔʀi] *nf* category; **catégorique** *adj* categorical

cathédrale [katedʀal] *nf* cathedral

catholique [katɔlik] *adj, nm/f* (Roman) Catholic; **pas très ~** a bit shady *ou* fishy

catimini [katimini]: **en ~** *adv* on the sly

cauchemar [koʃmaʀ] *nm* nightmare

cause [koz] *nf* cause; (JUR) lawsuit, case; **à ~ de** because of, owing to; **pour ~ de** on account of; **(et) pour ~** and for (a very) good reason; **être en ~** (*intérêts*) to be at stake; **remettre en ~** to challenge; **causer** *vt* to cause ♦ *vi* to chat, talk; **causerie** *nf* (*conférence*) talk; **causette** *nf*: **faire la causette** to have a chat

caution [kosjɔ̃] *nf* guarantee, security; (JUR) bail (bond); (*fig*) backing, support; **libéré sous ~** released on bail; **cautionner** *vt* (*répondre de*) to guarantee; (*soutenir*) to support

cavalcade [kavalkad] *nf* (*fig*) stampede

cavalier, -ière [kavalje, jɛʀ] *adj* (*désinvolte*) offhand ♦ *nm/f* rider; (*au bal*) partner ♦ *nm* (ÉCHECS) knight

cave [kav] *nf* cellar

caveau, x [kavo] *nm* vault

caverne [kavɛʀn] *nf* cave

CCP *sigle m* = **compte chèques postaux**

CD *sigle m* (= *compact disc*) CD

CD-ROM [sedeʀɔm] *sigle m* CD-ROM

CE *n abr* (= *Communauté Européenne*) EC

MOT-CLÉ

ce, cette [sə, sɛt] (*devant nm* **cet** + *voyelle ou h aspiré*; *pl* **ces**) *dét* (*proximité*) this; these *pl*; (*non-proximité*) that; those *pl*; **cette maison(-ci/là)** this/that house; **cette nuit** (*qui vient*) tonight; (*passée*) last night

♦ *pron* **1**: **c'est** it's *ou* it is; **c'est un peintre** he's *ou* he is a painter; **ce sont des peintres** they're *ou* they are painters; **c'est le facteur** (*à la porte*) it's the postman; **qui est-ce?** who is it?; (*en désignant*) who is he/she?; **qu'est-ce?** what is it?

2: **ce qui, ce que** what; (*chose qui*): **il est bête, ce qui me chagrine** he's stupid, which saddens me; **tout ce qui bouge** everything that *ou* which moves; **tout ce que je sais** all I know; **ce dont j'ai parlé** what I talked about; **ce que c'est grand!** it's so big!; *voir aussi* **-ci**; **est-ce que**; **n'est-ce pas**; **c'est-à-dire**

ceci [səsi] *pron* this

cécité [sesite] *nf* blindness

céder [sede] *vt* (*donner*) to give up ♦ *vi* (*chaise, barrage*) to give way; (*personne*) to give in; **~ à** to yield to, give in to

CEDEX [sedɛks] *sigle m* (= *courrier d'entreprise à distribution exceptionnelle*) *postal service for bulk users*

cédille [sedij] *nf* cedilla

cèdre [sɛdʀ] *nm* cedar

CEI *abr m* (= *Communauté des États Indépendants*) CIS

ceinture [sɛ̃tyʀ] *nf* belt; (*taille*) waist; **~ de sécurité** safety *ou* seat belt

cela [s(ə)la] *pron* that; (*comme sujet indéfini*) it; **quand/où ~?** when/where (was that)?

célèbre [selɛbʀ] *adj* famous; **célébrer** *vt* to celebrate

céleri [sɛlʀi] *nm*: **~(-rave)** celeriac; **~ (en branche)** celery

célibat [seliba] *nm* (*homme*) bachelorhood; (*femme*) spinsterhood; (*prêtre*) celibacy; **célibataire** *adj* single, unmarried ♦ *nm* bachelor ♦ *nf* unmarried woman

celle(s) [sɛl] *pron voir* **celui**
cellier [selje] *nm* storeroom (*for wine*)
cellule [selyl] *nf* (*gén*) cell
cellulite [selylit] *nf* excess fat, cellulite

MOT-CLÉ

celui, celle [səlɥi, sɛl] (*mpl* **ceux**, *fpl* **celles**) *pron* **1**: **celui-ci/là, celle-ci/là** this one/that one; **ceux-ci, celles-ci** these (ones); **ceux-là, celles-là** those (ones); **celui de mon frère** my brother's; **celui du salon/du dessous** the one in (*ou* from) the lounge/below
2: **celui qui bouge** the one which *ou* that moves; (*personne*) the one who moves; **celui que je vois** the one (which *ou* that) I see; the one (whom) I see; **celui dont je parle** the one I'm talking about
3 (*valeur indéfinie*): **celui qui veut** whoever wants

cendre [sɑ̃dʀ] *nf* ash; **~s** *nfpl* (*d'un défunt*) ashes; **sous la ~** (CULIN) in (the) embers; **cendrier** *nm* ashtray
cène [sɛn] *nf*: **la ~** (Holy) Communion
censé, e [sɑ̃se] *adj*: **être ~ faire** to be supposed to do
censeur [sɑ̃sœʀ] *nm* (SCOL) deputy-head (BRIT), vice-principal (US)
censure [sɑ̃syʀ] *nf* censorship; **censurer** *vt* (CINÉMA, PRESSE) to censor; (POL) to censure
cent [sɑ̃] *num* a hundred, one hundred ♦ *nm* (US, Canada etc) cent; (*partie de l'euro*) cent; **centaine** *nf*: **une centaine (de)** about a hundred, a hundred or so; **des centaines (de)** hundreds (of); **centenaire** *adj* hundred-year-old ♦ *nm* (*anniversaire*) centenary; **centième** *num* hundredth; **centigrade** *nm* centigrade; **centilitre** *nm* centilitre; **centime** *nm* centime; **centime d'euro** cent; **centimètre** *nm* centimetre; (*ruban*) tape measure, measuring tape
central, e, -aux [sɑ̃tʀal, o] *adj* central ♦ *nm*: **~ (téléphonique)** (telephone) exchange; **centrale** *nf* power station
centre [sɑ̃tʀ] *nm* centre; **~ commercial** shopping centre; **~ d'appels** call centre; **~ de loisirs** leisure centre; **centre-ville** *nm* town centre, downtown (area) (US)
centuple [sɑ̃typl] *nm*: **le ~ de qch** a hundred times sth; **au ~** a hundredfold
cep [sɛp] *nm* (vine) stock
cèpe [sɛp] *nm* (edible) boletus
cependant [s(ə)pɑ̃dɑ̃] *adv* however
céramique [seʀamik] *nf* ceramics *sg*
cercle [sɛʀkl] *nm* circle
cercueil [sɛʀkœj] *nm* coffin
céréale [seʀeal] *nf* cereal; **~s** *nfpl* breakfast cereal
cérémonie [seʀemɔni] *nf* ceremony
cerf [sɛʀ] *nm* stag
cerfeuil [sɛʀfœj] *nm* chervil
cerf-volant [sɛʀvɔlɑ̃] *nm* kite
cerise [s(ə)ʀiz] *nf* cherry; **cerisier** *nm* cherry (tree)
cerne [sɛʀn] *nm*: **avoir des ~s** to have shadows *ou* dark rings under one's eyes
cerner [sɛʀne] *vt* (MIL *etc*) to surround; (*fig*: *problème*) to delimit, define
certain, e [sɛʀtɛ̃, ɛn] *adj* certain ♦ *dét* certain; **d'un ~ âge** past one's prime, not so young; **un ~ temps** (quite) some time; **~s** ♦ *pron* some; **certainement** *adv* (*probablement*) most probably *ou* likely; (*bien sûr*) certainly, of course
certes [sɛʀt] *adv* (*sans doute*) admittedly; (*bien sûr*) of course
certificat [sɛʀtifika] *nm* certificate
certifier [sɛʀtifje] *vt*: **~ qch à qn** to assure sb of sth; **copie certifiée conforme** certified copy of the original
certitude [sɛʀtityd] *nf* certainty
cerveau, x [sɛʀvo] *nm* brain
cervelas [sɛʀvəla] *nm* saveloy
cervelle [sɛʀvɛl] *nf* (ANAT) brain; (CULIN) brains
ces [se] *dét voir* **ce**
CES *sigle m* (= *Collège d'enseignement*

secondaire) ≃ (junior) secondary school (*BRIT*)
cesse [sɛs]: **sans ~** *adv* (*tout le temps*) continually, constantly; (*sans interruption*) continuously; **il n'a eu de ~ que** he did not rest until; **cesser** *vt* to stop ♦ *vi* to stop, cease; **cesser de faire** to stop doing; **cessez-le-feu** *nm inv* ceasefire
c'est-à-dire [sɛtadiʀ] *adv* that is (to say)
cet, cette [sɛt] *dét voir* **ce**
ceux [sø] *pron voir* **celui**
CFC *abr* (= *chlorofluorocarbon*) CFC
CFDT *sigle f* (= *Confédération française démocratique du travail*) *French trade union*
CGT *sigle f* (= *Confédération générale du travail*) *French trade union*
chacun, e [ʃakœ̃, yn] *pron* each; (*indéfini*) everyone, everybody
chagrin [ʃagʀɛ̃] *nm* grief, sorrow; **avoir du ~** to be grieved; **chagriner** *vt* to grieve
chahut [ʃay] *nm* uproar; **chahuter** *vt* to rag, bait ♦ *vi* to make an uproar
chaîne [ʃɛn] *nf* chain; (*RADIO, TV: stations*) channel; **~s** *nfpl* (*AUTO*) (snow) chains; **travail à la ~** production line work; **~ (de montage)** production *ou* assembly line; **~ de montagnes** mountain range; **~ (hi-fi)** hi-fi system; **~ laser** CD player; **~ (stéréo)** stereo (system); **chaînette** *nf* (small) chain
chair [ʃɛʀ] *nf* flesh; **avoir la ~ de poule** to have goosepimples *ou* gooseflesh; **bien en ~** plump, well-padded; **en ~ et en os** in the flesh; **~ à saucisse** sausage meat
chaire [ʃɛʀ] *nf* (*d'église*) pulpit; (*d'université*) chair
chaise [ʃɛz] *nf* chair; **~ longue** deckchair
châle [ʃal] *nm* shawl
chaleur [ʃalœʀ] *nf* heat; (*fig: accueil*) warmth; **chaleureux, -euse** *adj* warm
chaloupe [ʃalup] *nf* launch; (*de sauvetage*) lifeboat
chalumeau, x [ʃalymo] *nm* blowlamp, blowtorch
chalutier [ʃalytje] *nm* trawler
chamailler [ʃamɑje]: **se ~** *vi* to squabble, bicker
chambouler [ʃɑ̃bule] (*fam*) *vt* to disrupt, turn upside down
chambre [ʃɑ̃bʀ] *nf* bedroom; (*POL, COMM*) chamber; **faire ~ à part** to sleep in separate rooms; **~ à air** (*de pneu*) (inner) tube; **~ à coucher** bedroom; **~ à un lit/deux lits** (*à l'hôtel*) single-/twin-bedded room; **~ d'amis** spare *ou* guest room; **~ noire** (*PHOTO*) dark room; **chambrer** *vt* (*vin*) to bring to room temperature
chameau, x [ʃamo] *nm* camel
chamois [ʃamwa] *nm* chamois
champ [ʃɑ̃] *nm* field; **~ de bataille** battlefield; **~ de courses** racecourse; **~ de tir** rifle range
champagne [ʃɑ̃paɲ] *nm* champagne
champêtre [ʃɑ̃pɛtʀ] *adj* country *cpd*, rural
champignon [ʃɑ̃piɲɔ̃] *nm* mushroom; (*terme générique*) fungus; **~ de Paris** button mushroom
champion, ne [ʃɑ̃pjɔ̃, jɔn] *adj, nm/f* champion; **championnat** *nm* championship
chance [ʃɑ̃s] *nf*: **la ~** luck; **~s** *nfpl* (*probabilités*) chances; **avoir de la ~** to be lucky; **il a des ~s de réussir** he's got a good chance of passing
chanceler [ʃɑ̃s(ə)le] *vi* to totter
chancelier [ʃɑ̃səlje] *nm* (*allemand*) chancellor
chanceux, -euse [ʃɑ̃sø, øz] *adj* lucky
chandail [ʃɑ̃daj] *nm* (thick) sweater
Chandeleur [ʃɑ̃dlœʀ] *nf*: **la ~** Candlemas
chandelier [ʃɑ̃dəlje] *nm* candlestick
chandelle [ʃɑ̃dɛl] *nf* (tallow) candle; **dîner aux ~s** candlelight dinner
change [ʃɑ̃ʒ] *nm* (*devises*) exchange
changement [ʃɑ̃ʒmɑ̃] *nm* change; **~**

de vitesses gears *pl*

changer [ʃɑ̃ʒe] *vt* (*modifier*) to change, alter; (*remplacer,* COMM) to change ♦ *vi* to change, alter; **se ~** *vi* to change (o.s.); **~ de** (*remplacer: adresse, nom, voiture etc*) to change one's; (*échanger: place, train etc*) to change; **~ d'avis** to change one's mind; **~ de vitesse** to change gear

chanson [ʃɑ̃sɔ̃] *nf* song

chant [ʃɑ̃] *nm* song; (*art vocal*) singing; (*d'église*) hymn

chantage [ʃɑ̃taʒ] *nm* blackmail; **faire du ~** to use blackmail

chanter [ʃɑ̃te] *vt, vi* to sing; **si cela lui chante** (*fam*) if he feels like it; **chanteur, -euse** *nm/f* singer

chantier [ʃɑ̃tje] *nm* (building) site; (*sur une route*) roadworks *pl*; **mettre en ~** to put in hand; **~ naval** shipyard

chantilly [ʃɑ̃tiji] *nf voir* **crème**

chantonner [ʃɑ̃tɔne] *vi, vt* to sing to oneself, hum

chanvre [ʃɑ̃vʀ] *nm* hemp

chaparder [ʃapaʀde] (*fam*) *vt* to pinch

chapeau, x [ʃapo] *nm* hat; **~!** well done!

chapelet [ʃaplɛ] *nm* (REL) rosary

chapelle [ʃapɛl] *nf* chapel

chapelure [ʃaplyʀ] *nf* (dried) breadcrumbs *pl*

chapiteau, x [ʃapito] *nm* (*de cirque*) marquee, big top

chapitre [ʃapitʀ] *nm* chapter

chaque [ʃak] *dét* each, every; (*indéfini*) every

char [ʃaʀ] *nm* (MIL): **~ (d'assaut)** tank; **~ à voile** sand yacht

charabia [ʃaʀabja] (*péj*) *nm* gibberish

charade [ʃaʀad] *nf* riddle; (*mimée*) charade

charbon [ʃaʀbɔ̃] *nm* coal; **~ de bois** charcoal

charcuterie [ʃaʀkytʀi] *nf* (*magasin*) pork butcher's shop and delicatessen; (*produits*) cooked pork meats *pl*; **charcutier, -ière** *nm/f* pork butcher

chardon [ʃaʀdɔ̃] *nm* thistle

charge [ʃaʀʒ] *nf* (*fardeau*) load, burden; (*explosif, ÉLEC, MIL,* JUR) charge; (*rôle, mission*) responsibility; **~s** *nfpl* (*du loyer*) service charges; **à la ~ de** (*dépendant de*) dependent upon; (*aux frais de*) chargeable to; **prendre en ~** to take charge of; (*suj: véhicule*) to take on; (*dépenses*) to take care of; **~s sociales** social security contributions

chargé, e [ʃaʀʒe] *adj* (*emploi du temps, journée*) full, heavy

chargement [ʃaʀʒəmɑ̃] *nm* (*objets*) load

charger [ʃaʀʒe] *vt* (*voiture, fusil, caméra*) to load; (*batterie*) to charge ♦ *vi* (MIL *etc*) to charge; **se ~ de** *vt* to see to; **~ qn de (faire) qch** to put sb in charge of (doing) sth

chariot [ʃaʀjo] *nm* trolley; (*charrette*) waggon

charité [ʃaʀite] *nf* charity

charmant, e [ʃaʀmɑ̃, ɑ̃t] *adj* charming

charme [ʃaʀm] *nm* charm; **charmer** *vt* to charm

charnel, le [ʃaʀnɛl] *adj* carnal

charnière [ʃaʀnjɛʀ] *nf* hinge; (*fig*) turning-point

charnu, e [ʃaʀny] *adj* fleshy

charpente [ʃaʀpɑ̃t] *nf* frame(work); **charpentier** *nm* carpenter

charpie [ʃaʀpi] *nf*: **en ~** (*fig*) in shreds *ou* ribbons

charrette [ʃaʀɛt] *nf* cart

charrier [ʃaʀje] *vt* (*entraîner: fleuve*) to carry (along); (*transporter*) to cart, carry

charrue [ʃaʀy] *nf* plough (*BRIT*), plow (*US*)

charter [ʃaʀtɛʀ] *nm* (*vol*) charter flight

chasse [ʃas] *nf* hunting; (*au fusil*) shooting; (*poursuite*) chase; (*aussi:* **~ d'eau**) flush; **~ gardée** private hunting grounds *pl*; **prendre en ~** to give chase to; **tirer la ~ (d'eau)** to flush the toilet, pull the chain; **~ à courre** hunting; **chasse-neige** *nm inv* snowplough (*BRIT*), snowplow (*US*); **chasser** *vt* to hunt; (*expulser*) to chase away *ou* out, drive away *ou* out; **chasseur, -euse** *nm/f* hunter ♦ *nm* (*avion*) fighter

châssis [ʃɑsi] *nm* (AUTO) chassis; (*cadre*) frame

chat [ʃa] *nm* cat

châtaigne [ʃɑtɛɲ] *nf* chestnut; **châtaignier** *nm* chestnut (tree)

châtain [ʃɑtɛ̃] *adj inv* (*cheveux*) chestnut (brown); (*personne*) chestnut-haired

château, x [ʃɑto] *nm* (*forteresse*) castle; (*résidence royale*) palace; (*manoir*) mansion; ~ **d'eau** water tower; ~ **fort** stronghold, fortified castle

châtier [ʃɑtje] *vt* to punish; **châtiment** *nm* punishment

chaton [ʃatɔ̃] *nm* (ZOOL) kitten

chatouiller [ʃatuje] *vt* to tickle; **chatouilleux, -euse** *adj* ticklish; (*fig*) touchy, over-sensitive

chatoyer [ʃatwaje] *vi* to shimmer

châtrer [ʃɑtʀe] *vt* (*mâle*) to castrate; (: *cheval*) to geld; (*femelle*) to spay

chatte [ʃat] *nf* (she-)cat

chaud, e [ʃo, ʃod] *adj* (*gén*) warm; (*très* ~) hot; **il fait** ~ it's warm; it's hot; **avoir** ~ to be warm; to be hot; **ça me tient** ~ it keeps me warm; **rester au** ~ to stay in the warm

chaudière [ʃodjɛʀ] *nf* boiler

chaudron [ʃodʀɔ̃] *nm* cauldron

chauffage [ʃofaʒ] *nm* heating; ~ **central** central heating

chauffard [ʃofaʀ] *nm* (*péj*) reckless driver

chauffe-eau [ʃofo] *nm inv* water-heater

chauffer [ʃofe] *vt* to heat ♦ *vi* to heat up, warm up; (*trop* ~: *moteur*) to overheat; **se** ~ *vi* (*au soleil*) to warm o.s

chauffeur [ʃofœʀ] *nm* driver; (*privé*) chauffeur

chaume [ʃom] *nm* (*du toit*) thatch; **chaumière** *nf* (thatched) cottage

chaussée [ʃose] *nf* road(way)

chausse-pied [ʃospje] *nm* shoe-horn

chausser [ʃose] *vt* (*bottes, skis*) to put on; (*enfant*) to put shoes on; ~ **du 38/42** to take size 38/42

chaussette [ʃosɛt] *nf* sock

chausson [ʃosɔ̃] *nm* slipper; (*de bébé*) bootee; ~ **(aux pommes)** (apple) turnover

chaussure [ʃosyʀ] *nf* shoe; **~s à talon** high-heeled shoes; **~s de marche** walking shoes/boots; **~s de ski** ski boots

chauve [ʃov] *adj* bald; **chauve-souris** *nf* bat

chauvin, e [ʃovɛ̃, in] *adj* chauvinistic

chaux [ʃo] *nf* lime; **blanchi à la** ~ whitewashed

chavirer [ʃaviʀe] *vi* to capsize

chef [ʃɛf] *nm* head, leader; (*de cuisine*) chef; ~ **d'accusation** charge; ~ **d'entreprise** company head; ~ **d'état** head of state; ~ **de famille** head of the family; ~ **de gare** station master; ~ **d'orchestre** conductor; ~ **de service** department head; **chef-d'œuvre** *nm* masterpiece; **chef-lieu** *nm* county town

chemin [ʃ(ə)mɛ̃] *nm* path; (*itinéraire, direction, trajet*) way; **en** ~ on the way; ~ **de fer** railway (BRIT), railroad (US); **par** ~ **de fer** by rail

cheminée [ʃ(ə)mine] *nf* chimney; (*à l'intérieur*) chimney piece, fireplace; (*de bateau*) funnel

cheminement [ʃ(ə)minmɑ̃] *nm* progress

cheminot [ʃ(ə)mino] *nm* railwayman

chemise [ʃ(ə)miz] *nf* shirt; (*dossier*) folder; ~ **de nuit** nightdress

chemisier [ʃ(ə)mizje, jɛʀ] *nm* blouse

chenal, -aux [ʃənal, o] *nm* channel

chêne [ʃɛn] *nm* oak (tree); (*bois*) oak

chenil [ʃ(ə)nil] *nm* kennels *pl*

chenille [ʃ(ə)nij] *nf* (ZOOL) caterpillar

chèque [ʃɛk] *nm* cheque (BRIT), check (US); ~ **sans provision** bad cheque; ~ **de voyage** traveller's cheque; **chéquier** [ʃekje] *nm* cheque book

cher, -ère [ʃɛʀ] *adj* (*aimé*) dear; (*coûteux*) expensive, dear ♦ *adv*: **ça**

coûte ~ it's expensive

chercher [ʃɛʀʃe] *vt* to look for; (*gloire etc*) to seek; **aller ~** to go for, go and fetch; **~ à faire** to try to do; **chercheur, -euse** *nm/f* researcher, research worker

chère [ʃɛʀ] *adj voir* **cher**

chéri, e [ʃeʀi] *adj* beloved, dear; **(mon) ~** darling

chérir [ʃeʀiʀ] *vt* to cherish

cherté [ʃɛʀte] *nf*: **la ~ de la vie** the high cost of living

chétif, -ive [ʃetif, iv] *adj* (*enfant*) puny

cheval, -aux [ʃ(ə)val, o] *nm* horse; (AUTO): **~ (vapeur)** horsepower *no pl*; **faire du ~** to ride; **à ~** on horseback; **à ~ sur** astride; (*fig*) overlapping; **~ de course** racehorse

chevalet [ʃ(ə)valɛ] *nm* easel

chevalier [ʃ(ə)valje] *nm* knight

chevalière [ʃ(ə)valjɛʀ] *nf* signet ring

chevalin, e [ʃ(ə)valɛ̃, in] *adj*: **boucherie ~e** horse-meat butcher's

chevaucher [ʃ(ə)voʃe] *vi* (*aussi*: **se ~**) to overlap (each other) ♦ *vt* to be astride, straddle

chevaux [ʃəvo] *nmpl de* **cheval**

chevelu, e [ʃəv(ə)ly] (*péj*) *adj* long-haired

chevelure [ʃəv(ə)lyʀ] *nf* hair *no pl*

chevet [ʃ(ə)vɛ] *nm*: **au ~ de qn** at sb's bedside; **lampe de ~** bedside lamp

cheveu, x [ʃ(ə)vø] *nm* hair; **~x** *nmpl* (*chevelure*) hair *sg*; **avoir les ~x courts** to have short hair

cheville [ʃ(ə)vij] *nf* (ANAT) ankle; (*de bois*) peg; (*pour une vis*) plug

chèvre [ʃɛvʀ] *nf* (she-)goat

chevreau, x [ʃəvʀo] *nm* kid

chèvrefeuille [ʃɛvʀəfœj] *nm* honeysuckle

chevreuil [ʃəvʀœj] *nm* roe deer *inv*; (CULIN) venison

chevronné, e [ʃəvʀɔne] *adj* seasoned

MOT-CLÉ

chez [ʃe] *prép* **1** (*à la demeure de*) at; (: *direction*) to; **chez qn** at/to sb's house *ou* place; **chez moi** at home; (*direction*) home

2 (*+profession*) at; (: *direction*) to; **chez le boulanger/dentiste** at *ou* to the baker's/dentist's

3 (*dans le caractère, l'œuvre de*) in; **chez les renards/Racine** in foxes/Racine

chez-soi [ʃeswa] *nm inv* home

chic [ʃik] *adj inv* chic, smart; (*fam*: *généreux*) nice, decent ♦ *nm* stylishness; **~ (alors)!** (*fam*) great!; **avoir le ~ de** to have the knack of

chicane [ʃikan] *nf* (*querelle*) squabble; **chicaner** *vi* (*ergoter*): **chicaner sur** to quibble about

chiche [ʃiʃ] *adj* niggardly, mean ♦ *excl* (*à un défi*) you're on!

chichis [ʃiʃi] (*fam*) *nmpl* fuss *sg*

chicorée [ʃikɔʀe] *nf* (*café*) chicory; (*salade*) endive

chien [ʃjɛ̃] *nm* dog; **~ de garde** guard dog; **chien-loup** *nm* wolfhound

chiendent [ʃjɛ̃dɑ̃] *nm* couch grass

chienne [ʃjɛn] *nf* dog, bitch

chier [ʃje] (*fam!*) *vi* to crap (*!*)

chiffon [ʃifɔ̃] *nm* (piece of) rag; **chiffonner** *vt* to crumple; (*fam*: *tracasser*) to concern

chiffre [ʃifʀ] *nm* (*représentant un nombre*) figure, numeral; (*montant, total*) total, sum; **en ~s ronds** in round figures; **~ d'affaires** turnover; **chiffrer** *vt* (*dépense*) to put a figure to, assess; (*message*) to (en)code, cipher; **se chiffrer à** to add up to, amount to

chignon [ʃiɲɔ̃] *nm* chignon, bun

Chili [ʃili] *nm*: **le ~** Chile; **chilien, ne** *adj* Chilean ♦ *nm/f*: **Chilien, ne** Chilean

chimie [ʃimi] *nf* chemistry; **chimique** *adj* chemical; **produits chimiques** chemicals

chimpanzé [ʃɛ̃pɑ̃ze] *nm* chimpanzee

Chine [ʃin] *nf*: **la ~** China; **chinois, e** *adj* Chinese ♦ *nm/f*: **Chinois, e** Chinese

♦ *nm* (*LING*) Chinese

chiot [ʃjo] *nm* pup(py)

chiper [ʃipe] (*fam*) *vt* to pinch

chipoter [ʃipɔte] (*fam*) *vi* (*ergoter*) to quibble

chips [ʃips] *nfpl* crisps (*BRIT*), (potato) chips (*US*)

chiquenaude [ʃiknod] *nf* flick, flip

chirurgical, e, -aux [ʃiʀyʀʒikal, o] *adj* surgical

chirurgie [ʃiʀyʀʒi] *nf* surgery; **~ esthétique** plastic surgery; **chirurgien, ne** *nm/f* surgeon

chlore [klɔʀ] *nm* chlorine

choc [ʃɔk] *nm* (*heurt*) impact, shock; (*collision*) crash; (*moral*) shock; (*affrontement*) clash

chocolat [ʃɔkɔla] *nm* chocolate; **~ au lait** milk chocolate; **~ (chaud)** hot chocolate

chœur [kœʀ] *nm* (*chorale*) choir; (*OPÉRA, THÉÂTRE*) chorus; **en ~** in chorus

choisir [ʃwaziʀ] *vt* to choose, select

choix [ʃwa] *nm* choice, selection; **avoir le ~** to have the choice; **premier ~** (*COMM*) class one; **de ~** choice, selected; **au ~** as you wish

chômage [ʃomaʒ] *nm* unemployment; **mettre au ~** to make redundant, put out of work; **être au ~** to be unemployed *ou* out of work; **chômeur, -euse** *nm/f* unemployed person

chope [ʃɔp] *nf* tankard

choper [ʃɔpe] (*fam*) *vt* (*objet, maladie*) to catch

choquer [ʃɔke] *vt* (*offenser*) to shock; (*deuil*) to shake

chorale [kɔʀal] *nf* choir

choriste [kɔʀist] *nm/f* choir member; (*OPÉRA*) chorus member

chose [ʃoz] *nf* thing; **c'est peu de ~** it's nothing (really)

chou, x [ʃu] *nm* cabbage; **mon petit ~** (my) sweetheart; **~ à la crème** choux bun; **~x de Bruxelles** Brussels sprouts; **chouchou, te** (*fam*) *nm/f* darling; (*SCOL*) teacher's pet; **choucroute** *nf* sauerkraut

chouette [ʃwɛt] *nf* owl ♦ *adj* (*fam*) great, smashing

chou-fleur [ʃuflœʀ] *nm* cauliflower

choyer [ʃwaje] *vt* (*dorloter*) to cherish; (: *excessivement*) to pamper

chrétien, ne [kʀetjɛ̃, jɛn] *adj, nm/f* Christian

Christ [kʀist] *nm*: **le ~** Christ; **christianisme** *nm* Christianity

chrome [kʀom] *nm* chromium; **chromé, e** *adj* chromium-plated

chronique [kʀɔnik] *adj* chronic ♦ *nf* (*de journal*) column, page; (*historique*) chronicle; (*RADIO, TV*): **la ~ sportive** the sports review

chronologique [kʀɔnɔlɔʒik] *adj* chronological

chronomètre [kʀɔnɔmɛtʀ] *nm* stopwatch; **chronométrer** *vt* to time

chrysanthème [kʀizɑ̃tɛm] *nm* chrysanthemum

chuchotement [ʃyʃɔtmɑ̃] *nm* whisper

chuchoter [ʃyʃɔte] *vt, vi* to whisper

chut [ʃyt] *excl* sh!

chute [ʃyt] *nf* fall; (*déchet*) scrap; **faire une ~ (de 10 m)** to fall (10 m); **~ (d'eau)** waterfall; **la ~ des cheveux** hair loss; **~ libre** free fall; **~s de pluie/neige** rain/snowfalls

Chypre [ʃipʀ] *nm/f* Cyprus

-ci [si] *adv voir* **par** ♦ *dét*: **ce garçon-~/-là** this/that boy; **ces femmes-~/-là** these/those women

cible [sibl] *nf* target

ciboulette [sibulɛt] *nf* (small) chive

cicatrice [sikatʀis] *nf* scar; **cicatriser** *vt* to heal

ci-contre [sikɔ̃tʀ] *adv* opposite

ci-dessous [sidəsu] *adv* below

ci-dessus [sidəsy] *adv* above

cidre [sidʀ] *nm* cider

Cie *abr* (= *compagnie*) Co.

ciel [sjɛl] *nm* sky; (*REL*) heaven; **cieux** *nmpl* (*REL*) heaven *sg*; **à ~ ouvert** open-air; (*mine*) open-cast

cierge [sjɛʀʒ] *nm* candle

cieux [sjø] *nmpl de* **ciel**
cigale [sigal] *nf* cicada
cigare [sigaʀ] *nm* cigar
cigarette [sigaʀɛt] *nf* cigarette
ci-gît [siʒi] *adv +vb* here lies
cigogne [sigɔɲ] *nf* stork
ci-inclus, e [siɛ̃kly, yz] *adj, adv* enclosed
ci-joint, e [siʒwɛ̃, ɛ̃t] *adj, adv* enclosed
cil [sil] *nm* (eye)lash
cime [sim] *nf* top; (*montagne*) peak
ciment [simɑ̃] *nm* cement
cimetière [simtjɛʀ] *nm* cemetery; (*d'église*) churchyard
cinéaste [sineast] *nm/f* film-maker
cinéma [sinema] *nm* cinema; **cinématographique** *adj* film *cpd*, cinema *cpd*
cinglant, e [sɛ̃glɑ̃, ɑ̃t] *adj* (*remarque*) biting
cinglé, e [sɛ̃gle] (*fam*) *adj* crazy
cinq [sɛ̃k] *num* five; **cinquantaine** *nf*: **une cinquantaine (de)** about fifty; **avoir la cinquantaine** (*âge*) to be around fifty; **cinquante** *num* fifty; **cinquantenaire** *adj, nm/f* fifty-year-old; **cinquième** *num* fifth
cintre [sɛ̃tʀ] *nm* coat-hanger
cintré, e [sɛ̃tʀe] *adj* (*chemise*) fitted
cirage [siʀaʒ] *nm* (shoe) polish
circonflexe [siʀkɔ̃flɛks] *adj*: **accent ~** circumflex accent
circonscription [siʀkɔ̃skʀipsjɔ̃] *nf* district; **~ électorale** (*d'un député*) constituency
circonscrire [siʀkɔ̃skʀiʀ] *vt* (*sujet*) to define, delimit; (*incendie*) to contain
circonstance [siʀkɔ̃stɑ̃s] *nf* circumstance; (*occasion*) occasion; **~s atténuantes** mitigating circumstances
circuit [siʀkɥi] *nm* (ÉLEC, TECH) circuit; (*trajet*) tour, (round) trip
circulaire [siʀkylɛʀ] *adj, nf* circular
circulation [siʀkylasjɔ̃] *nf* circulation; (AUTO): **la ~** (the) traffic
circuler [siʀkyle] *vi* (*sang, devises*) to circulate; (*véhicules*) to drive (along); (*passants*) to walk along; (*train, bus*) to run; **faire ~** (*nouvelle*) to spread (about), circulate; (*badauds*) to move on
cire [siʀ] *nf* wax; **ciré** *nm* oilskin; **cirer** *vt* to wax, polish
cirque [siʀk] *nm* circus; (*fig*) chaos, bedlam; **quel ~!** what a carry-on!
cisaille(s) [sizɑj] *nf(pl)* (gardening) shears *pl*
ciseau, x [sizo] *nm*: **~ (à bois)** chisel; **~x** *nmpl* (*paire de ~x*) (pair of) scissors
ciseler [siz(ə)le] *vt* to chisel, carve
citadin, e [sitadɛ̃, in] *nm/f* city dweller
citation [sitasjɔ̃] *nf* (*d'auteur*) quotation; (JUR) summons *sg*
cité [site] *nf* town; (*plus grande*) city; **~ universitaire** students' residences *pl*
citer [site] *vt* (*un auteur*) to quote (from); (*nommer*) to name; (JUR) to summon
citerne [sitɛʀn] *nf* tank
citoyen, ne [sitwajɛ̃, jɛn] *nm/f* citizen
citron [sitʀɔ̃] *nm* lemon; **~ vert** lime; **citronnade** *nf* still lemonade
citrouille [sitʀuj] *nf* pumpkin
civet [sivɛ] *nm*: **~ de lapin** rabbit stew
civière [sivjɛʀ] *nf* stretcher
civil, e [sivil] *adj* (*mariage, poli*) civil; (*non militaire*) civilian; **en ~** in civilian clothes; **dans le ~** in civilian life
civilisation [sivilizasjɔ̃] *nf* civilization
clair, e [klɛʀ] *adj* light; (*pièce*) light, bright; (*eau, son, fig*) clear ♦ *adv*: **voir ~** to see clearly; **tirer qch au ~** to clear sth up, clarify sth; **mettre au ~** (*notes etc*) to tidy up; **~ de lune** ♦ *nm* moonlight; **clairement** *adv* clearly
clairière [klɛʀjɛʀ] *nf* clearing
clairon [klɛʀɔ̃] *nm* bugle; **claironner** *vt* (*fig*) to trumpet, shout from the rooftops
clairsemé, e [klɛʀsəme] *adj* sparse
clairvoyant, e [klɛʀvwajɑ̃, ɑ̃t] *adj* perceptive, clear-sighted
clandestin, e [klɑ̃dɛstɛ̃, in] *adj* clandestine, secret; (*mouvement*) underground; (*travailleur*) illegal; **passager ~**

stowaway

clapier [klapje] *nm* (rabbit) hutch

clapoter [klapɔte] *vi* to lap

claque [klak] *nf* (*gifle*) slap; **claquer** *vi* (*porte*) to bang, slam; (*fam: mourir*) to snuff it ♦ *vt* (*porte*) to slam, bang; (*doigts*) to snap; (*fam: dépenser*) to blow; **il claquait des dents** his teeth were chattering; **être claqué** (*fam*) to be dead tired; **se claquer un muscle** to pull *ou* strain a muscle; **claquettes** *nfpl* tap-dancing *sg*; (*chaussures*) flip-flops

clarinette [klaʀinɛt] *nf* clarinet

clarté [klaʀte] *nf* (*luminosité*) brightness; (*d'un son, de l'eau*) clearness; (*d'une explication*) clarity

classe [klɑs] *nf* class; (SCOL: *local*) class(room); (: *leçon, élèves*) class; **aller en ~** to go to school; **classement** *nm* (*rang*: SCOL) place; (: SPORT) placing; (*liste*: SCOL) class list (in order of merit); (: SPORT) placings *pl*

classer [klɑse] *vt* (*idées, livres*) to classify; (*papiers*) to file; (*candidat, concurrent*) to grade; (JUR: *affaire*) to close; **se ~ premier/dernier** to come first/last; (SPORT) to finish first/last; **classeur** *nm* (*cahier*) file

classique [klasik] *adj* classical; (*sobre: coupe etc*) classic(al); (*habituel*) standard, classic

clause [kloz] *nf* clause

clavecin [klav(ə)sɛ̃] *nm* harpsichord

clavicule [klavikyl] *nf* collarbone

clavier [klavje] *nm* keyboard

clé [kle] *nf* key; (MUS) clef; (*de mécanicien*) spanner (BRIT), wrench (US); **prix ~s en main** (*d'une voiture*) on-the-road price; **~ anglaise** (monkey) wrench; **~ de contact** ignition key

clef [kle] *nf* = **clé**

clément, e [klemɑ̃, ɑ̃t] *adj* (*temps*) mild; (*indulgent*) lenient

clerc [klɛʀ] *nm*: **~ de notaire** solicitor's clerk

clergé [klɛʀʒe] *nm* clergy

cliché [kliʃe] *nm* (*fig*) cliché; (*négatif*) negative; (*photo*) print

client, e [klijɑ̃, klijɑ̃t] *nm/f* (*acheteur*) customer, client; (*d'hôtel*) guest, patron; (*du docteur*) patient; (*de l'avocat*) client; **clientèle** *nf* (*du magasin*) customers *pl*, clientèle; (*du docteur, de l'avocat*) practice

cligner [kliɲe] *vi*: **~ des yeux** to blink (one's eyes); **~ de l'œil** to wink; **clignotant** *nm* (AUTO) indicator; **clignoter** *vi* (*étoiles etc*) to twinkle; (*lumière*) to flicker

climat [klima] *nm* climate

climatisation [klimatizasjɔ̃] *nf* air conditioning; **climatisé, e** *adj* air-conditioned

clin d'œil [klɛ̃dœj] *nm* wink; **en un ~** in a flash

clinique [klinik] *nf* private hospital

clinquant, e [klɛ̃kɑ̃, ɑ̃t] *adj* flashy

clip [klip] *nm* (*boucle d'oreille*) clip-on; **(vidéo) ~** (pop) video

cliqueter [klik(ə)te] *vi* (*ferraille*) to jangle; (*clés*) to jingle

clochard, e [klɔʃaʀ, aʀd] *nm/f* tramp

cloche [klɔʃ] *nf* (*d'église*) bell; (*fam*) clot; **cloche-pied**: **à cloche-pied** *adv* on one leg, hopping (along); **clocher** *nm* church tower; (*en pointe*) steeple ♦ *vi* (*fam*) to be *ou* go wrong; **de clocher** (*péj*) parochial

cloison [klwazɔ̃] *nf* partition (wall)

cloître [klwatʀ] *nm* cloister; **cloîtrer** *vt*: **se cloîtrer** to shut o.s. up *ou* away

cloque [klɔk] *nf* blister

clore [klɔʀ] *vt* to close; **clos, e** *adj* voir **maison**; **huis**

clôture [klotyʀ] *nf* closure; (*barrière*) enclosure; **clôturer** *vt* (*terrain*) to enclose; (*débats*) to close

clou [klu] *nm* nail; **~s** *nmpl* (*passage ~té*) pedestrian crossing; **pneus à ~s** studded tyres; **le ~ du spectacle** the highlight of the show; **~ de girofle** clove; **clouer** *vt* to nail down *ou* up; **clouer le bec à qn** (*fam*) to shut sb up

clown [klun] *nm* clown
club [klœb] *nm* club
CMU *sigle f* (*= couverture maladie universelle*) *system of free health care for those on low incomes*
CNRS *sigle m* (*= Centre nationale de la recherche scientifique*) ≃ SERC (*BRIT*), ≃ NSF (*US*)
coaguler [kɔagyle] *vt, vi* (*aussi:* **se ~**: *sang*) to coagulate
coasser [kɔase] *vi* to croak
cobaye [kɔbaj] *nm* guinea-pig
coca [kɔka] *nm* Coke ®
cocaïne [kɔkain] *nf* cocaine
cocasse [kɔkas] *adj* comical, funny
coccinelle [kɔksinɛl] *nf* ladybird (*BRIT*), ladybug (*US*)
cocher [kɔʃe] *vt* to tick off
cochère [kɔʃɛʀ] *adj f*: **porte ~** carriage entrance
cochon, ne [kɔʃɔ̃, ɔn] *nm* pig ♦ *adj* (*fam*) dirty, smutty; **~ d'Inde** guinea pig; **cochonnerie** (*fam*) *nf* (*saleté*) filth; (*marchandise*) rubbish, trash
cocktail [kɔktɛl] *nm* cocktail; (*réception*) cocktail party
coco [kɔko] *nm voir* **noix**
cocorico [kɔkɔʀiko] *excl, nm* cock-a-doodle-do
cocotier [kɔkɔtje] *nm* coconut palm
cocotte [kɔkɔt] *nf* (*en fonte*) casserole; **~ (minute)** pressure cooker; **ma ~** (*fam*) sweetie (pie)
cocu [kɔky] (*fam*) *nm* cuckold
code [kɔd] *nm* code ♦ *adj*: **phares ~s** dipped lights; **se mettre en ~(s)** to dip one's (head)lights; **~ à barres** bar code; **~ civil** Common Law; **~ de la route** highway code; **~ pénal** penal code; **~ postal** (*numéro*) post (*BRIT*) *ou* zip (*US*) code
cœur [kœʀ] *nm* heart; (*CARTES: couleur*) hearts *pl*; (*: carte*) heart; **avoir bon ~** to be kind-hearted; **avoir mal au ~** to feel sick; **par ~** by heart; **de bon ~** willingly; **cela lui tient à ~** that's (very) close to his heart
coffre [kɔfʀ] *nm* (*meuble*) chest; (*d'auto*) boot (*BRIT*), trunk (*US*); **coffre(-fort)** *nm* safe; **coffret** *nm* casket
cognac [kɔɲak] *nm* brandy, cognac
cogner [kɔɲe] *vi* to knock; **se ~ la tête** to bang one's head
cohérent, e [kɔeʀɑ̃, ɑ̃t] *adj* coherent, consistent
cohorte [kɔɔʀt] *nf* troop
cohue [kɔy] *nf* crowd
coi, coite [kwa, kwat] *adj*: **rester ~** to remain silent
coiffe [kwaf] *nf* headdress
coiffé, e [kwafe] *adj*: **bien/mal ~** with tidy/untidy hair
coiffer [kwafe] *vt* (*fig: surmonter*) to cover, top; **se ~** *vi* to do one's hair; **~ qn** to do sb's hair; **coiffeur, -euse** *nm/f* hairdresser; **coiffeuse** *nf* (*table*) dressing table; **coiffure** *nf* (*cheveux*) hairstyle, hairdo; (*art*): **la coiffure** hairdressing
coin [kwɛ̃] *nm* corner; (*pour ~cer*) wedge; **l'épicerie du ~** the local grocer; **dans le ~** (*aux alentours*) in the area, around about; (*habiter*) locally; **je ne suis pas du ~** I'm not from here; **au ~ du feu** by the fireside; **regard en ~** sideways glance
coincé, e [kwɛ̃se] *adj* stuck, jammed; (*fig: inhibé*) inhibited, hung up (*fam*)
coincer [kwɛ̃se] *vt* to jam; (*fam: attraper*) to pinch
coïncidence [kɔɛ̃sidɑ̃s] *nf* coincidence
coïncider [kɔɛ̃side] *vi* to coincide
coing [kwɛ̃] *nm* quince
col [kɔl] *nm* (*de chemise*) collar; (*encolure, cou*) neck; (*de montagne*) pass; **~ de l'utérus** cervix; **~ roulé** polo-neck
colère [kɔlɛʀ] *nf* anger; **une ~** a fit of anger; **(se mettre) en ~** (to get) angry; **coléreux, -euse** *adj,* **colérique** *adj* quick-tempered, irascible
colifichet [kɔlifiʃɛ] *nm* trinket
colimaçon [kɔlimasɔ̃] *nm*: **escalier en**

~ spiral staircase
colin [kɔlɛ̃] *nm* hake
colique [kɔlik] *nf* diarrhoea
colis [kɔli] *nm* parcel
collaborateur, -trice [kɔ(l)labɔRatœR, tRis] *nm/f* (*aussi* POL) collaborator; (*d'une revue*) contributor
collaborer [kɔ(l)labɔRe] *vi* to collaborate; ~ **à** to collaborate on; (*revue*) to contribute to
collant, e [kɔlɑ̃, ɑ̃t] *adj* sticky; (*robe etc*) clinging, skintight; (*péj*) clinging ♦ *nm* (*bas*) tights *pl*; (*de danseur*) leotard
collation [kɔlasjɔ̃] *nf* light meal
colle [kɔl] *nf* glue; (*à papiers peints*) (wallpaper) paste; (*fam: devinette*) teaser, riddle; (SCOL: *fam*) detention
collecte [kɔlɛkt] *nf* collection; **collectif, -ive** *adj* collective; (*visite, billet*) group *cpd*
collection [kɔlɛksjɔ̃] *nf* collection; (ÉDITION) series; **collectionner** *vt* to collect; **collectionneur, -euse** *nm/f* collector
collectivité [kɔlɛktivite] *nf* group; **~s locales** (ADMIN) local authorities
collège [kɔlɛʒ] *nm* (*école*) (secondary) school; (*assemblée*) body; **collégien** *nm* schoolboy; **collégienne** *nf* schoolgirl

collège

The **collège** *is a state secondary school for children aged between eleven and fifteen. Pupils follow a nationally prescribed curriculum consisting of a common core and various options. Before leaving the collège, pupils are assessed by examination and course work for their* **brevet des collèges.**

collègue [kɔ(l)lɛg] *nm/f* colleague
coller [kɔle] *vt* (*papier, timbre*) to stick (on); (*affiche*) to stick up; (*enveloppe*) to stick down; (*morceaux*) to stick *ou* glue together; (*fam: mettre, fourrer*) to stick, shove; (SCOL: *fam*) to keep in ♦ *vi* (*être collant*) to be sticky; (*adhérer*) to stick; ~ **à** to stick to; **être collé à un examen** (*fam*) to fail an exam
collet [kɔlɛ] *nm* (*piège*) snare, noose; (*cou*): **prendre qn au ~** to grab sb by the throat
collier [kɔlje] *nm* (*bijou*) necklace; (*de chien*, TECH) collar
collimateur [kɔlimatœR] *nm*: **avoir qn/qch dans le ~** (*fig*) to have sb/sth in one's sights; **être dans le ~ de qn** to be in sb's sights
colline [kɔlin] *nf* hill
collision [kɔlizjɔ̃] *nf* collision, crash; **entrer en ~ (avec)** to collide (with)
colloque [kɔ(l)lɔk] *nm* symposium
collyre [kɔliR] *nm* eye drops
colmater [kɔlmate] *vt* (*fuite*) to seal off; (*brèche*) to plug, fill in
colombe [kɔlɔ̃b] *nf* dove
Colombie [kɔlɔ̃bi] *nf*: **la ~** Colombia
colon [kɔlɔ̃] *nm* settler
colonie [kɔlɔni] *nf* colony; **~ (de vacances)** holiday camp (*for children*)
colonne [kɔlɔn] *nf* column; **se mettre en ~ par deux** to get into twos; **~ (vertébrale)** spine, spinal column
colorant [kɔlɔRɑ̃, ɑ̃t] *nm* colouring
colorer [kɔlɔRe] *vt* to colour
colorier [kɔlɔRje] *vt* to colour (in)
coloris [kɔlɔRi] *nm* colour, shade
colporter [kɔlpɔRte] *vt* to hawk, peddle
colza [kɔlza] *nm* rape(seed)
coma [kɔma] *nm* coma; **être dans le ~** to be in a coma
combat [kɔ̃ba] *nm* fight, fighting *no pl*; **~ de boxe** boxing match; **combattant** *nm*: **ancien combattant** war veteran; **combattre** *vt* to fight; (*épidémie, ignorance*) to combat, fight against
combien [kɔ̃bjɛ̃] *adv* (*quantité*) how much; (*nombre*) how many; **~ de** (*quantité*) how much; (*nombre*) how many; **~ de temps** how long; **~ ça coûte/pèse?** how much does it cost/

weigh?; **on est le ~ aujourd'hui?** (*fam*) what's the date today?

combinaison [kɔ̃binɛzɔ̃] *nf* combination; (*astuce*) scheme; (*de femme*) slip; (*de plongée*) wetsuit; (*bleu de travail*) boiler suit (*BRIT*), coveralls *pl* (*US*)

combine [kɔ̃bin] *nf* trick; (*péj*) scheme, fiddle (*BRIT*)

combiné [kɔ̃bine] *nm* (*aussi:* **~ téléphonique**) receiver

combiner [kɔ̃bine] *vt* (*grouper*) to combine; (*plan, horaire*) to work out, devise

comble [kɔ̃bl] *adj* (*salle*) packed (full) ♦ *nm* (*du bonheur, plaisir*) height; **~s** *nmpl* (*CONSTR*) attic *sg*, loft *sg*; **c'est le ~!** that beats everything!

combler [kɔ̃ble] *vt* (*trou*) to fill in; (*besoin, lacune*) to fill; (*déficit*) to make good; (*satisfaire*) to fulfil

combustible [kɔ̃bystibl] *nm* fuel

comédie [kɔmedi] *nf* comedy; (*fig*) playacting *no pl*; **faire la ~** (*fam*) to make a fuss; **~ musicale** musical; **comédien, ne** *nm/f* actor(-tress)

Comédie française

Founded in 1680 by Louis XIV, the **Comédie française** *is the French national theatre. Subsidized by the state, the company performs mainly in the Palais Royal in Paris and stages mainly classical French plays.*

comestible [kɔmɛstibl] *adj* edible

comique [kɔmik] *adj* (*drôle*) comical; (*THÉÂTRE*) comic ♦ *nm* (*artiste*) comic, comedian

comité [kɔmite] *nm* committee; **~ d'entreprise** works council

commandant [kɔmɑ̃dɑ̃] *nm* (*gén*) commander, commandant; (*NAVIG, AVIAT*) captain

commande [kɔmɑ̃d] *nf* (*COMM*) order; **~s** *nfpl* (*AVIAT etc*) controls; **sur ~** to order; **commandement** *nm* command; (*REL*) commandment; **commander** *vt* (*COMM*) to order; (*diriger, ordonner*) to command; **commander à qn de faire** to command *ou* order sb to do

commando [kɔmɑ̃do] *nm* commando (squad)

MOT-CLÉ

comme [kɔm] *prép* **1** (*comparaison*) like; **tout comme son père** just like his father; **fort comme un bœuf** as strong as an ox; **joli comme tout** ever so pretty

2 (*manière*) like; **faites-le comme ça** do it like this, do it this way; **comme ci, comme ça** so-so, middling

3 (*en tant que*) as a; **donner comme prix** to give as a prize; **travailler comme secrétaire** to work as a secretary

♦ *conj* **1** (*ainsi que*) as; **elle écrit comme elle parle** she writes as she talks; **comme si** as if

2 (*au moment où, alors que*) as; **il est parti comme j'arrivais** he left as I arrived

3 (*parce que, puisque*) as; **comme il était en retard, il ...** as he was late, he ...

♦ *adv*: **comme il est fort/c'est bon!** he's so strong/it's so good!

commémorer [kɔmemɔʀe] *vt* to commemorate

commencement [kɔmɑ̃smɑ̃] *nm* beginning, start

commencer [kɔmɑ̃se] *vt, vi* to begin, start; **~ à** *ou* **de faire** to begin *ou* start doing

comment [kɔmɑ̃] *adv* how; **~?** (*que dites-vous*) pardon?

commentaire [kɔmɑ̃tɛʀ] *nm* (*remarque*) comment, remark; (*exposé*) commentary

commenter [kɔmɑ̃te] *vt* (*jugement, événement*) to comment (up)on; (*RADIO, TV: match, manifestation*) to cover

commérages [kɔmeʀaʒ] *nmpl* gossip *sg*

commerçant, e [kɔmɛʀsɑ̃, ɑ̃t] *nm/f* shopkeeper, trader
commerce [kɔmɛʀs] *nm* (*activité*) trade, commerce; (*boutique*) business; **~ électronique** e-commerce; **commercial, e, -aux** *adj* commercial, trading; (*péj*) commercial; **les commerciaux** the sales people; **commercialiser** *vt* to market
commère [kɔmɛʀ] *nf* gossip
commettre [kɔmɛtʀ] *vt* to commit
commis [kɔmi] *nm* (*de magasin*) (shop) assistant; (*de banque*) clerk
commissaire [kɔmisɛʀ] *nm* (*de police*) ≃ (police) superintendent; **commissaire-priseur** *nm* auctioneer; **commissariat** *nm* police station
commission [kɔmisjɔ̃] *nf* (*comité, pourcentage*) commission; (*message*) message; (*course*) errand; **~s** *nfpl* (*achats*) shopping *sg*
commode [kɔmɔd] *adj* (*pratique*) convenient, handy; (*facile*) easy; (*personne*): **pas ~** awkward (to deal with) ♦ *nf* chest of drawers; **commodité** *nf* convenience
commotion [komosjɔ̃] *nf*: **~ (cérébrale)** concussion; **commotionné, e** *adj* shocked, shaken
commun, e [kɔmœ̃, yn] *adj* common; (*pièce*) communal, shared; (*effort*) joint; **ça sort du ~** it's out of the ordinary; **le ~ des mortels** the common run of people; **en ~** (*faire*) jointly; **mettre en ~** to pool, share; *voir aussi* **communs**
communauté [kɔmynote] *nf* community
commune [kɔmyn] *nf* (ADMIN) commune, ≃ district; (: *urbaine*) ≃ borough
communicatif, -ive [kɔmynikatif, iv] *adj* (*rire*) infectious; (*personne*) communicative
communication [kɔmynikasjɔ̃] *nf* communication; **~ (téléphonique)** (telephone) call
communier [kɔmynje] *vi* (REL) to receive communion
communion [kɔmynjɔ̃] *nf* communion
communiquer [kɔmynike] *vt* (*nouvelle, dossier*) to pass on, convey; (*peur etc*) to communicate ♦ *vi* to communicate; **se ~ à** (*se propager*) to spread to
communisme [kɔmynism] *nm* communism; **communiste** *adj, nm/f* communist
communs [kɔmœ̃] *nmpl* (*bâtiments*) outbuildings
commutateur [kɔmytatœʀ] *nm* (ÉLEC) (change-over) switch, commutator
compact, e [kɔ̃pakt] *adj* (*dense*) dense; (*appareil*) compact
compagne [kɔ̃paɲ] *nf* companion
compagnie [kɔ̃paɲi] *nf* (*firme,* MIL) company; **tenir ~ à qn** to keep sb company; **fausser ~ à qn** to give sb the slip, slip *ou* sneak away from sb; **~ aérienne** airline (company)
compagnon [kɔ̃paɲɔ̃] *nm* companion
comparable [kɔ̃paʀabl] *adj*: **~ (à)** comparable (to)
comparaison [kɔ̃paʀɛzɔ̃] *nf* comparison
comparaître [kɔ̃paʀɛtʀ] *vi*: **~ (devant)** to appear (before)
comparer [kɔ̃paʀe] *vt* to compare; **~ qch/qn à** *ou* **et** (*pour choisir*) to compare sth/sb with *ou* and; (*pour établir une similitude*) to compare sth/sb to
compartiment [kɔ̃paʀtimɑ̃] *nm* compartment
comparution [kɔ̃paʀysjɔ̃] *nf* (JUR) appearance
compas [kɔ̃pɑ] *nm* (GÉOM) (pair of) compasses *pl*; (NAVIG) compass
compatible [kɔ̃patibl] *adj* compatible
compatir [kɔ̃patiʀ] *vi* to sympathize
compatriote [kɔ̃patʀijɔt] *nm/f* compatriot
compensation [kɔ̃pɑ̃sasjɔ̃] *nf* compensation
compenser [kɔ̃pɑ̃se] *vt* to compensate for, make up for
compère [kɔ̃pɛʀ] *nm* accomplice
compétence [kɔ̃petɑ̃s] *nf* competence

compétent, e [kɔ̃petɑ̃, ɑ̃t] *adj* (*apte*) competent, capable
compétition [kɔ̃petisjɔ̃] *nf* (*gén*) competition; (*SPORT*: *épreuve*) event; **la ~ automobile** motor racing
complainte [kɔ̃plɛ̃t] *nf* lament
complaire [kɔ̃plɛʀ]: **se ~** *vi*: **se ~ dans** to take pleasure in
complaisance [kɔ̃plɛzɑ̃s] *nf* kindness; **pavillon de ~** flag of convenience
complaisant, e [kɔ̃plɛzɑ̃, ɑ̃t] *adj* (*aimable*) kind, obliging
complément [kɔ̃plemɑ̃] *nm* complement; (*reste*) remainder; **~ d'information** (*ADMIN*) supplementary *ou* further information; **complémentaire** *adj* complementary; (*additionnel*) supplementary
complet, -ète [kɔ̃plɛ, ɛt] *adj* complete; (*plein*: *hôtel etc*) full ♦ *nm* (*aussi*: **~-veston**) suit; **pain ~** wholemeal bread; **complètement** *adv* completely; **compléter** *vt* (*porter à la quantité voulue*) to complete; (*augmenter*: *connaissances, études*) to complement, supplement; (: *garde-robe*) to add to; **se compléter** (*caractères*) to complement one another
complexe [kɔ̃plɛks] *adj, nm* complex; **complexé, e** *adj* mixed-up, hung-up
complication [kɔ̃plikasjɔ̃] *nf* complexity, intricacy; (*difficulté, ennui*) complication
complice [kɔ̃plis] *nm* accomplice; **complicité** *nf* complicity
compliment [kɔ̃plimɑ̃] *nm* (*louange*) compliment; **~s** *nmpl* (*félicitations*) congratulations
compliqué, e [kɔ̃plike] *adj* complicated, complex; (*personne*) complicated
compliquer [kɔ̃plike] *vt* to complicate; **se ~** to become complicated
complot [kɔ̃plo] *nm* plot
comportement [kɔ̃pɔʀtəmɑ̃] *nm* behaviour
comporter [kɔ̃pɔʀte] *vt* (*consister en*) to consist of, comprise; (*inclure*) to have; **se ~** *vi* to behave
composant [kɔ̃pozɑ̃] *nm*, **composante** [kɔ̃pozɑ̃t] *nf* component
composé [kɔ̃poze] *nm* compound
composer [kɔ̃poze] *vt* (*musique, texte*) to compose; (*mélange, équipe*) to make up; (*numéro*) to dial; (*constituer*) to make up, form ♦ *vi* (*transiger*) to come to terms; **se ~ de** to be composed of, be made up of; **compositeur, -trice** *nm/f* (*MUS*) composer; **composition** *nf* composition; (*SCOL*) test
composter [kɔ̃pɔste] *vt* (*billet*) to punch
compote [kɔ̃pɔt] *nf* stewed fruit *no pl*; **~ de pommes** stewed apples
compréhensible [kɔ̃pʀeɑ̃sibl] *adj* comprehensible; (*attitude*) understandable
compréhensif, -ive [kɔ̃pʀeɑ̃sif, iv] *adj* understanding
comprendre [kɔ̃pʀɑ̃dʀ] *vt* to understand; (*se composer de*) to comprise, consist of
compresse [kɔ̃pʀɛs] *nf* compress
compression [kɔ̃pʀesjɔ̃] *nf* compression; (*de personnes*) reduction
comprimé [kɔ̃pʀime] *nm* tablet
comprimer [kɔ̃pʀime] *vt* to compress; (*fig*: *crédit etc*) to reduce, cut down
compris, e [kɔ̃pʀi, iz] *pp de* **comprendre** ♦ *adj* (*inclus*) included; **~ entre** (*situé*) contained between; **l'électricité ~e/non ~e, y/non ~ l'électricité** including/excluding electricity; **100 F tout ~** 100 F all inclusive *ou* all-in
compromettre [kɔ̃pʀɔmɛtʀ] *vt* to compromise; **compromis** *nm* compromise
comptabilité [kɔ̃tabilite] *nf* (*activité*) accounting, accountancy; (*comptes*) accounts *pl*, books *pl*; (*service*) accounts office
comptable [kɔ̃tabl] *nm/f* accountant
comptant [kɔ̃tɑ̃] *adv*: **payer ~** to pay cash; **acheter ~** to buy for cash
compte [kɔ̃t] *nm* count; (*total, mon-*

tant) count, (right) number; (*bancaire, facture*) account; **~s** *nmpl* (FINANCE) accounts, books; (*fig*) explanation *sg*; **en fin de ~** all things considered; **s'en tirer à bon ~** to get off lightly; **pour le ~ de** on behalf of; **pour son propre ~** for one's own benefit; **tenir ~ de** to take account of; **travailler à son ~** to work for oneself; **rendre ~ (à qn) de qch** to give (sb) an account of sth; *voir aussi* **rendre ~ à rebours** countdown; **~ chèques postaux** Post Office account; **~ courant** current account; **~ rendu** account, report; (*de film, livre*) review; **compte-gouttes** *nm inv* dropper

compter [kɔ̃te] *vt* to count; (*facturer*) to charge for; (*avoir à son actif, comporter*) to have; (*prévoir*) to allow, reckon; (*penser, espérer*): **~ réussir** to expect to succeed ♦ *vi* to count; (*être économe*) to economize; (*figurer*): **~ parmi** to be *ou* rank among; **~ sur** to count (up)on; **~ avec qch/qn** to reckon with *ou* take account of sth/sb; **sans ~ que** besides which

compteur [kɔ̃tœʀ] *nm* meter; **~ de vitesse** speedometer

comptine [kɔ̃tin] *nf* nursery rhyme

comptoir [kɔ̃twaʀ] *nm* (*de magasin*) counter; (*bar*) bar

compulser [kɔ̃pylse] *vt* to consult

comte [kɔ̃t] *nm* count; **comtesse** *nf* countess

con, ne [kɔ̃, kɔn] (*fam!*) *adj* damned *ou* bloody (BRIT) stupid (*!*)

concéder [kɔ̃sede] *vt* to grant; (*défaite, point*) to concede

concentré, e [kɔ̃sɑ̃tʀe] *adj* (*lait*) condensed ♦ *nm*: **~ de tomates** tomato purée

concentrer [kɔ̃sɑ̃tʀe] *vt* to concentrate; **se ~** *vi* to concentrate

concept [kɔ̃sɛpt] *nm* concept

conception [kɔ̃sɛpsjɔ̃] *nf* conception; (*d'une machine etc*) design; (*d'un problème, de la vie*) approach

concerner [kɔ̃sɛʀne] *vt* to concern; **en ce qui me concerne** as far as I am concerned

concert [kɔ̃sɛʀ] *nm* concert; **de ~** (*décider*) unanimously; **concerter: se concerter** *vi* to put their *etc* heads together

concession [kɔ̃sesjɔ̃] *nf* concession; **concessionnaire** *nm/f* agent, dealer

concevoir [kɔ̃s(ə)vwaʀ] *vt* (*idée, projet*) to conceive (of); (*comprendre*) to understand; (*enfant*) to conceive; **bien/mal conçu** well-/badly-designed

concierge [kɔ̃sjɛʀʒ] *nm/f* caretaker

conciliabules [kɔ̃siljabyl] *nmpl* (private) discussions, confabulations

concilier [kɔ̃silje] *vt* to reconcile; **se ~** *vt* to win over

concis, e [kɔ̃si, iz] *adj* concise

concitoyen, ne [kɔ̃sitwajɛ̃, jɛn] *nm/f* fellow citizen

concluant, e [kɔ̃klyɑ̃, ɑ̃t] *adj* conclusive

conclure [kɔ̃klyʀ] *vt* to conclude; **conclusion** *nf* conclusion

conçois *etc* [kɔ̃swa] *vb voir* **concevoir**

concombre [kɔ̃kɔ̃bʀ] *nm* cucumber

concorder [kɔ̃kɔʀde] *vi* to tally, agree

concourir [kɔ̃kuʀiʀ] *vi* (SPORT) to compete; **~ à** (*effet etc*) to work towards

concours [kɔ̃kuʀ] *nm* competition; (SCOL) competitive examination; (*assistance*) aid, help; **~ de circonstances** combination of circumstances; **~ hippique** horse show

concret, -ète [kɔ̃kʀɛ, ɛt] *adj* concrete

concrétiser [kɔ̃kʀetize]: **se ~** *vi* to materialize

conçu, e [kɔ̃sy] *pp de* **concevoir**

concubinage [kɔ̃kybinaʒ] *nm* (JUR) cohabitation

concurrence [kɔ̃kyʀɑ̃s] *nf* competition; **faire ~ à** to be in competition with; **jusqu'à ~ de** up to

concurrent, e [kɔ̃kyʀɑ̃, ɑ̃t] *nm/f* (SPORT, ÉCON *etc*) competitor; (SCOL) candidate

condamner [kɔ̃dɑne] *vt* (*blâmer*) to

condemn; (*JUR*) to sentence; (*porte, ouverture*) to fill in, block up; **~ qn à 2 ans de prison** to sentence sb to 2 years' imprisonment

condensation [kɔ̃dɑ̃sasjɔ̃] *nf* condensation

condenser [kɔ̃dɑ̃se] *vt* to condense; **se ~** *vi* to condense

condisciple [kɔ̃disipl] *nm/f* fellow student

condition [kɔ̃disjɔ̃] *nf* condition; **~s** *nfpl* (*tarif, prix*) terms; (*circonstances*) conditions; **à ~ de** *ou* **que** provided that; **conditionnel, le** *nm* conditional (tense)

conditionnement [kɔ̃disjɔnmɑ̃] *nm* (*emballage*) packaging

conditionner [kɔ̃disjɔne] *vt* (*déterminer*) to determine; (*COMM*: *produit*) to package; **air conditionné** air conditioning

condoléances [kɔ̃dɔleɑ̃s] *nfpl* condolences

conducteur, -trice [kɔ̃dyktœʀ, tʀis] *nm/f* driver ♦ *nm* (*ÉLEC etc*) conductor

conduire [kɔ̃dɥiʀ] *vt* to drive; (*délégation, troupeau*) to lead; **se ~** *vi* to behave; **~ à** to lead to; **~ qn quelque part** to take sb somewhere; to drive sb somewhere

conduite [kɔ̃dɥit] *nf* (*comportement*) behaviour; (*d'eau, de gaz*) pipe; **sous la ~ de** led by; **~ à gauche** left-hand drive

cône [kon] *nm* cone

confection [kɔ̃fɛksjɔ̃] *nf* (*fabrication*) making; (*COUTURE*): **la ~** the clothing industry

confectionner [kɔ̃fɛksjɔne] *vt* to make

conférence [kɔ̃feʀɑ̃s] *nf* conference; (*exposé*) lecture; **~ de presse** press conference; **conférencier, -ière** *nm/f* speaker, lecturer

confesser [kɔ̃fese] *vt* to confess; **se ~** *vi* (*REL*) to go to confession; **confession** *nf* confession; (*culte*: *catholique etc*) denomination

confiance [kɔ̃fjɑ̃s] *nf* (*en l'honnêteté de qn*) confidence, trust; (*en la valeur de qch*) faith; **avoir ~ en** to have confidence *ou* faith in, trust; **faire ~ à qn** to trust sb; **mettre qn en ~** to win sb's trust; **~ en soi** self-confidence

confiant, e [kɔ̃fjɑ̃, jɑ̃t] *adj* confident; trusting

confidence [kɔ̃fidɑ̃s] *nf* confidence; **confidentiel, le** *adj* confidential

confier [kɔ̃fje] *vt*: **~ à qn** (*objet, travail*) to entrust to sb; (*secret, pensée*) to confide to sb; **se ~ à qn** to confide in sb

confins [kɔ̃fɛ̃] *nmpl*: **aux ~ de** on the borders of

confirmation [kɔ̃fiʀmasjɔ̃] *nf* confirmation

confirmer [kɔ̃fiʀme] *vt* to confirm

confiserie [kɔ̃fizʀi] *nf* (*magasin*) confectioner's *ou* sweet shop; **~s** *nfpl* (*bonbons*) confectionery *sg*

confisquer [kɔ̃fiske] *vt* to confiscate

confit, e [kɔ̃fi, it] *adj*: **fruits ~s** crystallized fruits ♦ *nm*: **~ d'oie** conserve of goose

confiture [kɔ̃fityʀ] *nf* jam; **~ d'oranges** (orange) marmalade

conflit [kɔ̃fli] *nm* conflict

confondre [kɔ̃fɔ̃dʀ] *vt* (*jumeaux, faits*) to confuse, mix up; (*témoin, menteur*) to confound; **se ~** *vi* to merge; **se ~ en excuses** to apologize profusely; **confondu, e** *adj* (*stupéfait*) speechless, overcome

conforme [kɔ̃fɔʀm] *adj*: **~ à** (*loi, règle*) in accordance with; **conformément** *adv*: **conformément à** in accordance with; **conformer** *vt*: **se conformer à** to conform to

confort [kɔ̃fɔʀ] *nm* comfort; **tout ~** (*COMM*) with all modern conveniences; **confortable** *adj* comfortable

confrère [kɔ̃fʀɛʀ] *nm* colleague

confronter [kɔ̃fʀɔ̃te] *vt* to confront

confus, e [kɔ̃fy, yz] *adj* (*vague*) confused; (*embarrassé*) embarrassed; **confusion** *nf* (*voir confus*) confusion;

embarrassment; (*voir confondre*) confusion, mixing up

congé [kɔ̃ʒe] *nm* (*vacances*) holiday; **en ~** on holiday; **semaine de ~** week off; **prendre ~ de qn** to take one's leave of sb; **donner son ~ à** to give in one's notice to; **~ de maladie** sick leave; **~ de maternité** maternity leave; **~s payés** paid holiday

congédier [kɔ̃ʒedje] *vt* to dismiss

congélateur [kɔ̃ʒelatœʀ] *nm* freezer

congeler [kɔ̃ʒ(ə)le] *vt* to freeze; **les produits congelés** frozen foods

congestion [kɔ̃ʒɛstjɔ̃] *nf* congestion; **~ cérébrale** stroke; **congestionner** *vt* (*rue*) to congest; (*visage*) to flush

congrès [kɔ̃gʀɛ] *nm* congress

conifère [kɔnifɛʀ] *nm* conifer

conjecture [kɔ̃ʒɛktyʀ] *nf* conjecture

conjoint, e [kɔ̃ʒwɛ̃, wɛ̃t] *adj* joint ♦ *nm/f* spouse

conjonction [kɔ̃ʒɔ̃ksjɔ̃] *nf* (LING) conjunction

conjonctivite [kɔ̃ʒɔ̃ktivit] *nf* conjunctivitis

conjoncture [kɔ̃ʒɔ̃ktyʀ] *nf* circumstances *pl*; **la ~ actuelle** the present (economic) situation

conjugaison [kɔ̃ʒygɛzɔ̃] *nf* (LING) conjugation

conjuguer [kɔ̃ʒyge] *vt* (LING) to conjugate; (*efforts etc*) to combine

conjuration [kɔ̃ʒyʀasjɔ̃] *nf* conspiracy

conjurer [kɔ̃ʒyʀe] *vt* (*sort, maladie*) to avert; (*implorer*) to beseech, entreat

connaissance [kɔnɛsɑ̃s] *nf* (*savoir*) knowledge *no pl*; (*personne connue*) acquaintance; **être sans ~** to be unconscious; **perdre/reprendre ~** to lose/regain consciousness; **à ma/sa ~** to (the best of) my/his knowledge; **faire la ~ de qn** to meet sb

connaisseur [kɔnɛsœʀ, øz] *nm* connoisseur

connaître [kɔnɛtʀ] *vt* to know; (*éprouver*) to experience; (*avoir: succès*) to have, enjoy; **~ de nom/vue** to know by name/sight; **ils se sont connus à Genève** they (first) met in Geneva; **s'y ~ en qch** to know a lot about sth

connecter [kɔnɛkte] *vt* to connect

connerie [kɔnʀi] (*fam!*) *nf* stupid thing (to do/say)

connu, e [kɔny] *adj* (*célèbre*) well-known

conquérir [kɔ̃keʀiʀ] *vt* to conquer; **conquête** *nf* conquest

consacrer [kɔ̃sakʀe] *vt* (*employer*) to devote, dedicate; (REL) to consecrate

conscience [kɔ̃sjɑ̃s] *nf* conscience; **avoir/prendre ~ de** to be/become aware of; **perdre ~** to lose consciousness; **avoir bonne/mauvaise ~** to have a clear/guilty conscience; **consciencieux, -euse** *adj* conscientious; **conscient, e** *adj* conscious

conscrit [kɔ̃skʀi] *nm* conscript

consécutif, -ive [kɔ̃sekytif, iv] *adj* consecutive; **~ à** following upon

conseil [kɔ̃sɛj] *nm* (*avis*) piece of advice; (*assemblée*) council; **des ~s** advice; **prendre ~ (auprès de qn)** to take advice (from sb); **~ d'administration** board (of directors); **le ~ des ministres** ≃ the Cabinet; **~ municipal** town council

conseiller, -ère [kɔ̃seje, ɛʀ] *nm/f* adviser ♦ *vt* (*personne*) to advise; (*méthode, action*) to recommend, advise; **~ à qn de** to advise sb to; **~ municipal** town councillor

consentement [kɔ̃sɑ̃tmɑ̃] *nm* consent

consentir [kɔ̃sɑ̃tiʀ] *vt* to agree, consent

conséquence [kɔ̃sekɑ̃s] *nf* consequence; **en ~** (*donc*) consequently; (*de façon appropriée*) accordingly; **conséquent, e** *adj* logical, rational; (*fam: important*) substantial; **par conséquent** consequently

conservateur, -trice [kɔ̃sɛʀvatœʀ, tʀis] *nm/f* (POL) conservative; (*de musée*) curator ♦ *nm* (*pour aliments*) preservative

conservatoire [kɔ̃sɛrvatwar] *nm* academy

conserve [kɔ̃sɛrv] *nf* (*gén pl*) canned *ou* tinned (*BRIT*) food; **en ~** canned, tinned (*BRIT*)

conserver [kɔ̃sɛrve] *vt* (*faculté*) to retain, keep; (*amis, livres*) to keep; (*préserver, aussi CULIN*) to preserve

considérable [kɔ̃siderabl] *adj* considerable, significant, extensive

considération [kɔ̃siderasjɔ̃] *nf* consideration; (*estime*) esteem

considérer [kɔ̃sidere] *vt* to consider; **~ qch comme** to regard sth as

consigne [kɔ̃siɲ] *nf* (*de gare*) left luggage (office) (*BRIT*), checkroom (*US*); (*ordre, instruction*) instructions *pl*; **~ (automatique)** left-luggage locker; **consigner** *vt* (*note, pensée*) to record; (*punir: élève*) to put in detention; (*COMM*) to put a deposit on

consistant, e [kɔ̃sistɑ̃, ɑ̃t] *adj* (*mélange*) thick; (*repas*) solid

consister [kɔ̃siste] *vi*: **~ en/à faire** to consist of/in doing

consœur [kɔ̃sœr] *nf* (lady) colleague

console [kɔ̃sɔl] *nf*: **~ de jeux** games console

consoler [kɔ̃sɔle] *vt* to console

consolider [kɔ̃sɔlide] *vt* to strengthen; (*fig*) to consolidate

consommateur, -trice [kɔ̃sɔmatœr, tris] *nm/f* (*ÉCON*) consumer; (*dans un café*) customer

consommation [kɔ̃sɔmasjɔ̃] *nf* (*boisson*) drink; (*ÉCON*) consumption

consommer [kɔ̃sɔme] *vt* (*suj: personne*) to eat *ou* drink, consume; (: *voiture, machine*) to use, consume; (*mariage*) to consummate ♦ *vi* (*dans un café*) to (have a) drink

consonne [kɔ̃sɔn] *nf* consonant

conspirer [kɔ̃spire] *vi* to conspire

constamment [kɔ̃stamɑ̃] *adv* constantly

constant, e [kɔ̃stɑ̃, ɑ̃t] *adj* constant; (*personne*) steadfast

constat [kɔ̃sta] *nm* (*de police, d'accident*) report; **~ (à l')amiable** *jointly-agreed statement for insurance purposes*; **~ d'échec** acknowledgement of failure

constatation [kɔ̃statasjɔ̃] *nf* (*observation*) (observed) fact, observation

constater [kɔ̃state] *vt* (*remarquer*) to note; (*ADMIN, JUR: attester*) to certify

consterner [kɔ̃stɛrne] *vt* to dismay

constipé, e [kɔ̃stipe] *adj* constipated

constitué, e [kɔ̃stitɥe] *adj*: **~ de** made up *ou* composed of

constituer [kɔ̃stitɥe] *vt* (*équipe*) to set up; (*dossier, collection*) to put together; (*suj: éléments: composer*) to make up, constitute; (*représenter, être*) to constitute; **se ~ prisonnier** to give o.s. up; **constitution** *nf* (*composition*) composition; (*santé, POL*) constitution

constructeur [kɔ̃stryktœr] *nm* manufacturer, builder

constructif, -ive [kɔ̃stryktif, iv] *adj* constructive

construction [kɔ̃stryksjɔ̃] *nf* construction, building

construire [kɔ̃strɥir] *vt* to build, construct

consul [kɔ̃syl] *nm* consul; **consulat** *nm* consulate

consultant, e [kɔ̃syltɑ̃, ɑ̃t] *adj, nm* consultant

consultation [kɔ̃syltasjɔ̃] *nf* consultation; **~s** *nfpl* (*POL*) talks; **heures de ~** (*MÉD*) surgery (*BRIT*) *ou* office (*US*) hours

consulter [kɔ̃sylte] *vt* to consult ♦ *vi* (*médecin*) to hold surgery (*BRIT*), be in (the office) (*US*); **se ~** *vi* to confer

consumer [kɔ̃syme] *vt* to consume; **se ~** *vi* to burn

contact [kɔ̃takt] *nm* contact; **au ~ de** (*air, peau*) on contact with; (*gens*) through contact with; **mettre/couper le ~** (*AUTO*) to switch on/off the ignition; **entrer en** *ou* **prendre ~ avec** to get in touch *ou* contact with; **contacter** *vt* to contact, get in touch with

contagieux, -euse [kɔ̃taʒjø, jøz] *adj* infectious; (*par le contact*) contagious
contaminer [kɔ̃tamine] *vt* to contaminate
conte [kɔ̃t] *nm* tale; **~ de fées** fairy tale
contempler [kɔ̃tɑ̃ple] *vt* to contemplate, gaze at
contemporain, e [kɔ̃tɑ̃pɔʀɛ̃, ɛn] *adj, nm/f* contemporary
contenance [kɔ̃t(ə)nɑ̃s] *nf* (*d'un récipient*) capacity; (*attitude*) bearing, attitude; **perdre ~** to lose one's composure
conteneur [kɔ̃t(ə)nœʀ] *nm* container
contenir [kɔ̃t(ə)niʀ] *vt* to contain; (*avoir une capacité de*) to hold; **se ~** *vi* to contain o.s.
content, e [kɔ̃tɑ̃, ɑ̃t] *adj* pleased, glad; **~ de** pleased with; **contenter** *vt* to satisfy, please; **se contenter de** to content o.s. with
contentieux [kɔ̃tɑ̃sjø] *nm* (COMM) litigation; (*service*) litigation department
contenu [kɔ̃t(ə)ny] *nm* (*d'un récipient*) contents *pl*; (*d'un texte*) content
conter [kɔ̃te] *vt* to recount, relate
contestable [kɔ̃tɛstabl] *adj* questionable
contestation [kɔ̃tɛstasjɔ̃] *nf* (POL) protest
conteste [kɔ̃tɛst]: **sans ~** *adv* unquestionably, indisputably; **contester** *vt* to question ♦ *vi* (POL, *gén*) to rebel (against established authority)
contexte [kɔ̃tɛkst] *nm* context
contigu, ë [kɔ̃tigy] *adj*: **~ (à)** adjacent (to)
continent [kɔ̃tinɑ̃] *nm* continent
continu, e [kɔ̃tiny] *adj* continuous; **faire la journée ~e** to work without taking a full lunch break; **(courant) ~** direct current, DC
continuel, le [kɔ̃tinɥɛl] *adj* (*qui se répète*) constant, continual; (*continu*) continuous
continuer [kɔ̃tinɥe] *vt* (*travail, voyage etc*) to continue (with), carry on (with), go on (with); (*prolonger: alignement, rue*) to continue ♦ *vi* (*vie, bruit*) to continue, go on; **~ à** *ou* **de faire** to go on *ou* continue doing
contorsionner [kɔ̃tɔʀsjɔne]: **se ~** *vi* to contort o.s., writhe about
contour [kɔ̃tuʀ] *nm* outline, contour; **contourner** *vt* to go round; (*difficulté*) to get round
contraceptif, -ive [kɔ̃tʀasɛptif, iv] *adj, nm* contraceptive; **contraception** *nf* contraception
contracté, e [kɔ̃tʀakte] *adj* tense
contracter [kɔ̃tʀakte] *vt* (*muscle etc*) to tense, contract; (*maladie, dette*) to contract; (*assurance*) to take out; **se ~** *vi* (*muscles*) to contract
contractuel, le [kɔ̃tʀaktɥɛl] *nm/f* (*agent*) traffic warden
contradiction [kɔ̃tʀadiksjɔ̃] *nf* contradiction; **contradictoire** *adj* contradictory, conflicting
contraignant, e [kɔ̃tʀɛɲɑ̃, ɑ̃t] *adj* restricting
contraindre [kɔ̃tʀɛ̃dʀ] *vt*: **~ qn à faire** to compel sb to do; **contrainte** *nf* constraint
contraire [kɔ̃tʀɛʀ] *adj, nm* opposite; **~ à** contrary to; **au ~** on the contrary
contrarier [kɔ̃tʀaʀje] *vt* (*personne: irriter*) to annoy; (*fig: projets*) to thwart, frustrate; **contrariété** *nf* annoyance
contraste [kɔ̃tʀast] *nm* contrast
contrat [kɔ̃tʀa] *nm* contract; **~ de travail** employment contract
contravention [kɔ̃tʀavɑ̃sjɔ̃] *nf* parking ticket
contre [kɔ̃tʀ] *prép* against; (*en échange*) (in exchange) for; **par ~** on the other hand
contrebande [kɔ̃tʀəbɑ̃d] *nf* (*trafic*) contraband, smuggling; (*marchandise*) contraband, smuggled goods *pl*; **faire la ~ de** to smuggle; **contrebandier, -ière** *nm/f* smuggler
contrebas [kɔ̃tʀəbɑ]: **en ~** *adv* (down) below

contrebasse [kɔ̃tʀəbɑs] *nf* (double) bass

contre...: **contrecarrer** *vt* to thwart; **contrecœur**: **à contrecœur** *adv* (be)grudgingly, reluctantly; **contrecoup** *nm* repercussions *pl*; **contredire** *vt* (*personne*) to contradict; (*faits*) to refute

contrée [kɔ̃tʀe] *nf* (*région*) region; (*pays*) land

contrefaçon [kɔ̃tʀəfasɔ̃] *nf* forgery

contrefaire [kɔ̃tʀəfɛʀ] *vt* (*document, signature*) to forge, counterfeit

contre...: **contre-indication** (*pl* **contre-indications**) *nf* (MÉD) contra-indication; **"contre-indication en cas d'eczéma"** "should not be used by people with eczema"; **contre-indiqué, e** *adj* (MÉD) contraindicated; (*déconseillé*) unadvisable, ill-advised; **contre-jour**: **à contre-jour** *adv* against the sunlight

contremaître [kɔ̃tʀəmɛtʀ] *nm* foreman

contrepartie [kɔ̃tʀəpaʀti] *nf*: **en ~** in return

contre-pied [kɔ̃tʀəpje] *nm*: **prendre le ~-~ de** (*opinion*) to take the opposing view of; (*action*) to take the opposite course to

contre-plaqué [kɔ̃tʀəplake] *nm* plywood

contrepoids [kɔ̃tʀəpwɑ] *nm* counterweight, counterbalance

contrepoison [kɔ̃tʀəpwazɔ̃] *nm* antidote

contrer [kɔ̃tʀe] *vt* to counter

contresens [kɔ̃tʀəsɑ̃s] *nm* (*erreur*) misinterpretation; (*de traduction*) mistranslation; **à ~** the wrong way

contretemps [kɔ̃tʀətɑ̃] *nm* hitch; **à ~** (*fig*) at an inopportune moment

contrevenir [kɔ̃tʀəv(ə)niʀ]: **~ à** *vt* to contravene

contribuable [kɔ̃tʀibɥabl] *nm/f* taxpayer

contribuer [kɔ̃tʀibɥe]: **~ à** *vt* to contribute towards; **contribution** *nf* contribution; **contributions directes/indirectes** direct/indirect taxation; **mettre à contribution** to call upon

contrôle [kɔ̃tʀol] *nm* checking *no pl*, check; (*des prix*) monitoring, control; (*test*) test, examination; **perdre le ~ de** (*véhicule*) to lose control of; **~ continu** (SCOL) continuous assessment; **~ d'identité** identity check

contrôler [kɔ̃tʀole] *vt* (*vérifier*) to check; (*surveiller*: *opérations*) to supervise; (: *prix*) to monitor, control; (*maîtriser*, COMM: *firme*) to control; **se ~** *vi* to control o.s.; **contrôleur, -euse** *nm/f* (*de train*) (ticket) inspector; (*de bus*) (bus) conductor(-tress)

contrordre [kɔ̃tʀɔʀdʀ] *nm*: **sauf ~** unless otherwise directed

controversé, e [kɔ̃tʀɔvɛʀse] *adj* (*personnage, question*) controversial

contusion [kɔ̃tyzjɔ̃] *nf* bruise, contusion

convaincre [kɔ̃vɛ̃kʀ] *vt*: **~ qn (de qch)** to convince sb (of sth); **~ qn (de faire)** to persuade sb (to do)

convalescence [kɔ̃valesɑ̃s] *nf* convalescence

convenable [kɔ̃vnabl] *adj* suitable; (*assez bon, respectable*) decent

convenance [kɔ̃vnɑ̃s] *nf*: **à ma/votre ~** to my/your liking; **~s** *nfpl* (*normes sociales*) proprieties

convenir [kɔ̃vniʀ] *vi* to be suitable; **~ à** to suit; **~ de** (*bien-fondé de qch*) to admit (to), acknowledge; (*date, somme etc*) to agree upon; **~ que** (*admettre*) to admit that; **~ de faire** to agree to do

convention [kɔ̃vɑ̃sjɔ̃] *nf* convention; **~s** *nfpl* (*convenances*) convention *sg*; **~ collective** (ÉCON) collective agreement; **conventionné, e** *adj* (ADMIN) *applying charges laid down by the state*

convenu, e [kɔ̃vny] *pp de* **convenir** ♦ *adj* agreed

conversation [kɔ̃vɛʀsasjɔ̃] *nf* conversation

convertir [kɔ̃vɛʀtiʀ] *vt*: **~ qn (à)** to convert sb (to); **se ~ (à)** to be converted (to); **~ qch en** to convert sth into

conviction [kɔ̃viksjɔ̃] *nf* conviction

convienne *etc* [kɔ̃vjɛn] *vb voir* **convenir**

convier [kɔ̃vje] *vt*: **~ qn à** (*dîner etc*) to (cordially) invite sb to

convive [kɔ̃viv] *nm/f* guest (*at table*)

convivial, e, -aux [kɔ̃vivjal, jo] *adj* (INFORM) user-friendly

convocation [kɔ̃vɔkasjɔ̃] *nf* (*document*) notification to attend; (: JUR) summons *sg*

convoi [kɔ̃vwa] *nm* convoy; (*train*) train

convoiter [kɔ̃vwate] *vt* to covet

convoquer [kɔ̃vɔke] *vt* (*assemblée*) to convene; (*subordonné*) to summon; (*candidat*) to ask to attend

convoyeur [kɔ̃vwajœʀ] *nm*: **~ de fonds** security guard

coopération [kɔɔpeʀasjɔ̃] *nf* co-operation; (ADMIN): **la C~** ≃ Voluntary Service Overseas (BRIT), ≃ Peace Corps (US)

coopérer [kɔɔpeʀe] *vi*: **~ (à)** to co-operate (in)

coordonnées [kɔɔʀdɔne] *nfpl*: **donnez-moi vos ~** (*fam*) can I have your details please?

coordonner [kɔɔʀdɔne] *vt* to coordinate

copain [kɔpɛ̃] (*fam*) *nm* mate, pal; (*petit ami*) boyfriend

copeau, x [kɔpo] *nm* shaving

copie [kɔpi] *nf* copy; (SCOL) script, paper; **copier** *vt, vi* to copy; **copier sur** to copy from; **copieur** *nm* (photo)copier

copieux, -euse [kɔpjø, jøz] *adj* copious

copine [kɔpin] (*fam*) *nf* mate, pal; (*petite amie*) girlfriend

copropriété [kopʀɔpʀijete] *nf* co-ownership, joint ownership

coq [kɔk] *nm* cock, rooster; **coq-à-l'âne** *nm inv* abrupt change of subject

coque [kɔk] *nf* (*de noix, mollusque*) shell; (*de bateau*) hull; **à la ~** (CULIN) (soft-)boiled

coquelicot [kɔkliko] *nm* poppy

coqueluche [kɔklyʃ] *nf* whooping-cough

coquet, te [kɔkɛ, ɛt] *adj* appearance-conscious; (*logement*) smart, charming

coquetier [kɔk(ə)tje] *nm* egg-cup

coquillage [kɔkijaʒ] *nm* (*mollusque*) shellfish *inv*; (*coquille*) shell

coquille [kɔkij] *nf* shell; (TYPO) misprint; **~ St Jacques** scallop

coquin, e [kɔkɛ̃, in] *adj* mischievous, roguish; (*polisson*) naughty

cor [kɔʀ] *nm* (MUS) horn; (MÉD): **~ (au pied)** corn

corail, -aux [kɔʀaj, o] *nm* coral *no pl*

Coran [kɔʀɑ̃] *nm*: **le ~** the Koran

corbeau, x [kɔʀbo] *nm* crow

corbeille [kɔʀbɛj] *nf* basket; **~ à papier** waste paper basket *ou* bin

corbillard [kɔʀbijaʀ] *nm* hearse

corde [kɔʀd] *nf* rope; (*de violon, raquette*) string; **usé jusqu'à la ~** threadbare; **~ à linge** washing *ou* clothes line; **~ à sauter** skipping rope; **~s vocales** vocal cords

cordée *nf* (*d'alpinistes*) rope, roped party

cordialement [kɔʀdjalmɑ̃] *adv* (*formule épistolaire*) (kind) regards

cordon [kɔʀdɔ̃] *nm* cord, string; **~ ombilical** umbilical cord; **~ sanitaire/de police** sanitary/police cordon

cordonnerie [kɔʀdɔnʀi] *nf* shoe repairer's (shop); **cordonnier** *nm* shoe repairer

Corée [kɔʀe] *nf*: **la ~ du Sud/du Nord** South/North Korea

coriace [kɔʀjas] *adj* tough

corne [kɔʀn] *nf* horn; (*de cerf*) antler

cornée [kɔʀne] *nf* cornea

corneille [kɔʀnɛj] *nf* crow

cornemuse [kɔʀnəmyz] *nf* bagpipes *pl*

cornet [kɔʀnɛ] *nm* (paper) cone; (*de*

glace) cornet, cone
corniche [kɔʀniʃ] *nf* (*route*) coast road
cornichon [kɔʀniʃɔ̃] *nm* gherkin
Cornouailles [kɔʀnwaj] *nf* Cornwall
corporation [kɔʀpɔʀasjɔ̃] *nf* corporate body
corporel, le [kɔʀpɔʀɛl] *adj* bodily; (*punition*) corporal
corps [kɔʀ] *nm* body; **à ~ perdu** headlong; **prendre ~** to take shape; **~ à ~** ♦ *adv* hand-to-hand ♦ *nm* clinch; **le ~ électoral** the electorate; **le ~ enseignant** the teaching profession
corpulent, e [kɔʀpylɑ̃, ɑ̃t] *adj* stout
correct, e [kɔʀɛkt] *adj* correct; (*fam: acceptable: salaire, hôtel*) reasonable, decent; **correcteur, -trice** *nm/f* (SCOL) examiner; **correction** *nf* (*voir corriger*) correction; (*voir correct*) correctness; (*coups*) thrashing; **correctionnel, le** *adj* (JUR): **tribunal correctionnel** ≃ criminal court
correspondance [kɔʀɛspɔ̃dɑ̃s] *nf* correspondence; (*de train, d'avion*) connection; **cours par ~** correspondence course; **vente par ~** mail-order business
correspondant, e [kɔʀɛspɔ̃dɑ̃, ɑ̃t] *nm/f* correspondent; (TÉL) person phoning (*ou* being phoned)
correspondre [kɔʀɛspɔ̃dʀ] *vi* to correspond, tally; **~ à** to correspond to; **~ avec qn** to correspond with sb
corrida [kɔʀida] *nf* bullfight
corridor [kɔʀidɔʀ] *nm* corridor
corrigé [kɔʀiʒe] *nm* (SCOL: *d'exercise*) correct version
corriger [kɔʀiʒe] *vt* (*devoir*) to correct; (*punir*) to thrash; **~ qn de** (*défaut*) to cure sb of
corroborer [kɔʀɔbɔʀe] *vt* to corroborate
corrompre [kɔʀɔ̃pʀ] *vt* to corrupt; (*acheter: témoin etc*) to bribe
corruption [kɔʀypsjɔ̃] *nf* corruption; (*de témoins*) bribery
corsage [kɔʀsaʒ] *nm* bodice; (*chemisier*) blouse
corsaire [kɔʀsɛʀ] *nm* pirate
corse [kɔʀs] *adj, nm/f* Corsican ♦ *nf*: **la C~** Corsica
corsé, e [kɔʀse] *adj* (*café*) full-flavoured; (*sauce*) spicy; (*problème*) tough
corset [kɔʀsɛ] *nm* corset
cortège [kɔʀtɛʒ] *nm* procession
cortisone [kɔʀtizɔn] *nf* cortisone
corvée [kɔʀve] *nf* chore, drudgery *no pl*
cosmétique [kɔsmetik] *nm* beauty care product
cosmopolite [kɔsmɔpɔlit] *adj* cosmopolitan
cossu, e [kɔsy] *adj* (*maison*) opulent(-looking)
costaud, e [kɔsto, od] (*fam*) *adj* strong, sturdy
costume [kɔstym] *nm* (*d'homme*) suit; (*de théâtre*) costume; **costumé, e** *adj* dressed up; **bal costumé** fancy dress ball
cote [kɔt] *nf* (*en Bourse*) quotation; **~ d'alerte** danger *ou* flood level
côte [kot] *nf* (*rivage*) coast(line); (*pente*) hill; (ANAT) rib; (*d'un tricot, tissu*) rib, ribbing *no pl*; **~ à ~** side by side; **la C~ (d'Azur)** the (French) Riviera
coté, e [kɔte] *adj*: **être bien ~** to be highly rated
côté [kote] *nm* (*gén*) side; (*direction*) way, direction; **de chaque ~ (de)** on each side (of); **de tous les ~s** from all directions; **de quel ~ est-il parti?** which way did he go?; **de ce/de l'autre ~** this/the other way; **du ~ de** (*provenance*) from; (*direction*) towards; (*proximité*) near; **de ~** (*regarder*) sideways; (*mettre*) aside; **mettre de l'argent de ~** to save some money; **à ~** (right) nearby; (*voisins*) next door; **à ~ de** beside, next to; (*en comparaison*) compared to; **être aux ~s de** to be by the side of
coteau, x [kɔto] *nm* hill
côtelette [kotlɛt] *nf* chop
côtier, -ière [kotje, jɛʀ] *adj* coastal

cotisation [kɔtizasjɔ̃] *nf* subscription, dues *pl*; (*pour une pension*) contributions *pl*
cotiser [kɔtize] *vi*: **~ (à)** to pay contributions (to); **se ~** *vi* to club together
coton [kɔtɔ̃] *nm* cotton; **~ hydrophile** cotton wool (BRIT), absorbent cotton (US); **Coton-Tige** ® *nm* cotton bud
côtoyer [kotwaje] *vt* (*fréquenter*) to rub shoulders with
cou [ku] *nm* neck
couchant [kuʃɑ̃] *adj*: **soleil ~** setting sun
couche [kuʃ] *nf* layer; (*de peinture, vernis*) coat; (*de bébé*) nappy (BRIT), diaper (US); **~ d'ozone** ozone layer; **~s sociales** social levels *ou* strata
couché, e [kuʃe] *adj* lying down; (*au lit*) in bed
coucher [kuʃe] *nm* (*du soleil*) setting ♦ *vt* (*personne*) to put to bed; (: *loger*) to put up; (*objet*) to lay on its side ♦ *vi* to sleep; **se ~** *vi* (*pour dormir*) to go to bed; (*pour se reposer*) to lie down; (*soleil*) to set; **~ de soleil** sunset
couchette [kuʃɛt] *nf* couchette; (*pour voyageur, sur bateau*) berth
coucou [kuku] *nm* cuckoo
coude [kud] *nm* (ANAT) elbow; (*de tuyau, de la route*) bend; **~ à ~** shoulder to shoulder, side by side
coudre [kudʀ] *vt* (*bouton*) to sew on ♦ *vi* to sew
couenne [kwan] *nf* (*de lard*) rind
couette [kwɛt] *nf* duvet, quilt; **~s** *nfpl* (*cheveux*) bunches
couffin [kufɛ̃] *nm* Moses basket
couler [kule] *vi* to flow, run; (*fuir: stylo, récipient*) to leak; (*nez*) to run; (*sombrer: bateau*) to sink ♦ *vt* (*cloche, sculpture*) to cast; (*bateau*) to sink; (*faire échouer: personne*) to bring down
couleur [kulœʀ] *nf* colour (BRIT), color (US); (CARTES) suit; **film/télévision en ~s** colo(u)r film/television
couleuvre [kulœvʀ] *nf* grass snake
coulisse [kulis] *nf*: **~s** ♦ *nfpl* (THÉÂTRE) wings; (*fig*): **dans les ~s** behind the scenes; **coulisser** *vi* to slide, run
couloir [kulwaʀ] *nm* corridor, passage; (*d'avion*) aisle; (*de bus*) gangway; **~ aérien/de navigation** air/shipping lane
coup [ku] *nm* (*heurt, choc*) knock; (*affectif*) blow, shock; (*agressif*) blow; (*avec arme à feu*) shot; (*de l'horloge*) stroke; (*tennis, golf*) stroke; (*boxe*) blow; (*fam: fois*) time; **~ de coude** nudge (with the elbow); **~ de tonnerre** clap of thunder; **~ de sonnette** ring of the bell; **donner un ~ de balai** to give the floor a sweep; **boire un ~** (*fam*) to have a drink; **être dans le ~** to be in on it; **du ~ ...** as a result; **d'un seul ~** (*subitement*) suddenly; (*à la fois*) at one go; **du premier ~** first time; **du même ~** at the same time; **à tous les ~s** (*fam*) every time; **tenir le ~** to hold out; **après ~** afterwards; **à ~ sûr** definitely, without fail; **~ sur ~** in quick succession; **sur le ~** outright; **sous le ~ de** (*surprise etc*) under the influence of; **en ~ de vent** in a tearing hurry; **~ de chance** stroke of luck; **~ de couteau** stab (of a knife); **~ d'État** coup; **~ de feu** shot; **~ de fil** (*fam*) phone call; **~ de frein** (sharp) braking *no pl*; **~ de main**: **donner un ~ de main à qn** to give sb a (helping) hand; **~ d'œil** glance; **~ de pied** kick; **~ de poing** punch; **~ de soleil** sunburn *no pl*; **~ de téléphone** phone call; **~ de tête** (*fig*) (sudden) impulse
coupable [kupabl] *adj* guilty ♦ *nm/f* (*gén*) culprit; (JUR) guilty party
coupe [kup] *nf* (*verre*) goblet; (*à fruits*) dish; (SPORT) cup; (*de cheveux, de vêtement*) cut; (*graphique, plan*) (cross) section
coupe-papier [kuppapje] *nm inv* paper knife
couper [kupe] *vt* to cut; (*retrancher*) to cut (out); (*route, courant*) to cut off; (*appétit*) to take away; (*vin à table*) to

dilute ♦ *vi* to cut; (*prendre un raccourci*) to take a short-cut; **se ~** *vi* (*se blesser*) to cut o.s.; **~ la parole à qn** to cut sb short

couple [kupl] *nm* couple

couplet [kuplɛ] *nm* verse

coupole [kupɔl] *nf* dome

coupon [kupɔ̃] *nm* (*ticket*) coupon; (*reste de tissu*) remnant; **coupon-réponse** *nm* reply coupon

coupure [kupyʀ] *nf* cut; (*billet de banque*) note; (*de journal*) cutting; **~ de courant** power cut

cour [kuʀ] *nf* (*de ferme, jardin*) (court)yard; (*d'immeuble*) back yard; (*JUR, royale*) court; **faire la ~ à qn** to court sb; **~ d'assises** court of assizes; **~ de récréation** playground; **~ martiale** court-martial

courage [kuʀaʒ] *nm* courage, bravery; **courageux, -euse** *adj* brave, courageous

couramment [kuʀamɑ̃] *adv* commonly; (*parler*) fluently

courant, e [kuʀɑ̃, ɑ̃t] *adj* (*fréquent*) common; (*COMM, gén: normal*) standard; (*en cours*) current ♦ *nm* current; (*fig*) movement; (*: d'opinion*) trend; **être au ~ (de)** (*fait, nouvelle*) to know (about); **mettre qn au ~ (de)** to tell sb (about); (*nouveau travail etc*) to teach sb the basics (of); **se tenir au ~ (de)** (*techniques etc*) to keep o.s. up-to-date (on); **dans le ~ de** (*pendant*) in the course of; **le 10 ~** (*COMM*) the 10th inst.; **~ d'air** draught; **~ électrique** (electric) current, power

courbature [kuʀbatyʀ] *nf* ache

courbe [kuʀb] *adj* curved ♦ *nf* curve; **courber** *vt* to bend; **se courber** *vi* (*personne*) to bend (down), stoop

coureur, -euse [kuʀœʀ, øz] *nm/f* (*SPORT*) runner (*ou* driver); (*péj*) womanizer; manhunter; **~ automobile** racing driver

courge [kuʀʒ] *nf* (*CULIN*) marrow; **courgette** *nf* courgette (*BRIT*), zucchini (*US*)

courir [kuʀiʀ] *vi* to run ♦ *vt* (*SPORT: épreuve*) to compete in; (*risque*) to run; (*danger*) to face; **~ les magasins** to go round the shops; **le bruit court que** the rumour is going round that

couronne [kuʀɔn] *nf* crown; (*de fleurs*) wreath, circlet

courons *etc* [kuʀɔ̃] *vb voir* **courir**

courrier [kuʀje] *nm* mail, post; (*lettres à écrire*) letters *pl*; **~ électronique** E-mail

courroie [kuʀwa] *nf* strap; (*TECH*) belt

courrons *etc* [kuʀɔ̃] *vb voir* **courir**

cours [kuʀ] *nm* (*leçon*) class; (*: particulier*) lesson; (*série de leçons, cheminement*) course; (*écoulement*) flow; (*COMM: de devises*) rate; (*: de denrées*) price; **donner libre ~ à** to give free expression to; **avoir ~** (*SCOL*) to have a class *ou* lecture; **en ~** (*année*) current; (*travaux*) in progress; **en ~ de route** on the way; **au ~ de** in the course of, during; **~ d'eau** waterway; **~ du soir** night school; **~ intensif** crash course

course [kuʀs] *nf* running; (*SPORT: épreuve*) race; (*d'un taxi*) journey, trip; (*commission*) errand; **~s** *nfpl* (*achats*) shopping *sg*; **faire des ~s** to do some shopping

court, e [kuʀ, kuʀt(ə)] *adj* short ♦ *adv* short ♦ *nm*: **~ (de tennis)** (tennis) court; **à ~ de** short of; **prendre qn de ~** to catch sb unawares; **court-circuit** *nm* short-circuit

courtier, -ère [kuʀtje, jɛʀ] *nm/f* broker

courtiser [kuʀtize] *vt* to court, woo

courtois, e [kuʀtwa, waz] *adj* courteous; **courtoisie** *nf* courtesy

couru, e [kuʀy] *pp de* **courir**

cousais *etc* [kuzɛ] *vb voir* **coudre**

couscous [kuskus] *nm* couscous

cousin, e [kuzɛ̃, in] *nm/f* cousin

coussin [kusɛ̃] *nm* cushion

cousu, e [kuzy] *pp de* **coudre**

coût [ku] *nm* cost; **le ~ de la vie** the cost of living; **coûtant** *adj m*: **au prix coûtant** at cost price

couteau, x [kuto] *nm* knife
coûter [kute] *vt, vi* to cost; **combien ça coûte?** how much is it?, what does it cost?; **coûte que coûte** at all costs; **coûteux, -euse** *adj* costly, expensive
coutume [kutym] *nf* custom
couture [kutyʀ] *nf* sewing; (*profession*) dressmaking; (*points*) seam; **couturier** *nm* fashion designer; **couturière** *nf* dressmaker
couvée [kuve] *nf* brood, clutch
couvent [kuvɑ̃] *nm* (*de sœurs*) convent; (*de frères*) monastery
couver [kuve] *vt* to hatch; (*maladie*) to be coming down with ♦ *vi* (*feu*) to smoulder; (*révolte*) to be brewing
couvercle [kuvɛʀkl] *nm* lid; (*de bombe aérosol etc, qui se visse*) cap, top
couvert, e [kuvɛʀ, ɛʀt] *pp de* **couvrir** ♦ *adj* (*ciel*) overcast ♦ *nm* place setting; (*place à table*) place; **~s** *nmpl* (*ustensiles*) cutlery *sg*; **~ de** covered with *ou* in; **mettre le ~** to lay the table
couverture [kuvɛʀtyʀ] *nf* blanket; (*de livre, assurance, fig*) cover; (*presse*) coverage; **~ chauffante** electric blanket
couveuse [kuvøz] *nf* (*de maternité*) incubator
couvre-feu [kuvʀəfø] *nm* curfew
couvre-lit [kuvʀəli] *nm* bedspread
couvreur [kuvʀœʀ] *nm* roofer
couvrir [kuvʀiʀ] *vt* to cover; **se ~** *vi* (*s'habiller*) to cover up; (*se coiffer*) to put on one's hat; (*ciel*) to cloud over
cow-boy [kobɔj] *nm* cowboy
crabe [kʀɑb] *nm* crab
cracher [kʀaʃe] *vi, vt* to spit
crachin [kʀaʃɛ̃] *nm* drizzle
crack [kʀak] *nm* (*fam: as*) ace
craie [kʀɛ] *nf* chalk
craindre [kʀɛ̃dʀ] *vt* to fear, be afraid of; (*être sensible à: chaleur, froid*) to be easily damaged by
crainte [kʀɛ̃t] *nf* fear; **de ~ de/que** for fear of/that; **craintif, -ive** *adj* timid
cramoisi, e [kʀamwazi] *adj* crimson
crampe [kʀɑ̃p] *nf* cramp
crampon [kʀɑ̃pɔ̃] *nm* (*de chaussure de football*) stud; (*de chaussure de course*) spike; (*d'alpinisme*) crampon; **cramponner** *vb*: **se cramponner (à)** to hang *ou* cling on (to)
cran [kʀɑ̃] *nm* (*entaille*) notch; (*de courroie*) hole; (*fam: courage*) guts *pl*; **~ d'arrêt** safety catch
crâne [kʀɑn] *nm* skull
crâner [kʀɑne] (*fam*) *vi* to show off
crapaud [kʀapo] *nm* toad
crapule [kʀapyl] *nf* villain
craquement [kʀakmɑ̃] *nm* crack, snap; (*du plancher*) creak, creaking *no pl*
craquer [kʀake] *vi* (*bois, plancher*) to creak; (*fil, branche*) to snap; (*couture*) to come apart; (*fig: accusé*) to break down; (*: fam*) to crack up ♦ *vt* (*allumette*) to strike; **j'ai craqué** (*fam*) I couldn't resist it
crasse [kʀas] *nf* grime, filth; **crasseux, -euse** *adj* grimy, filthy
cravache [kʀavaʃ] *nf* (riding) crop
cravate [kʀavat] *nf* tie
crawl [kʀol] *nm* crawl; **dos ~é** backstroke
crayon [kʀɛjɔ̃] *nm* pencil; **~ à bille** ball-point pen; **~ de couleur** crayon, colouring pencil; **crayon-feutre** (*pl* **crayons-feutres**) *nm* felt(-tip) pen
créancier, -ière [kʀeɑ̃sje, jɛʀ] *nm/f* creditor
création [kʀeasjɔ̃] *nf* creation
créature [kʀeatyʀ] *nf* creature
crèche [kʀɛʃ] *nf* (*de Noël*) crib; (*garderie*) crèche, day nursery
crédit [kʀedi] *nm* (*gén*) credit; **~s** *nmpl* (*fonds*) funds; **payer/acheter à ~** to pay/buy on credit *ou* on easy terms; **faire ~ à qn** to give sb credit; **créditer** *vt*: **créditer un compte (de)** to credit an account (with)
crédule [kʀedyl] *adj* credulous, gullible
créer [kʀee] *vt* to create
crémaillère [kʀemajɛʀ] *nf*: **pendre la ~** to have a house-warming party
crématoire [kʀematwaʀ] *adj*: **four ~**

crematorium

crème [kʀɛm] *nf* cream; (*entremets*) cream dessert ♦ *adj inv* cream(-coloured); **un (café) ~** ≃ a white coffee; **~ anglaise** (egg) custard; **~ chantilly** whipped cream; **~ fouettée** = **crème chantilly**; **crémerie** *nf* dairy; **crémeux, -euse** *adj* creamy

créneau, x [kʀeno] *nm* (*de fortification*) crenel(le); (*dans marché*) gap, niche; (AUTO): **faire un ~** to reverse into a parking space (*between two cars alongside the kerb*)

crêpe [kʀɛp] *nf* (*galette*) pancake ♦ *nm* (*tissu*) crêpe; **crêpé, e** *adj* (*cheveux*) backcombed; **crêperie** *nf* pancake shop *ou* restaurant

crépiter [kʀepite] *vi* (*friture*) to sputter, splutter; (*fire*) to crackle

crépu, e [kʀepy] *adj* frizzy, fuzzy

crépuscule [kʀepyskyl] *nm* twilight, dusk

cresson [kʀesɔ̃] *nm* watercress

crête [kʀɛt] *nf* (*de coq*) comb; (*de vague, montagne*) crest

creuser [kʀøze] *vt* (*trou, tunnel*) to dig; (*sol*) to dig a hole in; (*fig*) to go (deeply) into; **ça creuse** that gives you a real appetite; **se ~ la cervelle** (*fam*) to rack one's brains

creux, -euse [kʀø, kʀøz] *adj* hollow ♦ *nm* hollow; **heures creuses** slack periods; (*électricité, téléphone*) off-peak periods; **avoir un ~** (*fam*) to be hungry

crevaison [kʀəvɛzɔ̃] *nf* puncture

crevasse [kʀəvas] *nf* (*dans le sol, la peau*) crack; (*de glacier*) crevasse

crevé, e [kʀəve] (*fam*) *adj* (*fatigué*) all in, exhausted

crever [kʀəve] *vt* (*ballon*) to burst ♦ *vi* (*pneu*) to burst; (*automobiliste*) to have a puncture (BRIT) *ou* a flat (tire) (US); (*fam*) to die

crevette [kʀəvɛt] *nf*: **~ (rose)** prawn; **~ grise** shrimp

cri [kʀi] *nm* cry, shout; (*d'animal*: *spécifique*) cry, call; **c'est le dernier ~** (*fig*) it's the latest fashion

criant, e [kʀijɑ̃, kʀijɑ̃t] *adj* (*injustice*) glaring

criard, e [kʀijaʀ, kʀijaʀd] *adj* (*couleur*) garish, loud; (*voix*) yelling

crible [kʀibl] *nm* riddle; **passer qch au ~** (*fig*) to go over sth with a fine-tooth comb; **criblé, e** *adj*: **criblé de** riddled with; (*de dettes*) crippled with

cric [kʀik] *nm* (AUTO) jack

crier [kʀije] *vi* (*pour appeler*) to shout, cry (out); (*de douleur etc*) to scream, yell ♦ *vt* (*injure*) to shout (out), yell (out)

crime [kʀim] *nm* crime; (*meurtre*) murder; **criminel, le** *nm/f* criminal; (*assassin*) murderer

crin [kʀɛ̃] *nm* (*de cheval*) hair *no pl*

crinière [kʀinjɛʀ] *nf* mane

crique [kʀik] *nf* creek, inlet

criquet [kʀikɛ] *nm* grasshopper

crise [kʀiz] *nf* crisis; (MÉD) attack; (: *d'épilepsie*) fit; **piquer une ~ de nerfs** to go hysterical; **~ cardiaque** heart attack; **~ de foie** bilious attack

crisper [kʀispe] *vt* (*poings*) to clench; **se ~** *vi* (*visage*) to tense; (*personne*) to get tense

crisser [kʀise] *vi* (*neige*) to crunch, (*pneu*) to screech

cristal, -aux [kʀistal, o] *nm* crystal; **cristallin, e** *adj* crystal-clear

critère [kʀitɛʀ] *nm* criterion

critiquable [kʀitikabl] *adj* open to criticism

critique [kʀitik] *adj* critical ♦ *nm/f* (*de théâtre, musique*) critic ♦ *nf* criticism; (THÉÂTRE *etc*: *article*) review

critiquer [kʀitike] *vt* (*dénigrer*) to criticize; (*évaluer*) to assess, examine (critically)

croasser [kʀɔase] *vi* to caw

Croatie [kʀɔasi] *nf* Croatia

croc [kʀo] *nm* (*dent*) fang; (*de boucher*) hook; **croc-en-jambe** *nm*: **faire un croc-en-jambe à qn** to trip sb up

croche [kʀɔʃ] *nf* (MUS) quaver (BRIT),

eighth note (*US*); **croche-pied** *nm* = **croc-en-jambe**
crochet [kʀɔʃɛ] *nm* hook; (*détour*) detour; (*TRICOT: aiguille*) crochet hook; (*: technique*) crochet; **vivre aux ~s de qn** to live *ou* sponge off sb
crochu, e [kʀɔʃy] *adj* (*nez*) hooked; (*doigts*) claw-like
crocodile [kʀɔkɔdil] *nm* crocodile
croire [kʀwaʀ] *vt* to believe; **se ~ fort** to think one is strong; **~ que** to believe *ou* think that; **~ à, ~ en** to believe in
croîs [kʀwa] *vb voir* **croître**
croisade [kʀwazad] *nf* crusade
croisé, e [kʀwaze] *adj* (*veste*) double-breasted
croisement [kʀwazmɑ̃] *nm* (*carrefour*) crossroads *sg*; (*BIO*) crossing; (*: résultat*) crossbreed
croiser [kʀwaze] *vt* (*personne, voiture*) to pass; (*route*) to cross, cut across; (*BIO*) to cross; **se ~** *vi* (*personnes, véhicules*) to pass each other; (*routes, lettres*) to cross; (*regards*) to meet; **~ les jambes/bras** to cross one's legs/fold one's arms
croisière [kʀwazjɛʀ] *nf* cruise
croissance [kʀwasɑ̃s] *nf* growth
croissant [kʀwasɑ̃] *nm* (*à manger*) croissant; (*motif*) crescent
croître [kʀwatʀ] *vi* to grow
croix [kʀwa] *nf* cross; **~ gammée** swastika; **la C~ Rouge** the Red Cross
croque-monsieur [kʀɔkməsjø] *nm inv* toasted ham and cheese sandwich
croquer [kʀɔke] *vt* (*manger*) to crunch; (*: fruit*) to munch; (*dessiner*) to sketch; **chocolat à ~** plain dessert chocolate
croquis [kʀɔki] *nm* sketch
cross [kʀɔs] *nm*: **faire du ~ (à pied)** to do cross-country running
crosse [kʀɔs] *nf* (*de fusil*) butt; (*de revolver*) grip
crotte [kʀɔt] *nf* droppings *pl*; **crotté, e** *adj* muddy, mucky; **crottin** *nm* dung, manure; (*fromage*) (small round) cheese (*made of goat's milk*)
crouler [kʀule] *vi* (*s'effondrer*) to collapse; (*être délabré*) to be crumbling
croupe [kʀup] *nf* rump; **en ~** pillion
croupir [kʀupiʀ] *vi* to stagnate
croustillant, e [kʀustijɑ̃, ɑ̃t] *adj* crisp
croûte [kʀut] *nf* crust; (*du fromage*) rind; (*MÉD*) scab; **en ~** (*CULIN*) in pastry
croûton [kʀutɔ̃] *nm* (*CULIN*) crouton; (*bout du pain*) crust, heel
croyable [kʀwajabl] *adj* credible
croyant, e [kʀwajɑ̃, ɑ̃t] *nm/f* believer
CRS *sigle fpl* (= *Compagnies républicaines de sécurité*) *state security police force* ♦ *sigle m* member of the CRS
cru, e [kʀy] *pp de* **croire** ♦ *adj* (*non cuit*) raw; (*lumière, couleur*) harsh; (*paroles*) crude ♦ *nm* (*vignoble*) vineyard; (*vin*) wine; **un grand ~** a great vintage; **jambon ~** Parma ham
crû [kʀy] *pp de* **croître**
cruauté [kʀyote] *nf* cruelty
cruche [kʀyʃ] *nf* pitcher, jug
crucifix [kʀysifi] *nm* crucifix; **crucifixion** *nf* crucifixion
crudités [kʀydite] *nfpl* (*CULIN*) salads
crue [kʀy] *nf* (*inondation*) flood
cruel, le [kʀyɛl] *adj* cruel
crus *etc* [kʀy] *vb voir* **croire**; **croître**
crûs *etc* [kʀy] *vb voir* **croître**
crustacés [kʀystase] *nmpl* shellfish
Cuba [kyba] *nf* Cuba; **cubain, e** *adj* Cuban ♦ *nm/f*: **Cubain, e** Cuban
cube [kyb] *nm* cube; (*jouet*) brick; **mètre ~** cubic metre; **2 au ~** 2 cubed
cueillette [kœjɛt] *nf* picking; (*quantité*) crop, harvest
cueillir [kœjiʀ] *vt* (*fruits, fleurs*) to pick, gather; (*fig*) to catch
cuiller [kɥijɛʀ], **cuillère** [kɥijɛʀ] *nf* spoon; **~ à café** coffee spoon; (*CULIN*) teaspoonful; **~ à soupe** soup-spoon; (*CULIN*) tablespoonful; **cuillerée** *nf* spoonful
cuir [kɥiʀ] *nm* leather; **~ chevelu** scalp
cuire [kɥiʀ] *vt* (*aliments*) to cook; (*au four*) to bake ♦ *vi* to cook; **bien cuit** (*viande*) well done; **trop cuit** overdone

cuisant, e [kɥizɑ̃, ɑ̃t] *adj* (*douleur*) stinging; (*fig*: *souvenir, échec*) bitter
cuisine [kɥizin] *nf* (*pièce*) kitchen; (*art culinaire*) cookery, cooking; (*nourriture*) cooking, food; **faire la ~** to cook; **cuisiné, e** *adj*: **plat cuisiné** ready-made meal *ou* dish; **cuisiner** *vt* to cook; (*fam*) to grill ♦ *vi* to cook; **cuisinier, -ière** *nm/f* cook; **cuisinière** *nf* (*poêle*) cooker
cuisse [kɥis] *nf* thigh; (CULIN) leg
cuisson [kɥisɔ̃] *nf* cooking
cuit, e [kɥi, kɥit] *pp de* **cuire**
cuivre [kɥivʀ] *nm* copper; **les ~s** (MUS) the brass
cul [ky] (*fam!*) *nm* arse (*!*)
culbute [kylbyt] *nf* somersault; (*accidentelle*) tumble, fall
culminant, e [kylminɑ̃, ɑ̃t] *adj*: **point ~** highest point
culminer [kylmine] *vi* to reach its highest point
culot [kylo] (*fam*) *nm* (*effronterie*) cheek
culotte [kylɔt] *nf* (*de femme*) knickers *pl* (BRIT), panties *pl*
culpabilité [kylpabilite] *nf* guilt
culte [kylt] *nm* (*religion*) religion; (*hommage, vénération*) worship; (*protestant*) service
cultivateur, -trice [kyltivatœʀ, tʀis] *nm/f* farmer
cultivé, e [kyltive] *adj* (*personne*) cultured, cultivated
cultiver [kyltive] *vt* to cultivate; (*légumes*) to grow, cultivate
culture [kyltyʀ] *nf* cultivation; (*connaissances etc*) culture; **les ~s intensives** intensive farming; **~ physique** physical training; **culturel, le** *adj* cultural; **culturisme** *nm* body-building
cumin [kymɛ̃] *nm* cumin
cumuler [kymyle] *vt* (*emplois*) to hold concurrently; (*salaires*) to draw concurrently
cupide [kypid] *adj* greedy, grasping
cure [kyʀ] *nf* (MÉD) course of treatment
curé [kyʀe] *nm* parish priest
cure-dent [kyʀdɑ̃] *nm* toothpick
cure-pipe [kyʀpip] *nm* pipe cleaner
curer [kyʀe] *vt* to clean out
curieusement [kyʀjøzmɑ̃] *adv* curiously
curieux, -euse [kyʀjø, jøz] *adj* (*indiscret*) curious, inquisitive; (*étrange*) strange, curious ♦ *nmpl* (*badauds*) onlookers; **curiosité** *nf* curiosity; (*site*) unusual feature
curriculum vitae [kyʀikylɔmvite] *nm inv* curriculum vitae
curseur [kyʀsœʀ] *nm* (INFORM) cursor
cutané, e [kytane] *adj* skin
cuti-réaction [kytiʀeaksjɔ̃] *nf* (MÉD) skin-test
cuve [kyv] *nf* vat; (*à mazout etc*) tank
cuvée [kyve] *nf* vintage
cuvette [kyvɛt] *nf* (*récipient*) bowl, basin; (GÉO) basin
CV *sigle m* (AUTO) = **cheval vapeur**; (COMM) = **curriculum vitae**
cyanure [sjanyʀ] *nm* cyanide
cybercafé [sibɛʀkafe] *nm* cybercafé
cyclable [siklabl] *adj*: **piste ~** cycle track
cycle [sikl] *nm* cycle; **cyclisme** *nm* cycling; **cycliste** *nm/f* cyclist ♦ *adj* cycle *cpd*; **coureur cycliste** racing cyclist
cyclomoteur [siklomɔtœʀ] *nm* moped
cyclone [siklon] *nm* hurricane
cygne [siɲ] *nm* swan
cylindre [silɛ̃dʀ] *nm* cylinder; **cylindrée** *nf* (AUTO) (cubic) capacity
cymbale [sɛ̃bal] *nf* cymbal
cynique [sinik] *adj* cynical
cystite [sistit] *nf* cystitis

D, d

d' [d] *prép voir* **de**
dactylo [daktilo] *nf* (*aussi:* **~graphe**) typist; (*aussi:* **~graphie**) typing; **dactylographier** *vt* to type (out)
dada [dada] *nm* hobby-horse
daigner [deɲe] *vt* to deign

daim [dɛ̃] *nm* (fallow) deer *inv*; (*cuir suédé*) suede
dalle [dal] *nf* paving stone, slab
daltonien, ne [daltɔnjɛ̃, jɛn] *adj* colour-blind
dam [dɑ̃] *nm*: **au grand ~ de** much to the detriment (*ou* annoyance) of
dame [dam] *nf* lady; (CARTES, ÉCHECS) queen; **~s** *nfpl* (*jeu*) draughts *sg* (BRIT), checkers *sg* (US)
damner [dɑne] *vt* to damn
dancing [dɑ̃siŋ] *nm* dance hall
Danemark [danmaʀk] *nm* Denmark
danger [dɑ̃ʒe] *nm* danger; **dangereux, -euse** *adj* dangerous
danois, e [danwa, waz] *adj* Danish ♦ *nm/f*: **D~, e** Dane ♦ *nm* (LING) Danish

MOT-CLÉ

dans [dɑ̃] *prép* **1** (*position*) in; (*à l'intérieur de*) inside; **c'est dans le tiroir/le salon** it's in the drawer/lounge; **dans la boîte** in *ou* inside the box; **marcher dans la ville** to walk about the town
2 (*direction*) into; **elle a couru dans le salon** she ran into the lounge
3 (*provenance*) out of, from; **je l'ai pris dans le tiroir/salon** I took it out of *ou* from the drawer/lounge; **boire dans un verre** to drink out of *ou* from a glass
4 (*temps*) in; **dans 2 mois** in 2 months, in 2 months' time
5 (*approximation*) about; **dans les 20 F** about 20F

danse [dɑ̃s] *nf*: **la ~** dancing; **une ~** a dance; **la ~ classique** ballet; **danser** *vi, vt* to dance; **danseur, -euse** *nm/f* ballet dancer; (*au bal etc*) dancer; (: *cavalier*) partner
dard [daʀ] *nm* (*d'animal*) sting
date [dat] *nf* date; **de longue ~** long-standing; **~ de naissance** date of birth; **~ de péremption** expiry date; **~ limite** deadline; **dater** *vt, vi* to date; **dater de** to date from; **à dater de** (as) from
datte [dat] *nf* date
dauphin [dofɛ̃] *nm* (ZOOL) dolphin
davantage [davɑ̃taʒ] *adv* more; (*plus longtemps*) longer; **~ de** more

MOT-CLÉ

de, d' [də] (*de* + *le* = **du,** *de* + *les* = **des**) *prép* **1** (*appartenance*) of; **le toit de la maison** the roof of the house; **la voiture d'Ann/de mes parents** Ann's/my parents' car
2 (*provenance*) from; **il vient de Londres** he comes from London; **elle est sortie du cinéma** she came out of the cinema
3 (*caractérisation, mesure*): **un mur de brique/bureau d'acajou** a brick wall/ mahogany desk; **un billet de 50 F** a 50F note; **une pièce de 2 m de large** *ou* **large de 2 m** a room 2m wide, a 2m-wide room; **un bébé de 10 mois** a 10-month-old baby; **12 mois de crédit/travail** 12 months' credit/work; **augmenter de 10 F** to increase by 10F; **de 14 à 18** from 14 to 18
♦ *dét* **1** (*phrases affirmatives*) some (*souvent omis*); **du vin, de l'eau, des pommes** (some) wine, (some) water, (some) apples; **des enfants sont venus** some children came; **pendant des mois** for months
2 (*phrases interrogatives et négatives*) any; **a-t-il du vin?** has he got any wine?; **il n'a pas de pommes/ d'enfants** he hasn't (got) any apples/ children, he has no apples/children

dé [de] *nm* (*à jouer*) die *ou* dice; (*aussi:* **~ à coudre**) thimble
dealer [dilœʀ] (*fam*) *nm* (drug) pusher
déambuler [deɑ̃byle] *vi* to stroll about
débâcle [debɑkl] *nf* rout
déballer [debale] *vt* to unpack
débandade [debɑ̃dad] *nf* (*dispersion*) scattering

débarbouiller [debaʀbuje] *vt* to wash; **se ~** *vi* to wash (one's face)
débarcadère [debaʀkadɛʀ] *nm* wharf
débardeur [debaʀdœʀ] *nm* (*maillot*) tank top
débarquer [debaʀke] *vt* to unload, land ♦ *vi* to disembark; (*fig*: *fam*) to turn up
débarras [debaʀɑ] *nm* (*pièce*) lumber room; (*placard*) junk cupboard; **bon ~!** good riddance!; **débarrasser** *vt* to clear; **se débarrasser de** *vt* to get rid of; **débarrasser qn de** (*vêtements, paquets*) to relieve sb of
débat [deba] *nm* discussion, debate; **débattre** *vt* to discuss, debate; **se débattre** *vi* to struggle
débaucher [deboʃe] *vt* (*licencier*) to lay off, dismiss; (*entraîner*) to lead astray, debauch
débile [debil] (*fam*) *adj* (*idiot*) dim-witted
débit [debi] *nm* (*d'un liquide, fleuve*) flow; (*d'un magasin*) turnover (of goods); (*élocution*) delivery; (*bancaire*) debit; **~ de boissons** drinking establishment; **~ de tabac** tobacconist's; **débiter** *vt* (*compte*) to debit; (*couper*: *bois, viande*) to cut up; (*péj*: *dire*) to churn out; **débiteur, -trice** *nm/f* debtor ♦ *adj* in debit; (*compte*) debit *cpd*
déblayer [debleje] *vt* to clear
débloquer [deblɔke] *vt* (*prix, crédits*) to free
déboires [debwaʀ] *nmpl* setbacks
déboiser [debwaze] *vt* to deforest
déboîter [debwate] *vt* (*AUTO*) to pull out; **se ~ le genou** *etc* to dislocate one's knee *etc*
débonnaire [debɔnɛʀ] *adj* easy-going, good-natured
débordé, e [debɔʀde] *adj*: **être ~ (de)** (*travail, demandes*) to be snowed under (with)
déborder [debɔʀde] *vi* to overflow; (*lait etc*) to boil over; **~ (de) qch** (*dépasser*) to extend beyond sth
débouché [debuʃe] *nm* (*pour vendre*) outlet; (*perspective d'emploi*) opening
déboucher [debuʃe] *vt* (*évier, tuyau etc*) to unblock; (*bouteille*) to uncork ♦ *vi*: **~ de** to emerge from; **~ sur** (*études*) to lead on to
débourser [debuʀse] *vt* to pay out
déboussolé, e [debusɔle] (*fam*) *adj* disorientated
debout [d(ə)bu] *adv*: **être ~** (*personne*) to be standing, stand; (: *levé, éveillé*) to be up; **se mettre ~** to stand up; **se tenir ~** to stand; **~!** stand up!; (*du lit*) get up!; **cette histoire ne tient pas ~** this story doesn't hold water
déboutonner [debutɔne] *vt* to undo, unbutton
débraillé, e [debʀɑje] *adj* slovenly, untidy
débrancher [debʀɑ̃ʃe] *vt* to disconnect; (*appareil électrique*) to unplug
débrayage [debʀɛjaʒ] *nm* (*AUTO*) clutch; **débrayer** *vi* (*AUTO*) to declutch; (*cesser le travail*) to stop work
débris [debʀi] *nmpl* fragments; **des ~ de verre** bits of glass
débrouillard, e [debʀujaʀ, aʀd] (*fam*) *adj* smart, resourceful
débrouiller [debʀuje] *vt* to disentangle, untangle; **se ~** *vi* to manage; **débrouillez-vous** you'll have to sort things out yourself
début [deby] *nm* beginning, start; **~s** *nmpl* (*de carrière*) début *sg*; **~ juin** in early June; **débutant, e** *nm/f* beginner, novice; **débuter** *vi* to begin, start; (*faire ses débuts*) to start out
deçà [dəsa]: **en ~ de** *prép* this side of
décadence [dekadɑ̃s] *nf* decline
décaféiné, e [dekafeine] *adj* decaffeinated
décalage [dekalaʒ] *nm* gap; **~ horaire** time difference
décaler [dekale] *vt* to shift
décalquer [dekalke] *vt* to trace
décamper [dekɑ̃pe] (*fam*) *vi* to clear out *ou* off

décaper [dekape] *vt* (*surface peinte*) to strip

décapiter [dekapite] *vt* to behead; (*par accident*) to decapitate

décapotable [dekapɔtabl] *adj* convertible

décapsuleur [dekapsylœʀ] *nm* bottle-opener

décarcasser [dekaʀkase]: **se ~** (*fam*) *vi* to flog o.s. to death

décédé, e [desede] *adj* deceased

décéder [desede] *vi* to die

déceler [des(ə)le] *vt* (*trouver*) to discover, detect

décembre [desɑ̃bʀ] *nm* December

décemment [desamɑ̃] *adv* decently

décennie [deseni] *nf* decade

décent, e [desɑ̃, ɑ̃t] *adj* decent

déception [desɛpsjɔ̃] *nf* disappointment

décerner [desɛʀne] *vt* to award

décès [desɛ] *nm* death

décevant, e [des(ə)vɑ̃, ɑ̃t] *adj* disappointing

décevoir [des(ə)vwaʀ] *vt* to disappoint

déchaîner [deʃene] *vt* (*violence*) to unleash; (*enthousiasme*) to arouse; **se ~** (*tempête*) to rage; (*personne*) to fly into a rage

déchanter [deʃɑ̃te] *vi* to become disillusioned

décharge [deʃaʀʒ] *nf* (*dépôt d'ordures*) rubbish tip *ou* dump; (*électrique*) electrical discharge; **décharger** *vt* (*marchandise, véhicule*) to unload; (*tirer*) to discharge; **se décharger** *vi* (*batterie*) to go flat; **décharger qn de** (*responsabilité*) to release sb from

décharné, e [deʃaʀne] *adj* emaciated

déchausser [deʃose] *vt* (*skis*) to take off; **se ~** *vi* to take off one's shoes; (*dent*) to come *ou* work loose

déchéance [deʃeɑ̃s] *nf* (*physique*) degeneration; (*morale*) decay

déchet [deʃɛ] *nm* (*reste*) scrap; **~s** *nmpl* (*ordures*) refuse *sg*, rubbish *sg*; **~s nucléaires** nuclear waste

déchiffrer [deʃifʀe] *vt* to decipher

déchiqueter [deʃik(ə)te] *vt* to tear *ou* pull to pieces

déchirant, e [deʃiʀɑ̃, ɑ̃t] *adj* heart-rending

déchirement [deʃiʀmɑ̃] *nm* (*chagrin*) wrench, heartbreak; (*gén pl*: *conflit*) rift, split

déchirer [deʃiʀe] *vt* to tear; (*en morceaux*) to tear up; (*arracher*) to tear out; (*fig*: *conflit*) to tear (apart); **se ~** *vi* to tear, rip; **se ~ un muscle** to tear a muscle

déchirure [deʃiʀyʀ] *nf* (*accroc*) tear, rip; **~ musculaire** torn muscle

déchoir [deʃwaʀ] *vi* (*personne*) to lower o.s., demean o.s.

déchu, e [deʃy] *adj* (*roi*) deposed

décidé, e [deside] *adj* (*personne, air*) determined; **c'est ~** it's decided; **décidément** *adv* really

décider [deside] *vt*: **~ qch** to decide on sth; **se ~ (à faire)** to decide (to do), make up one's mind (to do); **se ~ pour** to decide on *ou* in favour of; **~ de faire/que** to decide to do/that; **~ qn (à faire qch)** to persuade sb (to do sth)

décimal, e, -aux [desimal, o] *adj* decimal; **décimale** *nf* decimal

décimètre [desimɛtʀ] *nm* decimetre

décisif, -ive [desizif, iv] *adj* decisive

décision [desizjɔ̃] *nf* decision

déclaration [deklaʀasjɔ̃] *nf* declaration; (*discours*: POL *etc*) statement; **~ (d'impôts)** ≈ tax return

déclarer [deklaʀe] *vt* to declare; (*décès, naissance*) to register; **se ~** *vi* (*feu*) to break out

déclencher [deklɑ̃ʃe] *vt* (*mécanisme etc*) to release; (*sonnerie*) to set off; (*attaque, grève*) to launch; (*provoquer*) to trigger off; **se ~** *vi* (*sonnerie*) to go off

déclic [deklik] *nm* (*bruit*) click

décliner [dekline] *vi* to decline ♦ *vt* (*invitation*) to decline; (*nom, adresse*) to state

décocher [dekɔʃe] *vt* (*coup de poing*) to throw; (*flèche, regard*) to shoot

décoiffer [dekwafe] *vt*: **~ qn** to mess up sb's hair; **je suis toute décoiffée** my hair is in a real mess

déçois *etc* [deswa] *vb voir* **décevoir**

décollage [dekɔlaʒ] *nm* (AVIAT) takeoff

décoller [dekɔle] *vt* to unstick ♦ *vi* (*avion*) to take off; **se ~** *vi* to come unstuck

décolleté, e [dekɔlte] *adj* low-cut ♦ *nm* low neck(line); (*plongeant*) cleavage

décolorer [dekɔlɔʀe]: **se ~** *vi* to fade; **se faire ~ les cheveux** to have one's hair bleached

décombres [dekɔ̃bʀ] *nmpl* rubble *sg*, debris *sg*

décommander [dekɔmɑ̃de] *vt* to cancel; **se ~** *vi* to cry off

décomposé, e [dekɔ̃poze] *adj* (*pourri*) decomposed; (*visage*) haggard, distorted

décompte [dekɔ̃t] *nm* deduction; (*facture*) detailed account

déconcerter [dekɔ̃sɛʀte] *vt* to disconcert, confound

déconfit, e [dekɔ̃fi, it] *adj* crestfallen

décongeler [dekɔ̃ʒ(ə)le] *vt* to thaw

déconner [dekɔne] (*fam*) *vi* to talk rubbish

déconseiller [dekɔ̃seje] *vt*: **~ qch (à qn)** to advise (sb) against sth; **c'est déconseillé** it's not recommended

décontracté, e [dekɔ̃tʀakte] *adj* relaxed, laid-back (*fam*)

décontracter [dekɔ̃tʀakte]: **se ~** *vi* to relax

déconvenue [dekɔ̃v(ə)ny] *nf* disappointment

décor [dekɔʀ] *nm* décor; (*paysage*) scenery; **~s** *nmpl* (THÉÂTRE) scenery *sg*, décor *sg*; (CINÉMA) set *sg*; **décorateur** *nm* (interior) decorator; **décoration** *nf* decoration; **décorer** *vt* to decorate

décortiquer [dekɔʀtike] *vt* to shell; (*fig*: *texte*) to dissect

découcher [dekuʃe] *vi* to spend the night away from home

découdre [dekudʀ]: **se ~** *vi* to come unstitched

découler [dekule] *vi*: **~ de** to ensue *ou* follow from

découper [dekupe] *vt* (*papier, tissu etc*) to cut up; (*viande*) to carve; (*article*) to cut out; **se ~ sur** to stand out against

décourager [dekuʀaʒe] *vt* to discourage; **se ~** *vi* to lose heart, become discouraged

décousu, e [dekuzy] *adj* unstitched; (*fig*) disjointed, disconnected

découvert, e [dekuvɛʀ, ɛʀt] *adj* (*tête*) bare, uncovered; (*lieu*) open, exposed ♦ *nm* (*bancaire*) overdraft; **découverte** *nf* discovery; **faire la découverte de** to discover

découvrir [dekuvʀiʀ] *vt* to discover; (*enlever ce qui couvre*) to uncover; (*dévoiler*) to reveal; **se ~** *vi* (*chapeau*) to take off one's hat; (*vêtement*) to take something off; (*ciel*) to clear

décret [dekʀɛ] *nm* decree; **décréter** *vt* to decree

décrié, e [dekʀije] *adj* disparaged

décrire [dekʀiʀ] *vt* to describe

décrocher [dekʀɔʃe] *vt* (*détacher*) to take down; (*téléphone*) to take off the hook; (: *pour répondre*) to lift the receiver; (*fam*: *contrat etc*) to get, land ♦ *vi* (*fam*: *abandonner*) to drop out; (: *cesser d'écouter*) to switch off

décroître [dekʀwɑtʀ] *vi* to decrease, decline

décrypter [dekʀipte] *vt* to decipher

déçu, e [desy] *pp de* **décevoir**

décupler [dekyple] *vt, vi* to increase tenfold

dédaigner [dedeɲe] *vt* to despise, scorn; (*négliger*) to disregard, spurn; **dédaigneux, -euse** *adj* scornful, disdainful; **dédain** *nm* scorn, disdain

dédale [dedal] *nm* maze

dedans [dədɑ̃] *adv* inside; (*pas en plein air*) indoors, inside ♦ *nm* inside; **au ~** inside

dédicacer [dedikase] *vt*: **~ (à qn)** to sign (for sb), autograph (for sb)
dédier [dedje] *vt* to dedicate
dédire [dediʀ]: **se ~** *vi* to go back on one's word, retract
dédommagement [dedɔmaʒmɑ̃] *nm* compensation
dédommager [dedɔmaʒe] *vt*: **~ qn (de)** to compensate sb (for)
dédouaner [dedwane] *vt* to clear through customs
dédoubler [deduble] *vt* (*classe, effectifs*) to split (into two)
déduire [dedɥiʀ] *vt*: **~ qch (de)** (*ôter*) to deduct sth (from); (*conclure*) to deduce *ou* infer sth (from)
déesse [deɛs] *nf* goddess
défaillance [defajɑ̃s] *nf* (*syncope*) blackout; (*fatigue*) (sudden) weakness *no pl*; (*technique*) fault, failure; **~ cardiaque** heart failure
défaillir [defajiʀ] *vi* to feel faint; (*mémoire etc*) to fail
défaire [defɛʀ] *vt* to undo; (*installation*) to take down, dismantle; **se ~** *vi* to come undone; **se ~ de** to get rid of
défait, e [defɛ, ɛt] *adj* (*visage*) haggard, ravaged; **défaite** *nf* defeat
défalquer [defalke] *vt* to deduct
défaut [defo] *nm* (*moral*) fault, failing, defect; (*tissus*) fault, flaw; (*manque, carence*): **~ de** shortage of; **prendre qn en ~** to catch sb out; **faire ~** (*manquer*) to be lacking; **à ~ de** for lack *ou* want of
défavorable [defavɔʀabl] *adj* unfavourable (*BRIT*), unfavorable (*US*)
défavoriser [defavɔʀize] *vt* to put at a disadvantage
défection [defɛksjɔ̃] *nf* defection, failure to give support
défectueux, -euse [defɛktɥø, øz] *adj* faulty, defective
défendre [defɑ̃dʀ] *vt* to defend; (*interdire*) to forbid; **se ~** *vi* to defend o.s.; **~ à qn qch/de faire** to forbid sb sth/to do; **il se défend** (*fam*: *se débrouille*) he can hold his own; **se ~ de/contre** (*se protéger*) to protect o.s. from/against; **se ~ de** (*se garder de*) to refrain from
défense [defɑ̃s] *nf* defence; (*d'éléphant etc*) tusk; **"~ de fumer"** "no smoking"
déférer [defeʀe] *vt* (*JUR*) to refer; **~ à** (*requête, décision*) to defer to
déferler [defɛʀle] *vi* (*vagues*) to break; (*fig*: *foule*) to surge
défi [defi] *nm* challenge; **lancer un ~ à qn** to challenge sb; **sur un ton de ~** defiantly
déficit [defisit] *nm* (*COMM*) deficit; **déficitaire** *adj* in deficit
défier [defje] *vt* (*provoquer*) to challenge; (*mort, autorité*) to defy
défigurer [defigyʀe] *vt* to disfigure
défilé [defile] *nm* (*GÉO*) (narrow) gorge *ou* pass; (*soldats*) parade; (*manifestants*) procession, march; **~ de mode** fashion parade
défiler [defile] *vi* (*troupes*) to march past; (*sportifs*) to parade; (*manifestants*) to march; (*visiteurs*) to pour, stream; **se ~** *vi*: **il s'est défilé** (*fam*) he wriggled out of it
définir [definiʀ] *vt* to define
définitif, -ive [definitif, iv] *adj* (*final*) final, definitive; (*pour longtemps*) permanent, definitive; (*refus*) definite; **définitive** *nf*: **en définitive** eventually; (*somme toute*) in fact; **définitivement** *adv* (*partir, s'installer*) for good
défoncer [defɔ̃se] *vt* (*porte*) to smash in *ou* down; **se ~** (*fam*) *vi* (*travailler*) to work like a dog; (*drogué*) to get high
déformer [defɔʀme] *vt* to put out of shape; (*pensée, fait*) to distort; **se ~** *vi* to lose its shape
défouler [defule]: **se ~** *vi* to unwind, let off steam
défraîchir [defʀeʃiʀ]: **se ~** *vi* to fade
défricher [defʀiʃe] *vt* to clear (for cultivation)
défunt, e [defœ̃, œ̃t] *nm/f* deceased
dégagé, e [degaʒe] *adj* (*route, ciel*) clear; **sur un ton ~** casually

dégagement [degaʒmɑ̃] *nm*: **voie de ~** slip road
dégager [degaʒe] *vt* (*exhaler*) to give off; (*délivrer*) to free, extricate; (*désencombrer*) to clear; (*isoler: idée, aspect*) to bring out; **se ~** *vi* (*passage, ciel*) to clear
dégarnir [degaʀniʀ] *vt* (*vider*) to empty, clear; **se ~** *vi* (*tempes, crâne*) to go bald
dégâts [degɑ] *nmpl* damage *sg*
dégel [deʒɛl] *nm* thaw; **dégeler** *vt* to thaw (out)
dégénérer [deʒeneʀe] *vi* to degenerate
dégingandé, e [deʒɛ̃gɑ̃de] *adj* gangling
dégivrer [deʒivʀe] *vt* (*frigo*) to defrost; (*vitres*) to de-ice
dégonflé, e [degɔ̃fle] *adj* (*pneu*) flat
dégonfler [degɔ̃fle] *vt* (*pneu, ballon*) to let down, deflate; **se ~** *vi* (*fam*) to chicken out
dégouliner [deguline] *vi* to trickle, drip
dégourdi, e [deguʀdi] *adj* smart, resourceful
dégourdir [deguʀdiʀ] *vt*: **se ~ les jambes** to stretch one's legs (*fig*)
dégoût [degu] *nm* disgust, distaste; **dégoûtant, e** *adj* disgusting; **dégoûté, e** *adj* disgusted; **dégoûté de** sick of; **dégoûter** *vt* to disgust; **dégoûter qn de qch** to put sb off sth
dégrader [degʀade] *vt* (MIL: *officier*) to degrade; (*abîmer*) to damage, deface; **se ~** *vi* (*relations, situation*) to deteriorate
dégrafer [degʀafe] *vt* to unclip, unhook
degré [dəgʀe] *nm* degree
dégressif, -ive [degʀesif, iv] *adj* on a decreasing scale
dégringoler [degʀɛ̃gɔle] *vi* to tumble (down)
dégrossir [degʀosiʀ] *vt* (*fig: projet*) to work out roughly
déguenillé, e [deg(ə)nije] *adj* ragged, tattered
déguerpir [degɛʀpiʀ] *vi* to clear off
dégueulasse [degœlas] (*fam*) *adj* disgusting
dégueuler [degœle] (*fam*) *vi* to throw up
déguisement [degizmɑ̃] *nm* (*pour s'amuser*) fancy dress
déguiser [degize]: **se ~** *vi* (*se costumer*) to dress up; (*pour tromper*) to disguise o.s.
dégustation [degystasjɔ̃] *nf* (*de fromages etc*) sampling; **~ de vins** winetasting session
déguster [degyste] *vt* (*vins*) to taste; (*fromages etc*) to sample; (*savourer*) to enjoy, savour
dehors [dəɔʀ] *adv* outside; (*en plein air*) outdoors ♦ *nm* outside ♦ *nmpl* (*apparences*) appearances; **mettre** *ou* **jeter ~** (*expulser*) to throw out; **au ~** outside; **au ~ de** outside; **en ~ de** (*hormis*) apart from
déjà [deʒa] *adv* already; (*auparavant*) before, already
déjeuner [deʒœne] *vi* to (have) lunch; (*le matin*) to have breakfast ♦ *nm* lunch
déjouer [deʒwe] *vt* (*complot*) to foil
delà [dəla] *adv*: **en ~ (de), au ~ (de)** beyond
délabrer [delɑbʀe]: **se ~** *vi* to fall into decay, become dilapidated
délacer [delase] *vt* (*chaussures*) to undo
délai [delɛ] *nm* (*attente*) waiting period; (*sursis*) extension (of time); (*temps accordé*) time limit; **sans ~** without delay; **dans les ~s** within the time limit
délaisser [delese] *vt* to abandon, desert
délasser [delɑse] *vt* to relax; **se ~** *vi* to relax
délavé, e [delave] *adj* faded
délayer [deleje] *vt* (CULIN) to mix (with water *etc*); (*peinture*) to thin down
delco [dɛlko] *nm* (AUTO) distributor
délecter [delɛkte]: **se ~** *vi* to revel *ou* delight in

délégué, e [delege] *nm/f* representative
déléguer [delege] *vt* to delegate
délibéré, e [delibeʀe] *adj* (*conscient*) deliberate
délibérer [delibeʀe] *vi* to deliberate
délicat, e [delika, at] *adj* delicate; (*plein de tact*) tactful; (*attention*) thoughtful; **délicatement** *adv* delicately; (*avec douceur*) gently
délice [delis] *nm* delight
délicieux, -euse [delisjø, jøz] *adj* (*au goût*) delicious; (*sensation*) delightful
délimiter [delimite] *vt* (*terrain*) to delimit, demarcate
délinquance [delɛ̃kɑ̃s] *nf* criminality; **délinquant, e** *adj, nm/f* delinquent
délirant, e [deliʀɑ̃, ɑ̃t] (*fam*) *adj* wild
délirer [deliʀe] *vi* to be delirious; **tu délires!** (*fam*) you're crazy!
délit [deli] *nm* (criminal) offence
délivrer [delivʀe] *vt* (*prisonnier*) to (set) free, release; (*passeport*) to issue
déloger [delɔʒe] *vt* (*objet coincé*) to dislodge
déloyal, e, -aux [delwajal, o] *adj* (*ami*) disloyal; (*procédé*) unfair
deltaplane [dɛltaplan] *nm* hang-glider
déluge [delyʒ] *nm* (*pluie*) downpour; (*biblique*) Flood
déluré, e [delyʀe] (*péj*) *adj* forward, pert
demain [d(ə)mɛ̃] *adv* tomorrow
demande [d(ə)mɑ̃d] *nf* (*requête*) request; (*revendication*) demand; (*d'emploi*) application; (*ÉCON*): **la ~** demand; **"~s d'emploi"** (*annonces*) "situations wanted"; **~ en mariage** proposal (of marriage)
demandé, e [d(ə)mɑ̃de] *adj* (*article etc*): **très ~** (very) much in demand
demander [d(ə)mɑ̃de] *vt* to ask for; (*chemin, heure etc*) to ask; (*nécessiter*) to require, demand; **se ~ si/pourquoi** *etc* to wonder whether/why *etc*; **~ qch à qn** to ask sb for sth; **~ un service à qn** to ask sb a favour; **~ à qn de faire** to ask sb to do; **demandeur, -euse** *nm/f*: **demandeur d'emploi** job-seeker
démangeaison [demɑ̃ʒɛzɔ̃] *nf* itching; **avoir des ~s** to be itching
démanger [demɑ̃ʒe] *vi* to itch
démanteler [demɑ̃t(ə)le] *vt* to break up
démaquillant [demakijɑ̃] *nm* make-up remover
démaquiller [demakije] *vt*: **se ~** to remove one's make-up
démarche [demaʀʃ] *nf* (*allure*) gait, walk; (*intervention*) step; (*fig*: *intellectuelle*) thought processes *pl*; **faire les ~s nécessaires (pour obtenir qch)** to take the necessary steps (to obtain sth)
démarcheur, -euse [demaʀʃœʀ, øz] *nm/f* (*COMM*) door-to-door salesman(-woman)
démarque [demaʀk] *nf* (*article*) markdown
démarrage [demaʀaʒ] *nm* start
démarrer [demaʀe] *vi* (*conducteur*) to start (up); (*véhicule*) to move off; (*travaux*) to get moving; **démarreur** *nm* (*AUTO*) starter
démêlant [demɛlɑ̃] *nm* conditioner
démêler [demele] *vt* to untangle; **démêlés** *nmpl* problems
déménagement [demenaʒmɑ̃] *nm* move; **camion de ~** removal van
déménager [demenaʒe] *vt* (*meubles*) to (re)move ♦ *vi* to move (house); **déménageur** *nm* removal man
démener [dem(ə)ne]: **se ~** *vi* (*se dépenser*) to exert o.s.; (*pour obtenir qch*) to go to great lengths
dément, e [demɑ̃, ɑ̃t] *adj* (*fou*) mad, crazy; (*fam*) brilliant, fantastic
démentiel, le [demɑ̃sjɛl] *adj* insane
démentir [demɑ̃tiʀ] *vt* to refute; **~ que** to deny that
démerder [demɛʀde] (*fam*): **se ~** *vi* to sort things out for o.s.
démesuré, e [dem(ə)zyʀe] *adj* immoderate
démettre [demɛtʀ] *vt*: **~ qn de** (*fonction, poste*) to dismiss sb from; **se ~**

l'épaule *etc* to dislocate one's shoulder *etc*

demeurant [d(ə)mœʀɑ̃]: **au ~** *adv* for all that

demeure [d(ə)mœʀ] *nf* residence; **demeurer** *vi* (*habiter*) to live; (*rester*) to remain

demi, e [dəmi] *adj* half ♦ *nm* (*bière*) ≃ half-pint (*0,25 litres*) ♦ *préfixe*: **~...** half-, semi..., demi-; **trois heures/bouteilles et ~es** three and a half hours/bottles, three hours/bottles and a half; **il est 2 heures et ~e/midi et ~** it's half past 2/half past 12; **à ~** half-; **à la ~e** (*heure*) on the half-hour; **demi-cercle** *nm* semicircle; **en demi-cercle** ♦ *adj* semicircular ♦ *adv* in a half circle; **demi-douzaine** *nf* half-dozen, half a dozen; **demi-finale** *nf* semifinal; **demi-frère** *nm* half-brother; **demi-heure** *nf* half-hour, half an hour; **demi-journée** *nf* half-day, half a day; **demi-litre** *nm* half-litre, half a litre; **demi-livre** *nf* half-pound, half a pound; **demi-mot** *adv*: **à demi-mot** without having to spell things out; **demi-pension** *nf* (*à l'hôtel*) half-board; **demi-pensionnaire** *nm/f*: **être demi-pensionnaire** to take school lunches; **demi-place** *nf* half-fare

démis, e [demi, iz] *adj* (*épaule etc*) dislocated

demi-sel [dəmisɛl] *adj inv* (*beurre, fromage*) slightly salted

demi-sœur [dəmisœʀ] *nf* half-sister

démission [demisjɔ̃] *nf* resignation; **donner sa ~** to give *ou* hand in one's notice; **démissionner** *vi* to resign

demi-tarif [dəmitaʀif] *nm* half-price; **voyager à ~-~** to travel half-fare

demi-tour [dəmituʀ] *nm* about-turn; **faire ~-~** to turn (and go) back

démocratie [demɔkʀasi] *nf* democracy; **démocratique** *adj* democratic

démodé, e [demɔde] *adj* old-fashioned

demoiselle [d(ə)mwazɛl] *nf* (*jeune fille*) young lady; (*célibataire*) single lady, maiden lady; **~ d'honneur** bridesmaid

démolir [demɔliʀ] *vt* to demolish

démon [demɔ̃] *nm* (*enfant turbulent*) devil, demon; **le D~** the Devil

démonstration [demɔ̃stʀasjɔ̃] *nf* demonstration

démonté, e [demɔ̃te] *adj* (*mer*) raging, wild

démonter [demɔ̃te] *vt* (*machine etc*) to take down, dismantle

démontrer [demɔ̃tʀe] *vt* to demonstrate

démordre [demɔʀdʀ] *vi*: **ne pas ~ de** to refuse to give up, stick to

démouler [demule] *vt* to turn out

démuni, e [demyni] *adj* (*sans argent*) impoverished; **~ de** without

démunir [demyniʀ] *vt*: **~ qn de** to deprive sb of; **se ~ de** to part with, give up

dénaturer [denatyʀe] *vt* (*goût*) to alter; (*pensée, fait*) to distort

dénicher [deniʃe] (*fam*) *vt* (*objet*) to unearth; (*restaurant etc*) to discover

dénier [denje] *vt* to deny

dénigrer [denigʀe] *vt* to denigrate, run down

dénivellation [denivelasjɔ̃] *nf* (*pente*) slope

dénombrer [denɔ̃bʀe] *vt* to count

dénomination [denɔminasjɔ̃] *nf* designation, appellation

dénommé, e [denɔme] *adj*: **un ~ Dupont** a certain Mr Dupont

dénoncer [denɔ̃se] *vt* to denounce

dénouement [denumɑ̃] *nm* outcome

dénouer [denwe] *vt* to unknot, undo; **se ~** *vi* (*nœud*) to come undone

dénoyauter [denwajote] *vt* to stone

denrée [dɑ̃ʀe] *nf*: **~s (alimentaires)** foodstuffs

dense [dɑ̃s] *adj* dense; **densité** *nf* density

dent [dɑ̃] *nf* tooth; **~ de lait/sagesse** milk/wisdom tooth; **dentaire** *adj* dental

dentelé, e [dɑ̃t(ə)le] *adj* jagged, in-

dented
dentelle [dɑ̃tɛl] *nf* lace *no pl*
dentier [dɑ̃tje] *nm* denture
dentifrice [dɑ̃tifʀis] *nm* toothpaste
dentiste [dɑ̃tist] *nm/f* dentist
dentition [dɑ̃tisjɔ̃] *nf* teeth
dénuder [denyde] *vt* to bare
dénué, e [denɥe] *adj*: **~ de** devoid of; **dénuement** *nm* destitution
déodorant [deɔdɔʀɑ̃] *nm* deodorant
déontologie [deɔ̃tɔlɔʒi] *nf* code of practice
dépannage [depanaʒ] *nm*: **service de ~** (AUTO) breakdown service
dépanner [depane] *vt* (*voiture, télévision*) to fix, repair; (*fig*) to bail out, help out; **dépanneuse** *nf* breakdown lorry (BRIT), tow truck (US)
dépareillé, e [depaʀeje] *adj* (*collection, service*) incomplete; (*objet*) odd
départ [depaʀ] *nm* departure; (SPORT) start; **au ~** at the start; **la veille de son ~** the day before he leaves/left
départager [depaʀtaʒe] *vt* to decide between
département [depaʀtəmɑ̃] *nm* department

département

France is divided into 96 administrative units called **départements.** *These local government divisions are headed by a state-appointed* **préfet,** *and administered by an elected* **Conseil général.** *Départements are usually named after prominent geographical features such as rivers or mountain ranges; see also* **DOM-TOM.**

dépassé, e [depɑse] *adj* superseded, outmoded; **il est complètement ~** he's completely out of his depth, he can't cope
dépasser [depɑse] *vt* (*véhicule, concurrent*) to overtake; (*endroit*) to pass, go past; (*somme, limite*) to exceed; (*fig: en beauté etc*) to surpass, outshine ♦ *vi* (*jupon etc*) to show
dépaysé, e [depeize] *adj* disoriented
dépaysement [depeizmɑ̃] *nm* (*changement*) change of scenery
dépecer [depəse] *vt* to joint, cut up
dépêche [depɛʃ] *nf* dispatch
dépêcher [depeʃe]: **se ~** *vi* to hurry
dépeindre [depɛ̃dʀ] *vt* to depict
dépendance [depɑ̃dɑ̃s] *nf* dependence; (*bâtiment*) outbuilding
dépendre [depɑ̃dʀ]: **~ de** *vt* to depend on; (*financièrement etc*) to be dependent on
dépens [depɑ̃] *nmpl*: **aux ~ de** at the expense of
dépense [depɑ̃s] *nf* spending *no pl*, expense, expenditure *no pl*; **dépenser** *vt* to spend; (*energie*) to expend, use up; **se dépenser** *vi* to exert o.s.; **dépensier, -ière** *adj*: **il est dépensier** he's a spendthrift
dépérir [depeʀiʀ] *vi* (*personne*) to waste away; (*plante*) to wither
dépêtrer [depetʀe] *vt*: **se ~ de** to extricate o.s. from
dépeupler [depœple]: **se ~** *vi* to become depopulated
dépilatoire [depilatwaʀ] *adj* depilatory, hair-removing
dépister [depiste] *vt* to detect; (*voleur*) to track down
dépit [depi] *nm* vexation, frustration; **en ~ de** in spite of; **en ~ du bon sens** contrary to all good sense; **dépité, e** *adj* vexed, frustrated
déplacé, e [deplase] *adj* (*propos*) out of place, uncalled-for
déplacement [deplasmɑ̃] *nm* (*voyage*) trip, travelling *no pl*
déplacer [deplase] *vt* (*table, voiture*) to move, shift; **se ~** *vi* to move; (*voyager*) to travel; **se ~ une vertèbre** to slip a disc
déplaire [deplɛʀ] *vt*: **ça me déplaît** I don't like this, I dislike this; **se ~** *vi* to be unhappy; **déplaisant, e** *adj* disagreeable

dépliant [deplijɑ̃] *nm* leaflet
déplier [deplije] *vt* to unfold
déplorer [deplɔʀe] *vt* to deplore
déployer [deplwaje] *vt* (*carte*) to open out; (*ailes*) to spread; (*troupes*) to deploy
déporter [depɔʀte] *vt* (*exiler*) to deport; (*dévier*) to carry off course
déposer [depoze] *vt* (*gén*: *mettre, poser*) to lay *ou* put down; (*à la banque, à la consigne*) to deposit; (*passager*) to drop (off), set down; (*roi*) to depose; (*plainte*) to lodge; (*marque*) to register; **se ~** *vi* to settle; **dépositaire** *nm/f* (COMM) agent; **déposition** *nf* statement
dépôt [depo] *nm* (*à la banque, sédiment*) deposit; (*entrepôt*) warehouse, store
dépotoir [depɔtwaʀ] *nm* dumping ground, rubbish dump
dépouiller [depuje] *vt* (*documents*) to go through, peruse; **~ qn/qch de** to strip sb/sth of; **~ le scrutin** to count the votes
dépourvu, e [depuʀvy] *adj*: **~ de** lacking in, without; **prendre qn au ~** to catch sb unprepared
déprécier [depʀesje]: **se ~** *vi* to depreciate
dépression [depʀesjɔ̃] *nf* depression; **~ (nerveuse)** (nervous) breakdown
déprimant, e [depʀimɑ̃, ɑ̃t] *adj* depressing
déprimer [depʀime] *vi* to be/get depressed

MOT-CLÉ

depuis [dəpɥi] *prép* **1** (*point de départ dans le temps*) since; **il habite Paris depuis 1983/l'an dernier** he has been living in Paris since 1983/last year; **depuis quand le connaissez-vous?** how long have you known him?
2 (*temps écoulé*) for; **il habite Paris depuis 5 ans** he has been living in Paris for 5 years; **je le connais depuis 3 ans** I've known him for 3 years
3 (*lieu*): **il a plu depuis Metz** it's been raining since Metz; **elle a téléphoné depuis Valence** she rang from Valence
4 (*quantité, rang*) from; **depuis les plus petits jusqu'aux plus grands** from the youngest to the oldest
♦ *adv* (*temps*) since (then); **je ne lui ai pas parlé depuis** I haven't spoken to him since (then)
depuis que *conj* (ever) since; **depuis qu'il m'a dit ça** (ever) since he said that to me

député, e [depyte] *nm/f* (POL) ≃ Member of Parliament (BRIT), ≃ Member of Congress (US)
députer [depyte] *vt* to delegate
déraciner [deʀasine] *vt* to uproot
dérailler [deʀɑje] *vi* (*train*) to be derailed; **faire ~** to derail
déraisonner [deʀɛzɔne] *vi* to talk nonsense, rave
dérangement [deʀɑ̃ʒmɑ̃] *nm* (*gêne*) trouble; (*gastrique etc*) disorder; **en ~** (*téléphone, machine*) out of order
déranger [deʀɑ̃ʒe] *vt* (*personne*) to trouble, bother; (*projets*) to disrupt, upset; (*objets, vêtements*) to disarrange; **se ~** *vi*: **surtout ne vous dérangez pas pour moi** please don't put yourself out on my account; **est-ce que cela vous dérange si ...?** do you mind if ...?
déraper [deʀape] *vi* (*voiture*) to skid; (*personne, semelles*) to slip
dérégler [deʀegle] *vt* (*mécanisme*) to put out of order; (*estomac*) to upset
dérider [deʀide]: **se ~** *vi* to brighten up
dérision [deʀizjɔ̃] *nf*: **tourner en ~** to deride; **dérisoire** *adj* derisory
dérive [deʀiv] *nf*: **aller à la ~** (NAVIG, *fig*) to drift
dérivé, e [deʀive] *nm* (TECH) by-product
dériver [deʀive] *vt* (MATH) to derive;

(*cours d'eau etc*) to divert ♦ *vi* (*bateau*) to drift; ~ **de** to derive from
dermatologue [dɛʀmatɔlɔg] *nm/f* dermatologist
dernier, -ière [dɛʀnje, jɛʀ] *adj* last; (*le plus récent*) latest, last; **lundi/le mois ~** last Monday/month; **c'est le ~ cri** it's the very latest thing; **en ~** last; **ce ~** the latter; **dernièrement** *adv* recently
dérobé, e [deʀɔbe] *adj*: **à la ~e** surreptitiously
dérober [deʀɔbe] *vt* to steal; **se ~** *vi* (*s'esquiver*) to slip away; **se ~ à** (*justice, regards*) to hide from; (*obligation*) to shirk
dérogation [deʀɔgasjɔ̃] *nf* (special) dispensation
déroger [deʀɔʒe]: **~ à** *vt* to go against, depart from
dérouiller [deʀuje] *vt*: **se ~ les jambes** to stretch one's legs (*fig*)
déroulement [deʀulmɑ̃] *nm* (*d'une opération etc*) progress
dérouler [deʀule] *vt* (*ficelle*) to unwind; **se ~** *vi* (*avoir lieu*) to take place; (*se passer*) to go (off); **tout s'est déroulé comme prévu** everything went as planned
dérouter [deʀute] *vt* (*avion, train*) to reroute, divert; (*étonner*) to disconcert, throw (out)
derrière [dɛʀjɛʀ] *adv, prép* behind ♦ *nm* (*d'une maison*) back; (*postérieur*) behind, bottom; **les pattes de ~** the back *ou* hind legs; **par ~** from behind; (*fig*) behind one's back
des [de] *dét voir* **de** ♦ *prép +dét* = **de +les**
dès [dɛ] *prép* from; **~ que** as soon as; **~ son retour** as soon as he was (*ou* is) back
désabusé, e [dezabyze] *adj* disillusioned
désaccord [dezakɔʀ] *nm* disagreement; **désaccordé, e** *adj* (*MUS*) out of tune
désaffecté, e [dezafɛkte] *adj* disused
désagréable [dezagʀeabl] *adj* unpleasant
désagréger [dezagʀeʒe]: **se ~** *vi* to disintegrate, break up
désagrément [dezagʀemɑ̃] *nm* annoyance, trouble *no pl*
désaltérer [dezalteʀe] *vt*: **se ~** to quench one's thirst
désapprobateur, -trice [dezapʀɔbatœʀ, tʀis] *adj* disapproving
désapprouver [dezapʀuve] *vt* to disapprove of
désarmant, e [dezaʀmɑ̃, ɑ̃t] *adj* disarming
désarroi [dezaʀwa] *nm* disarray
désastre [dezastʀ] *nm* disaster; **désastreux, -euse** *adj* disastrous
désavantage [dezavɑ̃taʒ] *nm* disadvantage; **désavantager** *vt* to put at a disadvantage
descendre [desɑ̃dʀ] *vt* (*escalier, montagne*) to go (*ou* come) down; (*valise, paquet*) to take *ou* get down; (*étagère etc*) to lower; (*fam*: *abattre*) to shoot down ♦ *vi* to go (*ou* come) down; (*passager*: *s'arrêter*) to get out, alight; **~ à pied/en voiture** to walk/drive down; **~ du train** to get out of *ou* get off the train; **~ de cheval** to dismount; **~ à l'hôtel** to stay at a hotel
descente [desɑ̃t] *nf* descent, going down; (*chemin*) way down; (*SKI*) downhill (race); **~ de lit** bedside rug; **~ (de police)** (police) raid
description [dɛskʀipsjɔ̃] *nf* description
désemparé, e [dezɑ̃paʀe] *adj* bewildered, distraught
désemplir [dezɑ̃pliʀ] *vi*: **ne pas ~** to be always full
déséquilibre [dezekilibʀ] *nm* (*position*): **en ~** unsteady; (*fig*: *des forces, du budget*) imbalance; **déséquilibré, e** *nm/f* (*PSYCH*) unbalanced person; **déséquilibrer** *vt* to throw off balance
désert, e [dezɛʀ, ɛʀt] *adj* deserted ♦ *nm* desert; **déserter** *vi, vt* to desert; **désertique** *adj* desert *cpd*
désespéré, e [dezɛspeʀe] *adj* desper-

ate

désespérer [dezɛspeʀe] *vi*: **~ (de)** to despair (of); **désespoir** *nm* despair; **en désespoir de cause** in desperation

déshabiller [dezabije] *vt* to undress; **se ~** *vi* to undress (o.s.)

déshériter [dezeʀite] *vt* to disinherit; **déshérités** *nmpl*: **les déshérités** the underprivileged

déshonneur [dezɔnœʀ] *nm* dishonour

déshydraté, e [dezidʀate] *adj* dehydrated

desiderata [dezideʀata] *nmpl* requirements

désigner [deziɲe] *vt* (*montrer*) to point out, indicate; (*dénommer*) to denote; (*candidat etc*) to name

désinfectant, e [dezɛ̃fɛktɑ̃, ɑ̃t] *adj, nm* disinfectant

désinfecter [dezɛ̃fɛkte] *vt* to disinfect

désintégrer [dezɛ̃tegʀe]: **se ~** *vi* to disintegrate

désintéressé, e [dezɛ̃teʀese] *adj* disinterested, unselfish

désintéresser [dezɛ̃teʀese] *vt*: **se ~ (de)** to lose interest (in)

désintoxication [dezɛ̃tɔksikasjɔ̃] *nf*: **faire une cure de ~** to undergo treatment for alcoholism (*ou* drug addiction)

désinvolte [dezɛ̃vɔlt] *adj* casual, offhand; **désinvolture** *nf* casualness

désir [deziʀ] *nm* wish; (*sensuel*) desire; **désirer** *vt* to want, wish for; (*sexuellement*) to desire; **je désire ...** (*formule de politesse*) I would like ...

désister [deziste]: **se ~** *vi* to stand down, withdraw

désobéir [dezɔbeiʀ] *vi*: **~ (à qn/qch)** to disobey (sb/sth); **désobéissant, e** *adj* disobedient

désobligeant, e [dezɔbliʒɑ̃, ɑ̃t] *adj* disagreeable

désodorisant [dezɔdɔʀizɑ̃] *nm* air freshener, deodorizer

désœuvré, e [dezœvʀe] *adj* idle

désolé, e [dezɔle] *adj* (*paysage*) desolate; **je suis ~** I'm sorry

désoler [dezɔle] *vt* to distress, grieve

désopilant, e [dezɔpilɑ̃, ɑ̃t] *adj* hilarious

désordonné, e [dezɔʀdɔne] *adj* untidy

désordre [dezɔʀdʀ] *nm* disorder(liness), untidiness; (*anarchie*) disorder; **en ~** in a mess, untidy

désorienté, e [dezɔʀjɑ̃te] *adj* disorientated

désormais [dezɔʀmɛ] *adv* from now on

désossé, e [dezɔse] *adj* (*viande*) boned

desquelles [dekɛl] *prép +pron* = **de +lesquelles**

desquels [dekɛl] *prép +pron* = **de +lesquels**

desséché, e [deseʃe] *adj* dried up

dessécher [deseʃe]: **se ~** *vi* to dry out

dessein [desɛ̃] *nm*: **à ~** intentionally, deliberately

desserrer [deseʀe] *vt* to loosen; (*frein*) to release

dessert [desɛʀ] *nm* dessert, pudding

desserte [desɛʀt] *nf* (*table*) side table; (*transport*): **la ~ du village est assurée par autocar** there is a coach service to the village

desservir [desɛʀviʀ] *vt* (*ville, quartier*) to serve; (*débarrasser*): **~ (la table)** to clear the table

dessin [desɛ̃] *nm* (*œuvre, art*) drawing; (*motif*) pattern, design; **~ animé** cartoon (film); **~ humoristique** cartoon; **dessinateur, -trice** *nm/f* drawer; (*de bandes dessinées*) cartoonist; (*industriel*) draughtsman(-woman) (*BRIT*), draftsman(-woman) (*US*); **dessiner** *vt* to draw; (*concevoir*) to design

dessous [d(ə)su] *adv* underneath, beneath ♦ *nm* underside ♦ *nmpl* (*sous-vêtements*) underwear *sg*; **en ~, par ~** underneath; **au-~ (de)** below; (*peu digne de*) beneath; **avoir le ~** to get the worst of it; **les voisins du ~** the downstairs neighbours; **dessous-de-plat** *nm inv* tablemat

dessus [d(ə)sy] *adv* on top; (*collé, écrit*)

on it ♦ *nm* top; **en ~** above; **par ~** ♦ *adv* over it ♦ *prép* over; **au-~ (de)** above; **avoir le ~** to get the upper hand; **dessus-de-lit** *nm inv* bedspread

destin [dɛstɛ̃] *nm* fate; (*avenir*) destiny

destinataire [dɛstinatɛʀ] *nm/f* (POSTES) addressee; (*d'un colis*) consignee

destination [dɛstinasjɔ̃] *nf* (*lieu*) destination; (*usage*) purpose; **à ~ de** bound for, travelling to

destinée [dɛstine] *nf* fate; (*existence, avenir*) destiny

destiner [dɛstine] *vt*: **~ qch à qn** (*envisager de donner*) to intend sb to have sth; (*adresser*) to intend sth for sb; **être destiné à** (*usage*) to be meant for

désuet, -ète [dezɥɛ, ɛt] *adj* outdated, outmoded

détachant [detaʃɑ̃] *nm* stain remover

détachement [detaʃmɑ̃] *nm* detachment

détacher [detaʃe] *vt* (*enlever*) to detach, remove; (*délier*) to untie; (ADMIN): **~ qn (auprès de** *ou* **à)** to post sb (to); **se ~** *vi* (*se séparer*) to come off; (: *page*) to come out; (*se défaire*) to come undone; **se ~ sur** to stand out against; **se ~ de** (*se désintéresser*) to grow away from

détail [detaj] *nm* detail; (COMM): **le ~** retail; **en ~** in detail; **au ~** (COMM) retail; **détaillant** *nm* retailer; **détaillé, e** *adj* (*plan, explications*) detailed; (*facture*) itemized; **détailler** *vt* (*expliquer*) to explain in detail

détaler [detale] (*fam*) *vi* (*personne*) to take off

détartrant [detaʀtʀɑ̃] *nm* scale remover

détaxé, e [detakse] *adj*: **produits ~s** tax-free goods

détecter [detɛkte] *vt* to detect

détective [detɛktiv] *nm*: **~ (privé)** private detective

déteindre [detɛ̃dʀ] *vi* (*au lavage*) to run, lose its colour

détendre [detɑ̃dʀ] *vt* (*corps, esprit*) to relax; **se ~** *vi* (*ressort*) to lose its tension; (*personne*) to relax

détenir [det(ə)niʀ] *vt* (*record, pouvoir, secret*) to hold; (*prisonnier*) to detain, hold

détente [detɑ̃t] *nf* relaxation

détention [detɑ̃sjɔ̃] *nf* (*d'armes*) possession; (*captivité*) detention; **~ préventive** custody

détenu, e [det(ə)ny] *nm/f* prisoner

détergent [detɛʀʒɑ̃] *nm* detergent

détériorer [deteʀjɔʀe] *vt* to damage; **se ~** *vi* to deteriorate

déterminé, e [detɛʀmine] *adj* (*résolu*) determined; (*précis*) specific, definite

déterminer [detɛʀmine] *vt* (*fixer*) to determine; **se ~ à faire qch** to make up one's mind to do sth

déterrer [deteʀe] *vt* to dig up

détestable [detɛstabl] *adj* foul, detestable

détester [detɛste] *vt* to hate, detest

détonner [detɔne] *vi* (*fig*) to clash

détour [detuʀ] *nm* detour; (*tournant*) bend, curve; **ça vaut le ~** it's worth the trip; **sans ~** (*fig*) plainly

détourné, e [detuʀne] *adj* (*moyen*) roundabout

détournement [detuʀnəmɑ̃] *nm*: **~ d'avion** hijacking

détourner [detuʀne] *vt* to divert; (*par la force*) to hijack; (*yeux, tête*) to turn away; (*de l'argent*) to embezzle; **se ~** *vi* to turn away

détracteur, -trice [detʀaktœʀ, tʀis] *nm/f* disparager, critic

détraquer [detʀake] *vt* to put out of order; (*estomac*) to upset; **se ~** *vi* (*machine*) to go wrong

détrempé, e [detʀɑ̃pe] *adj* (*sol*) sodden, waterlogged

détresse [detʀɛs] *nf* distress

détriment [detʀimɑ̃] *nm*: **au ~ de** to the detriment of

détritus [detʀity(s)] *nmpl* rubbish *sg*, refuse *sg*

détroit [detʀwa] *nm* strait

détromper [detʀɔ̃pe] *vt* to disabuse

détruire [detʀɥiʀ] *vt* to destroy

dette [dɛt] *nf* debt

DEUG *sigle m (= diplôme d'études universitaires générales) diploma taken after 2 years at university*

deuil [dœj] *nm* (*perte*) bereavement; (*période*) mourning; **être en ~** to be in mourning

deux [dø] *num* two; **tous les ~** both; **ses ~ mains** both his hands, his two hands; **~ fois** twice; **deuxième** *num* second; **deuxièmement** *adv* secondly; **deux-pièces** *nm inv* (*tailleur*) two-piece suit; (*de bain*) two-piece (swimsuit); (*appartement*) two-roomed flat (*BRIT*) *ou* apartment (*US*); **deux-points** *nm inv* colon *sg*; **deux-roues** *nm inv* two-wheeled vehicle

devais *etc* [dəvɛ] *vb voir* **devoir**

dévaler [devale] *vt* to hurtle down

dévaliser [devalize] *vt* to rob, burgle

dévaloriser [devalɔʀize] *vt* to depreciate; **se ~** *vi* to depreciate

dévaluation [devalɥasjɔ̃] *nf* devaluation

devancer [d(ə)vɑ̃se] *vt* (*coureur, rival*) to get ahead of; (*arriver*) to arrive before; (*prévenir: questions, désirs*) to anticipate

devant [d(ə)vɑ̃] *adv* in front; (*à distance: en avant*) ahead ♦ *prép* in front of; (*en avant*) ahead of; (*avec mouvement: passer*) past; (*en présence de*) before, in front of; (*étant donné*) in view of ♦ *nm* front; **prendre les ~s** to make the first move; **les pattes de ~** the front legs, the forelegs; **par ~** (*boutonner*) at the front; (*entrer*) the front way; **aller au-~ de qn** to go out to meet sb; **aller au-~ de** (*désirs de qn*) to anticipate

devanture [d(ə)vɑ̃tyʀ] *nf* (*étalage*) display; (*vitrine*) (shop) window

déveine [devɛn] (*fam*) *nf* rotten luck *no pl*

développement [dev(ə)lɔpmɑ̃] *nm* development; **pays en voie de ~** developing countries

développer [dev(ə)lɔpe] *vt* to develop; **se ~** *vi* to develop

devenir [dəv(ə)niʀ] *vb +attrib* to become; **que sont-ils devenus?** what has become of them?

dévergondé, e [devɛʀgɔ̃de] *adj* wild, shameless

déverser [devɛʀse] *vt* (*liquide*) to pour (out); (*ordures*) to tip (out); **se ~ dans** (*fleuve*) to flow into

dévêtir [devetiʀ]: **se ~** *vi* to undress

devez *etc* [dəve] *vb voir* **devoir**

déviation [devjasjɔ̃] *nf* (*AUTO*) diversion (*BRIT*), detour (*US*)

devienne *etc* [dəvjɛn] *vb voir* **devenir**

dévier [devje] *vt* (*fleuve, circulation*) to divert; (*coup*) to deflect ♦ *vi* to veer (off course)

devin [dəvɛ̃] *nm* soothsayer, seer

deviner [d(ə)vine] *vt* to guess; (*apercevoir*) to distinguish; **devinette** *nf* riddle

devins *etc* [dəvɛ̃] *vb voir* **devenir**

devis [d(ə)vi] *nm* estimate, quotation

dévisager [devizaʒe] *vt* to stare at

devise [dəviz] *nf* (*formule*) motto, watchword; **~s** *nfpl* (*argent*) currency *sg*

deviser [dəvize] *vi* to converse

dévisser [devise] *vt* to unscrew, undo

dévoiler [devwale] *vt* to unveil

devoir [d(ə)vwaʀ] *nm* duty; (*SCOL*) homework *no pl*; (*: en classe*) exercise ♦ *vt* (*argent, respect*): **~ qch (à qn)** to owe (sb) sth; (*+infin: obligation*): **il doit le faire** he has to do it, he must do it; (*: intention*): **le nouveau centre commercial doit ouvrir en mai** the new shopping centre is due to open in May; (*: probabilité*): **il doit être tard** it must be late

dévolu [devɔly] *nm*: **jeter son ~ sur** to fix one's choice on

dévorer [devɔʀe] *vt* to devour

dévot, e [devo, ɔt] *adj* devout, pious; **dévotion** *nf* devoutness

dévoué, e [devwe] *adj* devoted
dévouement [devumɑ̃] *nm* devotion
dévouer [devwe]: **se ~** *vi* (*se sacrifier*): **se ~ (pour)** to sacrifice o.s. (for); (*se consacrer*): **se ~ à** to devote *ou* dedicate o.s. to
dévoyé, e [devwaje] *adj* delinquent
devrai *etc* [dəvʀe] *vb voir* **devoir**
diabète [djabɛt] *nm* diabetes *sg*; **diabétique** *nm/f* diabetic
diable [djɑbl] *nm* devil
diabolo [djabɔlo] *nm* (*boisson*) *lemonade with fruit cordial*
diagnostic [djagnɔstik] *nm* diagnosis *sg*; **diagnostiquer** *vt* to diagnose
diagonal, e, -aux [djagɔnal, o] *adj* diagonal; **diagonale** *nf* diagonal; **en diagonale** diagonally
diagramme [djagʀam] *nm* chart, graph
dialecte [djalɛkt] *nm* dialect
dialogue [djalɔg] *nm* dialogue
diamant [djamɑ̃] *nm* diamond
diamètre [djamɛtʀ] *nm* diameter
diapason [djapazɔ̃] *nm* tuning fork
diaphragme [djafʀagm] *nm* diaphragm
diapo [djapo] (*fam*) *nf* slide
diapositive [djapozitiv] *nf* transparency, slide
diarrhée [djaʀe] *nf* diarrhoea
dictateur [diktatœʀ] *nm* dictator; **dictature** *nf* dictatorship
dictée [dikte] *nf* dictation
dicter [dikte] *vt* to dictate
dictionnaire [diksjɔnɛʀ] *nm* dictionary
dicton [diktɔ̃] *nm* saying, dictum
dièse [djez] *nm* sharp
diesel [djezɛl] *nm* diesel ♦ *adj inv* diesel
diète [djɛt] *nf* (*jeûne*) starvation diet; (*régime*) diet; **diététique** *adj*: **magasin diététique** health food shop
dieu, x [djø] *nm* god; **D~** God; **mon D~!** good heavens!
diffamation [difamasjɔ̃] *nf* slander; (*écrite*) libel
différé [difeʀe] *nm* (TV): **en ~** (pre-)recorded
différemment [difeʀamɑ̃] *adv* differently
différence [difeʀɑ̃s] *nf* difference; **à la ~ de** unlike; **différencier** *vt* to differentiate; **différend** *nm* difference (of opinion), disagreement
différent, e [difeʀɑ̃, ɑ̃t] *adj* (*dissemblable*) different; **~ de** different from; (*divers*) different, various
différer [difeʀe] *vt* to postpone, put off ♦ *vi*: **~ (de)** to differ (from)
difficile [difisil] *adj* difficult; (*exigeant*) hard to please; **difficilement** *adv* with difficulty
difficulté [difikylte] *nf* difficulty; **en ~** (*bateau, alpiniste*) in difficulties
difforme [difɔʀm] *adj* deformed, misshapen
diffuser [difyze] *vt* (*chaleur*) to diffuse; (*émission, musique*) to broadcast; (*nouvelle*) to circulate; (COMM) to distribute
digérer [diʒeʀe] *vt* to digest; (*fam: accepter*) to stomach, put up with; **digestif** *nm* (after-dinner) liqueur; **digestion** *nf* digestion
digne [diɲ] *adj* dignified; **~ de** worthy of; **~ de foi** trustworthy; **dignité** *nf* dignity
digue [dig] *nf* dike, dyke
dilapider [dilapide] *vt* to squander
dilemme [dilɛm] *nm* dilemma
dilettante [diletɑ̃t] *nm/f*: **faire qch en ~** to dabble in sth
diligence [diliʒɑ̃s] *nf* stagecoach
diluer [dilɥe] *vt* to dilute
diluvien, ne [dilyvjɛ̃, jɛn] *adj*: **pluie ~ne** torrential rain
dimanche [dimɑ̃ʃ] *nm* Sunday
dimension [dimɑ̃sjɔ̃] *nf* (*grandeur*) size; (~*s*) dimensions
diminué, e [diminɥe] *adj*: **il est très ~ depuis son accident** he's not at all the man he was since his accident
diminuer [diminɥe] *vt* to reduce, decrease; (*ardeur etc*) to lessen; (*dénigrer*) to belittle ♦ *vi* to decrease, diminish;

diminutif *nm* (*surnom*) pet name; **diminution** *nf* decreasing, diminishing
dinde [dɛ̃d] *nf* turkey
dindon [dɛ̃dɔ̃] *nm* turkey
dîner [dine] *nm* dinner ♦ *vi* to have dinner
dingue [dɛ̃g] (*fam*) *adj* crazy
dinosaure [dinɔzɔʀ] *nm* dinosaur
diplomate [diplɔmat] *adj* diplomatic ♦ *nm* diplomat; (*fig*) diplomatist; **diplomatie** *nf* diplomacy
diplôme [diplom] *nm* diploma; **avoir des ~s** to have qualifications; **diplômé, e** *adj* qualified
dire [diʀ] *nm*: **au ~ de** according to ♦ *vt* to say; (*secret, mensonge, heure*) to tell; **~ qch à qn** to tell sb sth; **~ à qn qu'il fasse** *ou* **de faire** to tell sb to do; **on dit que** they say that; **ceci dit** that being said; **si cela lui dit** (*plaire*) if he fancies it; **que dites-vous de** (*penser*) what do you think of; **on dirait que** it looks (*ou* sounds *etc*) as if; **dis/dites (donc)!** I say!
direct, e [diʀɛkt] *adj* direct ♦ *nm* (*TV*): **en ~** live; **directement** *adv* directly
directeur, -trice [diʀɛktœʀ, tʀis] *nm/f* (*d'entreprise*) director; (*de service*) manager(-eress); (*d'école*) head(teacher) (*BRIT*), principal (*US*)
direction [diʀɛksjɔ̃] *nf* (*sens*) direction; (*d'entreprise*) management; (*AUTO*) steering; **"toutes ~s"** "all routes"
dirent [diʀ] *vb voir* **dire**
dirigeant, e [diʀiʒɑ̃, ɑ̃t] *adj* (*classe*) ruling ♦ *nm/f* (*d'un parti etc*) leader
diriger [diʀiʒe] *vt* (*entreprise*) to manage, run; (*véhicule*) to steer; (*orchestre*) to conduct; (*recherches, travaux*) to supervise; **se ~** *vi* (*s'orienter*) to find one's way; **se ~ vers** *ou* **sur** to make *ou* head for
dis *etc* [di] *vb voir* **dire**
discernement [disɛʀnəmɑ̃] *nm* (*bon sens*) discernment, judgement
discerner [disɛʀne] *vt* to discern, make out
discipline [disiplin] *nf* discipline; **discipliner** *vt* to discipline
discontinu, e [diskɔ̃tiny] *adj* intermittent
discontinuer [diskɔ̃tinɥe] *vi*: **sans ~** without stopping, without a break
discordant, e [diskɔʀdɑ̃, ɑ̃t] *adj* discordant
discothèque [diskɔtɛk] *nf* (*boîte de nuit*) disco(thèque)
discours [diskuʀ] *nm* speech
discret, -ète [diskʀɛ, ɛt] *adj* discreet; (*parfum, maquillage*) unobtrusive; **discrétion** *nf* discretion; **à discrétion** as much as one wants
discrimination [diskʀiminasjɔ̃] *nf* discrimination; **sans ~** indiscriminately
disculper [diskylpe] *vt* to exonerate
discussion [diskysjɔ̃] *nf* discussion
discutable [diskytabl] *adj* debatable
discuté, e [diskyte] *adj* controversial
discuter [diskyte] *vt* (*débattre*) to discuss; (*contester*) to question, dispute ♦ *vi* to talk; (*protester*) to argue; **~ de** to discuss
dise *etc* [diz] *vb voir* **dire**
diseuse [dizøz] *nf*: **~ de bonne aventure** fortuneteller
disgracieux, -euse [disgʀasjø, jøz] *adj* ungainly, awkward
disjoindre [disʒwɛ̃dʀ] *vt* to take apart; **se ~** *vi* to come apart
disjoncteur [disʒɔ̃ktœʀ] *nm* (*ÉLEC*) circuit breaker
disloquer [dislɔke]: **se ~** *vi* (*parti, empire*) to break up
disons [dizɔ̃] *vb voir* **dire**
disparaître [dispaʀɛtʀ] *vi* to disappear; (*se perdre*: *traditions etc*) to die out; **faire ~** (*tache*) to remove; (*douleur*) to get rid of
disparition [dispaʀisjɔ̃] *nf* disappearance; **espèce en voie de ~** endangered species
disparu, e [dispaʀy] *nm/f* missing person ♦ *adj*: **être porté ~** to be reported missing

dispensaire [dispɑ̃sɛʀ] *nm* community clinic
dispenser [dispɑ̃se] *vt*: **~ qn de** to exempt sb from; **se ~ de** *vt* (*corvée*) to get out of
disperser [dispɛʀse] *vt* to scatter; **se ~** *vi* to break up
disponibilité [disponibilite] *nf* availability; **disponible** *adj* available
dispos [dispo] *adj m*: **(frais et) ~** fresh (as a daisy)
disposé, e [dispoze] *adj*: **bien/mal ~** (*humeur*) in a good/bad mood; **~ à** (*prêt à*) willing *ou* prepared to
disposer [dispoze] *vt* to arrange ♦ *vi*: **vous pouvez ~** you may leave; **~ de** to have (at one's disposal); **se ~ à faire** to prepare to do, be about to do
dispositif [dispozitif] *nm* device; (*fig*) system, plan of action
disposition [dispozisjɔ̃] *nf* (*arrangement*) arrangement, layout; (*humeur*) mood; **prendre ses ~s** to make arrangements; **avoir des ~s pour la musique** *etc* to have a special aptitude for music *etc*; **à la ~ de qn** at sb's disposal; **je suis à votre ~** I am at your service
disproportionné, e [dispʀɔpɔʀsjɔne] *adj* disproportionate, out of all proportion
dispute [dispyt] *nf* quarrel, argument; **disputer** *vt* (*match*) to play; (*combat*) to fight; **se disputer** *vi* to quarrel
disquaire [diskɛʀ] *nm/f* record dealer
disqualifier [diskalifje] *vt* to disqualify
disque [disk] *nm* (MUS) record; (*forme, pièce*) disc; (SPORT) discus; **~ compact** compact disc; **~ dur** hard disk; **disquette** *nf* floppy disk, diskette
disséminer [disemine] *vt* to scatter
disséquer [diseke] *vt* to dissect
dissertation [disɛʀtasjɔ̃] *nf* (SCOL) essay
dissimuler [disimyle] *vt* to conceal
dissipé, e [disipe] *adj* (*élève*) undisciplined, unruly
dissiper [disipe] *vt* to dissipate; (*fortune*) to squander; **se ~** *vi* (*brouillard*) to clear, disperse
dissolvant [disɔlvɑ̃] *nm* nail polish remover
dissonant, e [disɔnɑ̃, ɑ̃t] *adj* discordant
dissoudre [disudʀ] *vt* to dissolve; **se ~** *vi* to dissolve
dissuader [disɥade] *vt*: **~ qn de faire** to dissuade sb from doing; **dissuasion** *nf*: **force de dissuasion** deterrent power
distance [distɑ̃s] *nf* distance; (*fig*: *écart*) gap; **à ~** at *ou* from a distance; **distancer** *vt* to outdistance
distant, e [distɑ̃, ɑ̃t] *adj* (*réservé*) distant; **~ de** (*lieu*) far away from
distendre [distɑ̃dʀ]: **se ~** *vi* to distend
distillerie [distilʀi] *nf* distillery
distinct, e [distɛ̃(kt), ɛ̃kt] *adj* distinct; **distinctement** *adv* distinctly, clearly; **distinctif, -ive** *adj* distinctive
distingué, e [distɛ̃ge] *adj* distinguished
distinguer [distɛ̃ge] *vt* to distinguish
distraction [distʀaksjɔ̃] *nf* (*inattention*) absent-mindedness; (*passe-temps*) distraction, entertainment
distraire [distʀɛʀ] *vt* (*divertir*) to entertain, divert; (*déranger*) to distract; **se ~** *vi* to amuse *ou* enjoy o.s.; **distrait, e** *adj* absent-minded
distrayant, e [distʀɛjɑ̃, ɑ̃t] *adj* entertaining
distribuer [distʀibɥe] *vt* to distribute, hand out; (CARTES) to deal (out); (*courrier*) to deliver; **distributeur** *nm* (COMM) distributor; (*automatique*) (vending) machine; (: *de billets*) (cash) dispenser; **distribution** *nf* distribution; (*postale*) delivery; (*choix d'acteurs*) casting, cast
dit, e [di, dit] *pp de* **dire** ♦ *adj* (*fixé*): **le jour ~** the arranged day; (*surnommé*): **X, ~ Pierrot** X, known as Pierrot
dites [dit] *vb voir* **dire**
divaguer [divage] *vi* to ramble; (*fam*) to rave

divan [divɑ̃] *nm* divan
diverger [divɛʀʒe] *vi* to diverge
divers, e [divɛʀ, ɛʀs] *adj* (*varié*) diverse, varied; (*différent*) different, various; **~es personnes** various *ou* several people
diversifier [divɛʀsifje] *vt* to vary
diversité [divɛʀsite] *nf* (*variété*) diversity
divertir [divɛʀtiʀ]: **se ~** *vi* to amuse *ou* enjoy o.s.; **divertissement** *nm* distraction, entertainment
divin, e [divɛ̃, in] *adj* divine
diviser [divize] *vt* to divide; **division** *nf* division
divorce [divɔʀs] *nm* divorce; **divorcé, e** *nm/f* divorcee; **divorcer** *vi* to get a divorce, get divorced
divulguer [divylge] *vt* to disclose
dix [dis] *num* ten; **dixième** *num* tenth
dizaine [dizɛn] *nf*: **une ~ (de)** about ten, ten or so
do [do] *nm* (*note*) C; (*en chantant la gamme*) do(h)
docile [dɔsil] *adj* docile
dock [dɔk] *nm* dock; **docker** *nm* docker
docteur [dɔktœʀ] *nm* doctor; **doctorat** *nm* doctorate; **doctoresse** *nf* lady doctor
doctrine [dɔktʀin] *nf* doctrine
document [dɔkymɑ̃] *nm* document; **documentaire** *adj, nm* documentary; **documentaliste** *nm/f* (*SCOL*) librarian; **documentation** *nf* documentation, literature; **documenter** *vt*: **se documenter (sur)** to gather information (on)
dodo [dodo] *nm* (*langage enfantin*): **aller faire ~** to go to beddy-byes
dodu, e [dɔdy] *adj* plump
dogue [dɔg] *nm* mastiff
doigt [dwa] *nm* finger; **à deux ~s de** within an inch of; **~ de pied** toe; **doigté** *nm* (*MUS*) fingering; (*fig*: *habileté*) diplomacy, tact
doit *etc* [dwa] *vb voir* **devoir**
doléances [dɔleɑ̃s] *nfpl* grievances
dollar [dɔlaʀ] *nm* dollar
domaine [dɔmɛn] *nm* estate, property; (*fig*) domain, field
domestique [dɔmɛstik] *adj* domestic ♦ *nm/f* servant, domestic; **domestiquer** *vt* to domesticate
domicile [dɔmisil] *nm* home, place of residence; **à ~** at home; **livrer à ~** to deliver; **domicilié, e** *adj*: **"domicilié à ..."** "address ..."
dominant, e [dɔminɑ̃, ɑ̃t] *adj* (*opinion*) predominant
dominer [dɔmine] *vt* to dominate; (*sujet*) to master; (*surpasser*) to outclass, surpass; (*surplomber*) to tower above, dominate ♦ *vi* to be in the dominant position; **se ~** *vi* to control o.s.
domino [dɔmino] *nm* domino
dommage [dɔmaʒ] *nm*: **~s** (*dégâts*) damage *no pl*; **c'est ~!** what a shame!; **c'est ~ que** it's a shame *ou* pity that; **dommages-intérêts** *nmpl* damages
dompter [dɔ̃(p)te] *vt* to tame; **dompteur, -euse** *nm/f* trainer
DOM-TOM [dɔmtɔm] *sigle m* (= *départements et territoires d'outre-mer*) *French overseas departments and territories*
don [dɔ̃] *nm* gift; (*charité*) donation; **avoir des ~s pour** to have a gift *ou* talent for; **elle a le ~ de m'énerver** she's got a knack of getting on my nerves
donc [dɔ̃k] *conj* therefore, so; (*après une digression*) so, then
donjon [dɔ̃ʒɔ̃] *nm* keep
donné, e [dɔne] *adj* (*convenu*: *lieu, heure*) given; (*pas cher*: *fam*): **c'est ~** it's a gift; **étant ~ ...** given ...; **données** *nfpl* data
donner [dɔne] *vt* to give; (*vieux habits etc*) to give away; (*spectacle*) to put on; **~ qch à qn** to give sb sth, give sth to sb; **~ sur** (*suj*: *fenêtre, chambre*) to look (out) onto; **ça donne soif/faim** it makes you (feel) thirsty/hungry; **se ~ à fond** to give one's all; **se ~ du mal** to take (great) trouble; **s'en ~ à cœur**

joie (*fam*) to have a great time

MOT-CLÉ

dont [dɔ̃] *pron relatif* **1** (*appartenance: objets*) whose, of which; (*appartenance: êtres animés*) whose; **la maison dont le toit est rouge** the house the roof of which is red, the house whose roof is red; **l'homme dont je connais la sœur** the man whose sister I know
2 (*parmi lesquel(le)s*): **2 livres, dont l'un est ...** 2 books, one of which is ...; **il y avait plusieurs personnes, dont Gabrielle** there were several people, among them Gabrielle; **10 blessés, dont 2 grièvement** 10 injured, 2 of them seriously
3 (*complément d'adjectif, de verbe*): **le fils dont il est si fier** the son he's so proud of; **ce dont je parle** what I'm talking about

doré, e [dɔʀe] *adj* golden; (*avec dorure*) gilt, gilded
dorénavant [dɔʀenavɑ̃] *adv* henceforth
dorer [dɔʀe] *vt* to gild; **(faire) ~** (CULIN) to brown
dorloter [dɔʀlɔte] *vt* to pamper
dormir [dɔʀmiʀ] *vi* to sleep; (*être endormi*) to be asleep
dortoir [dɔʀtwaʀ] *nm* dormitory
dorure [dɔʀyʀ] *nf* gilding
dos [do] *nm* back; (*de livre*) spine; **"voir au ~"** "see over"; **de ~** from the back
dosage [dozaʒ] *nm* mixture
dose [doz] *nf* dose; **doser** *vt* to measure out; **il faut savoir doser ses efforts** you have to be able to pace yourself
dossard [dosaʀ] *nm* number (*worn by competitor*)
dossier [dosje] *nm* (*documents*) file; (*de chaise*) back; (PRESSE) feature; **un ~ scolaire** a school report
dot [dɔt] *nf* dowry
doter [dɔte] *vt*: **~ de** to equip with
douane [dwan] *nf* customs *pl*; **douanier, -ière** *adj* customs *cpd* ♦ *nm* customs officer
double [dubl] *adj, adv* double ♦ *nm* (*2 fois plus*): **le ~ (de)** twice as much (*ou* many) (as); (*autre exemplaire*) duplicate, copy; (*sosie*) double; (TENNIS) doubles *sg*; **en ~ (exemplaire)** in duplicate; **faire ~ emploi** to be redundant
double-cliquer [dublklike] *vi* (INFORM) to double-click
doubler [duble] *vt* (*multiplier par 2*) to double; (*vêtement*) to line; (*dépasser*) to overtake, pass; (*film*) to dub; (*acteur*) to stand in for ♦ *vi* to double
doublure [dublyʀ] *nf* lining; (CINÉMA) stand-in
douce [dus] *adj voir* **doux**; **douceâtre** *adj* sickly sweet; **doucement** *adv* gently; (*lentement*) slowly; **doucereux, -euse** (*péj*) *adj* sugary; **douceur** *nf* softness; (*de quelqu'un*) gentleness; (*de climat*) mildness
douche [duʃ] *nf* shower; **doucher**: **se doucher** *vi* to have *ou* take a shower
doudoune [dudun] *nf* padded jacket
doué, e [dwe] *adj* gifted, talented; **être ~ pour** to have a gift for
douille [duj] *nf* (ÉLEC) socket
douillet, te [dujɛ, ɛt] *adj* cosy; (*péj: à la douleur*) soft
douleur [dulœʀ] *nf* pain; (*chagrin*) grief, distress; **douloureux, -euse** *adj* painful
doute [dut] *nm* doubt; **sans ~** no doubt; (*probablement*) probably; **sans aucun ~** without a doubt; **douter** *vt* to doubt; **douter de** (*sincérité de qn*) to have (one's) doubts about; (*réussite*) to be doubtful of; **se douter de qch/que** to suspect sth/that; **je m'en doutais** I suspected as much; **douteux, -euse** *adj* (*incertain*) doubtful; (*péj*) dubious-looking
Douvres [duvʀ] *n* Dover
doux, douce [du, dus] *adj* soft; (*sucré*) sweet; (*peu fort: moutarde, clément: cli-*

mat) mild; (*pas brusque*) gentle

douzaine [duzɛn] *nf* (*12*) dozen; (*environ 12*): **une ~ (de)** a dozen or so

douze [duz] *num* twelve; **douzième** *num* twelfth

doyen, ne [dwajɛ̃, jɛn] *nm/f* (*en âge*) most senior member; (*de faculté*) dean

dragée [dʀaʒe] *nf* sugared almond

dragon [dʀagɔ̃] *nm* dragon

draguer [dʀage] *vt* (*rivière*) to dredge; (*fam*) to try to pick up

dramatique [dʀamatik] *adj* dramatic; (*tragique*) tragic ♦ *nf* (TV) (television) drama

dramaturge [dʀamatyʀʒ] *nm* dramatist, playwright

drame [dʀam] *nm* drama

drap [dʀa] *nm* (*de lit*) sheet; (*tissu*) woollen fabric

drapeau, x [dʀapo] *nm* flag

drap-housse [dʀaus] *nm* fitted sheet

dresser [dʀese] *vt* (*mettre vertical, monter*) to put up, erect; (*liste*) to draw up; (*animal*) to train; **se ~** *vi* (*obstacle*) to stand; (*personne*) to draw o.s. up; **~ qn contre qn** to set sb against sb; **~ l'oreille** to prick up one's ears

drogue [dʀɔg] *nf* drug; **la ~** drugs *pl*; **drogué, e** *nm/f* drug addict; **droguer** *vt* (*victime*) to drug; **se droguer** *vi* (*aux stupéfiants*) to take drugs; (*péj: de médicaments*) to dose o.s. up; **droguerie** *nf* hardware shop; **droguiste** *nm* keeper/owner of a hardware shop

droit, e [dʀwa, dʀwat] *adj* (*non courbe*) straight; (*vertical*) upright, straight; (*fig: loyal*) upright, straight(forward); (*opposé à gauche*) right, right-hand ♦ *adv* straight ♦ *nm* (*prérogative*) right; (*taxe*) duty, tax; (: *d'inscription*) fee; (JUR): **le ~** law; **avoir le ~ de** to be allowed to; **avoir ~ à** to be entitled to; **être dans son ~** to be within one's rights; **à ~e** on the right; (*direction*) (to the) right; **~s d'auteur** royalties; **~s de l'homme** human rights; **~s d'inscription** enrolment fee; **droite** *nf* (POL): **la droite** the right (wing); **droitier, -ière** *nm/f* right-handed person; **droiture** *nf* uprightness, straightness

drôle [dʀol] *adj* funny; **une ~ d'idée** a funny idea; **drôlement** (*fam*) *adv* (*très*) terribly, awfully

dromadaire [dʀɔmadɛʀ] *nm* dromedary

dru, e [dʀy] *adj* (*cheveux*) thick, bushy; (*pluie*) heavy

du [dy] *dét voir* **de** ♦ *prép +dét* = **de + le**

dû, due [dy] *vb voir* **devoir** ♦ *adj* (*somme*) owing, owed; (*causé par*): **~ à** due to ♦ *nm* due

duc [dyk] *nm* duke; **duchesse** *nf* duchess

dûment [dymɑ̃] *adv* duly

dune [dyn] *nf* dune

Dunkerque [dœ̃kɛʀk] *n* Dunkirk

duo [dɥo] *nm* (MUS) duet

dupe [dyp] *nf* dupe ♦ *adj*: **(ne pas) être ~ de** (not) to be taken in by

duplex [dyplɛks] *nm* (*appartement*) split-level apartment, duplex

duplicata [dyplikata] *nm* duplicate

duquel [dykɛl] *prép +pron* = **de +lequel**

dur, e [dyʀ] *adj* (*pierre, siège, travail, problème*) hard; (*voix, climat*) harsh; (*sévère*) hard, harsh; (*cruel*) hard(-hearted); (*porte, col*) stiff; (*viande*) tough ♦ *adv* hard ♦ *nm* (*fam: meneur*) tough nut; **~ d'oreille** hard of hearing

durant [dyʀɑ̃] *prép* (*au cours de*) during; (*pendant*) for; **des mois ~** for months

durcir [dyʀsiʀ] *vt, vi* to harden; **se ~** *vi* to harden

durée [dyʀe] *nf* length; (*d'une pile etc*) life; **de courte ~** (*séjour*) short

durement [dyʀmɑ̃] *adv* harshly

durer [dyʀe] *vi* to last

dureté [dyʀte] *nf* hardness; harshness; stiffness; toughness

durit ® [dyʀit] *nf* (car radiator) hose

dus *etc* [dy] *vb voir* **devoir**

duvet [dyvɛ] *nm* down; (*sac de couchage*) down-filled sleeping bag

DVD *sigle m* (= *digital versatile disc*) DVD

dynamique [dinamik] *adj* dynamic; **dynamisme** *nm* dynamism

dynamite [dinamit] *nf* dynamite

dynamo [dinamo] *nf* dynamo

dyslexie [dislɛksi] *nf* dyslexia, word-blindness

E, e

eau, x [o] *nf* water; **~x** *nfpl* (MÉD) waters; **prendre l'~** to leak, let in water; **tomber à l'~** (*fig*) to fall through; **~ courante** running water; **~ de Javel** bleach; **~ de toilette** toilet water; **~ douce** fresh water; **~ gazeuse** sparkling (mineral) water; **~ minérale** mineral water; **~ plate** still water; **~ potable** drinking water; **eau-de-vie** *nf* brandy; **eau-forte** *nf* etching

ébahi, e [ebai] *adj* dumbfounded

ébattre [ebatʀ]: **s'~** *vi* to frolic

ébaucher [eboʃe] *vt* to sketch out, outline; **s'~** *vi* to take shape

ébène [ebɛn] *nf* ebony; **ébéniste** *nm* cabinetmaker

éberlué, e [ebɛʀlɥe] *adj* astounded

éblouir [ebluiʀ] *vt* to dazzle

éborgner [ebɔʀɲe] *vt* to blind in one eye

éboueur [ebwœʀ] *nm* dustman (BRIT), garbageman (US)

ébouillanter [ebujɑ̃te] *vt* to scald; (CULIN) to blanch

éboulement [ebulmɑ̃] *nm* rock fall

ébouler [ebule]: **s'~** *vi* to crumble, collapse; **éboulis** *nmpl* fallen rocks

ébouriffé, e [ebuʀife] *adj* tousled

ébranler [ebʀɑ̃le] *vt* to shake; (*affaiblir*) to weaken; **s'~** *vi* (*partir*) to move off

ébrécher [ebʀeʃe] *vt* to chip

ébriété [ebʀijete] *nf*: **en état d'~** in a state of intoxication

ébrouer [ebʀue]: **s'~** *vi* to shake o.s.

ébruiter [ebʀɥite] *vt* to spread, disclose

ébullition [ebylisjɔ̃] *nf* boiling point

écaille [ekɑj] *nf* (*de poisson*) scale; (*matière*) tortoiseshell; **écailler** *vt* (*poisson*) to scale; **s'écailler** *vi* to flake *ou* peel (off)

écarlate [ekaʀlat] *adj* scarlet

écarquiller [ekaʀkije] *vt*: **~ les yeux** to stare wide-eyed

écart [ekaʀ] *nm* gap; **à l'~** out of the way; **à l'~ de** away from; **faire un ~** (*voiture*) to swerve; **~ de conduite** misdemeanour

écarté, e [ekaʀte] *adj* (*lieu*) out-of-the-way, remote; (*ouvert*): **les jambes ~es** legs apart; **les bras ~s** arms outstretched

écarter [ekaʀte] *vt* (*séparer*) to move apart, separate; (*éloigner*) to push back, move away; (*ouvrir*: *bras, jambes*) to spread, open; (: *rideau*) to draw (back); (*éliminer*: *candidat, possibilité*) to dismiss; **s'~** *vi* to part; (*s'éloigner*) to move away; **s'~ de** to wander from

écervelé, e [esɛʀvəle] *adj* scatterbrained, featherbrained

échafaud [eʃafo] *nm* scaffold

échafaudage [eʃafodaʒ] *nm* scaffolding

échafauder [eʃafode] *vt* (*plan*) to construct

échalote [eʃalɔt] *nf* shallot

échancrure [eʃɑ̃kʀyʀ] *nf* (*de robe*) scoop neckline

échange [eʃɑ̃ʒ] *nm* exchange; **en ~ de** in exchange *ou* return for; **échanger** *vt*: **échanger qch (contre)** to exchange sth (for); **échangeur** *nm* (AUTO) interchange

échantillon [eʃɑ̃tijɔ̃] *nm* sample

échappement [eʃapmɑ̃] *nm* (AUTO) exhaust

échapper [eʃape]: **~ à** *vt* (*gardien*) to escape (from); (*punition, péril*) to escape; **s'~** *vi* to escape; **~ à qn** (*détail, sens*) to escape sb; (*objet qu'on tient*) to slip out of sb's hands; **laisser ~** (*cri etc*) to let out; **l'~ belle** to have a narrow escape

écharde [eʃaʀd] *nf* splinter (of wood)

écharpe [eʃaʀp] *nf* scarf; **avoir le bras en ~** to have one's arm in a sling

échasse [eʃas] *nf* stilt

échassier [eʃasje] *nm* wader

échauffer [eʃofe] *vt* (*moteur*) to overheat; **s'~** *vi* (SPORT) to warm up; (*dans la discussion*) to become heated

échéance [eʃeɑ̃s] *nf* (*d'un paiement: date*) settlement date; (*fig*) deadline; **à brève ~** in the short term; **à longue ~** in the long run

échéant [eʃeɑ̃]: **le cas ~** *adv* if the case arises

échec [eʃɛk] *nm* failure; (ÉCHECS): **~ et mat/au roi** checkmate/check; **~s** *nmpl* (*jeu*) chess *sg*; **tenir en ~** to hold in check

échelle [eʃɛl] *nf* ladder; (*fig, d'une carte*) scale

échelon [eʃ(ə)lɔ̃] *nm* (*d'échelle*) rung; (ADMIN) grade; **échelonner** *vt* to space out

échevelé, e [eʃəv(ə)le] *adj* tousled, dishevelled

échine [eʃin] *nf* backbone, spine

échiquier [eʃikje] *nm* chessboard

écho [eko] *nm* echo; **échographie** *nf*: **passer une échographie** to have a scan

échoir [eʃwaʀ] *vi* (*dette*) to fall due; (*délais*) to expire; **~ à** to fall to

échouer [eʃwe] *vi* to fail; **s'~** *vi* to run aground

échu, e [eʃy] *pp de* **échoir**

éclabousser [eklabuse] *vt* to splash

éclair [eklɛʀ] *nm* (*d'orage*) flash of lightning, lightning *no pl*; (*gâteau*) éclair

éclairage [eklɛʀaʒ] *nm* lighting

éclaircie [eklɛʀsi] *nf* bright interval

éclaircir [eklɛʀsiʀ] *vt* to lighten; (*fig: mystère*) to clear up; (*: point*) to clarify; **s'~** *vi* (*ciel*) to clear; **s'~ la voix** to clear one's throat; **éclaircissement** *nm* (*sur un point*) clarification

éclairer [ekleʀe] *vt* (*lieu*) to light (up); (*personne: avec une lampe etc*) to light the way for; (*fig: problème*) to shed light on ♦ *vi*: **~ mal/bien** to give a poor/good light; **s'~ à la bougie** to use candlelight

éclaireur, -euse [eklɛʀœʀ, øz] *nm/f* (*scout*) (boy) scout/(girl) guide ♦ *nm* (MIL) scout

éclat [ekla] *nm* (*de bombe, de verre*) fragment; (*du soleil, d'une couleur etc*) brightness, brilliance; (*d'une cérémonie*) splendour; (*scandale*): **faire un ~** to cause a commotion; **~s de voix** shouts; **~ de rire** roar of laughter

éclatant, e [eklatɑ̃, ɑ̃t] *adj* brilliant

éclater [eklate] *vi* (*pneu*) to burst; (*bombe*) to explode; (*guerre*) to break out; (*groupe, parti*) to break up; **~ en sanglots/de rire** to burst out sobbing/laughing

éclipser [eklipse]: **s'~** *vi* to slip away

éclore [eklɔʀ] *vi* (*œuf*) to hatch; (*fleur*) to open (out)

écluse [eklyz] *nf* lock

écœurant, e [ekœʀɑ̃, ɑ̃t] *adj* (*gâteau etc*) sickly; (*fig*) sickening

écœurer [ekœʀe] *vt*: **~ qn** (*nourriture*) to make sb feel sick; (*conduite, personne*) to disgust sb

école [ekɔl] *nf* school; **aller à l'~** to go to school; **~ maternelle/primaire** nursery/primary school; **~ publique** state school; **écolier, -ière** *nm/f* schoolboy(-girl)

école maternelle

*Nursery school (***l'école maternelle***) is publicly funded in France and, though not compulsory, is attended by most children between the ages of two and six. Statutory education begins with primary school (***l'école primaire***) from the age of six to ten or eleven.*

écologie [ekɔlɔʒi] *nf* ecology; **écologique** *adj* environment-friendly; **écolo-**

giste *nm/f* ecologist
éconduire [ekɔ̃dɥiʀ] *vt* to dismiss
économe [ekɔnɔm] *adj* thrifty ♦ *nm/f* (*de lycée etc*) bursar (BRIT), treasurer (US)
économie [ekɔnɔmi] *nf* economy; (*gain: d'argent, de temps etc*) saving; (*science*) economics *sg*; **~s** *nfpl* (*pécule*) savings; **économique** *adj* (*avantageux*) economical; (ÉCON) economic; **économiser** *vt, vi* to save; **économiseur** *nm*: **économiseur d'écran** screen saver
écoper [ekɔpe] *vi* to bale out; **~ de 3 ans de prison** (*fig: fam*) to get sentenced to 3 years
écorce [ekɔʀs] *nf* bark; (*de fruit*) peel
écorcher [ekɔʀʃe] *vt*: **s'~ le genou/la main** to graze one's knee/one's hand; **écorchure** *nf* graze
écossais, e [ekɔsɛ, ɛz] *adj* Scottish ♦ *nm/f*: **É~, e** Scot
Écosse [ekɔs] *nf*: **l'~** Scotland
écosser [ekɔse] *vt* to shell
écoulement [ekulmɑ̃] *nm* (*d'eau*) flow
écouler [ekule] *vt* (*marchandise*) to sell; **s'~** *vi* (*eau*) to flow (out); (*jours, temps*) to pass (by)
écourter [ekuʀte] *vt* to curtail, cut short
écoute [ekut] *nf* (RADIO, TV): **temps/heure d'~** listening (*ou* viewing) time/hour; **rester à l'~ (de)** to stay tuned in (to); **~s téléphoniques** phone tapping *sg*
écouter [ekute] *vt* to listen to; **écouteur** *nm* (TÉL) receiver; (RADIO) headphones *pl*, headset
écoutille [ekutij] *nf* hatch
écran [ekʀɑ̃] *nm* screen; **petit ~** television; **~ total** sunblock
écrasant, e [ekʀazɑ̃, ɑ̃t] *adj* overwhelming
écraser [ekʀaze] *vt* to crush; (*piéton*) to run over; **s'~** *vi* to crash; **s'~ contre** to crash into
écrémé, e [ekʀeme] *adj* (*lait*) skimmed
écrevisse [ekʀəvis] *nf* crayfish *inv*
écrier [ekʀije]: **s'~** *vi* to exclaim
écrin [ekʀɛ̃] *nm* case, box
écrire [ekʀiʀ] *vt* to write; **s'~** to write to each other; **ça s'écrit comment?** how is it spelt?; **écrit** *nm* (*examen*) written paper; **par écrit** in writing
écriteau, x [ekʀito] *nm* notice, sign
écriture [ekʀityʀ] *nf* writing; **l'É~, les É~s** the Scriptures
écrivain [ekʀivɛ̃] *nm* writer
écrou [ekʀu] *nm* nut
écrouer [ekʀue] *vt* to imprison
écrouler [ekʀule]: **s'~** *vi* to collapse
écru, e [ekʀy] *adj* off-white, écru
ECU [eky] *sigle m* ECU
écueil [ekœj] *nm* reef; (*fig*) pitfall
éculé, e [ekyle] *adj* (*chaussure*) down-at-heel; (*fig: péj*) hackneyed
écume [ekym] *nf* foam; **écumer** *vt* (CULIN) to skim; **écumoire** *nf* skimmer
écureuil [ekyʀœj] *nm* squirrel
écurie [ekyʀi] *nf* stable
écusson [ekysɔ̃] *nm* badge
écuyer, -ère [ekɥije, jɛʀ] *nm/f* rider
eczéma [ɛgzema] *nm* eczema
édenté, e [edɑ̃te] *adj* toothless
EDF *sigle f* (= *Électricité de France*) *national electricity company*
édifice [edifis] *nm* edifice, building
édifier [edifje] *vt* to build, erect; (*fig*) to edify
Édimbourg [edɛ̃buʀ] *n* Edinburgh
éditer [edite] *vt* (*publier*) to publish; (*annoter*) to edit; **éditeur, -trice** *nm/f* publisher; **édition** *nf* edition; (*industrie du livre*) publishing
édredon [edʀədɔ̃] *nm* eiderdown
éducateur, -trice [edykatœʀ, tʀis] *nm/f* teacher; (*in special school*) instructor
éducatif, -ive [edykatif, iv] *adj* educational
éducation [edykasjɔ̃] *nf* education; (*familiale*) upbringing; (*manières*) (good) manners *pl*; **~ physique** physical education
édulcorant [edylkɔʀɑ̃] *nm* sweetener
éduquer [edyke] *vt* to educate; (*élever*)

to bring up
effacé, e [efase] *adj* unassuming
effacer [efase] *vt* to erase, rub out; **s'~** *vi* (*inscription etc*) to wear off; (*pour laisser passer*) to step aside
effarant, e [efaʀɑ̃, ɑ̃t] *adj* alarming
effarer [efaʀe] *vt* to alarm
effaroucher [efaʀuʃe] *vt* to frighten *ou* scare away
effectif, -ive [efɛktif, iv] *adj* real ♦ *nm* (SCOL) (pupil) numbers *pl*; (*entreprise*) staff, workforce; **effectivement** *adv* (*réellement*) actually, really; (*en effet*) indeed
effectuer [efɛktɥe] *vt* (*opération*) to carry out; (*trajet*) to make
efféminé, e [efemine] *adj* effeminate
effervescent, e [efɛʀvesɑ̃, ɑ̃t] *adj* effervescent
effet [efɛ] *nm* effect; (*impression*) impression; **~s** *nmpl* (*vêtements etc*) things; **faire ~** (*médicament*) to take effect; **faire bon/mauvais ~ sur qn** to make a good/bad impression on sb; **en ~** indeed; **~ de serre** greenhouse effect
efficace [efikas] *adj* (*personne*) efficient; (*action, médicament*) effective; **efficacité** *nf* efficiency; effectiveness
effilocher [efilɔʃe]: **s'~** *vi* to fray
efflanqué, e [eflɑ̃ke] *adj* emaciated
effleurer [eflœʀe] *vt* to brush (against); (*sujet*) to touch upon; (*suj. idée, pensée*): **ça ne m'a pas effleuré** it didn't cross my mind
effluves [eflyv] *nmpl* exhalation(s)
effondrer [efɔ̃dʀe]: **s'~** *vi* to collapse
efforcer [efɔʀse]: **s'~ de** *vt*: **s'~ de faire** to try hard to do
effort [efɔʀ] *nm* effort
effraction [efʀaksjɔ̃] *nf*: **s'introduire par ~ dans** to break into
effrayant, e [efʀɛjɑ̃, ɑ̃t] *adj* frightening
effrayer [efʀeje] *vt* to frighten, scare
effréné, e [efʀene] *adj* wild
effriter [efʀite]: **s'~** *vi* to crumble
effroi [efʀwa] *nm* terror, dread *no pl*
effronté, e [efʀɔ̃te] *adj* cheeky
effroyable [efʀwajabl] *adj* horrifying, appalling
effusion [efyzjɔ̃] *nf* effusion; **sans ~ de sang** without bloodshed
égal, e, -aux [egal, o] *adj* equal; (*constant*: *vitesse*) steady ♦ *nm/f* equal; **être ~ à** (*prix, nombre*) to be equal to; **ça lui est ~** it's all the same to him, he doesn't mind; **sans ~** matchless, unequalled; **d'~ à ~** as equals; **également** *adv* equally; (*aussi*) too, as well; **égaler** *vt* to equal; **égaliser** *vt* (*sol, salaires*) to level (out); (*chances*) to equalize ♦ *vi* (SPORT) to equalize; **égalité** *nf* equality; **être à égalité** to be level
égard [egaʀ] *nm*: **~s** consideration *sg*; **à cet ~** in this respect; **par ~ pour** out of consideration for; **à l'~ de** towards
égarement [egaʀmɑ̃] *nm* distraction
égarer [egaʀe] *vt* to mislay; **s'~** *vi* to get lost, lose one's way; (*objet*) to go astray
égayer [egeje] *vt* to cheer up; (*pièce*) to brighten up
églantine [eglɑ̃tin] *nf* wild *ou* dog rose
églefin [egləfɛ̃] *nm* haddock
église [egliz] *nf* church; **aller à l'~** to go to church
égoïsme [egɔism] *nm* selfishness; **égoïste** *adj* selfish
égorger [egɔʀʒe] *vt* to cut the throat of
égosiller [egozije]: **s'~** *vi* to shout o.s. hoarse
égout [egu] *nm* sewer
égoutter [egute] *vi* to drip; **s'~** *vi* to drip; **égouttoir** *nm* draining board; (*mobile*) draining rack
égratigner [egʀatiɲe] *vt* to scratch; **égratignure** *nf* scratch
Égypte [eʒipt] *nf*: **l'~** Egypt; **égyptien, ne** *adj* Egyptian ♦ *nm/f*: **Égyptien, ne** Egyptian
eh [e] *excl* hey!; **~ bien** well
éhonté, e [eɔ̃te] *adj* shameless, brazen

éjecter [eʒɛkte] *vt* (TECH) to eject; (*fam*) to kick *ou* chuck out
élaborer [elabɔʀe] *vt* to elaborate; (*projet, stratégie*) to work out; (*rapport*) to draft
élan [elɑ̃] *nm* (ZOOL) elk, moose; (SPORT) run up; (*fig*: *de tendresse etc*) surge; **prendre de l'~** to gather speed
élancé, e [elɑ̃se] *adj* slender
élancement [elɑ̃smɑ̃] *nm* shooting pain
élancer [elɑ̃se]: **s'~** *vi* to dash, hurl o.s.
élargir [elaʀʒiʀ] *vt* to widen; **s'~** *vi* to widen; (*vêtement*) to stretch
élastique [elastik] *adj* elastic ♦ *nm* (*de bureau*) rubber band; (*pour la couture*) elastic *no pl*
électeur, -trice [elɛktœʀ, tʀis] *nm/f* elector, voter
élection [elɛksjɔ̃] *nf* election
électorat [elɛktɔʀa] *nm* electorate
électricien, ne [elɛktʀisjɛ̃, jɛn] *nm/f* electrician
électricité [elɛktʀisite] *nf* electricity; **allumer/éteindre l'~** to put on/off the light
électrique [elɛktʀik] *adj* electric(al)
électrocuter [elɛktʀɔkyte] *vt* to electrocute
électroménager [elɛktʀomenaʒe] *adj, nm*: **appareils ~s, l'~** domestic (electrical) appliances
électronique [elɛktʀɔnik] *adj* electronic ♦ *nf* electronics *sg*
électrophone [elɛktʀɔfɔn] *nm* record player
élégance [elegɑ̃s] *nf* elegance
élégant, e [elegɑ̃, ɑ̃t] *adj* elegant
élément [elemɑ̃] *nm* element; (*pièce*) component, part; **~s de cuisine** kitchen units; **élémentaire** *adj* elementary
éléphant [elefɑ̃] *nm* elephant
élevage [el(ə)vaʒ] *nm* breeding; (*de bovins*) cattle rearing; **truite d'~** farmed trout
élévation [elevasjɔ̃] *nf* (*hausse*) rise
élevé, e [el(ə)ve] *adj* high; **bien/mal ~** well-/ill-mannered
élève [elɛv] *nm/f* pupil
élever [el(ə)ve] *vt* (*enfant*) to bring up, raise; (*animaux*) to breed; (*hausser*: *taux, niveau*) to raise; (*édifier*: *monument*) to put up, erect; **s'~** *vi* (*avion*) to go up; (*niveau, température*) to rise; **s'~ à** (*suj*: *frais, dégâts*) to amount to, add up to; **s'~ contre qch** to rise up against sth; **~ la voix** to raise one's voice; **éleveur, -euse** *nm/f* breeder
élimé, e [elime] *adj* threadbare
éliminatoire [eliminatwaʀ] *nf* (SPORT) heat
éliminer [elimine] *vt* to eliminate
élire [eliʀ] *vt* to elect
elle [ɛl] *pron* (*sujet*) she; (: *chose*) it; (*complément*) her; it; **~s** (*sujet*) they; (*complément*) them; **~-même** herself; itself; **~s-mêmes** themselves; *voir aussi* **il**
élocution [elɔkysjɔ̃] *nf* delivery; **défaut d'~** speech impediment
éloge [elɔʒ] *nm* (*gén no pl*) praise; **faire l'~ de** to praise; **élogieux, -euse** *adj* laudatory, full of praise
éloigné, e [elwaɲe] *adj* distant, far-off; (*parent*) distant; **éloignement** *nm* (*distance, aussi fig*) distance
éloigner [elwaɲe] *vt* (*échéance*) to put off, postpone; (*soupçons, danger*) to ward off; (*objet*): **~ qch (de)** to move *ou* take sth away (from); (*personne*): **~ qn (de)** to take sb away *ou* remove sb (from); **s'~ (de)** (*personne*) to go away (from); (*véhicule*) to move away (from); (*affectivement*) to become estranged (from); **ne vous éloignez pas!** don't go far away!
élu, e [ely] *pp de* **élire** ♦ *nm/f* (POL) elected representative
éluder [elyde] *vt* to evade
Élysée [elize] *nm*: **(le palais de) l'~** the Élysée Palace (*the French president's residence*)

émacié, e [emasje] *adj* emaciated
émail, -aux [emaj, o] *nm* enamel
e-mail [imɛl] *nm* e-mail; **envoyer qch par ~** to e-mail sth
émaillé, e [emaje] *adj* (*fig*): **~ de** dotted with
émanciper [emɑ̃sipe]: **s'~** *vi* (*fig*) to become emancipated *ou* liberated
émaner [emane]: **~ de** *vt* to come from
emballage [ɑ̃balaʒ] *nm* (*papier*) wrapping; (*boîte*) packaging
emballer [ɑ̃bale] *vt* to wrap (up); (*dans un carton*) to pack (up); (*fig*: *fam*) to thrill (to bits); **s'~** *vi* (*moteur*) to race; (*cheval*) to bolt; (*fig*: *personne*) to get carried away
embarcadère [ɑ̃baʀkadɛʀ] *nm* wharf, pier
embarcation [ɑ̃baʀkasjɔ̃] *nf* (small) boat, (small) craft *inv*
embardée [ɑ̃baʀde] *nf*: **faire une ~** to swerve
embarquement [ɑ̃baʀkəmɑ̃] *nm* (*de passagers*) boarding; (*de marchandises*) loading
embarquer [ɑ̃baʀke] *vt* (*personne*) to embark; (*marchandise*) to load; (*fam*) to cart off ♦ *vi* (*passager*) to board; **s'~** *vi* to board; **s'~ dans** (*affaire, aventure*) to embark upon
embarras [ɑ̃baʀa] *nm* (*gêne*) embarrassment; **mettre qn dans l'~** to put sb in an awkward position; **vous n'avez que l'~ du choix** the only problem is choosing
embarrassant, e [ɑ̃baʀasɑ̃, ɑ̃t] *adj* embarrassing
embarrasser [ɑ̃baʀase] *vt* (*encombrer*) to clutter (up); (*gêner*) to hinder, hamper; **~ qn** to put sb in an awkward position; **s'~ de** to burden o.s. with
embauche [ɑ̃boʃ] *nf* hiring; **embaucher** *vt* to take on, hire
embaumer [ɑ̃bome] *vt*: **~ la lavande** *etc* to be fragrant with lavender *etc*
embellie [ɑ̃beli] *nf* brighter period
embellir [ɑ̃beliʀ] *vt* to make more attractive; (*une histoire*) to embellish ♦ *vi* to grow lovelier *ou* more attractive
embêtements [ɑ̃bɛtmɑ̃] *nmpl* trouble *sg*
embêter [ɑ̃bete] *vt* to bother; **s'~** *vi* (*s'ennuyer*) to be bored
emblée [ɑ̃ble]: **d'~** *adv* straightaway
embobiner [ɑ̃bɔbine] *vt* (*fam*) to get round
emboîter [ɑ̃bwate] *vt* to fit together; **s'~ (dans)** to fit (into); **~ le pas à qn** to follow in sb's footsteps
embonpoint [ɑ̃bɔ̃pwɛ̃] *nm* stoutness
embouchure [ɑ̃buʃyʀ] *nf* (GÉO) mouth
embourber [ɑ̃buʀbe]: **s'~** *vi* to get stuck in the mud
embourgeoiser [ɑ̃buʀʒwaze]: **s'~** *vi* to become middle-class
embouteillage [ɑ̃butɛjaʒ] *nm* traffic jam
emboutir [ɑ̃butiʀ] *vt* (*heurter*) to crash into, ram
embranchement [ɑ̃bʀɑ̃ʃmɑ̃] *nm* (*routier*) junction
embraser [ɑ̃bʀaze]: **s'~** *vi* to flare up
embrassades [ɑ̃bʀasad] *nfpl* hugging and kissing
embrasser [ɑ̃bʀase] *vt* to kiss; (*sujet, période*) to embrace, encompass; **s'~** to kiss (each other)
embrasure [ɑ̃bʀazyʀ] *nf*: **dans l'~ de la porte** in the door(way)
embrayage [ɑ̃bʀɛjaʒ] *nm* clutch
embrayer [ɑ̃bʀeje] *vi* (AUTO) to let in the clutch
embrocher [ɑ̃bʀɔʃe] *vt* to put on a spit
embrouiller [ɑ̃bʀuje] *vt* to muddle up; (*fils*) to tangle (up); **s'~** *vi* (*personne*) to get in a muddle
embruns [ɑ̃bʀœ̃] *nmpl* sea spray *sg*
embûches [ɑ̃byʃ] *nfpl* pitfalls, traps
embué, e [ɑ̃bɥe] *adj* misted up
embuscade [ɑ̃byskad] *nf* ambush
éméché, e [emeʃe] *adj* tipsy, merry
émeraude [em(ə)ʀod] *nf* emerald
émerger [emɛʀʒe] *vi* to emerge; (*faire*

saillie, aussi fig) to stand out

émeri [em(ə)ʀi] *nm*: **toile** *ou* **papier ~** emery paper

émerveillement [emɛʀvɛjmɑ̃] *nm* wonder

émerveiller [emɛʀveje] *vt* to fill with wonder; **s'~ de** to marvel at

émettre [emɛtʀ] *vt* (*son, lumière*) to give out, emit; (*message etc*: RADIO) to transmit; (*billet, timbre, emprunt*) to issue; (*hypothèse, avis*) to voice, put forward ♦ *vi* to broadcast

émeus *etc* [emø] *vb voir* **émouvoir**

émeute [emøt] *nf* riot

émietter [emjete] *vt* to crumble

émigrer [emigʀe] *vi* to emigrate

émincer [emɛ̃se] *vt* to cut into thin slices

éminent, e [eminɑ̃, ɑ̃t] *adj* distinguished

émission [emisjɔ̃] *nf* (RADIO, TV) programme, broadcast; (*d'un message*) transmission; (*de timbre*) issue

emmagasiner [ɑ̃magazine] *vt* (*amasser*) to store up

emmanchure [ɑ̃mɑ̃ʃyʀ] *nf* armhole

emmêler [ɑ̃mele] *vt* to tangle (up); (*fig*) to muddle up; **s'~** *vi* to get in a tangle

emménager [ɑ̃menaʒe] *vi* to move in; **~ dans** to move into

emmener [ɑ̃m(ə)ne] *vt* to take (with one); (*comme otage, capture*) to take away; **~ qn au cinéma** to take sb to the cinema

emmerder [ɑ̃mɛʀde] (*fam!*) *vt* to bug, bother; **s'~** *vi* to be bored stiff

emmitoufler [ɑ̃mitufle]: **s'~** *vi* to wrap up (warmly)

émoi [emwa] *nm* commotion

émotif, -ive [emɔtif, iv] *adj* emotional

émotion [emosjɔ̃] *nf* emotion

émousser [emuse] *vt* to blunt; (*fig*) to dull

émouvoir [emuvwaʀ] *vt* to move; **s'~** *vi* to be moved; (*s'indigner*) to be roused

empailler [ɑ̃paje] *vt* to stuff

empaqueter [ɑ̃pakte] *vt* to parcel up

emparer [ɑ̃paʀe]: **s'~ de** *vt* (*objet*) to seize, grab; (*comme otage,* MIL) to seize; (*suj*: *peur etc*) to take hold of

empâter [ɑ̃pate]: **s'~** *vi* to thicken out

empêchement [ɑ̃pɛʃmɑ̃] *nm* (unexpected) obstacle, hitch

empêcher [ɑ̃peʃe] *vt* to prevent; **~ qn de faire** to prevent *ou* stop sb (from) doing; **il n'empêche que** nevertheless; **il n'a pas pu s'~ de rire** he couldn't help laughing

empereur [ɑ̃pʀœʀ] *nm* emperor

empester [ɑ̃pɛste] *vi* to stink, reek

empêtrer [ɑ̃petʀe] *vt*: **s'~ dans** (*fils etc*) to get tangled up in

emphase [ɑ̃fɑz] *nf* pomposity, bombast

empiéter [ɑ̃pjete] *vi*: **~ sur** to encroach upon

empiffrer [ɑ̃pifʀe]: **s'~** (*fam*) *vi* to stuff o.s.

empiler [ɑ̃pile] *vt* to pile (up)

empire [ɑ̃piʀ] *nm* empire; (*fig*) influence

empirer [ɑ̃piʀe] *vi* to worsen, deteriorate

emplacement [ɑ̃plasmɑ̃] *nm* site

emplettes [ɑ̃plɛt] *nfpl* shopping *sg*

emplir [ɑ̃pliʀ] *vt* to fill; **s'~ (de)** to fill (with)

emploi [ɑ̃plwa] *nm* use; (COMM, ÉCON) employment; (*poste*) job, situation; **mode d'~** directions for use; **~ du temps** timetable, schedule

employé, e [ɑ̃plwaje] *nm/f* employee; **~ de bureau** office employee *ou* clerk

employer [ɑ̃plwaje] *vt* to use; (*ouvrier, main-d'œuvre*) to employ; **s'~ à faire** to apply *ou* devote o.s. to doing; **employeur, -euse** *nm/f* employer

empocher [ɑ̃pɔʃe] *vt* to pocket

empoigner [ɑ̃pwaɲe] *vt* to grab

empoisonner [ɑ̃pwazɔne] *vt* to poison; (*empester*: *air, pièce*) to stink out; (*fam*): **~ qn** to drive sb mad

emporté, e [ɑ̃pɔʀte] *adj* quick-tempered

emporter [ɑ̃pɔʀte] *vt* to take (with one); (*en dérobant ou enlevant, emmener: blessés, voyageurs*) to take away; (*entraîner*) to carry away; **s'~** *vi* (*de colère*) to lose one's temper; **l'~ (sur)** to get the upper hand (of); **plats à ~** take-away meals

empreint, e [ɑ̃pʀɛ̃, ɛ̃t] *adj*: **~ de** (*regret, jalousie*) marked with; **empreinte** *nf*: **empreinte (de pas)** footprint; **empreinte (digitale)** fingerprint

empressé, e [ɑ̃pʀese] *adj* attentive

empressement [ɑ̃pʀesmɑ̃] *nm* (*hâte*) eagerness

empresser [ɑ̃pʀese]: **s'~** *vi*: **s'~ auprès de qn** to surround sb with attentions; **s'~ de faire** (*se hâter*) to hasten to do

emprise [ɑ̃pʀiz] *nf* hold, ascendancy

emprisonnement [ɑ̃pʀizɔnmɑ̃] *nm* imprisonment

emprisonner [ɑ̃pʀizɔne] *vt* to imprison

emprunt [ɑ̃pʀœ̃] *nm* loan

emprunté, e [ɑ̃pʀœ̃te] *adj* (*fig*) ill-at-ease, awkward

emprunter [ɑ̃pʀœ̃te] *vt* to borrow; (*itinéraire*) to take, follow

ému, e [emy] *pp de* **émouvoir** ♦ *adj* (*gratitude*) touched; (*compassion*) moved

MOT-CLÉ

en [ɑ̃] *prép* **1** (*endroit, pays*) in; (*direction*) to; **habiter en France/ville** to live in France/town; **aller en France/ville** to go to France/town

2 (*moment, temps*) in; **en été/juin** in summer/June

3 (*moyen*) by; **en avion/taxi** by plane/taxi

4 (*composition*) made of; **c'est en verre** it's (made of) glass; **un collier en argent** a silver necklace

5 (*description, état*): **une femme (habillée) en rouge** a woman (dressed) in red; **peindre qch en rouge** to paint sth red; **en T/étoile** T/star-shaped; **en chemise/chaussettes** in one's shirt-sleeves/socks; **en soldat** as a soldier; **cassé en plusieurs morceaux** broken into several pieces; **en réparation** being repaired, under repair; **en vacances** on holiday; **en deuil** in mourning; **le même en plus grand** the same but *ou* only bigger

6 (*avec gérondif*) while, on, by; **en dormant** while sleeping, as one sleeps; **en sortant** on going out, as he *etc* went out; **sortir en courant** to run out

♦ *pron* **1** (*indéfini*): **j'en ai/veux** I have/want some; **en as-tu?** have you got any?; **je n'en veux pas** I don't want any; **j'en ai 2** I've got 2; **combien y en a-t-il?** how many (of them) are there?; **j'en ai assez** I've got enough (of it *ou* them); (*j'en ai marre*) I've had enough

2 (*provenance*) from there; **j'en viens** I've come from there

3 (*cause*): **il en est malade/perd le sommeil** he is ill/can't sleep because of it

4 (*complément de nom, d'adjectif, de verbe*): **j'en connais les dangers** I know its *ou* the dangers; **j'en suis fier/ai besoin** I am proud of it/need it

ENA *sigle f* (= *École Nationale d'Administration*) *one of the Grandes Écoles*

encadrement [ɑ̃kadʀəmɑ̃] *nm* (*cadres*) managerial staff

encadrer [ɑ̃kadʀe] *vt* (*tableau, image*) to frame; (*fig: entourer*) to surround; (*personnel, soldats etc*) to train

encaissé, e [ɑ̃kese] *adj* (*vallée*) steep-sided; (*rivière*) with steep banks

encaisser [ɑ̃kese] *vt* (*chèque*) to cash; (*argent*) to collect; (*fam: coup, défaite*) to take

encart [ɑ̃kaʀ] *nm* insert

en-cas [ɑ̃kɑ] *nm* snack

encastré, e [ɑ̃kastʀe] *adj*: **four ~** built-in oven
enceinte [ɑ̃sɛ̃t] *adj f*: **~ (de 6 mois)** (6 months) pregnant ♦ *nf* (*mur*) wall; (*espace*) enclosure; (*aussi*: **~ acoustique**) (loud)speaker
encens [ɑ̃sɑ̃] *nm* incense
encercler [ɑ̃sɛʀkle] *vt* to surround
enchaîner [ɑ̃ʃene] *vt* to chain up; (*mouvements, séquences*) to link (together) ♦ *vi* to carry on
enchanté, e [ɑ̃ʃɑ̃te] *adj* (*ravi*) delighted; (*magique*) enchanted; **~ (de faire votre connaissance)** pleased to meet you
enchantement [ɑ̃ʃɑ̃tmɑ̃] *nm* delight; (*magie*) enchantment
enchère [ɑ̃ʃɛʀ] *nf* bid; **mettre/vendre aux ~s** to put up for (sale by)/sell by auction
enchevêtrer [ɑ̃ʃ(ə)vetʀe]: **s'~** *vi* to get in a tangle
enclencher [ɑ̃klɑ̃ʃe] *vt* (*mécanisme*) to engage; **s'~** *vi* to engage
enclin, e [ɑ̃klɛ̃, in] *adj*: **~ à** inclined *ou* prone to
enclos [ɑ̃klo] *nm* enclosure
enclume [ɑ̃klym] *nf* anvil
encoche [ɑ̃kɔʃ] *nf* notch
encoignure [ɑ̃kɔɲyʀ] *nf* corner
encolure [ɑ̃kɔlyʀ] *nf* (*cou*) neck
encombrant, e [ɑ̃kɔ̃bʀɑ̃, ɑ̃t] *adj* cumbersome, bulky
encombre [ɑ̃kɔ̃bʀ]: **sans ~** *adv* without mishap *ou* incident; **encombrement** *nm*: **être pris dans un encombrement** to be stuck in a traffic jam
encombrer [ɑ̃kɔ̃bʀe] *vt* to clutter (up); (*gêner*) to hamper; **s'~ de** (*bagages etc*) to load *ou* burden o.s. with
encontre [ɑ̃kɔ̃tʀ]: **à l'~ de** *prép* against, counter to

MOT-CLÉ

encore [ɑ̃kɔʀ] *adv* **1** (*continuation*) still; **il y travaille encore** he's still working on it; **pas encore** not yet
2 (*de nouveau*) again; **j'irai encore demain** I'll go again tomorrow; **encore une fois** (once) again; **encore deux jours** two more days
3 (*intensif*) even, still; **encore plus fort/mieux** even louder/better, louder/better still
4 (*restriction*) even so *ou* then, only; **encore pourrais-je le faire si ...** even so, I might be able to do it if ...; **si encore** if only
encore que *conj* although

encouragement [ɑ̃kuʀaʒmɑ̃] *nm* encouragement
encourager [ɑ̃kuʀaʒe] *vt* to encourage
encourir [ɑ̃kuʀiʀ] *vt* to incur
encrasser [ɑ̃kʀase] *vt* to make filthy
encre [ɑ̃kʀ] *nf* ink; **encrier** *nm* inkwell
encroûter [ɑ̃kʀute]: **s'~** (*fam*) *vi* (*fig*) to get into a rut, get set in one's ways
encyclopédie [ɑ̃siklɔpedi] *nf* encyclopaedia
endetter [ɑ̃dete]: **s'~** *vi* to get into debt
endiablé, e [ɑ̃djɑble] *adj* (*danse*) furious
endimanché, e [ɑ̃dimɑ̃ʃe] *adj* in one's Sunday best
endive [ɑ̃div] *nf* chicory *no pl*
endoctriner [ɑ̃dɔktʀine] *vt* to indoctrinate
endommager [ɑ̃dɔmaʒe] *vt* to damage
endormi, e [ɑ̃dɔʀmi] *adj* asleep
endormir [ɑ̃dɔʀmiʀ] *vt* to put to sleep; (*suj*: *chaleur etc*) to send to sleep; (MÉD: *dent, nerf*) to anaesthetize; (*fig*: *soupçons*) to allay; **s'~** *vi* to fall asleep, go to sleep
endosser [ɑ̃dose] *vt* (*responsabilité*) to take, shoulder; (*chèque*) to endorse; (*uniforme, tenue*) to put on, don
endroit [ɑ̃dʀwa] *nm* place; (*opposé à l'envers*) right side; **à l'~** (*vêtement*) the right way out; (*objet posé*) the right way round

enduire [ɑ̃dɥiʀ] *vt* to coat
enduit [ɑ̃dɥi] *nm* coating
endurance [ɑ̃dyʀɑ̃s] *nf* endurance
endurant, e [ɑ̃dyʀɑ̃, ɑ̃t] *adj* tough, hardy
endurcir [ɑ̃dyʀsiʀ]: **s'~** *vi* (*physiquement*) to become tougher; (*moralement*) to become hardened
endurer [ɑ̃dyʀe] *vt* to endure, bear
énergétique [enɛʀʒetik] *adj* (*aliment*) energy-giving
énergie [enɛʀʒi] *nf* (PHYSIQUE) energy; (TECH) power; (*morale*) vigour, spirit; **énergique** *adj* energetic, vigorous; (*mesures*) drastic, stringent
énervant, e [enɛʀvɑ̃, ɑ̃t] *adj* irritating, annoying
énerver [enɛʀve] *vt* to irritate, annoy; **s'~** *vi* to get excited, get worked up
enfance [ɑ̃fɑ̃s] *nf* childhood
enfant [ɑ̃fɑ̃] *nm/f* child; **~ de chœur** ♦ *nm* (REL) altar boy; **enfantillage** (*péj*) *nm* childish behaviour *no pl*; **enfantin, e** *adj* (*puéril*) childlike; (*langage, jeu etc*) children's *cpd*
enfer [ɑ̃fɛʀ] *nm* hell
enfermer [ɑ̃fɛʀme] *vt* to shut up; (*à clef, interner*) to lock up
enfiévré, e [ɑ̃fjevʀe] *adj* feverish
enfiler [ɑ̃file] *vt* (*vêtement*) to slip on, slip into; (*perles*) to string; (*aiguille*) to thread
enfin [ɑ̃fɛ̃] *adv* at last; (*en énumérant*) lastly; (*toutefois*) still; (*pour conclure*) in a word; (*somme toute*) after all
enflammer [ɑ̃flɑme]: **s'~** *vi* to catch fire; (MÉD) to become inflamed
enflé, e [ɑ̃fle] *adj* swollen
enfler [ɑ̃fle] *vi* to swell (up)
enfoncer [ɑ̃fɔ̃se] *vt* (*clou*) to drive in; (*faire pénétrer*): **~ qch dans** to push (*ou* drive) sth into; (*forcer: porte*) to break open; **s'~** *vi* to sink; **s'~ dans** to sink into; (*forêt, ville*) to disappear into
enfouir [ɑ̃fwiʀ] *vt* (*dans le sol*) to bury; (*dans un tiroir etc*) to tuck away
enfourcher [ɑ̃fuʀʃe] *vt* to mount
enfreindre [ɑ̃fʀɛ̃dʀ] *vt* to infringe, break
enfuir [ɑ̃fɥiʀ]: **s'~** *vi* to run away *ou* off
enfumer [ɑ̃fyme] *vt* (*pièce*) to fill with smoke
engageant, e [ɑ̃gaʒɑ̃, ɑ̃t] *adj* attractive, appealing
engagement [ɑ̃gaʒmɑ̃] *nm* commitment
engager [ɑ̃gaʒe] *vt* (*embaucher*) to take on; (: *artiste*) to engage; (*commencer*) to start; (*lier*) to bind, commit; (*impliquer*) to involve; (*investir*) to invest, lay out; (*inciter*) to urge; (*introduire: clé*) to insert; **s'~** *vi* (*promettre*) to commit o.s.; (MIL) to enlist; (*débuter: conversation etc*) to start (up); **s'~ à faire** to undertake to do; **s'~ dans** (*rue, passage*) to turn into; (*fig: affaire, discussion*) to enter into, embark on
engelures [ɑ̃ʒlyʀ] *nfpl* chilblains
engendrer [ɑ̃ʒɑ̃dʀe] *vt* to breed, create
engin [ɑ̃ʒɛ̃] *nm* machine; (*outil*) instrument; (AUT) vehicle; (AVIAT) aircraft *inv*
englober [ɑ̃glɔbe] *vt* to include
engloutir [ɑ̃glutiʀ] *vt* to swallow up
engoncé, e [ɑ̃gɔ̃se] *adj*: **~ dans** cramped in
engorger [ɑ̃gɔʀʒe] *vt* to obstruct, block
engouement [ɑ̃gumɑ̃] *nm* (sudden) passion
engouffrer [ɑ̃gufʀe] *vt* to swallow up, devour; **s'~ dans** to rush into
engourdir [ɑ̃guʀdiʀ] *vt* to numb; (*fig*) to dull, blunt; **s'~** *vi* to go numb
engrais [ɑ̃gʀɛ] *nm* manure; **~ (chimique)** (chemical) fertilizer
engraisser [ɑ̃gʀese] *vt* to fatten (up)
engrenage [ɑ̃gʀənaʒ] *nm* gears *pl*, gearing; (*fig*) chain
engueuler [ɑ̃gœle] (*fam*) *vt* to bawl at
enhardir [ɑ̃aʀdiʀ]: **s'~** *vi* to grow bolder
énigme [enigm] *nf* riddle
enivrer [ɑ̃nivʀe] *vt*: **s'~** to get drunk
enjambée [ɑ̃ʒɑ̃be] *nf* stride

enjamber [ɑ̃ʒɑ̃be] *vt* to stride over
enjeu, x [ɑ̃ʒø] *nm* stakes *pl*
enjôler [ɑ̃ʒole] *vt* to coax, wheedle
enjoliver [ɑ̃ʒɔlive] *vt* to embellish; **enjoliveur** *nm* (AUTO) hub cap
enjoué, e [ɑ̃ʒwe] *adj* playful
enlacer [ɑ̃lase] *vt* (*étreindre*) to embrace, hug
enlaidir [ɑ̃ledir] *vt* to make ugly ♦ *vi* to become ugly
enlèvement [ɑ̃lɛvmɑ̃] *nm* (*rapt*) abduction, kidnapping
enlever [ɑ̃l(ə)ve] *vt* (*ôter: gén*) to remove; (: *vêtement, lunettes*) to take off; (*emporter: ordures etc*) to take away; (*kidnapper*) to abduct, kidnap; (*obtenir: prix, contrat*) to win; (*prendre*): **~ qch à qn** to take sth (away) from sb
enliser [ɑ̃lize]: **s'~** *vi* to sink, get stuck
enneigé, e [ɑ̃neʒe] *adj* (*route, maison*) snowed-up; (*paysage*) snowy
ennemi, e [ɛnmi] *adj* hostile; (MIL) enemy *cpd* ♦ *nm/f* enemy
ennui [ɑ̃nɥi] *nm* (*lassitude*) boredom; (*difficulté*) trouble *no pl*; **avoir des ~s** to have problems; **ennuyer** *vt* to bother; (*lasser*) to bore; **s'ennuyer** *vi* to be bored; **ennuyeux, -euse** *adj* boring, tedious; (*embêtant*) annoying
énoncé [enɔ̃se] *nm* (*de problème*) terms *pl*
énoncer [enɔ̃se] *vt* (*faits*) to set out, state
enorgueillir [ɑ̃nɔrgœjir]: **s'~ de** *vt* to pride o.s. on
énorme [enɔrm] *adj* enormous, huge; **énormément** *adv* enormously; **énormément de neige/gens** an enormous amount of snow/number of people; **énormité** *nf* (*propos*) outrageous remark
enquérir [ɑ̃kerir]: **s'~ de** *vt* to inquire about
enquête [ɑ̃kɛt] *nf* (*de journaliste, de police*) investigation; (*judiciaire, administrative*) inquiry; (*sondage d'opinion*) survey; **enquêter** *vi* to investigate
enquiers *etc* [ɑ̃kje] *vb voir* **enquérir**
enquiquiner [ɑ̃kikine] (*fam*) *vt* to annoy, irritate, bother
enraciné, e [ɑ̃rasine] *adj* deep-rooted
enragé, e [ɑ̃raʒe] *adj* (MÉD) rabid, with rabies; (*fig*) fanatical
enrageant, e [ɑ̃raʒɑ̃, ɑ̃t] *adj* infuriating
enrager [ɑ̃raʒe] *vi* to be in a rage
enrayer [ɑ̃reje] *vt* to check, stop
enregistrement [ɑ̃r(ə)ʒistrəmɑ̃] *nm* recording; **~ des bagages** (*à l'aéroport*) baggage check-in
enregistrer [ɑ̃r(ə)ʒistre] *vt* (MUS *etc*) to record; (*fig: mémoriser*) to make a mental note of; (*bagages: à l'aéroport*) to check in
enrhumer [ɑ̃ryme] *vt*: **s'~, être enrhumé** to catch a cold
enrichir [ɑ̃riʃir] *vt* to make rich(er); (*fig*) to enrich; **s'~** *vi* to get rich(er)
enrober [ɑ̃rɔbe] *vt*: **~ qch de** to coat sth with
enrôler [ɑ̃role] *vt* to enlist; **s'~ (dans)** to enlist (in)
enrouer [ɑ̃rwe]: **s'~** *vi* to go hoarse
enrouler [ɑ̃rule] *vt* (*fil, corde*) to wind (up)
ensanglanté, e [ɑ̃sɑ̃glɑ̃te] *adj* covered with blood
enseignant, e [ɑ̃sɛɲɑ̃, ɑ̃t] *nm/f* teacher
enseigne [ɑ̃sɛɲ] *nf* sign; **~ lumineuse** neon sign
enseignement [ɑ̃sɛɲ(ə)mɑ̃] *nm* teaching; (ADMIN) education
enseigner [ɑ̃seɲe] *vt, vi* to teach; **~ qch à qn** to teach sb sth
ensemble [ɑ̃sɑ̃bl] *adv* together ♦ *nm* (*groupement*) set; (*vêtements*) outfit; (*totalité*): **l'~ du/de la** the whole *ou* entire; (*unité, harmonie*) unity; **impression/idée d'~** overall *ou* general impression/idea; **dans l'~** (*en gros*) on the whole
ensemencer [ɑ̃s(ə)mɑ̃se] *vt* to sow
ensevelir [ɑ̃səv(ə)lir] *vt* to bury
ensoleillé, e [ɑ̃sɔleje] *adj* sunny

ensommeillé, e [ɑ̃sɔmeje] *adj* drowsy
ensorceler [ɑ̃sɔʀsəle] *vt* to enchant, bewitch
ensuite [ɑ̃sɥit] *adv* then, next; (*plus tard*) afterwards, later
ensuivre [ɑ̃sɥivʀ]: **s'~** *vi* to follow, ensue; **et tout ce qui s'ensuit** and all that goes with it
entaille [ɑ̃taj] *nf* cut; (*sur un objet*) notch
entamer [ɑ̃tame] *vt* (*pain, bouteille*) to start; (*hostilités, pourparlers*) to open
entasser [ɑ̃tase] *vt* (*empiler*) to pile up, heap up; **s'~** *vi* (*s'amonceler*) to pile up; **s'~ dans** (*personnes*) to cram into
entendre [ɑ̃tɑ̃dʀ] *vt* to hear; (*comprendre*) to understand; (*vouloir dire*) to mean; **s'~** *vi* (*sympathiser*) to get on; (*se mettre d'accord*) to agree; **j'ai entendu dire que** I've heard (it said) that
entendu, e [ɑ̃tɑ̃dy] *adj* (*réglé*) agreed; (*au courant: air*) knowing; **(c'est) ~** all right, agreed; **bien ~** of course
entente [ɑ̃tɑ̃t] *nf* understanding; (*accord, traité*) agreement; **à double ~** (*sens*) with a double meaning
entériner [ɑ̃teʀine] *vt* to ratify, confirm
enterrement [ɑ̃tɛʀmɑ̃] *nm* (*cérémonie*) funeral, burial
enterrer [ɑ̃teʀe] *vt* to bury
entêtant, e [ɑ̃tɛtɑ̃, ɑ̃t] *adj* heady
entêté, e [ɑ̃tete] *adj* stubborn
en-tête [ɑ̃tɛt] *nm* heading; **papier à ~-~** headed notepaper
entêter [ɑ̃tete]: **s'~** *vi*: **s'~ (à faire)** to persist (in doing)
enthousiasme [ɑ̃tuzjasm] *nm* enthusiasm; **enthousiasmer** *vt* to fill with enthusiasm; **s'enthousiasmer (pour qch)** to get enthusiastic (about sth); **enthousiaste** *adj* enthusiastic
enticher [ɑ̃tiʃe]: **s'~ de** *vt* to become infatuated with
entier, -ère [ɑ̃tje, jɛʀ] *adj* whole; (*total: satisfaction etc*) complete; (*fig: caractère*) unbending ♦ *nm* (*MATH*) whole; **en ~** totally; **lait ~** full-cream milk; **entièrement** *adv* entirely, wholly
entonner [ɑ̃tɔne] *vt* (*chanson*) to strike up
entonnoir [ɑ̃tɔnwaʀ] *nm* funnel
entorse [ɑ̃tɔʀs] *nf* (*MÉD*) sprain; (*fig*): **~ au règlement** infringement of the rule
entortiller [ɑ̃tɔʀtije] *vt* (*enrouler*) to twist, wind; (*fam: cajoler*) to get round
entourage [ɑ̃tuʀaʒ] *nm* circle; (*famille*) circle of family/friends; (*ce qui enclôt*) surround
entourer [ɑ̃tuʀe] *vt* to surround; (*apporter son soutien à*) to rally round; **~ de** to surround with
entracte [ɑ̃tʀakt] *nm* interval
entraide [ɑ̃tʀɛd] *nf* mutual aid; **s'~r** *vi* to help each other
entrain [ɑ̃tʀɛ̃] *nm* spirit; **avec/sans ~** spiritedly/half-heartedly
entraînement [ɑ̃tʀɛnmɑ̃] *nm* training
entraîner [ɑ̃tʀene] *vt* (*charrier*) to carry *ou* drag along; (*TECH*) to drive; (*emmener: personne*) to take (off); (*influencer*) to lead; (*SPORT*) to train; (*impliquer*) to entail; **s'~** *vi* (*SPORT*) to train; **s'~ à qch/à faire** to train o.s. for sth/to do; **~ qn à faire** (*inciter*) to lead sb to do; **entraîneur, -euse** *nm/f* (*SPORT*) coach, trainer ♦ *nm* (*HIPPISME*) trainer
entraver [ɑ̃tʀave] *vt* (*action, progrès*) to hinder
entre [ɑ̃tʀ] *prép* between; (*parmi*) among(st); **l'un d'~ eux/nous** one of them/us; **~ eux** among(st) themselves; **entrebâillé, e** *adj* half-open, ajar; **entrechoquer**: **s'entrechoquer** *vi* to knock *ou* bang together; **entrecôte** *nf* entrecôte *ou* rib steak; **entrecouper** *vt*: **entrecouper qch de** to intersperse sth with; **entrecroiser**: **s'entrecroiser** *vi* to intertwine
entrée [ɑ̃tʀe] *nf* entrance; (*accès: au cinéma etc*) admission; (*billet*) (admission) ticket; (*CULIN*) first course
entre...: **entrefaites**: **sur ces entrefaites** *adv* at this juncture; **entrefilet** *nm* paragraph (*short article*); **entrejam-**

bes *nm* crotch; **entrelacer** *vt* to intertwine; **entremêler**: **s'entremêler** *vi* to become entangled; **entremets** *nm* (cream) dessert; **entremise** *nf* intervention; **par l'entremise de** through
entreposer [ɑ̃tʀəpoze] *vt* to store, put into storage
entrepôt [ɑ̃tʀəpo] *nm* warehouse
entreprenant, e [ɑ̃tʀəpʀənɑ̃, ɑ̃t] *adj* (*actif*) enterprising; (*trop galant*) forward
entreprendre [ɑ̃tʀəpʀɑ̃dʀ] *vt* (*se lancer dans*) to undertake; (*commencer*) to begin *ou* start (upon)
entrepreneur [ɑ̃tʀəpʀənœʀ, øz] *nm*: **~ (en bâtiment)** (building) contractor
entreprise [ɑ̃tʀəpʀiz] *nf* (*société*) firm, concern; (*action*) undertaking, venture
entrer [ɑ̃tʀe] *vi* to go (*ou* come) in, enter ♦ *vt* (*INFORM*) to enter, input; **(faire) ~ qch dans** to get sth into; **~ dans** (*gén*) to enter; (*pièce*) to go (*ou* come) into, enter; (*club*) to join; (*heurter*) to run into; **~ à l'hôpital** to go into hospital; **faire ~** (*visiteur*) to show in
entresol [ɑ̃tʀəsɔl] *nm* mezzanine
entre-temps [ɑ̃tʀətɑ̃] *adv* meanwhile
entretenir [ɑ̃tʀət(ə)niʀ] *vt* to maintain; (*famille, maîtresse*) to support, keep; **~ qn (de)** to speak to sb (about)
entretien [ɑ̃tʀətjɛ̃] *nm* maintenance; (*discussion*) discussion, talk; (*pour un emploi*) interview
entrevoir [ɑ̃tʀəvwaʀ] *vt* (*à peine*) to make out; (*brièvement*) to catch a glimpse of
entrevue [ɑ̃tʀəvy] *nf* (*audience*) interview
entrouvert, e [ɑ̃tʀuvɛʀ, ɛʀt] *adj* half-open
énumérer [enymeʀe] *vt* to list
envahir [ɑ̃vaiʀ] *vt* to invade; (*suj: inquiétude, peur*) to come over; **envahissant, e** (*péj*) *adj* (*personne*) intrusive
enveloppe [ɑ̃v(ə)lɔp] *nf* (*de lettre*) envelope; (*crédits*) budget; **envelopper** *vt* to wrap; (*fig*) to envelop, shroud
envenimer [ɑ̃v(ə)nime] *vt* to aggravate
envergure [ɑ̃vɛʀgyʀ] *nf* (*fig*) scope; (*personne*) calibre
enverrai *etc* [ɑ̃veʀɛ] *vb voir* **envoyer**
envers [ɑ̃vɛʀ] *prép* towards, to ♦ *nm* other side; (*d'une étoffe*) wrong side; **à l'~** (*verticalement*) upside down; (*pull*) back to front; (*chaussettes*) inside out
envie [ɑ̃vi] *nf* (*sentiment*) envy; (*souhait*) desire, wish; **avoir ~ de (faire)** to feel like (doing); (*plus fort*) to want (to do); **avoir ~ que** to wish that; **cette glace me fait ~** I fancy some of that ice cream; **envier** *vt* to envy; **envieux, -euse** *adj* envious
environ [ɑ̃viʀɔ̃] *adv*: **~ 3 h/2 km** (around) about 3 o'clock/2 km; *voir aussi* **environs**
environnant, e [ɑ̃viʀɔnɑ̃, ɑ̃t] *adj* surrounding
environnement [ɑ̃viʀɔnmɑ̃] *nm* environment
environs [ɑ̃viʀɔ̃] *nmpl* surroundings; **aux ~ de** (round) about
envisager [ɑ̃vizaʒe] *vt* to contemplate, envisage; **~ de faire** to consider doing
envoi [ɑ̃vwa] *nm* (*paquet*) parcel, consignment; **coup d'~** (*SPORT*) kick-off
envoler [ɑ̃vɔle]: **s'~** *vi* (*oiseau*) to fly away *ou* off; (*avion*) to take off; (*papier, feuille*) to blow away; (*fig*) to vanish (into thin air)
envoûter [ɑ̃vute] *vt* to bewitch
envoyé, e [ɑ̃vwaje] *nm/f* (*POL*) envoy; (*PRESSE*) correspondent
envoyer [ɑ̃vwaje] *vt* to send; (*lancer*) to hurl, throw; **~ chercher** to send for; **~ promener qn** (*fam*) to send sb packing
Éole [eɔl] *sigle m* (= *est-ouest-liaison-express*) *Paris high-speed, east-west subway service*
épagneul, e [epaɲœl] *nm/f* spaniel
épais, se [epɛ, ɛs] *adj* thick; **épaisseur** *nf* thickness
épancher [epɑ̃ʃe]: **s'~** *vi* to open one's heart
épanouir [epanwiʀ]: **s'~** *vi* (*fleur*) to

bloom, open out; (*visage*) to light up; (*personne*) to blossom
épargne [epaʀɲ] *nf* saving
épargner [epaʀɲe] *vt* to save; (*ne pas tuer ou endommager*) to spare ♦ *vi* to save; **~ qch à qn** to spare sb sth
éparpiller [epaʀpije] *vt* to scatter; **s'~** *vi* to scatter; (*fig*) to dissipate one's efforts
épars, e [epaʀ, aʀs] *adj* scattered
épatant, e [epatɑ̃, ɑ̃t] (*fam*) *adj* super
épater [epate] (*fam*) *vt* (*étonner*) to amaze; (*impressionner*) to impress
épaule [epol] *nf* shoulder
épauler [epole] *vt* (*aider*) to back up, support; (*arme*) to raise (to one's shoulder) ♦ *vi* to (take) aim
épaulette [epolɛt] *nf* (MIL) epaulette; (*rembourrage*) shoulder pad
épave [epav] *nf* wreck
épée [epe] *nf* sword
épeler [ep(ə)le] *vt* to spell
éperdu, e [epɛʀdy] *adj* distraught, overcome; (*amour*) passionate
éperon [epʀɔ̃] *nm* spur
épervier [epɛʀvje] *nm* sparrowhawk
épi [epi] *nm* (*de blé, d'orge*) ear; (*de maïs*) cob
épice [epis] *nf* spice
épicé, e [epise] *adj* spicy
épicer [epise] *vt* to spice
épicerie [episʀi] *nf* grocer's shop; (*denrées*) groceries *pl*; **~ fine** delicatessen;
épicier, -ière *nm/f* grocer
épidémie [epidemi] *nf* epidemic
épiderme [epidɛʀm] *nm* skin
épier [epje] *vt* to spy on, watch closely
épilepsie [epilɛpsi] *nf* epilepsy
épiler [epile] *vt* (*jambes*) to remove the hair from; (*sourcils*) to pluck
épilogue [epilɔg] *nm* (*fig*) conclusion, dénouement; **épiloguer** *vi*: **épiloguer sur** to hold forth on
épinards [epinaʀ] *nmpl* spinach *sg*
épine [epin] *nf* thorn, prickle; (*d'oursin etc*) spine; **~ dorsale** backbone; **épineux, -euse** *adj* thorny
épingle [epɛ̃gl] *nf* pin; **~ à cheveux** hairpin; **~ de nourrice** *ou* **de sûreté** safety pin; **épingler** *vt* (*badge, décoration*): **épingler qch sur** to pin sth on(to); (*fam*) to catch, nick
épique [epik] *adj* epic
épisode [epizɔd] *nm* episode; **film/roman à ~s** serial; **épisodique** *adj* occasional
éploré, e [eplɔʀe] *adj* tearful
épluche-légumes [eplyʃlegym] *nm inv* (potato) peeler
éplucher [eplyʃe] *vt* (*fruit, légumes*) to peel; (*fig*) to go over with a fine-tooth comb; **épluchures** *nfpl* peelings
éponge [epɔ̃ʒ] *nf* sponge; **éponger** *vt* (*liquide*) to mop up; (*surface*) to sponge; (*fig: déficit*) to soak up
épopée [epɔpe] *nf* epic
époque [epɔk] *nf* (*de l'histoire*) age, era; (*de l'année, la vie*) time; **d'~** (*meuble*) period *cpd*
époumoner [epumɔne]: **s'~** *vi* to shout o.s. hoarse
épouse [epuz] *nf* wife; **épouser** *vt* to marry
épousseter [epuste] *vt* to dust
époustouflant, e [epustuflɑ̃, ɑ̃t] (*fam*) *adj* staggering, mind-boggling
épouvantable [epuvɑ̃tabl] *adj* appalling, dreadful
épouvantail [epuvɑ̃taj] *nm* scarecrow
épouvante [epuvɑ̃t] *nf* terror; **film d'** horror film; **épouvanter** *vt* to terrify
époux [epu] *nm* husband ♦ *nmpl* (married) couple
éprendre [epʀɑ̃dʀ]: **s'~ de** *vt* to fall in love with
épreuve [epʀœv] *nf* (*d'examen*) test; (*malheur, difficulté*) trial, ordeal; (PHOTO) print; (TYPO) proof; (SPORT) event; **à toute ~** unfailing; **mettre à l'~** to put to the test
épris, e [epʀi, iz] *pp de* **éprendre**
éprouvant, e [epʀuvɑ̃, ɑ̃t] *adj* trying, testing
éprouver [epʀuve] *vt* (*tester*) to test;

(*marquer, faire souffrir*) to afflict, distress; (*ressentir*) to experience
éprouvette [epʀuvɛt] *nf* test tube
épuisé, e [epɥize] *adj* exhausted; (*livre*) out of print; **épuisement** *nm* exhaustion
épuiser [epɥize] *vt* (*fatiguer*) to exhaust, wear *ou* tire out; (*stock, sujet*) to exhaust; **s'~** *vi* to wear *ou* tire o.s. out, exhaust o.s.
épuisette [epɥizɛt] *nf* shrimping net
épurer [epyʀe] *vt* (*liquide*) to purify; (*parti etc*) to purge
équateur [ekwatœʀ] *nm* equator; **(la république de) l'É~** Ecuador
équation [ekwasjɔ̃] *nf* equation
équerre [ekɛʀ] *nf* (*à dessin*) (set) square
équilibre [ekilibʀ] *nm* balance; **garder/perdre l'~** to keep/lose one's balance; **être en ~** to be balanced; **équilibré, e** *adj* well-balanced; **équilibrer** *vt* to balance; **s'équilibrer** *vi* (*poids*) to balance; (*fig: défauts etc*) to balance each other out
équipage [ekipaʒ] *nm* crew
équipe [ekip] *nf* team
équipé, e [ekipe] *adj*: **bien/mal ~** well-/poorly-equipped; **équipée** *nf* escapade
équipement [ekipmɑ̃] *nm* equipment; **~s** *nmpl* (*installations*) amenities, facilities
équiper [ekipe] *vt* to equip; **~ qn/qch de** to equip sb/sth with
équipier, -ière [ekipje, jɛʀ] *nm/f* team member
équitable [ekitabl] *adj* fair
équitation [ekitasjɔ̃] *nf* (horse-)riding; **faire de l'~** to go riding
équivalent, e [ekivalɑ̃, ɑ̃t] *adj, nm* equivalent
équivaloir [ekivalwaʀ]: **~ à** *vt* to be equivalent to
équivoque [ekivɔk] *adj* equivocal, ambiguous; (*louche*) dubious ♦ *nf* (*incertitude*) doubt
érable [eʀabl] *nm* maple
érafler [eʀɑfle] *vt* to scratch; **éraflure** *nf* scratch
éraillé, e [eʀɑje] *adj* (*voix*) rasping
ère [ɛʀ] *nf* era; **en l'an 1050 de notre ~** in the year 1050 A.D.
érection [eʀɛksjɔ̃] *nf* erection
éreinter [eʀɛ̃te] *vt* to exhaust, wear out; (*critiquer*) to pull to pieces
ériger [eʀiʒe] *vt* (*monument*) to erect
ermite [ɛʀmit] *nm* hermit
éroder [eʀɔde] *vt* to erode
érotique [eʀɔtik] *adj* erotic
errer [eʀe] *vi* to wander
erreur [eʀœʀ] *nf* mistake, error; **faire ~** to be mistaken; **par ~** by mistake; **~ judiciaire** miscarriage of justice
érudit, e [eʀydi, it] *adj* erudite, learned
éruption [eʀypsjɔ̃] *nf* eruption; (*MÉD*) rash
es [ɛ] *vb voir* **être**
ès [ɛs] *prép*: **licencié ~ lettres/sciences** ≃ Bachelor of Arts/Science
escabeau, x [ɛskabo] *nm* (*tabouret*) stool; (*échelle*) stepladder
escadron [ɛskadʀɔ̃] *nm* squadron
escalade [ɛskalad] *nf* climbing *no pl*; (*POL etc*) escalation; **escalader** *vt* to climb
escale [ɛskal] *nf* (*NAVIG: durée*) call; (*endroit*) port of call; (*AVIAT*) stop(over); **faire ~ à** (*NAVIG*) to put in at; (*AVIAT*) to stop over at; **vol sans ~** nonstop flight
escalier [ɛskalje] *nm* stairs *pl*; **dans l'~** on the stairs; **~ roulant** escalator
escamoter [ɛskamɔte] *vt* (*esquiver*) to get round, evade; (*faire disparaître*) to conjure away
escapade [ɛskapad] *nf*: **faire une ~** to go on a jaunt; (*s'enfuir*) to run away *ou* off
escargot [ɛskaʀgo] *nm* snail
escarpé, e [ɛskaʀpe] *adj* steep
escarpin [ɛskaʀpɛ̃] *nm* low-fronted shoe, court shoe (*BRIT*)
escient [esjɑ̃] *nm*: **à bon ~** advisedly
esclaffer [ɛsklafe]: **s'~** *vi* to guffaw

esclandre [ɛsklɑ̃dʀ] *nm* scene, fracas
esclavage [ɛsklavaʒ] *nm* slavery
esclave [ɛsklav] *nm/f* slave
escompte [ɛskɔ̃t] *nm* discount; **escompter** *vt* (*fig*) to expect
escorte [ɛskɔʀt] *nf* escort; **escorter** *vt* to escort
escrime [ɛskʀim] *nf* fencing
escrimer [ɛskʀime]: **s'~** *vi*: **s'~ à faire** to wear o.s. out doing
escroc [ɛskʀo] *nm* swindler, conman; **escroquer** [ɛskʀɔke] *vt*: **escroquer qch (à qn)** to swindle sth (out of sb); **escroquerie** *nf* swindle
espace [ɛspas] *nm* space
espacer *vt* to space out; **s'~** *vi* (*visites etc*) to become less frequent
espadon [ɛspadɔ̃] *nm* swordfish *inv*
espadrille [ɛspadʀij] *nf* rope-soled sandal
Espagne [ɛspaɲ] *nf*: **l'~** Spain; **espagnol, e** *adj* Spanish ♦ *nm/f*: **Espagnol, e** Spaniard ♦ *nm* (LING) Spanish
escouade [ɛskwad] *nf* squad
espèce [ɛspɛs] *nf* (BIO, BOT, ZOOL) species *inv*; (*gén*: *sorte*) sort, kind, type; (*péj*): **~ de maladroit!** you clumsy oaf!; **~s** *nfpl* (COMM) cash *sg*; **en ~** in cash
espérance [ɛspeʀɑ̃s] *nf* hope; **~ de vie** life expectancy
espérer [ɛspeʀe] *vt* to hope for; **j'espère (bien)** I hope so; **~ que/faire** to hope that/to do
espiègle [ɛspjɛgl] *adj* mischievous
espion, ne [ɛspjɔ̃, jɔn] *nm/f* spy; **espionnage** *nm* espionage, spying; **espionner** *vt* to spy (up)on
esplanade [ɛsplanad] *nf* esplanade
espoir [ɛspwaʀ] *nm* hope
esprit [ɛspʀi] *nm* (*intellect*) mind; (*humour*) wit; (*mentalité, d'une loi etc, fantôme etc*) spirit; **faire de l'~** to try to be witty; **reprendre ses ~s** to come to; **perdre l'~** to lose one's mind
esquimau, de, x [ɛskimo, od] *adj* Eskimo ♦ *nm/f*: **E~, de** Eskimo ♦ *nm*: **E~** ® ice lolly (BRIT), popsicle (US)
esquinter [ɛskɛ̃te] (*fam*) *vt* to mess up
esquisse [ɛskis] *nf* sketch; **esquisser** *vt* to sketch; **esquisser un sourire** to give a vague smile
esquiver [ɛskive] *vt* to dodge; **s'~** *vi* to slip away
essai [esɛ] *nm* (*tentative*) attempt, try; (*de produit*) testing; (RUGBY) try; (LITTÉRATURE) essay; **~s** *nmpl* (AUTO) trials; **~ gratuit** (COMM) free trial; **à l'~** on a trial basis
essaim [esɛ̃] *nm* swarm
essayer [eseje] *vt* to try; (*vêtement, chaussures*) to try (on); (*méthode, voiture*) to try (out) ♦ *vi* to try; **~ de faire** to try *ou* attempt to do
essence [esɑ̃s] *nf* (*de voiture*) petrol (BRIT), gas(oline) (US); (*extrait de plante*) essence; (*espèce*: *d'arbre*) species *inv*
essentiel, le [esɑ̃sjɛl] *adj* essential; **c'est l'~** (*ce qui importe*) that's the main thing; **l'~ de** the main part of
essieu, x [esjø] *nm* axle
essor [esɔʀ] *nm* (*de l'économie etc*) rapid expansion
essorer [esɔʀe] *vt* (*en tordant*) to wring (out); (*par la force centrifuge*) to spin-dry; **essoreuse** *nf* spin-dryer
essouffler [esufle]: **s'~** *vi* to get out of breath
essuie-glace [esɥiglas] *nm inv* windscreen (BRIT) *ou* windshield (US) wiper
essuyer [esɥije] *vt* to wipe; (*fig*: *échec*) to suffer; **s'~** *vi* (*après le bain*) to dry o.s.; **~ la vaisselle** to dry up
est[1] [ɛ] *vb voir* **être**
est[2] [ɛst] *nm* east ♦ *adj inv* east, (*région*) east(ern); **à l'~** in the east; (*direction*) to the east, east(wards); **à l'~ de** (to the) east of
estampe [ɛstɑ̃p] *nf* print, engraving
est-ce que [ɛskə] *adv*: **~ c'est cher/c'était bon?** is it expensive/was it good?; **quand est-ce qu'il part?** when does he leave?, when is he leaving?; *voir aussi* **que**
esthéticienne [ɛstetisjɛn] *nf* beauti-

cian

esthétique [ɛstetik] *adj* attractive

estimation [ɛstimasjɔ̃] *nf* valuation; (*chiffre*) estimate

estime [ɛstim] *nf* esteem, regard; **estimer** *vt* (*respecter*) to esteem; (*expertiser: bijou etc*) to value; (*évaluer: coût etc*) to assess, estimate; (*penser*): **estimer que/être** to consider that/o.s. to be

estival, e, -aux [ɛstival, o] *adj* summer *cpd*

estivant, e [ɛstivɑ̃, ɑ̃t] *nm/f* (summer) holiday-maker

estomac [ɛstɔma] *nm* stomach

estomaqué, e [ɛstɔmake] (*fam*) *adj* flabbergasted

estomper [ɛstɔ̃pe]: **s'~** *vi* (*sentiments*) to soften; (*contour*) to become blurred

estrade [ɛstʀad] *nf* platform, rostrum

estragon [ɛstʀagɔ̃] *nm* tarragon

estuaire [ɛstɥɛʀ] *nm* estuary

et [e] *conj* and; **~ lui?** what about him?; **~ alors!** so what!

étable [etabl] *nf* cowshed

établi [etabli] *nm* (work)bench

établir [etabliʀ] *vt* (*papiers d'identité, facture*) to make out; (*liste, programme*) to draw up; (*entreprise*) to set up; (*réputation, usage, fait, culpabilité*) to establish; **s'~** *vi* to be established; **s'~ (à son compte)** to set up in business; **s'~ à/près de** to settle in/near

établissement [etablismɑ̃] *nm* (*entreprise, institution*) establishment; **~ scolaire** school, educational establishment

étage [etaʒ] *nm* (*d'immeuble*) storey, floor; **à l'~** upstairs; **au 2ème ~** on the 2nd (*BRIT*) *ou* 3rd (*US*) floor

étagère [etaʒɛʀ] *nf* (*rayon*) shelf; (*meuble*) shelves *pl*

étai [etɛ] *nm* stay, prop

étain [etɛ̃] *nm* pewter *no pl*

étais *etc* [etɛ] *vb voir* **être**

étal [etal] *nm* stall

étalage [etalaʒ] *nm* display; (*devanture*) display window; **faire ~ de** to show off, parade

étaler [etale] *vt* (*carte, nappe*) to spread (out); (*peinture*) to spread; (*échelonner: paiements, vacances*) to spread, stagger; (*marchandises*) to display; (*connaissances*) to parade; **s'~** *vi* (*liquide*) to spread out; (*fam*) to fall flat on one's face; **s'~ sur** (*suj: paiements etc*) to be spread out over

étalon [etalɔ̃] *nm* (*cheval*) stallion

étanche [etɑ̃ʃ] *adj* (*récipient*) watertight; (*montre, vêtement*) waterproof; **étancher** *vt*: **étancher sa soif** to quench one's thirst

étang [etɑ̃] *nm* pond

étant [etɑ̃] *vb voir* **être**; **donné**

étape [etap] *nf* stage; (*lieu d'arrivée*) stopping place; (: *CYCLISME*) staging point

état [eta] *nm* (*POL, condition*) state; **en mauvais ~** in poor condition; **en ~ (de marche)** in (working) order; **remettre en ~** to repair; **hors d'~** out of order; **être en ~/hors d'~ de faire** to be in a/in no fit state to do; **être dans tous ses ~s** to be in a state; **faire ~ de** (*alléguer*) to put forward; **l'É~** the State; **~ civil** civil status; **~ des lieux** inventory of fixtures; **étatiser** *vt* to bring under state control; **état-major** *nm* (*MIL*) staff; **États-Unis** *nmpl*: **les États-Unis** the United States

étau, x [eto] *nm* vice (*BRIT*), vise (*US*)

étayer [eteje] *vt* to prop *ou* shore up

etc. [ɛtseteʀa] *adv* etc

et c(a)etera [ɛtseteʀa] *adv* et cetera, and so on

été [ete] *pp de* **être** ♦ *nm* summer

éteindre [etɛ̃dʀ] *vt* (*lampe, lumière, radio*) to turn *ou* switch off; (*cigarette, feu*) to put out, extinguish; **s'~** *vi* (*feu, lumière*) to go out; (*mourir*) to pass away; **éteint, e** *adj* (*fig*) lacklustre, dull; (*volcan*) extinct

étendard [etɑ̃daʀ] *nm* standard

étendre [etɑ̃dʀ] *vt* (*pâte, liquide*) to spread; (*carte etc*) to spread out; (*linge*) to hang up; (*bras, jambes*) to stretch out; (*fig*: *agrandir*) to extend; **s'~** *vi* (*augmenter, se propager*) to spread; (*terrain, forêt etc*) to stretch; (*s'allonger*) to stretch out; (*se coucher*) to lie down; (*fig*: *expliquer*) to elaborate

étendu, e [etɑ̃dy] *adj* extensive; **étendue** *nf* (*d'eau, de sable*) stretch, expanse; (*importance*) extent

éternel, le [etɛʀnɛl] *adj* eternal

éterniser [etɛʀnize]: **s'~** *vi* to last for ages; (*visiteur*) to stay for ages

éternité [etɛʀnite] *nf* eternity; **ça a duré une ~** it lasted for ages

éternuement [etɛʀnymɑ̃] *nm* sneeze

éternuer [etɛʀnɥe] *vi* to sneeze

êtes [ɛt(z)] *vb voir* **être**

éthique [etik] *adj* ethical

ethnie [ɛtni] *nf* ethnic group

éthylisme [etilism] *nm* alcoholism

étiez [etjɛ] *vb voir* **être**

étinceler [etɛ̃s(ə)le] *vi* to sparkle

étincelle [etɛ̃sɛl] *nf* spark

étiqueter [etik(ə)te] *vt* to label

étiquette [etikɛt] *nf* label; (*protocole*): **l'~** etiquette

étirer [etiʀe]: **s'~** *vi* (*personne*) to stretch; (*convoi, route*): **s'~ sur** to stretch out over

étoffe [etɔf] *nf* material, fabric

étoffer [etɔfe] *vt* to fill out

étoile [etwal] *nf* star; **à la belle ~** in the open; **~ de mer** starfish; **~ filante** shooting star; **étoilé, e** *adj* starry

étonnant, e [etɔnɑ̃, ɑ̃t] *adj* amazing

étonnement [etɔnmɑ̃] *nm* surprise, amazement

étonner [etɔne] *vt* to surprise, amaze; **s'~ que/de** to be amazed that/at; **cela m'~ait (que)** (*j'en doute*) I'd be very surprised (if)

étouffant, e [etufɑ̃, ɑ̃t] *adj* stifling

étouffée [etufe]: **à l'~** *adv* (CULIN: *légumes*) steamed; (: *viande*) braised

étouffer [etufe] *vt* to suffocate; (*bruit*) to muffle; (*scandale*) to hush up ♦ *vi* to suffocate; **s'~** *vi* (*en mangeant etc*) to choke; **on étouffe** it's stifling

étourderie [etuʀdəʀi] *nf* (*caractère*) absent-mindedness *no pl*; (*faute*) thoughtless blunder

étourdi, e [etuʀdi] *adj* (*distrait*) scatterbrained, heedless

étourdir [etuʀdiʀ] *vt* (*assommer*) to stun, daze; (*griser*) to make dizzy *ou* giddy; **étourdissement** *nm* dizzy spell

étourneau, x [etuʀno] *nm* starling

étrange [etʀɑ̃ʒ] *adj* strange

étranger, -ère [etʀɑ̃ʒe, ɛʀ] *adj* foreign; (*pas de la famille, non familier*) strange ♦ *nm/f* foreigner; stranger ♦ *nm*: **à l'~** abroad

étrangler [etʀɑ̃gle] *vt* to strangle; **s'~** *vi* (*en mangeant etc*) to choke

MOT-CLÉ

être [ɛtʀ] *nm* being; **être humain** human being

♦ *vb +attrib* **1** (*état, description*) to be; **il est instituteur** he is *ou* he's a teacher; **vous êtes grand/intelligent/fatigué** you are *ou* you're tall/clever/tired

2 (*+à*: *appartenir*) to be; **le livre est à Paul** the book is Paul's *ou* belongs to Paul; **c'est à moi/eux** it is *ou* it's mine/theirs

3 (*+de*: *provenance*): **il est de Paris** he is from Paris; (: *appartenance*): **il est des nôtres** he is one of us

4 (*date*): **nous sommes le 10 janvier** it's the 10th of January (today)

♦ *vi* to be; **je ne serai pas ici demain** I won't be here tomorrow

♦ *vb aux* **1** to have; to be; **être arrivé/allé** to have arrived/gone; **il est parti** he has left, he has gone

2 (*forme passive*) to be; **être fait par** to be made by; **il a été promu** he has been promoted

3 (*+à*: *obligation*): **c'est à réparer** it needs repairing; **c'est à essayer** it should be tried

♦ *vb impers* **1**: **il est** *+adjectif* it is *+adjective*; **il est impossible de le faire** it's

impossible to do it
2 (*heure, date*): **il est 10 heures, c'est 10 heures** it is *ou* it's 10 o'clock
3 (*emphatique*): **c'est moi** it's me; **c'est à lui de le faire** it's up to him to do it

étreindre [etʀɛ̃dʀ] *vt* to clutch, grip; (*amoureusement, amicalement*) to embrace; **s'~** *vi* to embrace
étrenner [etʀene] *vt* to use (*ou* wear) for the first time; **étrennes** *nfpl* Christmas box *sg*
étrier [etʀije] *nm* stirrup
étriqué, e [etʀike] *adj* skimpy
étroit, e [etʀwa, wat] *adj* narrow; (*vêtement*) tight; (*fig: liens, collaboration*) close; **à l'~** cramped; **~ d'esprit** narrow-minded
étude [etyd] *nf* studying; (*ouvrage, rapport*) study; (*SCOL: salle de travail*) study room; **~s** *nfpl* (*SCOL*) studies; **être à l'~** (*projet etc*) to be under consideration; **faire des ~s (de droit/médecine)** to study (law/medicine)
étudiant, e [etydjɑ̃, jɑ̃t] *nm/f* student
étudier [etydje] *vt, vi* to study
étui [etɥi] *nm* case
étuve [etyv] *nf* steamroom
étuvée [etyve]: **à l'~** *adv* braised
eu, eue [y] *pp de* **avoir**
euh [ø] *excl* er
euro [øʀo] *nm* euro
Euroland [øʀɔlɑ̃d] *nm* Euroland
Europe [øʀɔp] *nf*: **l'~** Europe; **européen, ne** *adj* European ♦ *nm/f*: **Européen, ne** European
eus *etc* [y] *vb voir* **avoir**
eux [ø] *pron* (*sujet*) they; (*objet*) them
évacuer [evakɥe] *vt* to evacuate
évader [evade]: **s'~** *vi* to escape
évaluer [evalɥe] *vt* (*expertiser*) to appraise, evaluate; (*juger approximativement*) to estimate
évangile [evɑ̃ʒil] *nm* gospel
évanouir [evanwiʀ]: **s'~** *vi* to faint; (*disparaître*) to vanish, disappear; **évanouissement** *nm* (*syncope*) fainting fit
évaporer [evapɔʀe]: **s'~** *vi* to evaporate
évasé, e [evɑze] *adj* (*manches, jupe*) flared
évasif, -ive [evazif, iv] *adj* evasive
évasion [evazjɔ̃] *nf* escape
évêché [eveʃe] *nm* bishop's palace
éveil [evɛj] *nm* awakening; **être en ~** to be alert; **éveillé, e** *adj* awake; (*vif*) alert, sharp; **éveiller** *vt* to (a)waken; (*soupçons etc*) to arouse; **s'éveiller** *vi* to (a)waken; (*fig*) to be aroused
événement [evɛnmɑ̃] *nm* event
éventail [evɑ̃taj] *nm* fan; (*choix*) range
éventaire [evɑ̃tɛʀ] *nm* stall, stand
éventer [evɑ̃te] *vt* (*secret*) to uncover; **s'~** *vi* (*parfum*) to go stale
éventualité [evɑ̃tɥalite] *nf* eventuality; possibility; **dans l'~ de** in the event of
éventuel, le [evɑ̃tɥɛl] *adj* possible; **éventuellement** *adv* possibly
évêque [evɛk] *nm* bishop
évertuer [evɛʀtɥe]: **s'~** *vi*: **s'~ à faire** to try very hard to do
éviction [eviksjɔ̃] *nf* (*de locataire*) eviction
évidemment [evidamɑ̃] *adv* (*bien sûr*) of course; (*certainement*) obviously
évidence [evidɑ̃s] *nf* obviousness; (*fait*) obvious fact; **de toute ~** quite obviously *ou* evidently; **être en ~** to be clearly visible; **mettre en ~** (*fait*) to highlight; **évident, e** *adj* obvious, evident; **ce n'est pas évident!** (*fam*) it's not that easy!
évider [evide] *vt* to scoop out
évier [evje] *nm* (kitchen) sink
évincer [evɛ̃se] *vt* to oust
éviter [evite] *vt* to avoid; **~ de faire** to avoid doing; **~ qch à qn** to spare sb sth
évolué, e [evɔlɥe] *adj* advanced
évoluer [evɔlɥe] *vi* (*enfant, maladie*) to develop; (*situation, moralement*) to evolve, develop; (*aller et venir*) to move about; **évolution** *nf* development,

evolution

évoquer [evɔke] *vt* to call to mind, evoke; (*mentionner*) to mention

ex... [ɛks] *préfixe* ex-

exact, e [ɛgza(kt), ɛgzakt] *adj* exact; (*correct*) correct; (*ponctuel*) punctual; **l'heure ~e** the right *ou* exact time; **exactement** *adv* exactly

ex aequo [ɛgzeko] *adj* equally placed; **arriver ~** to finish neck and neck

exagéré, e [ɛgzaʒeʀe] *adj* (*prix etc*) excessive

exagérer [ɛgzaʒeʀe] *vt* to exaggerate ♦ *vi* to exaggerate; (*abuser*) to go too far

exalter [ɛgzalte] *vt* (*enthousiasmer*) to excite, elate

examen [ɛgzamɛ̃] *nm* examination; (*SCOL*) exam, examination; **à l'~** under consideration

examinateur, -trice [ɛgzaminatœʀ, tʀis] *nm/f* examiner

examiner [ɛgzamine] *vt* to examine

exaspérant, e [ɛgzaspeʀɑ̃, ɑ̃t] *adj* exasperating

exaspérer [ɛgzaspeʀe] *vt* to exasperate

exaucer [egzose] *vt* (*vœu*) to grant

excédent [ɛksedɑ̃] *nm* surplus; **en ~** surplus; **~ de bagages** excess luggage

excéder [ɛksede] *vt* (*dépasser*) to exceed; (*agacer*) to exasperate

excellent, e [ɛkselɑ̃, ɑ̃t] *adj* excellent

excentrique [ɛksɑ̃tʀik] *adj* eccentric

excepté, e [ɛksɛpte] *adj prép*: **les élèves ~s, ~ les élèves** except for the pupils

exception [ɛksɛpsjɔ̃] *nf* exception; **à l'~ de** except for, with the exception of; **d'~** (*mesure, loi*) special, exceptional; **exceptionnel, le** *adj* exceptional; **exceptionnellement** *adv* exceptionally

excès [ɛksɛ] *nm* surplus ♦ *nmpl* excesses; **faire des ~** to overindulge; **~ de vitesse** speeding *no pl*; **excessif, -ive** *adj* excessive

excitant, e [ɛksitɑ̃, ɑ̃t] *adj* exciting ♦ *nm* stimulant; **excitation** *nf* (*état*) excitement

exciter [ɛksite] *vt* to excite; (*suj*: *café etc*) to stimulate; **s'~** *vi* to get excited

exclamation [ɛksklamasjɔ̃] *nf* exclamation

exclamer [ɛksklame]: **s'~** *vi* to exclaim

exclure [ɛksklyʀ] *vt* (*faire sortir*) to expel; (*ne pas compter*) to exclude, leave out; (*rendre impossible*) to exclude, rule out; **il est exclu que** it's out of the question that ...; **il n'est pas exclu que ...** it's not impossible that ...; **exclusif, -ive** *adj* exclusive; **exclusion** *nf* exclusion; **à l'exclusion de** with the exclusion *ou* exception of; **exclusivité** *nf* (*COMM*) exclusive rights *pl*; **film passant en exclusivité à** film showing only at

excursion [ɛkskyʀsjɔ̃] *nf* (*en autocar*) excursion, trip; (*à pied*) walk, hike

excuse [ɛkskyz] *nf* excuse; **~s** *nfpl* (*regret*) apology *sg*, apologies; **excuser** *vt* to excuse; **s'excuser (de)** to apologize (for); **"excusez-moi"** "I'm sorry"; (*pour attirer l'attention*) "excuse me"

exécrable [ɛgzekʀabl] *adj* atrocious

exécuter [ɛgzekyte] *vt* (*tuer*) to execute; (*tâche etc*) to execute, carry out; (*MUS*: *jouer*) to perform, execute; **s'~** *vi* to comply; **exécutif, -ive** *adj, nm* (*POL*) executive; **exécution** *nf* execution; **mettre à exécution** to carry out

exemplaire [ɛgzɑ̃plɛʀ] *nm* copy

exemple [ɛgzɑ̃pl] *nm* example; **par ~** for instance, for example; **donner l'~** to set an example

exempt, e [ɛgzɑ̃, ɑ̃(p)t] *adj*: **~ de** (*dispensé de*) exempt from; (*sans*) free from

exercer [ɛgzɛʀse] *vt* (*pratiquer*) to exercise, practise; (*influence, contrôle*) to exert; (*former*) to exercise, train; **s'~** *vi* (*sportif, musicien*) to practise

exercice [ɛgzɛʀsis] *nm* exercise

exhaustif, -ive [ɛgzostif, iv] *adj* exhaustive

exhiber [ɛgzibe] *vt* (*montrer: papiers, certificat*) to present, produce; (*péj*) to display, flaunt; **s'~** *vi* to parade; (*suj: exhibitionniste*) to expose o.s; **exhibitionniste** [ɛgzibisjɔnist] *nm/f* flasher
exhorter [ɛgzɔʀte] *vt* to urge
exigeant, e [ɛgziʒɑ̃, ɑ̃t] *adj* demanding; (*péj*) hard to please
exigence [ɛgziʒɑ̃s] *nf* demand, requirement
exiger [ɛgziʒe] *vt* to demand, require
exigu, ë [ɛgzigy] *adj* cramped, tiny
exil [ɛgzil] *nm* exile; **exiler** *vt* to exile; **s'exiler** *vi* to go into exile
existence [ɛgzistɑ̃s] *nf* existence
exister [ɛgziste] *vi* to exist; **il existe un/des** there is a/are (some)
exonérer [ɛgzɔneʀe] *vt*: **~ de** to exempt from
exorbitant, e [ɛgzɔʀbitɑ̃, ɑ̃t] *adj* exorbitant
exorbité, e [ɛgzɔʀbite] *adj*: **yeux ~s** bulging eyes
exotique [ɛgzɔtik] *adj* exotic; **yaourt aux fruits ~s** tropical fruit yoghurt
expatrier [ɛkspatʀije] *vt*: **s'~** to leave one's country
expectative [ɛkspɛktativ] *nf*: **être dans l'~** to be still waiting
expédient [ɛkspedjɑ̃, jɑ̃t] (*péj*) *nm*: **vivre d'~s** to live by one's wits
expédier [ɛkspedje] *vt* (*lettre, paquet*) to send; (*troupes*) to dispatch; (*fam: travail etc*) to dispose of, dispatch; **expéditeur, -trice** *nm/f* sender; **expédition** *nf* sending; (*scientifique, sportive*, MIL) expedition
expérience [ɛkspeʀjɑ̃s] *nf* (*de la vie*) experience; (*scientifique*) experiment
expérimenté, e [ɛkspeʀimɑ̃te] *adj* experienced
expérimenter [ɛkspeʀimɑ̃te] *vt* to test out, experiment with
expert, e [ɛkspɛʀ, ɛʀt] *adj, nm* expert; **expert-comptable** *nm* ≃ chartered accountant (BRIT), ≃ certified public accountant (US)
expertise [ɛkspɛʀtiz] *nf* (*évaluation*) expert evaluation
expertiser [ɛkspɛʀtize] *vt* (*objet de valeur*) to value; (*voiture accidentée etc*) to assess damage to
expier [ɛkspje] *vt* to expiate, atone for
expirer [ɛkspiʀe] *vi* (*prendre fin, mourir*) to expire; (*respirer*) to breathe out
explicatif, -ive [ɛksplikatif, iv] *adj* explanatory
explication [ɛksplikasjɔ̃] *nf* explanation; (*discussion*) discussion; (*dispute*) argument; **~ de texte** (SCOL) critical analysis
explicite [ɛksplisit] *adj* explicit
expliquer [ɛksplike] *vt* to explain; **s'~** to explain (o.s.); **s'~ avec qn** (*discuter*) to explain o.s. to sb; **son erreur s'explique** one can understand his mistake
exploit [ɛksplwa] *nm* exploit, feat; **exploitant, e** *nm/f*: **exploitant (agricole)** farmer
exploitation *nf* exploitation; (*d'une entreprise*) running; **~ agricole** farming concern; **exploiter** *vt* (*personne, don*) to exploit; (*entreprise, ferme*) to run, operate; (*mine*) to exploit, work
explorer [ɛksplɔʀe] *vt* to explore
exploser [ɛksploze] *vi* to explode, blow up; (*engin explosif*) to go off; (*personne: de colère*) to flare up; **explosif, -ive** *adj, nm* explosive; **explosion** *nf* explosion
exportateur, -trice [ɛkspɔʀtatœʀ, tʀis] *adj* export *cpd*, exporting ♦ *nm* exporter
exportation [ɛkspɔʀtasjɔ̃] *nf* (*action*) exportation; (*produit*) export
exporter [ɛkspɔʀte] *vt* to export
exposant [ɛkspozɑ̃] *nm* exhibitor
exposé, e [ɛkspoze] *nm* talk ♦ *adj*: **~ au sud** facing south
exposer [ɛkspoze] *vt* (*marchandise*) to display; (*peinture*) to exhibit, show; (*parler de*) to explain, set out; (*mettre en danger, orienter*, PHOTO) to expose;

exposition *nf* (*manifestation*) exhibition; (*PHOTO*) exposure
exprès[1] [ɛkspʀɛ] *adv* (*délibérément*) on purpose; (*spécialement*) specially
exprès[2], -esse [ɛkspʀɛs] *adj* (*ordre, défense*) express, formal ♦ *adj inv* (*PTT*) express ♦ *adv* express
express [ɛkspʀɛs] *adj, nm*: **(café) ~** espresso (coffee); **(train) ~** fast train
expressément [ɛkspʀesemɑ̃] *adv* (*spécialement*) specifically
expressif, -ive [ɛkspʀesif, iv] *adj* expressive
expression [ɛkspʀesjɔ̃] *nf* expression
exprimer [ɛkspʀime] *vt* (*sentiment, idée*) to express; (*jus, liquide*) to press out; **s'~** *vi* (*personne*) to express o.s
exproprier [ɛkspʀɔpʀije] *vt* to buy up by compulsory purchase, expropriate
expulser [ɛkspylse] *vt* to expel; (*locataire*) to evict; (*SPORT*) to send off
exquis, e [ɛkski, iz] *adj* exquisite
extase [ɛkstɑz] *nf* ecstasy; **extasier**: **s'extasier sur** *vt* to go into raptures over
extension [ɛkstɑ̃sjɔ̃] *nf* (*fig*) extension
exténuer [ɛkstenɥe] *vt* to exhaust
extérieur, e [ɛksteʀjœʀ] *adj* (*porte, mur etc*) outer, outside; (*au dehors*: *escalier, w.-c.*) outside; (*commerce*) foreign; (*influences*) external; (*apparent*: *calme, gaieté etc*) surface *cpd* ♦ *nm* (*d'une maison, d'un récipient etc*) outside, exterior; (*apparence*) exterior; **à l'~** outside; (*à l'étranger*) abroad; **extérieurement** *adv* on the outside; (*en apparence*) on the surface
exterminer [ɛkstɛʀmine] *vt* to exterminate, wipe out
externat [ɛkstɛʀna] *nm* day school
externe [ɛkstɛʀn] *adj* external, outer ♦ *nm/f* (*MÉD*) non-resident medical student (*BRIT*), extern (*US*); (*SCOL*) day pupil
extincteur [ɛkstɛ̃ktœʀ] *nm* (fire) extinguisher
extinction [ɛkstɛ̃ksjɔ̃] *nf*: **~ de voix** loss of voice
extorquer [ɛkstɔʀke] *vt* to extort
extra [ɛkstʀa] *adj inv* first-rate; (*fam*) fantastic ♦ *nm inv* extra help
extracommunautaire [ɛkstʀakɔmynotɛʀ] *adj* non-EU
extrader [ɛkstʀade] *vt* to extradite
extraire [ɛkstʀɛʀ] *vt* to extract; **extrait** *nm* extract
extraordinaire [ɛkstʀaɔʀdinɛʀ] *adj* extraordinary; (*POL*: *mesures etc*) special
extravagant, e [ɛkstʀavagɑ̃, ɑ̃t] *adj* extravagant
extraverti, e [ɛkstʀavɛʀti] *adj* extrovert
extrême [ɛkstʀɛm] *adj, nm* extreme; **extrêmement** *adv* extremely; **extrême-onction** *nf* last rites *pl*; **Extrême-Orient** *nm* Far East
extrémité [ɛkstʀemite] *nf* end; (*situation*) straits *pl*, plight; (*geste désespéré*) extreme action; **~s** *nfpl* (*pieds et mains*) extremities
exubérant, e [ɛgzybeʀɑ̃, ɑ̃t] *adj* exuberant
exutoire [ɛgzytwaʀ] *nm* outlet, release

F, f

F *abr* = **franc**
fa [fɑ] *nm inv* (*MUS*) F; (*en chantant la gamme*) fa
fable [fɑbl] *nf* fable
fabricant [fabʀikɑ̃, ɑ̃t] *nm* manufacturer
fabrication [fabʀikasjɔ̃] *nf* manufacture
fabrique [fabʀik] *nf* factory; **fabriquer** *vt* to make; (*industriellement*) to manufacture; (*fig*): **qu'est-ce qu'il fabrique?** (*fam*) what is he doing?
fabulation [fabylasjɔ̃] *nf* fantasizing
fac [fak] (*fam*) *abr f* (*SCOL*) = **faculté**
façade [fasad] *nf* front, façade
face [fas] *nf* face; (*fig*: *aspect*) side ♦ *adj*: **le côté ~** heads; **en ~ de** opposite; (*fig*) in front of; **de ~** (*voir*) face on; **~ à** facing; (*fig*) faced with, in the face of; **faire ~ à** to face; **~ à ~** *adv* facing

each other ♦ *nm inv* encounter

fâché, e [fɑʃe] *adj* angry; (*désolé*) sorry

fâcher [fɑʃe] *vt* to anger; **se ~** *vi* to get angry; **se ~ avec** (*se brouiller*) to fall out with

fâcheux, -euse [fɑʃø, øz] *adj* unfortunate, regrettable

facile [fasil] *adj* easy; (*caractère*) easy-going; **facilement** *adv* easily

facilité *nf* easiness; (*disposition, don*) aptitude; **facilités de paiement** easy terms; **faciliter** *vt* to make easier

façon [fasɔ̃] *nf* (*manière*) way; (*d'une robe etc*) making-up, cut; **~s** *nfpl* (*péj*) fuss *sg*; **de ~ à/à ce que** so as to/that; **de toute ~** anyway, in any case; **façonner** [fasɔne] *vt* (*travailler: matière*) to shape, fashion

facteur, -trice [faktœʀ] *nm/f* postman(-woman) (*BRIT*), mailman(-woman) (*US*) ♦ *nm* (*MATH, fig: élément*) factor

factice [faktis] *adj* artificial

faction [faksjɔ̃] *nf* faction; **être de ~** to be on guard (duty)

facture [faktyʀ] *nf* (*à payer: gén*) bill; invoice; **facturer** *vt* to invoice

facultatif, -ive [fakyltatif, iv] *adj* optional

faculté [fakylte] *nf* (*intellectuelle, d'université*) faculty; (*pouvoir, possibilité*) power

fade [fad] *adj* insipid

fagot [fago] *nm* bundle of sticks

faible [fɛbl] *adj* weak; (*voix, lumière, vent*) faint; (*rendement, revenu*) low ♦ *nm* (*pour quelqu'un*) weakness, soft spot; **faiblesse** *nf* weakness; **faiblir** *vi* to weaken; (*lumière*) to dim; (*vent*) to drop

faïence [fajɑ̃s] *nf* earthenware *no pl*

faignant, e [fɛɲɑ̃, ɑ̃t] *nm/f* = **fainéant, e**

faille [faj] *vb voir* **falloir** ♦ *nf* (*GÉO*) fault; (*fig*) flaw, weakness

faillir [fajiʀ] *vi*: **j'ai failli tomber** I almost *ou* very nearly fell

faillite [fajit] *nf* bankruptcy

faim [fɛ̃] *nf* hunger; **avoir ~** to be hungry; **rester sur sa ~** (*aussi fig*) to be left wanting more

fainéant, e [fɛneɑ̃, ɑ̃t] *nm/f* idler, loafer

MOT-CLÉ

faire [fɛʀ] *vt* **1** (*fabriquer, être l'auteur de*) to make; **faire du vin/une offre/un film** to make wine/an offer/a film; **faire du bruit** to make a noise

2 (*effectuer: travail, opération*) to do; **que faites-vous?** (*quel métier etc*) what do you do?; (*quelle activité: au moment de la question*) what are you doing?; **faire la lessive** to do the washing

3 (*études*) to do; (*sport, musique*) to play; **faire du droit/du français** to do law/French; **faire du rugby/piano** to play rugby/the piano

4 (*simuler*): **faire le malade/l'ignorant** to act the invalid/the fool

5 (*transformer, avoir un effet sur*): **faire de qn un frustré/avocat** to make sb frustrated/a lawyer; **ça ne me fait rien** (*m'est égal*) I don't care *ou* mind; (*me laisse froid*) it has no effect on me; **ça ne fait rien** it doesn't matter; **faire que** (*impliquer*) to mean that

6 (*calculs, prix, mesures*): **2 et 2 font 4** 2 and 2 are *ou* make 4; **ça fait 10 m/15 F** it's 10 m/15F; **je vous le fais 10 F** I'll let you have it for 10F

7: **qu'a-t-il fait de sa valise?** what has he done with his case?

8: **ne faire que**: **il ne fait que critiquer** (*sans cesse*) all he (ever) does is criticize; (*seulement*) he's only criticizing

9 (*dire*) to say; **"vraiment?" fit-il** "really?" he said

10 (*maladie*) to have; **faire du diabète** to have diabetes *sg*

♦ *vi* **1** (*agir, s'y prendre*) to act, do; **il faut faire vite** we (*ou* you *etc*) must act quickly; **comment a-t-il fait pour?** how did he manage to?; **faites**

comme chez vous make yourself at home

2 (*paraître*) to look; **faire vieux/démodé** to look old/old-fashioned; **ça fait bien** it looks good

♦ *vb substitut* to do; **ne le casse pas comme je l'ai fait** don't break it as I did; **je peux le voir? - faites!** can I see it? - please do!

♦ *vb impers* **1**: **il fait beau** *etc* the weather is fine *etc*; *voir aussi* **jour**; **froid** *etc*

2 (*temps écoulé, durée*): **ça fait 2 ans qu'il est parti** it's 2 years since he left; **ça fait 2 ans qu'il y est** he's been there for 2 years

♦ *vb semi-aux* **1**: **faire** *+infinitif* (*action directe*) to make; **faire tomber/bouger qch** to make sth fall/move; **faire démarrer un moteur/chauffer de l'eau** to start up an engine/heat some water; **cela fait dormir** it makes you sleep; **faire travailler les enfants** to make the children work *ou* get the children to work

2 (*indirectement, par un intermédiaire*): **faire réparer qch** to get *ou* have sth repaired; **faire punir les enfants** to have the children punished; **se faire** *vi*

1 (*vin, fromage*) to mature

2: **cela se fait beaucoup/ne se fait pas** it's done a lot/not done

3: **se faire** *+nom ou pron*: **se faire une jupe** to make o.s. a skirt; **se faire des amis** to make friends; **se faire du souci** to worry; **il ne s'en fait pas** he doesn't worry

4: **se faire** *+adj* (*devenir*): **se faire vieux** to be getting old; (*délibérément*): **se faire beau** to do o.s. up

5: **se faire à** (*s'habituer*) to get used to; **je n'arrive pas à me faire à la nourriture/au climat** I can't get used to the food/climate

6: **se faire** *+infinitif*: **se faire examiner la vue/opérer** to have one's eyes tested/to have an operation; **se faire couper les cheveux** to get one's hair cut; **il va se faire tuer/punir** he's going to get himself killed/get (himself) punished; **il s'est fait aider** he got somebody to help him; **il s'est fait aider par Simon** he got Simon to help him; **se faire faire un vêtement** to get a garment made for o.s.

7 (*impersonnel*): **comment se fait-il/faisait-il que?** how is it/was it that?

faire-part [fɛʀpaʀ] *nm inv* announcement (*of birth, marriage etc*)

faisable [fəzabl] *adj* feasible

faisan, e [fəzɑ̃, an] *nm/f* pheasant; **faisandé, e** *adj* high (*bad*)

faisceau, x [fɛso] *nm* (*de lumière etc*) beam

faisons [fəzɔ̃] *vb voir* **faire**

fait, e [fɛ, fɛt] *adj* (*mûr: fromage, melon*) ripe ♦ *nm* (*événement*) event, occurrence; (*réalité, donnée*) fact; **être au ~ (de)** to be informed (of); **au ~** (*à propos*) by the way; **en venir au ~** to get to the point; **du ~ de ceci/qu'il a menti** because of *ou* on account of this/his having lied; **de ce ~** for this reason; **en ~** in fact; **prendre qn sur le ~** to catch sb in the act; **~ divers** news item

faîte [fɛt] *nm* top; (*fig*) pinnacle, height

faites [fɛt] *vb voir* **faire**

faitout [fɛtu] *nm*, **fait-tout** [fɛtu] *nm inv* stewpot

falaise [falɛz] *nf* cliff

falloir [falwaʀ] *vb impers*: **il faut qu'il parte/a fallu qu'il parte** (*obligation*) he has to *ou* must leave/had to leave; **il a fallu le faire** it had to be done; **il faut faire attention** you have to be careful; **il me faudrait 100 F** I would need 100 F; **il vous faut tourner à gauche après l'église** you have to turn left past the church; **nous avons ce qu'il (nous) faut** we have what we need; **s'en ~**: **il s'en est fallu de 100 F/5 minutes** we/they *etc* were 100 F

short/5 minutes late (*ou* early); **il s'en faut de beaucoup qu'il soit** he is far from being; **il s'en est fallu de peu que cela n'arrive** it very nearly happened
falsifier [falsifje] *vt* to falsify, doctor
famé, e [fame] *adj*: **mal ~** disreputable, of ill repute
famélique [famelik] *adj* half-starved
fameux, -euse [famø, øz] *adj* (*illustre*) famous; (*bon*: *repas, plat etc*) first-rate, first-class; (*valeur intensive*) real, downright
familial, e, -aux [familjal, jo] *adj* family *cpd*
familiarité [familjaʀite] *nf* familiarity; **~s** *nfpl* (*privautés*) familiarities
familier, -ère [familje, jɛʀ] *adj* (*connu*) familiar; (*atmosphère*) informal, friendly; (LING) informal, colloquial ♦ *nm* regular (visitor)
famille [famij] *nf* family; **il a de la ~ à Paris** he has relatives in Paris
famine [famin] *nf* famine
fanatique [fanatik] *adj* fanatical ♦ *nm/f* fanatic; **fanatisme** *nm* fanaticism
faner [fane]: **se ~** *vi* to fade
fanfare [fɑ̃faʀ] *nf* (*orchestre*) brass band; (*musique*) fanfare
fanfaron, ne [fɑ̃faʀɔ̃, ɔn] *nm/f* braggart
fantaisie [fɑ̃tezi] *nf* (*spontanéité*) fancy, imagination; (*caprice*) whim ♦ *adj*: **bijou ~** costume jewellery; **fantaisiste** (*péj*) *adj* unorthodox, eccentric
fantasme [fɑ̃tasm] *nm* fantasy
fantasque [fɑ̃task] *adj* whimsical, capricious
fantastique [fɑ̃tastik] *adj* fantastic
fantôme [fɑ̃tom] *nm* ghost, phantom
faon [fɑ̃] *nm* fawn
farce [faʀs] *nf* (*viande*) stuffing; (*blague*) (practical) joke; (THÉÂTRE) farce; **farcir** *vt* (*viande*) to stuff
fardeau, x [faʀdo] *nm* burden
farder [faʀde]: **se ~** *vi* to make (o.s.) up
farfelu, e [faʀfəly] *adj* hare-brained
farine [faʀin] *nf* flour; **farineux, -euse** *adj* (*sauce, pomme*) floury
farouche [faʀuʃ] *adj* (*timide*) shy, timid
fart [faʀt] *nm* (ski) wax
fascicule [fasikyl] *nm* volume
fascination [fasinasjɔ̃] *nf* fascination
fasciner [fasine] *vt* to fascinate
fascisme [faʃism] *nm* fascism
fasse *etc* [fas] *vb voir* **faire**
faste [fast] *nm* splendour
fastidieux, -euse [fastidjø, jøz] *adj* tedious, tiresome
fastueux, -euse [fastɥø, øz] *adj* sumptuous, luxurious
fatal, e [fatal] *adj* fatal; (*inévitable*) inevitable; **fatalité** *nf* (*destin*) fate; (*coïncidence*) fateful coincidence
fatidique [fatidik] *adj* fateful
fatigant, e [fatigɑ̃, ɑ̃t] *adj* tiring; (*agaçant*) tiresome
fatigue [fatig] *nf* tiredness, fatigue; **fatigué, e** *adj* tired; **fatiguer** *vt* to tire, make tired; (*fig*: *agacer*) to annoy ♦ *vi* (*moteur*) to labour, strain; **se fatiguer** to get tired
fatras [fatʀɑ] *nm* jumble, hotchpotch
faubourg [fobuʀ] *nm* suburb
fauché, e [foʃe] (*fam*) *adj* broke
faucher [foʃe] *vt* (*herbe*) to cut; (*champs, blés*) to reap; (*fig*: *véhicule*) to mow down; (*fam*: *voler*) to pinch
faucille [fosij] *nf* sickle
faucon [fokɔ̃] *nm* falcon, hawk
faudra [fodʀa] *vb voir* **falloir**
faufiler [fofile]: **se ~** *vi*: **se ~ dans** to edge one's way into; **se ~ parmi/entre** to thread one's way among/between
faune [fon] *nf* (ZOOL) wildlife, fauna
faussaire [fosɛʀ] *nm* forger
fausse [fos] *adj voir* **faux**; **faussement** *adv* (*accuser*) wrongly, wrongfully; (*croire*) falsely
fausser [fose] *vt* (*objet*) to bend, buckle, (*fig*) to distort; **~ compagnie à qn** to give sb the slip

faut [fo] *vb voir* **falloir**
faute [fot] *nf* (*erreur*) mistake, error; (*mauvaise action*) misdemeanour; (*FOOTBALL etc*) offence; (*TENNIS*) fault; **c'est de sa/ma ~** it's his/my fault; **être en ~** to be in the wrong; **~ de** (*temps, argent*) for *ou* through lack of; **sans ~** without fail; **~ de frappe** typing error; **~ de goût** error of taste; **~ professionnelle** professional misconduct *no pl*
fauteuil [fotœj] *nm* armchair; **~ roulant** wheelchair
fauteur [fotœʀ] *nm*: **~ de troubles** trouble-maker
fautif, -ive [fotif, iv] *adj* (*responsable*) at fault, in the wrong; (*incorrect*) incorrect, inaccurate; **il se sentait ~** he felt guilty
fauve [fov] *nm* wildcat ♦ *adj* (*couleur*) fawn
faux[1] [fo] *nf* scythe
faux[2], fausse [fo, fos] *adj* (*inexact*) wrong; (*voix*) out of tune; (*billet*) fake, forged; (*sournois, postiche*) false ♦ *adv* (*MUS*) out of tune ♦ *nm* (*copie*) fake, forgery; (*opposé au vrai*): **le ~** falsehood; **faire ~ bond à qn** to stand sb up; **fausse alerte** false alarm; **fausse couche** miscarriage; **~ frais** ♦ *nmpl* extras, incidental expenses; **~ pas** tripping *no pl*; (*fig*) faux pas; **~ témoignage** (*délit*) perjury; **faux-filet** *nm* sirloin; **faux-monnayeur** *nm* counterfeiter, forger
faveur [favœʀ] *nf* favour; **traitement de ~** preferential treatment; **en ~ de** in favour of
favorable [favɔʀabl] *adj* favourable
favori, te [favɔʀi, it] *adj, nm/f* favourite
favoriser [favɔʀize] *vt* to favour
fax [faks] *nm* fax; **faxer** *vt* to fax
fébrile [febʀil] *adj* feverish, febrile
fécond, e [fekɔ̃, ɔ̃d] *adj* fertile; **féconder** *vt* to fertilize; **fécondité** *nf* fertility
fécule [fekyl] *nf* potato flour; **féculent** *nm* starchy food
fédéral, e, -aux [fedeʀal, o] *adj* federal
fédération [fedeʀasjɔ̃] *nf* federation; **la F~ française de football** *the French football association*
fée [fe] *nf* fairy; **féerique** *adj* magical, fairytale *cpd*
feignant, e [fɛɲɑ̃, ɑ̃t] *nm/f* = **fainéant, e**
feindre [fɛ̃dʀ] *vt* to feign; **~ de faire** to pretend to do
feinte [fɛ̃t] *nf* (*SPORT*) dummy
fêler [fele] *vt* to crack
félicitations [felisitasjɔ̃] *nfpl* congratulations
féliciter [felisite] *vt*: **~ qn (de)** to congratulate sb (on)
félin, e [felɛ̃, in] *nm* (big) cat
fêlure [felyʀ] *nf* crack
femelle [fəmɛl] *adj, nf* female
féminin, e [feminɛ̃, in] *adj* feminine; (*sexe*) female; (*équipe, vêtements etc*) women's ♦ *nm* (*LING*) feminine; **féministe** [feminist] *adj* feminist
femme [fam] *nf* woman; (*épouse*) wife; **~ au foyer** housewife; **~ de chambre** chambermaid; **~ de ménage** cleaning lady
fémur [femyʀ] *nm* femur, thighbone
fendre [fɑ̃dʀ] *vt* (*couper en deux*) to split; (*fissurer*) to crack; (*traverser: foule, air*) to cleave through; **se ~** *vi* to crack
fenêtre [f(ə)nɛtʀ] *nf* window
fenouil [fənuj] *nm* fennel
fente [fɑ̃t] *nf* (*fissure*) crack; (*de boîte à lettres etc*) slit
fer [fɛʀ] *nm* iron; **~ à cheval** horseshoe; **~ (à repasser)** iron; **~ forgé** wrought iron
ferai *etc* [fəʀe] *vb voir* **faire**
fer-blanc [fɛʀblɑ̃] *nm* tin(plate)
férié, e [feʀje] *adj*: **jour ~** public holiday
ferions *etc* [fəʀjɔ̃] *vb voir* **faire**
ferme [fɛʀm] *adj* firm ♦ *adv* (*travailler etc*) hard ♦ *nf* (*exploitation*) farm; (*maison*) farmhouse
fermé, e [fɛʀme] *adj* closed, shut; (*gaz, eau etc*) off; (*fig: milieu*) exclusive

fermenter [fɛʀmɑ̃te] *vi* to ferment
fermer [fɛʀme] *vt* to close, shut; (*cesser l'exploitation de*) to close down, shut down; (*eau, électricité, robinet*) to put off, turn off; (*aéroport, route*) to close ♦ *vi* to close, shut; (*magasin: definitivement*) to close down, shut down; **se ~** *vi* to close, shut
fermeté [fɛʀmǝte] *nf* firmness
fermeture [fɛʀmǝtyʀ] *nf* closing; (*dispositif*) catch; **heures de ~** closing times; **~ éclair** ® zip (fastener) (BRIT), zipper (US)
fermier [fɛʀmje, jɛʀ] *nm* farmer; **fermière** *nf* woman farmer; (*épouse*) farmer's wife
fermoir [fɛʀmwaʀ] *nm* clasp
féroce [feʀɔs] *adj* ferocious, fierce
ferons [fǝʀɔ̃] *vb voir* **faire**
ferraille [feʀɑj] *nf* scrap iron; **mettre à la ~** to scrap
ferrer [feʀe] *vt* (*cheval*) to shoe
ferronnerie [feʀɔnʀi] *nf* ironwork
ferroviaire [feʀɔvjɛʀ] *adj* rail(way) *cpd* (BRIT), rail(road) *cpd* (US)
ferry(boat) [fɛʀe(bot)] *nm* ferry
fertile [fɛʀtil] *adj* fertile; **~ en incidents** eventful, packed with incidents
féru, e [feʀy] *adj*: **~ de** with a keen interest in
fesse [fɛs] *nf* buttock; **fessée** *nf* spanking
festin [fɛstɛ̃] *nm* feast
festival [fɛstival] *nm* festival
festivités [fɛstivite] *nfpl* festivities
festoyer [fɛstwaje] *vi* to feast
fêtard [fɛtaʀ, aʀd] (*fam*) *nm* high liver, merry-maker
fête [fɛt] *nf* (*religieuse*) feast; (*publique*) holiday; (*réception*) party; (*kermesse*) fête, fair; (*du nom*) feast day, name day; **faire la ~** to live it up; **faire ~ à qn** to give sb a warm welcome; **les ~s (de fin d'année)** the festive season; **la salle des ~s** the village hall; **~ foraine** (fun) fair; **fêter** *vt* to celebrate; (*personne*) to have a celebration for
feu, x [fø] *nm* (*gén*) fire; (*signal lumineux*) light; (*de cuisinière*) ring; **~x** *nmpl* (AUTO) (traffic) lights; **au ~!** (*incendie*) fire!; **à ~ doux/vif** over a slow/brisk heat; **à petit ~** (CULIN) over a gentle heat; (*fig*) slowly; **faire ~** to fire; **prendre ~** to catch fire; **mettre le ~ à** to set fire to; **faire du ~** to make a fire; **avez-vous du ~?** (*pour cigarette*) have you (got) a light?; **~ arrière** rear light; **~ d'artifice** (*spectacle*) fireworks *pl*; **~ de joie** bonfire; **~ rouge/vert/orange** red/green/amber (BRIT) *ou* yellow (US) light; **~x de brouillard** fog-lamps; **~x de croisement** dipped (BRIT) *ou* dimmed (US) headlights; **~x de position** sidelights; **~x de route** headlights
feuillage [fœjaʒ] *nm* foliage, leaves *pl*
feuille [fœj] *nf* (*d'arbre*) leaf; (*de papier*) sheet; **~ de maladie** *medical expenses claim form*; **~ de paie** pay slip
feuillet [fœjɛ] *nm* leaf
feuilleté, e [fœjte] *adj*: **pâte ~** flaky pastry
feuilleter [fœjte] *vt* (*livre*) to leaf through
feuilleton [fœjtɔ̃] *nm* serial
feutre [føtʀ] *nm* felt; (*chapeau*) felt hat; (*aussi:* **stylo-~**) felt-tip pen; **feutré, e** *adj* (*atmosphère*) muffled
fève [fɛv] *nf* broad bean
février [fevʀije] *nm* February
FF *abr* (= *franc français*) FF
FFF *sigle f* = **Fédération française de football**
fiable [fjabl] *adj* reliable
fiançailles [fjɑ̃saj] *nfpl* engagement *sg*
fiancé, e [fjɑ̃se] *nm/f* fiancé(e) ♦ *adj*: **être ~ (à)** to be engaged (to)
fiancer [fjɑ̃se]: **se ~** *vi* to become engaged
fibre [fibʀ] *nf* fibre; **~ de verre** fibreglass, glass fibre
ficeler [fis(ǝ)le] *vt* to tie up
ficelle [fisɛl] *nf* string *no pl*; (*morceau*) piece *ou* length of string
fiche [fiʃ] *nf* (*pour fichier*) (index) card; (*formulaire*) form; (ÉLEC) plug

ficher [fiʃe] *vt* (*dans un fichier*) to file; (*POLICE*) to put on file; (*fam*: *faire*) to do; (: *donner*) to give; (: *mettre*) to stick *ou* shove; **se ~ de** (*fam*: *se gausser*) to make fun of; **fiche-(moi) le camp** (*fam*) clear off; **fiche-moi la paix** (*fam*) leave me alone; **je m'en fiche!** (*fam*) I don't care!

fichier [fiʃje] *nm* file

fichu, e [fiʃy] *pp de* **ficher** (*fam*) ♦ *adj* (*fam*: *fini, inutilisable*) bust, done for; (: *intensif*) wretched, darned ♦ *nm* (*foulard*) (head)scarf; **mal ~** (*fam*) feeling lousy

fictif, -ive [fiktif, iv] *adj* fictitious

fiction [fiksjɔ̃] *nf* fiction; (*fait imaginé*) invention

fidèle [fidɛl] *adj* faithful ♦ *nm/f* (*REL*): **les ~s** (*à l'église*) the congregation *sg*; **fidélité** *nf* fidelity

fier¹ [fje]: **se ~ à** *vt* to trust

fier², fière [fjɛʀ] *adj* proud; **fierté** *nf* pride

fièvre [fjɛvʀ] *nf* fever; **avoir de la ~/39 de ~** to have a high temperature/a temperature of 39ºC; **fiévreux, -euse** *adj* feverish

figé, e [fiʒe] *adj* (*manières*) stiff; (*société*) rigid; (*sourire*) set

figer [fiʒe]: **se ~** *vi* (*huile*) to congeal; (*personne*) to freeze

fignoler [fiɲɔle] (*fam*) *vt* to polish up

figue [fig] *nf* fig; **figuier** *nm* fig tree

figurant, e [figyʀɑ̃, ɑ̃t] *nm/f* (*THÉÂTRE*) walk-on; (*CINÉMA*) extra

figure [figyʀ] *nf* (*visage*) face; (*forme, personnage*) figure; (*illustration*) picture, diagram

figuré, e [figyʀe] *adj* (*sens*) figurative

figurer [figyʀe] *vi* to appear ♦ *vt* to represent; **se ~ que** to imagine that

fil [fil] *nm* (*brin, fig*: *d'une histoire*) thread; (*électrique*) wire; (*d'un couteau*) edge; **au ~ des années** with the passing of the years; **au ~ de l'eau** with the stream *ou* current; **coup de ~** (*fam*) phone call; **~ à coudre** (sewing) thread; **~ de fer** wire; **~ de fer barbelé** barbed wire

filament [filamɑ̃] *nm* (*ÉLEC*) filament

filandreux, -euse [filɑ̃dʀø, øz] *adj* stringy

filature [filatyʀ] *nf* (*fabrique*) mill; (*policière*) shadowing *no pl*, tailing *no pl*

file [fil] *nf* line; (*AUTO*) lane; **en ~ indienne** in single file; **à la ~** (*d'affilée*) in succession; **~ (d'attente)** queue (*BRIT*), line (*US*)

filer [file] *vt* (*tissu, toile*) to spin; (*prendre en filature*) to shadow, tail; (*fam*: *donner*): **~ qch à qn** to slip sb sth ♦ *vi* (*bas*) to run; (*aller vite*) to fly past; (*fam*: *partir*) to make *ou* be off; **~ doux** to toe the line

filet [filɛ] *nm* net; (*CULIN*) fillet; (*d'eau, de sang*) trickle; **~ (à provisions)** string bag

filiale [filjal] *nf* (*COMM*) subsidiary

filière [filjɛʀ] *nf* (*carrière*) path; **suivre la ~** (*dans sa carrière*) to work one's way up (through the hierarchy)

filiforme [filifɔʀm] *adj* spindly

filigrane [filigʀan] *nm* (*d'un billet, timbre*) watermark

fille [fij] *nf* girl; (*opposé à fils*) daughter; **vieille ~** old maid; **fillette** *nf* (little) girl

filleul, e [fijœl] *nm/f* godchild, godson/daughter

film [film] *nm* (*pour photo*) (roll of) film; (*œuvre*) film, picture, movie; **~ d'épouvante** horror film; **~ policier** thriller

filon [filɔ̃] *nm* vein, lode; (*fig*) lucrative line, money spinner

fils [fis] *nm* son; **~ à papa** daddy's boy

filtre [filtʀ] *nm* filter; **filtrer** *vt* to filter; (*fig*: *candidats, visiteurs*) to screen

fin¹ [fɛ̃] *nf* end; **~s** *nfpl* (*but*) ends; **prendre ~** to come to an end; **mettre ~ à** to put an end to; **à la ~** in the end, eventually; **en ~ de compte** in the end; **sans ~** endless; **~ juin** at the end of June

fin², e [fɛ̃, fin] *adj* (*papier, couche, fil*)

thin; (*cheveux, visage*) fine; (*taille*) neat, slim; (*esprit, remarque*) subtle ♦ *adv* (*couper*) finely; **~ prêt** quite ready; **~es herbes** mixed herbs

final, e [final, o] *adj* final ♦ *nm* (MUS) finale; **finale** *nf* final; **quarts de finale** quarter finals; **finalement** *adv* finally, in the end; (*après tout*) after all

finance [finɑ̃s]: **~s** *nfpl* (*situation*) finances; (*activités*) finance *sg*; **moyennant ~** for a fee; **financer** *vt* to finance; **financier, -ière** *adj* financial

finaud, e [fino, od] *adj* wily

finesse [finɛs] *nf* thinness; (*raffinement*) fineness; (*subtilité*) subtlety

fini, e [fini] *adj* finished; (MATH) finite ♦ *nm* (*d'un objet manufacturé*) finish

finir [finiʀ] *vt* to finish ♦ *vi* to finish, end; **~ par faire** to end up *ou* finish up doing; **~ de faire** to finish doing; (*cesser*) to stop doing; **il finit par m'agacer** he's beginning to get on my nerves; **en ~ avec** to be *ou* have done with; **il va mal ~** he will come to a bad end

finition [finisjɔ̃] *nf* (*résultat*) finish

finlandais, e [fɛ̃lɑ̃dɛ, ɛz] *adj* Finnish ♦ *nm/f*: **F~, e** Finn

Finlande [fɛ̃lɑ̃d] *nf*: **la ~** Finland

fiole [fjɔl] *nf* phial

firme [fiʀm] *nf* firm

fis [fi] *vb voir* **faire**

fisc [fisk] *nm* tax authorities *pl*; **fiscal, e, -aux** *adj* tax *cpd*, fiscal; **fiscalité** *nf* tax system

fissure [fisyʀ] *nf* crack; **fissurer** *vt* to crack; **se fissurer** *vi* to crack

fiston [fistɔ̃] (*fam*) *nm* son, lad

fit [fi] *vb voir* **faire**

fixation [fiksasjɔ̃] *nf* (*attache*) fastening; (PSYCH) fixation

fixe [fiks] *adj* fixed; (*emploi*) steady, regular ♦ *nm* (*salaire*) basic salary; **à heure ~** at a set time; **menu à prix ~** set menu

fixé, e [fikse] *adj*: **être ~ (sur)** (*savoir à quoi s'en tenir*) to have made up one's mind (about)

fixer [fikse] *vt* (*attacher*): **~ qch (à/sur)** to fix *ou* fasten sth (to/onto); (*déterminer*) to fix, set; (*regarder*) to stare at; **se ~** *vi* (*s'établir*) to settle down; **se ~ sur** (*suj*: *attention*) to focus on

flacon [flakɔ̃] *nm* bottle

flageoler [flaʒɔle] *vi* (*jambes*) to sag

flageolet [flaʒɔlɛ] *nm* (CULIN) dwarf kidney bean

flagrant, e [flagʀɑ̃, ɑ̃t] *adj* flagrant, blatant; **en ~ délit** in the act

flair [flɛʀ] *nm* sense of smell; (*fig*) intuition; **flairer** *vt* (*humer*) to sniff (at); (*détecter*) to scent

flamand, e [flamɑ̃, ɑ̃d] *adj* Flemish ♦ *nm* (LING) Flemish ♦ *nm/f*: **F~, e** Fleming; **les F~s** the Flemish

flamant [flamɑ̃] *nm* flamingo

flambant [flɑ̃bɑ̃, ɑ̃t] *adv*: **~ neuf** brand new

flambé, e [flɑ̃be] *adj* (CULIN) flambé

flambeau, x [flɑ̃bo] *nm* (flaming) torch

flambée [flɑ̃be] *nf* blaze; (*fig*: *des prix*) explosion

flamber [flɑ̃be] *vi* to blaze (up)

flamboyer [flɑ̃bwaje] *vi* to blaze (up)

flamme [flɑm] *nf* flame; (*fig*) fire, fervour; **en ~s** on fire, ablaze

flan [flɑ̃] *nm* (CULIN) custard tart *ou* pie

flanc [flɑ̃] *nm* side; (MIL) flank

flancher [flɑ̃ʃe] (*fam*) *vi* to fail, pack up

flanelle [flanɛl] *nf* flannel

flâner [flɑne] *vi* to stroll; **flânerie** *nf* stroll

flanquer [flɑ̃ke] *vt* to flank; (*fam*: *mettre*) to chuck, shove; (: *jeter*): **~ par terre/à la porte** to fling to the ground/chuck out

flaque [flak] *nf* (*d'eau*) puddle; (*d'huile, de sang etc*) pool

flash [flaʃ] (*pl* **~es**) *nm* (PHOTO) flash; **~ (d'information)** newsflash

flasque [flask] *adj* flabby

flatter [flate] *vt* to flatter; **se ~ de qch** to pride o.s. on sth; **flatterie** *nf* flattery *no pl*; **flatteur, -euse** *adj* flattering

fléau, x [fleo] *nm* scourge
flèche [flɛʃ] *nf* arrow; (*de clocher*) spire; **monter en ~** (*fig*) to soar, rocket; **partir en ~** to be off like a shot; **fléchette** *nf* dart
fléchir [fleʃiʀ] *vt* (*corps, genou*) to bend; (*fig*) to sway, weaken ♦ *vi* (*fig*) to weaken, flag
flemmard, e [flemaʀ, aʀd] (*fam*) *nm/f* lazybones *sg*, loafer
flemme [flɛm] *nf* (*fam*) laziness; **j'ai la ~ de le faire** I can't be bothered doing it
flétrir [fletʀiʀ]: **se ~** *vi* to wither
fleur [flœʀ] *nf* flower; (*d'un arbre*) blossom; **en ~** (*arbre*) in blossom; **à ~s** flowery
fleuri, e [flœʀi] *adj* (*jardin*) in flower *ou* bloom; (*tissu, papier*) flowery
fleurir [flœʀiʀ] *vi* (*rose*) to flower; (*arbre*) to blossom; (*fig*) to flourish ♦ *vt* (*tombe*) to put flowers on; (*chambre*) to decorate with flowers
fleuriste [flœʀist] *nm/f* florist
fleuve [flœv] *nm* river
flexible [flɛksibl] *adj* flexible
flic [flik] (*fam*: *péj*) *nm* cop
flipper [flipœʀ] *nm* pinball (machine)
flirter [flœʀte] *vi* to flirt
flocon [flɔkɔ̃] *nm* flake
flopée [flɔpe] (*fam*) *nf*: **une ~ de** loads of, masses of
floraison [flɔʀezɔ̃] *nf* flowering
flore [flɔʀ] *nf* flora
florissant, e [flɔʀisɑ̃, ɑ̃t] *adj* (*économie*) flourishing
flot [flo] *nm* flood, stream; **~s** *nmpl* (*de la mer*) waves; **être à ~** (NAVIG) to be afloat; **entrer à ~s** to stream *ou* pour in
flottant, e [flɔtɑ̃, ɑ̃t] *adj* (*vêtement*) loose
flotte [flɔt] *nf* (NAVIG) fleet; (*fam*: *eau*) water; (: *pluie*) rain
flottement [flɔtmɑ̃] *nm* (*fig*) wavering, hesitation
flotter [flɔte] *vi* to float; (*nuage, odeur*) to drift; (*drapeau*) to fly; (*vêtements*) to hang loose; (*fam*: *pleuvoir*) to rain; **faire ~** to float; **flotteur** *nm* float
flou, e [flu] *adj* fuzzy, blurred; (*fig*) woolly, vague
fluctuation [flyktɥasjɔ̃] *nf* fluctuation
fluet, te [flyɛ, ɛt] *adj* thin, slight
fluide [flɥid] *adj* fluid; (*circulation etc*) flowing freely ♦ *nm* fluid
fluor [flyɔʀ] *nm*: **dentifrice au ~** fluoride toothpaste
fluorescent, e [flyɔʀesɑ̃, ɑ̃t] *adj* fluorescent
flûte [flyt] *nf* flute; (*verre*) flute glass; (*pain*) long loaf; **~!** drat it!; **~ à bec** recorder
flux [fly] *nm* incoming tide; (*écoulement*) flow; **le ~ et le reflux** the ebb and flow
FM *sigle f* (= *fréquence modulée*) FM
foc [fɔk] *nm* jib
foi [fwa] *nf* faith; **digne de ~** reliable; **être de bonne/mauvaise ~** to be sincere/insincere; **ma ~ ...** well ...
foie [fwa] *nm* liver; **crise de ~** stomach upset
foin [fwɛ̃] *nm* hay; **faire du ~** (*fig*: *fam*) to kick up a row
foire [fwaʀ] *nf* fair; (*fête foraine*) (fun) fair; **faire la ~** (*fig*: *fam*) to whoop it up; **~ (exposition)** trade fair
fois [fwa] *nf* time; **une/deux ~** once/twice; **2 ~ 2** 2 times 2; **une ~** (*passé*) once; (*futur*) sometime; **une ~ pour toutes** once and for all; **une ~ que** once; **des ~** (*parfois*) sometimes; **à la ~** (*ensemble*) at once
foison [fwazɔ̃] *nf*: **à ~** in plenty; **foisonner** *vi* to abound
fol [fɔl] *adj voir* **fou**
folie [fɔli] *nf* (*d'une décision, d'un acte*) madness, folly; (*état*) madness, insanity; **la ~ des grandeurs** delusions of grandeur; **faire des ~s** (*en dépenses*) to be extravagant
folklorique [fɔlklɔʀik] *adj* folk *cpd*; (*fam*) weird
folle [fɔl] *adj, nf voir* **fou**; **follement**

adv (*très*) madly, wildly

foncé, e [fɔ̃se] *adj* dark

foncer [fɔ̃se] *vi* to go darker; (*fam: aller vite*) to tear *ou* belt along; **~ sur** to charge at

foncier, -ère [fɔ̃sje, jɛʀ] *adj* (*honnêteté etc*) basic, fundamental; (COMM) real estate *cpd*

fonction [fɔ̃ksjɔ̃] *nf* function; (*emploi, poste*) post, position; **~s** *nfpl* (*professionnelles*) duties; **voiture de ~** company car; **en ~ de** (*par rapport à*) according to; **faire ~ de** to serve as; **la ~ publique** the state *ou* civil (BRIT) service; **fonctionnaire** *nm/f* state employee, local authority employee; (*dans l'administration*) ≈ civil servant; **fonctionner** *vi* to work, function

fond [fɔ̃] *nm* (*d'un récipient, trou*) bottom; (*d'une salle, scène*) back; (*d'un tableau, décor*) background; (*opposé à la forme*) content; (SPORT): **le ~** long distance (running); **au ~ de** at the bottom of; at the back of; **à ~** (*connaître, soutenir*) thoroughly; (*appuyer, visser*) right down *ou* home; **à ~ (de train)** (*fam*) full tilt; **dans le ~, au ~** (*en somme*) basically, really; **de ~ en comble** from top to bottom; *voir aussi* **fonds; ~ de teint** foundation (cream)

fondamental, e, -aux [fɔ̃damɑ̃tal, o] *adj* fundamental

fondant, e [fɔ̃dɑ̃, ɑ̃t] *adj* (*neige*) melting; (*poire*) that melts in the mouth

fondateur, -trice [fɔ̃datœʀ, tʀis] *nm/f* founder

fondation [fɔ̃dasjɔ̃] *nf* founding; (*établissement*) foundation; **~s** *nfpl* (*d'une maison*) foundations

fondé, e [fɔ̃de] *adj* (*accusation etc*) well-founded; **être ~ à** to have grounds for *ou* good reason to

fondement [fɔ̃dmɑ̃] *nm*: **sans ~** (*rumeur etc*) groundless, unfounded

fonder [fɔ̃de] *vt* to found; (*fig*) to base; **se ~ sur** (*suj: personne*) to base o.s. on

fonderie [fɔ̃dʀi] *nf* smelting works *sg*

fondre [fɔ̃dʀ] *vt* (*aussi:* **faire ~**) to melt; (*dans l'eau*) to dissolve; (*fig: mélanger*) to merge, blend ♦ *vi* (*à la chaleur*) to melt; (*dans l'eau*) to dissolve; (*fig*) to melt away; (*se précipiter*): **~ sur** to swoop down on; **~ en larmes** to burst into tears

fonds [fɔ̃] *nm* (COMM): **~ (de commerce)** business ♦ *nmpl* (*argent*) funds

fondu, e [fɔ̃dy] *adj* (*beurre, neige*) melted; (*métal*) molten; **fondue** *nf* (CULIN) fondue

font [fɔ̃] *vb voir* **faire**

fontaine [fɔ̃tɛn] *nf* fountain; (*source*) spring

fonte [fɔ̃t] *nf* melting; (*métal*) cast iron; **la ~ des neiges** the (spring) thaw

foot [fut] (*fam*) *nm* football

football [futbol] *nm* football, soccer; **footballeur** *nm* footballer

footing [futiŋ] *nm* jogging; **faire du ~** to go jogging

for [fɔʀ] *nm*: **dans son ~ intérieur** in one's heart of hearts

forain, e [fɔʀɛ̃, ɛn] *adj* fairground *cpd* ♦ *nm* (*marchand*) stallholder; (*acteur*) fairground entertainer

forçat [fɔʀsa] *nm* convict

force [fɔʀs] *nf* strength; (PHYSIQUE, MÉCANIQUE) force; **~s** *nfpl* (*physiques*) strength *sg*; (MIL) forces; **à ~ d'insister** by dint of insisting; as he (*ou* I *etc*) kept on insisting; **de ~** forcibly, by force; **les ~s de l'ordre** the police

forcé, e [fɔʀse] *adj* forced; **c'est ~** (*fam*) it's inevitable; **forcément** *adv* inevitably; **pas forcément** not necessarily

forcené, e [fɔʀsəne] *nm/f* maniac

forcer [fɔʀse] *vt* to force; (*voix*) to strain ♦ *vi* (SPORT) to overtax o.s.; **~ la dose** (*fam*) to overdo it; **se ~ (à faire)** to force o.s. (to do)

forcir [fɔʀsiʀ] *vi* (*grossir*) to broaden out

forer [fɔʀe] *vt* to drill, bore

forestier, -ère [fɔʀɛstje, jɛʀ] *adj* forest

cpd
forêt [fɔʀɛ] *nf* forest
forfait [fɔʀfɛ] *nm* (*COMM*) all-in deal *ou* price; **forfaitaire** *adj* inclusive
forge [fɔʀʒ] *nf* forge, smithy; **forger** *vt* to forge; (*fig*: *prétexte*) to contrive, make up; **forgeron** *nm* (black)smith
formaliser [fɔʀmalize]: **se ~** *vi*: **se ~ (de)** to take offence (at)
formalité [fɔʀmalite] *nf* formality; **simple ~** mere formality
format [fɔʀma] *nm* size; **formater** *vt* (*disque*) to format
formation [fɔʀmasjɔ̃] *nf* (*développement*) forming; (*apprentissage*) training; **~ permanente** continuing education; **~ professionnelle** vocational training
forme [fɔʀm] *nf* (*gén*) form; (*d'un objet*) shape, form; **~s** *nfpl* (*bonnes manières*) proprieties; (*d'une femme*) figure *sg*; **être en ~** (*SPORT etc*) to be on form; **en bonne et due ~** in due form
formel, le [fɔʀmɛl] *adj* (*catégorique*) definite, positive; **formellement** *adv* (*absolument*) positively; **formellement interdit** strictly forbidden
former [fɔʀme] *vt* to form; (*éduquer*) to train; **se ~** *vi* to form
formidable [fɔʀmidabl] *adj* tremendous
formulaire [fɔʀmylɛʀ] *nm* form
formule [fɔʀmyl] *nf* (*gén*) formula; (*expression*) phrase; **~ de politesse** polite phrase; (*en fin de lettre*) letter ending; **formuler** *vt* (*émettre*) to formulate
fort, e [fɔʀ, fɔʀt] *adj* strong; (*intensité, rendement*) high, great; (*corpulent*) stout; (*doué*) good, able ♦ *adv* (*serrer, frapper*) hard; (*parler*) loud(ly); (*beaucoup*) greatly, very much; (*très*) very ♦ *nm* (*édifice*) fort; (*point* ~) strong point, forte; **~e tête** rebel; **forteresse** *nf* stronghold
fortifiant [fɔʀtifjɑ̃, jɑ̃t] *nm* tonic
fortifier [fɔʀtifje] *vt* to strengthen
fortiori [fɔʀsjɔʀi]: **à ~** *adv* all the more so
fortuit, e [fɔʀtɥi, it] *adj* fortuitous, chance *cpd*
fortune [fɔʀtyn] *nf* fortune; **faire ~** to make one's fortune; **de ~** makeshift; **fortuné, e** *adj* wealthy
fosse [fos] *nf* (*grand trou*) pit; (*tombe*) grave
fossé [fose] *nm* ditch; (*fig*) gulf, gap
fossette [fosɛt] *nf* dimple
fossile [fosil] *nm* fossil
fossoyeur [foswajœʀ] *nm* gravedigger
fou (fol), folle [fu, fɔl] *adj* mad; (*déréglé etc*) wild, erratic; (*fam*: *extrême, très grand*) terrific, tremendous ♦ *nm/f* madman(-woman) ♦ *nm* (*du roi*) jester; **être ~de** to be mad *ou* crazy about; **avoir le ~rire** to have the giggles
foudre [fudʀ] *nf*: **la ~** lightning
foudroyant, e [fudʀwajɑ̃, ɑ̃t] *adj* (*progrès*) lightning *cpd*; (*succès*) stunning; (*maladie, poison*) violent
foudroyer [fudʀwaje] *vt* to strike down; **être foudroyé** to be struck by lightning; **~ qn du regard** to glare at sb
fouet [fwɛ] *nm* whip; (*CULIN*) whisk; **de plein ~** (*se heurter*) head on; **fouetter** *vt* to whip; (*crème*) to whisk
fougère [fuʒɛʀ] *nf* fern
fougue [fug] *nf* ardour, spirit; **fougueux, -euse** *adj* fiery
fouille [fuj] *nf* search; **~s** *nfpl* (*archéologiques*) excavations; **fouiller** *vt* to search; (*creuser*) to dig ♦ *vi* to rummage; **fouillis** *nm* jumble, muddle
fouiner [fwine] (*péj*) *vi*: **~ dans** to nose around *ou* about in
foulard [fulaʀ] *nm* scarf
foule [ful] *nf* crowd; **la ~** crowds *pl*; **une ~ de** masses of
foulée [fule] *nf* stride
fouler [fule] *vt* to press; (*sol*) to tread upon; **se ~ la cheville** to sprain one's ankle; **ne pas se ~** not to overexert o.s.; **il ne se foule pas** he doesn't put himself out; **foulure** *nf* sprain
four [fuʀ] *nm* oven; (*de potier*) kiln;

(*THÉÂTRE*: *échec*) flop
fourbe [fuʀb] *adj* deceitful
fourbu, e [fuʀby] *adj* exhausted
fourche [fuʀʃ] *nf* pitchfork
fourchette [fuʀʃɛt] *nf* fork; (*STATISTIQUE*) bracket, margin
fourgon [fuʀgɔ̃] *nm* van; (*RAIL*) wag(g)on; **fourgonnette** *nf* (small) van
fourmi [fuʀmi] *nf* ant; **~s** *nfpl* (*fig*) pins and needles; **fourmilière** *nf* ant-hill; **fourmiller** *vi* to swarm
fournaise [fuʀnɛz] *nf* blaze; (*fig*) furnace, oven
fourneau, x [fuʀno] *nm* stove
fournée [fuʀne] *nf* batch
fourni, e [fuʀni] *adj* (*barbe, cheveux*) thick; (*magasin*): **bien ~ (en)** well stocked (with)
fournir [fuʀniʀ] *vt* to supply; (*preuve, exemple*) to provide, supply; (*effort*) to put in; **fournisseur, -euse** *nm/f* supplier; (*INTERNET*): **fournisseur d'accès à Internet** (Internet) service provider, ISP; **fourniture** *nf* supply(ing); **fournitures scolaires** school stationery
fourrage [fuʀaʒ] *nm* fodder
fourré, e [fuʀe] *adj* (*bonbon etc*) filled; (*manteau etc*) fur-lined ♦ *nm* thicket
fourrer [fuʀe] (*fam*) *vt* to stick, shove; **se ~ dans/sous** to get into/under; **fourre-tout** *nm inv* (*sac*) holdall; (*fig*) rag-bag
fourrière [fuʀjɛʀ] *nf* pound
fourrure [fuʀyʀ] *nf* fur; (*sur l'animal*) coat
fourvoyer [fuʀvwaje]: **se ~** *vi* to go astray, stray
foutre [futʀ] (*fam!*) *vt* = **ficher**; **foutu, e** (*fam!*) *adj* = **fichu, e**
foyer [fwaje] *nm* (*maison*) home; (*famille*) family; (*de cheminée*) hearth; (*de jeunes etc*) (social) club; (*résidence*) hostel; (*salon*) foyer; **lunettes à double ~** bi-focal glasses
fracas [fʀaka] *nm* (*d'objet qui tombe*) crash; **fracassant, e** *adj* (*succès*) thundering; **fracasser** *vt* to smash
fraction [fʀaksjɔ̃] *nf* fraction; **fractionner** *vt* to divide (up), split (up)
fracture [fʀaktyʀ] *nf* fracture; **~ du crâne** fractured skull; **fracturer** *vt* (*coffre, serrure*) to break open; (*os, membre*) to fracture
fragile [fʀaʒil] *adj* fragile, delicate; (*fig*) frail; **fragilité** *nf* fragility
fragment [fʀagmɑ̃] *nm* (*d'un objet*) fragment, piece
fraîche [fʀɛʃ] *adj voir* **frais**; **fraîcheur** *nf* coolness; (*d'un aliment*) freshness; **fraîchir** *vi* to get cooler; (*vent*) to freshen
frais, fraîche [fʀɛ, fʀɛʃ] *adj* fresh; (*froid*) cool ♦ *adv* (*récemment*) newly, fresh(ly) ♦ *nm*: **mettre au ~** to put in a cool place ♦ *nmpl* (*gén*) expenses; (*COMM*) costs; **il fait ~** it's cool; **servir ~** serve chilled; **prendre le ~** to take a breath of cool air; **faire des ~** to go to a lot of expense; **~ de scolarité** school fees (*BRIT*), tuition (*US*); **~ généraux** overheads
fraise [fʀɛz] *nf* strawberry; **~ des bois** wild strawberry
framboise [fʀɑ̃bwaz] *nf* raspberry
franc, franche [fʀɑ̃, fʀɑ̃ʃ] *adj* (*personne*) frank, straightforward; (*visage*) open; (*net*: *refus*) clear; (: *coupure*) clean; (*intensif*) downright ♦ *nm* franc
français, e [fʀɑ̃sɛ, ɛz] *adj* French ♦ *nm/f*: **F~, e** Frenchman(-woman) ♦ *nm* (*LING*) French; **les F~** the French
France [fʀɑ̃s] *nf*: **la ~** France
franche [fʀɑ̃ʃ] *adj voir* **franc**; **franchement** *adv* frankly; (*nettement*) definitely; (*tout à fait*: *mauvais etc*) downright
franchir [fʀɑ̃ʃiʀ] *vt* (*obstacle*) to clear, get over; (*seuil, ligne, rivière*) to cross; (*distance*) to cover
franchise [fʀɑ̃ʃiz] *nf* frankness; (*douanière*) exemption; (*ASSURANCES*) excess
franc-maçon [fʀɑ̃masɔ̃] *nm* freemason
franco [fʀɑ̃ko] *adv* (*COMM*): **~ (de port)**

postage paid

francophone [fʀɑ̃kɔfɔn] *adj* French-speaking

franc-parler [fʀɑ̃paʀle] *nm inv* outspokenness; **avoir son ~-~** to speak one's mind

frange [fʀɑ̃ʒ] *nf* fringe

frangipane [fʀɑ̃ʒipan] *nf* almond paste

franquette [fʀɑ̃kɛt]: **à la bonne ~** *adv* without any fuss

frappant, e [fʀapɑ̃, ɑ̃t] *adj* striking

frappé, e [fʀape] *adj* iced

frapper [fʀape] *vt* to hit, strike; (*étonner*) to strike; **~ dans ses mains** to clap one's hands; **frappé de stupeur** dumbfounded

frasques [fʀask] *nfpl* escapades

fraternel, le [fʀatɛʀnɛl] *adj* brotherly, fraternal; **fraternité** *nf* brotherhood

fraude [fʀod] *nf* fraud; (*SCOL*) cheating; **passer qch en ~** to smuggle sth in (*ou* out); **~ fiscale** tax evasion; **frauder** *vi, vt* to cheat; **frauduleux, -euse** *adj* fraudulent

frayer [fʀeje] *vt* to open up, clear ♦ *vi* to spawn; **se ~ un chemin dans la foule** to force one's way through the crowd

frayeur [fʀɛjœʀ] *nf* fright

fredonner [fʀədɔne] *vt* to hum

freezer [fʀizœʀ] *nm* freezing compartment

frein [fʀɛ̃] *nm* brake; **mettre un ~ à** (*fig*) to curb, check; **~ à main** handbrake; **freiner** *vi* to brake ♦ *vt* (*progrès etc*) to check

frêle [fʀɛl] *adj* frail, fragile

frelon [fʀəlɔ̃] *nm* hornet

frémir [fʀemiʀ] *vi* (*de peur, d'horreur*) to shudder; (*de colère*) to shake; (*feuillage*) to quiver

frêne [fʀɛn] *nm* ash

frénétique [fʀenetik] *adj* frenzied, frenetic

fréquemment [fʀekamɑ̃] *adv* frequently

fréquent, e [fʀekɑ̃, ɑ̃t] *adj* frequent

fréquentation [fʀekɑ̃tasjɔ̃] *nf* frequenting; **~s** *nfpl* (*relations*) company *sg*

fréquenté, e [fʀekɑ̃te] *adj*: **très ~** (very) busy; **mal ~** patronized by disreputable elements

fréquenter [fʀekɑ̃te] *vt* (*lieu*) to frequent; (*personne*) to see; **se ~** to see each other

frère [fʀɛʀ] *nm* brother

fresque [fʀɛsk] *nf* (*ART*) fresco

fret [fʀɛ(t)] *nm* freight

frétiller [fʀetije] *vi* (*poisson*) to wriggle

fretin [fʀətɛ̃] *nm*: **menu ~** small fry

friable [fʀijabl] *adj* crumbly

friand, e [fʀijɑ̃, fʀijɑ̃d] *adj*: **~ de** very fond of ♦ *nm*: **~ au fromage** cheese puff

friandise [fʀijɑ̃diz] *nf* sweet

fric [fʀik] (*fam*) *nm* cash, bread

friche [fʀiʃ]: **en ~** *adj, adv* (lying) fallow

friction [fʀiksjɔ̃] *nf* (*massage*) rub, rub-down; (*TECH, fig*) friction; **frictionner** *vt* to rub (down)

frigidaire ® [fʀiʒidɛʀ] *nm* refrigerator

frigide [fʀiʒid] *adj* frigid

frigo [fʀigo] (*fam*) *nm* fridge

frigorifié, e [fʀigɔʀifje] (*fam*) *adj*: **être ~** to be frozen stiff

frigorifique [fʀigɔʀifik] *adj* refrigerating

frileux, -euse [fʀilø, øz] *adj* sensitive to (the) cold

frime [fʀim] (*fam*) *nf*: **c'est de la ~** it's a lot of eyewash, it's all put on; **frimer** (*fam*) *vi* to show off

frimousse [fʀimus] *nf* (sweet) little face

fringale [fʀɛ̃gal] (*fam*) *nf*: **avoir la ~** to be ravenous

fringant, e [fʀɛ̃gɑ̃, ɑ̃t] *adj* dashing

fringues [fʀɛ̃g] (*fam*) *nfpl* clothes

fripé, e [fʀipe] *adj* crumpled

fripon, ne [fʀipɔ̃, ɔn] *adj* roguish, mischievous ♦ *nm/f* rascal, rogue

fripouille [fʀipuj] *nf* scoundrel

frire [fʀiʀ] *vt, vi*: **faire ~** to fry

frisé, e [fʀize] *adj* (*cheveux*) curly; (*personne*) curly-haired
frisson [fʀisɔ̃] *nm* (*de froid*) shiver; (*de peur*) shudder; **frissonner** *vi* (*de fièvre, froid*) to shiver; (*d'horreur*) to shudder
frit, e [fʀi, fʀit] *pp de* **frire**; **frite** *nf*: **(pommes) frites** chips (BRIT), French fries; **friteuse** *nf* chip pan; **friture** *nf* (*huile*) (deep) fat; (*plat*): **friture (de poissons)** fried fish
frivole [fʀivɔl] *adj* frivolous
froid, e [fʀwa, fʀwad] *adj, nm* cold; **il fait ~** it's cold; **avoir/prendre ~** to be/catch cold; **être en ~ avec** to be on bad terms with; **froidement** *adv* (*accueillir*) coldly; (*décider*) coolly
froideur [fʀwadœʀ] *nf* coldness
froisser [fʀwase] *vt* to crumple (up), crease; (*fig*) to hurt, offend; **se ~** *vi* to crumple, crease; (*personne*) to take offence; **se ~ un muscle** to strain a muscle
frôler [fʀole] *vt* to brush against; (*suj: projectile*) to skim past; (*fig*) to come very close to
fromage [fʀɔmaʒ] *nm* cheese; **~ blanc** soft white cheese
froment [fʀɔmɑ̃] *nm* wheat
froncer [fʀɔ̃se] *vt* to gather; **~ les sourcils** to frown
frondaisons [fʀɔ̃dɛzɔ̃] *nfpl* foliage *sg*
front [fʀɔ̃] *nm* forehead, brow; (MIL) front; **de ~** (*se heurter*) head-on; (*rouler*) together (*i.e. 2 or 3 abreast*); (*simultanément*) at once; **faire ~ à** to face up to
frontalier, -ère [fʀɔ̃talje, jɛʀ] *adj* border *cpd*, frontier *cpd*
frontière [fʀɔ̃tjɛʀ] *nf* frontier, border
frotter [fʀɔte] *vi* to rub, scrape ♦ *vt* to rub; (*pommes de terre, plancher*) to scrub; **~ une allumette** to strike a match
fructifier [fʀyktifje] *vi* to yield a profit
fructueux, -euse [fʀyktɥø, øz] *adj* fruitful
frugal, e, -aux [fʀygal, o] *adj* frugal
fruit [fʀɥi] *nm* fruit *gen no pl*; **~ de la passion** passion fruit; **~s de mer** seafood(s); **~s secs** dried fruit *sg*; **fruité, e** *adj* fruity; **fruitier, -ère** *adj*: **arbre fruitier** fruit tree
fruste [fʀyst] *adj* unpolished, uncultivated
frustrer [fʀystʀe] *vt* to frustrate
FS *abr* (= *franc suisse*) SF
fuel(-oil) [fjul(ɔjl)] *nm* fuel oil; (*domestique*) heating oil
fugace [fygas] *adj* fleeting
fugitif, -ive [fyʒitif, iv] *adj* (*fugace*) fleeting ♦ *nm/f* fugitive
fugue [fyg] *nf*: **faire une ~** to run away, abscond
fuir [fɥiʀ] *vt* to flee from; (*éviter*) to shun ♦ *vi* to run away; (*gaz, robinet*) to leak
fuite [fɥit] *nf* flight; (*écoulement, divulgation*) leak; **être en ~** to be on the run; **mettre en ~** to put to flight
fulgurant, e [fylgyʀɑ̃, ɑ̃t] *adj* lightning *cpd*, dazzling
fulminer [fylmine] *vi* to thunder forth
fumé, e [fyme] *adj* (CULIN) smoked; (*verre*) tinted; **fumée** *nf* smoke
fumer [fyme] *vi* to smoke; (*soupe*) to steam ♦ *vt* to smoke
fûmes *etc* [fym] *vb voir* **être**
fumet [fymɛ] *nm* aroma
fumeur, -euse [fymœʀ, øz] *nm/f* smoker
fumeux, -euse [fymø, øz] (*péj*) *adj* woolly, hazy
fumier [fymje] *nm* manure
fumiste [fymist] *nm/f* (*péj: paresseux*) shirker
funèbre [fynɛbʀ] *adj* funeral *cpd*; (*fig: atmosphère*) gloomy
funérailles [fyneʀɑj] *nfpl* funeral *sg*
funeste [fynɛst] *adj* (*erreur*) disastrous
fur [fyʀ]: **au ~ et à mesure** *adv* as one goes along; **au ~ et à mesure que** as
furet [fyʀɛ] *nm* ferret
fureter [fyʀ(ə)te] (*péj*) *vi* to nose about
fureur [fyʀœʀ] *nf* fury; **être en ~** to

be infuriated; **faire ~** to be all the rage
furibond, e [fyʀibɔ̃, ɔ̃d] *adj* furious
furie [fyʀi] *nf* fury; (*femme*) shrew, vixen; **en ~** (*mer*) raging; **furieux, -euse** *adj* furious
furoncle [fyʀɔ̃kl] *nm* boil
furtif, -ive [fyʀtif, iv] *adj* furtive
fus [fy] *vb voir* **être**
fusain [fyzɛ̃] *nm* (ART) charcoal
fuseau, x [fyzo] *nm* (*pour filer*) spindle; (*pantalon*) (ski) pants; **~ horaire** time zone
fusée [fyze] *nf* rocket; **~ éclairante** flare
fuser [fyze] *vi* (*rires etc*) to burst forth
fusible [fyzibl] *nm* (ÉLEC: *fil*) fuse wire; (: *fiche*) fuse
fusil [fyzi] *nm* (*de guerre, à canon rayé*) rifle, gun; (*de chasse, à canon lisse*) shotgun, gun; **fusillade** *nf* gunfire *no pl*, shooting *no pl*; **fusiller** *vt* to shoot; **fusil-mitrailleur** *nm* machine gun
fusionner [fyzjɔne] *vi* to merge
fut [fy] *vb voir* **être**
fût [fy] *vb voir* **être** ♦ *nm* (*tonneau*) barrel, cask
futé, e [fyte] *adj* crafty; **Bison ~** ® *TV and radio traffic monitoring service*
futile [fytil] *adj* futile; frivolous
futur, e [fytyʀ] *adj, nm* future
fuyant, e [fɥijɑ̃, ɑ̃t] *vb voir* **fuir** ♦ *adj* (*regard etc*) evasive; (*lignes etc*) receding
fuyard, e [fɥijaʀ, aʀd] *nm/f* runaway

G, g

gâcher [gɑʃe] *vt* (*gâter*) to spoil; (*gaspiller*) to waste; **gâchis** *nm* waste *no pl*
gadoue [gadu] *nf* sludge
gaffe [gaf] *nf* blunder; **faire ~** (*fam*) to be careful
gage [gaʒ] *nm* (*dans un jeu*) forfeit; (*fig*: *de fidélité, d'amour*) token
gageure [gaʒyʀ] *nf*: **c'est une ~** it's attempting the impossible
gagnant, e [gaɲɑ̃, ɑ̃t] *nm/f* winner
gagne-pain [gaɲpɛ̃] *nm inv* job
gagner [gaɲe] *vt* to win; (*somme d'argent, revenu*) to earn; (*aller vers, atteindre*) to reach; (*envahir*: *sommeil, peur*) to overcome; (: *mal*) to spread to ♦ *vi* to win; (*fig*) to gain; **~ du temps/de la place** to gain time/save space; **~ sa vie** to earn one's living
gai, e [ge] *adj* cheerful; (*un peu ivre*) merry; **gaiement** *adv* cheerfully; **gaieté** *nf* cheerfulness; **de gaieté de cœur** with a light heart
gaillard [gajaʀ, aʀd] *nm* (strapping) fellow
gain [gɛ̃] *nm* (*revenu*) earnings *pl*; (*bénéfice*: *gén pl*) profits *pl*
gaine [gɛn] *nf* (*corset*) girdle; (*fourreau*) sheath
gala [gala] *nm* official reception; **de ~** (*soirée etc*) gala
galant, e [galɑ̃, ɑ̃t] *adj* (*courtois*) courteous, gentlemanly; (*entreprenant*) flirtatious, gallant; (*scène, rendez-vous*) romantic
galère [galɛʀ] *nf* galley; **quelle ~!** (*fam*) it's a real grind!; **galérer** (*fam*) *vi* to slog away, work hard; (*rencontrer les difficultés*) to have a hassle
galerie [galʀi] *nf* gallery; (THÉÂTRE) circle; (*de voiture*) roof rack; (*fig*: *spectateurs*) audience; **~ de peinture** (private) art gallery; **~ marchande** shopping arcade
galet [galɛ] *nm* pebble
galette [galɛt] *nf* flat cake; **~ des Rois** *cake eaten on Twelfth Night*
galipette [galipɛt] *nf* somersault
Galles [gal] *nfpl*: **le pays de ~** Wales; **gallois, e** *adj* Welsh ♦ *nm/f*: **Gallois, e** Welshman(-woman) ♦ *nm* (LING) Welsh
galon [galɔ̃] *nm* (MIL) stripe; (*décoratif*) piece of braid
galop [galo] *nm* gallop; **galoper** *vi* to gallop
galopin [galɔpɛ̃] *nm* urchin, ragamuffin
gambader [gɑ̃bade] *vi* (*animal, enfant*)

to leap about
gambas [gɑ̃bas] *nfpl* Mediterranean prawns
gamin, e [gamɛ̃, in] *nm/f* kid ♦ *adj* childish
gamme [gam] *nf* (MUS) scale; (*fig*) range
gammé, e [game] *adj*: **croix ~e** swastika
gang [gɑ̃g] *nm* (*de criminels*) gang
gant [gɑ̃] *nm* glove; **~ de toilette** face flannel (BRIT), face cloth
garage [gaʀaʒ] *nm* garage; **garagiste** *nm/f* garage owner; (*employé*) garage mechanic
garantie [gaʀɑ̃ti] *nf* guarantee; **(bon de) ~** guarantee *ou* warranty slip
garantir [gaʀɑ̃tiʀ] *vt* to guarantee
garce [gaʀs] (*fam*) *nf* bitch
garçon [gaʀsɔ̃] *nm* boy; (*célibataire*): **vieux ~** bachelor; (*serveur*): **~ (de café)** waiter; **~ de courses** messenger; **~ d'honneur** best man; **garçonnière** *nf* bachelor flat
garde [gaʀd(ə)] *nm* (*de prisonnier*) guard; (*de domaine etc*) warden; (*soldat, sentinelle*) guardsman ♦ *nf* (*soldats*) guard; **de ~** on duty; **monter la ~** to stand guard; **mettre en ~** to warn; **prendre ~ (à)** to be careful (of); **~ champêtre** ♦ *nm* rural policeman; **~ du corps** ♦ *nm* bodyguard; **~ des enfants** ♦ *nf* (*après divorce*) custody of the children; **~ à vue** ♦ *nf* (JUR) ≈ police custody; **garde-à-vous** *nm*: **être/se mettre au garde-à-vous** to be at/stand to attention; **garde-barrière** *nm/f* level-crossing keeper; **garde-boue** *nm inv* mudguard; **garde-chasse** *nm* gamekeeper; **garde-malade** *nf* home nurse; **garde-manger** *nm inv* (*armoire*) meat safe; (*pièce*) pantry, larder
garder [gaʀde] *vt* (*conserver*) to keep; (*surveiller*: *enfants*) to look after; (: *immeuble, lieu, prisonnier*) to guard; **se ~** *vi* (*aliment*: *se conserver*) to keep; **se ~ de faire** to be careful not to do; **~ le lit/la chambre** to stay in bed/indoors; **pêche/chasse gardée** private fishing/hunting (ground)
garderie [gaʀdəʀi] *nf* day nursery, crèche
garde-robe [gaʀdəʀɔb] *nf* wardrobe
gardien, ne [gaʀdjɛ̃, jɛn] *nm/f* (*garde*) guard; (*de prison*) warder; (*de domaine, réserve*) warden; (*de musée etc*) attendant; (*de phare, cimetière*) keeper; (*d'immeuble*) caretaker; (*fig*) guardian; **~ de but** goalkeeper; **~ de la paix** policeman; **~ de nuit** night watchman
gare [gaʀ] *nf* station; **~ routière** bus station
garer [gaʀe] *vt* to park; **se ~** *vi* to park
gargariser [gaʀgaʀize]: **se ~** *vi* to gargle
gargote [gaʀgɔt] *nf* cheap restaurant
gargouille [gaʀguj] *nf* gargoyle
gargouiller [gaʀguje] *vi* to gurgle
garnement [gaʀnəmɑ̃] *nm* rascal, scallywag
garni, e [gaʀni] *adj* (*plat*) served with vegetables (*and chips or rice etc*)
garnison [gaʀnizɔ̃] *nf* garrison
garniture [gaʀnityʀ] *nf* (CULIN) vegetables *pl*; **~ de frein** brake lining
gars [gɑ] (*fam*) *nm* guy
Gascogne [gaskɔɲ] *nf* Gascony; **le golfe de ~** the Bay of Biscay
gas-oil [gazɔjl] *nm* diesel (oil)
gaspiller [gaspije] *vt* to waste
gastronome [gastʀɔnɔm] *nm/f* gourmet; **gastronomie** *nf* gastronomy; **gastronomique** *adj* gastronomic
gâteau, x [gɑto] *nm* cake; **~ sec** biscuit
gâter [gɑte] *vt* to spoil; **se ~** *vi* (*dent, fruit*) to go bad; (*temps, situation*) to change for the worse
gâterie [gɑtʀi] *nf* little treat
gâteux, -euse [gɑtø, øz] *adj* senile
gauche [goʃ] *adj* left, left-hand; (*maladroit*) awkward, clumsy ♦ *nf* (POL) left (wing); **le bras ~** the left arm; **le côté ~** the left-hand side; **à ~** on the left;

(*direction*) (to the) left; **gaucher, -ère** *adj* left-handed; **gauchiste** *nm/f* leftist
gaufre [gofʀ] *nf* waffle
gaufrette [gofʀɛt] *nf* wafer
gaulois, e [golwa, waz] *adj* Gallic ♦ *nm/f*: **G~, e** Gaul
gaver [gave] *vt* to force-feed; **se ~ de** to stuff o.s. with
gaz [gɑz] *nm inv* gas
gaze [gɑz] *nf* gauze
gazer [gɑze] (*fam*) *vi*: **ça gaze?** how's things?
gazette [gazɛt] *nf* news sheet
gazeux, -euse [gɑzø, øz] *adj* (*boisson*) fizzy; (*eau*) sparkling
gazoduc [gɑzodyk] *nm* gas pipeline
gazon [gɑzɔ̃] *nm* (*herbe*) grass; (*pelouse*) lawn
gazouiller [gazuje] *vi* to chirp; (*enfant*) to babble
geai [ʒɛ] *nm* jay
géant, e [ʒeɑ̃, ɑ̃t] *adj* gigantic; (COMM) giant-size ♦ *nm/f* giant
geindre [ʒɛ̃dʀ] *vi* to groan, moan
gel [ʒɛl] *nm* frost; **~ douche** shower gel
gélatine [ʒelatin] *nf* gelatine
gelée [ʒ(ə)le] *nf* jelly; (*gel*) frost
geler [ʒ(ə)le] *vt, vi* to freeze; **il gèle** it's freezing
gélule [ʒelyl] *nf* (MÉD) capsule
gelures [ʒəlyʀ] *nfpl* frostbite *sg*
Gémeaux [ʒemo] *nmpl*: **les ~** Gemini
gémir [ʒemiʀ] *vi* to groan, moan
gênant, e [ʒɛnɑ̃, ɑ̃t] *adj* (*irritant*) annoying; (*embarrassant*) embarrassing
gencive [ʒɑ̃siv] *nf* gum
gendarme [ʒɑ̃daʀm] *nm* gendarme; **gendarmerie** *nf military police force in countryside and small towns; their police station or barracks*
gendre [ʒɑ̃dʀ] *nm* son-in-law
gêné, e [ʒene] *adj* embarrassed
gêner [ʒene] *vt* (*incommoder*) to bother; (*encombrer*) to be in the way; (*embarrasser*): **~ qn** to make sb feel ill-at-ease
général, e, -aux [ʒeneʀal, o] *adj, nm* general; **en ~** usually, in general; **générale** *nf*: **(répétition) générale** final dress rehearsal; **généralement** *adv* generally; **généraliser** *vt, vi* to generalize; **se généraliser** *vi* to become widespread; **généraliste** *nm/f* general practitioner, G.P.
génération [ʒeneʀasjɔ̃] *nf* generation
généreux, -euse [ʒeneʀø, øz] *adj* generous
générique [ʒeneʀik] *nm* (CINÉMA) credits *pl*
générosité [ʒeneʀozite] *nf* generosity
genêt [ʒ(ə)nɛ] *nm* broom *no pl* (*shrub*)
génétique [ʒenetik] *adj* genetic; **génétiquement** *adv*: **~ment modifié** genetically modified, GM
Genève [ʒ(ə)nɛv] *n* Geneva
génial, e, -aux [ʒenjal, jo] *adj* of genius; (*fam: formidable*) fantastic, brilliant
génie [ʒeni] *nm* genius; (MIL): **le ~** the Engineers *pl*; **~ civil** civil engineering
genièvre [ʒənjɛvʀ] *nm* juniper
génisse [ʒenis] *nf* heifer
génital, e, -aux [ʒenital, o] *adj* genital; **les parties ~es** the genitals
génoise [ʒenwaz] *nf* sponge cake
genou, x [ʒ(ə)nu] *nm* knee; **à ~x** on one's knees; **se mettre à ~x** to kneel down
genre [ʒɑ̃ʀ] *nm* kind, type, sort; (LING) gender; **avoir bon ~** to look a nice sort; **avoir mauvais ~** to be coarse-looking; **ce n'est pas son ~** it's not like him
gens [ʒɑ̃] *nmpl* (*f in some phrases*) people *pl*
gentil, le [ʒɑ̃ti, ij] *adj* kind; (*enfant: sage*) good; (*endroit etc*) nice; **gentillesse** *nf* kindness; **gentiment** *adv* kindly
géographie [ʒeɔgʀafi] *nf* geography
geôlier [ʒolje, jɛʀ] *nm* jailer
géologie [ʒeɔlɔʒi] *nf* geology
géomètre [ʒeɔmɛtʀ] *nm/f* (*arpenteur*) (land) surveyor
géométrie [ʒeɔmetʀi] *nf* geometry; **géométrique** *adj* geometric
gérant, e [ʒeʀɑ̃, ɑ̃t] *nm/f* manager(-

eress)
gerbe [ʒɛʀb] *nf* (*de fleurs*) spray; (*de blé*) sheaf
gercé, e [ʒɛʀse] *adj* chapped
gerçure [ʒɛʀsyʀ] *nf* crack
gérer [ʒeʀe] *vt* to manage
germain, e [ʒɛʀmɛ̃, ɛn] *adj*: **cousin ~** first cousin
germe [ʒɛʀm] *nm* germ; **germer** *vi* to sprout; (*semence*) to germinate
geste [ʒɛst] *nm* gesture
gestion [ʒɛstjɔ̃] *nf* management
ghetto [geto] *nm* ghetto
gibet [ʒibɛ] *nm* gallows *pl*
gibier [ʒibje] *nm* (*animaux*) game
giboulée [ʒibule] *nf* sudden shower
gicler [ʒikle] *vi* to spurt, squirt
gifle [ʒifl] *nf* slap (in the face); **gifler** *vt* to slap (in the face)
gigantesque [ʒigɑ̃tɛsk] *adj* gigantic
gigogne [ʒigɔɲ] *adj*: **lits ~s** truckle (BRIT) *ou* trundle beds
gigot [ʒigo] *nm* leg (of mutton *ou* lamb)
gigoter [ʒigɔte] *vi* to wriggle (about)
gilet [ʒilɛ] *nm* waistcoat; (*pull*) cardigan; **~ de sauvetage** life jacket
gin [dʒin] *nm* gin; **~-tonic** gin and tonic
gingembre [ʒɛ̃ʒɑ̃bʀ] *nm* ginger
girafe [ʒiʀaf] *nf* giraffe
giratoire [ʒiʀatwaʀ] *adj*: **sens ~** roundabout
girofle [ʒiʀɔfl] *nf*: **clou de ~** clove
girouette [ʒiʀwɛt] *nf* weather vane *ou* cock
gitan, e [ʒitɑ̃, an] *nm/f* gipsy
gîte [ʒit] *nm* (*maison*) home; (*abri*) shelter; **~ (rural)** holiday cottage *ou* apartment
givre [ʒivʀ] *nm* (hoar) frost; **givré, e** *adj* covered in frost; (*fam*: *fou*) nuts; **orange givrée** orange sorbet (*served in peel*)
glace [glas] *nf* ice; (*crème glacée*) ice cream; (*miroir*) mirror; (*de voiture*) window
glacé, e [glase] *adj* (*mains, vent, pluie*) freezing; (*lac*) frozen; (*boisson*) iced
glacer [glase] *vt* to freeze; (*gâteau*) to ice; (*fig*): **~ qn** (*intimider*) to chill sb; (*paralyser*) to make sb's blood run cold
glacial, e [glasjal, jo] *adj* icy
glacier [glasje] *nm* (GÉO) glacier; (*marchand*) ice-cream maker
glacière [glasjɛʀ] *nf* icebox
glaçon [glasɔ̃] *nm* icicle; (*pour boisson*) ice cube
glaïeul [glajœl] *nm* gladiolus
glaise [glɛz] *nf* clay
gland [glɑ̃] *nm* acorn; (*décoration*) tassel
glande [glɑ̃d] *nf* gland
glander [glɑ̃de] (*fam*) *vi* to fart around (*!*)
glauque [glok] *adj* dull blue-green
glissade [glisad] *nf* (*par jeu*) slide; (*chute*) slip; **faire des ~s sur la glace** to slide on the ice
glissant, e [glisɑ̃, ɑ̃t] *adj* slippery
glissement [glismɑ̃] *nm*: **~ de terrain** landslide
glisser [glise] *vi* (*avancer*) to glide *ou* slide along; (*coulisser, tomber*) to slide; (*déraper*) to slip; (*être glissant*) to be slippery ♦ *vt* to slip; **se ~ dans** to slip into
global, e, -aux [glɔbal, o] *adj* overall
globe [glɔb] *nm* globe
globule [glɔbyl] *nm* (*du sang*) corpuscle
globuleux, -euse [glɔbylø, øz] *adj*: **yeux ~** protruding eyes
gloire [glwaʀ] *nf* glory; **glorieux, -euse** *adj* glorious
glousser [gluse] *vi* to cluck; (*rire*) to chuckle; **gloussement** *nm* cluck; chuckle
glouton, ne [glutɔ̃, ɔn] *adj* gluttonous
gluant, e [glyɑ̃, ɑ̃t] *adj* sticky, gummy
glucose [glykoz] *nm* glucose
glycine [glisin] *nf* wisteria
goal [gol] *nm* goalkeeper
GO *sigle* (= *grandes ondes*) LW
gobelet [gɔblɛ] *nm* (*en étain, verre, ar-*

gent) tumbler; (*d'enfant, de pique-nique*) beaker; (*à dés*) cup
gober [gɔbe] *vt* to swallow (whole)
godasse [gɔdas] (*fam*) *nf* shoe
godet [gɔdɛ] *nm* pot
goéland [gɔelɑ̃] *nm* (sea)gull
goélette [gɔelɛt] *nf* schooner
gogo [gɔgo]: **à ~** *adv* galore
goguenard, e [gɔg(ə)naʀ, aʀd] *adj* mocking
goinfre [gwɛ̃fʀ] *nm* glutton
golf [gɔlf] *nm* golf; (*terrain*) golf course
golfe [gɔlf] *nm* gulf; (*petit*) bay
gomme [gɔm] *nf* (*à effacer*) rubber (*BRIT*), eraser; **gommer** *vt* to rub out (*BRIT*), erase
gond [gɔ̃] *nm* hinge; **sortir de ses ~s** (*fig*) to fly off the handle
gondoler [gɔ̃dɔle]: **se ~** *vi* (*planche*) to warp; (*métal*) to buckle
gonflé, e [gɔ̃fle] *adj* swollen; **il est ~** (*fam: courageux*) he's got some nerve; (*impertinent*) he's got a nerve
gonfler [gɔ̃fle] *vt* (*pneu, ballon: en soufflant*) to blow up; (*: avec une pompe*) to pump up; (*nombre, importance*) to inflate ♦ *vi* to swell (up); (*CULIN: pâte*) to rise; **gonfleur** *nm* pump
gonzesse [gɔ̃zɛs] (*fam*) *nf* chick, bird (*BRIT*)
goret [gɔʀɛ] *nm* piglet
gorge [gɔʀʒ] *nf* (*ANAT*) throat; (*vallée*) gorge
gorgé, e [gɔʀʒe] *adj*: **~ de** filled with; (*eau*) saturated with; **gorgée** *nf* (*petite*) sip; (*grande*) gulp
gorille [gɔʀij] *nm* gorilla; (*fam*) bodyguard
gosier [gozje] *nm* throat
gosse [gɔs] (*fam*) *nm/f* kid
goudron [gudʀɔ̃] *nm* tar; **goudronner** *vt* to tar(mac) (*BRIT*), asphalt (*US*)
gouffre [gufʀ] *nm* abyss, gulf
goujat [guʒa] *nm* boor
goulot [gulo] *nm* neck; **boire au ~** to drink from the bottle
goulu, e [guly] *adj* greedy
gourd, e [guʀ, guʀd] *adj* numb (with cold)
gourde [guʀd] *nf* (*récipient*) flask; (*fam*) (clumsy) clot *ou* oaf ♦ *adj* oafish
gourdin [guʀdɛ̃] *nm* club, bludgeon
gourer [guʀe] (*fam*): **se ~** *vi* to boob
gourmand, e [guʀmɑ̃, ɑ̃d] *adj* greedy; **gourmandise** [guʀmɑ̃diz] *nf* greed; (*bonbon*) sweet
gourmet [guʀmɛ] *nm* gourmet
gourmette [guʀmɛt] *nf* chain bracelet
gousse [gus] *nf*: **~ d'ail** clove of garlic
goût [gu] *nm* taste; **avoir bon ~** to taste good; **de bon ~** tasteful; **de mauvais ~** tasteless; **prendre ~ à** to develop a taste *ou* a liking for
goûter [gute] *vt* (*essayer*) to taste; (*apprécier*) to enjoy ♦ *vi* to have (afternoon) tea ♦ *nm* (afternoon) tea
goutte [gut] *nf* drop; (*MÉD*) gout; (*alcool*) brandy; **tomber ~ à ~** to drip; **goutte-à-goutte** *nm* (*MÉD*) drip
gouttelette [gut(ə)lɛt] *nf* droplet
gouttière [gutjɛʀ] *nf* gutter
gouvernail [guvɛʀnaj] *nm* rudder; (*barre*) helm, tiller
gouvernante [guvɛʀnɑ̃t] *nf* governess
gouvernement [guvɛʀnəmɑ̃] *nm* government
gouverner [guvɛʀne] *vt* to govern
grabuge [gʀabyʒ] (*fam*) *nm* mayhem
grâce [gʀɑs] *nf* (*charme*) grace; (*faveur*) favour; (*JUR*) pardon; **~s** *nfpl* (*REL*) grace *sg*; **faire ~ à qn de qch** to spare sb sth; **rendre ~(s) à** to give thanks to; **demander ~** to beg for mercy; **~ à** thanks to; **gracier** *vt* to pardon; **gracieux, -euse** *adj* graceful
grade [gʀad] *nm* rank; **monter en ~** to be promoted
gradin [gʀadɛ̃] *nm* tier; step; **~s** *nmpl* (*de stade*) terracing *sg*
gradué, e [gʀadɥe] *adj*: **verre ~** measuring jug
graduel, le [gʀadɥɛl] *adj* gradual
graduer [gʀadɥe] *vt* (*effort etc*) to increase gradually; (*règle, verre*) to gradu-

ate
graffiti [grafiti] *nmpl* graffiti
grain [grɛ̃] *nm* (*gén*) grain; (NAVIG) squall; **~ de beauté** beauty spot; **~ de café** coffee bean; **~ de poivre** peppercorn; **~ de poussière** speck of dust; **~ de raisin** grape
graine [grɛn] *nf* seed
graissage [grɛsaʒ] *nm* lubrication, greasing
graisse [grɛs] *nf* fat; (*lubrifiant*) grease; **graisser** *vt* to lubricate, grease; (*tacher*) to make greasy; **graisseux, -euse** *adj* greasy
grammaire [gra(m)mɛr] *nf* grammar; **grammatical, e, -aux** *adj* grammatical
gramme [gram] *nm* gramme
grand, e [grɑ̃, grɑ̃d] *adj* (*haut*) tall; (*gros, vaste, large*) big, large; (*long*) long; (*plus âgé*) big; (*adulte*) grown-up; (*sens abstraits*) great ♦ *adv*: **~ ouvert** wide open; **au ~ air** in the open (air); **les ~s blessés** the severely injured; **~ ensemble** housing scheme; **~ magasin** department store; **~e personne** grown-up; **~e surface** hypermarket; **~es écoles** *prestige schools of university level*; **~es lignes** (RAIL) main lines; **~es vacances** summer holidays; **grand-chose** [grɑ̃ʃoz] *nm/f inv*: **pas grand-chose** not much; **Grande-Bretagne** *nf* (Great) Britain; **grandeur** *nf* (*dimension*) size; **grandeur nature** life-size; **grandiose** *adj* imposing; **grandir** *vi* to grow ♦ *vt*: **grandir qn** (*suj*: *vêtement, chaussure*) to make sb look taller; **grand-mère** *nf* grandmother; **grand-messe** *nf* high mass; **grand-peine**: **à grand-peine** *adv* with difficulty; **grand-père** *nm* grandfather; **grand-route** *nf* main road; **grands-parents** *nmpl* grandparents
grange [grɑ̃ʒ] *nf* barn
granit(e) [granit] *nm* granite
graphique [grafik] *adj* graphic ♦ *nm* graph
grappe [grap] *nf* cluster; **~ de raisin** bunch of grapes
gras, se [grɑ, grɑs] *adj* (*viande, soupe*) fatty; (*personne*) fat; (*surface, main*) greasy; (*plaisanterie*) coarse; (TYPO) bold ♦ *nm* (CULIN) fat; **faire la ~se matinée** to have a lie-in (BRIT), sleep late (US); **grassement** *adv*: **grassement payé** handsomely paid; **grassouillet, te** *adj* podgy, plump
gratifiant, e [gratifjɑ̃, jɑ̃t] *adj* gratifying, rewarding
gratin [gratɛ̃] *nm* (*plat*) cheese-topped dish; (*croûte*) cheese topping; **gratiné, e** *adj* (CULIN) au gratin
gratis [gratis] *adv* free
gratitude [gratityd] *nf* gratitude
gratte-ciel [gratsjɛl] *nm inv* skyscraper
gratte-papier [gratpapje] (*péj*) *nm inv* penpusher
gratter [grate] *vt* (*avec un outil*) to scrape; (*enlever: avec un outil*) to scrape off; (*: avec un ongle*) to scratch; (*enlever avec un ongle*) to scratch off ♦ *vi* (*irriter*) to be scratchy; (*démanger*) to itch; **se ~** to scratch (o.s.)
gratuit, e [gratɥi, ɥit] *adj* (*entrée, billet*) free; (*fig*) gratuitous
gravats [gravɑ] *nmpl* rubble *sg*
grave [grav] *adj* (*maladie, accident*) serious, bad; (*sujet, problème*) serious, grave; (*air*) grave, solemn; (*voix, son*) deep, low-pitched; **gravement** *adv* seriously; (*parler, regarder*) gravely
graver [grave] *vt* to engrave
gravier [gravje] *nm* gravel *no pl*; **gravillons** *nmpl* loose chippings *ou* gravel *sg*
gravir [gravir] *vt* to climb (up)
gravité [gravite] *nf* (*de maladie, d'accident*) seriousness; (*de sujet, problème*) gravity
graviter [gravite] *vi* to revolve
gravure [gravyr] *nf* engraving; (*reproduction*) print
gré [gre] *nm*: **de bon ~** willingly; **contre le ~ de qn** against sb's will; **de**

son (plein) ~ of one's own free will; **bon ~ mal ~** like it or not; **de ~ ou de force** whether one likes it or not; **savoir ~ à qn de qch** to be grateful to sb for sth

grec, grecque [gʀɛk] *adj* Greek; (*classique*: *vase etc*) Grecian ♦ *nm/f*: **G~, Grecque** Greek ♦ *nm* (LING) Greek

Grèce [gʀɛs] *nf*: **la ~** Greece

greffe [gʀɛf] *nf* (BOT, MÉD: *de tissu*) graft; (MÉD: *d'organe*) transplant; **greffer** *vt* (BOT, MÉD: *tissu*) to graft; (MÉD: *organe*) to transplant

greffier [gʀefje, jɛʀ] *nm* clerk of the court

grêle [gʀɛl] *adj* (very) thin ♦ *nf* hail; **grêler** *vb impers*: **il grêle** it's hailing; **grêlon** *nm* hailstone

grelot [gʀəlo] *nm* little bell

grelotter [gʀəlɔte] *vi* to shiver

grenade [gʀənad] *nf* (*explosive*) grenade; (BOT) pomegranate; **grenadine** *nf* grenadine

grenat [gʀəna] *adj inv* dark red

grenier [gʀənje] *nm* attic; (*de ferme*) loft

grenouille [gʀənuj] *nf* frog

grès [gʀɛ] *nm* sandstone; (*poterie*) stoneware

grésiller [gʀezije] *vi* to sizzle; (RADIO) to crackle

grève [gʀɛv] *nf* (*d'ouvriers*) strike; (*plage*) shore; **se mettre en/faire ~** to go on/be on strike; **~ de la faim** hunger strike; **~ du zèle** work-to-rule (BRIT), slowdown (US); **~ sauvage** wildcat strike

gréviste [gʀevist] *nm/f* striker

gribouiller [gʀibuje] *vt* to scribble, scrawl

grièvement [gʀijɛvmɑ̃] *adv* seriously

griffe [gʀif] *nf* claw; (*de couturier*) label; **griffer** *vt* to scratch

griffonner [gʀifɔne] *vt* to scribble

grignoter [gʀiɲɔte] *vt* (*personne*) to nibble at; (*souris*) to gnaw at ♦ *vi* to nibble

gril [gʀil] *nm* steak *ou* grill pan; **faire cuire au ~** to grill; **grillade** *nf* (*viande etc*) grill

grillage [gʀijaʒ] *nm* (*treillis*) wire netting; (*clôture*) wire fencing

grille [gʀij] *nf* (*clôture*) wire fence; (*portail*) (metal) gate; (*d'égout*) (metal) grate; (*fig*) grid

grille-pain [gʀijpɛ̃] *nm inv* toaster

griller [gʀije] *vt* (*pain*) to toast; (*viande*) to grill; (*fig*: *ampoule etc*) to blow; **faire ~** to toast; to grill; (*châtaignes*) to roast; **~ un feu rouge** to jump the lights

grillon [gʀijɔ̃] *nm* cricket

grimace [gʀimas] *nf* grimace; (*pour faire rire*): **faire des ~s** to pull *ou* make faces

grimper [gʀɛ̃pe] *vi, vt* to climb

grincer [gʀɛ̃se] *vi* (*objet métallique*) to grate; (*plancher, porte*) to creak; **~ des dents** to grind one's teeth

grincheux, -euse [gʀɛ̃ʃø, øz] *adj* grumpy

grippe [gʀip] *nf* flu, influenza; **grippé, e** *adj*: **être grippé** to have flu

gris, e [gʀi, gʀiz] *adj* grey; (*ivre*) tipsy

grisaille [gʀizɑj] *nf* greyness, dullness

griser [gʀize] *vt* to intoxicate

grisonner [gʀizɔne] *vi* to be going grey

grisou [gʀizu] *nm* firedamp

grive [gʀiv] *nf* thrush

grivois, e [gʀivwa, waz] *adj* saucy

Groenland [gʀɔɛnlɑ̃d] *nm* Greenland

grogner [gʀɔɲe] *vi* to growl; (*fig*) to grumble; **grognon, ne** *adj* grumpy

groin [gʀwɛ̃] *nm* snout

grommeler [gʀɔm(ə)le] *vi* to mutter to o.s.

gronder [gʀɔ̃de] *vi* to rumble; (*fig*: *révolte*) to be brewing ♦ *vt* to scold; **se faire ~** to get a telling-off

groom [gʀum] *nm* bellboy

gros, se [gʀo, gʀos] *adj* big, large; (*obèse*) fat; (*travaux, dégâts*) extensive; (*épais*) thick; (*rhume, averse*) heavy

♦ *adv*: **risquer/gagner ~** to risk/win a lot ♦ *nm/f* fat man/woman ♦ *nm* (*COMM*): **le ~** the wholesale business; **prix de ~** wholesale price; **par ~ temps/grosse mer** in rough weather/ heavy seas; **en ~** roughly; (*COMM*) wholesale; **~ lot** jackpot; **~ mot** coarse word; **~ plan** (*PHOTO*) close-up; **~ sel** cooking salt; **~ titre** headline; **~se caisse** big drum

groseille [gʀozɛj] *nf*: **~ (rouge/ blanche)** red/white currant; **~ à maquereau** gooseberry

grosse [gʀos] *adj voir* **gros**; **grossesse** *nf* pregnancy; **grosseur** *nf* size; (*tumeur*) lump

grossier, -ière [gʀosje, jɛʀ] *adj* coarse; (*insolent*) rude; (*dessin*) rough; (*travail*) roughly done; (*imitation, instrument*) crude; (*évident*: *erreur*) gross; **grossièrement** *adv* (*sommairement*) roughly; (*vulgairement*) coarsely; **grossièretés** *nfpl*: **dire des grossièretés** to use coarse language

grossir [gʀosiʀ] *vi* (*personne*) to put on weight ♦ *vt* (*exagérer*) to exaggerate; (*au microscope*) to magnify; (*suj*: *vêtement*): **~ qn** to make sb look fatter

grossiste [gʀosist] *nm/f* wholesaler

grosso modo [gʀosomɔdo] *adv* roughly

grotesque [gʀɔtɛsk] *adj* (*extravagant*) grotesque; (*ridicule*) ludicrous

grotte [gʀɔt] *nf* cave

grouiller [gʀuje] *vi*: **~ de** to be swarming with; **se ~** (*fam*) ♦ *vi* to get a move on; **grouillant, e** *adj* swarming

groupe [gʀup] *nm* group; **le ~ des 8** Group of 8; **~ de parole** support group; **~ sanguin** blood group; **groupement** *nm* (*action*) grouping; (*groupe*) group; **grouper** *vt* to group; **se grouper** *vi* to gather

grue [gʀy] *nf* crane

grumeaux [gʀymo] *nmpl* lumps

guenilles [gənij] *nfpl* rags

guenon [gənɔ̃] *nf* female monkey

guépard [gepaʀ] *nm* cheetah

guêpe [gɛp] *nf* wasp

guêpier [gepje] *nm* (*fig*) trap

guère [gɛʀ] *adv* (*avec adjectif, adverbe*): **ne ... ~** hardly; (*avec verbe*): **ne ... ~** (*pas beaucoup*) *tournure négative* +*much*; (*pas souvent*) hardly ever; (*pas longtemps*) *tournure négative* +(*very*) *long*; **il n'y a ~ que/de** there's hardly anybody (*ou* anything) but/hardly any; **ce n'est ~ difficile** it's hardly difficult; **nous n'avons ~ de temps** we have hardly any time

guéridon [geʀidɔ̃] *nm* pedestal table

guérilla [geʀija] *nf* guerrilla warfare

guérillero [geʀijeʀo] *nm* guerrilla

guérir [geʀiʀ] *vt* (*personne, maladie*) to cure; (*membre, plaie*) to heal ♦ *vi* (*malade, maladie*) to be cured; (*blessure*) to heal; **guérison** *nf* (*de maladie*) curing; (*de membre, plaie*) healing; (*de malade*) recovery; **guérisseur, -euse** *nm/f* healer

guerre [gɛʀ] *nf* war; **~ civile** civil war; **en ~** at war; **faire la ~ à** to wage war against; **guerrier, -ière** *adj* warlike ♦ *nm/f* warrior

guet [gɛ] *nm*: **faire le ~** to be on the look-out; **guet-apens** [gɛtapɑ̃] *nm* ambush; **guetter** *vt* (*épier*) to watch (intently); (*attendre*) to watch (out) for; (*hostilement*) to be lying in wait for

gueule [gœl] *nf* (*d'animal*) mouth; (*fam*: *figure*) face; (: *bouche*) mouth; **ta ~!** (*fam*) shut up!; **~ de bois** (*fam*) hangover; **gueuler** (*fam*) *vi* to bawl; **gueuleton** (*fam*) *nm* blow-out

gui [gi] *nm* mistletoe

guichet [giʃɛ] *nm* (*de bureau, banque*) counter; **les ~s** (*à la gare, au théâtre*) the ticket office *sg*; **~ automatique** cash dispenser (*BRIT*), automatic telling machine (*US*)

guide [gid] *nm* guide ♦ *nf* (*éclaireuse*) girl guide; **guider** *vt* to guide

guidon [gidɔ̃] *nm* handlebars *pl*

guignol [giɲɔl] *nm* ≃ Punch and Judy

show; (*fig*) clown

guillemets [gijmɛ] *nmpl*: **entre ~** in inverted commas

guillotiner [gijɔtine] *vt* to guillotine

guindé, e [gɛ̃de] *adj* (*personne, air*) stiff, starchy; (*style*) stilted

guirlande [giʀlɑ̃d] *nf* (*fleurs*) garland; **~ de Noël** tinsel garland; **~ lumineuse** string of fairy lights; **~ de papier** paper chain

guise [giz] *nf*: **à votre ~** as you wish *ou* please; **en ~ de** by way of

guitare [gitaʀ] *nf* guitar

gym [ʒim] *nf* (*exercices*) gym; **gymnase** *nm* gym(nasium); **gymnaste** *nm/f* gymnast; **gymnastique** *nf* gymnastics *sg*; (*au réveil etc*) keep-fit exercises *pl*

gynécologie [ʒinekɔlɔʒi] *nf* gynaecology; **gynécologique** *adj* gynaecological; **gynécologue** *nm/f* gynaecologist

H, h

habile [abil] *adj* skilful; (*malin*) clever; **habileté** [abilte] *nf* skill, skilfulness; cleverness

habillé, e [abije] *adj* dressed; (*chic*) dressy

habillement [abijmɑ̃] *nm* clothes *pl*

habiller [abije] *vt* to dress; (*fournir en vêtements*) to clothe; **s'~** *vi* to dress (o.s.), (*se déguiser, mettre des vêtements chic*) to dress up

habit [abi] *nm* outfit; **~s** *nmpl* (*vêtements*) clothes; **~ (de soirée)** evening dress; (*pour homme*) tails *pl*

habitant, e [abitɑ̃, ɑ̃t] *nm/f* inhabitant; (*d'une maison*) occupant; **loger chez l'~** to stay with the locals

habitation [abitasjɔ̃] *nf* house; **~s à loyer modéré** (block of) council flats

habiter [abite] *vt* to live in ♦ *vi*: **~ à/dans** to live in

habitude [abityd] *nf* habit; **avoir l'~ de faire** to be in the habit of doing; (*expérience*) to be used to doing; **d'~** usually; **comme d'~** as usual

habitué, e [abitɥe] *nm/f* (*de maison*) regular visitor; (*de café*) regular (customer)

habituel, le [abitɥɛl] *adj* usual

habituer [abitɥe] *vt*: **~ qn à** to get sb used to; **s'~ à** to get used to

'hache ['aʃ] *nf* axe

'hacher ['aʃe] *vt* (*viande*) to mince; (*persil*) to chop; **'hachis** *nm* mince *no pl*; **hachis Parmentier** ≃ shepherd's pie

'hachisch ['aʃiʃ] *nm* hashish

'hachoir ['aʃwaʀ] *nm* (*couteau*) chopper; (*appareil*) (meat) mincer; (*planche*) chopping board

'hagard, e ['agaʀ, aʀd] *adj* wild, distraught

'haie ['ɛ] *nf* hedge; (SPORT) hurdle

'haillons ['ɑjɔ̃] *nmpl* rags

'haine ['ɛn] *nf* hatred

'haïr ['aiʀ] *vt* to detest, hate

'hâlé, e ['ɑle] *adj* (sun)tanned, sunburnt

haleine [alɛn] *nf* breath; **hors d'~** out of breath; **tenir en ~** (*attention*) to hold spellbound; (*incertitude*) to keep in suspense; **de longue ~** long-term

'haleter ['alte] *vt* to pant

'hall ['ol] *nm* hall

'halle ['al] *nf* (covered) market; **~s** *nfpl* (*d'une grande ville*) central food market *sg*

hallucinant, e [alysinɑ̃, ɑ̃t] *adj* staggering

hallucination [alysinasjɔ̃] *nf* hallucination

'halte ['alt] *nf* stop, break; (*endroit*) stopping place ♦ *excl* stop!; **faire ~** to stop

haltère [altɛʀ] *nm* dumbbell, barbell; **~s** *nmpl*: **(poids et) ~s** (*activité*) weightlifting *sg*; **haltérophilie** *nf* weightlifting

'hamac ['amak] *nm* hammock

'hamburger ['ɑ̃buʀgœʀ] *nm* hamburger

'hameau, x ['amo] *nm* hamlet

hameçon [amsɔ̃] *nm* (fish) hook

'hanche ['ɑ̃ʃ] *nf* hip

'hand-ball ['ɑ̃dbal] *nm* handball
'handicapé, e ['ɑ̃dikape] *nm/f* physically (*ou* mentally) handicapped person; ~ **moteur** spastic
hangar ['ɑ̃gaʀ] *nm* shed; (AVIAT) hangar
'hanneton ['antɔ̃] *nm* cockchafer
'hanter ['ɑ̃te] *vt* to haunt
'hantise ['ɑ̃tiz] *nf* obsessive fear
'happer ['ape] *vt* to snatch; (*suj: train etc*) to hit
'haras ['aʀɑ] *nm* stud farm
'harassant, e ['aʀasɑ̃, ɑ̃t] *adj* exhausting
'harcèlement ['aʀsɛlmɑ̃] *nm* harassment; ~ **sexuel** sexual harassment
'harceler ['aʀsəle] *vt* to harass; ~ **qn de questions** to plague sb with questions
'hardi, e ['aʀdi] *adj* bold, daring
'hareng ['aʀɑ̃] *nm* herring
'hargne ['aʀɲ] *nf* aggressiveness; **'hargneux, -euse** *adj* aggressive
'haricot ['aʀiko] *nm* bean; ~ **blanc** haricot bean; ~ **vert** green bean; ~ **rouge** kidney bean
harmonica [aʀmɔnika] *nm* mouth organ
harmonie [aʀmɔni] *nf* harmony; **harmonieux, -euse** *adj* harmonious; (*couleurs, couple*) well-matched
'harnacher ['aʀnaʃe] *vt* to harness
'harnais ['aʀnɛ] *nm* harness
'harpe ['aʀp] *nf* harp
'harponner ['aʀpɔne] *vt* to harpoon; (*fam*) to collar
'hasard ['azaʀ] *nm*: **le** ~ chance, fate; **un** ~ a coincidence; **au** ~ (*aller*) aimlessly; (*choisir*) at random; **par** ~ by chance; **à tout** ~ (*en cas de besoin*) just in case; (*en espérant trouver ce qu'on cherche*) on the off chance (BRIT); **'hasarder** *vt* (*mot*) to venture; **se hasarder à faire** to risk doing
'hâte ['ɑt] *nf* haste; **à la** ~ hurriedly, hastily; **en** ~ posthaste, with all possible speed; **avoir** ~ **de** to be eager *ou* anxious to; **'hâter** *vt* to hasten; **se hâter** *vi* to hurry; **'hâtif, -ive** *adj* (*travail*) hurried; (*décision, jugement*) hasty
'hausse ['os] *nf* rise, increase; **être en** ~ to be going up; **'hausser** *vt* to raise; **hausser les épaules** to shrug (one's shoulders)
'haut, e ['o, 'ot] *adj* high; (*grand*) tall ♦ *adv* high ♦ *nm* top (part); **de 3 m de** ~ 3 m high, 3 m in height; **des ~s et des bas** ups and downs; **en** ~ **lieu** in high places; **à ~e voix, (tout)** ~ aloud, out loud; **du** ~ **de** from the top of; **de** ~ **en bas** from top to bottom; **plus** ~ higher up, further up; (*dans un texte*) above; (*parler*) louder; **en** ~ (*être/aller*) at/to the top; (*dans une maison*) upstairs; **en** ~ **de** at the top of
'hautain, e ['otɛ̃, ɛn] *adj* haughty
'hautbois ['obwɑ] *nm* oboe
'haut-de-forme ['odfɔʀm] *nm* top hat
'hauteur ['otœʀ] *nf* height; **à la** ~ **de** (*accident*) near; (*fig: tâche, situation*) equal to; **à la** ~ (*fig*) up to it
'haut...: 'haut-fourneau *nm* blast *ou* smelting furnace; **'haut-le-cœur** *nm inv* retch, heave; **'haut-parleur** *nm* (loud)speaker
'havre ['ɑvʀ] *nm* haven
'Haye ['ɛ] *n*: **la** ~ the Hague
'hayon ['ɛjɔ̃] *nm* hatchback
hebdo [ɛbdo] (*fam*) *nm* weekly
hebdomadaire [ɛbdɔmadɛʀ] *adj, nm* weekly
hébergement [ebɛʀʒəmɑ̃] *nm* accommodation
héberger [ebɛʀʒe] *vt* (*touristes*) to accommodate, lodge; (*amis*) to put up; (*réfugiés*) to take in
hébété, e [ebete] *adj* dazed
hébreu, x [ebʀø] *adj m, nm* Hebrew
hécatombe [ekatɔ̃b] *nf* slaughter
hectare [ɛktaʀ] *nm* hectare
'hein ['ɛ̃] *excl* eh?
'hélas ['elɑs] *excl* alas! ♦ *adv* unfortunately
'héler ['ele] *vt* to hail
hélice [elis] *nf* propeller
hélicoptère [elikɔptɛʀ] *nm* helicopter

helvétique [ɛlvetik] *adj* Swiss
hématome [ematom] *nm* nasty bruise
hémicycle [emisikl] *nm* (*POL*): **l'~** ≃ the benches (of the Commons) (*BRIT*), ≃ the floor (of the House of Representatives) (*US*)
hémisphère [emisfɛʀ] *nm*: **l'~ nord/sud** the northern/southern hemisphere
hémorragie [emɔʀaʒi] *nf* bleeding *no pl*, haemorrhage
hémorroïdes [emɔʀɔid] *nfpl* piles, haemorrhoids
'hennir ['eniʀ] *vi* to neigh, whinny; **'hennissement** *nm* neigh, whinny
hépatite [epatit] *nf* hepatitis
herbe [ɛʀb] *nf* grass; (*CULIN, MÉD*) herb; **~s de Provence** mixed herbs; **en ~** unripe; (*fig*) budding; **herbicide** *nm* weed-killer; **herboriste** *nm/f* herbalist
'hère ['ɛʀ] *nm*: **pauvre ~** poor wretch
héréditaire [eʀeditɛʀ] *adj* hereditary
'hérisser ['eʀise] *vt*: **~ qn** (*fig*) to ruffle sb; **se ~** *vi* to bristle, bristle up; **'hérisson** *nm* hedgehog
héritage [eʀitaʒ] *nm* inheritance; (*coutumes, système*) heritage, legacy
hériter [eʀite] *vi*: **~ de qch (de qn)** to inherit sth (from sb); **héritier, -ière** [eʀitje, jɛʀ] *nm/f* heir(-ess)
hermétique [ɛʀmetik] *adj* airtight; watertight; (*fig*: *obscur*) abstruse; (: *impénétrable*) impenetrable
hermine [ɛʀmin] *nf* ermine
'hernie ['ɛʀni] *nf* hernia
héroïne [eʀɔin] *nf* heroine; (*drogue*) heroin
héroïque [eʀɔik] *adj* heroic
'héron ['eʀɔ̃] *nm* heron
'héros ['eʀo] *nm* hero
hésitant [ezitɑ̃, ɑ̃t] *adj* hesitant
hésitation [ezitasjɔ̃] *nf* hesitation
hésiter [ezite] *vi*: **~ (à faire)** to hesitate (to do)
hétéroclite [eteʀɔklit] *adj* heterogeneous; (*objets*) sundry
hétérogène [eteʀɔʒɛn] *adj* heterogeneous
hétérosexuel, le [eteʀɔsɛksɥɛl] *adj* heterosexual
'hêtre ['ɛtʀ] *nm* beech
heure [œʀ] *nf* hour; (*SCOL*) period; (*moment*) time; **c'est l'~** it's time; **quelle ~ est-il?** what time is it?; **2 ~s (du matin)** 2 o'clock (in the morning); **être à l'~** to be on time; (*montre*) to be right; **mettre à l'~** to set right; **à une ~ avancée (de la nuit)** at a late hour of the night; **à toute ~** at any time; **24 ~s sur 24** round the clock, 24 hours a day; **à l'~ qu'il est** at this time (of day); by now; **sur l'~** at once; **~ de pointe** rush hour; (*téléphone*) peak period; **~ d'affluence** rush hour; **~s creuses** slack periods; (*pour électricité, téléphone etc*) off-peak periods; **~s supplémentaires** overtime *sg*
heureusement [œʀøzmɑ̃] *adv* (*par bonheur*) fortunately, luckily
heureux, -euse [œʀø, øz] *adj* happy; (*chanceux*) lucky, fortunate
'heurter ['œʀte] *vt* (*mur*) to strike, hit; (*personne*) to collide with; **se ~ à** *vt* (*fig*) to come up against
'heurts ['œʀ] *nmpl* (*fig*) clashes
hexagone [ɛgzagɔn] *nm* hexagon; (*la France*) France (*because of its shape*)
hiberner [ibɛʀne] *vi* to hibernate
'hibou, x ['ibu] *nm* owl
'hideux, -euse ['idø, øz] *adj* hideous
hier [jɛʀ] *adv* yesterday; **~ soir** last night, yesterday evening; **toute la journée d'~** all day yesterday; **toute la matinée d'~** all yesterday morning
'hiérarchie ['jeʀaʀʃi] *nf* hierarchy
'hi-fi ['ifi] *adj inv* hi-fi ♦ *nf* hi-fi
hilare [ilaʀ] *adj* mirthful
hindou, e [ɛ̃du] *adj* Hindu ♦ *nm/f*: **H~, e** Hindu
hippique [ipik] *adj* equestrian, horse *cpd*; **un club ~** a riding centre; **un concours ~** a horse show; **hippisme** *nm* (horse)riding
hippodrome [ipɔdʀom] *nm* racecourse
hippopotame [ipɔpɔtam] *nm* hippo-

potamus

hirondelle [irɔ̃dɛl] *nf* swallow

hirsute [irsyt] *adj* (*personne*) shaggy-haired; (*barbe*) shaggy; (*tête*) tousled

'hisser ['ise] *vt* to hoist, haul up; **se ~** *vi* to heave o.s. up

histoire [istwaʀ] *nf* (*science, événements*) history; (*anecdote, récit, mensonge*) story; (*affaire*) business *no pl*; **~s** *nfpl* (*chichis*) fuss *no pl*; (*ennuis*) trouble *sg*; **historique** *adj* historical; (*important*) historic

'hit-parade ['itpaʀad] *nm*: **le ~-~** the charts

hiver [ivɛʀ] *nm* winter; **hivernal, e, -aux** *adj* winter *cpd*; (*glacial*) wintry; **hiverner** *vi* to winter

HLM *nm ou f* (= *habitation à loyer modéré*) council flat; **des HLM** council housing

'hobby ['ɔbi] *nm* hobby

'hocher ['ɔʃe] *vt*: **~ la tête** to nod; (*signe négatif ou dubitatif*) to shake one's head

'hochet ['ɔʃɛ] *nm* rattle

'hockey ['ɔkɛ] *nm*: **~ (sur glace/gazon)** (ice/field) hockey

'hold-up ['ɔldœp] *nm inv* hold-up

'hollandais, e ['ɔlɑ̃dɛ, ɛz] *adj* Dutch ♦ *nm* (LING) Dutch ♦ *nm/f*: **H~, e** Dutchman(-woman); **les H~** the Dutch

'Hollande ['ɔlɑ̃d] *nf*: **la ~** Holland

'homard ['ɔmaʀ] *nm* lobster

homéopathique [ɔmeɔpatik] *adj* homoeopathic

homicide [ɔmisid] *nm* murder; **~ involontaire** manslaughter

hommage [ɔmaʒ] *nm* tribute; **~s** *nmpl*: **présenter ses ~s** to pay one's respects; **rendre ~ à** to pay tribute *ou* homage to

homme [ɔm] *nm* man; **~ d'affaires** businessman; **~ d'État** statesman; **~ de main** hired man; **~ de paille** stooge; **~ politique** politician; **homme-grenouille** *nm* frogman

homo...: **homogène** *adj* homogeneous; **homologue** *nm/f* counterpart; **homologué, e** *adj* (SPORT) ratified; (*tarif*) authorized; **homonyme** *nm* (LING) homonym; (*d'une personne*) namesake; **homosexuel, le** *adj* homosexual

'Hongrie ['ɔ̃gʀi] *nf*: **la ~** Hungary; **'hongrois, e** *adj* Hungarian ♦ *nm/f*: **Hongrois, e** Hungarian ♦ *nm* (LING) Hungarian

honnête [ɔnɛt] *adj* (*intègre*) honest; (*juste, satisfaisant*) fair; **honnêtement** *adv* honestly; **honnêteté** *nf* honesty

honneur [ɔnœʀ] *nm* honour; (*mérite*) credit; **en l'~ de** in honour of; (*événement*) on the occasion of; **faire ~ à** (*engagements*) to honour; (*famille*) to be a credit to; (*fig: repas etc*) to do justice to

honorable [ɔnɔʀabl] *adj* worthy, honourable; (*suffisant*) decent

honoraire [ɔnɔʀɛʀ] *adj* honorary; **professeur ~** professor emeritus; **honoraires** [ɔnɔʀɛʀ] *nmpl* fees *pl*

honorer [ɔnɔʀe] *vt* to honour; (*estimer*) to hold in high regard; (*faire honneur à*) to do credit to; **honorifique** [ɔnɔʀifik] *adj* honorary

'honte ['ɔ̃t] *nf* shame; **avoir ~ de** to be ashamed of; **faire ~ à qn** to make sb (feel) ashamed; **'honteux, -euse** *adj* ashamed; (*conduite, acte*) shameful, disgraceful

hôpital, -aux [ɔpital, o] *nm* hospital

'hoquet ['ɔkɛ] *nm*: **avoir le ~** to have (the) hiccoughs; **'hoqueter** *vi* to hiccough

horaire [ɔʀɛʀ] *adj* hourly ♦ *nm* timetable, schedule; **~s** *nmpl* (*d'employé*) hours; **~ souple** flexitime

horizon [ɔʀizɔ̃] *nm* horizon

horizontal, e, -aux [ɔʀizɔ̃tal, o] *adj* horizontal

horloge [ɔʀlɔʒ] *nf* clock; **l'~ parlante** the speaking clock; **horloger, -ère**

nm/f watchmaker; clockmaker
'hormis ['ɔʀmi] *prép* save
horoscope [ɔʀɔskɔp] *nm* horoscope
horreur [ɔʀœʀ] *nf* horror; **quelle ~!** how awful!; **avoir ~ de** to loathe *ou* detest; **horrible** *adj* horrible; **horrifier** *vt* to horrify
horripiler [ɔʀipile] *vt* to exasperate
'hors ['ɔʀ] *prép*: **~ de** out of; **~ pair** outstanding; **~ de propos** inopportune; **être ~ de soi** to be beside o.s.; **~ d'usage** out of service; **'hors-bord** *nm inv* speedboat (*with outboard motor*); **'hors-d'œuvre** *nm inv* hors d'œuvre; **'hors-jeu** *nm inv* offside; **'hors-la-loi** *nm inv* outlaw; **'hors-taxe** *adj* (*boutique, articles*) duty-free
hortensia [ɔʀtɑ̃sja] *nm* hydrangea
hospice [ɔspis] *nm* (*de vieillards*) home
hospitalier, -ière [ɔspitalje, jɛʀ] *adj* (*accueillant*) hospitable; (*MÉD: service, centre*) hospital *cpd*
hospitaliser [ɔspitalize] *vt* to take/send to hospital, hospitalize
hospitalité [ɔspitalite] *nf* hospitality
hostie [ɔsti] *nf* host (*REL*)
hostile [ɔstil] *adj* hostile; **hostilité** *nf* hostility
hosto [ɔsto] (*fam*) *nm* hospital
hôte [ot] *nm* (*maître de maison*) host; (*invité*) guest
hôtel [otɛl] *nm* hotel; **aller à l'~** to stay in a hotel; **~ de ville** town hall; **~ (particulier)** (private) mansion; **hôtelier, -ière** *adj* hotel *cpd* ♦ *nm/f* hotelier; **hôtellerie** *nf* hotel business
hôtesse [otɛs] *nf* hostess; **~ de l'air** air stewardess; **~ (d'accueil)** receptionist
'hotte ['ɔt] *nf* (*panier*) basket (*carried on the back*); **~ aspirante** cooker hood
'houblon ['ublɔ̃] *nm* (*BOT*) hop; (*pour la bière*) hops *pl*
'houille ['uj] *nf* coal; **~ blanche** hydroelectric power
'houle ['ul] *nf* swell; **'houleux, -euse** *adj* stormy
'houligan ['uligɑ̃] *nm* hooligan
'hourra ['uʀa] *excl* hurrah!
'houspiller ['uspije] *vt* to scold
'housse ['us] *nf* cover
'houx ['u] *nm* holly
'hublot ['yblo] *nm* porthole
'huche ['yʃ] *nf*: **~ à pain** bread bin
'huer ['ɥe] *vt* to boo
huile [ɥil] *nf* oil; **~ solaire** suntan oil; **huiler** *vt* to oil; **huileux, -euse** *adj* oily
huis [ɥi] *nm*: **à ~ clos** in camera
huissier [ɥisje] *nm* usher; (*JUR*) ≃ bailiff
'huit ['ɥi(t)] *num* eight; **samedi en ~** a week on Saturday; **dans ~ jours** in a week; **'huitaine** *nf*: **une huitaine (de jours)** a week or so; **'huitième** *num* eighth
huître [ɥitʀ] *nf* oyster
humain, e [ymɛ̃, ɛn] *adj* human; (*compatissant*) humane ♦ *nm* human (being); **humanitaire** *adj* humanitarian; **humanité** *nf* humanity
humble [œ̃bl] *adj* humble
humecter [ymɛkte] *vt* to dampen
'humer ['yme] *vt* (*plat*) to smell; (*parfum*) to inhale
humeur [ymœʀ] *nf* mood; **de bonne/mauvaise ~** in a good/bad mood
humide [ymid] *adj* damp; (*main, yeux*) moist; (*climat, chaleur*) humid; (*saison, route*) wet
humilier [ymilje] *vt* to humiliate
humilité [ymilite] *nf* humility, humbleness
humoristique [ymɔʀistik] *adj* humorous
humour [ymuʀ] *nm* humour; **avoir de l'~** to have a sense of humour; **~ noir** black humour
'huppé, e ['ype] (*fam*) *adj* posh
'hurlement ['yʀləmɑ̃] *nm* howling *no pl*, howl, yelling *no pl*, yell
'hurler ['yʀle] *vi* to howl, yell
hurluberlu [yʀlybɛʀly] (*péj*) *nm* crank
'hutte ['yt] *nf* hut
hybride [ibʀid] *adj, nm* hybrid

hydratant, e [idʀatɑ̃, ɑ̃t] *adj* (*crème*) moisturizing
hydraulique [idʀolik] *adj* hydraulic
hydravion [idʀavjɔ̃] *nm* seaplane
hydrogène [idʀɔʒɛn] *nm* hydrogen
hydroglisseur [idʀɔglisœʀ] *nm* hydroplane
hyène [jɛn] *nf* hyena
hygiénique [iʒenik] *adj* hygienic
hymne [imn] *nm* hymn; **~ national** national anthem
hypermarché [ipɛʀmaʀʃe] *nm* hypermarket
hypermétrope [ipɛʀmetʀɔp] *adj* long-sighted
hypertension [ipɛʀtɑ̃sjɔ̃] *nf* high blood pressure
hypertexte [ipɛʀtɛkst] *nm* (INFORM) hypertext
hypnose [ipnoz] *nf* hypnosis; **hypnotiser** *vt* to hypnotize; **hypnotiseur** *nm* hypnotist
hypocrisie [ipɔkʀizi] *nf* hypocrisy; **hypocrite** *adj* hypocritical
hypothèque [ipɔtɛk] *nf* mortgage
hypothèse [ipɔtɛz] *nf* hypothesis
hystérique [isteʀik] *adj* hysterical

I, i

iceberg [ajsbɛʀg] *nm* iceberg
ici [isi] *adv* here; **jusqu'~** as far as this; (*temps*) so far; **d'~ demain** by tomorrow; **d'~ là** by then, in the meantime; **d'~ peu** before long
icône [ikon] *nf* icon
idéal, e, -aux [ideal, o] *adj* ideal ♦ *nm* ideal; **idéaliste** *adj* idealistic ♦ *nm/f* idealist
idée [ide] *nf* idea; **avoir dans l'~ que** to have an idea that; **~ fixe** obsession; **~ reçue** generally accepted idea
identifier [idɑ̃tifje] *vt* to identify; **s'~ à** (*héros etc*) to identify with
identique [idɑ̃tik] *adj*: **~ (à)** identical (to)
identité [idɑ̃tite] *nf* identity
idiot, e [idjo, idjɔt] *adj* idiotic ♦ *nm/f* idiot; **idiotie** *nf* idiotic thing
idole [idɔl] *nf* idol
if [if] *nm* yew
igloo [iglu] *nm* igloo
ignare [iɲaʀ] *adj* ignorant
ignifugé, e [iɲifyʒe] *adj* fireproof
ignoble [iɲɔbl] *adj* vile
ignorant, e [iɲɔʀɑ̃, ɑ̃t] *adj* ignorant
ignorer [iɲɔʀe] *vt* not to know; (*personne*) to ignore
il [il] *pron* he; (*animal, chose, en tournure impersonnelle*) it; **~s** they; *voir* **avoir**
île [il] *nf* island; **l'~ Maurice** Mauritius; **les ~s anglo-normandes** the Channel Islands; **les ~s Britanniques** the British Isles
illégal, e, -aux [i(l)legal, o] *adj* illegal
illégitime [i(l)leʒitim] *adj* illegitimate
illettré, e [i(l)letʀe] *adj, nm/f* illiterate
illimité, e [i(l)limite] *adj* unlimited
illisible [i(l)lizibl] *adj* illegible; (*roman*) unreadable
illogique [i(l)lɔʒik] *adj* illogical
illumination [i(l)lyminasjɔ̃] *nf* illumination; (*idée*) flash of inspiration
illuminer [i(l)lymine] *vt* to light up; (*monument, rue: pour une fête*) to illuminate; (*: au moyen de projecteurs*) to floodlight
illusion [i(l)lyzjɔ̃] *nf* illusion; **se faire des ~s** to delude o.s.; **faire ~** to delude *ou* fool people; **illusionniste** *nm/f* conjuror
illustration [i(l)lystʀasjɔ̃] *nf* illustration
illustre [i(l)lystʀ] *adj* illustrious
illustré, e [i(l)lystʀe] *adj* illustrated ♦ *nm* comic
illustrer [i(l)lystʀe] *vt* to illustrate; **s'~** to become famous, win fame
îlot [ilo] *nm* small island, islet
ils [il] *pron voir* **il**
image [imaʒ] *nf* (*gén*) picture; (*métaphore*) image; **~ de marque** brand image; (*fig*) public image; **imagé, e** *adj* (*texte*) full of imagery; (*langage*)

colourful

imaginaire [imaʒinɛʀ] *adj* imaginary

imagination [imaʒinasjɔ̃] *nf* imagination; **avoir de l'~** to be imaginative

imaginer [imaʒine] *vt* to imagine; (*inventer: expédient*) to devise, think up; **s'~** *vt* (*se figurer: scène etc*) to imagine, picture; **s'~ que** to imagine that

imbattable [ɛ̃batabl] *adj* unbeatable

imbécile [ɛ̃besil] *adj* idiotic ♦ *nm/f* idiot; **imbécillité** *nf* idiocy; (*action*) idiotic thing; (*film, livre, propos*) rubbish

imbiber [ɛ̃bibe] *vt* to soak; **s'~ de** to become saturated with

imbu, e [ɛ̃by] *adj*: **~ de** full of

imbuvable [ɛ̃byvabl] *adj* undrinkable; (*personne: fam*) unbearable

imitateur, -trice [imitatœʀ, tʀis] *nm/f* (*gén*) imitator; (MUSIC-HALL) impersonator

imitation [imitasjɔ̃] *nf* imitation; (*de personnalité*) impersonation

imiter [imite] *vt* to imitate; (*contrefaire*) to forge; (*ressembler à*) to look like

immaculé, e [imakyle] *adj* (*linge, surface, réputation*) spotless; (*blancheur*) immaculate

immangeable [ɛ̃mɑ̃ʒabl] *adj* inedible

immatriculation [imatʀikylasjɔ̃] *nf* registration

immatriculer [imatʀikyle] *vt* to register; **faire/se faire ~** to register

immédiat, e [imedja, jat] *adj* immediate ♦ *nm*: **dans l'~** for the time being; **immédiatement** *adv* immediately

immense [i(m)mɑ̃s] *adj* immense

immerger [imɛʀʒe] *vt* to immerse, submerge

immeuble [imœbl] *nm* building; (*à usage d'habitation*) block of flats

immigration [imigʀasjɔ̃] *nf* immigration

immigré, e [imigʀe] *nm/f* immigrant

imminent, e [iminɑ̃, ɑ̃t] *adj* imminent

immiscer [imise]: **s'~** *vi*: **s'~ dans** to interfere in *ou* with

immobile [i(m)mɔbil] *adj* still, motionless

immobilier, -ière [imɔbilje, jɛʀ] *adj* property *cpd* ♦ *nm*: **l'~** the property business

immobiliser [imɔbilize] *vt* (*gén*) to immobilize; (*circulation, véhicule, affaires*) to bring to a standstill; **s'~** (*personne*) to stand still; (*machine, véhicule*) to come to a halt

immonde [i(m)mɔ̃d] *adj* foul

immoral, e, -aux [i(m)mɔʀal, o] *adj* immoral

immortel, le [imɔʀtɛl] *adj* immortal

immuable [imɥabl] *adj* unchanging

immunisé, e [im(m)ynize] *adj*: **~ contre** immune to

immunité [imynite] *nf* immunity

impact [ɛ̃pakt] *nm* impact

impair, e [ɛ̃pɛʀ] *adj* odd ♦ *nm* faux pas, blunder

impardonnable [ɛ̃paʀdɔnabl] *adj* unpardonable, unforgivable

imparfait, e [ɛ̃paʀfɛ, ɛt] *adj* imperfect

impartial, e, -aux [ɛ̃paʀsjal, jo] *adj* impartial, unbiased

impasse [ɛ̃pɑs] *nf* dead end, cul-de-sac; (*fig*) deadlock

impassible [ɛ̃pasibl] *adj* impassive

impatience [ɛ̃pasjɑ̃s] *nf* impatience

impatient, e [ɛ̃pasjɑ̃, jɑ̃t] *adj* impatient; **impatienter**: **s'impatienter** *vi* to get impatient

impeccable [ɛ̃pekabl] *adj* (*parfait*) perfect; (*propre*) impeccable; (*fam*) smashing

impensable [ɛ̃pɑ̃sabl] *adj* (*événement hypothétique*) unthinkable; (*événement qui a eu lieu*) unbelievable

imper [ɛ̃pɛʀ] (*fam*) *nm* raincoat

impératif, -ive [ɛ̃peʀatif, iv] *adj* imperative ♦ *nm* (LING) imperative; **~s** *nmpl* (*exigences: d'une fonction, d'une charge*) requirements; (*: de la mode*) demands

impératrice [ɛ̃peʀatʀis] *nf* empress

imperceptible [ɛ̃pɛʀsɛptibl] *adj* imperceptible

impérial, e, -aux [ɛ̃peʀjal, jo] *adj* imperial; **impériale** *nf* top deck

impérieux, -euse [ɛ̃peʀjø, jøz] *adj* (*caractère, ton*) imperious; (*obligation, besoin*) pressing, urgent

impérissable [ɛ̃peʀisabl] *adj* undying

imperméable [ɛ̃pɛʀmeabl] *adj* waterproof; (*fig*): **~ à** impervious to ♦ *nm* raincoat

impertinent, e [ɛ̃pɛʀtinɑ̃, ɑ̃t] *adj* impertinent

imperturbable [ɛ̃pɛʀtyʀbabl] *adj* (*personne, caractère*) unperturbable; (*sang-froid, gaieté, sérieux*) unshakeable

impétueux, -euse [ɛ̃petɥø, øz] *adj* impetuous

impitoyable [ɛ̃pitwajabl] *adj* pitiless, merciless

implanter [ɛ̃plɑ̃te]: **s'~** *vi* to be set up

impliquer [ɛ̃plike] *vt* to imply; **~ qn (dans)** to implicate sb (in)

impoli, e [ɛ̃pɔli] *adj* impolite, rude

impopulaire [ɛ̃pɔpylɛʀ] *adj* unpopular

importance [ɛ̃pɔʀtɑ̃s] *nf* importance; **sans ~** unimportant

important, e [ɛ̃pɔʀtɑ̃, ɑ̃t] *adj* important; (*en quantité: somme, retard*) considerable, sizeable; (*: dégâts*) extensive; (*péj: airs, ton*) self-important ♦ *nm*: **l'~** the important thing

importateur, -trice [ɛ̃pɔʀtatœʀ, tʀis] *nm/f* importer

importation [ɛ̃pɔʀtasjɔ̃] *nf* importation; (*produit*) import

importer [ɛ̃pɔʀte] *vt* (COMM) to import; (*maladies, plantes*) to introduce ♦ *vi* (*être important*) to matter; **il importe qu'il fasse** it is important that he should do; **peu m'importe** (*je n'ai pas de préférence*) I don't mind; (*je m'en moque*) I don't care; **peu importe (que)** it doesn't matter (if); *voir aussi* **n'importe**

importun, e [ɛ̃pɔʀtœ̃, yn] *adj* irksome, importunate; (*arrivée, visite*) inopportune, ill-timed ♦ *nm* intruder; **importuner** *vt* to bother

imposable [ɛ̃pozabl] *adj* taxable

imposant, e [ɛ̃pozɑ̃, ɑ̃t] *adj* imposing

imposer [ɛ̃poze] *vt* (*taxer*) to tax; **s'~** (*être nécessaire*) to be imperative; **~ qch à qn** to impose sth on sb; **en ~ à** to impress; **s'~ comme** to emerge as; **s'~ par** to win recognition through

impossibilité [ɛ̃pɔsibilite] *nf* impossibility; **être dans l'~ de faire qch** to be unable to do sth

impossible [ɛ̃pɔsibl] *adj* impossible; **il m'est ~ de le faire** it is impossible for me to do it, I can't possibly do it; **faire l'~** to do one's utmost

imposteur [ɛ̃pɔstœʀ] *nm* impostor

impôt [ɛ̃po] *nm* tax; **~s** *nmpl* (*contributions*) (income) tax *sg*; **payer 1000 F d'~s** to pay 1,000F in tax; **~ foncier** land tax; **~ sur le chiffre d'affaires** corporation (BRIT) *ou* corporate (US) tax; **~ sur le revenu** income tax

impotent, e [ɛ̃pɔtɑ̃, ɑ̃t] *adj* disabled

impraticable [ɛ̃pʀatikabl] *adj* (*projet*) impracticable, unworkable; (*piste*) impassable

imprécis, e [ɛ̃pʀesi, iz] *adj* imprecise

imprégner [ɛ̃pʀeɲe] *vt* (*tissu*) to impregnate; (*lieu, air*) to fill; **s'~ de** (*fig*) to absorb

imprenable [ɛ̃pʀənabl] *adj* (*forteresse*) impregnable; **vue ~** unimpeded outlook

imprésario [ɛ̃pʀesaʀjo] *nm* manager

impression [ɛ̃pʀesjɔ̃] *nf* impression; (*d'un ouvrage, tissu*) printing; **faire bonne ~** to make a good impression; **impressionnant, e** *adj* (*imposant*) impressive; (*bouleversant*) upsetting; **impressionner** *vt* (*frapper*) to impress; (*bouleverser*) to upset

imprévisible [ɛ̃pʀevizibl] *adj* unforeseeable

imprévoyant, e [ɛ̃pʀevwajɑ̃, ɑ̃t] *adj* lacking in foresight; (*en matière d'argent*) improvident

imprévu, e [ɛ̃pʀevy] *adj* unforeseen, unexpected ♦ *nm* (*incident*) unexpected incident; **des vacances pleines d'~** holidays full of surprises; **en cas d'~** if anything unexpected happens; **sauf ~** unless anything unexpected crops up

imprimante [ɛ̃pRimɑ̃t] *nf* printer

imprimé [ɛ̃pRime] *nm* (*formulaire*) printed form; (*POSTES*) printed matter *no pl*; (*tissu*) printed fabric; **~ à fleur** floral print

imprimer [ɛ̃pRime] *vt* to print; (*publier*) to publish; **imprimerie** *nf* printing; (*établissement*) printing works *sg*; **imprimeur** *nm* printer

impromptu, e [ɛ̃pRɔ̃pty] *adj* (*repas, discours*) impromptu; (*départ*) sudden; (*visite*) surprise

impropre [ɛ̃pRɔpR] *adj* inappropriate; **~ à** unfit for

improviser [ɛ̃pRɔvize] *vt, vi* to improvise

improviste [ɛ̃pRɔvist]: **à l'~** *adv* unexpectedly, without warning

imprudence [ɛ̃pRydɑ̃s] *nf* (*d'une personne, d'une action*) carelessness *no pl*; (*d'une remarque*) imprudence *no pl*; **commettre une ~** to do something foolish

imprudent, e [ɛ̃pRydɑ̃, ɑ̃t] *adj* (*conducteur, geste, action*) careless; (*remarque*) unwise, imprudent; (*projet*) foolhardy

impudent, e [ɛ̃pydɑ̃, ɑ̃t] *adj* impudent

impudique [ɛ̃pydik] *adj* shameless

impuissant, e [ɛ̃pɥisɑ̃, ɑ̃t] *adj* helpless; (*sans effet*) ineffectual; (*sexuellement*) impotent

impulsif, -ive [ɛ̃pylsif, iv] *adj* impulsive

impulsion [ɛ̃pylsjɔ̃] *nf* (*ÉLEC, instinct*) impulse; (*élan, influence*) impetus

impunément [ɛ̃pynemɑ̃] *adv* with impunity

inabordable [inabɔRdabl] *adj* (*cher*) prohibitive

inacceptable [inaksɛptabl] *adj* unacceptable

inaccessible [inaksesibl] *adj* inaccessible

inachevé, e [inaʃ(ə)ve] *adj* unfinished

inactif, -ive [inaktif, iv] *adj* inactive; (*remède*) ineffective; (*BOURSE: marché*) slack ♦ *nm*: **les ~s** the non-working population

inadapté, e [inadapte] *adj* (*gén*): **~ à** not adapted to, unsuited to; (*PSYCH*) maladjusted

inadéquat, e [inadekwa(t), kwat] *adj* inadequate

inadmissible [inadmisibl] *adj* inadmissible

inadvertance [inadvɛRtɑ̃s]: **par ~** *adv* inadvertently

inaltérable [inalteRabl] *adj* (*matière*) stable; (*fig*) unfailing; **~ à** unaffected by

inanimé, e [inanime] *adj* (*matière*) inanimate; (*évanoui*) unconscious; (*sans vie*) lifeless

inanition [inanisjɔ̃] *nf*: **tomber d'~** to faint with hunger (and exhaustion)

inaperçu, e [inapɛRsy] *adj*: **passer ~** to go unnoticed

inapte [inapt] *adj*: **~ à** incapable of; (*MIL*) unfit for

inattaquable [inatakabl] *adj* (*texte, preuve*) irrefutable

inattendu, e [inatɑ̃dy] *adj* unexpected

inattentif, -ive [inatɑ̃tif, iv] *adj* inattentive; **~ à** (*dangers, détails*) heedless of; **inattention** *nf*: **faute d'inattention** careless mistake

inauguration [inogyRasjɔ̃] *nf* inauguration

inaugurer [inogyRe] *vt* (*monument*) to unveil; (*exposition, usine*) to open; (*fig*) to inaugurate

inavouable [inavwabl] *adj* shameful; (*bénéfices*) undisclosable

incalculable [ɛ̃kalkylabl] *adj* incalculable

incandescence [ɛ̃kɑ̃desɑ̃s] *nf*: **porter à ~** to heat white-hot

incapable [ɛ̃kapabl] *adj* incapable; **~ de faire** incapable of doing; (*empêché*)

unable to do
incapacité [ɛ̃kapasite] *nf* (*incompétence*) incapability; (*impossibilité*) incapacity; **dans l'~ de faire** unable to do
incarcérer [ɛ̃kaʀseʀe] *vt* to incarcerate, imprison
incarné, e [ɛ̃kaʀne] *adj* (*ongle*) ingrown
incarner [ɛ̃kaʀne] *vt* to embody, personify; (*THÉÂTRE*) to play
incassable [ɛ̃kɑsabl] *adj* unbreakable
incendiaire [ɛ̃sɑ̃djɛʀ] *adj* incendiary; (*fig: discours*) inflammatory
incendie [ɛ̃sɑ̃di] *nm* fire; **~ criminel** arson *no pl*; **~ de forêt** forest fire; **incendier** *vt* (*mettre le feu à*) to set fire to, set alight; (*brûler complètement*) to burn down; **se faire incendier** (*fam*) to get a rocket
incertain, e [ɛ̃sɛʀtɛ̃, ɛn] *adj* uncertain; (*temps*) unsettled; (*imprécis: contours*) indistinct, blurred; **incertitude** *nf* uncertainty
incessamment [ɛ̃sesamɑ̃] *adv* very shortly
incident [ɛ̃sidɑ̃, ɑ̃t] *nm* incident; **~ de parcours** minor hitch *ou* setback; **~ technique** technical difficulties *pl*
incinérer [ɛ̃sineʀe] *vt* (*ordures*) to incinerate; (*mort*) to cremate
incisive [ɛ̃siziv] *nf* incisor
inciter [ɛ̃site] *vt*: **~ qn à (faire) qch** to encourage sb to do sth; (*à la révolte etc*) to incite sb to do sth
inclinable [ɛ̃klinabl] *adj*: **siège à dossier ~** reclining seat
inclinaison [ɛ̃klinɛzɔ̃] *nf* (*déclivité: d'une route etc*) incline; (*: d'un toit*) slope; (*état penché*) tilt
inclination [ɛ̃klinasjɔ̃] *nf* (*penchant*) inclination; **~ de (la) tête** nod (of the head); **~ (de buste)** bow
incliner [ɛ̃kline] *vt* (*pencher*) to tilt ♦ *vi*: **~ à qch/à faire** to incline towards sth/ doing; **s'~ (devant)** to bow (before); (*céder*) to give in *ou* yield (to); **~ la tête** to give a slight bow
inclure [ɛ̃klyʀ] *vt* to include; (*joindre à un envoi*) to enclose; **jusqu'au 10 mars inclus** until 10th March inclusive
incognito [ɛ̃kɔɲito] *adv* incognito ♦ *nm*: **garder l'~** to remain incognito
incohérent, e [ɛ̃kɔeʀɑ̃, ɑ̃t] *adj* (*comportement*) inconsistent; (*geste, langage, texte*) incoherent
incollable [ɛ̃kɔlabl] *adj* (*riz*) non-stick; **il est ~** (*fam*) he's got all the answers
incolore [ɛ̃kɔlɔʀ] *adj* colourless
incommoder [ɛ̃kɔmɔde] *vt* (*chaleur, odeur*): **~ qn** to bother sb
incomparable [ɛ̃kɔ̃paʀabl] *adj* incomparable
incompatible [ɛ̃kɔ̃patibl] *adj* incompatible
incompétent, e [ɛ̃kɔ̃petɑ̃, ɑ̃t] *adj* incompetent
incomplet, -ète [ɛ̃kɔ̃plɛ, ɛt] *adj* incomplete
incompréhensible [ɛ̃kɔ̃pʀeɑ̃sibl] *adj* incomprehensible
incompris, e [ɛ̃kɔ̃pʀi, iz] *adj* misunderstood
inconcevable [ɛ̃kɔ̃s(ə)vabl] *adj* inconceivable
inconciliable [ɛ̃kɔ̃siljabl] *adj* irreconcilable
inconditionnel, le [ɛ̃kɔ̃disjɔnɛl] *adj* unconditional; (*partisan*) unquestioning ♦ *nm/f* (*d'un homme politique*) ardent supporter; (*d'un écrivain, d'un chanteur*) ardent admirer; (*d'une activité*) fanatic
inconfort [ɛ̃kɔ̃fɔʀ] *nm* discomfort; **inconfortable** *adj* uncomfortable
incongru, e [ɛ̃kɔ̃gʀy] *adj* unseemly
inconnu, e [ɛ̃kɔny] *adj* unknown ♦ *nm/f* stranger ♦ *nm*: **l'~** the unknown; **inconnue** *nf* unknown factor
inconsciemment [ɛ̃kɔ̃sjamɑ̃] *adv* unconsciously
inconscient, e [ɛ̃kɔ̃sjɑ̃, jɑ̃t] *adj* unconscious; (*irréfléchi*) thoughtless, reckless; (*sentiment*) subconscious ♦ *nm* (*PSYCH*): **l'~** the unconscious; **~ de** unaware of
inconsidéré, e [ɛ̃kɔ̃sideʀe] *adj* ill-

considered

inconsistant, e [ɛ̃kɔ̃sistɑ̃, ɑ̃t] *adj* (*fig*) flimsy, weak

inconsolable [ɛ̃kɔ̃sɔlabl] *adj* inconsolable

incontestable [ɛ̃kɔ̃tɛstabl] *adj* indisputable

incontinent, e [ɛ̃kɔ̃tinɑ̃, ɑ̃t] *adj* incontinent

incontournable [ɛ̃kɔ̃tuʀnabl] *adj* unavoidable

incontrôlable [ɛ̃kɔ̃tʀolabl] *adj* unverifiable; (*irrépressible*) uncontrollable

inconvenant, e [ɛ̃kɔ̃v(ə)nɑ̃, ɑ̃t] *adj* unseemly, improper

inconvénient [ɛ̃kɔ̃venjɑ̃] *nm* disadvantage, drawback; **si vous n'y voyez pas d'~** if you have no objections

incorporer [ɛ̃kɔʀpɔʀe] *vt*: **~ (à)** to mix in (with); **~ (dans)** (*paragraphe etc*) to incorporate (in); (*MIL: appeler*) to recruit (into); **il a très bien su s'~ à notre groupe** he was very easily incorporated into our group

incorrect, e [ɛ̃kɔʀɛkt] *adj* (*impropre, inconvenant*) improper; (*défectueux*) faulty; (*inexact*) incorrect; (*impoli*) impolite; (*déloyal*) underhand

incorrigible [ɛ̃kɔʀiʒibl] *adj* incorrigible

incrédule [ɛ̃kʀedyl] *adj* incredulous; (*REL*) unbelieving

increvable [ɛ̃kʀəvabl] (*fam*) *adj* tireless

incriminer [ɛ̃kʀimine] *vt* (*personne*) to incriminate; (*action, conduite*) to bring under attack; (*bonne foi, honnêteté*) to call into question

incroyable [ɛ̃kʀwajabl] *adj* incredible

incruster [ɛ̃kʀyste] *vt* (*ART*) to inlay; **s'~** *vi* (*invité*) to take root

inculpé, e [ɛ̃kylpe] *nm/f* accused

inculper [ɛ̃kylpe] *vt*: **~ (de)** to charge (with)

inculquer [ɛ̃kylke] *vt*: **~ qch à** to inculcate sth in *ou* instil sth into

inculte [ɛ̃kylt] *adj* uncultivated; (*esprit, peuple*) uncultured

Inde [ɛ̃d] *nf*: **l'~** India

indécent, e [ɛ̃desɑ̃, ɑ̃t] *adj* indecent

indéchiffrable [ɛ̃deʃifʀabl] *adj* indecipherable

indécis, e [ɛ̃desi, iz] *adj* (*par nature*) indecisive; (*temporairement*) undecided

indéfendable [ɛ̃defɑ̃dabl] *adj* indefensible

indéfini, e [ɛ̃defini] *adj* (*imprécis, incertain*) undefined; (*illimité, LING*) indefinite; **indéfiniment** *adv* indefinitely; **indéfinissable** *adj* indefinable

indélébile [ɛ̃delebil] *adj* indelible

indélicat, e [ɛ̃delika, at] *adj* tactless

indemne [ɛ̃dɛmn] *adj* unharmed; **indemniser** *vt*: **indemniser qn (de)** to compensate sb (for)

indemnité [ɛ̃dɛmnite] *nf* (*dédommagement*) compensation *no pl*; (*allocation*) allowance; **indemnité de licenciement** redundancy payment

indépendamment [ɛ̃depɑ̃damɑ̃] *adv* independently; **~ de** (*abstraction faite de*) irrespective of; (*en plus de*) over and above

indépendance [ɛ̃depɑ̃dɑ̃s] *nf* independence

indépendant, e [ɛ̃depɑ̃dɑ̃, ɑ̃t] *adj* independent; **~ de** independent of

indescriptible [ɛ̃dɛskʀiptibl] *adj* indescribable

indésirable [ɛ̃deziʀabl] *adj* undesirable

indestructible [ɛ̃dɛstʀyktibl] *adj* indestructible

indétermination [ɛ̃detɛʀminasjɔ̃] *nf* (*irrésolution: chronique*) indecision; (*: temporaire*) indecisiveness

indéterminé, e [ɛ̃detɛʀmine] *adj* (*date, cause, nature*) unspecified; (*forme, longueur, quantité*) indeterminate

index [ɛ̃dɛks] *nm* (*doigt*) index finger; (*d'un livre etc*) index; **mettre à l'~** to blacklist; **indexé, e** *adj* (*ÉCON*): **indexé (sur)** index-linked (to)

indic [ɛ̃dik] (*fam*) *nm* (*POLICE*) grass

indicateur [ɛ̃dikatœʀ] *nm* (*POLICE*) informer; (*TECH*) gauge, indicator

indicatif, -ive [ɛ̃dikatif, iv] *adj*: **à titre**

~ for (your) information ♦ *nm* (LING) indicative; (RADIO) theme *ou* signature tune; (TÉL) dialling code
indication [ɛ̃dikasjɔ̃] *nf* indication; (*renseignement*) information *no pl*; **~s** *nfpl* (*directives*) instructions
indice [ɛ̃dis] *nm* (*marque, signe*) indication, sign; (POLICE: *lors d'une enquête*) clue; (JUR: *présomption*) piece of evidence; (SCIENCE, ÉCON, TECH) index
indicible [ɛ̃disibl] *adj* inexpressible
indien, ne [ɛ̃djɛ̃, jɛn] *adj* Indian ♦ *nm/f*: **I~, ne** Indian
indifféremment [ɛ̃difeʀamɑ̃] *adv* (*sans distinction*) equally (well)
indifférence [ɛ̃difeʀɑ̃s] *nf* indifference
indifférent, e [ɛ̃difeʀɑ̃, ɑ̃t] *adj* (*peu intéressé*) indifferent; **ça m'est ~** it doesn't matter to me; **elle m'est ~e** I am indifferent to her
indigence [ɛ̃diʒɑ̃s] *nf* poverty
indigène [ɛ̃diʒɛn] *adj* native, indigenous; (*des gens du pays*) local ♦ *nm/f* native
indigeste [ɛ̃diʒɛst] *adj* indigestible
indigestion [ɛ̃diʒɛstjɔ̃] *nf* indigestion *no pl*
indigne [ɛ̃diɲ] *adj* unworthy
indigner [ɛ̃diɲe] *vt*: **s'~ (de *ou* contre)** to get indignant (at)
indiqué, e [ɛ̃dike] *adj* (*date, lieu*) agreed; (*traitement*) appropriate; (*conseillé*) advisable
indiquer [ɛ̃dike] *vt* (*suj*: *pendule, aiguille*) to show; (: *étiquette, panneau*) to show, indicate; (*renseigner sur*) to point out, tell; (*déterminer*: *date, lieu*) to give, state; (*signaler, dénoter*) to indicate, point to; **~ qch/qn à qn** (*montrer du doigt*) to point sth/sb out to sb; (*faire connaître*: *médecin, restaurant*) to tell sb of sth/sb
indirect, e [ɛ̃diʀɛkt] *adj* indirect
indiscipliné, e [ɛ̃disipline] *adj* undisciplined
indiscret, -ète [ɛ̃diskʀɛ, ɛt] *adj* indiscreet
indiscutable [ɛ̃diskytabl] *adj* indisputable
indispensable [ɛ̃dispɑ̃sabl] *adj* indispensable, essential
indisposé, e [ɛ̃dispoze] *adj* indisposed
indisposer [ɛ̃dispoze] *vt* (*incommoder*) to upset; (*déplaire à*) to antagonize; (*énerver*) to irritate
indistinct, e [ɛ̃distɛ̃(kt), ɛ̃kt] *adj* indistinct; **indistinctement** *adv* (*voir, prononcer*) indistinctly; (*sans distinction*) indiscriminately
individu [ɛ̃dividy] *nm* individual; **individuel, le** *adj* (*gén*) individual; (*responsabilité, propriété, liberté*) personal; **chambre individuelle** single room; **maison individuelle** detached house
indolore [ɛ̃dɔlɔʀ] *adj* painless
indomptable [ɛ̃dɔ̃(p)tabl] *adj* untameable; (*fig*) invincible
Indonésie [ɛ̃dɔnezi] *nf* Indonesia
indu, e [ɛ̃dy] *adj*: **à une heure ~e** at some ungodly hour
induire [ɛ̃dɥiʀ] *vt*: **~ qn en erreur** to lead sb astray, mislead sb
indulgent, e [ɛ̃dylʒɑ̃, ɑ̃t] *adj* (*parent, regard*) indulgent; (*juge, examinateur*) lenient
industrialisé, e [ɛ̃dystʀijalize] *adj* industrialized
industrie [ɛ̃dystʀi] *nf* industry; **industriel, le** *adj* industrial ♦ *nm* industrialist
inébranlable [inebʀɑ̃labl] *adj* (*masse, colonne*) solid; (*personne, certitude, foi*) unshakeable
inédit, e [inedi, it] *adj* (*correspondance, livre*) hitherto unpublished; (*spectacle, moyen*) novel, original; (*film*) unreleased
ineffaçable [inefasabl] *adj* indelible
inefficace [inefikas] *adj* (*remède, moyen*) ineffective; (*machine, employé*) inefficient
inégal, e, -aux [inegal, o] *adj* unequal; (*irrégulier*) uneven; **inégalable** *adj* matchless; **inégalé, e** *adj* (*record*) unequalled; (*beauté*) unrivalled; **inégalité** *nf* inequality

inépuisable [inepɥizabl] *adj* inexhaustible
inerte [inɛʀt] *adj* (*immobile*) lifeless; (*sans réaction*) passive
inespéré, e [inɛspeʀe] *adj* unexpected, unhoped-for
inestimable [inɛstimabl] *adj* priceless; (*fig*: *bienfait*) invaluable
inévitable [inevitabl] *adj* unavoidable; (*fatal, habituel*) inevitable
inexact, e [inɛgza(kt), akt] *adj* inaccurate
inexcusable [inɛkskyzabl] *adj* unforgivable
inexplicable [inɛksplikabl] *adj* inexplicable
in extremis [inɛkstʀemis] *adv* at the last minute ♦ *adj* last-minute
infaillible [ɛ̃fajibl] *adj* infallible
infâme [ɛ̃fɑm] *adj* vile
infarctus [ɛ̃faʀktys] *nm*: **~ (du myocarde)** coronary (thrombosis)
infatigable [ɛ̃fatigabl] *adj* tireless
infect, e [ɛ̃fɛkt] *adj* revolting; (*personne*) obnoxious; (*temps*) foul
infecter [ɛ̃fɛkte] *vt* (*atmosphère, eau*) to contaminate; (*MÉD*) to infect; **s'~** to become infected *ou* septic; **infection** *nf* infection; (*puanteur*) stench
inférieur, e [ɛ̃feʀjœʀ] *adj* lower; (*en qualité, intelligence*) inferior; **~ à** (*somme, quantité*) less *ou* smaller than; (*moins bon que*) inferior to
infernal, e, -aux [ɛ̃fɛʀnal, o] *adj* (*insupportable*: *chaleur, rythme*) infernal; (: *enfant*) horrid; (*satanique, effrayant*) diabolical
infidèle [ɛ̃fidɛl] *adj* unfaithful
infiltrer [ɛ̃filtʀe] *vb*: **s'~ dans** to get into; (*liquide*) to seep through; (*fig*: *groupe, ennemi*) to infiltrate
infime [ɛ̃fim] *adj* minute, tiny
infini, e [ɛ̃fini] *adj* infinite ♦ *nm* infinity; **à l'~** endlessly; **infiniment** *adv* infinitely; **infinité** *nf*: **une infinité de** an infinite number of
infinitif [ɛ̃finitif, iv] *nm* infinitive
infirme [ɛ̃fiʀm] *adj* disabled ♦ *nm/f* disabled person
infirmerie [ɛ̃fiʀməʀi] *nf* medical room
infirmier, -ière [ɛ̃fiʀmje] *nm/f* nurse; **infirmière chef** sister
infirmité [ɛ̃fiʀmite] *nf* disability
inflammable [ɛ̃flamabl] *adj* (in)flammable
inflation [ɛ̃flasjɔ̃] *nf* inflation
infliger [ɛ̃fliʒe] *vt*: **~ qch (à qn)** to inflict sth (on sb); (*amende, sanction*) to impose sth (on sb)
influençable [ɛ̃flyɑ̃sabl] *adj* easily influenced
influence [ɛ̃flyɑ̃s] *nf* influence; **influencer** *vt* to influence; **influent, e** *adj* influential
informateur, -trice [ɛ̃fɔʀmatœʀ, tʀis] *nm/f* (*POLICE*) informer
informaticien, ne [ɛ̃fɔʀmatisjɛ̃, jɛn] *nm/f* computer scientist
information [ɛ̃fɔʀmasjɔ̃] *nf* (*renseignement*) piece of information; (*PRESSE, TV*: *nouvelle*) item of news; (*diffusion de renseignements , INFORM*) information; (*JUR*) inquiry, investigation; **~s** *nfpl* (*TV*) news *sg*
informatique [ɛ̃fɔʀmatik] *nf* (*technique*) data processing; (*science*) computer science ♦ *adj* computer *cpd*; **informatiser** *vt* to computerize
informe [ɛ̃fɔʀm] *adj* shapeless
informer [ɛ̃fɔʀme] *vt*: **~ qn (de)** to inform sb (of); **s'~ (de/si)** to inquire *ou* find out (about/whether *ou* if)
infos [ɛ̃fo] *nfpl*: **les ~** the news *sg*
infraction [ɛ̃fʀaksjɔ̃] *nf* offence; **~ à** violation *ou* breach of; **être en ~** to be in breach of the law
infranchissable [ɛ̃fʀɑ̃ʃisabl] *adj* impassable; (*fig*) insuperable
infrarouge [ɛ̃fʀaʀuʒ] *adj* infrared
infrastructure [ɛ̃fʀastʀyktyʀ] *nf* (*AVIAT, MIL*) ground installations *pl*; (*ÉCON*: *touristique etc*) infrastructure
infuser [ɛ̃fyze] *vt, vi* (*thé*) to brew; (*tisane*) to infuse; **infusion** *nf* (*tisane*)

herb tea
ingénier [ɛ̃ʒenje]: **s'~** *vi*: **s'~ à faire** to strive to do
ingénierie [ɛ̃ʒeniʀi] *nf* engineering; **~ génétique** genetic engineering
ingénieur [ɛ̃ʒenjœʀ] *nm* engineer; **ingénieur du son** sound engineer
ingénieux, -euse [ɛ̃ʒenjø, jøz] *adj* ingenious, clever
ingénu, e [ɛ̃ʒeny] *adj* ingenuous, artless
ingérer [ɛ̃ʒeʀe] *vb*: **s'~ dans** to interfere in
ingrat, e [ɛ̃gʀa, at] *adj* (*personne*) ungrateful; (*travail, sujet*) thankless; (*visage*) unprepossessing
ingrédient [ɛ̃gʀedjɑ̃] *nm* ingredient
ingurgiter [ɛ̃gyʀʒite] *vt* to swallow
inhabitable [inabitabl] *adj* uninhabitable
inhabité, e [inabite] *adj* uninhabited
inhabituel, le [inabitɥɛl] *adj* unusual
inhibition [inibisjɔ̃] *nf* inhibition
inhumain, e [inymɛ̃, ɛn] *adj* inhuman
inhumation [inymasjɔ̃] *nf* burial
inhumer [inyme] *vt* to inter, bury
inimaginable [inimaʒinabl] *adj* unimaginable
ininterrompu, e [inɛ̃teʀɔ̃py] *adj* (*file, série*) unbroken; (*flot, vacarme*) uninterrupted, non-stop; (*effort*) unremitting, continuous; (*suite, ligne*) unbroken
initial, e, -aux [inisjal, jo] *adj* initial; **initiale** *nf* initial; **initialiser** *vt* to initialize
initiation [inisjasjɔ̃] *nf*: **~ à** introduction to
initiative [inisjativ] *nf* initiative
initier [inisje] *vt*: **~ qn à** to initiate sb into; (*faire découvrir*: *art, jeu*) to introduce sb to
injecté, e [ɛ̃ʒɛkte] *adj*: **yeux ~s de sang** bloodshot eyes
injecter [ɛ̃ʒɛkte] *vt* to inject; **injection** *nf* injection; **à injection** (AUTO) fuel injection *cpd*
injure [ɛ̃ʒyʀ] *nf* insult, abuse *no pl*; **injurier** *vt* to insult, abuse; **injurieux, -euse** *adj* abusive, insulting
injuste [ɛ̃ʒyst] *adj* unjust, unfair; **injustice** *nf* injustice
inlassable [ɛ̃lɑsabl] *adj* tireless
inné, e [i(n)ne] *adj* innate, inborn
innocent, e [inɔsɑ̃, ɑ̃t] *adj* innocent; **innocenter** *vt* to clear, prove innocent
innombrable [i(n)nɔ̃bʀabl] *adj* innumerable
innommable [i(n)nɔmabl] *adj* unspeakable
innover [inɔve] *vi* to break new ground
inoccupé, e [inɔkype] *adj* unoccupied
inodore [inɔdɔʀ] *adj* (*gaz*) odourless; (*fleur*) scentless
inoffensif, -ive [inɔfɑ̃sif, iv] *adj* harmless, innocuous
inondation [inɔ̃dasjɔ̃] *nf* flood
inonder [inɔ̃de] *vt* to flood; **~ de** to flood with
inopiné, e [inɔpine] *adj* unexpected; (*mort*) sudden
inopportun, e [inɔpɔʀtœ̃, yn] *adj* ill-timed, untimely
inoubliable [inublijabl] *adj* unforgettable
inouï, e [inwi] *adj* unheard-of, extraordinary
inox [inɔks] *nm* stainless steel
inqualifiable [ɛ̃kalifjabl] *adj* unspeakable
inquiet, -ète [ɛ̃kjɛ, ɛ̃kjɛt] *adj* anxious; **inquiétant, e** *adj* worrying, disturbing; **inquiéter** *vt* to worry; **s'inquiéter** to worry; **s'inquiéter de** to worry about; (*s'enquérir de*) to inquire about; **inquiétude** *nf* anxiety
insaisissable [ɛ̃sezisabl] *adj* (*fugitif, ennemi*) elusive; (*différence, nuance*) imperceptible
insalubre [ɛ̃salybʀ] *adj* insalubrious
insatisfaisant, e [ɛ̃satisfəzɑ̃, ɑ̃t] *adj* unsatisfactory
insatisfait, e [ɛ̃satisfɛ, ɛt] *adj* (*non comblé*) unsatisfied; (*mécontent*) dissat-

isfied

inscription [ɛ̃skʀipsjɔ̃] *nf* inscription; (*immatriculation*) enrolment

inscrire [ɛ̃skʀiʀ] *vt* (*marquer: sur son calepin etc*) to note *ou* write down; (*: sur un mur, une affiche etc*) to write; (*: dans la pierre, le métal*) to inscribe; (*mettre: sur une liste, un budget etc*) to put down; **s'~** (*pour une excursion etc*) to put one's name down; **s'~ (à)** (*club, parti*) to join; (*université*) to register *ou* enrol (at); (*examen, concours*) to register (for); **~ qn à** (*club, parti*) to enrol sb at

insecte [ɛ̃sɛkt] *nm* insect; **insecticide** *nm* insecticide

insensé, e [ɛ̃sɑ̃se] *adj* mad

insensibiliser [ɛ̃sɑ̃sibilize] *vt* to anaesthetize

insensible [ɛ̃sɑ̃sibl] *adj* (*nerf, membre*) numb; (*dur, indifférent*) insensitive

inséparable [ɛ̃sepaʀabl] *adj* inseparable ♦ *nm*: **~s** (*oiseaux*) lovebirds

insigne [ɛ̃siɲ] *nm* (*d'un parti, club*) badge; (*d'une fonction*) insignia ♦ *adj* distinguished

insignifiant, e [ɛ̃siɲifjɑ̃, jɑ̃t] *adj* insignificant; trivial

insinuer [ɛ̃sinɥe] *vt* to insinuate; **s'~ dans** (*fig*) to worm one's way into

insipide [ɛ̃sipid] *adj* insipid

insister [ɛ̃siste] *vi* to insist; (*continuer à sonner*) to keep on trying; **~ sur** (*détail, sujet*) to lay stress on

insolation [ɛ̃sɔlasjɔ̃] *nf* (*MÉD*) sunstroke *no pl*

insolent, e [ɛ̃sɔlɑ̃, ɑ̃t] *adj* insolent

insolite [ɛ̃sɔlit] *adj* strange, unusual

insomnie [ɛ̃sɔmni] *nf* insomnia *no pl*

insonoriser [ɛ̃sɔnɔʀize] *vt* to soundproof

insouciant, e [ɛ̃susjɑ̃, jɑ̃t] *adj* carefree; **~ du danger** heedless of (the) danger

insoumis, e [ɛ̃sumi, iz] *adj* (*caractère, enfant*) rebellious, refractory; (*contrée, tribu*) unsubdued

insoupçonnable [ɛ̃supsɔnabl] *adj* unsuspected; (*personne*) above suspicion

insoupçonné, e [ɛ̃supsɔne] *adj* unsuspected

insoutenable [ɛ̃sut(ə)nabl] *adj* (*argument*) untenable; (*chaleur*) unbearable

inspecter [ɛ̃spɛkte] *vt* to inspect; **inspecteur, -trice** *nm/f* inspector; **inspecteur d'Académie** (regional) director of education; **inspecteur des finances** ≃ tax inspector (*BRIT*), ≃ Internal Revenue Service agent (*US*); **inspection** *nf* inspection

inspirer [ɛ̃spiʀe] *vt* (*gén*) to inspire ♦ *vi* (*aspirer*) to breathe in; **s'~ de** (*suj: artiste*) to draw one's inspiration from

instable [ɛ̃stabl] *adj* unstable; (*meuble, équilibre*) unsteady; (*temps*) unsettled

installation [ɛ̃stalasjɔ̃] *nf* installation; **~s** *nfpl* facilities

installer [ɛ̃stale] *vt* (*loger, placer*) to put; (*meuble, gaz, électricité*) to put in; (*rideau, étagère, tente*) to put up; (*appartement*) to fit out; **s'~** (*s'établir: artisan, dentiste etc*) to set o.s. up; (*se loger*) to settle; (*emménager*) to settle in; (*sur un siège, à un emplacement*) to settle (down); (*fig: maladie, grève*) to take a firm hold

instance [ɛ̃stɑ̃s] *nf* (*ADMIN: autorité*) authority; **affaire en ~** matter pending; **être en ~ de divorce** to be awaiting a divorce

instant [ɛ̃stɑ̃] *nm* moment, instant; **dans un ~** in a moment; **à l'~** this instant; **pour l'~** for the moment, for the time being

instantané, e [ɛ̃stɑ̃tane] *adj* (*lait, café*) instant; (*explosion, mort*) instantaneous ♦ *nm* snapshot

instar [ɛ̃staʀ]: **à l'~ de** *prép* following the example of, like

instaurer [ɛ̃stɔʀe] *vt* to institute; (*couvre-feu*) to impose

instinct [ɛ̃stɛ̃] *nm* instinct; **instinctivement** *adv* instinctively

instit [ɛ̃stit] (*fam*) *nm/f* (primary school) teacher

instituer [ɛ̃stitɥe] *vt* to establish
institut [ɛ̃stity] *nm* institute; **~ de beauté** beauty salon; **Institut universitaire de technologie** ≈ polytechnic
instituteur, -trice [ɛ̃stitytœʀ, tʀis] *nm/f* (primary school) teacher
institution [ɛ̃stitysjɔ̃] *nf* institution; (*collège*) private school
instructif, -ive [ɛ̃stʀyktif, iv] *adj* instructive
instruction [ɛ̃stʀyksjɔ̃] *nf* (*enseignement, savoir*) education; (JUR) (preliminary) investigation and hearing; **~s** *nfpl* (*ordres, mode d'emploi*) instructions; **~ civique** civics *sg*
instruire [ɛ̃stʀɥiʀ] *vt* (*élèves*) to teach; (*recrues*) to train; (JUR: *affaire*) to conduct the investigation for; **s'~** to educate o.s.; **instruit, e** *adj* educated
instrument [ɛ̃stʀymɑ̃] *nm* instrument; **~ à cordes/vent** stringed/wind instrument; **~ de mesure** measuring instrument; **~ de musique** musical instrument; **~ de travail** (working) tool
insu [ɛ̃sy] *nm*: **à l'~ de qn** without sb knowing (it)
insubmersible [ɛ̃sybmɛʀsibl] *adj* unsinkable
insuffisant, e [ɛ̃syfizɑ̃, ɑ̃t] *adj* (*en quantité*) insufficient; (*en qualité*) inadequate; (*sur une copie*) poor
insulaire [ɛ̃sylɛʀ] *adj* island *cpd*; (*attitude*) insular
insuline [ɛ̃sylin] *nf* insulin
insulte [ɛ̃sylt] *nf* insult; **insulter** *vt* to insult
insupportable [ɛ̃sypɔʀtabl] *adj* unbearable
insurger [ɛ̃syʀʒe] *vb*: **s'~ (contre)** to rise up *ou* rebel (against)
insurmontable [ɛ̃syʀmɔ̃tabl] *adj* (*difficulté*) insuperable; (*aversion*) unconquerable
insurrection [ɛ̃syʀɛksjɔ̃] *nf* insurrection
intact, e [ɛ̃takt] *adj* intact
intangible [ɛ̃tɑ̃ʒibl] *adj* intangible; (*principe*) inviolable
intarissable [ɛ̃taʀisabl] *adj* inexhaustible
intégral, e, -aux [ɛ̃tegʀal, o] *adj* complete; **texte ~** unabridged version; **bronzage ~** all-over suntan; **intégralement** *adv* in full; **intégralité** *nf* whole; **dans son intégralité** in full; **intégrant, e** *adj*: **faire partie intégrante de** to be an integral part of
intègre [ɛ̃tɛgʀ] *adj* upright
intégrer [ɛ̃tegʀe] *vt*: **bien s'~** to integrate well
intégrisme [ɛ̃tegʀism] *nm* fundamentalism
intellectuel, le [ɛ̃telɛktɥɛl] *adj* intellectual ♦ *nm/f* intellectual; (*péj*) highbrow
intelligence [ɛ̃teliʒɑ̃s] *nf* intelligence; (*compréhension*): **l'~ de** the understanding of; (*complicité*): **regard d'~** glance of complicity; (*accord*): **vivre en bonne ~ avec qn** to be on good terms with sb
intelligent, e [ɛ̃teliʒɑ̃, ɑ̃t] *adj* intelligent
intelligible [ɛ̃teliʒibl] *adj* intelligible
intempéries [ɛ̃tɑ̃peʀi] *nfpl* bad weather *sg*
intempestif, -ive [ɛ̃tɑ̃pɛstif, iv] *adj* untimely
intenable [ɛ̃t(ə)nabl] *adj* (*chaleur*) unbearable
intendant, e [ɛ̃tɑ̃dɑ̃] *nm/f* (MIL) quartermaster; (SCOL) bursar
intense [ɛ̃tɑ̃s] *adj* intense; **intensif, -ive** *adj* intensive; **un cours intensif** a crash course
intenter [ɛ̃tɑ̃te] *vt*: **~ un procès contre** *ou* **à** to start proceedings against
intention [ɛ̃tɑ̃sjɔ̃] *nf* intention; (JUR) intent; **avoir l'~ de faire** to intend to do; **à l'~ de** for; (*renseignement*) for the benefit of; (*film, ouvrage*) aimed at; **à cette ~** with this aim in view; **intentionné, e** *adj*: **bien intentionné** well-meaning *ou* -intentioned; **mal inten-**

tionné ill-intentioned
interactif, -ive [ɛ̃tɛʀaktif, iv] *adj* (*COMPUT*) interactive
intercalaire [ɛ̃tɛʀkalɛʀ] *nm* divider
intercaler [ɛ̃tɛʀkale] *vt* to insert
intercepter [ɛ̃tɛʀsɛpte] *vt* to intercept; (*lumière, chaleur*) to cut off
interchangeable [ɛ̃tɛʀʃɑ̃ʒabl] *adj* interchangeable
interclasse [ɛ̃tɛʀklɑs] *nm* (*SCOL*) break (between classes)
interdiction [ɛ̃tɛʀdiksjɔ̃] *nf* ban; **~ de stationner** no parking; **~ de fumer** no smoking
interdire [ɛ̃tɛʀdiʀ] *vt* to forbid; (*ADMIN*) to ban, prohibit; (: *journal, livre*) to ban; **~ à qn de faire** to forbid sb to do; (*suj: empêchement*) to prevent sb from doing
interdit, e [ɛ̃tɛʀdi, it] *adj* (*stupéfait*) taken aback
intéressant, e [ɛ̃teʀesɑ̃, ɑ̃t] *adj* interesting; (*avantageux*) attractive
intéressé, e [ɛ̃teʀese] *adj* (*parties*) involved, concerned; (*amitié, motifs*) self-interested
intéresser [ɛ̃teʀese] *vt* (*captiver*) to interest; (*toucher*) to be of interest to; (*ADMIN: concerner*) to affect, concern; **s'~ à** to be interested in
intérêt [ɛ̃teʀɛ] *nm* interest; (*égoïsme*) self-interest; **tu as ~ à accepter** it's in your interest to accept; **tu as ~ à te dépêcher** you'd better hurry
intérieur, e [ɛ̃teʀjœʀ] *adj* (*mur, escalier, poche*) inside; (*commerce, politique*) domestic; (*cour, calme, vie*) inner; (*navigation*) inland ♦ *nm* (*d'une maison, d'un récipient etc*) inside; (*d'un pays, aussi décor, mobilier*) interior; **à l'~ (de)** inside; **intérieurement** *adv* inwardly
intérim [ɛ̃teʀim] *nm* interim period; **faire de l'~** to temp; **assurer l'~ (de)** to deputize (for); **par ~** interim
intérimaire [ɛ̃teʀimɛʀ] *adj* (*directeur, ministre*) acting; (*secrétaire, personnel*) temporary ♦ *nm/f* (*secrétaire*) temporary secretary, temp (*BRIT*)
interlocuteur, -trice [ɛ̃tɛʀlɔkytœʀ, tʀis] *nm/f* speaker; **son ~** the person he was speaking to
interloquer [ɛ̃tɛʀlɔke] *vt* to take aback
intermède [ɛ̃tɛʀmɛd] *nm* interlude
intermédiaire [ɛ̃tɛʀmedjɛʀ] *adj* intermediate; (*solution*) temporary ♦ *nm/f* intermediary; (*COMM*) middleman; **sans ~** directly; **par l'~ de** through
interminable [ɛ̃tɛʀminabl] *adj* endless
intermittence [ɛ̃tɛʀmitɑ̃s] *nf*: **par ~** sporadically, intermittently
internat [ɛ̃tɛʀna] *nm* boarding school
international, e, -aux [ɛ̃tɛʀnasjɔnal, o] *adj, nm/f* international
interne [ɛ̃tɛʀn] *adj* internal ♦ *nm/f* (*SCOL*) boarder; (*MÉD*) houseman
interner [ɛ̃tɛʀne] *vt* (*POL*) to intern; (*MÉD*) to confine to a mental institution
Internet [ɛ̃tɛʀnɛt] *nm*: **l'~** the Internet
interpeller [ɛ̃tɛʀpəle] *vt* (*appeler*) to call out to; (*apostropher*) to shout at; (*POLICE, POL*) to question; (*concerner*) to concern
interphone [ɛ̃tɛʀfɔn] *nm* intercom; (*d'immeuble*) entry phone
interposer [ɛ̃tɛʀpoze] *vt*: **s'~** to intervene; **par personnes interposées** through a third party
interprétation [ɛ̃tɛʀpʀetasjɔ̃] *nf* interpretation
interprète [ɛ̃tɛʀpʀɛt] *nm/f* interpreter; (*porte-parole*) spokesperson
interpréter [ɛ̃tɛʀpʀete] *vt* to interpret; (*jouer*) to play; (*chanter*) to sing
interrogateur, -trice [ɛ̃teʀɔgatœʀ, tʀis] *adj* questioning, inquiring
interrogatif, -ive [ɛ̃teʀɔgatif, iv] *adj* (*LING*) interrogative
interrogation [ɛ̃teʀɔgasjɔ̃] *nf* question; (*action*) questioning; (*SCOL*) (written *ou* oral) test
interrogatoire [ɛ̃teʀɔgatwaʀ] *nm* (*POLICE*) questioning *no pl*; (*JUR, aussi fig*) cross-examination
interroger [ɛ̃teʀɔʒe] *vt* to question; (*IN-*

FORM) to consult; (*SCOL*) to test
interrompre [ɛ̃teʀɔ̃pʀ] *vt* (*gén*) to interrupt; (*négociations*) to break off; (*match*) to stop; **s'~** to break off; **interrupteur** *nm* switch; **interruption** *nf* interruption; (*pause*) break; **sans interruption** without stopping
intersection [ɛ̃tɛʀsɛksjɔ̃] *nf* intersection
interstice [ɛ̃tɛʀstis] *nm* crack; (*de volet*) slit
interurbain, e [ɛ̃teʀyʀbɛ̃, ɛn] *adj* (*TÉL*) long-distance
intervalle [ɛ̃tɛʀval] *nm* (*espace*) space; (*de temps*) interval; **à deux jours d'~** two days apart
intervenir [ɛ̃tɛʀvəniʀ] *vi* (*gén*) to intervene; **~ auprès de qn** to intervene with sb
intervention [ɛ̃tɛʀvɑ̃sjɔ̃] *nf* intervention; (*discours*) speech; **intervention chirurgicale** (surgical) operation
intervertir [ɛ̃tɛʀvɛʀtiʀ] *vt* to invert (the order of), reverse
interview [ɛ̃tɛʀvju] *nf* interview
intestin [ɛ̃tɛstɛ̃, in] *nm* intestine
intime [ɛ̃tim] *adj* intimate; (*vie*) private; (*conviction*) inmost; (*dîner, cérémonie*) quiet ♦ *nm/f* close friend; **un journal ~** a diary
intimider [ɛ̃timide] *vt* to intimidate
intimité [ɛ̃timite] *nf*: **dans l'~** in private; (*sans formalités*) with only a few friends, quietly
intitulé, e [ɛ̃tityle] *adj* entitled
intolérable [ɛ̃tɔleʀabl] *adj* intolerable
intox [ɛ̃tɔks] (*fam*) *nf* brainwashing
intoxication [ɛ̃tɔksikasjɔ̃] *nf*: **~ alimentaire** food poisoning
intoxiquer [ɛ̃tɔksike] *vt* to poison; (*fig*) to brainwash
intraduisible [ɛ̃tʀadɥizibl] *adj* untranslatable; (*fig*) inexpressible
intraitable [ɛ̃tʀɛtabl] *adj* inflexible, uncompromising
intranet [ɛ̃tʀanɛt] *nm* intranet
intransigeant, e [ɛ̃tʀɑ̃ziʒɑ̃, ɑ̃t] *adj* intransigent
intransitif, -ive [ɛ̃tʀɑ̃zitif, iv] *adj* (*LING*) intransitive
intrépide [ɛ̃tʀepid] *adj* dauntless
intrigue [ɛ̃tʀig] *nf* (*scénario*) plot; **intriguer** *vt* to puzzle, intrigue
intrinsèque [ɛ̃tʀɛ̃sɛk] *adj* intrinsic
introduction [ɛ̃tʀɔdyksjɔ̃] *nf* introduction
introduire [ɛ̃tʀɔdɥiʀ] *vt* to introduce; (*visiteur*) to show in; (*aiguille, clef*): **~ qch dans** to insert *ou* introduce sth into; **s'~ (dans)** to get in(to); (*dans un groupe*) to get o.s. accepted (into)
introuvable [ɛ̃tʀuvabl] *adj* which cannot be found; (*COMM*) unobtainable
introverti, e [ɛ̃tʀɔvɛʀti] *nm/f* introvert
intrus, e [ɛ̃tʀy, yz] *nm/f* intruder
intrusion [ɛ̃tʀyzjɔ̃] *nf* intrusion
intuition [ɛ̃tɥisjɔ̃] *nf* intuition
inusable [inyzabl] *adj* hard-wearing
inusité, e [inyzite] *adj* rarely used
inutile [inytil] *adj* useless; (*superflu*) unnecessary; **inutilement** *adv* unnecessarily; **inutilisable** *adj* unusable
invalide [ɛ̃valid] *adj* disabled ♦ *nm*: **~ de guerre** disabled ex-serviceman
invariable [ɛ̃vaʀjabl] *adj* invariable
invasion [ɛ̃vazjɔ̃] *nf* invasion
invectiver [ɛ̃vɛktive] *vt* to hurl abuse at
invendable [ɛ̃vɑ̃dabl] *adj* unsaleable; (*COMM*) unmarketable; **invendus** *nmpl* unsold goods
inventaire [ɛ̃vɑ̃tɛʀ] *nm* inventory; (*COMM*: *liste*) stocklist; (: *opération*) stocktaking *no pl*
inventer [ɛ̃vɑ̃te] *vt* to invent; (*subterfuge*) to devise, invent; (*histoire, excuse*) to make up, invent; **inventeur** *nm* inventor; **inventif, -ive** *adj* inventive; **invention** *nf* invention
inverse [ɛ̃vɛʀs] *adj* opposite ♦ *nm* opposite; **dans l'ordre ~** in the reverse order; **en sens ~** in (*ou* from) the opposite direction; **dans le sens ~ des aiguilles d'une montre** anticlockwise;

tu t'es trompé, c'est l'~ you've got it wrong, it's the other way round; **inversement** *adv* conversely; **inverser** *vt* to invert, reverse; (*ÉLEC*) to reverse
investigation [ɛ̃vɛstigasjɔ̃] *nf* investigation
investir [ɛ̃vɛstiʀ] *vt* to invest; **investissement** *nm* investment; **investiture** *nf* nomination
invétéré, e [ɛ̃veteʀe] *adj* inveterate
invisible [ɛ̃vizibl] *adj* invisible
invitation [ɛ̃vitasjɔ̃] *nf* invitation
invité, e [ɛ̃vite] *nm/f* guest
inviter [ɛ̃vite] *vt* to invite
invivable [ɛ̃vivabl] *adj* unbearable
involontaire [ɛ̃vɔlɔ̃tɛʀ] *adj* (*mouvement*) involuntary; (*insulte*) unintentional; (*complice*) unwitting
invoquer [ɛ̃vɔke] *vt* (*Dieu, muse*) to call upon, invoke; (*prétexte*) to put forward (as an excuse); (*loi, texte*) to refer to
invraisemblable [ɛ̃vʀɛsɑ̃blabl] *adj* (*fait, nouvelle*) unlikely, improbable; (*insolence, habit*) incredible
iode [jɔd] *nm* iodine
irai *etc* [iʀe] *vb voir* **aller**
Irak [iʀak] *nm* Iraq; **irakien, ne** *adj* Iraqi ♦ *nm/f*: **Irakien, ne** Iraqi
Iran [iʀɑ̃] *nm* Iran; **iranien, ne** *adj* Iranian ♦ *nm/f*: **Iranien, ne** Iranian
irascible [iʀasibl] *adj* short-tempered
irions *etc* [iʀjɔ̃] *vb voir* **aller**
iris [iʀis] *nm* iris
irlandais, e [iʀlɑ̃dɛ, ɛz] *adj* Irish ♦ *nm/f*: **Irlandais, e** Irishman(-woman); **les Irlandais** the Irish
Irlande [iʀlɑ̃d] *nf* Ireland; **~ du Nord** Northern Ireland; **la République d'~** the Irish Republic
ironie [iʀɔni] *nf* irony; **ironique** *adj* ironical; **ironiser** *vi* to be ironical
irons *etc* [iʀɔ̃] *vb voir* **aller**
irradier [iʀadje] *vt* to irradiate
irraisonné, e [iʀɛzɔne] *adj* irrational
irrationnel, le [iʀasjɔnɛl] *adj* irrational
irréalisable [iʀealizabl] *adj* unrealizable; (*projet*) impracticable
irrécupérable [iʀekypeʀabl] *adj* beyond repair; (*personne*) beyond redemption
irréductible [iʀedyktibl] *adj* (*volonté*) indomitable; (*ennemi*) implacable
irréel, le [iʀeɛl] *adj* unreal
irréfléchi, e [iʀefleʃi] *adj* thoughtless
irrégularité [iʀegylaʀite] *nf* irregularity; (*de travail, d'effort, de qualité*) unevenness *no pl*
irrégulier, -ière [iʀegylje, jɛʀ] *adj* irregular; (*travail, effort, qualité*) uneven; (*élève, athlète*) erratic
irrémédiable [iʀemedjabl] *adj* irreparable
irremplaçable [iʀɑ̃plasabl] *adj* irreplaceable
irréparable [iʀepaʀabl] *adj* (*objet*) beyond repair; (*dommage etc*) irreparable
irréprochable [iʀepʀɔʃabl] *adj* irreproachable, beyond reproach; (*tenue*) impeccable
irrésistible [iʀezistibl] *adj* irresistible; (*besoin, désir, preuve, logique*) compelling; (*amusant*) hilarious
irrésolu, e [iʀezɔly] *adj* (*personne*) irresolute; (*problème*) unresolved
irrespectueux, -euse [iʀɛspɛktɥø, øz] *adj* disrespectful
irrespirable [iʀɛspiʀabl] *adj* unbreathable; (*fig*) oppressive
irresponsable [iʀɛspɔ̃sabl] *adj* irresponsible
irriguer [iʀige] *vt* to irrigate
irritable [iʀitabl] *adj* irritable
irriter [iʀite] *vt* to irritate
irruption [iʀypsjɔ̃] *nf*: **faire ~ (chez qn)** to burst in (on sb)
Islam [islam] *nm* Islam; **islamique** *adj* Islamic; **islamiste** *adj* (*militant*) Islamic; (*mouvement*) Islamic fundamentalist ♦ *nm/f* Islamic fundamentalist
Islande [islɑ̃d] *nf* Iceland
isolant, e [izɔlɑ̃, ɑ̃t] *adj* insulating; (*insonorisant*) soundproofing
isolation [izɔlasjɔ̃] *nf* insulation
isolé, e [izɔle] *adj* isolated; (*contre le*

froid) insulated
isoler [izɔle] *vt* to isolate; (*prisonnier*) to put in solitary confinement; (*ville*) to cut off, isolate; (*contre le froid*) to insulate; **s'~** *vi* to isolate o.s.; **isoloir** [izɔlwaʀ] *nm* polling booth
Israël [isʀaɛl] *nm* Israel; **israélien, ne** *adj* Israeli ♦ *nm/f*: **Israélien, ne** Israeli; **israélite** *adj* Jewish ♦ *nm/f*: **Israélite** Jew (Jewess)
issu, e [isy] *adj*: **~ de** (*né de*) descended from; (*résultant de*) stemming from; **issue** *nf* (*ouverture, sortie*) exit; (*solution*) way out, solution; (*dénouement*) outcome; **à l'issue de** at the conclusion *ou* close of; **voie sans issue** dead end; **issue de secours** emergency exit
Italie [itali] *nf* Italy; **italien, ne** *adj* Italian ♦ *nm/f*: **Italien, ne** Italian ♦ *nm* (LING) Italian
italique [italik] *nm*: **en ~** in italics
itinéraire [itineʀɛʀ] *nm* itinerary, route; **~ bis** diversion
IUT *sigle m* = **Institut universitaire de technologie**
IVG *sigle f* (= *interruption volontaire de grossesse*) abortion
ivoire [ivwaʀ] *nm* ivory
ivre [ivʀ] *adj* drunk; **~ de** (*colère, bonheur*) wild with; **ivresse** *nf* drunkenness; **ivrogne** *nm/f* drunkard

J, j

j' [ʒ] *pron voir* **je**
jacasser [ʒakase] *vi* to chatter
jacinthe [ʒasɛ̃t] *nf* hyacinth
jadis [ʒɑdis] *adv* long ago
jaillir [ʒajiʀ] *vi* (*liquide*) to spurt out; (*cris, responses*) to burst forth
jais [ʒɛ] *nm* jet; **(d'un noir) de ~** jet-black
jalousie [ʒaluzi] *nf* jealousy; (*store*) slatted blind
jaloux, -ouse [ʒalu, uz] *adj* jealous
jamais [ʒamɛ] *adv* never; (*sans négation*) ever; **ne ... ~** never; **à ~** for ever
jambe [ʒɑ̃b] *nf* leg
jambon [ʒɑ̃bɔ̃] *nm* ham; **~ blanc** boiled *ou* cooked ham; **jambonneau, x** *nm* knuckle of ham
jante [ʒɑ̃t] *nf* (wheel) rim
janvier [ʒɑ̃vje] *nm* January
Japon [ʒapɔ̃] *nm* Japan; **japonais, e** *adj* Japanese ♦ *nm/f*: **Japonais, e** Japanese ♦ *nm* (LING) Japanese
japper [ʒape] *vi* to yap, yelp
jaquette [ʒakɛt] *nf* (*de cérémonie*) morning coat
jardin [ʒaʀdɛ̃] *nm* garden; **~ d'enfants** nursery school; **jardinage** *nm* gardening; **jardiner** *vi* to do some gardening; **jardinier, -ière** *nm/f* gardener; **jardinière** *nf* planter; (*de fenêtre*) window box; **jardinière de légumes** mixed vegetables
jargon [ʒaʀgɔ̃] *nm* (*baragouin*) gibberish; (*langue professionnelle*) jargon
jarret [ʒaʀɛ] *nm* back of knee; (CULIN) knuckle, shin
jarretelle [ʒaʀtɛl] *nf* suspender (BRIT), garter (US)
jarretière [ʒaʀtjɛʀ] *nf* garter
jaser [ʒɑze] *vi* (*médire*) to gossip
jatte [ʒat] *nf* basin, bowl
jauge [ʒoʒ] *nf* (*instrument*) gauge; **~ d'essence** petrol gauge; **~ d'huile** (oil) dipstick
jaune [ʒon] *adj, nm* yellow ♦ *adv* (*fam*): **rire ~** to laugh on the other side of one's face; **~ d'œuf** (egg) yolk; **jaunir** *vi, vt* to turn yellow; **jaunisse** *nf* jaundice
Javel [ʒavɛl] *nf voir* **eau**
javelot [ʒavlo] *nm* javelin
J.-C. *abr* = **Jésus-Christ**
je, j' [ʒə] *pron* I
jean [dʒin] *nm* jeans *pl*
Jésus-Christ [ʒezykʀi(st)] *n* Jesus Christ; **600 avant/après ~-~** *ou* **J.-C.** 600 B.C./A.D.
jet[1] [ʒɛ] *nm* (*lancer: action*) throwing *no*

pl; (: *résultat*) throw; (*jaillissement*: *d'eaux*) jet; (: *de sang*) spurt; **~ d'eau** spray

jet² [dʒɛt] *nm* (*avion*) jet

jetable [ʒ(ə)tabl] *adj* disposable

jetée [ʒəte] *nf* jetty; (*grande*) pier

jeter [ʒ(ə)te] *vt* (*gén*) to throw; (*se défaire de*) to throw away *ou* out; **se ~ dans** to flow into; **~ qch à qn** to throw sth to sb; (*de façon agressive*) to throw sth at sb; **~ un coup d'œil (à)** to take a look (at); **~ un sort à qn** to cast a spell on sb; **se ~ sur qn** to rush at sb

jeton [ʒ(ə)tɔ̃] *nm* (*au jeu*) counter

jette *etc* [ʒɛt] *vb voir* **jeter**

jeu, x [ʒø] *nm* (*divertissement*, TECH: *d'une pièce*) play; (TENNIS: *partie*, FOOTBALL *etc*: *façon de jouer*) game; (THÉÂTRE *etc*) acting; (*série d'objets, jouet*) set; (CARTES) hand; (*au casino*): **le ~** gambling; **être en ~** to be at stake; **entrer/mettre en ~** to come/bring into play; **~ de cartes** pack of cards; **~ d'échecs** chess set; **~ de hasard** game of chance; **~ de mots** pun; **~ de société** parlour game; **~ télévisé** television quiz; **~ vidéo** video game

jeudi [ʒødi] *nm* Thursday

jeun [ʒœ̃]: **à ~** *adv* on an empty stomach; **être à ~** to have eaten nothing; **rester à ~** not to eat anything

jeune [ʒœn] *adj* young; **les ~s** young people; **~ fille** girl; **~ homme** young man; **~s mariés** newly-weds

jeûne [ʒøn] *nm* fast

jeunesse [ʒœnɛs] *nf* youth; (*aspect*) youthfulness

joaillerie [ʒɔajʀi] *nf* jewellery; (*magasin*) jeweller's; **joaillier, -ière** *nm/f* jeweller

jogging [dʒɔgiŋ] *nm* jogging; (*survêtement*) tracksuit; **faire du ~** to go jogging

joie [ʒwa] *nf* joy

joindre [ʒwɛ̃dʀ] *vt* to join; (*à une lettre*): **~ qch à** to enclose sth with; (*contacter*) to contact, get in touch with; **se ~ à** to join; **~ les mains** to put one's hands together

joint, e [ʒwɛ̃, ɛ̃t] *adj*: **pièce ~e** enclosure ♦ *nm* joint; (*ligne*) join; **~ de culasse** cylinder head gasket; **~ de robinet** washer

joker [(d)ʒɔkɛʀ] *nm* (INFORM): (*caractère m*) ~ wildcard

joli, e [ʒɔli] *adj* pretty, attractive; **c'est du ~!** (*ironique*) that's very nice!; **c'est bien ~, mais ...** that's all very well but ...

jonc [ʒɔ̃] *nm* (bul)rush

jonction [ʒɔ̃ksjɔ̃] *nf* junction

jongleur, -euse [ʒɔ̃glœʀ, øz] *nm/f* juggler

jonquille [ʒɔ̃kij] *nf* daffodil

Jordanie [ʒɔʀdani] *nf*: **la ~** Jordan

joue [ʒu] *nf* cheek

jouer [ʒwe] *vt* to play; (*somme d'argent, réputation*) to stake, wager; (*simuler*: *sentiment*) to affect, feign ♦ *vi* to play; (*THÉÂTRE, CINÉMA*) to act; (*au casino*) to gamble; (*bois, porte*: *se voiler*) to warp; (*clef, pièce*: *avoir du jeu*) to be loose; **~ sur** (*miser*) to gamble on; **~ de** (*MUS*) to play; **~ à** (*jeu, sport, roulette*) to play; **~ un tour à qn** to play a trick on sb; **~ serré** to play a close game; **~ la comédie** to put on an act; **bien joué!** well done!; **on joue Hamlet au théâtre X** Hamlet is on at the X theatre

jouet [ʒwɛ] *nm* toy; **être le ~ de** (*illusion etc*) to be the victim of

joueur, -euse [ʒwœʀ, øz] *nm/f* player; **être beau ~** to be a good loser

joufflu, e [ʒufly] *adj* chubby-cheeked

joug [ʒu] *nm* yoke

jouir [ʒwiʀ] *vi* (*sexe*: *fam*) to come ♦ *vt*: **~ de** to enjoy; **jouissance** *nf* pleasure; (*JUR*) use

joujou [ʒuʒu] (*fam*) *nm* toy

jour [ʒuʀ] *nm* day; (*opposé à la nuit*) day, daytime; (*clarté*) daylight; (*fig*: *aspect*) light; (*ouverture*) gap; **au ~ le ~**

from day to day; **de nos ~s** these days; **du ~ au lendemain** overnight; **il fait ~** it's daylight; **au grand ~** (*fig*) in the open; **mettre au ~** to disclose; **mettre à ~** to update; **donner le ~ à** to give birth to; **voir le ~** to be born; **~ férié** public holiday; **~ de fête** holiday; **~ ouvrable** working day

journal, -aux [ʒuʀnal, o] *nm* (news)paper; (*spécialisé*) journal; (*intime*) diary; **~ de bord** log; **~ télévisé** television news *sg*

journalier, -ière [ʒuʀnalje, jɛʀ] *adj* daily; (*banal*) everyday

journalisme [ʒuʀnalism] *nm* journalism; **journaliste** *nm/f* journalist

journée [ʒuʀne] *nf* day; **faire la ~ continue** to work over lunch

journellement [ʒuʀnɛlmɑ̃] *adv* daily

joyau, x [ʒwajo] *nm* gem, jewel

joyeux, -euse [ʒwajø, øz] *adj* joyful, merry; **~ Noël!** merry Christmas!; **~ anniversaire!** happy birthday!

jubiler [ʒybile] *vi* to be jubilant, exult

jucher [ʒyʃe] *vt, vi* to perch

judas [ʒyda] *nm* (*trou*) spy-hole

judiciaire [ʒydisjɛʀ] *adj* judicial

judicieux, -euse [ʒydisjø, jøz] *adj* judicious

judo [ʒydo] *nm* judo

juge [ʒyʒ] *nm* judge; **~ d'instruction** examining (*BRIT*) *ou* committing (*US*) magistrate; **~ de paix** justice of the peace; **~ de touche** linesman

jugé [ʒyʒe]: **au ~** *adv* by guesswork

jugement [ʒyʒmɑ̃] *nm* judgment; (*JUR: au pénal*) sentence; (: *au civil*) decision

jugeote [ʒyʒɔt] (*fam*) *nf* commonsense

juger [ʒyʒe] *vt* to judge; (*estimer*) to consider; **~ qn/qch satisfaisant** to consider sb/sth (to be) satisfactory; **~ bon de faire** to see fit to do; **~ de** to appreciate

juif, -ive [ʒɥif, ʒɥiv] *adj* Jewish ♦ *nm/f*: **J~, ive** Jew (Jewess)

juillet [ʒɥijɛ] *nm* July

> **14 juillet**
>
> *In France,* **le 14 juillet** *is a national holiday commemorating the storming of the Bastille during the French Revolution, celebrated by parades, music, dancing and firework displays. In Paris, there is a military parade along the Champs-Élysées, attended by the President.*

juin [ʒɥɛ̃] *nm* June

jumeau, -elle, x [ʒymo, ɛl] *adj, nm/f* twin

jumeler [ʒym(ə)le] *vt* to twin

jumelle [ʒymɛl] *adj, nf voir* **jumeau**; **~s** *nfpl* (*appareil*) binoculars

jument [ʒymɑ̃] *nf* mare

jungle [ʒœ̃gl] *nf* jungle

jupe [ʒyp] *nf* skirt

jupon [ʒypɔ̃] *nm* waist slip

juré, e [ʒyʀe] *nm/f* juror

jurer [ʒyʀe] *vt* (*obéissance etc*) to swear, vow ♦ *vi* (*dire des jurons*) to swear, curse; (*dissoner*): **~ (avec)** to clash (with); **~ de faire/que** to swear to do/that; **~ de qch** (*s'en porter garant*) to swear to sth

juridique [ʒyʀidik] *adj* legal

juron [ʒyʀɔ̃] *nm* curse, swearword

jury [ʒyʀi] *nm* jury; (*ART, SPORT*) panel of judges; (*SCOL*) board of examiners

jus [ʒy] *nm* juice; (*de viande*) gravy, (meat) juice; **~ de fruit** fruit juice

jusque [ʒysk]: **jusqu'à** *prép* (*endroit*) as far as, (up) to; (*moment*) until, till; (*limite*) up to; **~ sur/dans** up to; (*y compris*) even on/in; **jusqu'à ce que** until; **jusqu'à présent** so far; **jusqu'où?** how far?

justaucorps [ʒystokɔʀ] *nm* leotard

juste [ʒyst] *adj* (*équitable*) just, fair; (*légitime*) just; (*exact*) right; (*pertinent*) apt; (*étroit*) tight; (*insuffisant*) on the short side ♦ *adv* rightly, correctly; (*chanter*) in tune; (*exactement, seulement*) just; **~ assez/au-dessus** just

enough/above; **au ~** exactly; **le ~ milieu** the happy medium; **c'était ~** it was a close thing; **justement** *adv* justly; (*précisément*) just, precisely; **justesse** *nf* (*précision*) accuracy; (*d'une remarque*) aptness; (*d'une opinion*) soundness; **de justesse** only just
justice [ʒystis] *nf* (*équité*) fairness, justice; (ADMIN) justice; **rendre ~ à qn** to do sb justice; **justicier, -ière** *nm/f* righter of wrongs
justificatif, -ive [ʒystifikatif, iv] *adj* (*document*) supporting; **pièce justificative** written proof
justifier [ʒystifje] *vt* to justify; **~ de** to prove
juteux, -euse [ʒytø, øz] *adj* juicy
juvénile [ʒyvenil] *adj* youthful

K, k

K [kɑ] *nm* (INFORM) K
kaki [kaki] *adj inv* khaki
kangourou [kɑ̃guʀu] *nm* kangaroo
karaté [kaʀate] *nm* karate
karting [kaʀtiŋ] *nm* go-carting, karting
kascher [kaʃɛʀ] *adj* kosher
kayak [kajak] *nm* canoe, kayak; **faire du ~** to go canoeing
kermesse [kɛʀmɛs] *nf* fair; (*fête de charité*) bazaar, (charity) fête
kidnapper [kidnape] *vt* to kidnap
kilo [kilo] *nm* = **kilogramme**
kilo...: kilobit *nm* kilobit; **kilogramme** *nm* kilogramme; **kilométrage** *nm* number of kilometres travelled, ≃ mileage; **kilomètre** *nm* kilometre; **kilométrique** *adj* (*distance*) in kilometres
kinésithérapeute [kineziteʀapøt] *nm/f* physiotherapist
kiosque [kjɔsk] *nm* kiosk, stall; **~ à musique** bandstand
kir [kiʀ] *nm* kir (*white wine with blackcurrant liqueur*)
kit [kit] *nm*: **en ~** in kit form
klaxon [klaksɔn] *nm* horn; **klaxonner** *vi, vt* to hoot (BRIT), honk (US)
km *abr* = **kilomètre**
km/h *abr* (= *kilomètres/heure*) ≃ mph
K.-O. (*fam*) *adj inv* shattered, knackered
Kosovo [kɔsɔvo] *nm* Kosovo
k-way ® [kawɛ] *nm* (lightweight nylon) cagoule
kyste [kist] *nm* cyst

L, l

l' [l] *art déf voir* **le**
la [la] *art déf voir* **le** ♦ *nm* (MUS) A; (*en chantant la gamme*) la
là [la] *adv* there; (*ici*) here; (*dans le temps*) then; **elle n'est pas ~** she isn't here; **c'est ~ que** this is where; **~ où** where; **de ~** (*fig*) hence; **par ~** (*fig*) by that; *voir aussi* **-ci**; **ce**; **celui**; **là-bas** *adv* there
label [labɛl] *nm* stamp, seal
labeur [labœʀ] *nm* toil *no pl*, toiling *no pl*
labo [labo] (*fam*) *nm* (= *laboratoire*) lab
laboratoire [labɔʀatwaʀ] *nm* laboratory; **~ de langues** language laboratory
laborieux, -euse [labɔʀjø, jøz] *adj* (*tâche*) laborious
labour [labuʀ] *nm* ploughing *no pl*; **~s** *nmpl* (*champs*) ploughed fields; **cheval de ~** plough- *ou* cart-horse; **labourer** *vt* to plough
labyrinthe [labiʀɛ̃t] *nm* labyrinth, maze
lac [lak] *nm* lake
lacer [lase] *vt* to lace *ou* do up
lacérer [laseʀe] *vt* to tear to shreds
lacet [lasɛ] *nm* (*de chaussure*) lace; (*de route*) sharp bend; (*piège*) snare
lâche [lɑʃ] *adj* (*poltron*) cowardly; (*desserré*) loose, slack ♦ *nm/f* coward
lâcher [lɑʃe] *vt* to let go of; (*ce qui tombe, abandonner*) to drop; (*oiseau, animal: libérer*) to release, set free; (*fig: mot, remarque*) to let slip, come out

with ♦ *vi* (*freins*) to fail; **~ les amarres** (*NAVIG*) to cast off (the moorings); **~ prise** to let go
lâcheté [lɑʃte] *nf* cowardice
lacrymogène [lakʀimɔʒɛn] *adj*: **gaz ~** teargas
lacté, e [lakte] *adj* (*produit, régime*) milk *cpd*
lacune [lakyn] *nf* gap
là-dedans [ladədɑ̃] *adv* inside (there), in it; (*fig*) in that
là-dessous [ladsu] *adv* underneath, under there; (*fig*) behind that
là-dessus [ladsy] *adv* on there; (*fig: sur ces mots*) at that point; (: *à ce sujet*) about that
ladite [ladit] *dét voir* **ledit**
lagune [lagyn] *nf* lagoon
là-haut [lao] *adv* up there
laïc [laik] *adj, nm/f* = **laïque**
laid, e [lɛ, lɛd] *adj* ugly; **laideur** *nf* ugliness *no pl*
lainage [lɛnaʒ] *nm* (*vêtement*) woollen garment; (*étoffe*) woollen material
laine [lɛn] *nf* wool
laïque [laik] *adj* lay, civil; (*SCOL*) state *cpd* ♦ *nm/f* layman(-woman)
laisse [lɛs] *nf* (*de chien*) lead, leash; **tenir en ~** to keep on a lead *ou* leash
laisser [lese] *vt* to leave ♦ *vb aux*: **~ qn faire** to let sb do; **se ~ aller** to let o.s. go; **laisse-toi faire** let me (*ou* him *etc*) do it; **laisser-aller** *nm* carelessness, slovenliness; **laissez-passer** *nm inv* pass
lait [lɛ] *nm* milk; **frère/sœur de ~** foster brother/sister; **~ condensé/concentré** evaporated/condensed milk; **~ démaquillant** cleansing milk; **laitage** *nm* dairy product; **laiterie** *nf* dairy; **laitier, -ière** *adj* dairy *cpd* ♦ *nm/f* milkman (dairywoman)
laiton [lɛtɔ̃] *nm* brass
laitue [lety] *nf* lettuce
laïus [lajys] (*péj*) *nm* spiel
lambeau, x [lɑ̃bo] *nm* scrap; **en ~x** in tatters, tattered
lambris [lɑ̃bʀi] *nm* panelling *no pl*
lame [lam] *nf* blade; (*vague*) wave; (*~lle*) strip; **~ de fond** ground swell *no pl*; **~ de rasoir** razor blade; **lamelle** *nf* thin strip *ou* blade
lamentable [lamɑ̃tabl] *adj* appalling
lamenter [lamɑ̃te] *vb*: **se ~ (sur)** to moan (over)
lampadaire [lɑ̃padɛʀ] *nm* (*de salon*) standard lamp; (*dans la rue*) street lamp
lampe [lɑ̃p] *nf* lamp; (*TECH*) valve; **~ à souder** blowlamp; **~ de chevet** bedside lamp; **~ de poche** torch (*BRIT*), flashlight (*US*)
lampion [lɑ̃pjɔ̃] *nm* Chinese lantern
lance [lɑ̃s] *nf* spear; **~ d'incendie** fire hose
lancée [lɑ̃se] *nf*: **être/continuer sur sa ~** to be under way/keep going
lancement [lɑ̃smɑ̃] *nm* launching
lance-pierres [lɑ̃spjɛʀ] *nm inv* catapult
lancer [lɑ̃se] *nm* (*SPORT*) throwing *no pl*, throw ♦ *vt* to throw; (*émettre, projeter*) to throw out, send out; (*produit, fusée, bateau, artiste*) to launch; (*injure*) to hurl, fling; **se ~** *vi* (*prendre de l'élan*) to build up speed; (*se précipiter*): **se ~ sur** *ou* **contre** to rush at; **se ~ dans** (*discussion*) to launch into; (*aventure*) to embark on; **~ qch à qn** to throw sth to sb; (*de façon agressive*) to throw sth at sb; **~ du poids** putting the shot
lancinant, e [lɑ̃sinɑ̃, ɑ̃t] *adj* (*douleur*) shooting
landau [lɑ̃do] *nm* pram (*BRIT*), baby carriage (*US*)
lande [lɑ̃d] *nf* moor
langage [lɑ̃gaʒ] *nm* language
langouste [lɑ̃gust] *nf* crayfish *inv*; **langoustine** *nf* Dublin Bay prawn
langue [lɑ̃g] *nf* (*ANAT, CULIN*) tongue; (*LING*) language; **tirer la ~ (à)** to stick out one's tongue (at); **de ~ française** French-speaking; **~ maternelle** native language, mother tongue; **~ vivante/étrangère** modern/foreign language

langueur [lɑ̃gœʀ] *nf* languidness
languir [lɑ̃giʀ] *vi* to languish; (*conversation*) to flag; **faire ~ qn** to keep sb waiting
lanière [lanjɛʀ] *nf* (*de fouet*) lash; (*de sac, bretelle*) strap
lanterne [lɑ̃tɛʀn] *nf* (*portable*) lantern; (*électrique*) light, lamp; (*de voiture*) (side)light
laper [lape] *vt* to lap up
lapidaire [lapidɛʀ] *adj* (*fig*) terse
lapin [lapɛ̃] *nm* rabbit; (*peau*) rabbitskin; (*fourrure*) cony; **poser un ~ à qn** (*fam*) to stand sb up
Laponie [laponi] *nf* Lapland
laps [laps] *nm*: **~ de temps** space of time, time *no pl*
laque [lak] *nf* (*vernis*) lacquer; (*pour cheveux*) hair spray
laquelle [lakɛl] *pron voir* **lequel**
larcin [laʀsɛ̃] *nm* theft
lard [laʀ] *nm* (*bacon*) (streaky) bacon; (*graisse*) fat
lardon [laʀdɔ̃] *nm*: **~s** chopped bacon
large [laʀʒ] *adj* wide, broad; (*fig*) generous ♦ *adv*: **calculer/voir ~** to allow extra/think big ♦ *nm* (*largeur*): **5 m de ~** 5 m wide *ou* in width; (*mer*): **le ~** the open sea; **au ~ de** off; **~ d'esprit** broad-minded; **largement** *adv* widely; (*de loin*) greatly; (*au moins*) easily; (*généreusement*) generously; **c'est largement suffisant** that's ample; **largesse** *nf* generosity; **largesses** *nfpl* (*dons*) liberalities; **largeur** *nf* (*qu'on mesure*) width; (*impression visuelle*) wideness, width; (*d'esprit*) broadness
larguer [laʀge] *vt* to drop; **~ les amarres** to cast off (the moorings)
larme [laʀm] *nf* tear; (*fam: goutte*) drop; **en ~s** in tears; **larmoyer** *vi* (*yeux*) to water; (*se plaindre*) to whimper
larvé, e [laʀve] *adj* (*fig*) latent
laryngite [laʀɛ̃ʒit] *nf* laryngitis
las, lasse [lɑ, lɑs] *adj* weary
laser [lazɛʀ] *nm*: **(rayon) ~** laser (beam); **chaîne ~** compact disc (player); **disque ~** compact disc
lasse [lɑs] *adj voir* **las**
lasser [lɑse] *vt* to weary, tire; **se ~ de** *vt* to grow weary *ou* tired of
latéral, e, -aux [lateʀal, o] *adj* side *cpd*, lateral
latin, e [latɛ̃, in] *adj* Latin ♦ *nm/f*: **L~, e** Latin ♦ *nm* (LING) Latin
latitude [latityd] *nf* latitude
latte [lat] *nf* lath, slat; (*de plancher*) board
lauréat, e [lɔʀea, at] *nm/f* winner
laurier [lɔʀje] *nm* (BOT) laurel; (CULIN) bay leaves *pl*
lavable [lavabl] *adj* washable
lavabo [lavabo] *nm* washbasin; **~s** *nmpl* (*toilettes*) toilet *sg*
lavage [lavaʒ] *nm* washing *no pl*, wash; **~ de cerveau** brainwashing *no pl*
lavande [lavɑ̃d] *nf* lavender
lave [lav] *nf* lava *no pl*
lave-linge [lavlɛ̃ʒ] *nm inv* washing machine
laver [lave] *vt* to wash; (*tache*) to wash off; **se ~** *vi* to have a wash, wash; **se ~ les mains/dents** to wash one's hands/clean one's teeth; **~ qn de** (*accusation*) to clear sb of; **laverie** *nf*: **laverie (automatique)** launderette; **lavette** *nf* dish cloth; (*fam*) drip; **laveur, -euse** *nm/f* cleaner; **lave-vaisselle** *nm inv* dishwasher; **lavoir** *nm* wash house; (*évier*) sink
laxatif, -ive [laksatif, iv] *adj, nm* laxative
layette [lɛjɛt] *nf* baby clothes

MOT-CLÉ

le [lə], **la, l'** (*pl* **les**) *art déf* **1** the; **le livre/la pomme/l'arbre** the book/the apple/the tree; **les étudiants** the students

2 (*noms abstraits*): **le courage/l'amour/la jeunesse** courage/love/youth

3 (*indiquant la possession*): **se casser la**

jambe *etc* to break one's leg *etc*; **levez la main** put your hand up; **avoir les yeux gris/le nez rouge** to have grey eyes/a red nose

4 (*temps*): **le matin/soir** in the morning/evening; mornings/evenings; **le jeudi** *etc* (*d'habitude*) on Thursdays *etc*; (*ce jeudi-là etc*) on (the) Thursday

5 (*distribution, évaluation*) a, an; **10 F le mètre/kilo** 10F a *ou* per metre/kilo; **le tiers/quart de** a third/quarter of

♦ *pron* **1** (*personne*: *mâle*) him; (*personne*: *femelle*) her; (: *pluriel*) them; **je le/la/les vois** I can see him/her/them

2 (*animal, chose*: *singulier*) it; (: *pluriel*) them; **je le** (*ou* **la**) **vois** I can see it; **je les vois** I can see them

3 (*remplaçant une phrase*): **je ne le savais pas** I didn't know (about it); **il était riche et ne l'est plus** he was once rich but no longer is

lécher [leʃe] *vt* to lick; (*laper*: *lait, eau*) to lick *ou* lap up; **lèche-vitrines** *nm*: **faire du lèche-vitrines** to go window-shopping

leçon [l(ə)sɔ̃] *nf* lesson; **faire la ~ à** (*fig*) to give a lecture to; **~s de conduite** driving lessons

lecteur, -trice [lɛktœʀ, tʀis] *nm/f* reader; (*d'université*) foreign language assistant ♦ *nm* (*TECH*): **~ de cassettes/CD** cassette/CD player; **~ de disquette** disk drive

lecture [lɛktyʀ] *nf* reading

ledit [lədi], **ladite** (*mpl* **lesdits**, *fpl* **lesdites**) *dét* the aforesaid

légal, e, -aux [legal, o] *adj* legal; **légaliser** *vt* to legalize; **légalité** *nf* law

légendaire [leʒɑ̃dɛʀ] *adj* legendary

légende [leʒɑ̃d] *nf* (*mythe*) legend; (*de carte, plan*) key; (*de dessin*) caption

léger, -ère [leʒe, ɛʀ] *adj* light; (*bruit, retard*) slight; (*personne*: *superficiel*) thoughtless; (: *volage*) free and easy; **à la légère** (*parler, agir*) rashly, thoughtlessly; **légèrement** *adv* (*s'habiller, bouger*) lightly; (*un peu*) slightly; **manger légèrement** to eat a light meal; **légèreté** *nf* lightness; (*d'une remarque*) flippancy

Légion d'honneur

Created by Napoleon in 1802 to reward service to the state, **la Légion d'honneur** *is a prestigious French order headed by the President of the Republic, the Grand Maître. Members receive an annual tax-free payment.*

législatif, -ive [leʒislatif, iv] *adj* legislative; **législatives** *nfpl* general election *sg*

légitime [leʒitim] *adj* (*JUR*) lawful, legitimate; (*fig*) rightful, legitimate; **en état de ~ défense** in self-defence

legs [lɛg] *nm* legacy

léguer [lege] *vt*: **~ qch à qn** (*JUR*) to bequeath sth to sb

légume [legym] *nm* vegetable

lendemain [lɑ̃dmɛ̃] *nm*: **le ~** the next *ou* following day; **le ~ matin/soir** the next *ou* following morning/evening; **le ~ de** the day after

lent, e [lɑ̃, lɑ̃t] *adj* slow; **lentement** *adv* slowly; **lenteur** *nf* slowness *no pl*

lentille [lɑ̃tij] *nf* (*OPTIQUE*) lens *sg*; (*CULIN*) lentil

léopard [leɔpaʀ] *nm* leopard

lèpre [lɛpʀ] *nf* leprosy

MOT-CLÉ

lequel, laquelle [ləkɛl, lakɛl] (*mpl* **lesquels**, *fpl* **lesquelles**) (*à + lequel* = **auquel**, *de + lequel* = **duquel** *etc*) *pron* **1** (*interrogatif*) which, which one

2 (*relatif*: *personne*: *sujet*) who; (: *objet, après préposition*) whom; (: *chose*) which

♦ *adj*: **auquel cas** in which case

les [le] *dét voir* **le**

lesbienne [lɛsbjɛn] *nf* lesbian

lesdites [ledit], **lesdits** [ledi] *dét pl*

voir **ledit**

léser [leze] *vt* to wrong

lésiner [lezine] *vi*: **ne pas ~ sur les moyens** (*pour mariage etc*) to push the boat out

lésion [lezjɔ̃] *nf* lesion, damage *no pl*

lesquelles, lesquels [lekɛl] *pron pl voir* **lequel**

lessive [lesiv] *nf* (*poudre*) washing powder; (*linge*) washing *no pl*, wash; **lessiver** *vt* to wash; (*fam*: *fatiguer*) to tire out, exhaust

lest [lɛst] *nm* ballast

leste [lɛst] *adj* sprightly, nimble

lettre [lɛtʀ] *nf* letter; **~s** *nfpl* (*littérature*) literature *sg*; (SCOL) arts (subjects); **à la ~** literally; **en toutes ~s** in full

leucémie [løsemi] *nf* leukaemia

MOT-CLÉ

leur [lœʀ] *adj possessif* their; **leur maison** their house; **leurs amis** their friends

♦ *pron* **1** (*objet indirect*) (to) them; **je leur ai dit la vérité** I told them the truth; **je le leur ai donné** I gave it to them, I gave them it

2 (*possessif*): **le(la) leur, les leurs** theirs

---

leurre [lœʀ] *nm* (*fig*: *illusion*) delusion; (: *duperie*) deception; **leurrer** *vt* to delude, deceive

leurs [lœʀ] *adj voir* **leur**

levain [ləvɛ̃] *nm* leaven

levé, e [ləve] *adj*: **être ~** to be up; **levée** *nf* (POSTES) collection

lever [l(ə)ve] *vt* (*vitre, bras etc*) to raise; (*soulever de terre, supprimer*: *interdiction, siège*) to lift; (*impôts, armée*) to levy ♦ *vi* to rise ♦ *nm*: **au ~** on getting up; **se ~** *vi* to get up; (*soleil*) to rise; (*jour*) to break; (*brouillard*) to lift; **~ de soleil** sunrise; **~ du jour** daybreak

levier [ləvje] *nm* lever

lèvre [lɛvʀ] *nf* lip

lévrier [levʀije] *nm* greyhound

levure [l(ə)vyʀ] *nf* yeast; **~ chimique** baking powder

lexique [lɛksik] *nm* vocabulary; (*glossaire*) lexicon

lézard [lezaʀ] *nm* lizard

lézarde [lezaʀd] *nf* crack

liaison [ljɛzɔ̃] *nf* (*rapport*) connection; (*transport*) link; (*amoureuse*) affair; (PHONÉTIQUE) liaison; **entrer/être en ~ avec** to get/be in contact with

liane [ljan] *nf* creeper

liant, e [ljɑ̃, ljɑ̃t] *adj* sociable

liasse [ljas] *nf* wad, bundle

Liban [libɑ̃] *nm*: **le ~** (the) Lebanon; **libanais, e** *adj* Lebanese ♦ *nm/f*: **Libanais, e** Lebanese

libeller [libele] *vt* (*chèque, mandat*): **~ (au nom de)** to make out (to); (*lettre*) to word

libellule [libelyl] *nf* dragonfly

libéral, e, -aux [libeʀal, o] *adj, nm/f* liberal; **profession ~e** (liberal) profession

libérer [libeʀe] *vt* (*délivrer*) to free, liberate; (*relâcher*: *prisonnier*) to discharge, release; (: *d'inhibitions*) to liberate; (*gaz*) to release; **se ~** *vi* (*de rendez-vous*) to get out of previous engagements

liberté [libɛʀte] *nf* freedom; (*loisir*) free time; **~s** *nfpl* (*privautés*) liberties; **mettre/être en ~** to set/be free; **en ~ provisoire/surveillée/conditionnelle** on bail/probation/parole

libraire [libʀɛʀ] *nm/f* bookseller

librairie [libʀeʀi] *nf* bookshop

libre [libʀ] *adj* free; (*route, voie*) clear; (*place, salle*) free; (*ligne*) not engaged; (SCOL) non-state; **~ de qch/de faire** free from sth/to do; **~ arbitre** free will; **libre-échange** *nm* free trade; **libre-service** *nm* self-service store

Libye [libi] *nf*: **la ~** Libya

licence [lisɑ̃s] *nf* (*permis*) permit; (*diplôme*) degree; (*liberté*) liberty; **licencié, e** *nm/f* (SCOL): **licencié ès lettres/en droit** ≃ Bachelor of Arts/Law

licenciement [lisɑ̃simɑ̃] *nm* redundancy
licencier [lisɑ̃sje] *vt* (*débaucher*) to make redundant; (*renvoyer*) to dismiss
licite [lisit] *adj* lawful
lie [li] *nf* dregs *pl*, sediment
lié, e [lje] *adj*: **très ~ avec** very friendly with *ou* close to
liège [ljɛʒ] *nm* cork
lien [ljɛ̃] *nm* (*corde, fig: affectif*) bond; (*rapport*) link, connection; **~ de parenté** family tie
lier [lje] *vt* (*attacher*) to tie up; (*joindre*) to link up; (*fig: unir, engager*) to bind; **se ~ avec** to make friends with; **~ qch à** to tie *ou* link sth to; **~ conversation avec** to strike up a conversation with
lierre [ljɛʀ] *nm* ivy
liesse [ljɛs] *nf*: **être en ~** to be celebrating *ou* jubilant
lieu, x [ljø] *nm* place; **~x** *nmpl* (*locaux*) premises; (*endroit: d'un accident etc*) scene *sg*; **en ~ sûr** in a safe place; **en premier ~** in the first place; **en dernier ~** lastly; **avoir ~** to take place; **tenir ~ de** to serve as; **donner ~ à** to give rise to; **au ~ de** instead of; **lieu-dit** (*pl* **lieux-dits**) *nm* locality
lieutenant [ljøt(ə)nɑ̃] *nm* lieutenant
lièvre [ljɛvʀ] *nm* hare
ligament [ligamɑ̃] *nm* ligament
ligne [liɲ] *nf* (*gén*) line; (*TRANSPORTS: liaison*) service; (*: trajet*) route; (*silhouette*) figure; **entrer en ~ de compte** to come into it; **en ~** (*INFORM*) online; **~ fixe** (*TEL*) fixed line (phone)
lignée [liɲe] *nf* line, lineage
ligoter [ligɔte] *vt* to tie up
ligue [lig] *nf* league; **liguer** *vt*: **se liguer contre** (*fig*) to combine against
lilas [lila] *nm* lilac
limace [limas] *nf* slug
limande [limɑ̃d] *nf* dab
lime [lim] *nf* file; **~ à ongles** nail file; **limer** *vt* to file
limier [limje] *nm* bloodhound; (*détective*) sleuth
limitation [limitasjɔ̃] *nf*: **~ de vitesse** speed limit
limite [limit] *nf* (*de terrain*) boundary; (*partie ou point extrême*) limit; **vitesse/charge ~** maximum speed/load; **cas ~** borderline case; **date ~** deadline; **limiter** *vt* (*restreindre*) to limit, restrict; (*délimiter*) to border; **limitrophe** *adj* border *cpd*
limoger [limɔʒe] *vt* to dismiss
limon [limɔ̃] *nm* silt
limonade [limɔnad] *nf* lemonade
lin [lɛ̃] *nm* (*tissu*) linen
linceul [lɛ̃sœl] *nm* shroud
linge [lɛ̃ʒ] *nm* (*serviettes etc*) linen; (*lessive*) washing; (*aussi:* **~ de corps**) underwear; **lingerie** *nf* lingerie, underwear
lingot [lɛ̃go] *nm* ingot
linguistique [lɛ̃gɥistik] *adj* linguistic ♦ *nf* linguistics *sg*
lion, ne [ljɔ̃, ljɔn] *nm/f* lion (lioness); (*signe*): **le L~** Leo; **lionceau, x** *nm* lion cub
liqueur [likœʀ] *nf* liqueur
liquidation [likidasjɔ̃] *nf* (*vente*) sale
liquide [likid] *adj* liquid ♦ *nm* liquid; (*COMM*): **en ~** in ready money *ou* cash; **liquider** *vt* to liquidate; (*COMM: articles*) to clear, sell off; **liquidités** *nfpl* (*COMM*) liquid assets
lire [liʀ] *nf* (*monnaie*) lira ♦ *vt, vi* to read
lis [lis] *nm* = **lys**
lisible [lizibl] *adj* legible
lisière [lizjɛʀ] *nf* (*de forêt*) edge
lisons [lizɔ̃] *vb voir* **lire**
lisse [lis] *adj* smooth
liste [list] *nf* list; **faire la ~ de** to list; **~ électorale** electoral roll; **listing** *nm* (*INFORM*) printout
lit [li] *nm* bed; **petit ~, lit à une place** single bed; **grand ~, lit à deux places** double bed; **faire son ~** to make one's bed; **aller/se mettre au ~** to go to/get into bed; **~ de camp** campbed, **~ d'enfant** cot (*BRIT*), crib (*US*)

literie [litʀi] *nf* bedding, bedclothes *pl*
litière [litjɛʀ] *nf* litter
litige [litiʒ] *nm* dispute
litre [litʀ] *nm* litre
littéraire [liteʀɛʀ] *adj* literary ♦ *nm/f* arts student; **elle est très ~** (*she's very literary*)
littéral, e, -aux [liteʀal, o] *adj* literal
littérature [liteʀatyʀ] *nf* literature
littoral, -aux [litɔʀal, o] *nm* coast
liturgie [lityʀʒi] *nf* liturgy
livide [livid] *adj* livid, pallid
livraison [livʀɛzɔ̃] *nf* delivery
livre [livʀ] *nm* book ♦ *nf* (*poids, monnaie*) pound; **~ de bord** logbook; **~ de poche** paperback
livré, e [livʀe] *adj*: **~ à soi-même** left to o.s. *ou* one's own devices; **livrée** *nf* livery
livrer [livʀe] *vt* (COMM) to deliver; (*otage, coupable*) to hand over; (*secret, information*) to give away; **se ~ à** (*se confier*) to confide in; (*se rendre, s'abandonner*) to give o.s. up to; (*faire: pratiques, actes*) to indulge in; (*enquête*) to carry out
livret [livʀɛ] *nm* booklet; (*d'opéra*) libretto; **~ de caisse d'épargne** (savings) bank-book; **~ de famille** (official) family record book; **~ scolaire** (school) report book
livreur, -euse [livʀœʀ, øz] *nm/f* delivery boy *ou* man/girl *ou* woman
local, e, -aux [lɔkal] *adj* local ♦ *nm* (*salle*) premises *pl*; *voir aussi* **locaux**; **localiser** *vt* (*repérer*) to locate, place; (*limiter*) to confine; **localité** *nf* locality
locataire [lɔkatɛʀ] *nm/f* tenant; (*de chambre*) lodger
location [lɔkasjɔ̃] *nf* (*par le locataire, le loueur*) renting; (*par le propriétaire*) renting out, letting; (THÉÂTRE) booking office; **"~ de voitures"** "car rental"; **habiter en ~** to live in rented accommodation; **prendre une ~ (pour les vacances)** to rent a house *etc* (for the holidays)
locaux [lɔko] *nmpl* premises
locomotive [lɔkɔmɔtiv] *nf* locomotive, engine
locution [lɔkysjɔ̃] *nf* phrase
loge [lɔʒ] *nf* (THÉÂTRE: *d'artiste*) dressing room; (: *de spectateurs*) box; (*de concierge, franc-maçon*) lodge
logement [lɔʒmɑ̃] *nm* accommodation *no pl* (BRIT), accommodations *pl* (US); (*appartement*) flat (BRIT), apartment (US); (*hébergement*) housing *no pl*
loger [lɔʒe] *vt* to accommodate ♦ *vi* to live; **se ~ dans** (*suj: balle, flèche*) to lodge itself in; **trouver à se ~** to find accommodation; **logeur, -euse** *nm/f* landlord(-lady)
logiciel [lɔʒisjɛl] *nm* software
logique [lɔʒik] *adj* logical ♦ *nf* logic
logis [lɔʒi] *nm* abode, dwelling
logo [lɔgo] *nm* logo
loi [lwa] *nf* law; **faire la ~** to lay down the law
loin [lwɛ̃] *adv* far; (*dans le temps: futur*) a long way off; (: *passé*) a long time ago; **plus ~** further; **~ de** far from; **au ~** far off; **de ~** from a distance; (*fig: de beaucoup*) by far
lointain, e [lwɛ̃tɛ̃, ɛn] *adj* faraway, distant; (*dans le futur, passé*) distant; (*cause, parent*) remote, distant ♦ *nm*: **dans le ~** in the distance
loir [lwaʀ] *nm* dormouse
loisir [lwaziʀ] *nm*: **heures de ~** spare time; **~s** *nmpl* (*temps libre*) leisure *sg*; (*activités*) leisure activities; **avoir le ~ de faire** to have the time *ou* opportunity to do; **à ~** at leisure
londonien, ne [lɔ̃dɔnjɛ̃, jɛn] *adj* London *cpd*, of London ♦ *nm/f*: **L~, ne** Londoner
Londres [lɔ̃dʀ] *n* London
long, longue [lɔ̃, lɔ̃g] *adj* long ♦ *adv*: **en savoir ~** to know a great deal ♦ *nm*: **de 3 m de ~** 3 m long, 3 m in length; **ne pas faire ~ feu** not to last long; **(tout) le ~ de** (all) along; **tout au ~ de** (*année, vie*) throughout; **de ~**

en large (*marcher*) to and fro, up and down; *voir aussi* **longue**

longer [lɔ̃ʒe] *vt* to go (*ou* walk *ou* drive) along(side); (*suj*: *mur, route*) to border

longiligne [lɔ̃ʒiliɲ] *adj* long-limbed

longitude [lɔ̃ʒityd] *nf* longitude

longtemps [lɔ̃tɑ̃] *adv* (for) a long time, (for) long; **avant ~** before long; **pour** *ou* **pendant ~** for a long time; **mettre ~ à faire** to take a long time to do

longue [lɔ̃g] *adj voir* **long** ♦ *nf*: **à la ~** in the end; **longuement** *adv* (*longtemps*) for a long time; (*en détail*) at length

longueur [lɔ̃gœʀ] *nf* length; **~s** *nfpl* (*fig*: *d'un film etc*) tedious parts; **en ~** lengthwise; **tirer en ~** to drag on; **à ~ de journée** all day long; **~ d'onde** wavelength

longue-vue [lɔ̃gvy] *nf* telescope

look [luk] (*fam*) *nm* look, image

lopin [lɔpɛ̃] *nm*: **~ de terre** patch of land

loque [lɔk] *nf* (*personne*) wreck; **~s** *nfpl* (*habits*) rags

loquet [lɔkɛ] *nm* latch

lorgner [lɔʀɲe] *vt* to eye; (*fig*) to have one's eye on

lors [lɔʀ]: **~ de** *prép* at the time of; during

lorsque [lɔʀsk] *conj* when, as

losange [lɔzɑ̃ʒ] *nm* diamond

lot [lo] *nm* (*part*) share, (*de ~erie*) prize; (*fig*: *destin*) fate, lot; (COMM, INFORM) batch; **le gros ~** the jackpot

loterie [lɔtʀi] *nf* lottery

loti, e [lɔti] *adj*: **bien/mal ~** well-/ badly off

lotion [losjɔ̃] *nf* lotion

lotissement [lɔtismɑ̃] *nm* housing development; (*parcelle*) plot, lot

loto [lɔto] *nm* lotto

Loto

Le Loto is a state-run national lottery with large cash prizes. Participants select 7 numbers out of 49. The more correct numbers, the greater the prize. The draw is televised twice weekly.

lotte [lɔt] *nf* monkfish

louable [lwabl] *adj* commendable

louanges [lwɑ̃ʒ] *nfpl* praise *sg*

loubard [lubaʀ] (*fam*) *nm* lout

louche [luʃ] *adj* shady, fishy, dubious ♦ *nf* ladle; **loucher** *vi* to squint

louer [lwe] *vt* (*maison*: *suj*: *propriétaire*) to let, rent (out); (: *locataire*) to rent; (*voiture etc*: *entreprise*) to hire out (BRIT), rent (out); (: *locataire*) to hire, rent; (*réserver*) to book; (*faire l'éloge de*) to praise; **"à ~"** "to let" (BRIT), "for rent" (US)

loup [lu] *nm* wolf

loupe [lup] *nf* magnifying glass

louper [lupe] (*fam*) *vt* (*manquer*) to miss; (*examen*) to flunk

lourd, e [luʀ, luʀd] *adj, adv* heavy; **~ de** (*conséquences, menaces*) charged with; **il fait ~** the weather is close, it's sultry; **lourdaud, e** (*péj*) *adj* clumsy; **lourdement** *adv* heavily; **lourdeur** *nf* weight; **lourdeurs d'estomac** indigestion

loutre [lutʀ] *nf* otter

louveteau, x [luv(ə)to] *nm* wolf-cub; (*scout*) cub (scout)

louvoyer [luvwaje] *vi* (*fig*) to hedge, evade the issue

loyal, e, -aux [lwajal, o] *adj* (*fidèle*) loyal, faithful; (*fair-play*) fair; **loyauté** *nf* loyalty, faithfulness; fairness

loyer [lwaje] *nm* rent

lu, e [ly] *pp de* **lire**

lubie [lybi] *nf* whim, craze

lubrifiant [lybʀifjɑ̃, jɑ̃t] *nm* lubricant

lubrifier [lybʀifje] *vt* to lubricate

lubrique [lybʀik] *adj* lecherous

lucarne [lykaʀn] *nf* skylight

lucide [lysid] *adj* lucid; (*accidenté*) conscious

lucratif, -ive [lykʀatif, iv] *adj* lucrative, profitable; **à but non ~** non profit-making

lueur [lɥœʀ] *nf* (*pâle*) (faint) light; (*chatoyante*) glimmer *no pl*; (*fig*) glimmer; gleam

luge [lyʒ] *nf* sledge (BRIT), sled (US)

lugubre [lygybʀ] *adj* gloomy, dismal

MOT-CLÉ

lui [lɥi] *pron* **1** (*objet indirect: mâle*) (to) him; (: *femelle*) (to) her; (: *chose, animal*) (to) it; **je lui ai parlé** I have spoken to him (*ou* to her); **il lui a offert un cadeau** he gave him (*ou* her) a present

2 (*après préposition, comparatif: personne*) him; (: *chose, animal*) it; **elle est contente de lui** she is pleased with him; **je la connais mieux que lui** I know her better than he does; I know her better than him

3 (*sujet, forme emphatique*) he; **lui, il est à Paris** HE is in Paris

4: lui-même himself; itself

luire [lɥiʀ] *vi* to shine; (*en rougeoyant*) to glow

lumière [lymjɛʀ] *nf* light; **mettre en ~** (*fig*) to highlight; **~ du jour** daylight

luminaire [lyminɛʀ] *nm* lamp, light

lumineux, -euse [lyminø, øz] *adj* luminous; (*éclairé*) illuminated; (*ciel, couleur*) bright; (*rayon*) of light, light *cpd*; (*fig: regard*) radiant

lunatique [lynatik] *adj* whimsical, temperamental

lundi [lœ̃di] *nm* Monday; **~ de Pâques** Easter Monday

lune [lyn] *nf* moon; **~ de miel** honeymoon

lunette [lynɛt] *nf*: **~s** ♦ *nfpl* glasses, spectacles; (*protectrices*) goggles; **~ arrière** (AUTO) rear window; **~s de soleil** sunglasses

lus *etc* [ly] *vb voir* **lire**

lustre [lystʀ] *nm* (*de plafond*) chandelier; (*fig: éclat*) lustre; **lustrer** *vt* to shine

lut [ly] *vb voir* **lire**

luth [lyt] *nm* lute

lutin [lytɛ̃] *nm* imp, goblin

lutte [lyt] *nf* (*conflit*) struggle; (*sport*) wrestling; **lutter** *vi* to fight, struggle

luxe [lyks] *nm* luxury; **de ~** luxury *cpd*

Luxembourg [lyksɑ̃buʀ] *nm*: **le ~** Luxembourg

luxer [lykse] *vt*: **se ~ l'épaule** to dislocate one's shoulder

luxueux, -euse [lyksɥø, øz] *adj* luxurious

luxure [lyksyʀ] *nf* lust

luxuriant, e [lyksyʀjɑ̃, jɑ̃t] *adj* luxuriant

lycée [lise] *nm* secondary school; **lycéen, ne** *nm/f* secondary school pupil

lyophilisé, e [ljɔfilize] *adj* (*café*) freeze-dried

lyrique [liʀik] *adj* lyrical; (OPÉRA) lyric; **artiste ~** opera singer

lys [lis] *nm* lily

M, m

M *abr* = **Monsieur**

m' [m] *pron voir* **me**

ma [ma] *adj voir* **mon**

macaron [makaʀɔ̃] *nm* (*gâteau*) macaroon; (*insigne*) (round) badge

macaronis [makaʀɔni] *nmpl* macaroni *sg*

macédoine [masedwan] *nf*: **~ de fruits** fruit salad; **~ de légumes** mixed vegetables

macérer [maseʀe] *vi, vt* to macerate; (*dans du vinaigre*) to pickle

mâcher [mɑʃe] *vt* to chew; **ne pas ~ ses mots** not to mince one's words

machin [maʃɛ̃] (*fam*) *nm* thing(umajig)

machinal, e, -aux [maʃinal, o] *adj* mechanical, automatic; **machinalement** *adv* mechanically, automatically

machination [maʃinasjɔ̃] *nf* frame-up

machine [maʃin] *nf* machine; (*locomotive*) engine; **~ à écrire** typewriter; **~ à laver/coudre** washing/sewing

machine; **~ à sous** fruit machine
macho [matʃo] *(fam) nm* male chauvinist
mâchoire [mɑʃwaʀ] *nf* jaw
mâchonner [mɑʃɔne] *vt* to chew (at)
maçon [masɔ̃] *nm* builder; *(poseur de briques)* bricklayer; **maçonnerie** *nf* *(murs)* brickwork; *(pierres)* masonry, stonework
maculer [makyle] *vt* to stain
Madame [madam] *(pl* **Mesdames**) *nf*: **~ X** Mrs X; **occupez-vous de ~/Monsieur/Mademoiselle** please serve this lady/gentleman/(young) lady; **bonjour ~/Monsieur/Mademoiselle** good morning; *(ton déférent)* good morning Madam/Sir/Madam; *(le nom est connu)* good morning Mrs/Mr/Miss X; **~/Monsieur/Mademoiselle!** *(pour appeler)* Madam/Sir/Miss!; **~/Monsieur/Mademoiselle** *(sur lettre)* Dear Madam/Sir/Madam; **chère ~/cher Monsieur/chère Mademoiselle** Dear Mrs/Mr/Miss X; **Mesdames** Ladies
madeleine [madlɛn] *nf* madeleine; *small sponge cake*
Mademoiselle [madmwazɛl] *(pl* **Mesdemoiselles**) *nf* Miss; *voir aussi* **Madame**
madère [madɛʀ] *nm* Madeira (wine)
magasin [magazɛ̃] *nm (boutique)* shop; *(entrepôt)* warehouse; **en ~** (COMM) in stock
magazine [magazin] *nm* magazine
Maghreb [magʀɛb] *nm*: **le ~** North Africa; **maghrébin, e** *adj* North African ♦ *nm/f*: **Maghrébin, e** North African
magicien, ne [maʒisjɛ̃, jɛn] *nm/f* magician
magie [maʒi] *nf* magic; **magique** *adj* magic; *(enchanteur)* magical
magistral, e, -aux [maʒistʀal, o] *adj* *(œuvre, adresse)* masterly; *(ton)* authoritative; **cours ~** lecture
magistrat [maʒistʀa] *nm* magistrate
magnat [magna] *nm* tycoon
magnétique [maɲetik] *adj* magnetic
magnétiser [maɲetize] *vt* to magnetize; *(fig)* to mesmerize, hypnotize
magnétophone [maɲetɔfɔn] *nm* tape recorder; **~ à cassettes** cassette recorder
magnétoscope [maɲetɔskɔp] *nm* video-tape recorder
magnifique [maɲifik] *adj* magnificent
magot [mago] *(fam) nm (argent)* pile (of money); *(économies)* nest egg
magouille [maguj] *(fam) nf* scheming; **magouiller** *(fam) vi* to scheme
magret [magʀɛ] *nm*: **~ de canard** duck steaklet
mai [mɛ] *nm* May

mai

Le premier mai *is a public holiday in France marking union demonstrations in the United States in 1886 to secure the eight-hour working day. It is traditional to exchange and wear sprigs of lily of the valley.* **Le 8 mai** *is a public holiday in France commemorating the surrender of the German army to Eisenhower on May 7, 1945. There are parades of ex-servicemen in most towns. The social upheavals of May and June 1968, marked by student demonstrations, strikes and rioting, are generally referred to as "les événements de* **mai 68**". *De Gaulle's government survived, but reforms in education and a move towards decentralization ensued.*

maigre [mɛgʀ] *adj* (very) thin, skinny; *(viande)* lean; *(fromage)* low-fat; *(végétation)* thin, sparse; *(fig)* poor, meagre, skimpy; **jours ~s** days of abstinence, fish days; **maigreur** *nf* thinness; **maigrir** *vi* to get thinner, lose weight; **maigrir de 2 kilos** to lose 2 kilos
maille [mɑj] *nf* stitch; **avoir ~ à partir avec qn** to have a brush with sb; **~ à l'endroit/à l'envers** plain/purl stitch

maillet [majɛ] *nm* mallet
maillon [mɑjɔ̃] *nm* link
maillot [majo] *nm* (*aussi:* **~ de corps**) vest; (*de sportif*) jersey; **~ de bain** swimsuit; (*d'homme*) bathing trunks *pl*
main [mɛ̃] *nf* hand; **à la ~** in one's hand; **se donner la ~** to hold hands; **donner** *ou* **tendre la ~ à qn** to hold out one's hand to sb; **serrer la ~ à qn** to shake hands with sb; **sous la ~** to *ou* at hand; **à remettre en ~s propres** to be delivered personally; **mettre la dernière ~ à** to put the finishing touches to; **se faire/perdre la ~** to get one's hand in/lose one's touch; **avoir qch bien en ~** to have (got) the hang of sth; **main-d'œuvre** *nf* manpower, labour; **main-forte** *nf*: **prêter main-forte à qn** to come to sb's assistance; **mainmise** *nf* (*fig*): **mainmise sur** complete hold on
maint, e [mɛ̃, mɛ̃t] *adj* many a; **~s** many; **à ~es reprises** time and (time) again
maintenant [mɛ̃t(ə)nɑ̃] *adv* now; (*actuellement*) nowadays
maintenir [mɛ̃t(ə)niʀ] *vt* (*retenir, soutenir*) to support; (*contenir: foule etc*) to hold back; (*conserver, affirmer*) to maintain; **se ~** *vi* (*prix*) to keep steady; (*amélioration*) to persist
maintien [mɛ̃tjɛ̃] *nm* (*sauvegarde*) maintenance; (*attitude*) bearing
maire [mɛʀ] *nm* mayor; **mairie** *nf* (*bâtiment*) town hall; (*administration*) town council
mais [mɛ] *conj* but; **~ non!** of course not!; **~ enfin** but after all; (*indignation*) look here!
maïs [mais] *nm* maize (BRIT), corn (US)
maison [mɛzɔ̃] *nf* house; (*chez-soi*) home; (COMM) firm ♦ *adj inv* (CULIN) home-made; (*fig*) in-house, own; **à la ~** at home; (*direction*) home; **~ close** *ou* **de passe** brothel; **~ de repos** convalescent home; **~ de retraite** old people's home; **~ de santé** mental home; **~ des jeunes** ≃ youth club; **~ mère** parent company; **maisonnée** *nf* household, family; **maisonnette** *nf* small house, cottage

maisons des jeunes et de la culture

Maisons des jeunes et de la culture *are centres for young people which organize a wide range of sporting and cultural activities, and are also engaged in welfare work. The centres are, in part, publicly financed.*

maître, -esse [mɛtʀ, mɛtʀɛs] *nm/f* master (mistress); (SCOL) teacher, schoolmaster(-mistress) ♦ *nm* (*peintre etc*) master; (*titre*): **M~** Maître, *term of address gen for a barrister* ♦ *adj* (*principal, essentiel*) main; **être ~ de** (*soi, situation*) to be in control of; **une maîtresse femme** a managing woman; **~ chanteur** blackmailer; **~ d'école** schoolmaster; **~ d'hôtel** (*domestique*) butler; (*d'hôtel*) head waiter; **~ nageur** lifeguard; **maîtresse** *nf* (*amante*) mistress; **maîtresse (d'école)** teacher, (school)mistress; **maîtresse de maison** hostess; (*ménagère*) housewife
maîtrise [mɛtʀiz] *nf* (*aussi:* **~ de soi**) self-control, self-possession; (*habileté*) skill, mastery; (*suprématie*) mastery, command; (*diplôme*) ≃ master's degree; **maîtriser** *vt* (*cheval, incendie*) to (bring under) control; (*sujet*) to master; (*émotion*) to control, master; **se maîtriser** to control o.s.
maïzena ® [maizena] *nf* cornflour
majestueux, -euse [maʒɛstɥø, øz] *adj* majestic
majeur, e [maʒœʀ] *adj* (*important*) major; (JUR) of age ♦ *nm* (*doigt*) middle finger; **en ~e partie** for the most part; **la ~e partie de** most of
majoration [maʒɔʀasjɔ̃] *nf* rise, increase
majorer [maʒɔʀe] *vt* to increase
majoritaire [maʒɔʀitɛʀ] *adj* majority

majorité [maʒɔʀite] *nf* (*gén*) majority; (*parti*) party in power; **en ~** mainly

majuscule [maʒyskyl] *adj, nf*: **(lettre) ~** capital (letter)

mal [mal, mo] (*pl* **maux**) *nm* (*opposé au bien*) evil; (*tort, dommage*) harm; (*douleur physique*) pain, ache; (*~adie*) illness, sickness *no pl* ♦ *adv* badly ♦ *adj* bad, wrong; **être ~ à l'aise** to be uncomfortable; **être ~ avec qn** to be on bad terms with sb; **il a ~ compris** he misunderstood; **dire/penser du ~ de** to speak/think ill of; **ne voir aucun ~ à** to see no harm in, see nothing wrong in; **faire ~ à qn** to hurt sb; **se faire ~** to hurt o.s.; **se donner du ~ pour faire qch** to go to a lot of trouble to do sth; **ça fait ~** it hurts; **j'ai ~ au dos** my back hurts; **avoir ~ à la tête/à la gorge/aux dents** to have a headache/a sore throat/toothache; **avoir le ~ du pays** to be homesick; *voir aussi* **cœur**; **maux**; **~ de mer** seasickness; **~ en point** in a bad state

malade [malad] *adj* ill, sick; (*poitrine, jambe*) bad; (*plante*) diseased ♦ *nm/f* invalid, sick person; (*à l'hôpital etc*) patient; **tomber ~** to fall ill; **être ~ du cœur** to have heart trouble *ou* a bad heart; **~ mental** mentally sick *ou* ill person; **maladie** *nf* (*spécifique*) disease, illness; (*mauvaise santé*) illness, sickness; **maladif, -ive** *adj* sickly; (*curiosité, besoin*) pathological

maladresse [maladʀɛs] *nf* clumsiness *no pl*; (*gaffe*) blunder

maladroit, e [maladʀwa, wat] *adj* clumsy

malaise [malɛz] *nm* (MÉD) feeling of faintness; (*fig*) uneasiness, malaise; **avoir un ~** to feel faint

malaisé, e [maleze] *adj* difficult

malaxer [malakse] *vt* (*pétrir*) to knead; (*mélanger*) to mix

malbouffe [malbuf] (*fam*) *nf*: **la ~** junk food

malchance [malʃɑ̃s] *nf* misfortune, ill luck *no pl*; **par ~** unfortunately; **malchanceux, -euse** *adj* unlucky

mâle [mɑl] *adj* (*aussi* ÉLEC, TECH) male; (*viril*: *voix, traits*) manly ♦ *nm* male

malédiction [malediksjɔ̃] *nf* curse

mal...: malencontreux, -euse *adj* unfortunate, untoward; **mal-en-point** *adj inv* in a sorry state; **malentendant, e** *nm/f*: **les malentendants** the hard of hearing; **malentendu** *nm* misunderstanding; **malfaçon** *nf* fault; **malfaisant, e** *adj* evil, harmful; **malfaiteur** *nm* lawbreaker, criminal; (*voleur*) burglar, thief; **malfamé, e** *adj* disreputable

malgache [malgaʃ] *adj* Madagascan, Malagasy ♦ *nm/f*: **M~** Madagascan, Malagasy ♦ *nm* (LING) Malagasy

malgré [malgʀe] *prép* in spite of, despite; **~ tout** all the same

malhabile [malabil] *adj* clumsy, awkward

malheur [malœʀ] *nm* (*situation*) adversity, misfortune; (*événement*) misfortune; (*: très grave*) disaster, tragedy; **faire un ~** to be a smash hit; **malheureusement** *adv* unfortunately; **malheureux, -euse** *adj* (*triste*) unhappy, miserable; (*infortuné, regrettable*) unfortunate; (*malchanceux*) unlucky; (*insignifiant*) wretched ♦ *nm/f* poor soul; **les malheureux** the destitute

malhonnête [malɔnɛt] *adj* dishonest; **malhonnêteté** *nf* dishonesty

malice [malis] *nf* mischievousness; (*méchanceté*): **par ~** out of malice *ou* spite; **sans ~** guileless; **malicieux, -euse** *adj* mischievous

malin, -igne [malɛ̃, maliɲ] *adj* (*futé*: *f gén*: *~e*) smart, shrewd; (MÉD) malignant

malingre [malɛ̃gʀ] *adj* puny

malle [mal] *nf* trunk; **mallette** *nf* (small) suitcase; (*porte-documents*) attaché case

malmener [malməne] *vt* to manhandle; (*fig*) to give a rough handling to

malodorant, e [malɔdɔʀɑ̃, ɑ̃t] *adj* foul- *ou* ill-smelling
malotru [malɔtʀy] *nm* lout, boor
malpoli, e [malpɔli] *adj* impolite
malpropre [malpʀɔpʀ] *adj* dirty
malsain, e [malsɛ̃, ɛn] *adj* unhealthy
malt [malt] *nm* malt
Malte [malt] *nf* Malta
maltraiter [maltʀete] *vt* to manhandle, ill-treat
malveillance [malvɛjɑ̃s] *nf* (*animosité*) ill will; (*intention de nuire*) malevolence
malversation [malvɛʀsasjɔ̃] *nf* embezzlement
maman [mamɑ̃] *nf* mum(my), mother
mamelle [mamɛl] *nf* teat
mamelon [mam(ə)lɔ̃] *nm* (ANAT) nipple
mamie [mami] (*fam*) *nf* granny
mammifère [mamifɛʀ] *nm* mammal
mammouth [mamut] *nm* mammoth
manche [mɑ̃ʃ] *nf* (*de vêtement*) sleeve; (*d'un jeu, tournoi*) round; (GÉO): **la M~** the Channel ♦ *nm* (*d'outil, casserole*) handle; (*de pelle, pioche etc*) shaft; **à ~s courtes/longues** short-/long-sleeved
manchette [mɑ̃ʃɛt] *nf* (*de chemise*) cuff; (*coup*) forearm blow; (*titre*) headline
manchot [mɑ̃ʃo, ɔt] *nm* one-armed man; armless man; (ZOOL) penguin
mandarine [mɑ̃daʀin] *nf* mandarin (orange), tangerine
mandat [mɑ̃da] *nm* (*postal*) postal *ou* money order; (*d'un député etc*) mandate; (*procuration*) power of attorney, proxy; (POLICE) warrant; **~ d'arrêt** warrant for arrest; **mandataire** *nm/f* (*représentant*) representative; (JUR) proxy
manège [manɛʒ] *nm* riding school; (*à la foire*) roundabout, merry-go-round; (*fig*) game, ploy
manette [manɛt] *nf* lever, tap; **~ de jeu** joystick
mangeable [mɑ̃ʒabl] *adj* edible, eatable
mangeoire [mɑ̃ʒwaʀ] *nf* trough, manger
manger [mɑ̃ʒe] *vt* to eat; (*ronger: suj: rouille etc*) to eat into *ou* away ♦ *vi* to eat; **donner à ~ à** (*enfant*) to feed; **mangeur, -euse** *nm/f* eater; **gros mangeur** big eater
mangue [mɑ̃g] *nf* mango
maniable [manjabl] *adj* (*outil*) handy; (*voiture, voilier*) easy to handle
maniaque [manjak] *adj* finicky, fussy ♦ *nm/f* (*méticuleux*) fusspot; (*fou*) maniac
manie [mani] *nf* (*tic*) odd habit; (*obsession*) mania; **avoir la ~ de** to be obsessive about
manier [manje] *vt* to handle
manière [manjɛʀ] *nf* (*façon*) way, manner; **~s** *nfpl* (*attitude*) manners; (*chichis*) fuss *sg*; **de ~ à** so as to; **de cette ~** in this way *ou* manner; **d'une certaine ~** in a way; **de toute ~** in any case
maniéré, e [manjeʀe] *adj* affected
manif [manif] (*fam*) *nf* demo
manifestant, e [manifɛstɑ̃, ɑ̃t] *nm/f* demonstrator
manifestation [manifɛstasjɔ̃] *nf* (*de joie, mécontentement*) expression, demonstration; (*symptôme*) outward sign; (*culturelle etc*) event; (POL) demonstration
manifeste [manifɛst] *adj* obvious, evident ♦ *nm* manifesto; **manifester** *vt* (*volonté, intentions*) to show, indicate; (*joie, peur*) to express, show ♦ *vi* to demonstrate; **se manifester** *vi* (*émotion*) to show *ou* express itself; (*difficultés*) to arise; (*symptômes*) to appear
manigance [manigɑ̃s] *nf* scheme; **manigancer** *vt* to plot
manipulation [manipylasjɔ̃] *nf* handling; (POL, *génétique*) manipulation
manipuler [manipyle] *vt* to handle; (*fig*) to manipulate
manivelle [manivɛl] *nf* crank
mannequin [mankɛ̃] *nm* (COUTURE) dummy; (MODE) model
manœuvre [manœvʀ] *nf* (*gén*) manoeuvre (BRIT), maneuver (US) ♦ *nm* labourer; **manœuvrer** *vt* to manoeuvre

(*BRIT*), maneuver (*US*); (*levier, machine*) to operate ♦ *vi* to manoeuvre

manoir [manwaʀ] *nm* manor *ou* country house

manque [mɑ̃k] *nm* (*insuffisance*): **~ de** lack of; (*vide*) emptiness, gap; (*MÉD*) withdrawal; **être en état de ~** to suffer withdrawal symptoms

manqué, e [mɑ̃ke] *adj* failed; **garçon ~** tomboy

manquer [mɑ̃ke] *vi* (*faire défaut*) to be lacking; (*être absent*) to be missing; (*échouer*) to fail ♦ *vt* to miss ♦ *vb impers*: **il (nous) manque encore 100 F** we are still 100 F short; **il manque des pages (au livre)** there are some pages missing (from the book); **il/cela me manque** I miss him/this; **~ à** (*règles etc*) to be in breach of, fail to observe; **~ de** to lack; **je ne ~ai pas de le lui dire** I'll be sure to tell him; **il a manqué (de) se tuer** he very nearly got killed

mansarde [mɑ̃saʀd] *nf* attic; **mansardé, e** *adj*: **chambre mansardée** attic room

manteau, x [mɑ̃to] *nm* coat

manucure [manykyʀ] *nf* manicurist

manuel, le [manɥɛl] *adj* manual ♦ *nm* (*ouvrage*) manual, handbook

manufacture [manyfaktyʀ] *nf* factory; **manufacturé, e** *adj* manufactured

manuscrit, e [manyskʀi, it] *adj* handwritten ♦ *nm* manuscript

manutention [manytɑ̃sjɔ̃] *nf* (*COMM*) handling

mappemonde [mapmɔ̃d] *nf* (*plane*) map of the world; (*sphère*) globe

maquereau, x [makʀo] *nm* (*ZOOL*) mackerel *inv*; (*fam*) pimp

maquette [makɛt] *nf* (*à échelle réduite*) (scale) model; (*d'une page illustrée*) paste-up

maquillage [makijaʒ] *nm* making up; (*crème etc*) make-up

maquiller [makije] *vt* (*personne, visage*) to make up; (*truquer: passeport, statistique*) to fake; (*: voiture volée*) to do over (*respray etc*); **se ~** *vi* to make up (one's face)

maquis [maki] *nm* (*GÉO*) scrub; (*MIL*) maquis, underground fighting *no pl*

maraîcher, -ère [maʀeʃe, ɛʀ] *adj*: **cultures maraîchères** market gardening *sg* ♦ *nm/f* market gardener

marais [maʀɛ] *nm* marsh, swamp

marasme [maʀasm] *nm* stagnation, slump

marathon [maʀatɔ̃] *nm* marathon

maraudeur [maʀodœʀ, øz] *nm* prowler

marbre [maʀbʀ] *nm* marble

marc [maʀ] *nm* (*de raisin, pommes*) marc; **~ de café** coffee grounds *pl ou* dregs *pl*

marchand, e [maʀʃɑ̃, ɑ̃d] *nm/f* shopkeeper, tradesman(-woman); (*au marché*) stallholder; (*de vins, charbon*) merchant ♦ *adj*: **prix/valeur ~(e)** market price/value; **~(e) de fruits** fruiterer (*BRIT*), fruit seller (*US*); **~(e) de journaux** newsagent; **~(e) de légumes** greengrocer (*BRIT*), produce dealer (*US*); **~(e) de poissons** fishmonger; **marchander** *vi* to bargain, haggle; **marchandise** *nf* goods *pl*, merchandise *no pl*

marche [maʀʃ] *nf* (*d'escalier*) step; (*activité*) walking; (*promenade, trajet, allure*) walk; (*démarche*) walk, gait; (*MIL etc*) march; (*fonctionnement*) running; (*des événements*) course; **dans le sens de la ~** (*RAIL*) facing the engine; **en ~** (*monter etc*) while the vehicle is moving *ou* in motion; **mettre en ~** to start; **se mettre en ~** (*personne*) to get moving; (*machine*) to start; **être en état de ~** to be in working order; **~ à suivre** (correct) procedure; **~ arrière** reverse (gear); **faire ~ arrière** to reverse; (*fig*) to backtrack, back-pedal

marché [maʀʃe] *nm* market; (*transaction*) bargain, deal; **faire du ~ noir** to buy and sell on the black market; **~ aux puces** flea market; **M~ commun**

Common Market

marchepied [maʀʃəpje] *nm* (*RAIL*) step

marcher [maʀʃe] *vi* to walk; (*MIL*) to march; (*aller: voiture, train, affaires*) to go; (*prospérer*) to go well; (*fonctionner*) to work, run; (*fam: consentir*) to go along, agree; (*: croire naïvement*) to be taken in; **faire ~ qn** (*taquiner*) to pull sb's leg; (*tromper*) to lead sb up the garden path; **marcheur, -euse** *nm/f* walker

mardi [maʀdi] *nm* Tuesday; **M~ gras** Shrove Tuesday

mare [maʀ] *nf* pond; (*flaque*) pool

marécage [maʀekaʒ] *nm* marsh, swamp; **marécageux, -euse** *adj* marshy

maréchal, -aux [maʀeʃal, o] *nm* marshal; **maréchal-ferrant** [maʀeʃalfɛʀɑ̃, maʀeʃo-] (*pl* **maréchaux-ferrants**) *nm* blacksmith, farrier

marée [maʀe] *nf* tide; (*poissons*) fresh (sea) fish; **~ haute/basse** high/low tide; **~ montante/descendante** rising/ebb tide; **~ noire** oil slick

marelle [maʀɛl] *nf* hopscotch

margarine [maʀgaʀin] *nf* margarine

marge [maʀʒ] *nf* margin; **en ~ de** (*fig*) on the fringe of; **~ bénéficiaire** profit margin

marginal, e, -aux [maʀʒinal, o] *nm/f* (*original*) eccentric; (*déshérité*) dropout

marguerite [maʀgəʀit] *nf* marguerite, (*BOT*) daisy; (*d'imprimante*) daisy-wheel

mari [maʀi] *nm* husband

mariage [maʀjaʒ] *nm* marriage; (*noce*) wedding; **~ civil/religieux** registry office (*BRIT*) *ou* civil/church wedding

marié, e [maʀje] *adj* married ♦ *nm* (bride)groom; **les ~s** the bride and groom; **les (jeunes) ~s** the newly-weds; **mariée** *nf* bride

marier [maʀje] *vt* to marry; (*fig*) to blend; **se ~** *vr* to get married; **se ~ (avec)** to marry

marin, e [maʀɛ̃, in] *adj* sea *cpd*, marine ♦ *nm* sailor

marine [maʀin] *adj voir* **marin** ♦ *adj inv* navy (blue) ♦ *nm* (*MIL*) marine ♦ *nf* navy; **~ de guerre** navy; **~ marchande** merchant navy

mariner [maʀine] *vt*: **faire ~** to marinade

marionnette [maʀjɔnɛt] *nf* puppet

maritalement [maʀitalmɑ̃] *adv*: **vivre ~** to live as husband and wife

maritime [maʀitim] *adj* sea *cpd*, maritime

mark [maʀk] *nm* mark

marmelade [maʀməlad] *nf* stewed fruit, compote; **~ d'oranges** marmalade

marmite [maʀmit] *nf* (cooking-)pot

marmonner [maʀmɔne] *vt, vi* to mumble, mutter

marmot [maʀmo] (*fam*) *nm* kid

marmotter [maʀmɔte] *vt* to mumble

Maroc [maʀɔk] *nm*: **le ~** Morocco; **marocain, e** [maʀɔkɛ̃, ɛn] *adj* Moroccan ♦ *nm/f*: **Marocain, e** Moroccan

maroquinerie [maʀɔkinʀi] *nf* (*articles*) fine leather goods *pl*; (*boutique*) shop selling fine leather goods

marquant, e [maʀkɑ̃, ɑ̃t] *adj* outstanding

marque [maʀk] *nf* mark; (*COMM: de nourriture*) brand; (*: de voiture, produits manufacturés*) make; (*de disques*) label; **de ~** (*produits*) high-class; (*visiteur etc*) distinguished, well-known; **une grande ~ de vin** a well-known brand of wine; **~ de fabrique** trademark; **~ déposée** registered trademark

marquer [maʀke] *vt* to mark; (*inscrire*) to write down; (*bétail*) to brand; (*SPORT: but etc*) to score; (*: joueur*) to mark; (*accentuer: taille etc*) to emphasize; (*manifester: refus, intérêt*) to show ♦ *vi* (*événement*) to stand out, be outstanding; (*SPORT*) to score

marqueterie [maʀkɛtʀi] *nf* inlaid work, marquetry

marquis [maʀki] *nm* marquis, mar-

quess; **marquise** *nf* marchioness; (*auvent*) glass canopy *ou* awning
marraine [maʀɛn] *nf* godmother
marrant, e [maʀɑ̃, ɑ̃t] (*fam*) *adj* funny
marre [maʀ] (*fam*) *adv*: **en avoir ~ de** to be fed up with
marrer [maʀe]: **se ~** (*fam*) *vi* to have a (good) laugh
marron [maʀɔ̃] *nm* (*fruit*) chestnut ♦ *adj inv* brown; **~s glacés** candied chestnuts; **marronnier** *nm* chestnut (tree)
mars [maʀs] *nm* March
Marseille [maʀsɛj] *n* Marseilles

Marseillaise

***La Marseillaise** has been France's national anthem since 1879. The words of the "Chant de guerre de l'armée du Rhin", as the song was originally called, were written to an anonymous tune by the army captain Rouget de Lisle in 1792. Adopted as a marching song by the battalion of Marseilles, it was finally popularized as the Marseillaise.*

marsouin [maʀswɛ̃] *nm* porpoise
marteau, x [maʀto] *nm* hammer; **être ~** (*fam*) to be nuts; **marteau-piqueur** *nm* pneumatic drill
marteler [maʀtəle] *vt* to hammer
martien, ne [maʀsjɛ̃, jɛn] *adj* Martian, of *ou* from Mars
martyr, e [maʀtiʀ] *nm/f* martyr; **martyre** *nm* martyrdom; (*fig*: *sens affaibli*) agony, torture; **martyriser** *vt* (*REL*) to martyr; (*fig*) to bully; (*enfant*) to batter, beat
marxiste [maʀksist] *adj, nm/f* Marxist
mascara [maskaʀa] *nm* mascara
masculin, e [maskylɛ̃, in] *adj* masculine; (*sexe, population*) male; (*équipe, vêtements*) men's; (*viril*) manly ♦ *nm* masculine; **masculinité** *nf* masculinity
masochiste [mazɔʃist] *adj* masochistic
masque [mask] *nm* mask; **masquer** *vt* (*cacher*: *paysage, porte*) to hide, conceal; (*dissimuler*: *vérité, projet*) to mask, obscure
massacre [masakʀ] *nm* massacre, slaughter; **massacrer** *vt* to massacre, slaughter; (*fam*: *texte etc*) to murder
massage [masaʒ] *nm* massage
masse [mas] *nf* mass; (*ÉLEC*) earth; (*maillet*) sledgehammer; (*péj*): **la ~** the masses *pl*; **une ~ de** (*fam*) masses *ou* loads of; **en ~** ♦ *adv* (*acheter*) in bulk; (*en foule*) en masse ♦ *adj* (*exécutions, production*) mass *cpd*
masser [mase] *vt* (*assembler*: *gens*) to gather; (*pétrir*) to massage; **se ~** *vi* (*foule*) to gather; **masseur, -euse** *nm/f* masseur(-euse)
massif, -ive [masif, iv] *adj* (*porte*) solid, massive; (*visage*) heavy, large; (*bois, or*) solid; (*dose*) massive; (*déportations etc*) mass *cpd* ♦ *nm* (*montagneux*) massif; (*de fleurs*) clump, bank
massue [masy] *nf* club, bludgeon
mastic [mastik] *nm* (*pour vitres*) putty; (*pour fentes*) filler
mastiquer [mastike] *vt* (*aliment*) to chew, masticate
mat, e [mat] *adj* (*couleur, métal*) mat(t); (*bruit, son*) dull ♦ *adj inv* (*ÉCHECS*): **être ~** to be checkmate
mât [mɑ] *nm* (*NAVIG*) mast; (*poteau*) pole, post
match [matʃ] *nm* match; **faire ~ nul** to draw; **~ aller** first leg; **~ retour** second leg, return match
matelas [mat(ə)lɑ] *nm* mattress; **~ pneumatique** air bed *ou* mattress; **matelassé, e** *adj* (*vêtement*) padded; (*tissu*) quilted
matelot [mat(ə)lo] *nm* sailor, seaman
mater [mate] *vt* (*personne*) to bring to heel, subdue; (*révolte*) to put down
matérialiser [mateʀjalize]: **se ~** *vi* to materialize
matérialiste [mateʀjalist] *adj* materialistic
matériaux [mateʀjo] *nmpl* material(s)

matériel, le [materjɛl] *adj* material ♦ *nm* equipment *no pl*; (*de camping etc*) gear *no pl*; (*INFORM*) hardware

maternel, le [matɛrnɛl] *adj* (*amour, geste*) motherly, maternal; (*grand-père, oncle*) maternal; **maternelle** *nf* (*aussi*: **école maternelle**) (state) nursery school

maternité [matɛrnite] *nf* (*établissement*) maternity hospital; (*état de mère*) motherhood, maternity; (*grossesse*) pregnancy; **congé de ~** maternity leave

mathématique [matematik] *adj* mathematical; **mathématiques** *nfpl* (*science*) mathematics *sg*

maths [mat] (*fam*) *nfpl* maths

matière [matjɛr] *nf* matter; (*COMM, TECH*) material, matter *no pl*; (*fig: d'un livre etc*) subject matter, material; (*SCOL*) subject; **en ~ de** as regards; **~s grasses** fat content *sg*; **~s premières** raw materials

hôtel Matignon

L'hôtel **Matignon** *is the Paris office and residence of the French Prime Minister. By extension, the term "Matignon" is often used to refer to the Prime Minister or his staff.*

matin [matɛ̃] *nm, adv* morning; **du ~ au soir** from morning till night; **de bon** *ou* **grand ~** early in the morning; **matinal, e, -aux** *adj* (*toilette, gymnastique*) morning *cpd*; **être matinal** (*personne*) to be up early; to be an early riser; **matinée** *nf* morning; (*spectacle*) matinée

matou [matu] *nm* tom(cat)

matraque [matrak] *nf* (*de policier*) truncheon (*BRIT*), billy (*US*)

matricule [matrikyl] *nm* (*MIL*) regimental number; (*ADMIN*) reference number

matrimonial, e, -aux [matrimɔnjal, jo] *adj* marital, marriage *cpd*

maudire [modir] *vt* to curse; **maudit, e** (*fam*) *adj* (*satané*) blasted, confounded

maugréer [mogree] *vi* to grumble

maussade [mosad] *adj* sullen; (*temps*) gloomy

mauvais, e [mɔvɛ, ɛz] *adj* bad; (*faux*): **le ~ numéro/moment** the wrong number/moment; (*méchant, malveillant*) malicious, spiteful; **il fait ~** the weather is bad; **la mer est ~e** the sea is rough; **~ plaisant** hoaxer; **~e herbe** weed; **~e langue** gossip, scandalmonger (*BRIT*); **~e passe** bad patch

mauve [mov] *adj* mauve

maux [mo] *nmpl de* **mal; ~ de ventre** stomachache *sg*

maximum [maksimɔm] *adj, nm* maximum; **au ~** (*le plus possible*) as much as one can; (*tout au plus*) at the (very) most *ou* maximum; **faire le ~** to do one's level best

mayonnaise [majɔnɛz] *nf* mayonnaise

mazout [mazut] *nm* (fuel) oil

Me *abr* = **Maître**

me, m' [m(ə)] *pron* (*direct: téléphoner, attendre etc*) me; (*indirect: parler, donner etc*) (to) me; (*réfléchi*) myself

mec [mɛk] (*fam*) *nm* bloke, guy

mécanicien, ne [mekanisjɛ̃, jɛn] *nm/f* mechanic; (*RAIL*) (train *ou* engine) driver

mécanique [mekanik] *adj* mechanical ♦ *nf* (*science*) mechanics *sg*; (*mécanisme*) mechanism; **ennui ~** engine trouble *no pl*

mécanisme [mekanism] *nm* mechanism

méchamment [meʃamɑ̃] *adv* nastily, maliciously, spitefully

méchanceté [meʃɑ̃ste] *nf* nastiness, maliciousness; **dire des ~s à qn** to say spiteful things to sb

méchant, e [meʃɑ̃, ɑ̃t] *adj* nasty, malicious, spiteful; (*enfant: pas sage*) naughty; (*animal*) vicious

mèche [mɛʃ] *nf* (*de cheveux*) lock; (*de lampe, bougie*) wick; (*d'un explosif*) fuse;

de ~ avec in league with
méchoui [meʃwi] *nm* barbecue of a whole roast sheep
méconnaissable [mekɔnɛsabl] *adj* unrecognizable
méconnaître [mekɔnɛtʀ] *vt* (*ignorer*) to be unaware of; (*mésestimer*) to misjudge
mécontent, e [mekɔ̃tɑ̃, ɑ̃t] *adj*: **~ (de)** discontented *ou* dissatisfied *ou* displeased (with); (*contrarié*) annoyed (at); **mécontentement** *nm* dissatisfaction, discontent, displeasure; (*irritation*) annoyance
médaille [medaj] *nf* medal
médaillon [medajɔ̃] *nm* (*bijou*) locket
médecin [med(ə)sɛ̃] *nm* doctor; **~ légiste** forensic surgeon
médecine [med(ə)sin] *nf* medicine
média [medja] *nmpl*: **les ~** the media; **médiatique** *adj* media *cpd*; **médiatisé, e** *adj* reported in the media; **ce procès a été très médiatisé** (*péj*) this trial was turned into a media event
médical, e, -aux [medikal, o] *adj* medical; **passer une visite ~e** to have a medical
médicament [medikamɑ̃] *nm* medicine, drug
médiéval, e, -aux [medjeval, o] *adj* medieval
médiocre [medjɔkʀ] *adj* mediocre, poor
médire [mediʀ] *vi*: **~ de** to speak ill of; **médisance** *nf* scandalmongering (BRIT)
méditer [medite] *vi* to meditate
Méditerranée [mediteʀane] *nf*: **la (mer) ~** the Mediterranean (Sea); **méditerranéen, ne** *adj* Mediterranean ♦ *nm/f*: **Méditerranéen, ne** native *ou* inhabitant of a Mediterranean country
méduse [medyz] *nf* jellyfish
meeting [mitiŋ] *nm* (POL, SPORT) rally
méfait [mefɛ] *nm* (*faute*) misdemeanour, wrongdoing; **~s** *nmpl* (*ravages*) ravages, damage *sg*
méfiance [mefjɑ̃s] *nf* mistrust, distrust
méfiant, e [mefjɑ̃, jɑ̃t] *adj* mistrustful, distrustful
méfier [mefje]: **se ~** *vi* to be wary; to be careful; **se ~ de** to mistrust, distrust, be wary of
mégarde [megaʀd] *nf*: **par ~** (*accidentellement*) accidentally; (*par erreur*) by mistake
mégère [meʒɛʀ] *nf* shrew
mégot [mego] (*fam*) *nm* cigarette end
meilleur, e [mɛjœʀ] *adj, adv* better ♦ *nm*: **le ~** the best; **le ~ des deux** the better of the two; **~ marché** (*inv*) cheaper; **meilleure** *nf*: **la meilleure** the best (one)
mélancolie [melɑ̃kɔli] *nf* melancholy, gloom; **mélancolique** *adj* melancholic, melancholy
mélange [melɑ̃ʒ] *nm* mixture; **mélanger** *vt* to mix; (*vins, couleurs*) to blend; (*mettre en désordre*) to mix up, muddle (up)
mélasse [melas] *nf* treacle, molasses *sg*
mêlée [mele] *nf* mêlée, scramble; (RUGBY) scrum(mage)
mêler [mele] *vt* (*unir*) to mix; (*embrouiller*) to muddle (up), mix up; **se ~** *vi* to mix, mingle; **se ~ à** (*personne*: *se joindre*) to join; (: *s'associer à*) to mix with; **se ~ de** (*suj*: *personne*) to meddle with, interfere in; **mêle-toi de ce qui te regarde!** mind your own business!
mélodie [melɔdi] *nf* melody; **mélodieux, -euse** *adj* melodious
melon [m(ə)lɔ̃] *nm* (BOT) (honeydew) melon; (*aussi*: **chapeau ~**) bowler (hat)
membre [mɑ̃bʀ] *nm* (ANAT) limb; (*personne, pays, élément*) member ♦ *adj* member *cpd*
mémé [meme] (*fam*) *nf* granny

MOT-CLÉ

même [mɛm] *adj* **1** (*avant le nom*) same; **en même temps** at the same time
2 (*après le nom*: *renforcement*): **il est la loyauté même** he is loyalty itself; **ce**

sont ses paroles/celles-là mêmes they are his very words/the very ones ♦ *pron*: **le(la) même** the same one ♦ *adv* 1 (*renforcement*): **il n'a même pas pleuré** he didn't even cry; **même lui l'a dit** even HE said it; **ici même** at this very place
2: **à même**: **à même la bouteille** straight from the bottle; **à même la peau** next to the skin; **être à même de faire** to be in a position to do, be able to do
3: **de même**: **faire de même** to do likewise; **lui de même** so does (*ou* did *ou* is) he; **de même que** just as; **il en va de même pour** the same goes for

mémo [memo] (*fam*) *nm* memo
mémoire [memwaʀ] *nf* memory ♦ *nm* (SCOL) dissertation, paper; **~s** *nmpl* (*souvenirs*) memoirs; **à la ~ de** to the *ou* in memory of; **de ~** from memory; **~ morte/vive** (INFORM) ROM/RAM
mémorable [memɔʀabl] *adj* memorable, unforgettable
menace [mənas] *nf* threat; **menacer** *vt* to threaten
ménage [menaʒ] *nm* (*travail*) housework; (*couple*) (married) couple; (*famille*, ADMIN) household; **faire le ~** to do the housework; **ménagement** *nm* care and attention; **ménager, -ère** *adj* household *cpd*, domestic ♦ *vt* (*traiter: personne*) to handle with tact; (*utiliser*) to use sparingly; (*prendre soin de*) to take (great) care of, look after; (*organiser*) to arrange; **ménager qch à qn** (*réserver*) to have sth in store for sb; **ménagère** *nf* housewife
mendiant, e [mɑ̃djɑ̃, jɑ̃t] *nm/f* beggar
mendier [mɑ̃dje] *vi* to beg ♦ *vt* to beg (for)
mener [m(ə)ne] *vt* to lead; (*enquête*) to conduct; (*affaires*) to manage ♦ *vi*: **~ à/dans** (*emmener*) to take to/into; **~ qch à bien** to see sth through (to a successful conclusion), complete sth successfully
meneur, -euse [mənœʀ, øz] *nm/f* leader; (*péj*) agitator
méningite [menɛ̃ʒit] *nf* meningitis *no pl*
ménopause [menopoz] *nf* menopause
menottes [mənɔt] *nfpl* handcuffs
mensonge [mɑ̃sɔ̃ʒ] *nm* lie; (*action*) lying *no pl*; **mensonger, -ère** *adj* false
mensualité [mɑ̃sɥalite] *nf* (*traite*) monthly payment
mensuel, le [mɑ̃sɥɛl] *adj* monthly
mensurations [mɑ̃syʀasjɔ̃] *nfpl* measurements
mental, e, -aux [mɑ̃tal, o] *adj* mental; **mentalité** *nf* mentality
menteur, -euse [mɑ̃tœʀ, øz] *nm/f* liar
menthe [mɑ̃t] *nf* mint
mention [mɑ̃sjɔ̃] *nf* (*annotation*) note, comment; (SCOL) grade; **~ bien** *etc* ≃ grade B *etc* (*ou* upper 2nd class *etc*) pass (BRIT), ≃ pass with (high) honors (US); (ADMIN): **"rayer les ~s inutiles"** "delete as appropriate"; **mentionner** *vt* to mention
mentir [mɑ̃tiʀ] *vi* to lie
menton [mɑ̃tɔ̃] *nm* chin
menu, e [məny] *adj* (*personne*) slim, slight; (*frais, difficulté*) minor ♦ *adv* (*couper, hacher*) very fine ♦ *nm* menu; **~ touristique/gastronomique** economy/gourmet's menu
menuiserie [mənɥizʀi] *nf* (*métier*) joinery, carpentry; (*passe-temps*) woodwork; **menuisier** *nm* joiner, carpenter
méprendre [mepʀɑ̃dʀ]: **se ~** *vi*: **se ~ sur** to be mistaken (about)
mépris [mepʀi] *nm* (*dédain*) contempt, scorn; **au ~ de** regardless of, in defiance of; **méprisable** *adj* contemptible, despicable; **méprisant, e** *adj* scornful; **méprise** *nf* mistake, error; **mépriser** *vt* to scorn, despise; (*gloire, danger*) to scorn, spurn
mer [mɛʀ] *nf* sea; (*marée*) tide; **en ~** at sea; **en haute** *ou* **pleine ~** off shore, on the open sea; **la ~ du Nord/Rouge**

the North/Red Sea

mercenaire [mɛʀsənɛʀ] *nm* mercenary, hired soldier

mercerie [mɛʀsəʀi] *nf* (*boutique*) haberdasher's shop (*BRIT*), notions store (*US*)

merci [mɛʀsi] *excl* thank you ♦ *nf*: **à la ~ de qn/qch** at sb's mercy/the mercy of sth; **~ beaucoup** thank you very much; **~ de** thank you for; **sans ~** merciless(ly)

mercredi [mɛʀkʀədi] *nm* Wednesday

mercure [mɛʀkyʀ] *nm* mercury

merde [mɛʀd] (*fam!*) *nf* shit (*!*) ♦ *excl* (bloody) hell (*!*)

mère [mɛʀ] *nf* mother; **~ célibataire** unmarried mother

merguez [mɛʀgɛz] *nf* merguez sausage (*type of spicy sausage from N Africa*)

méridional, e, -aux [meʀidjɔnal, o] *adj* southern ♦ *nm/f* Southerner

meringue [məʀɛ̃g] *nf* meringue

mérite [meʀit] *nm* merit; **avoir du ~ (à faire qch)** to deserve credit (for doing sth); **mériter** *vt* to deserve

merlan [mɛʀlɑ̃] *nm* whiting

merle [mɛʀl] *nm* blackbird

merveille [mɛʀvɛj] *nf* marvel, wonder; **faire ~** to work wonders; **à ~** perfectly, wonderfully; **merveilleux, -euse** *adj* marvellous, wonderful

mes [me] *adj voir* **mon**

mésange [mezɑ̃ʒ] *nf* tit(mouse)

mésaventure [mezavɑ̃tyʀ] *nf* misadventure, misfortune

Mesdames [medam] *nfpl de* **Madame**

Mesdemoiselles [medmwazɛl] *nfpl de* **Mademoiselle**

mesquin, e [mɛskɛ̃, in] *adj* mean, petty; **mesquinerie** *nf* meanness; (*procédé*) mean trick

message [mesaʒ] *nm* message; **messager, -ère** *nm/f* messenger; **messagerie** *nf* (*INTERNET*) **messagerie électronique** bulletin board

messe [mɛs] *nf* mass

Messieurs [mesjø] *nmpl de* **Monsieur**

mesure [m(ə)zyʀ] *nf* (*évaluation, dimension*) measurement; (*récipient*) measure; (*MUS*: *cadence*) time, tempo; (: *division*) bar; (*retenue*) moderation; (*disposition*) measure, step; **sur ~** (*costume*) made-to-measure; **dans la ~ où** insofar as, inasmuch as; **à ~ que** as; **être en ~ de** to be in a position to; **dans une certaine ~** to a certain extent

mesurer [məzyʀe] *vt* to measure; (*juger*) to weigh up, assess; (*modérer*: *ses paroles etc*) to moderate; **se ~ avec** to have a confrontation with; **il mesure 1 m 80** he's 1 m 80 tall

met [mɛ] *vb voir* **mettre**

métal, -aux [metal, o] *nm* metal; **métallique** *adj* metallic

météo [meteo] *nf* (*bulletin*) weather report

météorologie [meteɔʀɔlɔʒi] *nf* meteorology

méthode [metɔd] *nf* method; (*livre, ouvrage*) manual, tutor

méticuleux, -euse [metikylø, øz] *adj* meticulous

métier [metje] *nm* (*profession*: *gén*) job; (: *manuel*) trade; (*artisanal*) craft; (*technique, expérience*) (acquired) skill *ou* technique; (*aussi*: **~ à tisser**) (weaving) loom; **avoir du ~** to have practical experience

métis, se [metis] *adj, nm/f* half-caste, half-breed

métrage [metʀaʒ] *nm*: **long/moyen/court ~** full-length/medium-length/short film

mètre [mɛtʀ] *nm* metre; (*règle*) (metre) rule; (*ruban*) tape measure; **métrique** *adj* metric

métro [metʀo] *nm* underground (*BRIT*), subway

métropole [metʀɔpɔl] *nf* (*capitale*) metropolis; (*pays*) home country

mets [mɛ] *nm* dish

metteur [metœʀ] *nm*: **~ en scène** (*THÉÂTRE*) producer; (*CINÉMA*) director

MOT-CLÉ

mettre [mɛtʀ] *vt* **1** (*placer*) to put; **mettre en bouteille/en sac** to bottle/put in bags *ou* sacks; **mettre en charge (pour)** to charge (with), indict (for)

2 (*vêtements*: *revêtir*) to put on; (: *porter*) to wear; **mets ton gilet** put your cardigan on; **je ne mets plus mon manteau** I no longer wear my coat

3 (*faire fonctionner*: *chauffage, électricité*) to put on; (: *reveil, minuteur*) to set; (*installer*: *gaz, eau*) to put in, lay on; **mettre en marche** to start up

4 (*consacrer*): **mettre du temps à faire qch** to take time to do sth *ou* over sth

5 (*noter, écrire*) to say, put (down); **qu'est-ce qu'il a mis sur la carte?** what did he say *ou* write on the card?; **mettez au pluriel** ... put ... into the plural

6 (*supposer*): **mettons que** ... let's suppose *ou* say that ...

7: **y mettre du sien** to pull one's weight

se mettre *vi* **1** (*se placer*): **vous pouvez vous mettre là** you can sit (*ou* stand) there; **où ça se met?** where does it go?; **se mettre au lit** to get into bed; **se mettre au piano** to sit down at the piano; **se mettre de l'encre sur les doigts** to get ink on one's fingers

2 (*s'habiller*): **se mettre en maillot de bain** to get into *ou* put on a swimsuit; **n'avoir rien à se mettre** to have nothing to wear

3: **se mettre à** to begin, start; **se mettre à faire** to begin *ou* start doing *ou* to do; **se mettre au piano** to start learning the piano; **se mettre au travail/à l'étude** to get down to work/one's studies

meuble [mœbl] *nm* piece of furniture; **des ~s** furniture; **meublé** *nm* furnished flatlet (*BRIT*) *ou* room; **meubler** *vt* to furnish

meugler [møgle] *vi* to low, moo

meule [møl] *nf* (*de foin, blé*) stack; (*de fromage*) round; (*à broyer*) millstone

meunier [mønje, jɛʀ] *nm* miller; **meunière** *nf* miller's wife

meure *etc* [mœʀ] *vb voir* **mourir**

meurtre [mœʀtʀ] *nm* murder; **meurtrier, -ière** *adj* (*arme etc*) deadly; (*fureur, instincts*) murderous ♦ *nm/f* murderer(-eress)

meurtrir [mœʀtʀiʀ] *vt* to bruise; (*fig*) to wound; **meurtrissure** *nf* bruise

meus *etc* [mœ] *vb voir* **mouvoir**

meute [møt] *nf* pack

mexicain, e [mɛksikɛ̃, ɛn] *adj* Mexican ♦ *nm/f*: **M~, e** Mexican

Mexico [mɛksiko] *n* Mexico City

Mexique [mɛksik] *nm*: **le ~** Mexico

Mgr *abr* = **Monseigneur**

mi [mi] *nm* (*MUS*) E; (*en chantant la gamme*) mi ♦ *préfixe*: **~...** half(-); mid-; **à la ~-janvier** in mid-January; **à ~-hauteur** halfway up; **mi-bas** *nm inv* knee sock

miauler [mjole] *vi* to mew

miche [miʃ] *nf* round *ou* cob loaf

mi-chemin [miʃmɛ̃]: **à ~-~** *adv* halfway, midway

mi-clos, e [miklo, kloz] *adj* half-closed

micro [mikʀo] *nm* mike, microphone; (*INFORM*) micro

microbe [mikʀɔb] *nm* germ, microbe

micro...: **micro-onde** *nf*: **four à micro-ondes** microwave oven; **micro-ordinateur** *nm* microcomputer; **microscope** *nm* microscope; **microscopique** *adj* microscopic

midi [midi] *nm* midday, noon; (*moment du déjeuner*) lunchtime; (*sud*) south; **à ~** at 12 (o'clock) *ou* midday *ou* noon; **le M~** the South (of France), the Midi

mie [mi] *nf* crumb (of the loaf)

miel [mjɛl] *nm* honey; **mielleux, -euse** *adj* (*personne*) unctuous, syrupy

mien, ne [mjɛ̃, mjɛn] *pron*: **le(la)**

~(ne), les ~(ne)s mine; **les ~s** my family

miette [mjɛt] *nf* (*de pain, gâteau*) crumb; (*fig*: *de la conversation etc*) scrap; **en ~s** in pieces *ou* bits

MOT-CLÉ

mieux [mjø] *adv* **1** (*d'une meilleure façon*): **mieux (que)** better (than); **elle travaille/mange mieux** she works/eats better; **elle va mieux** she is better

2 (*de la meilleure façon*) best; **ce que je sais le mieux** what I know best; **les livres les mieux faits** the best made books

3: de mieux en mieux better and better

♦ *adj* **1** (*plus à l'aise, en meilleure forme*) better; **se sentir mieux** to feel better

2 (*plus satisfaisant*) better; **c'est mieux ainsi** it's better like this; **c'est le mieux des deux** it's the better of the two; **le(la) mieux, les mieux** the best; **demandez-lui, c'est le mieux** ask him, it's the best thing

3 (*plus joli*) better-looking

4: au mieux at best; **au mieux avec** on the best of terms with; **pour le mieux** for the best

♦ *nm* **1** (*progrès*) improvement

2: de mon/ton mieux as best I/you can (*ou* could); **faire de son mieux** to do one's best

mièvre [mjɛvʀ] *adj* mawkish (BRIT), sickly sentimental

mignon, ne [miɲɔ̃, ɔn] *adj* sweet, cute

migraine [migʀɛn] *nf* headache; (MÉD) migraine

mijoter [miʒɔte] *vt* to simmer; (*préparer avec soin*) to cook lovingly; (*fam*: *tramer*) to plot, cook up ♦ *vi* to simmer

mil [mil] *num* = **mille**

milieu, x [miljø] *nm* (*centre*) middle; (BIO, GÉO) environment; (*entourage social*) milieu; (*provenance*) background; (*pègre*): **le ~** the underworld; **au ~ de** in the middle of; **au beau** *ou* **en plein ~ (de)** right in the middle (of); **un juste ~** a happy medium

militaire [militɛʀ] *adj* military, army *cpd* ♦ *nm* serviceman

militant, e [militɑ̃, ɑ̃t] *adj, nm/f* militant

militer [milite] *vi* to be a militant

mille [mil] *num* a *ou* one thousand ♦ *nm* (*mesure*): **~ (marin)** nautical mile; **mettre dans le ~** (*fig*) to be bang on target; **millefeuille** *nm* cream *ou* vanilla slice; **millénaire** *nm* millennium ♦ *adj* thousand-year-old; (*fig*) ancient; **mille-pattes** *nm inv* centipede

millésimé, e [milezime] *adj* vintage *cpd*

millet [mijɛ] *nm* millet

milliard [miljaʀ] *nm* milliard, thousand million (BRIT), billion (US); **milliardaire** *nm/f* multimillionaire (BRIT), billionaire (US)

millier [milje] *nm* thousand; **un ~ (de)** a thousand or so, about a thousand; **par ~s** in (their) thousands, by the thousand

milligramme [miligʀam] *nm* milligramme

millimètre [milimɛtʀ] *nm* millimetre

million [miljɔ̃] *nm* million; **deux ~s de** two million; **millionnaire** *nm/f* millionaire

mime [mim] *nm/f* (*acteur*) mime(r) ♦ *nm* (*art*) mime, miming; **mimer** *vt* to mime; (*singer*) to mimic, take off

mimique [mimik] *nf* (*grimace*) (funny) face; (*signes*) gesticulations *pl*, sign language *no pl*

minable [minabl] *adj* (*décrépit*) shabby(-looking); (*médiocre*) pathetic

mince [mɛ̃s] *adj* thin; (*personne, taille*) slim, slender; (*fig*: *profit, connaissances*) slight, small, weak ♦ *excl*: **~ alors!** drat it!, darn it! (US); **minceur** *nf* thinness; (*d'une personne*) slimness, slenderness; **mincir** *vi* to get slimmer

mine [min] *nf* (*physionomie*) expression,

look; (*allure*) exterior, appearance; (*de crayon*) lead; (*gisement, explosif, fig: source*) mine; **avoir bonne ~** (*personne*) to look well; (*ironique*) to look an utter idiot; **avoir mauvaise ~** to look unwell *ou* poorly; **faire ~ de faire** to make a pretence of doing; **~ de rien** although you wouldn't think so
miner [mine] *vt* (*saper*) to undermine, erode; (MIL) to mine
minerai [minʀɛ] *nm* ore
minéral, e, -aux [mineʀal, o] *adj, nm* mineral
minéralogique [mineʀalɔʒik] *adj*: **numéro ~** registration number
minet, te [minɛ, ɛt] *nm/f* (*chat*) pussy-cat; (*péj*) young trendy
mineur, e [minœʀ] *adj* minor ♦ *nm/f* (JUR) minor, person under age ♦ *nm* (*travailleur*) miner
miniature [minjatyʀ] *adj, nf* miniature
minibus [minibys] *nm* minibus
mini-cassette [minikasɛt] *nf* cassette (recorder)
minier, -ière [minje, jɛʀ] *adj* mining
mini-jupe [miniʒyp] *nf* mini-skirt
minime [minim] *adj* minor, minimal
minimiser [minimize] *vt* to minimize; (*fig*) to play down
minimum [minimɔm] *adj, nm* minimum; **au ~** (*au moins*) at the very least
ministère [ministɛʀ] *nm* (*aussi* REL) ministry; (*cabinet*) government
ministre [ministʀ] *nm* (*aussi* REL) minister
Minitel ® [minitɛl] *nm videotext terminal and service*

Minitel

Minitel **is a personal computer terminal supplied free of change by France-Télécom to telephone subscribers. It serves as a computerized telephone directory as well as giving access to various services, including information on train timetables, the stock market and situations vacant. Services are accessed by phoning the relevant number and charged to the subscriber's phone bill.**

minoritaire [minɔʀitɛʀ] *adj* minority
minorité [minɔʀite] *nf* minority; **être en ~** to be in the *ou* a minority
minuit [minɥi] *nm* midnight
minuscule [minyskyl] *adj* minute, tiny ♦ *nf*: **(lettre) ~** small letter
minute [minyt] *nf* minute; **à la ~** (just) this instant; (*faire*) there and then; **minuter** *vt* to time; **minuterie** *nf* time switch
minutieux, -euse [minysjø, jøz] *adj* (*personne*) meticulous; (*travail*) minutely detailed
mirabelle [miʀabɛl] *nf* (cherry) plum
miracle [miʀɑkl] *nm* miracle
mirage [miʀaʒ] *nm* mirage
mire [miʀ] *nf*: **point de ~** (*fig*) focal point
miroir [miʀwaʀ] *nm* mirror
miroiter [miʀwate] *vi* to sparkle, shimmer; **faire ~ qch à qn** to paint sth in glowing colours for sb, dangle sth in front of sb's eyes
mis, e [mi, miz] *pp de* **mettre** ♦ *adj*: **bien ~** well-dressed
mise [miz] *nf* (*argent: au jeu*) stake; (*tenue*) clothing, attire; **être de ~** to be acceptable *ou* in season; **~ au point** (*fig*) clarification; **~ de fonds** capital outlay; **~ en examen** charging, indictment; **~ en plis** set; **~ en scène** production
miser [mize] *vt* (*enjeu*) to stake, bet; **~ sur** (*cheval, numéro*) to bet on; (*fig*) to bank *ou* count on
misérable [mizeʀabl] *adj* (*lamentable, malheureux*) pitiful, wretched; (*pauvre*) poverty-stricken; (*insignifiant, mesquin*) miserable ♦ *nm/f* wretch
misère [mizɛʀ] *nf* (extreme) poverty, destitution; **~s** *nfpl* (*malheurs*) woes, miseries; (*ennuis*) little troubles; **salaire**

de ~ starvation wage
missile [misil] *nm* missile
mission [misjɔ̃] *nf* mission; **partir en ~** (ADMIN, POL) to go on an assignment; **missionnaire** *nm/f* missionary
mit [mi] *vb voir* **mettre**
mité, e [mite] *adj* moth-eaten
mi-temps [mitɑ̃] *nf inv* (SPORT: *période*) half; (: *pause*) half-time; **à ~-~** part-time
miteux, -euse [mitø, øz] *adj* (*lieu*) seedy
mitigé, e [mitiʒe] *adj*: **sentiments ~s** mixed feelings
mitonner [mitɔne] *vt* to cook with loving care; (*fig*) to cook up quietly
mitoyen, ne [mitwajɛ̃, jɛn] *adj* (*mur*) common, party *cpd*
mitrailler [mitʀɑje] *vt* to machine-gun; (*fig*) to pelt, bombard; (: *photographier*) to take shot after shot of; **mitraillette** *nf* submachine gun; **mitrailleuse** *nf* machine gun
mi-voix [mivwa]: **à ~-~** *adv* in a low *ou* hushed voice
mixage [miksaʒ] *nm* (CINÉMA) (sound) mixing
mixer [miksœʀ] *nm* (food) mixer
mixte [mikst] *adj* (*gén*) mixed; (SCOL) mixed, coeducational
mixture [mikstyʀ] *nf* mixture; (*fig*) concoction
Mlle (*pl* **Mlles**) *abr* = **Mademoiselle**
MM *abr* = **Messieurs**
Mme (*pl* **Mmes**) *abr* = **Madame**
mobile [mɔbil] *adj* mobile; (*pièce de machine*) moving ♦ *nm* (*motif*) motive; (*œuvre d'art*) mobile
mobilier, -ière [mɔbilje, jɛʀ] *nm* furniture
mobiliser [mɔbilize] *vt* to mobilize
mocassin [mɔkasɛ̃] *nm* moccasin
moche [mɔʃ] (*fam*) *adj* (*laid*) ugly; (*mauvais*) rotten
modalité [mɔdalite] *nf* form, mode; **~s de paiement** methods of payment
mode [mɔd] *nf* fashion ♦ *nm* (*manière*) form, mode; **à la ~** fashionable, in fashion; **~ d'emploi** directions *pl* (for use)
modèle [mɔdɛl] *adj, nm* model; (*qui pose*: *de peintre*) sitter; **~ déposé** registered design; **~ réduit** small-scale model; **modeler** *vt* to model
modem [mɔdɛm] *nm* modem
modéré, e [mɔdeʀe] *adj, nm/f* moderate
modérer [mɔdeʀe] *vt* to moderate; **se ~** *vi* to restrain o.s.
moderne [mɔdɛʀn] *adj* modern ♦ *nm* (*style*) modern style; (*meubles*) modern furniture; **moderniser** *vt* to modernize
modeste [mɔdɛst] *adj* modest; **modestie** *nf* modesty
modifier [mɔdifje] *vt* to modify, alter; **se ~** *vi* to alter
modique [mɔdik] *adj* modest
modiste [mɔdist] *nf* milliner
module [mɔdyl] *nm* module
moelle [mwal] *nf* marrow; **~ épinière** spinal cord
moelleux, -euse [mwalø, øz] *adj* soft; (*gâteau*) light and moist
mœurs [mœʀ] *nfpl* (*conduite*) morals; (*manières*) manners; (*pratiques sociales, mode de vie*) habits
mohair [mɔɛʀ] *nm* mohair
moi [mwa] *pron* me; (*emphatique*): **~, je** ... for my part, I ..., I myself ...; **à ~** mine; **moi-même** *pron* myself; (*emphatique*) I myself
moindre [mwɛ̃dʀ] *adj* lesser; lower; **le(la) ~, les ~s** the least, the slightest; **merci – c'est la ~ des choses!** thank you – it's a pleasure!
moine [mwan] *nm* monk, friar
moineau, x [mwano] *nm* sparrow

MOT-CLÉ

moins [mwɛ̃] *adv* **1** (*comparatif*): **moins (que)** less (than); **moins grand que** less tall than, not as tall as; **moins je travaille, mieux je me porte** the less I work, the better I feel

2 (*superlatif*): **le moins** (the) least; **c'est ce que j'aime le moins** it's what I like (the) least; **le(la) moins doué(e)** the least gifted; **au moins, du moins** at least; **pour le moins** at the very least

3: **moins de** (*quantité*) less (than); (*nombre*) fewer (than); **moins de sable/d'eau** less sand/water; **moins de livres/gens** fewer books/people; **moins de 2 ans** less than 2 years; **moins de midi** not yet midday

4: **de moins, en moins**: **100 F/3 jours de moins** 100F/3 days less; **3 livres en moins** 3 books fewer; 3 books too few; **de l'argent en moins** less money; **le soleil en moins** but for the sun, minus the sun; **de moins en moins** less and less

5: **à moins de, à moins que** unless; **à moins de faire** unless we do (*ou* he does *etc*); **à moins que tu ne fasses** unless you do; **à moins d'un accident** barring any accident

♦ *prép*: **4 moins 2** 4 minus 2; **il est moins 5** it's 5 to; **il fait moins 5** it's 5 (degrees) below (freezing), it's minus 5

mois [mwa] *nm* month

moisi [mwazi] *nm* mould, mildew; **odeur de ~** musty smell; **moisir** *vi* to go mouldy; **moisissure** *nf* mould *no pl*

moisson [mwasɔ̃] *nf* harvest; **moissonner** *vt* to harvest, reap; **moissonneuse** *nf* (*machine*) harvester

moite [mwat] *adj* sweaty, sticky

moitié [mwatje] *nf* half; **la ~** half; **la ~ de** half (of); **la ~ du temps** half the time; **à la ~ de** halfway through, **à ~** (*avant le verbe*) half; (*avant l'adjectif*) half-; **à ~ prix** (at) half-price; **~ moitié** half-and-half

moka [mɔka] *nm* coffee gateau

mol [mɔl] *adj voir* **mou**

molaire [mɔlɛʀ] *nf* molar

molester [mɔlɛste] *vt* to manhandle, maul (about)

molle [mɔl] *adj voir* **mou; mollement** *adv* (*péj*: *travailler*) sluggishly; (*protester*) feebly

mollet [mɔlɛ] *nm* calf ♦ *adj m*: **œuf ~** soft-boiled egg

molletonné, e [mɔltɔne] *adj* fleece-lined

mollir [mɔliʀ] *vi* (*fléchir*) to relent; (*substance*) to go soft

mollusque [mɔlysk] *nm* mollusc

môme [mom] (*fam*) *nm/f* (*enfant*) brat

moment [mɔmɑ̃] *nm* moment; **ce n'est pas le ~** this is not the (right) time; **pour un bon ~** for a good while; **pour le ~** for the moment, for the time being; **au ~ de** at the time of; **au ~ où** just as; **à tout ~** (*peut arriver etc*) at any time *ou* moment; (*constamment*) constantly, continually; **en ce ~** at the moment; at present; **sur le ~** at the time; **par ~s** now and then, at times; **du ~ où** *ou* **que** seeing that, since; **momentané, e** *adj* temporary, momentary; **momentanément** *adv* (*court instant*) for a short while

momie [mɔmi] *nf* mummy

mon, ma [mɔ̃, ma] (*pl* **mes**) *adj* my

Monaco [mɔnako] *nm* Monaco

monarchie [mɔnaʀʃi] *nf* monarchy

monastère [mɔnastɛʀ] *nm* monastery

monceau, x [mɔ̃so] *nm* heap

mondain, e [mɔ̃dɛ̃, ɛn] *adj* (*vie*) society *cpd*

monde [mɔ̃d] *nm* world; (*haute société*): **le ~** (high) society; **il y a du ~** (*beaucoup de gens*) there are a lot of people; (*quelques personnes*) there are some people; **beaucoup/peu de ~** many/few people; **mettre au ~** to bring into the world; **pas le moins du ~** not in the least; **se faire un ~ de qch** to make a great deal of fuss about sth; **mondial, e, -aux** *adj* (*population*) world *cpd*; (*influence*) world-wide; **mondialement** *adv* throughout the world

monégasque [mɔnegask] *adj* Monegasque, of *ou* from Monaco

monétaire [mɔnetɛʀ] *adj* monetary

moniteur, -trice [mɔnitœʀ, tʀis] *nm/f* (*SPORT*) instructor(-tress); (*de colonie de vacances*) supervisor ♦ *nm* (*écran*) monitor

monnaie [mɔnɛ] *nf* (*ÉCON, gén*: *moyen d'échange*) currency; (*petites pièces*): **avoir de la ~** to have (some) change; **une pièce de ~** a coin; **faire de la ~** to get (some) change; **avoir/faire la ~ de 20 F** to have change of/get change for 20 F; **rendre à qn la ~ (sur 20 F)** to give sb the change (out of *ou* from 20 F); **monnayer** *vt* to convert into cash; (*talent*) to capitalize on

monologue [mɔnɔlɔg] *nm* monologue, soliloquy; **monologuer** *vi* to soliloquize

monopole [mɔnɔpɔl] *nm* monopoly

monotone [mɔnɔtɔn] *adj* monotonous

Monsieur [məsjø] (*pl* **Messieurs**) *titre* Mr ♦ *nm* (*homme quelconque*): **un/le m~** a/the gentleman; **~, ...** (*en tête de lettre*) Dear Sir, ...; *voir aussi* **Madame**

monstre [mɔ̃stʀ] *nm* monster ♦ *adj* (*fam*: *colossal*) monstrous; **un travail ~** a fantastic amount of work; **monstrueux, -euse** *adj* monstrous

mont [mɔ̃] *nm*: **par ~s et par vaux** up hill and down dale; **le M~ Blanc** Mont Blanc

montage [mɔ̃taʒ] *nm* (*assemblage*: *d'appareil*) assembly; (*PHOTO*) photomontage; (*CINÉMA*) editing

montagnard, e [mɔ̃taɲaʀ, aʀd] *adj* mountain *cpd* ♦ *nm/f* mountain-dweller

montagne [mɔ̃taɲ] *nf* (*cime*) mountain; (*région*): **la ~** the mountains *pl*; **~s russes** big dipper *sg*, switchback *sg*; **montagneux, -euse** *adj* mountainous; (*basse montagne*) hilly

montant, e [mɔ̃tɑ̃, ɑ̃t] *adj* rising; **pull à col ~** high-necked jumper ♦ *nm* (*somme, total*) (sum) total, (total) amount; (*de fenêtre*) upright; (*de lit*) post

monte-charge [mɔ̃tʃaʀʒ] *nm inv* goods lift, hoist

montée [mɔ̃te] *nf* (*des prix, hostilités*) rise; (*escalade*) climb; (*côte*) hill; **au milieu de la ~** halfway up

monter [mɔ̃te] *vt* (*escalier, côte*) to go (*ou* come) up; (*valise, paquet*) to take (*ou* bring) up; (*étagère*) to raise; (*tente, échafaudage*) to put up; (*machine*) to assemble; (*CINÉMA*) to edit; (*THÉÂTRE*) to put on, stage; (*société etc*) to set up ♦ *vi* to go (*ou* come) up; (*prix, niveau, température*) to go up, rise; (*passager*) to get on; **se ~ à** (*frais etc*) to add up to, come to; **~ à pied** to walk up, go up on foot; **~ dans le train/l'avion** to get into the train/plane, board the train/plane; **~ sur** to climb up onto; **~ à cheval** (*faire du cheval*) to ride, go riding

montre [mɔ̃tʀ] *nf* watch; **contre la ~** (*SPORT*) against the clock; **montre-bracelet** *nf* wristwatch

montrer [mɔ̃tʀe] *vt* to show; **~ qch à qn** to show sb sth

monture [mɔ̃tyʀ] *nf* (*cheval*) mount; (*de lunettes*) frame; (*d'une bague*) setting

monument [mɔnymɑ̃] *nm* monument; **~ aux morts** war memorial

moquer [mɔke]: **se ~ de** *vt* to make fun of, laugh at; (*fam*: *se désintéresser de*) not to care about; (*tromper*): **se ~ de qn** to take sb for a ride; **moquerie** *nf* mockery

moquette [mɔkɛt] *nf* fitted carpet

moqueur, -euse [mɔkœʀ, øz] *adj* mocking

moral, e, -aux [mɔʀal, o] *adj* moral ♦ *nm* morale; **avoir le ~** (*fam*) to be in good spirits; **avoir le ~ à zéro** (*fam*) to be really down; **morale** *nf* (*mœurs*) morals *pl*; (*valeurs*) moral standards *pl*, morality; (*d'une fable etc*) moral; **faire la morale à** to lecture, preach at; **moralité** *nf* morality; (*de fable*) moral

morceau, x [mɔʀso] *nm* piece, bit;

(*d'une œuvre*) passage, extract; (*MUS*) piece; (*CULIN*: *de viande*) cut; (*de sucre*) lump; **mettre en ~x** to pull to pieces *ou* bits; **manger un ~** to have a bite (to eat)

morceler [mɔʀsəle] *vt* to break up, divide up

mordant, e [mɔʀdɑ̃, ɑ̃t] *adj* (*ton, remarque*) scathing, cutting; (*ironie, froid*) biting ♦ *nm* (*style*) bite, punch

mordiller [mɔʀdije] *vt* to nibble at, chew at

mordre [mɔʀdʀ] *vt* to bite ♦ *vi* (*poisson*) to bite; **~ sur** (*fig*) to go over into, overlap into; **~ à l'hameçon** to bite, rise to the bait

mordu, e [mɔʀdy] (*fam*) *nm/f* enthusiast; **un ~ de jazz** a jazz fanatic

morfondre [mɔʀfɔ̃dʀ]: **se ~** *vi* to mope

morgue [mɔʀg] *nf* (*arrogance*) haughtiness; (*lieu*: *de la police*) morgue; (: *à l'hôpital*) mortuary

morne [mɔʀn] *adj* dismal, dreary

morose [mɔʀoz] *adj* sullen, morose

mors [mɔʀ] *nm* bit

morse [mɔʀs] *nm* (*ZOOL*) walrus; (*TÉL*) Morse (code)

morsure [mɔʀsyʀ] *nf* bite

mort[1] [mɔʀ] *nf* death

mort[2]**, e** [mɔʀ, mɔʀt] *pp de* **mourir** ♦ *adj* dead ♦ *nm/f* (*défunt*) dead man/woman; (*victime*): **il y a eu plusieurs ~s** several people were killed, there were several killed; **~ de peur/fatigue** frightened to death/dead tired

mortalité [mɔʀtalite] *nf* mortality, death rate

mortel, le [mɔʀtɛl] *adj* (*poison etc*) deadly, lethal; (*accident, blessure*) fatal; (*silence, ennemi*) deadly; (*péché*) mortal; (*fam*: *ennuyeux*) deadly boring

mortier [mɔʀtje] *nm* (*gén*) mortar

mort-né, e [mɔʀne] *adj* (*enfant*) stillborn

mortuaire [mɔʀtɥɛʀ] *adj*: **avis ~** death announcement

morue [mɔʀy] *nf* (*ZOOL*) cod *inv*

mosaïque [mɔzaik] *nf* mosaic

Moscou [mɔsku] *n* Moscow

mosquée [mɔske] *nf* mosque

mot [mo] *nm* word; (*message*) line, note; **~ à ~** word for word; **~ d'ordre** watchword; **~ de passe** password; **~s croisés** crossword (puzzle) *sg*

motard [mɔtaʀ, aʀd] *nm* biker; (*policier*) motorcycle cop

motel [mɔtɛl] *nm* motel

moteur, -trice [mɔtœʀ, tʀis] *adj* (*ANAT, PHYSIOL*) motor; (*TECH*) driving; (*AUTO*): **à 4 roues motrices** 4-wheel drive ♦ *nm* engine, motor; **à ~** power-driven, motor *cpd*

motif [mɔtif] *nm* (*cause*) motive; (*décoratif*) design, pattern, motif; **sans ~** groundless

motivation [mɔtivasjɔ̃] *nf* motivation

motiver [mɔtive] *vt* to motivate; (*justifier*) to justify, account for

moto [moto] *nf* (motor)bike; **motocycliste** *nm/f* motorcyclist

motorisé, e [mɔtɔʀize] *adj* (*personne*) having transport *ou* a car

motrice [mɔtʀis] *adj voir* **moteur**

motte [mɔt] *nf*: **~ de terre** lump of earth, clod (of earth); **~ de beurre** lump of butter

mou (mol), molle [mu, mɔl] *adj* soft; (*personne*) lethargic; (*protestations*) weak ♦ *nm*: **avoir du mou** to be slack

moucharder [muʃaʀde] (*fam*) *vt* (*SCOL*) to sneak on; (*POLICE*) to grass on

mouche [muʃ] *nf* fly

moucher [muʃe]: **se ~** *vi* to blow one's nose

moucheron [muʃʀɔ̃] *nm* midge

mouchoir [muʃwaʀ] *nm* handkerchief, hanky; **~ en papier** tissue, paper hanky

moudre [mudʀ] *vt* to grind

moue [mu] *nf* pout; **faire la ~** to pout; (*fig*) to pull a face

mouette [mwɛt] *nf* (sea)gull

moufle [mufl] *nf* (*gant*) mitt(en)

mouillé, e [muje] *adj* wet

mouiller [muje] *vt* (*humecter*) to wet, moisten; (*tremper*): **~ qn/qch** to make sb/sth wet ♦ *vi* (*NAVIG*) to lie *ou* be at anchor; **se ~** to get wet; (*fam*: *prendre des risques*) to commit o.s.

moulant, e [mulɑ̃, ɑ̃t] *adj* figure-hugging

moule [mul] *nf* mussel ♦ *nm* (*CULIN*) mould; **~ à gâteaux** ♦ *nm* cake tin (*BRIT*) *ou* pan (*US*)

moulent [mul] *voir* **moudre; mouler**

mouler [mule] *vt* (*suj*: *vêtement*) to hug, fit closely round

moulin [mulɛ̃] *nm* mill; **~ à café/à poivre** coffee/pepper mill; **~ à légumes** (vegetable) shredder; **~ à paroles** (*fig*) chatterbox; **~ à vent** windmill

moulinet [mulinɛ] *nm* (*de canne à pêche*) reel; (*mouvement*): **faire des ~s avec qch** to whirl sth around

moulinette ® [mulinɛt] *nf* (vegetable) shredder

moulu, e [muly] *pp de* **moudre**

mourant, e [muʀɑ̃, ɑ̃t] *adj* dying

mourir [muʀiʀ] *vi* to die; (*civilisation*) to die out; **~ de froid/faim** to die of exposure/hunger; **~ de faim/d'ennui** (*fig*) to be starving/be bored to death; **~ d'envie de faire** to be dying to do

mousse [mus] *nf* (*BOT*) moss; (*de savon*) lather; (*écume*: *sur eau, bière*) froth, foam; (*CULIN*) mousse ♦ *nm* (*NAVIG*) ship's boy; **~ à raser** shaving foam

mousseline [muslin] *nf* muslin; **pommes ~** mashed potatoes

mousser [muse] *vi* (*bière, détergent*) to foam; (*savon*) to lather; **mousseux, -euse** *adj* frothy ♦ *nm*: **(vin) mousseux** sparkling wine

mousson [musɔ̃] *nf* monsoon

moustache [mustaʃ] *nf* moustache; **~s** *nfpl* (*du chat*) whiskers *pl*; **moustachu, e** *adj* with a moustache

moustiquaire [mustikɛʀ] *nf* mosquito net

moustique [mustik] *nm* mosquito

moutarde [mutaʀd] *nf* mustard

mouton [mutɔ̃] *nm* sheep *inv*; (*peau*) sheepskin; (*CULIN*) mutton

mouvement [muvmɑ̃] *nm* movement; (*fig*: *impulsion*) gesture; **avoir un bon ~** to make a nice gesture; **en ~** in motion; on the move; **mouvementé, e** *adj* (*vie, poursuite*) eventful; (*réunion*) turbulent

mouvoir [muvwaʀ]: **se ~** *vi* to move

moyen, ne [mwajɛ̃, jɛn] *adj* average; (*tailles, prix*) medium; (*de grandeur moyenne*) medium-sized ♦ *nm* (*façon*) means *sg*, way; **~s** *nmpl* (*capacités*) means; **très ~** (*résultats*) pretty poor; **je n'en ai pas les ~s** I can't afford it; **au ~ de** by means of; **par tous les ~s** by every possible means, every possible way; **par ses propres ~s** all by oneself; **~ âge** Middle Ages; **~ de transport** means of transport

moyennant [mwajɛnɑ̃] *prép* (*somme*) for; (*service, conditions*) in return for; (*travail, effort*) with

moyenne [mwajɛn] *nf* average; (*MATH*) mean; (*SCOL*) pass mark; **en ~** on (an) average; **~ d'âge** average age

Moyen-Orient [mwajɛnɔʀjɑ̃] *nm*: **le ~-~** the Middle East

moyeu, x [mwajø] *nm* hub

MST *sigle f* (= *maladie sexuellement transmissible*) STD

MTC *sigle m* (= *mécanisme du taux de change*) ERM

mû, mue [my] *pp de* **mouvoir**

muer [mɥe] *vi* (*oiseau, mammifère*) to moult; (*serpent*) to slough; (*jeune garçon*): **il mue** his voice is breaking; **se ~ en** to transform into

muet, te [mɥɛ, mɥɛt] *adj* dumb; (*fig*): **~ d'admiration** *etc* speechless with admiration *etc*; (*CINÉMA*) silent ♦ *nm/f* mute

mufle [myfl] *nm* muzzle; (*fam*: *goujat*) boor

mugir [myʒiʀ] *vi* (*taureau*) to bellow; (*vache*) to low; (*fig*) to howl

muguet [mygɛ] *nm* lily of the valley

mule [myl] *nf* (*ZOOL*) (she-)mule

mulet [mylɛ] *nm* (ZOOL) (he-)mule
multinationale [myltinasjɔnal] *nf* multinational
multiple [myltipl] *adj* multiple, numerous; (*varié*) many, manifold; **multiplication** *nf* multiplication; **multiplier** *vt* to multiply; **se multiplier** *vi* to multiply
municipal, e, -aux [mynisipal, o] *adj* (*élections, stade*) municipal; (*conseil*) town *cpd*; **piscine/bibliothèque ~e** public swimming pool/library; **municipalité** *nf* (*ville*) municipality; (*conseil*) town council
munir [myniʀ] *vt*: **~ qch de** to equip sth with; **se ~ de** to arm o.s. with
munitions [mynisjɔ̃] *nfpl* ammunition *sg*
mur [myʀ] *nm* wall; **~ du son** sound barrier
mûr, e [myʀ] *adj* ripe; (*personne*) mature
muraille [myʀɑj] *nf* (high) wall
mural, e, -aux [myʀal, o] *adj* wall *cpd*; (*art*) mural
mûre [myʀ] *nf* blackberry
muret [myʀɛ] *nm* low wall
mûrir [myʀiʀ] *vi* (*fruit, blé*) to ripen; (*abcès*) to come to a head; (*fig: idée, personne*) to mature ♦ *vt* (*projet*) to nurture; (*personne*) to (make) mature
murmure [myʀmyʀ] *nm* murmur; **murmurer** *vi* to murmur
muscade [myskad] *nf* (*aussi:* **noix (de) ~**) nutmeg
muscat [myska] *nm* (*raisins*) muscat grape; (*vin*) muscatel (wine)
muscle [myskl] *nm* muscle; **musclé, e** *adj* muscular; (*fig*) strong-arm
museau, x [myzo] *nm* muzzle; (CULIN) brawn
musée [myze] *nm* museum; (*de peinture*) art gallery
museler [myz(ə)le] *vt* to muzzle; **muselière** *nf* muzzle
musette [myzɛt] *nf* (*sac*) lunchbag
musical, e, -aux [myzikal, o] *adj* musical
music-hall [myzikol] *nm* (*salle*) variety theatre; (*genre*) variety
musicien, ne [myzisjɛ̃, jɛn] *adj* musical ♦ *nm/f* musician
musique [myzik] *nf* music; **~ d'ambiance** background music
musulman, e [myzylmɑ̃, an] *adj, nm/f* Moslem, Muslim
mutation [mytasjɔ̃] *nf* (ADMIN) transfer
muter [myte] *vt* to transfer, move
mutilé, e [mytile] *nm/f* disabled person (*through loss of limbs*)
mutiler [mytile] *vt* to mutilate, maim
mutin, e [mytɛ̃, in] *adj* (*air, ton*) mischievous, impish ♦ *nm/f* (MIL, NAVIG) mutineer; **mutinerie** *nf* mutiny
mutisme [mytism] *nm* silence
mutuel, le [mytɥɛl] *adj* mutual; **mutuelle** *nf voluntary insurance premiums for back-up health cover*
myope [mjɔp] *adj* short-sighted
myosotis [mjɔzɔtis] *nm* forget-me-not
myrtille [miʀtij] *nf* bilberry
mystère [mistɛʀ] *nm* mystery; **mystérieux, -euse** *adj* mysterious
mystifier [mistifje] *vt* to fool
mythe [mit] *nm* myth
mythologie [mitɔlɔʒi] *nf* mythology

N, n

n' [n] *adv voir* **ne**
nacre [nakʀ] *nf* mother of pearl
nage [naʒ] *nf* swimming; (*manière*) style of swimming, stroke; **traverser/s'éloigner à la ~** to swim across/away; **en ~** bathed in sweat; **nageoire** *nf* fin; **nager** *vi* to swim; **nageur, -euse** *nm/f* swimmer
naguère [nagɛʀ] *adv* formerly
naïf, -ïve [naif, naiv] *adj* naïve
nain, e [nɛ̃, nɛn] *nm/f* dwarf
naissance [nɛsɑ̃s] *nf* birth; **donner ~ à** to give birth to; (*fig*) to give rise to
naître [nɛtʀ] *vi* to be born; (*fig*): **~ de** to arise from, be born out of; **il est né**

en 1960 he was born in 1960; **faire ~** (*fig*) to give rise to, arouse
naïve [naiv] *adj voir* **naïf**
naïveté [naivte] *nf* naïvety
nana [nana] (*fam*) *nf* (*fille*) chick, bird (*BRIT*)
nantir [nɑ̃tiʀ] *vt*: **~ qn de** to provide sb with; **les nantis** (*péj*) the well-to-do
nappe [nap] *nf* tablecloth; (*de pétrole, gaz*) layer; **~ phréatique** ground water; **napperon** *nm* table-mat
naquit *etc* [naki] *vb voir* **naître**
narcodollars [naʀkodɔlaʀ] *nmpl* drug money *sg*
narguer [naʀge] *vt* to taunt
narine [naʀin] *nf* nostril
narquois, e [naʀkwa, waz] *adj* mocking
natal, e [natal] *adj* native; **natalité** *nf* birth rate
natation [natasjɔ̃] *nf* swimming
natif, -ive [natif, iv] *adj* native
nation [nasjɔ̃] *nf* nation; **national, e, -aux** *adj* national; **nationale** *nf*: **(route) nationale** ≃ A road (*BRIT*), ≃ state highway (*US*); **nationaliser** *vt* to nationalize; **nationalisme** *nm* nationalism; **nationalité** *nf* nationality
natte [nat] *nf* (*cheveux*) plait; (*tapis*) mat
naturaliser [natyʀalize] *vt* to naturalize
nature [natyʀ] *nf* nature ♦ *adj, adv* (*CULIN*) plain, without seasoning or sweetening; (*café, thé*) black, without sugar; (*yaourt*) natural; **payer en ~** to pay in kind; **~ morte** still-life; **naturel, le** *adj* (*gén, aussi enfant*) natural ♦ *nm* (*absence d'affectation*) naturalness; (*caractère*) disposition, nature; **naturellement** *adv* naturally; (*bien sûr*) of course
naufrage [nofʀaʒ] *nm* (ship)wreck; **faire ~** to be shipwrecked
nauséabond, e [nozeabɔ̃, ɔ̃d] *adj* foul
nausée [noze] *nf* nausea
nautique [notik] *adj* nautical, water *cpd*; **sports ~s** water sports
naval, e [naval] *adj* naval; (*industrie*) shipbuilding
navet [navɛ] *nm* turnip; (*péj*: *film*) rubbishy film
navette [navɛt] *nf* shuttle; **faire la ~ (entre)** to go to and fro *ou* shuttle (between)
navigateur [navigatœʀ, tʀis] *nm* (*NAVIG*) seafarer; (*INFORM*) browser
navigation [navigasjɔ̃] *nf* navigation, sailing
naviguer [navige] *vi* to navigate, sail; **~ sur Internet** to browse the Internet
navire [naviʀ] *nm* ship
navrer [navʀe] *vt* to upset, distress; **je suis navré** I'm so sorry
ne, n' [n(ə)] *adv voir* **pas**; **plus**; **jamais** *etc*; (*sans valeur négative*: *non traduit*): **c'est plus loin que je ~ le croyais** it's further than I thought
né, e [ne] *pp* (*voir naître*): **~ en 1960** born in 1960; **~e Scott** née Scott
néanmoins [neɑ̃mwɛ̃] *adv* nevertheless
néant [neɑ̃] *nm* nothingness; **réduire à ~** to bring to nought; (*espoir*) to dash
nécessaire [nesesɛʀ] *adj* necessary ♦ *nm* necessary; (*sac*) kit; **je vais faire le ~** I'll see to it; **~ de couture** sewing kit; **nécessité** *nf* necessity; **nécessiter** *vt* to require
nécrologique [nekʀɔlɔʒik] *adj*: **rubrique ~** obituary column
néerlandais, e [neɛʀlɑ̃dɛ, ɛz] *adj* Dutch
nef [nɛf] *nf* (*d'église*) nave
néfaste [nefast] *adj* (*nuisible*) harmful; (*funeste*) ill-fated
négatif, -ive [negatif, iv] *adj* negative ♦ *nm* (*PHOTO*) negative
négligé, e [negliʒe] *adj* (*en désordre*) slovenly ♦ *nm* (*tenue*) negligee
négligeable [negliʒabl] *adj* negligible
négligent, e [negliʒɑ̃, ɑ̃t] *adj* careless, negligent
négliger [negliʒe] *vt* (*tenue*) to be careless about; (*avis, précautions*) to disregard; (*épouse, jardin*) to neglect; **~ de**

faire to fail to do, not bother to do
négoce [negɔs] *nm* trade
négociant [negɔsjɑ̃, jɑ̃t] *nm* merchant
négociation [negɔsjasjɔ̃] *nf* negotiation; **négocier** *vi, vt* to negotiate
nègre [nɛgʀ] (*péj*) *nm* (*écrivain*) ghost (writer)
neige [nɛʒ] *nf* snow; **neiger** *vi* to snow
nénuphar [nenyfaʀ] *nm* water-lily
néon [neɔ̃] *nm* neon
néo-zélandais, e [neoʒelɑ̃dɛ, ɛz] *adj* New Zealand *cpd* ♦ *nm/f*: **N~-Z~, e** New Zealander
nerf [nɛʀ] *nm* nerve; **être sur les ~s** to be all keyed up; **allons, du ~!** come on, buck up!; **nerveux, -euse** *adj* nervous; (*irritable*) touchy, nervy; (*voiture*) nippy, responsive; **nervosité** *nf* excitability, tenseness; (*irritabilité passagère*) irritability, nerviness
nervure [nɛʀvyʀ] *nf* vein
n'est-ce pas [nɛspɑ] *adv* isn't it?, won't you? *etc, selon le verbe qui précède*
Net [nɛt] *nm* (*Internet*): **le ~** the Net
net, nette [nɛt] *adj* (*sans équivoque, distinct*) clear; (*évident: amélioration, différence*) marked, distinct; (*propre*) neat, clean; (COMM: *prix, salaire*) net ♦ *adv* (*refuser*) flatly ♦ *nm*: **mettre au ~** to copy out; **s'arrêter ~** to stop dead; **nettement** *adv* clearly, distinctly; (*incontestablement*) decidedly, distinctly; **netteté** *nf* clearness
nettoyage [netwajaʒ] *nm* cleaning; **~ à sec** dry cleaning
nettoyer [netwaje] *vt* to clean
neuf[1] [nœf] *num* nine
neuf[2], neuve [nœf, nœv] *adj* new ♦ *nm*: **remettre à ~** to do up (as good as new), refurbish; **quoi de ~?** what's new?
neutre [nøtʀ] *adj* neutral; (LING) neuter
neuve [nœv] *adj voir* **neuf[2]**
neuvième [nœvjɛm] *num* ninth
neveu, x [n(ə)vø] *nm* nephew
névrosé, e [nevʀoze] *adj, nm/f* neurotic
nez [ne] *nm* nose; **~ à ~ avec** face to face with; **avoir du ~** to have flair
ni [ni] *conj*: **~ ... ~** neither ... nor; **je n'aime ~ les lentilles ~ les épinards** I like neither lentils nor spinach; **il n'a dit ~ oui ~ non** he didn't say either yes or no; **elles ne sont venues ~ l'une ~ l'autre** neither of them came
niais, e [njɛ, njɛz] *adj* silly, thick
niche [niʃ] *nf* (*du chien*) kennel; (*de mur*) recess, niche; **nicher** *vi* to nest
nid [ni] *nm* nest; **~ de poule** pothole
nièce [njɛs] *nf* niece
nier [nje] *vt* to deny
nigaud, e [nigo, od] *nm/f* booby, fool
Nil [nil] *nm*: **le ~** the Nile
n'importe [nɛ̃pɔʀt] *adv*: **~ qui/quoi/où** anybody/anything/anywhere; **~ quand** any time; **~ quel/quelle** any; **~ lequel/laquelle** any (one); **~ comment** (*sans soin*) carelessly
niveau, x [nivo] *nm* level; (*des élèves, études*) standard; **~ de vie** standard of living
niveler [niv(ə)le] *vt* to level
NN *abr* (= *nouvelle norme*) *revised standard of hotel classification*
noble [nɔbl] *adj* noble; **noblesse** *nf* nobility; (*d'une action etc*) nobleness
noce [nɔs] *nf* wedding; (*gens*) wedding party (*ou* guests *pl*); **faire la ~** (*fam*) to go on a binge
nocif, -ive [nɔsif, iv] *adj* harmful
nocturne [nɔktyʀn] *adj* nocturnal ♦ *nf* late-night opening
Noël [nɔɛl] *nm* Christmas
nœud [nø] *nm* knot; (*ruban*) bow; **~ papillon** bow tie
noir, e [nwaʀ] *adj* black; (*obscur, sombre*) dark ♦ *nm/f* black man/woman ♦ *nm*: **dans le ~** in the dark; **travail au ~** moonlighting; **travailler au ~** to work on the side; **noircir** *vt, vi* to blacken; **noire** *nf* (MUS) crotchet (BRIT), quarter note (US)
noisette [nwazɛt] *nf* hazelnut
noix [nwa] *nf* walnut; (CULIN): **une ~ de**

beurre a knob of butter; ~ **de cajou** cashew nut; ~ **de coco** coconut; **à la ~** (*fam*) worthless

nom [nɔ̃] *nm* name; (LING) noun; ~ **de famille** surname; ~ **de jeune fille** maiden name; ~ **déposé** trade name; ~ **propre** proper noun

nomade [nɔmad] *nm/f* nomad

nombre [nɔ̃bʀ] *nm* number; **venir en ~** to come in large numbers; **depuis ~ d'années** for many years; **au ~ de mes amis** among my friends; **nombreux, -euse** *adj* many, numerous; (*avec nom sg*: *foule etc*) large; **peu nombreux** few

nombril [nɔ̃bʀi(l)] *nm* navel

nommer [nɔme] *vt* to name; (*élire*) to appoint, nominate; **se ~**: **il se nomme Pascal** his name's Pascal, he's called Pascal

non [nɔ̃] *adv* (*réponse*) no; (*avec loin, sans, seulement*) not; ~ **(pas) que** not that; **moi ~ plus** neither do I, I don't either; **c'est bon ~?** (*exprimant le doute*) it's good, isn't it?

non-alcoolisé, e [nɔ̃alkɔlize] *adj* non-alcoholic

nonante [nɔnɑ̃t] (BELGIQUE, SUISSE) *num* ninety

non-fumeur [nɔ̃fymœʀ, øz] *nm* non-smoker

non-sens [nɔ̃sɑ̃s] *nm* absurdity

nonchalant, e [nɔ̃ʃalɑ̃, ɑ̃t] *adj* nonchalant

nord [nɔʀ] *nm* North ♦ *adj* northern; north; **au ~** (*situation*) in the north; (*direction*) to the north; **au ~ de** (to the) north of; **nord-est** *nm* North-East; **nord-ouest** *nm* North-West

normal, e, -aux [nɔʀmal, o] *adj* normal; **c'est tout à fait ~** it's perfectly natural; **vous trouvez ça ~?** does it seem right to you?; **normale** *nf*: **la normale** the norm, the average; **normalement** *adv* (*en général*) normally

normand, e [nɔʀmɑ̃, ɑ̃d] *adj* of Normandy

Normandie [nɔʀmɑ̃di] *nf* Normandy

norme [nɔʀm] *nf* norm; (TECH) standard

Norvège [nɔʀvɛʒ] *nf* Norway; **norvégien, ne** *adj* Norwegian ♦ *nm/f*: **Norvégien, ne** Norwegian ♦ *nm* (LING) Norwegian

nos [no] *adj voir* **notre**

nostalgie [nɔstalʒi] *nf* nostalgia; **nostalgique** *adj* nostalgic

notable [nɔtabl] *adj* (*fait*) notable, noteworthy; (*marqué*) noticeable, marked ♦ *nm* prominent citizen

notaire [nɔtɛʀ] *nm* solicitor

notamment [nɔtamɑ̃] *adv* in particular, among others

note [nɔt] *nf* (*écrite*, MUS) note; (SCOL) mark (BRIT), grade; (*facture*) bill; ~ **de service** memorandum

noté, e [nɔte] *adj*: **être bien/mal ~** (*employé etc*) to have a good/bad record

noter [nɔte] *vt* (*écrire*) to write down; (*remarquer*) to note, notice; (*devoir*) to mark, grade

notice [nɔtis] *nf* summary, short article; (*brochure*) leaflet, instruction book

notifier [nɔtifje] *vt*: ~ **qch à qn** to notify sb of sth, notify sth to sb

notion [nosjɔ̃] *nf* notion, idea

notoire [nɔtwaʀ] *adj* widely known; (*en mal*) notorious

notre [nɔtʀ] (*pl* **nos**) *adj* our

nôtre [notʀ] *pron*: **le ~, la ~, les ~s** ours ♦ *adj* ours; **les ~s** ours; (*alliés etc*) our own people; **soyez des ~s** join us

nouer [nwe] *vt* to tie, knot; (*fig*: *alliance etc*) to strike up

noueux, -euse [nwø, øz] *adj* gnarled

nouilles [nuj] *nfpl* noodles

nourrice [nuʀis] *nf* (*gardienne*) child-minder

nourrir [nuʀiʀ] *vt* to feed; (*fig*: *espoir*) to harbour, nurse; **se ~** to eat; **se ~ de** to feed (o.s.) on; **nourrissant, e** *adj* nourishing, nutritious; **nourrisson** *nm* (unweaned) infant; **nourriture** *nf* food

nous [nu] *pron* (*sujet*) we; (*objet*) us; **nous-mêmes** *pron* ourselves

nouveau (nouvel), -elle, x [nuvo, nuvɛl] *adj* new ♦ *nm*: **y a-t-il du ~?** is there anything new on this? ♦ *nm/f* new pupil (*ou* employee); **de ~, à ~** again; **~ venu, nouvelle venue** newcomer; **~x mariés** newly-weds; **nouveau-né, e** *nm/f* newborn baby; **nouveauté** *nf* novelty; (*objet*) new thing *ou* article

nouvel [nuvɛl] *adj voir* **nouveau**; **N~ An** New Year

nouvelle [nuvɛl] *adj voir* **nouveau** ♦ *nf* (piece of) news *sg*; (LITTÉRATURE) short story; **les ~s** the news; **je suis sans ~s de lui** I haven't heard from him; **Nouvelle-Calédonie** *nf* New Caledonia; **nouvellement** *adv* recently, newly; **Nouvelle-Zélande** *nf* New Zealand

novembre [nɔvɑ̃bʀ] *nm* November

novice [nɔvis] *adj* inexperienced

noyade [nwajad] *nf* drowning *no pl*

noyau, x [nwajo] *nm* (*de fruit*) stone; (BIO, PHYSIQUE) nucleus; (*fig: centre*) core; **noyauter** *vt* (POL) to infiltrate

noyer [nwaje] *nm* walnut (tree); (*bois*) walnut ♦ *vt* to drown; (*moteur*) to flood; **se ~** *vi* to be drowned, drown; (*suicide*) to drown o.s.

nu, e [ny] *adj* naked; (*membres*) naked, bare; (*pieds, mains, chambre, fil électrique*) bare ♦ *nm* (ART) nude; **tout ~** stark naked; **se mettre ~** to strip; **mettre à ~** to bare

nuage [nɥaʒ] *nm* cloud; **nuageux, -euse** *adj* cloudy

nuance [nɥɑ̃s] *nf* (*de couleur, sens*) shade; **il y a une ~ (entre)** there's a slight difference (between); **nuancer** *vt* (*opinion*) to bring some reservations *ou* qualifications to

nucléaire [nykleeʀ] *adj* nuclear ♦ *nm*: **le ~** nuclear energy

nudiste [nydist] *nm/f* nudist

nuée [nɥe] *nf*: **une ~ de** a cloud *ou* host *ou* swarm of

nues [ny] *nfpl*: **tomber des ~** to be taken aback; **porter qn aux ~** to praise sb to the skies

nuire [nɥiʀ] *vi* to be harmful; **~ à** to harm, do damage to; **nuisible** *adj* harmful; **animal nuisible** pest

nuit [nɥi] *nf* night; **il fait ~** it's dark; **cette ~** (*hier*) last night; (*aujourd'hui*) tonight; **~ blanche** sleepless night

nul, nulle [nyl] *adj* (*aucun*) no; (*minime*) nil, non-existent; (*non valable*) null; (*péj*) useless, hopeless ♦ *pron* none, no one; **match** *ou* **résultat ~** draw; **~le part** nowhere; **nullement** *adv* by no means; **nullité** *nf* (*personne*) nonentity

numérique [nymeʀik] *adj* numerical; (*affichage*) digital

numéro [nymeʀo] *nm* number; (*spectacle*) act, turn; (PRESSE) issue, number; **~ de téléphone** (tele)phone number; **~ vert** ≃ freefone ® number (BRIT), ≃ toll-free number (US); **numéroter** *vt* to number

nu-pieds [nypje] *adj inv, adv* barefoot

nuque [nyk] *nf* nape of the neck

nu-tête [nytɛt] *adj inv, adv* bareheaded

nutritif, -ive [nytʀitif, iv] *adj* (*besoins, valeur*) nutritional; (*nourrissant*) nutritious

nylon [nilɔ̃] *nm* nylon

O, o

oasis [ɔazis] *nf* oasis

obéir [ɔbeiʀ] *vi* to obey; **~ à** to obey; **obéissance** *nf* obedience; **obéissant, e** *adj* obedient

obèse [ɔbɛz] *adj* obese; **obésité** *nf* obesity

objecter [ɔbʒɛkte] *vt* (*prétexter*) to plead, put forward as an excuse; **~ (à qn) que** to object (to sb) that; **objecteur** *nm*: **objecteur de conscience** conscientious objector

objectif, -ive [ɔbʒɛktif, iv] *adj* objective ♦ *nm* objective; (PHOTO) lens *sg*, objective; **objectivité** *nf* objectivity

objection [ɔbʒɛksjɔ̃] *nf* objection

objet [ɔbʒɛ] *nm* object; (*d'une discussion, recherche*) subject; **être** *ou* **faire l'~ de** (*discussion*) to be the subject of; (*soins*) to be given *ou* shown; **sans ~** purposeless; groundless; **~ d'art** objet d'art; **~s trouvés** lost property *sg* (*BRIT*), lost-and-found *sg* (*US*); **~s de valeur** valuables

obligation [ɔbligasjɔ̃] *nf* obligation; (*COMM*) bond, debenture; **obligatoire** *adj* compulsory, obligatory; **obligatoirement** *adv* necessarily; (*fam: sans aucun doute*) inevitably

obligé, e [ɔbliʒe] *adj* (*redevable*): **être très ~ à qn** to be most obliged to sb

obligeance [ɔbliʒɑ̃s] *nf*: **avoir l'~ de ...** to be kind *ou* good enough to ...; **obligeant, e** *adj* (*personne*) obliging, kind

obliger [ɔbliʒe] *vt* (*contraindre*): **~ qn à faire** to force *ou* oblige sb to do; **je suis bien obligé** I have to

oblique [ɔblik] *adj* oblique; **en ~** diagonally; **obliquer** *vi*: **obliquer vers** to turn off towards

oblitérer [ɔbliteʀe] *vt* (*timbre-poste*) to cancel

obnubiler [ɔbnybile] *vt* to obsess

obscène [ɔpsɛn] *adj* obscene

obscur, e [ɔpskyʀ] *adj* dark; (*méconnu*) obscure; **obscurcir** *vt* to darken; (*fig*) to obscure; **s'obscurcir** *vi* to grow dark; **obscurité** *nf* darkness; **dans l'obscurité** in the dark, in darkness

obsédé, e [ɔpsede] *nm/f*: **un ~ (sexuel)** a sex maniac

obséder [ɔpsede] *vt* to obsess, haunt

obsèques [ɔpsɛk] *nfpl* funeral *sg*

observateur, -trice [ɔpsɛʀvatœʀ, tʀis] *adj* observant, perceptive ♦ *nm/f* observer

observation [ɔpsɛʀvasjɔ̃] *nf* observation; (*d'un règlement etc*) observance; (*reproche*) reproof; **être en ~** (*MÉD*) to be under observation

observatoire [ɔpsɛʀvatwaʀ] *nm* observatory

observer [ɔpsɛʀve] *vt* (*regarder*) to observe, watch; (*scientifiquement; aussi règlement etc*) to observe; (*surveiller*) to watch; (*remarquer*) to observe, notice; **faire ~ qch à qn** (*dire*) to point out sth to sb

obsession [ɔpsesjɔ̃] *nf* obsession

obstacle [ɔpstakl] *nm* obstacle; (*ÉQUITATION*) jump, hurdle; **faire ~ à** (*projet*) to hinder, put obstacles in the path of

obstiné, e [ɔpstine] *adj* obstinate

obstiner [ɔpstine]: **s'~** *vi* to insist, dig one's heels in; **s'~ à faire** to persist (obstinately) in doing

obstruer [ɔpstʀye] *vt* to block, obstruct

obtenir [ɔptəniʀ] *vt* to obtain, get; (*résultat*) to achieve, obtain; **~ de pouvoir faire** to obtain permission to do

obturateur [ɔptyʀatœʀ, tʀis] *nm* (*PHOTO*) shutter

obus [ɔby] *nm* shell

occasion [ɔkazjɔ̃] *nf* (*aubaine, possibilité*) opportunity; (*circonstance*) occasion; (*COMM: article non neuf*) secondhand buy; (*: acquisition avantageuse*) bargain; **à plusieurs ~s** on several occasions; **à l'~** sometimes, on occasions; **d'~** secondhand; **occasionnel, le** *adj* (*non régulier*) occasional; **occasionnellement** *adv* occasionally, from time to time

occasionner [ɔkazjɔne] *vt* to cause

occident [ɔksidɑ̃] *nm*: **l'O~** the West; **occidental, e, -aux** *adj* western; (*POL*) Western ♦ *nm/f* Westerner

occupation [ɔkypasjɔ̃] *nf* occupation

occupé, e [ɔkype] *adj* (*personne*) busy; (*place, sièges*) taken; (*toilettes*) engaged; (*ligne*) engaged (*BRIT*), busy (*US*); (*MIL, POL*) occupied

occuper [ɔkype] *vt* to occupy; (*poste*) to hold; **s'~ de** (*être responsable de*) to be in charge of; (*se charger de: affaire*) to take charge of, deal with; (*: clients*

etc) to attend to; **s'~ (à qch)** to occupy o.s. *ou* keep o.s. busy (with sth)
occurrence [ɔkyʀɑ̃s] *nf*: **en l'~** in this case
océan [ɔseɑ̃] *nm* ocean
octante [ɔktɑ̃t] *adj* (*regional*) eighty
octet [ɔktɛ] *nm* byte
octobre [ɔktɔbʀ] *nm* October
octroyer [ɔktʀwaje]: **s'~** *vt* (*vacances etc*) to treat o.s. to
oculiste [ɔkylist] *nm/f* eye specialist
odeur [ɔdœʀ] *nf* smell
odieux, -euse [ɔdjø, jøz] *adj* hateful
odorant, e [ɔdɔʀɑ̃, ɑ̃t] *adj* sweet-smelling, fragrant
odorat [ɔdɔʀa] *nm* (sense of) smell
œil [œj] (*pl* **yeux**) *nm* eye; **à l'œil** (*fam*) for free; **à l'œil nu** with the naked eye; **tenir qn à l'œil** to keep an eye *ou* a watch on sb; **avoir l'œil à** to keep an eye on; **fermer les yeux (sur)** (*fig*) to turn a blind eye (to); **voir qch d'un bon/mauvais œil** to look on sth favourably/unfavourably
œillères [œjɛʀ] *nfpl* blinkers (*BRIT*), blinders (*US*)
œillet [œjɛ] *nm* (*BOT*) carnation
œuf [œf, *pl* ø] *nm* egg; **œuf à la coque/sur le plat/dur** boiled/fried/hard-boiled egg; **œuf de Pâques** Easter egg; **œufs brouillés** scrambled eggs
œuvre [œvʀ] *nf* (*tâche*) task, undertaking; (*livre, tableau etc*) work; (*ensemble de la production artistique*) works *pl* ♦ *nm* (*CONSTR*): **le gros œuvre** the shell; **œuvre (de bienfaisance)** charity; **mettre en œuvre** (*moyens*) to make use of; **œuvre d'art** work of art
offense [ɔfɑ̃s] *nf* insult; **offenser** *vt* to offend, hurt
offert, e [ɔfɛʀ, ɛʀt] *pp de* **offrir**
office [ɔfis] *nm* (*agence*) bureau, agency; (*REL*) service ♦ *nm ou nf* (*pièce*) pantry; **faire ~ de** to act as; **d'~** automatically; **~ du tourisme** tourist bureau
officiel, le [ɔfisjɛl] *adj, nm/f* official
officier [ɔfisje] *nm* officer
officieux, -euse [ɔfisjø, jøz] *adj* unofficial
offrande [ɔfʀɑ̃d] *nf* offering
offre [ɔfʀ] *nf* offer; (*aux enchères*) bid; (*ADMIN*: *soumission*) tender; (*ÉCON*): **l'~ et la demande** supply and demand; **"~s d'emploi"** "situations vacant"; **~ d'emploi** job advertised
offrir [ɔfʀiʀ] *vt*: **~ (à qn)** to offer (to sb); (*faire cadeau de*) to give (to sb) **s'~** *vt* (*vacances, voiture*) to treat o.s. to; **~ (à qn) de faire qch** to offer to do sth (for sb); **~ à boire à qn** (*chez soi*) to offer sb a drink
offusquer [ɔfyske] *vt* to offend
OGM *sigle m* (= *organisme génétiquement modifié*) GMO
oie [wa] *nf* (*ZOOL*) goose
oignon [ɔɲɔ̃] *nm* onion; (*de tulipe etc*) bulb
oiseau, x [wazo] *nm* bird; **~ de proie** bird of prey
oisif, -ive [wazif, iv] *adj* idle
oléoduc [ɔleɔdyk] *nm* (oil) pipeline
olive [ɔliv] *nf* (*BOT*) olive; **olivier** *nm* olive (tree)
OLP *sigle f* (= *Organisation de libération de la Palestine*) PLO
olympique [ɔlɛ̃pik] *adj* Olympic
ombragé, e [ɔ̃bʀaʒe] *adj* shaded, shady; **ombrageux, -euse** *adj* (*personne*) touchy, easily offended
ombre [ɔ̃bʀ] *nf* (*espace non ensoleillé*) shade; (*~ portée, tache*) shadow; **à l'~** in the shade; **dans l'~** (*fig*) in the dark; **~ à paupières** eyeshadow; **ombrelle** *nf* parasol, sunshade
omelette [ɔmlɛt] *nf* omelette; **~ norvégienne** baked Alaska
omettre [ɔmɛtʀ] *vt* to omit, leave out
omnibus [ɔmnibys] *nm* slow *ou* stopping train
omoplate [ɔmɔplat] *nf* shoulder blade

MOT-CLÉ

on [ɔ̃] *pron* **1** (*indéterminé*) you, one; **on peut le faire ainsi** you *ou* one can do

it like this, it can be done like this
2 (*quelqu'un*): **on les a attaqués** they were attacked; **on vous demande au téléphone** there's a phone call for you, you're wanted on the phone
3 (*nous*) we; **on va y aller demain** we're going tomorrow
4 (*les gens*) they; **autrefois, on croyait ...** they used to believe ...
5: on ne peut plus
♦ *adv*: **on ne peut plus stupide** as stupid as can be

oncle [ɔ̃kl] *nm* uncle
onctueux, -euse [ɔ̃ktɥø, øz] *adj* creamy, smooth
onde [ɔ̃d] *nf* wave; **sur les ~s** on the radio; **sur ~s courtes** on short wave *sg*; **moyennes/longues ~s** medium/long wave *sg*
ondée [ɔ̃de] *nf* shower
on-dit [ɔ̃di] *nm inv* rumour
onduler [ɔ̃dyle] *vi* to undulate; (*cheveux*) to wave
onéreux, -euse [ɔnerø, øz] *adj* costly
ongle [ɔ̃gl] *nm* nail
ont [ɔ̃] *vb voir* **avoir**
ONU *sigle f* (= *Organisation des Nations Unies*) UN
onze ['ɔ̃z] *num* eleven; **onzième** *num* eleventh
OPA *sigle f* = **offre publique d'achat**
opaque [ɔpak] *adj* opaque
opéra [ɔpera] *nm* opera; (*édifice*) opera house
opérateur, -trice [ɔperatœr, tris] *nm/f* operator; **~ (de prise de vues)** cameraman
opération [ɔperasjɔ̃] *nf* operation; (COMM) dealing
opératoire [ɔperatwar] *adj* (*choc etc*) post-operative
opérer [ɔpere] *vt* (*personne*) to operate on; (*faire, exécuter*) to carry out, make ♦ *vi* (*remède: faire effet*) to act, work; (MÉD) to operate; **s'~** *vi* (*avoir lieu*) to occur, take place; **se faire ~** to have an operation
opérette [ɔperɛt] *nf* operetta, light opera
ophtalmologiste [ɔftalmɔlɔʒist] *nm/f* ophthalmologist, optician
opiner [ɔpine] *vi*: **~ de la tête** to nod assent
opinion [ɔpinjɔ̃] *nf* opinion; **l'~ (publique)** public opinion
opportun, e [ɔpɔrtœ̃, yn] *adj* timely, opportune; **opportuniste** *nm/f* opportunist
opposant, e [ɔpozɑ̃, ɑ̃t] *nm/f* opponent
opposé, e [ɔpoze] *adj* (*direction*) opposite; (*faction*) opposing; (*opinions, intérêts*) conflicting; (*contre*): **~ à** opposed to, against ♦ *nm*: **l'~** the other *ou* opposite side (*ou* direction); (*contraire*) the opposite; **à l'~** (*fig*) on the other hand; **à l'~ de** (*fig*) contrary to, unlike
opposer [ɔpoze] *vt* (*personnes, équipes*) to oppose; (*couleurs*) to contrast; **s'~** *vi* (*équipes*) to confront each other; (*opinions*) to conflict; (*couleurs, styles*) to contrast; **s'~ à** (*interdire*) to oppose; **~ qch à** (*comme obstacle, défense*) to set sth against; (*comme objection*) to put sth forward against
opposition [ɔpozisjɔ̃] *nf* opposition; **par ~ à** as opposed to, **entrer en ~ avec** to come into conflict with; **faire ~ à un chèque** to stop a cheque
oppressant, e [ɔpresɑ̃, ɑ̃t] *adj* oppressive
oppresser [ɔprese] *vt* to oppress; **oppression** *nf* oppression
opprimer [ɔprime] *vt* to oppress
opter [ɔpte] *vi*: **~ pour** to opt for
opticien, ne [ɔptisjɛ̃, jɛn] *nm/f* optician
optimisme [ɔptimism] *nm* optimism; **optimiste** *nm/f* optimist ♦ *adj* optimistic
option [ɔpsjɔ̃] *nf* option; **matière à ~** (SCOL) optional subject
optique [ɔptik] *adj* (*nerf*) optic; (*verres*) optical ♦ *nf* (*fig: manière de voir*) per-

spective

opulent, e [ɔpylɑ̃, ɑ̃t] *adj* wealthy, opulent; (*formes, poitrine*) ample, generous

or [ɔʀ] *nm* gold ♦ *conj* now, but; **en ~** (*objet*) gold *cpd*; **une affaire en ~** a real bargain; **il croyait gagner ~ il a perdu** he was sure he would win and yet he lost

orage [ɔʀaʒ] *nm* (thunder)storm; **orageux, -euse** *adj* stormy

oral, e, -aux [ɔʀal, o] *adj, nm* oral; **par voie ~e** (MÉD) orally

orange [ɔʀɑ̃ʒ] *nf* orange ♦ *adj inv* orange; **orangeade** *nf* orangeade; **orangé, e** *adj* orangey, orange-coloured; **oranger** *nm* orange tree

orateur [ɔʀatœʀ, tʀis] *nm* speaker

orbite [ɔʀbit] *nf* (ANAT) (eye-)socket; (PHYSIQUE) orbit

orchestre [ɔʀkɛstʀ] *nm* orchestra; (*de jazz*) band; (*places*) stalls *pl* (BRIT), orchestra (US); **orchestrer** *vt* to orchestrate

orchidée [ɔʀkide] *nf* orchid

ordinaire [ɔʀdinɛʀ] *adj* ordinary; (*qualité*) standard; (*péj: commun*) common ♦ *nm* ordinary; (*menus*) everyday fare ♦ *nf* (*essence*) ≃ two-star (petrol) (BRIT), ≃ regular gas (US); **d'~** usually, normally; **comme à l'~** as usual

ordinateur [ɔʀdinatœʀ] *nm* computer

ordonnance [ɔʀdɔnɑ̃s] *nf* (MÉD) prescription; (MIL) orderly, batman (BRIT)

ordonné, e [ɔʀdɔne] *adj* tidy, orderly

ordonner [ɔʀdɔne] *vt* (*agencer*) to organize, arrange; (*donner un ordre*): **~ à qn de faire** to order sb to do; (REL) to ordain; (MÉD) to prescribe

ordre [ɔʀdʀ] *nm* order; (*propreté et soin*) orderliness, tidiness; (*nature*): **d'~ pratique** of a practical nature; **~s** *nmpl* (REL) holy orders; **mettre en ~** to tidy (up), put in order; **à l'~ de qn** payable to sb; **être aux ~s de qn/sous les ~s de qn** to be at sb's disposal/under sb's command; **jusqu'à nouvel ~** until further notice; **de premier ~** first-rate; **~ du jour** (*d'une réunion*) agenda; **à l'~ du jour** (*fig*) topical

ordure [ɔʀdyʀ] *nf* filth *no pl*; **~s** *nfpl* (*balayures, déchets*) rubbish *sg*, refuse *sg*; **~s ménagères** household refuse

oreille [ɔʀɛj] *nf* ear; **avoir de l'~** to have a good ear (for music)

oreiller [ɔʀeje] *nm* pillow

oreillons [ɔʀɛjɔ̃] *nmpl* mumps *sg*

ores [ɔʀ]: **d'~ et déjà** *adv* already

orfèvrerie [ɔʀfɛvʀəʀi] *nf* goldsmith's (*ou* silversmith's) trade; (*ouvrage*) gold (*ou* silver) plate

organe [ɔʀgan] *nm* organ; (*porte-parole*) representative, mouthpiece

organigramme [ɔʀganigʀam] *nm* (*tableau hiérarchique*) organization chart; (*schéma*) flow chart

organique [ɔʀganik] *adj* organic

organisateur, -trice [ɔʀganizatœʀ, tʀis] *nm/f* organizer

organisation [ɔʀganizasjɔ̃] *nf* organization

organiser [ɔʀganize] *vt* to organize; (*mettre sur pied: service etc*) to set up; **s'~** to get organized

organisme [ɔʀganism] *nm* (BIO) organism; (*corps, ADMIN*) body

organiste [ɔʀganist] *nm/f* organist

orgasme [ɔʀgasm] *nm* orgasm, climax

orge [ɔʀʒ] *nf* barley

orgue [ɔʀg] *nm* organ; **~s** *nfpl* (MUS) organ *sg*

orgueil [ɔʀgœj] *nm* pride; **orgueilleux, -euse** *adj* proud

Orient [ɔʀjɑ̃] *nm*: **l'~** the East, the Orient; **oriental, e, -aux** *adj* (*langue, produit*) oriental; (*frontière*) eastern

orientation [ɔʀjɑ̃tasjɔ̃] *nf* (*de recherches*) orientation; (*d'une maison etc*) aspect; (*d'un journal*) leanings *pl*; **avoir le sens de l'~** to have a (good) sense of direction; **~ professionnelle** careers advisory service

orienté, e [ɔʀjɑ̃te] *adj* (*fig: article, journal*) slanted; **bien/mal ~** (*apparte-*

ment) well/badly positioned; **~ au sud** facing south, with a southern aspect

orienter [ɔʀjɑ̃te] *vt* (*tourner*: *antenne*) to direct, turn; (*personne, recherches*) to direct; (*fig*: *élève*) to orientate; **s'~** (*se repérer*) to find one's bearings; **s'~ vers** (*fig*) to turn towards

origan [ɔʀigɑ̃] *nm* oregano

originaire [ɔʀiʒinɛʀ] *adj*: **être ~ de** to be a native of

original, e, -aux [ɔʀiʒinal, o] *adj* original; (*bizarre*) eccentric ♦ *nm/f* eccentric ♦ *nm* (*document etc*, ART) original

origine [ɔʀiʒin] *nf* origin; **dès l'~** at *ou* from the outset; **à l'~** originally; **originel, le** *adj* original

orme [ɔʀm] *nm* elm

ornement [ɔʀnəmɑ̃] *nm* ornament

orner [ɔʀne] *vt* to decorate, adorn

ornière [ɔʀnjɛʀ] *nf* rut

orphelin, e [ɔʀfəlɛ̃, in] *adj* orphan(ed) ♦ *nm/f* orphan; **~ de père/mère** fatherless/motherless; **orphelinat** *nm* orphanage

orteil [ɔʀtɛj] *nm* toe; **gros ~** big toe

orthographe [ɔʀtɔgʀaf] *nf* spelling

ortie [ɔʀti] *nf* (stinging) nettle

os [ɔs] *nm* bone; **tomber sur un ~** (*fam*) to hit a snag

osciller [ɔsile] *vi* (*au vent etc*) to rock; (*fig*): **~ entre** to waver *ou* fluctuate between

osé, e [oze] *adj* daring, bold

oseille [ozɛj] *nf* sorrel

oser [oze] *vi, vt* to dare; **~ faire** to dare (to) do

osier [ozje] *nm* willow; **d'~, en ~** wicker(work)

ossature [ɔsatyʀ] *nf* (ANAT) frame, skeletal structure; (*fig*) framework

osseux, -euse [ɔsø, øz] *adj* bony; (*tissu, maladie, greffe*) bone *cpd*

ostensible [ɔstɑ̃sibl] *adj* conspicuous

otage [ɔtaʒ] *nm* hostage; **prendre qn comme ~** to take sb hostage

OTAN *sigle f* (= *Organisation du traité de l'Atlantique Nord*) NATO

otarie [ɔtaʀi] *nf* sea-lion

ôter [ote] *vt* to remove; (*soustraire*) to take away; **~ qch à qn** to take sth (away) from sb; **~ qch de** to remove sth from

otite [ɔtit] *nf* ear infection

ou [u] *conj* or; **~ ... ~** either ... or; **~ bien** or (else)

MOT-CLÉ

où [u] *pron relatif* **1** (*position, situation*) where, that (*souvent omis*); **la chambre où il était** the room (that) he was in, the room where he was; **la ville où je l'ai rencontré** the town where I met him; **la pièce d'où il est sorti** the room he came out of; **le village d'où je viens** the village I come from; **les villes par où il est passé** the towns he went through

2 (*temps, état*) that (*souvent omis*); **le jour où il est parti** the day (that) he left; **au prix où c'est** at the price it is

♦ *adv* **1** (*interrogation*) where; **où est-il/va-t-il?** where is he/is he going?; **par où?** which way?; **d'où vient que ...?** how come ...?

2 (*position*) where; **je sais où il est** I know where he is; **où que l'on aille** wherever you go

ouate ['wat] *nf* cotton wool (BRIT), cotton (US)

oubli [ubli] *nm* (*acte*): **l'~ de** forgetting; (*trou de mémoire*) lapse of memory; (*négligence*) omission, oversight; **tomber dans l'~** to sink into oblivion

oublier [ublije] *vt* to forget; (*laisser quelque part*: *chapeau etc*) to leave behind; (*ne pas voir*: *erreurs etc*) to miss

oubliettes [ublijɛt] *nfpl* dungeon *sg*

ouest [wɛst] *nm* west ♦ *adj inv* west; (*région*) western; **à l'~** in the west; (*direction*) (to the) west, westwards; **à l'~ de** (to the) west of

ouf ['uf] *excl* phew!

oui ['wi] *adv* yes

ouï-dire ['widiʀ]: **par ~-~** *adv* by hearsay

ouïe [wi] *nf* hearing; **~s** *nfpl* (*de poisson*) gills

ouille ['uj] *excl* ouch!

ouragan [uʀagɑ̃] *nm* hurricane

ourlet [uʀlɛ] *nm* hem

ours [uʀs] *nm* bear; **~ brun/blanc** brown/polar bear; **~ (en peluche)** teddy (bear)

oursin [uʀsɛ̃] *nm* sea urchin

ourson [uʀsɔ̃] *nm* (bear-)cub

ouste [ust] *excl* hop it!

outil [uti] *nm* tool; **outiller** *vt* to equip

outrage [utʀaʒ] *nm* insult; **~ à la pudeur** indecent conduct *no pl*; **outrager** *vt* to offend gravely

outrance [utʀɑ̃s]: **à ~** *adv* excessively, to excess

outre [utʀ] *prép* besides ♦ *adv*: **passer ~ à** to disregard, take no notice of; **en ~** besides, moreover; **~ mesure** to excess; (*manger, boire*) immoderately; **outre-Atlantique** *adv* across the Atlantic; **outre-Manche** *adv* across the Channel; **outre-mer** *adv* overseas; **outrepasser** *vt* to go beyond, exceed

ouvert, e [uvɛʀ, ɛʀt] *pp de* **ouvrir** ♦ *adj* open; (*robinet, gaz etc*) on; **ouvertement** *adv* openly; **ouverture** *nf* opening; (*MUS*) overture; **ouverture d'esprit** open-mindedness

ouvrable [uvʀabl] *adj*: **jour ~** working day, weekday

ouvrage [uvʀaʒ] *nm* (*tâche, de tricot etc*) work *no pl*; (*texte, livre*) work; **ouvragé, e** *adj* finely embroidered (*ou* worked *ou* carved)

ouvre-boîte(s) [uvʀəbwat] *nm inv* tin (*BRIT*) *ou* can opener

ouvre-bouteille(s) [uvʀəbutɛj] *nm inv* bottle-opener

ouvreuse [uvʀøz] *nf* usherette

ouvrier, -ière [uvʀije, ijɛʀ] *nm/f* worker ♦ *adj* working-class; (*conflit*) industrial; (*mouvement*) labour *cpd*; **classe ouvrière** working class

ouvrir [uvʀiʀ] *vt* (*gén*) to open; (*brèche, passage, MÉD: abcès*) to open up; (*commencer l'exploitation de, créer*) to open (up); (*eau, électricité, chauffage, robinet*) to turn on ♦ *vi* to open; to open up; **s'~** *vi* to open; **s'~ à qn** to open one's heart to sb; **~ l'appétit à qn** to whet sb's appetite

ovaire [ɔvɛʀ] *nm* ovary

ovale [ɔval] *adj* oval

ovni [ɔvni] *sigle m* (= *objet volant non identifié*) UFO

oxyder [ɔkside]: **s'~** *vi* to become oxidized

oxygène [ɔksiʒɛn] *nm* oxygen

oxygéné, e [ɔksiʒene] *adj*: **eau ~e** hydrogen peroxide

oxygéner [ɔksiʒene]: **s'~** (*fam*) *vi* to get some fresh air

ozone [ozon] *nf* ozone; **la couche d'~** the ozone layer

P, p

pacifique [pasifik] *adj* peaceful ♦ *nm*: **le P~, l'océan P~** the Pacific (Ocean)

pacotille [pakɔtij] *nf* cheap junk

pack [pak] *nm* pack

pacte [pakt] *nm* pact, treaty

pagaie [pagɛ] *nf* paddle

pagaille [pagaj] *nf* mess, shambles *sg*

pagayer *vi* to paddle

page [paʒ] *nf* page ♦ *nm* page (boy); **à la ~** (*fig*) up-to date; **~ d'accueil** (*INFORM*) home page

paiement [pɛmɑ̃] *nm* payment

païen, ne [pajɛ̃, pajɛn] *adj, nm/f* pagan, heathen

paillasson [pajasɔ̃] *nm* doormat

paille [pɑj] *nf* straw

paillettes [pɑjɛt] *nfpl* (*décoratives*) sequins, spangles

pain [pɛ̃] *nm* (*substance*) bread; (*unité*) loaf (of bread); (*morceau*): **~ de savon** *etc* bar of soap *etc*; **~ au chocolat** chocolate-filled pastry; **~ aux raisins**

currant bun; ~ **bis/complet** brown/ wholemeal (*BRIT*) *ou* wholewheat (*US*) bread; ~ **d'épice** gingerbread; ~ **de mie** sandwich loaf; ~ **grillé** toast
pair, e [pɛʀ] *adj* (*nombre*) even ♦ *nm* peer; **aller de** ~ to go hand in hand *ou* together; **jeune fille au** ~ au pair; **paire** *nf* pair
paisible [pezibl] *adj* peaceful, quiet
paître [pɛtʀ] *vi* to graze
paix [pɛ] *nf* peace; **faire/avoir la** ~ to make/have peace; **fiche-lui la ~!** (*fam*) leave him alone!
Pakistan [pakistɑ̃] *nm*: **le** ~ Pakistan
palace [palas] *nm* luxury hotel
palais [palɛ] *nm* palace; (*ANAT*) palate
pâle [pɑl] *adj* pale; **bleu** ~ pale blue
Palestine [palɛstin] *nf*: **la** ~ Palestine
palet [palɛ] *nm* disc; (*HOCKEY*) puck
paletot [palto] *nm* (thick) cardigan
palette [palɛt] *nf* (*de peintre*) palette; (*produits*) range
pâleur [pɑlœʀ] *nf* paleness
palier [palje] *nm* (*d'escalier*) landing; (*fig*) level, plateau; **par ~s** in stages
pâlir [pɑliʀ] *vi* to turn *ou* go pale; (*couleur*) to fade
palissade [palisad] *nf* fence
pallier [palje]: *vt* to offset, make up for
palmarès [palmaʀɛs] *nm* record (of achievements); (*SPORT*) list of winners
palme [palm] *nf* (*de plongeur*) flipper; **palmé, e** *adj* (*pattes*) webbed
palmier [palmje] *nm* palm tree; (*gâteau*) *heart-shaped biscuit made of flaky pastry*
pâlot, te [pɑlo, ɔt] *adj* pale, peaky
palourde [paluʀd] *nf* clam
palper [palpe] *vt* to feel, finger
palpitant, e [palpitɑ̃, ɑ̃t] *adj* thrilling
palpiter [palpite] *vi* (*cœur, pouls*) to beat; (: *plus fort*) to pound, throb
paludisme [palydism] *nm* malaria
pamphlet [pɑ̃flɛ] *nm* lampoon, satirical tract
pamplemousse [pɑ̃pləmus] *nm* grapefruit
pan [pɑ̃] *nm* section, piece ♦ *excl* bang!
panache [panaʃ] *nm* plume; (*fig*) spirit, panache
panaché, e [panaʃe] *adj*: **glace ~e** mixed-flavour ice cream ♦ *nm* (*bière*) shandy
pancarte [pɑ̃kaʀt] *nf* sign, notice
pancréas [pɑ̃kʀeɑs] *nm* pancreas
pané, e [pane] *adj* fried in breadcrumbs
panier [panje] *nm* basket; **mettre au** ~ to chuck away; ~ **à provisions** shopping basket; **panier-repas** *nm* packed lunch
panique [panik] *nf, adj* panic; **paniquer** *vi* to panic
panne [pan] *nf* breakdown; **être/tomber en** ~ to have broken down/break down; **être en ~ d'essence** *ou* **sèche** to have run out of petrol (*BRIT*) *ou* gas (*US*); ~ **d'électricité** *ou* **de courant** power *ou* electrical failure
panneau, x [pano] *nm* (*écriteau*) sign, notice; ~ **d'affichage** notice board; ~ **de signalisation** roadsign
panoplie [panɔpli] *nf* (*jouet*) outfit; (*fig*) array
panorama [panɔʀama] *nm* panorama
panse [pɑ̃s] *nf* paunch
pansement [pɑ̃smɑ̃] *nm* dressing, bandage; ~ **adhésif** sticking plaster
panser [pɑ̃se] *vt* (*plaie*) to dress, bandage; (*bras*) to put a dressing on, bandage; (*cheval*) to groom
pantalon [pɑ̃talɔ̃] *nm* trousers *pl*, pair of trousers; ~ **de ski** ski pants *pl*
panthère [pɑ̃tɛʀ] *nf* panther
pantin [pɑ̃tɛ̃] *nm* puppet
pantois [pɑ̃twa] *adj m*: **rester** ~ to be flabbergasted
pantoufle [pɑ̃tufl] *nf* slipper
paon [pɑ̃] *nm* peacock
papa [papa] *nm* dad(dy)
pape [pap] *nm* pope
paperasse [papʀas] (*péj*) *nf* bumf *no pl*, papers *pl*; **paperasserie** (*péj*) *nf* paperwork *no pl*; (*tracasserie*) red tape *no pl*

papeterie [papɛtʀi] *nf* (*magasin*) stationer's (shop)
papi *nm* (*fam*) granddad
papier [papje] *nm* paper; (*article*) article; **~s** *nmpl* (*aussi:* **~s d'identité**) (identity) papers; **~ à lettres** writing paper, notepaper; **~ carbone** carbon paper; **~ (d')aluminium** aluminium (BRIT) *ou* aluminum (US) foil, tinfoil; **~ de verre** sandpaper; **~ hygiénique** *ou* **de toilette** toilet paper; **~ journal** newspaper; **~ peint** wallpaper
papillon [papijɔ̃] *nm* butterfly; (*fam: contravention*) (parking) ticket; **~ de nuit** moth
papillote [papijɔt] *nf*: **en ~** cooked in tinfoil
papoter [papɔte] *vi* to chatter
paquebot [pak(ə)bo] *nm* liner
pâquerette [pɑkʀɛt] *nf* daisy
Pâques [pɑk] *nm, nfpl* Easter
paquet [pakɛ] *nm* packet; (*colis*) parcel; (*fig: tas*): **~ de** pile *ou* heap of; **paquet-cadeau** *nm*: **faites-moi un paquet-cadeau** gift-wrap it for me
par [paʀ] *prép* by; **finir** *etc* **~** to end *etc* with; **~ amour** out of love; **passer ~ Lyon/la côte** to go via *ou* through Lyons/along by the coast; **~ la fenêtre** (*jeter, regarder*) out of the window; **3 ~ jour/personne** 3 a *ou* per day/head; **2 ~ 2** in twos; **~ ici** this way; (*dans le coin*) round here; **~-ci, ~-là** here and there; **~ temps de pluie** in wet weather
parabolique [paʀabɔlik] *adj*: **antenne ~** parabolic *ou* dish aerial
parachever [paʀaʃ(ə)ve] *vt* to perfect
parachute [paʀaʃyt] *nm* parachute; **parachutiste** *nm/f* parachutist; (MIL) paratrooper
parade [paʀad] *nf* (*spectacle, défilé*) parade; (ESCRIME, BOXE) parry
paradis [paʀadi] *nm* heaven, paradise
paradoxe [paʀadɔks] *nm* paradox
paraffine [paʀafin] *nf* paraffin
parages [paʀaʒ] *nmpl*: **dans les ~ (de)** in the area *ou* vicinity (of)
paragraphe [paʀagʀaf] *nm* paragraph
paraître [paʀɛtʀ] *vb +attrib* to seem, look, appear ♦ *vi* to appear; (*être visible*) to show; (PRESSE, ÉDITION) to be published, come out, appear ♦ *vb impers*: **il paraît que** it seems *ou* appears that, they say that; **chercher à ~** to show off
parallèle [paʀalɛl] *adj* parallel; (*non officiel*) unofficial ♦ *nm* (*comparaison*): **faire un ~ entre** to draw a parallel between ♦ *nf* parallel (line)
paralyser [paʀalize] *vt* to paralyse
paramédical, e, -aux [paʀamedikal, o] *adj*: **personnel ~** paramedics *pl*, paramedical workers *pl*
paraphrase [paʀafʀɑz] *nf* paraphrase
parapluie [paʀaplɥi] *nm* umbrella
parasite [paʀazit] *nm* parasite; **~s** *nmpl* (TÉL) interference *sg*
parasol [paʀasɔl] *nm* parasol, sunshade
paratonnerre [paʀatɔnɛʀ] *nm* lightning conductor
paravent [paʀavɑ̃] *nm* folding screen
parc [paʀk] *nm* (public) park, gardens *pl*; (*de château etc*) grounds *pl*; (*d'enfant*) playpen; (*ensemble d'unités*) stock; (*de voitures etc*) fleet; **~ d'attractions** theme park; **~ de stationnement** car park
parcelle [paʀsɛl] *nf* fragment, scrap; (*de terrain*) plot, parcel
parce que [paʀsk(ə)] *conj* because
parchemin [paʀʃəmɛ̃] *nm* parchment
parcmètre [paʀkmɛtʀ] *nm* parking meter
parcourir [paʀkuʀiʀ] *vt* (*trajet, distance*) to cover; (*article, livre*) to skim *ou* glance through; (*lieu*) to go all over, travel up and down; (*suj: frisson*) to run through
parcours [paʀkuʀ] *nm* (*trajet*) journey; (*itinéraire*) route
par-derrière [paʀdɛʀjɛʀ] *adv* round the back; **dire du mal de qn ~-~** to speak ill of sb behind his back

par-dessous [paʀd(ə)su] *prép, adv* under(neath)

pardessus [paʀdəsy] *nm* overcoat

par-dessus [paʀd(ə)sy] *prép* over (the top of) ♦ *adv* over (the top); **~-~ le marché** on top of all that; **~-~ tout** above all; **en avoir ~-~ la tête** to have had enough

par-devant [paʀd(ə)vɑ̃] *adv* (*passer*) round the front

pardon [paʀdɔ̃] *nm* forgiveness *no pl* ♦ *excl* sorry!; (*pour interpeller etc*) excuse me!; **demander ~ à qn (de)** to apologize to sb (for); **je vous demande ~** I'm sorry; (*pour interpeller*) excuse me; **pardonner** *vt* to forgive; **pardonner qch à qn** to forgive sb for sth

pare...: pare-balles *adj inv* bulletproof; **pare-brise** *nm inv* windscreen (*BRIT*), windshield (*US*); **pare-chocs** *nm inv* bumper

paré, e [paʀe] *adj* ready, all set

pareil, le [paʀɛj] *adj* (*identique*) the same, alike; (*similaire*) similar; (*tel*): **un courage/livre ~** such courage/a book, courage/a book like this; **de ~s livres** such books; **ne pas avoir son(sa) ~(le)** to be second to none; **~ à** the same as; (*similaire*) similar to; **sans ~** unparalleled, unequalled

parent, e [paʀɑ̃, ɑ̃t] *nm/f*: **un(e) ~(e)** a relative *ou* relation; **~s** *nmpl* (*père et mère*) parents; **parenté** *nf* (*lien*) relationship

parenthèse [paʀɑ̃tɛz] *nf* (*ponctuation*) bracket, parenthesis; (*digression*) parenthesis, digression; **entre ~s** in brackets; (*fig*) incidentally

parer [paʀe] *vt* to adorn; (*éviter*) to ward off; **~ au plus pressé** to attend to the most urgent things first

paresse [paʀɛs] *nf* laziness; **paresseux, -euse** *adj* lazy

parfaire [paʀfɛʀ] *vt* to perfect

parfait, e [paʀfɛ, ɛt] *adj* perfect ♦ *nm* (*LING*) perfect (tense); **parfaitement** *adv* perfectly ♦ *excl* (most) certainly

parfois [paʀfwa] *adv* sometimes

parfum [paʀfœ̃] *nm* (*produit*) perfume, scent; (*odeur: de fleur*) scent, fragrance; (*goût*) flavour; **parfumé, e** *adj* (*fleur, fruit*) fragrant; (*femme*) perfumed; **parfumé au café** coffee-flavoured; **parfumer** *vt* (*suj: odeur, bouquet*) to perfume; (*crème, gâteau*) to flavour; **parfumerie** *nf* (*produits*) perfumes *pl*; (*boutique*) perfume shop

pari [paʀi] *nm* bet; **parier** *vt* to bet

Paris [paʀi] *n* Paris; **parisien, ne** *adj* Parisian; (*GÉO, ADMIN*) Paris *cpd* ♦ *nm/f*: **Parisien, ne** Parisian

parjure [paʀʒyʀ] *nm* perjury

parking [paʀkiŋ] *nm* (*lieu*) car park

parlant, e [paʀlɑ̃, ɑ̃t] *adj* (*regard*) eloquent; (*CINÉMA*) talking; **les chiffres sont ~s** the figures speak for themselves

parlement [paʀləmɑ̃] *nm* parliament; **parlementaire** *adj* parliamentary ♦ *nm/f* member of parliament; **parlementer** *vi* to negotiate, parley

parler [paʀle] *vi* to speak, talk; (*avouer*) to talk; **~ (à qn) de** to talk *ou* speak (to sb) about; **~ le/en français** to speak French/in French; **~ affaires** to talk business; **sans ~ de** (*fig*) not to mention, to say nothing of; **tu parles!** (*fam: bien sûr*) you bet!

parloir [paʀlwaʀ] *nm* (*de prison, d'hôpital*) visiting room

parmi [paʀmi] *prép* among(st)

paroi [paʀwa] *nf* wall; (*cloison*) partition; **~ rocheuse** rock face

paroisse [paʀwas] *nf* parish

parole [paʀɔl] *nf* (*faculté*): **la ~** speech; (*mot, promesse*) word; **~s** *nfpl* (*MUS*) words, lyrics; **tenir ~** to keep one's word; **prendre la ~** to speak; **demander la ~** to ask for permission to speak; **je te crois sur ~** I'll take your word for it

parquer [paʀke] *vt* (*voiture, matériel*) to park; (*bestiaux*) to pen (in *ou* up)

parquet [paʀkɛ] *nm* (parquet) floor;

(*JUR*): **le ~** the Public Prosecutor's department

parrain [paʀɛ̃] *nm* godfather; **parrainer** *vt* (*suj*: *entreprise*) to sponsor

pars [paʀ] *vb voir* **partir**

parsemer [paʀsəme] *vt* (*suj*: *feuilles, papiers*) to be scattered over; **~ qch de** to scatter sth with

part [paʀ] *nf* (*qui revient à qn*) share; (*fraction, ~ie*) part; **prendre ~ à** (*débat etc*) to take part in; (*soucis, douleur de qn*) to share in; **faire ~ de qch à qn** to announce sth to sb, inform sb of sth; **pour ma ~** as for me, as far as I'm concerned; **à ~ entière** full; **de la ~ de** (*au nom de*) on behalf of; (*donné par*) from; **de toute(s) ~(s)** from all sides *ou* quarters; **de ~ et d'autre** on both sides, on either side; **d'une ~ ... d'autre ~** on the one hand ... on the other hand; **d'autre ~** (*de plus*) moreover; **à ~** ♦ *adv* (*séparément*) separately; (*de côté*) aside ♦ *prép* apart from, except for; **faire la ~ des choses** to make allowances

partage [paʀtaʒ] *nm* (*fractionnement*) dividing up; (*répartition*) sharing (out) *no pl*, share-out

partager [paʀtaʒe] *vt* to share; (*distribuer, répartir*) to share (out); (*morceler, diviser*) to divide (up); **se ~** *vt* (*héritage etc*) to share between themselves (*ou* ourselves)

partance [paʀtɑ̃s]: **en ~** *adv*: **en ~ pour** (bound) for

partenaire [paʀtənɛʀ] *nm/f* partner

parterre [paʀtɛʀ] *nm* (*de fleurs*) (flower) bed; (*THÉÂTRE*) stalls *pl*

parti [paʀti] *nm* (*POL*) party; (*décision*) course of action; (*personne à marier*) match; **tirer ~ de** to take advantage of, turn to good account; **prendre ~ (pour/contre)** to take sides *ou* a stand (for/against); **~ pris** bias

partial, e, -aux [paʀsjal, jo] *adj* biased, partial

participant, e [paʀtisipɑ̃, ɑ̃t] *nm/f* participant; (*à un concours*) entrant

participation [paʀtisipasjɔ̃] *nf* participation; (*financière*) contribution

participer [paʀtisipe]: **~ à** *vt* (*course, réunion*) to take part in; (*frais etc*) to contribute to; (*chagrin, succès de qn*) to share (in)

particularité [paʀtikylaʀite] *nf* (distinctive) characteristic

particulier, -ière [paʀtikylje, jɛʀ] *adj* (*spécifique*) particular; (*spécial*) special, particular; (*personnel, privé*) private; (*étrange*) peculiar, odd ♦ *nm* (*individu*: *ADMIN*) private individual; **~ à** peculiar to; **en ~** (*surtout*) in particular, particularly; (*en privé*) in private; **particulièrement** *adv* particularly

partie [paʀti] *nf* (*gén*) part; (*JUR etc*: *protagonistes*) party; (*de cartes, tennis etc*) game; **une ~ de pêche** a fishing party *ou* trip; **en ~** partly, in part; **faire ~ de** (*suj*: *chose*) to be part of; **prendre qn à ~** to take sb to task; **en grande ~** largely, in the main; **~ civile** (*JUR*) *party claiming damages in a criminal case*

partiel, le [paʀsjɛl] *adj* partial ♦ *nm* (*SCOL*) class exam

partir [paʀtiʀ] *vi* (*gén*) to go; (*quitter*) to go, leave; (*tache*) to go, come out; **~ de** (*lieu*: *quitter*) to leave; (: *commencer à*) to start from; **à ~ de** from

partisan, e [paʀtizɑ̃, an] *nm/f* partisan ♦ *adj*: **être ~ de qch/de faire** to be in favour of sth/doing

partition [paʀtisjɔ̃] *nf* (*MUS*) score

partout [paʀtu] *adv* everywhere; **~ où il allait** everywhere *ou* wherever he went

paru [paʀy] *pp de* **paraître**

parure [paʀyʀ] *nf* (*bijoux etc*) finery *no pl*; jewellery *no pl*; (*assortiment*) set

parution [paʀysjɔ̃] *nf* publication

parvenir [paʀvəniʀ]: **~ à** *vt* (*atteindre*) to reach; (*réussir*): **~ à faire** to manage to do, succeed in doing; **~ à ses fins** to achieve one's ends

pas[1] [pɑ] *nm* (*enjambée, DANSE*) step;

(*allure, mesure*) pace; (*bruit*) (foot)step; (*trace*) footprint; **~ à ~** step by step; **au ~** at walking pace; **faire les cent ~** to pace up and down; **faire les premiers ~** to make the first move; **sur le ~ de la porte** on the doorstep

MOT-CLÉ

pas[2] [pɑ] *adv* **1** (*en corrélation avec ne, non etc*) not; **il ne pleure pas** he does not *ou* doesn't cry; he's not *ou* isn't crying; **il n'a pas pleuré/ne pleurera pas** he did not *ou* didn't/will not *ou* won't cry; **ils n'ont pas de voiture/d'enfants** they haven't got a car/any children, they have no car/children; **il m'a dit de ne pas le faire** he told me not to do it; **non pas que** ... not that ...

2 (*employé sans ne etc*): **pas moi** not me; not I, I don't (*ou* can't *etc*); **une pomme pas mûre** an apple which isn't ripe; **pas plus tard qu'hier** only yesterday; **pas du tout** not at all

3: pas mal not bad; not badly; **pas mal de** quite a lot of

passage [pɑsaʒ] *nm* (*fait de passer*) *voir* **passer**; (*lieu, prix de la traversée, extrait*) passage; (*chemin*) way; **de ~** (*touristes*) passing through; **~ à niveau** level crossing; **~ clouté** pedestrian crossing; **"~ interdit"** "no entry"; **~ souterrain** subway (*BRIT*), underpass

passager, -ère [pɑsaʒe, ɛʀ] *adj* passing ♦ *nm/f* passenger; **~ clandestin** stowaway

passant, e [pɑsɑ̃, ɑ̃t] *adj* (*rue, endroit*) busy ♦ *nm/f* passer-by; **en ~** in passing

passe[1] [pɑs] *nf* (*SPORT, NAVIG*) pass; **être en ~ de faire** to be on the way to doing; **être dans une mauvaise ~** to be going through a rough patch

passe[2] [pɑs] *nm* (*~-partout*) master *ou* skeleton key

passé, e [pɑse] *adj* (*révolu*) past, (*dernier: semaine etc*) last; (*couleur*) faded ♦ *prép* after ♦ *nm* past; (*LING*) past (tense); **~ de mode** out of fashion; **~ composé** perfect (tense); **~ simple** past historic

passe-partout [pɑspaʀtu] *nm inv* master *ou* skeleton key ♦ *adj inv* all-purpose

passeport [pɑspɔʀ] *nm* passport

passer [pɑse] *vi* (*aller*) to go; (*voiture, piétons: défiler*) to pass (by), go by; (*facteur, laitier etc*) to come, call; (*pour rendre visite*) to call *ou* drop in; (*film, émission*) to be on; (*temps, jours*) to pass, go by; (*couleur*) to fade; (*mode*) to die out; (*douleur*) to pass, go away; (*SCOL*) to go up (to the next class) ♦ *vt* (*frontière, rivière etc*) to cross; (*douane*) to go through; (*examen*) to sit, take; (*visite médicale etc*) to have; (*journée, temps*) to spend; (*enfiler: vêtement*) to slip on; (*film, pièce*) to show, put on; (*disque*) to play, put on; (*marché, accord*) to agree on; **se ~** *vi* (*avoir lieu: scène, action*) to take place; (*se dérouler: entretien etc*) to go; (*s'écouler: semaine etc*) to pass, go by; (*arriver*): **que s'est-il passé?** what happened?; **~ qch à qn** (*sel etc*) to pass sth to sb; (*prêter*) to lend sb sth; (*lettre, message*) to pass sth on to sb; (*tolérer*) to let sb get away with sth; **~ par** to go through; **~ avant qch/qn** (*fig*) to come before sth/sb; **~ un coup de fil à qn** (*fam*) to give sb a ring; **laisser ~** (*air, lumière, personne*) to let through; (*occasion*) to let slip, miss; (*erreur*) to overlook; **~ la seconde** (*AUTO*) to change into second; **~ le balai/l'aspirateur** to sweep up/hoover; **je vous passe M. X** (*je vous mets en communication avec lui*) I'm putting you through to Mr X; (*je lui passe l'appareil*) here is Mr X, I'll hand you over to Mr X; **se ~ de** to go *ou* do without

passerelle [pɑsʀɛl] *nf* footbridge; (*de navire, avion*) gangway

passe-temps [pɑstɑ̃] *nm inv* pastime

passible [pasibl] *adj*: **~ de** liable to

passif, -ive [pasif, iv] *adj* passive

passion [pasjɔ̃] *nf* passion; **passionnant, e** *adj* fascinating; **passionné, e** *adj* (*personne*) passionate; (*récit*) impassioned; **être passionné de** to have a passion for; **passionner** *vt* (*personne*) to fascinate, grip; **se passionner pour** (*sport*) to have a passion for

passoire [paswaʀ] *nf* sieve; (*à légumes*) colander; (*à thé*) strainer

pastèque [pastɛk] *nf* watermelon

pasteur [pastœʀ] *nm* (*protestant*) minister, pastor

pasteurisé, e [pastœʀize] *adj* pasteurized

pastille [pastij] *nf* (*à sucer*) lozenge, pastille

patate [patat] *nf* (*fam*: *pomme de terre*) spud; **~ douce** sweet potato

patauger [patoʒe] *vi* to splash about

pâte [pɑt] *nf* (*à tarte*) pastry; (*à pain*) dough; (*à frire*) batter; **~s** *nfpl* (*macaroni etc*) pasta *sg*; **~ à modeler** modelling clay, Plasticine ® (*BRIT*); **~ brisée** shortcrust pastry; **~ d'amandes** almond paste; **~ de fruits** crystallized fruit *no pl*; **~ feuilletée** puff *ou* flaky pastry

pâté [pɑte] *nm* (*charcuterie*) pâté; (*tache*) ink blot; (*de sable*) sandpie; **~ de maisons** block (of houses); **~ en croûte** ≃ pork pie

pâtée [pɑte] *nf* mash, feed

patente [patɑ̃t] *nf* (*COMM*) trading licence

paternel, le [patɛʀnɛl] *adj* (*amour, soins*) fatherly; (*ligne, autorité*) paternal

pâteux, -euse [pɑtø, øz] *adj* pasty; (*langue*) coated

pathétique [patetik] *adj* moving

patience [pasjɑ̃s] *nf* patience

patient, e [pasjɑ̃, jɑ̃t] *adj, nm/f* patient; **patienter** *vi* to wait

patin [patɛ̃] *nm* skate; (*sport*) skating; **~s (à glace)** (ice) skates; **~s à roulettes** roller skates

patinage [patinaʒ] *nm* skating

patiner [patine] *vi* to skate; (*roue, voiture*) to spin; **se ~** *vi* (*meuble, cuir*) to acquire a sheen; **patineur, -euse** *nm/f* skater; **patinoire** *nf* skating rink, (ice) rink

pâtir [pɑtiʀ]: **~ de** *vt* to suffer because of

pâtisserie [pɑtisʀi] *nf* (*boutique*) cake shop; (*gâteau*) cake, pastry; (*à la maison*) pastry- *ou* cake-making, baking; **pâtissier, -ière** *nm/f* pastrycook

patois [patwa, waz] *nm* dialect, patois

patraque [patʀak] (*fam*) *adj* peaky, off-colour

patrie [patʀi] *nf* homeland

patrimoine [patʀimwan] *nm* (*culture*) heritage

patriotique [patʀijɔtik] *adj* patriotic

patron, ne [patʀɔ̃, ɔn] *nm/f* boss; (*REL*) patron saint ♦ *nm* (*COUTURE*) pattern; **patronat** *nm* employers *pl*; **patronner** *vt* to sponsor, support

patrouille [patʀuj] *nf* patrol

patte [pat] *nf* (*jambe*) leg; (*pied*: *de chien, chat*) paw; (: *d'oiseau*) foot

pâturage [pɑtyʀaʒ] *nm* pasture

paume [pom] *nf* palm

paumé, e [pome] (*fam*) *nm/f* drop-out

paumer [pome] (*fam*) *vt* to lose

paupière [popjɛʀ] *nf* eyelid

pause [poz] *nf* (*arrêt*) break; (*en parlant, MUS*) pause

pauvre [povʀ] *adj* poor; **pauvreté** *nf* (*état*) poverty

pavaner [pavane]: **se ~** *vi* to strut about

pavé, e [pave] *adj* (*cour*) paved; (*chaussée*) cobbled ♦ *nm* (*bloc*) paving stone; cobblestone

pavillon [pavijɔ̃] *nm* (*de banlieue*) small (detached) house; pavilion; (*drapeau*) flag

pavoiser [pavwaze] *vi* (*fig*) to rejoice, exult

pavot [pavo] *nm* poppy

payant, e [pɛjɑ̃, ɑ̃t] *adj* (*spectateurs etc*) paying; (*fig*: *entreprise*) profitable; (*effort*) which pays off; **c'est ~** you have to pay, there is a charge

paye [pɛj] *nf* pay, wages *pl*

payer [peje] *vt* (*créancier, employé, loyer*) to pay; (*achat, réparations, fig*: *faute*) to pay for ♦ *vi* to pay; (*métier*) to be well-paid; (*tactique etc*) to pay off; **il me l'a fait ~ 10 F** he charged me 10 F for it; **~ qch à qn** to buy sth for sb, buy sb sth; **se ~ la tête de qn** (*fam*) to take the mickey out of sb

pays [pei] *nm* country; (*région*) region; **du ~** local

paysage [peizaʒ] *nm* landscape

paysan, ne [peizɑ̃, an] *nm/f* farmer; (*péj*) peasant ♦ *adj* (*agricole*) farming; (*rural*) country

Pays-Bas [peiba] *nmpl*: **les ~-~** the Netherlands

PC *nm* (INFORM) PC ♦ *sigle m* = **parti communiste**

P.D.G. *sigle m* = **président directeur général**

péage [peaʒ] *nm* toll; (*endroit*) tollgate

peau, x [po] *nf* skin; **gants de ~** fine leather gloves; **être bien/mal dans sa ~** to be quite at ease/ill-at-ease; **~ de chamois** (*chiffon*) chamois leather, shammy; **Peau-Rouge** *nm/f* Red Indian, redskin

pêche [pɛʃ] *nf* (*sport, activité*) fishing; (*poissons pêchés*) catch; (*fruit*) peach; **~ à la ligne** (*en rivière*) angling

péché [peʃe] *nm* sin

pécher [peʃe] *vi* (RÉL) to sin

pêcher [peʃe] *nm* peach tree ♦ *vi* to go fishing ♦ *vt* (*attraper*) to catch; (*être pêcheur de*) to fish for

pécheur, -eresse [peʃœʀ, peʃʀɛs] *nm/f* sinner

pêcheur [pɛʃœʀ] *nm* fisherman; (*à la ligne*) angler

pécule [pekyl] *nm* savings *pl*, nest egg

pédagogie [pedagɔʒi] *nf* educational methods *pl*, pedagogy; **pédagogique** *adj* educational

pédale [pedal] *nf* pedal

pédalo [pedalo] *nm* pedal-boat

pédant, e [pedɑ̃, ɑ̃t] (*péj*) *adj* pedantic

pédestre [pedɛstʀ] *adj*: **randonnée ~** ramble; **sentier ~** pedestrian footpath

pédiatre [pedjatʀ] *nm/f* paediatrician, child specialist

pédicure [pedikyʀ] *nm/f* chiropodist

pègre [pɛgʀ] *nf* underworld

peignais *etc* [pɛɲɛ] *vb voir* **peindre**; **peigner**

peigne [pɛɲ] *nm* comb; **peigner** *vt* to comb (the hair of); **se peigner** *vi* to comb one's hair

peignoir *nm* dressing gown; **peignoir de bain** bathrobe

peindre [pɛ̃dʀ] *vt* to paint; (*fig*) to portray, depict

peine [pɛn] *nf* (*affliction*) sorrow, sadness *no pl*; (*mal, effort*) trouble *no pl*, effort; (*difficulté*) difficulty; (JUR) sentence; **avoir de la ~** to be sad; **faire de la ~ à qn** to distress *ou* upset sb; **prendre la ~ de faire** to go to the trouble of doing; **se donner de la ~** to make an effort; **ce n'est pas la ~ de faire** there's no point in doing, it's not worth doing; **à ~** scarcely, hardly, barely; **à ~ ... que** hardly ... than; **~ capitale** *ou* **de mort** capital punishment, death sentence; **peiner** *vi* (*personne*) to work hard; (*moteur, voiture*) to labour ♦ *vt* to grieve, sadden

peintre [pɛ̃tʀ] *nm* painter; **~ en bâtiment** house painter

peinture [pɛ̃tyʀ] *nf* painting; (*matière*) paint; (*surfaces peintes: aussi*: **~s**) paintwork; **"~ fraîche"** "wet paint"

péjoratif, -ive [peʒɔʀatif, iv] *adj* pejorative, derogatory

pelage [pəlaʒ] *nm* coat, fur

pêle-mêle [pɛlmɛl] *adv* higgledy-piggledy

peler [pəle] *vt, vi* to peel

pèlerin [pɛlʀɛ̃] *nm* pilgrim

pèlerinage [pɛlʀinaʒ] *nm* pilgrimage

pelle [pɛl] *nf* shovel; (*d'enfant, de terrassier*) spade

pellicule [pelikyl] *nf* film; **~s** *nfpl* (MÉD)

dandruff *sg*
pelote [p(ə)lɔt] *nf* (*de fil, laine*) ball
peloton [p(ə)lɔtɔ̃] *nm* group, squad; (*CYCLISME*) pack; **~ d'exécution** firing squad
pelotonner [p(ə)lɔtɔne]: **se ~** *vi* to curl (o.s.) up
pelouse [p(ə)luz] *nf* lawn
peluche [p(ə)lyʃ] *nf*: **(animal en) ~** fluffy animal, soft toy; **chien/lapin en ~** fluffy dog/rabbit
pelure [p(ə)lyʀ] *nf* peeling, peel *no pl*
pénal, e, -aux [penal, o] *adj* penal; **pénalité** *nf* penalty
penaud, e [pəno, od] *adj* sheepish, contrite
penchant [pɑ̃ʃɑ̃] *nm* (*tendance*) tendency, propensity; (*faible*) liking, fondness
pencher [pɑ̃ʃe] *vi* to tilt, lean over ♦ *vt* to tilt; **se ~** *vi* to lean over; (*se baisser*) to bend down; **se ~ sur** (*fig: problème*) to look into; **~ pour** to be inclined to favour
pendaison [pɑ̃dɛzɔ̃] *nf* hanging
pendant [pɑ̃dɑ̃] *prép* (*au cours de*) during; (*indique la durée*) for; **~ que** while
pendentif [pɑ̃dɑ̃tif] *nm* pendant
penderie [pɑ̃dʀi] *nf* wardrobe
pendre [pɑ̃dʀ] *vt, vi* to hang; **se ~** (*se suicider*) to hang o.s.; **~ la crémaillère** to have a house-warming party
pendule [pɑ̃dyl] *nf* clock ♦ *nm* pendulum
pénétrer [penetʀe] *vi, vt* to penetrate; **~ dans** to enter
pénible [penibl] *adj* (*travail*) hard; (*sujet*) painful; (*personne*) tiresome; **péniblement** *adv* with difficulty
péniche [peniʃ] *nf* barge
pénicilline [penisilin] *nf* penicillin
péninsule [penɛ̃syl] *nf* peninsula
pénis [penis] *nm* penis
pénitence [penitɑ̃s] *nf* (*peine*) penance; (*repentir*) penitence; **pénitencier** *nm* penitentiary
pénombre [penɔ̃bʀ] *nf* (*faible clarté*) half-light; (*obscurité*) darkness
pensée [pɑ̃se] *nf* thought; (*démarche, doctrine*) thinking *no pl*; (*fleur*) pansy; **en ~** in one's mind
penser [pɑ̃se] *vi, vt* to think; **~ à** (*ami, vacances*) to think of *ou* about; (*réfléchir à: problème, offre*) to think about *ou* over; (*prévoir*) to think of; **faire ~ à** to remind one of; **~ faire qch** to be thinking of doing sth, intend to do sth; **pensif, -ive** *adj* pensive, thoughtful
pension [pɑ̃sjɔ̃] *nf* (*allocation*) pension; (*prix du logement*) board and lodgings, bed and board; (*école*) boarding school; **~ alimentaire** (*de divorcée*) maintenance allowance, alimony; **~ complète** full board; **~ (de famille)** boarding house, guesthouse; **pensionnaire** *nm/f* (*SCOL*) boarder; **pensionnat** *nm* boarding school
pente [pɑ̃t] *nf* slope; **en ~** sloping
Pentecôte [pɑ̃tkot] *nf*: **la ~** Whitsun (*BRIT*), Pentecost
pénurie [penyʀi] *nf* shortage
pépé [pepe] (*fam*) *nm* grandad
pépin [pepɛ̃] *nm* (*BOT: graine*) pip; (*ennui*) snag, hitch
pépinière [pepinjɛʀ] *nf* nursery
perçant, e [pɛʀsɑ̃, ɑ̃t] *adj* (*cri*) piercing, shrill; (*regard*) piercing
percée [pɛʀse] *nf* (*trouée*) opening; (*MIL, technologique*) breakthrough
perce-neige [pɛʀsənɛʒ] *nf inv* snowdrop
percepteur [pɛʀsɛptœʀ, tʀis] *nm* tax collector
perception [pɛʀsɛpsjɔ̃] *nf* perception; (*bureau*) tax office
percer [pɛʀse] *vt* to pierce; (*ouverture etc*) to make; (*mystère, énigme*) to penetrate ♦ *vi* to break through; **perceuse** *nf* drill
percevoir [pɛʀsəvwaʀ] *vt* (*distinguer*) to perceive, detect; (*taxe, impôt*) to collect; (*revenu, indemnité*) to receive
perche [pɛʀʃ] *nf* (*bâton*) pole
percher [pɛʀʃe] *vt, vi* to perch; **se ~** *vi*

to perch; **perchoir** *nm* perch

perçois *etc* [pɛʀswa] *vb voir* **percevoir**

percolateur [pɛʀkɔlatœʀ] *nm* percolator

perçu, e [pɛʀsy] *pp de* **percevoir**

percussion [pɛʀkysjɔ̃] *nf* percussion

percuter [pɛʀkyte] *vt* to strike; (*suj*: *véhicule*) to crash into

perdant, e [pɛʀdɑ̃, ɑ̃t] *nm/f* loser

perdre [pɛʀdʀ] *vt* to lose; (*gaspiller*: *temps, argent*) to waste; (*personne*: *moralement etc*) to ruin ♦ *vi* to lose; (*sur une vente etc*) to lose out; **se ~** *vi* (*s'égarer*) to get lost, lose one's way; (*denrées*) to go to waste

perdrix [pɛʀdʀi] *nf* partridge

perdu, e [pɛʀdy] *pp de* **perdre** ♦ *adj* (*isolé*) out-of-the-way; (COMM: *emballage*) non-returnable; (*malade*): **il est ~** there's no hope left for him; **à vos moments ~s** in your spare time

père [pɛʀ] *nm* father; **~ de famille** father; **le ~ Noël** Father Christmas

perfection [pɛʀfɛksjɔ̃] *nf* perfection; **à la ~** to perfection; **perfectionné, e** *adj* sophisticated; **perfectionner** *vt* to improve, perfect

perforatrice [pɛʀfɔʀatʀis] *nf* (*de bureau*) punch

perforer [pɛʀfɔʀe] *vt* (*poinçonner*) to punch

performant, e [pɛʀfɔʀmɑ̃, ɑ̃t] *adj*: **très ~** high-performance *cpd*

perfusion [pɛʀfyzjɔ̃] *nf*: **faire une ~ à qn** to put sb on a drip

péricliter [peʀiklite] *vi* to collapse

péril [peʀil] *nm* peril

périmé, e [peʀime] *adj* (ADMIN) out-of-date, expired

périmètre [peʀimɛtʀ] *nm* perimeter

période [peʀjɔd] *nf* period; **périodique** *adj* periodic ♦ *nm* periodical

péripéties [peʀipesi] *nfpl* events, episodes

périphérique [peʀifeʀik] *adj* (*quartiers*) outlying ♦ *nm* (AUTO) ring road

périple [peʀipl] *nm* journey

périr [peʀiʀ] *vi* to die, perish

périssable [peʀisabl] *adj* perishable

perle [pɛʀl] *nf* pearl; (*de plastique, métal, sueur*) bead

permanence [pɛʀmanɑ̃s] *nf* permanence; (*local*) (duty) office; **assurer une ~** (*service public, bureaux*) to operate *ou* maintain a basic service; **être de ~** to be on call *ou* duty; **en ~** continuously

permanent, e [pɛʀmanɑ̃, ɑ̃t] *adj* permanent; (*spectacle*) continuous; **permanente** *nf* perm

perméable [pɛʀmeabl] *adj* (*terrain*) permeable; **~ à** (*fig*) receptive *ou* open to

permettre [pɛʀmɛtʀ] *vt* to allow, permit; **~ à qn de faire/qch** to allow sb to do/sth; **se ~ de faire** to take the liberty of doing

permis [pɛʀmi, iz] *nm* permit, licence; **~ de chasse** hunting permit; **~ (de conduire)** (driving) licence (BRIT), (driver's) license (US); **~ de construire** planning permission (BRIT), building permit (US); **~ de séjour** residence permit; **~ de travail** work permit

permission [pɛʀmisjɔ̃] *nf* permission; (MIL) leave; **avoir la ~ de faire** to have permission to do; **en ~** on leave

permuter [pɛʀmyte] *vt* to change around, permutate ♦ *vi* to change, swap

Pérou [peʀu] *nm* Peru

perpétuel, le [pɛʀpetɥɛl] *adj* perpetual; **perpétuité** *nf*: **à perpétuité** for life; **être condamné à perpétuité** to receive a life sentence

perplexe [pɛʀplɛks] *adj* perplexed, puzzled

perquisitionner [pɛʀkizisjɔne] *vi* to carry out a search

perron [peʀɔ̃] *nm* steps *pl* (*leading to entrance*)

perroquet [peʀɔkɛ] *nm* parrot

perruche [peʀyʃ] *nf* budgerigar (BRIT), budgie (BRIT), parakeet (US)

perruque [peʀyk] *nf* wig
persan, e [pɛʀsɑ̃, an] *adj* Persian
persécuter [pɛʀsekyte] *vt* to persecute
persévérer [pɛʀsevere] *vi* to persevere
persiennes [pɛʀsjɛn] *nfpl* shutters
persil [pɛʀsi] *nm* parsley
Persique [pɛʀsik] *adj*: **le golfe ~** the (Persian) Gulf
persistant, e [pɛʀsistɑ̃, ɑ̃t] *adj* persistent
persister [pɛʀsiste] *vi* to persist; **~ à faire qch** to persist in doing sth
personnage [pɛʀsɔnaʒ] *nm* (*individu*) character, individual; (*célébrité*) important person; (*de roman, film*) character; (PEINTURE) figure
personnalité [pɛʀsɔnalite] *nf* personality; (*personnage*) prominent figure
personne [pɛʀsɔn] *nf* person ♦ *pron* nobody, no one; (*avec négation en anglais*) anybody, anyone; **~s** *nfpl* (*gens*) people *pl*; **il n'y a ~** there's nobody there, there isn't anybody there; **~ âgée** elderly person; **personnel, le** *adj* personal; (*égoïste*) selfish ♦ *nm* staff, personnel; **personnellement** *adv* personally
perspective [pɛʀspɛktiv] *nf* (ART) perspective; (*vue*) view; (*point de vue*) viewpoint, angle; (*chose envisagée*) prospect; **en ~** in prospect
perspicace [pɛʀspikas] *adj* clear-sighted, gifted with (*ou* showing) insight; **perspicacité** *nf* clear-sightedness
persuader [pɛʀsɥade] *vt*: **~ qn (de faire)** to persuade sb (to do); **persuasif, -ive** *adj* persuasive
perte [pɛʀt] *nf* loss; (*de temps*) waste; (*fig: morale*) ruin; **à ~ de vue** as far as the eye can (*ou* could) see; **~s blanches** (vaginal) discharge *sg*
pertinemment [pɛʀtinamɑ̃] *adv* (*savoir*) full well
pertinent, e [pɛʀtinɑ̃, ɑ̃t] *adj* apt, relevant
perturbation [pɛʀtyʀbasjɔ̃] *nf*: **~ (atmosphérique)** atmospheric disturbance
perturber [pɛʀtyʀbe] *vt* to disrupt; (PSYCH) to perturb, disturb
pervers, e [pɛʀvɛʀ, ɛʀs] *adj* perverted
pervertir [pɛʀvɛʀtiʀ] *vt* to pervert
pesant, e [pəzɑ̃, ɑ̃t] *adj* heavy; (*fig: présence*) burdensome
pèse-personne [pɛzpɛʀsɔn] *nm* (bathroom) scales *pl*
peser [pəze] *vt* to weigh ♦ *vi* to weigh; (*fig: avoir de l'importance*) to carry weight; **~ lourd** to be heavy
pessimisme [pesimism] *nm* pessimism
pessimiste [pesimist] *adj* pessimistic ♦ *nm/f* pessimist
peste [pɛst] *nf* plague
pester [pɛste] *vi*: **~ contre** to curse
pétale [petal] *nm* petal
pétanque [petɑ̃k] *nf type of bowls*

pétanque

Pétanque, *which originated in the south of France, is a version of the game of* **boules** *played on a variety of hard surfaces. Standing with their feet together, players throw steel bowls towards a wooden jack.*

pétarader [petaʀade] *vi* to backfire
pétard [petaʀ] *nm* banger (BRIT), firecracker
péter [pete] *vi* (*fam: casser*) to bust; (*fam!*) to fart (*!*)
pétillant, e [petijɑ̃, ɑ̃t] *adj* (*eau etc*) sparkling
pétiller [petije] *vi* (*feu*) to crackle; (*champagne*) to bubble; (*yeux*) to sparkle
petit, e [p(ə)ti, it] *adj* small; (*avec nuance affective*) little; (*voyage*) short, little; (*bruit etc*) faint, slight; **~s** *nmpl* (*d'un animal*) young *pl*; **les tout-~s** the little ones, the tiny tots; **~ à ~** bit by bit, gradually; **~(e) ami(e)** boyfriend/girlfriend; **~ déjeuner** breakfast; **~ pain** (bread) roll; **les ~es annonces** the

small ads; **~s pois** garden peas; **petite-fille** *nf* granddaughter; **petit-fils** *nm* grandson

pétition [petisjɔ̃] *nf* petition

petits-enfants [pətizɑ̃fɑ̃] *nmpl* grandchildren

petit-suisse [pətisɥis] (*pl* **~s-~s**) *nm* *small individual pot of cream cheese*

pétrin [petʀɛ̃] *nm* (*fig*): **dans le ~** (*fam*) in a jam *ou* fix

pétrir [petʀiʀ] *vt* to knead

pétrole [petʀɔl] *nm* oil; (*pour lampe, réchaud etc*) paraffin (oil); **pétrolier, -ière** *nm* oil tanker

MOT-CLÉ

peu [pø] *adv* **1** (*modifiant verbe, adjectif, adverbe*): **il boit peu** he doesn't drink (very) much; **il est peu bavard** he's not very talkative; **peu avant/après** shortly before/afterwards

2 (*modifiant nom*): **peu de**: **peu de gens/d'arbres** few *ou* not (very) many people/trees; **il a peu d'espoir** he hasn't (got) much hope, he has little hope; **pour peu de temps** for (only) a short while

3: **peu à peu** little by little; **à peu près** just about, more or less; **à peu près 10 kg/10 F** approximately 10 kg/10F

♦ *nm* **1**: **le peu de gens qui** the few people who; **le peu de sable qui** what little sand, the little sand which

2: **un peu** a little; **un petit peu** a little bit; **un peu d'espoir** a little hope

♦ *pron*: **peu le savent** few know (it); **avant** *ou* **sous peu** shortly, before long; **de peu** (only) just

peuple [pœpl] *nm* people; **peupler** *vt* (*pays, région*) to populate; (*étang*) to stock; (*suj*: *hommes, poissons*) to inhabit

peuplier [pøplije] *nm* poplar (tree)

peur [pœʀ] *nf* fear; **avoir ~ (de/de faire/que)** to be frightened *ou* afraid (of/of doing/that); **faire ~ à** to frighten; **de ~ de/que** for fear of/that; **peureux, -euse** *adj* fearful, timorous

peut [pø] *vb voir* **pouvoir**

peut-être [pøtɛtʀ] *adv* perhaps, maybe; **~-~ que** perhaps, maybe; **~-~ bien qu'il fera/est** he may well do/be

peux *etc* [pø] *vb voir* **pouvoir**

phare [faʀ] *nm* (*en mer*) lighthouse; (*de véhicule*) headlight; **~s de recul** reversing lights

pharmacie [faʀmasi] *nf* (*magasin*) chemist's (*BRIT*), pharmacy; (*de salle de bain*) medicine cabinet; **pharmacien, ne** *nm/f* pharmacist, chemist (*BRIT*)

phénomène [fenɔmɛn] *nm* phenomenon

philatélie [filateli] *nf* philately, stamp collecting

philosophe [filɔzɔf] *nm/f* philosopher ♦ *adj* philosophical

philosophie [filɔzɔfi] *nf* philosophy

phobie [fɔbi] *nf* phobia

phonétique [fɔnetik] *nf* phonetics *sg*

phoque [fɔk] *nm* seal

phosphorescent, e [fɔsfɔʀesɑ̃, ɑ̃t] *adj* luminous

photo [fɔto] *nf* photo(graph); **prendre en ~** to take a photo of; **faire de la ~** to take photos; **~ d'identité** passport photograph; **photocopie** *nf* photocopy; **photocopier** *vt* to photocopy; **photocopieuse** *nf* photocopier; **photographe** *nm/f* photographer; **photographie** *nf* (*technique*) photography; (*cliché*) photograph; **photographier** *vt* to photograph

phrase [fʀɑz] *nf* sentence

physicien, ne [fizisjɛ̃, jɛn] *nm/f* physicist

physionomie [fizjɔnɔmi] *nf* face

physique [fizik] *adj* physical ♦ *nm* physique ♦ *nf* physics *sg*; **au ~** physically; **physiquement** *adv* physically

piailler [pjɑje] *vi* to squawk

pianiste [pjanist] *nm/f* pianist

piano [pjano] *nm* piano; **pianoter** *vi* to tinkle away (at the piano)

pic [pik] *nm* (*instrument*) pick(axe);

(*montagne*) peak; (*ZOOL*) woodpecker; **à ~** vertically; (*fig*: *tomber, arriver*) just at the right time

pichet [piʃɛ] *nm* jug

picorer [pikɔʀe] *vt* to peck

picoter [pikɔte] *vt* (*suj*: *oiseau*) to peck ♦ *vi* (*irriter*) to smart, prickle

pie [pi] *nf* magpie

pièce [pjɛs] *nf* (*d'un logement*) room; (*THÉÂTRE*) play; (*de machine*) part; (*de monnaie*) coin; (*document*) document; (*fragment, de collection*) piece; **dix francs ~** ten francs each; **vendre à la ~** to sell separately; **travailler à la ~** to do piecework; **un maillot une ~** a one-piece swimsuit; **un deux-~s cuisine** a two-room(ed) flat (*BRIT*) *ou* apartment (*US*) with kitchen; **~ à conviction** exhibit; **~ d'identité: avez-vous une ~ d'identité?** have you got any (means of) identification?; **~ montée** tiered cake; **~s détachées** spares, (spare) parts; **~s justificatives** supporting documents

pied [pje] *nm* foot; (*de table*) leg; (*de lampe*) base; **à ~** on foot; **au ~ de la lettre** literally; **avoir ~** to be able to touch the bottom, not to be out of one's depth; **avoir le ~ marin** to be a good sailor; **sur ~** (*debout, rétabli*) up and about; **mettre sur ~** (*entreprise*) to set up; **c'est le ~** (*fam*) it's brilliant; **mettre les ~s dans le plat** (*fam*) to put one's foot in it; **il se débrouille comme un ~** (*fam*) he's completely useless; **pied-noir** *nm Algerian-born Frenchman*

piège [pjɛʒ] *nm* trap; **prendre au ~** to trap; **piéger** *vt* (*avec une bombe*) to booby-trap; **lettre/voiture piégée** letter-/car-bomb

pierre [pjɛʀ] *nf* stone; **~ précieuse** precious stone, gem; **~ tombale** tombstone; **pierreries** *nfpl* gems, precious stones

piétiner [pjetine] *vi* (*trépigner*) to stamp (one's foot); (*fig*) to be at a standstill ♦ *vt* to trample on

piéton, ne [pjetɔ̃, ɔn] *nm/f* pedestrian; **piétonnier, -ière** *adj*: **rue** *ou* **zone piétonnière** pedestrian precinct

pieu, x [pjø] *nm* post; (*pointu*) stake

pieuvre [pjœvʀ] *nf* octopus

pieux, -euse [pjø, pjøz] *adj* pious

piffer [pife] (*fam*) *vt*: **je ne peux pas le ~** I can't stand him

pigeon [piʒɔ̃] *nm* pigeon

piger [piʒe] (*fam*) *vi, vt* to understand

pigiste [piʒist] *nm/f* freelance(r)

pignon [piɲɔ̃] *nm* (*de mur*) gable

pile [pil] *nf* (*tas*) pile; (*ÉLEC*) battery ♦ *adv* (*fam*: *s'arrêter etc*) dead; **à deux heures ~** at two on the dot; **jouer à ~ ou face** to toss up (for it); **~ ou face?** heads or tails?

piler [pile] *vt* to crush, pound

pilier [pilje] *nm* pillar

piller [pije] *vt* to pillage, plunder, loot

pilote [pilɔt] *nm* pilot; (*de voiture*) driver ♦ *adj* pilot *cpd*; **~ de course** racing driver; **~ de ligne/d'essai/de chasse** airline/test/fighter pilot; **piloter** *vt* (*avion*) to pilot, fly; (*voiture*) to drive

pilule [pilyl] *nf* pill; **prendre la ~** to be on the pill

piment [pimɑ̃] *nm* (*aussi:* **~ rouge**) chilli; (*fig*) spice, piquancy; **~ doux** pepper, capsicum; **pimenté, e** *adj* (*plat*) hot, spicy

pimpant, e [pɛ̃pɑ̃, ɑ̃t] *adj* spruce

pin [pɛ̃] *nm* pine

pinard [pinaʀ] (*fam*) *nm* (cheap) wine, plonk (*BRIT*)

pince [pɛ̃s] *nf* (*outil*) pliers *pl*; (*de homard, crabe*) pincer, claw; (*COUTURE*: *pli*) dart; **~ à épiler** tweezers *pl*; **~ à linge** clothes peg (*BRIT*) *ou* pin (*US*)

pincé, e [pɛ̃se] *adj* (*air*) stiff

pinceau, x [pɛ̃so] *nm* (paint)brush

pincée [pɛ̃se] *nf*: **une ~ de** a pinch of

pincer [pɛ̃se] *vt* to pinch; (*fam*) to nab

pinède [pinɛd] *nf* pinewood, pine forest

pingouin [pɛ̃gwɛ̃] *nm* penguin

ping-pong ® [piŋpɔ̃g] *nm* table tennis
pingre [pɛ̃gʀ] *adj* niggardly
pinson [pɛ̃sɔ̃] *nm* chaffinch
pintade [pɛ̃tad] *nf* guinea-fowl
pioche [pjɔʃ] *nf* pickaxe; **piocher** *vt* to dig up (with a pickaxe); **piocher dans** (*le tas, ses économies*) to dig into
pion [pjɔ̃] *nm* (*ÉCHECS*) pawn; (*DAMES*) piece; (*SCOL*) supervisor
pionnier [pjɔnje] *nm* pioneer
pipe [pip] *nf* pipe; **fumer la ~** to smoke a pipe
pipeau, x [pipo] *nm* (reed-)pipe
piquant, e [pikɑ̃, ɑ̃t] *adj* (*barbe, rosier etc*) prickly; (*saveur, sauce*) hot, pungent; (*détail*) titillating; (*froid*) biting ♦ *nm* (*épine*) thorn, prickle; (*fig*) spiciness, spice
pique [pik] *nf* pike; (*fig*) cutting remark ♦ *nm* (*CARTES*) spades *pl*
pique-nique [piknik] *nm* picnic; **pique-niquer** *vi* to have a picnic
piquer [pike] *vt* (*suj: guêpe, fumée, orties*) to sting; (*: moustique*) to bite; (*: barbe*) to prick; (*: froid*) to bite; (*MÉD*) to give a jab to; (*: chien, chat*) to put to sleep; (*intérêt*) to arouse; (*fam: voler*) to pinch ♦ *vi* (*avion*) to go into a dive; **se ~** (*avec une aiguille*) to prick o.s.; (*dans les orties*) to get stung; (*suj: toxicomane*) to shoot up; **~ une colère** to fly into a rage
piquet [pikɛ] *nm* (*pieu*) post, stake; (*de tente*) peg; **~ de grève** (strike-)picket
piqûre [pikyʀ] *nf* (*d'épingle*) prick; (*d'ortie*) sting; (*de moustique*) bite; (*MÉD*) injection, shot (*US*); **faire une ~ à qn** to give sb an injection
pirate [piʀat] *nm, adj* pirate; **~ de l'air** hijacker
pire [piʀ] *adj* worse; (*superlatif*): **le(la) ~ ...** the worst ... ♦ *nm*: **le ~ (de)** the worst (of); **au ~** at (the very) worst
pis [pi] *nm* (*de vache*) udder; (*pire*): **le ~** the worst ♦ *adj, adv* worse; **de mal en ~** from bad to worse
piscine [pisin] *nf* (swimming) pool; **~ couverte** indoor (swimming) pool
pissenlit [pisɑ̃li] *nm* dandelion
pistache [pistaʃ] *nf* pistachio (nut)
piste [pist] *nf* (*d'un animal, sentier*) track, trail; (*indice*) lead; (*de stade*) track; (*de cirque*) ring; (*de danse*) floor; (*de patinage*) rink; (*de ski*) run; (*AVIAT*) runway; **~ cyclable** cycle track
pistolet [pistɔlɛ] *nm* (*arme*) pistol, gun; (*à peinture*) spray gun; **pistolet-mitrailleur** *nm* submachine gun
piston [pistɔ̃] *nm* (*TECH*) piston; **avoir du ~** (*fam*) to have friends in the right places; **pistonner** *vt* (*candidat*) to pull strings for
piteux, -euse [pitø, øz] *adj* pitiful, sorry (*avant le nom*)
pitié [pitje] *nf* pity; **il me fait ~** I feel sorry for him; **avoir ~ de** (*compassion*) to pity, feel sorry for; (*merci*) to have pity *ou* mercy on
pitoyable [pitwajabl] *adj* pitiful
pitre [pitʀ] *nm* clown; **pitrerie** *nf* tomfoolery *no pl*
pittoresque [pitɔʀɛsk] *adj* picturesque
pivot [pivo] *nm* pivot; **pivoter** *vi* to revolve; (*fauteuil*) to swivel
P.J. *sigle f* (= *police judiciaire*) ≃ CID (*BRIT*), ≃ FBI (*US*)
placard [plakaʀ] *nm* (*armoire*) cupboard; (*affiche*) poster, notice
place [plas] *nf* (*emplacement, classement*) place; (*de ville, village*) square; (*espace libre*) room, space; (*de parking*) space; (*siège: de train, cinéma, voiture*) seat; (*emploi*) job; **en ~** (*mettre*) in its place; **sur ~** on the spot; **faire ~ à** to give way to; **ça prend de la ~** it takes up a lot of room *ou* space; **à la ~ de** in place of, instead of; **à ta ~ ...** if I were you ...; **se mettre à la ~ de qn** to put o.s. in sb's place *ou* in sb's shoes
placé, e [plase] *adj*: **être bien/mal ~** (*spectateur*) to have a good/a poor seat; (*concurrent*) to be in a good/bad position; **il est bien ~ pour le savoir**

he is in a position to know

placement [plasmɑ̃] *nm* (*FINANCE*) investment; **bureau de ~** employment agency

placer [plase] *vt* to place; (*convive, spectateur*) to seat; (*argent*) to place, invest; **il n'a pas pu ~ un mot** he couldn't get a word in; **se ~ au premier rang** to go and stand (*ou* sit) in the first row

plafond [plafɔ̃] *nm* ceiling

plage [plaʒ] *nf* beach

plagiat [plaʒja] *nm* plagiarism

plaid [plɛd] *nm* (tartan) car rug

plaider [plede] *vi* (*avocat*) to plead ♦ *vt* to plead; **~ pour** (*fig*) to speak for; **plaidoyer** *nm* (*JUR*) speech for the defence; (*fig*) plea

plaie [plɛ] *nf* wound

plaignant, e [plɛɲɑ̃, ɑ̃t] *nm/f* plaintiff

plaindre [plɛ̃dʀ] *vt* to pity, feel sorry for; **se ~** *vi* (*gémir*) to moan; (*protester*): **se ~ (à qn) (de)** to complain (to sb) (about); (*souffrir*): **se ~ de** to complain of

plaine [plɛn] *nf* plain

plain-pied [plɛ̃pje] *adv*: **de ~-~ (avec)** on the same level (as)

plainte [plɛ̃t] *nf* (*gémissement*) moan, groan; (*doléance*) complaint; **porter ~** to lodge a complaint

plaire [plɛʀ] *vi* to be a success, be successful; **ça plaît beaucoup aux jeunes** it's very popular with young people; **~ à: cela me plaît** I like it; **se ~ quelque part** to like being somewhere *ou* like it somewhere; **j'irai si ça me plaît** I'll go if I feel like it; **s'il vous plaît** please

plaisance [plɛzɑ̃s] *nf* (*aussi*: **navigation de ~**) (pleasure) sailing, yachting

plaisant, e [plɛzɑ̃, ɑ̃t] *adj* pleasant; (*histoire, anecdote*) amusing

plaisanter [plɛzɑ̃te] *vi* to joke; **plaisanterie** *nf* joke

plaise *etc* [plɛz] *vb voir* **plaire**

plaisir [pleziʀ] *nm* pleasure; **faire ~ à qn** (*délibérément*) to be nice to sb, please sb; **ça me fait ~** I like (doing) it; **j'espère que ça te fera ~** I hope you'll like it; **pour le ~** for pleasure

plaît [plɛ] *vb voir* **plaire**

plan, e [plɑ̃, an] *adj* flat ♦ *nm* plan; (*fig*) level, plane; (*CINÉMA*) shot; **au premier/second ~** in the foreground/middle distance; **à l'arrière ~** in the background; **rester en ~** (*fam*) to be left stranded; **laisser en ~** (*fam*: *travail*) to drop, abandon; **~ d'eau** lake

planche [plɑ̃ʃ] *nf* (*pièce de bois*) plank, (wooden) board; (*illustration*) plate; **~ à repasser** ironing board; **~ à roulettes** skateboard; **~ à voile** (*sport*) windsurfing

plancher [plɑ̃ʃe] *nm* floor; floorboards *pl* ♦ *vi* (*fam*) to work hard

planer [plane] *vi* to glide; (*fam*: *rêveur*) to have one's head in the clouds; **~ sur** (*fig*: *danger*) to hang over

planète [planɛt] *nf* planet

planeur [planœʀ] *nm* glider

planification [planifikasjɔ̃] *nf* (economic) planning

planifier [planifje] *vt* to plan

planning [planiŋ] *nm* programme, schedule

planque [plɑ̃k] (*fam*) *nf* (*emploi peu fatigant*) cushy (*BRIT*) *ou* easy number; (*cachette*) hiding place

plant [plɑ̃] *nm* seedling, young plant

plante [plɑ̃t] *nf* plant; **~ d'appartement** house *ou* pot plant; **~ des pieds** sole (of the foot)

planter [plɑ̃te] *vt* (*plante*) to plant; (*enfoncer*) to hammer *ou* drive in; (*tente*) to put up, pitch; (*fam*: *personne*) to dump; **se ~** (*fam*: *se tromper*) to get it wrong

plantureux, -euse [plɑ̃tyʀø, øz] *adj* copious, lavish; (*femme*) buxom

plaque [plak] *nf* plate; (*de verglas, d'eczéma*) patch; (*avec inscription*) plaque; **~ chauffante** hotplate; **~ de chocolat** bar of chocolate; **~ (minéralogique *ou* d'immatriculation)** number

(*BRIT*) *ou* license (*US*) plate; ~ **tournante** (*fig*) centre

plaqué, e [plake] *adj*: ~ **or/argent** gold-/silver-plated

plaquer [plake] *vt* (*aplatir*): ~ **qch sur** *ou* **contre** to make sth stick *ou* cling to; (*RUGBY*) to bring down; (*fam: laisser tomber*) to drop

plaquette [plakɛt] *nf* (*de chocolat*) bar; (*beurre*) pack(et); ~ **de frein** brake pad

plastique [plastik] *adj, nm* plastic; **plastiquer** *vt* to blow up (*with a plastic bomb*)

plat, e [pla, -at] *adj* flat; (*cheveux*) straight; (*style*) flat, dull ♦ *nm* (*récipient, CULIN*) dish; (*d'un repas*) course; **à** ~ **ventre** face down; **à** ~ (*pneu, batterie*) flat; (*fam: personne*) dead beat; ~ **cuisiné** pre-cooked meal; ~ **de résistance** main course; ~ **du jour** dish of the day

platane [platan] *nm* plane tree

plateau, x [plato] *nm* (*support*) tray; (*GÉO*) plateau; (*CINÉMA*) set; ~ **de fromages** cheeseboard

plate-bande [platbɑ̃d] *nf* flower bed

plate-forme [platfɔʀm] *nf* platform; ~-~ **de forage/pétrolière** drilling/oil rig

platine [platin] *nm* platinum ♦ *nf* (*d'un tourne-disque*) turntable

plâtre [plɑtʀ] *nm* (*matériau*) plaster; (*statue*) plaster statue; (*MÉD*) (plaster) cast; **avoir un bras dans le** ~ to have an arm in plaster

plein, e [plɛ̃, plɛn] *adj* full ♦ *nm*: **faire le** ~ **(d'essence)** to fill up (with petrol); **à** ~**es mains** (*ramasser*) in handfuls; **à** ~ **temps** full-time; **en** ~ **air** in the open air; **en** ~ **soleil** in direct sunlight; **en** ~**e nuit/rue** in the middle of the night/street; **en** ~ **jour** in broad daylight

pleurer [plœʀe] *vi* to cry; (*yeux*) to water ♦ *vt* to mourn (for); ~ **sur** to lament (over), to bemoan

pleurnicher [plœʀniʃe] *vi* to snivel, whine

pleurs [plœʀ] *nmpl*: **en** ~ in tears

pleut [plø] *vb voir* **pleuvoir**

pleuvoir [pløvwaʀ] *vb impers* to rain ♦ *vi* (*coups*) to rain down; (*critiques, invitations*) to shower down; **il pleut** it's raining

pli [pli] *nm* fold; (*de jupe*) pleat; (*de pantalon*) crease; **prendre le** ~ **de faire** to get into the habit of doing; **un mauvais** ~ a bad habit

pliant, e [plijɑ̃, plijɑ̃t] *adj* folding

plier [plije] *vt* to fold; (*pour ranger*) to fold up; (*genou, bras*) to bend ♦ *vi* to bend; (*fig*) to yield; **se** ~ *vi* to fold; **se** ~ **à** to submit to

plinthe [plɛ̃t] *nf* skirting board

plisser [plise] *vt* (*jupe*) to put pleats in; (*yeux*) to screw up; (*front*) to crease

plomb [plɔ̃] *nm* (*métal*) lead; (*d'une cartouche*) (lead) shot; (*PÊCHE*) sinker; (*ÉLEC*) fuse; **sans** ~ (*essence etc*) unleaded

plombage [plɔ̃baʒ] *nm* (*de dent*) filling

plomberie [plɔ̃bʀi] *nf* plumbing

plombier [plɔ̃bje] *nm* plumber

plonge [plɔ̃ʒ] *nf* washing-up

plongeant, e [plɔ̃ʒɑ̃, ɑ̃t] *adj* (*vue*) from above; (*décolleté*) plunging

plongée [plɔ̃ʒe] *nf* (*SPORT*) diving *no pl*; (*sans scaphandre*) skin diving; ~ **sous-marine** diving

plongeoir [plɔ̃ʒwaʀ] *nm* diving board

plongeon [plɔ̃ʒɔ̃] *nm* dive

plonger [plɔ̃ʒe] *vi* to dive ♦ *vt*: ~ **qch dans** to plunge sth into; **se** ~ **dans** (*études, lecture*) to bury *ou* immerse o.s. in; **plongeur** *nm* diver

ployer [plwaje] *vt, vi* to bend

plu [ply] *pp de* **plaire**; **pleuvoir**

pluie [plɥi] *nf* rain

plume [plym] *nf* feather; (*pour écrire*) (pen) nib; (*fig*) pen

plupart [plypaʀ]: **la** ~ *pron* the majority, most (of them); **la** ~ **des** most, the majority of; **la** ~ **du temps/d'entre nous** most of the time/of us; **pour la** ~ for the most part, mostly

pluriel [plyʀjɛl] *nm* plural

plus¹ [ply] *vb voir* **plaire**

MOT-CLÉ

plus² [ply] *adv* **1** (*forme négative*): **ne ... plus** no more, no longer; **je n'ai plus d'argent** I've got no more money *ou* no money left; **il ne travaille plus** he's no longer working, he doesn't work any more
2 (*comparatif*) more, ...+er; (*superlatif*): **le plus** the most, the ...+est; **plus grand/intelligent (que)** bigger/more intelligent (than); **le plus grand/intelligent** the biggest/most intelligent; **tout au plus** at the very most
3 (*davantage*) more; **il travaille plus (que)** he works more (than); **plus il travaille, plus il est heureux** the more he works, the happier he is; **plus de pain** more bread; **plus de 10 personnes** more than 10 people, over 10 people; **3 heures de plus que** 3 hours more than; **de plus** what's more, moreover; **3 kilos en plus** 3 kilos more; **en plus de** in addition to; **de plus en plus** more and more; **plus ou moins** more or less; **ni plus ni moins** no more, no less
♦ *prép*: **4 plus 2** 4 plus 2

plusieurs [plyzjœʀ] *dét, pron* several; **ils sont ~** there are several of them
plus-value [plyvaly] *nf* (*bénéfice*) surplus
plut [ply] *vb voir* **plaire**
plutôt [plyto] *adv* rather; **je préfère ~ celui-ci** I'd rather have this one; **~ que (de) faire** rather than *ou* instead of doing
pluvieux, -euse [plyvjø, jøz] *adj* rainy, wet
PME *sigle f* (= *petite(s) et moyenne(s) entreprise(s)*) small business(es)
PMU *sigle m* (= *Pari mutuel urbain*) *system of betting on horses*; (*café*) betting agency
PNB *sigle m* (= *produit national brut*) GNP
pneu [pnø] *nm* tyre (*BRIT*), tire (*US*)
pneumonie [pnømɔni] *nf* pneumonia
poche [pɔʃ] *nf* pocket; (*sous les yeux*) bag, pouch; **argent de ~** pocket money
pocher [pɔʃe] *vt* (*CULIN*) to poach
pochette [pɔʃɛt] *nf* (*d'aiguilles etc*) case; (*mouchoir*) breast pocket handkerchief; (*sac à main*) clutch bag; **~ de disque** record sleeve
poêle [pwal] *nm* stove ♦ *nf*: **~ (à frire)** frying pan
poème [pɔɛm] *nm* poem
poésie [pɔezi] *nf* (*poème*) poem; (*art*): **la ~** poetry
poète [pɔɛt] *nm* poet
poids [pwa] *nm* weight; (*SPORT*) shot; **vendre au ~** to sell by weight; **prendre du ~** to put on weight; **~ lourd** (*camion*) lorry (*BRIT*), truck (*US*)
poignant, e [pwaɲɑ̃, ɑ̃t] *adj* poignant
poignard [pwaɲaʀ] *nm* dagger; **poignarder** *vt* to stab, knife
poigne [pwaɲ] *nf* grip; **avoir de la ~** (*fig*) to rule with a firm hand
poignée [pwaɲe] *nf* (*de sel etc, fig*) handful; (*de couvercle, porte*) handle; **~ de main** handshake
poignet [pwaɲɛ] *nm* (*ANAT*) wrist; (*de chemise*) cuff
poil [pwal] *nm* (*ANAT*) hair; (*de pinceau, brosse*) bristle; (*de tapis*) strand; (*pelage*) coat; **à ~** (*fam*) starkers; **au ~** (*fam*) hunky-dory; **poilu, e** *adj* hairy
poinçon [pwɛ̃sɔ̃] *nm* (*marque*) hallmark; **poinçonner** [pwɛ̃sɔne] *vt* (*bijou*) to hallmark; (*billet*) to punch
poing [pwɛ̃] *nm* fist; **coup de ~** punch
point [pwɛ̃] *nm* point; (*endroit*) spot; (*marque, signe*) dot; (: *de ponctuation*) full stop, period (*US*); (*COUTURE, TRICOT*) stitch ♦ *adv* = **pas²**; **faire le ~** (*fig*) to take stock (of the situation); **sur le ~ de faire** (just) about to do; **à tel ~ que** so much so that; **mettre au ~** (*procédé*) to develop; (*affaire*) to settle; **à ~**

(CULIN: *viande*) medium; **à ~ (nommé)** just at the right time; **deux ~s** colon; **~ (de côté)** stitch (*pain*); **~ d'exclamation/d'interrogation** exclamation/ question mark; **~ de repère** landmark; (*dans le temps*) point of reference; **~ de suture** (MÉD) stitch; **~ de vente** retail outlet; **~ de vue** viewpoint; (*fig*: *opinion*) point of view; **~ d'honneur**: **mettre un ~ d'honneur à faire qch** to make it a point of honour to do sth; **~ faible/fort** weak/strong point; **~ noir** blackhead; **~s de suspension** suspension points

pointe [pwɛ̃t] *nf* point; (*clou*) tack; (*fig*): **une ~ de** a hint of; **être à la ~ de** (*fig*) to be in the forefront of; **sur la ~ des pieds** on tiptoe; **en ~** pointed, tapered; **de ~** (*technique etc*) leading; **heures de ~** peak hours

pointer [pwɛ̃te] *vt* (*diriger*: *canon, doigt*): **~ sur qch** to point at sth ♦ *vi* (*employé*) to clock in

pointillé [pwɛ̃tije] *nm* (*trait*) dotted line

pointilleux, -euse [pwɛ̃tijø, øz] *adj* particular, pernickety

pointu, e [pwɛ̃ty] *adj* pointed; (*voix*) shrill; (*analyse*) precise

pointure [pwɛ̃tyʀ] *nf* size

point-virgule [pwɛ̃viʀgyl] *nm* semicolon

poire [pwaʀ] *nf* pear; (*fam*: *péj*) mug

poireau, x [pwaʀo] *nm* leek

poireauter [pwaʀote] *vi* (*fam*) to be left kicking one's heels

poirier [pwaʀje] *nm* pear tree

pois [pwɑ] *nm* (BOT) pea; (*sur une étoffe*) dot, spot; **~ chiche** chickpea; **à ~** (*cravate etc*) spotted, polka-dot *cpd*

poison [pwazɔ̃] *nm* poison

poisse [pwas] (*fam*) *nf* rotten luck

poisseux, -euse [pwasø, øz] *adj* sticky

poisson [pwasɔ̃] *nm* fish *gén inv*; **les P~s** (*signe*) Pisces; **~ d'avril!** April fool!; **~ rouge** goldfish; **poissonnerie** *nf* fish-shop; **poissonnier, ière** *nm/f* fishmonger (BRIT), fish merchant (US)

poitrine [pwatʀin] *nf* chest; (*seins*) bust, bosom; (CULIN) breast

poivre [pwavʀ] *nm* pepper

poivron [pwavʀɔ̃] *nm* pepper, capsicum

polaire [pɔlɛʀ] *adj* polar

polar [pɔlaʀ] (*fam*) *nm* detective novel

pôle [pol] *nm* (GÉO, ÉLEC) pole

poli, e [pɔli] *adj* polite; (*lisse*) smooth

police [pɔlis] *nf* police; **~ d'assurance** insurance policy; **~ judiciaire** ≃ Criminal Investigation Department (BRIT), ≃ Federal Bureau of Investigation (US); **~ secours** ≃ emergency services *pl* (BRIT), ≃ paramedics *pl* (US); **policier, -ière** *adj* police *cpd* ♦ *nm* policeman; (*aussi: **roman policier***) detective novel

polir [pɔliʀ] *vt* to polish

polisson, ne [pɔlisɔ̃, ɔn] *nm/f* (*enfant*) (little) rascal

politesse [pɔlitɛs] *nf* politeness

politicien, ne [pɔlitisjɛ̃, jɛn] (*péj*) *nm/f* politician

politique [pɔlitik] *adj* political ♦ *nf* politics *sg*; (*mesures, méthode*) policies *pl*

pollen [pɔlɛn] *nm* pollen

polluant, e [pɔlɥɑ̃, ɑ̃t] *adj* polluting ♦ *nm*: **(produit) ~** pollutant; **non ~** non-polluting

polluer [pɔlɥe] *vt* to pollute; **pollution** *nf* pollution

polo [pɔlo] *nm* (*chemise*) polo shirt

Pologne [pɔlɔɲ] *nf*: **la ~** Poland, **polonais, e** *adj* Polish ♦ *nm/f*: **Polonais, e** Pole ♦ *nm* (LING) Polish

poltron, ne [pɔltʀɔ̃, ɔn] *adj* cowardly

polycopier [pɔlikɔpje] *vt* to duplicate

Polynésie [pɔlinezi] *nf*: **la ~** Polynesia

polyvalent, e [pɔlivalɑ̃, ɑ̃t] *adj* (*rôle*) varied; (*salle*) multi-purpose

pommade [pɔmad] *nf* ointment, cream

pomme [pɔm] *nf* apple; **tomber dans les ~s** (*fam*) to pass out; **~ d'Adam** Adam's apple; **~ de pin** pine *ou* fir cone; **~ de terre** potato

pommeau, x [pɔmo] *nm* (*boule*) knob; (*de selle*) pommel
pommette [pɔmɛt] *nf* cheekbone
pommier [pɔmje] *nm* apple tree
pompe [pɔ̃p] *nf* pump; (*faste*) pomp (and ceremony); **~ à essence** petrol pump; **~s funèbres** funeral parlour *sg*, undertaker's *sg*; **pomper** *vt* to pump; (*aspirer*) to pump up; (*absorber*) to soak up
pompeux, -euse [pɔ̃pø, øz] *adj* pompous
pompier [pɔ̃pje] *nm* fireman
pompiste [pɔ̃pist] *nm/f* petrol (BRIT) *ou* gas (US) pump attendant
poncer [pɔ̃se] *vt* to sand (down)
ponctuation [pɔ̃ktɥasjɔ̃] *nf* punctuation
ponctuel, le [pɔ̃ktɥɛl] *adj* punctual
pondéré, e [pɔ̃deʀe] *adj* level-headed, composed
pondre [pɔ̃dʀ] *vt* to lay
poney [pɔnɛ] *nm* pony
pont [pɔ̃] *nm* bridge; (NAVIG) deck; **faire le ~** to take the extra day off; **~ suspendu** suspension bridge; **pont-levis** *nm* drawbridge

faire le pont

The expression **"faire le pont"** *refers to the practice of taking a Monday or Friday off to make a long weekend if a public holiday falls on a Tuesday or Thursday. The French often do this at* **l'Ascension, l'Assomption** *and* **le 14 juillet.**

pop [pɔp] *adj inv* pop
populace [pɔpylas] (*péj*) *nf* rabble
populaire [pɔpylɛʀ] *adj* popular; (*manifestation*) mass *cpd*; (*milieux, quartier*) working-class; (*expression*) vernacular
popularité [pɔpylaʀite] *nf* popularity
population [pɔpylasjɔ̃] *nf* population; **~ active** working population
populeux, -euse [pɔpylø, øz] *adj* densely populated
porc [pɔʀ] *nm* pig; (CULIN) pork
porcelaine [pɔʀsəlɛn] *nf* porcelain, china; piece of china(ware)
porc-épic [pɔʀkepik] *nm* porcupine
porche [pɔʀʃ] *nm* porch
porcherie [pɔʀʃəʀi] *nf* pigsty
pore [pɔʀ] *nm* pore
porno [pɔʀno] *adj* porno ♦ *nm* porn
port [pɔʀ] *nm* harbour, port; (*ville*) port; (*de l'uniforme etc*) wearing; (*pour lettre*) postage; (*pour colis, aussi: posture*) carriage; **~ de pêche/de plaisance** fishing/sailing harbour
portable [pɔʀtabl] *nm* (COMPUT) laptop (computer)
portail [pɔʀtaj] *nm* gate
portant, e [pɔʀtɑ̃, ɑ̃t] *adj*: **bien/mal ~** in good/poor health
portatif, -ive [pɔʀtatif, iv] *adj* portable
porte [pɔʀt] *nf* door; (*de ville, jardin*) gate; **mettre à la ~** to throw out; **~ à ~** ♦ *nm* door-to-door selling; **~ d'entrée** front door; **porte-avions** *nm inv* aircraft carrier; **porte-bagages** *nm inv* luggage rack; **porte-bonheur** *nm inv* lucky charm; **porte-clefs** *nm inv* key ring; **porte-documents** *nm inv* attaché *ou* document case
porté, e [pɔʀte] *adj*: **être ~ à faire** to be inclined to do; **être ~ sur qch** to be keen on sth; **portée** *nf* (*d'une arme*) range; (*fig: effet*) impact, import; (*: capacité*) scope, capability; (*de chatte etc*) litter; (MUS) stave, staff; **à/hors de portée (de)** within/out of reach (of); **à portée de (la) main** within (arm's) reach; **à la portée de qn** (*fig*) at sb's level, within sb's capabilities
porte...: porte-fenêtre *nf* French window; **portefeuille** *nm* wallet; **portemanteau, x** *nm* (*cintre*) coat hanger; (*au mur*) coat rack; **porte-monnaie** *nm inv* purse; **porte-parole** *nm inv* spokesman
porter [pɔʀte] *vt* to carry; (*sur soi: vêtement, barbe, bague*) to wear; (*fig: responsabilité etc*) to bear, carry; (*ins-

cription, nom, fruits) to bear; (*coup*) to deal; (*attention*) to turn; (*apporter*): ~ **qch à qn** to take sth to sb ♦ *vi* (*voix*) to carry; (*coup, argument*) to hit home; **se ~** *vi* (*se sentir*): **se ~ bien/mal** to be well/unwell; **~ sur** (*recherches*) to be concerned with; **se faire ~ malade** to report sick

porteur [pɔrtœr, øz] *nm* (*de bagages*) porter; (*de chèque*) bearer

porte-voix [pɔrtəvwa] *nm inv* megaphone

portier [pɔrtje] *nm* doorman

portière [pɔrtjɛr] *nf* door

portillon [pɔrtijɔ̃] *nm* gate

portion [pɔrsjɔ̃] *nf* (*part*) portion, share; (*partie*) portion, section

porto [pɔrto] *nm* port (wine)

portrait [pɔrtrɛ] *nm* (*peinture*) portrait; (*photo*) photograph; **portrait-robot** *nm* Identikit ® *ou* photo-fit ® picture

portuaire [pɔrtɥɛr] *adj* port *cpd*, harbour *cpd*

portugais, e [pɔrtygɛ, ɛz] *adj* Portuguese ♦ *nm/f*: **P~, e** Portuguese ♦ *nm* (LING) Portuguese

Portugal [pɔrtygal] *nm*: **le ~** Portugal

pose [poz] *nf* (*de moquette*) laying; (*attitude, d'un modèle*) pose; (PHOTO) exposure

posé, e [poze] *adj* serious

poser [poze] *vt* to put; (*installer: moquette, carrelage*) to lay; (*rideaux, papier peint*) to hang; (*question*) to ask; (*principe, conditions*) to lay *ou* set down; (*problème*) to formulate; (*difficulté*) to pose ♦ *vi* (*modèle*) to pose; **se ~** *vi* (*oiseau, avion*) to land; (*question*) to arise; **~ qch (sur)** (*déposer*) to put sth down (on); **~ qch sur/quelque part** (*placer*) to put sth on/somewhere; **~ sa candidature à un poste** to apply for a post

positif, -ive [pozitif, iv] *adj* positive

position [pozisjɔ̃] *nf* position; **prendre ~** (*fig*) to take a stand

posologie [pozɔlɔʒi] *nf* dosage

posséder [pɔsede] *vt* to own, possess; (*qualité, talent*) to have, possess; (*sexuellement*) to possess; **possession** *nf* ownership *no pl*, possession

possibilité [pɔsibilite] *nf* possibility; **~s** *nfpl* (*potentiel*) potential *sg*

possible [pɔsibl] *adj* possible; (*projet, entreprise*) feasible ♦ *nm*: **faire son ~** to do all one can, do one's utmost; **le plus/moins de livres ~** as many/few books as possible; **le plus vite ~** as quickly as possible; **dès que ~** as soon as possible

postal, e, -aux [pɔstal, o] *adj* postal

poste [pɔst] *nf* (*service*) post, postal service; (*administration, bureau*) post office ♦ *nm* (*fonction*, MIL) post; (TÉL) extension; (*de radio etc*) set; **mettre à la ~** to post; **~ (de police)** *nm* police station; **~ de secours** *nm* first-aid post; **~ restante** *nf* poste restante (BRIT), general delivery (US)

poster[1] [pɔste] *vt* to post

poster[2] [pɔstɛr] *nm* poster

postérieur, e [pɔsterjœr] *adj* (*date*) later; (*partie*) back ♦ *nm* (*fam*) behind

posthume [pɔstym] *adj* posthumous

postulant, e [pɔstylɑ̃, ɑ̃t] *nm/f* applicant

postuler [pɔstyle] *vi*: **~ à** *ou* **pour un emploi** to apply for a job

posture [pɔstyr] *nf* position

pot [po] *nm* (*en verre*) jar; (*en terre*) pot; (*en plastique, carton*) carton; (*en métal*) tin; (*fam: chance*) luck; **avoir du ~** (*fam*) to be lucky; **boire** *ou* **prendre un ~** (*fam*) to have a drink; **petit ~ (pour bébé)** (jar of) baby food; **~ catalytique** catalytic converter; **~ d'échappement** exhaust pipe; **~ de fleurs** plant pot, flowerpot; (*plante*) pot plant

potable [pɔtabl] *adj*: **eau (non) ~** (non-)drinking water

potage [pɔtaʒ] *nm* soup; **potager, -ère** *adj*: **(jardin) potager** kitchen *ou* vegetable garden

pot-au-feu [pɔtofø] *nm inv* (beef) stew

pot-de-vin [podvɛ̃] *nm* bribe
pote [pɔt] (*fam*) *nm* pal
poteau, x [pɔto] *nm* post; **~ indicateur** signpost
potelé, e [pɔt(ə)le] *adj* plump, chubby
potence [pɔtɑ̃s] *nf* gallows *sg*
potentiel, le [pɔtɑ̃sjɛl] *adj, nm* potential
poterie [pɔtʀi] *nf* pottery; (*objet*) piece of pottery
potier [pɔtje, jɛʀ] *nm* potter
potins [pɔtɛ̃] (*fam*) *nmpl* gossip *sg*
potiron [pɔtiʀɔ̃] *nm* pumpkin
pou, x [pu] *nm* louse
poubelle [pubɛl] *nf* (dust)bin
pouce [pus] *nm* thumb
poudre [pudʀ] *nf* powder; (*fard*) (face) powder; (*explosif*) gunpowder; **en ~: café en ~** instant coffee; **lait en ~** dried *ou* powdered milk; **poudreuse** *nf* powder snow; **poudrier** *nm* (powder) compact
pouffer [pufe] *vi*: **~ (de rire)** to burst out laughing
poulailler [pulɑje] *nm* henhouse
poulain [pulɛ̃] *nm* foal; (*fig*) protégé
poule [pul] *nf* hen; (CULIN) (boiling) fowl
poulet [pulɛ] *nm* chicken; (*fam*) cop
poulie [puli] *nf* pulley
pouls [pu] *nm* pulse; **prendre le ~ de qn** to feel sb's pulse
poumon [pumɔ̃] *nm* lung
poupe [pup] *nf* stern; **en ~** astern
poupée [pupe] *nf* doll
pouponnière [pupɔnjɛʀ] *nf* crèche, day nursery
pour [puʀ] *prép* for ♦ *nm*: **le ~ et le contre** the pros and cons; **~ faire** (so as) to do, in order to do; **~ avoir fait** for having done; **~ que** so that, in order that; **~ 100 francs d'essence** 100 francs' worth of petrol; **~ cent** per cent; **~ ce qui est de** as for
pourboire [puʀbwaʀ] *nm* tip
pourcentage [puʀsɑ̃taʒ] *nm* percentage
pourchasser [puʀʃase] *vt* to pursue
pourparlers [puʀpaʀle] *nmpl* talks, negotiations
pourpre [puʀpʀ] *adj* crimson
pourquoi [puʀkwa] *adv, conj* why ♦ *nm inv*: **le ~ (de)** the reason (for)
pourrai *etc* [puʀe] *vb voir* **pouvoir**
pourri, e [puʀi] *adj* rotten
pourrir [puʀiʀ] *vi* to rot; (*fruit*) to go rotten *ou* bad ♦ *vt* to rot; (*fig*) to spoil thoroughly; **pourriture** *nf* rot
pourrons *etc* [puʀɔ̃] *vb voir* **pouvoir**
poursuite [puʀsɥit] *nf* pursuit, chase; **~s** *nfpl* (JUR) legal proceedings
poursuivre [puʀsɥivʀ] *vt* to pursue, chase (after); (*obséder*) to haunt; (JUR) to bring proceedings against, prosecute; (*: au civil*) to sue; (*but*) to strive towards; (*continuer: études etc*) to carry on with, continue; **se ~** *vi* to go on, continue
pourtant [puʀtɑ̃] *adv* yet; **c'est ~ facile** (and) yet it's easy
pourtour [puʀtuʀ] *nm* perimeter
pourvoir [puʀvwaʀ] *vt*: **~ qch/qn de** to equip sth/sb with ♦ *vi*: **~ à** to provide for; **pourvoyeur** *nm* supplier; **pourvu, e** *adj*: **pourvu de** equipped with; **pourvu que** (*si*) provided that, so long as; (*espérons que*) let's hope (that)
pousse [pus] *nf* growth; (*bourgeon*) shoot
poussé, e [puse] *adj* (*enquête*) exhaustive; (*études*) advanced; **poussée** *nf* thrust; (*d'acné*) eruption; (*fig: prix*) upsurge
pousser [puse] *vt* to push; (*émettre: cri, soupir*) to give; (*stimuler: élève*) to urge on; (*poursuivre: études, discussion*) to carry on (further) ♦ *vi* to push; (*croître*) to grow; **se ~** *vi* to move over; **~ qn à** (*inciter*) to urge *ou* press sb to; (*acculer*) to drive sb to; **faire ~** (*plante*) to grow
poussette [pusɛt] *nf* push chair (BRIT), stroller (US)
poussière [pusjɛʀ] *nf* dust; **poussié-**

reux, -euse *adj* dusty
poussin [pusɛ̃] *nm* chick
poutre [putʀ] *nf* beam

MOT-CLÉ

pouvoir [puvwaʀ] *nm* power; (*POL: dirigeants*): **le pouvoir** those in power; **les pouvoirs publics** the authorities; **pouvoir d'achat** purchasing power
♦ *vb semi-aux* **1** (*être en état de*) can, be able to; **je ne peux pas le réparer** I can't *ou* I am not able to repair it; **déçu de ne pas pouvoir le faire** disappointed not to be able to do it
2 (*avoir la permission*) can, may, be allowed to; **vous pouvez aller au cinéma** you can *ou* may go to the pictures
3 (*probabilité, hypothèse*) may, might, could; **il a pu avoir un accident** he may *ou* might *ou* could have had an accident; **il aurait pu le dire!** he might *ou* could have said (so)!
♦ *vb impers* may, might, could; **il peut arriver que** it may *ou* might *ou* could happen that
♦ *vt* can, be able to; **j'ai fait tout ce que j'ai pu** I did all I could; **je n'en peux plus** (*épuisé*) I'm exhausted; (*à bout*) I can't take any more; **se pouvoir** *vi*: **il se peut que** it may *ou* might be that; **cela se pourrait** that's quite possible

prairie [pʀeʀi] *nf* meadow
praline [pʀalin] *nf* sugared almond
praticable [pʀatikabl] *adj* passable, practicable
pratiquant, e [pʀatikɑ̃, ɑ̃t] *nm/f* (regular) churchgoer
pratique [pʀatik] *nf* practice ♦ *adj* practical; **pratiquement** *adv* (*pour ainsi dire*) practically, virtually; **pratiquer** *vt* to practise; (*l'équitation, la pêche*) to go in for; (*le golf, football*) to play; (*intervention, opération*) to carry out
pré [pʀe] *nm* meadow
préados [pʀeado] *nmpl* preteens
préalable [pʀealabl] *adj* preliminary; **au ~** beforehand
préambule [pʀeɑ̃byl] *nm* preamble; (*fig*) prelude; **sans ~** straight away
préau [pʀeo] *nm* (*SCOL*) covered playground
préavis [pʀeavi] *nm* notice
précaution [pʀekosjɔ̃] *nf* precaution; **avec ~** cautiously; **par ~** as a precaution
précédemment [pʀesedamɑ̃] *adv* before, previously
précédent, e [pʀesedɑ̃, ɑ̃t] *adj* previous ♦ *nm* precedent
précéder [pʀesede] *vt* to precede
précepteur, -trice [pʀesɛptœʀ, tʀis] *nm/f* (private) tutor
prêcher [pʀeʃe] *vt* to preach
précieux, -euse [pʀesjø, jøz] *adj* precious; (*aide, conseil*) invaluable
précipice [pʀesipis] *nm* drop, chasm
précipitamment [pʀesipitamɑ̃] *adv* hurriedly, hastily
précipitation [pʀesipitasjɔ̃] *nf* (*hâte*) haste; **~s** *nfpl* (*pluie*) rain *sg*
précipité, e [pʀesipite] *adj* hasty
précipiter [pʀesipite] *vt* (*hâter: départ*) to hasten; (*faire tomber*): **~ qn/qch du haut de** to throw *ou* hurl sb/sth off *ou* from; **se ~** *vi* to speed up; **se ~ sur/vers** to rush at/towards
précis, e [pʀesi, iz] *adj* precise; (*mesures*) accurate, precise; **à 4 heures ~es** at 4 o'clock sharp; **précisément** *adv* precisely; **préciser** *vt* (*expliquer*) to be more specific about, clarify; (*spécifier*) to state, specify; **se préciser** *vi* to become clear(er); **précision** *nf* precision; (*détail*) point *ou* detail; **demander des précisions** to ask for further explanation
précoce [pʀekɔs] *adj* early; (*enfant*) precocious
préconçu, e [pʀekɔ̃sy] *adj* preconceived
préconiser [pʀekɔnize] *vt* to advocate
prédécesseur [pʀedesesœʀ] *nm* pre-

decessor

prédilection [pʀedilɛksjɔ̃] *nf*: **avoir une ~ pour** to be partial to

prédire [pʀediʀ] *vt* to predict

prédominer [pʀedɔmine] *vi* to predominate

préface [pʀefas] *nf* preface

préfecture [pʀefɛktyʀ] *nf* prefecture; **~ de police** police headquarters *pl*

préférable [pʀefeʀabl] *adj* preferable

préféré, e [pʀefeʀe] *adj, nm/f* favourite

préférence [pʀefeʀɑ̃s] *nf* preference; **de ~** preferably

préférer [pʀefeʀe] *vt*: **~ qn/qch (à)** to prefer sb/sth (to), like sb/sth better (than); **~ faire** to prefer to do; **je ~ais du thé** I would rather have tea, I'd prefer tea

préfet [pʀefɛ] *nm* prefect

préhistorique [pʀeistɔʀik] *adj* prehistoric

préjudice [pʀeʒydis] *nm* (*matériel*) loss; (*moral*) harm *no pl*; **porter ~ à** to harm, be detrimental to; **au ~ de** at the expense of

préjugé [pʀeʒyʒe] *nm* prejudice; **avoir un ~ contre** to be prejudiced *ou* biased against

préjuger [pʀeʒyʒe]: **~ de** *vt* to prejudge

prélasser [pʀelɑse]: **se ~** *vi* to lounge

prélèvement [pʀelɛvmɑ̃] *nm* (*montant*) deduction; **faire un ~ de sang** to take a blood sample

prélever [pʀel(ə)ve] *vt* (*échantillon*) to take; **~ (sur)** (*montant*) to deduct (from); (*argent*: *sur son compte*) to withdraw (from)

prématuré, e [pʀematyʀe] *adj* premature ♦ *nm* premature baby

premier, -ière [pʀəmje, jɛʀ] *adj* first; (*rang*) front; (*fig*: *objectif*) basic; **le ~ venu** the first person to come along; **de ~ ordre** first-rate; **P~ Ministre** Prime Minister; **première** *nf* (SCOL) lower sixth form; (THÉÂTRE) first night; (AUTO) first (gear); (AVIAT, RAIL *etc*) first class; (CINÉMA) première; (*exploit*) first;

premièrement *adv* firstly

prémonition [pʀemɔnisjɔ̃] *nf* premonition

prémunir [pʀemyniʀ]: **se ~** *vi*: **se ~ contre** to guard against

prenant, e [pʀənɑ̃, ɑ̃t] *adj* absorbing, engrossing

prénatal, e [pʀenatal] *adj* (MÉD) antenatal

prendre [pʀɑ̃dʀ] *vt* to take; (*repas*) to have; (*se procurer*) to get; (*malfaiteur, poisson*) to catch; (*passager*) to pick up; (*personnel*) to take on; (*traiter*: *personne*) to handle; (*voix, ton*) to put on; (*ôter*): **~ qch à** to take sth from; (*coincer*): **se ~ les doigts dans** to get one's fingers caught in ♦ *vi* (*liquide, ciment*) to set; (*greffe, vaccin*) to take; (*feu*: *foyer*) to go; (*se diriger*): **~ à gauche** to turn (to the) left; **~ froid** to catch cold; **se ~ pour** to think one is; **s'en ~ à** to attack; **se ~ d'amitié pour** to befriend; **s'y ~** (*procéder*) to set about it

preneur [pʀənœʀ, øz] *nm*: **être/trouver ~** to be willing to buy/find a buyer

preniez [pʀənje] *vb voir* **prendre**

prenne *etc* [pʀɛn] *vb voir* **prendre**

prénom [pʀenɔ̃] *nm* first *ou* Christian name

préoccupation [pʀeɔkypasjɔ̃] *nf* (*souci*) concern; (*idée fixe*) preoccupation

préoccuper [pʀeɔkype] *vt* (*inquiéter*) to worry; (*absorber*) to preoccupy; **se ~ de** to be concerned with

préparatifs [pʀepaʀatif] *nmpl* preparations

préparation [pʀepaʀasjɔ̃] *nf* preparation

préparer [pʀepaʀe] *vt* to prepare; (*café, thé*) to make; (*examen*) to prepare for; (*voyage, entreprise*) to plan; **se ~** *vi* (*orage, tragédie*) to brew, be in the air; **~ qch à qn** (*surprise etc*) to have sth in store for sb; **se ~ (à qch/faire)** to prepare (o.s.) *ou* get ready (for sth/to do)

prépondérant, e [prepɔ̃derɑ̃, ɑ̃t] *adj* major, dominating

préposé, e [prepoze] *nm/f* employee; (*facteur*) postman

préposition [prepozisjɔ̃] *nf* preposition

près [prɛ] *adv* near, close; **~ de** near (to), close to; (*environ*) nearly, almost; **de ~** closely; **à 5 kg ~** to within about 5 kg; **à cela ~ que** apart from the fact that; **il n'est pas à 10 minutes ~** he can spare 10 minutes

présage [prezaʒ] *nm* omen; **présager** *vt* to foresee

presbyte [prɛsbit] *adj* long-sighted

presbytère [prɛsbitɛr] *nm* presbytery

prescription [prɛskripsjɔ̃] *nf* prescription

prescrire [prɛskrir] *vt* to prescribe

présence [prezɑ̃s] *nf* presence; (*au bureau, à l'école*) attendance

présent, e [prezɑ̃, ɑ̃t] *adj, nm* present; **à ~ (que)** now (that)

présentation [prezɑ̃tasjɔ̃] *nf* presentation; (*de nouveau venu*) introduction; (*allure*) appearance; **faire les ~s** to do the introductions

présenter [prezɑ̃te] *vt* to present; (*excuses, condoléances*) to offer; (*invité, conférencier*): **~ qn (à)** to introduce sb (to) ♦ *vi*: **~ bien** to have a pleasing appearance; **se ~** *vi* (*occasion*) to arise; **se ~ à** (*examen*) to sit; (*élection*) to stand at, run for

préservatif [prezɛrvatif, iv] *nm* sheath, condom

préserver [prezɛrve] *vt*: **~ de** (*protéger*) to protect from

président [prezidɑ̃] *nm* (POL) president; (*d'une assemblée,* COMM) chairman; **~ directeur général** chairman and managing director; **présidentielles** *nfpl* presidential elections

présider [prezide] *vt* to preside over; (*dîner*) to be the guest of honour at

présomptueux, -euse [prezɔ̃ptɥø, øz] *adj* presumptuous

presque [prɛsk] *adv* almost, nearly; **~ personne** hardly anyone; **~ rien** hardly anything; **~ pas** hardly (at all); **~ pas (de)** hardly any

presqu'île [prɛskil] *nf* peninsula

pressant, e [prɛsɑ̃, ɑ̃t] *adj* urgent

presse [prɛs] *nf* press; (*affluence*): **heures de ~** busy times

pressé, e [prese] *adj* in a hurry; (*travail*) urgent; **orange ~e** freshly-squeezed orange juice

pressentiment [prɛsɑ̃timɑ̃] *nm* foreboding, premonition

pressentir [prɛsɑ̃tir] *vt* to sense

presse-papiers [prɛspapje] *nm inv* paperweight

presser [prese] *vt* (*fruit, éponge*) to squeeze; (*bouton*) to press; (*allure*) to speed up; (*inciter*): **~ qn de faire** to urge *ou* press sb to do ♦ *vi* to be urgent; **se ~** *vi* (*se hâter*) to hurry (up); **se ~ contre qn** to squeeze up against sb; **rien ne presse** there's no hurry

pressing [presiŋ] *nm* (*magasin*) dry-cleaner's

pression [prɛsjɔ̃] *nf* pressure; (*bouton*) press stud; (*fam: bière*) draught beer; **faire ~ sur** to put pressure on; **~ artérielle** blood pressure

prestance [prɛstɑ̃s] *nf* presence, imposing bearing

prestataire [prɛstatɛr] *nm/f* supplier

prestation [prɛstasjɔ̃] *nf* (*allocation*) benefit; (*d'une entreprise*) service provided; (*d'un artiste*) performance

prestidigitateur, -trice [prɛstidiʒitatœr, tris] *nm/f* conjurer

prestige [prɛstiʒ] *nm* prestige; **prestigieux, -euse** *adj* prestigious

présumer [prezyme] *vt*: **~ que** to presume *ou* assume that

prêt, e [prɛ, prɛt] *adj* ready ♦ *nm* (*somme*) loan; **prêt-à-porter** *nm* ready-to-wear *ou* off-the-peg (BRIT) clothes *pl*

prétendre [pretɑ̃dr] *vt* (*affirmer*): **~**

que to claim that; (*avoir l'intention de*): **~ faire qch** to mean *ou* intend to do sth; **prétendu, e** *adj* (*supposé*) so-called

prétentieux, -euse [pʀetɑ̃sjø, jøz] *adj* pretentious

prétention [pʀetɑ̃sjɔ̃] *nf* claim; (*vanité*) pretentiousness; **~s** *nfpl* (*salaire*) expected salary

prêter [pʀete] *vt* (*livres, argent*): **~ qch (à)** to lend sth (to); (*supposer*): **~ à qn** (*caractère, propos*) to attribute to sb; **se ~ à** to lend o.s. (*ou* itself) to; (*manigances etc*) to go along with; **~ à** (*critique, commentaires etc*) to be open to, give rise to; **~ attention à** to pay attention to; **~ serment** to take the oath

prétexte [pʀetɛkst] *nm* pretext, excuse; **sous aucun ~** on no account; **prétexter** *vt* to give as a pretext *ou* an excuse

prêtre [pʀɛtʀ] *nm* priest

preuve [pʀœv] *nf* proof; (*indice*) proof, evidence *no pl*; **faire ~ de** to show; **faire ses ~s** to prove o.s. (*ou* itself)

prévaloir [pʀevalwaʀ] *vi* to prevail

prévenant, e [pʀev(ə)nɑ̃, ɑ̃t] *adj* thoughtful, kind

prévenir [pʀev(ə)niʀ] *vt* (*éviter*: *catastrophe etc*) to avoid, prevent; (*anticiper*: *désirs, besoins*) to anticipate; **~ qn (de)** (*avertir*) to warn sb (about); (*informer*) to tell *ou* inform sb (about)

préventif, -ive [pʀevɑ̃tif, iv] *adj* preventive

prévention [pʀevɑ̃sjɔ̃] *nf* prevention; **~ routière** road safety

prévenu, e [pʀev(ə)ny] *nm/f* (*JUR*) defendant, accused

prévision [pʀevizjɔ̃] *nf*: **~s** predictions; (*ÉCON*) forecast *sg*; **en ~ de** in anticipation of; **~s météorologiques** weather forecast *sg*

prévoir [pʀevwaʀ] *vt* (*anticiper*) to foresee; (*s'attendre à*) to expect, reckon on; (*organiser*: *voyage etc*) to plan; (*envisager*) to allow; **comme prévu** as planned; **prévoyant, e** *adj* gifted with (*ou* showing) foresight; **prévu, e** *pp de* **prévoir**

prier [pʀije] *vi* to pray ♦ *vt* (*Dieu*) to pray to; (*implorer*) to beg; (*demander*): **~ qn de faire** to ask sb to do; **se faire ~** to need coaxing *ou* persuading; **je vous en prie** (*allez-y*) please do; (*de rien*) don't mention it; **prière** *nf* prayer; **"prière de ..."** "please ..."

primaire [pʀimɛʀ] *adj* primary ♦ *nm* (*SCOL*) primary education

prime [pʀim] *nf* (*bonus*) bonus; (*subvention*) premium; (*COMM*: *cadeau*) free gift; (*ASSURANCES, BOURSE*) premium ♦ *adj*: **de ~ abord** at first glance; **primer** *vt* (*récompenser*) to award a prize to ♦ *vi* to dominate; to be most important

primeurs [pʀimœʀ] *nfpl* early fruits and vegetables

primevère [pʀimvɛʀ] *nf* primrose

primitif, -ive [pʀimitif, iv] *adj* primitive; (*originel*) original

primordial, e, -iaux [pʀimɔʀdjal, jo] *adj* essential

prince [pʀɛ̃s] *nm* prince; **princesse** *nf* princess

principal, e, -aux [pʀɛ̃sipal, o] *adj* principal, main ♦ *nm* (*SCOL*) principal, head(master); (*essentiel*) main thing

principe [pʀɛ̃sip] *nm* principle; **par ~** on principle; **en ~** (*habituellement*) as a rule; (*théoriquement*) in principle

printemps [pʀɛ̃tɑ̃] *nm* spring

priorité [pʀijɔʀite] *nf* priority; (*AUTO*) right of way; **~ à droite** right of way to vehicles coming from the right

pris, e [pʀi, pʀiz] *pp de* **prendre** ♦ *adj* (*place*) taken; (*mains*) full; (*personne*) busy; **avoir le nez/la gorge ~(e)** to have a stuffy nose/a hoarse throat; **être ~ de panique** to be panic-stricken

prise [pʀiz] *nf* (*d'une ville*) capture; (*PÊCHE, CHASSE*) catch; (*point d'appui ou pour empoigner*) hold; (*ÉLEC*: *fiche*) plug; (: *femelle*) socket; **être aux ~s avec** to be grappling with; **~ de conscience**

awareness, realization; **~ de contact** (*rencontre*) initial meeting, first contact; **~ de courant** power point; **~ de sang** blood test; **~ de vue** (*photo*) shot; **~ multiple** adaptor

priser [pRize] *vt* (*estimer*) to prize, value

prison [pRizɔ̃] *nf* prison; **aller/être en ~** to go to/be in prison *ou* jail; **prisonnier, -ière** *nm/f* prisoner ♦ *adj* captive

prit [pRi] *vb voir* **prendre**

privé, e [pRive] *adj* private ♦ *nm* (COMM) private sector; **en ~** in private

priver [pRive] *vt*: **~ qn de** to deprive sb of; **se ~ de** to go *ou* do without

privilège [pRivilɛʒ] *nm* privilege

prix [pRi] *nm* price; (*récompense*, SCOL) prize; **hors de ~** exorbitantly priced; **à aucun ~** not at any price; **à tout ~** at all costs; **~ d'achat/de vente/de revient** purchasing/selling/cost price

probable [pRɔbabl] *adj* likely, probable; **probablement** *adv* probably

probant, e [pRɔbɑ̃, ɑ̃t] *adj* convincing

problème [pRɔblɛm] *nm* problem

procédé [pRɔsede] *nm* (*méthode*) process; (*comportement*) behaviour *no pl*

procéder [pRɔsede] *vi* to proceed; (*moralement*) to behave; **~ à** to carry out

procès [pRɔsɛ] *nm* trial; (*poursuites*) proceedings *pl*; **être en ~ avec** to be involved in a lawsuit with

processus [pRɔsesys] *nm* process

procès-verbal, -aux [pRɔsɛvɛRbal, o] *nm* (*de réunion*) minutes *pl*; (*aussi*: **P.V.**) parking ticket

prochain, e [pRɔʃɛ̃, ɛn] *adj* next; (*proche*: *départ, arrivée*) impending ♦ *nm* fellow man; **la ~e fois/semaine ~e** next time/week; **prochainement** *adv* soon, shortly

proche [pRɔʃ] *adj* nearby; (*dans le temps*) imminent; (*parent, ami*) close; **~s** *nmpl* (*parents*) close relatives; **être ~ (de)** to be near, be close (to); **le P~ Orient** the Middle East

proclamer [pRɔklame] *vt* to proclaim

procuration [pRɔkyRasjɔ̃] *nf* proxy

procurer [pRɔkyRe] *vt*: **~ qch à qn** (*fournir*) to obtain sth for sb; (*causer*: *plaisir etc*) to bring sb sth; **se ~** *vt* to get; **procureur** *nm* public prosecutor

prodige [pRɔdiʒ] *nm* marvel, wonder; (*personne*) prodigy; **prodiguer** *vt* (*soins, attentions*): **prodiguer qch à qn** to give sb sth

producteur, -trice [pRɔdyktœR, tRis] *nm/f* producer

productif, -ive [pRɔdyktif, iv] *adj* productive

production [pRɔdyksjɔ̃] *nf* production; (*rendement*) output

productivité [pRɔdyktivite] *nf* productivity

produire [pRɔdɥiR] *vt* to produce; **se ~** *vi* (*événement*) to happen, occur; (*acteur*) to perform, appear

produit [pRɔdɥi] *nm* product; **~ chimique** chemical; **~ d'entretien** cleaning product; **~ national brut** gross national product; **~s alimentaires** foodstuffs

prof [pRɔf] (*fam*) *nm* teacher

profane [pRɔfan] *adj* (REL) secular ♦ *nm/f* layman(-woman)

proférer [pRɔfeRe] *vt* to utter

professeur, e [pRɔfesœR] *nm/f* teacher; (*de faculté*) (university) lecturer; (*: titulaire d'une chaire*) professor

profession [pRɔfesjɔ̃] *nf* occupation; **~ libérale** (liberal) profession; **sans ~** unemployed; **professionnel, le** *adj, nm/f* professional

profil [pRɔfil] *nm* profile; **de ~** in profile

profit [pRɔfi] *nm* (*avantage*) benefit, advantage; (COMM, FINANCE) profit; **au ~ de** in aid of; **tirer ~ de** to profit from; **profitable** *adj* (*utile*) beneficial; (*lucratif*) profitable; **profiter** *vi*: **profiter de** (*situation, occasion*) to take advantage of; (*vacances, jeunesse etc*) to make the most of

profond, e [pRɔfɔ̃, ɔ̃d] *adj* deep; (*senti-*

ment, intérêt) profound; **profondément** *adv* deeply; **il dort profondément** he is sound asleep; **profondeur** *nf* depth

progéniture [pʀɔʒenityʀ] *nf* offspring *inv*

programme [pʀɔgʀam] *nm* programme; (*SCOL*) syllabus, curriculum; (*INFORM*) program; **programmer** *vt* (*émission*) to schedule; (*INFORM*) to program; **programmeur, -euse** *nm/f* programmer

progrès [pʀɔgʀɛ] *nm* progress *no pl*; **faire des ~** to make progress; **progresser** *vi* to progress; **progressif, -ive** *adj* progressive

prohiber [pʀɔibe] *vt* to prohibit, ban

proie [pʀwa] *nf* prey *no pl*

projecteur [pʀɔʒɛktœʀ] *nm* (*pour film*) projector; (*de théâtre, cirque*) spotlight

projectile [pʀɔʒɛktil] *nm* missile

projection [pʀɔʒɛksjɔ̃] *nf* projection; (*séance*) showing

projet [pʀɔʒɛ] *nm* plan; (*ébauche*) draft; **~ de loi** bill; **projeter** *vt* (*envisager*) to plan; (*film, photos*) to project; (*ombre, lueur*) to throw, cast; (*jeter*) to throw up (*ou* off *ou* out)

prolétaire [pʀɔletɛʀ] *adj, nmf* proletarian

prolongement [pʀɔlɔ̃ʒmɑ̃] *nm* extension; **dans le ~ de** running on from

prolonger [pʀɔlɔ̃ʒe] *vt* (*débat, séjour*) to prolong; (*délai, billet, rue*) to extend; **se ~** *vi* to go on

promenade [pʀɔm(ə)nad] *nf* walk (*ou* drive *ou* ride); **faire une ~** to go for a walk; **une ~ en voiture/à vélo** a drive/(bicycle) ride

promener [pʀɔm(ə)ne] *vt* (*chien*) to take out for a walk; (*doigts, regard*): **~ qch sur** to run sth over; **se ~** *vi* to go for (*ou* be out for) a walk

promesse [pʀɔmɛs] *nf* promise

promettre [pʀɔmɛtʀ] *vt* to promise ♦ *vi* to be *ou* look promising; **~ à qn de faire** to promise sb that one will do

promiscuité [pʀɔmiskɥite] *nf* (*chambre*) lack of privacy

promontoire [pʀɔmɔ̃twaʀ] *nm* headland

promoteur, -trice [pʀɔmɔtœʀ, tʀis] *nm/f*: **~ (immobilier)** property developer (*BRIT*), real estate promoter (*US*)

promotion [pʀɔmosjɔ̃] *nf* promotion; **en ~** on special offer

promouvoir [pʀɔmuvwaʀ] *vt* to promote

prompt, e [pʀɔ̃(pt), pʀɔ̃(p)t] *adj* swift, rapid

prôner [pʀone] *vt* (*préconiser*) to advocate

pronom [pʀɔnɔ̃] *nm* pronoun

prononcer [pʀɔnɔ̃se] *vt* to pronounce; (*dire*) to utter; (*discours*) to deliver; **se ~** *vi* to be pronounced; **se ~ (sur)** (*se décider*) to reach a decision (on *ou* about), give a verdict (on); **prononciation** *nf* pronunciation

pronostic [pʀɔnɔstik] *nm* (*MÉD*) prognosis; (*fig: aussi:* **~s**) forecast

propagande [pʀɔpagɑ̃d] *nf* propaganda

propager [pʀɔpaʒe] *vt* to spread; **se ~** *vi* to spread

prophète [pʀɔfɛt] *nm* prophet

prophétie [pʀɔfesi] *nf* prophecy

propice [pʀɔpis] *adj* favourable

proportion [pʀɔpɔʀsjɔ̃] *nf* proportion; **toute(s) ~(s) gardée(s)** making due allowance(s)

propos [pʀɔpo] *nm* (*intention*) intention, aim; (*sujet*): **à quel ~?** what about? ♦ *nmpl* (*paroles*) talk *no pl*, remarks; **à ~ de** about, regarding; **à tout ~** for the slightest thing *ou* reason; **à ~** by the way; (*opportunément*) at the right moment

proposer [pʀɔpoze] *vt* to propose; **~ qch (à qn)** (*suggérer*) to suggest sth (to sb), propose sth (to sb); (*offrir*) to offer (sb) sth; **se ~** to offer one's services; **se ~ de faire** to intend *ou* propose to do; **proposition** (*suggestion*) *nf* propo-

sal, suggestion; (*LING*) clause
propre [pʀɔpʀ] *adj* clean; (*net*) neat, tidy; (*possessif*) own; (*sens*) literal; (*particulier*): ~ **à** peculiar to; (*approprié*): ~ **à** suitable for ♦ *nm*: **recopier au** ~ to make a fair copy of; **proprement** *adv* (*avec propreté*) cleanly; **le village proprement dit** the village itself; **à proprement parler** strictly speaking; **propreté** *nf* cleanliness
propriétaire [pʀɔpʀijetɛʀ] *nm/f* owner; (*pour le locataire*) landlord(-lady)
propriété [pʀɔpʀijete] *nf* property; (*droit*) ownership
propulser [pʀɔpylse] *vt* to propel
proroger [pʀɔʀɔʒe] *vt* (*prolonger*) to extend
proscrire [pʀɔskʀiʀ] *vt* (*interdire*) to ban, prohibit
prose [pʀoz] *nf* (*style*) prose
prospecter [pʀɔspɛkte] *vt* to prospect; (*COMM*) to canvass
prospectus [pʀɔspɛktys] *nm* leaflet
prospère [pʀɔspɛʀ] *adj* prosperous; **prospérer** *vi* to prosper
prosterner [pʀɔstɛʀne]: **se** ~ *vi* to bow low, prostrate o.s.
prostituée [pʀɔstitɥe] *nf* prostitute
prostitution [pʀɔstitysjɔ̃] *nf* prostitution
protecteur, -trice [pʀɔtɛktœʀ, tʀis] *adj* protective; (*air, ton*: *péj*) patronizing ♦ *nm/f* protector
protection [pʀɔtɛksjɔ̃] *nf* protection; (*d'un personnage influent*: *aide*) patronage
protéger [pʀɔteʒe] *vt* to protect; **se** ~ **de** *ou* **contre** to protect o.s. from
protéine [pʀɔtein] *nf* protein
protestant, e [pʀɔtɛstɑ̃, ɑ̃t] *adj, nm/f* Protestant
protestation [pʀɔtɛstasjɔ̃] *nf* (*plainte*) protest
protester [pʀɔtɛste] *vi*: ~ **(contre)** to protest (against *ou* about); ~ **de** (*son innocence*) to protest
prothèse [pʀɔtɛz] *nf*: ~ **dentaire** denture
protocole [pʀɔtɔkɔl] *nm* (*fig*) etiquette
proue [pʀu] *nf* bow(s *pl*), prow
prouesse [pʀuɛs] *nf* feat
prouver [pʀuve] *vt* to prove
provenance [pʀɔv(ə)nɑ̃s] *nf* origin; **avion en** ~ **de** plane (arriving) from
provenir [pʀɔv(ə)niʀ]: ~ **de** *vt* to come from
proverbe [pʀɔvɛʀb] *nm* proverb
province [pʀɔvɛ̃s] *nf* province
proviseur [pʀɔvizœʀ] *nm* ≃ head(teacher) (*BRIT*), ≃ principal (*US*)
provision [pʀɔvizjɔ̃] *nf* (*réserve*) stock, supply; **~s** *nfpl* (*vivres*) provisions, food *no pl*
provisoire [pʀɔvizwaʀ] *adj* temporary; **provisoirement** *adv* temporarily
provocant, e [pʀɔvɔkɑ̃, ɑ̃t] *adj* provocative
provoquer [pʀɔvɔke] *vt* (*défier*) to provoke; (*causer*) to cause, bring about; (*inciter*): ~ **qn à** to incite sb to
proxénète [pʀɔksenɛt] *nm* procurer
proximité [pʀɔksimite] *nf* nearness, closeness; (*dans le temps*) imminence, closeness; **à** ~ near *ou* close by; **à** ~ **de** near (to), close to
prudemment [pʀydamɑ̃] *adv* carefully; wisely, sensibly
prudence [pʀydɑ̃s] *nf* carefulness; **avec** ~ carefully; **par** ~ as a precaution
prudent, e [pʀydɑ̃, ɑ̃t] *adj* (*pas téméraire*) careful; (: *en général*) safety-conscious; (*sage, conseillé*) wise, sensible; **c'est plus** ~ it's wiser
prune [pʀyn] *nf* plum
pruneau, x [pʀyno] *nm* prune
prunelle [pʀynɛl] *nf* (*BOT*) sloe; **il y tient comme à la** ~ **de ses yeux** he treasures *ou* cherishes it
prunier [pʀynje] *nm* plum tree
PS *sigle m* = **parti socialiste**
psaume [psom] *nm* psalm
pseudonyme [psødɔnim] *nm* (*gén*) fictitious name; (*d'écrivain*) pseudonym,

pen name

psychanalyse [psikanaliz] *nf* psychoanalysis

psychiatre [psikjatʀ] *nm/f* psychiatrist; **psychiatrique** *adj* psychiatric

psychique [psiʃik] *adj* psychological

psychologie [psikɔlɔʒi] *nf* psychology; **psychologique** *adj* psychological; **psychologue** *nm/f* psychologist

P.T.T. *sigle fpl* = **Postes, Télécommunications et Télédiffusion**

pu [py] *pp de* **pouvoir**

puanteur [pɥɑ̃tœʀ] *nf* stink, stench

pub [pyb] *nf* (*fam: annonce*) ad, advert; (*pratique*) advertising

public, -ique [pyblik] *adj* public; (*école, instruction*) state *cpd* ♦ *nm* public; (*assistance*) audience; **en ~** in public

publicitaire [pyblisitɛʀ] *adj* advertising *cpd*; (*film*) publicity *cpd*

publicité [pyblisite] *nf* (*méthode, profession*) advertising; (*annonce*) advertisement; (*révélations*) publicity

publier [pyblije] *vt* to publish

publique [pyblik] *adj voir* **public**

puce [pys] *nf* flea; (INFORM) chip; **carte à ~** smart card; **~s** *nfpl* (*marché*) flea market *sg*

pudeur [pydœʀ] *nf* modesty; **pudique** *adj* (*chaste*) modest; (*discret*) discreet

puer [pɥe] (*péj*) *vi* to stink

puéricultrice [pɥeʀikyltʀis] *nf* p(a)ediatric nurse

puéril, e [pɥeʀil] *adj* childish

puis [pɥi] *vb voir* **pouvoir** ♦ *adv* then

puiser [pɥize] *vt*: **~ (dans)** to draw (from)

puisque [pɥisk] *conj* since

puissance [pɥisɑ̃s] *nf* power; **en ~** ♦ *adj* potential

puissant, e [pɥisɑ̃, ɑ̃t] *adj* powerful

puisse *etc* [pɥis] *vb voir* **pouvoir**

puits [pɥi] *nm* well

pull(-over) [pyl(ɔvɛʀ)] *nm* sweater

pulluler [pylyle] *vi* to swarm

pulvérisateur [pylveʀizatœʀ] *nm* spray

pulvériser [pylveʀize] *vt* to pulverize; (*liquide*) to spray

punaise [pynɛz] *nf* (ZOOL) bug; (*clou*) drawing pin (BRIT), thumbtack (US)

punch¹ [pɔ̃ʃ] *nm* (*boisson*) punch

punch² [pœnʃ] *nm* (BOXE, *fig*) punch

punir [pyniʀ] *vt* to punish; **punition** *nf* punishment

pupille [pypij] *nf* (ANAT) pupil ♦ *nm/f* (*enfant*) ward

pupitre [pypitʀ] *nm* (SCOL) desk

pur, e [pyʀ] *adj* pure; (*vin*) undiluted; (*whisky*) neat; **en ~e perte** to no avail; **c'est de la folie ~e** it's sheer madness; **purement** *adv* purely

purée [pyʀe] *nf*: **~ (de pommes de terre)** mashed potatoes *pl*; **~ de marrons** chestnut purée

purgatoire [pyʀgatwaʀ] *nm* purgatory

purger [pyʀʒe] *vt* (MÉD, POL) to purge; (JUR: *peine*) to serve

purin [pyʀɛ̃] *nm* liquid manure

pur-sang [pyʀsɑ̃] *nm inv* thoroughbred

putain [pytɛ̃] (*fam!*) *nf* whore (!)

puzzle [pœzl] *nm* jigsaw (puzzle)

P.-V. *sigle m* = **procès-verbal**

pyjama [piʒama] *nm* pyjamas *pl* (BRIT), pajamas *pl* (US)

Pyrénées [piʀene] *nfpl*: **les ~** the Pyrenees

Q, q

QI *sigle m* (= *quotient intellectuel*) IQ

quadra [k(w)adʀa] *nm/f* man/woman in his/her forties; **les ~s** forty somethings (*fam*)

quadragénaire [k(w)adʀaʒenɛʀ] *nm/f* man/woman in his/her forties

quadriller [kadʀije] *vt* (POLICE) to keep under tight control

quadruple [k(w)adʀypl] *nm*: **le ~ de** four times as much as; **quadruplés, -ées** *nm/fpl* quadruplets, quads

quai [ke] *nm* (*de port*) quay; (*de gare*) platform; **être à ~** (*navire*) to be alongside

qualification [kalifikasjɔ̃] *nf* (*aptitude*) qualification

qualifié, e [kalifje] *adj* qualified; (*main d'œuvre*) skilled

qualifier [kalifje] *vt* to qualify; **se ~** *vi* to qualify; **~ qch/qn de** to describe sth/sb as

qualité [kalite] *nf* quality

quand [kɑ̃] *conj, adv* when; **~ je serai riche** when I'm rich; **~ même** all the same; **~ même, il exagère!** really, he overdoes it!; **~ bien même** even though

quant [kɑ̃]: **~ à** *prép* (*pour ce qui est de*) as for, as to; (*au sujet de*) regarding; **quant-à-soi** *nm*: **rester sur son quant-à-soi** to remain aloof

quantité [kɑ̃tite] *nf* quantity, amount; (*grand nombre*): **une** *ou* **des ~(s) de** a great deal of

quarantaine [kaʀɑ̃tɛn] *nf* (MÉD) quarantine; **avoir la ~** (*âge*) to be around forty; **une ~ (de)** forty or so, about forty

quarante [kaʀɑ̃t] *num* forty

quart [kaʀ] *nm* (*fraction*) quarter; (*surveillance*) watch; **un ~ de vin** a quarter litre of wine; **le ~ de** a quarter of; **~ d'heure** quarter of an hour; **~s de finale** quarter finals

quartier [kaʀtje] *nm* (*de ville*) district, area; (*de bœuf*) quarter; (*de fruit*) piece; **cinéma de ~** local cinema; **avoir ~ libre** (*fig*) to be free; **~ général** headquarters *pl*

quartz [kwaʀts] *nm* quartz

quasi [kazi] *adv* almost, nearly; **quasiment** *adv* almost, nearly; **quasiment jamais** hardly ever

quatorze [katɔʀz] *num* fourteen

quatre [katʀ] *num* four; **à ~ pattes** on all fours; **se mettre en ~ pour qn** to go out of one's way for sb; **~ à ~** (*monter, descendre*) four at a time; **quatre-quarts** *nm inv* pound cake, **quatre-vingt-dix** *num* ninety; **quatre-vingts** *num* eighty; **quatre-vingt-un** *num* eighty-one; **quatrième** *num* fourth ♦ *nf* (SCOL) third form *ou* year

quatuor [kwatɥɔʀ] *nm* quartet(te)

MOT-CLÉ

que [kə] *conj* **1** (*introduisant complétive*) that; **il sait que tu es là** he knows (that) you're here; **je veux que tu acceptes** I want you to accept; **il a dit que oui** he said he would (*ou* it was *etc*)

2 (*reprise d'autres conjonctions*): **quand il rentrera et qu'il aura mangé** when he gets back and (when) he has eaten; **si vous y allez ou que vous ...** if you go there or if you ...

3 (*en tête de phrase*: *hypothèse, souhait etc*): **qu'il le veuille ou non** whether he likes it or not; **qu'il fasse ce qu'il voudra!** let him do as he pleases!

4 (*après comparatif*) than, as; *voir aussi* **plus**; **aussi**; **autant** *etc*

5 (*seulement*): **ne ... que** only; **il ne boit que de l'eau** he only drinks water

♦ *adv* (*exclamation*): **qu'il** *ou* **qu'est-ce qu'il est bête/court vite!** he's so silly!/he runs so fast!; **que de livres!** what a lot of books!

♦ *pron* **1** (*relatif*: *personne*) whom; (: *chose*) that, which; **l'homme que je vois** the man (whom) I see; **le livre que tu vois** the book (that *ou* which) you see; **un jour que j'étais ...** a day when I was ...

2 (*interrogatif*) what; **que fais-tu?, qu'est-ce que tu fais?** what are you doing?; **qu'est-ce que c'est?** what is it?, what's that?; **que faire?** what can one do?

Québec [kebɛk] *n*: **le ~** Quebec; **québecois, e** *adj* Quebec ♦ *nm/f*: **Québecois, e** Quebecker ♦ *nm* (LING) Quebec French

MOT-CLÉ

quel, quelle [kɛl] *adj* **1** (*interrogatif*: *personne*) who; (: *chose*) what; which; **quel est cet homme?** who is this man?; **quel est ce livre?** what is this book?; **quel livre/homme?** what book/man?; (*parmi un certain choix*) which book/man?; **quels acteurs préférez-vous?** which actors do you prefer?; **dans quels pays êtes-vous allé?** which *ou* what countries did you go to?

2 (*exclamatif*): **quelle surprise!** what a surprise!

3: quel que soit le coupable whoever is guilty; **quel que soit votre avis** whatever your opinion

quelconque [kɛlkɔ̃k] *adj* (*indéfini*): **un ami/prétexte ~** some friend/pretext or other; (*médiocre*: *repas*) indifferent, poor; (*laid*: *personne*) plain-looking

MOT-CLÉ

quelque [kɛlk] *adj* **1** some; a few; (*tournure interrogative*) any; **quelque espoir** some hope; **il a quelques amis** he has a few *ou* some friends; **a-t-il quelques amis?** has he any friends?; **les quelques livres qui** the few books which; **20 kg et quelque(s)** a bit over 20 kg

2: quelque ... que: **quelque livre qu'il choisisse** whatever (*ou* whichever) book he chooses

3: quelque chose something; (*tournure interrogative*) anything; **quelque chose d'autre** something else; anything else; **quelque part** somewhere; anywhere; **en quelque sorte** as it were

♦ *adv* **1** (*environ*): **quelque 100 mètres** some 100 metres

2: quelque peu rather, somewhat

quelquefois [kɛlkəfwa] *adv* sometimes

quelques-uns, -unes [kɛlkəzœ̃, yn] *pron* a few, some

quelqu'un [kɛlkœ̃] *pron* someone, somebody; (+*tournure interrogative*) anyone, anybody; **~ d'autre** someone *ou* somebody else; (+ *tournure interrogative*) anybody else

quémander [kemɑ̃de] *vt* to beg for

qu'en dira-t-on [kɑ̃diʀatɔ̃] *nm inv*: **le ~-~-~-~** gossip, what people say

querelle [kəʀɛl] *nf* quarrel; **quereller**: **se quereller** *vi* to quarrel

qu'est-ce que [kɛskə] *voir* **que**

qu'est-ce qui [kɛski] *voir* **qui**

question [kɛstjɔ̃] *nf* question; (*fig*) matter, issue; **il a été ~ de** we (*ou* they) spoke about; **de quoi est-il ~?** what is it about?; **il n'en est pas ~** there's no question of it; **hors de ~** out of the question; **remettre en ~** to question; **questionnaire** *nm* questionnaire; **questionner** *vt* to question

quête [kɛt] *nf* collection; (*recherche*) quest, search; **faire la ~** (*à l'église*) to take the collection; (*artiste*) to pass the hat round

quetsche [kwɛtʃ] *nf kind of dark-red plum*

queue [kø] *nf* tail; (*fig*: *du classement*) bottom; (: *de poêle*) handle; (: *de fruit, feuille*) stalk; (: *de train, colonne, file*) rear; **faire la ~** to queue (up) (BRIT), line up (US); **~ de cheval** ponytail; **~ de poisson** (AUT): **faire une ~ de poisson à qn** to cut in front of sb

qui [ki] *pron* (*personne*) who; (+*prép*) whom; (*chose, animal*) which, that; **qu'est-ce ~ est sur la table?** what is on the table?; **~ est-ce ~?** who?; **~ est-ce que?** who?; **à ~ est ce sac?** whose bag is this?; **à ~ parlais-tu?** who were you talking to?, to whom were you talking?; **amenez ~ vous voulez** bring who you like; **~ que ce soit** whoever it may be

quiconque [kikɔ̃k] *pron* (*celui qui*) whoever, anyone who; (*n'importe qui*) anyone, anybody

quiétude [kjetyd] *nf*: **en toute ~** in complete peace

quille [kij] *nf*: **(jeu de) ~s** skittles *sg* (*BRIT*), bowling (*US*)

quincaillerie [kɛ̃kajʀi] *nf* (*ustensiles*) hardware; (*magasin*) hardware shop; **quincaillier, -ière** *nm/f* hardware dealer

quinquagénaire [kɛ̃kaʒenɛʀ] *nm/f* man/woman in his/her fifties

quintal, -aux [kɛ̃tal, o] *nm* quintal (*100 kg*)

quinte [kɛ̃t] *nf*: **~ (de toux)** coughing fit

quintuple [kɛ̃typl] *nm*: **le ~ de** five times as much as; **quintuplés, -ées** *nm/fpl* quintuplets, quins

quinzaine [kɛ̃zɛn] *nf*: **une ~ (de)** about fifteen, fifteen or so; **une ~ (de jours)** a fortnight (*BRIT*), two weeks

quinze [kɛ̃z] *num* fifteen; **dans ~ jours** in a fortnight('s time), in two weeks(' time)

quiproquo [kipʀɔko] *nm* misunderstanding

quittance [kitɑ̃s] *nf* (*reçu*) receipt

quitte [kit] *adj*: **être ~ envers qn** to be no longer in sb's debt; (*fig*) to be quits with sb; **~ à faire** even if it means doing

quitter [kite] *vt* to leave; (*vêtement*) to take off; **se ~** *vi* (*couples, interlocuteurs*) to part; **ne quittez pas** (*au téléphone*) hold the line

qui-vive [kiviv] *nm*: **être sur le ~-~** to be on the alert

quoi [kwa] *pron* (*interrogatif*) what; **~ de neuf?** what's the news?; **as-tu de ~ écrire?** have you anything to write with?; **~ qu'il arrive** whatever happens; **~ qu'il en soit** be that as it may; **~ que ce soit** anything at all; **"il n'y a pas de ~"** "(please) don't mention it"; **il n'y a pas de ~ rire** there's nothing to laugh about; **à ~ bon?** what's the use?; **en ~ puis-je vous aider?** how can I help you?

quoique [kwak] *conj* (al)though

quote-part [kɔtpaʀ] *nf* share

quotidien, ne [kɔtidjɛ̃, jɛn] *adj* daily; (*banal*) everyday ♦ *nm* (*journal*) daily (paper); **quotidiennement** *adv* daily

R, r

r. *abr* = **route**; **rue**

rab [ʀab] (*fam*) *nm* (*nourriture*) extra; **est-ce qu'il y a du ~?** is there any extra (left)?

rabâcher [ʀabɑʃe] *vt* to keep on repeating

rabais [ʀabɛ] *nm* reduction, discount; **rabaisser** *vt* (*dénigrer*) to belittle; (*rabattre*: *prix*) to reduce

rabat-joie [ʀabaʒwa] *nm inv* killjoy

rabattre [ʀabatʀ] *vt* (*couvercle, siège*) to pull down; (*déduire*) to reduce; **se ~** *vi* (*se refermer*: *couvercle*) to fall shut; (*véhicule, coureur*) to cut in; **se ~ sur** to fall back on

rabbin [ʀabɛ̃] *nm* rabbi

râblé, e [ʀɑble] *adj* stocky

rabot [ʀabo] *nm* plane

rabougri, e [ʀabugʀi] *adj* stunted

rabrouer [ʀabʀue] *vt* to snub

racaille [ʀakɑj] (*péj*) *nf* rabble, riffraff

raccommoder [ʀakɔmɔde] *vt* to mend, repair; **se ~** *vi* (*fam*) to make it up

raccompagner [ʀakɔ̃paɲe] *vt* to take *ou* see back

raccord [ʀakɔʀ] *nm* link; (*retouche*) touch up; **raccorder** *vt* to join (up), link up; (*suj*: *pont etc*) to connect, link

raccourci [ʀakuʀsi] *nm* short cut

raccourcir [ʀakuʀsiʀ] *vt* to shorten ♦ *vi* (*jours*) to grow shorter, draw in

raccrocher [ʀakʀɔʃe] *vt* (*tableau*) to hang back up; (*récepteur*) to put down ♦ *vi* (*TÉL*) to hang up, ring off; **se ~ à** *vt* to cling to, hang on to

race [ʀas] *nf* race; (*d'animaux, fig*) breed; **de ~** purebred, pedigree

rachat [raʃa] *nm* buying; (*du même objet*) buying back

racheter [raʃ(ə)te] *vt* (*article perdu*) to buy another; (*après avoir vendu*) to buy back; (*d'occasion*) to buy; (COMM: *part, firme*) to buy up; (*davantage*): **~ du lait/3 œufs** to buy more milk/another 3 eggs *ou* 3 more eggs; **se ~** *vi* (*fig*) to make amends

racial, e, -aux [rasjal, jo] *adj* racial

racine [rasin] *nf* root; **~ carrée/cubique** square/cube root

raciste [rasist] *adj, nm/f* raci(al)ist

racket [rakɛt] *nm* racketeering *no pl*

raclée [rɑkle] (*fam*) *nf* hiding, thrashing

racler [rɑkle] *vt* (*surface*) to scrape; **se ~ la gorge** to clear one's throat

racoler [rakɔle] *vt* (*suj: prostituée*) to solicit; (: *parti, marchand*) to tout for

racontars [rakɔ̃taʀ] *nmpl* story, lie

raconter [rakɔ̃te] *vt*: **~ (à qn)** (*décrire*) to relate (to sb), tell (sb) about; (*dire de mauvaise foi*) to tell (sb); **~ une histoire** to tell a story

racorni, e [rakɔʀni] *adj* hard(ened)

radar [radaʀ] *nm* radar

rade [rad] *nf* (natural) harbour; **rester en ~** (*fig*) to be left stranded

radeau, x [rado] *nm* raft

radiateur [radjatœʀ] *nm* radiator, heater; (AUTO) radiator; **~ électrique/à gaz** electric/gas heater *ou* fire

radiation [radjasjɔ̃] *nf* (PHYSIQUE) radiation

radical, e, -aux [radikal, o] *adj* radical

radier [radje] *vt* to strike off

radieux, -euse [radjø, jøz] *adj* radiant

radin, e [radɛ̃, in] (*fam*) *adj* stingy

radio [radjo] *nf* radio; (MÉD) X-ray ♦ *nm* radio operator; **à la ~** on the radio; **radioactif, -ive** *adj* radioactive; **radiocassette** *nm* cassette radio, radio cassette player; **radiodiffuser** *vt* to broadcast; **radiographie** *nf* radiography; (*photo*) X-ray photograph; **radiophonique** *adj* radio *cpd*; **radio-réveil** (*pl* **radios-réveils**) *nm* radio alarm clock

radis [radi] *nm* radish

radoter [radɔte] *vi* to ramble on

radoucir [radusiʀ]: **se ~** *vi* (*temps*) to become milder; (*se calmer*) to calm down

rafale [rafal] *nf* (*vent*) gust (of wind); (*tir*) burst of gunfire

raffermir [rafɛʀmiʀ] *vt* to firm up; **se ~** *vi* (*fig: autorité, prix*) to strengthen

raffiner [rafine] *vt* to refine; **raffinerie** *nf* refinery

raffoler [rafɔle]: **~ de** *vt* to be very keen on

rafistoler [rafistɔle] (*fam*) *vt* to patch up

rafle [rɑfl] *nf* (*de police*) raid; **rafler** (*fam*) *vt* to swipe, nick

rafraîchir [rafʀeʃiʀ] *vt* (*atmosphère, température*) to cool (down); (*aussi: mettre à ~*) to chill; (*fig: rénover*) to brighten up; **se ~** *vi* (*temps*) to grow cooler; (*en se lavant*) to freshen up; (*en buvant*) to refresh o.s.; **rafraîchissant, e** *adj* refreshing; **rafraîchissement** *nm* (*boisson*) cool drink; **rafraîchissements** *nmpl* (*boissons, fruits etc*) refreshments

rage [raʒ] *nf* (MÉD): **la ~** rabies; (*fureur*) rage, fury; **faire ~** to rage; **~ de dents** (raging) toothache

ragot [rago] (*fam*) *nm* malicious gossip *no pl*

ragoût [ragu] *nm* stew

raide [rɛd] *adj* stiff; (*câble*) taut, tight; (*escarpé*) steep; (*droit: cheveux*) straight; (*fam: sans argent*) flat broke; (*osé*) daring, bold ♦ *adv* (*en pente*) steeply; **~ mort** stone dead; **raidir** *vt* (*muscles*) to stiffen; **se raidir** *vi* (*tissu*) to stiffen; (*personne*) to tense up; (: *se préparer moralement*) to brace o.s.; (*fig: position*) to harden; **raideur** *nf* (*rigidité*) stiffness; **avec raideur** (*répondre*) stiffly, abruptly

raie [rɛ] *nf* (ZOOL) skate, ray; (*rayure*) stripe; (*des cheveux*) parting

raifort [rɛfɔʀ] *nm* horseradish

rail [rɑj] *nm* rail; (*chemins de fer*) railways *pl*; **par ~** by rail
railler [rɑje] *vt* to scoff at, jeer at
rainure [renyr] *nf* groove
raisin [rezɛ̃] *nm* (*aussi:* **~s**) grapes *pl*; **~s secs** raisins
raison [rezɔ̃] *nf* reason; **avoir ~** to be right; **donner ~ à qn** to agree with sb; (*événement*) to prove sb right; **perdre la ~** to become insane; **~ de plus** all the more reason; **à plus forte ~** all the more so; **en ~ de** because of; **à ~ de** at the rate of; **sans ~** for no reason; **raisonnable** *adj* reasonable, sensible
raisonnement [rezɔnmɑ̃] *nm* (*façon de réfléchir*) reasoning; (*argumentation*) argument
raisonner [rezɔne] *vi* (*penser*) to reason; (*argumenter, discuter*) to argue ♦ *vt* (*personne*) to reason with
rajeunir [raʒœnir] *vt* (*suj: coiffure, robe*): **~ qn** to make sb look younger; (*fig: personnel*) to inject new blood into ♦ *vi* to become (*ou* look) younger
rajouter [raʒute] *vt* to add
rajuster [raʒyste] *vt* (*vêtement*) to straighten, tidy; (*salaires*) to adjust
ralenti [ralɑ̃ti] *nm*: **au ~** (*fig*) at a slower pace; **tourner au ~** (*AUTO*) to tick over (*AUTO*), idle
ralentir [ralɑ̃tir] *vt* to slow down
râler [rɑle] *vi* to groan; (*fam*) to grouse, moan (and groan)
rallier [ralje] *vt* (*rejoindre*) to rejoin; (*gagner à sa cause*) to win over; **se ~ à** (*avis*) to come over *ou* round to
rallonge [ralɔ̃ʒ] *nf* (*de table*) (extra) leaf
rallonger [ralɔ̃ʒe] *vt* to lengthen
rallye [rali] *nm* rally; (*POL*) march
ramassage [ramɑsaʒ] *nm*: **~ scolaire** school bus service
ramassé, e [ramɑse] *adj* (*trapu*) squat
ramasser [ramɑse] *vt* (*objet tombé ou par terre, fam*) to pick up; (*recueillir: copies, ordures*) to collect; (*récolter*) to gather; **se ~** *vi* (*sur soi-même*) to huddle up; **ramassis** (*péj*) *nm* (*de voyous*) bunch; (*d'objets*) jumble
rambarde [rɑ̃bard] *nf* guardrail
rame [ram] *nf* (*aviron*) oar; (*de métro*) train; (*de papier*) ream
rameau, x [ramo] *nm* (small) branch; **les R~x** (*REL*) Palm Sunday *sg*
ramener [ram(ə)ne] *vt* to bring back; (*reconduire*) to take back; **~ qch à** (*réduire à*) to reduce sth to
ramer [rame] *vi* to row
ramollir [ramɔlir] *vt* to soften; **se ~** *vi* to go soft
ramoner [ramɔne] *vt* to sweep
rampe [rɑ̃p] *nf* (*d'escalier*) banister(s *pl*); (*dans un garage*) ramp; (*THÉÂTRE*): **la ~** the footlights *pl*; **~ de lancement** launching pad
ramper [rɑ̃pe] *vi* to crawl
rancard [rɑ̃kar] (*fam*) *nm* (*rendez-vous*) date
rancart [rɑ̃kar] *nm*: **mettre au ~** (*fam*) to scrap
rance [rɑ̃s] *adj* rancid
rancœur [rɑ̃kœr] *nf* rancour
rançon [rɑ̃sɔ̃] *nf* ransom
rancune [rɑ̃kyn] *nf* grudge, rancour; **garder ~ à qn (de qch)** to bear sb a grudge (for sth); **sans ~!** no hard feelings!; **rancunier, -ière** *adj* vindictive, spiteful
randonnée [rɑ̃dɔne] *nf* ride; (*pédestre*) walk, ramble; (*: en montagne*) hike, hiking *no pl*
rang [rɑ̃] *nm* (*rangée*) row; (*grade, classement*) rank; **~s** *nmpl* (*MIL*) ranks; **se mettre en ~s** to get into *ou* form rows; **au premier ~** in the first row; (*fig*) ranking first
rangé, e [rɑ̃ʒe] *adj* (*vie*) well-ordered; (*personne*) steady
rangée [rɑ̃ʒe] *nf* row
ranger [rɑ̃ʒe] *vt* (*mettre de l'ordre dans*) to tidy up; (*classer, grouper*) to order, arrange; (*mettre à sa place*) to put away; (*fig: classer*): **~ qn/qch parmi** to

rank sb/sth among; **se ~** *vi* (*véhicule, conducteur*) to pull over *ou* in; (*piéton*) to step aside; (*s'assagir*) to settle down; **se ~ à** (*avis*) to come round to

ranimer [Ranime] *vt* (*personne*) to bring round; (*douleur, souvenir*) to revive; (*feu*) to rekindle

rap [Rap] *nm* rap (music)

rapace [Rapas] *nm* bird of prey

râpe [Rɑp] *nf* (CULIN) grater; **râper** *vt* (CULIN) to grate

rapetisser [Rap(ə)tise] *vt* to shorten

rapide [Rapid] *adj* fast; (*prompt*: *coup d'œil, mouvement*) quick ♦ *nm* express (train); (*de cours d'eau*) rapid; **rapidement** *adv* fast; quickly

rapiécer [Rapjese] *vt* to patch

rappel [Rapɛl] *nm* (THÉÂTRE) curtain call; (MÉD: *vaccination*) booster; (*deuxième avis*) reminder; **rappeler** *vt* to call back; (*ambassadeur*, MIL) to recall; (*faire se souvenir*): **rappeler qch à qn** to remind sb of sth; **se rappeler** *vt* (*se souvenir de*) to remember, recall

rapport [Rapɔʀ] *nm* (*lien, analogie*) connection; (*compte rendu*) report; (*profit*) yield, return; **~s** *nmpl* (*entre personnes, pays*) relations; **avoir ~ à** to have something to do with; **être/se mettre en ~ avec qn** to be/get in touch with sb; **par ~ à** in relation to; **~s (sexuels)** (sexual) intercourse *sg*

rapporter [Rapɔʀte] *vt* (*rendre, ramener*) to bring back; (*bénéfice*) to yield, bring in; (*mentionner, répéter*) to report ♦ *vi* (*investissement*) to give a good return *ou* yield; (: *activité*) to be very profitable; **se ~ à** *vt* (*correspondre à*) to relate to; **rapporteur, -euse** *nm/f* (*péj*) telltale ♦ *nm* (GÉOM) protractor

rapprochement [RapRɔʃmɑ̃] *nm* (*de nations*) reconciliation; (*rapport*) parallel

rapprocher [RapRɔʃe] *vt* (*deux objets*) to bring closer together; (*fig*: *ennemis, partis etc*) to bring together; (*comparer*) to establish a parallel between; (*chaise d'une table*): **~ qch (de)** to bring sth closer (to); **se ~** *vi* to draw closer *ou* nearer; **se ~ de** to come closer to; (*présenter une analogie avec*) to be close to

rapt [Rapt] *nm* abduction

raquette [Rakɛt] *nf* (*de tennis*) racket; (*de ping-pong*) bat

rare [RɑR] *adj* rare; **se faire ~** to become scarce; **rarement** *adv* rarely, seldom

ras, e [Rɑ, Rɑz] *adj* (*poil, herbe*) short; (*tête*) close-cropped ♦ *adv* short; **en ~e campagne** in open country; **à ~ bords** to the brim; **en avoir ~ le bol** (*fam*) to be fed up; **~ du cou** ♦ *adj* (*pull, robe*) crew-neck

rasade [Rɑzad] *nf* glassful

raser [Rɑze] *vt* (*barbe, cheveux*) to shave off; (*menton, personne*) to shave; (*fam*: *ennuyer*) to bore; (*démolir*) to raze (to the ground); (*frôler*) to graze, skim; **se ~** *vi* to shave; (*fam*) to be bored (to tears); **rasoir** *nm* razor

rassasier [Rasazje] *vt*: **être rassasié** to have eaten one's fill

rassemblement [Rasɑ̃bləmɑ̃] *nm* (*groupe*) gathering; (POL) union

rassembler [Rasɑ̃ble] *vt* (*réunir*) to assemble, gather; (*documents, notes*) to gather together, collect; **se ~** *vi* to gather

rassis, e [Rasi, iz] *adj* (*pain*) stale

rassurer [RasyRe] *vt* to reassure; **se ~** *vi* to reassure o.s.; **rassure-toi** don't worry

rat [Ra] *nm* rat

rate [Rat] *nf* spleen

raté, e [Rate] *adj* (*tentative*) unsuccessful, failed ♦ *nm/f* (*fam*: *personne*) failure

râteau, x [Rɑto] *nm* rake

rater [Rate] *vi* (*affaire, projet etc*) to go wrong, fail ♦ *vt* (*fam*: *cible, train, occasion*) to miss; (*plat*) to spoil; (*fam*: *examen*) to fail

ration [Rasjɔ̃] *nf* ration

ratisser [Ratise] *vt* (*allée*) to rake; (*feuilles*) to rake up; (*suj*: *armée, police*) to comb

RATP *sigle f* (= *Régie autonome des transports parisiens*) *Paris transport authority*

rattacher [ratafe] *vt* (*animal, cheveux*) to tie up again; (*fig*: *relier*): **~ qch à** to link sth with

rattrapage [ratrapaʒ] *nm*: **cours de ~** remedial class

rattraper [ratrape] *vt* (*fugitif*) to recapture; (*empêcher de tomber*) to catch (hold of); (*atteindre, rejoindre*) to catch up with; (*réparer*: *erreur*) to make up for; **se ~** *vi* to make up for it; **se ~ (à)** (*se raccrocher*) to stop o.s. falling (by catching hold of)

rature [ratyr] *nf* deletion, erasure

rauque [rok] *adj* (*voix*) hoarse

ravages [ravaʒ] *nmpl*: **faire des ~** to wreak havoc

ravaler [ravale] *vt* (*mur, façade*) to restore; (*déprécier*) to lower

ravi, e [ravi] *adj*: **être ~ de/que** to be delighted with/that

ravigoter [ravigɔte] (*fam*) *vt* to buck up

ravin [ravɛ̃] *nm* gully, ravine

ravir [ravir] *vt* (*enchanter*) to delight; **à ~** *adv* beautifully

raviser [ravize]: **se ~** *vi* to change one's mind

ravissant, e [ravisɑ̃, ɑ̃t] *adj* delightful

ravisseur, -euse [ravisœr, øz] *nm/f* abductor, kidnapper

ravitaillement [ravitajmɑ̃] *nm* (*réserves*) supplies *pl*

ravitailler [ravitaje] *vt* (*en vivres, ammunitions*) to provide with fresh supplies; (*avion*) to refuel; **se ~** *vi* to get fresh supplies; (*avion*) to refuel

raviver [ravive] *vt* (*feu, douleur*) to revive; (*couleurs*) to brighten up

rayé, e [reje] *adj* (*à rayures*) striped

rayer [reje] *vt* (*érafler*) to scratch; (*barrer*) to cross out; (*d'une liste*) to cross off

rayon [rɛjɔ̃] *nm* (*de soleil etc*) ray; (*GÉOM*) radius; (*de roue*) spoke; (*étagère*) shelf; (*de grand magasin*) department; **dans un ~ de** within a radius of; **~ de soleil** sunbeam; **~s X** X-rays

rayonnement [rɛjɔnmɑ̃] *nm* (*fig*: *d'une culture*) influence

rayonner [rɛjɔne] *vi* (*fig*) to shine forth; (*personne*: *de joie, de beauté*) to be radiant; (*touriste*) to go touring (*from one base*)

rayure [rejyr] *nf* (*motif*) stripe; (*éraflure*) scratch; **à ~s** striped

raz-de-marée [rɑdmare] *nm inv* tidal wave

ré [re] *nm* (*MUS*) D; (*en chantant la gamme*) re

réacteur [reaktœr] *nm* (*d'avion*) jet engine; (*nucléaire*) reactor

réaction [reaksjɔ̃] *nf* reaction

réadapter [readapte]: **se ~ (à)** *vi* to readjust (to)

réagir [reaʒir] *vi* to react

réalisateur, -trice [realizatœr, tris] *nm/f* (*TV, CINÉMA*) director

réalisation [realizasjɔ̃] *nf* realization; (*cinéma*) production; **en cours de ~** under way

réaliser [realize] *vt* (*projet, opération*) to carry out, realize; (*rêve, souhait*) to realize, fulfil; (*exploit*) to achieve; (*film*) to produce; (*se rendre compte de*) to realize; **se ~** *vi* to be realized

réaliste [realist] *adj* realistic

réalité [realite] *nf* reality; **en ~** in (actual) fact; **dans la ~** in reality

réanimation [reanimasjɔ̃] *nf* resuscitation; **service de ~** intensive care unit

rébarbatif, -ive [rebarbatif, iv] *adj* forbidding

rebattu, e [r(ə)baty] *adj* hackneyed

rebelle [rəbɛl] *nm/f* rebel ♦ *adj* (*troupes*) rebel; (*enfant*) rebellious; (*mèche etc*) unruly

rebeller [r(ə)bele]: **se ~** *vi* to rebel

rebondi, e [r(ə)bɔ̃di] *adj* (*joues*) chubby

rebondir [r(ə)bɔ̃dir] *vi* (*ballon*: *au sol*) to bounce; (: *contre un mur*) to re-

bound; (*fig*) to get moving again; **rebondissement** *nm* new development
rebord [R(ə)bɔR] *nm* edge; **le ~ de la fenêtre** the windowsill
rebours [R(ə)buR]: **à ~** *adv* the wrong way
rebrousser [R(ə)bRuse] *vt*: **~ chemin** to turn back
rebut [Rəby] *nm*: **mettre au ~** to scrap; **rebutant, e** *adj* off-putting; **rebuter** *vt* to put off
récalcitrant, e [Rekalsitʀɑ̃, ɑ̃t] *adj* refractory
recaler [R(ə)kale] *vt* (SCOL) to fail; **se faire ~** to fail
récapituler [Rekapityle] *vt* to recapitulate, sum up
receler [R(ə)səle] *vt* (*produit d'un vol*) to receive; (*fig*) to conceal; **receleur, -euse** *nm/f* receiver
récemment [Resamɑ̃] *adv* recently
recensement [R(ə)sɑ̃smɑ̃] *nm* (population) census
recenser [R(ə)sɑ̃se] *vt* (*population*) to take a census of; (*inventorier*) to list
récent, e [Resɑ̃, ɑ̃t] *adj* recent
récépissé [Resepise] *nm* receipt
récepteur [ResɛptœR, tRis] *nm* receiver
réception [Resɛpsjɔ̃] *nf* receiving *no pl*; (*accueil*) reception, welcome; (*bureau*) reception desk; (*réunion mondaine*) reception, party; **réceptionniste** *nm/f* receptionist
recette [R(ə)sɛt] *nf* recipe; (COMM) takings *pl*; **~s** *nfpl* (COMM: *rentrées*) receipts
receveur, -euse [R(ə)səvœR, øz] *nm/f* (*des contributions*) tax collector; (*des postes*) postmaster(-mistress)
recevoir [R(ə)səvwaR] *vt* to receive; (*client, patient*) to see; **être reçu** (*à un examen*) to pass
rechange [R(ə)ʃɑ̃ʒ]: **de ~** *adj* (*pièces*) spare; (*fig*: *solution*) alternative; **des vêtements de ~** a change of clothes
réchapper [Reʃape]: **~ de** *ou* **à** *vt* (*accident, maladie*) to come through
recharge [R(ə)ʃaRʒ] *nf* refill; **rechargeable** *adj* (*stylo etc*) refillable; **recharger** *vt* (*stylo*) to refill; (*batterie*) to recharge
réchaud [Reʃo] *nm* (portable) stove
réchauffement [Reʃofmɑ̃] *nm*: **le ~ climatique** global warming
réchauffer [Reʃofe] *vt* (*plat*) to reheat; (*mains, personne*) to warm; **se ~** *vi* (*température*) to get warmer; (*personne*) to warm o.s. (up)
rêche [Rɛʃ] *adj* rough
recherche [R(ə)ʃɛRʃ] *nf* (*action*) search; (*raffinement*) studied elegance; (*scientifique etc*): **la ~** research; **~s** *nfpl* (*de la police*) investigations; (*scientifiques*) research *sg*; **la ~ de** the search for; **être à la ~ de qch** to be looking for sth
recherché, e [R(ə)ʃɛRʃe] *adj* (*rare, demandé*) much sought-after; (*raffiné*: *style*) mannered; (: *tenue*) elegant
rechercher [R(ə)ʃɛRʃe] *vt* (*objet égaré, personne*) to look for; (*causes, nouveau procédé*) to try to find; (*bonheur, compliments*) to seek
rechigner [R(ə)ʃiɲe] *vi*: **~ à faire qch** to balk *ou* jib at doing sth
rechute [R(ə)ʃyt] *nf* (MÉD) relapse
récidiver [Residive] *vi* to commit a subsequent offence; (*fig*) to do it again
récif [Resif] *nm* reef
récipient [Resipjɑ̃] *nm* container
récit [Resi] *nm* story; **récital** *nm* recital; **réciter** *vt* to recite
réclamation [Reklɑmasjɔ̃] *nf* complaint; **~s** *nfpl* (*bureau*) complaints department *sg*
réclame [Reklɑm] *nf* ad, advert(isement); **en ~** on special offer; **réclamer** *vt* to ask for; (*revendiquer*) to claim, demand ♦ *vi* to complain
réclusion [Reklyzjɔ̃] *nf* imprisonment
recoin [Rəkwɛ̃] *nm* nook, corner
reçois *etc* [Rəswa] *vb voir* **recevoir**
récolte [Rekɔlt] *nf* harvesting, gathering; (*produits*) harvest, crop; **récolter** *vt* to harvest, gather (in); (*fig*) to collect
recommandé [R(ə)kɔmɑ̃de] *nm*

(*POSTES*): **en ~** by registered mail

recommander [R(ə)kɔmɑ̃de] *vt* to recommend; (*POSTES*) to register

recommencer [R(ə)kɔmɑ̃se] *vt* (*reprendre: lutte, séance*) to resume, start again; (*refaire: travail, explications*) to start afresh, start (over) again ♦ *vi* to start again; (*récidiver*) to do it again

récompense [Rekɔ̃pɑ̃s] *nf* reward; (*prix*) award; **récompenser** *vt*: **récompenser qn (de** *ou* **pour)** to reward sb (for)

réconcilier [Rekɔ̃silje] *vt* to reconcile; **se ~ (avec)** to be reconciled (with)

reconduire [R(ə)kɔ̃dɥiR] *vt* (*raccompagner*) to take *ou* see back; (*renouveler*) to renew

réconfort [Rekɔ̃fɔR] *nm* comfort; **réconforter** *vt* (*consoler*) to comfort

reconnaissance [R(ə)kɔnɛsɑ̃s] *nf* (*gratitude*) gratitude, gratefulness; (*action de reconnaître*) recognition; (*MIL*) reconnaissance, recce; **reconnaissant, e** *adj* grateful

reconnaître [R(ə)kɔnɛtR] *vt* to recognize; (*MIL: lieu*) to reconnoitre; (*JUR: enfant, torts*) to acknowledge; **~ que** to admit *ou* acknowledge that; **reconnu, e** *adj* (*indiscuté, connu*) recognized

reconstituant, e [R(ə)kɔ̃stitɥɑ̃, ɑ̃t] *adj* (*aliment, régime*) strength-building

reconstituer [R(ə)kɔ̃stitɥe] *vt* (*événement, accident*) to reconstruct; (*fresque, vase brisé*) to piece together, reconstitute

reconstruction [R(ə)kɔ̃stRyksjɔ̃] *nf* rebuilding

reconstruire [R(ə)kɔ̃stRɥiR] *vt* to rebuild

reconvertir [R(ə)kɔ̃vɛRtiR]: **se ~ dans** *vr* (*un métier, une branche*) to go into

record [R(ə)kɔR] *nm, adj* record

recoupement [R(ə)kupmɑ̃] *nm*: **par ~** by cross-checking

recouper [R(ə)kupe]: **se ~** *vi* (*témoignages*) to tie *ou* match up

recourber [R(ə)kuRbe]: **se ~** *vi* to curve (up), bend (up)

recourir [R(ə)kuRiR]: **~ à** *vt* (*ami, agence*) to turn *ou* appeal to; (*force, ruse, emprunt*) to resort to

recours [R(ə)kuR] *nm*: **avoir ~ à = recourir à; en dernier ~** as a last resort

recouvrer [R(ə)kuvRe] *vt* (*vue, santé etc*) to recover, regain

recouvrir [R(ə)kuvRiR] *vt* (*couvrir à nouveau*) to re-cover; (*couvrir entièrement, aussi fig*) to cover

récréation [RekReasjɔ̃] *nf* (*SCOL*) break

récrier [RekRije]: **se ~** *vi* to exclaim

récriminations [RekRiminasjɔ̃] *nfpl* remonstrations, complaints

recroqueviller [R(ə)kRɔk(ə)vije]: **se ~** *vi* (*personne*) to huddle up

recrudescence [R(ə)kRydesɑ̃s] *nf* fresh outbreak

recrue [RəkRy] *nf* recruit

recruter [R(ə)kRyte] *vt* to recruit

rectangle [Rɛktɑ̃gl] *nm* rectangle; **rectangulaire** *adj* rectangular

rectificatif [Rɛktifikatif, iv] *nm* correction

rectifier [Rɛktifje] *vt* (*calcul, adresse, paroles*) to correct; (*erreur*) to rectify

rectiligne [Rɛktiliɲ] *adj* straight

recto [Rɛkto] *nm* front (of a page); **~ verso** on both sides (of the page)

reçu, e [R(ə)sy] *pp de* **recevoir** ♦ *adj* (*candidat*) successful; (*admis, consacré*) accepted ♦ *nm* (*COMM*) receipt

recueil [Rəkœj] *nm* collection; **recueillir** *vt* to collect; (*voix, suffrages*) to win; (*accueillir: réfugiés, chat*) to take in; **se recueillir** *vi* to gather one's thoughts, meditate

recul [R(ə)kyl] *nm* (*éloignement*) distance; (*déclin*) decline; **être en ~** to be on the decline; **avec du ~** with hindsight; **avoir un mouvement de ~** to recoil; **prendre du ~** to stand back; **reculé, e** *adj* remote; **reculer** *vi* to move back, back away; (*AUTO*) to reverse, back (up); (*fig*) to (be on the) decline ♦ *vt* to move back; (*véhicule*) to reverse, back (up); (*date, décision*) to postpone; **reculons**: **à reculons** *adv* backwards

récupérer [ʀekypeʀe] *vt* to recover, get back; (*heures de travail*) to make up; (*déchets*) to salvage ♦ *vi* to recover

récurer [ʀekyʀe] *vt* to scour

récuser [ʀekyze] *vt* to challenge; **se ~** *vi* to decline to give an opinion

reçut [ʀəsy] *vb voir* **recevoir**

recycler [ʀ(ə)sikle] *vt* (TECH) to recycle; **se ~** *vi* to retrain

rédacteur, -trice [ʀedaktœʀ, tʀis] *nm/f* (*journaliste*) writer; subeditor; (*d'ouvrage de référence*) editor, compiler; **~ en chef** chief editor

rédaction [ʀedaksjɔ̃] *nf* writing; (*rédacteurs*) editorial staff; (SCOL: *devoir*) essay, composition

redemander [ʀədmɑ̃de] *vt* (*une nouvelle fois*) to ask again for; (*davantage*) to ask for more of

redescendre [ʀ(ə)desɑ̃dʀ] *vi* to go back down ♦ *vt* (*pente etc*) to go down

redevance [ʀ(ə)dəvɑ̃s] *nf* (TÉL) rental charge; (TV) licence fee

rédiger [ʀediʒe] *vt* to write; (*contrat*) to draw up

redire [ʀ(ə)diʀ] *vt* to repeat; **trouver à ~ à** to find fault with

redonner [ʀ(ə)dɔne] *vt* (*rendre*) to give back; (*resservir*: *nourriture*) to give more

redoubler [ʀ(ə)duble] *vi* (*tempête, violence*) to intensify; (SCOL) to repeat a year; **~ de patience/prudence** to be doubly patient/careful

redoutable [ʀ(ə)dutabl] *adj* formidable, fearsome

redouter [ʀ(ə)dute] *vt* to dread

redressement [ʀ(ə)dʀɛsmɑ̃] *nm* (*économique*) recovery

redresser [ʀ(ə)dʀese] *vt* (*relever*) to set upright; (*pièce tordue*) to straighten out; (*situation, économie*) to put right; **se ~** *vi* (*personne*) to sit (*ou* stand) up (straight); (*économie*) to recover

réduction [ʀedyksjɔ̃] *nf* reduction

réduire [ʀedɥiʀ] *vt* to reduce; (*prix, dépenses*) to cut, reduce; **se ~ à** (*revenir à*) to boil down to; **réduit** *nm* (*pièce*) tiny room

rééducation [ʀeedykasjɔ̃] *nf* (*d'un membre*) re-education; (*de délinquants, d'un blessé*) rehabilitation

réel, le [ʀeɛl] *adj* real; **réellement** *adv* really

réexpédier [ʀeɛkspedje] *vt* (*à l'envoyeur*) to return, send back; (*au destinataire*) to send on, forward

refaire [ʀ(ə)fɛʀ] *vt* to do again; (*faire de nouveau*: *sport*) to take up again; (*réparer, restaurer*) to do up

réfection [ʀefɛksjɔ̃] *nf* repair

réfectoire [ʀefɛktwaʀ] *nm* refectory

référence [ʀefeʀɑ̃s] *nf* reference; **~s** *nfpl* (*recommandations*) reference *sg*

référer [ʀefeʀe]: **se ~ à** *vt* to refer to

refermer [ʀ(ə)fɛʀme] *vt* to close *ou* shut again; **se ~** *vi* (*porte*) to close *ou* shut (again)

refiler [ʀ(ə)file] *vi* (*fam*) to palm off

réfléchi, e [ʀefleʃi] *adj* (*caractère*) thoughtful; (*action*) well-thought-out; (LING) reflexive; **c'est tout ~** my mind's made up

réfléchir [ʀefleʃiʀ] *vt* to reflect ♦ *vi* to think; **~ à** to think about

reflet [ʀ(ə)flɛ] *nm* reflection; (*sur l'eau etc*) sheen *no pl*, glint; **refléter** *vt* to reflect; **se refléter** *vi* to be reflected

réflexe [ʀeflɛks] *nm, adj* reflex

réflexion [ʀeflɛksjɔ̃] *nf* (*de la lumière etc*) reflection; (*fait de penser*) thought; (*remarque*) remark; **~ faite, à la ~** on reflection

refluer [ʀ(ə)flye] *vi* to flow back; (*foule*) to surge back

reflux [ʀəfly] *nm* (*de la mer*) ebb

réforme [ʀefɔʀm] *nf* reform; (REL): **la R~** the Reformation; **réformer** *vt* to reform; (MIL) to declare unfit for service

refouler [ʀ(ə)fule] *vt* (*envahisseurs*) to drive back; (*larmes*) to force back; (*désir, colère*) to repress

refrain [ʀ(ə)fʀɛ̃] *nm* refrain, chorus
refréner [ʀəfʀene] *vt*, **réfréner** [ʀefʀene] *vt* to curb, check
réfrigérateur [ʀefʀiʒeʀatœʀ] *nm* refrigerator, fridge
refroidir [ʀ(ə)fʀwadiʀ] *vt* to cool; (*fig*: *personne*) to put off ♦ *vi* to cool (down); **se ~** *vi* (*temps*) to get cooler *ou* colder; (*fig*: *ardeur*) to cool (off); **refroidissement** *nm* (*grippe etc*) chill
refuge [ʀ(ə)fyʒ] *nm* refuge; **réfugié, e** *adj, nm/f* refugee; **réfugier**: **se réfugier** *vi* to take refuge
refus [ʀ(ə)fy] *nm* refusal; **ce n'est pas de ~** I won't say no, it's welcome; **refuser** *vt* to refuse; (*SCOL*: *candidat*) to fail; **refuser qch à qn** to refuse sb sth; **se refuser à faire** to refuse to do
réfuter [ʀefyte] *vt* to refute
regagner [ʀ(ə)gaɲe] *vt* (*faveur*) to win back; (*lieu*) to get back to
regain [ʀəgɛ̃] *nm* (*renouveau*): **un ~ de** renewed *+nom*
régal [ʀegal] *nm* treat; **régaler**: **se régaler** *vi* to have a delicious meal; (*fig*) to enjoy o.s.
regard [ʀ(ə)gaʀ] *nm* (*coup d'œil*) look, glance; (*expression*) look (in one's eye); **au ~ de** (*loi, morale*) from the point of view of; **en ~ de** in comparison with
regardant, e [ʀ(ə)gaʀdɑ̃, ɑ̃t] *adj* (*économe*) tight-fisted; **peu ~ (sur)** very free (about)
regarder [ʀ(ə)gaʀde] *vt* to look at, (*film, télévision, match*) to watch; (*concerner*) to concern ♦ *vi* to look; **ne pas ~ à la dépense** to spare no expense; **~ qn/qch comme** to regard sb/sth as
régie [ʀeʒi] *nf* (*COMM, INDUSTRIE*) state-owned company; (*THÉÂTRE, CINÉMA*) production; (*RADIO, TV*) control room
regimber [ʀ(ə)ʒɛ̃be] *vi* to balk, jib
régime [ʀeʒim] *nm* (*POL*) régime; (*MÉD*) diet; (*ADMIN*: *carcéral, fiscal etc*) system; (*de bananes, dattes*) bunch; **se mettre au/suivre un ~** to go on/be on a diet
régiment [ʀeʒimɑ̃] *nm* regiment
région [ʀeʒjɔ̃] *nf* region; **régional, e, -aux** *adj* regional
régir [ʀeʒiʀ] *vt* to govern
régisseur [ʀeʒisœʀ] *nm* (*d'un domaine*) steward; (*CINÉMA, TV*) assistant director; (*THÉÂTRE*) stage manager
registre [ʀəʒistʀ] *nm* register
réglage [ʀeglaʒ] *nm* adjustment
règle [ʀɛgl] *nf* (*instrument*) ruler; (*loi*) rule; **~s** *nfpl* (*menstruation*) period *sg*; **en ~** (*papiers d'identité*) in order; **en ~ générale** as a (general) rule
réglé, e [ʀegle] *adj* (*vie*) well-ordered; (*arrangé*) settled
règlement [ʀɛgləmɑ̃] *nm* (*paiement*) settlement; (*arrêté*) regulation; (*règles, statuts*) regulations *pl*, rules *pl*; **~ de compte(s)** settling of old scores; **réglementaire** *adj* conforming to the regulations; (*tenue*) regulation *cpd*; **réglementation** *nf* (*règles*) regulations; **réglementer** *vt* to regulate
régler [ʀegle] *vt* (*conflit, facture*) to settle; (*personne*) to settle up with; (*mécanisme, machine*) to regulate, adjust; (*thermostat etc*) to set, adjust
réglisse [ʀeglis] *nf* liquorice
règne [ʀɛɲ] *nm* (*d'un roi etc, fig*) reign; **régner** *vi* (*roi*) to rule, reign; (*fig*) to reign
regorger [ʀ(ə)gɔʀʒe] *vi*: **~ de** to overflow with, be bursting with
regret [ʀ(ə)gʀɛ] *nm* regret; **à ~** with regret; **sans ~** with no regrets; **regrettable** *adj* regrettable; **regretter** *vt* to regret; (*personne*) to miss; **je regrette mais ...** I'm sorry but ...
regrouper [ʀ(ə)gʀupe] *vt* (*grouper*) to group together; (*contenir*) to include, comprise; **se ~** *vi* to gather (together)
régulier, -ière [ʀegylje, jɛʀ] *adj* (*gén*) regular; (*vitesse, qualité*) steady; (*égal*: *couche, ligne*) even, (*TRANSPORTS*: *ligne, service*), scheduled, regular; (*légal*) lawful, in order; (*honnête*) straight, on the level; **régulièrement** *adv* regularly, (*uniformément*) evenly

rehausser [ʀəose] *vt* (*relever*) to heighten, raise; (*fig: souligner*) to set off, enhance
rein [ʀɛ̃] *nm* kidney; **~s** *nmpl* (*dos*) back *sg*
reine [ʀɛn] *nf* queen
reine-claude [ʀɛnklod] *nf* greengage
réinsertion [ʀeɛ̃sɛʀsjɔ̃] *nf* (*de délinquant*) reintegration, rehabilitation
réintégrer [ʀeɛ̃tegʀe] *vt* (*lieu*) to return to; (*fonctionnaire*) to reinstate
rejaillir [ʀ(ə)ʒajiʀ] *vi* to splash up; **~ sur** (*fig: scandale*) to rebound on; (*: gloire*) to be reflected on
rejet [ʀəʒɛ] *nm* rejection; **rejeter** *vt* (*relancer*) to throw back; (*écarter*) to reject; (*déverser*) to throw out, discharge; (*vomir*) to bring *ou* throw up; **rejeter la responsabilité de qch sur qn** to lay the responsibility for sth at sb's door
rejoindre [ʀ(ə)ʒwɛ̃dʀ] *vt* (*famille, régiment*) to rejoin, return to; (*lieu*) to get (back) to; (*suj: route etc*) to meet, join; (*rattraper*) to catch up (with); **se ~** *vi* to meet; **je te rejoins à la gare** I'll see *ou* meet you at the station
réjouir [ʀeʒwiʀ] *vt* to delight; **se ~ (de)** *vi* to be delighted (about); **réjouissances** *nfpl* (*fête*) festivities
relâche [ʀəlɑʃ] *nm ou nf*: **sans ~** without respite *ou* a break; **relâché, e** *adj* loose, lax; **relâcher** *vt* (*libérer*) to release; (*desserrer*) to loosen; **se relâcher** *vi* (*discipline*) to become slack *ou* lax; (*élève etc*) to slacken off
relais [ʀ(ə)lɛ] *nm* (SPORT): **(course de) ~** relay (race); **prendre le ~ (de)** to take over (from); **~ routier** ≈ transport café (BRIT), ≈ truck stop (US)
relancer [ʀ(ə)lɑ̃se] *vt* (*balle*) to throw back; (*moteur*) to restart; (*fig*) to boost, revive; (*harceler*): **~ qn** to pester sb
relatif, -ive [ʀ(ə)latif, iv] *adj* relative
relation [ʀ(ə)lasjɔ̃] *nf* (*rapport*) relation(ship); (*connaissance*) acquaintance; **~s** *nfpl* (*rapports*) relations; (*connaissances*) connections; **être/entrer en ~(s) avec** to be/get in contact with
relaxe [ʀəlaks] (*fam*) *adj* (*tenue*) informal; (*personne*) relaxed; **relaxer: se relaxer** *vi* to relax
relayer [ʀ(ə)leje] *vt* (*collaborateur, coureur etc*) to relieve; **se ~** *vi* (*dans une activité*) to take it in turns
reléguer [ʀ(ə)lege] *vt* to relegate
relent(s) [ʀəlɑ̃] *nm(pl)* (foul) smell
relevé, e [ʀəl(ə)ve] *adj* (*manches*) rolled-up; (*sauce*) highly-seasoned ♦ *nm* (*de compteur*) reading; (*bancaire*) statement
relève [ʀəlɛv] *nf* (*personne*) relief; **prendre la ~** to take over
relever [ʀəl(ə)ve] *vt* (*meuble*) to stand up again; (*personne tombée*) to help up; (*vitre, niveau de vie*) to raise; (*col*) to turn up; (*style*) to elevate; (*plat, sauce*) to season; (*sentinelle, équipe*) to relieve; (*fautes*) to pick out; (*défi*) to accept, take up; (*noter: adresse etc*) to take down, note; (*: plan*) to sketch; (*compteur*) to read; (*ramasser: cahiers*) to collect, take in; **se ~** *vi* (*se remettre debout*) to get up; **~ de** (*maladie*) to be recovering from; (*être du ressort de*) to be a matter for; (*fig*) to pertain to; **~ qn de** (*fonctions*) to relieve sb of
relief [ʀəljɛf] *nm* relief; **mettre en ~** (*fig*) to bring out, highlight
relier [ʀəlje] *vt* to link up; (*livre*) to bind; **~ qch à** to link sth to
religieuse [ʀ(ə)liʒjøz] *nf* nun; (*gâteau*) cream bun
religieux, -euse [ʀ(ə)liʒjø, jøz] *adj* religious ♦ *nm* monk
religion [ʀ(ə)liʒjɔ̃] *nf* religion
relire [ʀ(ə)liʀ] *vt* (*à nouveau*) to reread, read again; (*vérifier*) to read over
reliure [ʀəljyʀ] *nf* binding
reluire [ʀ(ə)lɥiʀ] *vi* to gleam
remanier [ʀ(ə)manje] *vt* to reshape, recast; (POL) to reshuffle
remarquable [ʀ(ə)maʀkabl] *adj* remarkable
remarque [ʀ(ə)maʀk] *nf* remark;

(*écrite*) note

remarquer [R(ə)maRke] *vt* (*voir*) to notice; **se ~** *vi* to be noticeable; **faire ~ (à qn) que** to point out (to sb) that; **faire ~ qch (à qn)** to point sth out (to sb); **remarquez, ...** mind you ...; **se faire ~** to draw attention to o.s.

rembourrer [Rɑ̃buRe] *vt* to stuff

remboursement [Rɑ̃buRsəmɑ̃] *nm* (*de dette, d'emprunt*) repayment; (*de frais*) refund; **rembourser** *vt* to pay back, repay; (*frais, billet etc*) to refund; **se faire rembourser** to get a refund

remède [R(ə)mɛd] *nm* (*médicament*) medicine; (*traitement, fig*) remedy, cure

remémorer [R(ə)memɔRe]: **se ~** *vt* to recall, recollect

remerciements [RəmɛRsimɑ̃] *nmpl* thanks

remercier [R(ə)mɛRsje] *vt* to thank; (*congédier*) to dismiss; **~ qn de/d'avoir fait** to thank sb for/for having done

remettre [R(ə)mɛtR] *vt* (*replacer*) to put back; (*vêtement*) to put back on; (*ajouter*) to add; (*ajourner*): **~ qch (à)** to postpone sth (until); **se ~** *vi*: **se ~ (de)** to recover (from); **~ qch à qn** (*donner: lettre, clé etc*) to hand over sth to sb; (: *prix, décoration*) to present sb with sth; **se ~ à faire qch** to start doing sth again

remise [R(ə)miz] *nf* (*rabais*) discount; (*local*) shed; **~ de peine** reduction of sentence; **~ en jeu** (*FOOTBALL*) throw-in

remontant [R(ə)mɔ̃tɑ̃, ɑ̃t] *nm* tonic, pick-me-up

remonte-pente [R(ə)mɔ̃tpɑ̃t] *nm* ski-lift

remonter [R(ə)mɔ̃te] *vi* to go back up; (*prix, température*) to go up again ♦ *vt* (*pente*) to go up; (*fleuve*) to sail (*ou* swim *etc*) up; (*manches, pantalon*) to roll up; (*col*) to turn up; (*niveau, limite*) to raise; (*fig: personne*) to buck up; (*qch de démonté*) to put back together, reassemble; (*montre*) to wind up; **~ le moral à qn** to raise sb's spirits; **~ à** (*dater de*) to date *ou* go back to

remontrance [R(ə)mɔ̃tRɑ̃s] *nf* reproof, reprimand

remontrer [R(ə)mɔ̃tRe] *vt* (*fig*): **en ~ à** to prove one's superiority over

remords [R(ə)mɔR] *nm* remorse *no pl*; **avoir des ~** to feel remorse

remorque [R(ə)mɔRk] *nf* trailer; **remorquer** *vt* to tow; **remorqueur** *nm* tug(boat)

remous [Rəmu] *nm* (*d'un navire*) (back)wash *no pl*; (*de rivière*) swirl, eddy ♦ *nmpl* (*fig*) stir *sg*

remparts [Rɑ̃paR] *nmpl* walls, ramparts

remplaçant, e [Rɑ̃plasɑ̃, ɑ̃t] *nm/f* replacement, stand-in; (*SCOL*) supply teacher

remplacement [Rɑ̃plasmɑ̃] *nm* replacement; **faire des ~s** (*professeur*) to do supply teaching; (*secrétaire*) to temp

remplacer [Rɑ̃plase] *vt* to replace; **~ qch/qn par** to replace sth/sb with

rempli, e [Rɑ̃pli] *adj* (*emploi du temps*) full, busy; **~ de** full of, filled with

remplir [Rɑ̃pliR] *vt* to fill (up); (*questionnaire*) to fill out *ou* up; (*obligations, fonction, condition*) to fulfil; **se ~** *vi* to fill up

remporter [Rɑ̃pɔRte] *vt* (*marchandise*) to take away; (*fig*) to win, achieve

remuant, e [Rəmɥɑ̃, ɑ̃t] *adj* restless

remue-ménage [R(ə)mymenaʒ] *nm inv* commotion

remuer [Rəmɥe] *vt* to move; (*café, sauce*) to stir ♦ *vi* to move; **se ~** *vi* to move; (*fam: s'activer*) to get a move on

rémunérer [RemyneRe] *vt* to remunerate

renard [R(ə)naR] *nm* fox

renchérir [Rɑ̃ʃeRiR] *vi* (*fig*): **~ (sur)** (*en paroles*) to add something (to)

rencontre [Rɑ̃kɔ̃tR] *nf* meeting; (*imprévue*) encounter; **aller à la ~ de qn** to go and meet sb; **rencontrer** *vt* to meet; (*mot, expression*) to come across; (*difficultés*) to meet with; **se rencontrer** *vi* to meet

rendement [rɑ̃dmɑ̃] *nm* (*d'un travailleur, d'une machine*) output; (*d'un champ*) yield

rendez-vous [rɑ̃devu] *nm* appointment; (*d'amoureux*) date; (*lieu*) meeting place; **donner ~-~ à qn** to arrange to meet sb; **avoir/prendre ~-~ (avec)** to have/make an appointment (with)

rendre [rɑ̃dʀ] *vt* (*restituer*) to give back, return; (*invitation*) to return, repay; (*vomir*) to bring up; (*exprimer, traduire*) to render; (*faire devenir*): **~ qn célèbre/qch possible** to make sb famous/sth possible; **se ~** *vi* (*capituler*) to surrender, give o.s. up; (*aller*): **se ~ quelque part** to go somewhere; **~ la monnaie à qn** to give sb his change; **se ~ compte de qch** to realize sth

rênes [ʀɛn] *nfpl* reins

renfermé, e [ʀɑ̃fɛʀme] *adj* (*fig*) withdrawn ♦ *nm*: **sentir le ~** to smell stuffy

renfermer [ʀɑ̃fɛʀme] *vt* to contain

renflouer [ʀɑ̃flue] *vt* to refloat; (*fig*) to set back on its (*ou* his/her *etc*) feet

renfoncement [ʀɑ̃fɔ̃smɑ̃] *nm* recess

renforcer [ʀɑ̃fɔʀse] *vt* to reinforce; **renfort**: **renforts** *nmpl* reinforcements; **à grand renfort de** with a great deal of

renfrogné, e [ʀɑ̃fʀɔɲe] *adj* sullen

rengaine [ʀɑ̃gɛn] (*péj*) *nf* old tune

renier [ʀənje] *vt* (*personne*) to disown, repudiate; (*foi*) to renounce

renifler [ʀ(ə)nifle] *vi, vt* to sniff

renne [ʀɛn] *nm* reindeer *inv*

renom [ʀənɔ̃] *nm* reputation; (*célébrité*) renown; **renommé, e** *adj* celebrated, renowned; **renommée** *nf* fame

renoncer [ʀ(ə)nɔ̃se]: **~ à** *vt* to give up; **~ à faire** to give up the idea of doing

renouer [ʀənwe] *vt*: **~ avec** (*habitude*) to take up again

renouvelable [ʀ(ə)nuv(ə)labl] *adj* (*énergie etc*) renewable

renouveler [ʀ(ə)nuv(ə)le] *vt* to renew; (*exploit, méfait*) to repeat; **se ~** *vi* (*incident*) to recur, happen again; **renouvellement** *nm* (*remplacement*) renewal

rénover [ʀenɔve] *vt* (*immeuble*) to renovate, do up; (*quartier*) to redevelop

renseignement [ʀɑ̃sɛɲmɑ̃] *nm* information *no pl*, piece of information; **(bureau des) ~s** information office

renseigner [ʀɑ̃seɲe] *vt*: **~ qn (sur)** to give information to sb (about); **se ~** *vi* to ask for information, make inquiries

rentabilité [ʀɑ̃tabilite] *nf* profitability

rentable [ʀɑ̃tabl] *adj* profitable

rente [ʀɑ̃t] *nf* private income; (*pension*) pension

rentrée [ʀɑ̃tʀe] *nf*: **~ (d'argent)** cash *no pl* coming in; **la ~ (des classes)** the start of the new school year

> **rentrée (des classes)**
>
> **La rentrée (des classes)** *in September marks an important point in the French year. Children and teachers return to school, and political and social life begin again after the long summer break.*

rentrer [ʀɑ̃tʀe] *vi* (*revenir chez soi*) to go (*ou* come) (back) home; (*entrer de nouveau*) to go (*ou* come) back in; (*entrer*) to go (*ou* come) in; (*air, clou: pénétrer*) to go in; (*revenu*) to come in ♦ *vt* to bring in; (: *véhicule*) to put away; (*chemise dans pantalon etc*) to tuck in; (*griffes*) to draw in; **~ le ventre** to pull in one's stomach; **~ dans** (*heurter*) to crash into; **~ dans l'ordre** to be back to normal; **~ dans ses frais** to recover one's expenses

renverse [ʀɑ̃vɛʀs]: **à la ~** *adv* backwards

renverser [ʀɑ̃vɛʀse] *vt* (*faire tomber: chaise, verre*) to knock over, overturn; (*liquide, contenu*) to spill, upset; (*piéton*) to knock down; (*retourner*) to turn upside down; (: *ordre des mots etc*) to reverse; (*fig: gouvernement etc*) to overthrow; (*fam: stupéfier*) to bowl over; **se ~** *vi* (*verre, vase*) to fall over; (*contenu*) to spill

renvoi [rɑ̃vwa] *nm* (*d'employé*) dismissal; (*d'élève*) expulsion; (*référence*) cross-reference; (*éructation*) belch; **renvoyer** *vt* to send back; (*congédier*) to dismiss; (*élève*: *définitivement*) to expel; (*lumière*) to reflect; (*ajourner*): **renvoyer qch (à)** to put sth off *ou* postpone sth (until)

repaire [r(ə)pɛr] *nm* den

répandre [repɑ̃dr] *vt* (*renverser*) to spill; (*étaler, diffuser*) to spread; (*odeur*) to give off; **se ~** *vi* to spill; (*se propager*) to spread; **répandu, e** *adj* (*opinion, usage*) widespread

réparation [reparasjɔ̃] *nf* repair

réparer [repare] *vt* to repair; (*fig*: *offense*) to make up for, atone for; (: *oubli, erreur*) to put right

repartie [reparti] *nf* retort; **avoir de la ~** to be quick at repartee

repartir [r(ə)partir] *vi* to leave again; (*voyageur*) to set off again; (*fig*) to get going again; **~ à zéro** to start from scratch (again)

répartir [repartir] *vt* (*pour attribuer*) to share out; (*pour disperser, disposer*) to divide up; (*poids*) to distribute; **se ~** *vt* (*travail, rôles*) to share out between themselves; **répartition** *nf* (*des richesses etc*) distribution

repas [r(ə)pɑ] *nm* meal

repassage [r(ə)pɑsaʒ] *nm* ironing

repasser [r(ə)pɑse] *vi* to come (*ou* go) back ♦ *vt* (*vêtement, tissu*) to iron; (*examen*) to retake, resit; (*film*) to show again; (*leçon*: *revoir*) to go over (again)

repêcher [r(ə)peʃe] *vt* to fish out; (*candidat*) to pass (*by inflating marks*)

repentir [rəpɑ̃tir] *nm* repentance; **se ~** *vi* to repent; **se ~ d'avoir fait qch** (*regretter*) to regret having done sth

répercussions [repɛrkysjɔ̃] *nfpl* (*fig*) repercussions

répercuter [repɛrkyte]: **se ~** *vi* (*bruit*) to reverberate; (*fig*): **se ~ sur** to have repercussions on

repère [r(ə)pɛr] *nm* mark; (*monument, événement*) landmark

repérer [r(ə)pere] *vt* (*fam*: *erreur, personne*) to spot; (: *endroit*) to locate; **se ~** *vi* to find one's way about

répertoire [repɛrtwar] *nm* (*liste*) (alphabetical) list; (*carnet*) index notebook; (*INFORM*) folder, directory; (*d'un artiste*) repertoire

répéter [repete] *vt* to repeat; (*préparer*: *leçon*) to learn, go over; (*THÉÂTRE*) to rehearse; **se ~** *vi* (*redire*) to repeat o.s.; (*se reproduire*) to be repeated, recur

répétition [repetisjɔ̃] *nf* repetition; (*THÉÂTRE*) rehearsal

répit [repi] *nm* respite

replier [r(ə)plije] *vt* (*rabattre*) to fold down *ou* over; **se ~** *vi* (*troupes, armée*) to withdraw, fall back; (*sur soi-même*) to withdraw into o.s.

réplique [replik] *nf* (*repartie, fig*) reply; (*THÉÂTRE*) line; (*copie*) replica; **répliquer** *vi* to reply; (*riposter*) to retaliate

répondeur [repɔ̃dœr, øz] *nm*: **~ automatique** (*TÉL*) answering machine

répondre [repɔ̃dr] *vi* to answer, reply; (*freins*) to respond; **~ à** to reply to, answer; (*affection, salut*) to return; (*provocation*) to respond to; (*correspondre à*: *besoin*) to answer; (: *conditions*) to meet; (: *description*) to match; (*avec impertinence*): **~ à qn** to answer sb back; **~ de** to answer for

réponse [repɔ̃s] *nf* answer, reply; **en ~ à** in reply to

reportage [r(ə)pɔrtaʒ] *nm* report; **~ en direct** (live) commentary

reporter¹ [rəpɔrtɛr] *nm* reporter

reporter² [rəpɔrte] *vt* (*ajourner*): **~ qch (à)** to postpone sth (until); (*transférer*): **~ qch sur** to transfer sth to; **se ~ à** (*époque*) to think back to; (*document*) to refer to

repos [r(ə)po] *nm* rest; (*tranquillité*) peace (and quiet); (*MIL*): **~!** stand at ease!; **ce n'est pas de tout ~!** it's no picnic!

reposant, e [r(ə)pozɑ̃, ɑ̃t] *adj* restful

reposer [R(ə)poze] *vt* (*verre, livre*) to put down; (*délasser*) to rest ♦ *vi*: **laisser ~** (*pâte*) to leave to stand; **se ~** *vi* to rest; **se ~ sur qn** to rely on sb; **~ sur** (*fig*) to rest on

repoussant, e [R(ə)pusɑ̃, ɑ̃t] *adj* repulsive

repousser [R(ə)puse] *vi* to grow again ♦ *vt* to repel, repulse; (*offre*) to turn down, reject; (*personne*) to push back; (*différer*) to put back

reprendre [R(ə)pRɑ̃dR] *vt* (*objet prêté, donné*) to take back; (*prisonnier, ville*) to recapture; (*firme, entreprise*) to take over; (*le travail*) to resume; (*emprunter: argument, idée*) to take up, use; (*refaire: article etc*) to go over again; (*vêtement*) to alter; (*réprimander*) to tell off; (*corriger*) to correct; (*chercher*): **je viendrai te ~ à 4 h** I'll come and fetch you at 4; (*se resservir de*): **~ du pain/un œuf** to take (*ou* eat) more bread/another egg ♦ *vi* (*classes, pluie*) to start (up) again; (*activités, travaux, combats*) to resume, start (up) again; (*affaires*) to pick up; (*dire*): **reprit-il** he went on; **se ~** *vi* (*se ressaisir*) to recover; **~ des forces** to recover one's strength; **~ courage** to take new heart; **~ la route** to set off again; **~ haleine** *ou* **son souffle** to get one's breath back

représailles [R(ə)pRezɑj] *nfpl* reprisals

représentant, e [R(ə)pRezɑ̃tɑ̃, ɑ̃t] *nm/f* representative

représentation [R(ə)pRezɑ̃tasjɔ̃] *nf* (*symbole, image*) representation; (*spectacle*) performance

représenter [R(ə)pRezɑ̃te] *vt* to represent; (*donner: pièce, opéra*) to perform; **se ~** *vt* (*se figurer*) to imagine

répression [RepResjɔ̃] *nf* repression

réprimer [RepRime] *vt* (*émotions*) to suppress; (*peuple etc*) to repress

repris [R(ə)pRi, iz] *nm*: **~ de justice** ex-prisoner, ex-convict

reprise [R(ə)pRiz] *nf* (*recommencement*) resumption; (*économique*) recovery; (*TV*) repeat; (*COMM*) trade-in, part exchange; (*raccommodage*) mend; **à plusieurs ~s** on several occasions

repriser [R(ə)pRize] *vt* (*chaussette, lainage*) to darn; (*tissu*) to mend

reproche [R(ə)pRɔʃ] *nm* (*remontrance*) reproach; **faire des ~s à qn** to reproach sb; **sans ~(s)** beyond reproach; **reprocher** *vt*: **reprocher qch à qn** to reproach *ou* blame sb for sth; **reprocher qch à** (*critiquer*) to have sth against

reproduction [R(ə)pRɔdyksjɔ̃] *nf* reproduction

reproduire [R(ə)pRɔdɥiR] *vt* to reproduce; **se ~** *vi* (*BIO*) to reproduce; (*recommencer*) to recur, re-occur

réprouver [RepRuve] *vt* to reprove

reptile [Rɛptil] *nm* reptile

repu, e [Rəpy] *adj* satisfied, sated

république [Repyblik] *nf* republic

répugnant, e [Repyɲɑ̃, ɑ̃t] *adj* disgusting

répugner [Repyɲe]: **~ à** *vt*: **~ à qn** to repel *ou* disgust sb; **~ à faire** to be loath *ou* reluctant to do

réputation [Repytasjɔ̃] *nf* reputation; **réputé, e** *adj* renowned

requérir [RəkeRiR] *vt* (*nécessiter*) to require, call for

requête [Rəkɛt] *nf* request

requin [Rəkɛ̃] *nm* shark

requis, e [Rəki, iz] *adj* required

RER *sigle m* (= *réseau express régional*) *Greater Paris high-speed train service*

rescapé, e [Rɛskape] *nm/f* survivor

rescousse [Rɛskus] *nf*: **aller à la ~ de qn** to go to sb's aid *ou* rescue

réseau, x [Rezo] *nm* network

réservation [RezɛRvasjɔ̃] *nf* booking, reservation

réserve [RezɛRv] *nf* (*retenue*) reserve; (*entrepôt*) storeroom; (*restriction, d'Indiens*) reservation; (*de pêche, chasse*) preserve; **de ~** (*provisions etc*) in reserve

réservé, e [RezɛRve] *adj* reserved;

chasse/pêche ~e private hunting/ fishing
réserver [ʀezɛʀve] *vt* to reserve; (*chambre, billet etc*) to book, reserve; (*fig: destiner*) to have in store; (*garder*): **~ qch pour/à** to keep *ou* save sth for
réservoir [ʀezɛʀvwaʀ] *nm* tank
résidence [ʀezidɑ̃s] *nf* residence; **~ secondaire** second home; **résidentiel, le** *adj* residential; **résider** *vi*: **résider à/dans/en** to reside in; **résider dans** (*fig*) to lie in
résidu [ʀezidy] *nm* residue *no pl*
résigner [ʀeziɲe]: **se ~** *vi*: **se ~ (à qch/à faire)** to resign o.s. (to sth/to doing)
résilier [ʀezilje] *vt* to terminate
résistance [ʀezistɑ̃s] *nf* resistance; (*de réchaud, bouilloire: fil*) element
résistant, e [ʀezistɑ̃, ɑ̃t] *adj* (*personne*) robust, tough; (*matériau*) strong, hard-wearing
résister [ʀeziste] *vi* to resist; **~ à** (*assaut, tentation*) to resist; (*supporter: gel etc*) to withstand; (*désobéir à*) to stand up to, oppose
résolu, e [ʀezɔly] *pp de* **résoudre** ♦ *adj*: **être ~ à qch/faire** to be set upon sth/doing
résolution [ʀezɔlysjɔ̃] *nf* (*fermeté, décision*) resolution; (*d'un problème*) solution
résolve *etc* [ʀesɔlv] *vb voir* **résoudre**
résonner [ʀezɔne] *vi* (*cloche, pas*) to reverberate, resound; (*salle*) to be resonant
résorber [ʀezɔʀbe]: **se ~** *vi* (*fig: chômage*) to be reduced; (*: déficit*) to be absorbed
résoudre [ʀezudʀ] *vt* to solve; **se ~ à faire** to bring o.s. to do
respect [ʀɛspɛ] *nm* respect; **tenir en ~** to keep at bay; **respecter** *vt* to respect; **respectueux, -euse** *adj* respectful
respiration [ʀɛspiʀasjɔ̃] *nf* breathing *no pl*
respirer [ʀɛspiʀe] *vi* to breathe; (*fig: se détendre*) to get one's breath; (*: se rassurer*) to breathe again ♦ *vt* to breathe (in), inhale; (*manifester: santé, calme etc*) to exude
resplendir [ʀɛsplɑ̃diʀ] *vi* to shine; (*fig*): **~ (de)** to be radiant (with)
responsabilité [ʀɛspɔ̃sabilite] *nf* responsibility; (*légale*) liability
responsable [ʀɛspɔ̃sabl] *adj* responsible ♦ *nm/f* (*coupable*) person responsible; (*personne compétente*) person in charge; (*de parti, syndicat*) official; **~ de** responsible for
resquiller [ʀɛskije] (*fam*) *vi* to get in without paying; (*ne pas faire la queue*) to jump the queue
ressaisir [ʀ(ə)seziʀ]: **se ~** *vi* to regain one's self-control
ressasser [ʀ(ə)sase] *vt* to keep going over
ressemblance [ʀ(ə)sɑ̃blɑ̃s] *nf* resemblance, similarity, likeness
ressemblant, e [ʀ(ə)sɑ̃blɑ̃, ɑ̃t] *adj* (*portrait*) lifelike, true to life
ressembler [ʀ(ə)sɑ̃ble]: **~ à** *vt* to be like, resemble; (*visuellement*) to look like; **se ~** *vi* to be (*ou* look) alike
ressemeler [ʀ(ə)səm(ə)le] *vt* to (re)sole
ressentiment [ʀ(ə)sɑ̃timɑ̃] *nm* resentment
ressentir [ʀ(ə)sɑ̃tiʀ] *vt* to feel
resserrer [ʀ(ə)seʀe] *vt* (*nœud, boulon*) to tighten (up); (*fig: liens*) to strengthen
resservir [ʀ(ə)sɛʀviʀ] *vi* to do *ou* serve again; **se ~** *vi* to help o.s. again
ressort [ʀəsɔʀ] *nm* (*pièce*) spring; (*énergie*) spirit; (*recours*): **en dernier ~** as a last resort; (*compétence*): **être du ~ de** to fall within the competence of
ressortir [ʀəsɔʀtiʀ] *vi* to go (*ou* come) out (again); (*contraster*) to stand out; **~ de** to emerge from; **faire ~** (*fig: souligner*) to bring out
ressortissant, e [ʀ(ə)sɔʀtisɑ̃, ɑ̃t] *nm/f*

national

ressources [R(ə)suRs] *nfpl* (*moyens*) resources

ressusciter [Resysite] *vt* (*fig*) to revive, bring back ♦ *vi* to rise (from the dead)

restant, e [Rɛstɑ̃, ɑ̃t] *adj* remaining ♦ *nm*: **le ~ (de)** the remainder (of); **un ~ de** (*de trop*) some left-over

restaurant [RɛstɔRɑ̃] *nm* restaurant

restauration [RɛstɔRasjɔ̃] *nf* restoration; (*hôtellerie*) catering; **~ rapide** fast food

restaurer [RɛstɔRe] *vt* to restore; **se ~** *vi* to have something to eat

reste [Rɛst] *nm* (*restant*): **le ~ (de)** the rest (of); (*de trop*): **un ~ (de)** some left-over; **~s** *nmpl* (*nourriture*) left-overs; (*d'une cité etc, dépouille mortelle*) remains; **du ~, au ~** besides, moreover

rester [Rɛste] *vi* to stay, remain; (*subsister*) to remain, be left; (*durer*) to last, live on ♦ *vb impers*: **il reste du pain/2 œufs** there's some bread/there are 2 eggs left (over); **restons-en là** let's leave it at that; **il me reste assez de temps** I have enough time left; **il ne me reste plus qu'à** ... I've just got to ...

restituer [Rɛstitɥe] *vt* (*objet, somme*): **~ qch (à qn)** to return sth (to sb)

restreindre [RɛstRɛ̃dR] *vt* to restrict, limit

restriction [RɛstRiksjɔ̃] *nf* restriction

résultat [Rezylta] *nm* result; (*d'examen, d'élection*) results *pl*

résulter [Rezylte]: **~ de** *vt* to result from, be the result of

résumé [Rezyme] *nm* summary, résumé

résumer [Rezyme] *vt* (*texte*) to summarize; (*récapituler*) to sum up

résurrection [RezyRɛksjɔ̃] *nf* resurrection

rétablir [RetabliR] *vt* to restore, re-establish; **se ~** *vi* (*guérir*) to recover; (*silence, calme*) to return, be restored; **rétablissement** *nm* restoring; (*guérison*) recovery

retaper [R(ə)tape] (*fam*) *vt* (*maison, voiture etc*) to do up; (*revigorer*) to buck up

retard [R(ə)taR] *nm* (*d'une personne attendue*) lateness *no pl*; (*sur l'horaire, un programme*) delay; (*fig*: *scolaire, mental etc*) backwardness; **en ~ (de 2 heures)** (2 hours) late; **avoir du ~** to be late; (*sur un programme*) to be behind (schedule); **prendre du ~** (*train, avion*) to be delayed; **sans ~** without delay

retardataire [R(ə)taRdatɛR] *nmf* latecomer

retardement [R(ə)taRdəmɑ̃]: **à ~** *adj* delayed action *cpd*; **bombe à ~** time bomb

retarder [R(ə)taRde] *vt* to delay; (*montre*) to put back ♦ *vi* (*montre*) to be slow; **~ qn (d'une heure)** (*sur un horaire*) to delay sb (an hour); **~ qch (de 2 jours)** (*départ, date*) to put sth back (2 days)

retenir [Rət(ə)niR] *vt* (*garder, retarder*) to keep, detain; (*maintenir*: *objet qui glisse, fig*: *colère, larmes*) to hold back; (*se rappeler*) to retain; (*réserver*) to reserve; (*accepter*: *proposition etc*) to accept; (*fig*: *empêcher d'agir*): **~ qn (de faire)** to hold sb back (from doing); (*prélever*): **~ qch (sur)** to deduct sth (from); **se ~** *vi* (*se raccrocher*): **se ~ à** to hold onto; (*se contenir*): **se ~ de faire** to restrain o.s. from doing; **~ son souffle** to hold one's breath

retentir [R(ə)tɑ̃tiR] *vi* to ring out; (*salle*): **~ de** to ring *ou* resound with; **retentissant, e** *adj* resounding; **retentissement** *nm* repercussion

retenu, e [Rət(ə)ny] *adj* (*place*) reserved; (*personne*: *empêché*) held up; **retenue** *nf* (*prélèvement*) deduction; (*SCOL*) detention; (*modération*) (self-) restraint

réticence [Retisɑ̃s] *nf* hesitation, reluctance *no pl*; **réticent, e** *adj* hesitant, reluctant

rétine [Retin] *nf* retina
retiré, e [R(ə)tiRe] *adj* (*vie*) secluded; (*lieu*) remote
retirer [R(ə)tiRe] *vt* (*vêtement, lunettes*) to take off, remove; (*argent, plainte*) to withdraw; (*reprendre*: *bagages, billets*) to collect, pick up; (*extraire*): **~ qch de** to take sth out of, remove sth from
retombées [Rətɔ̃be] *nfpl* (*radioactives*) fallout *sg*; (*fig*: *répercussions*) effects
retomber [R(ə)tɔ̃be] *vi* (*à nouveau*) to fall again; (*atterrir*: *après un saut etc*) to land; (*échoir*): **~ sur qn** to fall on sb
rétorquer [RetɔRke] *vt*: **~ (à qn) que** to retort (to sb) that
retouche [R(ə)tuʃ] *nf* (*sur vêtement*) alteration; **retoucher** *vt* (*photographie*) to touch up; (*texte, vêtement*) to alter
retour [R(ə)tuR] *nm* return; **au ~** (*en route*) on the way back; **à mon ~** when I get/got back; **être de ~ (de)** to be back (from); **par ~ du courrier** by return of post
retourner [R(ə)tuRne] *vt* (*dans l'autre sens*: *matelas, crêpe etc*) to turn (over); (: *sac, vêtement*) to turn inside out; (*fam*: *bouleverser*) to shake; (*renvoyer, restituer*): **~ qch à qn** to return sth to sb ♦ *vi* (*aller, revenir*): **~ quelque part/ à** to go back *ou* return somewhere/to; **se ~** *vi* (*tourner la tête*) to turn round; **~ à** (*état, activité*) to return to, go back to; **se ~ contre** (*fig*) to turn against
retrait [R(ə)tRɛ] *nm* (*d'argent*) withdrawal; **en ~** set back; **~ du permis (de conduire)** disqualification from driving (*BRIT*), revocation of driver's license (*US*)
retraite [R(ə)tRɛt] *nf* (*d'un employé*) retirement; (*revenu*) pension; (*d'une armée, REL*) retreat; **prendre sa ~** to retire; **~ anticipée** early retirement; **retraité, e** *adj* retired ♦ *nm/f* pensioner
retrancher [R(ə)tRɑ̃ʃe] *vt* (*nombre, somme*): **~ qch de** to take *ou* deduct sth from; **se ~ derrière/dans** to take refuge behind/in
retransmettre [R(ə)tRɑ̃smɛtR] *vt* (*RADIO*) to broadcast; (*TV*) to show
rétrécir [RetResiR] *vt* (*vêtement*) to take in ♦ *vi* to shrink
rétribution [Retribysj ɔ̃] *nf* payment
rétro [RetRo] *adj inv*: **la mode ~** the nostalgia vogue
rétrograde [RetRɔgRad] *adj* reactionary, backward-looking
rétroprojecteur [RetRopRɔʒɛktœR] *nm* overhead projector
rétrospective [RetRɔspɛktiv] *nf* retrospective exhibition/season; **rétrospectivement** *adv* in retrospect
retrousser [R(ə)tRuse] *vt* to roll up
retrouvailles [R(ə)tRuvɑj] *nfpl* reunion *sg*
retrouver [R(ə)tRuve] *vt* (*fugitif, objet perdu*) to find; (*calme, santé*) to regain; (*revoir*) to see again; (*rejoindre*) to meet (again), join; **se ~** *vi* to meet; (*s'orienter*) to find one's way; **se ~ quelque part** to find o.s. somewhere; **s'y ~** (*y voir clair*) to make sense of it; (*rentrer dans ses frais*) to break even
rétroviseur [RetRɔvizœR] *nm* (rear-view) mirror
réunion [Reynjɔ̃] *nf* (*séance*) meeting
réunir [ReyniR] *vt* (*rassembler*) to gather together; (*inviter*: *amis, famille*) to have round, have in; (*cumuler*: *qualités etc*) to combine; (*rapprocher*: *ennemis*) to bring together (again), reunite; (*rattacher*: *parties*) to join (together); **se ~** *vi* (*se rencontrer*) to meet
réussi, e [Reysi] *adj* successful
réussir [ReysiR] *vi* to succeed, be successful; (*à un examen*) to pass ♦ *vt* to make a success of; **~ à faire** to succeed in doing; **~ à qn** (*être bénéfique à*) to agree with sb; **réussite** *nf* success; (*CARTES*) patience
revaloir [R(ə)valwaR] *vt*: **je vous revaudrai cela** I'll repay you some day; (*en mal*) I'll pay you back for this
revanche [R(ə)vɑ̃ʃ] *nf* revenge; (*sport*) revenge match; **en ~** on the other

hand

rêve [RɛV] *nm* dream; **de ~** dream *cpd*; **faire un ~** to have a dream

revêche [Rəvɛʃ] *adj* surly, sour-tempered

réveil [Revɛj] *nm* waking up *no pl*; (*fig*) awakening; (*pendule*) alarm (clock); **au ~** on waking (up); **réveille-matin** *nm inv* alarm clock; **réveiller** *vt* (*personne*) to wake up; (*fig*) to awaken, revive; **se réveiller** *vi* to wake up

réveillon [Revɛjɔ̃] *nm* Christmas Eve; (*de la Saint-Sylvestre*) New Year's Eve; **réveillonner** *vi* to celebrate Christmas Eve (*ou* New Year's Eve)

révélateur, -trice [RevelatœR, tRis] *adj*: **~ (de qch)** revealing (sth)

révéler [Revele] *vt* to reveal; **se ~** *vi* to be revealed, reveal itself ♦ *vb +attrib*: **se ~ difficile/aisé** to prove difficult/easy

revenant, e [R(ə)vənɑ̃, ɑ̃t] *nm/f* ghost

revendeur, -euse [R(ə)vɑ̃dœR, øz] *nm/f* (*détaillant*) retailer; (*de drogue*) (drug-)dealer

revendication [R(ə)vɑ̃dikasjɔ̃] *nf* claim, demand

revendiquer [R(ə)vɑ̃dike] *vt* to claim, demand; (*responsabilité*) to claim

revendre [R(ə)vɑ̃dR] *vt* (*d'occasion*) to resell; (*détailler*) to sell; **à ~** (*en abondance*) to spare

revenir [Rəv(ə)niR] *vi* to come back; (*coûter*): **~ cher/à 100 F (à qn)** to cost (sb) a lot/100 F; **~ à** (*reprendre*: *études, projet*) to return to, go back to; (*équivaloir à*) to amount to; **~ à qn** (*part, honneur*) to go to sb, be sb's; (*souvenir, nom*) to come back to sb; **~ sur** (*question, sujet*) to go back over; (*engagement*) to go back on; **~ à soi** to come round; **n'en pas ~**: **je n'en reviens pas** I can't get over it; **~ sur ses pas** to retrace one's steps; **cela revient à dire que/au même** it amounts to saying that/the same thing; **faire ~** (CULIN) to brown

revenu [Rəv(ə)ny] *nm* income; **~s** *nmpl* income *sg*

rêver [Reve] *vi, vt* to dream; **~ de/à** to dream of

réverbère [RevɛRbɛR] *nm* street lamp *ou* light; **réverbérer** *vt* to reflect

révérence [RevɛRɑ̃s] *nf* (*salut*) bow; (: *de femme*) curtsey

rêverie [RɛvRi] *nf* daydreaming *no pl*, daydream

revers [R(ə)vɛR] *nm* (*de feuille, main*) back; (*d'étoffe*) wrong side; (*de pièce, médaille*) back, reverse; (TENNIS, PING-PONG) backhand; (*de veste*) lapel; (*fig*: *échec*) setback

revêtement [R(ə)vɛtmɑ̃] *nm* (*des sols*) flooring; (*de chaussée*) surface

revêtir [R(ə)vetiR] *vt* (*habit*) to don, put on; (*prendre*: *importance, apparence*) to take on; **~ qch de** to cover sth with

rêveur, -euse [RɛvœR, øz] *adj* dreamy ♦ *nm/f* dreamer

revient [Rəvjɛ̃] *vb voir* **revenir**

revigorer [R(ə)vigɔRe] *vt* (*air frais*) to invigorate, brace up; (*repas, boisson*) to revive, buck up

revirement [R(ə)viRmɑ̃] *nm* change of mind; (*d'une situation*) reversal

réviser [Revize] *vt* to revise; (*machine*) to overhaul, service

révision [Revizjɔ̃] *nf* revision; (*de voiture*) servicing *no pl*

revivre [R(ə)vivR] *vi* (*reprendre des forces*) to come alive again ♦ *vt* (*épreuve, moment*) to relive

revoir [RəvwaR] *vt* to see again; (*réviser*) to revise ♦ *nm*: **au ~** goodbye

révoltant, e [Revɔltɑ̃, ɑ̃t] *adj* revolting, appalling

révolte [Revɔlt] *nf* rebellion, revolt

révolter [Revɔlte] *vt* to revolt; **se ~ (contre)** to rebel (against); **ça me révolte (de voir que ...)** I'm revolted *ou* appalled (to see that ...)

révolu, e [Revɔly] *adj* past; (ADMIN): **âgé de 18 ans ~s** over 18 years of age

révolution [Revɔlysjɔ̃] *nf* revolution; **révolutionnaire** *adj, nm/f* revolutionary

revolver [ʀevɔlvɛʀ] *nm* gun; (*à barillet*) revolver

révoquer [ʀevɔke] *vt* (*fonctionnaire*) to dismiss; (*arrêt, contrat*) to revoke

revue [ʀ(ə)vy] *nf* review; (*périodique*) review, magazine; (*de music-hall*) variety show; **passer en ~** (*mentalement*) to go through

rez-de-chaussée [ʀed(ə)ʃose] *nm inv* ground floor

RF *sigle f* = **République française**

Rhin [ʀɛ̃] *nm* Rhine

rhinocéros [ʀinɔseʀɔs] *nm* rhinoceros

Rhône [ʀon] *nm* Rhone

rhubarbe [ʀybaʀb] *nf* rhubarb

rhum [ʀɔm] *nm* rum

rhumatisme [ʀymatism] *nm* rheumatism *no pl*

rhume [ʀym] *nm* cold; **~ de cerveau** head cold; **le ~ des foins** hay fever

ri [ʀi] *pp de* **rire**

riant, e [ʀ(i)jɑ̃, ʀ(i)jɑ̃t] *adj* smiling, cheerful

ricaner [ʀikane] *vi* (*avec méchanceté*) to snigger; (*bêtement*) to giggle

riche [ʀiʃ] *adj* rich; (*personne, pays*) rich, wealthy; **~ en** rich in; **richesse** *nf* wealth; (*fig: de sol, musée etc*) richness; **richesses** *nfpl* (*ressources, argent*) wealth *sg*; (*fig: trésors*) treasures

ricochet [ʀikɔʃɛ] *nm*: **faire des ~s** to skip stones; **par ~** (*fig*) as an indirect result

rictus [ʀiktys] *nm* grin

ride [ʀid] *nf* wrinkle

rideau, x [ʀido] *nm* curtain; **~ de fer** (*boutique*) metal shutter(s)

rider [ʀide] *vt* to wrinkle; **se ~** *vi* to become wrinkled

ridicule [ʀidikyl] *adj* ridiculous ♦ *nm*: **le ~** ridicule; **ridiculiser**: **se ridiculiser** *vi* to make a fool of o.s.

MOT-CLÉ

rien [ʀjɛ̃] *pron* **1**: **(ne) ... rien** nothing; *tournure negative + anything*; **qu'est-ce que vous avez? – rien** what have you got? – nothing; **il n'a rien dit/fait** he said/did nothing; he hasn't said/done anything; **il n'a rien** (*n'est pas blessé*) he's all right; **de rien!** not at all!

2 (*quelque chose*): **a-t-il jamais rien fait pour nous?** has he ever done anything for us?

3: **rien de**: **rien d'intéressant** nothing interesting; **rien d'autre** nothing else; **rien du tout** nothing at all

4: **rien que** just, only; nothing but; **rien que pour lui faire plaisir** only *ou* just to please him; **rien que la vérité** nothing but the truth; **rien que cela** that alone

♦ *nm*: **un petit rien** (*cadeau*) a little something; **des riens** trivia *pl*; **un rien de** a hint of; **en un rien de temps** in no time at all

rieur, -euse [ʀ(i)jœʀ, ʀ(i)jøz] *adj* cheerful

rigide [ʀiʒid] *adj* stiff; (*fig*) rigid; strict

rigole [ʀigɔl] *nf* (*conduit*) channel

rigoler [ʀigɔle] *vi* (*fam: rire*) to laugh; (*s'amuser*) to have (some) fun; (*plaisanter*) to be joking *ou* kidding; **rigolo, -ote** (*fam*) *adj* funny ♦ *nm/f* comic; (*péj*) fraud, phoney

rigoureusement [ʀiguʀøzmɑ̃] *adv* (*vrai*) absolutely; (*interdit*) strictly

rigoureux, -euse [ʀiguʀø, øz] *adj* rigorous; (*hiver*) hard, harsh

rigueur [ʀigœʀ] *nf* rigour; **être de ~** to be the rule; **à la ~** at a pinch; **tenir ~ à qn de qch** to hold sth against sb

rillettes [ʀijɛt] *nfpl* potted meat (*made from pork or goose*)

rime [ʀim] *nf* rhyme

rinçage [ʀɛ̃saʒ] *nm* rinsing (out); (*opération*) rinse

rincer [ʀɛ̃se] *vt* to rinse; (*récipient*) to rinse out

ring [ʀiŋ] *nm* (boxing) ring

ringard, e [ʀɛ̃gaʀ, aʀd] (*fam*) *adj* old-fashioned

rions [ʀjɔ̃] *vb voir* **rire**

riposter [ʀipɔste] *vi* to retaliate ♦ *vt*: **~ que** to retort that

rire [ʀiʀ] *vi* to laugh; (*se divertir*) to have fun ♦ *nm* laugh; **le ~** laughter; **~ de** to laugh at; **pour ~** (*pas sérieusement*) for a joke *ou* a laugh

risée [ʀize] *nf*: **être la ~ de** to be the laughing stock of

risible [ʀizibl] *adj* laughable

risque [ʀisk] *nm* risk; **le ~** danger; **à ses ~s et périls** at his own risk; **risqué, e** *adj* risky; (*plaisanterie*) risqué, daring; **risquer** *vt* to risk; (*allusion, question*) to venture, hazard; **ça ne risque rien** it's quite safe; **risquer de: il risque de se tuer** he could get himself killed; **ce qui risque de se produire** what might *ou* could well happen; **il ne risque pas de recommencer** there's no chance of him doing that again; **se risquer à faire** (*tenter*) to venture *ou* dare to do

rissoler [ʀisɔle] *vi, vt*: **(faire) ~** to brown

ristourne [ʀistuʀn] *nf* discount

rite [ʀit] *nm* rite; (*fig*) ritual

rivage [ʀivaʒ] *nm* shore

rival, e, -aux [ʀival, o] *adj, nm/f* rival; **rivaliser** *vi*: **rivaliser avec** (*personne*) to rival, vie with; **rivalité** *nf* rivalry

rive [ʀiv] *nf* shore; (*de fleuve*) bank; **riverain, e** *nm/f* riverside (*ou* lakeside) resident; (*d'une route*) local resident

rivet [ʀivɛ] *nm* rivet

rivière [ʀivjɛʀ] *nf* river

rixe [ʀiks] *nf* brawl, scuffle

riz [ʀi] *nm* rice; **rizière** *nf* paddy-field, ricefield

RMI *sigle m* (= *revenu minimum d'insertion*) ≃ income support (*BRIT*), welfare (*US*)

RN *sigle f* = **route nationale**

robe [ʀɔb] *nf* dress; (*de juge*) robe; (*pelage*) coat; **~ de chambre** dressing gown; **~ de soirée/de mariée** evening/wedding dress

robinet [ʀɔbinɛ] *nm* tap

robot [ʀɔbo] *nm* robot

robuste [ʀɔbyst] *adj* robust, sturdy; **robustesse** *nf* robustness, sturdiness

roc [ʀɔk] *nm* rock

rocade [ʀɔkad] *nf* bypass

rocaille [ʀɔkaj] *nf* loose stones *pl*; (*jardin*) rockery, rock garden

roche [ʀɔʃ] *nf* rock

rocher [ʀɔʃe] *nm* rock

rocheux, -euse [ʀɔʃø, øz] *adj* rocky

rodage [ʀɔdaʒ] *nm*: **en ~** running in

roder [ʀɔde] *vt* (*AUTO*) to run in

rôder [ʀode] *vi* to roam about; (*de façon suspecte*) to lurk (about *ou* around); **rôdeur, -euse** *nm/f* prowler

rogne [ʀɔɲ] (*fam*) *nf*: **être en ~** to be in a temper

rogner [ʀɔɲe] *vt* to clip; **~ sur** (*fig*) to cut down *ou* back on

rognons [ʀɔɲɔ̃] *nmpl* (*CULIN*) kidneys

roi [ʀwa] *nm* king; **la fête des R~s, les R~s** Twelfth Night

fête des Rois

La fête des Rois *is celebrated on January 6. Figurines representing the magi are traditionally added to the Christmas crib and people eat* **la galette des Rois**, *a plain, flat cake in which a porcelain charm (***la fève***) is hidden. Whoever finds the charm is king or queen for the day and chooses a partner.*

rôle [ʀol] *nm* role, part

romain, e [ʀɔmɛ̃, ɛn] *adj* Roman ♦ *nm/f*: **R~, e** Roman

roman, e [ʀɔmɑ̃, an] *adj* (*ARCHIT*) Romanesque ♦ *nm* novel; **~ d'espionnage** spy novel *ou* story; **~ policier** detective story

romance [ʀɔmɑ̃s] *nf* ballad

romancer [ʀɔmɑ̃se] *vt* (*agrémenter*) to romanticize; **romancier, -ière** *nm/f* novelist; **romanesque** *adj* (*amours, aventures*) storybook *cpd*; (*sentimental:*

personne) romantic
roman-feuilleton [ʀɔmɑ̃fœjtɔ̃] *nm* serialized novel
romanichel, le [ʀɔmaniʃɛl] (*péj*) *nm/f* gipsy
romantique [ʀɔmɑ̃tik] *adj* romantic
romarin [ʀɔmaʀɛ̃] *nm* rosemary
rompre [ʀɔ̃pʀ] *vt* to break; (*entretien, fiançailles*) to break off ♦ *vi* (*fiancés*) to break it off; **se ~** *vi* to break; **rompu, e** *adj* (*fourbu*) exhausted
ronces [ʀɔ̃s] *nfpl* brambles
ronchonner [ʀɔ̃ʃɔne] (*fam*) *vi* to grouse, grouch
rond, e [ʀɔ̃, ʀɔ̃d] *adj* round; (*joues, mollets*) well-rounded; (*fam: ivre*) tight ♦ *nm* (*cercle*) ring; (*fam: sou*): **je n'ai plus un ~** I haven't a penny left; **en ~** (*s'asseoir, danser*) in a ring; **ronde** *nf* (*gén: de surveillance*) rounds *pl*, patrol; (*danse*) round (dance); (*MUS*) semibreve (*BRIT*), whole note (*US*); **à la ronde** (*alentour*): **à 10 km à la ronde** for 10 km round; **rondelet, te** *adj* plump
rondelle [ʀɔ̃dɛl] *nf* (*tranche*) slice, round; (*TECH*) washer
rondement [ʀɔ̃dmɑ̃] *adv* (*efficacement*) briskly
rondin [ʀɔ̃dɛ̃] *nm* log
rond-point [ʀɔ̃pwɛ̃] *nm* roundabout
ronflant, e [ʀɔ̃flɑ̃, ɑ̃t] (*péj*) *adj* high-flown, grand
ronflement [ʀɔ̃fləmɑ̃] *nm* snore, snoring
ronfler [ʀɔ̃fle] *vi* to snore; (*moteur, poêle*) to hum
ronger [ʀɔ̃ʒe] *vt* to gnaw (at); (*suj: vers, rouille*) to eat into; **se ~ les ongles** to bite one's nails; **se ~ les sangs** to worry o.s. sick; **rongeur** *nm* rodent
ronronner [ʀɔ̃ʀɔne] *vi* to purr
rosace [ʀozas] *nf* (*vitrail*) rose window
rosbif [ʀɔsbif] *nm*: **du ~** roasting beef; (*cuit*) roast beef
rose [ʀoz] *nf* rose ♦ *adj* pink
rosé, e [ʀoze] *adj* pinkish; **(vin) ~** rosé
roseau, x [ʀozo] *nm* reed
rosée [ʀoze] *nf* dew
rosette [ʀozɛt] *nf* (*nœud*) bow
rosier [ʀozje] *nm* rosebush, rose tree
rosse [ʀɔs] (*fam*) *adj* nasty, vicious
rossignol [ʀɔsiɲɔl] *nm* (*ZOOL*) nightingale
rot [ʀo] *nm* belch; (*de bébé*) burp
rotatif, -ive [ʀɔtatif, iv] *adj* rotary
rotation [ʀɔtasjɔ̃] *nf* rotation
roter [ʀɔte] (*fam*) *vi* to burp, belch
rôti [ʀoti] *nm*: **du ~** roasting meat; (*cuit*) roast meat; **~ de bœuf/porc** joint of beef/pork
rotin [ʀɔtɛ̃] *nm* rattan (cane); **fauteuil en ~** cane (arm)chair
rôtir [ʀotiʀ] *vi, vt* (*aussi:* **faire ~**) to roast; **rôtisserie** *nf* (*restaurant*) steakhouse; (*traiteur*) roast meat shop; **rôtissoire** *nf* (roasting) spit
rotule [ʀɔtyl] *nf* kneecap
roturier, -ière [ʀɔtyʀje, jɛʀ] *nm/f* commoner
rouage [ʀwaʒ] *nm* cog(wheel), gearwheel; **les ~s de l'État** the wheels of State
roucouler [ʀukule] *vi* to coo
roue [ʀu] *nf* wheel; **~ de secours** spare wheel
roué, e [ʀwe] *adj* wily
rouer [ʀwe] *vt*: **~ qn de coups** to give sb a thrashing
rouge [ʀuʒ] *adj, nm/f* red ♦ *nm* red; **(vin) ~** red wine; **sur la liste ~** ex-directory (*BRIT*), unlisted (*US*); **passer au ~** (*signal*) to go red; (*automobiliste*) to go through a red light; **~ (à lèvres)** lipstick; **rouge-gorge** *nm* robin (redbreast)
rougeole [ʀuʒɔl] *nf* measles *sg*
rougeoyer [ʀuʒwaje] *vi* to glow red
rouget [ʀuʒɛ] *nm* mullet
rougeur [ʀuʒœʀ] *nf* redness; (*MÉD: tache*) red blotch
rougir [ʀuʒiʀ] *vi* to turn red; (*de honte, timidité*) to blush, flush; (*de plaisir, colère*) to flush
rouille [ʀuj] *nf* rust; **rouillé, e** *adj*

rusty; **rouiller** *vt* to rust ♦ *vi* to rust, go rusty; **se rouiller** *vi* to rust

roulant, e [rulɑ̃, ɑ̃t] *adj* (*meuble*) on wheels; (*tapis etc*) moving; **escalier ~** escalator

rouleau, x [rulo] *nm* roll; (*à mise en plis, à peinture, vague*) roller; **~ à pâtisserie** rolling pin

roulement [rulmɑ̃] *nm* (*rotation*) rotation; (*bruit*) rumbling *no pl*, rumble; **travailler par ~** to work on a rota (*BRIT*) *ou* rotation (*US*) basis; **~ (à billes)** ball bearings *pl*; **~ de tambour** drum roll

rouler [rule] *vt* to roll; (*papier, tapis*) to roll up; (*CULIN*: *pâte*) to roll out; (*fam*: *duper*) to do, con ♦ *vi* (*bille, boule*) to roll; (*voiture, train*) to go, run; (*automobiliste*) to drive; (*bateau*) to roll; **se ~ dans** (*boue*) to roll in; (*couverture*) to roll o.s. (up) in

roulette [rulɛt] *nf* (*de table, fauteuil*) castor; (*de dentiste*) drill; (*jeu*) roulette; **à ~s** on castors; **ça a marché comme sur des ~s** (*fam*) it went off very smoothly

roulis [ruli] *nm* roll(ing)

roulotte [rulɔt] *nf* caravan

roumain, e [rumɛ̃, ɛn] *adj* Rumanian ♦ *nm/f*: **R~, e** Rumanian

Roumanie [rumani] *nf* Rumania

rouquin, e [rukɛ̃, in] (*péj*) *nm/f* redhead

rouspéter [ruspete] (*fam*) *vi* to moan

rousse [rus] *adj voir* **roux**

roussir [rusir] *vt* to scorch ♦ *vi* (*CULIN*): **faire ~** to brown

route [rut] *nf* road; (*fig*: *chemin*) way; (*itinéraire, parcours*) route; (*fig*: *voie*) road, path; **il y a 3h de ~** it's a 3-hour ride *ou* journey; **en ~** on the way; **mettre en ~** to start up; **se mettre en ~** to set off; **~ nationale** ≃ A road (*BRIT*), ≃ state highway (*US*); **routier, -ière** *adj* road *cpd* ♦ *nm* (*camionneur*) (long-distance) lorry (*BRIT*) *ou* truck (*US*) driver; (*restaurant*) ≃ transport café (*BRIT*), ≃ truck stop (*US*)

routine [rutin] *nf* routine; **routinier, -ière** (*péj*) *adj* (*activité*) humdrum; (*personne*) addicted to routine

rouvrir [ruvrir] *vt, vi* to reopen, open again; **se ~** *vi* to reopen, open again

roux, rousse [ru, rus] *adj* red; (*personne*) red-haired ♦ *nm/f* redhead

royal, e, -aux [rwajal, o] *adj* royal; (*cadeau etc*) fit for a king

royaume [rwajom] *nm* kingdom; (*fig*) realm; **le R~-Uni** the United Kingdom

royauté [rwajote] *nf* (*régime*) monarchy

RPR *sigle m*: **Rassemblement pour la République** *French right-wing political party*

ruban [rybɑ̃] *nm* ribbon; **~ adhésif** adhesive tape

rubéole [rybeɔl] *nf* German measles *sg*, rubella

rubis [rybi] *nm* ruby

rubrique [rybrik] *nf* (*titre, catégorie*) heading; (*PRESSE*: *article*) column

ruche [ryʃ] *nf* hive

rude [ryd] *adj* (*au toucher*) rough; (*métier, tâche*) hard, tough; (*climat*) severe, harsh; (*bourru*) harsh, rough; (*fruste*: *manières*) rugged, tough; (*fam*: *fameux*) jolly good; **rudement** (*fam*) *adv* (*très*) terribly

rudimentaire [rydimɑ̃tɛr] *adj* rudimentary, basic

rudiments [rydimɑ̃] *nmpl*: **avoir des ~ d'anglais** to have a smattering of English

rudoyer [rydwaje] *vt* to treat harshly

rue [ry] *nf* street

ruée [rɥe] *nf* rush

ruelle [rɥɛl] *nf* alley(-way)

ruer [rɥe] *vi* (*cheval*) to kick out; **se ~** *vi*: **se ~ sur** to pounce on; **se ~ vers/dans/hors de** to rush *ou* dash towards/into/out of

rugby [rygbi] *nm* rugby (football)

rugir [ryʒir] *vi* to roar

rugueux, -euse [rygø, øz] *adj* rough

ruine [ʀɥin] *nf* ruin; **ruiner** *vt* to ruin; **ruineux, -euse** *adj* ruinous
ruisseau, x [ʀɥiso] *nm* stream, brook
ruisseler [ʀɥis(ə)le] *vi* to stream
rumeur [ʀymœʀ] *nf* (*nouvelle*) rumour; (*bruit confus*) rumbling
ruminer [ʀymine] *vt* (*herbe*) to ruminate; (*fig*) to ruminate on *ou* over, chew over
rupture [ʀyptyʀ] *nf* (*séparation, désunion*) break-up, split; (*de négociations etc*) breakdown; (*de contrat*) breach; (*dans continuité*) break
rural, e, -aux [ʀyʀal, o] *adj* rural, country *cpd*
ruse [ʀyz] *nf*: **la ~** cunning, craftiness; (*pour tromper*) trickery; **une ~** a trick, a ruse; **rusé, e** *adj* cunning, crafty
russe [ʀys] *adj* Russian ♦ *nm/f*: **R~** Russian ♦ *nm* (*LING*) Russian
Russie [ʀysi] *nf*: **la ~** Russia
rustine ® [ʀystin] *nf* rubber repair patch (*for bicycle tyre*)
rustique [ʀystik] *adj* rustic
rustre [ʀystʀ] *nm* boor
rutilant, e [ʀytilɑ̃, ɑ̃t] *adj* gleaming
rythme [ʀitm] *nm* rhythm; (*vitesse*) rate; (: *de la vie*) pace, tempo; **rythmé, e** *adj* rhythmic(al)

S, s

s' [s] *pron voir* **se**
sa [sa] *adj voir* **son**[1]
SA *sigle* (= *société anonyme*) ≃ Ltd (*BRIT*), ≃ Inc. (*US*)
sable [sɑbl] *nm* sand; **~s mouvants** quicksand(s)
sablé [sɑble] *nm* shortbread biscuit
sabler [sɑble] *vt* (*contre le verglas*) to grit; **~ le champagne** to drink champagne
sablier [sɑblije] *nm* hourglass; (*de cuisine*) egg timer
sablonneux, -euse [sɑblɔnø, øz] *adj* sandy
saborder [sabɔʀde] *vt* (*navire*) to scuttle; (*fig*: *projet*) to put paid to, scupper
sabot [sabo] *nm* clog; (*de cheval*) hoof; **~ de frein** brake shoe
saboter [sabɔte] *vt* to sabotage; (*bâcler*) to make a mess of, botch
sac [sak] *nm* bag; (*à charbon etc*) sack; **~ à dos** rucksack; **~ à main** handbag; **~ de couchage** sleeping bag; **~ de voyage** travelling bag; **~ poubelle** bin liner
saccadé, e [sakade] *adj* jerky; (*respiration*) spasmodic
saccager [sakaʒe] *vt* (*piller*) to sack; (*dévaster*) to create havoc in
saccharine [sakaʀin] *nf* saccharin
sacerdoce [sasɛʀdɔs] *nm* priesthood; (*fig*) calling, vocation
sache *etc* [saʃ] *vb voir* **savoir**
sachet [saʃɛ] *nm* (small) bag; (*de sucre, café*) sachet; **du potage en ~** packet soup; **~ de thé** tea bag
sacoche [sakɔʃ] *nf* (*gén*) bag; (*de bicyclette*) saddlebag
sacquer [sake] (*fam*) *vt* (*employé*) to fire; (*détester*): **je ne peux pas le ~** I can't stand him
sacre [sakʀ] *nm* (*roi*) coronation
sacré, e [sakʀe] *adj* sacred; (*fam*: *satané*) blasted; (: *fameux*): **un ~ toupé** a heck of a cheek
sacrement [sakʀəmɑ̃] *nm* sacrament
sacrifice [sakʀifis] *nm* sacrifice; **sacrifier** *vt* to sacrifice
sacristie [sakʀisti] *nf* (*catholique*) sacristy; (*protestante*) vestry
sadique [sadik] *adj* sadistic
safran [safʀɑ̃] *nm* saffron
sage [saʒ] *adj* wise; (*enfant*) good
sage-femme [saʒfam] *nf* midwife
sagesse [saʒɛs] *nf* wisdom
Sagittaire [saʒitɛʀ] *nm*: **le ~** Sagittarius
Sahara [saaʀa] *nm*: **le ~** the Sahara (desert)
saignant, e [sɛɲɑ̃, ɑ̃t] *adj* (*viande*) rare
saignée [seɲe] *nf* (*fig*) heavy losses *pl*

saigner [seɲe] *vi* to bleed ♦ *vt* to bleed; (*animal*) to kill (by bleeding); **~ du nez** to have a nosebleed

saillie [saji] *nf* (*sur un mur etc*) projection

saillir [sajiʀ] *vi* to project, stick out; (*veine, muscle*) to bulge

sain, e [sɛ̃, sɛn] *adj* healthy; **~ d'esprit** sound in mind, sane; **~ et sauf** safe and sound, unharmed

saindoux [sɛ̃du] *nm* lard

saint, e [sɛ̃, sɛ̃t] *adj* holy ♦ *nm/f* saint; **le S~ Esprit** the Holy Spirit *ou* Ghost; **la S~e Vierge** the Blessed Virgin; **la S~-Sylvestre** New Year's Eve; **sainteté** *nf* holiness

sais *etc* [sɛ] *vb voir* **savoir**

saisi, e [sezi] *adj*: **~ de panique** panic-stricken; **être ~ (par le froid)** to be struck by the sudden cold; **saisie** *nf* seizure; **~e (de données)** (data) capture

saisir [seziʀ] *vt* to take hold of, grab; (*fig*: *occasion*) to seize; (*comprendre*) to grasp; (*entendre*) to get, catch; (*données*) to capture; (CULIN) to fry quickly; (JUR: *biens, publication*) to seize; **se ~ de** *vt* to seize; **saisissant, e** *adj* startling, striking

saison [sɛzɔ̃] *nf* season; **morte ~** slack season; **saisonnier, -ière** *adj* seasonal

sait [sɛ] *vb voir* **savoir**

salade [salad] *nf* (BOT) lettuce *etc*; (CULIN) (green) salad; (*fam*: *confusion*) tangle, muddle; **~ composée** mixed salad; **~ de fruits** fruit salad; **saladier** *nm* (salad) bowl

salaire [salɛʀ] *nm* (*annuel, mensuel*) salary; (*hebdomadaire, journalier*) pay, wages *pl*; **~ minimum interprofessionnel de croissance** *index-linked guaranteed minimum wage*

salarié, e [salaʀje] *nm/f* salaried employee; wage-earner

salaud [salo] (*fam!*) *nm* sod (*!*), bastard (*!*)

sale [sal] *adj* dirty, filthy; (*fam*: *mauvais*) nasty

salé, e [sale] *adj* (*mer, goût*) salty; (CULIN: *amandes, beurre etc*) salted; (: *gâteaux*) savoury; (*fam*: *grivois*) spicy; (: *facture*) steep

saler [sale] *vt* to salt

saleté [salte] *nf* (*état*) dirtiness; (*crasse*) dirt, filth; (*tache etc*) dirt *no pl*; (*fam*: *méchanceté*) dirty trick; (: *camelote*) rubbish *no pl*; (: *obscénité*) filthy thing (to say)

salière [saljɛʀ] *nf* saltcellar

salir [saliʀ] *vt* to (make) dirty; (*fig*: *quelqu'un*) to soil the reputation of; **se ~** *vi* to get dirty; **salissant, e** *adj* (*tissu*) which shows the dirt; (*travail*) dirty, messy

salle [sal] *nf* room; (*d'hôpital*) ward; (*de restaurant*) dining room; (*d'un cinéma*) auditorium; (: *public*) audience; **~ à manger** dining room; **~ d'attente** waiting room; **~ de bain(s)** bathroom; **~ de classe** classroom; **~ de concert** concert hall; **~ d'eau** shower-room; **~ d'embarquement** (*à l'aéroport*) departure lounge; **~ de jeux** (*pour enfants*) playroom; **~ d'opération** (*d'hôpital*) operating theatre; **~ de séjour** living room; **~ des ventes** saleroom

salon [salɔ̃] *nm* lounge, sitting room; (*mobilier*) lounge suite; (*exposition*) exhibition, show; **~ de beauté** beauty salon; **~ de coiffure** hairdressing salon; **~ de thé** tearoom

salope [salɔp] (*fam!*) *nf* bitch (*!*); **saloperie** (*fam!*) *nf* (*action*) dirty trick; (*chose sans valeur*) rubbish *no pl*

salopette [salɔpɛt] *nf* dungarees *pl*; (*d'ouvrier*) overall(s)

salsifis [salsifi] *nm* salsify

salubre [salybʀ] *adj* healthy, salubrious

saluer [salɥe] *vt* (*pour dire bonjour, fig*) to greet; (*pour dire au revoir*) to take one's leave; (MIL) to salute

salut [saly] *nm* (*geste*) wave; (*parole*) greeting; (MIL) salute; (*sauvegarde*) safety; (REL) salvation ♦ *excl* (*fam*: *bonjour*) hi (there); (: *au revoir*) see you, bye

salutations [salytasjɔ̃] *nfpl* greetings; **Veuillez agréer, Monsieur, mes ~ distinguées** yours faithfully

samedi [samdi] *nm* Saturday

SAMU [samy] *sigle m* (= *service d'assistance médicale d'urgence*) ≃ ambulance (service) (*BRIT*), ≃ paramedics *pl* (*US*)

sanction [sɑ̃ksjɔ̃] *nf* sanction; **sanctionner** *vt* (*loi, usage*) to sanction; (*punir*) to punish

sandale [sɑ̃dal] *nf* sandal; **~s à lanières** strappy sandals

sandwich [sɑ̃dwi(t)ʃ] *nm* sandwich

sang [sɑ̃] *nm* blood; **en ~** covered in blood; **se faire du mauvais ~** to fret, get in a state; **sang-froid** *nm* calm, sangfroid; **de sang-froid** in cold blood; **sanglant, e** *adj* bloody

sangle [sɑ̃gl] *nf* strap

sanglier [sɑ̃glije] *nm* (wild) boar

sanglot [sɑ̃glo] *nm* sob; **sangloter** *vi* to sob

sangsue [sɑ̃sy] *nf* leech

sanguin, e [sɑ̃gɛ̃, in] *adj* blood *cpd*; **sanguinaire** *adj* bloodthirsty

sanitaire [sanitɛʀ] *adj* health *cpd*; **~s** *nmpl* (*lieu*) bathroom *sg*

sans [sɑ̃] *prép* without; **un pull ~ manches** a sleeveless jumper; **~ faute** without fail; **~ arrêt** without a break; **~ ça** (*fam*) otherwise; **~ qu'il s'en aperçoive** without him *ou* his noticing; **sans-abri** *nmpl* homeless; **sans-emploi** *nm/f inv* unemployed person; **les sans-emploi** the unemployed; **sans-gêne** *adj inv* inconsiderate

santé [sɑ̃te] *nf* health; **en bonne ~** in good health; **boire à la ~ de qn** to drink (to) sb's health; **à ta/votre ~!** cheers!

saoudien, ne [saudjɛ̃, jɛn] *adj* Saudi Arabian ♦ *nm/f*: **S~, ne** Saudi Arabian

saoul, e [su, sul] *adj* = **soûl**

saper [sape] *vt* to undermine, sap

sapeur-pompier [sapœʀpɔ̃pje] *nm* fireman

saphir [safiʀ] *nm* sapphire

sapin [sapɛ̃] *nm* fir (tree); (*bois*) fir; **~ de Noël** Christmas tree

sarcastique [saʀkastik] *adj* sarcastic

sarcler [saʀkle] *vt* to weed

Sardaigne [saʀdɛɲ] *nf*: **la ~** Sardinia

sarrasin [saʀazɛ̃] *nm* buckwheat

SARL *sigle f* (= *société à responsabilité limitée*) ≃ plc (*BRIT*), ≃ Inc. (*US*)

sas [sɑs] *nm* (*de sous-marin, d'engin spatial*) airlock; (*d'écluse*) lock

satané, e [satane] (*fam*) *adj* confounded

satellite [satelit] *nm* satellite

satin [satɛ̃] *nm* satin

satire [satiʀ] *nf* satire; **satirique** *adj* satirical

satisfaction [satisfaksjɔ̃] *nf* satisfaction

satisfaire [satisfɛʀ] *vt* to satisfy; **~ à** (*conditions*) to meet; **satisfaisant, e** *adj* (*acceptable*) satisfactory; **satisfait, e** *adj* satisfied; **satisfait de** happy *ou* satisfied with

saturer [satyʀe] *vt* to saturate

sauce [sos] *nf* sauce; (*avec un rôti*) gravy; **saucière** *nf* sauceboat

saucisse [sosis] *nf* sausage

saucisson [sosisɔ̃] *nm* (slicing) sausage

sauf, sauve [sof, sov] *adj* unharmed, unhurt; (*fig*: *honneur*) intact, saved ♦ *prép* except; **laisser la vie sauve à qn** to spare sb's life; **~ si** (*à moins que*) unless; **~ erreur** if I'm not mistaken; **~ avis contraire** unless you hear to the contrary

sauge [soʒ] *nf* sage

saugrenu, e [sogʀəny] *adj* preposterous

saule [sol] *nm* willow (tree)

saumon [somɔ̃] *nm* salmon *inv*

saumure [somyʀ] *nf* brine

saupoudrer [sopudʀe] *vt*: **~ qch de** to sprinkle sth with

saur [sɔʀ] *adj m*: **hareng ~** smoked *ou* red herring, kipper

saurai *etc* [sɔʀe] *vb voir* **savoir**

saut [so] *nm* jump; (*discipline sportive*) jumping; **faire un ~ chez qn** to pop over to sb's (place); **~ à l'élastique** bungee jumping; **~ à la perche** pole vaulting; **~ en hauteur/longueur** high/long jump; **~ périlleux** somersault

saute [sot] *nf*: **~ d'humeur** sudden change of mood

sauter [sote] *vi* to jump, leap; (*exploser*) to blow up, explode; (: *fusibles*) to blow; (*se détacher*) to pop out (*ou* off) ♦ *vt* to jump (over), leap (over); (*fig*: *omettre*) to skip, miss (out); **faire ~** to blow up; (CULIN) to sauté; **~ au cou de qn** to fly into sb's arms; **~ sur une occasion** to jump at an opportunity; **~ aux yeux** to be (quite) obvious

sauterelle [sotʀɛl] *nf* grasshopper

sautiller [sotije] *vi* (*oiseau*) to hop; (*enfant*) to skip

sauvage [sovaʒ] *adj* (*gén*) wild; (*peuplade*) savage; (*farouche*: *personne*) unsociable; (*barbare*) wild, savage; (*non officiel*) unauthorized, unofficial; **faire du camping ~** to camp in the wild ♦ *nm/f* savage; (*timide*) unsociable type

sauve [sov] *adj f voir* **sauf**

sauvegarde [sovgaʀd] *nf* safeguard; (INFORM) backup; **sauvegarder** *vt* to safeguard; (INFORM: *enregistrer*) to save; (: *copier*) to back up

sauve-qui-peut [sovkipø] *excl* run for your life!

sauver [sove] *vt* to save; (*porter secours à*) to rescue; (*récupérer*) to salvage, rescue; **se ~** *vi* (*s'enfuir*) to run away; (*fam*: *partir*) to be off; **sauvetage** *nm* rescue; **sauveteur** *nm* rescuer; **sauvette**: **à la sauvette** *adv* (*se marier etc*) hastily, hurriedly; **sauveur** *nm* saviour (BRIT), savior (US)

savais *etc* [save] *vb voir* **savoir**

savamment [savamɑ̃] *adv* (*avec érudition*) learnedly; (*habilement*) skilfully, cleverly

savant, e [savɑ̃, ɑ̃t] *adj* scholarly, learned ♦ *nm* scientist

saveur [savœʀ] *nf* flavour; (*fig*) savour

savoir [savwaʀ] *vt* to know; (*être capable de*): **il sait nager** he can swim ♦ *nm* knowledge; **se ~** *vi* (*être connu*) to be known; **à ~** that is, namely; **faire ~ qch à qn** to let sb know sth; **pas que je sache** not as far as I know

savon [savɔ̃] *nm* (*produit*) soap; (*morceau*) bar of soap; (*fam*): **passer un ~ à qn** to give sb a good dressing-down; **savonner** *vt* to soap; **savonnette** *nf* bar of soap

savons [savɔ̃] *vb voir* **savoir**

savourer [savuʀe] *vt* to savour; **savoureux, -euse** *adj* tasty; (*fig*: *anecdote*) spicy, juicy

saxo(phone) [saksɔ(fɔn)] *nm* sax(ophone)

scabreux, -euse [skabʀø, øz] *adj* risky; (*indécent*) improper, shocking

scandale [skɑ̃dal] *nm* scandal; (*tapage*): **faire un ~** to make a scene, create a disturbance; **faire ~** to scandalize people; **scandaleux, -euse** *adj* scandalous, outrageous

scandinave [skɑ̃dinav] *adj* Scandinavian ♦ *nm/f*: **S~** Scandinavian

Scandinavie [skɑ̃dinavi] *nf* Scandinavia

scaphandre [skafɑ̃dʀ] *nm* (*de plongeur*) diving suit

scarabée [skaʀabe] *nm* beetle

scarlatine [skaʀlatin] *nf* scarlet fever

scarole [skaʀɔl] *nf* endive

sceau, x [so] *nm* seal

scélérat, e [seleʀa, at] *nm/f* villain

sceller [sele] *vt* to seal

scénario [senaʀjo] *nm* scenario

scène [sɛn] *nf* (*gén*) scene; (*estrade, fig*: *théâtre*) stage; **entrer en ~** to come on stage; **mettre en ~** (THÉÂTRE) to stage; (CINÉMA) to direct; **~ de ménage** domestic scene

sceptique [sɛptik] *adj* sceptical

schéma [ʃema] *nm* (*diagramme*) diagram, sketch; **schématique** *adj* diagrammatic(al), schematic; (*fig*) oversimplified

sciatique [sjatik] *nf* sciatica

scie [si] *nf* saw; **~ à métaux** hacksaw

sciemment [sjamɑ̃] *adv* knowingly

science [sjɑ̃s] *nf* science; (*savoir*) knowledge; **~s naturelles** (SCOL) natural science *sg*, biology *sg*; **~s po** political science *ou* studies *pl*; **science-fiction** *nf* science fiction; **scientifique** *adj* scientific ♦ *nm/f* scientist; (*étudiant*) science student

scier [sje] *vt* to saw; (*retrancher*) to saw off; **scierie** *nf* sawmill

scinder [sɛ̃de] *vt* to split up; **se ~** *vi* to split up

scintiller [sɛ̃tije] *vi* to sparkle; (*étoile*) to twinkle

scission [sisjɔ̃] *nf* split

sciure [sjyʀ] *nf*: **~ (de bois)** sawdust

sclérose [skleʀoz] *nf*: **~ en plaques** multiple sclerosis

scolaire [skɔlɛʀ] *adj* school *cpd*; **scolariser** *vt* to provide with schooling/schools; **scolarité** *nf* schooling

scooter [skutœʀ] *nm* (motor) scooter

score [skɔʀ] *nm* score

scorpion [skɔʀpjɔ̃] *nm* (*signe*): **le S~** Scorpio

Scotch ® [skɔtʃ] *nm* adhesive tape

scout, e [skut] *adj, nm* scout

script [skʀipt] *nm* (*écriture*) printing; (CINÉMA) (shooting) script

scrupule [skʀypyl] *nm* scruple

scruter [skʀyte] *vt* to scrutinize; (*l'obscurité*) to peer into

scrutin [skʀytɛ̃] *nm* (*vote*) ballot; (*ensemble des opérations*) poll

sculpter [skylte] *vt* to sculpt; (*bois*) to carve; **sculpteur** *nm* sculptor; **sculpture** *nf* sculpture; **sculpture sur bois** wood carving

SDF *sigle m* (= *sans domicile fixe*) homeless person; **les SDF** the homeless

MOT-CLÉ

se [sə], s' *pron* **1** (*emploi réfléchi*) oneself; (: *masc*) himself; (: *fém*) herself; (: *sujet non humain*) itself; (: *pl*) themselves; **se voir comme l'on est** to see o.s. as one is

2 (*réciproque*) one another, each other; **ils s'aiment** they love one another *ou* each other

3 (*passif*): **cela se répare facilement** it is easily repaired

4 (*possessif*): **se casser la jambe/laver les mains** to break one's leg/wash one's hands

séance [seɑ̃s] *nf* (*d'assemblée*) meeting, session; (*de tribunal*) sitting, session; (*musicale*, CINÉMA, THÉÂTRE) performance; **~ tenante** forthwith

seau, x [so] *nm* bucket, pail

sec, sèche [sɛk, sɛʃ] *adj* dry; (*raisins, figues*) dried; (*cœur*: *insensible*) hard, cold ♦ *nm*: **tenir au ~** to keep in a dry place ♦ *adv* hard; **je le bois ~** I drink it straight *ou* neat; **à ~** (*puits*) dried up

sécateur [sekatœʀ] *nm* secateurs *pl* (BRIT), shears *pl*

sèche [sɛʃ] *adj f voir* **sec**; **sèche-cheveux** *nm inv* hair-drier; **sèche-linge** *nm inv* tumble dryer; **sèchement** *adv* (*répondre*) drily

sécher [seʃe] *vt* to dry; (*dessécher*: *peau, blé*) to dry (out); (: *étang*) to dry up; (*fam*: *cours*) to skip ♦ *vi* to dry; to dry out; to dry up; (*fam*: *candidat*) to be stumped; **se ~** (*après le bain*) to dry o.s.; **sécheresse** *nf* dryness; (*absence de pluie*) drought; **séchoir** *nm* drier

second, e [s(ə)gɔ̃, ɔ̃d] *adj* second ♦ *nm* (*assistant*) second in command; (NAVIG) first mate; **voyager en ~e** to travel second-class; **secondaire** *adj* secondary; **seconde** *nf* second; **seconder** *vt* to assist

secouer [s(ə)kwe] *vt* to shake; (*passagers*) to rock; (*traumatiser*) to shake (up); **se ~** *vi* (*fam*: *faire un effort*) to shake o.s. up; (: *se dépêcher*) to get a move on

secourir [s(ə)kuʀiʀ] *vt* (*venir en aide à*) to assist, aid; **secourisme** *nm* first aid; **secouriste** *nmf* first-aid worker

secours [s(ə)kuʀ] *nm* help, aid, assistance ♦ *nmpl* aid *sg*; **au ~!** help!; **appeler au ~** to shout *ou* call for help; **porter ~ à qn** to give sb assistance, help sb; **les premiers ~** first aid *sg*

secousse [s(ə)kus] *nf* jolt, bump; (*électrique*) shock; (*fig*: *psychologique*) jolt, shock; **~ sismique** earth tremor

secret, -ète [səkʀɛ, ɛt] *adj* secret; (*fig*: *renfermé*) reticent, reserved ♦ *nm* secret; (*discrétion absolue*): **le ~** secrecy

secrétaire [s(ə)kʀetɛʀ] *nm/f* secretary ♦ *nm* (*meuble*) writing desk; **~ de direction** private *ou* personal secretary; **~ d'État** junior minister; **~ général** (COMM) company secretary; **secrétariat** *nm* (*profession*) secretarial work; (*bureau*) office; (: *d'organisation internationale*) secretariat

secteur [sɛktœʀ] *nm* sector; (*zone*) area; (ÉLEC): **branché sur ~** plugged into the mains (supply)

section [sɛksjɔ̃] *nf* section; (*de parcours d'autobus*) fare stage; (MIL: *unité*) platoon; **sectionner** *vt* to sever

Sécu [seky] *abr f* = **sécurité sociale**

séculaire [sekylɛʀ] *adj* (*très vieux*) age-old

sécuriser [sekyʀize] *vt* to give (a feeling of) security to

sécurité [sekyʀite] *nf* (*absence de danger*) safety; (*absence de troubles*) security; **système de ~** security system; **être en ~** to be safe; **la ~ routière** road safety; **la ~ sociale** ≃ (the) Social Security (BRIT), ≃ Welfare (US)

sédentaire [sedɑ̃tɛʀ] *adj* sedentary

séduction [sedyksjɔ̃] *nf* seduction; (*charme, attrait*) appeal, charm

séduire [sedɥiʀ] *vt* to charm; (*femme*: *abuser de*) to seduce; **séduisant, e** *adj* (*femme*) seductive; (*homme, offre*) very attractive

ségrégation [segʀegasjɔ̃] *nf* segregation

seigle [sɛgl] *nm* rye

seigneur [sɛɲœʀ] *nm* lord

sein [sɛ̃] *nm* breast; (*entrailles*) womb; **au ~ de** (*équipe, institution*) within

séisme [seism] *nm* earthquake

seize [sɛz] *num* sixteen; **seizième** *num* sixteenth

séjour [seʒuʀ] *nm* stay; (*pièce*) living room; **séjourner** *vi* to stay

sel [sɛl] *nm* salt; (*fig*: *piquant*) spice

sélection [selɛksjɔ̃] *nf* selection; **sélectionner** *vt* to select

self-service [sɛlfsɛʀvis] *adj, nm* self-service

selle [sɛl] *nf* saddle; **~s** *nfpl* (MÉD) stools; **seller** *vt* to saddle

sellette [sɛlɛt] *nf*: **être sur la ~** to be in the hot seat

selon [s(ə)lɔ̃] *prép* according to; (*en se conformant à*) in accordance with; **~ que** according to whether; **~ moi** as I see it

semaine [s(ə)mɛn] *nf* week; **en ~** during the week, on weekdays

semblable [sɑ̃blabl] *adj* similar; (*de ce genre*): **de ~s mésaventures** such mishaps ♦ *nm* fellow creature *ou* man; **~ à** similar to, like

semblant [sɑ̃blɑ̃] *nm*: **un ~ de ...** a semblance of ...; **faire ~ (de faire)** to pretend (to do)

sembler [sɑ̃ble] *vb +attrib* to seem ♦ *vb impers*: **il semble (bien) que/inutile de** it (really) seems *ou* appears that/ useless to; **il me semble que** it seems to me that; **comme bon lui semble** as he sees fit

semelle [s(ə)mɛl] *nf* sole; (*intérieure*) insole, inner sole

semence [s(ə)mɑ̃s] *nf* (*graine*) seed

semer [s(ə)me] *vt* to sow; (*fig*: *éparpiller*) to scatter; (: *confusion*) to spread; (*fam*: *poursuivants*) to lose, shake off; **semé de** (*difficultés*) riddled with

semestre [s(ə)mɛstʀ] *nm* half-year; (SCOL) semester

séminaire [seminɛʀ] *nm* seminar
semi-remorque [səmiʀəmɔʀk] *nm* articulated lorry (*BRIT*), semi(trailer) (*US*)
semoule [s(ə)mul] *nf* semolina
sempiternel, le [sɑ̃pitɛʀnɛl] *adj* eternal, never-ending
sénat [sena] *nm* senate; **sénateur** *nm* senator
sens [sɑ̃s] *nm* (*PHYSIOL, instinct*) sense; (*signification*) meaning, sense; (*direction*) direction; **à mon ~** to my mind; **dans le ~ des aiguilles d'une montre** clockwise; **~ dessus dessous** upside down; **~ interdit** one-way street; **~ unique** one-way street
sensation [sɑ̃sasjɔ̃] *nf* sensation; **à ~** (*péj*) sensational; **faire ~** to cause *ou* create a sensation; **sensationnel, le** *adj* (*fam*) fantastic, terrific
sensé, e [sɑ̃se] *adj* sensible
sensibiliser [sɑ̃sibilize] *vt*: **~ qn à** to make sb sensitive to
sensibilité [sɑ̃sibilite] *nf* sensitivity
sensible [sɑ̃sibl] *adj* sensitive; (*aux sens*) perceptible; (*appréciable*: *différence, progrès*) appreciable, noticeable; **sensiblement** *adv* (*à peu près*): **ils sont sensiblement du même âge** they are approximately the same age; **sensiblerie** *nf* sentimentality
sensuel, le [sɑ̃sɥɛl] *adj* (*personne*) sensual; (*musique*) sensuous
sentence [sɑ̃tɑ̃s] *nf* (*jugement*) sentence
sentier [sɑ̃tje] *nm* path
sentiment [sɑ̃timɑ̃] *nm* feeling; **sentimental, e, -aux** *adj* sentimental; (*vie, aventure*) love *cpd*
sentinelle [sɑ̃tinɛl] *nf* sentry
sentir [sɑ̃tiʀ] *vt* (*par l'odorat*) to smell; (*par le goût*) to taste; (*au toucher, fig*) to feel; (*répandre une odeur de*) to smell of; (*: ressemblance*) to smell like ♦ *vi* to smell; **~ mauvais** to smell bad; **se ~ bien** to feel good; **se ~ mal** (*être indisposé*) to feel unwell *ou* ill; **se ~ le courage/la force de faire** to feel brave/strong enough to do; **il ne peut pas le ~** (*fam*) he can't stand him
séparation [sepaʀasjɔ̃] *nf* separation; (*cloison*) division, partition
séparé, e [sepaʀe] *adj* (*distinct*) separate; (*époux*) separated; **séparément** *adv* separately
séparer [sepaʀe] *vt* to separate; (*désunir*) to drive apart; (*détacher*): **~ qch de** to pull sth (off) from; **se ~** *vi* (*époux, amis*) to separate, part; (*se diviser*: *route etc*) to divide; **se ~ de** (*époux*) to separate *ou* part from; (*employé, objet personnel*) to part with
sept [sɛt] *num* seven; **septante** (*BELGIQUE, SUISSE*) *adj inv* seventy
septembre [sɛptɑ̃bʀ] *nm* September
septennat [sɛptena] *nm seven year term of office (of French President)*
septentrional, e, -aux [sɛptɑ̃tʀijɔnal, o] *adj* northern
septicémie [sɛptisemi] *nf* blood poisoning, septicaemia
septième [sɛtjɛm] *num* seventh
septique [sɛptik] *adj*: **fosse ~** septic tank
sépulture [sepyltyʀ] *nf* (*tombeau*) burial place, grave
séquelles [sekɛl] *nfpl* after-effects; (*fig*) aftermath *sg*
séquestrer [sekɛstʀe] *vt* (*personne*) to confine illegally; (*biens*) to impound
serai *etc* [səʀe] *vb voir* **être**
serein, e [səʀɛ̃, ɛn] *adj* serene
serez [səʀe] *vb voir* **être**
sergent [sɛʀʒɑ̃] *nm* sergeant
série [seʀi] *nf* series *inv*; (*de clés, casseroles, outils*) set; (*catégorie*: *SPORT*) rank; **en ~** in quick succession; (*COMM*) mass *cpd*; **hors ~** (*COMM*) custom-built
sérieusement [seʀjøzmɑ̃] *adv* seriously
sérieux, -euse [seʀjø, jøz] *adj* serious; (*élève, employé*) reliable, responsible; (*client, maison*) reliable, dependable ♦ *nm* seriousness; (*d'une entreprise etc*) reliability; **garder son ~** to keep a

straight face; **prendre qch/qn au ~** to take sth/sb seriously

serin [s(ə)ʀɛ̃] *nm* canary

seringue [s(ə)ʀɛ̃g] *nf* syringe

serions [səʀjɔ̃] *vb voir* **être**

serment [sɛʀmɑ̃] *nm* (*juré*) oath; (*promesse*) pledge, vow

séronégatif, -ive [seʀonegatif, iv] *adj* (*MÉD*) HIV negative

séropositif, -ive [seʀopozitif, iv] *adj* (*MÉD*) HIV positive

serpent [sɛʀpɑ̃] *nm* snake; **serpenter** *vi* to wind

serpillière [sɛʀpijɛʀ] *nf* floorcloth

serre [sɛʀ] *nf* (*AGR*) greenhouse; **~s** *nfpl* (*griffes*) claws, talons

serré, e [seʀe] *adj* (*habits*) tight; (*fig: lutte, match*) tight, close-fought; (*passagers etc*) (tightly) packed; (*réseau*) dense; **avoir le cœur ~** to have a heavy heart

serrer [seʀe] *vt* (*tenir*) to grip *ou* hold tight; (*comprimer, coincer*) to squeeze; (*poings, mâchoires*) to clench; (*suj: vêtement*) to be too tight for; (*ceinture, nœud, vis*) to tighten ♦ *vi*: **~ à droite** to keep *ou* get over to the right; **se ~** *vi* (*se rapprocher*) to squeeze up; **se ~ contre qn** to huddle up to sb; **~ la main à qn** to shake sb's hand; **~ qn dans ses bras** to hug sb, clasp sb in one's arms

serrure [seʀyʀ] *nf* lock; **serrurier** *nm* locksmith

sert *etc* [sɛʀ] *vb voir* **servir**

servante [sɛʀvɑ̃t] *nf* (maid)servant

serveur, -euse [sɛʀvœʀ, øz] *nm/f* waiter (waitress)

serviable [sɛʀvjabl] *adj* obliging, willing to help

service [sɛʀvis] *nm* service; (*assortiment de vaisselle*) set, service; (*bureau: de la vente etc*) department, section; (*travail*) duty; **premier ~** (*série de repas*) first sitting; **être de ~** to be on duty; **faire le ~** to serve; **rendre un ~ à qn** to do sb a favour; (*objet: s'avérer utile*) to come in useful *ou* handy for sb; **mettre en ~** to put into service *ou* operation; **~ compris/non compris** service included/not included; **hors ~** out of order; **~ après-vente** after-sales service; **~ d'ordre** police (*ou* stewards) in charge of maintaining order; **~ militaire** military service; **~s secrets** secret service *sg*

service militaire

French men over eighteen are required to do ten months' **service militaire** *if pronounced fit. The call-up can be delayed if the conscript is in full-time higher education. Conscientious objectors are required to do two years' public service. Since 1970, women have been able to do military service, though few do.*

serviette [sɛʀvjɛt] *nf* (*de table*) (table) napkin, serviette; (*de toilette*) towel; (*porte-documents*) briefcase; **~ de plage** beach towel; **~ hygiénique** sanitary towel

servir [sɛʀviʀ] *vt* to serve; (*au restaurant*) to wait on; (*au magasin*) to serve, attend to ♦ *vi* (*TENNIS*) to serve; (*CARTES*) to deal; **se ~** *vi* (*prendre d'un plat*) to help o.s.; **vous êtes servi?** are you being served?; **~ à qn** (*diplôme, livre*) to be of use to sb; **~ à qch/faire** (*outil etc*) to be used for sth/doing; **ça ne sert à rien** it's no use; **~ (à qn) de** to serve as (for sb); **se ~ de** (*plat*) to help o.s. to; (*voiture, outil, relations*) to use

serviteur [sɛʀvitœʀ] *nm* servant

ses [se] *adj voir* **son**[1]

set [sɛt] *nm*: **~ (de table)** tablemat, place mat

seuil [sœj] *nm* doorstep; (*fig*) threshold

seul, e [sœl] *adj* (*sans compagnie*) alone; (*unique*): **un ~ livre** only one book, a single book ♦ *adv* (*vivre*) alone, on one's own ♦ *nm, nf*: **il en reste un(e) ~(e)** there's only one left; **le ~ li-**

vre the only book; **parler tout ~** to talk to oneself; **faire qch (tout) ~** to do sth (all) on one's own *ou* (all) by oneself; **à lui (tout) ~** single-handed, on his own; **se sentir ~** to feel lonely; **seulement** *adv* only; **non seulement ... mais aussi** *ou* **encore** not only ... but also

sève [sɛv] *nf* sap

sévère [sevɛʀ] *adj* severe

sévices [sevis] *nmpl* (physical) cruelty *sg*, ill treatment *sg*

sévir [seviʀ] *vi* (*punir*) to use harsh measures, crack down; (*suj: fléau*) to rage, be rampant

sevrer [səvʀe] *vt* (*enfant etc*) to wean

sexe [sɛks] *nm* sex; (*organes génitaux*) genitals, sex organs; **sexuel, le** *adj* sexual

seyant, e [sɛjɑ̃, ɑ̃t] *adj* becoming

shampooing [ʃɑ̃pwɛ̃] *nm* shampoo

short [ʃɔʀt] *nm* (pair of) shorts *pl*

MOT-CLÉ

si [si] *nm* (MUS) B; (*en chantant la gamme*) ti

♦ *adv* **1** (*oui*) yes

2 (*tellement*) so; **si gentil/rapidement** so kind/fast; **(tant et) si bien que** so much so that; **si rapide qu'il soit** however fast he may be

♦ *conj* if; **si tu veux** if you want; **je me demande si** I wonder if *ou* whether; **si seulement** if only

Sicile [sisil] *nf*: **la ~** Sicily

SIDA [sida] *sigle m* (= *syndrome immuno-déficitaire acquis*) AIDS *sg*

sidéré, e [sideʀe] *adj* staggered

sidérurgie [sideʀyʀʒi] *nf* steel industry

siècle [sjɛkl] *nm* century

siège [sjɛʒ] *nm* seat; (*d'entreprise*) head office; (*d'organisation*) headquarters *pl*; (MIL) siege; **~ social** registered office; **siéger** *vi* to sit

sien, ne [sjɛ̃, sjɛn] *pron*: **le(la) ~(ne), les ~(ne)s** (*homme*) his; (*femme*) hers; (*chose, animal*) its; **les ~s** (*sa famille*) one's family; **faire des ~nes** (*fam*) to be up to one's (usual) tricks

sieste [sjɛst] *nf* (afternoon) snooze *ou* nap; **faire la ~** to have a snooze *ou* nap

sifflement [sifləmɑ̃] *nm*: **un ~** a whistle

siffler [sifle] *vi* (*gén*) to whistle; (*en respirant*) to wheeze; (*serpent, vapeur*) to hiss ♦ *vt* (*chanson*) to whistle; (*chien etc*) to whistle for; (*fille*) to whistle at; (*pièce, orateur*) to hiss, boo; (*fin du match, départ*) to blow one's whistle for; (*fam: verre*) to guzzle

sifflet [siflɛ] *nm* whistle; **coup de ~** whistle

siffloter [siflɔte] *vi, vt* to whistle

sigle [sigl] *nm* acronym

signal, -aux [siɲal, o] *nm* signal; (*indice, écriteau*) sign; **donner le ~ de** to give the signal for; **~ d'alarme** alarm signal; **signaux (lumineux)** (AUTO) traffic signals; **signalement** *nm* description, particulars *pl*

signaler [siɲale] *vt* to indicate; (*personne: faire un signe*) to signal; (*vol, perte*) to report; (*faire remarquer*): **~ qch à qn/(à qn) que** to point out sth to sb/(to sb) that; **se ~ (par)** to distinguish o.s. (by)

signature [siɲatyʀ] *nf* signature; (*action*) signing

signe [siɲ] *nm* sign; (TYPO) mark; **faire un ~ de la main** to give a sign with one's hand; **faire ~ à qn** (*fig: contacter*) to get in touch with sb; **faire ~ à qn d'entrer** to motion (to) sb to come in; **signer** *vt* to sign; **se signer** *vi* to cross o.s.

significatif, -ive [siɲifikatif, iv] *adj* significant

signification [siɲifikasjɔ̃] *nf* meaning

signifier [siɲifje] *vt* (*vouloir dire*) to mean; (*faire connaître*): **~ qch (à qn)** to make sth known (to sb)

silence [silɑ̃s] *nm* silence; (MUS) rest;

garder le ~ to keep silent, say nothing; **silencieux, -euse** *adj* quiet, silent ♦ *nm* silencer

silex [silɛks] *nm* flint

silhouette [silwɛt] *nf* outline, silhouette; (*allure*) figure

silicium [silisjɔm] *nm* silicon

sillage [sijaʒ] *nm* wake

sillon [sijɔ̃] *nm* furrow; (*de disque*) groove; **sillonner** *vt* to criss-cross

simagrées [simagʀe] *nfpl* fuss *sg*

similaire [similɛʀ] *adj* similar; **similicuir** *nm* imitation leather; **similitude** *nf* similarity

simple [sɛ̃pl] *adj* simple; (*non multiple*) single; **~ messieurs** *nm* (*TENNIS*) men's singles *sg*; **~ soldat** private

simplicité [sɛ̃plisite] *nf* simplicity

simplifier [sɛ̃plifje] *vt* to simplify

simulacre [simylakʀ] *nm* (*péj*): **un ~ de** a pretence of

simuler [simyle] *vt* to sham, simulate

simultané, e [simyltane] *adj* simultaneous

sincère [sɛ̃sɛʀ] *adj* sincere; **sincèrement** *adv* sincerely; (*pour parler franchement*) honestly, really; **sincérité** *nf* sincerity

sine qua non [sinekwanɔn] *adj*: **condition ~** indispensable condition

singe [sɛ̃ʒ] *nm* monkey; (*de grande taille*) ape; **singer** *vt* to ape, mimic; **singeries** *nfpl* antics

singulariser [sɛ̃gylaʀize]: **se ~** *vi* to call attention to o.s.

singularité [sɛ̃gylaʀite] *nf* peculiarity

singulier, -ière [sɛ̃gylje, jɛʀ] *adj* remarkable, singular ♦ *nm* singular

sinistre [sinistʀ] *adj* sinister ♦ *nm* (*incendie*) blaze; (*catastrophe*) disaster; (*ASSURANCES*) damage (*giving rise to a claim*); **sinistré, e** *adj* disaster-stricken ♦ *nm/f* disaster victim

sinon [sinɔ̃] *conj* (*autrement, sans quoi*) otherwise, or else; (*sauf*) except, other than; (*si ce n'est*) if not

sinueux, -euse [sinɥø, øz] *adj* winding

sinus [sinys] *nm* (*ANAT*) sinus; (*GÉOM*) sine; **sinusite** *nf* sinusitis

siphon [sifɔ̃] *nm* (*tube, d'eau gazeuse*) siphon; (*d'évier etc*) U-bend

sirène [siʀɛn] *nf* siren; **~ d'alarme** fire alarm; (*en temps de guerre*) air-raid siren

sirop [siʀo] *nm* (*à diluer: de fruit etc*) syrup; (*pharmaceutique*) syrup, mixture; **~ pour la toux** cough mixture

siroter [siʀɔte] *vt* to sip

sismique [sismik] *adj* seismic

site [sit] *nm* (*paysage, environnement*) setting; (*d'une ville etc: emplacement*) site; **~ (pittoresque)** beauty spot; **~s touristiques** places of interest; **~ Web** (*INFORM*) website

sitôt [sito] *adv*: **~ parti** as soon as he *etc* had left; **~ que** as soon as; **pas de ~** not for a long time

situation [sitɥasjɔ̃] *nf* situation; (*d'un édifice, d'une ville*) position, location; **~ de famille** marital status

situé, e [sitɥe] *adj* situated

situer [sitɥe] *vt* to site, situate; (*en pensée*) to set, place; **se ~** *vi* to be situated

six [sis] *num* six; **sixième** *num* sixth ♦ *nf* (*SCOL*) first form

Skaï ® [skaj] *nm* Leatherette ®

ski [ski] *nm* (*objet*) ski; (*sport*) skiing; **faire du ~** to ski; **~ de fond** cross-country skiing; **~ nautique** water-skiing; **~ de piste** downhill skiing; **~ de randonnée** cross-country skiing; **skier** *vi* to ski; **skieur, -euse** *nm/f* skier

slip [slip] *nm* (*sous-vêtement*) pants *pl*, briefs *pl*; (*de bain: d'homme*) trunks *pl*; (*: du bikini*) (bikini) briefs *pl*

slogan [slɔgɑ̃] *nm* slogan

SMIC [smik] *sigle m* = **salaire minimum interprofessionnel de croissance**

SMIC

In France, the SMIC *is the minimum*

legal hourly rate for workers over eighteen. It is index-linked and is raised each time the cost of living rises by 2%.

smicard, e [smikaR, aRd] (*fam*) *nm/f* minimum wage earner
smoking [smɔkiŋ] *nm* dinner *ou* evening suit
SNCF *sigle f* (= *Société nationale des chemins de fer français*) *French railways*
snob [snɔb] *adj* snobbish ♦ *nm/f* snob; **snobisme** *nm* snobbery, snobbishness
sobre [sɔbR] *adj* (*personne*) temperate, abstemious; (*élégance, style*) sober
sobriquet [sɔbRikɛ] *nm* nickname
social, e, -aux [sɔsjal, jo] *adj* social
socialisme [sɔsjalism] *nm* socialism; **socialiste** *nm/f* socialist
société [sɔsjete] *nf* society; (*sportive*) club; (COMM) company; **la ~ de consommation** the consumer society; **~ anonyme** ≈ limited (BRIT) *ou* incorporated (US) company
sociologie [sɔsjɔlɔʒi] *nf* sociology
socle [sɔkl] *nm* (*de colonne, statue*) plinth, pedestal; (*de lampe*) base
socquette [sɔkɛt] *nf* ankle sock
sœur [sœR] *nf* sister; (*religieuse*) nun, sister
soi [swa] *pron* oneself; **en ~** (*intrinsèquement*) in itself; **cela va de ~** that *ou* it goes without saying; **soi-disant** *adj inv* so-called ♦ *adv* supposedly
soie [swa] *nf* silk; **soierie** *nf* (*tissu*) silk
soif [swaf] *nf* thirst; **avoir ~** to be thirsty; **donner ~ à qn** to make sb thirsty
soigné, e [swaɲe] *adj* (*tenue*) well-groomed, neat; (*travail*) careful, meticulous
soigner [swaɲe] *vt* (*malade, maladie*: *suj*: *docteur*) to treat; (*suj*: *infirmière, mère*) to nurse, look after; (*travail, détails*) to take care over; (*jardin, invités*) to look after; **soigneux, -euse** *adj* (*propre*) tidy, neat; (*appliqué*) painstaking, careful
soi-même [swamɛm] *pron* oneself
soin [swɛ̃] *nm* (*application*) care; (*propreté, ordre*) tidiness, neatness; **~s** *nmpl* (*à un malade, blessé*) treatment *sg*, medical attention *sg*; (*hygiène*) care *sg*; **prendre ~ de** to take care of, look after; **prendre ~ de faire** to take care to do; **les premiers ~s** first aid *sg*
soir [swaR] *nm* evening; **ce ~** this evening, tonight; **demain ~** tomorrow evening, tomorrow night; **soirée** *nf* evening; (*réception*) party
soit [swa] *vb voir* **être** ♦ *conj* (*à savoir*) namely; (*ou*): **~ ... ~** either ... or ♦ *adv* so be it, very well; **~ que ... ~ que** *ou* **ou que** whether ... or whether
soixantaine [swasɑ̃tɛn] *nf*: **une ~ (de)** sixty or so, about sixty; **avoir la ~** (*âge*) to be around sixty
soixante [swasɑ̃t] *num* sixty; **soixante-dix** *num* seventy
soja [sɔʒa] *nm* soya; (*graines*) soya beans *pl*; **germes de ~** beansprouts
sol [sɔl] *nm* ground; (*de logement*) floor; (AGR) soil; (MUS) G; (: *en chantant la gamme*) so(h)
solaire [sɔlɛR] *adj* (*énergie etc*) solar; (*crème etc*) sun *cpd*
soldat [sɔlda] *nm* soldier
solde [sɔld] *nf* pay ♦ *nm* (COMM) balance; **~s** *nm ou f pl* (*articles*) sale goods; (*vente*) sales; **en ~** at sale price; **solder** *vt* (*marchandise*) to sell at sale price, sell off; **se solder par** (*fig*) to end in; **article soldé (à) 10 F** item reduced to 10 F
sole [sɔl] *nf* sole *inv* (*fish*)
soleil [sɔlɛj] *nm* sun; (*lumière*) sun(light); (*temps ensoleillé*) sun(shine); **il fait du ~** it's sunny; **au ~** in the sun
solennel, le [sɔlanɛl] *adj* solemn
solfège [sɔlfɛʒ] *nm* musical theory
solidaire [sɔlidɛR] *adj*: **être ~s** to show solidarity, stand *ou* stick together; **être ~ de** (*collègues*) to stand by; **solidarité** *nf* solidarity; **par solidarité (avec)** in sympathy (with)

solide [sɔlid] *adj* solid; (*mur, maison, meuble*) solid, sturdy; (*connaissances, argument*) sound; (*personne, estomac*) robust, sturdy ♦ *nm* solid

soliste [sɔlist] *nm/f* soloist

solitaire [sɔlitɛʀ] *adj* (*sans compagnie*) solitary, lonely; (*lieu*) lonely ♦ *nm/f* (*ermite*) recluse; (*fig*: *ours*) loner

solitude [sɔlityd] *nf* loneliness; (*tranquillité*) solitude

solive [sɔliv] *nf* joist

solliciter [sɔlisite] *vt* (*personne*) to appeal to; (*emploi, faveur*) to seek

sollicitude [sɔlisityd] *nf* concern

soluble [sɔlybl] *adj* soluble

solution [sɔlysjɔ̃] *nf* solution; **~ de facilité** easy way out

solvable [sɔlvabl] *adj* solvent

sombre [sɔ̃bʀ] *adj* dark; (*fig*) gloomy; **sombrer** *vi* (*bateau*) to sink; **sombrer dans** (*misère, désespoir*) to sink into

sommaire [sɔmɛʀ] *adj* (*simple*) basic; (*expéditif*) summary ♦ *nm* summary

sommation [sɔmasjɔ̃] *nf* (*JUR*) summons *sg*; (*avant de faire feu*) warning

somme [sɔm] *nf* (*MATH*) sum; (*quantité*) amount; (*argent*) sum, amount ♦ *nm*: **faire un ~** to have a (short) nap; **en ~** all in all; **~ toute** all in all

sommeil [sɔmɛj] *nm* sleep; **avoir ~** to be sleepy; **sommeiller** *vi* to doze

sommer [sɔme] *vt*: **~ qn de faire** to command *ou* order sb to do

sommes [sɔm] *vb voir* **être**

sommet [sɔmɛ] *nm* top; (*d'une montagne*) summit, top; (*fig*: *de la perfection, gloire*) height

sommier [sɔmje] *nm* (bed) base

somnambule [sɔmnɑ̃byl] *nm/f* sleepwalker

somnifère [sɔmnifɛʀ] *nm* sleeping drug *no pl* (*ou* pill)

somnoler [sɔmnɔle] *vi* to doze

somptueux, -euse [sɔ̃ptɥø, øz] *adj* sumptuous

son[1], sa [sɔ̃, sa] (*pl* **ses**) *adj* (*antécédent humain*: *mâle*) his; (: *femelle*) her; (: *valeur indéfinie*) one's, his/her; (*antécédent non humain*) its

son[2] [sɔ̃] *nm* sound; (*de blé*) bran

sondage [sɔ̃daʒ] *nm*: **~ (d'opinion)** (opinion) poll

sonde [sɔ̃d] *nf* (*NAVIG*) lead *ou* sounding line; (*MÉD*) probe; (*TECH*: *de forage*) borer, driller

sonder [sɔ̃de] *vt* (*NAVIG*) to sound; (*TECH*) to bore, drill; (*fig*: *personne*) to sound out; **~ le terrain** (*fig*) to test the ground

songe [sɔ̃ʒ] *nm* dream; **songer** *vi*: **songer à** (*penser à*) to think over; (*envisager*) to consider, think of; **songer que** to think that; **songeur, -euse** *adj* pensive

sonnant, e [sɔnɑ̃, ɑ̃t] *adj*: **à 8 heures ~es** on the stroke of 8

sonné, e [sɔne] *adj* (*fam*) cracked; **il est midi ~** it's gone twelve

sonner [sɔne] *vi* to ring ♦ *vt* (*cloche*) to ring; (*glas, tocsin*) to sound; (*portier, infirmière*) to ring for; **~ faux** (*instrument*) to sound out of tune; (*rire*) to ring false

sonnerie [sɔnʀi] *nf* (*son*) ringing; (*sonnette*) bell; **~ d'alarme** alarm bell

sonnette [sɔnɛt] *nf* bell; **~ d'alarme** alarm bell

sono [sɔno] *abr f* = **sonorisation**

sonore [sɔnɔʀ] *adj* (*voix*) sonorous, ringing; (*salle*) resonant; (*film, signal*) sound *cpd*; **sonorisation** *nf* (*équipement*: *de salle de conférences*) public address system, P.A. system; (: *de discothèque*) sound system; **sonorité** *nf* (*de piano, violon*) tone; (*d'une salle*) acoustics *pl*

sont [sɔ̃] *vb voir* **être**

sophistiqué, e [sɔfistike] *adj* sophisticated

sorbet [sɔʀbɛ] *nm* water ice, sorbet

sorcellerie [sɔʀsɛlʀi] *nf* witchcraft *no pl*

sorcier [sɔʀsje] *nm* sorcerer; **sorcière** *nf* witch *ou* sorceress

sordide [sɔʀdid] *adj* (*lieu*) squalid; (*action*) sordid

sornettes [sɔʀnɛt] *nfpl* twaddle *sg*

sort [sɔʀ] *nm* (*destinée*) fate; (*condition*) lot; (*magique*) curse, spell; **tirer au ~** to draw lots

sorte [sɔʀt] *nf* sort, kind; **de la ~** in that way; **de (telle) ~ que** so that; **en quelque ~** in a way; **faire en ~ que** to see to it that

sortie [sɔʀti] *nf* (*issue*) way out, exit; (*remarque drôle*) sally; (*promenade*) outing; (*le soir: au restaurant etc*) night out; (COMM: *d'un disque*) release; (: *d'un livre*) publication; (: *d'un modèle*) launching; **~s** *nfpl* (COMM: *somme*) items of expenditure, outgoings; **~ de bain** (*vêtement*) bathrobe; **~ de secours** emergency exit

sortilège [sɔʀtilɛʒ] *nm* (magic) spell

sortir [sɔʀtiʀ] *vi* (*gén*) to come out; (*partir, se promener, aller au spectacle*) to go out; (*numéro gagnant*) to come up ♦ *vt* (*gén*) to take out; (*produit, modèle*) to bring out; (*fam: dire*) to come out with; **~ avec qn** to be going out with sb; **s'en ~** (*malade*) to pull through; (*d'une difficulté etc*) to get through; **~ de** (*endroit*) to go (*ou* come) out of, leave; (*provenir de*) to come from; (*compétence*) to be outside

sosie [sɔzi] *nm* double

sot, sotte [so, sɔt] *adj* silly, foolish ♦ *nm/f* fool, **sottise** *nf* (*caractère*) silliness, foolishness; (*action*) silly *ou* foolish thing

sou [su] *nm*: **près de ses ~s** tight-fisted; **sans le ~** penniless

soubresaut [subʀəso] *nm* start; (*cahot*) jolt

souche [suʃ] *nf* (*d'arbre*) stump; (*de carnet*) counterfoil (BRIT), stub

souci [susi] *nm* (*inquiétude*) worry; (*préoccupation*) concern; (BOT) marigold; **se faire du ~** to worry; **soucier: se soucier de** *vt* to care about; **soucieux, -euse** *adj* concerned, worried

soucoupe [sukup] *nf* saucer; **~ volante** flying saucer

soudain, e [sudɛ̃, ɛn] *adj* (*douleur, mort*) sudden ♦ *adv* suddenly, all of a sudden

soude [sud] *nf* soda

souder [sude] *vt* (*avec fil à ~*) to solder; (*par soudure autogène*) to weld; (*fig*) to bind together

soudoyer [sudwaje] (*péj*) *vt* to bribe

soudure [sudyʀ] *nf* soldering; welding; (*joint*) soldered joint; weld

souffert, e [sufɛʀ, ɛʀt] *pp de* **souffrir**

souffle [sufl] *nm* (*en expirant*) breath; (*en soufflant*) puff, blow; (*respiration*) breathing; (*d'explosion, de ventilateur*) blast; (*du vent*) blowing; **être à bout de ~** to be out of breath; **un ~ d'air** a breath of air

soufflé, e [sufle] *adj* (*fam: stupéfié*) staggered ♦ *nm* (CULIN) soufflé

souffler [sufle] *vi* (*gén*) to blow; (*haleter*) to puff (and blow) ♦ *vt* (*feu, bougie*) to blow out; (*chasser: poussière etc*) to blow away; (TECH: *verre*) to blow; (*dire*): **~ qch à qn** to whisper sth to sb; **soufflet** *nm* (*instrument*) bellows *pl*; (*gifle*) slap (in the face); **souffleur** *nm* (THÉÂTRE) prompter

souffrance [sufʀɑ̃s] *nf* suffering; **en ~** (*affaire*) pending

souffrant, e [sufʀɑ̃, ɑ̃t] *adj* unwell

souffre-douleur [sufʀədulœʀ] *nm inv* butt, underdog

souffrir [sufʀiʀ] *vi* to suffer, be in pain ♦ *vt* to suffer, endure; (*supporter*) to bear, stand; **~ de** (*maladie, froid*) to suffer from; **elle ne peut pas le ~** she can't stand *ou* bear him

soufre [sufʀ] *nm* sulphur

souhait [swɛ] *nm* wish; **tous nos ~s de** good wishes *ou* our best wishes for; **à vos ~s!** bless you!; **souhaitable** *adj* desirable

souhaiter [swete] *vt* to wish for; **~ la bonne année à qn** to wish sb a happy New Year; **~ que** to hope that

souiller [suje] *vt* to dirty, soil; (*fig: réputation etc*) to sully, tarnish

soûl, e [su, sul] *adj* drunk ♦ *nm*: **tout**

son ~ to one's heart's content
soulagement [sulaʒmɑ̃] *nm* relief
soulager [sulaʒe] *vt* to relieve
soûler [sule] *vt*: **~ qn** to get sb drunk; (*suj*: *boisson*) to make sb drunk; (*fig*) to make sb's head spin *ou* reel; **se ~** *vi* to get drunk
soulever [sul(ə)ve] *vt* to lift; (*poussière*) to send up; (*enthousiasme*) to arouse; (*question, débat*) to raise; **se ~** *vi* (*peuple*) to rise up; (*personne couchée*) to lift o.s. up
soulier [sulje] *nm* shoe
souligner [suliɲe] *vt* to underline; (*fig*) to emphasize, stress
soumettre [sumɛtʀ] *vt* (*pays*) to subject, subjugate; (*rebelle*) to put down, subdue; **se ~ (à)** to submit (to); **~ qch à qn** (*projet etc*) to submit sth to sb
soumis, e [sumi, iz] *adj* submissive; **soumission** *nf* submission
soupape [supap] *nf* valve
soupçon [supsɔ̃] *nm* suspicion; (*petite quantité*): **un ~ de** a hint *ou* touch of; **soupçonner** *vt* to suspect; **soupçonneux, -euse** *adj* suspicious
soupe [sup] *nf* soup
souper [supe] *vi* to have supper ♦ *nm* supper
soupeser [supəze] *vt* to weigh in one's hand(s); (*fig*) to weigh up
soupière [supjɛʀ] *nf* (soup) tureen
soupir [supiʀ] *nm* sigh; **pousser un ~ de soulagement** to heave a sigh of relief
soupirail, -aux [supiʀaj, o] *nm* (small) basement window
soupirer [supiʀe] *vi* to sigh
souple [supl] *adj* supple; (*fig*: *règlement, caractère*) flexible; (: *démarche, taille*) lithe, supple; **souplesse** *nf* suppleness; (*de caractère*) flexibility
source [suʀs] *nf* (*point d'eau*) spring; (*d'un cours d'eau, fig*) source; **de bonne ~** on good authority
sourcil [suʀsi] *nm* (eye)brow; **sourciller** *vi*: **sans sourciller** without turning a hair *ou* batting an eyelid
sourd, e [suʀ, suʀd] *adj* deaf; (*bruit*) muffled; (*douleur*) dull ♦ *nm/f* deaf person; **faire la ~e oreille** to turn a deaf ear; **sourdine** *nf* (*MUS*) mute; **en sourdine** softly, quietly; **sourd-muet, sourde-muette** *adj* deaf-and-dumb ♦ *nm/f* deaf-mute
souriant, e [suʀjɑ̃, jɑ̃t] *adj* cheerful
souricière [suʀisjɛʀ] *nf* mousetrap; (*fig*) trap
sourire [suʀiʀ] *nm* smile ♦ *vi* to smile; **~ à qn** to smile at sb; (*fig*: *plaire à*) to appeal to sb; (*suj*: *chance*) to smile on sb; **garder le ~** to keep smiling
souris [suʀi] *nf* mouse
sournois, e [suʀnwa, waz] *adj* deceitful, underhand
sous [su] *prép* under; **~ la pluie** in the rain; **~ terre** underground; **~ peu** shortly, before long; **sous-bois** *nm inv* undergrowth
souscrire [suskʀiʀ]: **~ à** *vt* to subscribe to
sous...: **sous-directeur, -trice** *nm/f* assistant manager(-manageress); **sous-entendre** *vt* to imply, infer; **sous-entendu, e** *adj* implied ♦ *nm* innuendo, insinuation; **sous-estimer** *vt* to underestimate; **sous-jacent, e** *adj* underlying; **sous-louer** *vt* to sublet; **sous-marin, e** *adj* (*flore, faune*) submarine; (*pêche*) underwater ♦ *nm* submarine; **sous-officier** *nm* ≃ non-commissioned officer (N.C.O.); **sous-produit** *nm* by-product; **sous-pull** *nm* thin poloneck jersey; **soussigné, e** *adj*: **je soussigné** I the undersigned; **sous-sol** *nm* basement; **sous-titre** *nm* subtitle
soustraction [sustʀaksjɔ̃] *nf* subtraction
soustraire [sustʀɛʀ] *vt* to subtract, take away; (*dérober*): **~ qch à qn** to remove sth from sb; **se ~ à** (*autorité etc*) to elude, escape from
sous...: **sous-traitant** *nm* sub-

contractor; **sous-traiter** *vt* to sub-contract; **sous-vêtements** *nmpl* underwear *sg*

soutane [sutan] *nf* cassock, soutane

soute [sut] *nf* hold

soutenir [sut(ə)niʀ] *vt* to support; (*assaut, choc*) to stand up to, withstand; (*intérêt, effort*) to keep up; (*assurer*): **~ que** to maintain that; **soutenu, e** *adj* (*efforts*) sustained, unflagging; (*style*) elevated

souterrain, e [suteʀɛ̃, ɛn] *adj* underground ♦ *nm* underground passage

soutien [sutjɛ̃] *nm* support; **soutien-gorge** *nm* bra

soutirer [sutiʀe] *vt*: **~ qch à qn** to squeeze *ou* get sth out of sb

souvenir [suv(ə)niʀ] *nm* memory; (*objet*) souvenir ♦ *vb*: **se ~ de** to remember; **se ~ que** to remember that; **en ~ de** in memory *ou* remembrance of

souvent [suvɑ̃] *adv* often; **peu ~** seldom, infrequently

souverain, e [suv(ə)ʀɛ̃, ɛn] *nm/f* sovereign, monarch

soyeux, -euse [swajø, øz] *adj* silky

soyons *etc* [swajɔ̃] *vb voir* **être**

spacieux, -euse [spasjø, jøz] *adj* spacious, roomy

spaghettis [spageti] *nmpl* spaghetti *sg*

sparadrap [spaʀadʀa] *nm* sticking plaster (*BRIT*), Bandaid ® (*US*)

spatial, e, -aux [spasjal, jo] *adj* (*AVIAT*) space *cpd*

speaker, ine [spikœʀ, kʀin] *nm/f* announcer

spécial, e, -aux [spesjal, jo] *adj* special; (*bizarre*) peculiar; **spécialement** *adv* especially, particularly; (*tout exprès*) specially; **spécialiser**: **se spécialiser** *vi* to specialize; **spécialiste** *nm/f* specialist; **spécialité** *nf* speciality; (*branche*) special field

spécifier [spesifje] *vt* to specify, state

spécimen [spesimɛn] *nm* specimen

spectacle [spɛktakl] *nm* (*scène*) sight; (*représentation*) show; (*industrie*) show business; **spectaculaire** *adj* spectacular

spectateur, -trice [spɛktatœʀ, tʀis] *nm/f* (*CINÉMA etc*) member of the audience; (*SPORT*) spectator; (*d'un événement*) onlooker, witness

spéculer [spekyle] *vi* to speculate

spéléologie [speleɔlɔʒi] *nf* potholing

sperme [spɛʀm] *nm* semen, sperm

sphère [sfɛʀ] *nf* sphere

spirale [spiʀal] *nf* spiral

spirituel, le [spiʀitɥɛl] *adj* spiritual; (*fin, piquant*) witty

splendide [splɑ̃did] *adj* splendid

sponsoring [spɔ̃sɔʀiŋ] *nm* sponsorship

sponsoriser [spɔ̃sɔʀize] *vt* to sponsor

spontané, e [spɔ̃tane] *adj* spontaneous; **spontanéité** *nf* spontaneity

sport [spɔʀ] *nm* sport ♦ *adj inv* (*vêtement*) casual; **faire du ~** to do sport; **~s d'hiver** winter sports; **sportif, -ive** *adj* (*journal, association, épreuve*) sports *cpd*; (*allure, démarche*) athletic; (*attitude, esprit*) sporting

spot [spɔt] *nm* (*lampe*) spot(light); **~ (publicitaire)** commercial (break)

square [skwaʀ] *nm* public garden(s)

squelette [skəlɛt] *nm* skeleton; **squelettique** *adj* scrawny

stabiliser [stabilize] *vt* to stabilize

stable [stabl] *adj* stable, steady

stade [stad] *nm* (*SPORT*) stadium; (*phase, niveau*) stage; **stadier** *nm* steward (*working in a stadium*)

stage [staʒ] *nm* (*cours*) training course; **~ de formation (professionnelle)** vocational (training) course; **~ de perfectionnement** advanced training course; **stagiaire** *nm/f, adj* trainee

stagner [stagne] *vi* to stagnate

stalle [stal] *nf* stall, box

stand [stɑ̃d] *nm* (*d'exposition*) stand; (*de foire*) stall; **~ de tir** (*à la foire, SPORT*) shooting range

standard [stɑ̃daʀ] *adj inv* standard ♦ *nm* switchboard; **standardiste** *nm/f* switchboard operator

standing [stɑ̃diŋ] *nm* standing; **de grand ~** luxury
starter [startɛr] *nm* (*AUTO*) choke
station [stasjɔ̃] *nf* station; (*de bus*) stop; (*de villégiature*) resort; **~ balnéaire** seaside resort; **~ de ski** ski resort; **~ de taxis** taxi rank (*BRIT*) *ou* stand (*US*); **stationnement** *nm* parking; **stationner** *vi* to park; **station-service** *nf* service station
statistique [statistik] *nf* (*science*) statistics *sg*; (*rapport, étude*) statistic ♦ *adj* statistical
statue [staty] *nf* statue
statu quo [statykwo] *nm* status quo
statut [staty] *nm* status; **~s** *nmpl* (*JUR, ADMIN*) statutes; **statutaire** *adj* statutory
Sté *abr* = **société**
steak [stɛk] *nm* steak; **~ haché** hamburger
sténo(dactylo) [steno(daktilo)] *nf* shorthand typist (*BRIT*), stenographer (*US*)
sténo(graphie) [steno(grafi)] *nf* shorthand
stéréo [stereo] *adj* stereo
stérile [steril] *adj* sterile
stérilet [sterilɛ] *nm* coil, loop
stériliser [sterilize] *vt* to sterilize
stigmates [stigmat] *nmpl* scars, marks
stimulant [stimylɑ̃] *nm* (*fig*) stimulus, incentive; (*physique*) stimulant
stimuler [stimyle] *vt* to stimulate
stipuler [stipyle] *vt* to stipulate
stock [stɔk] *nm* stock; **stocker** *vt* to stock
stop [stɔp] *nm* (*AUTO*: *écriteau*) stop sign; (: *feu arrière*) brake-light; **faire du ~** (*fam*) to hitch(hike); **stopper** *vt, vi* to stop, halt
store [stɔr] *nm* blind; (*de magasin*) shade, awning
strabisme [strabism] *nm* squinting
strapontin [strapɔ̃tɛ̃] *nm* jump *ou* foldaway seat
stratégie [strateʒi] *nf* strategy; **stratégique** *adj* strategic
stress [strɛs] *nm* stress; **stressant, e** *adj* stressful; **stresser** *vt*: **stresser qn** to make sb (feel) tense
strict, e [strikt] *adj* strict; (*tenue, décor*) severe, plain; **le ~ nécessaire/minimum** the bare essentials/minimum
strident, e [stridɑ̃, ɑ̃t] *adj* shrill, strident
strophe [strɔf] *nf* verse, stanza
structure [stryktyr] *nf* structure
studieux, -euse [stydjø, jøz] *adj* studious
studio [stydjo] *nm* (*logement*) (one-roomed) flatlet (*BRIT*) *ou* apartment (*US*); (*d'artiste, TV etc*) studio
stupéfait, e [stypefɛ, ɛt] *adj* astonished
stupéfiant [stypefjɑ̃, jɑ̃t] *adj* (*étonnant*) stunning, astounding ♦ *nm* (*MÉD*) drug, narcotic
stupéfier [stypefje] *vt* (*étonner*) to stun, astonish
stupeur [stypœr] *nf* astonishment
stupide [stypid] *adj* stupid; **stupidité** *nf* stupidity; (*parole, acte*) stupid thing (to do *ou* say)
style [stil] *nm* style
stylé, e [stile] *adj* well-trained
styliste [stilist] *nm/f* designer
stylo [stilo] *nm*: **~ (à encre)** (fountain) pen; **~ (à) bille** ball-point pen; **~-feutre** felt-tip pen
su, e [sy] *pp de* **savoir** ♦ *nm*: **au ~ de** with the knowledge of
suave [sɥav] *adj* sweet
subalterne [sybaltɛrn] *adj* (*employé, officier*) junior; (*rôle*) subordinate, subsidiary ♦ *nm/f* subordinate
subconscient [sypkɔ̃sjɑ̃] *nm* subconscious
subir [sybir] *vt* (*affront, dégâts*) to suffer; (*opération, châtiment*) to undergo
subit, e [sybi, it] *adj* sudden; **subitement** *adv* suddenly, all of a sudden
subjectif, -ive [sybʒɛktif, iv] *adj* subjective

subjonctif [sybʒɔ̃ktif] *nm* subjunctive
subjuguer [sybʒyge] *vt* to captivate
submerger [sybmɛʀʒe] *vt* to submerge; (*fig*) to overwhelm
subordonné, e [sybɔʀdɔne] *adj, nm/f* subordinate
subrepticement [sybʀɛptismɑ̃] *adv* surreptitiously
subside [sybzid] *nm* grant
subsidiaire [sybzidjɛʀ] *adj*: **question ~** deciding question
subsister [sybziste] *vi* (*rester*) to remain, subsist; (*survivre*) to live on
substance [sypstɑ̃s] *nf* substance
substituer [sypstitɥe] *vt*: **~ qn/qch à** to substitute sb/sth for; **se ~ à qn** (*évincer*) to substitute o.s. for sb
substitut [sypstity] *nm* (*succédané*) substitute
subterfuge [sypteʀfyʒ] *nm* subterfuge
subtil, e [syptil] *adj* subtle
subtiliser [syptilize] *vt*: **~ qch (à qn)** to spirit sth away (from sb)
subvenir [sybvəniʀ]: **~ à** *vt* to meet
subvention [sybvɑ̃sjɔ̃] *nf* subsidy, grant; **subventionner** *vt* to subsidize
suc [syk] *nm* (*BOT*) sap; (*de viande, fruit*) juice
succédané [syksedane] *nm* substitute
succéder [syksede]: **~ à** *vt* to succeed; **se ~** *vi* (*accidents, années*) to follow one another
succès [syksɛ] *nm* success; **avoir du ~** to be a success, be successful; **à ~** successful; **~ de librairie** bestseller; **~ (féminins)** conquests
successif, -ive [syksesif, iv] *adj* successive
successeur [syksesœʀ] *nm* successor
succession [syksesjɔ̃] *nf* (*série, POL*) succession; (*JUR: patrimoine*) estate, inheritance
succomber [sykɔ̃be] *vi* to die, succumb; (*fig*): **~ à** to succumb to
succulent, e [sykylɑ̃, ɑ̃t] *adj* (*repas, mets*) delicious
succursale [sykyʀsal] *nf* branch
sucer [syse] *vt* to suck; **sucette** *nf* (*bonbon*) lollipop; (*de bébé*) dummy (*BRIT*), pacifier (*US*)
sucre [sykʀ] *nm* (*substance*) sugar; (*morceau*) lump of sugar, sugar lump *ou* cube; **~ d'orge** barley sugar; **~ en morceaux/en poudre** lump/caster sugar; **~ glace/roux** icing/brown sugar; **sucré, e** *adj* (*produit alimentaire*) sweetened; (*au goût*) sweet; **sucrer** *vt* (*thé, café*) to sweeten, put sugar in; **sucreries** *nfpl* (*bonbons*) sweets, sweet things; **sucrier** *nm* (*récipient*) sugar bowl
sud [syd] *nm*: **le ~** the south ♦ *adj inv* south; (*côte*) south, southern; **au ~** (*situation*) in the south; (*direction*) to the south; **au ~ de** (to the) south of; **sud-africain, e** *adj* South African ♦ *nm/f*: **Sud-Africain, e** South African; **sud-américain, e** *adj* South American ♦ *nm/f*: **Sud-Américain, e** South American; **sud-est** *nm, adj inv* south-east, **sud-ouest** *nm, adj inv* south-west
Suède [sɥɛd] *nf*: **la ~** Sweden; **suédois, e** *adj* Swedish ♦ *nm/f*: **Suédois, e** Swede ♦ *nm* (*LING*) Swedish
suer [sɥe] *vi* to sweat; (*suinter*) to ooze; **sueur** *nf* sweat; **en sueur** sweating, in a sweat; **donner des sueurs froids à qn** to put sb in(to) a cold sweat
suffire [syfiʀ] *vi* (*être assez*): **~ (à qn/pour qch/pour faire)** to be enough *ou* sufficient (for sb/for sth/to do); **il suffit d'une négligence ...** it only takes one act of carelessness ...; **il suffit qu'on oublie pour que ...** one only needs to forget for ...; **ça suffit!** that's enough!
suffisamment [syfizamɑ̃] *adv* sufficiently, enough; **~ de** sufficient, enough
suffisant, e [syfizɑ̃, ɑ̃t] *adj* sufficient; (*résultats*) satisfactory; (*vaniteux*) self-important, bumptious
suffixe [syfiks] *nm* suffix
suffoquer [syfɔke] *vt* to choke, suffocate; (*stupéfier*) to stagger, astound ♦ *vi*

to choke, suffocate

suffrage [syfʀaʒ] *nm* (*POL*: *voix*) vote

suggérer [sygʒeʀe] *vt* to suggest; **suggestion** *nf* suggestion

suicide [sɥisid] *nm* suicide; **suicider**: **se suicider** *vi* to commit suicide

suie [sɥi] *nf* soot

suinter [sɥɛ̃te] *vi* to ooze

suis [sɥi] *vb voir* **être**; **suivre**

suisse [sɥis] *adj* Swiss ♦ *nm*: **S~** Swiss *pl inv* ♦ *nf*: **la S~** Switzerland; **la S~ romande/allemande** French-speaking/German-speaking Switzerland; **Suissesse** *nf* Swiss (woman *ou* girl)

suite [sɥit] *nf* (*continuation*: *d'énumération etc*) rest, remainder; (: *de feuilleton*) continuation; (: *film etc sur le même thème*) sequel; (*série*) series, succession; (*conséquence*) result; (*ordre, liaison logique*) coherence; (*appartement, MUS*) suite; (*escorte*) retinue, suite; **~s** *nfpl* (*d'une maladie etc*) effects; **prendre la ~ de** (*directeur etc*) to succeed, take over from; **donner ~ à** (*requête, projet*) to follow up; **faire ~ à** to follow; **(faisant) ~ à votre lettre du ...** further to your letter of the ...; **de ~** (*d'affilée*) in succession; (*immédiatement*) at once; **par la ~** afterwards, subsequently; **à la ~** one after the other; **à la ~ de** (*derrière*) behind; (*en conséquence de*) following

suivant, e [sɥivɑ̃, ɑ̃t] *adj* next, following ♦ *prép* (*selon*) according to; **au ~!** next!

suivi, e [sɥivi] *adj* (*effort, qualité*) consistent; (*cohérent*) coherent; **très/peu ~** (*cours*) well-/poorly-attended

suivre [sɥivʀ] *vt* (*gén*) to follow; (*SCOL*: *cours*) to attend; (*comprendre*) to keep up with; (*COMM*: *article*) to continue to stock ♦ *vi* to follow; (*élève*: *assimiler*) to keep up; **se ~** *vi* (*accidents etc*) to follow one after the other; **faire ~** (*lettre*) to forward; **"à ~"** "to be continued"

sujet, te [syʒɛ, ɛt] *adj*: **être ~ à** (*vertige etc*) to be liable *ou* subject to ♦ *nm/f* (*d'un souverain*) subject ♦ *nm* subject; **au ~ de** about; **~ de conversation** topic *ou* subject of conversation; **~ d'examen** (*SCOL*) examination question

summum [sɔ(m)mɔm] *nm*: **le ~ de** the height of

super [sypɛʀ] (*fam*) *adj inv* terrific, great, fantastic, super

superbe [sypɛʀb] *adj* magnificent, superb

super(carburant) [sypɛʀ(kaʀbyʀɑ̃)] *nm* ≃ 4-star petrol (*BRIT*), ≃ high-octane gasoline (*US*)

supercherie [sypɛʀʃəʀi] *nf* trick

supérette [sypeʀɛt] *nf* (*COMM*) minimarket, superette (*US*)

superficie [sypɛʀfisi] *nf* (surface) area

superficiel, le [sypɛʀfisjɛl] *adj* superficial

superflu, e [sypɛʀfly] *adj* superfluous

supérieur, e [sypeʀjœʀ] *adj* (*lèvre, étages, classes*) upper; (*plus élevé*: *température, niveau, enseignement*): **~ (à)** higher (than); (*meilleur*: *qualité, produit*): **~ (à)** superior (to); (*excellent, hautain*) superior ♦ *nm, nf* superior; **supériorité** *nf* superiority

superlatif [sypɛʀlatif] *nm* superlative

supermarché [sypɛʀmaʀʃe] *nm* supermarket

superposer [sypɛʀpoze] *vt* (*faire chevaucher*) to superimpose; **lits superposés** bunk beds

superproduction [sypɛʀpʀɔdyksjɔ̃] *nf* (*film*) spectacular

superpuissance [sypɛʀpɥisɑ̃s] *nf* super-power

superstitieux, -euse [sypɛʀstisjø, jøz] *adj* superstitious

superviser [sypɛʀvize] *vt* to supervise

supplanter [syplɑ̃te] *vt* to supplant

suppléance [sypleɑ̃s] *nf*: **faire des ~s** (*professeur*) to do supply teaching; **suppléant, e** *adj* (*professeur*) supply *cpd*; (*juge, fonctionnaire*) deputy *cpd* ♦ *nm/f* (*professeur*) supply teacher

suppléer [syplee] *vt* (*ajouter*: *mot manquant etc*) to supply, provide; (*compenser*: *lacune*) to fill in; **~ à** to make up for

supplément [syplemɑ̃] *nm* supplement; (*de frites etc*) extra portion; **un ~ de travail** extra *ou* additional work; **payer un ~** to pay an additional charge; **le vin est en ~** wine is extra; **supplémentaire** *adj* additional, further; (*train, bus*) relief *cpd*, extra

supplications [syplikasjɔ̃] *nfpl* pleas, entreaties

supplice [syplis] *nm* torture *no pl*

supplier [syplije] *vt* to implore, beseech

support [sypɔʀ] *nm* support; (*publicitaire*) medium; (*audio-visuel*) aid

supportable [sypɔʀtabl] *adj* (*douleur*) bearable

supporter¹ [sypɔʀtœʀ] *nm* supporter, fan

supporter² [sypɔʀte] *vt* (*conséquences, épreuve*) to bear, endure; (*défauts, personne*) to put up with; (*suj*: *chose*: *chaleur etc*) to withstand; (*suj*: *personne*: *chaleur, vin*) to be able to take

supposer [sypoze] *vt* to suppose; (*impliquer*) to presuppose; **à ~ que** supposing (that)

suppositoire [sypozitwaʀ] *nm* suppository

suppression [sypʀesjɔ̃] *nf* (*voir supprimer*) cancellation; removal; deletion

supprimer [sypʀime] *vt* (*congés, service d'autobus etc*) to cancel; (*emplois, privilèges, témoin gênant*) to do away with; (*cloison, cause, anxiété*) to remove; (*clause, mot*) to delete

suprême [sypʀɛm] *adj* supreme

MOT-CLÉ

sur [syʀ] *prép* **1** (*position*) on; (*pardessus*) over; (*au-dessus*) above; **pose-le sur la table** put it on the table; **je n'ai pas d'argent sur moi** I haven't any money on me

2 (*direction*) towards; **en allant sur Paris** going towards Paris; **sur votre droite** on *ou* to your right

3 (*à propos de*) on, about; **un livre/une conférence sur Balzac** a book/lecture on *ou* about Balzac

4 (*proportion, mesures*) out of, by; **un sur 10** one in 10; (SCOL) one out of 10; **4 m sur 2** 4 m by 2

sur ce *adv* hereupon

sûr, e [syʀ] *adj* sure, certain; (*digne de confiance*) reliable; (*sans danger*) safe; (*diagnostic, goût*) reliable; **le plus ~ est de** the safest thing is to; **~ de soi** self-confident; **~ et certain** absolutely certain

surcharge [syʀʃaʀʒ] *nf* (*de passagers, marchandises*) excess load; **surcharger** *vt* to overload

surchoix [syʀʃwa] *adj inv* top-quality

surclasser [syʀklɑse] *vt* to outclass

surcroît [syʀkʀwa] *nm*: **un ~ de** additional *+nom*; **par ou de ~** moreover; **en ~** in addition

surdité [syʀdite] *nf* deafness

surélever [syʀel(ə)ve] *vt* to raise, heighten

sûrement [syʀmɑ̃] *adv* (*certainement*) certainly; (*sans risques*) safely

surenchère [syʀɑ̃ʃɛʀ] *nf* (*aux enchères*) higher bid; **surenchérir** *vi* to bid higher; (*fig*) to try and outbid each other

surent [syʀ] *vb voir* **savoir**

surestimer [syʀɛstime] *vt* to overestimate

sûreté [syʀte] *nf* (*sécurité*) safety; (*exactitude*: *de renseignements etc*) reliability; (*d'un geste*) steadiness; **mettre en ~** to put in a safe place; **pour plus de ~** as an extra precaution, to be on the safe side

surf [sœʀf] *nm* surfing

surface [syʀfas] *nf* surface; (*superficie*) surface area; **une grande ~** a supermarket; **faire ~** to surface; **en ~** near the surface; (*fig*) superficially

surfait, e [syʀfɛ, ɛt] *adj* overrated
surfer [syʀfe] *vi*: **~ sur Internet** to surf *ou* browse the Internet
surgelé, e [syʀʒəle] *adj* (deep-)frozen ♦ *nm*: **les ~s** (deep-)frozen food
surgir [syʀʒiʀ] *vi* to appear suddenly; (*fig*: *problème, conflit*) to arise
sur...: **surhumain, e** *adj* superhuman; **sur-le-champ** *adv* immediately; **surlendemain** *nm*: **le surlendemain (soir)** two days later (in the evening); **le surlendemain de** two days after; **surmenage** *nm* overwork(ing); **surmener**: **se surmener** *vi* to overwork
surmonter [syʀmɔ̃te] *vt* (*vaincre*) to overcome; (*être au-dessus de*) to top
surnaturel, le [syʀnatyʀɛl] *adj, nm* supernatural
surnom [syʀnɔ̃] *nm* nickname
surnombre [syʀnɔ̃bʀ] *nm*: **être en ~** to be too many (*ou* one too many)
surpeuplé, e [syʀpœple] *adj* overpopulated
sur-place [syʀplas] *nm* **faire du ~-~** to mark time
surplomber [syʀplɔ̃be] *vt, vi* to overhang
surplus [syʀply] *nm* (*COMM*) surplus; (*reste*): **~ de bois** wood left over
surprenant, e [syʀpʀənɑ̃, ɑ̃t] *adj* amazing
surprendre [syʀpʀɑ̃dʀ] *vt* (*étonner*) to surprise; (*tomber sur*: *intrus etc*) to catch; (*entendre*) to overhear
surpris, e [syʀpʀi, iz] *adj*: **~ (de/que)** surprised (at/that); **surprise** *nf* surprise; **faire une surprise à qn** to give sb a surprise; **surprise-partie** *nf* party
surréservation [syʀʀezɛʀvasjɔ̃] *nf* double booking, overbooking
sursaut [syʀso] *nm* start, jump; **~ de** (*énergie, indignation*) sudden fit *ou* burst of; **en ~** with a start; **sursauter** *vi* to (give a) start, jump
sursis [syʀsi] *nm* (*JUR*: *gén*) suspended sentence; (*fig*) reprieve
surtaxe [syʀtaks] *nf* surcharge
surtout [syʀtu] *adv* (*avant tout, d'abord*) above all; (*spécialement, particulièrement*) especially; **~, ne dites rien!** whatever you do don't say anything!; **~ pas!** certainly *ou* definitely not!; **~ que ...** especially as ...
surveillance [syʀvɛjɑ̃s] *nf* watch; (*POLICE, MIL*) surveillance; **sous ~ médicale** under medical supervision
surveillant, e [syʀvɛjɑ̃, ɑ̃t] *nm/f* (*de prison*) warder; (*SCOL*) monitor
surveiller [syʀveje] *vt* (*enfant, bagages*) to watch, keep an eye on; (*prisonnier, suspect*) to keep (a) watch on; (*territoire, bâtiment*) to (keep) watch over; (*travaux*) to supervise; (*SCOL*: *examen*) to invigilate; **~ son langage/sa ligne** to watch one's language/figure
survenir [syʀvəniʀ] *vi* (*incident, retards*) to occur, arise; (*événement*) to take place
survêt(ement) [syʀvɛt(mɑ̃)] *nm* tracksuit
survie [syʀvi] *nf* survival; **survivant, e** *nm/f* survivor; **survivre** *vi* to survive; **survivre à** (*accident etc*) to survive
survoler [syʀvɔle] *vt* to fly over; (*fig*: *livre*) to skim through
survolté, e [syʀvɔlte] *adj* (*fig*) worked up
sus [sy(s)]: **en ~ de** *prép* in addition to, over and above; **en ~** in addition
susceptible [sysɛptibl] *adj* touchy, sensitive; **~ de faire** liable to do
susciter [sysite] *vt* (*admiration*) to arouse; (*ennuis*): **~ (à qn)** to create (for sb)
suspect, e [syspɛ(kt), ɛkt] *adj* suspicious; (*témoignage, opinions*) suspect ♦ *nm/f* suspect; **suspecter** *vt* to suspect; (*honnêteté de qn*) to question, have one's suspicions about
suspendre [syspɑ̃dʀ] *vt* (*accrocher*: *vêtement*): **~ qch (à)** to hang sth up (on); (*interrompre, démettre*) to suspend; **se ~ à** to hang from
suspendu, e [syspɑ̃dy] *adj* (*accroché*):

~ **à** hanging on (*ou* from); (*perché*): ~ **au-dessus de** suspended over

suspens [syspɑ̃]: **en ~** *adv* (*affaire*) in abeyance; **tenir en ~** to keep in suspense

suspense [syspɛns, syspɑ̃s] *nm* suspense

suspension [syspɑ̃sjɔ̃] *nf* suspension; (*lustre*) light fitting *ou* fitment

sut [sy] *vb voir* **savoir**

suture [sytyʀ] *nf* (*MÉD*): **point de ~** stitch

svelte [svɛlt] *adj* slender, svelte

SVP *abr* (= *s'il vous plaît*) please

sweat-shirt [switʃœʀt] (*pl* **~-~s**) *nm* sweatshirt

syllabe [si(l)lab] *nf* syllable

symbole [sɛ̃bɔl] *nm* symbol; **symbolique** *adj* symbolic(al); (*geste, offrande*) token *cpd*; **symboliser** *vt* to symbolize

symétrique [simetʀik] *adj* symmetrical

sympa [sɛ̃pa] (*fam*) *adj inv* nice; **sois ~, prête-le moi** be a pal and lend it to me

sympathie [sɛ̃pati] *nf* (*inclination*) liking; (*affinité*) friendship, (*condoléances*) sympathy; **j'ai beaucoup de ~ pour lui** I like him a lot; **sympathique** *adj* nice, friendly

sympathisant, e [sɛ̃patizɑ̃, ɑ̃t] *nm/f* sympathizer

sympathiser [sɛ̃patize] *vi* (*voisins etc: s'entendre*) to get on (*BRIT*) *ou* along (*US*) (well)

symphonie [sɛ̃fɔni] *nf* symphony

symptôme [sɛ̃ptom] *nm* symptom

synagogue [sinagɔg] *nf* synagogue

syncope [sɛ̃kɔp] *nf* (*MÉD*) blackout; **tomber en ~** to faint, pass out

syndic [sɛ̃dik] *nm* (*d'immeuble*) managing agent

syndical, e, -aux [sɛ̃dikal, o] *adj* (trade) union *cpd*; **syndicaliste** *nm/f* trade unionist

syndicat [sɛ̃dika] *nm* (*d'ouvriers, employés*) (trade) union; **~ d'initiative** tourist office; **syndiqué, e** *adj* belonging to a (trade) union; **syndiquer: se syndiquer** *vi* to form a trade union; (*adhérer*) to join a trade union

synonyme [sinɔnim] *adj* synonymous ♦ *nm* synonym; **~ de** synonymous with

syntaxe [sɛ̃taks] *nf* syntax

synthèse [sɛ̃tɛz] *nf* synthesis

synthétique [sɛ̃tetik] *adj* synthetic

Syrie [siʀi] *nf*: **la ~** Syria

systématique [sistematik] *adj* systematic

système [sistɛm] *nm* system; **~ D** (*fam*) resourcefulness

T, t

t' [t] *pron voir* **te**

ta [ta] *adj voir* **ton**[1]

tabac [taba] *nm* tobacco; (*magasin*) tobacconist's (shop); **~ blond/brun** light/dark tobacco

tabagisme [tabaʒism] *nm*: **~ passif** passive smoking

tabasser [tabase] (*fam*) *vt* to beat up

table [tabl] *nf* table; **à ~!** dinner *etc* is ready!; **se mettre à ~** to sit down to eat; **mettre la ~** to lay the table; **faire ~ rase de** to make a clean sweep of; **~ à repasser** ironing board; **~ de cuisson** (*à l'électricité*) hotplate; (*au gaz*) gas ring; **~ de nuit** *ou* **de chevet** bedside table; **~ des matières** (table of) contents *pl*; **~ d'orientation** viewpoint indicator; **~ roulante** trolley

tableau, x [tablo] *nm* (*peinture*) painting; (*reproduction, fig*) picture; (*panneau*) board; (*schéma*) table, chart; **~ d'affichage** notice board; **~ de bord** dashboard; (*AVIAT*) instrument panel; **~ noir** blackboard

tabler [table] *vi*: **~ sur** to bank on

tablette [tablɛt] *nf* (*planche*) shelf; **~ de chocolat** bar of chocolate

tableur [tablœʀ] *nm* spreadsheet

tablier [tablije] *nm* apron

tabou [tabu] *nm* taboo

tabouret [tabuʀɛ] *nm* stool
tac [tak] *nm*: **il m'a répondu du ~ au ~** he answered me right back
tache [taʃ] *nf* (*saleté*) stain, mark; (*ART, de couleur, lumière*) spot; **~ de rousseur** freckle
tâche [tɑʃ] *nf* task
tacher [taʃe] *vt* to stain, mark
tâcher [tɑʃe] *vi*: **~ de faire** to try *ou* endeavour to do
tacheté, e [taʃte] *adj* spotted
tacot [tako] (*péj*) *nm* banger (*BRIT*), (old) heap
tact [takt] *nm* tact; **avoir du ~** to be tactful
tactique [taktik] *adj* tactical ♦ *nf* (*technique*) tactics *sg*; (*plan*) tactic
taie [tɛ] *nf*: **~ (d'oreiller)** pillowslip, pillowcase
taille [taj] *nf* cutting; (*d'arbre etc*) pruning; (*milieu du corps*) waist; (*hauteur*) height; (*grandeur*) size; **de ~ à faire** capable of doing; **de ~** sizeable; **taille-crayon(s)** *nm* pencil sharpener
tailler [taje] *vt* (*pierre, diamant*) to cut; (*arbre, plante*) to prune; (*vêtement*) to cut out; (*crayon*) to sharpen
tailleur [tajœʀ] *nm* (*couturier*) tailor; (*vêtement*) suit; **en ~** (*assis*) cross-legged
taillis [taji] *nm* copse
taire [tɛʀ] *vi*: **faire ~ qn** to make sb be quiet; **se ~** *vi* to be silent *ou* quiet
talc [talk] *nm* talc, talcum powder
talent [talɑ̃] *nm* talent
talkie-walkie [tokiwoki] *nm* walkie-talkie
taloche [talɔʃ] (*fam*) *nf* clout, cuff
talon [talɔ̃] *nm* heel; (*de chèque, billet*) stub, counterfoil (*BRIT*); **~s plats/aiguilles** flat/stiletto heels
talonner [talɔne] *vt* (*suivre*) to follow hot on the heels of; (*harceler*) to hound
talus [taly] *nm* embankment
tambour [tɑ̃buʀ] *nm* (*MUS, aussi*) drum; (*musicien*) drummer; (*porte*) revolving door(s *pl*); **tambourin** *nm* tambourine; **tambouriner** *vi* to drum; **tambouriner à/sur** to drum on
tamis [tami] *nm* sieve
Tamise [tamiz] *nf*: **la ~** the Thames
tamisé, e [tamize] *adj* (*fig*) subdued, soft
tampon [tɑ̃pɔ̃] *nm* (*de coton, d'ouate*) wad, pad; (*amortisseur*) buffer; (*bouchon*) plug, stopper; (*cachet, timbre*) stamp; **(mémoire) ~** (*INFORM*) buffer; **~ (hygiénique)** tampon; **tamponner** *vt* (*timbres*) to stamp; (*heurter*) to crash *ou* ram into; **tamponneuse** *adj f*: **autos tamponneuses** dodgems
tandem [tɑ̃dɛm] *nm* tandem
tandis [tɑ̃di]: **~ que** *conj* while
tanguer [tɑ̃ge] *vi* to pitch (and toss)
tanière [tanjɛʀ] *nf* lair, den
tanné, e [tane] *adj* weather-beaten
tanner [tane] *vt* to tan; (*fam: harceler*) to badger
tant [tɑ̃] *adv* so much; **~ de** (*sable, eau*) so much; (*gens, livres*) so many; **~ que** as long as; (*autant que*) as much as; **~ mieux** that's great; (*avec une certaine réserve*) so much the better; **~ pis** too bad; (*conciliant*) never mind
tante [tɑ̃t] *nf* aunt
tantôt [tɑ̃to] *adv* (*parfois*): **~ ... ~** now ... now; (*cet après-midi*) this afternoon
taon [tɑ̃] *nm* horsefly
tapage [tapaʒ] *nm* uproar, din
tapageur, -euse [tapaʒœʀ, øz] *adj* noisy; (*voyant*) loud, flashy
tape [tap] *nf* slap
tape-à-l'œil [tapalœj] *adj inv* flashy, showy
taper [tape] *vt* (*porte*) to bang, slam; (*enfant*) to slap; (*dactylographier*) to type (out); (*fam: emprunter*): **~ qn de 10 F** to touch sb for 10 F ♦ *vi* (*soleil*) to beat down; **se ~** *vt* (*repas*) to put away; (*fam: corvée*) to get landed with; **~ sur qn** to thump sb; (*fig*) to run sb down; **~ sur un clou** to hit a nail; **~ sur la table** to bang on the table; **~ à** (*porte etc*) to knock on; **~ dans** (*se ser-*

vir) to dig into; **~ des mains/pieds** to clap one's hands/stamp one's feet; **~ (à la machine)** to type; **se ~ un travail** (*fam*) to land o.s. a job

tapi, e [tapi] *adj* (*blotti*) crouching; (*caché*) hidden away

tapis [tapi] *nm* carpet; (*petit*) rug; **mettre sur le ~** (*fig*) to bring up for discussion; **~ de bain** bath mat; **~ de sol** (*de tente*) groundsheet; **~ de souris** (INFORM) mouse mat; **~ roulant** (*pour piétons*) moving walkway; (*pour bagages*) carousel

tapisser [tapise] *vt* (*avec du papier peint*) to paper; (*recouvrir*): **~ qch (de)** to cover sth (with); **tapisserie** *nf* (*tenture, broderie*) tapestry; (*papier peint*) wallpaper; **tapissier-décorateur** *nm* interior decorator

tapoter [tapɔte] *vt* (*joue, main*) to pat; (*objet*) to tap

taquin, e [takɛ̃, in] *adj* teasing; **taquiner** *vt* to tease

tarabiscoté, e [taʀabiskɔte] *adj* over-ornate, fussy

tard [taʀ] *adv* late; **plus ~** later (on); **au plus ~** at the latest; **sur le ~** late in life

tarder [taʀde] *vi* (*chose*) to be a long time coming; (*personne*): **~ à faire** to delay doing; **il me tarde d'être** I am longing to be; **sans (plus) ~** without (further) delay

tardif, -ive [taʀdif, iv] *adj* late

taré, e [taʀe] *nm/f* cretin

tarif [taʀif] *nm*: **~ des consommations** price list; **~s postaux/douaniers** postal/customs rates; **~ des taxis** taxi fares; **~ plein/réduit** (*train*) full/reduced fare; (*téléphone*) peak/off-peak rate

tarir [taʀiʀ] *vi* to dry up, run dry

tarte [taʀt] *nf* tart; **~ aux fraises** strawberry tart; **~ Tatin** ≃ apple upside-down tart

tartine [taʀtin] *nf* slice of bread; **~ de miel** slice of bread and honey; **tartiner** *vt* to spread; **fromage à tartiner** cheese spread

tartre [taʀtʀ] *nm* (*des dents*) tartar; (*de bouilloire*) fur, scale

tas [tɑ] *nm* heap, pile; (*fig*): **un ~ de** heaps of, lots of; **en ~** in a heap *ou* pile; **formé sur le ~** trained on the job

tasse [tɑs] *nf* cup; **~ à café** coffee cup

tassé, e [tɑse] *adj*: **bien ~** (*café etc*) strong

tasser [tɑse] *vt* (*terre, neige*) to pack down; (*entasser*): **~ qch dans** to cram sth into; **se ~** *vi* (*se serrer*) to squeeze up; (*s'affaisser*) to settle; (*fig*) to settle down

tata [tata] *nf* auntie

tâter [tɑte] *vt* to feel; (*fig*) to try out; **se ~** (*hésiter*) to be in two minds; **~ de** (*prison etc*) to have a taste of

tatillon, ne [tatijɔ̃, ɔn] *adj* pernickety

tâtonnement [tɑtɔnmɑ̃] *nm*: **par ~s** (*fig*) by trial and error

tâtonner [tɑtɔne] *vi* to grope one's way along

tâtons [tɑtɔ̃]: **à ~** *adv*: **chercher/avancer à ~** to grope around for/grope one's way forward

tatouage [tatwaʒ] *nm* tattoo

tatouer [tatwe] *vt* to tattoo

taudis [todi] *nm* hovel, slum

taule [tol] (*fam*) *nf* nick (*fam*), prison

taupe [top] *nf* mole

taureau, x [tɔʀo] *nm* bull; (*signe*): **le T~** Taurus

tauromachie [tɔʀɔmaʃi] *nf* bullfighting

taux [to] *nm* rate; (*d'alcool*) level; **~ de change** exchange rate; **~ d'intérêt** interest rate

taxe [taks] *nf* tax; (*douanière*) duty; **toutes ~s comprises** inclusive of tax; **la boutique hors ~s** the duty free shop; **~ à la valeur ajoutée** value added tax

taxer [takse] *vt* (*personne*) to tax; (*produit*) to put a tax on, tax

taxi [taksi] *nm* taxi; (*chauffeur: fam*) taxi

driver

Tchécoslovaquie [tʃekɔslɔvaki] *nf* Czechoslovakia; **tchèque** *adj* Czech ♦ *nm/f*: **Tchèque** Czech ♦ *nm* (*LING*) Czech; **la République tchèque** the Czech Republic

te, t' [tə] *pron* you; (*réfléchi*) yourself

technicien, ne [tɛknisjɛ̃, jɛn] *nm/f* technician

technico-commercial, e, -aux [tɛknikokɔmɛʀsjal, jo] *adj*: **agent ~-~** sales technician

technique [tɛknik] *adj* technical ♦ *nf* technique; **techniquement** *adv* technically

technologie [tɛknɔlɔʒi] *nf* technology; **technologique** *adj* technological

teck [tɛk] *nm* teak

tee-shirt [tiʃœʀt] *nm* T-shirt, tee-shirt

teignais *etc* [tɛɲɛ] *vb voir* **teindre**

teindre [tɛ̃dʀ] *vt* to dye; **se ~ les cheveux** to dye one's hair; **teint, e** *adj* dyed ♦ *nm* (*du visage*) complexion; (*momentané*) colour ♦ *nf* shade; **grand teint** colourfast

teinté, e [tɛ̃te] *adj*: **~ de** (*fig*) tinged with

teinter [tɛ̃te] *vt* (*verre, papier*) to tint; (*bois*) to stain

teinture [tɛ̃tyʀ] *nf* dye; **~ d'iode** tincture of iodine; **teinturerie** *nf* dry cleaner's; **teinturier** *nm* dry cleaner

tel, telle [tɛl] *adj* (*pareil*) such; (*comme*): **~ un/des ...** like a/like ...; (*indéfini*) such-and-such a; (*intensif*): **un ~/de tels ...** such (a)/such ...; **rien de ~** nothing like it; **~ que** like, such as; **~ quel** as it is *ou* stands (*ou* was *etc*); **venez ~ jour** come on such-and-such a day

télé [tele] (*fam*) *nf* TV

télé...: télécabine *nf* (*benne*) cable car; **télécarte** *nf* phonecard; **télécommande** *nf* remote control; **télécopie** *nf* fax; **envoyer qch par télécopie** to fax sth; **télécopieur** *nm* fax machine; **télédistribution** *nf* cable TV; **téléférique** *nm* = **téléphérique**; **télégramme** *nm* telegram; **télégraphier** *vt* to telegraph, cable; **téléguider** *vt* to radio-control; **télématique** *nf* telematics *sg*; **téléobjectif** *nm* telephoto lens *sg*; **télépathie** *nf* telepathy; **téléphérique** *nm* cable car

téléphone [telefɔn] *nm* telephone; **avoir le ~** to be on the (tele)phone; **au ~** on the phone; **~ mobile** mobile phone; **~ rouge** hot line; **~ sans fil** cordless (tele)phone; **~ de voiture** car phone; **téléphoner** *vi* to make a phone call; **téléphoner à** to phone, call up; **téléphonique** *adj* (tele)phone *cpd*

télescope [telɛskɔp] *nm* telescope

télescoper [telɛskɔpe] *vt* to smash up; **se ~** (*véhicules*) to concertina

télé...: téléscripteur *nm* teleprinter; **télésiège** *nm* chairlift; **téléski** *nm* ski-tow; **téléspectateur, -trice** *nm/f* (television) viewer; **télévente** *nf* telesales; **téléviseur** *nm* television set; **télévision** *nf* television; **à la télévision** on television; **télévision numérique** digital TV

télex [telɛks] *nm* telex

telle [tɛl] *adj voir* **tel**; **tellement** *adv* (*tant*) so much; (*si*) so; **tellement de** (*sable, eau*) so much; (*gens, livres*) so many; **il s'est endormi tellement il était fatigué** he was so tired (that) he fell asleep; **pas tellement** not (all) that much; not (all) that *+adjectif*

téméraire [temeʀɛʀ] *adj* reckless, rash; **témérité** *nf* recklessness, rashness

témoignage [temwaɲaʒ] *nm* (*JUR*: *déclaration*) testimony *no pl*, evidence *no pl*; (*rapport, récit*) account; (*fig*: *d'affection etc*: *cadeau*) token, mark; (: *geste*) expression

témoigner [temwaɲe] *vt* (*intérêt, gratitude*) to show ♦ *vi* (*JUR*) to testify, give evidence; **~ de** to bear witness to, testify to

témoin [temwɛ̃] *nm* witness ♦ *adj*: **appartement ~** show flat (*BRIT*); **être ~**

de to witness; **~ oculaire** eyewitness

tempe [tɑ̃p] *nf* temple

tempérament [tɑ̃peʀamɑ̃] *nm* temperament, disposition; **à ~** (*vente*) on deferred (payment) terms; (*achat*) by instalments, hire purchase *cpd*

température [tɑ̃peʀatyʀ] *nf* temperature; **avoir** *ou* **faire de la ~** to be running *ou* have a temperature

tempéré, e [tɑ̃peʀe] *adj* temperate

tempête [tɑ̃pɛt] *nf* storm; **~ de sable/neige** sand/snowstorm

temple [tɑ̃pl] *nm* temple; (*protestant*) church

temporaire [tɑ̃pɔʀɛʀ] *adj* temporary

temps [tɑ̃] *nm* (*atmosphérique*) weather; (*durée*) time; (*époque*) time, times *pl*; (LING) tense; (MUS) beat; (TECH) stroke; **un ~ de chien** (*fam*) rotten weather; **quel ~ fait-il?** what's the weather like?; **il fait beau/mauvais ~** the weather is fine/bad; **avoir le ~/tout son ~** to have time/plenty of time; **en ~ de paix/guerre** in peacetime/wartime; **en ~ utile** *ou* **voulu** in due time *ou* course; **ces derniers ~** lately; **dans quelque ~** in a (little) while; **de ~ en ~, de ~ à autre** from time to time; **à ~** (*partir, arriver*) in time; **à ~ complet, à plein ~** full-time; **à ~ partiel** part-time; **dans le ~** at one time; **~ d'arrêt** pause, halt; **~ mort** (COMM) slack period

tenable [t(ə)nabl] *adj* bearable

tenace [tənas] *adj* persistent

tenailler [tənɑje] *vt* (*fig*) to torment

tenailles [tənɑj] *nfpl* pincers

tenais *etc* [t(ə)nɛ] *vb voir* **tenir**

tenancier, -ière [tənɑ̃sje] *nm/f* manager/manageress

tenant, e [tənɑ̃, ɑ̃t] *nm/f* (SPORT): **~ du titre** title-holder

tendance [tɑ̃dɑ̃s] *nf* tendency; (*opinions*) leanings *pl*, sympathies *pl*; (*évolution*) trend; **avoir ~ à** to have a tendency to, tend to

tendeur [tɑ̃dœʀ] *nm* (*attache*) elastic strap

tendre [tɑ̃dʀ] *adj* tender; (*bois, roche, couleur*) soft ♦ *vt* (*élastique, peau*) to stretch; (*corde*) to tighten; (*muscle*) to tense; (*fig*: *piège*) to set, lay; (*donner*): **~ qch à qn** to hold sth out to sb; (*offrir*) to offer sb sth; **se ~** *vi* (*corde*) to tighten; (*relations*) to become strained; **~ à qch/à faire** to tend towards sth/to do; **~ l'oreille** to prick up one's ears; **~ la main/le bras** to hold out one's hand/stretch out one's arm; **tendrement** *adv* tenderly; **tendresse** *nf* tenderness

tendu, e [tɑ̃dy] *pp de* **tendre** ♦ *adj* (*corde*) tight; (*muscles*) tensed; (*relations*) strained

ténèbres [tenɛbʀ] *nfpl* darkness *sg*

teneur [tənœʀ] *nf* content; (*d'une lettre*) terms *pl*, content

tenir [t(ə)niʀ] *vt* to hold; (*magasin, hôtel*) to run; (*promesse*) to keep ♦ *vi* to hold; (*neige, gel*) to last; **se ~** *vi* (*avoir lieu*) to be held, take place; (*être*: *personne*) to stand; **~ à** (*personne, objet*) to be attached to; (*réputation*) to care about; **~ à faire** to be determined to do; **~ de** (*ressembler à*) to take after; **ça ne tient qu'à lui** it is entirely up to him; **~ qn pour** to regard sb as; **~ qch de qn** (*histoire*) to have heard *ou* learnt sth from sb; (*qualité, défaut*) to have inherited *ou* got sth from sb; **~ dans** to fit into; **~ compte de qch** to take sth into account; **~ les comptes** to keep the books; **~ bon** to stand fast; **~ le coup** to hold out; **~ au chaud** to keep hot; **tiens/tenez, voilà le stylo** there's the pen!; **tiens, voilà Alain!** look, here's Alain!; **tiens?** (*surprise*) really?; **se ~ droit** to stand (*ou* sit) up straight; **bien se ~** to behave well; **se ~ à qch** to hold on to sth; **s'en ~ à qch** to confine o.s. to sth

tennis [tenis] *nm* tennis; (*court*) tennis court ♦ *nm ou f pl* (*aussi:* **chaussures de ~**) tennis *ou* gym shoes; **~ de table** table tennis; **tennisman** *nm* tennis player

tension [tɑ̃sjɔ̃] *nf* tension; (*MÉD*) blood pressure; **avoir de la ~** to have high blood pressure

tentation [tɑ̃tasjɔ̃] *nf* temptation

tentative [tɑ̃tativ] *nf* attempt

tente [tɑ̃t] *nf* tent

tenter [tɑ̃te] *vt* (*éprouver, attirer*) to tempt; (*essayer*): **~ qch/de faire** to attempt *ou* try sth/to do; **~ sa chance** to try one's luck

tenture [tɑ̃tyʀ] *nf* hanging

tenu, e [t(ə)ny] *pp de* **tenir** ♦ *adj* (*maison, comptes*): **bien ~** well-kept; (*obligé*): **~ de faire** obliged to do ♦ *nf* (*vêtements*) clothes *pl*; (*comportement*) (good) manners *pl*, good behaviour; (*d'une maison*) upkeep; **en petite ~e** scantily dressed *ou* clad; **~e de route** (*AUTO*) road-holding; **~e de soirée** evening dress

ter [tɛʀ] *adj*: **16 ~** 16b *ou* B

térébenthine [teʀebɑ̃tin] *nf*: **(essence de) ~** (oil of) turpentine

Tergal ® [tɛʀgal] *nm* Terylene ®

terme [tɛʀm] *nm* term; (*fin*) end; **à court/long ~** ♦ *adj* short-/long-term ♦ *adv* in the short/long term; **avant ~** (*MÉD*) prematurely; **mettre un ~ à** to put an end *ou* a stop to; **en bons ~s** on good terms

terminaison [tɛʀminɛzɔ̃] *nf* (*LING*) ending

terminal [tɛʀminal, o] *nm* terminal; **terminale** *nf* (*SCOL*) ≃ sixth form *ou* year (*BRIT*), ≃ twelfth grade (*US*)

terminer [tɛʀmine] *vt* to finish; **se ~** *vi* to end

terne [tɛʀn] *adj* dull

ternir [tɛʀniʀ] *vt* to dull; (*fig*) to sully, tarnish; **se ~** *vi* to become dull

terrain [teʀɛ̃] *nm* (*sol, fig*) ground; (*COMM*: *étendue de terre*) land *no pl*; (*parcelle*) plot (of land); (*à bâtir*) site; **sur le ~** (*fig*) on the field; **~ d'aviation** airfield; **~ de camping** campsite; **~ de football/rugby** football/rugby pitch (*BRIT*) *ou* field (*US*); **~ de golf** golf course; **~ de jeu** games field; (*pour les petits*) playground; **~ de sport** sports ground; **~ vague** waste ground *no pl*

terrasse [teʀas] *nf* terrace; **à la ~** (*café*) outside; **terrasser** *vt* (*adversaire*) to floor; (*suj*: *maladie etc*) to strike down

terre [tɛʀ] *nf* (*gén, aussi ÉLEC*) earth; (*substance*) soil, earth; (*opposé à mer*) land *no pl*; (*contrée*) land; **~s** *nfpl* (*terrains*) lands, land *sg*; **en ~** (*pipe, poterie*) clay *cpd*; **à ~** *ou* **par ~** (*mettre, être, s'asseoir*) on the ground (*ou* floor); (*jeter, tomber*) to the ground, down; **~ à ~** *adj inv* down-to-earth; **~ cuite** terracotta; **la ~ ferme** dry land; **~ glaise** clay

terreau [teʀo] *nm* compost

terre-plein [tɛʀplɛ̃] *nm* platform; (*sur chaussée*) central reservation

terrer [teʀe]: **se ~** *vi* to hide away

terrestre [teʀɛstʀ] *adj* (*surface*) earth's, of the earth; (*BOT, ZOOL, MIL*) land *cpd*; (*REL*) earthly

terreur [teʀœʀ] *nf* terror *no pl*

terrible [teʀibl] *adj* terrible, dreadful; (*fam*) terrific; **pas ~** nothing special

terrien, ne [teʀjɛ̃, jɛn] *adj*: **propriétaire ~** landowner ♦ *nm/f* (*non martien etc*) earthling

terrier [teʀje] *nm* burrow, hole; (*chien*) terrier

terrifier [teʀifje] *vt* to terrify

terrine [teʀin] *nf* (*récipient*) terrine; (*CULIN*) pâté

territoire [teʀitwaʀ] *nm* territory

terroir [teʀwaʀ] *nm*: **accent du ~** country accent

terroriser [teʀɔʀize] *vt* to terrorize

terrorisme [teʀɔʀism] *nm* terrorism; **terroriste** *nm/f* terrorist

tertiaire [tɛʀsjɛʀ] *adj* tertiary ♦ *nm* (*ÉCON*) service industries *pl*

tertre [tɛʀtʀ] *nm* hillock, mound

tes [te] *adj voir* **ton**[1]

tesson [tesɔ̃] *nm*: **~ de bouteille** piece

of broken bottle
test [tɛst] *nm* test
testament [tɛstamɑ̃] *nm* (*JUR*) will; (*REL*) Testament; (*fig*) legacy
tester [tɛste] *vt* to test
testicule [tɛstikyl] *nm* testicle
têtard [tɛtaʀ] *nm* tadpole
tête [tɛt] *nf* head; (*cheveux*) hair *no pl*; (*visage*) face; **de ~** *adj* (*wagon etc*) front *cpd* ♦ *adv* (*calculer*) in one's head, mentally; **tenir ~ à qn** to stand up to sb; **la ~ en bas** with one's head down; **la ~ la première** (*tomber*) headfirst; **faire une ~** (*FOOTBALL*) to head the ball; **faire la ~** (*fig*) to sulk; **en ~** at the front; (*SPORT*) in the lead; **à la ~ de** at the head of; **à ~ reposée** in a more leisurely moment; **n'en faire qu'à sa ~** to do as one pleases; **en avoir par-dessus la ~** to be fed up; **en ~ à ~** in private, alone together; **de la ~ aux pieds** from head to toe; **~ de lecture** (playback) head; **~ de liste** (*POL*) chief candidate; **~ de série** (*TENNIS*) seeded player, seed; **tête à queue** *nm inv*: **faire un tête-à-queue** to spin round
téter [tete] *vt*: **~ (sa mère)** to suck at one's mother's breast, feed
tétine [tetin] *nf* teat; (*sucette*) dummy (*BRIT*), pacifier (*US*)
têtu, e [tety] *adj* stubborn, pigheaded
texte [tɛkst] *nm* text; (*morceau choisi*) passage
textile [tɛkstil] *adj* textile *cpd* ♦ *nm* textile; **le ~** the textile industry
Texto ® [tɛksto] *nm* text message
texto [tɛksto] (*fam*) *adj* word for word ♦ *nm* text message
texture [tɛkstyʀ] *nf* texture
thaïlandais, e [tajlɑ̃dɛ, ɛz] *adj* Thai ♦ *nm/f*: **T~, e** Thai
Thaïlande [tailɑ̃d] *nf* Thailand
TGV *sigle m* (= *train à grande vitesse*) high-speed train
thé [te] *nm* tea; **~ au citron** lemon tea; **~ au lait** tea with milk; **prendre le ~** to have tea; **faire le ~** to make the tea
théâtral, e, -aux [teɑtʀal, o] *adj* theatrical
théâtre [teɑtʀ] *nm* theatre; (*péj*: *simulation*) playacting; (*fig*: *lieu*): **le ~ de** the scene of; **faire du ~** to act
théière [tejɛʀ] *nf* teapot
thème [tɛm] *nm* theme; (*SCOL*: *traduction*) prose (composition)
théologie [teɔlɔʒi] *nf* theology
théorie [teɔʀi] *nf* theory; **théorique** *adj* theoretical
thérapie [teʀapi] *nf* therapy
thermal, e, -aux [tɛʀmal, o] *adj*: **station ~e** spa; **cure ~e** water cure
thermes [tɛʀm] *nmpl* thermal baths
thermomètre [tɛʀmɔmɛtʀ] *nm* thermometer
thermos ® [tɛʀmos] *nm ou nf*: **(bouteille) ~** vacuum *ou* Thermos ® flask
thèse [tɛz] *nf* thesis
thon [tɔ̃] *nm* tuna (fish)
thym [tɛ̃] *nm* thyme
tibia [tibja] *nm* shinbone, tibia; (*partie antérieure de la jambe*) shin
TIC [teise] *sigle f* (= *technologies de l'information et de la communication*) ICT
tic [tik] *nm* tic, (nervous) twitch; (*de langage etc*) mannerism
ticket [tikɛ] *nm* ticket; **~ de caisse** receipt; **~ de quai** platform ticket
tic-tac [tiktak] *nm* ticking; **faire ~-~** to tick
tiède [tjɛd] *adj* lukewarm; (*vent, air*) mild, warm; **tiédir** *vi* to cool; (*se réchauffer*) to grow warmer
tien, ne [tjɛ̃, tjɛn] *pron*: **le(la) ~(ne), les ~(ne)s** yours; **à la ~ne!** cheers!
tiens [tjɛ̃] *vb, excl voir* **tenir**
tierce [tjɛʀs] *adj voir* **tiers**
tiercé [tjɛʀse] *nm system of forecast betting giving first 3 horses*
tiers, tierce [tjɛʀ, tjɛʀs] *adj* third ♦ *nm* (*JUR*) third party; (*fraction*) third; **le ~ monde** the Third World
tifs [tif] (*fam*) *nmpl* hair
tige [tiʒ] *nf* stem; (*baguette*) rod
tignasse [tiɲas] (*péj*) *nf* mop of hair
tigre [tigʀ] *nm* tiger; **tigresse** *nf* ti-

gress; **tigré, e** *adj* (*rayé*) striped; (*tacheté*) spotted; (*chat*) tabby
tilleul [tijœl] *nm* lime (tree), linden (tree); (*boisson*) lime(-blossom) tea
timbale [tɛ̃bal] *nf* (metal) tumbler; **~s** *nfpl* (MUS) timpani, kettledrums
timbre [tɛ̃bʀ] *nm* (*tampon*) stamp; (*aussi*: **~-poste**) (postage) stamp; (MUS: *de voix, instrument*) timbre, tone
timbré, e [tɛ̃bʀe] (*fam*) *adj* cracked
timide [timid] *adj* shy; (*timoré*) timid; **timidement** *adv* shyly; timidly; **timidité** *nf* shyness; timidity
tins *etc* [tɛ̃] *vb voir* **tenir**
tintamarre [tɛ̃tamaʀ] *nm* din, uproar
tinter [tɛ̃te] *vi* to ring, chime; (*argent, clefs*) to jingle
tique [tik] *nf* (*parasite*) tick
tir [tiʀ] *nm* (*sport*) shooting; (*fait ou manière de ~er*) firing *no pl*; (*rafale*) fire; (*stand*) shooting gallery; **~ à l'arc** archery; **~ au pigeon** clay pigeon shooting
tirage [tiʀaʒ] *nm* (*action*) printing; (PHOTO) print; (*de journal*) circulation; (*de livre*: *nombre d'exemplaires*) (print) run; (: *édition*) edition; (*de loterie*) draw; **par ~ au sort** by drawing lots
tirailler [tiʀɑje] *vt*: **être tiraillé entre** to be torn between
tire [tiʀ] *nf*: **vol à la ~** pickpocketing
tiré, e [tiʀe] *adj* (*traits*) drawn; **~ par les cheveux** far-fetched
tire-au-flanc [tiʀoflɑ̃] (*péj*) *nm inv* skiver
tire-bouchon [tiʀbuʃɔ̃] *nm* corkscrew
tirelire [tiʀliʀ] *nf* moneybox
tirer [tiʀe] *vt* (*gén*) to pull; (*extraire*): **~ qch de** to take *ou* pull sth out of; (*trait, rideau, carte, conclusion, chèque*) to draw; (*langue*) to stick out; (*en faisant feu*: *balle, coup*) to fire; (: *animal*) to shoot; (*journal, livre, photo*) to print; (FOOTBALL: *corner etc*) to take ♦ *vi* (*faire feu*) to fire; (*faire du tir* , FOOTBALL) to shoot; **se ~** *vi* (*fam*) to push off; **s'en ~** (*éviter le pire*) to get off; (*survivre*) to pull through; (*se débrouiller*) to manage; **~ sur** (*corde*) to pull on *ou* at; (*faire feu sur*) to shoot *ou* fire at; (*pipe*) to draw on; (*approcher de*: *couleur*) to verge *ou* border on; **~ qn de** (*embarras etc*) to help *ou* get sb out of; **~ à l'arc/la carabine** to shoot with a bow and arrow/with a rifle; **~ à sa fin** to be drawing to a close; **~ qch au clair** to clear sth up; **~ au sort** to draw lots; **~ parti de** to take advantage of; **~ profit de** to profit from
tiret [tiʀɛ] *nm* dash
tireur [tiʀœʀ] *nm* gunman; **~ d'élite** marksman
tiroir [tiʀwaʀ] *nm* drawer; **tiroir-caisse** *nm* till
tisane [tizan] *nf* herb tea
tisonnier [tizɔnje] *nm* poker
tisser [tise] *vt* to weave; **tisserand** *nm* weaver
tissu [tisy] *nm* fabric, material, cloth *no pl*; (ANAT, BIO) tissue; **tissu-éponge** *nm* (terry) towelling *no pl*
titre [titʀ] *nm* (*gén*) title; (*de journal*) headline; (*diplôme*) qualification; (COMM) security; **en ~** (*champion*) official; **à juste ~** rightly; **à quel ~?** on what grounds?; **à aucun ~** on no account; **au même ~ (que)** in the same way (as); **à ~ d'information** for (your) information; **à ~ gracieux** free of charge; **à ~ d'essai** on a trial basis; **à ~ privé** in a private capacity; **~ de propriété** title deed; **~ de transport** ticket
tituber [titybe] *vi* to stagger (along)
titulaire [titylɛʀ] *adj* (ADMIN) with tenure ♦ *nm/f* (*de permis*) holder
toast [tost] *nm* slice *ou* piece of toast; (*de bienvenue*) (welcoming) toast; **porter un ~ à qn** to propose *ou* drink a toast to sb
toboggan [tɔbɔgɑ̃] *nm* slide; (AUTO) flyover
toc [tɔk] *excl*: **~, toc** knock knock ♦ *nm*: **en ~** fake
tocsin [tɔksɛ̃] *nm* alarm (bell)

toge [tɔʒ] *nf* toga; (*de juge*) gown
tohu-bohu [tɔybɔy] *nm* hubbub
toi [twa] *pron* you
toile [twal] *nf* (*tableau*) canvas; **de** *ou* **en ~** (*pantalon*) cotton; (*sac*) canvas; **~ cirée** oilcloth; **~ d'araignée** cobweb; **~ de fond** (*fig*) backdrop
toilette [twalɛt] *nf* (*habits*) outfit; **~s** *nfpl* (*w.-c.*) toilet *sg*; **faire sa ~** to have a wash, get washed; **articles de ~** toiletries
toi-même [twamɛm] *pron* yourself
toiser [twaze] *vt* to eye up and down
toison [twazɔ̃] *nf* (*de mouton*) fleece
toit [twa] *nm* roof; **~ ouvrant** sunroof
toiture [twatyʀ] *nf* roof
tôle [tol] *nf* (*plaque*) steel *ou* iron sheet; **~ ondulée** corrugated iron
tolérable [tɔleʀabl] *adj* tolerable
tolérant, e [tɔleʀɑ̃, ɑ̃t] *adj* tolerant
tolérer [tɔleʀe] *vt* to tolerate; (*ADMIN: hors taxe etc*) to allow
tollé [tɔ(l)le] *nm* outcry
tomate [tɔmat] *nf* tomato; **~s farcies** stuffed tomatoes
tombe [tɔ̃b] *nf* (*sépulture*) grave; (*avec monument*) tomb
tombeau, x [tɔ̃bo] *nm* tomb
tombée [tɔ̃be] *nf*: **à la ~ de la nuit** at nightfall
tomber [tɔ̃be] *vi* to fall; (*fièvre, vent*) to drop; **laisser ~** (*objet*) to drop; (*personne*) to let down; (*activité*) to give up; **laisse ~!** forget it!; **faire ~** to knock over; **~ sur** (*rencontrer*) to bump into; **~ de fatigue/sommeil** to drop from exhaustion/be falling asleep on one's feet; **ça tombe bien** that's come at the right time; **il est bien tombé** he's been lucky; **~ à l'eau** (*projet*) to fall through; **~ en panne** to break down
tombola [tɔ̃bɔla] *nf* raffle
tome [tɔm] *nm* volume
ton¹, ta [tɔ̃, ta] (*pl* **tes**) *adj* your
ton² [tɔ̃] *nm* (*gén*) tone; (*couleur*) shade, tone; **de bon ~** in good taste
tonalité [tɔnalite] *nf* (*au téléphone*) dialling tone
tondeuse [tɔ̃døz] *nf* (*à gazon*) (lawn)mower; (*du coiffeur*) clippers *pl*; (*pour les moutons*) shears *pl*
tondre [tɔ̃dʀ] *vt* (*pelouse, herbe*) to mow; (*haie*) to cut, clip; (*mouton, toison*) to shear; (*cheveux*) to crop
tongs [tɔ̃g] *nfpl* flip-flops
tonifier [tɔnifje] *vt* (*peau, organisme*) to tone up
tonique [tɔnik] *adj* fortifying ♦ *nm* tonic
tonne [tɔn] *nf* metric ton, tonne
tonneau, x [tɔno] *nm* (*à vin, cidre*) barrel; **faire des ~x** (*voiture, avion*) to roll over
tonnelle [tɔnɛl] *nf* bower, arbour
tonner [tɔne] *vi* to thunder; **il tonne** it is thundering, there's some thunder
tonnerre [tɔnɛʀ] *nm* thunder
tonton [tɔ̃tɔ̃] *nm* uncle
tonus [tɔnys] *nm* energy
top [tɔp] *nm*: **au 3ème ~** at the 3rd stroke
topinambour [tɔpinɑ̃buʀ] *nm* Jerusalem artichoke
topo [tɔpo] (*fam*) *nm* rundown; **c'est le même ~** it's the same old story
toque [tɔk] *nf* (*de fourrure*) fur hat; **~ de cuisinier** chef's hat; **~ de jockey/juge** jockey's/judge's cap
toqué, e [tɔke] (*fam*) *adj* cracked
torche [tɔʀʃ] *nf* torch
torchon [tɔʀʃɔ̃] *nm* cloth; (*à vaisselle*) tea towel *ou* cloth
tordre [tɔʀdʀ] *vt* (*chiffon*) to wring; (*barre, fig: visage*) to twist; **se ~** *vi*: **se ~ le poignet/la cheville** to twist one's wrist/ankle; **se ~ de douleur/rire** to be doubled up with pain/laughter; **tordu, e** *adj* bent; (*fig*) crazy
tornade [tɔʀnad] *nf* tornado
torpille [tɔʀpij] *nf* torpedo
torréfier [tɔʀefje] *vt* to roast
torrent [tɔʀɑ̃] *nm* mountain stream
torsade [tɔʀsad] *nf*: **un pull à ~s** a

cable sweater

torse [tɔʀs] *nm* chest; (*ANAT, SCULPTURE*) torso; **~ nu** stripped to the waist

tort [tɔʀ] *nm* (*défaut*) fault; **~s** *nmpl* (*JUR*) fault *sg*; **avoir ~** to be wrong; **être dans son ~** to be in the wrong; **donner ~ à qn** to lay the blame on sb; **causer du ~ à** to harm; **à ~** wrongly; **à ~ et à travers** wildly

torticolis [tɔʀtikɔli] *nm* stiff neck

tortiller [tɔʀtije] *vt* to twist; (*moustache*) to twirl; **se ~** *vi* to wriggle; (*en dansant*) to wiggle

tortionnaire [tɔʀsjɔnɛʀ] *nm* torturer

tortue [tɔʀty] *nf* tortoise; (*d'eau douce*) terrapin; (*d'eau de mer*) turtle

tortueux, -euse [tɔʀtɥø, øz] *adj* (*rue*) twisting; (*fig*) tortuous

torture [tɔʀtyʀ] *nf* torture; **torturer** *vt* to torture; (*fig*) to torment

tôt [to] *adv* early; **~ ou tard** sooner or later; **si ~** so early; (*déjà*) so soon; **plus ~** earlier; **au plus ~** at the earliest; **il eut ~ fait de faire** he soon did

total, e, -aux [tɔtal, o] *adj, nm* total; **au ~** in total; (*fig*) on the whole; **faire le ~** to work out the total; **totalement** *adv* totally; **totaliser** *vt* to total; **totalitaire** *adj* totalitarian; **totalité** *nf*: **la totalité de** all (of); the whole *+sg*; **en totalité** entirely

toubib [tubib] (*fam*) *nm* doctor

touchant, e [tuʃɑ̃, ɑ̃t] *adj* touching

touche [tuʃ] *nf* (*de piano, de machine à écrire*) key; (*de téléphone*) button; (*PEINTURE etc*) stroke, touch; (*fig: de nostalgie*) touch; (*FOOTBALL: aussi:* **remise en ~**) throw-in; (*aussi:* **ligne de ~**) touch-line

toucher [tuʃe] *nm* touch ♦ *vt* to touch; (*palper*) to feel; (*atteindre: d'un coup de feu etc*) to hit; (*concerner*) to concern, affect; (*contacter*) to reach, contact; (*recevoir: récompense*) to receive, get; (*: salaire*) to draw, get; (*: chèque*) to cash; **se ~** (*être en contact*) to touch; **au ~** to the touch; **~ à** to touch; (*concerner*) to have to do with, concern; **je vais lui en ~ un mot** I'll have a word with him about it; **~ à sa fin** to be drawing to a close

touffe [tuf] *nf* tuft

touffu, e [tufy] *adj* thick, dense

toujours [tuʒuʀ] *adv* always; (*encore*) still; (*constamment*) forever; **~ plus** more and more; **pour ~** forever; **~ est-il que** the fact remains that; **essaie ~** (you can) try anyway

toupet [tupɛ] (*fam*) *nm* cheek

toupie [tupi] *nf* (spinning) top

tour [tuʀ] *nf* tower; (*immeuble*) high-rise block (*BRIT*) *ou* building (*US*); (*ÉCHECS*) castle, rook ♦ *nm* (*excursion*) trip; (*à pied*) stroll, walk; (*en voiture*) run, ride; (*SPORT: aussi:* **~ de piste**) lap; (*d'être servi ou de jouer etc*) turn; (*de roue etc*) revolution; (*POL: aussi:* **~ de scrutin**) ballot; (*ruse, de prestidigitation*) trick; (*de potier*) wheel; (*à bois, métaux*) lathe; (*circonférence*): **de 3 m de ~** 3 m round, with a circumference *ou* girth of 3 m; **faire le ~ de** to go round; (*à pied*) to walk round; **c'est au ~ de Renée** it's Renée's turn; **à ~ de rôle, ~ à ~** in turn; **~ de chant** *nm* song recital; **~ de contrôle** *nf* control tower; **~ de garde** *nm* spell of duty; **~ d'horizon** *nm* (*fig*) general survey; **~ de taille/tête** *nm* waist/head measurement; **un 33 ~s** an LP; **un 45 ~s** a single

tourbe [tuʀb] *nf* peat

tourbillon [tuʀbijɔ̃] *nm* whirlwind; (*d'eau*) whirlpool; (*fig*) whirl, swirl; **tourbillonner** *vi* to whirl (round)

tourelle [tuʀɛl] *nf* turret

tourisme [tuʀism] *nm* tourism; **agence de ~** tourist agency; **faire du ~** to go touring; (*en ville*) to go sightseeing; **touriste** *nm/f* tourist; **touristique** *adj* tourist *cpd*; (*région*) touristic

tourment [tuʀmɑ̃] *nm* torment; **tourmenter** *vt* to torment; **se tourmenter** *vi* to fret, worry o.s.

tournage [turnaʒ] *nm* (CINÉMA) shooting
tournant [turnɑ̃] *nm* (*de route*) bend; (*fig*) turning point
tournebroche [turnəbrɔʃ] *nm* roasting spit
tourne-disque [turnədisk] *nm* record player
tournée [turne] *nf* (*du facteur etc*) round; (*d'artiste, politicien*) tour; (*au café*) round (of drinks)
tournemain [turnəmɛ̃]: **en un ~** *adv* (as) quick as a flash
tourner [turne] *vt* to turn; (*sauce, mélange*) to stir; (CINÉMA: *faire les prises de vues*) to shoot; (: *produire*) to make ♦ *vi* to turn; (*moteur*) to run; (*taximètre*) to tick away; (*lait etc*) to turn (sour); **se ~** *vi* to turn round; **mal ~** to go wrong; **~ autour de** to go round; (*péj*) to hang round; **~ à/en** to turn into; **~ à gauche/droite** to turn left/right; **~ le dos à** to turn one's back on; to have one's back to; **~ de l'œil** to pass out; **se ~ vers** to turn towards; (*fig*) to turn to
tournesol [turnəsɔl] *nm* sunflower
tournevis [turnəvis] *nm* screwdriver
tourniquet [turnikɛ] *nm* (*pour arroser*) sprinkler; (*portillon*) turnstile; (*présentoir*) revolving stand
tournoi [turnwa] *nm* tournament
tournoyer [turnwaje] *vi* to swirl (round)
tournure [turnyr] *nf* (LING) turn of phrase; (*évolution*): **la ~ de qch** the way sth is developing; **~ d'esprit** turn *ou* cast of mind; **la ~ des événements** the turn of events
tourte [turt] *nf* pie
tourterelle [turtərɛl] *nf* turtledove
tous [tu] *adj, pron voir* **tout**
Toussaint [tusɛ̃] *nf*: **la ~** All Saints' Day

Toussaint

La Toussaint, *November 1, is a public holiday in France. People traditionally visit the graves of friends and relatives to lay wreaths of heather and chrysanthemums.*

tousser [tuse] *vi* to cough

MOT-CLÉ

tout, e [tu, tut] (*mpl* **tous**, *fpl* **toutes**) *adj* **1** (*avec article singulier*) all; **tout le lait** all the milk; **toute la nuit** all night, the whole night; **tout le livre** the whole book; **tout un pain** a whole loaf; **tout le temps** all the time; the whole time; **c'est tout le contraire** it's quite the opposite
2 (*avec article pluriel*) every, all; **tous les livres** all the books; **toutes les nuits** every night; **toutes les fois** every time; **toutes les trois/deux semaines** every third/other *ou* second week, every three/two weeks; **tous les deux** both *ou* each of us (*ou* them *ou* you); **toutes les trois** all three of us (*ou* them *ou* you)
3 (*sans article*): **à tout âge** at any age; **pour toute nourriture, il avait ...** his only food was ...
♦ *pron* everything, all; **il a tout fait** he's done everything; **je les vois tous** I can see them all *ou* all of them; **nous y sommes tous allés** all of us went, we all went; **en tout** in all; **tout ce qu'il sait** all he knows
♦ *nm* whole; **le tout** all of it (*ou* them); **le tout est de ...** the main thing is to ...; **pas du tout** not at all
♦ *adv* **1** (*très, complètement*) very; **tout près** very near; **le tout premier** the very first; **tout seul** all alone; **le livre tout entier** the whole book; **tout en haut** right at the top; **tout droit** straight ahead
2: tout en while; **tout en travaillant** while working, as he *etc* works
3: tout d'abord first of all; **tout à coup** suddenly; **tout à fait** absolutely;

tout à l'heure a short while ago; (*futur*) in a short while, shortly; **à tout à l'heure!** see you later!; **tout de même** all the same; **tout le monde** everybody; **tout de suite** immediately, straight away; **tout terrain** *ou* **tous terrains** all-terrain

toutefois [tutfwa] *adv* however
toutes [tut] *adj, pron voir* **tout**
toux [tu] *nf* cough
toxicomane [tɔksikɔman] *nm/f* drug addict
toxique [tɔksik] *adj* toxic
trac [tʀak] *nm* (*au théâtre, en public*) stage fright; (*aux examens*) nerves *pl*; **avoir le ~** (*au théâtre, en public*) to have stage fright; (*aux examens*) to be feeling nervous
tracasser [tʀakase] *vt* to worry, bother; **se ~** to worry
trace [tʀas] *nf* (*empreintes*) tracks *pl*; (*marques, aussi fig*) mark; (*quantité infime, indice, vestige*) trace; **~s de pas** footprints
tracé [tʀase] *nm* (*parcours*) line; (*plan*) layout
tracer [tʀase] *vt* to draw; (*piste*) to open up
tract [tʀakt] *nm* tract, pamphlet
tractations [tʀaktasjɔ̃] *nfpl* dealings, bargaining *sg*
tracteur [tʀaktœʀ] *nm* tractor
traction [tʀaksjɔ̃] *nf*: **~ avant/arrière** front-wheel/rear-wheel drive
tradition [tʀadisjɔ̃] *nf* tradition; **traditionnel, le** *adj* traditional
traducteur, -trice [tʀadyktœʀ, tʀis] *nm/f* translator
traduction [tʀadyksjɔ̃] *nf* translation
traduire [tʀadɥiʀ] *vt* to translate; (*exprimer*) to convey; **~ qn en justice** to bring sb before the courts
trafic [tʀafik] *nm* traffic; **~ d'armes** arms dealing; **trafiquant, e** *nm/f* trafficker; (*d'armes*) dealer; **trafiquer** (*péj*) *vt* (*vin*) to doctor; (*moteur, document*) to tamper with
tragédie [tʀaʒedi] *nf* tragedy; **tragique** *adj* tragic
trahir [tʀaiʀ] *vt* to betray; **trahison** *nf* betrayal; (*JUR*) treason
train [tʀɛ̃] *nm* (*RAIL*) train; (*allure*) pace; **être en ~ de faire qch** to be doing sth; **mettre qn en ~** to put sb in good spirits; **se sentir en ~** to feel in good form; **~ d'atterrissage** undercarriage; **~ de vie** style of living; **~ électrique** (*jouet*) (electric) train set; **~-autos-couchettes** car-sleeper train
traîne [tʀɛn] *nf* (*de robe*) train; **être à la ~** to lag behind
traîneau, x [tʀɛno] *nm* sleigh, sledge
traînée [tʀene] *nf* trail; (*sur un mur, dans le ciel*) streak; (*péj*) slut
traîner [tʀene] *vt* (*remorque*) to pull; (*enfant, chien*) to drag *ou* trail along ♦ *vi* (*robe, manteau*) to trail; (*être en désordre*) to lie around; (*aller lentement*) to dawdle (along); (*vagabonder, agir lentement*) to hang about; (*durer*) to drag on; **se ~** *vi* to drag o.s. along; **~ les pieds** to drag one's feet
train-train [tʀɛ̃tʀɛ̃] *nm* humdrum routine
traire [tʀɛʀ] *vt* to milk
trait [tʀɛ] *nm* (*ligne*) line; (*de dessin*) stroke; (*caractéristique*) feature, trait; **~s** *nmpl* (*du visage*) features; **d'un ~** (*boire*) in one gulp; **de ~** (*animal*) draught; **avoir ~ à** to concern; **~ d'union** hyphen
traitant, e [tʀɛtɑ̃, ɑ̃t] *adj* (*shampooing*) medicated; **votre médecin ~** your usual *ou* family doctor
traite [tʀɛt] *nf* (*COMM*) draft; (*AGR*) milking; **d'une ~** without stopping; **la ~ des noirs** the slave trade
traité [tʀete] *nm* treaty
traitement [tʀɛtmɑ̃] *nm* treatment; (*salaire*) salary; **~ de données** data processing; **~ de texte** word processing; (*logiciel*) word processing package
traiter [tʀete] *vt* to treat; (*qualifier*): **~**

qn d'idiot to call sb a fool ♦ *vi* to deal; **~ de** to deal with

traiteur [tʀɛtœʀ] *nm* caterer

traître, -esse [tʀɛtʀ, tʀɛtʀɛs] *adj* (*dangereux*) treacherous ♦ *nm* traitor

trajectoire [tʀaʒɛktwaʀ] *nf* path

trajet [tʀaʒɛ] *nm* (*parcours, voyage*) journey; (*itinéraire*) route; (*distance à parcourir*) distance

trame [tʀam] *nf* (*de tissu*) weft; (*fig*) framework; **usé jusqu'à la ~** threadbare

tramer [tʀame] *vt*: **il se trame quelque chose** there's something brewing

trampoline [tʀɑ̃pɔlin] *nm* trampoline

tramway [tʀamwɛ] *nm* tram(way); (*voiture*) tram(car) (*BRIT*), streetcar (*US*)

tranchant, e [tʀɑ̃ʃɑ̃, ɑ̃t] *adj* sharp; (*fig*) peremptory ♦ *nm* (*d'un couteau*) cutting edge; (*de la main*) edge; **à double ~** double-edged

tranche [tʀɑ̃ʃ] *nf* (*morceau*) slice; (*arête*) edge; **~ d'âge/de salaires** age/wage bracket

tranché, e [tʀɑ̃ʃe] *adj* (*couleurs*) distinct; (*opinions*) clear-cut; **tranchée** *nf* trench

trancher [tʀɑ̃ʃe] *vt* to cut, sever ♦ *vi* to take a decision; **~ avec** to contrast sharply with

tranquille [tʀɑ̃kil] *adj* quiet; (*rassuré*) easy in one's mind, with one's mind at rest; **se tenir ~** (*enfant*) to be quiet; **laisse-moi/laisse-ça ~** leave me/it alone; **avoir la conscience ~** to have a clear conscience; **tranquillisant** *nm* tranquillizer; **tranquillité** *nf* peace (and quiet); (*d'esprit*) peace of mind

transat [tʀɑ̃zat] *nm* deckchair

transborder [tʀɑ̃sbɔʀde] *vt* to tran(s)ship

transcription [tʀɑ̃skʀipsjɔ̃] *nf* transcription; (*copie*) transcript

transférer [tʀɑ̃sfeʀe] *vt* to transfer; **transfert** *nm* transfer

transformation [tʀɑ̃sfɔʀmasjɔ̃] *nf* change; transformation; alteration; (*RUGBY*) conversion

transformer [tʀɑ̃sfɔʀme] *vt* to change; (*radicalement*) to transform; (*vêtement*) to alter; (*matière première, appartement, RUGBY*) to convert; **(se) ~ en** to turn into

transfusion [tʀɑ̃sfyzjɔ̃] *nf*: **~ sanguine** blood transfusion

transgresser [tʀɑ̃sgʀese] *vt* to contravene

transi, e [tʀɑ̃zi] *adj* numb (with cold), chilled to the bone

transiger [tʀɑ̃ziʒe] *vi* to compromise

transit [tʀɑ̃zit] *nm* transit; **transiter** *vi* to pass in transit

transitif, -ive [tʀɑ̃zitif, iv] *adj* transitive

transition [tʀɑ̃zisjɔ̃] *nf* transition; **transitoire** *adj* transitional

translucide [tʀɑ̃slysid] *adj* translucent

transmettre [tʀɑ̃smɛtʀ] *vt* (*passer*): **~ qch à qn** to pass sth on to sb; (*TECH, TÉL, MÉD*) to transmit; (*TV, RADIO*: *retransmettre*) to broadcast; **transmission** *nf* transmission

transparent, e [tʀɑ̃spaʀɑ̃, ɑ̃t] *adj* transparent

transpercer [tʀɑ̃spɛʀse] *vt* (*froid, pluie*) to go through, pierce; (*balle*) to go through

transpiration [tʀɑ̃spiʀasjɔ̃] *nf* perspiration

transpirer [tʀɑ̃spiʀe] *vi* to perspire

transplanter [tʀɑ̃splɑ̃te] *vt* (*MÉD, BOT*) to transplant; **transplantation** *nf* (*MÉD*) transplant

transport [tʀɑ̃spɔʀ] *nm* transport; **~s en commun** public transport *sg*; **transporter** *vt* to carry, move; (*COMM*) to transport, convey; **transporteur** *nm* haulage contractor (*BRIT*), trucker (*US*)

transvaser [tʀɑ̃svɑze] *vt* to decant

transversal, e, -aux [tʀɑ̃svɛʀsal, o] *adj* (*rue*) which runs across; **coupe ~e** cross section

trapèze [tʀapɛz] *nm* (*au cirque*) trapeze

trappe [tʀap] *nf* trap door

trapu, e [trapy] *adj* squat, stocky
traquenard [traknar] *nm* trap
traquer [trake] *vt* to track down; (*harceler*) to hound
traumatiser [tromatize] *vt* to traumatize
travail, -aux [travaj] *nm* (*gén*) work; (*tâche, métier*) work *no pl*, job; (*ÉCON, MÉD*) labour; **être sans ~** (*employé*) to be unemployed; *voir aussi* **travaux; ~ (au) noir** moonlighting
travailler [travaje] *vi* to work; (*bois*) to warp ♦ *vt* (*bois, métal*) to work; (*objet d'art, discipline*) to work on; **cela le travaille** it is on his mind; **travailleur, -euse** *adj* hard-working ♦ *nm/f* worker; **travailliste** *adj* ≃ Labour *cpd*
travaux [travo] *nmpl* (*de réparation, agricoles etc*) work *sg*; (*sur route*) roadworks *pl*; (*de construction*) building (work); **travaux des champs** farmwork *sg*; **travaux dirigés** (*SCOL*) tutorial; **travaux forcés** hard labour *sg*; **travaux manuels** (*SCOL*) handicrafts; **travaux ménagers** housework *sg*; **travaux pratiques** (*SCOL*) practical work; (*en laboratoire*) lab work
travers [traver] *nm* fault, failing; **en ~ (de)** across; **au ~ (de)/à ~** through; **de ~** (*nez, bouche*) crooked; (*chapeau*) askew; **comprendre de ~** to misunderstand; **regarder de ~** (*fig*) to look askance at
traverse [travers] *nf* (*de voie ferrée*) sleeper; **chemin de ~** shortcut
traversée [traverse] *nf* crossing
traverser [traverse] *vt* (*gén*) to cross; (*ville, tunnel, aussi: percer, fig*) to go through; (*suj: ligne, trait*) to run across
traversin [traversɛ̃] *nm* bolster
travesti [travesti] *nm* transvestite
trébucher [trebyʃe] *vi*: **~ (sur)** to stumble (over), trip (against)
trèfle [trɛfl] *nm* (*BOT*) clover; (*CARTES: couleur*) clubs *pl*; (: *carte*) club
treille [trɛj] *nf* vine arbour
treillis [treji] *nm* (*métallique*) wire-mesh; (*MIL: tenue*) combat uniform; (*pantalon*) combat trousers *pl*
treize [trɛz] *num* thirteen; **treizième** *num* thirteenth

treizième mois

Le treizième mois *is an end-of-year bonus roughly equal to one month's salary. For many employees it is a standard part of their salary package.*

tréma [trema] *nm* diaeresis
tremblement [trɑ̃bləmɑ̃] *nm*: **~ de terre** earthquake
trembler [trɑ̃ble] *vi* to tremble, shake; **~ de** (*froid, fièvre*) to shiver *ou* tremble with; (*peur*) to shake *ou* tremble with; **~ pour qn** to fear for sb
trémousser [tremuse]: **se ~** *vi* to jig about, wriggle about
trempe [trɑ̃p] *nf* (*fig*): **de cette/sa ~** of this/his calibre
trempé, e [trɑ̃pe] *adj* soaking (wet), drenched; (*TECH*) tempered
tremper [trɑ̃pe] *vt* to soak, drench; (*aussi:* **faire ~, mettre à ~**) to soak; (*plonger*): **~ qch dans** to dip sth in(to) ♦ *vi* to soak; (*fig*): **~ dans** to be involved *ou* have a hand in; **se ~** *vi* to have a quick dip; **trempette** *nf*: **faire trempette** to go paddling
tremplin [trɑ̃plɛ̃] *nm* springboard; (*SKI*) ski-jump
trentaine [trɑ̃tɛn] *nf*: **une ~ (de)** thirty or so, about thirty; **avoir la ~** (*âge*) to be around thirty
trente [trɑ̃t] *num* thirty; **être sur son ~ et un** to be wearing one's Sunday best; **trentième** *num* thirtieth
trépidant, e [trepidɑ̃, ɑ̃t] *adj* (*fig: rythme*) pulsating; (: *vie*) hectic
trépied [trepje] *nm* tripod
trépigner [trepiɲe] *vi* to stamp (one's feet)
très [trɛ] *adv* very; much *+pp*, highly *+pp*
trésor [trezɔr] *nm* treasure; **T~ (pu-**

blic) public revenue; **trésorerie** *nf* (*gestion*) accounts *pl*; (*bureaux*) accounts department; **difficultés de trésorerie** cash problems, shortage of cash *ou* funds; **trésorier, -ière** *nm/f* treasurer

tressaillir [tʀesajiʀ] *vi* to shiver, shudder

tressauter [tʀesote] *vi* to start, jump

tresse [tʀɛs] *nf* braid, plait; **tresser** *vt* (*cheveux*) to braid, plait; (*fil, jonc*) to plait; (*corbeille*) to weave; (*corde*) to twist

tréteau, x [tʀeto] *nm* trestle

treuil [tʀœj] *nm* winch

trêve [tʀɛv] *nf* (MIL, POL) truce; (*fig*) respite; **~ de ...** enough of this ...

tri [tʀi] *nm*: **faire le ~ (de)** to sort out; **le (bureau de) ~** (POSTES) the sorting office

triangle [tʀijɑ̃gl] *nm* triangle; **triangulaire** *adj* triangular

tribord [tʀibɔʀ] *nm*: **à ~** to starboard, on the starboard side

tribu [tʀiby] *nf* tribe

tribunal, -aux [tʀibynal, o] *nm* (JUR) court; (MIL) tribunal

tribune [tʀibyn] *nf* (*estrade*) platform, rostrum; (*débat*) forum; (*d'église, de tribunal*) gallery; (*de stade*) stand

tribut [tʀiby] *nm* tribute

tributaire [tʀibytɛʀ] *adj*: **être ~ de** to be dependent on

tricher [tʀiʃe] *vi* to cheat; **tricheur, -euse** *nm/f* cheat(er)

tricolore [tʀikɔlɔʀ] *adj* three-coloured; (*français*) red, white and blue

tricot [tʀiko] *nm* (*technique, ouvrage*) knitting *no pl*; (*vêtement*) jersey, sweater; **~ de peau** vest; **tricoter** *vt* to knit

trictrac [tʀiktʀak] *nm* backgammon

tricycle [tʀisikl] *nm* tricycle

triennal, e, -aux [tʀijenal, o] *adj* three-year

trier [tʀije] *vt* to sort out; (POSTES, *fruits*) to sort

trimestre [tʀimɛstʀ] *nm* (SCOL) term; (COMM) quarter; **trimestriel, le** *adj* quarterly; (SCOL) end-of-term

tringle [tʀɛ̃gl] *nf* rod

trinquer [tʀɛ̃ke] *vi* to clink glasses

triomphe [tʀijɔ̃f] *nm* triumph; **triompher** *vi* to triumph, win; **triompher de** to triumph over, overcome

tripes [tʀip] *nfpl* (CULIN) tripe *sg*

triple [tʀipl] *adj* triple ♦ *nm*: **le ~ (de)** (*comparaison*) three times as much (as); **en ~ exemplaire** in triplicate; **tripler** *vi, vt* to triple, treble

triplés, -ées [tʀiple] *nm/fpl* triplets

tripoter [tʀipɔte] *vt* to fiddle with

triste [tʀist] *adj* sad; (*couleur, temps, journée*) dreary; (*péj*): **~ personnage/affaire** sorry individual/affair; **tristesse** *nf* sadness

trivial, e, -aux [tʀivjal, jo] *adj* coarse, crude; (*commun*) mundane

troc [tʀɔk] *nm* barter

troène [tʀɔɛn] *nm* privet

trognon [tʀɔɲɔ̃] *nm* (*de fruit*) core; (*de légume*) stalk

trois [tʀwɑ] *num* three; **troisième** *num* third; **trois quarts** *nmpl*: **les trois quarts de** three-quarters of

trombe [tʀɔ̃b] *nf*: **des ~s d'eau** a downpour; **en ~** like a whirlwind

trombone [tʀɔ̃bɔn] *nm* (MUS) trombone; (*de bureau*) paper clip

trompe [tʀɔ̃p] *nf* (*d'éléphant*) trunk; (MUS) trumpet, horn

tromper [tʀɔ̃pe] *vt* to deceive; (*vigilance, poursuivants*) to elude; **se ~** *vi* to make a mistake, be mistaken; **se ~ de voiture/jour** to take the wrong car/get the day wrong; **se ~ de 3 cm/20 F** to be out by 3 cm/20 F; **tromperie** *nf* deception, trickery *no pl*

trompette [tʀɔ̃pɛt] *nf* trumpet; **en ~** (*nez*) turned-up

trompeur, -euse [tʀɔ̃pœʀ, øz] *adj* deceptive

tronc [tʀɔ̃] *nm* (BOT, ANAT) trunk; (*d'église*) collection box

tronçon [tʀɔ̃sɔ̃] *nm* section; **tron-**

çonner *vt* to saw up
trône [tRon] *nm* throne
trop [tRo] *adv (+vb)* too much; (*+adjectif, adverbe*) too; **~ (nombreux)** too many; **~ peu (nombreux)** too few; **~ (souvent)** too often; **~ (longtemps)** (for) too long; **~ de** (*nombre*) too many; (*quantité*) too much; **de ~, en ~**: **des livres en ~** a few books too many; **du lait en ~** too much milk; **3 livres/3 F de ~** 3 books too many/3 F too much
tropical, e, -aux [tRɔpikal, o] *adj* tropical
tropique [tRɔpik] *nm* tropic
trop-plein [tRoplɛ̃] *nm* (*tuyau*) overflow *ou* outlet (pipe); (*liquide*) overflow
troquer [tRɔke] *vt*: **~ qch contre** to barter *ou* trade sth for; (*fig*) to swap sth for
trot [tRo] *nm* trot; **trotter** *vi* to trot
trotteuse [tRɔtøz] *nf* (sweep) second hand
trottinette [tRɔtinɛt] *nf* (child's) scooter
trottoir [tRɔtwaR] *nm* pavement; **faire le ~** (*péj*) to walk the streets; **~ roulant** moving walkway, travellator
trou [tRu] *nm* hole; (*fig*) gap; (COMM) deficit; **~ d'air** air pocket; **~ d'ozone** ozone hole; **le ~ de la serrure** the keyhole; **~ de mémoire** blank, lapse of memory
troublant, e [tRublɑ̃, ɑ̃t] *adj* disturbing
trouble [tRubl] *adj* (*liquide*) cloudy; (*image, photo*) blurred; (*affaire*) shady, murky ♦ *nm* agitation; **~s** *nmpl* (POL) disturbances, troubles, unrest *sg*; (MÉD) trouble *sg*, disorders; **trouble-fête** *nm* spoilsport
troubler [tRuble] *vt* to disturb; (*liquide*) to make cloudy; (*intriguer*) to bother; **se ~** *vi* (*personne*) to become flustered *ou* confused
trouer [tRue] *vt* to make a hole (*ou* holes) in
trouille [tRuj] (*fam*) *nf*: **avoir la ~** to be scared to death
troupe [tRup] *nf* troop; **~ (de théâtre)** (theatrical) company
troupeau, x [tRupo] *nm* (*de moutons*) flock; (*de vaches*) herd
trousse [tRus] *nf* case, kit; (*d'écolier*) pencil case; **aux ~s de** (*fig*) on the heels *ou* tail of; **~ à outils** toolkit; **~ de toilette** toilet bag
trousseau, x [tRuso] *nm* (*de mariée*) trousseau; **~ de clefs** bunch of keys
trouvaille [tRuvɑj] *nf* find
trouver [tRuve] *vt* to find; (*rendre visite*): **aller/venir ~ qn** to go/come and see sb; **se ~** *vi* (*être*) to be; **je trouve que** I find *ou* think that; **~ à boire/critiquer** to find something to drink/criticize; **se ~ bien** to feel well; **se ~ mal** to pass out
truand [tRyɑ̃] *nm* gangster; **truander** *vt*: **se faire truander** to be swindled
truc [tRyk] *nm* (*astuce*) way, trick; (*de cinéma, prestidigitateur*) trick, effect; (*chose*) thing, thingumajig; **avoir le ~** to have the knack
truelle [tRyɛl] *nf* trowel
truffe [tRyf] *nf* truffle; (*nez*) nose
truffé, e [tRyfe] *adj*: **~ de** (*fig*) peppered with; (*fautes*) riddled with; (*pièges*) bristling with
truie [tRɥi] *nf* sow
truite [tRɥit] *nf* trout *inv*
truquage [tRykaʒ] *nm* special effects
truquer [tRyke] *vt* (*élections, serrure, dés*) to fix
TSVP *sigle* (= *tournez svp*) PTO
TTC *sigle* (= *toutes taxes comprises*) inclusive of tax
tu[1] [ty] *pron* you
tu[2]**, e** [ty] *pp de* **taire**
tuba [tyba] *nm* (MUS) tuba; (SPORT) snorkel
tube [tyb] *nm* tube; (*chanson*) hit
tuberculose [tybɛRkyloz] *nf* tuberculosis
tuer [tɥe] *vt* to kill; **se ~** *vi* to be killed;

(*suicide*) to kill o.s.; **tuerie** *nf* slaughter *no pl*

tue-tête [tytɛt]: **à ~-~** *adv* at the top of one's voice

tueur [tɥœʀ] *nm* killer; **~ à gages** hired killer

tuile [tɥil] *nf* tile; (*fam*) spot of bad luck, blow

tulipe [tylip] *nf* tulip

tuméfié, e [tymefje] *adj* puffed-up, swollen

tumeur [tymœʀ] *nf* growth, tumour

tumulte [tymylt] *nm* commotion; **tumultueux, -euse** *adj* stormy, turbulent

tunique [tynik] *nf* tunic

Tunisie [tynizi] *nf*: **la ~** Tunisia; **tunisien, ne** *adj* Tunisian ♦ *nm/f*: **Tunisien, ne** Tunisian

tunnel [tynɛl] *nm* tunnel; **le ~ sous la Manche** the Channel Tunnel

turbulences [tyʀbylɑ̃s] *nfpl* (AVIAT) turbulence *sg*

turbulent, e [tyʀbylɑ̃, ɑ̃t] *adj* boisterous, unruly

turc, turque [tyʀk] *adj* Turkish ♦ *nm/f*: **T~, -que** Turk/Turkish woman ♦ *nm* (LING) Turkish

turf [tyʀf] *nm* racing; **turfiste** *nm/f* racegoer

Turquie [tyʀki] *nf*: **la ~** Turkey

turquoise [tyʀkwaz] *nf* turquoise ♦ *adj inv* turquoise

tus *etc* [ty] *vb voir* **taire**

tutelle [tytɛl] *nf* (JUR) guardianship; (POL) trusteeship; **sous la ~ de** (*fig*) under the supervision of

tuteur [tytœʀ] *nm* (JUR) guardian; (*de plante*) stake, support

tutoyer [tytwaje] *vt*: **~ qn** to address sb as "tu"

tuyau, x [tɥijo] *nm* pipe; (*flexible*) tube; (*fam*) tip; **~ d'arrosage** hosepipe; **~ d'échappement** exhaust pipe; **tuyauterie** *nf* piping *no pl*

TVA *sigle f* (= *taxe à la valeur ajoutée*) VAT

tympan [tɛ̃pɑ̃] *nm* (ANAT) eardrum

type [tip] *nm* type; (*fam*) chap, guy ♦ *adj* typical, classic

typé, e [tipe] *adj* ethnic

typique [tipik] *adj* typical

tyran [tiʀɑ̃] *nm* tyrant; **tyrannique** *adj* tyrannical

tzigane [dzigan] *adj* gipsy, tzigane

U, u

UEM *sigle f* (= *union économique et monétaire*) EMU

ulcère [ylsɛʀ] *nm* ulcer; **ulcérer** *vt* (*fig*) to sicken, appal

ultérieur, e [ylteʀjœʀ] *adj* later, subsequent; **remis à une date ~e** postponed to a later date; **ultérieurement** *adv* later, subsequently

ultime [yltim] *adj* final

ultra... [yltʀa] *préfixe*: **~moderne/-rapide** ultra-modern/-fast

MOT-CLÉ

un, une [œ̃, yn] *art indéf* a; (*devant voyelle*) an; **un garçon/vieillard** a boy/an old man; **une fille** a girl

♦ *pron* one; **l'un des meilleurs** one of the best; **l'un ..., l'autre** (the) one ..., the other; **les uns ..., les autres** some ..., others; **l'un et l'autre** both (of them); **l'un ou l'autre** either (of them); **l'un l'autre, les uns les autres** each other, one another; **pas un seul** not a single one; **un par un** one by one

♦ *num* one; **une pomme seulement** one apple only

unanime [ynanim] *adj* unanimous; **unanimité** *nf*: **à l'unanimité** unanimously

uni, e [yni] *adj* (*ton, tissu*) plain; (*surface*) smooth, even; (*famille*) close (-knit); (*pays*) united

unifier [ynifje] *vt* to unite, unify

uniforme [ynifɔʀm] *adj* uniform; (*surface, ton*) even ♦ *nm* uniform; **uniformiser** *vt* (*systèmes*) to standardize
union [ynjɔ̃] *nf* union; **~ de consommateurs** consumers' association; **U~ européenne** European Union; **U~ soviétique** Soviet Union
unique [ynik] *adj* (*seul*) only; (*exceptionnel*) unique; (*le même*): **un prix/système ~** a single price/system; **fils/fille ~** only son/daughter, only child; **sens ~** one-way street; **uniquement** *adv* only, solely; (*juste*) only, merely
unir [yniʀ] *vt* (*nations*) to unite; (*en mariage*) to unite, join together; **s'~** *vi* to unite; (*en mariage*) to be joined together
unitaire [ynitɛʀ] *adj*: **prix ~** unit price
unité [ynite] *nf* unit; (*harmonie, cohésion*) unity
univers [ynivɛʀ] *nm* universe; **universel, le** *adj* universal
universitaire [ynivɛʀsitɛʀ] *adj* university *cpd*; (*diplôme, études*) academic, university *cpd* ♦ *nm/f* academic
université [ynivɛʀsite] *nf* university
urbain, e [yʀbɛ̃, ɛn] *adj* urban, city *cpd*, town *cpd*; **urbanisme** *nm* town planning
urgence [yʀʒɑ̃s] *nf* urgency; (*MÉD etc*) emergency; **d'~** *adj* emergency *cpd* ♦ *adv* as a matter of urgency; **(service des) ~s** casualty
urgent, e [yʀʒɑ̃, ɑ̃t] *adj* urgent
urine [yʀin] *nf* urine; **urinoir** *nm* (public) urinal
urne [yʀn] *nf* (*électorale*) ballot box; (*vase*) urn
urticaire [yʀtikɛʀ] *nf* nettle rash
us [ys] *nmpl*: **~ et coutumes** (habits and) customs
USA *sigle mpl*: **les USA** the USA
usage [yzaʒ] *nm* (*emploi, utilisation*) use; (*coutume*) custom; **à l'~** with use; **à l'~ de** (*pour*) for (use of); **hors d'~** out of service; **à ~ interne** (*MÉD*) to be taken; **à ~ externe** (*MÉD*) for external use only; **usagé, e** *adj* (*usé*) worn; **usager, -ère** *nm/f* user
usé, e [yze] *adj* worn; (*banal*: *argument etc*) hackneyed
user [yze] *vt* (*outil*) to wear down; (*vêtement*) to wear out; (*matière*) to wear away; (*consommer*: *charbon etc*) to use; **s'~** *vi* (*tissu, vêtement*) to wear out; **~ de** (*moyen, procédé*) to use, employ; (*droit*) to exercise
usine [yzin] *nf* factory
usité, e [yzite] *adj* common
ustensile [ystɑ̃sil] *nm* implement; **~ de cuisine** kitchen utensil
usuel, le [yzɥɛl] *adj* everyday, common
usure [yzyʀ] *nf* wear
utérus [yteʀys] *nm* uterus, womb
utile [ytil] *adj* useful
utilisation [ytilizasjɔ̃] *nf* use
utiliser [ytilize] *vt* to use
utilitaire [ytilitɛʀ] *adj* utilitarian
utilité [ytilite] *nf* usefulness *no pl*; **de peu d'~** of little use *ou* help
utopie [ytɔpi] *nf* utopia

V, v

va [va] *vb voir* **aller**
vacance [vakɑ̃s] *nf* (*ADMIN*) vacancy; **~s** *nfpl* holiday(s *pl*), vacation *sg*; **les grandes ~s** the summer holidays; **prendre des/ses ~s** to take a holiday/one's holiday(s); **aller en ~s** to go on holiday; **vacancier, -ière** *nm/f* holiday-maker
vacant, e [vakɑ̃, ɑ̃t] *adj* vacant
vacarme [vakaʀm] *nm* (*bruit*) racket
vaccin [vaksɛ̃] *nm* vaccine; (*opération*) vaccination; **vaccination** *nf* vaccination; **vacciner** *vt* to vaccinate; **être vacciné contre qch** (*fam*) to be cured of sth
vache [vaʃ] *nf* (*ZOOL*) cow; (*cuir*) cowhide ♦ *adj* (*fam*) rotten, mean; **vachement** (*fam*) *adv* (*très*) really; (*pleuvoir, travailler*) a hell of a lot; **vacherie** *nf* (*action*) dirty trick; (*remarque*) nasty re-

mark

vaciller [vasije] *vi* to sway, wobble; (*bougie, lumière*) to flicker; (*fig*) to be failing, falter

va-et-vient [vaevjɛ̃] *nm inv* (*de personnes, véhicules*) comings and goings *pl*, to-ings and fro-ings *pl*

vagabond [vagabɔ̃] *nm* (*rôdeur*) tramp, vagrant; (*voyageur*) wanderer; **vagabonder** *vi* to roam, wander

vagin [vaʒɛ̃] *nm* vagina

vague [vag] *nf* wave ♦ *adj* vague; (*regard*) faraway; (*manteau, robe*) loose (-fitting); (*quelconque*): **un ~ bureau/cousin** some office/cousin or other; **~ de fond** ground swell; **~ de froid** cold spell

vaillant, e [vajɑ̃, ɑ̃t] *adj* (*courageux*) gallant; (*robuste*) hale and hearty

vaille [vaj] *vb voir* **valoir**

vain, e [vɛ̃, vɛn] *adj* vain; **en ~** in vain

vaincre [vɛ̃kʀ] *vt* to defeat; (*fig*) to conquer, overcome; **vaincu, e** *nm/f* defeated party; **vainqueur** *nm* victor; (*SPORT*) winner

vais [vɛ] *vb voir* **aller**

vaisseau, x [vɛso] *nm* (*ANAT*) vessel; (*NAVIG*) ship, vessel; **~ spatial** spaceship

vaisselier [vɛsəlje] *nm* dresser

vaisselle [vɛsɛl] *nf* (*service*) crockery; (*plats etc à laver*) (dirty) dishes *pl*; **faire la ~** to do the washing-up (*BRIT*) *ou* the dishes

val [val, vo] (*pl* **vaux** *ou* **~s**) *nm* valley

valable [valabl] *adj* valid; (*acceptable*) decent, worthwhile

valent *etc* [val] *vb voir* **valoir**

valet [valɛ] *nm* manservant; (*CARTES*) jack

valeur [valœʀ] *nf* (*gén*) value; (*mérite*) worth, merit; (*COMM: titre*) security; **mettre en ~** (*détail*) to highlight; (*objet décoratif*) to show off to advantage; **avoir de la ~** to be valuable; **sans ~** worthless; **prendre de la ~** to go up *ou* gain in value

valide [valid] *adj* (*en bonne santé*) fit; (*valable*) valid; **valider** *vt* to validate

valions [valjɔ̃] *vb voir* **valoir**

valise [valiz] *nf* (suit)case; **faire ses ~s** to pack one's bags

vallée [vale] *nf* valley

vallon [valɔ̃] *nm* small valley; **vallonné, e** *adj* hilly

valoir [valwaʀ] *vi* (*être valable*) to hold, apply ♦ *vt* (*prix, valeur, effort*) to be worth; (*causer*): **~ qch à qn** to earn sb sth; **se ~** *vi* to be of equal merit; (*péj*) to be two of a kind; **faire ~** (*droits, prérogatives*) to assert; **faire ~ que** to point out that; **à ~ sur** to be deducted from; **vaille que vaille** somehow or other; **cela ne me dit rien qui vaille** I don't like the look of it at all; **ce climat ne me vaut rien** this climate doesn't suit me; **~ le coup** *ou* **la peine** to be worth the trouble *ou* worth it; **~ mieux: il vaut mieux se taire** it's better to say nothing; **ça ne vaut rien** it's worthless; **que vaut ce candidat?** how good is this applicant?

valse [vals] *nf* waltz

valu, e [valy] *pp de* **valoir**

vandalisme [vɑ̃dalism] *nm* vandalism

vanille [vanij] *nf* vanilla

vanité [vanite] *nf* vanity; **vaniteux, -euse** *adj* vain, conceited

vanne [van] *nf* gate; (*fig*) joke

vannerie [vanʀi] *nf* basketwork

vantard, e [vɑ̃taʀ, aʀd] *adj* boastful

vanter [vɑ̃te] *vt* to speak highly of, praise; **se ~** *vi* to boast, brag; **se ~ de** to pride o.s. on; (*péj*) to boast of

vapeur [vapœʀ] *nf* steam; (*émanation*) vapour, fumes *pl*; **~s** *nfpl* (*bouffées*) vapours; **à ~** steam-powered, steam *cpd*; **cuit à la ~** steamed; **vaporeux, -euse** *adj* (*flou*) hazy, misty; (*léger*) filmy; **vaporisateur** *nm* spray; **vaporiser** *vt* (*parfum etc*) to spray

varappe [vaʀap] *nf* rock climbing

vareuse [vaʀøz] *nf* (*blouson*) pea jacket; (*d'uniforme*) tunic

variable [vaʀjabl] *adj* variable; (*temps,*

humeur) changeable; (*divers: résultats*) varied, various

varice [vaʀis] *nf* varicose vein

varicelle [vaʀisɛl] *nf* chickenpox

varié, e [vaʀje] *adj* varied; (*divers*) various

varier [vaʀje] *vi* to vary; (*temps, humeur*) to change ♦ *vt* to vary; **variété** *nf* variety; **variétés** *nfpl*: **spectacle/émission de variétés** variety show

variole [vaʀjɔl] *nf* smallpox

vas [va] *vb voir* **aller**

vase [vɑz] *nm* vase ♦ *nf* silt, mud; **vaseux, -euse** *adj* silty, muddy; (*fig: confus*) woolly, hazy; (*: fatigué*) woozy

vasistas [vazistɑs] *nm* fanlight

vaste [vast] *adj* vast, immense

vaudrai *etc* [vodʀe] *vb voir* **valoir**

vaurien, ne [voʀjɛ̃, jɛn] *nm/f* good-for-nothing

vaut [vo] *vb voir* **valoir**

vautour [votuʀ] *nm* vulture

vautrer [votʀe] *vb*: **se ~ dans/sur** to wallow in/sprawl on

vaux [vo] *nmpl de* **val** ♦ *vb voir* **valoir**

va-vite [vavit]: **à la ~-~** *adv* in a rush *ou* hurry

VDQS

VDQS is the second highest French wine classification after AOC, indicating high-quality wine from an approved regional vineyard. It is followed by **vin de pays. Vin de table** *or* **vin ordinaire** *is table wine of unspecified origin, often blended.*

veau, x [vo] *nm* (ZOOL) calf; (CULIN) veal; (*peau*) calfskin

vécu, e [veky] *pp de* **vivre**

vedette [vədɛt] *nf* (*artiste etc*) star; (*canot*) motor boat; (*police*) launch

végétal, e, -aux [veʒetal, o] *adj* vegetable ♦ *nm* vegetable, plant; **végétalien, ne** *adj, nm/f* vegan

végétarien, ne [veʒetaʀjɛ̃, jɛn] *adj, nm/f* vegetarian

végétation [veʒetasjɔ̃] *nf* vegetation; **~s** *nfpl* (MÉD) adenoids

véhicule [veikyl] *nm* vehicle; **~ utilitaire** commercial vehicle

veille [vɛj] *nf* (*état*) wakefulness; (*jour*): **la ~ (de)** the day before; **la ~ au soir** the previous evening; **à la ~ de** on the eve of; **la ~ de Noël** Christmas Eve; **la ~ du jour de l'An** New Year's Eve

veillée [veje] *nf* (*soirée*) evening; (*réunion*) evening gathering; **~ (funèbre)** wake

veiller [veje] *vi* to stay up ♦ *vt* (*malade, mort*) to watch over, sit up with; **~ à** to attend to, see to; **~ à ce que** to make sure that; **~ sur** to watch over; **veilleur** *nm*: **veilleur de nuit** night watchman; **veilleuse** *nf* (*lampe*) night light; (AUTO) sidelight; (*flamme*) pilot light

veinard, e [vɛnaʀ, aʀd] *nm/f* lucky devil

veine [vɛn] *nf* (ANAT, *du bois etc*) vein; (*filon*) vein, seam; (*fam: chance*): **avoir de la ~** to be lucky

véliplanchiste [veliplɑ̃ʃist] *nm/f* windsurfer

vélo [velo] *nm* bike, cycle; **faire du ~** to go cycling; **~ tout-terrain** mountain bike; **vélomoteur** *nm* moped

velours [v(ə)luʀ] *nm* velvet; **~ côtelé** corduroy; **velouté, e** *adj* velvety ♦ *nm*: **velouté de tomates** cream of tomato soup

velu, e [vəly] *adj* hairy

venais *etc* [vənɛ] *vb voir* **venir**

venaison [vənɛzɔ̃] *nf* venison

vendange [vɑ̃dɑ̃ʒ] *nf* (*aussi:* **_s**) grape harvest; **vendanger** *vi* to harvest the grapes

vendeur, -euse [vɑ̃dœʀ, øz] *nm/f* shop assistant ♦ *nm* (JUR) vendor, seller; **~ de journaux** newspaper seller

vendre [vɑ̃dʀ] *vt* to sell; **~ qch à qn** to sell sb sth; **"à ~"** "for sale"

vendredi [vɑ̃dʀədi] *nm* Friday; **V~ saint** Good Friday

vénéneux, -euse [venenø, øz] *adj* poisonous

vénérien, ne [veneʀjɛ̃, jɛn] *adj* venereal

vengeance [vɑ̃ʒɑ̃s] *nf* vengeance *no pl*, revenge *no pl*

venger [vɑ̃ʒe] *vt* to avenge; **se ~** *vi* to avenge o.s.; **se ~ de qch** to avenge o.s. for sth, take one's revenge for sth; **se ~ de qn** to take revenge on sb; **se ~ sur** to take revenge on

venimeux, -euse [vənimø, øz] *adj* poisonous, venomous; (*fig: haineux*) venomous, vicious

venin [vənɛ̃] *nm* venom, poison

venir [v(ə)niʀ] *vi* to come; **~ de** to come from; **~ de faire**: **je viens d'y aller/de le voir** I've just been there/ seen him; **s'il vient à pleuvoir** if it should rain; **j'en viens à croire que** I have come to believe that; **faire ~** (*docteur, plombier*) to call (out)

vent [vɑ̃] *nm* wind; **il y a du ~** it's windy; **c'est du ~** it's all hot air; **au ~** to windward; **sous le ~** to leeward; **avoir le ~ debout/arrière** to head into the wind/have the wind astern; **dans le ~** (*fam*) trendy

vente [vɑ̃t] *nf* sale; **la ~** (*activité*) selling; (*secteur*) sales *pl*; **mettre en ~** (*produit*) to put on sale; (*maison, objet personnel*) to put up for sale; **~ aux enchères** auction sale; **~ de charité** jumble sale

venteux, -euse [vɑ̃tø, øz] *adj* windy

ventilateur [vɑ̃tilatœʀ] *nm* fan

ventiler [vɑ̃tile] *vt* to ventilate

ventouse [vɑ̃tuz] *nf* (*de caoutchouc*) suction pad

ventre [vɑ̃tʀ] *nm* (ANAT) stomach; (*légèrement péj*) belly; (*utérus*) womb; **avoir mal au ~** to have stomach ache (BRIT) *ou* a stomach ache (US)

ventriloque [vɑ̃tʀilɔk] *nm/f* ventriloquist

venu, e [v(ə)ny] *pp de* **venir** ♦ *adj*: **bien ~** timely; **mal ~** out of place; **être mal ~ à** *ou* **de faire** to have no grounds for doing, be in no position to do

ver [vɛʀ] *nm* worm; (*des fruits etc*) maggot; (*du bois*) woodworm *no pl*; *voir aussi* **vers**; **~ à soie** silkworm; **~ de terre** earthworm; **~ luisant** glow-worm; **~ solitaire** tapeworm

verbaliser [vɛʀbalize] *vi* (POLICE) to book *ou* report an offender

verbe [vɛʀb] *nm* verb

verdâtre [vɛʀdɑtʀ] *adj* greenish

verdict [vɛʀdik(t)] *nm* verdict

verdir [vɛʀdiʀ] *vi, vt* to turn green; **verdure** *nf* greenery

véreux, -euse [veʀø, øz] *adj* worm-eaten; (*malhonnête*) shady, corrupt

verge [vɛʀʒ] *nf* (ANAT) penis

verger [vɛʀʒe] *nm* orchard

verglacé, e [vɛʀglase] *adj* icy, iced-over

verglas [vɛʀglɑ] *nm* (black) ice

vergogne [vɛʀgɔɲ]: **sans ~** *adv* shamelessly

véridique [veʀidik] *adj* truthful

vérification [veʀifikasjɔ̃] *nf* (*action*) checking *no pl*, (*contrôle*) check

vérifier [veʀifje] *vt* to check; (*corroborer*) to confirm, bear out

véritable [veʀitabl] *adj* real; (*ami, amour*) true

vérité [veʀite] *nf* truth; **en ~** really, actually

vermeil, le [vɛʀmɛj] *adj* ruby red

vermine [vɛʀmin] *nf* vermin *pl*

vermoulu, e [vɛʀmuly] *adj* worm-eaten

verni, e [vɛʀni] *adj* (*fam*) lucky; **cuir ~** patent leather

vernir [vɛʀniʀ] *vt* (*bois, tableau, ongles*) to varnish; (*poterie*) to glaze

vernis *nm* (*enduit*) varnish; glaze; (*fig*) veneer; **~ à ongles** nail polish *ou* varnish; **vernissage** *nm* (*d'une exposition*) preview

vérole [veʀɔl] *nf* (*variole*) smallpox

verrai *etc* [veʀe] *vb voir* **voir**

verre [vɛʀ] *nm* glass; (*de lunettes*) lens *sg*; **boire** *ou* **prendre un ~** to have a drink; **~ dépoli** frosted glass; **~s de contact** contact lenses; **verrerie** *nf* (*fabrique*) glassworks *sg*; (*activité*) glass-making; (*objets*) glassware; **verrière** *nf* (*paroi vitrée*) glass wall; (*toit vitré*) glass roof

verrons *etc* [vɛʀɔ̃] *vb voir* **voir**

verrou [veʀu] *nm* (*targette*) bolt; **mettre qn sous les ~s** to put sb behind bars; **verrouillage** *nm* locking; **verrouillage centralisé** central locking; **verrouiller** *vt* (*porte*) to bolt; (*ordinateur*) to lock

verrue [veʀy] *nf* wart

vers [vɛʀ] *nm* line ♦ *nmpl* (*poésie*) verse *sg* ♦ *prép* (*en direction de*) toward(s); (*près de*) around (about); (*temporel*) about, around

versant [vɛʀsɑ̃] *nm* slopes *pl*, side

versatile [vɛʀsatil] *adj* fickle, changeable

verse [vɛʀs]: **à ~** *adv*: **il pleut à ~** it's pouring (with rain)

Verseau [vɛʀso] *nm*: **le ~** Aquarius

versement [vɛʀsəmɑ̃] *nm* payment; **en 3 ~s** in 3 instalments

verser [vɛʀse] *vt* (*liquide, grains*) to pour; (*larmes, sang*) to shed; (*argent*) to pay ♦ *vi* (*véhicule*) to overturn; (*fig*): **~ dans** to lapse into

verset [vɛʀsɛ] *nm* verse

version [vɛʀsjɔ̃] *nf* version; (*SCOL*) translation (*into the mother tongue*); **film en ~ originale** film in the original language

verso [vɛʀso] *nm* back; **voir au ~** see over(leaf)

vert, e [vɛʀ, vɛʀt] *adj* green; (*vin*) young; (*vigoureux*) sprightly ♦ *nm* green

vertèbre [vɛʀtɛbʀ] *nf* vertebra

vertement [vɛʀtəmɑ̃] *adv* (*réprimander*) sharply

vertical, e, -aux [vɛʀtikal, o] *adj* vertical; **verticale** *nf* vertical; **à la verticale** vertically; **verticalement** *adv* vertically

vertige [vɛʀtiʒ] *nm* (*peur du vide*) vertigo; (*étourdissement*) dizzy spell; (*fig*) fever; **vertigineux, -euse** *adj* breathtaking

vertu [vɛʀty] *nf* virtue; **en ~ de** in accordance with; **vertueux, -euse** *adj* virtuous

verve [vɛʀv] *nf* witty eloquence; **être en ~** to be in brilliant form

verveine [vɛʀvɛn] *nf* (*BOT*) verbena, vervain; (*infusion*) verbena tea

vésicule [vezikyl] *nf* vesicle; **~ biliaire** gall-bladder

vessie [vesi] *nf* bladder

veste [vɛst] *nf* jacket; **~ droite/croisée** single-/double-breasted jacket

vestiaire [vɛstjɛʀ] *nm* (*au théâtre etc*) cloakroom; (*de stade etc*) changing-room (*BRIT*), locker-room (*US*)

vestibule [vɛstibyl] *nm* hall

vestige [vɛstiʒ] *nm* relic; (*fig*) vestige; **~s** *nmpl* (*de ville*) remains

vestimentaire [vɛstimɑ̃tɛʀ] *adj* (*détail*) of dress; (*élégance*) sartorial; **dépenses ~s** clothing expenditure

veston [vɛstɔ̃] *nm* jacket

vêtement [vɛtmɑ̃] *nm* garment, item of clothing; **~s** *nmpl* clothes

vétérinaire [veteʀinɛʀ] *nm/f* vet, veterinary surgeon

vêtir [vetiʀ] *vt* to clothe, dress

veto [veto] *nm* veto; **opposer un ~ à** to veto

vêtu, e [vety] *pp de* **vêtir**

vétuste [vetyst] *adj* ancient, timeworn

veuf, veuve [vœf, vœv] *adj* widowed ♦ *nm* widower

veuille [vœj] *vb voir* **vouloir**

veuillez [vœje] *vb voir* **vouloir**

veule [vøl] *adj* spineless

veuve [vœv] *nf* widow

veux [vø] *vb voir* **vouloir**

vexant, e [vɛksɑ̃, ɑ̃t] *adj* (*contrariant*) annoying; (*blessant*) hurtful

vexation [vɛksasjɔ̃] *nf* humiliation

vexer [vɛkse] *vt*: **~ qn** to hurt sb's feelings; **se ~** *vi* to be offended

viable [vjabl] *adj* viable; (*économie, industrie etc*) sustainable
viaduc [vjadyk] *nm* viaduct
viager, -ère [vjaʒe, ɛʀ] *adj*: **rente viagère** life annuity
viande [vjɑ̃d] *nf* meat
vibrer [vibʀe] *vi* to vibrate; (*son, voix*) to be vibrant; (*fig*) to be stirred; **faire ~** to (cause to) vibrate; (*fig*) to stir, thrill
vice [vis] *nm* vice; (*défaut*) fault ♦ *préfixe*: **~...** vice-; **~ de forme** legal flaw *ou* irregularity
vichy [viʃi] *nm* (*toile*) gingham
vicié, e [visje] *adj* (*air*) polluted, tainted; (*JUR*) invalidated
vicieux, -euse [visjø, jøz] *adj* (*pervers*) lecherous; (*rétif*) unruly ♦ *nm/f* lecher
vicinal, e, -aux [visinal, o] *adj*: **chemin ~** by-road, byway
victime [viktim] *nf* victim; (*d'accident*) casualty
victoire [viktwaʀ] *nf* victory
victuailles [viktɥaj] *nfpl* provisions
vidange [vidɑ̃ʒ] *nf* (*d'un fossé, réservoir*) emptying; (*AUTO*) oil change; (*de lavabo: bonde*) waste outlet; **~s** *nfpl* (*matières*) sewage *sg*; **vidanger** *vt* to empty
vide [vid] *adj* empty ♦ *nm* (*PHYSIQUE*) vacuum; (*espace*) (empty) space, gap; (*futilité, néant*) void; **avoir peur du ~** to be afraid of heights; **emballé sous ~** vacuum packed; **à ~** (*sans occupants*) empty; (*sans charge*) unladen
vidéo [video] *nf* video ♦ *adj*: **cassette ~** video cassette; **jeu ~** video game; **vidéoclip** *nm* music video; **vidéoclub** *nm* video shop
vide-ordures [vidɔʀdyʀ] *nm inv* (rubbish) chute
vidéothèque [videɔtɛk] *nf* video library
vide-poches [vidpɔʃ] *nm inv* tidy; (*AUTO*) glove compartment
vider [vide] *vt* to empty; (*CULIN*: *volaille, poisson*) to gut, clean out; **se ~** *vi* to empty; **~ les lieux** to quit *ou* vacate the premises; **videur** *nm* (*de boîte de nuit*) bouncer, doorman
vie [vi] *nf* life; **être en ~** to be alive; **sans ~** lifeless; **à ~** for life
vieil [vjɛj] *adj m voir* **vieux**; **vieillard** *nm* old man; **les vieillards** old people, the elderly; **vieille** *adj, nf voir* **vieux**; **vieilleries** *nfpl* old things; **vieillesse** *nf* old age; **vieillir** *vi* (*prendre de l'âge*) to grow old; (*population, vin*) to age; (*doctrine, auteur*) to become dated ♦ *vt* to age; **vieillissement** *nm* growing old; ageing
Vienne [vjɛn] *nf* Vienna
viens [vjɛ̃] *vb voir* **venir**
vierge [vjɛʀʒ] *adj* virgin; (*page*) clean, blank ♦ *nf* virgin; (*signe*): **la V~** Virgo
Vietnam, Viet-Nam [vjɛtnam] *nm* Vietnam; **vietnamien, ne** *adj* Vietnamese ♦ *nm/f*: **Vietnamien, ne** Vietnamese
vieux (vieil), vieille [vjø, vjɛj] *adj* old ♦ *nm/f* old man (woman) ♦ *nmpl* old people; **mon ~/ma vieille** (*fam*) old man/girl; **prendre un coup de ~** to put years on; **vieille fille** spinster; **~ garçon** bachelor; **~ jeu** *adj inv* old-fashioned
vif, vive [vif, viv] *adj* (*animé*) lively; (*alerte, brusque, aigu*) sharp; (*lumière, couleur*) bright; (*air*) crisp; (*vent, émotion*) keen; (*fort: regret, déception*) great, deep; (*vivant*): **brûlé ~** burnt alive; **de vive voix** personally; **avoir l'esprit ~** to be quick-witted; **piquer qn au ~** to cut sb to the quick; **à ~** (*plaie*) open; **avoir les nerfs à ~** to be on edge
vigne [viɲ] *nf* (*plante*) vine; (*plantation*) vineyard; **vigneron** *nm* wine grower
vignette [viɲɛt] *nf* (*ADMIN*) ≃ (road) tax disc (*BRIT*), ≃ license plate sticker (*US*); (*de médicament*) price label (*used for reimbursement*)
vignoble [viɲɔbl] *nm* (*plantation*) vineyard; (*vignes d'une région*) vineyards *pl*
vigoureux, -euse [viguʀø, øz] *adj* vigorous, robust

vigueur [vigœʀ] *nf* vigour; **entrer en ~** to come into force; **en ~** current

vil, e [vil] *adj* vile, base

vilain, e [vilɛ̃, ɛn] *adj* (*laid*) ugly; (*affaire, blessure*) nasty; (*pas sage*: *enfant*) naughty

villa [villa] *nf* (detached) house; **~ en multipropriété** time-share villa

village [vilaʒ] *nm* village; **villageois, e** *adj* village *cpd* ♦ *nm/f* villager

ville [vil] *nf* town; (*importante*) city; (*administration*): **la ~** ≃ the Corporation; ≃ the (town) council; **~ d'eaux** spa

villégiature [vi(l)leʒjatyʀ] *nf* holiday; **(lieu de) ~** (holiday) resort

vin [vɛ̃] *nm* wine; **avoir le ~ gai** to get happy after a few drinks; **~ d'honneur** reception (*with wine and snacks*); **~ de pays** local wine; **~ ordinaire** table wine

vinaigre [vinɛgʀ] *nm* vinegar; **vinaigrette** *nf* vinaigrette, French dressing

vindicatif, -ive [vɛ̃dikatif, iv] *adj* vindictive

vineux, -euse [vinø, øz] *adj* win(e)y

vingt [vɛ̃] *num* twenty; **vingtaine** *nf*: **une vingtaine (de)** about twenty, twenty or so; **vingtième** *num* twentieth

vinicole [vinikɔl] *adj* wine *cpd*, wine-growing

vins *etc* [vɛ̃] *vb voir* **venir**

vinyle [vinil] *nm* vinyl

viol [vjɔl] *nm* (*d'une femme*) rape; (*d'un lieu sacré*) violation

violacé, e [vjɔlase] *adj* purplish, mauvish

violemment [vjɔlamɑ̃] *adv* violently

violence [vjɔlɑ̃s] *nf* violence

violent, e [vjɔlɑ̃, ɑ̃t] *adj* violent; (*remède*) drastic

violer [vjɔle] *vt* (*femme*) to rape; (*sépulture, loi, traité*) to violate

violet, te [vjɔlɛ, ɛt] *adj, nm* purple, mauve; **violette** *nf* (*fleur*) violet

violon [vjɔlɔ̃] *nm* violin; (*fam*: *prison*) lock-up; **~ d'Ingres** hobby; **violoncelle** *nm* cello; **violoniste** *nm/f* violinist

vipère [vipɛʀ] *nf* viper, adder

virage [viʀaʒ] *nm* (*d'un véhicule*) turn; (*d'une route, piste*) bend

virée [viʀe] *nf* trip; (*à pied*) walk; (*longue*) walking tour; (*dans les cafés*) tour

virement [viʀmɑ̃] *nm* (COMM) transfer

virent [viʀ] *vb voir* **voir**

virer [viʀe] *vt* (COMM): **~ qch (sur)** to transfer sth (into); (*fam*: *expulser*): **~ qn** to kick sb out ♦ *vi* to turn; (CHIMIE) to change colour; **~ de bord** to tack

virevolter [viʀvɔlte] *vi* to twirl around

virgule [viʀgyl] *nf* comma; (MATH) point

viril, e [viʀil] *adj* (*propre à l'homme*) masculine; (*énergique, courageux*) manly, virile

virtuel, le [viʀtɥɛl] *adj* potential; (*théorique*) virtual

virtuose [viʀtɥoz] *nm/f* (MUS) virtuoso; (*gén*) master

virus [viʀys] *nm* virus

vis¹ [vi] *vb voir* **voir**; **vivre**

vis² [vi] *nf* screw

visa [viza] *nm* (*sceau*) stamp; (*validation de passeport*) visa

visage [vizaʒ] *nm* face

vis-à-vis [vizavi] *prep*: **~-~-~ de qn** to(wards) sb; **en ~-~-~** facing each other

viscéral, e, -aux [viseʀal, o] *adj* (*fig*) deep-seated, deep-rooted

visées [vize] *nfpl* (*intentions*) designs

viser [vize] *vi* to aim ♦ *vt* to aim at; (*concerner*) to be aimed *ou* directed at; (*apposer un visa sur*) to stamp, visa; **~ à qch/faire** to aim at sth/at doing *ou* to do; **viseur** *nm* (*d'arme*) sights *pl*; (PHOTO) viewfinder

visibilité [vizibilite] *nf* visibility

visible [vizibl] *adj* visible; (*disponible*): **est-il ~?** can he see me?, will he see visitors?

visière [vizjɛʀ] *nf* (*de casquette*) peak; (*qui s'attache*) eyeshade

vision [vizjɔ̃] *nf* vision; (*sens*) (eye)sight,

vision; (*fait de voir*): **la ~ de** the sight of; **visionneuse** *nf* viewer

visite [vizit] *nf* visit; **~ médicale** medical examination; **~ accompagnée** *ou* **guidée** guided tour; **faire une ~ à qn** to call on sb, pay sb a visit; **rendre ~ à qn** to visit sb, pay sb a visit; **être en ~ (chez qn)** to be visiting (sb); **avoir de la ~** to have visitors; **heures de ~** (*hôpital, prison*) visiting hours

visiter [vizite] *vt* to visit; **visiteur, -euse** *nm/f* visitor

vison [vizɔ̃] *nm* mink

visser [vise] *vt*: **~ qch** (*fixer, serrer*) to screw sth on

visuel, le [vizɥɛl] *adj* visual

vit [vi] *vb voir* **voir**; **vivre**

vital, e, -aux [vital, o] *adj* vital

vitamine [vitamin] *nf* vitamin

vite [vit] *adv* (*rapidement*) quickly, fast; (*sans délai*) quickly; (*sous peu*) soon; **~!** quick!; **faire ~** to be quick; **le temps passe ~** time flies

vitesse [vitɛs] *nf* speed; (AUTO: *dispositif*) gear; **prendre de la ~** to pick up *ou* gather speed; **à toute ~** at full *ou* top speed; **en ~** (*rapidement*) quickly; (*en hâte*) in a hurry

viticole [vitikɔl] *adj* wine *cpd*, wine-growing; **viticulteur** *nm* wine grower

vitrage [vitʀaʒ] *nm*: **double ~** double glazing

vitrail, -aux [vitʀaj, o] *nm* stained-glass window

vitre [vitʀ] *nf* (window) pane; (*de portière, voiture*) window; **vitré, e** *adj* glass *cpd*; **vitrer** *vt* to glaze; **vitreux, -euse** *adj* (*terne*) glassy

vitrine [vitʀin] *nf* (shop) window; (*petite armoire*) display cabinet; **en ~** in the window; **~ publicitaire** display case, showcase

vivable [vivabl] *adj* (*personne*) livable-with; (*maison*) fit to live in

vivace [vivas] *adj* (*arbre, plante*) hardy; (*fig*) indestructible, inveterate

vivacité [vivasite] *nf* liveliness, vivacity

vivant, e [vivɑ̃, ɑ̃t] *adj* (*qui vit*) living, alive; (*animé*) lively; (*preuve, exemple*) living ♦ *nm*: **du ~ de qn** in sb's lifetime; **les ~s** the living

vive [viv] *adj voir* **vif** ♦ *vb voir* **vivre** ♦ *excl*: **~ le roi!** long live the king!; **vivement** *adv* deeply ♦ *excl*: **vivement les vacances!** roll on the holidays!

vivier [vivje] *nm* (*étang*) fish tank; (*réservoir*) fishpond

vivifiant, e [vivifjɑ̃, jɑ̃t] *adj* invigorating

vivions [vivjɔ̃] *vb voir* **vivre**

vivoter [vivɔte] *vi* (*personne*) to scrape a living, get by; (*fig*: *affaire etc*) to struggle along

vivre [vivʀ] *vi, vt* to live; (*période*) to live through; **~ de** to live on; **il vit encore** he is still alive; **se laisser ~** to take life as it comes; **ne plus ~** (*être anxieux*) to live on one's nerves; **il a vécu** (*eu une vie aventureuse*) he has seen life; **être facile à ~** to be easy to get on with; **faire ~ qn** (*pourvoir à sa subsistance*) to provide (a living) for sb; **vivres** *nmpl* provisions, food supplies

vlan [vlɑ̃] *excl* wham!, bang!

VO [veo] *nf*: **film en ~** film in the original version; **en ~ sous-titrée** in the original version with subtitles

vocable [vɔkabl] *nm* term

vocabulaire [vɔkabylɛʀ] *nm* vocabulary

vocation [vɔkasjɔ̃] *nf* vocation, calling

vociférer [vɔsifeʀe] *vi, vt* to scream

vœu, x [vø] *nm* wish; (*promesse*) vow; **faire ~ de** to take a vow of; **tous nos ~x de bonne année, meilleurs ~x** best wishes for the New Year

vogue [vɔg] *nf* fashion, vogue

voguer [vɔge] *vi* to sail

voici [vwasi] *prép* (*pour introduire, désigner*) here is *+sg*, here are *+pl*; **et ~ que ...** and now it (*ou* he) ...; *voir aussi* **voilà**

voie [vwa] *nf* way; (RAIL) track, line; (AUTO) lane; **être en bonne ~** to be going well; **mettre qn sur la ~** to put sb on the right track; **pays en ~ de développement** developing country; **être en ~ d'achèvement/de rénovation** to be nearing completion/in the process of renovation; **par ~ buccale** *ou* **orale** orally; **à ~ étroite** narrow-gauge; **~ d'eau** (*NAVIG*) leak; **~ de garage** (*RAIL*) siding; **~ ferrée** track; railway line; **la ~ publique** the public highway

voilà [vwala] *prép* (*en désignant*) there is *+sg*, there are *+pl*; **les ~** *ou* **voici** here *ou* there they are; **en ~** *ou* **voici un** here's one, there's one; **voici mon frère et ~ ma sœur** this is my brother and that's my sister; **~** *ou* **voici deux ans** two years ago; **~** *ou* **voici deux ans que** it's two years since; **et ~!** there we are!; **~ tout** that's all; **~** *ou* **voici** (*en offrant etc*) there *ou* here you are; **tiens! ~ Paul** look! there's Paul

voile [vwal] *nm* veil; (*tissu léger*) net ♦ *nf* sail; (*sport*) sailing; **voiler** *vt* to veil; (*fausser*: *roue*) to buckle; (: *bois*) to warp; **se voiler** *vi* (*lune, regard*) to mist over; (*voix*) to become husky; (*roue, disque*) to buckle; (*planche*) to warp; **voilier** *nm* sailing ship; (*de plaisance*) sailing boat; **voilure** *nf* (*de voilier*) sails *pl*

voir [vwaR] *vi, vt* to see; **se ~** *vt* (*être visible*) to show; (*se fréquenter*) to see each other; (*se produire*) to happen; **se ~ critiquer/transformer** to be criticized/transformed; **cela se voit** (*c'est visible*) that's obvious, it shows; **faire ~ qch à qn** to show sb sth; **en faire ~ à qn** (*fig*) to give sb a hard time; **ne pas pouvoir ~ qn** not to be able to stand sb; **voyons!** let's see now; (*indignation etc*) come on!; **avoir quelque chose à ~ avec** to have something to do with

voire [vwaR] *adv* even

voisin, e [vwazɛ̃, in] *adj* (*proche*) neighbouring; (*contigu*) next; (*ressemblant*) connected ♦ *nm/f* neighbour;

voisinage *nm* (*proximité*) proximity; (*environs*) vicinity; (*quartier, voisins*) neighbourhood

voiture [vwatyR] *nf* car; (*wagon*) coach, carriage; **~ de course** racing car; **~ de sport** sports car

voix [vwɑ] *nf* voice; (*POL*) vote; **à haute ~** aloud; **à ~ basse** in a low voice; **à 2/4 ~** (*MUS*) in 2/4 parts; **avoir ~ au chapitre** to have a say in the matter

vol [vɔl] *nm* (*d'oiseau, d'avion*) flight; (*larcin*) theft; **~ régulier** scheduled flight; **à ~ d'oiseau** as the crow flies; **au ~: attraper qch au ~** to catch sth as it flies past; **en ~** in flight; **~ à main armée** armed robbery; **~ à voile** gliding; **~ libre** hang-gliding

volage [vɔlaʒ] *adj* fickle

volaille [vɔlaj] *nf* (*oiseaux*) poultry *pl*; (*viande*) poultry *no pl*; (*oiseau*) fowl

volant, e [vɔlɑ̃, ɑ̃t] *adj voir* **feuille** *etc* ♦ *nm* (*d'automobile*) (steering) wheel; (*de commande*) wheel; (*objet lancé*) shuttlecock; (*bande de tissu*) flounce

volcan [vɔlkɑ̃] *nm* volcano

volée [vɔle] *nf* (*TENNIS*) volley; **à la ~: rattraper à la ~** to catch in mid-air; **à toute ~** (*sonner les cloches*) vigorously; (*lancer un projectile*) with full force; **~ de coups/de flèches** volley of blows/arrows

voler [vɔle] *vi* (*avion, oiseau, fig*) to fly; (*voleur*) to steal ♦ *vt* (*objet*) to steal; (*personne*) to rob; **~ qch à qn** to steal sth from sb; **il ne l'a pas volé!** he asked for it!

volet [vɔlɛ] *nm* (*de fenêtre*) shutter; (*de feuillet, document*) section

voleur, -euse [vɔlœR, øz] *nm/f* thief ♦ *adj* thieving; **"au ~!"** "stop thief!"

volière [vɔljɛR] *nf* aviary

volley [vɔlɛ] *nm* volleyball

volontaire [vɔlɔ̃tɛR] *adj* (*acte, enrôlement, prisonnier*) voluntary; (*oubli*) intentional; (*caractère, personne*: *décidé*) self-willed ♦ *nm/f* volunteer

volonté [vɔlɔ̃te] *nf* (*faculté de vouloir*)

will; (*énergie, fermeté*) will(power); (*souhait, désir*) wish; **à ~** as much as one likes; **bonne ~** goodwill, willingness; **mauvaise ~** lack of goodwill, unwillingness

volontiers [vɔlɔ̃tje] *adv* (*avec plaisir*) willingly, gladly; (*habituellement, souvent*) readily, willingly; **voulez-vous boire quelque chose? - ~!** would you like something to drink? - yes, please!

volt [vɔlt] *nm* volt

volte-face [vɔltəfas] *nf inv*: **faire ~-~** to turn round

voltige [vɔltiʒ] *nf* (ÉQUITATION) trick riding; (*au cirque*) acrobatics *sg*; **voltiger** *vi* to flutter (about)

volubile [vɔlybil] *adj* voluble

volume [vɔlym] *nm* volume; (GÉOM: *solide*) solid; **volumineux, -euse** *adj* voluminous, bulky

volupté [vɔlypte] *nf* sensual delight *ou* pleasure

vomi [vɔmi] *nm* vomit; **vomir** *vi* to vomit, be sick ♦ *vt* to vomit, bring up; (*fig*) to belch out, spew out; (*exécrer*) to loathe, abhor; **vomissements** *nmpl*: **être pris de vomissements** to (suddenly) start vomiting

vont [vɔ̃] *vb voir* **aller**

vorace [vɔʀas] *adj* voracious

vos [vo] *adj voir* **votre**

vote [vɔt] *nm* vote; **~ par correspondance/procuration** postal/proxy vote; **voter** *vi* to vote ♦ *vt* (*projet de loi*) to vote for; (*loi, réforme*) to pass

votre [vɔtʀ] (*pl* **vos**) *adj* your

vôtre [votʀ] *pron*: **le ~, la ~, les ~s** yours; **les ~s** (*fig*) your family *ou* folks; **à la ~** (*toast*) your (good) health!

voudrai *etc* [vudʀe] *vb voir* **vouloir**

voué, e [vwe] *adj*: **~ à** doomed to

vouer [vwe] *vt*: **~ qch à** (*Dieu, un saint*) to dedicate sth to; **~ sa vie à** (*étude, cause etc*) to devote one's life to; **~ une amitié éternelle à qn** to vow undying friendship to sb

MOT-CLÉ

vouloir [vulwaʀ] *nm*: **le bon vouloir de qn** sb's goodwill; sb's pleasure

♦ *vt* **1** (*exiger, désirer*) to want; **vouloir faire/que qn fasse** to want to do/sb to do; **voulez-vous du thé?** would you like *ou* do you want some tea?; **que me veut-il?** what does he want with me?; **sans le vouloir** (*involontairement*) without meaning to, unintentionally; **je voudrais ceci/faire** I would *ou* I'd like this/to do

2 (*consentir*): **je veux bien** (*bonne volonté*) I'll be happy to; (*concession*) fair enough, that's fine; **oui, si on veut** (*en quelque sorte*) yes, if you like; **veuillez attendre** please wait; **veuillez agréer ...** (*formule épistolaire*) yours faithfully

3: **en vouloir à qn** to bear sb a grudge; **s'en vouloir (de)** to be annoyed with o.s. (for); **il en veut à mon argent** he's after my money

4: **vouloir de**: **l'entreprise ne veut plus de lui** the firm doesn't want him any more; **elle ne veut pas de son aide** she doesn't want his help

5: **vouloir dire** to mean

voulu, e [vuly] *adj* (*requis*) required, requisite; (*délibéré*) deliberate, intentional; *voir aussi* **vouloir**

vous [vu] *pron* you; (*objet indirect*) (to) you; (*réfléchi*: *sg*) yourself; (: *pl*) yourselves; (*réciproque*) each other; **~-même** yourself; **~-mêmes** yourselves

voûte [vut] *nf* vault; **voûter**: **se voûter** *vi* (*dos, personne*) to become stooped

vouvoyer [vuvwaje] *vt*: **~ qn** to address sb as "vous"

voyage [vwajaʒ] *nm* journey, trip; (*fait de ~r*): **le ~** travel(ling); **partir/être en ~** to go off/be away on a journey *ou* trip; **faire bon ~** to have a good journey; **~ d'agrément/d'affaires** pleasure/business trip; **~ de noces** honeymoon; **~ organisé** package tour

voyager [vwajaʒe] *vi* to travel; **voyageur, -euse** *nm/f* traveller; (*passager*) passenger
voyant, e [vwajɑ̃, ɑ̃t] *adj* (*couleur*) loud, gaudy ♦ *nm* (*signal*) (warning) light; **voyante** *nf* clairvoyant
voyelle [vwajɛl] *nf* vowel
voyons *etc* [vwajɔ̃] *vb voir* **voir**
voyou [vwaju] *nm* hooligan
vrac [vʀak]: **en ~** *adv* (*au détail*) loose; (*en gros*) in bulk; (*en désordre*) in a jumble
vrai, e [vʀɛ] *adj* (*véridique*: *récit, faits*) true; (*non factice, authentique*) real; **à ~ dire** to tell the truth; **vraiment** *adv* really; **vraisemblable** *adj* likely; (*excuse*) convincing; **vraisemblablement** *adj* probably; **vraisemblance** *nf* likelihood; (*romanesque*) verisimilitude
vrille [vʀij] *nf* (*de plante*) tendril; (*outil*) gimlet; (*spirale*) spiral; (AVIAT) spin
vrombir [vʀɔ̃biʀ] *vi* to hum
VRP *sigle m* (= *voyageur, représentant, placier*) sales rep (*fam*)
VTT *sigle m* (= *vélo tout-terrain*) mountain bike
vu, e [vy] *pp de* **voir** ♦ *adj*: **bien/mal ~** (*fig*: *personne*) popular/unpopular; (: *chose*) approved/disapproved of ♦ *prép* (*en raison de*) in view of; **~ que** in view of the fact that
vue [vy] *nf* (*fait de voir*): **la ~ de** the sight of; (*sens, faculté*) (eye)sight; (*panorama, image, photo*) view; **~s** *nfpl* (*idées*) views; (*dessein*) designs; **hors de ~** out of sight; **avoir en ~** to have in mind; **tirer à ~** to shoot on sight; **à ~ d'œil** visibly; **de ~** by sight; **perdre de ~** to lose sight of; **en ~** (*visible*) in sight; (*célèbre*) in the public eye; **en ~ de faire** with a view to doing
vulgaire [vylgɛʀ] *adj* (*grossier*) vulgar, coarse; (*ordinaire*) commonplace; (*péj*: *quelconque*): **de ~s touristes** common tourists; (BOT, ZOOL: *non latin*) common; **vulgariser** *vt* to popularize
vulnérable [vylneʀabl] *adj* vulnerable

W, w

wagon [vagɔ̃] *nm* (*de voyageurs*) carriage; (*de marchandises*) truck, wagon; **wagon-lit** *nm* sleeper, sleeping car; **wagon-restaurant** *nm* restaurant *ou* dining car
wallon, ne [walɔ̃, ɔn] *adj* Walloon
waters [watɛʀ] *nmpl* toilet *sg*
watt [wat] *nm* watt
WC *sigle mpl* (= *water-closet(s)*) toilet
Web [wɛb] *nm inv*: **le ~** the (World Wide) Web
week-end [wikɛnd] *nm* weekend
western [wɛstɛʀn] *nm* western
whisky [wiski] (*pl* **whiskies**) *nm* whisky

X, x

xénophobe [gzenɔfɔb] *adj* xenophobic ♦ *nm/f* xenophobe
xérès [gzeʀɛs] *nm* sherry
xylophone [gzilɔfɔn] *nm* xylophone

Y, y

y [i] *adv* (*à cet endroit*) there; (*dessus*) on it (*ou* them); (*dedans*) in it (*ou* them) ♦ *pron* (about *ou* on *ou* of) it (*d'après le verbe employé*); **j'~ pense** I'm thinking about it; **ça ~ est!** that's it!; *voir aussi* **aller**; **avoir**
yacht [jɔt] *nm* yacht
yaourt [jauʀt] *nm* yoghourt; **~ nature/aux fruits** plain/fruit yogurt
yeux [jø] *nmpl de* **œil**
yoga [jɔga] *nm* yoga
yoghourt [jɔguʀt] *nm* = **yaourt**
yougoslave [jugɔslav] (HISTOIRE) *adj* Yugoslav(ian) ♦ *nm/f*: **Y~** Yugoslav
Yougoslavie [jugɔslavi] (HISTOIRE) *nf* Yugoslavia

Z, z

zapper [zape] *vi* to zap
zapping [zapiŋ] *nm*: **faire du ~** to flick through the channels
zèbre [zɛbʀ(ə)] *nm* (ZOOL) zebra; **zébré, e** *adj* striped, streaked
zèle [zɛl] *nm* zeal; **faire du ~** (*péj*) to be over-zealous; **zélé, e** *adj* zealous
zéro [zeʀo] *nm* zero, nought (BRIT); **au-dessous de ~** below zero (Centigrade) *ou* freezing; **partir de ~** to start from scratch; **trois (buts) à ~** 3 (goals to) nil
zeste [zɛst] *nm* peel, zest
zézayer [zezeje] *vi* to have a lisp
zigzag [zigzag] *nm* zigzag; **zigzaguer** *vi* to zigzag
zinc [zɛ̃g] *nm* (CHIMIE) zinc
zizanie [zizani] *nf*: **semer la ~** to stir up ill-feeling
zizi [zizi] *nm* (*langage enfantin*) willy
zodiaque [zɔdjak] *nm* zodiac
zona [zona] *nm* shingles *sg*
zone [zon] *nf* zone, area; **~ bleue** ≃ restricted parking area; **~ industrielle** industrial estate
zoo [zo(o)] *nm* zoo
zoologie [zɔɔlɔʒi] *nf* zoology; **zoologique** *adj* zoological
zut [zyt] *excl* dash (it)! (BRIT), nuts! (US)

ENGLISH – FRENCH
ANGLAIS – FRANÇAIS

A, a

A [eɪ] *n* (*MUS*) la *m*

KEYWORD

a [eɪ, ə] (*before vowel or silent h: an*) *indef art* **1** un(e); **a book** un livre; **an apple** une pomme; **she's a doctor** elle est médecin
2 (*instead of the number "one"*) un(e); **a year ago** il y a un an; **a hundred/thousand** *etc* **pounds** cent/mille *etc* livres
3 (*in expressing ratios, prices etc*): **3 a day/week** 3 par jour/semaine; **10 km an hour** 10 km à l'heure; **30p a kilo** 30p le kilo

A.A. *n abbr* = **Alcoholics Anonymous**; (*BRIT: Automobile Association*) ≃ TCF *m*
A.A.A. (*US*) *n abbr* (= *American Automobile Association*) ≃ TCF *m*
aback [ə'bæk] *adv*: **to be taken ~** être stupéfait(e), être décontenancé(e)
abandon [ə'bændən] *vt* abandonner
abate [ə'beɪt] *vi* s'apaiser, se calmer
abbey ['æbɪ] *n* abbaye *f*
abbot ['æbət] *n* père supérieur
abbreviation [əbriːvɪ'eɪʃən] *n* abréviation *f*
abdicate ['æbdɪkeɪt] *vt, vi* abdiquer
abdomen ['æbdəmen] *n* abdomen *m*
abduct [æb'dʌkt] *vt* enlever
aberration [æbə'reɪʃən] *n* anomalie *f*
abide [ə'baɪd] *vt*: **I can't ~ it/him** je ne peux pas le souffrir *or* supporter; **~ by** *vt fus* observer, respecter
ability [ə'bɪlɪtɪ] *n* compétence *f*; capacité *f*; (*skill*) talent *m*
abject ['æbdʒɛkt] *adj* (*poverty*) sordide; (*apology*) plat(e)
ablaze [ə'bleɪz] *adj* en feu, en flammes
able ['eɪbl] *adj* capable, compétent(e); **to be ~ to do sth** être capable de faire qch, pouvoir faire qch; **~-bodied** *adj* robuste; **ably** *adv* avec compétence *or* talent, habilement
abnormal [æb'nɔːməl] *adj* anormal(e)
aboard [ə'bɔːd] *adv* à bord ♦ *prep* à bord de
abode [ə'bəud] *n* (*LAW*): **of no fixed ~** sans domicile fixe
abolish [ə'bɔlɪʃ] *vt* abolir
aborigine [æbə'rɪdʒɪnɪ] *n* aborigène *m/f*
abort [ə'bɔːt] *vt* faire avorter; **~ion** *n* avortement *m*; **to have an ~ion** se faire avorter; **~ive** [ə'bɔːtɪv] *adj* manqué(e)

KEYWORD

about [ə'baut] *adv* **1** (*approximately*) environ, à peu près; **about a hundred/thousand** *etc* environ cent/mille *etc*, une centaine/un millier *etc*; **it takes about 10 hours** ça prend environ *or* à peu près 10 heures; **at about 2 o'clock** vers 2 heures; **I've just about finished** j'ai presque fini
2 (*referring to place*) çà et là, de côté et d'autre; **to run about** courir çà et là; **to walk about** se promener, aller et venir
3: to be about to do sth être sur le point de faire qch
♦ *prep* **1** (*relating to*) au sujet de, à propos de; **a book about London** un livre sur Londres; **what is it about?** de quoi s'agit-il?; **we talked about it** nous en avons parlé; **what** *or* **how about doing this?** et si nous faisions ceci?
2 (*referring to place*) dans; **to walk**

about the town se promener dans la ville

about-face [ə'baut'feɪs] *n* demi-tour *m*
about-turn [ə'baut'tə:n] *n* (*MIL*) demi-tour *m*; (*fig*) volte-face *f*
above [ə'bʌv] *adv* au-dessus ♦ *prep* au-dessus de; (*more*) plus de; **mentioned ~** mentionné ci-dessus; **~ all** par-dessus tout, surtout; **~board** *adj* franc (franche); honnête
abrasive [ə'breɪzɪv] *adj* abrasif(-ive); (*fig*) caustique, agressif(-ive)
abreast [ə'brɛst] *adv* de front; **to keep ~ of** se tenir au courant de
abroad [ə'brɔ:d] *adv* à l'étranger
abrupt [ə'brʌpt] *adj* (*steep, blunt*) abrupt(e); (*sudden, gruff*) brusque; **~ly** *adv* (*speak, end*) brusquement
abscess ['æbsɪs] *n* abcès *m*
absence ['æbsəns] *n* absence *f*
absent ['æbsənt] *adj* absent(e); **~ee** [æbsən'ti:] *n* absent(e); (*habitual*) absentéiste *m/f*; **~-minded** *adj* distrait(e)
absolute ['æbsəlu:t] *adj* absolu(e); **~ly** [æbsə'lu:tlɪ] *adv* absolument
absolve [əb'zɔlv] *vt*: **to ~ sb (from)** (*blame, responsibility, sin*) absoudre qn (de)
absorb [əb'zɔ:b] *vt* absorber; **to be ~ed in a book** être plongé(e) dans un livre; **~ent cotton** (*US*) *n* coton *m* hydrophile
abstain [əb'steɪn] *vi*: **to ~ (from)** s'abstenir (de)
abstract ['æbstrækt] *adj* abstrait(e)
absurd [əb'sə:d] *adj* absurde
abundant [ə'bʌndənt] *adj* abondant(e)
abuse [*n* ə'bju:s, *vb* ə'bju:z] *n* abus *m*; (*insults*) insultes *fpl*, injures *fpl* ♦ *vt* abuser de; (*insult*) insulter; **abusive** [ə'bju:sɪv] *adj* grossier(-ère), injurieux(-euse)
abysmal [ə'bɪzməl] *adj* exécrable; (*ignorance etc*) sans bornes
abyss [ə'bɪs] *n* abîme *m*, gouffre *m*
AC *abbr* (= *alternating current*) courant alternatif
academic [ækə'dɛmɪk] *adj* universitaire; (*person*: *scholarly*) intellectuel(le); (*pej*: *issue*) oiseux(-euse), purement théorique ♦ *n* universitaire *m/f*; **~ year** *n* année *f* universitaire
academy [ə'kædəmɪ] *n* (*learned body*) académie *f*; (*school*) collège *m*; **~ of music** conservatoire *m*
accelerate [æk'sɛləreɪt] *vt, vi* accélérer; **accelerator** *n* accélérateur *m*
accent ['æksɛnt] *n* accent *m*
accept [ək'sɛpt] *vt* accepter; **~able** *adj* acceptable; **~ance** *n* acceptation *f*
access ['æksɛs] *n* accès *m*; (*LAW*: *in divorce*) droit *m* de visite; **~ible** [æk'sɛsəbl] *adj* accessible
accessory [æk'sɛsərɪ] *n* accessoire *m*
accident ['æksɪdənt] *n* accident *m*; (*chance*) hasard *m*; **by ~** accidentellement; par hasard; **~al** [æksɪ'dɛntl] *adj* accidentel(le); **~ally** [æksɪ'dɛntəlɪ] *adv* accidentellement; **~ insurance** *n* assurance *f* accident; **~-prone** *adj* sujet(te) aux accidents
acclaim [ə'kleɪm] *n* acclamations *fpl* ♦ *vt* acclamer
accommodate [ə'kɔmədeɪt] *vt* loger, recevoir; (*oblige, help*) obliger; (*car etc*) contenir; **accommodating** *adj* obligeant(e), arrangeant(e); **accommodation** [əkɔmə'deɪʃən] (*US* **accommodations**) *n* logement *m*
accompany [ə'kʌmpənɪ] *vt* accompagner
accomplice [ə'kʌmplɪs] *n* complice *m/f*
accomplish [ə'kʌmplɪʃ] *vt* accomplir; **~ment** *n* accomplissement *m*; réussite *f*; (*skill*: *gen pl*) talent *m*
accord [ə'kɔ:d] *n* accord *m* ♦ *vt* accorder; **of his own ~** de son plein gré; **~ance** [ə'kɔ:dəns] *n*: **in ~ance with** conformément à; **~ing**: **~ing to** *prep* selon; **~ingly** *adv* en conséquence
accordion [ə'kɔ:dɪən] *n* accordéon *m*
account [ə'kaunt] *n* (*COMM*) compte *m*; (*report*) compte rendu; récit *m*; **~s** *npl*

(COMM) comptabilité *f*, comptes; **of no ~** sans importance; **on ~** en acompte; **on no ~** en aucun cas; **on ~ of** à cause de; **to take into ~, take ~ of** tenir compte de; **~ for** *vt fus* expliquer, rendre compte de; **~able** *adj*: **~able (to)** responsable (devant); **~ancy** *n* comptabilité *f*; **~ant** *n* comptable *m/f*; **~ number** *n* (*at bank etc*) numéro *m* de compte

accrued interest [ə'kru:d-] *n* intérêt *m* cumulé

accumulate [ə'kju:mjuleɪt] *vt* accumuler, amasser ♦ *vi* s'accumuler, s'amasser

accuracy ['ækjurəsɪ] *n* exactitude *f*, précision *f*

accurate ['ækjurɪt] *adj* exact(e), précis(e); **~ly** *adv* avec précision

accusation [ækju'zeɪʃən] *n* accusation *f*

accuse [ə'kju:z] *vt*: **to ~ sb (of sth)** accuser qn (de qch); **the ~d** l'accusé(e)

accustom [ə'kʌstəm] *vt* accoutumer, habituer; **~ed** *adj* (*usual*) habituel(le); (*in the habit*): **~ed to** habitué(e) *or* accoutumé(e) à

ace [eɪs] *n* as *m*

ache [eɪk] *n* mal *m*, douleur *f* ♦ *vi* (*yearn*): **to ~ to do sth** mourir d'envie de faire qch; **my head ~s** j'ai mal à la tête

achieve [ə'tʃi:v] *vt* (*aim*) atteindre; (*victory, success*) remporter, obtenir; **~ment** *n* exploit *m*, réussite *f*

acid ['æsɪd] *adj* acide ♦ *n* acide *m*; **~ rain** *n* pluies *fpl* acides

acknowledge [ək'nɔlɪdʒ] *vt* (*letter: also:* **~ receipt of**) accuser réception de; (*fact*) reconnaître; **~ment** *n* (*of letter*) accusé *m* de réception

acne ['æknɪ] *n* acné *m*

acorn ['eɪkɔ:n] *n* gland *m*

acoustic [ə'ku:stɪk] *adj* acoustique; **~s** *n, npl* acoustique *f*

acquaint [ə'kweɪnt] *vt*: **to ~ sb with sth** mettre qn au courant de qch; **to be ~ed with** connaître; **~ance** *n* connaissance *f*

acquire [ə'kwaɪəʳ] *vt* acquérir

acquit [ə'kwɪt] *vt* acquitter; **to ~ o.s. well** bien se comporter, s'en tirer très honorablement

acre ['eɪkəʳ] *n* acre *f* (= *4047 m²*)

acrid ['ækrɪd] *adj* âcre

acrobat ['ækrəbæt] *n* acrobate *m/f*

across [ə'krɔs] *prep* (*on the other side*) de l'autre côté de; (*crosswise*) en travers de ♦ *adv* de l'autre côté; en travers; **to run/swim ~** traverser en courant/à la nage; **~ from** en face de

acrylic [ə'krɪlɪk] *adj* acrylique

act [ækt] *n* acte *m*, action *f*; (*of play*) acte; (*in music-hall etc*) numéro *m*; (LAW) loi *f* ♦ *vi* agir; (THEATRE) jouer; (*pretend*) jouer la comédie ♦ *vt* (*part*) jouer, tenir; **in the ~ of** en train de; **to ~ as** servir de; **~ing** *adj* suppléant(e), par intérim ♦ *n* (*activity*): **to do some ~ing** faire du théâtre (*or* du cinéma)

action ['ækʃən] *n* action *f*; (MIL) combat(s) *m(pl)*; **out of ~** hors de combat; (*machine*) hors d'usage; **to take ~** agir, prendre des mesures; **~ replay** *n* (TV) ralenti *m*

activate ['æktɪveɪt] *vt* (*mechanism*) actionner, faire fonctionner

active ['æktɪv] *adj* actif(-ive); (*volcano*) en activité; **~ly** *adv* activement; **activity** [æk'tɪvɪtɪ] *n* activité *f*; **activity holiday** *n* vacances actives

actor ['æktəʳ] *n* acteur *m*

actress ['æktrɪs] *n* actrice *f*

actual ['æktjuəl] *adj* réel(le), véritable; **~ly** *adv* (*really*) réellement, véritablement; (*in fact*) en fait

acute [ə'kju:t] *adj* aigu(ë); (*mind, observer*) pénétrant(e), perspicace

ad [æd] *n abbr* = **advertisement**

A.D. *adv abbr* (= *anno Domini*) ap. J.-C.

adamant ['ædəmənt] *adj* inflexible

adapt [ə'dæpt] *vt* adapter ♦ *vi*: **to ~ (to)** s'adapter (à); **~able** *adj* (*device*) adaptable; (*person*) qui s'adapte facilement; **~er, ~or** *n* (*ELEC*) adaptateur *m*

add [æd] *vt* ajouter; (*figures: also:* **to ~ up**) additionner ♦ *vi*: **to ~ to** (*increase*) ajouter à, accroître

adder ['ædəʳ] *n* vipère *f*

addict ['ædɪkt] *n* intoxiqué(e); (*fig*) fanatique *m/f*; **~ed** [ə'dɪktɪd] *adj*: **to be ~ed to** (*drugs, drink etc*) être adonné(e) à; (*fig: football etc*) être un(e) fanatique de; **~ion** *n* (*MED*) dépendance *f*; **~ive** *adj* qui crée une dépendance

addition [ə'dɪʃən] *n* addition *f*; (*thing added*) ajout *m*; **in ~** de plus; de surcroît; **in ~ to** en plus de; **~al** *adj* supplémentaire

additive ['ædɪtɪv] *n* additif *m*

address [ə'drɛs] *n* adresse *f*; (*talk*) discours *m*, allocution *f* ♦ *vt* adresser; (*speak to*) s'adresser à; **to ~ (o.s. to) a problem** s'attaquer à un problème

adept ['ædɛpt] *adj*: **~ at** expert(e) à *or* en

adequate ['ædɪkwɪt] *adj* adéquat(e); suffisant(e)

adhere [əd'hɪəʳ] *vi*: **to ~ to** adhérer à; (*fig: rule, decision*) se tenir à

adhesive [əd'hi:zɪv] *n* adhésif *m*; **~ tape** *n* (*BRIT*) ruban adhésif; (*US: MED*) sparadrap *m*

ad hoc [æd'hɔk] *adj* improvisé(e), ad hoc

adjacent [ə'dʒeɪsənt] *adj*: **~ (to)** adjacent (à)

adjective ['ædʒɛktɪv] *n* adjectif *m*

adjoining [ə'dʒɔɪnɪŋ] *adj* voisin(e), adjacent(e), attenant(e)

adjourn [ə'dʒə:n] *vt* ajourner ♦ *vi* suspendre la séance; clore la session

adjust [ə'dʒʌst] *vt* (*machine*) ajuster, régler; (*prices, wages*) rajuster ♦ *vi*: **to ~ (to)** s'adapter (à); **~able** *adj* réglable; **~ment** *n* (*PSYCH*) adaptation *f*; (*to machine*) ajustage *m*, réglage *m*; (*of prices, wages*) rajustement *m*

ad-lib [æd'lɪb] *vt, vi* improviser; **ad lib** *adv* à volonté, à loisir

administer [əd'mɪnɪstəʳ] *vt* administrer; (*justice*) rendre; **administration** [ədmɪnɪs'treɪʃən] *n* administration *f*; **administrative** [əd'mɪnɪstrətɪv] *adj* administratif(-ive)

admiral ['ædmərəl] *n* amiral *m*; **A~ty** ['ædmərəltɪ] (*BRIT*) *n*: **the A~ty** ministère *m* de la Marine

admire [əd'maɪəʳ] *vt* admirer

admission [əd'mɪʃən] *n* admission *f*; (*to exhibition, night club etc*) entrée *f*; (*confession*) aveu *m*; **~ charge** *n* droits *mpl* d'admission

admit [əd'mɪt] *vt* laisser entrer; admettre; (*agree*) reconnaître, admettre; **~ to** *vt fus* reconnaître, avouer; **~tance** *n* admission *f*, (droit *m* d')entrée *f*; **~tedly** *adv* il faut en convenir

ado [ə'du:] *n*: **without (any) more ~** sans plus de cérémonies

adolescence [ædəu'lɛsns] *n* adolescence *f*; **adolescent** *adj, n* adolescent(e)

adopt [ə'dɔpt] *vt* adopter; **~ed** *adj* adoptif(-ive), adopté(e); **~ion** *n* adoption *f*

adore [ə'dɔ:ʳ] *vt* adorer

adorn [ə'dɔ:n] *vt* orner

Adriatic (Sea) [eɪdrɪ'ætɪk-] *n* Adriatique *f*

adrift [ə'drɪft] *adv* à la dérive

adult ['ædʌlt] *n* adulte *m/f* ♦ *adj* adulte; (*literature, education*) pour adultes

adultery [ə'dʌltərɪ] *n* adultère *m*

advance [əd'vɑ:ns] *n* avance *f* ♦ *adj*: **~ booking** réservation *f* ♦ *vt* avancer ♦ *vi* avancer, s'avancer; **~ notice** avertissement *m*; **to make ~s (to sb)** faire des propositions (à qn); (*amorously*) faire des avances (à qn); **in ~** à l'avance, d'avance; **~d** *adj* avancé(e); (*SCOL: studies*) supérieur(e)

advantage [əd'vɑ:ntɪdʒ] *n* (*also TENNIS*) avantage *m*; **to take ~ of** (*person*) exploiter

advent ['ædvənt] *n* avènement *m*, venue *f*; **A~** Avent *m*

adventure [əd'vɛntʃəʳ] *n* aventure *f*

adverb ['ædvə:b] *n* adverbe *m*

adverse ['ædvəːs] *adj* défavorable, contraire

advert ['ædvəːt] (*BRIT*) *n abbr* = **advertisement**

advertise ['ædvətaɪz] *vi, vt* faire de la publicité (pour); (*in classified ads etc*) mettre une annonce (pour vendre); **to ~ for** (*staff, accommodation*) faire paraître une annonce pour trouver; **~ment** [əd'vəːtɪsmənt] *n* (*COMM*) réclame *f*, publicité *f*; (*in classified ads*) annonce *f*; **advertising** *n* publicité *f*

advice [əd'vaɪs] *n* conseils *mpl*; (*notification*) avis *m*; **piece of ~** conseil; **to take legal ~** consulter un avocat

advisable [əd'vaɪzəbl] *adj* conseillé(e), indiqué(e)

advise [əd'vaɪz] *vt* conseiller; **to ~ sb of sth** aviser *or* informer qn de qch; **to ~ against sth/doing sth** déconseiller qch/conseiller de ne pas faire qch; **~r, advisor** *n* conseiller(-ère); **advisory** *adj* consultatif(-ive)

advocate [*n* 'ædvəkɪt, *vb* 'ædvəkeɪt] *n* (*upholder*) défenseur *m*, avocat(e); (*LAW*) avocat(e) ♦ *vt* recommander, prôner

Aegean (Sea) [iː'dʒiːən-] *n* (mer *f*) Égée *f*

aerial ['ɛərɪəl] *n* antenne *f* ♦ *adj* aérien(ne)

aerobics [ɛə'rəubɪks] *n* aérobic *f*

aeroplane ['ɛərəpleɪn] (*BRIT*) *n* avion *m*

aerosol ['ɛərəsɔl] *n* aérosol *m*

aesthetic [iːs'θɛtɪk] *adj* esthétique

afar [ə'fɑːʳ] *adv*: **from ~** de loin

affair [ə'fɛəʳ] *n* affaire *f*; (*also:* **love ~**) liaison *f*; aventure *f*

affect [ə'fɛkt] *vt* affecter; (*disease*) atteindre; **~ed** *adj* affecté(e); **~ion** *n* affection *f*; **~ionate** *adj* affectueux(-euse)

affinity [ə'fɪnɪtɪ] *n* (*bond, rapport*): **to have an ~ with/for** avoir une affinité avec/pour

afflict [ə'flɪkt] *vt* affliger

affluence ['æfluəns] *n* abondance *f*, opulence *f*

affluent ['æfluənt] *adj* (*person, family, surroundings*) aisé(e), riche; **the ~ society** la société d'abondance

afford [ə'fɔːd] *vt* se permettre; (*provide*) fournir, procurer

afloat [ə'fləut] *adj, adv* à flot; **to stay ~** surnager

afoot [ə'fut] *adv*: **there is something ~** il se prépare quelque chose

afraid [ə'freɪd] *adj* effrayé(e); **to be ~ of** *or* **to** avoir peur de; **I am ~ that ...** je suis désolé(e), mais ...; **I am ~ so/not** hélas oui/non

Africa ['æfrɪkə] *n* Afrique *f*; **~n** *adj* africain(e) ♦ *n* Africain(e)

after ['ɑːftəʳ] *prep, adv* après ♦ *conj* après que, après avoir *or* être *+pp*; **what/who are you ~?** que/qui cherchez-vous?; **~ he left/having done** après qu'il fut parti/après avoir fait; **ask ~ him** demandez de ses nouvelles; **to name sb ~ sb** donner à qn le nom de qn; **twenty ~ eight** (*US*) huit heures vingt; **~ all** après tout; **~ you!** après vous, Monsieur (*or* Madame *etc*); **~effects** *npl* (*of disaster, radiation, drink etc*) répercussions *fpl*; (*of illness*) séquelles *fpl*, suites *fpl*; **~math** *n* conséquences *fpl*, suites *fpl*; **~noon** *n* après-midi *m or f*; **~s** (*inf*) *n* (*dessert*) dessert *m*; **~-sales service** (*BRIT*) *n* (*for car, washing machine etc*) service *m* après-vente; **~-shave (lotion)** *n* after-shave *m*; **~sun** *n* après-soleil *m inv*; **~thought** *n*: **I had an ~thought** il m'est venu une idée après coup; **~wards** (*US* **afterward**) *adv* après

again [ə'gɛn] *adv* de nouveau; encore (une fois); **to do sth ~** refaire qch; **not ... ~** ne ... plus; **~ and ~** à plusieurs reprises

against [ə'gɛnst] *prep* contre; (*compared to*) par rapport à

age [eɪdʒ] *n* âge *m* ♦ *vt, vi* vieillir; **it's been ~s since** ça fait une éternité que ... ne; **he is 20 years of ~** il a 20 ans; **to come of ~** atteindre sa majorité; **~d** [*adj* eɪdʒd, *npl* 'eɪdʒɪd] *adj*: **~d 10**

âgé(e) de 10 ans ♦ *npl*: **the ~d** les personnes âgées; **~ group** *n* tranche *f* d'âge; **~ limit** *n* limite *f* d'âge

agency ['eɪdʒənsɪ] *n* agence *f*; (*government body*) organisme *m*, office *m*

agenda [ə'dʒɛndə] *n* ordre *m* du jour

agent ['eɪdʒənt] *n* agent *m*, représentant *m*; (*firm*) concessionnaire *m*

aggravate ['ægrəveɪt] *vt* aggraver; (*annoy*) exaspérer

aggressive [ə'grɛsɪv] *adj* agressif(-ive)

agitate ['ædʒɪteɪt] *vt* (*person*) agiter, émouvoir, troubler ♦ *vi*: **to ~ for/against** faire campagne pour/contre

AGM *n abbr* (= *annual general meeting*) AG *f*

ago [ə'gəu] *adv*: **2 days ~** il y a deux jours; **not long ~** il n'y a pas longtemps; **how long ~?** il y a combien de temps (de cela)?

agony ['ægənɪ] *n* (*pain*) douleur *f* atroce; **to be in ~** souffrir le martyre

agree [ə'gri:] *vt* (*price*) convenir de ♦ *vi*: **to ~ with** (*person*) être d'accord avec; (*statements etc*) concorder avec; (LING) s'accorder avec; **to ~ to do** accepter de *or* consentir à faire; **to ~ to sth** consentir à qch; **to ~ that** (*admit*) convenir *or* reconnaître que; **garlic doesn't ~ with me** je ne supporte pas l'ail; **~able** *adj* agréable; (*willing*) consentant(e), d'accord; **~d** *adj* (*time, place*) convenu(e); **~ment** *n* accord *m*; **in ~ment** d'accord

agricultural [ægrɪ'kʌltʃərəl] *adj* agricole

agriculture ['ægrɪkʌltʃə^r] *n* agriculture *f*

aground [ə'graund] *adv*: **to run ~** échouer, s'échouer

ahead [ə'hɛd] *adv* (*in front*: *of position, place*) devant; (: *at the head*) en avant; (*look, plan, think*) en avant; **~ of** devant; (*fig*: *schedule etc*) en avance sur; **~ of time** en avance; **go right** *or* **straight ~** allez tout droit; **go ~!** (*fig*: *permission*) allez-y!

aid [eɪd] *n* aide *f*; (*device*) appareil *m* ♦ *vt* aider; **in ~ of** en faveur de; *see also* **hearing**

aide [eɪd] *n* (*person*) aide *mf*, assistant(e)

AIDS [eɪdz] *n abbr* (= *acquired immune deficiency syndrome*) SIDA *m*; **AIDS-related** *adj* associé(e) au sida

aim [eɪm] *vt*: **to ~ sth (at)** (*gun, camera*) braquer *or* pointer qch (sur); (*missile*) lancer qch (à *or* contre *or* en direction de); (*blow*) allonger qch (à); (*remark*) destiner *or* adresser qch (à) ♦ *vi* (*also*: **to take ~**) viser ♦ *n* but *m*; (*skill*): **his ~ is bad** il vise mal; **to ~ at** viser; (*fig*) viser (à); **to ~ to do** avoir l'intention de faire; **~less** *adj* sans but

ain't [eɪnt] (*inf*) = **am not**; **aren't**; **isn't**

air [ɛə^r] *n* air *m* ♦ *vt* (*room, bed, clothes*) aérer; (*grievances, views, ideas*) exposer, faire connaître ♦ *cpd* (*currents, attack etc*) aérien(ne); **to throw sth into the ~** jeter qch en l'air; **by ~** (*travel*) par avion; **to be on the ~** (RADIO, TV: *programme*) être diffusé(e); (: *station*) diffuser; **~bed** *n* matelas *m* pneumatique; **~-conditioned** *adj* climatisé(e); **~ conditioning** *n* climatisation *f*; **~craft** *n inv* avion *m*; **~craft carrier** *n* porte-avions *m inv*; **~field** *n* terrain *m* d'aviation; **A~ Force** *n* armée *f* de l'air; **~ freshener** *n* désodorisant *m*; **~gun** *n* fusil *m* à air comprimé; **~ hostess** *n* (BRIT) hôtesse *f* de l'air; **~ letter** *n* (BRIT) aérogramme *m*; **~lift** *n* pont aérien; **~line** *n* ligne aérienne, compagnie *f* d'aviation; **~liner** *n* avion *m* de ligne; **~mail** *n*: **by ~mail** par avion; **~ mile** *n* air mile *m*; **~plane** *n* (US) avion *m*; **~port** *n* aéroport *m*; **~ raid** *n* attaque *or* raid aérien(ne); **~sick** *adj*: **to be ~sick** avoir le mal de l'air; **~tight** *adj* hermétique; **~-traffic controller** *n* aiguilleur *m* du ciel; **~y** *adj* bien aéré(e); (*manners*) dégagé(e)

aisle [aɪl] *n* (*of church*) allée centrale; nef latérale; (*of theatre etc*) couloir *m*, passage *m*, allée; ~ **seat** *n* place *f* côté couloir

ajar [ə'dʒɑːʳ] *adj* entrouvert(e)

akin [ə'kɪn] *adj*: ~ **to** (*similar*) qui tient de *or* ressemble à

alarm [ə'lɑːm] *n* alarme *f* ♦ *vt* alarmer; ~ **call** *n* coup de fil *m* pour réveiller; ~ **clock** *n* réveille-matin *m inv*, réveil *m*

alas [ə'læs] *excl* hélas!

album ['ælbəm] *n* album *m*

alcohol ['ælkəhɔl] *n* alcool *m*; **~-free** *adj* sans alcool; **~ic** [ælkə'hɔlɪk] *adj* alcoolique ♦ *n* alcoolique *m/f*; **A~ics Anonymous** Alcooliques anonymes

ale [eɪl] *n* bière *f*

alert [ə'ləːt] *adj* alerte, vif (vive); vigilant(e) ♦ *n* alerte *f* ♦ *vt* alerter; **on the ~** sur le qui-vive; (*MIL*) en état d'alerte

algebra ['ældʒɪbrə] *n* algèbre *m*

Algeria [æl'dʒɪərɪə] *n* Algérie *f*

alias ['eɪlɪəs] *adv* alias ♦ *n* faux nom, nom d'emprunt; (*writer*) pseudonyme *m*

alibi ['ælɪbaɪ] *n* alibi *m*

alien ['eɪlɪən] *n* étranger(-ère); (*from outer space*) extraterrestre *mf* ♦ *adj*: ~ **(to)** étranger(-ère) (à)

alight [ə'laɪt] *adj, adv* en feu ♦ *vi* mettre pied à terre; (*passenger*) descendre

alike [ə'laɪk] *adj* semblable, pareil(le) ♦ *adv* de même; **to look ~** se ressembler

alimony ['ælɪmənɪ] *n* (*payment*) pension *f* alimentaire

alive [ə'laɪv] *adj* vivant(e); (*lively*) plein(e) de vie

KEYWORD

all [ɔːl] *adj* (*singular*) tout(e); (*plural*) tous (toutes); **all day** toute la journée; **all night** toute la nuit; **all men** tous les hommes; **all five** tous les cinq; **all the food** toute la nourriture; **all the books** tous les livres; **all the time** tout le temps; **all his life** toute sa vie

♦ *pron* **1** tout; **I ate it all, I ate all of it** j'ai tout mangé; **all of us went** nous y sommes tous allés; **all of the boys went** tous les garçons y sont allés

2 (*in phrases*): **above all** surtout, par-dessus tout; **after all** après tout; **not at all** (*in answer to question*) pas du tout; (*in answer to thanks*) je vous en prie!; **I'm not at all tired** je ne suis pas du tout fatigué(e); **anything at all will do** n'importe quoi fera l'affaire; **all in all** tout bien considéré, en fin de compte

♦ *adv*: **all alone** tout(e) seul(e); **it's not as hard as all that** ce n'est pas si difficile que ça; **all the more/the better** d'autant plus/mieux; **all but** presque, pratiquement; **the score is 2 all** le score est de 2 partout

allege [ə'lɛdʒ] *vt* alléguer, prétendre; **~dly** [ə'lɛdʒɪdlɪ] *adv* à ce que l'on prétend, paraît-il

allegiance [ə'liːdʒəns] *n* allégeance *f*, fidélité *f*, obéissance *f*

allergic [ə'ləːdʒɪk] *adj*: ~ **to** allergique à

allergy ['ælədʒɪ] *n* allergie *f*

alleviate [ə'liːvɪeɪt] *vt* soulager, adoucir

alley ['ælɪ] *n* ruelle *f*

alliance [ə'laɪəns] *n* alliance *f*

allied ['ælaɪd] *adj* allié(e)

all-in ['ɔːlɪn] (*BRIT*) *adj* (*also adv*: *charge*) tout compris

all-night ['ɔːl'naɪt] *adj* ouvert(e) *or* qui dure toute la nuit

allocate ['æləkeɪt] *vt* (*share out*) répartir, distribuer; **to ~ sth to** (*duties*) assigner *or* attribuer qch à; (*sum, time*) allouer qch à

allot [ə'lɔt] *vt*: **to ~ (to)** (*money*) répartir (entre), distribuer (à); (*time*) allouer (à); **~ment** *n* (*share*) part *f*; (*garden*) lopin *m* de terre (*loué à la municipalité*)

all-out ['ɔːlaut] *adj* (*effort etc*) total(e) ♦ *adv*: **all out** à fond

allow [ə'lau] *vt* (*practice, behaviour*) permettre, autoriser; (*sum to spend etc*) accorder; allouer; (*sum, time estimated*) compter, prévoir; (*claim, goal*) admettre; (*concede*): **to ~ that** convenir que; **to ~ sb to do** permettre à qn de faire, autoriser qn à faire; **he is ~ed to** ... on lui permet de ...; **~ for** *vt fus* tenir compte de; **~ance** [ə'lauəns] *n* (*money received*) allocation *f*; subside *m*; indemnité *f*; (TAX) somme *f* déductible du revenu imposable, abattement *m*; **to make ~ances for** tenir compte de

alloy ['ælɔɪ] *n* alliage *m*

all: ~ right *adv* (*feel, work*) bien; (*as answer*) d'accord; **~-rounder** *n*: **to be a good ~-rounder** être doué(e) en tout; **~-time** *adj* (*record*) sans précédent, absolu(e)

ally [*n* 'ælaɪ, *vb* ə'laɪ] *n* allié *m* ♦ *vt*: **to ~ o.s. with** s'allier avec

almighty [ɔ:l'maɪtɪ] *adj* tout-puissant; (*tremendous*) énorme

almond ['ɑ:mənd] *n* amande *f*

almost ['ɔ:lməust] *adv* presque

alone [ə'ləun] *adj, adv* seul(e); **to leave sb ~** laisser qn tranquille; **to leave sth ~** ne pas toucher à qch; **let ~** ... sans parler de ...; encore moins ...

along [ə'lɔŋ] *prep* le long de ♦ *adv*: **is he coming ~ with us?** vient-il avec nous?; **he was hopping/limping ~** il avançait en sautillant/boitant; **~ with** (*together with*: *person*) en compagnie de; (: *thing*) avec, en plus de; **all ~** (*all the time*) depuis le début; **~side** *prep* le long de; à côté de ♦ *adv* bord à bord

aloof [ə'lu:f] *adj* distant(e) ♦ *adv*: **to stand ~** se tenir à distance *or* à l'écart

aloud [ə'laud] *adv* à haute voix

alphabet ['ælfəbɛt] *n* alphabet *m*; **~ical** [ælfə'bɛtɪkl] *adj* alphabétique

alpine ['ælpaɪn] *adj* alpin(e), alpestre

Alps [ælps] *npl*: **the ~** les Alpes *fpl*

already [ɔ:l'rɛdɪ] *adv* déjà

alright ['ɔ:l'raɪt] (BRIT) *adv* = **all right**

Alsatian [æl'seɪʃən] (BRIT) *n* (*dog*) berger allemand

also ['ɔ:lsəu] *adv* aussi

altar ['ɔltə^r] *n* autel *m*

alter ['ɔltə^r] *vt, vi* changer

alternate [*adj* ɔl'tə:nɪt, *vb* 'ɔltə:neɪt] *adj* alterné(e), alternant(e), alternatif(-ive) ♦ *vi* alterner; **on ~ days** un jour sur deux, tous les deux jours; **alternating current** *n* courant alternatif

alternative [ɔl'tə:nətɪv] *adj* (*solutions*) possible, au choix; (*plan*) autre, de rechange; (*lifestyle etc*) parallèle ♦ *n* (*choice*) alternative *f*; (*other possibility*) solution *f* de remplacement *or* de rechange, autre possibilité *f*; **~ medicine** médicines *fpl* parallèles *or* douces; **~ly** *adv*: **~ly one could** une autre *or* l'autre solution serait de, on pourrait aussi

alternator ['ɔltə:neɪtə^r] *n* (AUT) alternateur *m*

although [ɔ:l'ðəu] *conj* bien que *+sub*

altitude ['æltɪtju:d] *n* altitude *f*

alto ['æltəu] *n* (*female*) contralto *m*; (*male*) haute-contre *f*

altogether [ɔ:ltə'gɛðə^r] *adv* entièrement, tout à fait; (*on the whole*) tout compte fait; (*in all*) en tout

aluminium [ælju'mɪnɪəm] (BRIT), **aluminum** [ə'lu:mɪnəm] (US) *n* aluminium *m*

always ['ɔ:lweɪz] *adv* toujours

Alzheimer's (disease) ['æltshaɪməz-] *n* maladie *f* d'Alzheimer

AM *n abbr* (= *Assembly Member*) député *m* au Parlement gallois

am [æm] *vb see* **be**

a.m. *adv abbr* (= *ante meridiem*) du matin

amalgamate [ə'mælgəmeɪt] *vt, vi* fusionner

amateur ['æmətə^r] *n* amateur *m*; **~ish** (*pej*) *adj* d'amateur

amaze [ə'meɪz] *vt* stupéfier; **to be ~d (at)** être stupéfait(e) (de); **~ment** *n* stupéfaction *f*, stupeur *f*; **amazing** *adj* étonnant(e); exceptionnel(le)

ambassador [æm'bæsədə^r] *n* ambassadeur *m*

amber ['æmbə^r] *n* ambre *m*; **at ~** (BRIT: AUT) à l'orange

ambiguous [æm'bɪgjuəs] *adj* ambigu(ë)

ambition [æm'bɪʃən] *n* ambition *f*;

ambitious *adj* ambitieux(-euse)
ambulance ['æmbjuləns] *n* ambulance *f*
ambush ['æmbuʃ] *n* embuscade *f* ♦ *vt* tendre une embuscade à
amenable [ə'mi:nəbl] *adj*: **~ to** (*advice etc*) disposé(e) à écouter
amend [ə'mɛnd] *vt* (*law*) amender; (*text*) corriger; **to make ~s** réparer ses torts, faire amende honorable
amenities [ə'mi:nɪtɪz] *npl* aménagements *mpl*, équipements *mpl*
America [ə'mɛrɪkə] *n* Amérique *f*; **~n** *adj* américain(e) ♦ *n* Américain(e)
amiable ['eɪmɪəbl] *adj* aimable, affable
amicable ['æmɪkəbl] *adj* amical(e); (LAW) à l'amiable
amid(st) [ə'mɪd(st)] *prep* parmi, au milieu de
amiss [ə'mɪs] *adj, adv*: **there's something ~** il y a quelque chose qui ne va pas *or* qui cloche; **to take sth ~** prendre qch mal *or* de travers
ammonia [ə'məunɪə] *n* (*gas*) ammoniac *m*; (*liquid*) ammoniaque *f*
ammunition [æmju'nɪʃən] *n* munitions *fpl*
amok [ə'mɔk] *adv*: **to run ~** être pris(e) d'un accès de folie furieuse
among(st) [ə'mʌŋ(st)] *prep* parmi, entre
amorous ['æmərəs] *adj* amoureux(-euse)
amount [ə'maunt] *n* (*sum*) somme *f*, montant *m*; (*quantity*) quantité *f*, nombre *m* ♦ *vi*: **to ~ to** (*total*) s'élever à; (*be same as*) équivaloir à, revenir à
amp(ere) ['æmp(ɛə^r^)] *n* ampère *m*
ample ['æmpl] *adj* ample; spacieux(-euse); (*enough*): **this is ~** c'est largement suffisant; **to have ~ time/room** avoir bien assez de temps/place
amplifier ['æmplɪfaɪə^r^] *n* amplificateur *m*
amuse [ə'mju:z] *vt* amuser, divertir; **~ment** *n* amusement *m*; **~ment arcade** *n* salle *f* de jeu; **~ment park** *n* parc *m* d'attractions
an [æn, ən] *indef art see* **a**
anaemic [ə'ni:mɪk] (US **anemic**) *adj* anémique
anaesthetic [ænɪs'θɛtɪk] (US **anesthetic**) *n* anesthésique *m*
analog(ue) ['ænəlɔg] *adj* (*watch, computer*) analogique
analyse ['ænəlaɪz] (US **analyze**) *vt* analyser; **analysis** [ə'næləsɪs] (*pl* **analyses**) *n* analyse *f*; **analyst** ['ænəlɪst] *n* (POL *etc*) spécialiste *m/f*; (US) psychanalyste *m/f*
analyze ['ænəlaɪz] (US) *vt* = **analyse**
anarchist ['ænəkɪst] *n* anarchiste *m/f*
anarchy ['ænəkɪ] *n* anarchie *f*
anatomy [ə'nætəmɪ] *n* anatomie *f*
ancestor ['ænsɪstə^r^] *n* ancêtre *m*
anchor ['æŋkə^r^] *n* ancre *f* ♦ *vi* (*also*: **to drop ~**) jeter l'ancre, mouiller ♦ *vt* mettre à l'ancre; (*fig*): **to ~ sth to** fixer qch à
anchovy ['æntʃəvɪ] *n* anchois *m*
ancient ['eɪnʃənt] *adj* ancien(ne), antique; (*person*) d'un âge vénérable; (*car*) antédiluvien(ne)
ancillary [æn'sɪlərɪ] *adj* auxiliaire
and [ænd] *conj* et; **~ so on** et ainsi de suite; **try ~ come** tâchez de venir; **he talked ~ talked** il n'a pas arrêté de parler; **better ~ better** de mieux en mieux
anew [ə'nju:] *adv* à nouveau
angel ['eɪndʒəl] *n* ange *m*
anger ['æŋgə^r^] *n* colère *f*
angina [æn'dʒaɪnə] *n* angine *f* de poitrine
angle ['æŋgl] *n* angle *m*; **from their ~** de leur point de vue
angler ['æŋglə^r^] *n* pêcheur(-euse) à la ligne
Anglican ['æŋglɪkən] *adj, n* anglican(e)
angling ['æŋglɪŋ] *n* pêche *f* à la ligne
Anglo- ['æŋgləu] *prefix* anglo(-)
angrily ['æŋgrɪlɪ] *adv* avec colère
angry ['æŋgrɪ] *adj* en colère, furieux(-euse); (*wound*) enflammé(e); **to be ~**

with sb/at sth être furieux contre qn/ de qch; **to get ~** se fâcher, se mettre en colère

anguish ['æŋgwɪʃ] *n* (*mental*) angoisse *f*

animal ['ænɪməl] *n* animal *m* ♦ *adj* animal(e)

animate [*vb* 'ænɪmeɪt, *adj* 'ænɪmɪt] *vt* animer ♦ *adj* animé(e), vivant(e); **~d** *adj* animé(e)

aniseed ['ænɪsi:d] *n* anis *m*

ankle ['æŋkl] *n* cheville *f*; **~ sock** *n* socquette *f*

annex ['ænɛks] *n* (*BRIT*: *~e*) annexe *f*

anniversary [ænɪ'və:sərɪ] *n* anniversaire *m*

announce [ə'nauns] *vt* annoncer; (*birth, death*) faire part de; **~ment** *n* annonce *f*; (*for births etc: in newspaper*) avis *m* de faire-part; (: *letter, card*) faire-part *m*; **~r** *n* (*RADIO, TV*: *between programmes*) speaker(ine)

annoy [ə'nɔɪ] *vt* agacer, ennuyer, contrarier; **don't get ~ed!** ne vous fâchez pas!; **~ance** *n* mécontentement *m*, contrariété *f*; **~ing** *adj* agaçant(e), contrariant(e)

annual ['ænjuəl] *adj* annuel(le) ♦ *n* (*BOT*) plante annuelle; (*children's book*) album *m*

annul [ə'nʌl] *vt* annuler

annum ['ænəm] *n see* **per**

anonymous [ə'nɔnɪməs] *adj* anonyme

anorak ['ænəræk] *n* anorak *m*

anorexia [ænə'rɛksɪə] *n* anorexie *f*

another [ə'nʌðəʳ] *adj*: **~ book** (*one more*) un autre livre, encore un livre, un livre de plus; (*a different one*) un autre livre ♦ *pron* un(e) autre, encore un(e), un(e) de plus; *see also* **one**

answer ['ɑ:nsəʳ] *n* réponse *f*; (*to problem*) solution *f* ♦ *vi* répondre ♦ *vt* (*reply to*) répondre à; (*problem*) résoudre; (*prayer*) exaucer; **in ~ to your letter** en réponse à votre lettre; **to ~ the phone** répondre (au téléphone); **to ~ the bell** *or* **the door** aller *or* venir ouvrir (la porte); **~ back** *vi* répondre, répliquer; **~ for** *vt fus* (*person*) répondre de, se porter garant de; (*crime, one's actions*) être responsable de; **~ to** *vt fus* (*description*) répondre *or* correspondre à; **~able** *adj*: **~able (to sb/for sth)** responsable (devant qn/de qch); **~ing machine** *n* répondeur *m* automatique

ant [ænt] *n* fourmi *f*

antagonism [æn'tægənɪzəm] *n* antagonisme *m*

antagonize [æn'tægənaɪz] *vt* éveiller l'hostilité de, contrarier

Antarctic [ænt'ɑ:ktɪk] *n*: **the ~** l'Antarctique *m*

antenatal ['æntɪ'neɪtl] *adj* prénatal(e); **~ clinic** *n* service *m* de consultation prénatale

anthem ['ænθəm] *n*: **national ~** hymne national

anti: **~-aircraft** *adj* (*missile*) antiaérien(ne); **~biotic** ['æntɪbaɪ'ɔtɪk] *n* antibiotique *m*; **~body** *n* anticorps *m*

anticipate [æn'tɪsɪpeɪt] *vt* s'attendre à; prévoir; (*wishes, request*) aller au devant de, devancer

anticipation [æntɪsɪ'peɪʃən] *n* attente *f*; **in ~** par anticipation, à l'avance

anticlimax ['æntɪ'klaɪmæks] *n* déception *f*, douche froide (*fam*)

anticlockwise ['æntɪ'klɔkwaɪz] *adj, adv* dans le sens inverse des aiguilles d'une montre

antics ['æntɪks] *npl* singeries *fpl*

antidepressant ['æntɪdɪ'prɛsənt] *n* antidépresseur *m*

antifreeze ['æntɪfri:z] *n* antigel *m*

antihistamine ['æntɪ'hɪstəmɪn] *n* antihistaminique *m*

antiquated ['æntɪkweɪtɪd] *adj* vieilli(e), suranné(e), vieillot(te)

antique [æn'ti:k] *n* objet *m* d'art ancien, meuble ancien *or* d'époque, antiquité *f* ♦ *adj* ancien(ne); **~ dealer** *n* antiquaire *m*; **~ shop** *n* magasin *m* d'antiquités

anti: **~-Semitism** ['æntɪ'sɛmɪtɪzəm] *n*

antisémitisme *m*; **~septic** [æntɪ'sɛptɪk] *n* antiseptique *m*; **~social** ['æntɪ'səuʃəl] *adj* peu liant(e), sauvage, insociable; (*against society*) antisocial(e)

antlers ['æntləz] *npl* bois *mpl*, ramure *f*

anvil ['ænvɪl] *n* enclume *f*

anxiety [æŋ'zaɪətɪ] *n* anxiété *f*; (*keenness*): **~ to do** grand désir *or* impatience *f* de faire

anxious ['æŋkʃəs] *adj* anxieux(-euse), angoissé(e); (*worrying*: *time, situation*) inquiétant(e); (*keen*): **~ to do/that** qui tient beaucoup à faire/à ce que; impatient(e) de faire/que

KEYWORD

any ['ɛnɪ] *adj* **1** (*in questions etc*: *singular*) du, de l', de la; (: *plural*) des; **have you any butter/children/ink?** avez-vous du beurre/des enfants/de l'encre?
2 (*with negative*) de, d'; **I haven't any money/books** je n'ai pas d'argent/de livres
3 (*no matter which*) n'importe quel(le); **choose any book you like** vous pouvez choisir n'importe quel livre
4 (*in phrases*): **in any case** de toute façon; **any day now** d'un jour à l'autre; **at any moment** à tout moment, d'un instant à l'autre; **at any rate** en tout cas
♦ *pron* **1** (*in questions etc*) en; **have you got any?** est-ce que vous en avez?; **can any of you sing?** est-ce que parmi vous il y en a qui savent chanter?
2 (*with negative*) en; **I haven't any (of them)** je n'en ai pas, je n'en ai aucun
3 (*no matter which one(s)*) n'importe lequel (*or* laquelle); **take any of those books (you like)** vous pouvez prendre n'importe lequel de ces livres
♦ *adv* **1** (*in questions etc*): **do you want any more soup/sandwiches?** voulez-vous encore de la soupe/des sandwichs?; **are you feeling any better?** est-ce que vous vous sentez mieux?
2 (*with negative*): **I can't hear him any more** je ne l'entends plus; **don't wait any longer** n'attendez pas plus longtemps

any: ~body *pron* n'importe qui; (*in interrogative sentences*) quelqu'un; (*in negative sentences*): **I don't see ~body** je ne vois personne; **~how** *adv* (*at any rate*) de toute façon, quand même; (*haphazard*) n'importe comment; **~one** *pron* = **anybody**; **~thing** *pron* n'importe quoi, quelque chose, ne ... rien; **~way** *adv* de toute façon; **~where** *adv* n'importe où, quelque part; **I don't see him ~where** je ne le vois nulle part

apart [ə'pɑːt] *adv* (*to one side*) à part; de côté; à l'écart; (*separately*) séparément; **10 miles ~** à 10 miles l'un de l'autre; **to take ~** démonter; **~ from** à part, excepté

apartheid [ə'pɑːteɪt] *n* apartheid *m*

apartment [ə'pɑːtmənt] *n* (*US*) appartement *m*, logement *m*; (*room*) chambre *f*; **~ building** (*US*) *n* immeuble *m*; (*divided house*) maison divisée en appartements

ape [eɪp] *n* (grand) singe ♦ *vt* singer

apéritif [ə'pɛrɪtiːf] *n* apéritif *m*

aperture ['æpətʃjuə^r] *n* orifice *m*, ouverture *f*; (*PHOT*) ouverture (du diaphragme)

APEX ['eɪpɛks] *n abbr* (*AVIAT*) (= *advance purchase excursion*) APEX *m*

apologetic [əpɔlə'dʒɛtɪk] *adj* (*tone, letter*) d'excuse; (*person*): **to be ~** s'excuser

apologize [ə'pɔlədʒaɪz] *vi*: **to ~ (for sth to sb)** s'excuser (de qch auprès de qn), présenter des excuses (à qn pour qch)

apology [ə'pɔlədʒɪ] *n* excuses *fpl*

apostle [ə'pɔsl] *n* apôtre *m*

apostrophe [ə'pɔstrəfɪ] *n* apostrophe *f*

appalling [ə'pɔːlɪŋ] *adj* épouvantable; (*stupidity*) consternant(e)

apparatus [æpəˈreɪtəs] *n* appareil *m*, dispositif *m*; (*in gymnasium*) agrès *mpl*; (*of government*) dispositif *m*

apparel [əˈpærəl] (*US*) *n* habillement *m*

apparent [əˈpærənt] *adj* apparent(e); **~ly** *adv* apparemment

appeal [əˈpiːl] *vi* (*LAW*) faire *or* interjeter appel ♦ *n* appel *m*; (*request*) prière *f*; appel *m*; (*charm*) attrait *m*, charme *m*; **to ~ for** lancer un appel pour; **to ~ to** (*beg*) faire appel à; (*be attractive*) plaire à; **it doesn't ~ to me** cela ne m'attire pas; **~ing** *adj* (*attractive*) attrayant(e)

appear [əˈpɪəʳ] *vi* apparaître, se montrer; (*LAW*) comparaître; (*publication*) paraître, sortir, être publié(e); (*seem*) paraître, sembler; **it would ~ that** il semble que; **to ~ in Hamlet** jouer dans Hamlet; **to ~ on TV** passer à la télé; **~ance** *n* apparition *f*; parution *f*; (*look, aspect*) apparence *f*, aspect *m*

appease [əˈpiːz] *vt* apaiser, calmer

appendicitis [əpɛndɪˈsaɪtɪs] *n* appendicite *f*

appendix [əˈpɛndɪks] (*pl* **appendices**) *n* appendice *m*

appetite [ˈæpɪtaɪt] *n* appétit *m*; **appetizer** *n* amuse-gueule *m*; (*drink*) apéritif *m*

applaud [əˈplɔːd] *vt, vi* applaudir

applause [əˈplɔːz] *n* applaudissements *mpl*

apple [ˈæpl] *n* pomme *f*; **~ tree** *n* pommier *m*

appliance [əˈplaɪəns] *n* appareil *m*

applicable [əˈplɪkəbl] *adj* (*relevant*): **to be ~ to** valoir pour

applicant [ˈæplɪkənt] *n*: **~ (for)** candidat(e) (à)

application [æplɪˈkeɪʃən] *n* application *f*; (*for a job, a grant etc*) demande *f*; candidature *f*; **~ form** *n* formulaire *m* de demande

applied [əˈplaɪd] *adj* appliqué(e)

apply [əˈplaɪ] *vt*: **to ~ (to)** (*paint, ointment*) appliquer (sur); (*law etc*) appliquer (à) ♦ *vi*: **to ~ to** (*be suitable for, relevant to*) s'appliquer à; (*ask*) s'adresser à; **to ~ (for)** (*permit, grant*) faire une demande (en vue d'obtenir); (*job*) poser sa candidature (pour), faire une demande d'emploi (concernant); **to ~ o.s. to** s'appliquer à

appoint [əˈpɔɪnt] *vt* nommer, engager; **~ed** *adj*: **at the ~ed time** à l'heure dite; **~ment** *n* nomination *f*; (*meeting*) rendez-vous *m*; **to make an ~ment (with)** prendre rendez-vous (avec)

appraisal [əˈpreɪzl] *n* évaluation *f*

appreciate [əˈpriːʃɪeɪt] *vt* (*like*) apprécier; (*be grateful for*) être reconnaissant(e) de; (*understand*) comprendre; se rendre compte de ♦ *vi* (*FINANCE*) prendre de la valeur

appreciation [əpriːʃɪˈeɪʃən] *n* appréciation *f*; (*gratitude*) reconnaissance *f*; (*COMM*) hausse *f*, valorisation *f*

appreciative [əˈpriːʃɪətɪv] *adj* (*person*) sensible; (*comment*) élogieux(-euse)

apprehensive [æprɪˈhɛnsɪv] *adj* inquiet(-ète), appréhensif(-ive)

apprentice [əˈprɛntɪs] *n* apprenti *m*; **~ship** *n* apprentissage *m*

approach [əˈprəutʃ] *vi* approcher ♦ *vt* (*come near*) approcher de; (*ask, apply to*) s'adresser à; (*situation, problem*) aborder ♦ *n* approche *f*; (*access*) accès *m*; **~able** *adj* accessible

appropriate [*adj* əˈprəuprɪɪt, *vb* əˈprəuprɪeɪt] *adj* (*moment, remark*) opportun(e); (*tool etc*) approprié(e) ♦ *vt* (*take*) s'approprier

approval [əˈpruːvəl] *n* approbation *f*; **on ~** (*COMM*) à l'examen

approve [əˈpruːv] *vt* approuver; **~ of** *vt fus* approuver

approximate [*adj* əˈprɔksɪmɪt, *vb* əˈprɔksɪmeɪt] *adj* approximatif(-ive) ♦ *vt* se rapprocher de, être proche de; **~ly** *adv* approximativement

apricot [ˈeɪprɪkɔt] *n* abricot *m*

April [ˈeɪprəl] *n* avril *m*; **~ Fool's Day** le premier avril

April Fool's Day

April Fool's Day *est le 1er avril, à l'occasion duquel on fait des farces de toutes sortes. Les victimes de ces farces sont les "April fools". Les médias britanniques se prennent aussi au jeu, diffusant de fausses nouvelles, comme la découverte d'îles de la taille de l'Irlande, ou faisant des reportages bidon, montrant par exemple la culture d'arbres à spaghettis en Italie.*

apron ['eɪprən] *n* tablier *m*
apt [æpt] *adj* (*suitable*) approprié(e); (*likely*): **~ to do** susceptible de faire; qui a tendance à faire
Aquarius [ə'kwɛərɪəs] *n* le Verseau
Arab ['ærəb] *adj* arabe ♦ *n* Arabe *m/f*; **~ian** [ə'reɪbɪən] *adj* arabe; **~ic** *adj* arabe ♦ *n* arabe *m*
arbitrary ['ɑːbɪtrərɪ] *adj* arbitraire
arbitration [ɑːbɪ'treɪʃən] *n* arbitrage *m*
arcade [ɑː'keɪd] *n* arcade *f*; (*passage with shops*) passage *m*, galerie marchande; (*with video games*) salle *f* de jeu
arch [ɑːtʃ] *n* arc *m*; (*of foot*) cambrure *f*, voûte *f* plantaire ♦ *vt* arquer, cambrer
archaeologist [ɑːkɪ'ɔlədʒɪst] *n* archéologue *m/f*
archaeology [ɑːkɪ'ɔlədʒɪ] *n* archéologie *f*
archbishop [ɑːtʃ'bɪʃəp] *n* archevêque *m*
archeology *etc* (*US*) [ɑːkɪ'ɔlədʒɪ] = **archaeology** *etc*
archery ['ɑːtʃərɪ] *n* tir *m* à l'arc
architect ['ɑːkɪtɛkt] *n* architecte *m*; **~ure** *n* architecture *f*
archives ['ɑːkaɪvz] *npl* archives *fpl*
Arctic ['ɑːktɪk] *adj* arctique ♦ *n* Arctique *m*
ardent ['ɑːdənt] *adj* fervent(e)
are [ɑːʳ] *vb see* **be**
area ['ɛərɪə] *n* (GEOM) superficie *f*; (*zone*) région *f*; (: *smaller*) secteur *m*, partie *f*; (*in room*) coin *m*; (*knowledge, research*) domaine *m*; **~ code** (*US*) *n* (TEL) indicatif *m* téléphonique
aren't [ɑːnt] = **are not**
Argentina [ɑːdʒən'tiːnə] *n* Argentine *f*; **Argentinian** [ɑːdʒən'tɪnɪən] *adj* argentin(e) ♦ *n* Argentin(e)
arguably ['ɑːgjuəblɪ] *adv*: **it is ~** ... on peut soutenir que c'est ...
argue ['ɑːgjuː] *vi* (*quarrel*) se disputer; (*reason*) argumenter; **to ~ that** objecter *or* alléguer que
argument ['ɑːgjumənt] *n* (*reasons*) argument *m*; (*quarrel*) dispute *f*; **~ative** [ɑːgju'mɛntətɪv] *adj* ergoteur(-euse), raisonneur(-euse)
Aries ['ɛərɪz] *n* le Bélier
arise [ə'raɪz] (*pt* **arose**, *pp* **arisen**) *vi* survenir, se présenter
aristocrat ['ærɪstəkræt] *n* aristocrate *m/f*
arithmetic [ə'rɪθmətɪk] *n* arithmétique *f*
ark [ɑːk] *n*: **Noah's A~** l'Arche *f* de Noé
arm [ɑːm] *n* bras *m* ♦ *vt* armer; **~s** *npl* (*weapons*, HERALDRY) armes *fpl*; **~ in ~** bras dessus bras dessous
armaments ['ɑːməmənts] *npl* armement *m*
armchair ['ɑːmtʃɛəʳ] *n* fauteuil *m*
armed [ɑːmd] *adj* armé(e); **~ robbery** *n* vol *m* à main armée
armour ['ɑːməʳ] (*US* **armor**) *n* armure *f*; (MIL: *tanks*) blindés *mpl*; **~ed car** *n* véhicule blindé
armpit ['ɑːmpɪt] *n* aisselle *f*
armrest ['ɑːmrɛst] *n* accoudoir *m*
army ['ɑːmɪ] *n* armée *f*
A road (BRIT) *n* (AUT) route nationale
aroma [ə'rəumə] *n* arôme *m*; **~therapy** *n* aromathérapie *f*
arose [ə'rəuz] *pt of* **arise**
around [ə'raund] *adv* autour; (*nearby*) dans les parages ♦ *prep* autour de; (*near*) près de; (*fig: about*) environ; (: *date, time*) vers

arouse [ə'rauz] *vt* (*sleeper*) éveiller; (*curiosity, passions*) éveiller, susciter; (*anger*) exciter

arrange [ə'reɪndʒ] *vt* arranger; **to ~ to do sth** prévoir de faire qch; **~ment** *n* arrangement *m*; **~ments** *npl* (*plans etc*) arrangements *mpl*, dispositions *fpl*

array [ə'reɪ] *n*: **~ of** déploiement *m or* étalage *m* de

arrears [ə'rɪəz] *npl* arriéré *m*; **to be in ~ with one's rent** devoir un arriéré de loyer

arrest [ə'rest] *vt* arrêter; (*sb's attention*) retenir, attirer ♦ *n* arrestation *f*; **under ~** en état d'arrestation

arrival [ə'raɪvl] *n* arrivée *f*; **new ~** nouveau venu, nouvelle venue; (*baby*) nouveau-né(e)

arrive [ə'raɪv] *vi* arriver

arrogant ['ærəgənt] *adj* arrogant(e)

arrow ['ærəu] *n* flèche *f*

arse [ɑːs] (*BRIT: inf!*) *n* cul *m* (*!*)

arson ['ɑːsn] *n* incendie criminel

art [ɑːt] *n* art *m*; **A~s** *npl* (*SCOL*) les lettres *fpl*

artery ['ɑːtərɪ] *n* artère *f*

art gallery *n* musée *m* d'art; (*small and private*) galerie *f* de peinture

arthritis [ɑː'θraɪtɪs] *n* arthrite *f*

artichoke ['ɑːtɪtʃəuk] *n* (*also:* **globe ~**) artichaut *m*; (*also:* **Jerusalem ~**) topinambour *m*

article ['ɑːtɪkl] *n* article *m*; **~s** *npl* (*BRIT: LAW: training*) ≃ stage *m*; **~ of clothing** vêtement *m*

articulate [*adj* ɑː'tɪkjulɪt, *vb* ɑː'tɪkjuleɪt] *adj* (*person*) qui s'exprime bien; (*speech*) bien articulé(e), prononcé(e) clairement ♦ *vt* exprimer; **~d lorry** (*BRIT*) *n* (camion *m*) semi-remorque *m*

artificial [ɑːtɪ'fɪʃəl] *adj* artificiel(le); **~ respiration** *n* respiration artificielle

artist ['ɑːtɪst] *n* artiste *m/f*; **~ic** [ɑː'tɪstɪk] *adj* artistique; **~ry** *n* art *m*, talent *m*

art school *n* ≃ école *f* des beaux-arts

KEYWORD

as [æz, əz] *conj* **1** (*referring to time*) comme, alors que; à mesure que; **he came in as I was leaving** il est arrivé comme je partais; **as the years went by** à mesure que les années passaient; **as from tomorrow** à partir de demain

2 (*in comparisons*): **as big as** aussi grand que; **twice as big as** deux fois plus grand que; **as much** *or* **many as** autant que; **as much money/many books** autant d'argent/de livres que; **as soon as** dès que

3 (*since, because*) comme, puisque; **as he had to be home by 10 ...** comme il *or* puisqu'il devait être de retour avant 10 h ...

4 (*referring to manner, way*) comme; **do as you wish** faites comme vous voudrez

5 (*concerning*): **as for** *or* **to that** quant à cela, pour ce qui est de cela

6: **as if** *or* **though** comme si; **he looked as if he was ill** il avait l'air d'être malade; *see also* **long**; **such**; **well**

♦ *prep*: **he works as a driver** il travaille comme chauffeur; **as chairman of the company, he ...** en tant que président de la société, il ...; **dressed up as a cowboy** déguisé en cowboy; **he gave me it as a present** il me l'a offert, il m'en a fait cadeau

a.s.a.p. *abbr* (= *as soon as possible*) dès que possible

asbestos [æz'bestəs] *n* amiante *f*

ascend [ə'send] *vt* gravir; (*throne*) monter sur

ascertain [æsə'teɪn] *vt* vérifier

ash [æʃ] *n* (*dust*) cendre *f*; (*also:* **~ tree**) frêne *m*

ashamed [ə'ʃeɪmd] *adj* honteux(-euse), confus(e); **to be ~ of** avoir honte de

ashore [ə'ʃɔːʳ] *adv* à terre

ashtray ['æʃtreɪ] *n* cendrier *m*

Ash Wednesday *n* mercredi *m* des cendres
Asia ['eɪʃə] *n* Asie *f*; **~n** *n* Asiatique *m/f* ♦ *adj* asiatique
aside [ə'saɪd] *adv* de côté; à l'écart ♦ *n* aparté *m*
ask [ɑːsk] *vt* demander; (*invite*) inviter; **to ~ sb sth/to do sth** demander qch à qn/à qn de faire qch; **to ~ sb about sth** questionner qn sur qch; se renseigner auprès de qn sur qch; **to ~ (sb) a question** poser une question (à qn); **to ~ sb out to dinner** inviter qn au restaurant; **~ after** *vt fus* demander des nouvelles de; **~ for** *vt fus* demander; (*trouble*) chercher
asking price ['ɑːskɪŋ-] *n*: **the ~** le prix de départ
asleep [ə'sliːp] *adj* endormi(e); **to fall ~** s'endormir
asparagus [əs'pærəgəs] *n* asperges *fpl*
aspect ['æspɛkt] *n* aspect *m*; (*direction in which a building etc faces*) orientation *f*, exposition *f*
aspire [əs'paɪəʳ] *vi*: **to ~ to** aspirer à
aspirin ['æsprɪn] *n* aspirine *f*
ass [æs] *n* âne *m*; (*inf*) imbécile *m/f*; (*US: inf!*) cul *m* (*!*)
assailant [ə'seɪlənt] *n* agresseur *m*; assaillant *m*
assassinate [ə'sæsɪneɪt] *vt* assassiner; **assassination** [əsæsɪ'neɪʃən] *n* assassinat *m*
assault [ə'sɔːlt] *n* (*MIL*) assaut *m*; (*gen*: *attack*) agression *f* ♦ *vt* attaquer; (*sexually*) violenter
assemble [ə'sɛmbl] *vt* assembler ♦ *vi* s'assembler, se rassembler; **assembly** *n* assemblée *f*, réunion *f*; (*institution*) assemblée; (*construction*) assemblage *m*; **assembly line** *n* chaîne *f* de montage
assent [ə'sɛnt] *n* assentiment *m*, consentement *m*
assert [ə'səːt] *vt* affirmer, déclarer; (*one's authority*) faire valoir; (*one's innocence*) protester de
assess [ə'sɛs] *vt* évaluer; (*tax, payment*) établir *or* fixer le montant de; (*property etc: for tax*) calculer la valeur imposable de; (*person*) juger la valeur de; **~ment** *n* évaluation *f*, fixation *f*, calcul *m* de la valeur imposable de, jugement *m*; **~or** *n* expert *m* (*impôt et assurance*)
asset ['æsɛt] *n* avantage *m*, atout *m*; **~s** *npl* (*FINANCE*) capital *m*; avoir(s) *m(pl)*; actif *m*
assign [ə'saɪn] *vt* (*date*) fixer; (*task*) assigner à; (*resources*) affecter à; **~ment** *n* tâche *f*, mission *f*
assist [ə'sɪst] *vt* aider, assister; **~ance** *n* aide *f*, assistance *f*; **~ant** *n* assistant(e), adjoint(e); (*BRIT*: *also*: **shop ~ant**) vendeur(-euse)
associate [*n, adj* ə'səuʃɪɪt, *vb* ə'səuʃɪeɪt] *adj, n* associé(e) ♦ *vt* associer ♦ *vi*: **to ~ with sb** fréquenter qn; **association** [əsəusɪ'eɪʃən] *n* association *f*
assorted [ə'sɔːtɪd] *adj* assorti(e)
assortment [ə'sɔːtmənt] *n* assortiment *m*
assume [ə'sjuːm] *vt* supposer; (*responsibilities etc*) assumer; (*attitude, name*) prendre, adopter; **assumption** [ə'sʌmpʃən] *n* supposition *f*, hypothèse *f*; (*of power*) assomption *f*, prise *f*
assurance [ə'ʃuərəns] *n* assurance *f*
assure [ə'ʃuəʳ] *vt* assurer
asthma ['æsmə] *n* asthme *m*
astonish [ə'stɔnɪʃ] *vt* étonner, stupéfier; **~ment** *n* étonnement *m*
astound [ə'staund] *vt* stupéfier, sidérer
astray [ə'streɪ] *adv*: **to go ~** s'égarer; (*fig*) quitter le droit chemin; **to lead ~** détourner du droit chemin
astride [ə'straɪd] *prep* à cheval sur
astrology [əs'trɔlədʒɪ] *n* astrologie *f*
astronaut ['æstrənɔːt] *n* astronaute *m/f*
astronomy [əs'trɔnəmɪ] *n* astronomie *f*
asylum [ə'saɪləm] *n* asile *m*

KEYWORD

at [æt] *prep* **1** (*referring to position, direction*) à; **at the top** au sommet; **at home/school** à la maison *or* chez soi/à

l'école; **at the baker's** à la boulangerie, chez le boulanger; **to look at sth** regarder qch
2 (*referring to time*): **at 4 o'clock** à 4 heures; **at Christmas** à Noël; **at night** la nuit; **at times** par moments, parfois
3 (*referring to rates, speed etc*) à; **at £1 a kilo** une livre le kilo; **two at a time** deux à la fois; **at 50 km/h** à 50 km/h
4 (*referring to manner*): **at a stroke** d'un seul coup; **at peace** en paix
5 (*referring to activity*): **to be at work** être au travail, travailler; **to play at cowboys** jouer aux cowboys; **to be good at sth** être bon en qch
6 (*referring to cause*): **shocked/surprised/annoyed at sth** choqué par/étonné de/agacé par qch; **I went at his suggestion** j'y suis allé sur son conseil

ate [eɪt] *pt of* **eat**
atheist ['eɪθɪɪst] *n* athée *m/f*
Athens ['æθɪnz] *n* Athènes
athlete ['æθli:t] *n* athlète *m/f*; **athletic** [æθ'lɛtɪk] *adj* athlétique; **athletics** *n* athlétisme *m*
Atlantic [ət'læntɪk] *adj* atlantique ♦ *n*: **the ~ (Ocean)** l'(océan *m*) Atlantique *m*
atlas ['ætləs] *n* atlas *m*
ATM *n abbr* (= *automated telling machine*) guichet *m* automatique
atmosphere ['ætməsfɪə^r] *n* atmosphère *f*
atom ['ætəm] *n* atome *m*; **~ic** [ə'tɔmɪk] *adj* atomique; **~(ic) bomb** *n* bombe *f* atomique; **~izer** *n* atomiseur *m*
atone [ə'təun] *vi*: **to ~ for** expier, racheter
atrocious [ə'trəuʃəs] *adj* (*very bad*) atroce, exécrable
attach [ə'tætʃ] *vt* attacher; (*document, letter*) joindre; **to be ~ed to sb/sth** être attaché à qn/qch
attaché case [ə'tæʃeɪ] *n* mallette *f*, attaché-case *m*
attachment [ə'tætʃmənt] *n* (*tool*) accessoire *m*; (*love*): **~ (to)** affection *f* (pour), attachement *m* (à)
attack [ə'tæk] *vt* attaquer; (*task etc*) s'attaquer à ♦ *n* attaque *f*; (*also:* **heart ~**) crise *f* cardiaque
attain [ə'teɪn] *vt* (*also:* **to ~ to**) parvenir à, atteindre; (: *knowledge*) acquérir
attempt [ə'tɛmpt] *n* tentative *f* ♦ *vt* essayer, tenter; **to make an ~ on sb's life** attenter à la vie de qn; **~ed** *adj*: **~ed murder/suicide** tentative *f* de meurtre/suicide
attend [ə'tɛnd] *vt* (*course*) suivre; (*meeting, talk*) assister à; (*school, church*) aller à, fréquenter; (*patient*) soigner, s'occuper de; **~ to** *vt fus* (*needs, affairs etc*) s'occuper de; (*customer, patient*) s'occuper de; **~ance** *n* (*being present*) présence *f*; (*people present*) assistance *f*; **~ant** *n* employé(e) ♦ *adj* (*dangers*) inhérent(e), concomitant(e)
attention [ə'tɛnʃən] *n* attention *f*; **~!** (MIL) garde-à-vous!; **for the ~ of** (ADMIN) à l'attention de
attentive [ə'tɛntɪv] *adj* attentif(-ive); (*kind*) prévenant(e)
attest [ə'tɛst] *vi*: **to ~ to** (*demonstrate*) démontrer, (*confirm*) témoigner
attic ['ætɪk] *n* grenier *m*
attitude ['ætɪtju:d] *n* attitude *f*; pose *f*, maintien *m*
attorney [ə'tə:nɪ] *n* (US: *lawyer*) avoué *m*; **A~ General** *n* (BRIT) ≃ procureur général; (US) ≃ garde *m* des Sceaux, ministre *m* de la Justice
attract [ə'trækt] *vt* attirer; **~ion** *n* (*gen pl: pleasant things*) attraction *f*, attrait *m*; (PHYSICS) attraction *f*; (*fig: towards sb or sth*) attirance *f*; **~ive** *adj* attrayant(e); (*person*) séduisant(e)
attribute [*n* 'ætrɪbju:t, *vb* ə'trɪbju:t] *n* attribut *m* ♦ *vt*: **to ~ sth to** attribuer qch à
attrition [ə'trɪʃən] *n*: **war of ~** guerre *f* d'usure
aubergine ['əubəʒi:n] *n* aubergine *f*

auction ['ɔ:kʃən] *n* (*also:* **sale by ~**) vente *f* aux enchères ♦ *vt* (*also:* **sell by ~**) vendre aux enchères; (*also:* **put up for ~**) mettre aux enchères; **~eer** [ɔ:kʃə'nɪə^r] *n* commissaire-priseur *m*
audience ['ɔ:dɪəns] *n* (*people*) assistance *f*; public *m*; spectateurs *mpl*; (*interview*) audience *f*
audiovisual ['ɔ:dɪəu'vɪzjuəl] *adj* audiovisuel(le); **~ aids** *npl* supports *or* moyens audiovisuels
audit ['ɔ:dɪt] *vt* vérifier
audition [ɔ:'dɪʃən] *n* audition *f*
auditor ['ɔ:dɪtə^r] *n* vérificateur *m* des comptes
augur ['ɔ:gə^r] *vi*: **it ~s well** c'est bon signe *or* de bon augure
August ['ɔ:gəst] *n* août *m*
aunt [ɑ:nt] *n* tante *f*; **~ie, ~y** ['ɑ:ntɪ] *n dimin of* **aunt**
au pair ['əu'pɛə^r] *n* (*also:* **~ girl**) jeune fille *f* au pair
auspicious [ɔ:s'pɪʃəs] *adj* de bon augure, propice
Australia [ɔs'treɪlɪə] *n* Australie *f*; **~n** *adj* australien(ne) ♦ *n* Australien(ne)
Austria ['ɔstrɪə] *n* Autriche *f*; **~n** *adj* autrichien(ne) ♦ *n* Autrichien(ne)
authentic [ɔ:'θɛntɪk] *adj* authentique
author ['ɔ:θə^r] *n* auteur *m*
authoritarian [ɔ:θɔrɪ'tɛərɪən] *adj* autoritaire
authoritative [ɔ:'θɔrɪtətɪv] *adj* (*account*) digne de foi; (*study, treatise*) qui fait autorité; (*person, manner*) autoritaire
authority [ɔ:'θɔrɪtɪ] *n* autorité *f*; (*permission*) autorisation (formelle); **the authorities** *npl* (*ruling body*) les autorités *fpl*, l'administration *f*
authorize ['ɔ:θəraɪz] *vt* autoriser
auto ['ɔ:təu] (*US*) *n* auto *f*, voiture *f*
auto: ~biography [ɔ:təbaɪ'ɔgrəfɪ] *n* autobiographie *f*; **~graph** ['ɔ:təgrɑ:f] *n* autographe *m* ♦ *vt* signer, dédicacer; **~mated** ['ɔ:təmeɪtɪd] *adj* automatisé(e), automatique; **~matic** [ɔ:tə'mætɪk] *adj* automatique ♦ *n* (*gun*) automatique *m*; (*washing machine*) machine *f* à laver automatique; (*BRIT*: *AUT*) voiture *f* à transmission automatique; **~matically** *adv* automatiquement; **~mation** [ɔ:tə'meɪʃən] *n* automatisation *f* (électronique); **~mobile** ['ɔ:təməbi:l] (*US*) *n* automobile *f*; **~nomy** [ɔ:'tɔnəmɪ] *n* autonomie *f*
autumn ['ɔ:təm] *n* automne *m*; **in ~** en automne
auxiliary [ɔ:g'zɪlɪərɪ] *adj* auxiliaire ♦ *n* auxiliaire *m/f*
avail [ə'veɪl] *vt*: **to ~ o.s. of** profiter de ♦ *n*: **to no ~** sans résultat, en vain, en pure perte
availability [əveɪlə'bɪlɪtɪ] *n* disponibilité *f*
available [ə'veɪləbl] *adj* disponible
avalanche ['ævəlɑ:nʃ] *n* avalanche *f*
Ave *abbr* = **avenue**
avenge [ə'vɛndʒ] *vt* venger
avenue ['ævənju:] *n* avenue *f*; (*fig*) moyen *m*
average ['ævərɪdʒ] *n* moyenne *f*; (*fig*) moyen *m* ♦ *adj* moyen(ne) ♦ *vt* (*a certain figure*) atteindre *or* faire *etc* en moyenne; **on ~** en moyenne; **~ out** *vi*: **to ~ out at** représenter en moyenne, donner une moyenne de
averse [ə'və:s] *adj*: **to be ~ to sth/doing sth** éprouver une forte répugnance envers qch/à faire qch
avert [ə'və:t] *vt* (*danger*) prévenir, écarter; (*one's eyes*) détourner
aviary ['eɪvɪərɪ] *n* volière *f*
avocado [ævə'kɑ:dəu] *n* (*BRIT*: **~ pear**) avocat *m*
avoid [ə'vɔɪd] *vt* éviter
await [ə'weɪt] *vt* attendre
awake [ə'weɪk] (*pt* **awoke**, *pp* **awoken**) *adj* éveillé(e) ♦ *vt* éveiller ♦ *vi* s'éveiller; **~ to** (*dangers, possibilities*) conscient(e) de; **to be ~** être réveillé(e); **he was still ~** il ne dormait pas encore; **~ning** *n* réveil *m*
award [ə'wɔ:d] *n* récompense *f*, prix *m*;

(*LAW*: *damages*) dommages-intérêts *mpl* ♦ *vt* (*prize*) décerner; (*LAW*: *damages*) accorder

aware [ə'wɛəʳ] *adj*: **~ (of)** (*conscious*) conscient(e) (de); (*informed*) au courant (de); **to become ~ of/that** prendre conscience de/que; se rendre compte de/que; **~ness** *n* conscience *f*, connaissance *f*

away [ə'weɪ] *adj, adv* (au) loin; absent(e); **two kilometres ~** à (une distance de) deux kilomètres, à deux kilomètres de distance; **two hours ~ by car** à deux heures de voiture *or* de route; **the holiday was two weeks ~** il restait deux semaines jusqu'aux vacances; **~ from** loin de; **he's ~ for a week** il est parti (pour) une semaine; **to pedal/work/laugh ~** être en train de pédaler/travailler/rire; **to fade ~** (*sound*) s'affaiblir; (*colour*) s'estomper; **to wither ~** (*plant*) se dessécher; **to take ~** emporter; (*subtract*) enlever; **~ game** *n* (*SPORT*) match *m* à l'extérieur

awe [ɔː] *n* respect mêlé de crainte; **~-inspiring** ['ɔːɪnspaɪərɪŋ] *adj* impressionnant(e)

awful ['ɔːfəl] *adj* affreux(-euse); **an ~ lot (of)** un nombre incroyable (de); **~ly** *adv* (*very*) terriblement, vraiment

awkward ['ɔːkwəd] *adj* (*clumsy*) gauche, maladroit(e); (*inconvenient*) peu pratique; (*embarrassing*) gênant(e), délicat(e)

awning ['ɔːnɪŋ] *n* (*of tent*) auvent *m*; (*of shop*) store *m*; (*of hotel etc*) marquise *f*

awoke [ə'wəuk] *pt of* **awake**; **~n** [ə'wəukən] *pp of* **awake**

axe [æks] (*US* **ax**) *n* hache *f* ♦ *vt* (*project etc*) abandonner; (*jobs*) supprimer

axes¹ ['æksɪz] *npl of* **axe**

axes² ['æksiːz] *npl of* **axis**

axis ['æksɪs] (*pl* **axes**) *n* axe *m*

axle ['æksl] *n* (*also*: **~-tree**: *AUT*) essieu *m*

ay(e) [aɪ] *excl* (*yes*) oui

B, b

B [biː] *n* (*MUS*) si *m*; **~ road** (*BRIT*) route départmentale

B.A. *abbr* = **Bachelor of Arts**

babble ['bæbl] *vi* bredouiller; (*baby, stream*) gazouiller

baby ['beɪbɪ] *n* bébé *m*; (*US*: *inf*: *darling*): **come on, ~!** viens ma belle/mon gars!; **~ carriage** (*US*) *n* voiture *f* d'enfant; **~ food** *n* aliments *mpl* pour bébé(s); **~-sit** *vi* garder les enfants; **~-sitter** *n* baby-sitter *m/f*; **~ wipe** *n* lingette *f* (*pour bébé*)

bachelor ['bætʃələʳ] *n* célibataire *m*; **B~ of Arts/Science** ≃ licencié(e) ès *or* en lettres/sciences

back [bæk] *n* (*of person, horse, book*) dos *m*; (*of hand*) dos, revers *m*; (*of house*) derrière *m*; (*of car, train*) arrière *m*; (*of chair*) dossier *m*; (*of page*) verso *m*; (*of room, audience*) fond *m*; (*SPORT*) arrière *m* ♦ *vt* (*candidate*: *also*: **~ up**) soutenir, appuyer; (*horse*: *at races*) parier *or* miser sur; (*car*) (faire) reculer ♦ *vi* (*also*: **~ up**) reculer; (*also*: **~ up**: *car etc*) faire marche arrière ♦ *adj* (*in compounds*) de derrière, à l'arrière ♦ *adv* (*not forward*) en arrière; (*returned*): **he's ~** il est rentré, il est de retour; (*restitution*): **throw the ball ~** renvoie la balle; (*again*): **he called ~** il a rappelé; **~ seat/wheel** (*AUT*) siège *m*/roue *f* arrière *inv*; **~ payments/rent** arriéré *m* de paiements/loyer; **he ran ~** il est revenu en courant; **~ down** *vi* rabattre de ses prétentions; **~ out** *vi* (*of promise*) se dédire; **~ up** *vt* (*candidate etc*) soutenir, appuyer; (*COMPUT*) sauvegarder; **~ache** *n* mal *m* de dos; **~bencher** (*BRIT*) *n* membre du parlement sans portefeuille; **~bone** *n* colonne vertébrale, épine dorsale; **~date** *vt* (*letter*) antidater; **~dated pay rise** augmentation *f* avec effet rétroactif; **~fire** *vi* (*AUT*) pétarader;

(*plans*) mal tourner; **~ground** *n* arrière-plan *m*; (*of events*) situation *f*, conjoncture *f*; (*basic knowledge*) éléments *mpl* de base; (*experience*) formation *f*; **family ~ground** milieu familial; **~hand** *n* (TENNIS: *also:* **~hand stroke**) revers *m*; **~hander** (BRIT) *n* (*bribe*) pot-de-vin *m*; **~ing** *n* (*fig*) soutien *m*, appui *m*; **~lash** *n* contre-coup *m*, répercussion *f*; **~log** *n*: **~log of work** travail *m* en retard; **~ number** *n* (*of magazine etc*) vieux numéro; **~pack** *n* sac *m* à dos; **~packer** *n* randonneur(-euse); **~ pain** *n* mal *m* de dos; **~ pay** *n* rappel *m* de salaire; **~side** (*inf*) *n* derrière *m*, postérieur *m*; **~stage** *adv* ♦ *n* derrière la scène, dans la coulisse; **~stroke** *n* dos crawlé; **~up** *adj* (*train, plane*) supplémentaire, de réserve; (COMPUT) de sauvegarde ♦ *n* (*support*) appui *m*, soutien *m*; (*also:* **~up disk/file**) sauvegarde *f*; **~ward** *adj* (*movement*) en arrière; (*person, country*) arriéré(e); attardé(e); **~wards** *adv* (*move, go*) en arrière; (*read a list*) à l'envers, à rebours; (*fall*) à la renverse; (*walk*) à reculons; **~water** *n* (*fig*) coin reculé; bled perdu (*péj*); **~yard** *n* arrière-cour *f*

bacon ['beɪkən] *n* bacon *m*, lard *m*

bacteria [bæk'tɪərɪə] *npl* bactéries *fpl*

bad [bæd] *adj* mauvais(e); (*child*) vilain(e); (*mistake, accident etc*) grave; (*meat, food*) gâté(e), avarié(e); **his ~ leg** sa jambe malade; **to go ~** (*meat, food*) se gâter

badge [bædʒ] *n* insigne *m*; (*of policeman*) plaque *f*

badger ['bædʒə^r] *n* blaireau *m*

badly ['bædlɪ] *adv* (*work, dress etc*) mal; **~ wounded** grièvement blessé; **he needs it ~** il en a absolument besoin; **~ off** *adj, adv* dans la gêne

badminton ['bædmɪntən] *n* badminton *m*

bad-tempered ['bæd'tɛmpəd] *adj* (*person: by nature*) ayant mauvais caractère; (*: on one occasion*) de mauvaise humeur

baffle ['bæfl] *vt* (*puzzle*) déconcerter

bag [bæg] *n* sac *m* ♦ *vt* (*inf: take*) empocher; s'approprier; **~s of** (*inf: lots of*) des masses de; **~gage** *n* bagages *mpl*; **~gage allowance** *n* franchise *f* de bagages; **~gage reclaim** *n* livraison *f* de bagages; **~gy** *adj* avachi(e), qui fait des poches; **~pipes** *npl* cornemuse *f*

bail [beɪl] *n* (*payment*) caution *f*; (*release*) mise *f* en liberté sous caution ♦ *vt* (*prisoner: also:* **grant ~ to**) mettre en liberté sous caution; (*boat: also:* **~ out**) écoper; **on ~** (*prisoner*) sous caution; *see also* **bale**; **~ out** *vt* (*prisoner*) payer la caution de

bailiff ['beɪlɪf] *n* (BRIT) ≃ huissier *m*; (US) ≃ huissier-audiencier *m*

bait [beɪt] *n* appât *m* ♦ *vt* appâter; (*fig: tease*) tourmenter

bake [beɪk] *vt* (faire) cuire au four ♦ *vi* (*bread etc*) cuire (au four); (*make cakes etc*) faire de la pâtisserie; **~d beans** *npl* haricots blancs à la sauce tomate; **~d potato** *n* pomme *f* de terre en robe des champs; **~r** *n* boulanger *m*; **~ry** *n* boulangerie *f*; boulangerie industrielle; **baking** *n* cuisson *f*; **baking powder** *n* levure *f* (chimique)

balance ['bæləns] *n* équilibre *m*; (COMM: *sum*) solde *m*; (*remainder*) reste *m*; (*scales*) balance *f* ♦ *vt* mettre *or* faire tenir en équilibre; (*pros and cons*) peser; (*budget*) équilibrer; (*account*) balancer; **~ of trade/payments** balance commerciale/des comptes *or* paiements; **~d** *adj* (*personality, diet*) équilibré(e); (*report*) objectif(-ive); **~ sheet** *n* bilan *m*

balcony ['bælkənɪ] *n* balcon *m*; (*in theatre*) deuxième balcon

bald [bɔːld] *adj* chauve; (*tyre*) lisse

bale [beɪl] *n* balle *f*, ballot *m*; **~ out** *vi* (*of a plane*) sauter en parachute

ball [bɔːl] *n* boule *f*; (*football*) ballon *m*; (*for tennis, golf*) balle *f*; (*of wool*) pelote *f*; (*of string*) bobine *f*; (*dance*) bal *m*; **to**

play ~ (with sb) (*fig*) coopérer (avec qn)
ballast ['bæləst] *n* lest *m*
ball bearings *npl* roulement *m* à billes
ballerina [bælə'ri:nə] *n* ballerine *f*
ballet ['bæleɪ] *n* ballet *m*; (*art*) danse *f* (classique); **~ dancer** *n* danseur(-euse) *m/f* de ballet; **~ shoe** *n* chausson *m* de danse
balloon [bə'lu:n] *n* ballon *m*; (*in comic strip*) bulle *f*
ballot ['bælət] *n* scrutin *m*; **~ paper** *n* bulletin *m* de vote
ballpoint (pen) ['bɔ:lpɔɪnt(-)] *n* stylo *m* à bille
ballroom ['bɔ:lrum] *n* salle *f* de bal
ban [bæn] *n* interdiction *f* ♦ *vt* interdire
banana [bə'nɑ:nə] *n* banane *f*
band [bænd] *n* bande *f*; (*at a dance*) orchestre *m*; (*MIL*) musique *f*, fanfare *f*; **~ together** *vi* se liguer
bandage ['bændɪdʒ] *n* bandage *m*, pansement *m* ♦ *vt* bander
Bandaid ® ['bændeɪd] (*US*) *n* pansement adhésif
bandit *n* bandit *m*
bandy-legged ['bændɪ'lɛgɪd] *adj* aux jambes arquées
bang [bæŋ] *n* détonation *f*; (*of door*) claquement *m*; (*blow*) coup (violent) ♦ *vt* frapper (violemment); (*door*) claquer ♦ *vi* détoner; claquer ♦ *excl* pan!; **~s** (*US*) *npl* (*fringe*) frange *f*
banish ['bænɪʃ] *vt* bannir
banister(s) ['bænɪstə(z)] *n(pl)* rampe *f* (d'escalier)
bank [bæŋk] *n* banque *f*; (*of river, lake*) bord *m*, rive *f*; (*of earth*) talus *m*, remblai *m* ♦ *vi* (*AVIAT*) virer sur l'aile; **~ on** *vt fus* miser *or* tabler sur; **~ account** *n* compte *m* en banque; **~ card** *n* carte *f* d'identité bancaire; **~er** *n* banquier *m*; **~er's card** (*BRIT*) *n* = **bank card**; **~ holiday** (*BRIT*) *n* jour férié (*les banques sont fermées*); **~ing** *n* opérations *fpl* bancaires; profession *f* de banquier; **~note** *n* billet *m* de banque; **~ rate** *n* taux *m* de l'escompte

bank holiday

Un **bank holiday** *en Grande-Bretagne est un lundi férié et donc l'occasion d'un week-end prolongé. La circulation sur les routes et le trafic dans les gares et les aéroports augmentent considérablement à ces périodes. Les principaux bank holidays, à part Pâques et Noël, ont lieu au mois de mai et fin août.*

bankrupt ['bæŋkrʌpt] *adj* en faillite; **to go ~** faire faillite; **~cy** *n* faillite *f*
bank statement *n* relevé *m* de compte
banner ['bænə[r]] *n* bannière *f*
bannister(s) ['bænɪstə(z)] *n(pl)* = **banister(s)**
baptism ['bæptɪzəm] *n* baptême *m*
bar [bɑ:[r]] *n* (*pub*) bar *m*; (*counter: in pub*) comptoir *m*, bar; (*rod: of metal etc*) barre *f*; (*on window etc*) barreau *m*; (*of chocolate*) tablette *f*, plaque *f*; (*fig*) obstacle *m*; (*prohibition*) mesure *f* d'exclusion; (*MUS*) mesure *f* ♦ *vt* (*road*) barrer; (*window*) munir de barreaux; (*person*) exclure; (*activity*) interdire; **~ of soap** savonnette *f*; **the B~** (*LAW*) le barreau; **behind ~s** (*prisoner*) sous les verrous; **~ none** sans exception
barbaric [bɑ:'bærɪk] *adj* barbare
barbecue ['bɑ:bɪkju:] *n* barbecue *m*
barbed wire ['bɑ:bd-] *n* fil *m* de fer barbelé
barber ['bɑ:bə[r]] *n* coiffeur *m* (pour hommes)
bar code *n* (*on goods*) code *m* à barres
bare [bɛə[r]] *adj* nu(e) ♦ *vt* mettre à nu, dénuder; (*teeth*) montrer; **the ~ necessities** le strict nécessaire; **~back** *adv* à cru, sans selle; **~faced** *adj* impudent(e), effronté(e); **~foot** *adj, adv* nu-pieds, (les) pieds nus; **~ly** *adv* à peine
bargain ['bɑ:gɪn] *n* (*transaction*) marché *m*; (*good buy*) affaire *f*, occasion *f* ♦

vi (*haggle*) marchander; (*negotiate*): **to ~ (with sb)** négocier (avec qn), traiter (avec qn); **into the ~** par-dessus le marché; **~ for** *vt fus*: **he got more than he ~ed for** il ne s'attendait pas à un coup pareil

barge [bɑːdʒ] *n* péniche *f*; **~ in** *vi* (*walk in*) faire irruption; (*interrupt talk*) intervenir mal à propos

bark [bɑːk] *n* (*of tree*) écorce *f*; (*of dog*) aboiement *m* ♦ *vi* aboyer

barley ['bɑːlɪ] *n* orge *f*; **~ sugar** *n* sucre *m* d'orge

bar: ~maid *n* serveuse *f* de bar, barmaid *f*; **~man** (*irreg*) *n* barman *m*; **~ meal** *n* repas *m* de bistrot; **to go for a ~ meal** aller manger au bistrot

barn [bɑːn] *n* grange *f*

barometer [bə'rɔmɪtə^r] *n* baromètre *m*

baron ['bærən] *n* baron *m*; **~ess** ['bærənɪs] *n* baronne *f*

barracks ['bærəks] *npl* caserne *f*

barrage ['bærɑːʒ] *n* (*MIL*) tir *m* de barrage; (*dam*) barrage *m*; (*fig*) pluie *f*

barrel ['bærəl] *n* tonneau *m*; (*of oil*) baril *m*; (*of gun*) canon *m*

barren ['bærən] *adj* stérile

barricade [bærɪ'keɪd] *n* barricade *f*

barrier ['bærɪə^r] *n* barrière *f*; (*fig: to progress etc*) obstacle *m*

barring ['bɑːrɪŋ] *prep* sauf

barrister ['bærɪstə^r] (*BRIT*) *n* avocat (plaidant)

barrow ['bærəu] *n* (*wheelbarrow*) charrette *f* à bras

bartender ['bɑːtɛndə^r] (*US*) *n* barman *m*

barter ['bɑːtə^r] *vt*: **to ~ sth for** échanger qch contre

base [beɪs] *n* base *f*; (*of tree, post*) pied *m* ♦ *vt*: **to ~ sth on** baser *or* fonder qch sur ♦ *adj* vil(e), bas(se)

baseball ['beɪsbɔːl] *n* base-ball *m*

basement ['beɪsmənt] *n* sous-sol *m*

bases[1] ['beɪsɪz] *npl of* **base**

bases[2] ['beɪsiːz] *npl of* **basis**

bash [bæʃ] (*inf*) *vt* frapper, cogner

bashful ['bæʃful] *adj* timide; modeste

basic ['beɪsɪk] *adj* fondamental(e), de base; (*minimal*) rudimentaire; **~ally** *adv* fondamentalement, à la base; (*in fact*) en fait, au fond; **~s** *npl*: **the ~s** l'essentiel *m*

basil ['bæzl] *n* basilic *m*

basin ['beɪsn] *n* (*vessel, also GEO*) cuvette *f*, bassin *m*; (*also:* **washbasin**) lavabo *m*

basis ['beɪsɪs] (*pl* **bases**) *n* base *f*; **on a trial ~** à titre d'essai; **on a part-time ~** à temps partiel

bask [bɑːsk] *vi*: **to ~ in the sun** se chauffer au soleil

basket ['bɑːskɪt] *n* corbeille *f*; (*with handle*) panier *m*; **~ball** *n* basket-ball *m*

bass [beɪs] *n* (*MUS*) basse *f*; **~ drum** *n* grosse caisse *f*

bassoon [bə'suːn] *n* (*MUS*) basson *m*

bastard ['bɑːstəd] *n* enfant naturel(le), bâtard(e); (*inf!*) salaud *m* (*!*)

bat [bæt] *n* chauve-souris *f*; (*for baseball etc*) batte *f*; (*BRIT: for table tennis*) raquette *f* ♦ *vt*: **he didn't ~ an eyelid** il n'a pas sourcillé *or* bronché

batch [bætʃ] *n* (*of bread*) fournée *f*; (*of papers*) liasse *f*

bated ['beɪtɪd] *adj*: **with ~ breath** en retenant son souffle

bath [bɑːθ] *n* bain *m*; (*~tub*) baignoire *f* ♦ *vt* baigner, donner un bain à; **to have a ~** prendre un bain; *see also* **baths**

bathe [beɪð] *vi* se baigner ♦ *vt* (*wound*) laver; **bathing** *n* baignade *f*; **bathing costume, bathing suit** (*US*) *n* maillot *m* (de bain)

bath: ~robe *n* peignoir *m* de bain; **~room** *n* salle *f* de bains; **~s** *npl* (*also:* **swimming ~s**) piscine *f*; **~ towel** *n* serviette *f* de bain

baton ['bætən] *n* bâton *m*; (*MUS*) baguette *f*; (*club*) matraque *f*

batter ['bætə^r] *vt* battre ♦ *n* pâte *f* à frire; **~ed** ['bætəd] *adj* (*hat, pan*) cabossé(e)

battery ['bætəri] *n* batterie *f*; (*of torch*) pile *f*; **~ farming** *n* élevage *f* en batterie

battle ['bætl] *n* bataille *f*, combat *m* ♦ *vi* se battre, lutter; **~field** *n* champ *m* de bataille; **~ship** *n* cuirassé *m*

Bavaria [bə'vɛəriə] *n* Bavière *f*

bawl [bɔ:l] *vi* hurler; (*child*) brailler

bay [beɪ] *n* (*of sea*) baie *f*; **to hold sb at ~** tenir qn à distance *or* en échec; **~ leaf** *n* laurier *m*; **~ window** *n* baie vitrée

bazaar [bə'zɑ:ʳ] *n* bazar *m*; vente *f* de charité

B & B *n abbr* = **bed and breakfast**

BBC *n abbr* (= *British Broadcasting Corporation*) la BBC

B.C. *adv abbr* (= *before Christ*) av. J.-C.

KEYWORD

be [bi:] (*pt* **was, were**, *pp* **been**) *aux vb*
1 (*with present participle*: *forming continuous tenses*): **what are you doing?** que faites-vous?; **they're coming tomorrow** ils viennent demain; **I've been waiting for you for 2 hours** je t'attends depuis 2 heures
2 (*with pp*: *forming passives*) être; **to be killed** être tué(e); **he was nowhere to be seen** on ne le voyait nulle part
3 (*in tag questions*): **it was fun, wasn't it?** c'était drôle, n'est-ce pas?; **she's back, is she?** elle est rentrée, n'est-ce pas *or* alors?
4 (*+to +infinitive*): **the house is to be sold** la maison doit être vendue; **he's not to open it** il ne doit pas l'ouvrir
♦ *vb + complement* **1** (*gen*) être; **I'm English** je suis anglais(e); **I'm tired** je suis fatigué(e); **I'm hot/cold** j'ai chaud/froid; **he's a doctor** il est médecin; **2 and 2 are 4** 2 et 2 font 4
2 (*of health*) aller; **how are you?** comment allez-vous?; **he's fine now** il va bien maintenant; **he's very ill** il est très malade
3 (*of age*) avoir; **how old are you?** quel âge avez-vous?; **I'm sixteen (years old)** j'ai seize ans
4 (*cost*) coûter; **how much was the meal?** combien a coûté le repas?; **that'll be £5, please** ça fera 5 livres, s'il vous plaît
♦ *vi* **1** (*exist, occur etc*) être, exister; **the prettiest girl that ever was** la fille la plus jolie qui ait jamais existé; **be that as it may** quoi qu'il en soit; **so be it** soit
2 (*referring to place*) être, se trouver; **I won't be here tomorrow** je ne serai pas là demain; **Edinburgh is in Scotland** Édimbourg est *or* se trouve en Écosse
3 (*referring to movement*) aller; **where have you been?** où êtes-vous allé(s)?
♦ *impers vb* **1** (*referring to time, distance*) être; **it's 5 o'clock** il est 5 heures; **it's the 28th of April** c'est le 28 avril; **it's 10 km to the village** le village est à 10 km
2 (*referring to the weather*) faire; **it's too hot/cold** il fait trop chaud/froid; **it's windy** il y a du vent
3 (*emphatic*): **it's me/the postman** c'est moi/le facteur

beach [bi:tʃ] *n* plage *f* ♦ *vt* échouer; **~ towel** *n* serviette *f* de plage

beacon ['bi:kən] *n* (*lighthouse*) fanal *m*; (*marker*) balise *f*

bead [bi:d] *n* perle *f*

beak [bi:k] *n* bec *m*

beaker ['bi:kəʳ] *n* gobelet *m*

beam [bi:m] *n* poutre *f*; (*of light*) rayon *m* ♦ *vi* rayonner

bean [bi:n] *n* haricot *m*; (*of coffee*) grain *m*; **runner ~** haricot *m* (à rames); **broad ~** fève *f*; **~sprouts** *npl* germes *mpl* de soja

bear [bɛəʳ] (*pt* **bore**, *pp* **borne**) *n* ours *m* ♦ *vt* porter; (*endure*) supporter ♦ *vi*: **to ~ right/left** obliquer à droite/gauche, se diriger vers la droite/gauche; **~ out** *vt* corroborer, confirmer; **~ up** *vi* (*person*) tenir le coup

beard [bɪəd] *n* barbe *f*; **~ed** *adj* barbu(e)

bearer ['bɛərə[r]] *n* porteur *m*; (*of passport*) titulaire *m/f*

bearing ['bɛərɪŋ] *n* maintien *m*, allure *f*; (*connection*) rapport *m*; **~s** *npl* (*also:* **ball ~s**) roulement *m* (à billes); **to take a ~** faire le point

beast [bi:st] *n* bête *f*; (*inf: person*) brute *f*; **~ly** *adj* infect(e)

beat [bi:t] (*pt* **beat**, *pp* **beaten**) *n* battement *m*; (MUS) temps *m*, mesure *f*; (*of policeman*) ronde *f* ♦ *vt, vi* battre; **off the ~en track** hors des chemins *or* sentiers battus; **~ it!** (*inf*) fiche(-moi) le camp!; **~ off** *vt* repousser; **~ up** *vt* (*inf: person*) tabasser; (*eggs*) battre; **~ing** *n* raclée *f*

beautiful ['bju:tɪful] *adj* beau (belle); **~ly** *adv* admirablement

beauty ['bju:tɪ] *n* beauté *f*; **~ parlour** *n* institut *m* de beauté; **~ salon** *n*, **~ shop** *n* = **~ parlour**; **~ spot** (BRIT) *n* (TOURISM) site naturel (d'une grande beauté)

beaver ['bi:və[r]] *n* castor *m*

because [bɪ'kɔz] *conj* parce que; **~ of** *prep* à cause de

beck [bɛk] *n*: **to be at sb's ~ and call** être à l'entière disposition de qn

beckon ['bɛkən] *vt* (*also:* **~ to**) faire signe (de venir) à

become [bɪ'kʌm] (*irreg: like* **come**) *vi* devenir; **to ~ fat/thin** grossir/maigrir; **becoming** *adj* (*behaviour*) convenable, bienséant(e); (*clothes*) seyant(e)

bed [bɛd] *n* lit *m*; (*of flowers*) parterre *m*; (*of coal, clay*) couche *f*; (*of sea*) fond *m*; **to go to ~** aller se coucher; **~ and breakfast** *n* (*terms*) chambre et petit déjeuner; (*place*) *voir encadré*; **~clothes** *npl* couvertures *fpl* et draps *mpl*; **~ding** *n* literie *f*; **~ linen** *n* draps *mpl* de lit (et taies *fpl* d'oreillers), literie *f*

bed and breakfast

Un **bed and breakfast** *est une petite pension dans une maison particulière ou une ferme où l'on peut louer une chambre avec petit déjeuner compris pour un prix modique par rapport à ce que l'on paierait dans un hôtel. Ces établissements sont communément appelés B & B, et sont signalés par une pancarte dans le jardin ou audessus de la porte.*

bedraggled [bɪ'drægld] *adj* (*person, clothes*) débraillé(e); (*hair: wet*) trempé(e)

bed: ~ridden *adj* cloué(e) au lit; **~room** *n* chambre *f* (à coucher); **~side** *n*: **at sb's ~side** au chevet de qn; **~sit(ter)** *n* (BRIT) chambre meublée, studio *m*; **~spread** *n* couvre-lit *m*, dessus-de-lit *m inv*; **~time** *n* heure *f* du coucher

bee [bi:] *n* abeille *f*

beech [bi:tʃ] *n* hêtre *m*

beef [bi:f] *n* bœuf *m*; **roast ~** rosbif *m*; **~burger** *n* hamburger *m*; **~eater** *n* *hallebardier de la Tour de Londres*

bee: ~hive *n* ruche *f*; **~line** *n*: **to make a ~line for** se diriger tout droit vers

been [bi:n] *pp of* **be**

beer [bɪə[r]] *n* bière *f*

beet [bi:t] *n* (*vegetable*) betterave *f*; (US: *also:* **red ~**) betterave (potagère)

beetle ['bi:tl] *n* scarabée *m*

beetroot ['bi:tru:t] (BRIT) *n* betterave *f*

before [bɪ'fɔ:[r]] *prep* (*in time*) avant; (*in space*) devant ♦ *conj* avant que +*sub*; avant de ♦ *adv* avant; devant; **~ going** avant de partir; **~ she goes** avant qu'elle ne parte; **the week ~** la semaine précédente *or* d'avant; **I've seen it ~** je l'ai déjà vu; **~hand** *adv* au préalable, à l'avance

beg [bɛg] *vi* mendier ♦ *vt* mendier; (*forgiveness, mercy etc*) demander; (*entreat*) supplier; *see also* **pardon**

began [bɪ'gæn] *pt of* **begin**
beggar ['bɛgəʳ] *n* mendiant(e)
begin [bɪ'gɪn] (*pt* **began**, *pp* **begun**) *vt, vi* commencer; **to ~ doing** *or* **to do sth** commencer à *or* de faire qch; **~ner** *n* débutant(e); **~ning** *n* commencement *m*, début *m*
behalf [bɪ'hɑ:f] *n*: **on ~ of,** *(US)* **in ~ of** (*representing*) de la part de; (*for benefit of*) pour le compte de; **on my/his ~** pour moi/lui
behave [bɪ'heɪv] *vi* se conduire, se comporter; (*well*: *also:* **~ o.s.**) se conduire bien *or* comme il faut; **behaviour** (*US* **behavior**) [bɪ'heɪvjəʳ] *n* comportement *m*, conduite *f*
behead [bɪ'hɛd] *vt* décapiter
behind [bɪ'haɪnd] *prep* derrière; (*time, progress*) en retard sur; (*work, studies*) en retard dans ♦ *adv* derrière ♦ *n* derrière *m*; **to be ~ (schedule)** avoir du retard; **~ the scenes** dans les coulisses
behold [bɪ'həuld] (*irreg*: *like* **hold**) *vt* apercevoir, voir
beige [beɪʒ] *adj* beige
Beijing ['beɪ'dʒɪŋ] *n* Bei-jing, Pékin
being ['bi:ɪŋ] *n* être *m*
Beirut [beɪ'ru:t] *n* Beyrouth
Belarus [bɛlə'rus] *n* Bélarus *f*
belated [bɪ'leɪtɪd] *adj* tardif(-ive)
belch [bɛltʃ] *vi* avoir un renvoi, roter ♦ *vt* (*also:* **~ out**: *smoke etc*) vomir, cracher
Belgian ['bɛldʒən] *adj* belge, de Belgique ♦ *n* Belge *m/f*
Belgium ['bɛldʒəm] *n* Belgique *f*
belie [bɪ'laɪ] *vt* démentir
belief [bɪ'li:f] *n* (*opinion*) conviction *f*; (*trust, faith*) foi *f*
believe [bɪ'li:v] *vt, vi* croire; **to ~ in** (*God*) croire en; (*method, ghosts*) croire à; **~r** *n* (*in idea, activity*): **~r in** partisan(e) de; (*REL*) croyant(e)
belittle [bɪ'lɪtl] *vt* déprécier, rabaisser
bell [bɛl] *n* cloche *f*; (*small*) clochette *f*, grelot *m*; (*on door*) sonnette *f*; (*electric*) sonnerie *f*
belligerent [bɪ'lɪdʒərənt] *adj* (*person, attitude*) agressif(-ive)
bellow ['bɛləu] *vi* (*bull*) meugler; (*person*) brailler
belly ['bɛlɪ] *n* ventre *m*
belong [bɪ'lɔŋ] *vi*: **to ~ to** appartenir à; (*club etc*) faire partie de; **this book ~s here** ce livre va ici; **~ings** *npl* affaires *fpl*, possessions *fpl*
beloved [bɪ'lʌvɪd] *adj* (bien-)aimé(e)
below [bɪ'ləu] *prep* sous, au-dessous de ♦ *adv* en dessous; **see ~** voir plus bas *or* plus loin *or* ci-dessous
belt [bɛlt] *n* ceinture *f*; (*of land*) région *f*; (*TECH*) courroie *f* ♦ *vt* (*thrash*) donner une raclée à; **~way** (*US*) *n* (*AUT*) route *f* de ceinture; (: *motorway*) périphérique *m*
bemused [bɪ'mju:zd] *adj* stupéfié(e)
bench [bɛntʃ] *n* (*gen, also BRIT: POL*) banc *m*; (*in workshop*) établi *m*; **the B~** (*LAW: judge*) le juge; (: *judges collectively*) la magistrature, la Cour
bend [bɛnd] (*pt, pp* **bent**) *vt* courber; (*leg, arm*) plier ♦ *vi* se courber ♦ *n* (*BRIT: in road*) virage *m*, tournant *m*; (*in pipe, river*) coude *m*; **~ down** *vi* se baisser; **~ over** *vi* se pencher
beneath [bɪ'ni:θ] *prep* sous, au-dessous de; (*unworthy of*) indigne de ♦ *adv* dessous, au-dessous, en bas
benefactor ['bɛnɪfæktəʳ] *n* bienfaiteur *m*
beneficial [bɛnɪ'fɪʃəl] *adj* salutaire; avantageux(-euse); **~ to the health** bon(ne) pour la santé
benefit ['bɛnɪfɪt] *n* avantage *m*, profit *m*; (*allowance of money*) allocation *f* ♦ *vt* faire du bien à, profiter à ♦ *vi*: **he'll ~ from it** cela lui fera du bien, il y gagnera *or* s'en trouvera bien
Benelux ['bɛnɪlʌks] *n* Bénélux *m*
benevolent [bɪ'nɛvələnt] *adj* bienveillant(e); (*organization*) bénévole
benign [bɪ'naɪn] *adj* (*person, smile*) bienveillant(e), affable; (*MED*) bénin(-igne)

bent [bɛnt] *pt, pp of* **bend** ♦ *n* inclination *f*, penchant *m*; **to be ~ on** être résolu(e) à
bequest [bɪ'kwɛst] *n* legs *m*
bereaved [bɪ'ri:vd] *n*: **the ~** la famille du disparu
beret ['bɛreɪ] *n* béret *m*
Berlin [bə:'lɪn] *n* Berlin
berm [bə:m] (*US*) *n* (*AUT*) accotement *m*
Bermuda [bə:'mju:də] *n* Bermudes *fpl*
berry ['bɛrɪ] *n* baie *f*
berserk [bə'sə:k] *adj*: **to go ~** (*madman, crowd*) se déchaîner
berth [bə:θ] *n* (*bed*) couchette *f*; (*for ship*) poste *m* d'amarrage, mouillage *m* ♦ *vi* (*in harbour*) venir à quai; (*at anchor*) mouiller
beseech [bɪ'si:tʃ] (*pt, pp* **besought**) *vt* implorer, supplier
beset [bɪ'sɛt] (*pt, pp* **beset**) *vt* assaillir
beside [bɪ'saɪd] *prep* à côté de; **to be ~ o.s. (with anger)** être hors de soi; **that's ~ the point** cela n'a rien à voir; **~s** *adv* en outre, de plus; (*in any case*) d'ailleurs ♦ *prep* (*as well as*) en plus de
besiege [bɪ'si:dʒ] *vt* (*town*) assiéger; (*fig*) assaillir
best [bɛst] *adj* meilleur(e) ♦ *adv* le mieux; **the ~ part of** (*quantity*) le plus clair de, la plus grande partie de; **at ~** au mieux; **to make the ~ of sth** s'accommoder de qch (du mieux que l'on peut); **to do one's ~** faire de son mieux; **to the ~ of my knowledge** pour autant que je sache; **to the ~ of my ability** du mieux que je pourrai; **~ before date** *n* date *f* de limite d'utilisation *or* de consommation; **~ man** *n* garçon *m* d'honneur
bestow [bɪ'stəu] *vt*: **to ~ sth on sb** accorder qch à qn; (*title*) conférer qch à qn
bet [bɛt] (*pt, pp* **bet** *or* **betted**) *n* pari *m* ♦ *vt, vi* parier
betray [bɪ'treɪ] *vt* trahir
better ['bɛtəʳ] *adj* meilleur(e) ♦ *adv* mieux ♦ *vt* améliorer ♦ *n*: **to get the ~ of** triompher de, l'emporter sur; **you had ~ do it** vous feriez mieux de le faire; **he thought ~ of it** il s'est ravisé; **to get ~** aller mieux; s'améliorer; **~ off** *adj* plus à l'aise financièrement; (*fig*): **you'd be ~ off this way** vous vous en trouveriez mieux ainsi
betting ['bɛtɪŋ] *n* paris *mpl*; **~ shop** (*BRIT*) *n* bureau *m* de paris
between [bɪ'twi:n] *prep* entre ♦ *adv*: **(in) ~** au milieu; dans l'intervalle; (*in time*) dans l'intervalle
beverage ['bɛvərɪdʒ] *n* boisson *f* (*gén sans alcool*)
beware [bɪ'wɛəʳ] *vi*: **to ~ (of)** prendre garde (à); **"~ of the dog"** "(attention) chien méchant"
bewildered [bɪ'wɪldəd] *adj* dérouté(e), ahuri(e)
beyond [bɪ'jɔnd] *prep* (*in space, time*) au-delà de; (*exceeding*) au-dessus de ♦ *adv* au-delà; **~ doubt** hors de doute; **~ repair** irréparable
bias ['baɪəs] *n* (*prejudice*) préjugé *m*, parti pris; **~(s)ed** *adj* partial(e), montrant un parti pris
bib [bɪb] *n* bavoir *m*, bavette *f*
Bible ['baɪbl] *n* Bible *f*
bicarbonate of soda [baɪ'kɑ:bənɪt-] *n* bicarbonate *m* de soude
bicker ['bɪkəʳ] *vi* se chamailler
bicycle ['baɪsɪkl] *n* bicyclette *f*
bid [bɪd] (*pt* **bid** *or* **bade**, *pp* **bid(den)**) *n* offre *f*; (*at auction*) enchère *f*; (*attempt*) tentative *f* ♦ *vi* faire une enchère *or* offre ♦ *vt* faire une enchère *or* offre de; **to ~ sb good day** souhaiter le bonjour à qn; **~der** *n*: **the highest ~der** le plus offrant; **~ding** *n* enchères *fpl*
bide [baɪd] *vt*: **to ~ one's time** attendre son heure
bifocals [baɪ'fəuklz] *npl* verres *mpl* à double foyer, lunettes bifocales
big [bɪg] *adj* grand(e); gros(se); **~headed** *adj* prétentieux(-euse)
bigot ['bɪgət] *n* fanatique *m/f*, sectaire *m/f*; **~ed** *adj* fanatique, sectaire; **~ry** *n*

fanatisme *m*, sectarisme *m*
big top *n* grand chapiteau
bike [baɪk] *n* vélo *m*, bécane *f*
bikini [bɪ'ki:nɪ] *n* bikini *m*
bilingual [baɪ'lɪŋgwəl] *adj* bilingue
bill [bɪl] *n* note *f*, facture *f*; (POL) projet *m* de loi; (*US*: *banknote*) billet *m* (de banque); (*of bird*) bec *m*; (THEATRE): **on the ~** à l'affiche; **"post no ~s"** "défense d'afficher"; **to fit** *or* **fill the ~** (*fig*) faire l'affaire; **~board** *n* panneau *m* d'affichage
billet ['bɪlɪt] *n* cantonnement *m* (chez l'habitant)
billfold ['bɪlfəuld] (*US*) *n* portefeuille *m*
billiards ['bɪljədz] *n* (jeu *m* de) billard *m*
billion ['bɪljən] *n* (BRIT) billion *m* (*million de millions*); (*US*) milliard *m*
bimbo ['bɪmbəu] (*inf*) *n* ravissante idiote *f*, potiche *f*
bin [bɪn] *n* boîte *f*; (*also:* **dustbin**) poubelle *f*; (*for coal*) coffre *m*
bind [baɪnd] (*pt, pp* **bound**) *vt* attacher; (*book*) relier; (*oblige*) obliger, contraindre ♦ *n* (*inf*: *nuisance*) scie *f*; **~ing** *adj* (*contract*) constituant une obligation
binge [bɪndʒ] (*inf*) *n*: **to go on a/the ~** aller faire la bringue
bingo ['bɪŋgəu] *n jeu de loto pratiqué dans des établissements publics*
binoculars [bɪ'nɔkjuləz] *npl* jumelles *fpl*
bio *prefix*: **~chemistry** *n* biochimie *f*; **~degradable** *adj* biodégradable; **~graphy** *n* biographie *f*; **~logical** *adj* biologique; **~logy** *n* biologie *f*
birch [bə:tʃ] *n* bouleau *m*
bird [bə:d] *n* oiseau *m*; (BRIT: *inf*: *girl*) nana *f*; **~'s-eye view** *n* vue *f* à vol d'oiseau; (*fig*) vue d'ensemble *or* générale; **~-watcher** *n* ornithologue *m/f* amateur
Biro ['baɪərəu] ® *n* stylo *m* à bille
birth [bə:θ] *n* naissance *f*; **to give ~ to** (*subj*: *woman*) donner naissance à; (: *animal*) mettre bas; **~ certificate** *n* acte *m* de naissance; **~ control** *n* (*policy*) limitation *f* des naissances; (*method*) méthode(s) contraceptive(s); **~day** *n* anniversaire *m* ♦ *cpd* d'anniversaire; **~place** *n* lieu *m* de naissance; (*fig*) berceau *m*; **~ rate** *n* (taux *m* de) natalité *f*
biscuit ['bɪskɪt] *n* (BRIT) biscuit *m*; (*US*) petit pain au lait
bisect [baɪ'sɛkt] *vt* couper *or* diviser en deux
bishop ['bɪʃəp] *n* évêque *m*; (CHESS) fou *m*
bit [bɪt] *pt of* **bite** ♦ *n* morceau *m*; (*of tool*) mèche *f*; (*of horse*) mors *m*; (COMPUT) élément *m* binaire; **a ~ of** un peu de; **a ~ mad** un peu fou; **~ by ~** petit à petit
bitch [bɪtʃ] *n* (*dog*) chienne *f*; (*inf!*) salope *f* (*!*), garce *f*
bite [baɪt] (*pt* **bit**, *pp* **bitten**) *vt, vi* mordre; (*insect*) piquer ♦ *n* (*insect* ~) piqûre *f*; (*mouthful*) bouchée *f*; **let's have a ~ (to eat)** (*inf*) mangeons un morceau; **to ~ one's nails** se ronger les ongles
bitter ['bɪtə^r^] *adj* amer(-ère); (*weather, wind*) glacial(e); (*criticism*) cinglant(e); (*struggle*) acharné(e) ♦ *n* (BRIT: *beer*) bière *f* (*forte*); **~ness** *n* amertume *f*; (*taste*) goût amer
black [blæk] *adj* noir(e) ♦ *n* (*colour*) noir *m*; (*person*): **B~** noir(e) ♦ *vt* (BRIT: INDUSTRY) boycotter; **to give sb a ~ eye** pocher l'œil à qn, faire un œil au beurre noir à qn; **~ and blue** couvert(e) de bleus; **to be in the ~** (*in credit*) être créditeur(-trice); **~berry** *n* mûre *f*; **~bird** *n* merle *m*; **~board** *n* tableau noir; **~ coffee** *n* café noir; **~currant** *n* cassis *m*; **~en** *vt* noircir; **~ ice** *n* verglas *m*; **~leg** (BRIT) *n* briseur *m* de grève, jaune *m*; **~list** *n* liste noire; **~mail** *n* chantage *m* ♦ *vt* faire chanter, soumettre au chantage; **~ market** *n* marché noir; **~out** *n* panne *f* d'électricité; (*TV etc*) interruption *f* d'émission; (*fainting*) syncope *f*; **~ pudding** *n* boudin (noir); **B~ Sea** *n*: **the B~ Sea** la mer Noire; **~**

sheep *n* brebis galeuse; **~smith** *n* forgeron *m*; **~ spot** (*AUT*) *n* point noir
bladder ['blædər] *n* vessie *f*
blade [bleɪd] *n* lame *f*; (*of propeller*) pale *f*; **~ of grass** brin *m* d'herbe
blame [bleɪm] *n* faute *f*, blâme *m* ♦ *vt*: **to ~ sb/sth for sth** attribuer à qn/qch la responsabilité de qch; reprocher qch à qn/qch; **who's to ~?** qui est le fautif *or* coupable *or* responsable?
bland [blænd] *adj* (*taste, food*) doux (douce), fade
blank [blæŋk] *adj* blanc (blanche); (*look*) sans expression, dénué(e) d'expression ♦ *n* espace *m* vide, blanc *m*; (*cartridge*) cartouche *f* à blanc; **his mind was a ~** il avait la tête vide; **~ cheque** chèque *m* en blanc
blanket ['blæŋkɪt] *n* couverture *f*; (*of snow, cloud*) couche *f*
blare [bleər] *vi* beugler
blast [blɑːst] *n* souffle *m*; (*of explosive*) explosion *f* ♦ *vt* faire sauter *or* exploser; **~-off** *n* (*SPACE*) lancement *m*
blatant ['bleɪtənt] *adj* flagrant(e), criant(e)
blaze [bleɪz] *n* (*fire*) incendie *m*; (*fig*) flamboiement *m* ♦ *vi* (*fire*) flamber; (*fig: eyes*) flamboyer; (: *guns*) crépiter ♦ *vt*: **to ~ a trail** (*fig*) montrer la voie
blazer ['bleɪzər] *n* blazer *m*
bleach [bliːtʃ] *n* (*also:* **household ~**) eau *f* de Javel ♦ *vt* (*linen etc*) blanchir; **~ed** *adj* (*hair*) oxygéné(e), décoloré(e)
bleak [bliːk] *adj* morne; (*countryside*) désolé(e)
bleat [bliːt] *vi* bêler
bleed [bliːd] (*pt, pp* **bled**) *vt, vi* saigner; **my nose is ~ing** je saigne du nez
bleeper ['bliːpər] *n* (*device*) bip *m*
blemish ['blɛmɪʃ] *n* défaut *m*; (*on fruit, reputation*) tache *f*
blend [blɛnd] *n* mélange *m* ♦ *vt* mélanger ♦ *vi* (*colours etc: also:* **~ in**) se mélanger, se fondre; **~er** *n* mixeur *m*
bless [blɛs] (*pt, pp* **blessed** *or* **blest**) *vt* bénir; **~ you!** (*after sneeze*) à vos souhaits!; **~ing** *n* bénédiction *f*; (*godsend*) bienfait *m*
blew [bluː] *pt of* **blow**
blight [blaɪt] *vt* (*hopes etc*) anéantir; (*life*) briser
blimey ['blaɪmɪ] (*BRIT: inf*) *excl* mince alors!
blind [blaɪnd] *adj* aveugle ♦ *n* (*for window*) store *m* ♦ *vt* aveugler; **~ alley** *n* impasse *f*; **~ corner** (*BRIT*) *n* virage *m* sans visibilité; **~fold** *n* bandeau *m* ♦ *adj, adv* les yeux bandés ♦ *vt* bander les yeux à; **~ly** *adv* aveuglément; **~ness** *n* cécité *f*; **~ spot** *n* (*AUT etc*) angle mort; **that is her ~ spot** (*fig*) elle refuse d'y voir clair sur ce point
blink [blɪŋk] *vi* cligner des yeux; (*light*) clignoter; **~ers** *npl* œillères *fpl*
bliss [blɪs] *n* félicité *f*, bonheur *m* sans mélange
blister ['blɪstər] *n* (*on skin*) ampoule *f*, cloque *f*; (*on paintwork, rubber*) boursouflure *f* ♦ *vi* (*paint*) se boursoufler, se cloquer
blizzard ['blɪzəd] *n* blizzard *m*, tempête *f* de neige
bloated ['bləutɪd] *adj* (*face*) bouffi(e); (*stomach, person*) gonflé(e)
blob [blɔb] *n* (*drop*) goutte *f*; (*stain, spot*) tache *f*
block [blɔk] *n* bloc *m*; (*in pipes*) obstruction *f*; (*toy*) cube *m*; (*of buildings*) pâté *m* (de maisons) ♦ *vt* bloquer; (*fig*) faire obstacle à; **~ of flats** (*BRIT*) immeuble (locatif); **mental ~** trou *m* de mémoire; **~ade** [blɔ'keɪd] *n* blocus *m*; **~age** *n* obstruction *f*; **~buster** *n* (*film, book*) grand succès; **~ letters** *npl* majuscules *fpl*
bloke [bləuk] (*BRIT: inf*) *n* type *m*
blond(e) [blɔnd] *adj, n* blond(e)
blood [blʌd] *n* sang *m*; **~ donor** *n* donneur(-euse) de sang; **~ group** *n* groupe sanguin; **~hound** *n* limier *m*; **~ poisoning** *n* empoisonnement *m* du sang; **~ pressure** *n* tension *f* (artérielle); **~shed** *n* effusion *f* de sang, carna-

ge *m*; ~ **sports** *npl* sports *mpl* sanguinaires; **~shot** *adj*: **~shot eyes** yeux injectés de sang; **~stream** *n* sang *m*, système sanguin; ~ **test** *n* prise *f* de sang; **~thirsty** *adj* sanguinaire; ~ **vessel** *n* vaisseau sanguin; **~y** *adj* sanglant(e); (*nose*) en sang; (*BRIT*: *inf!*): **this ~y** ... ce foutu ... (*!*), ce putain de ... (*!*); **~y strong/good** vachement *or* sacrément fort/bon; **~y-minded** (*BRIT*: *inf*) *adj* contrariant(e), obstiné(e)

bloom [bluːm] *n* fleur *f* ♦ *vi* être en fleur

blossom [ˈblɔsəm] *n* fleur(s) *f(pl)* ♦ *vi* être en fleurs; (*fig*) s'épanouir; **to ~ into** devenir

blot [blɔt] *n* tache *f* ♦ *vt* tacher; ~ **out** *vt* (*memories*) effacer; (*view*) cacher, masquer

blotchy [ˈblɔtʃɪ] *adj* (*complexion*) couvert(e) de marbrures

blotting paper [ˈblɔtɪŋ-] *n* buvard *m*

blouse [blauz] *n* chemisier *m*, corsage *m*

blow [bləu] (*pt* **blew**, *pp* **blown**) *n* coup *m* ♦ *vi* souffler ♦ *vt* souffler; (*fuse*) faire sauter; (*instrument*) jouer de; **to ~ one's nose** se moucher; **to ~ a whistle** siffler; ~ **away** *vt* chasser, faire s'envoler; ~ **down** *vt* faire tomber, renverser; ~ **off** *vt* emporter; ~ **out** *vi* (*fire, flame*) s'éteindre; ~ **over** *vi* s'apaiser; ~ **up** *vt* faire sauter; (*tyre*) gonfler; (*PHOT*) agrandir ♦ *vi* exploser, sauter; **~-dry** *n* brushing *m*; **~lamp** (*BRIT*) *n* chalumeau *m*; **~-out** *n* (*of tyre*) éclatement *m*; **~-torch** *n* = **blowlamp**

blue [bluː] *adj* bleu(e); (*fig*) triste; **~s** *n* (*MUS*): **the ~s** le blues; ~ **film/joke** film *m*/histoire *f* pornographique; **to come out of the ~** (*fig*) être complètement inattendu; **~bell** *n* jacinthe *f* des bois; **~bottle** *n* mouche *f* à viande; **~print** *n* (*fig*) projet *m*, plan directeur

bluff [blʌf] *vi* bluffer ♦ *n* bluff *m*; **to call sb's ~** mettre qn au défi d'exécuter ses menaces

blunder [ˈblʌndə^r] *n* gaffe *f*, bévue *f* ♦ *vi* faire une gaffe *or* une bévue

blunt [blʌnt] *adj* (*person*) brusque, ne mâchant pas ses mots; (*knife*) émoussé(e), peu tranchant(e); (*pencil*) mal taillé

blur [bləː^r] *n* tache *or* masse floue *or* confuse ♦ *vt* brouiller

blush [blʌʃ] *vi* rougir ♦ *n* rougeur *f*

blustery [ˈblʌstərɪ] *adj* (*weather*) à bourrasques

boar [bɔː^r] *n* sanglier *m*

board [bɔːd] *n* planche *f*; (*on wall*) panneau *m*; (*for chess*) échiquier *m*; (*cardboard*) carton *m*; (*committee*) conseil *m*, comité *m*; (*in firm*) conseil d'administration; (*NAUT, AVIAT*): **on ~** à bord ♦ *vt* (*ship*) monter à bord de; (*train*) monter dans; **full ~** (*BRIT*) pension complète; **half ~** demi-pension *f*; ~ **and lodging** chambre *f* avec pension; **which goes by the ~** (*fig*) qu'on laisse tomber, qu'on abandonne; ~ **up** *vt* (*door, window*) boucher; **~er** *n* (*SCOL*) interne *m/f*, pensionnaire; ~ **game** *n* jeu *m* de société; **~ing card** *n* = **boarding pass**; **~ing house** *n* pension *f*; **~ing pass** *n* (*AVIAT, NAUT*) carte *f* d'embarquement; **~ing school** *n* internat *m*, pensionnat *m*; ~ **room** *n* salle *f* du conseil d'administration

boast [bəust] *vi*: **to ~ (about** *or* **of)** se vanter (de)

boat [bəut] *n* bateau *m*; (*small*) canot *m*; barque *f*; ~ **train** *n* train *m* (qui assue correspondance avec le ferry)

bob [bɔb] *vi* (*boat, cork on water*: *also*: ~ **up and down**) danser, se balancer

bobby [ˈbɔbɪ] (*BRIT*: *inf*) *n* ≃ agent *m* (de police)

bobsleigh [ˈbɔbsleɪ] *n* bob *m*

bode [bəud] *vi*: **to ~ well/ill (for)** être de bon/mauvais augure (pour)

bodily [ˈbɔdɪlɪ] *adj* corporel(le) ♦ *adv* dans ses bras

body [ˈbɔdɪ] *n* corps *m*; (*of car*) carrosserie *f*; (*of plane*) fuselage *m*; (*fig*: *soci-*

ety) organe *m*, organisme *m*; (: *quantity*) ensemble *m*, masse *f*; (*of wine*) corps; **~-building** *n* culturisme *m*; **~guard** *n* garde *m* du corps; **~work** *n* carrosserie *f*

bog [bɔg] *n* tourbière *f* ♦ *vt*: **to get ~ged down** (*fig*) s'enliser

bog-standard (*inf*) *adj* tout à fait ordinaire

bogus ['bəugəs] *adj* bidon *inv*; fantôme

boil [bɔɪl] *vt* (faire) bouillir ♦ *vi* bouillir ♦ *n* (MED) furoncle *m*; **to come to the** (*BRIT*) **~** *or* **a** (*US*) **~** bouillir; **~ down to** *vt fus* (*fig*) se réduire *or* ramener à; **~ over** *vi* déborder; **~ed egg** *n* œuf *m* à la coque; **~ed potatoes** *npl* pommes *fpl* à l'anglaise *or* à l'eau; **~er** *n* chaudière *f*; **~ing point** *n* point *m* d'ébullition

boisterous ['bɔɪstərəs] *adj* bruyant(e), tapageur(-euse)

bold [bəuld] *adj* hardi(e), audacieux(-euse); (*pej*) effronté(e); (*outline, colour*) franc (franche), tranché(e), marqué(e); (*pattern*) grand(e)

bollard ['bɔləd] (BRIT) *n* (AUT) borne lumineuse *or* de signalisation

bolt [bəult] *n* (*lock*) verrou *m*; (*with nut*) boulon *m* ♦ *adv*: **~ upright** droit(e) comme un piquet ♦ *vt* verrouiller; (TECH: *also*: **~ on, ~ together**) boulonner; (*food*) engloutir ♦ *vi* (*horse*) s'emballer

bomb [bɔm] *n* bombe *f* ♦ *vt* bombarder; **~ing** *n* (*by terrorist*) attentat *m* à la bombe; **~ disposal unit** *n* section *f* de déminage; **~er** *n* (AVIAT) bombardier *m*; **~shell** *n* (*fig*) bombe *f*

bond [bɔnd] *n* lien *m*; (*binding promise*) engagement *m*, obligation *f*; (COMM) obligation; **in ~** (*of goods*) en douane

bondage ['bɔndɪdʒ] *n* esclavage *m*

bone [bəun] *n* os *m*; (*of fish*) arête *f* ♦ *vt* désosser; ôter les arêtes de; **~ dry** *adj* complètement sec (sèche); **~ idle** *adj* fainéant(e); **~ marrow** *n* moelle *f* osseuse

bonfire ['bɔnfaɪə^r] *n* feu *m* (de joie); (*for rubbish*) feu

bonnet ['bɔnɪt] *n* bonnet *m*; (BRIT: *of car*) capot *m*

bonus ['bəunəs] *n* prime *f*, gratification *f*

bony ['bəunɪ] *adj* (*arm, face*, MED: *tissue*) osseux(-euse); (*meat*) plein(e) d'os; (*fish*) plein d'arêtes

boo [bu:] *excl* hou!, peuh! ♦ *vt* huer

booby trap ['bu:bɪ-] *n* engin piégé

book [buk] *n* livre *m*; (*of stamps, tickets*) carnet *m* ♦ *vt* (*ticket*) prendre; (*seat, room*) réserver; (*driver*) dresser un procès-verbal à; (*football player*) prendre le nom de; **~s** *npl* (*accounts*) comptes *mpl*, comptabilité *f*; **~case** *n* bibliothèque *f* (*meuble*); **~ing office** (BRIT) *n* bureau *m* de location; **~-keeping** *n* comptabilité *f*; **~let** *n* brochure *f*; **~maker** *n* bookmaker *m*; **~seller** *n* libraire *m/f*; **~shelf** *n* (*single*) étagère *f* (à livres); **~shop** *n* librairie *f*; **~store** *n* librairie *f*

boom [bu:m] *n* (*noise*) grondement *m*; (*in prices, population*) forte augmentation ♦ *vi* gronder; prospérer

boon [bu:n] *n* bénédiction *f*, grand avantage

boost [bu:st] *n* stimulant *m*, remontant *m* ♦ *vt* stimuler; **~er** *n* (MED) rappel *m*

boot [bu:t] *n* botte *f*; (*for hiking*) chaussure *f* (de marche); (*for football etc*) soulier *m*; (BRIT: *of car*) coffre *m* ♦ *vt* (COMPUT) amorcer, initialiser; **to ~** (*in addition*) par-dessus le marché

booth [bu:ð] *n* (*at fair*) baraque (foraine); (*telephone etc*) cabine *f*; (*also*: **voting ~**) isoloir *m*

booze [bu:z] (*inf*) *n* boissons *fpl* alcooliques, alcool *m*

border ['bɔ:də^r] *n* bordure *f*; bord *m*; (*of a country*) frontière *f* ♦ *vt* border; (*also*: **~ on**: *country*) être limitrophe de; **B~s** *n* (GEO): **the B~s** *la région frontière entre l'Écosse et l'Angleterre*; **~ on** *vt fus* être voisin(e) de, toucher à; **~line** *n* (*fig*) ligne *f* de démarcation; **~line case**

cas *m* limite

bore [bɔːʳ] *pt of* **bear** ♦ *vt* (*hole*) percer; (*oil well, tunnel*) creuser; (*person*) ennuyer, raser ♦ *n* raseur(-euse); (*of gun*) calibre *m*; **to be ~d** s'ennuyer; **~dom** *n* ennui *m*; **boring** *adj* ennuyeux(-euse)

born [bɔːn] *adj*: **to be ~** naître; **I was ~ in 1960** je suis né en 1960

borne [bɔːn] *pp of* **bear**

borough ['bʌrə] *n* municipalité *f*

borrow ['bɔrəu] *vt*: **to ~ sth (from sb)** emprunter qch (à qn)

Bosnia (and) Herzegovina ['bɔznɪə(ənd)həːtsəgəu'viːnə] *n* Bosnie-Herzégovine *f*; **Bosnian** *adj* bosniaque, bosnien(ne) ♦ *n* Bosniaque *m/f*

bosom ['buzəm] *n* poitrine *f*; (*fig*) sein *m*

boss [bɔs] *n* patron(ne) ♦ *vt* (*also:* **~ around/about**) mener à la baguette; **~y** *adj* autoritaire

bosun ['bəusn] *n* maître *m* d'équipage

botany ['bɔtənɪ] *n* botanique *f*

botch [bɔtʃ] *vt* (*also:* **~ up**) saboter, bâcler

both [bəuθ] *adj* les deux, l'un(e) et l'autre ♦ *pron*: **~ (of them)** les deux, tous (toutes) (les) deux, l'un(e) et l'autre; **they sell ~ the fabric and the finished curtains** ils vendent (et) le tissu et les rideaux (finis), ils vendent à la fois le tissu et les rideaux (finis); **~ of us went, we ~ went** nous y sommes allés (tous) les deux

bother ['bɔðəʳ] *vt* (*worry*) tracasser; (*disturb*) déranger ♦ *vi* (*also:* **~ o.s.**) se tracasser, se faire du souci ♦ *n*: **it is a ~ to have to do** c'est vraiment ennuyeux d'avoir à faire; **it's no ~** aucun problème; **to ~ doing** prendre la peine de faire

bottle ['bɔtl] *n* bouteille *f*; (*baby's*) biberon *m* ♦ *vt* mettre en bouteille(s); **~d beer** bière *f* en canette; **~d water** eau minérale; **~ up** *vt* refouler, contenir; **~ bank** *n* conteneur *m* à verre; **~neck** *n* étranglement *m*; **~-opener** *n* ouvre-bouteille *m*

bottom ['bɔtəm] *n* (*of container, sea etc*) fond *m*; (*buttocks*) derrière *m*; (*of page, list*) bas *m* ♦ *adj* du fond; du bas; **the ~ of the class** le dernier de la classe

bough [bau] *n* branche *f*, rameau *m*

bought [bɔːt] *pt, pp of* **buy**

boulder ['bəuldəʳ] *n* gros rocher

bounce [bauns] *vi* (*ball*) rebondir; (*cheque*) être refusé(e) (*étant sans provision*) ♦ *vt* faire rebondir ♦ *n* (*rebound*) rebond *m*; **~r** (*inf*) *n* (*at dance, club*) videur *m*

bound [baund] *pt, pp of* **bind** ♦ *n* (*gen pl*) limite *f*; (*leap*) bond *m* ♦ *vi* (*leap*) bondir ♦ *vt* (*limit*) borner ♦ *adj*: **to be ~ to do sth** (*obliged*) être obligé(e) *or* avoir obligation de faire qch; **he's ~ to fail** (*likely*) il est sûr d'échouer, son échec est inévitable *or* assuré; **~ by** (*law, regulation*) engagé(e) par; **~ for** à destination de; **out of ~s** dont l'accès est interdit

boundary ['baundrɪ] *n* frontière *f*

bout [baut] *n* période *f*; (*of malaria etc*) accès *m*, crise *f*, attaque *f*; (*BOXING etc*) combat *m*, match *m*

bow¹ [bəu] *n* nœud *m*; (*weapon*) arc *m*; (*MUS*) archet *m*

bow² [bau] *n* (*with body*) révérence *f*, inclination *f* (du buste *or* corps); (*NAUT: also:* **~s**) proue *f* ♦ *vi* faire une révérence, s'incliner; (*yield*): **to ~ to** *or* **before** s'incliner devant, se soumettre à

bowels ['bauəlz] *npl* intestins *mpl*; (*fig*) entrailles *fpl*

bowl [bəul] *n* (*for eating*) bol *m*; (*ball*) boule *f* ♦ *vi* (*CRICKET, BASEBALL*) lancer (la balle)

bow-legged ['bəu'lɛgɪd] *adj* aux jambes arquées

bowler ['bəuləʳ] *n* (*CRICKET, BASEBALL*) lanceur *m* (de la balle); (*BRIT: also:* **~ hat**) (chapeau *m*) melon *m*

bowling ['bəulɪŋ] *n* (*game*) jeu *m* de boules; jeu *m* de quilles; **~ alley** *n* bowling *m*; **~ green** *n* terrain *m* de boules (*gazonné et carré*)

bowls [bəulz] *n* (*game*) (jeu *m* de) boules *fpl*

bow tie [bəu-] *n* nœud *m* papillon

box [bɔks] *n* boîte *f*; (*also*: **cardboard ~**) carton *m*; (*THEATRE*) loge *f* ♦ *vt* mettre en boîte; (*SPORT*) boxer avec ♦ *vi* boxer, faire de la boxe; **~er** *n* (*person*) boxeur *m*; **~er shorts** *npl* caleçon *msg*; **~ing** *n* (*SPORT*) boxe *f*; **B~ing Day** (*BRIT*) *n* le lendemain de Noël; **~ing gloves** *npl* gants *mpl* de boxe; **~ing ring** *n* ring *m*; **~ office** *n* bureau *m* de location; **~room** *n* débarras *m*; chambrette *f*

Boxing Day

Boxing Day *est le lendemain de Noël, férié en Grande-Bretagne. Si Noël tombe un samedi, le jour férié est reculé jusqu'au lundi suivant. Ce nom vient d'une coutume du XIXe siècle qui consistait à donner des cadeaux de Noël (dans des boîtes) à ses employés etc le 26 décembre.*

boy [bɔɪ] *n* garçon *m*

boycott ['bɔɪkɔt] *n* boycottage *m* ♦ *vt* boycotter

boyfriend ['bɔɪfrɛnd] *n* (petit) ami

boyish ['bɔɪɪʃ] *adj* (*behaviour*) de garçon; (*girl*) garçonnier(-ière)

BR *n abbr* = **British Rail**

bra [brɑː] *n* soutien-gorge *m*

brace [breɪs] *n* (*on teeth*) appareil *m* (dentaire); (*tool*) vilbrequin *m* ♦ *vt* (*knees, shoulders*) appuyer; **~s** *npl* (*BRIT: for trousers*) bretelles *fpl*; **to ~ o.s.** (*lit*) s'arc-bouter; (*fig*) se préparer mentalement

bracelet ['breɪslɪt] *n* bracelet *m*

bracing ['breɪsɪŋ] *adj* tonifiant(e), tonique

bracket ['brækɪt] *n* (*TECH*) tasseau *m*, support *m*; (*group*) classe *f*, tranche *f*; (*also*: **brace ~**) accolade *f*; (*also*: **round ~**) parenthèse *f*; (*also*: **square ~**) crochet *m* ♦ *vt* mettre entre parenthèse(s); (*fig*: *also*: **~ together**) regrouper

brag [bræg] *vi* se vanter

braid [breɪd] *n* (*trimming*) galon *m*; (*of hair*) tresse *f*

brain [breɪn] *n* cerveau *m*; **~s** *npl* (*intellect, CULIN*) cervelle *f*; **he's got ~s** il est intelligent; **~wash** *vt* faire subir un lavage de cerveau à; **~wave** *n* idée géniale; **~y** *adj* intelligent(e), doué(e)

braise [breɪz] *vt* braiser

brake [breɪk] *n* (*on vehicle, also fig*) frein *m* ♦ *vi* freiner; **~ light** *n* feu *m* de stop

bran [bræn] *n* son *m*

branch [brɑːntʃ] *n* branche *f*; (*COMM*) succursale *f* ♦ *vi* bifurquer; **~ out** *vi* (*fig*): **to ~ out into** étendre ses activités à

brand [brænd] *n* marque (commerciale) ♦ *vt* (*cattle*) marquer (au fer rouge); **~-new** *adj* tout(e) neuf (neuve), flambant neuf (neuve)

brandy ['brændɪ] *n* cognac *m*, fine *f*

brash [bræʃ] *adj* effronté(e)

brass [brɑːs] *n* cuivre *m* (jaune), laiton *m*; **the ~** (*MUS*) les cuivres; **~ band** *n* fanfare *f*

brat [bræt] (*pej*) *n* mioche *m/f*, môme *m/f*

brave [breɪv] *adj* courageux(-euse), brave ♦ *n* guerrier indien ♦ *vt* braver, affronter; **~ry** *n* bravoure *f*, courage *m*

brawl [brɔːl] *n* rixe *f*, bagarre *f*

brazen ['breɪzn] *adj* impudent(e), effronté(e) ♦ *vt*: **to ~ it out** payer d'effronterie, crâner

brazier ['breɪzɪə^r] *n* brasero *m*

Brazil [brə'zɪl] *n* Brésil *m*

breach [briːtʃ] *vt* ouvrir une brèche dans ♦ *n* (*gap*) brèche *f*; (*breaking*): **~ of contract** rupture *f* de contrat; **~ of the peace** attentat *m* à l'ordre public

bread [brɛd] *n* pain *m*; **~ and butter** *n* tartines (beurrées); (*fig*) subsistance *f*; **~bin** (*BRIT*) *n* boîte *f* à pain; (*bigger*) huche *f* à pain; **~crumbs** *npl* miettes *fpl* de pain; (CULIN) chapelure *f*, panure *f*; **~line** *n*: **to be on the ~line** être sans le sou *or* dans l'indigence

breadth [brɛtθ] *n* largeur *f*; (*fig*) ampleur *f*

breadwinner ['brɛdwɪnəʳ] *n* soutien *m* de famille

break [breɪk] (*pt* **broke**, *pp* **broken**) *vt* casser, briser; (*promise*) rompre; (*law*) violer ♦ *vi* (se) casser, se briser; (*weather*) tourner; (*story, news*) se répandre; (*day*) se lever ♦ *n* (*gap*) brèche *f*; (*fracture*) cassure *f*; (*pause, interval*) interruption *f*, arrêt *m*; (: *short*) pause *f*; (: *at school*) récréation *f*; (*chance*) chance *f*, occasion *f* favorable; **to ~ one's leg** *etc* se casser la jambe *etc*; **to ~ a record** battre un record; **to ~ the news to sb** annoncer la nouvelle à qn; **~ even** rentrer dans ses frais; **~ free** *or* **loose** se dégager, s'échapper; **~ open** (*door etc*) forcer, fracturer; **~ down** *vt* (*figures, data*) décomposer, analyser ♦ *vi* s'effondrer; (MED) faire une dépression (nerveuse); (AUT) tomber en panne; **~ in** *vt* (*horse etc*) dresser ♦ *vi* (*burglar*) entrer par effraction; (*interrupt*) interrompre; **~ into** *vt fus* (*house*) s'introduire *or* pénétrer par effraction dans; **~ off** *vi* (*speaker*) s'interrompre; (*branch*) se rompre; **~ out** *vi* éclater, se déclarer; (*prisoner*) s'évader; **to ~ out in spots** *or* **a rash** avoir une éruption de boutons; **~ up** *vi* (*ship*) se disloquer; (*crowd, meeting*) se disperser, se séparer; (*marriage*) se briser; (SCOL) entrer en vacances ♦ *vt* casser; (*fight etc*) interrompre, faire cesser; **~age** *n* casse *f*; **~down** *n* (AUT) panne *f*; (*in communications, marriage*) rupture *f*; (MED: *also:* **nervous ~down**) dépression (nerveuse); (*of statistics*) ventilation *f*; **~down van** (BRIT) *n* dépanneuse *f*; **~er** *n* brisant *m*

breakfast ['brɛkfəst] *n* petit déjeuner

break: ~-in *n* cambriolage *m*; **~ing and entering** *n* (LAW) effraction *f*; **~through** *n* percée *f*; **~water** *n* brise-lames *m inv*, digue *f*

breast [brɛst] *n* (*of woman*) sein *m*; (*chest, of meat*) poitrine *f*; **~-feed** (*irreg: like* **feed**) *vt, vi* allaiter; **~stroke** *n* brasse *f*

breath [brɛθ] *n* haleine *f*; **out of ~** à bout de souffle, essoufflé(e); **B~alyser** ® ['brɛθəlaɪzəʳ] *n* Alcootest ® *m*

breathe [bri:ð] *vt, vi* respirer; **~ in** *vt, vi* aspirer, inspirer; **~ out** *vt, vi* expirer; **~r** *n* moment *m* de repos *or* de répit; **breathing** *n* respiration *f*

breathless ['brɛθlɪs] *adj* essoufflé(e), haletant(e)

breathtaking ['brɛθteɪkɪŋ] *adj* stupéfiant(e)

breed [bri:d] (*pt,pp* **bred**) *vt* élever, faire l'élevage de ♦ *vi* se reproduire ♦ *n* race *f*, variété *f*; **~ing** *n* (*upbringing*) éducation *f*

breeze [bri:z] *n* brise *f*; **breezy** *adj* frais (fraîche); aéré(e); (*manner etc*) désinvolte, jovial(e)

brevity ['brɛvɪtɪ] *n* brièveté *f*

brew [bru:] *vt* (*tea*) faire infuser; (*beer*) brasser ♦ *vi* (*fig*) se préparer, couver; **~ery** *n* brasserie *f* (*fabrique*)

bribe [braɪb] *n* pot-de-vin *m* ♦ *vt* acheter; soudoyer; **~ry** *n* corruption *f*

brick [brɪk] *n* brique *f*; **~layer** *n* maçon *m*

bridal ['braɪdl] *adj* nuptial(e)

bride [braɪd] *n* mariée *f*, épouse *f*; **~groom** *n* marié *m*, époux *m*; **~smaid** *n* demoiselle *f* d'honneur

bridge [brɪdʒ] *n* pont *m*; (NAUT) passerelle *f* (de commandement); (*of nose*) arête *f*; (CARDS, DENTISTRY) bridge *m* ♦ *vt* (*fig: gap, gulf*) combler

bridle ['braɪdl] *n* bride *f*; **~ path** *n* piste *or* allée cavalière

brief [bri:f] *adj* bref (brève) ♦ *n* (LAW) dossier *m*, cause *f*; (*gen*) tâche *f* ♦ *vt* mettre au courant; **~s** *npl* (*undergarment*) slip *m*; **~case** *n* serviette *f*; porte-documents *m inv*; **~ly** *adv* brièvement

bright [braɪt] *adj* brillant(e); (*room, weather*) clair(e); (*clever: person, idea*) intelligent(e); (*cheerful: colour, person*) vif (vive)
brighten ['braɪtn] (*also:* ~ **up**) *vt* (*room*) éclaircir, égayer; (*event*) égayer ♦ *vi* s'éclaircir; (*person*) retrouver un peu de sa gaieté; (*face*) s'éclairer; (*prospects*) s'améliorer
brilliance ['brɪljəns] *n* éclat *m*
brilliant ['brɪljənt] *adj* brillant(e); (*sunshine, light*) éclatant(e); (*inf: holiday etc*) super
brim [brɪm] *n* bord *m*
brine [braɪn] *n* (CULIN) saumure *f*
bring [brɪŋ] (*pt, pp* **brought**) *vt* apporter; (*person*) amener; ~ **about** *vt* provoquer, entraîner; ~ **back** *vt* rapporter; ramener; (*restore: hanging*) réinstaurer; ~ **down** *vt* (*price*) faire baisser; (*enemy plane*) descendre; (*government*) faire tomber; ~ **forward** *vt* avancer; ~ **off** *vt* (*task, plan*) réussir, mener à bien; ~ **out** *vt* (*meaning*) faire ressortir; (*book*) publier; (*object*) sortir; ~ **round** *vt* (*unconscious person*) ranimer; ~ **up** *vt* (*child*) élever; (*carry up*) monter; (*question*) soulever; (*food: vomit*) vomir, rendre
brink [brɪŋk] *n* bord *m*
brisk [brɪsk] *adj* vif (vive)
bristle ['brɪsl] *n* poil *m* ♦ *vi* se hérisser
Britain ['brɪtən] *n* (*also:* **Great** ~) Grande-Bretagne *f*
British ['brɪtɪʃ] *adj* britannique ♦ *npl*: **the** ~ les Britanniques *mpl*; ~ **Isles** *npl*: **the** ~ **Isles** les Iles *fpl* Britanniques; ~ **Rail** *n compagnie ferroviaire britannique*
Briton ['brɪtən] *n* Britannique *m/f*
Brittany ['brɪtənɪ] *n* Bretagne *f*
brittle ['brɪtl] *adj* cassant(e), fragile
broach [brəutʃ] *vt* (*subject*) aborder
broad [brɔːd] *adj* large; (*general: outlines*) grand(e); (: *distinction*) général(e); (*accent*) prononcé(e); **in** ~ **daylight** en plein jour; ~**cast** (*pt, pp* **broadcast**) *n* émission *f* ♦ *vt* radiodiffuser; téléviser ♦ *vi* émettre; ~**en** *vt* élargir ♦ *vi* s'élargir; **to** ~**en one's mind** élargir ses horizons; ~**ly** *adv* en gros, généralement; ~**-minded** *adj* large d'esprit
broccoli ['brɔkəlɪ] *n* brocoli *m*
brochure ['brəuʃjuə[r]] *n* prospectus *m*, dépliant *m*
broil [brɔɪl] *vt* griller
broke [brəuk] *pt of* **break** ♦ *adj* (*inf*) fauché(e)
broken ['brəukn] *pp of* **break** ♦ *adj* cassé(e); (*machine: also:* ~ **down**) fichu(e); **in** ~ **English/French** dans un anglais/ français approximatif *or* hésitant; ~ **leg** *etc* jambe *etc* cassée; ~**-hearted** *adj* (ayant) le cœur brisé
broker ['brəukə[r]] *n* courtier *m*
brolly ['brɔlɪ] (BRIT: *inf*) *n* pépin *m*, parapluie *m*
bronchitis [brɔŋ'kaɪtɪs] *n* bronchite *f*
bronze [brɔnz] *n* bronze *m*
brooch [brəutʃ] *n* broche *f*
brood [bruːd] *n* couvée *f* ♦ *vi* (*person*) méditer (sombrement), ruminer
broom [brum] *n* balai *m*; (BOT) genêt *m*; ~**stick** *n* manche *m* à balai
Bros. *abbr* = **Brothers**
broth [brɔθ] *n* bouillon *m* de viande et de légumes
brothel ['brɔθl] *n* maison close *m*
brother ['brʌðə[r]] *n* frère *m*; ~**-in-law** *n* beau-frère *m*
brought [brɔːt] *pt, pp of* **bring**
brow [brau] *n* front *m*; (*eyebrow*) sourcil *m*; (*of hill*) sommet *m*
brown [braun] *adj* brun(e), marron *inv*; (*hair*) châtain *inv*, brun; (*eyes*) marron *inv*; (*tanned*) bronzé(e) ♦ *n* (*colour*) brun *m* ♦ *vt* (CULIN) faire dorer; ~ **bread** *n* pain *m* bis; **B~ie** *n* (*also:* **B~ie Guide**) jeannette *f*, éclaireuse (cadette); ~**ie** (US) *n* (*cake*) gâteau *m* au chocolat et aux noix; ~ **paper** *n* papier *m* d'emballage; ~ **sugar** *n* cassonade *f*
browse [brauz] *vi* (*among books*) bouquiner, feuilleter les livres; (COMPUT) surfer *or* naviguer sur le Net; **to** ~

through a book feuilleter un livre
browser ['brauzər] *n* (COMPUT) navigateur *m*
bruise [bru:z] *n* bleu *m*, contusion *f* ♦ *vt* contusionner, meurtrir
brunette [bru:'nɛt] *n* (femme) brune
brunt [brʌnt] *n*: **the ~ of** (*attack, criticism etc*) le plus gros de
brush [brʌʃ] *n* brosse *f*; (*painting*) pinceau *m*; (*shaving*) blaireau *m*; (*quarrel*) accrochage *m*, prise *f* de bec ♦ *vt* brosser; (*also*: **~ against**) effleurer, frôler; **~ aside** *vt* écarter, balayer; **~ up** *vt* (*knowledge*) rafraîchir, réviser; **~wood** *n* broussailles *fpl*, taillis *m*
Brussels ['brʌslz] *n* Bruxelles; **~ sprout** *n* chou *m* de Bruxelles
brutal ['bru:tl] *adj* brutal(e)
brute [bru:t] *n* brute *f* ♦ *adj*: **by ~ force** par la force
BSc *abbr* = **Bachelor of Science**
BSE *n abbr* (= *bovine spongiform encephalopathy*) ESB *f*, BSE *f*
bubble ['bʌbl] *n* bulle *f* ♦ *vi* bouillonner, faire des bulles; (*sparkle*) pétiller; **~ bath** *n* bain moussant; **~ gum** *n* bubblegum *m*
buck [bʌk] *n* mâle *m* (*d'un lapin, daim etc*); (US: *inf*) dollar *m* ♦ *vi* ruer, lancer une ruade; **to pass the ~ (to sb)** se décharger de la responsabilité (sur qn); **~ up** *vi* (*cheer up*) reprendre du poil de la bête, se remonter
bucket ['bʌkɪt] *n* seau *m*

Buckingham Palace

Buckingham Palace est la résidence officielle londonienne du souverain britannique depuis 1762. Construit en 1703, il fut à l'origine le palais du duc de Buckingham. Il a été partiellement reconstruit au début du siècle.

buckle ['bʌkl] *n* boucle *f* ♦ *vt* (*belt etc*) boucler, attacher ♦ *vi* (*warp*) tordre, gauchir; (: *wheel*) se voiler; se déformer
bud [bʌd] *n* bourgeon *m*; (*of flower*) bouton *m* ♦ *vi* bourgeonner; (*flower*) éclore
Buddhism ['budɪzəm] *n* bouddhisme *m*
Buddhist *adj* bouddhiste ♦ *n* Bouddhiste *m/f*
budding ['bʌdɪŋ] *adj* (*poet etc*) en herbe; (*passion etc*) naissant(e)
buddy ['bʌdɪ] (US) *n* copain *m*
budge [bʌdʒ] *vt* faire bouger; (*fig*: *person*) faire changer d'avis ♦ *vi* bouger; changer d'avis
budgerigar ['bʌdʒərɪgɑ:r] (BRIT) *n* perruche *f*
budget ['bʌdʒɪt] *n* budget *m* ♦ *vi*: **to ~ for sth** inscrire qch au budget
budgie ['bʌdʒɪ] (BRIT) *n* = **budgerigar**
buff [bʌf] *adj* (couleur *f*) chamois *m* ♦ *n* (*inf*: *enthusiast*) mordu(e); **he's a ... ~** c'est un mordu de ...
buffalo ['bʌfələu] (*pl* **~** *or* **~es**) *n* buffle *m*; (US) bison *m*
buffer ['bʌfər] *n* tampon *m*; (COMPUT) mémoire *f* tampon
buffet¹ ['bʌfɪt] *vt* secouer, ébranler
buffet² ['bufeɪ] *n* (*food*, BRIT: *bar*) buffet *m*; **~ car** (BRIT) *n* (RAIL) voiture-buffet *f*
bug [bʌg] *n* (*insect*) punaise *f*; (: *gen*) insecte *m*, bestiole *f*; (*fig*: *germ*) virus *m*, microbe *m*; (COMPUT) erreur *f*; (*fig*: *spy device*) dispositif *m* d'écoute (électronique) ♦ *vt* garnir de dispositifs d'écoute; (*inf*: *annoy*) embêter; **~ged** *adj* sur écoute
bugle ['bju:gl] *n* clairon *m*
build [bɪld] (*pt, pp* **built**) *n* (*of person*) carrure *f*, charpente *f* ♦ *vt* construire, bâtir; **~ up** *vt* accumuler, amasser; accroître; **~er** *n* entrepreneur *m*; **~ing** *n* (*trade*) construction *f*; (*house, structure*) bâtiment *m*, construction; (*offices, flats*) immeuble *m*; **~ing society** (BRIT) *n* société *f* de crédit immobilier

building society

Une **building society** *est une mutuelle dont les épargnants et emprunteurs sont les propriétaires. Ces mu-*

tuelles offrent deux services principaux: on peut y avoir un compte d'épargne duquel on peut retirer son argent sur demande ou moyennant un court préavis; et on peut également y faire des emprunts à long terme, par exemple pour acheter une maison.

built [bɪlt] *pt, pp of* **build**; **~-in** ['bɪlt'ɪn] *adj* (*cupboard, oven*) encastré(e); (*device*) incorporé(e); intégré(e); **~-up area** ['bɪltʌp-] *n* zone urbanisée

bulb [bʌlb] *n* (BOT) bulbe *m*, oignon *m*; (ELEC) ampoule *f*

Bulgaria [bʌl'gɛərɪə] *n* Bulgarie *f*

bulge [bʌldʒ] *n* renflement *m*, gonflement *m* ♦ *vi* (*pocket, file etc*) être plein(e) à craquer; (*cheeks*) être gonflé(e)

bulk [bʌlk] *n* masse *f*, volume *m*; (*of person*) corpulence *f*; **in ~** (COMM) en vrac; **the ~ of** la plus grande *or* grosse partie de; **~y** *adj* volumineux(-euse), encombrant(e)

bull [bul] *n* taureau *m*; (*male elephant/whale*) mâle *m*; **~dog** *n* bouledogue *m*

bulldozer ['buldəuzə^r] *n* bulldozer *m*

bullet ['bulɪt] *n* balle *f* (*de fusil etc*)

bulletin ['bulɪtɪn] *n* bulletin *m*, communiqué *m*; (*news ~*) (bulletin d')informations *fpl*; **~ board** *n* (INTERNET) messagerie *f* électronique

bulletproof ['bulɪtpru:f] *adj* (*car*) blindé(e); (*vest etc*) pare-balles *inv*

bullfight ['bulfaɪt] *n* corrida *f*, course *f* de taureaux; **~er** *n* torero *m*; **~ing** *n* tauromachie *f*

bullion ['buljən] *n* or *m or* argent *m* en lingots

bullock ['bulək] *n* bœuf *m*

bullring ['bulrɪŋ] *n* arènes *fpl*

bull's-eye ['bulzaɪ] *n* centre *m* (*de la cible*)

bully ['bulɪ] *n* brute *f*, tyran *m* ♦ *vt* tyranniser, rudoyer

bum [bʌm] *n* (*inf*: *backside*) derrière *m*; (*esp US*: *tramp*) vagabond(e), traîne-savates *m/f inv*

bumblebee ['bʌmblbi:] *n* bourdon *m*

bump [bʌmp] *n* (*in car*: *minor accident*) accrochage *m*; (*jolt*) cahot *m*; (*on road etc, on head*) bosse *f* ♦ *vt* heurter, cogner; **~ into** *vt fus* rentrer dans, tamponner; (*meet*) tomber sur; **~er** *n* pare-chocs *m inv* ♦ *adj*: **~er crop/harvest** récolte/moisson exceptionnelle; **~er cars** (US) *npl* autos tamponneuses; **~y** *adj* cahoteux(-euse)

bun [bʌn] *n* petit pain au lait; (*of hair*) chignon *m*

bunch [bʌntʃ] *n* (*of flowers*) bouquet *m*; (*of keys*) trousseau *m*; (*of bananas*) régime *m*; (*of people*) groupe *m*; **~es** *npl* (*in hair*) couettes *fpl*; **~ of grapes** grappe *f* de raisin

bundle ['bʌndl] *n* paquet *m* ♦ *vt* (*also*: **~ up**) faire un paquet de; (*put*): **to ~ sth/sb into** fourrer *or* enfourner qch/qn dans

bungalow ['bʌŋgələu] *n* bungalow *m*

bungle ['bʌŋgl] *vt* bâcler, gâcher

bunion ['bʌnjən] *n* oignon *m* (*au pied*)

bunk [bʌŋk] *n* couchette *f*; **~ beds** *npl* lits superposés

bunker ['bʌŋkə^r] *n* (*coal store*) soute *f* à charbon; (MIL, GOLF) bunker *m*

bunting ['bʌntɪŋ] *n* pavoisement *m*, drapeaux *mpl*

buoy [bɔɪ] *n* bouée *f*; **~ up** *vt* faire flotter; (*fig*) soutenir, épauler; **~ant** *adj* capable de flotter; (*carefree*) gai(e), plein(e) d'entrain; (*economy*) ferme, actif

burden ['bə:dn] *n* fardeau *m* ♦ *vt* (*trouble*) accabler, surcharger

bureau ['bjuərəu] (*pl* **~x**) *n* (BRIT: *writing desk*) bureau *m*, secrétaire *m*; (US: *chest of drawers*) commode *f*; (*office*) bureau, office *m*; **~cracy** [bjuə'rɔkrəsɪ] *n* bureaucratie *f*

burglar ['bə:glə^r] *n* cambrioleur *m*; **~ alarm** *n* sonnerie *f* d'alarme

Burgundy ['bə:gəndɪ] *n* Bourgogne *f*

burial ['bɛrɪəl] *n* enterrement *m*

burly ['bəːlɪ] *adj* de forte carrure, costaud(e)

Burma ['bəːmə] *n* Birmanie *f*

burn [bəːn] (*pt, pp* **burned** *or* **burnt**) *vt, vi* brûler ♦ *n* brûlure *f*; **~ down** *vt* incendier, détruire par le feu; **~er** *n* brûleur *m*; **~ing** *adj* brûlant(e); (*house*) en flammes; (*ambition*) dévorant(e)

burrow ['bʌrəu] *n* terrier *m* ♦ *vt* creuser

bursary ['bəːsərɪ] (*BRIT*) *n* bourse *f* (d'études)

burst [bəːst] (*pt,pp* **burst**) *vt* crever; faire éclater; (*subj: river: banks etc*) rompre ♦ *vi* éclater; (*tyre*) crever ♦ *n* (*of gunfire*) rafale *f* (de tir); (*also:* **~ pipe**) rupture *f*; fuite *f*; **a ~ of enthusiasm/energy** un accès d'enthousiasme/d'énergie; **to ~ into flames** s'enflammer soudainement; **to ~ out laughing** éclater de rire; **to ~ into tears** fondre en larmes; **to be ~ing with** être plein (à craquer) de; (*fig*) être débordant(e) de; **~ into** *vt fus* (*room etc*) faire irruption dans

bury ['bɛrɪ] *vt* enterrer

bus [bʌs] (*pl* **~es**) *n* autobus *m*

bush [buʃ] *n* buisson *m*; (*scrubland*) brousse *f*; **to beat about the ~** tourner autour du pot; **~y** *adj* broussailleux(-euse), touffu(e)

busily ['bɪzɪlɪ] *adv* activement

business ['bɪznɪs] *n* (*matter, firm*) affaire *f*; (*trading*) affaires *fpl*; (*job, duty*) travail *m*; **to be away on ~** être en déplacement d'affaires; **it's none of my ~** cela ne me regarde pas, ce ne sont pas mes affaires; **he means ~** il ne plaisante pas, il est sérieux; **~like** *adj* (*firm*) sérieux(-euse); (*method*) efficace; **~man** (*irreg*) *n* homme *m* d'affaires; **~ trip** *n* voyage *m* d'affaires; **~woman** (*irreg*) *n* femme *f* d'affaires

busker ['bʌskəʳ] (*BRIT*) *n* musicien ambulant

bus: ~ shelter *n* abribus *m*; **~ station** *n* gare routière; **~ stop** *n* arrêt *m* d'autobus

bust [bʌst] *n* buste *m*; (*measurement*) tour *m* de poitrine ♦ *adj* (*inf: broken*) fichu(e), fini(e); **to go ~** faire faillite

bustle ['bʌsl] *n* remue-ménage *m*, affairement *m* ♦ *vi* s'affairer, se démener; **bustling** *adj* (*town*) bruyant(e), affairé(e)

busy ['bɪzɪ] *adj* occupé(e); (*shop, street*) très fréquenté(e) ♦ *vt*: **to ~ o.s.** s'occuper; **~body** *n* mouche *f* du coche, âme *f* charitable; **~ signal** (*US*) *n* (*TEL*) tonalité *f* occupé *inv*

KEYWORD

but [bʌt] *conj* mais; **I'd love to come, but I'm busy** j'aimerais venir mais je suis occupé

♦ *prep* (*apart from, except*) sauf, excepté; **we've had nothing but trouble** nous n'avons eu que des ennuis; **no-one but him can do it** lui seul peut le faire; **but for you/your help** sans toi/ton aide; **anything but that** tout sauf *or* excepté ça, tout mais pas ça

♦ *adv* (*just, only*) ne ... que; **she's but a child** elle n'est qu'une enfant; **had I but known** si seulement j'avais su; **all but finished** pratiquement terminé

butcher ['butʃəʳ] *n* boucher *m* ♦ *vt* massacrer; (*cattle etc for meat*) tuer; **~'s (shop)** *n* boucherie *f*

butler ['bʌtləʳ] *n* maître *m* d'hôtel

butt [bʌt] *n* (*large barrel*) gros tonneau; (*of gun*) crosse *f*; (*of cigarette*) mégot *m*; (*BRIT: fig: target*) cible *f* ♦ *vt* donner un coup de tête à; **~ in** *vi* (*interrupt*) s'immiscer dans la conversation

butter ['bʌtəʳ] *n* beurre *m* ♦ *vt* beurrer; **~cup** *n* bouton *m* d'or

butterfly ['bʌtəflaɪ] *n* papillon *m*; (*SWIMMING: also:* **~ stroke**) brasse *f* papillon

buttocks ['bʌtəks] *npl* fesses *fpl*

button ['bʌtn] *n* bouton *m*; (*US: badge*) pin *m* ♦ *vt* (*also:* **~ up**) boutonner ♦ *vi* se boutonner

buttress ['bʌtrɪs] *n* contrefort *m*

buy [baɪ] (*pt, pp* **bought**) *vt* acheter ♦ *n* achat *m*; **to ~ sb sth/sth from sb** acheter qch à qn; **to ~ sb a drink** offrir un verre *or* à boire à qn; **~er** *n* acheteur(-euse)

buzz [bʌz] *n* bourdonnement *m*; (*inf: phone call*): **to give sb a ~** passer un coup *m* de fil à qn ♦ *vi* bourdonner; **~er** *n* timbre *m* électrique; **~ word** *n* (*inf*) mot *m* à la mode

KEYWORD

by [baɪ] *prep* **1** (*referring to cause, agent*) par, de; **killed by lightning** tué par la foudre; **surrounded by a fence** entouré d'une barrière; **a painting by Picasso** un tableau de Picasso

2 (*referring to method, manner, means*): **by bus/car** en autobus/voiture; **by train** par le *or* en train; **to pay by cheque** payer par chèque; **by saving hard, he ...** à force d'économiser, il ...

3 (*via, through*) par; **we came by Dover** nous sommes venus par Douvres

4 (*close to, past*) à côté de; **the house by the school** la maison à côté de l'école; **a holiday by the sea** des vacances au bord de la mer; **she sat by his bed** elle était assise à son chevet; **she went by me** elle est passée à côté de moi; **I go by the post office every day** je passe devant la poste tous les jours

5 (*with time: not later than*) avant; (: *during*): **by daylight** à la lumière du jour; **by night** la nuit, de nuit; **by 4 o'clock** avant 4 heures; **by this time tomorrow** d'ici demain à la même heure; **by the time I got here it was too late** lorsque je suis arrivé il était déjà trop tard

6 (*amount*) à; **by the kilo/metre** au kilo/au mètre; **paid by the hour** payé à l'heure

7 (*MATH, measure*): **to divide/multiply by 3** diviser/multiplier par 3; **a room 3 metres by 4** une pièce de 3 mètres sur 4; **it's broader by a metre** c'est plus large d'un mètre; **one by one** un à un; **little by little** petit à petit, peu à peu

8 (*according to*) d'après, selon; **it's 3 o'clock by my watch** il est 3 heures à ma montre; **it's all right by me** je n'ai rien contre

9: (all) by oneself *etc* tout(e) seul(e)

10: by the way au fait, à propos

♦ *adv* **1** *see* **go**; **pass** *etc*

2: by and by un peu plus tard, bientôt; **by and large** dans l'ensemble

bye(-bye) ['baɪ('baɪ)] *excl* au revoir!, salut!

by(e)-law ['baɪlɔː] *n* arrêté municipal

by: ~-election (*BRIT*) *n* élection (législative) partielle; **~gone** *adj* passé(e) ♦ *n*: **let ~gones be ~gones** passons l'éponge, oublions le passé; **~pass** *n* (route *f* de) contournement *m*; (*MED*) pontage *m* ♦ *vt* éviter; **~-product** *n* sous-produit *m*, dérivé *m*; (*fig*) conséquence *f* secondaire, retombée *f*; **~stander** *n* spectateur(-trice), badaud(e)

byte [baɪt] *n* (*COMPUT*) octet *m*

byword ['baɪwəːd] *n*: **to be a ~ for** être synonyme de (*fig*)

C, c

C [siː] *n* (*MUS*) do *m*

CA *abbr* = **chartered accountant**

cab [kæb] *n* taxi *m*; (*of train, truck*) cabine *f*

cabaret ['kæbəreɪ] *n* (*show*) spectacle *m* de cabaret

cabbage ['kæbɪdʒ] *n* chou *m*

cabin ['kæbɪn] *n* (*house*) cabane *f*, hutte *f*; (*on ship*) cabine *f*; (*on plane*) compartiment *m*; **~ crew** *n* (*AVIAT*) équipage *m*; **~ cruiser** *n* cruiser *m*

cabinet ['kæbɪnɪt] *n* (*POL*) cabinet *m*; (*furniture*) petit meuble à tiroirs et

rayons; (*also:* **display ~**) vitrine *f*, petite armoire vitrée
cable ['keɪbl] *n* câble *m* ♦ *vt* câbler, télégraphier; **~-car** *n* téléphérique *m*; **~ television** *n* télévision *f* par câble
cache [kæʃ] *n* stock *m*
cackle ['kækl] *vi* caqueter
cactus ['kæktəs] (*pl* **cacti**) *n* cactus *m*
cadet [kə'dɛt] *n* (MIL) élève *m* officier
cadge [kædʒ] (*inf*) *vt*: **to ~ (from** *or* **off)** se faire donner (par)
Caesarian [sɪ'zɛərɪən] *n* (*also:* **~ section**) césarienne *f*
café ['kæfeɪ] *n* ≃ café(-restaurant) *m* (*sans alcool*)
cage [keɪdʒ] *n* cage *f*
cagey ['keɪdʒɪ] (*inf*) *adj* réticent(e); méfiant(e)
cagoule [kə'gu:l] *n* K-way ® *m*
Cairo ['kaɪərəu] *n* le Caire
cajole [kə'dʒəul] *vt* couvrir de flatteries *or* de gentillesses
cake [keɪk] *n* gâteau *m*; **~d** *adj*: **~d with** raidi(e) par, couvert(e) d'une croûte de
calculate ['kælkjuleɪt] *vt* calculer; (*estimate*: *chances, effect*) évaluer; **calculation** *n* calcul *m*; **calculator** *n* machine *f* à calculer, calculatrice *f*; (*pocket*) calculette *f*
calendar ['kæləndəʳ] *n* calendrier *m*; **~ year** *n* année civile
calf [kɑ:f] (*pl* **calves**) *n* (*of cow*) veau *m*; (*of other animals*) petit *m*; (*also:* **~skin**) veau *m*, vachette *f*; (ANAT) mollet *m*
calibre ['kælɪbəʳ] (US **caliber**) *n* calibre *m*
call [kɔ:l] *vt* appeler; (*meeting*) convoquer ♦ *vi* appeler; (*visit*: *also:* **~ in, ~ round**) passer ♦ *n* (*shout*) appel *m*, cri *m*; (*also:* **telephone ~**) coup *m* de téléphone; (*visit*) visite *f*; **she's ~ed Suzanne** elle s'appelle Suzanne; **to be on ~** être de permanence; **~ back** *vi* (*return*) repasser; (TEL) rappeler; **~ for** *vt fus* (*demand*) demander; (*fetch*) passer prendre; **~ off** *vt* annuler; **~ on** *vt fus* (*visit*) rendre visite à, passer voir; (*request*): **to ~ on sb to do** inviter qn à faire; **~ out** *vi* pousser un cri *or* des cris; **~ up** *vt* (MIL) appeler, mobiliser; (TEL) appeler; **~box** (BRIT) *n* (TEL) cabine *f* téléphonique; **~ centre** *n* centre *m* d'appels; **~er** *n* (TEL) personne *f* qui appelle; (*visitor*) visiteur *m*; **~ girl** *n* call-girl *f*; **~-in** (US) *n* (RADIO, TV: *phone-in*) programme *m* à ligne ouverte; **~ing** *n* vocation *f*; (*trade, occupation*) état *m*; **~ing card** (US) *n* carte *f* de visite
callous ['kæləs] *adj* dur(e), insensible
calm [kɑ:m] *adj* calme ♦ *n* calme *m* ♦ *vt* calmer, apaiser; **~ down** *vi* se calmer ♦ *vt* calmer, apaiser
Calor gas ® ['kæləʳ-] *n* butane *m*, butagaz *m* ®
calorie ['kælərɪ] *n* calorie *f*
calves [kɑ:vz] *npl of* **calf**
camber ['kæmbəʳ] *n* (*of road*) bombement *m*
Cambodia [kæm'bəudɪə] *n* Cambodge *m*
camcorder ['kæmkɔ:dəʳ] *n* caméscope *m*
came [keɪm] *pt of* **come**
camel ['kæməl] *n* chameau *m*
camera ['kæmərə] *n* (PHOT) appareil-photo *m*; (*also:* **cine-~, movie ~**) caméra *f*; **in ~** à huis clos; **~man** (*irreg*) *n* caméraman *m*
camouflage ['kæməflɑ:ʒ] *n* camouflage *m* ♦ *vt* camoufler
camp [kæmp] *n* camp *m* ♦ *vi* camper ♦ *adj* (*man*) efféminé(e)
campaign [kæm'peɪn] *n* (MIL, POL *etc*) campagne *f* ♦ *vi* faire campagne
camp: ~bed (BRIT) *n* lit *m* de camp; **~er** *n* campeur(-euse); (*vehicle*) camping-car *m*; **~ing** *n* camping *m*; **to go ~ing** faire du camping; **~ing gas** ® *n* butane *m*; **~site** *n* campement *m*, (terrain *m* de) camping *m*
campus ['kæmpəs] *n* campus *m*
can¹ [kæn] *n* (*of milk, oil, water*) bidon *m*; (*tin*) boîte *f* de conserve ♦ *vt* mettre en conserve

KEYWORD

can² [kæn] (*negative* **cannot, can't,** *conditional and pt* **could**) *aux vb* **1** (*be able to*) pouvoir; **you can do it if you try** vous pouvez le faire si vous essayez; **I can't hear you** je ne t'entends pas

2 (*know how to*) savoir; **I can swim/play tennis/drive** je sais nager/jouer au tennis/conduire; **can you speak French?** parlez-vous français?

3 (*may*) pouvoir; **can I use your phone?** puis-je me servir de votre téléphone?

4 (*expressing disbelief, puzzlement etc*): **it can't be true!** ce n'est pas possible!; **what CAN he want?** qu'est-ce qu'il peut bien vouloir?

5 (*expressing possibility, suggestion etc*): **he could be in the library** il est peut-être dans la bibliothèque; **she could have been delayed** il se peut qu'elle ait été retardée

Canada ['kænədə] *n* Canada *m*; **Canadian** [kə'neɪdɪən] *adj* canadien(ne) ♦ *n* Canadien(ne)

canal [kə'næl] *n* canal *m*

canapé ['kænəpeɪ] *n* canapé *m*

canary [kə'nɛərɪ] *n* canari *m*, serin *m*

cancel ['kænsəl] *vt* annuler; (*train*) supprimer; (*party, appointment*) décommander; (*cross out*) barrer, rayer; **~lation** [kænsə'leɪʃən] *n* annulation *f*; suppression *f*

cancer ['kænsə^r^] *n* (MED) cancer *m*; **C~** (ASTROLOGY) le Cancer

candid ['kændɪd] *adj* (très) franc (franche), sincère

candidate ['kændɪdeɪt] *n* candidat(e)

candle ['kændl] *n* bougie *f*; (*of tallow*) chandelle *f*; (*in church*) cierge *m*; **~light** *n*: **by ~light** à la lumière d'une bougie; (*dinner*) aux chandelles; **~stick** *n* (*also:* **~ holder**) bougeoir *m*; (*bigger, ornate*) chandelier *m*

candour ['kændə^r^] (US **candor**) *n* (grande) franchise *or* sincérité

candy ['kændɪ] *n* sucre candi; (US) bonbon *m*; **~-floss** (BRIT) *n* barbe *f* à papa

cane [keɪn] *n* canne *f*; (*for furniture, baskets etc*) rotin *m* ♦ *vt* (BRIT: SCOL) administrer des coups de bâton à

canister ['kænɪstə^r^] *n* boîte *f*; (*of gas, pressurized substance*) bombe *f*

cannabis ['kænəbɪs] *n* (*drug*) cannabis *m*

canned [kænd] *adj* (*food*) en boîte, en conserve

cannon ['kænən] (*pl* **~** *or* **~s**) *n* (*gun*) canon *m*

cannot ['kænɔt] = **can not**

canoe [kə'nu:] *n* pirogue *f*; (SPORT) canoë *m*; **~ing** *n*: **to go ~ing** faire du canoë

canon ['kænən] *n* (*clergyman*) chanoine *m*; (*standard*) canon *m*

can-opener ['kænəupnə^r^] *n* ouvre-boîte *m*

canopy ['kænəpɪ] *n* baldaquin *m*; dais *m*

can't [kænt] = **cannot**

canteen [kæn'ti:n] *n* cantine *f*; (BRIT: *of cutlery*) ménagère *f*

canter ['kæntə^r^] *vi* (*horse*) aller au petit galop

canvas ['kænvəs] *n* toile *f*

canvass ['kænvəs] *vi* (POL): **to ~ for** faire campagne pour ♦ *vt* (*investigate: opinions etc*) sonder

canyon ['kænjən] *n* cañon *m*, gorge (profonde)

cap [kæp] *n* casquette *f*; (*of pen*) capuchon *m*; (*of bottle*) capsule *f*; (*contraceptive: also:* **Dutch ~**) diaphragme *m*; (*for toy gun*) amorce *f* ♦ *vt* (*outdo*) surpasser; (*put limit on*) plafonner

capability [keɪpə'bɪlɪtɪ] *n* aptitude *f*, capacité *f*

capable ['keɪpəbl] *adj* capable

capacity [kə'pæsɪtɪ] *n* capacité *f*; (*capability*) aptitude *f*; (*of factory*) rendement *m*

cape [keɪp] *n* (*garment*) cape *f*; (GEO)

cap *m*
caper ['keɪpə^r] *n* (*CULIN*: *gen pl*) câpre *f*; (*prank*) farce *f*
capital ['kæpɪtl] *n* (*also:* **~ city**) capitale *f*; (*money*) capital *m*; (*also:* **~ letter**) majuscule *f*; **~ gains tax** *n* (*COMM*) impôt *m* sur les plus-values; **~ism** *n* capitalisme *m*; **~ist** *adj* capitaliste ♦ *n* capitaliste *m/f*; **~ize** ['kæpɪtəlaɪz] *vi*: **to ~ize on** tirer parti de; **~ punishment** *n* peine capitale

Capitol

Le Capitol *est le siège du* Congress, *à Washington. Il est situé sur Capitol Hill.*

Capricorn ['kæprɪkɔ:n] *n* le Capricorne
capsize [kæp'saɪz] *vt* faire chavirer ♦ *vi* chavirer
capsule ['kæpsju:l] *n* capsule *f*
captain ['kæptɪn] *n* capitaine *m*
caption ['kæpʃən] *n* légende *f*
captive ['kæptɪv] *adj*, *n* captif(-ive)
capture ['kæptʃə^r] *vt* capturer, prendre; (*attention*) capter; (*COMPUT*) saisir ♦ *n* capture *f*; (*data* ~) saisie *f* de données
car [kɑ:^r] *n* voiture *f*, auto *f*; (*RAIL*) wagon *m*, voiture
caramel ['kærəməl] *n* caramel *m*
caravan ['kærəvæn] *n* caravane *f*; **~ning** *n*: **to go ~ning** faire du caravaning; **~ site** (*BRIT*) *n* camping *m* pour caravanes
carbohydrate [kɑ:bəu'haɪdreɪt] *n* hydrate *m* de carbone; (*food*) féculent *m*
carbon ['kɑ:bən] *n* carbone *m*; **~ dioxide** *n* gaz *m* carbonique; **~ monoxide** *n* oxyde *m* de carbone; **~ paper** *n* papier *m* carbone
car boot sale *n marché aux puces où les particuliers vendent des objets entreposés dans le coffre de leur voiture*
carburettor [kɑ:bju'rɛtə^r] (*US* **carburetor**) *n* carburateur *m*
card [kɑ:d] *n* carte *f*; (*material*) carton *m*; **~board** *n* carton *m*; **~ game** *n* jeu *m* de cartes
cardiac ['kɑ:dɪæk] *adj* cardiaque
cardigan ['kɑ:dɪgən] *n* cardigan *m*
cardinal ['kɑ:dɪnl] *adj* cardinal(e) ♦ *n* cardinal *m*
card index *n* fichier *m*
cardphone *n* téléphone *m* à carte
care [kɛə^r] *n* soin *m*, attention *f*; (*worry*) souci *m*; (*charge*) charge *f*, garde *f* ♦ *vi*: **to ~ about** se soucier de, s'intéresser à; (*person*) être attaché(e) à; **~ of** chez, aux bons soins de; **in sb's ~** à la garde de qn, confié(e) à qn; **to take ~ (to do)** faire attention (à faire); **to take ~ of** s'occuper de; **I don't ~** ça m'est bien égal; **I couldn't ~ less** je m'en fiche complètement (*inf*); **~ for** *vt fus* s'occuper de; (*like*) aimer
career [kə'rɪə^r] *n* carrière *f* ♦ *vi* (*also:* **~ along**) aller à toute allure; **~ woman** (*irreg*) *n* femme ambitieuse
care: ~free *adj* sans souci, insouciant(e); **~ful** *adj* (*thorough*) soigneux(-euse); (*cautious*) prudent(e); **(be) ~ful!** (fais) attention!; **~fully** *adv* avec soin, soigneusement; prudemment; **~less** *adj* négligent(e); (*heedless*) insouciant(e); **~r** *n* (*MED*) aide *f*
caress [kə'rɛs] *n* caresse *f* ♦ *vt* caresser
caretaker ['kɛəteɪkə^r] *n* gardien(ne), concierge *m/f*
car-ferry ['kɑ:fɛrɪ] *n* (*on sea*) ferry(-boat) *m*
cargo ['kɑ:gəu] (*pl* **~es**) *n* cargaison *f*, chargement *m*
car hire *n* location *f* de voitures
Caribbean [kærɪ'bi:ən] *adj*: **the ~ (Sea)** la mer des Antilles *or* Caraïbes
caring ['kɛərɪŋ] *adj* (*person*) bienveillant(e); (*society, organization*) humanitaire
carnation [kɑ:'neɪʃən] *n* œillet *m*
carnival ['kɑ:nɪvl] *n* (*public celebration*) carnaval *m*; (*US*: *funfair*) fête foraine
carol ['kærəl] *n*: **(Christmas) ~** chant *m* de Noël
carp [kɑ:p] *n* (*fish*) carpe *f*

car park (*BRIT*) *n* parking *m*, parc *m* de stationnement

carpenter ['kɑːpɪntəʳ] *n* charpentier *m*; **carpentry** *n* menuiserie *f*

carpet ['kɑːpɪt] *n* tapis *m* ♦ *vt* recouvrir d'un tapis; **~ sweeper** *n* balai *m* mécanique

car phone *n* (*TEL*) téléphone *m* de voiture

car rental *n* location *f* de voitures

carriage ['kærɪdʒ] *n* voiture *f*; (*of goods*) transport *m*; (: *cost*) port *m*; **~way** (*BRIT*) *n* (*part of road*) chaussée *f*

carrier ['kærɪəʳ] *n* transporteur *m*, camionneur *m*; (*company*) entreprise *f* de transport; (*MED*) porteur(-euse); **~ bag** (*BRIT*) *n* sac *m* (en papier *or* en plastique)

carrot ['kærət] *n* carotte *f*

carry ['kærɪ] *vt* (*subj*: *person*) porter; (: *vehicle*) transporter; (*involve*: *responsibilities etc*) comporter, impliquer ♦ *vi* (*sound*) porter; **to get carried away** (*fig*) s'emballer, s'enthousiasmer; **~ on** *vi*: **to ~ on with sth/doing** continuer qch/de faire ♦ *vt* poursuivre; **~ out** *vt* (*orders*) exécuter; (*investigation*) mener; **~cot** (*BRIT*) *n* porte-bébé *m*; **~-on** (*inf*) *n* (*fuss*) histoires *fpl*

cart [kɑːt] *n* charrette *f* ♦ *vt* (*inf*) transporter, trimballer (*inf*)

carton ['kɑːtən] *n* (*box*) carton *m*; (*of yogurt*) pot *m*; (*of cigarettes*) cartouche *f*

cartoon [kɑː'tuːn] *n* (*PRESS*) dessin *m* (humoristique), caricature *f*; (*BRIT*: *comic strip*) bande dessinée; (*CINEMA*) dessin animé

cartridge ['kɑːtrɪdʒ] *n* cartouche *f*

carve [kɑːv] *vt* (*meat*) découper; (*wood, stone*) tailler, sculpter; **~ up** *vt* découper; (*fig*: *country*) morceler; **carving** *n* sculpture *f*; **carving knife** *n* couteau *m* à découper

car wash *n* station *f* de lavage (de voitures)

case [keɪs] *n* cas *m*; (*LAW*) affaire *f*, procès *m*; (*box*) caisse *f*, boîte *f*, étui *m*; (*BRIT*: *also*: **suitcase**) valise *f*; **in ~ of** en cas de; **in ~ he ...** au cas où il ...; **just in ~** à tout hasard; **in any ~** en tout cas, de toute façon

cash [kæʃ] *n* argent *m*; (*COMM*) argent liquide, espèces *fpl* ♦ *vt* encaisser; **to pay (in) ~** payer comptant; **~ on delivery** payable *or* paiement à la livraison; **~-book** *n* livre *m* de caisse; **~ card** (*BRIT*) *n* carte *f* de retrait; **~ desk** (*BRIT*) *n* caisse *f*; **~ dispenser** (*BRIT*) *n* distributeur *m* automatique de billets, billeterie *f*

cashew [kæ'ʃuː] *n* (*also*: **~ nut**) noix *f* de cajou

cashier [kæ'ʃɪəʳ] *n* caissier(-ère)

cashmere ['kæʃmɪəʳ] *n* cachemire *m*

cash register *n* caisse (enregistreuse)

casing ['keɪsɪŋ] *n* revêtement (protecteur), enveloppe (protectrice)

casino [kə'siːnəu] *n* casino *m*

casket ['kɑːskɪt] *n* coffret *m*; (*US*: *coffin*) cercueil *m*

casserole ['kæsərəul] *n* (*container*) cocotte *f*; (*food*) ragoût *m* (en cocotte)

cassette [kæ'sɛt] *n* cassette *f*, musicassette *f*; **~ player** *n* lecteur *m* de cassettes; **~ recorder** *n* magnétophone *m* à cassettes

cast [kɑːst] (*pt, pp* **cast**) *vt* (*throw*) jeter; (*shed*) perdre; se dépouiller de; (*statue*) mouler; (*THEATRE*): **to ~ sb as Hamlet** attribuer à qn le rôle de Hamlet ♦ *n* (*THEATRE*) distribution *f*; (*also*: **plaster ~**) plâtre *m*; **to ~ one's vote** voter; **~ off** *vi* (*NAUT*) larguer les amarres; (*KNITTING*) arrêter les mailles; **~ on** *vi* (*KNITTING*) monter les mailles

castaway ['kɑːstəweɪ] *n* naufragé(e)

caster sugar ['kɑːstə-] (*BRIT*) *n* sucre *m* semoule

casting vote (*BRIT*) *n* voix prépondérante (*pour départager*)

cast iron *n* fonte *f*

castle ['kɑːsl] *n* château (fort); (*CHESS*) tour *f*

castor ['kɑːstəʳ] *n* (*wheel*) roulette *f*; **~**

oil *n* huile *f* de ricin
castrate [kæs'treɪt] *vt* châtrer
casual ['kæʒjul] *adj* (*by chance*) de hasard, fait(e) au hasard, fortuit(e); (*irregular: work etc*) temporaire; (*unconcerned*) désinvolte; **~ly** *adv* avec désinvolture, négligemment; (*dress*) de façon décontractée
casualty ['kæʒjultɪ] *n* accidenté(e), blessé(e); (*dead*) victime *f*, mort(e); (MED: *department*) urgences *fpl*
casual wear *n* vêtements *mpl* décontractés
cat [kæt] *n* chat *m*
catalogue ['kætəlɔg] (US **catalog**) *n* catalogue *m* ♦ *vt* cataloguer
catalyst ['kætəlɪst] *n* catalyseur *m*
catalytic converter [kætə'lɪtɪk kən'vəːtə^r] *n* pot *m* catalytique
catapult ['kætəpʌlt] (BRIT) *n* (*sling*) lance-pierres *m inv*, fronde *m*
catarrh [kə'tɑː^r] *n* rhume *m* chronique, catarrhe *m*
catastrophe [kə'tæstrəfɪ] *n* catastrophe *f*
catch [kætʃ] (*pt, pp* **caught**) *vt* attraper; (*person: by surprise*) prendre, surprendre; (*understand, hear*) saisir ♦ *vi* (*fire*) prendre; (*become trapped*) se prendre, s'accrocher ♦ *n* prise *f*; (*trick*) attrape *f*; (*of lock*) loquet *m*; **to ~ sb's attention** *or* **eye** attirer l'attention de qn; **to ~ one's breath** retenir son souffle; **to ~ fire** prendre feu; **to ~ sight of** apercevoir; **~ on** *vi* saisir; (*grow popular*) prendre; **~ up** *vi* se rattraper, combler son retard ♦ *vt* (*also:* **~ up with**) rattraper; **~ing** *adj* (MED) contagieux(-euse); **~ment area** ['kætʃmənt-] (BRIT) *n* (SCOL) secteur *m* de recrutement; **~ phrase** *n* slogan *m*; expression *f* (à la mode); **~y** *adj* (*tune*) facile à retenir
category ['kætɪgərɪ] *n* catégorie *f*
cater ['keɪtə^r] *vi* (*provide food*): **to ~ (for)** préparer des repas (pour), se charger de la restauration (pour); **~ for** (BRIT) *vt fus* (*needs*) satisfaire, pourvoir à; (*readers, consumers*) s'adresser à, pourvoir aux besoins de; **~er** *n* traiteur *m*; fournisseur *m*; **~ing** *n* restauration *f*; approvisionnement *m*, ravitaillement *m*
caterpillar ['kætəpɪlə^r] *n* chenille *f*
cathedral [kə'θiːdrəl] *n* cathédrale *f*
catholic ['kæθəlɪk] *adj* (*tastes*) éclectique, varié(e); **C~** *adj* catholique ♦ *n* catholique *m/f*
Catseye ® ['kæts'aɪ] (BRIT) *n* (AUT) catadioptre *m*
cattle ['kætl] *npl* bétail *m*
catty ['kætɪ] *adj* méchant(e)
caucus ['kɔːkəs] *n* (POL: *group*) comité local d'un parti politique; (US: POL) comité électoral (pour désigner des candidats)
caught [kɔːt] *pt, pp of* **catch**
cauliflower ['kɔlɪflauə^r] *n* chou-fleur *m*
cause [kɔːz] *n* cause *f* ♦ *vt* causer
caution ['kɔːʃən] *n* prudence *f*; (*warning*) avertissement *m* ♦ *vt* avertir, donner un avertissement à; **cautious** *adj* prudent(e)
cavalry ['kævəlrɪ] *n* cavalerie *f*
cave [keɪv] *n* caverne *f*, grotte *f*; **~ in** *vi* (*roof etc*) s'effondrer; **~man** (*irreg*) *n* homme *m* des cavernes
caviar(e) ['kævɪɑː^r] *n* caviar *m*
CB *n abbr* (= *Citizens' Band (Radio)*) CB *f*
CBI *n abbr* (= *Confederation of British Industries*) *groupement du patronat*
cc *abbr* = **carbon copy**; **cubic centimetres**
CD *n abbr* (= *compact disc (player)*) CD *m*; **CDI** *n abbr* (= *Compact Disk Interactive*) CD-I *m*; **CD player** *n* platine *f* laser; **CD-ROM** [siːdiː'rɔm] *n abbr* (= *compact disc read-only memory*) CD-Rom *m*
CDT BRIT *abbr* SCOL (= *Craft, Design and Technology*) EMT *f*
cease [siːs] *vt, vi* cesser; **~fire** *n* cessez-le-feu *m*; **~less** *adj* incessant(e), continuel(le)
cedar ['siːdə^r] *n* cèdre *m*
ceiling ['siːlɪŋ] *n* plafond *m*

celebrate ['sɛlɪbreɪt] *vt, vi* célébrer; **~d** *adj* célèbre; **celebration** [sɛlɪ'breɪʃən] *n* célébration *f*; **celebrity** [sɪ'lɛbrɪtɪ] *n* célébrité *f*

celery ['sɛlərɪ] *n* céleri *m* (à côtes)

cell [sɛl] *n* cellule *f*; (ELEC) élément *m* (*de pile*)

cellar ['sɛlə^r] *n* cave *f*

cello ['tʃɛləu] *n* violoncelle *m*

cellphone ['sɛlfəun] *n* téléphone *m* cellulaire

Celt [kɛlt, sɛlt] *n* Celte *m/f*; **~ic** *adj* celte

cement [sə'mɛnt] *n* ciment *m*; **~ mixer** *n* bétonnière *f*

cemetery ['sɛmɪtrɪ] *n* cimetière *m*

censor ['sɛnsə^r] *n* censeur *m* ♦ *vt* censurer; **~ship** *n* censure *f*

censure ['sɛnʃə^r] *vt* blâmer, critiquer

census ['sɛnsəs] *n* recensement *m*

cent [sɛnt] *n* (*US, euro etc: coin*) cent *m* (= *un centième du dollar, de l'euro etc*); *see also* **per**

centenary [sɛn'tiːnərɪ] *n* centenaire *m*

center ['sɛntə^r] (*US*) *n* = **centre**

centigrade ['sɛntɪgreɪd] *adj* centigrade

centimetre ['sɛntɪmiːtə^r] (*US* **centimeter**) *n* centimètre *m*

centipede ['sɛntɪpiːd] *n* mille-pattes *m inv*

central ['sɛntrəl] *adj* central(e); **C~ America** *n* Amérique centrale; **~ heating** *n* chauffage central; **~ reservation** (BRIT) *n* (AUT) terre-plein central

centre ['sɛntə^r] (*US* **center**) *n* centre *m* ♦ *vt* centrer; **~-forward** *n* (SPORT) avant-centre *m*; **~-half** *n* (SPORT) demi-centre *m*

century ['sɛntjurɪ] *n* siècle *m*; **20th ~** XXe siècle

ceramic [sɪ'ræmɪk] *adj* céramique

cereal ['siːrɪəl] *n* céréale *f*

ceremony ['sɛrɪmənɪ] *n* cérémonie *f*; **to stand on ~** faire des façons

certain ['səːtən] *adj* certain(e); **for ~** certainement, sûrement; **~ly** *adv* certainement; **~ty** *n* certitude *f*

certificate [sə'tɪfɪkɪt] *n* certificat *m*

certified ['səːtɪfaɪd] *adj*: **by ~ mail** (*US*) en recommandé, avec avis de réception; **~ public accountant** (*US*) expert-comptable *m*

certify ['səːtɪfaɪ] *vt* certifier; (*award diploma to*) conférer un diplôme *etc* à; (*declare insane*) déclarer malade mental(e)

cervical ['səːvɪkl] *adj*: **~ cancer** cancer *m* du col de l'utérus; **~ smear** frottis vaginal

cervix ['səːvɪks] *n* col *m* de l'utérus

cf. *abbr* (= *compare*) cf., voir

CFC *n abbr* (= *chlorofluorocarbon*) CFC *m (gen pl)*

ch. *abbr* (= *chapter*) chap

chafe [tʃeɪf] *vt* irriter, frotter contre

chain [tʃeɪn] *n* chaîne *f* ♦ *vt* (*also:* **~ up**) enchaîner, attacher (avec une chaîne); **~ reaction** *n* réaction *f* en chaîne; **~-smoke** *vi* fumer cigarette sur cigarette; **~ store** *n* magasin *m* à succursales multiples

chair [tʃɛə^r] *n* chaise *f*; (*armchair*) fauteuil *m*; (*of university*) chaire *f*; (*of meeting, committee*) présidence *f* ♦ *vt* (*meeting*) présider; **~lift** *n* télésiège *m*; **~man** (*irreg*) *n* président *m*

chalet ['ʃæleɪ] *n* chalet *m*

chalk [tʃɔːk] *n* craie *f*

challenge ['tʃælɪndʒ] *n* défi *m* ♦ *vt* défier; (*statement, right*) mettre en question, contester; **to ~ sb to do** mettre qn au défi de faire; **challenging** *adj* (*tone, look*) de défi, provocateur(-trice); (*task, career*) qui représente un défi *or* une gageure

chamber ['tʃeɪmbə^r] *n* chambre *f*; **~ of commerce** chambre de commerce; **~maid** *n* femme *f* de chambre; **~ music** *n* musique *f* de chambre

champagne [ʃæm'peɪn] *n* champagne *m*

champion ['tʃæmpɪən] *n* champion(ne); **~ship** *n* championnat *m*

chance [tʃɑːns] *n* (*opportunity*) occasion *f*, possibilité *f*; (*hope, likelihood*) chance *f*; (*risk*) risque *m* ♦ *vt*: **to ~ it** risquer (le

coup), essayer ♦ *adj* fortuit(e), de hasard; **to take a ~** prendre un risque; **by ~** par hasard
chancellor ['tʃɑːnsələʳ] *n* chancelier *m*; **C~ of the Exchequer** (*BRIT*) *n* chancelier *m* de l'Échiquier; ≃ ministre *m* des Finances
chandelier [ʃændəˈlɪəʳ] *n* lustre *m*
change [tʃeɪndʒ] *vt* (*alter, replace*, COMM: *money*) changer; (*hands, trains, clothes, one's name*) changer de; (*transform*): **to ~ sb into** changer *or* transformer qn en ♦ *vi* (*gen*) changer; (*one's clothes*) se changer; (*be transformed*): **to ~ into** se changer *or* transformer en ♦ *n* changement *m*; (*money*) monnaie *f*; **to ~ gear** (*AUT*) changer de vitesse; **to ~ one's mind** changer d'avis; **a ~ of clothes** des vêtements de rechange; **for a ~** pour changer; **~able** *adj* (*weather*) variable; **~ machine** *n* distributeur *m* de monnaie; **~over** *n* (*to new system*) changement *m*, passage *m*; **changing** *adj* changeant(e); **changing room** (*BRIT*) *n* (*in shop*) salon *m* d'essayage; (*SPORT*) vestiaire *m*
channel ['tʃænl] *n* (*TV*) chaîne *f*; (*navigable passage*) chenal *m*; (*irrigation*) canal *m* ♦ *vt* canaliser; **the (English) C~** la Manche; **the C~ Islands** les îles de la Manche, les îles Anglo-Normandes; **the C~ Tunnel** le tunnel sous la Manche; **~-hopping** *n* (*TV*) zapping *m*
chant [tʃɑːnt] *n* chant *m*; (*REL*) psalmodie *f* ♦ *vt* chanter, scander
chaos ['keɪɔs] *n* chaos *m*
chap [tʃæp] (*BRIT*: *inf*) *n* (*man*) type *m*
chapel ['tʃæpl] *n* chapelle *f*; (*BRIT*: *non-conformist ~*) église *f*
chaplain ['tʃæplɪn] *n* aumônier *m*
chapped [tʃæpt] *adj* (*skin, lips*) gercé(e)
chapter ['tʃæptəʳ] *n* chapitre *m*
char [tʃɑːʳ] *vt* (*burn*) carboniser
character ['kærɪktəʳ] *n* caractère *m*; (*in novel, film*) personnage *m*; (*eccentric*) numéro *m*, phénomène *m*; **~istic** [kærɪktəˈrɪstɪk] *adj* caractéristique ♦ *n* caractéristique *f*
charcoal ['tʃɑːkəul] *n* charbon *m* de bois; (*for drawing*) charbon *m*
charge [tʃɑːdʒ] *n* (*cost*) prix (demandé); (*accusation*) accusation *f*; (*LAW*) inculpation *f* ♦ *vt*: **to ~ sb (with)** inculper qn (de); (*battery, enemy*) charger; (*customer, sum*) faire payer ♦ *vi* foncer; **~s** *npl* (*costs*) frais *mpl*; **to reverse the ~s** (*TEL*) téléphoner en P.C.V.; **to take ~ of** se charger de; **to be in ~ of** être responsable de, s'occuper de; **how much do you ~?** combien prenez-vous?; **to ~ an expense (up) to sb** mettre une dépense sur le compte de qn; **~ card** *n* carte *f* de client
charity ['tʃærɪtɪ] *n* charité *f*; (*organization*) institution *f* charitable *or* de bienfaisance, œuvre *f* (de charité)
charm [tʃɑːm] *n* charme *m*; (*on bracelet*) breloque *f* ♦ *vt* charmer, enchanter; **~ing** *adj* charmant(e)
chart [tʃɑːt] *n* tableau *m*, diagramme *m*; graphique *m*; (*map*) carte marine ♦ *vt* dresser *or* établir la carte de; **~s** *npl* (*hit parade*) hit-parade *m*
charter ['tʃɑːtəʳ] *vt* (*plane*) affréter ♦ *n* (*document*) charte *f*; **~ed accountant** (*BRIT*) *n* expert-comptable *m*; **~ flight** *n* charter *m*
chase [tʃeɪs] *vt* poursuivre, pourchasser; (*also:* **~ away**) chasser ♦ *n* poursuite *f*, chasse *f*
chasm ['kæzəm] *n* gouffre *m*, abîme *m*
chat [tʃæt] *vi* (*also:* **have a ~**) bavarder, causer ♦ *n* conversation *f*; **~ show** (*BRIT*) *n* causerie télévisée
chatter ['tʃætəʳ] *vi* (*person*) bavarder; (*animal*) jacasser ♦ *n* bavardage *m*; jacassement *m*; **my teeth are ~ing** je claque des dents; **~box** (*inf*) *n* moulin *m* à paroles
chatty ['tʃætɪ] *adj* (*style*) familier(-ère); (*person*) bavard(e)
chauffeur ['ʃəufəʳ] *n* chauffeur *m* (de maître)
chauvinist ['ʃəuvɪnɪst] *n* (*male ~*) phal-

locrate *m*; (*nationalist*) chauvin(e)

cheap [tʃi:p] *adj* bon marché *inv*, pas cher (chère); (*joke*) facile, d'un goût douteux; (*poor quality*) à bon marché, de qualité médiocre ♦ *adv* à bon marché, pour pas cher; ~ **day return** billet *m* d'aller et retour réduit (*valable pour la journée*); **~er** *adj* moins cher (chère); **~ly** *adv* à bon marché, à bon compte

cheat [tʃi:t] *vi* tricher ♦ *vt* tromper, duper; (*rob*): **to ~ sb out of sth** escroquer qch à qn ♦ *n* tricheur(-euse); escroc *m*

check [tʃɛk] *vt* vérifier; (*passport, ticket*) contrôler; (*halt*) arrêter; (*restrain*) maîtriser ♦ *n* vérification *f*; contrôle *m*; (*curb*) frein *m*; (*US*: *bill*) addition *f*; (*pattern*: *gen pl*) carreaux *mpl*; (*US*) = **cheque** ♦ *adj* (*pattern, cloth*) à carreaux; **~ in** *vi* (*in hotel*) remplir sa fiche (d'hôtel); (*at airport*) se présenter à l'enregistrement ♦ *vt* (*luggage*) (faire) enregistrer; **~ out** *vi* (*in hotel*) régler sa note; **~ up** *vi*: **to ~ up (on sth)** vérifier (qch); **to ~ up on sb** se renseigner sur le compte de qn; **~ered** (*US*) *adj* = **chequered**; **~ers** (*US*) *npl* jeu *m* de dames; **~-in (desk)** *n* enregistrement *m*; **~ing account** (*US*) *n* (*current account*) compte courant; **~mate** *n* échec et mat *m*; **~out** *n* (*in shop*) caisse *f*; **~point** *n* contrôle *m*; **~room** (*US*) *n* (*left-luggage office*) consigne *f*; **~up** *n* (*MED*) examen médical, check-up *m*

cheek [tʃi:k] *n* joue *f*; (*impudence*) toupet *m*, culot *m*; **~bone** *n* pommette *f*; **~y** *adj* effronté(e), culotté(e)

cheep [tʃi:p] *vi* piauler

cheer [tʃɪəʳ] *vt* acclamer, applaudir; (*gladden*) réjouir, réconforter ♦ *vi* applaudir ♦ *n* (*gen pl*) acclamations *fpl*, applaudissements *mpl*; bravos *mpl*, hourras *mpl*; **~s!** à la vôtre!; **~ up** *vi* se dérider, reprendre courage ♦ *vt* remonter le moral à *or* de, dérider; **~ful** *adj* gai(e), joyeux(-euse)

cheerio [tʃɪərɪ'əu] (*BRIT*) *excl* salut!, au revoir!

cheese [tʃi:z] *n* fromage *m*; **~board** *n* plateau *m* de fromages

cheetah ['tʃi:tə] *n* guépard *m*

chef [ʃɛf] *n* chef (cuisinier)

chemical ['kɛmɪkl] *adj* chimique ♦ *n* produit *m* chimique

chemist ['kɛmɪst] *n* (*BRIT*: *pharmacist*) pharmacien(ne); (*scientist*) chimiste *m/f*; **~ry** *n* chimie *f*; **~'s (shop)** (*BRIT*) *n* pharmacie *f*

cheque [tʃɛk] (*BRIT*) *n* chèque *m*; **~book** *n* chéquier *m*, carnet *m* de chèques; **~ card** *n* carte *f* (d'identité) bancaire

chequered ['tʃɛkəd] (*US* **checkered**) *adj* (*fig*) varié(e)

cherish ['tʃɛrɪʃ] *vt* chérir

cherry ['tʃɛrɪ] *n* cerise *f*; (*also*: **~ tree**) cerisier *m*

chess [tʃɛs] *n* échecs *mpl*; **~board** *n* échiquier *m*

chest [tʃɛst] *n* poitrine *f*; (*box*) coffre *m*, caisse *f*; **~ of drawers** *n* commode *f*

chestnut ['tʃɛsnʌt] *n* châtaigne *f*; (*also*: **~ tree**) châtaignier *m*

chew [tʃu:] *vt* mâcher; **~ing gum** *n* chewing-gum *m*

chic [ʃi:k] *adj* chic *inv*, élégant(e)

chick [tʃɪk] *n* poussin *m*; (*inf*) nana *f*

chicken ['tʃɪkɪn] *n* poulet *m*; (*inf*: *coward*) poule mouillée; **~ out** (*inf*) *vi* se dégonfler; **~pox** *n* varicelle *f*

chicory ['tʃɪkərɪ] *n* (*for coffee*) chicorée *f*; (*salad*) endive *f*

chief [tʃi:f] *n* chef ♦ *adj* principal(e); **~ executive** (*US* **chief executive officer**) *n* directeur(-trice) général(e); **~ly** *adv* principalement, surtout

chiffon ['ʃɪfɔn] *n* mousseline *f* de soie

chilblain ['tʃɪlbleɪn] *n* engelure *f*

child [tʃaɪld] (*pl* **~ren**) *n* enfant *m/f*; **~birth** *n* accouchement *m*; **~hood** *n* enfance *f*; **~ish** *adj* puéril(e), enfantin(e); **~like** *adj* d'enfant, innocent(e); **~ minder** (*BRIT*) *n* garde *f* d'enfants; **~ren** ['tʃɪldrən] *npl of* **child**

Chile ['tʃɪlɪ] *n* Chili *m*
chill [tʃɪl] *n* (*of water*) froid *m*; (*of air*) fraîcheur *f*; (MED) refroidissement *m*, coup *m* de froid ♦ *vt* (*person*) faire frissonner; (CULIN) mettre au frais, rafraîchir
chil(l)i ['tʃɪlɪ] *n* piment *m* (rouge)
chilly ['tʃɪlɪ] *adj* froid(e), glacé(e); (*sensitive to cold*) frileux(-euse); **to feel ~** avoir froid
chime [tʃaɪm] *n* carillon *m* ♦ *vi* carillonner, sonner
chimney ['tʃɪmnɪ] *n* cheminée *f*; **~ sweep** *n* ramonneur *m*
chimpanzee [tʃɪmpæn'zi:] *n* chimpanzé *m*
chin [tʃɪn] *n* menton *m*
China ['tʃaɪnə] *n* Chine *f*
china ['tʃaɪnə] *n* porcelaine *f*; (*crockery*) (vaisselle *f* en) porcelaine
Chinese [tʃaɪ'ni:z] *adj* chinois(e) ♦ *n inv* (*person*) Chinois(e); (LING) chinois *m*
chink [tʃɪŋk] *n* (*opening*) fente *f*, fissure *f*; (*noise*) tintement *m*
chip [tʃɪp] *n* (*gen pl*: CULIN: BRIT) frite *f*; (: US: *potato* ~) chip *m*; (*of wood*) copeau *m*; (*of glass, stone*) éclat *m*; (*also*: **microchip**) puce *f* ♦ *vt* (*cup, plate*) ébrécher

chip shop

Un **chip shop**, *que l'on appelle également un "fish-and-chip shop", est un magasin où l'on vend des plats à emporter. Les chip shops sont d'ailleurs à l'origine des* **takeaways**. *On y achète en particulier du poisson frit et des frites, mais on y trouve également des plats traditionnels britanniques (steak pies, saucisses, etc). Tous les plats étaient à l'origine emballés dans du papier journal. Dans certains de ces magasins, on peut s'asseoir pour consommer sur place.*

chiropodist [kɪ'rɔpədɪst] (BRIT) *n* pédicure *m/f*
chirp [tʃə:p] *vi* pépier, gazouiller
chisel ['tʃɪzl] *n* ciseau *m*
chit [tʃɪt] *n* mot *m*, note *f*
chitchat ['tʃɪttʃæt] *n* bavardage *m*
chivalry ['ʃɪvəlrɪ] *n* esprit *m* chevaleresque, galanterie *f*
chives [tʃaɪvz] *npl* ciboulette *f*, civette *f*
chock-a-block ['tʃɔkə'blɔk], **chock-full** [tʃɔk'ful] *adj* plein(e) à craquer
chocolate ['tʃɔklɪt] *n* chocolat *m*
choice [tʃɔɪs] *n* choix *m* ♦ *adj* de choix
choir ['kwaɪə^r^] *n* chœur *m*, chorale *f*; **~boy** *n* jeune choriste *m*
choke [tʃəuk] *vi* étouffer ♦ *vt* étrangler; étouffer ♦ *n* (AUT) starter *m*; **street ~d with traffic** rue engorgée *or* embouteillée
cholesterol [kə'lɛstərɔl] *n* cholestérol *m*
choose [tʃu:z] (*pt* **chose**, *pp* **chosen**) *vt* choisir; **to ~ to do** décider de faire, juger bon de faire; **choosy** *adj*: **(to be) choosy** (faire le/la) difficile
chop [tʃɔp] *vt* (*wood*) couper (à la hache); (CULIN: *also*: **~ up**) couper (fin), émincer, hacher (en morceaux) ♦ *n* (CULIN) côtelette *f*; **~s** *npl* (*jaws*) mâchoires *fpl*
chopper ['tʃɔpə^r^] *n* (*helicopter*) hélicoptère *m*, hélico *m*
choppy ['tʃɔpɪ] *adj* (*sea*) un peu agité(e)
chopsticks ['tʃɔpstɪks] *npl* baguettes *fpl*
chord [kɔ:d] *n* (MUS) accord *m*
chore [tʃɔ:^r^] *n* travail *m* de routine; **household ~s** travaux *mpl* du ménage
chortle ['tʃɔ:tl] *vi* glousser
chorus ['kɔ:rəs] *n* chœur *m*; (*repeated part of song*: *also fig*) refrain *m*
chose [tʃəuz] *pt of* **choose**; **~n** *pp of* **choose**
chowder ['tʃaudə^r^] *n* soupe *f* de poisson
Christ [kraɪst] *n* Christ *m*
christen ['krɪsn] *vt* baptiser
christening *n* baptême *m*
Christian ['krɪstɪən] *adj*, *n* chrétien(ne); **~ity** [krɪstɪ'ænɪtɪ] *n* christianisme *m*; **~**

name *n* prénom *m*

Christmas ['krɪsməs] *n* Noël *m or f*; **Happy** *or* **Merry ~!** joyeux Noël!; **~ card** *n* carte *f* de Noël; **~ Day** *n* le jour de Noël; **~ Eve** *n* la veille de Noël; la nuit de Noël; **~ tree** *n* arbre *m* de Noël

chrome [krəum] *n* chrome *m*

chromium ['krəumɪəm] *n* chrome *m*

chronic ['krɔnɪk] *adj* chronique

chronicle ['krɔnɪkl] *n* chronique *f*

chronological [krɔnə'lɔdʒɪkl] *adj* chronologique

chrysanthemum [krɪ'sænθəməm] *n* chrysanthème *m*

chubby ['tʃʌbɪ] *adj* potelé(e), rondelet(te)

chuck [tʃʌk] (*inf*) *vt* (*throw*) lancer, jeter; (*BRIT*: *person*) plaquer; (: *also:* **~ up**: *job*) lâcher; **~ out** *vt* flanquer dehors *or* à la porte; (*rubbish*) jeter

chuckle ['tʃʌkl] *vi* glousser

chug [tʃʌg] *vi* faire teuf-teuf; (*also:* **~ along**) avancer en faisant teuf-teuf

chum [tʃʌm] *n* copain (copine)

chunk [tʃʌŋk] *n* gros morceau

church [tʃə:tʃ] *n* église *f*; **~yard** *n* cimetière *m*

churn [tʃə:n] *n* (*for butter*) baratte *f*; (*also:* **milk ~**) (grand) bidon à lait; **~ out** *vt* débiter

chute [ʃu:t] *n* glissoire *f*; (*also:* **rubbish ~**) vide-ordures *m inv*

chutney ['tʃʌtnɪ] *n* condiment *m* à base de fruits au vinaigre

CIA *n abbr* (= *Central Intelligence Agency*) CIA *f*

CID (*BRIT*) *n abbr* (= *Criminal Investigation Department*) P.J. *f*

cider ['saɪdə^r^] *n* cidre *m*

cigar [sɪ'gɑ:^r^] *n* cigare *m*

cigarette [sɪgə'rɛt] *n* cigarette *f*; **~ case** *n* étui *m* à cigarettes; **~ end** *n* mégot *m*

Cinderella [sɪndə'rɛlə] *n* Cendrillon

cinders ['sɪndəz] *npl* cendres *fpl*

cine-camera ['sɪnɪ'kæmərə] (*BRIT*) *n* caméra *f*

cinema ['sɪnəmə] *n* cinéma *m*

cinnamon ['sɪnəmən] *n* cannelle *f*

circle ['sə:kl] *n* cercle *m*; (*in cinema, theatre*) balcon *m* ♦ *vi* faire *or* décrire des cercles ♦ *vt* (*move round*) faire le tour de, tourner autour de; (*surround*) entourer, encercler

circuit ['sə:kɪt] *n* circuit *m*; **~ous** [sə:'kjuɪtəs] *adj* indirect(e), qui fait un détour

circular ['sə:kjulə^r^] *adj* circulaire ♦ *n* circulaire *f*

circulate ['sə:kjuleɪt] *vi* circuler ♦ *vt* faire circuler; **circulation** [sə:kju'leɪʃən] *n* circulation *f*; (*of newspaper*) tirage *m*

circumflex ['sə:kəmflɛks] *n* (*also:* **~ accent**) accent *m* circonflexe

circumstances ['sə:kəmstənsɪz] *npl* circonstances *fpl*; (*financial condition*) moyens *mpl*, situation financière

circus ['sə:kəs] *n* cirque *m*

CIS *n abbr* (= *Commonwealth of Independent States*) CEI *f*

cistern ['sɪstən] *n* réservoir *m* (d'eau); (*in toilet*) réservoir de la chasse d'eau

citizen ['sɪtɪzn] *n* citoyen(ne); (*resident*): **the ~s of this town** les habitants de cette ville; **~ship** *n* citoyenneté *f*

citrus fruit ['sɪtrəs-] *n* agrume *m*

city ['sɪtɪ] *n* ville *f*, cité *f*; **the C~** la Cité de Londres (*centre des affaires*); **~ technology college** *n* établissement *m* d'enseignement technologique

civic ['sɪvɪk] *adj* civique; (*authorities*) municipal(e); **~ centre** (*BRIT*) *n* centre administratif (municipal)

civil ['sɪvɪl] *adj* civil(e); (*polite*) poli(e), courtois(e); (*disobedience, defence*) passif(-ive); **~ engineer** *n* ingénieur *m* des travaux publics; **~ian** [sɪ'vɪlɪən] *adj*, *n* civil(e)

civilization [sɪvɪlaɪ'zeɪʃən] *n* civilisation *f*

civilized ['sɪvɪlaɪzd] *adj* civilisé(e); (*fig*) où règnent les bonnes manières

civil: ~ law *n* code civil; (*study*) droit civil; **~ servant** *n* fonctionnaire *m/f*; **C~**

Service *n* fonction publique, administration *f*; **~ war** *n* guerre civile
clad [klæd] *adj*: **~ (in)** habillé(e) (de)
claim [kleɪm] *vt* revendiquer; (*rights, inheritance*) demander, prétendre à; (*assert*) déclarer, prétendre ♦ *vi* (*for insurance*) faire une déclaration de sinistre ♦ *n* revendication *f*; demande *f*; prétention *f*, déclaration *f*; (*right*) droit *m*, titre *m*; **~ant** *n* (ADMIN, LAW) requérant(e)
clairvoyant [klɛə'vɔɪənt] *n* voyant(e)
clam [klæm] *n* palourde *f*
clamber ['klæmbə^r] *vi* grimper, se hisser
clammy ['klæmɪ] *adj* humide (et froid(e)), moite
clamour ['klæmə^r] (US **clamor**) *vi*: **to ~ for** réclamer à grands cris
clamp [klæmp] *n* agrafe *f*, crampon *m* ♦ *vt* serrer; (*sth to sth*) fixer; (*wheel*) mettre un sabot à; **~ down on** *vt fus* sévir *or* prendre des mesures draconiennes contre
clan [klæn] *n* clan *m*
clang [klæŋ] *vi* émettre un bruit *or* fracas métallique
clap [klæp] *vi* applaudir; **~ping** *n* applaudissements *mpl*
claret ['klærət] *n* (vin *m* de) bordeaux *m* (rouge)
clarinet [klærɪ'nɛt] *n* clarinette *f*
clarity ['klærɪtɪ] *n* clarté *f*
clash [klæʃ] *n* choc *m*; (*fig*) conflit *m* ♦ *vi* se heurter; être *or* entrer en conflit; (*colours*) jurer; (*two events*) tomber en même temps
clasp [klɑːsp] *n* (*of necklace, bag*) fermoir *m*; (*hold, embrace*) étreinte *f* ♦ *vt* serrer, étreindre
class [klɑːs] *n* classe *f* ♦ *vt* classer, classifier
classic ['klæsɪk] *adj* classique ♦ *n* (*author, work*) classique *m*; **~al** *adj* classique
classified ['klæsɪfaɪd] *adj* (*information*) secret(-ète); **~ advertisement** *n* petite annonce
classmate ['klɑːsmeɪt] *n* camarade *m/f* de classe
classroom ['klɑːsrum] *n* (salle *f* de) classe *f*; **~ assistant** *n* aide-éducateur(-trice)
clatter ['klætə^r] *n* cliquetis *m* ♦ *vi* cliqueter
clause [klɔːz] *n* clause *f*; (LING) proposition *f*
claw [klɔː] *n* griffe *f*; (*of bird of prey*) serre *f*; (*of lobster*) pince *f*
clay [kleɪ] *n* argile *f*
clean [kliːn] *adj* propre; (*clear, smooth*) net(te); (*record, reputation*) sans tache; (*joke, story*) correct(e) ♦ *vt* nettoyer; **~ out** *vt* nettoyer (à fond); **~ up** *vt* nettoyer; (*fig*) remettre de l'ordre dans; **~-cut** *adj* (*person*) net(te), soigné(e); **~er** *n* (*person*) nettoyeur(-euse), femme *f* de ménage; (*product*) détachant *m*; **~er's** *n* (*also:* **dry ~er's**) teinturier *m*; **~ing** *n* nettoyage *m*; **~liness** ['klɛnlɪnɪs] *n* propreté *f*
cleanse [klɛnz] *vt* nettoyer; (*purify*) purifier; **~r** *n* (*for face*) démaquillant *m*
clean-shaven ['kliːn'ʃeɪvn] *adj* rasé(e) de près
cleansing department ['klɛnzɪŋ-] (BRIT) *n* service *m* de voirie
clear [klɪə^r] *adj* clair(e); (*glass, plastic*) transparent(e); (*road, way*) libre, dégagé(e); (*conscience*) net(te) ♦ *vt* (*room*) débarrasser; (*of people*) faire évacuer; (*cheque*) compenser; (LAW: *suspect*) innocenter; (*obstacle*) franchir *or* sauter sans heurter ♦ *vi* (*weather*) s'éclaircir; (*fog*) se dissiper ♦ *adv*: **~ of** à distance de, à l'écart de; **to ~ the table** débarrasser la table, desservir; **~ up** *vt* ranger, mettre en ordre; (*mystery*) éclaircir, résoudre; **~ance** *n* (*removal*) déblaiement *m*; (*permission*) autorisation *f*; **~-cut** *adj* clair(e), nettement défini(e); **~ing** *n* (*in forest*) clairière *f*; **~ing bank** (BRIT) *n* *banque qui appartient à une chambre de compensation*; **~ly** *adv* clairement; (*evidently*) de toute évidence;

~way (BRIT) *n* route *f* à stationnement interdit
clef [klɛf] *n* (MUS) clé *f*
cleft [klɛft] *n* (*in rock*) crevasse *f*, fissure *f*
clementine ['klɛməntaɪn] *n* clémentine *f*
clench [klɛntʃ] *vt* serrer
clergy ['klə:dʒɪ] *n* clergé *m*; **~man** (*irreg*) *n* ecclésiastique *m*
clerical ['klɛrɪkl] *adj* de bureau, d'employé de bureau; (REL) clérical(e), du clergé
clerk [klɑ:k, (US) klə:rk] *n* employé(e) de bureau; (US: *salesperson*) vendeur (-euse)
clever ['klɛvə^r] *adj* (*mentally*) intelligent(e); (*deft, crafty*) habile, adroit(e); (*device, arrangement*) ingénieux(-euse), astucieux(-euse)
click [klɪk] *vi* faire un bruit sec *or* un déclic
client ['klaɪənt] *n* client(e)
cliff [klɪf] *n* falaise *f*
climate ['klaɪmɪt] *n* climat *m*
climax ['klaɪmæks] *n* apogée *m*, point culminant; (*sexual*) orgasme *m*
climb [klaɪm] *vi* grimper, monter ♦ *vt* gravir, escalader, monter sur ♦ *n* montée *f*, escalade *f*; **~-down** *n* reculade *f*, dérobade *f*; **~er** *n* (*mountaineer*) grimpeur(-euse), varappeur(-euse); (*plant*) plante grimpante; **~ing** *n* (*mountaineering*) escalade *f*, varappe *f*
clinch [klɪntʃ] *vt* (*deal*) conclure, sceller
cling [klɪŋ] (*pt, pp* **clung**) *vi*: **to ~ (to)** se cramponner (à), s'accrocher (à); (*of clothes*) coller (à)
clinic ['klɪnɪk] *n* centre médical; **~al** *adj* clinique; (*attitude*) froid(e), détaché(e)
clink [klɪŋk] *vi* tinter, cliqueter
clip [klɪp] *n* (*for hair*) barrette *f*; (*also:* **paper ~**) trombone *m* ♦ *vt* (*fasten*) attacher; (*hair, nails*) couper; (*hedge*) tailler; **~pers** *npl* (*for hedge*) sécateur *m*; (*also:* **nail ~pers**) coupe-ongles *m inv*; **~ping** *n* (*from newspaper*) coupure *f* de journal
cloak [kləuk] *n* grande cape ♦ *vt* (*fig*) masquer, cacher; **~room** *n* (*for coats etc*) vestiaire *m*; (BRIT: *WC*) toilettes *fpl*
clock [klɔk] *n* (*large*) horloge *f*; (*small*) pendule *f*; **~ in** (BRIT) *vi* pointer (en arrivant); **~ off** (BRIT) *vi* pointer (en partant); **~ on** (BRIT) *vi* = **clock in**; **~ out** (BRIT) *vi* = **clock off**; **~wise** *adv* dans le sens des aiguilles d'une montre; **~work** *n* rouages *mpl*, mécanisme *m*; (*of clock*) mouvement *m* (d'horlogerie) ♦ *adj* mécanique
clog [klɔg] *n* sabot *m* ♦ *vt* boucher ♦ *vi* (*also:* **~ up**) se boucher
cloister ['klɔɪstə^r] *n* cloître *m*
close[1] [kləus] *adj* (*near*) près, proche; (*contact, link*) étroit(e); (*contest*) très serré(e); (*watch*) étroit(e), strict(e); (*examination*) attentif(-ive), minutieux (-euse); (*weather*) lourd(e), étouffant(e) ♦ *adv* près, à proximité; **~ to** près de, proche de; **~ by** *adj* proche ♦ *adv* tout(e) près; **~ at hand** = **close by**; **a ~ friend** un ami intime; **to have a ~ shave** (*fig*) l'échapper belle
close[2] [kləuz] *vt* fermer ♦ *vi* (*shop etc*) fermer; (*lid, door etc*) se fermer; (*end*) se terminer, se conclure ♦ *n* (*end*) conclusion *f*, fin *f*; **~ down** *vt, vi* fermer (*définitivement*); **~d** *adj* fermé(e); **~d shop** *n* organisation *f* qui n'admet que des travailleurs syndiqués
close-knit ['kləus'nɪt] *adj* (*family, community*) très uni(e)
closely ['kləuslɪ] *adv* (*examine, watch*) de près
closet ['klɔzɪt] *n* (*cupboard*) placard *m*, réduit *m*
close-up ['kləusʌp] *n* gros plan
closure ['kləuʒə^r] *n* fermeture *f*
clot [klɔt] *n* (*gen: blood ~*) caillot *m*; (*inf: person*) ballot *m* ♦ *vi* (*blood*) se coaguler; **~ted cream** *crème fraîche très épaisse*
cloth [klɔθ] *n* (*material*) tissu *m*, étoffe *f*; (*also:* **teacloth**) torchon *m*; lavette *f*
clothe [kləuð] *vt* habiller, vêtir; **~s** *npl*

vêtements *mpl*, habits *mpl*; **~s brush** *n* brosse *f* à habits; **~s line** *n* corde *f* (à linge); **~s peg** (*US* **clothes pin**) *n* pince *f* à linge; **clothing** *n* = **clothes**

cloud [klaud] *n* nuage *m*; **~burst** *n* grosse averse; **~y** *adj* nuageux(-euse), couvert(e); (*liquid*) trouble

clout [klaut] *vt* flanquer une taloche à

clove [kləuv] *n* (*CULIN*: *spice*) clou *m* de girofle; **~ of garlic** gousse *f* d'ail

clover ['kləuvər] *n* trèfle *m*

clown [klaun] *n* clown *m* ♦ *vi* (*also*: **~ about, ~ around**) faire le clown

cloying ['klɔɪɪŋ] *adj* (*taste, smell*) écœurant(e)

club [klʌb] *n* (*society, place*: *also*: **golf ~**) club *m*; (*weapon*) massue *f*, matraque *f* ♦ *vt* matraquer ♦ *vi*: **to ~ together** s'associer; **~s** *npl* (*CARDS*) trèfle *m*; **~ class** *n* (*AVIAT*) classe *f* club; **~house** *n* club *m*

cluck [klʌk] *vi* glousser

clue [klu:] *n* indice *m*; (*in crosswords*) définition *f*; **I haven't a ~** je n'en ai pas la moindre idée

clump [klʌmp] *n*: **~ of trees** bouquet *m* d'arbres

clumsy ['klʌmzɪ] *adj* gauche, maladroit(e)

clung [klʌŋ] *pt, pp of* **cling**

cluster ['klʌstər] *n* (*of people*) (petit) groupe; (*of flowers*) grappe *f*; (*of stars*) amas *m* ♦ *vi* se rassembler

clutch [klʌtʃ] *n* (*grip, grasp*) étreinte *f*, prise *f*; (*AUT*) embrayage *m* ♦ *vt* (*grasp*) agripper; (*hold tightly*) serrer fort; (*hold on to*) se cramponner à

clutter ['klʌtər] *vt* (*also*: **~ up**) encombrer

CND *n abbr* (= *Campaign for Nuclear Disarmament*) *mouvement pour le désarmement nucléaire*

Co. *abbr* = **county; company**

c/o *abbr* (= *care of*) aux bons soins de

coach [kəutʃ] *n* (*bus*) autocar *m*; (*horse-drawn*) diligence *f*; (*of train*) voiture *f*, wagon *m*; (*SPORT*: *trainer*) entraîneur(-euse); (*SCOL*: *tutor*) répétiteur(-trice) ♦ *vt* entraîner; (*student*) faire travailler; **~ trip** *n* excursion *f* en car

coal [kəul] *n* charbon *m*; **~ face** *n* front *m* de taille; **~field** *n* bassin houiller

coalition [kəuə'lɪʃən] *n* coalition *f*

coalman (*irreg*) *n* charbonnier *m*, marchand *m* de charbon

coalmine *n* mine *f* de charbon

coarse [kɔ:s] *adj* grossier(-ère), rude

coast [kəust] *n* côte *f* ♦ *vi* (*car, cycle etc*) descendre en roue libre; **~al** *adj* côtier(-ère); **~guard** *n* garde-côte *m*; (*service*) gendarmerie *f* maritime; **~line** *n* côte *f*, littoral *m*

coat [kəut] *n* manteau *m*; (*of animal*) pelage *m*, poil *m*; (*of paint*) couche *f* ♦ *vt* couvrir; **~ hanger** *n* cintre *m*; **~ing** *n* couche *f*, revêtement *m*; **~ of arms** *n* blason *m*, armoiries *fpl*

coax [kəuks] *vt* persuader par des cajoleries

cobbler ['kɔblər] *n* cordonnier *m*

cobbles ['kɔblz] (*also*: **~tones**) *npl* pavés (ronds)

cobweb ['kɔbwɛb] *n* toile *f* d'araignée

cocaine [kə'keɪn] *n* cocaïne *f*

cock [kɔk] *n* (*rooster*) coq *m*; (*male bird*) mâle *m* ♦ *vt* (*gun*) armer; **~erel** *n* jeune coq *m*

cockle ['kɔkl] *n* coque *f*

cockney ['kɔknɪ] *n* cockney *m*, *habitant des quartiers populaires de l'East End de Londres*, ≃ faubourien(ne)

cockpit ['kɔkpɪt] *n* (*in aircraft*) poste *m* de pilotage, cockpit *m*

cockroach ['kɔkrəutʃ] *n* cafard *m*

cocktail ['kɔkteɪl] *n* cocktail *m*; (*fruit ~ etc*) salade *f*; **~ cabinet** *n* (meuble-)bar *m*; **~ party** *n* cocktail *m*

cocoa ['kəukəu] *n* cacao *m*

coconut ['kəukənʌt] *n* noix *f* de coco

COD *abbr* = **cash on delivery**

cod [kɔd] *n* morue fraîche, cabillaud *m*

code [kəud] *n* code *m*; (*TEL*: *area code*) indicatif *m*

cod-liver oil *n* huile *f* de foie de morue
coercion [kəu'ə:ʃən] *n* contrainte *f*
coffee ['kɔfɪ] *n* café *m*; **~ bar** (*BRIT*) *n* café *m*; **~ bean** *n* grain *m* de café; **~ break** *n* pause-café *f*; **~pot** *n* cafetière *f*; **~ table** *n* (petite) table basse
coffin ['kɔfɪn] *n* cercueil *m*
cog [kɔg] *n* dent *f* (d'engrenage); (*wheel*) roue dentée
cogent ['kəudʒənt] *adj* puissant(e), convaincant(e)
coil [kɔɪl] *n* rouleau *m*, bobine *f*; (*contraceptive*) stérilet *m* ♦ *vt* enrouler
coin [kɔɪn] *n* pièce *f* de monnaie ♦ *vt* (*word*) inventer; **~age** *n* monnaie *f*, système *m* monétaire; **~ box** (*BRIT*) *n* cabine *f* téléphonique
coincide [kəuɪn'saɪd] *vi* coïncider; **~nce** [kəu'ɪnsɪdəns] *n* coïncidence *f*
Coke [kəuk] ® *n* coca *m*
coke [kəuk] *n* coke *m*
colander ['kɔləndə^r] *n* passoire *f*
cold [kəuld] *adj* froid(e) ♦ *n* froid *m*; (*MED*) rhume *m*; **it's ~** il fait froid; **to be** *or* **feel ~** (*person*) avoir froid; **to catch ~** prendre *or* attraper froid; **to catch a ~** attraper un rhume; **in ~ blood** de sang-froid; **~-shoulder** *vt* se montrer froid(e) envers, snober; **~ sore** *n* bouton *m* de fièvre
coleslaw ['kəulslɔ:] *n sorte de salade de chou cru*
colic ['kɔlɪk] *n* colique(s) *f(pl)*
collapse [kə'læps] *vi* s'effondrer, s'écrouler ♦ *n* effondrement *m*, écroulement *m*; **collapsible** *adj* pliant(e); télescopique
collar ['kɔlə^r] *n* (*of coat, shirt*) col *m*; (*for animal*) collier *m*; **~bone** *n* clavicule *f*
collateral [kə'lætərl] *n* nantissement *m*
colleague ['kɔli:g] *n* collègue *m/f*
collect [kə'lɛkt] *vt* rassembler; ramasser; (*as a hobby*) collectionner; (*BRIT*: *call and pick up*) (passer) prendre; (*mail*) faire la levée de, ramasser; (*money owed*) encaisser; (*donations, subscriptions*) recueillir ♦ *vi* (*people*) se rassembler; (*things*) s'amasser; **to call ~** (*US*: *TEL*) téléphoner en P.C.V.; **~ion** *n* collection *f*; (*of mail*) levée *f*; (*for money*) collecte *f*, quête *f*; **~or** *n* collectionneur *m*
college ['kɔlɪdʒ] *n* collège *m*
collide [kə'laɪd] *vi* entrer en collision
colliery ['kɔlɪərɪ] (*BRIT*) *n* mine *f* de charbon, houillère *f*
collision [kə'lɪʒən] *n* collision *f*
colloquial [kə'ləukwɪəl] *adj* familier (-ère)
colon ['kəulən] *n* (*sign*) deux-points *m inv*; (*MED*) côlon *m*
colonel ['kə:nl] *n* colonel *m*
colony ['kɔlənɪ] *n* colonie *f*
colour ['kʌlə^r] (*US* **color**) *n* couleur *f* ♦ *vt* (*paint*) peindre; (*dye*) teindre; (*news*) fausser, exagérer ♦ *vi* (*blush*) rougir; **~s** *npl* (*of party, club*) couleurs *fpl*; **~ in** *vt* colorier; **~ bar** *n* discrimination raciale (*dans un établissement*); **~-blind** *adj* daltonien(ne); **~ed** *adj* (*person*) de couleur; (*illustration*) en couleur; **~ film** *n* (*for camera*) pellicule *f* (en) couleur; **~ful** *adj* coloré(e), vif(-vive); (*personality*) pittoresque, haut(e) en couleurs; **~ing** ['kʌlərɪŋ] *n* colorant *m*; (*complexion*) teint *m*; **~ scheme** *n* combinaison *f* de(s) couleurs; **~ television** *n* télévision *f* (en) couleur
colt [kəult] *n* poulain *m*
column ['kɔləm] *n* colonne *f*; **~ist** ['kɔləmnɪst] *n* chroniqueur(-euse)
coma ['kəumə] *n* coma *m*
comb [kəum] *n* peigne *m* ♦ *vt* (*hair*) peigner; (*area*) ratisser, passer au peigne fin
combat ['kɔmbæt] *n* combat *m* ♦ *vt* combattre, lutter contre
combination [kɔmbɪ'neɪʃən] *n* combinaison *f*
combine [*vb* kəm'baɪn, *n* 'kɔmbaɪn] *vt*: **to ~ sth with sth** combiner qch avec qch; (*one quality with another*) joindre *or* allier qch à qch ♦ *vi* s'associer; (*CHEM*) se combiner ♦ *n* (*ECON*) trust *m*; **~ (har-**

vester) *n* moissonneuse-batteuse(-lieuse) *f*

come [kʌm] (*pt* **came**, *pp* **come**) *vi* venir, arriver; **to ~ to** (*decision etc*) parvenir *or* arriver à; **to ~ undone/loose** se défaire/desserrer; **~ about** *vi* se produire, arriver; **~ across** *vt fus* rencontrer par hasard, tomber sur; **~ along** *vi* = **come on**; **~ away** *vi* partir, s'en aller, se détacher; **~ back** *vi* revenir; **~ by** *vt fus* (*acquire*) obtenir, se procurer; **~ down** *vi* descendre; (*prices*) baisser; (*buildings*) s'écrouler, être démoli(e); **~ forward** *vi* s'avancer, se présenter, s'annoncer; **~ from** *vt fus* être originaire de, venir de; **~ in** *vi* entrer; **~ in for** *vi* (*criticism etc*) être l'objet de; **~ into** *vt fus* (*money*) hériter de; **~ off** *vi* (*button*) se détacher; (*stain*) s'enlever; (*attempt*) réussir; **~ on** *vi* (*pupil, work, project*) faire des progrès, s'avancer; (*lights, electricity*) s'allumer; (*central heating*) se mettre en marche; **~ on!** viens!, allons!, allez!; **~ out** *vi* sortir; (*book*) paraître; (*strike*) cesser le travail, se mettre en grève; **~ round** *vi* (*after faint, operation*) revenir à soi, reprendre connaissance; **~ to** *vi* revenir à soi; **~ up** *vi* monter; **~ up against** *vt fus* (*resistance, difficulties*) rencontrer; **~ up with** *vt fus*: **he came up with an idea** il a eu une idée, il a proposé quelque chose; **~ upon** *vt fus* tomber sur; **~back** *n* (THEATRE *etc*) rentrée *f*

comedian [kə'mi:dɪən] *n* (*in music hall etc*) comique *m*; (THEATRE) comédien *m*

comedy ['kɔmɪdɪ] *n* comédie *f*

comeuppance [kʌm'ʌpəns] *n*: **to get one's ~** recevoir ce qu'on mérite

comfort ['kʌmfət] *n* confort *m*, bien-être *m*; (*relief*) soulagement *m*, réconfort *m* ♦ *vt* consoler, réconforter; **the ~s of home** les commodités *fpl* de la maison; **~able** *adj* confortable; (*person*) à l'aise; (*patient*) dont l'état est stationnaire; (*walk etc*) facile; **~ably** *adv* (*sit*) confortablement; (*live*) à l'aise; **~ station** (US) *n* toilettes *fpl*

comic ['kɔmɪk] *adj* (*also:* **~al**) comique ♦ *n* comique *m*; (BRIT: *magazine*) illustré *m*; **~ strip** *n* bande dessinée

coming ['kʌmɪŋ] *n* arrivée *f* ♦ *adj* prochain(e), à venir; **~(s) and going(s)** *n(pl)* va-et-vient *m inv*

comma ['kɔmə] *n* virgule *f*

command [kə'mɑ:nd] *n* ordre *m*, commandement *m*; (MIL: *authority*) commandement; (*mastery*) maîtrise *f* ♦ *vt* (*troops*) commander; **to ~ sb to do** ordonner à qn de faire; **~eer** [kɔmən'dɪə^r] *vt* réquisitionner; **~er** *n* (MIL) commandant *m*

commando [kə'mɑ:ndəu] *n* commando *m*; membre *m* d'un commando

commemorate [kə'mɛməreɪt] *vt* commémorer

commence [kə'mɛns] *vt, vi* commencer

commend [kə'mɛnd] *vt* louer; (*recommend*) recommander

commensurate [kə'mɛnʃərɪt] *adj*: **~ with** *or* **to** en proportion de, proportionné(e) à

comment ['kɔmɛnt] *n* commentaire *m* ♦ *vi*: **to ~ (on)** faire des remarques (sur); **"no ~"** "je n'ai rien à dire"; **~ary** ['kɔməntərɪ] *n* commentaire *m*; (SPORT) reportage *m* (en direct); **~ator** ['kɔmənteɪtə^r] *n* commentateur *m*; reporter *m*

commerce ['kɔmə:s] *n* commerce *m*

commercial [kə'mə:ʃəl] *adj* commercial(e) ♦ *n* (TV, RADIO) annonce *f* publicitaire, spot *m* (publicitaire)

commiserate [kə'mɪzəreɪt] *vi*: **to ~ with sb** témoigner de la sympathie pour qn

commission [kə'mɪʃən] *n* (*order for work*) commande *f*; (*committee, fee*) commission *f* ♦ *vt* (*work of art*) commander, charger un artiste de l'exécution de; **out of ~** (*not working*) hors service; **~aire** [kəmɪʃə'nɛə^r] (BRIT) *n* (*at shop, cinema etc*) portier *m* (en uniforme); **~er** *n* (*POLICE*) préfet *m* (de police)

commit [kə'mɪt] *vt* (*act*) commettre; (*resources*) consacrer; (*to sb's care*) confier (à); **to ~ o.s. (to do)** s'engager (à faire); **to ~ suicide** se suicider; **~ment** *n* engagement *m*; (*obligation*) responsabilité(s) *f(pl)*

committee [kə'mɪtɪ] *n* comité *m*

commodity [kə'mɔdɪtɪ] *n* produit *m*, marchandise *f*, article *m*

common ['kɔmən] *adj* commun(e); (*usual*) courant(e) ♦ *n* terrain communal; **the C~s** (*BRIT*) *npl* la chambre des Communes; **in ~** en commun; **~er** *n* roturier(-ière); **~ law** *n* droit coutumier; **~ly** *adv* communément, généralement; couramment; **C~ Market** *n* Marché commun; **~place** *adj* banal(e), ordinaire; **~ room** *n* salle commune; **~ sense** *n* bon sens; **C~wealth** (*BRIT*) *n* Commonwealth *m*

commotion [kə'məuʃən] *n* désordre *m*, tumulte *m*

communal ['kɔmju:nl] *adj* (*life*) communautaire; (*for common use*) commun(e)

commune [*n* 'kɔmju:n, *vb* kə'mju:n] *n* (*group*) communauté *f* ♦ *vi*: **to ~ with** communier avec

communicate [kə'mju:nɪkeɪt] *vt, vi* communiquer; **communication** [kəmju:nɪ'keɪʃən] *n* communication *f*; **communication cord** (*BRIT*) *n* sonnette *f* d'alarme

communion [kə'mju:nɪən] *n* (*also:* **Holy C~**) communion *f*

communism ['kɔmjunɪzəm] *n* communisme *m*; **communist** *adj* communiste ♦ *n* communiste *m/f*

community [kə'mju:nɪtɪ] *n* communauté *f*; **~ centre** *n* centre *m* de loisirs; **~ chest** (*US*) *n* fonds commun

commutation ticket [kɔmju'teɪʃən-] (*US*) *n* carte *f* d'abonnement

commute [kə'mju:t] *vi* faire un trajet journalier pour se rendre à son travail ♦ *vt* (*LAW*) commuer; **~r** *n* banlieusard(e) (*qui fait un trajet journalier pour se rendre à son travail*)

compact [*adj* kəm'pækt, *n* 'kɔmpækt] *adj* compact(e) ♦ *n* (*also:* **powder ~**) poudrier *m*; **~ disc** *n* disque compact; **~ disc player** *n* lecteur *m* de disque compact

companion [kəm'pænjən] *n* compagnon (compagne); **~ship** *n* camaraderie *f*

company ['kʌmpənɪ] *n* compagnie *f*; **to keep sb ~** tenir compagnie à qn; **~ secretary** (*BRIT*) *n* (*COMM*) secrétaire général (*d'une société*)

comparative [kəm'pærətɪv] *adj* (*study*) comparatif(-ive); (*relative*) relatif(-ive); **~ly** *adv* (*relatively*) relativement

compare [kəm'pɛə[r]] *vt*: **to ~ sth/sb with/to** comparer qch/qn avec *or* et/à ♦ *vi*: **to ~ (with)** se comparer (à); être comparable (à); **comparison** [kəm'pærɪsn] *n* comparaison *f*

compartment [kəm'pɑ:tmənt] *n* compartiment *m*

compass ['kʌmpəs] *n* boussole *f*; **~es** *npl* (*GEOM*: *also:* **pair of ~es**) compas *m*

compassion [kəm'pæʃən] *n* compassion *f*; **~ate** *adj* compatissant(e)

compatible [kəm'pætɪbl] *adj* compatible

compel [kəm'pɛl] *vt* contraindre, obliger

compensate ['kɔmpənseɪt] *vt* indemniser, dédommager ♦ *vi*: **to ~ for** compenser; **compensation** [kɔmpən'seɪʃən] *n* compensation *f*; (*money*) dédommagement *m*, indemnité *f*

compère ['kɔmpɛə[r]] *n* (*TV*) animateur(-trice)

compete [kəm'pi:t] *vi*: **to ~ (with)** rivaliser (avec), faire concurrence (à)

competent ['kɔmpɪtənt] *adj* compétent(e), capable

competition [kɔmpɪ'tɪʃən] *n* (*contest*) compétition *f*, concours *m*; (*ECON*) concurrence *f*

competitive [kəm'pɛtɪtɪv] *adj* (*ECON*) concurrentiel(le); (*sport*) de compétition; (*person*) qui a l'esprit de compétition; **competitor** *n* concurrent(e)

complacency [kəm'pleɪsnsɪ] *n* suffisance *f*, vaine complaisance

complain [kəm'pleɪn] *vi*: **to ~ (about)** se plaindre (de); (*in shop etc*) réclamer (au sujet de); **to ~ of** (*pain*) se plaindre de; **~t** *n* plainte *f*; réclamation *f*; (*MED*) affection *f*

complement [*n* 'kɔmplɪmənt, *vb* 'kɔmplɪmɛnt] *n* complément *m*; (*especially of ship's crew etc*) effectif complet ♦ *vt* (*enhance*) compléter; **~ary** [kɔmplɪ'mɛntərɪ] *adj* complémentaire

complete [kəm'pli:t] *adj* complet(-ète) ♦ *vt* achever, parachever; (*set, group*) compléter; (*a form*) remplir; **~ly** *adv* complètement; **completion** *n* achèvement *m*; (*of contract*) exécution *f*

complex ['kɔmplɛks] *adj* complexe ♦ *n* complexe *m*

complexion [kəm'plɛkʃən] *n* (*of face*) teint *m*

compliance [kəm'plaɪəns] *n* (*submission*) docilité *f*; (*agreement*): **~ with** le fait de se conformer à; **in ~ with** en accord avec

complicate ['kɔmplɪkeɪt] *vt* compliquer; **~d** *adj* compliqué(e); **complication** [kɔmplɪ'keɪʃən] *n* complication *f*

compliment [*n* 'kɔmplɪmənt, *vb* 'kɔmplɪmɛnt] *n* compliment *m* ♦ *vt* complimenter; **~s** *npl* (*respects*) compliments *mpl*, hommages *mpl*; **to pay sb a ~** faire *or* adresser un compliment à qn; **~ary** [kɔmplɪ'mɛntərɪ] *adj* flatteur(-euse); (*free*) (offert(e)) à titre gracieux; **~ary ticket** *n* billet *m* de faveur

comply [kəm'plaɪ] *vi*: **to ~ with** se soumettre à, se conformer à

component [kəm'pəunənt] *n* composant *m*, élément *m*

compose [kəm'pəuz] *vt* composer; (*form*): **to be ~d of** se composer de; **to ~ o.s.** se calmer, se maîtriser; prendre une contenance; **~d** *adj* calme, posé(e); **~r** *n* (*MUS*) compositeur *m*; **composition** [kɔmpə'zɪʃən] *n* composition *f*;

composure [kəm'pəuʒə^r] *n* calme *m*, maîtrise *f* de soi

compound ['kɔmpaund] *n* composé *m*; (*enclosure*) enclos *m*, enceinte *f*; **~ fracture** *n* fracture compliquée; **~ interest** *n* intérêt composé

comprehend [kɔmprɪ'hɛnd] *vt* comprendre; **comprehension** *n* compréhension *f*

comprehensive [kɔmprɪ'hɛnsɪv] *adj* (très) complet(-ète); **~ policy** *n* (*INSURANCE*) assurance *f* tous risques; **~ (school)** (*BRIT*) *n école secondaire polyvalente*; ≃ C.E.S. *m*

compress [*vb* kəm'prɛs, *n* 'kɔmprɛs] *vt* comprimer; (*text, information*) condenser ♦ *n* (*MED*) compresse *f*

comprise [kəm'praɪz] *vt* (*also:* **be ~d of**) comprendre; (*constitute*) constituer, représenter

compromise ['kɔmprəmaɪz] *n* compromis *m* ♦ *vt* compromettre ♦ *vi* transiger, accepter un compromis

compulsion [kəm'pʌlʃən] *n* contrainte *f*, force *f*

compulsive [kəm'pʌlsɪv] *adj* (*PSYCH*) compulsif(-ive); (*book, film etc*) captivant(e)

compulsory [kəm'pʌlsərɪ] *adj* obligatoire

computer [kəm'pju:tə^r] *n* ordinateur *m*; **~ game** *n* jeu *m* vidéo; **~-generated** *adj* de synthèse; **~ize** *vt* informatiser; **~ programmer** *n* programmeur(-euse); **~ programming** *n* programmation *f*; **~ science** *n* informatique *f*; **computing** *n* = **computer science**

comrade ['kɔmrɪd] *n* camarade *m/f*

con [kɔn] *vt* duper; (*cheat*) escroquer ♦ *n* escroquerie *f*

conceal [kən'si:l] *vt* cacher, dissimuler

conceit [kən'si:t] *n* vanité *f*, suffisance *f*, prétention *f*; **~ed** *adj* vaniteux(-euse), suffisant(e)
conceive [kən'si:v] *vt, vi* concevoir
concentrate ['kɔnsəntreɪt] *vi* se concentrer ♦ *vt* concentrer; **concentration** *n* concentration *f*; **concentration camp** *n* camp *m* de concentration
concept ['kɔnsɛpt] *n* concept *m*
concern [kən'sə:n] *n* affaire *f*; (COMM) entreprise *f*, firme *f*; (*anxiety*) inquiétude *f*, souci *m* ♦ *vt* concerner; **to be ~ed (about)** s'inquiéter (de), être inquiet (-ète) (au sujet de); **~ing** *prep* en ce qui concerne, à propos de
concert ['kɔnsət] *n* concert *m*; **~ed** [kən'sə:tɪd] *adj* concerté(e); **~ hall** *n* salle *f* de concert
concerto [kən'tʃə:təu] *n* concerto *m*
concession [kən'sɛʃən] *n* concession *f*; **tax ~** dégrèvement fiscal
conclude [kən'klu:d] *vt* conclure; **conclusion** [kən'klu:ʒən] *n* conclusion *f*; **conclusive** [kən'klu:sɪv] *adj* concluant(e), définitif(-ive)
concoct [kən'kɔkt] *vt* confectionner, composer; (*fig*) inventer; **~ion** *n* mélange *m*
concourse ['kɔŋkɔ:s] *n* (*hall*) hall *m*, salle *f* des pas perdus
concrete ['kɔŋkri:t] *n* béton *m* ♦ *adj* concret(-ète); (*floor etc*) en béton
concur [kən'kə:ʳ] *vi* (*agree*) être d'accord
concurrently [kən'kʌrntlɪ] *adv* simultanément
concussion [kən'kʌʃən] *n* (MED) commotion (cérébrale)
condemn [kən'dɛm] *vt* condamner
condensation [kɔndɛn'seɪʃən] *n* condensation *f*
condense [kən'dɛns] *vi* se condenser ♦ *vt* condenser; **~d milk** *n* lait concentré (sucré)
condition [kən'dɪʃən] *n* condition *f*; (MED) état *m* ♦ *vt* déterminer, conditionner; **on ~ that** à condition que *+sub*, à condition de; **~al** *adj* conditionnel(le); **~er** *n* (*for hair*) baume après-shampooing *m*; (*for fabrics*) assouplissant *m*
condolences [kən'dəulənsɪz] *npl* condoléances *fpl*
condom ['kɔndəm] *n* préservatif *m*
condominium [kɔndə'mɪnɪəm] (US) *n* (*building*) immeuble *m* (en copropriété)
condone [kən'dəun] *vt* fermer les yeux sur, approuver (tacitement)
conducive [kən'dju:sɪv] *adj*: **~ to** favorable à, qui contribue à
conduct [*n* 'kɔndʌkt, *vb* kən'dʌkt] *n* conduite *f* ♦ *vt* conduire; (MUS) diriger; **to ~ o.s.** se conduire, se comporter; **~ed tour** *n* voyage organisé; (*of building*) visite guidée; **~or** *n* (*of orchestra*) chef *m* d'orchestre; (*on bus*) receveur *m*; (US: *on train*) chef *m* de train; (ELEC) conducteur *m*; **~ress** *n* (*on bus*) receveuse *f*
cone [kəun] *n* cône *m*; (*for ice-cream*) cornet *m*; (BOT) pomme *f* de pin, cône
confectioner [kən'fɛkʃənəʳ] *n* confiseur(-euse); **~'s (shop)** *n* confiserie *f*; **~y** *n* confiserie *f*
confer [kən'fə:ʳ] *vt*: **to ~ sth on** conférer qch à ♦ *vi* conférer, s'entretenir
conference ['kɔnfərəns] *n* conférence *f*
confess [kən'fɛs] *vt* confesser, avouer ♦ *vi* se confesser; **~ion** *n* confession *f*
confetti [kən'fɛtɪ] *n* confettis *mpl*
confide [kən'faɪd] *vi*: **to ~ in** se confier à
confidence ['kɔnfɪdns] *n* confiance *f*; (*also*: **self-~**) assurance *f*, confiance en soi; (*secret*) confidence *f*; **in ~** (*speak, write*) en confidence, confidentiellement; **~ trick** *n* escroquerie *f*; **confident** *adj* sûr(e), assuré(e); **confidential** [kɔnfɪ'dɛnʃəl] *adj* confidentiel(le)
confine [kən'faɪn] *vt* limiter, borner; (*shut up*) confiner, enfermer; **~d** *adj* (*space*) restreint(e), réduit(e); **~ment** *n* emprisonnement *m*, détention *f*; **~s**

['kɔnfaɪnz] *npl* confins *mpl*, bornes *fpl*

confirm [kən'fə:m] *vt* confirmer; (*appointment*) ratifier; **~ation** [kɔnfə'meɪʃən] *n* confirmation *f*; **~ed** *adj* invétéré(e), incorrigible

confiscate ['kɔnfɪskeɪt] *vt* confisquer

conflict [*n* 'kɔnflɪkt, *vb* kən'flɪkt] *n* conflit *m*, lutte *f* ♦ *vi* être *or* entrer en conflit; (*opinions*) s'opposer, se heurter; **~ing** [kən'flɪktɪŋ] *adj* contradictoire

conform [kən'fɔ:m] *vi*: **to ~ (to)** se conformer (à)

confound [kən'faund] *vt* confondre

confront [kən'frʌnt] *vt* confronter, mettre en présence; (*enemy, danger*) affronter, faire face à; **~ation** [kɔnfrən'teɪʃən] *n* confrontation *f*

confuse [kən'fju:z] *vt* (*person*) troubler; (*situation*) embrouiller; (*one thing with another*) confondre; **~d** *adj* (*person*) dérouté(e), désorienté(e); **confusing** *adj* peu clair(e), déroutant(e); **confusion** [kən'fju:ʒən] *n* confusion *f*

congeal [kən'dʒi:l] *vi* (*blood*) se coaguler; (*oil etc*) se figer

congenial [kən'dʒi:nɪəl] *adj* sympathique, agréable

congested [kən'dʒɛstɪd] *adj* (*MED*) congestionné(e); (*area*) surpeuplé(e); (*road*) bloqué(e); **congestion** *n* congestion *f*; (*fig*) encombrement *m*

congratulate [kən'grætjuleɪt] *vt*: **to ~ sb (on)** féliciter qn (de); **congratulations** [kəngrætju'leɪʃənz] *npl* félicitations *fpl*

congregate ['kɔŋgrɪgeɪt] *vi* se rassembler, se réunir; **congregation** [kɔŋgrɪ'geɪʃən] *n* assemblée *f* (des fidèles)

congress ['kɔŋgrɛs] *n* congrès *m*; **~man** (*irreg*) (*US*) *n* membre *m* du Congrès

conjunction [kən'dʒʌŋkʃən] *n* (*LING*) conjonction *f*

conjunctivitis [kəndʒʌŋktɪ'vaɪtɪs] *n* conjonctivite *f*

conjure ['kʌndʒər] *vi* faire des tours de passe-passe; **~ up** *vt* (*ghost, spirit*) faire apparaître; (*memories*) évoquer; **~r** *n* prestidigitateur *m*, illusionniste *m/f*

con man (*irreg*) *n* escroc *m*

connect [kə'nɛkt] *vt* joindre, relier; (*ELEC*) connecter; (*TEL*: *caller*) mettre en connection (*with* avec); (: *new subscriber*) brancher; (*fig*) établir un rapport entre, faire un rapprochement entre ♦ *vi* (*train*): **to ~ with** assurer la correspondance avec; **to be ~ed with** (*fig*) avoir un rapport avec, avoir des rapports avec, être en relation avec; **~ion** *n* relation *f*, lien *m*; (*ELEC*) connexion *f*; (*train, plane etc*) correspondance *f*; (*TEL*) branchement *m*, communication *f*

connive [kə'naɪv] *vi*: **to ~ at** se faire le complice de

conquer ['kɔŋkər] *vt* conquérir; (*feelings*) vaincre, surmonter; **conquest** ['kɔŋkwest] *n* conquête *f*

cons [kɔnz] *npl see* **convenience**; **pro**

conscience ['kɔnʃəns] *n* conscience *f*; **conscientious** [kɔnʃɪ'ɛnʃəs] *adj* consciencieux(-euse)

conscious ['kɔnʃəs] *adj* conscient(e); **~ness** *n* conscience *f*; (*MED*) connaissance *f*

conscript ['kɔnskrɪpt] *n* conscrit *m*

consent [kən'sɛnt] *n* consentement *m* ♦ *vi*: **to ~ (to)** consentir (à)

consequence ['kɔnsɪkwəns] *n* conséquence *f*, suites *fpl*; (*significance*) importance *f*; **consequently** *adv* par conséquent, donc

conservation [kɔnsə'veɪʃən] *n* préservation *f*, protection *f*

conservative [kən'sə:vətɪv] *adj* conservateur(-trice); **at a ~ estimate** au bas mot; **C~** (*BRIT*) *adj, n* (*POL*) conservateur(-trice)

conservatory [kən'sə:vətrɪ] *n* (*greenhouse*) serre *f*

conserve [kən'sə:v] *vt* conserver, préserver; (*supplies, energy*) économiser ♦ *n* confiture *f*

consider [kən'sɪdər] *vt* (*study*) considérer, réfléchir à; (*take into account*) penser à, prendre en considération; (*regard, judge*) considérer, estimer; **to ~ doing sth** envisager de faire qch; **~able** *adj* considérable; **~ably** *adv* nettement; **~ate** *adj* prévenant(e), plein(e) d'égards; **~ation** [kənsɪdə'reɪʃən] *n* considération *f*; **~ing** *prep* étant donné

consign [kən'saɪn] *vt* expédier; (*to sb's care*) confier; (*fig*) livrer; **~ment** *n* arrivage *m*, envoi *m*

consist [kən'sɪst] *vi*: **to ~ of** consister en, se composer de

consistency [kən'sɪstənsɪ] *n* consistance *f*; (*fig*) cohérence *f*

consistent [kən'sɪstənt] *adj* logique, cohérent(e)

consolation [kɔnsə'leɪʃən] *n* consolation *f*

console[1] [kən'səul] *vt* consoler

console[2] ['kɔnsəul] *n* (COMPUT) console *f*

consonant ['kɔnsənənt] *n* consonne *f*

conspicuous [kən'spɪkjuəs] *adj* voyant(e), qui attire l'attention

conspiracy [kən'spɪrəsɪ] *n* conspiration *f*, complot *m*

constable ['kʌnstəbl] (BRIT) *n* ≃ agent *m* de police, gendarme *m*; **chief ~** ≃ préfet *m* de police; **constabulary** [kən'stæbjulərɪ] (BRIT) *n* ≃ police *f*, gendarmerie *f*

constant ['kɔnstənt] *adj* constant(e); incessant(e); **~ly** *adv* constamment, sans cesse

constipated ['kɔnstɪpeɪtɪd] *adj* constipé(e); **constipation** [kɔnstɪ'peɪʃən] *n* constipation *f*

constituency [kən'stɪtjuənsɪ] *n* circonscription électorale

constituent [kən'stɪtjuənt] *n* (POL) électeur(-trice); (*part*) élément constitutif, composant *m*

constitution [kɔnstɪ'tju:ʃən] *n* constitution *f*; **~al** *adj* constitutionnel(le)

constraint [kən'streɪnt] *n* contrainte *f*

construct [kən'strʌkt] *vt* construire; **~ion** *n* construction *f*; **~ive** *adj* constructif(-ive); **~ive dismissal** démission forcée

consul ['kɔnsl] *n* consul *m*; **~ate** ['kɔnsjulɪt] *n* consulat *m*

consult [kən'sʌlt] *vt* consulter; **~ant** *n* (MED) médecin consultant; (*other specialist*) consultant *m*, (expert-)conseil *m*; **~ing room** (BRIT) *n* cabinet *m* de consultation

consume [kən'sju:m] *vt* consommer; **~r** *n* consommateur(-trice); **~r goods** *npl* biens *mpl* de consommation; **~r society** *n* société *f* de consommation

consummate ['kɔnsʌmeɪt] *vt* consommer

consumption [kən'sʌmpʃən] *n* consommation *f*

cont. *abbr* (= *continued*) suite

contact ['kɔntækt] *n* contact *m*; (*person*) connaissance *f*, relation *f* ♦ *vt* contacter, se mettre en contact *or* en rapport avec; **~ lenses** *npl* verres *mpl* de contact, lentilles *fpl*

contagious [kən'teɪdʒəs] *adj* contagieux(-euse)

contain [kən'teɪn] *vt* contenir; **to ~ o.s.** se contenir, se maîtriser; **~er** *n* récipient *m*; (*for shipping etc*) container *m*

contaminate [kən'tæmɪneɪt] *vt* contaminer

cont'd *abbr* (= *continued*) suite

contemplate ['kɔntəmpleɪt] *vt* contempler; (*consider*) envisager

contemporary [kən'tɛmpərərɪ] *adj* contemporain(e); (*design, wallpaper*) moderne ♦ *n* contemporain(e)

contempt [kən'tɛmpt] *n* mépris *m*, dédain *m*; **~ of court** (LAW) outrage *m* à l'autorité de la justice; **~uous** [kən'tɛmptjuəs] *adj* dédaigneux(-euse), méprisant(e)

contend [kən'tɛnd] *vt*: **to ~ that** soutenir *or* prétendre que ♦ *vi*: **to ~ with** (*compete*) rivaliser avec; (*struggle*) lutter avec; **~er** *n* concurrent(e); (POL) candidat(e)

content [*adj, vb* kən'tɛnt, *n* 'kɔntɛnt] *adj* content(e), satisfait(e) ♦ *vt* contenter, satisfaire ♦ *n* contenu *m*; (*of fat, moisture*) teneur *f*; **~s** *npl* (*of container etc*) contenu *m*; **(table of) ~s** table *f* des matières; **~ed** *adj* content(e), satisfait(e)

contention [kən'tɛnʃən] *n* dispute *f*, contestation *f*; (*argument*) assertion *f*, affirmation *f*

contest [*n* 'kɔntɛst, *vb* kən'tɛst] *n* combat *m*, lutte *f*; (*competition*) concours *m* ♦ *vt* (*decision, statement*) contester, discuter; (*compete for*) disputer; **~ant** [kən'tɛstənt] *n* concurrent(e); (*in fight*) adversaire *m/f*

context ['kɔntɛkst] *n* contexte *m*

continent ['kɔntɪnənt] *n* continent *m*; **the C~** (BRIT) l'Europe continentale; **~al** [kɔntɪ'nɛntl] *adj* continental(e); **~al breakfast** *n* petit déjeuner *m* à la française; **~al quilt** (BRIT) *n* couette *f*

contingency [kən'tɪndʒənsɪ] *n* éventualité *f*, événement imprévu

continual [kən'tɪnjuəl] *adj* continuel(le)

continuation [kəntɪnju'eɪʃən] *n* continuation *f*; (*after interruption*) reprise *f*; (*of story*) suite *f*

continue [kən'tɪnju:] *vi, vt* continuer; (*after interruption*) reprendre, poursuivre; **continuity** [kɔntɪ'nju:ɪtɪ] *n* continuité *f*; (TV *etc*) enchaînement *m*; **continuous** [kən'tɪnjuəs] *adj* continu(e); (LING) progressif(-ive)

contort [kən'tɔ:t] *vt* tordre, crisper

contour ['kɔntuəʳ] *n* contour *m*, profil *m*; (*on map*: *also*: **~ line**) courbe *f* de niveau

contraband ['kɔntrəbænd] *n* contrebande *f*

contraceptive [kɔntrə'sɛptɪv] *adj* contraceptif(-ive), anticonceptionnel(le) ♦ *n* contraceptif *m*

contract [*n* 'kɔntrækt, *vb* kən'trækt] *n* contrat *m* ♦ *vi* (*become smaller*) se contracter, se resserrer; (COMM): **to ~ to do sth** s'engager (par contrat) à faire qch; **~ion** [kən'trækʃən] *n* contraction *f*; **~or** [kən'træktəʳ] *n* entrepreneur *m*

contradict [kɔntrə'dɪkt] *vt* contredire

contraflow ['kɔntrəfləu] *n* (AUT): **~ lane** voie *f* à contresens; **there's a ~ system in operation on ...** une voie a été mise en sens inverse sur ...

contraption [kən'træpʃən] (*pej*) *n* machin *m*, truc *m*

contrary[1] ['kɔntrərɪ] *adj* contraire, opposé(e) ♦ *n* contraire *m*; **on the ~** au contraire; **unless you hear to the ~** sauf avis contraire

contrary[2] [kən'trɛərɪ] *adj* (*perverse*) contrariant(e), entêté(e)

contrast [*n* 'kɔntrɑ:st, *vb* kən'trɑ:st] *n* contraste *m* ♦ *vt* mettre en contraste, contraster; **in ~ to** *or* **with** contrairement à

contravene [kɔntrə'vi:n] *vt* enfreindre, violer, contrevenir à

contribute [kən'trɪbju:t] *vi* contribuer ♦ *vt*: **to ~ £10/an article to** donner 10 livres/un article à; **to ~ to** contribuer à; (*newspaper*) collaborer à; **contribution** [kɔntrɪ'bju:ʃən] *n* contribution *f*; **contributor** [kən'trɪbjutəʳ] *n* (*to newspaper*) collaborateur(-trice)

contrive [kən'traɪv] *vi*: **to ~ to do** s'arranger pour faire, trouver le moyen de faire

control [kən'trəul] *vt* maîtriser, commander; (*check*) contrôler ♦ *n* contrôle *m*, autorité *f*; maîtrise *f*; **~s** *npl* (*of machine etc*) commandes *fpl*; (*on radio,* TV) boutons *mpl* de réglage; **~led substance** narcotique *m*; **everything is under ~** tout va bien, j'ai (*or* il a *etc*) la situation en main; **to be in ~ of** être maître de, maîtriser; **the car went out of ~** j'ai (*or* il a *etc*) perdu le contrôle du véhicule; **~ panel** *n* tableau *m* de commande; **~ room** *n* salle *f* des commandes; **~ tower** *n* (AVIAT) tour *f* de contrôle

controversial [kɔntrə'və:ʃl] *adj* (*topic*)

discutable, controversé(e); (*person*) qui fait beaucoup parler de lui; **controversy** ['kɔntrəvəːsɪ] *n* controverse *f*, polémique *f*

convalesce [kɔnvə'lɛs] *vi* relever de maladie, se remettre (d'une maladie)

convector [kən'vɛktə[r]] *n* (*heater*) radiateur *m* (à convexion)

convene [kən'viːn] *vt* convoquer, assembler ♦ *vi* se réunir, s'assembler

convenience [kən'viːnɪəns] *n* commodité *f*; **at your ~** quand *or* comme cela vous convient; **all modern ~s**, (*BRIT*) **all mod cons** avec tout le confort moderne, tout confort

convenient [kən'viːnɪənt] *adj* commode

convent ['kɔnvənt] *n* couvent *m*; **~ school** *n* couvent *m*

convention [kən'vɛnʃən] *n* convention *f*; **~al** *adj* conventionnel(le)

conversant [kən'vəːsnt] *adj*: **to be ~ with** s'y connaître en; être au courant de

conversation [kɔnvə'seɪʃən] *n* conversation *f*

converse [*n* 'kɔnvəːs, *vb* kən'vəːs] *n* contraire *m*, inverse *m* ♦ *vi* s'entretenir; **~ly** [kɔn'vəːslɪ] *adv* inversement, réciproquement

convert [*vb* kən'vəːt, *n* 'kɔnvəːt] *vt* (*REL, COMM*) convertir; (*alter*) transformer; (*house*) aménager ♦ *n* converti(e); **~ible** [kən'vəːtəbl] *n* (voiture *f*) décapotable *f*

convey [kən'veɪ] *vt* transporter; (*thanks*) transmettre; (*idea*) communiquer; **~or belt** *n* convoyeur *m*, tapis roulant

convict [*vb* kən'vɪkt, *n* 'kɔnvɪkt] *vt* déclarer (*or* reconnaître) coupable ♦ *n* forçat *m*, détenu *m*; **~ion** *n* (*LAW*) condamnation *f*; (*belief*) conviction *f*

convince [kən'vɪns] *vt* convaincre, persuader; **convincing** *adj* persuasif(-ive), convaincant(e)

convoluted ['kɔnvəluːtɪd] *adj* (*argument*) compliqué(e)

convulse [kən'vʌls] *vt*: **to be ~d with laughter/pain** se tordre de rire/douleur

cook [kuk] *vt* (faire) cuire ♦ *vi* cuire; (*person*) faire la cuisine ♦ *n* cuisinier (-ière); **~book** *n* livre *m* de cuisine; **~er** *n* cuisinière *f*; **~ery** *n* cuisine *f*; **~ery book** (*BRIT*) *n* = **cookbook**; **~ie** (*US*) *n* biscuit *m*, petit gâteau sec; **~ing** *n* cuisine *f*

cool [kuːl] *adj* frais (fraîche); (*calm, unemotional*) calme; (*unfriendly*) froid(e) ♦ *vt, vi* rafraîchir, refroidir

coop [kuːp] *n* poulailler *m*; (*for rabbits*) clapier *m* ♦ *vt*: **to ~ up** (*fig*) cloîtrer, enfermer

cooperate [kəu'ɔpəreɪt] *vi* coopérer, collaborer; **cooperation** [kəuɔpə'reɪʃən] *n* coopération *f*, collaboration *f*; **cooperative** [kəu'ɔpərətɪv] *adj* coopératif(-ive) ♦ *n* coopérative *f*

coordinate [*vb* kəu'ɔːdɪneɪt, *n* kəu'ɔdɪnət] *vt* coordonner ♦ *n* (*MATH*) coordonnée *f*; **~s** *npl* (*clothes*) ensemble *m*, coordonnés *mpl*

co-ownership [kəu'əunəʃɪp] *n* copropriété *f*

cop [kɔp] (*inf*) *n* flic *m*

cope [kəup] *vi*: **to ~ with** faire face à; (*solve*) venir à bout de

copper ['kɔpə[r]] *n* cuivre *m*; (*BRIT*: *inf*: *policeman*) flic *m*; **~s** *npl* (*coins*) petite monnaie

copy ['kɔpɪ] *n* copie *f*; (*of book etc*) exemplaire *m* ♦ *vt* copier; **~right** *n* droit *m* d'auteur, copyright *m*

coral ['kɔrəl] *n* corail *m*

cord [kɔːd] *n* corde *f*; (*fabric*) velours côtelé; (*ELEC*) cordon *m*, fil *m*

cordial ['kɔːdɪəl] *adj* cordial(e), chaleureux(-euse) ♦ *n* cordial *m*

cordon ['kɔːdn] *n* cordon *m*; **~ off** *vt* boucler (*par cordon de police*)

corduroy ['kɔːdərɔɪ] *n* velours côtelé

core [kɔː[r]] *n* noyau *m*; (*of fruit*) trognon *m*, cœur *m*; (*of building, problem*) cœur

♦ *vt* enlever le trognon *or* le cœur de

cork [kɔːk] *n* liège *m*; (*of bottle*) bouchon *m*; **~screw** *n* tire-bouchon *m*

corn [kɔːn] *n* (*BRIT*: *wheat*) blé *m*; (*US*: *maize*) maïs *m*; (*on foot*) cor *m*; **~ on the cob** (*CULIN*) épi *m* de maïs; **~ed beef** *n* corned-beef *m*

corner ['kɔːnəʳ] *n* coin *m*; (*AUT*) tournant *m*, virage *m*; (*FOOTBALL*: *also*: **~ kick**) corner *m* ♦ *vt* acculer, mettre au pied du mur; coincer; (*COMM*: *market*) accaparer ♦ *vi* prendre un virage; **~stone** *n* pierre *f* angulaire

cornet ['kɔːnɪt] *n* (*MUS*) cornet *m* à pistons; (*BRIT*: *of ice-cream*) cornet (de glace)

cornflakes ['kɔːnfleɪks] *npl* corn-flakes *mpl*

cornflour ['kɔːnflauəʳ] (*BRIT*), **cornstarch** ['kɔːnstɑːtʃ] (*US*) *n* farine *f* de maïs, maïzena *f*®

Cornwall ['kɔːnwəl] *n* Cornouailles *f*

corny ['kɔːnɪ] (*inf*) *adj* rebattu(e)

coronary ['kɔrənərɪ] *n* (*also*: **~ thrombosis**) infarctus *m* (du myocarde), thrombose *f* coronarienne

coronation [kɔrə'neɪʃən] *n* couronnement *m*

coroner ['kɔrənəʳ] *n officiel chargé de déterminer les causes d'un décès*

corporal ['kɔːpərl] *n* caporal *m*, brigadier *m* ♦ *adj*: **~ punishment** châtiment corporel

corporate ['kɔːpərɪt] *adj* en commun, collectif(-ive); (*COMM*) de l'entreprise

corporation [kɔːpə'reɪʃən] *n* (*of town*) municipalité *f*, conseil municipal; (*COMM*) société *f*

corps [kɔːʳ] (*pl* ~) *n* corps *m*

corpse [kɔːps] *n* cadavre *m*

correct [kə'rɛkt] *adj* (*accurate*) correct(e), exact(e); (*proper*) correct, convenable ♦ *vt* corriger; **~ion** *n* correction *f*

correspond [kɔrɪs'pɔnd] *vi* correspondre; **~ence** *n* correspondance *f*; **~ence course** *n* cours *m* par correspondance; **~ent** *n* correspondant(e)

corridor ['kɔrɪdɔːʳ] *n* couloir *m*, corridor *m*

corrode [kə'rəud] *vt* corroder, ronger ♦ *vi* se corroder

corrugated ['kɔrəgeɪtɪd] *adj* plissé(e); ondulé(e); **~ iron** *n* tôle ondulée

corrupt [kə'rʌpt] *adj* corrompu(e) ♦ *vt* corrompre; **~ion** *n* corruption *f*

Corsica ['kɔːsɪkə] *n* Corse *f*

cosmetic [kɔz'mɛtɪk] *n* produit *m* de beauté, cosmétique *m*

cost [kɔst] (*pt, pp* **cost**) *n* coût *m* ♦ *vi* coûter ♦ *vt* établir *or* calculer le prix de revient de; **~s** *npl* (*COMM*) frais *mpl*; (*LAW*) dépens *mpl*; **it ~s £5/too much** cela coûte cinq livres/c'est trop cher; **at all ~s** coûte que coûte, à tout prix

co-star ['kəustɑːʳ] *n* partenaire *m/f*

cost: **~-effective** *adj* rentable; **~ly** *adj* coûteux(-euse); **~-of-living** *adj*: **~-of-living allowance** indemnité *f* de vie chère; **~-of-living index** index *m* du coût de la vie; **~ price** (*BRIT*) *n* prix coûtant *or* de revient

costume ['kɔstjuːm] *n* costume *m*; (*lady's suit*) tailleur *m*; (*BRIT*: *also*: **swimming ~**) maillot *m* (de bain); **~ jewellery** *n* bijoux *mpl* fantaisie

cosy ['kəuzɪ] (*US* **cozy**) *adj* douillet(te); (*person*) à l'aise, au chaud

cot [kɔt] *n* (*BRIT*: *child's*) lit *m* d'enfant, petit lit; (*US*: *campbed*) lit de camp

cottage ['kɔtɪdʒ] *n* petite maison (à la campagne), cottage *m*; **~ cheese** *n* fromage blanc (*maigre*)

cotton ['kɔtn] *n* coton *m*; **~ on** (*inf*) *vi*: **to ~ on to** piger; **~ candy** (*US*) *n* barbe *f* à papa; **~ wool** (*BRIT*) *n* ouate *f*, coton *m* hydrophile

couch [kautʃ] *n* canapé *m*; divan *m*

couchette [kuː'ʃɛt] *n* couchette *f*

cough [kɔf] *vi* tousser ♦ *n* toux *f*; **~ sweet** *n* pastille *f* pour *or* contre la toux

could [kud] *pt of* **can**[2]; **~n't = could not**

council ['kaunsl] *n* conseil *m*; **city** *or* **town ~** conseil municipal; **~ estate** (*BRIT*) *n* (zone *f* de) logements loués à/par la municipalité; **~ house** (*BRIT*) *n* maison *f* (à loyer modéré) louée par la municipalité; **~lor** *n* conseiller(-ère)

counsel ['kaunsl] *n* (*lawyer*) avocat(e); (*advice*) conseil *m*, consultation *f*; **~lor** *n* conseiller(-ère); (*US: lawyer*) avocat(e)

count [kaunt] *vt, vi* compter ♦ *n* compte *m*; (*nobleman*) comte *m*; **~ on** *vt fus* compter sur; **~down** *n* compte *m* à rebours

countenance ['kauntɪnəns] *n* expression *f* ♦ *vt* approuver

counter ['kauntəʳ] *n* comptoir *m*; (*in post office, bank*) guichet *m*; (*in game*) jeton *m* ♦ *vt* aller à l'encontre de, opposer ♦ *adv*: **~ to** contrairement à; **~act** *vt* neutraliser, contrebalancer; **~feit** *n* faux *m*, contrefaçon *f* ♦ *vt* contrefaire ♦ *adj* faux (fausse); **~foil** *n* talon *m*, souche *f*; **~part** *n* (*of person etc*) homologue *m/f*

countess ['kauntɪs] *n* comtesse *f*

countless ['kauntlɪs] *adj* innombrable

country ['kʌntrɪ] *n* pays *m*; (*native land*) patrie *f*; (*as opposed to town*) campagne *f*; (*region*) région *f*, pays; **~ dancing** (*BRIT*) *n* danse *f* folklorique; **~ house** *n* manoir *m*, (petit) château; **~man** (*irreg*) *n* (*compatriot*) compatriote *m*; (*country dweller*) habitant *m* de la campagne, campagnard *m*; **~side** *n* campagne *f*

county ['kauntɪ] *n* comté *m*

coup [ku:] (*pl* **~s**) *n* beau coup; (*also:* **~ d'état**) coup d'État

couple ['kʌpl] *n* couple *m*; **a ~ of** deux; (*a few*) quelques

coupon ['ku:pɔn] *n* coupon *m*, bon-prime *m*, bon-réclame *m*; (*COMM*) coupon

courage ['kʌrɪdʒ] *n* courage *m*

courier ['kurɪəʳ] *n* messager *m*, courrier *m*; (*for tourists*) accompagnateur(-trice), guide *m/f*

course [kɔ:s] *n* cours *m*; (*of ship*) route *f*; (*for golf*) terrain *m*; (*part of meal*) plat *m*; **first ~** entrée *f*; **of ~** bien sûr; **~ of action** parti *m*, ligne *f* de conduite; **~ of treatment** (*MED*) traitement *m*

court [kɔ:t] *n* cour *f*; (*LAW*) cour, tribunal *m*; (*TENNIS*) court *m* ♦ *vt* (*woman*) courtiser, faire la cour à; **to take to ~** actionner *or* poursuivre en justice

courteous ['kə:tɪəs] *adj* courtois(e), poli(e); **courtesy** ['kə:təsɪ] *n* courtoisie *f*, politesse *f*; **(by) courtesy of** avec l'aimable autorisation de; **courtesy bus** *or* **coach** *n* navette gratuite

court: ~-house (*US*) *n* palais *m* de justice; **~ier** *n* courtisan *m*, dame *f* de la cour; **~ martial** (*pl* **courts martial**) *n* cour martiale, conseil *m* de guerre; **~room** *n* salle *f* de tribunal; **~yard** *n* cour *f*

cousin ['kʌzn] *n* cousin(e); **first ~** cousin(e) germain(e)

cove [kəuv] *n* petite baie, anse *f*

covenant ['kʌvənənt] *n* engagement *m*

cover ['kʌvəʳ] *vt* couvrir ♦ *n* couverture *f*; (*of pan*) couvercle *m*; (*over furniture*) housse *f*; (*shelter*) abri *m*; **to take ~** se mettre à l'abri; **under ~** à l'abri; **under ~ of darkness** à la faveur de la nuit; **under separate ~** (*COMM*) sous pli séparé; **to ~ up for sb** couvrir qn; **~age** *n* (*TV, PRESS*) reportage *m*; **~ charge** *n* couvert *m* (*supplément à payer*); **~ing** *n* couche *f*; **~ing letter** (*US* **cover letter**) *n* lettre explicative; **~ note** *n* (*INSURANCE*) police *f* provisoire

covert ['kʌvət] *adj* (*threat*) voilé(e), caché(e); (*glance*) furtif(-ive)

cover-up ['kʌvərʌp] *n* tentative *f* pour étouffer une affaire

covet ['kʌvɪt] *vt* convoiter

cow [kau] *n* vache *f* ♦ *vt* effrayer, intimider

coward ['kauəd] *n* lâche *m/f*; **~ice** *n* lâcheté *f*; **~ly** *adj* lâche

cowboy ['kaubɔɪ] *n* cow-boy *m*

cower ['kauəʳ] *vi* se recroqueviller

coy [kɔɪ] *adj* faussement effarouché(e) *or* timide
cozy ['kəuzɪ] (*US*) *adj* = **cosy**
CPA (*US*) *n abbr* = **certified public accountant**
crab [kræb] *n* crabe *m*; **~ apple** *n* pomme *f* sauvage
crack [kræk] *n* (*split*) fente *f*, fissure *f*; (*in cup, bone etc*) fêlure *f*; (*in wall*) lézarde *f*; (*noise*) craquement *m*, coup (sec); (*drug*) crack *m* ♦ *vt* fendre, fissurer; fêler; lézarder; (*whip*) faire claquer; (*nut*) casser; (*code*) déchiffrer; (*problem*) résoudre ♦ *adj* (*athlete*) de première classe, d'élite; **~ down on** *vt fus* mettre un frein à; **~ up** *vi* être au bout du rouleau, s'effondrer; **~ed** *adj* (*cup, bone*) fêlé(e); (*broken*) cassé(e); (*wall*) lézardé(e); (*surface*) craquelé(e); (*inf: mad*) cinglé(e); **~er** *n* (*Christmas cracker*) pétard *m*; (*biscuit*) biscuit (salé)
crackle ['krækl] *vi* crépiter, grésiller
cradle ['kreɪdl] *n* berceau *m*
craft [krɑːft] *n* métier (artisanal); (*pl inv: boat*) embarcation *f*, barque *f*; (*: plane*) appareil *m*; **~sman** (*irreg*) *n* artisan *m*, ouvrier (qualifié); **~smanship** *n* travail *m*; **~y** *adj* rusé(e), malin(-igne)
crag [kræg] *n* rocher escarpé
cram [kræm] *vt* (*fill*): **to ~ sth with** bourrer qch de; (*put*): **to ~ sth into** fourrer qch dans ♦ *vi* (*for exams*) bachoter
cramp [kræmp] *n* crampe *f* ♦ *vt* gêner, entraver; **~ed** *adj* à l'étroit, très serré(e)
cranberry ['krænbərɪ] *n* canneberge *f*
crane [kreɪn] *n* grue *f*
crank [kræŋk] *n* manivelle *f*; (*person*) excentrique *m/f*
cranny ['krænɪ] *n see* **nook**
crash [kræʃ] *n* fracas *m*; (*of car*) collision *f*; (*of plane*) accident *m* ♦ *vt* avoir un accident avec ♦ *vi* (*plane*) s'écraser; (*two cars*) se percuter, s'emboutir; (*COMM*) s'effondrer; **to ~ into** se jeter *or* se fracasser contre; **~ course** *n* cours intensif; **~ helmet** *n* casque (protecteur); **~ landing** *n* atterrissage forcé *or* en catastrophe
crate [kreɪt] *n* cageot *m*; (*for bottles*) caisse *f*
cravat(e) [krə'væt] *n* foulard (noué autour du cou)
crave [kreɪv] *vt, vi*: **to ~ (for)** avoir une envie irrésistible de
crawl [krɔːl] *vi* ramper; (*vehicle*) avancer au pas ♦ *n* (*SWIMMING*) crawl *m*
crayfish ['kreɪfɪʃ] *n inv* (*freshwater*) écrevisse *f*; (*saltwater*) langoustine *f*
crayon ['kreɪən] *n* crayon *m* (de couleur)
craze [kreɪz] *n* engouement *m*
crazy ['kreɪzɪ] *adj* fou (folle)
creak [kriːk] *vi* grincer; craquer
cream [kriːm] *n* crème *f* ♦ *adj* (*colour*) crème *inv*; **~ cake** *n* (petit) gâteau à la crème; **~ cheese** *n* fromage *m* à la crème, fromage blanc; **~y** *adj* crémeux(-euse)
crease [kriːs] *n* pli *m* ♦ *vt* froisser, chiffonner ♦ *vi* se froisser, se chiffonner
create [kriː'eɪt] *vt* créer; **creation** *n* création *f*; **creative** *adj* (*artistic*) créatif(-ive); (*ingenious*) ingénieux (-euse)
creature ['kriːtʃə^{r}] *n* créature *f*
crèche [krɛʃ] *n* garderie *f*, crèche *f*
credence ['kriːdns] *n*: **to lend** *or* **give ~ to** ajouter foi à
credentials [krɪ'dɛnʃlz] *npl* (*references*) références *fpl*; (*papers of identity*) pièce *f* d'identité
credit ['krɛdɪt] *n* crédit *m*; (*recognition*) honneur *m* ♦ *vt* (*COMM*) créditer; (*believe: also:* **give ~ to**) ajouter foi à, croire; **~s** *npl* (*CINEMA, TV*) générique *m*; **to be in ~** (*person, bank account*) être créditeur(-trice); **to ~ sb with** (*fig*) prêter *or* attribuer à qn; **~ card** *n* carte *f* de crédit; **~or** *n* créancier(-ière)
creed [kriːd] *n* croyance *f*; credo *m*
creek [kriːk] *n* crique *f*, anse *f*; (*US: stream*) ruisseau *m*, petit cours d'eau
creep [kriːp] (*pt, pp* **crept**) *vi* ramper;

~er *n* plante grimpante; **~y** *adj* (*frightening*) qui fait frissonner, qui donne la chair de poule
cremate [krɪ'meɪt] *vt* incinérer; **crematorium** [krɛmə'tɔːrɪəm] (*pl* **crematoria**) *n* four *m* crématoire
crêpe [kreɪp] *n* crêpe *m*; **~ bandage** (*BRIT*) *n* bande *f* Velpeau ®
crept [krɛpt] *pt, pp of* **creep**
crescent ['krɛsnt] *n* croissant *m*; (*street*) rue *f* (*en arc de cercle*)
cress [krɛs] *n* cresson *m*
crest [krɛst] *n* crête *f*; **~fallen** *adj* déconfit(e), découragé(e)
Crete [kriːt] *n* Crète *f*
crevice ['krɛvɪs] *n* fissure *f*, lézarde *f*, fente *f*
crew [kruː] *n* équipage *m*; (*CINEMA*) équipe *f*; **~-cut** *n*: **to have a ~-cut** avoir les cheveux en brosse; **~-neck** *n* col ras du cou
crib [krɪb] *n* lit *m* d'enfant; (*for baby*) berceau *m* ♦ *vt* (*inf*) copier
crick [krɪk] *n*: **~ in the neck** torticolis *m*; **~ in the back** tour *m* de reins
cricket ['krɪkɪt] *n* (*insect*) grillon *m*, cri-cri *m inv*; (*game*) cricket *m*
crime [kraɪm] *n* crime *m*; **criminal** ['krɪmɪnl] *adj, n* criminel(le)
crimson ['krɪmzn] *adj* cramoisi(e)
cringe [krɪndʒ] *vi* avoir un mouvement de recul
crinkle ['krɪŋkl] *vt* froisser, chiffonner
cripple ['krɪpl] *n* boiteux(-euse), infirme *m/f* ♦ *vt* estropier
crisis ['kraɪsɪs] (*pl* **crises**) *n* crise *f*
crisp [krɪsp] *adj* croquant(e); (*weather*) vif (vive); (*manner etc*) brusque; **~s** (*BRIT*) *npl* (pommes) chips *fpl*
crisscross ['krɪskrɔs] *adj* entrecroisé(e)
criterion [kraɪ'tɪərɪən] (*pl* **criteria**) *n* critère *m*
critic ['krɪtɪk] *n* critique *m*; **~al** *adj* critique; **~ally** *adv* (*examine*) d'un œil critique; (*speak etc*) sévèrement; **~ally ill** gravement malade; **~ism** ['krɪtɪsɪzəm] *n* critique *f*; **~ize** ['krɪtɪsaɪz] *vt* critiquer

croak [krəuk] *vi* (*frog*) coasser; (*raven*) croasser; (*person*) parler d'une voix rauque
Croatia [krəu'eɪʃə] *n* Croatie *f*
crochet ['krəuʃeɪ] *n* travail *m* au crochet
crockery ['krɔkərɪ] *n* vaisselle *f*
crocodile ['krɔkədaɪl] *n* crocodile *m*
crocus ['krəukəs] *n* crocus *m*
croft [krɔft] (*BRIT*) *n* petite ferme
crony ['krəunɪ] (*inf: pej*) *n* copain (copine)
crook [kruk] *n* escroc *m*; (*of shepherd*) houlette *f*; **~ed** ['krukɪd] *adj* courbé(e), tordu(e); (*action*) malhonnête
crop [krɔp] *n* (*produce*) culture *f*; (*amount produced*) récolte *f*; (*riding ~*) cravache *f* ♦ *vt* (*hair*) tondre; **~ up** *vi* surgir, se présenter, survenir
cross [krɔs] *n* croix *f*; (*BIO etc*) croisement *m* ♦ *vt* (*street etc*) traverser; (*arms, legs, BIO*) croiser; (*cheque*) barrer ♦ *adj* en colère, fâché(e); **~ out** *vt* barrer, biffer; **~ over** *vi* traverser; **~bar** *n* barre (transversale); **~-country (race)** *n* cross(-country) *m*; **~-examine** *vt* (*LAW*) faire subir un examen contradictoire à; **~-eyed** *adj* qui louche; **~fire** *n* feux croisés; **~ing** *n* (*sea passage*) traversée *f*; (*also:* **pedestrian ~ing**) passage clouté; **~ing guard** (*US*) *n contractuel qui fait traverser la rue aux enfants*; **~ purposes** *npl*: **to be at ~ purposes with sb** comprendre qn de travers; **~-reference** *n* renvoi *m*, référence *f*; **~roads** *n* carrefour *m*; **~ section** *n* (*of object*) coupe transversale; (*in population*) échantillon *m*; **~walk** (*US*) *n* passage clouté; **~wind** *n* vent *m* de travers; **~word** *n* mots *mpl* croisés
crotch [krɔtʃ] *n* (*ANAT, of garment*) entre-jambes *m inv*
crouch [krautʃ] *vi* s'accroupir; se tapir
crow [krəu] *n* (*bird*) corneille *f*; (*of cock*) chant *m* du coq, cocorico *m* ♦ *vi* (*cock*) chanter
crowbar ['krəubaːʳ] *n* levier *m*

crowd [kraud] *n* foule *f* ♦ *vt* remplir ♦ *vi* affluer, s'attrouper, s'entasser; **to ~ in** entrer en foule; **~ed** *adj* bondé(e), plein(e)
crown [kraun] *n* couronne *f*; (*of head*) sommet *m* de la tête; (*of hill*) sommet ♦ *vt* couronner; **~ jewels** *npl* joyaux *mpl* de la Couronne
crow's-feet ['krəuzfi:t] *npl* pattes *fpl* d'oie
crucial ['kru:ʃl] *adj* crucial(e), décisif (-ive)
crucifix ['kru:sɪfɪks] *n* (REL) crucifix *m*; **~ion** [kru:sɪ'fɪkʃən] *n* (REL) crucifixion *f*
crude [kru:d] *adj* (*materials*) brut(e); non raffiné(e); (*fig*: *basic*) rudimentaire, sommaire; (: *vulgar*) cru(e), grossier (-ère); **~ (oil)** *n* (pétrole) brut *m*
cruel ['kruəl] *adj* cruel(le); **~ty** *n* cruauté *f*
cruise [kru:z] *n* croisière *f* ♦ *vi* (*ship*) croiser; (*car*) rouler; **~r** *n* croiseur *m*; (*motorboat*) yacht *m* de croisière
crumb [krʌm] *n* miette *f*
crumble ['krʌmbl] *vt* émietter ♦ *vi* (*plaster etc*) s'effriter; (*land, earth*) s'ébouler; (*building*) s'écrouler, crouler; (*fig*) s'effondrer; **crumbly** *adj* friable
crumpet ['krʌmpɪt] *n* petite crêpe (épaisse)
crumple ['krʌmpl] *vt* froisser, friper
crunch [krʌntʃ] *vt* croquer; (*underfoot*) faire craquer *or* crisser, écraser ♦ *n* (*fig*) instant *m* *or* moment *m* critique, moment de vérité; **~y** *adj* croquant(e), croustillant(e)
crusade [kru:'seɪd] *n* croisade *f*
crush [krʌʃ] *n* foule *f*, cohue *f*; (*love*): **to have a ~ on sb** avoir le béguin pour qn (*inf*); (*drink*): **lemon ~** citron pressé ♦ *vt* écraser; (*crumple*) froisser; (*fig*: *hopes*) anéantir
crust [krʌst] *n* croûte *f*
crutch [krʌtʃ] *n* béquille *f*
crux [krʌks] *n* point crucial
cry [kraɪ] *vi* pleurer; (*shout*: *also*: **~ out**) crier ♦ *n* cri *m*; **~ off** (*inf*) *vi* se dédire; se décommander
cryptic ['krɪptɪk] *adj* énigmatique
crystal ['krɪstl] *n* cristal *m*; **~-clear** *adj* clair(e) comme de l'eau de roche
CSA *n abbr* (= *Child Support Agency*) *organisme pour la protection des enfants de parents séparés, qui contrôle le versement des pensions alimentaires*
CTC *n abbr* = **city technology college**
cub [kʌb] *n* petit *m* (*d'un animal*); (*also*: **C~ scout**) louveteau *m*
Cuba ['kju:bə] *n* Cuba *m*
cube [kju:b] *n* cube *m* ♦ *vt* (MATH) élever au cube; **cubic** *adj* cubique; **cubic metre** *etc* mètre *m etc* cube; **cubic capacity** *n* cylindrée *f*
cubicle ['kju:bɪkl] *n* (*in hospital*) box *m*; (*at pool*) cabine *f*
cuckoo ['kuku:] *n* coucou *m*; **~ clock** *n* (pendule *f* à) coucou *m*
cucumber ['kju:kʌmbə^r] *n* concombre *m*
cuddle ['kʌdl] *vt* câliner, caresser ♦ *vi* se blottir l'un contre l'autre
cue [kju:] *n* (*snooker ~*) queue *f* de billard; (THEATRE *etc*) signal *m*
cuff [kʌf] *n* (BRIT: *of shirt, coat etc*) poignet *m*, manchette *f*; (US: *of trousers*) revers *m*; (*blow*) tape *f*; **off the ~** à l'improviste; **~ links** *npl* boutons *mpl* de manchette
cul-de-sac ['kʌldəsæk] *n* cul-de-sac *m*, impasse *f*
cull [kʌl] *vt* sélectionner ♦ *n* (*of animals*) massacre *m*
culminate ['kʌlmɪneɪt] *vi*: **to ~ in** finir *or* se terminer par; (*end in*) mener à; **culmination** [kʌlmɪ'neɪʃən] *n* point culminant
culottes [kju:'lɔts] *npl* jupe-culotte *f*
culprit ['kʌlprɪt] *n* coupable *m/f*
cult [kʌlt] *n* culte *m*
cultivate ['kʌltɪveɪt] *vt* cultiver; **cultivation** [kʌltɪ'veɪʃən] *n* culture *f*
cultural ['kʌltʃərəl] *adj* culturel(le)
culture ['kʌltʃə^r] *n* culture *f*; **~d** *adj* (*person*) cultivé(e)

cumbersome ['kʌmbəsəm] *adj* encombrant(e), embarrassant(e)

cunning ['kʌnɪŋ] *n* ruse *f*, astuce *f* ♦ *adj* rusé(e), malin(-igne); (*device, idea*) astucieux(-euse)

cup [kʌp] *n* tasse *f*; (*as prize*) coupe *f*; (*of bra*) bonnet *m*

cupboard ['kʌbəd] *n* armoire *f*; (*built-in*) placard *m*

cup tie (BRIT) *n* match *m* de coupe

curate ['kjuərɪt] *n* vicaire *m*

curator [kjuə'reɪtə^r] *n* conservateur *m* (*d'un musée etc*)

curb [kə:b] *vt* refréner, mettre un frein à ♦ *n* (*fig*) frein *m*, restriction *f*; (US: *kerb*) bord *m* du trottoir

curdle ['kə:dl] *vi* se cailler

cure [kjuə^r] *vt* guérir; (CULIN: *salt*) saler; (: *smoke*) fumer; (: *dry*) sécher ♦ *n* remède *m*

curfew ['kə:fju:] *n* couvre-feu *m*

curiosity [kjuərɪ'ɔsɪtɪ] *n* curiosité *f*

curious ['kjuərɪəs] *adj* curieux(-euse)

curl [kə:l] *n* boucle *f* (de cheveux) ♦ *vt, vi* boucler; (*tightly*) friser; **~ up** *vi* s'enrouler; se pelotonner; **~er** *n* bigoudi *m*, rouleau *m*; **~y** *adj* bouclé(e); frisé(e)

currant ['kʌrnt] *n* (*dried*) raisin *m* de Corinthe, raisin sec; (*bush*) groseiller *m*; (*fruit*) groseille *f*

currency ['kʌrnsɪ] *n* monnaie *f*; **to gain ~** (*fig*) s'accréditer

current ['kʌrnt] *n* courant *m* ♦ *adj* courant(e); **~ account** (BRIT) *n* compte courant; **~ affairs** *npl* (questions *fpl* d')actualité *f*; **~ly** *adv* actuellement

curriculum [kə'rɪkjuləm] (*pl* **~s** *or* **curricula**) *n* programme *m* d'études; **~ vitae** *n* curriculum vitae *m*

curry ['kʌrɪ] *n* curry *m* ♦ *vt*: **to ~ favour with** chercher à s'attirer les bonnes grâces de

curse [kə:s] *vi* jurer, blasphémer ♦ *vt* maudire ♦ *n* (*spell*) malédiction *f*; (*problem, scourge*) fléau *m*; (*swearword*) juron *m*

cursor ['kə:sə^r] *n* (COMPUT) curseur *m*

cursory ['kə:sərɪ] *adj* superficiel(le), hâtif(-ive)

curt [kə:t] *adj* brusque, sec (sèche)

curtail [kə:'teɪl] *vt* (*visit etc*) écourter; (*expenses, freedom etc*) réduire

curtain ['kə:tn] *n* rideau *m*

curts(e)y ['kə:tsɪ] *vi* faire une révérence

curve [kə:v] *n* courbe *f*; (*in the road*) tournant *m*, virage *m* ♦ *vi* se courber; (*road*) faire une courbe

cushion ['kuʃən] *n* coussin *m* ♦ *vt* (*fall, shock*) amortir

custard ['kʌstəd] *n* (*for pouring*) crème anglaise

custody ['kʌstədɪ] *n* (*of child*) garde *f*; **to take sb into ~** (*suspect*) placer qn en détention préventive

custom ['kʌstəm] *n* coutume *f*, usage *m*; (COMM) clientèle *f*; **~ary** *adj* habituel(le)

customer ['kʌstəmə^r] *n* client(e)

customized ['kʌstəmaɪzd] *adj* (*car etc*) construit(e) sur commande

custom-made ['kʌstəm'meɪd] *adj* (*clothes*) fait(e) sur mesure; (*other goods*) hors série, fait(e) sur commande

customs ['kʌstəmz] *npl* douane *f*; **~ officer** *n* douanier(-ière)

cut [kʌt] (*pt, pp* **cut**) *vt* couper; (*meat*) découper; (*reduce*) réduire ♦ *vi* couper ♦ *n* coupure *f*; (*of clothes*) coupe *f*; (*in salary etc*) réduction *f*; (*of meat*) morceau *m*; **to ~ one's hand** se couper la main; **to ~ a tooth** percer une dent; **~ down** *vt fus* (*tree etc*) couper, abattre; (*consumption*) réduire; **~ off** *vt* couper; (*fig*) isoler; **~ out** *vt* découper; (*stop*) arrêter; (*remove*) ôter; **~ up** *vt* (*paper, meat*) découper; **~back** *n* réduction *f*

cute [kju:t] *adj* mignon(ne), adorable

cutlery ['kʌtlərɪ] *n* couverts *mpl*

cutlet ['kʌtlɪt] *n* côtelette *f*

cut: ~out *n* (*switch*) coupe-circuit *m inv*; (*cardboard cutout*) découpage *m*; **~-price** (US **cut-rate**) *adj* au rabais, à prix réduit; **~-throat** *n* assassin *m* ♦ *adj* acharné(e); **~ting** *adj* tranchant(e), coupant(e); (*fig*) cinglant(e), mordant(e) ♦ *n* (*BRIT*: *from newspaper*) coupure *f* (de journal); (*from plant*) bouture *f*

CV *n abbr* = **curriculum vitae**

cwt *abbr* = **hundredweight(s)**

cyanide ['saɪənaɪd] *n* cyanure *m*

cybercafé ['saɪbəkæfeɪ] *n* cybercafé *m*

cyberspace ['saɪbəspeɪs] *n* cyberspace *m*

cycle ['saɪkl] *n* cycle *m*; (*bicycle*) bicyclette *f*, vélo *m* ♦ *vi* faire de la bicyclette; **~ hire** *n* location *f* de vélos; **~ lane** *or* **path** *n* piste *f* cyclable; **cycling** *n* cyclisme *m*; **cyclist** ['saɪklɪst] *n* cycliste *m/f*

cygnet ['sɪgnɪt] *n* jeune cygne *m*

cylinder ['sɪlɪndə^r] *n* cylindre *m*; **~-head gasket** *n* joint *m* de culasse

cymbals ['sɪmblz] *npl* cymbales *fpl*

cynic ['sɪnɪk] *n* cynique *m/f*; **~al** *adj* cynique; **~ism** ['sɪnɪsɪzəm] *n* cynisme *m*

Cypriot ['sɪprɪət] *adj* cypriote, chypriote ♦ *n* Cypriote *m/f*, Chypriote *m/f*

Cyprus ['saɪprəs] *n* Chypre *f*

cyst [sɪst] *n* kyste *m*

cystitis [sɪs'taɪtɪs] *n* cystite *f*

czar [zɑː^r] *n* tsar *m*

Czech [tʃɛk] *adj* tchèque ♦ *n* Tchèque *m/f*; (*LING*) tchèque *m*

Czechoslovak [tʃɛkə'sləuvæk] *adj* tchécoslovaque ♦ *n* Tchécoslovaque *m/f*

Czechoslovakia [tʃɛkəslə'vækɪə] *n* Tchécoslovaquie *f*

D, d

D [diː] *n* (*MUS*) ré *m*

dab [dæb] *vt* (*eyes, wound*) tamponner; (*paint, cream*) appliquer (par petites touches *or* rapidement)

dabble ['dæbl] *vi*: **to ~ in** faire *or* se mêler *or* s'occuper un peu de

dad [dæd] *n*, **daddy** [dædɪ] *n* papa *m*

daffodil ['dæfədɪl] *n* jonquille *f*

daft [dɑːft] *adj* idiot(e), stupide

dagger ['dægə^r] *n* poignard *m*

daily ['deɪlɪ] *adj* quotidien(ne), journalier(-ère) ♦ *n* quotidien *m* ♦ *adv* tous les jours

dainty ['deɪntɪ] *adj* délicat(e), mignon(ne)

dairy ['dɛərɪ] *n* (*BRIT*: *shop*) crémerie *f*, laiterie *f*; (*on farm*) laiterie; **~ products** *npl* produits laitiers; **~ store** (*US*) *n* crémerie *f*, laiterie *f*

daisy ['deɪzɪ] *n* pâquerette *f*

dale [deɪl] *n* vallon *m*

dam [dæm] *n* barrage *m* ♦ *vt* endiguer

damage ['dæmɪdʒ] *n* dégâts *mpl*, dommages *mpl*; (*fig*) tort *m* ♦ *vt* endommager, abîmer; (*fig*) faire du tort à; **~s** *npl* (*LAW*) dommages-intérêts *mpl*

damn [dæm] *vt* condamner; (*curse*) maudire ♦ *n* (*inf*): **I don't give a ~** je m'en fous ♦ *adj* (*inf*: *also*: **~ed**): **this ~ ...** ce sacré *or* foutu ...; **~ (it)!** zut!; **~ing** *adj* accablant(e)

damp [dæmp] *adj* humide ♦ *n* humidité *f* ♦ *vt* (*also*: **~en**: *cloth, rag*) humecter; (: *enthusiasm*) refroidir

damson ['dæmzən] *n* prune *f* de Damas

dance [dɑːns] *n* danse *f*; (*social event*) bal *m* ♦ *vi* danser; **~ hall** *n* salle *f* de bal, dancing *m*; **~r** *n* danseur(-euse); **dancing** *n* danse *f*

dandelion ['dændɪlaɪən] *n* pissenlit *m*

dandruff ['dændrəf] *n* pellicules *fpl*

Dane [deɪn] *n* Danois(e)

danger ['deɪndʒə^r] *n* danger *m*; **there is a ~ of fire** il y a (un) risque d'incendie; **in ~** en danger; **he was in ~ of falling** il risquait de tomber; **~ous** *adj* dangereux(-euse)

dangle ['dæŋgl] *vt* balancer ♦ *vi* pendre

Danish ['deɪnɪʃ] *adj* danois(e) ♦ *n* (*LING*) danois *m*

dare [dɛə^r] *vt*: **to ~ sb to do** défier qn de faire ♦ *vi*: **to ~ (to) do sth** oser faire qch; **I ~ say** (*I suppose*) il est probable (que); **daring** *adj* hardi(e), audacieux(-euse); (*dress*) osé(e) ♦ *n* audace *f*, hardiesse *f*

dark [dɑːk] *adj* (*night, room*) obscur(e), sombre; (*colour, complexion*) foncé(e), sombre ♦ *n*: **in the ~** dans le noir; **in the ~ about** (*fig*) ignorant tout de; **after ~** après la tombée de la nuit; **~en** *vt* obscurcir, assombrir ♦ *vi* s'obscurcir, s'assombrir; **~ glasses** *npl* lunettes noires; **~ness** *n* obscurité *f*; **~room** *n* chambre noire

darling ['dɑːlɪŋ] *adj* chéri(e) ♦ *n* chéri(e); (*favourite*): **to be the ~ of** être la coqueluche de

darn [dɑːn] *vt* repriser, raccommoder

dart [dɑːt] *n* fléchette *f*; (*sewing*) pince *f* ♦ *vi*: **to ~ towards** (*also:* **make a ~ towards**) se précipiter *or* s'élancer vers; **to ~ away/along** partir/passer comme une flèche; **~board** *n* cible *f* (de jeu de fléchettes); **~s** *n* (jeu *m* de) fléchettes *fpl*

dash [dæʃ] *n* (*sign*) tiret *m*; (*small quantity*) goutte *f*, larme *f* ♦ *vt* (*missile*) jeter *or* lancer violemment; (*hopes*) anéantir ♦ *vi*: **to ~ towards** (*also:* **make a ~ towards**) se précipiter *or* se ruer vers; **~ away** *vi* partir à toute allure, filer; **~ off** *vi* = **dash away**

dashboard ['dæʃbɔːd] *n* (AUT) tableau *m* de bord

dashing ['dæʃɪŋ] *adj* fringant(e)

data ['deɪtə] *npl* données *fpl*; **~base** *n* (COMPUT) base *f* de données; **~ processing** *n* traitement *m* de données

date [deɪt] *n* date *f*; (*with sb*) rendez-vous *m*; (*fruit*) datte *f* ♦ *vt* dater; (*person*) sortir avec; **~ of birth** date de naissance; **to ~** (*until now*) à ce jour; **out of ~** (*passport*) périmé(e); (*theory etc*) dépassé(e); (*clothes etc*) démodé(e); **up to ~** moderne; (*news*) très récent; **~d** ['deɪtɪd] *adj* démodé(e); **~ rape** *n* viol *m* (*à l'issue d'un rendez-vous galant*)

daub [dɔːb] *vt* barbouiller

daughter ['dɔːtə^r] *n* fille *f*; **~-in-law** *n* belle-fille *f*, bru *f*

daunting ['dɔːntɪŋ] *adj* décourageant(e)

dawdle ['dɔːdl] *vi* traîner, lambiner

dawn [dɔːn] *n* aube *f*, aurore *f* ♦ *vi* (*day*) se lever, poindre; (*fig*): **it ~ed on him that ...** il lui vint à l'esprit que ...

day [deɪ] *n* jour *m*; (*as duration*) journée *f*; (*period of time, age*) époque *f*, temps *m*; **the ~ before** la veille, le jour précédent; **the ~ after, the following ~** le lendemain, le jour suivant; **the ~ after tomorrow** après-demain; **the ~ before yesterday** avant-hier; **by ~** de jour; **~break** *n* point *m* du jour; **~dream** *vi* rêver (tout éveillé); **~light** *n* (lumière *f* du) jour *m*; **~ return** (BRIT) *n* billet *m* d'aller-retour (valable pour la journée); **~time** *n* jour *m*, journée *f*; **~-to-~** *adj* quotidien(ne); (*event*) journalier(-ère)

daze [deɪz] *vt* (*stun*) étourdir ♦ *n*: **in a ~** étourdi(e), hébété(e)

dazzle ['dæzl] *vt* éblouir, aveugler

DC *abbr* (= *direct current*) courant continu

D-day ['diːdeɪ] *n* le jour J

dead [dɛd] *adj* mort(e); (*numb*) engourdi(e), insensible; (*battery*) à plat; (*telephone*): **the line is ~** la ligne est coupée ♦ *adv* absolument, complètement ♦ *npl*: **the ~** les morts; **he was shot ~** il a été tué d'un coup de revolver; **~ on time** à l'heure pile; **~ tired** éreinté(e), complètement fourbu(e); **to stop ~** s'arrêter pile *or* net; **~en** *vt* (*blow, sound*) amortir; (*pain*) calmer; **~ end** *n* impasse *f*; **~ heat** *n* (SPORT): **to finish in a ~ heat** terminer ex-æquo; **~line** *n* date *f or* heure *f* limite; **~lock** (*fig*) *n* impasse *f*; **~ loss** *n*: **to be a ~ loss** (*inf: person*) n'être bon(ne) à rien; **~ly** *adj* mortel(le); (*weapon*) meurtrier(-ère); (*accuracy*) extrême; **~pan** *adj* impassible; **D~ Sea** *n*: **the D~ Sea** la mer Morte

deaf [dɛf] *adj* sourd(e); **~en** *vt* rendre sourd; **~ening** *adj* assourdisant(e); **~-**

mute *n* sourd(e)-muet(te); **~ness** *n* surdité *f*

deal [di:l] (*pt, pp* **dealt**) *n* affaire *f*, marché *m* ♦ *vt* (*blow*) porter; (*cards*) donner, distribuer; **a great ~ (of)** beaucoup (de); **~ in** *vt fus* faire le commerce de; **~ with** *vt fus* (*person, problem*) s'occuper *or* se charger de; (*be about: book etc*) traiter de; **~er** *n* marchand *m*; **~ings** *npl* (COMM) transactions *fpl*; (*relations*) relations *fpl*, rapports *mpl*

dean [di:n] *n* (*REL, BRIT: SCOL*) doyen *m*; (*US: SCOL*) conseiller(-ère) (principal(e)) d'éducation

dear [dɪəʳ] *adj* cher (chère); (*expensive*) cher, coûteux(-euse) ♦ *n*: **my ~** mon cher/ma chère; **~ me!** mon Dieu!; **D~ Sir/Madam** (*in letter*) Monsieur/Madame; **D~ Mr/Mrs X** Cher Monsieur/Chère Madame; **~ly** *adv* (*love*) tendrement; (*pay*) cher

death [dɛθ] *n* mort *f*; (*fatality*) mort *m*; (ADMIN) décès *m*; **~ certificate** *n* acte *m* de décès; **~ly** *adj* de mort; **~ penalty** *n* peine *f* de mort; **~ rate** *n* (taux *m* de) mortalité *f*; **~ toll** *n* nombre *m* de morts

debase [dɪ'beɪs] *vt* (*value*) déprécier, dévaloriser

debatable [dɪ'beɪtəbl] *adj* discutable

debate [dɪ'beɪt] *n* discussion *f*, débat *m* ♦ *vt* discuter, débattre

debit ['dɛbɪt] *n* débit *m* ♦ *vt*: **to ~ a sum to sb** *or* **to sb's account** porter une somme au débit de qn, débiter qn d'une somme; *see also* **direct**

debt [dɛt] *n* dette *f*; **to be in ~** avoir des dettes, être endetté(e); **~or** *n* débiteur(-trice)

decade ['dɛkeɪd] *n* décennie *f*, décade *f*

decadence ['dɛkədəns] *n* décadence *f*

decaff ['di:kæf] (*inf*) *n* déca *m*

decaffeinated [dɪ'kæfɪneɪtɪd] *adj* décaféiné(e)

decanter [dɪ'kæntəʳ] *n* carafe *f*

decay [dɪ'keɪ] *n* (*of building*) délabrement *m*; (*also:* **tooth ~**) carie *f* (dentaire) ♦ *vi* (*rot*) se décomposer, pourrir; (: *teeth*) se carier

deceased [dɪ'si:st] *n* défunt(e)

deceit [dɪ'si:t] *n* tromperie *f*, supercherie *f*; **~ful** *adj* trompeur(-euse); **deceive** *vt* tromper

December [dɪ'sɛmbəʳ] *n* décembre *m*

decent ['di:sənt] *adj* décent(e), convenable

deception [dɪ'sɛpʃən] *n* tromperie *f*

deceptive [dɪ'sɛptɪv] *adj* trompeur (-euse)

decide [dɪ'saɪd] *vt* (*person*) décider; (*question, argument*) trancher, régler ♦ *vi* se décider, décider; **to ~ to do/that** décider de faire/que; **to ~ on** décider, se décider pour; **~d** *adj* (*resolute*) résolu(e), décidé(e); (*clear, definite*) net(te), marqué(e); **~dly** *adv* résolument; (*distinctly*) incontestablement, nettement

deciduous [dɪ'sɪdjuəs] *adj* à feuilles caduques

decimal ['dɛsɪməl] *adj* décimal(e) ♦ *n* décimale *f*; **~ point** *n* ≃ virgule *f*

decipher [dɪ'saɪfəʳ] *vt* déchiffrer

decision [dɪ'sɪʒən] *n* décision *f*

decisive [dɪ'saɪsɪv] *adj* décisif(-ive); (*person*) décidé(e)

deck [dɛk] *n* (NAUT) pont *m*; (*verandah*) véranda *f*; (*of bus*): **top ~** impériale *f*; (*of cards*) jeu *m*; (*record ~*) platine *f*; **~chair** *n* chaise longue

declare [dɪ'klɛəʳ] *vt* déclarer

decline [dɪ'klaɪn] *n* (*decay*) déclin *m*; (*lessening*) baisse *f* ♦ *vt* refuser, décliner ♦ *vi* décliner; (*business*) baisser

decoder [di:'kəudəʳ] *n* (TV) décodeur *m*

decorate ['dɛkəreɪt] *vt* (*adorn, give a medal to*) décorer; (*paint and paper*) peindre et tapisser; **decoration** [dɛkə'reɪʃən] *n* (*medal etc, adornment*) décoration *f*; **decorator** *n* peintre-décorateur *m*

decoy ['di:kɔɪ] *n* piège *m*; (*person*) compère *m*

decrease [*n* 'di:kri:s, *vb* di:'kri:s] *n*: **~ (in)** diminution *f* (de) ♦ *vt, vi* diminuer

dentures ['dɛntʃəz] *npl* dentier *m sg*
deny [dɪ'naɪ] *vt* nier; (*refuse*) refuser
deodorant [di:'əudərənt] *n* déodorant *m*, désodorisant *m*
depart [dɪ'pɑ:t] *vi* partir; **to ~ from** (*fig: differ from*) s'écarter de
department [dɪ'pɑ:tmənt] *n* (COMM) rayon *m*; (SCOL) section *f*; (POL) ministère *m*, département *m*; **~ store** *n* grand magasin
departure [dɪ'pɑ:tʃə^r] *n* départ *m*; **a new ~** une nouvelle voie; **~ lounge** *n* (*at airport*) salle *f* d'embarquement
depend [dɪ'pɛnd] *vi*: **to ~ on** dépendre de; (*rely on*) compter sur; **it ~s** cela dépend; **~ing on the result** selon le résultat; **~able** *adj* (*person*) sérieux (-euse), sûr(e); (*car, watch*) solide, fiable; **~ant** *n* personne *f* à charge; **~ent** *adj*: **to be ~ent (on)** dépendre (de) ♦ *n* = **dependant**
depict [dɪ'pɪkt] *vt* (*in picture*) représenter; (*in words*) (dé)peindre, décrire
depleted [dɪ'pli:tɪd] *adj* (considérablement) réduit(e) *or* diminué(e)
deport [dɪ'pɔ:t] *vt* expulser
deposit [dɪ'pɔzɪt] *n* (CHEM, COMM, GEO) dépôt *m*; (*of ore, oil*) gisement *m*; (*part payment*) arrhes *fpl*, acompte *m*; (*on bottle etc*) consigne *f*; (*for hired goods etc*) cautionnement *m*, garantie *f* ♦ *vt* déposer; **~ account** *n* compte *m* sur livret
depot ['dɛpəu] *n* dépôt *m*; (US: RAIL) gare *f*
depress [dɪ'prɛs] *vt* déprimer; (*press down*) appuyer sur, abaisser; (*prices, wages*) faire baisser; **~ed** *adj* (*person*) déprimé(e); (*area*) en déclin, touché(e) par le sous-emploi; **~ing** *adj* déprimant(e); **~ion** *n* dépression *f*; (*hollow*) creux *m*
deprivation [dɛprɪ'veɪʃən] *n* privation *f*; (*loss*) perte *f*
deprive [dɪ'praɪv] *vt*: **to ~ sb of** priver qn de; **~d** *adj* déshérité(e)
depth [dɛpθ] *n* profondeur *f*; **in the ~s of despair** au plus profond du désespoir; **to be out of one's ~** avoir perdu pied, nager
deputize ['dɛpjutaɪz] *vi*: **to ~ for** assurer l'intérim de
deputy ['dɛpjutɪ] *adj* adjoint(e) ♦ *n* (*second in command*) adjoint(e); (US: *also:* **~ sheriff**) shérif adjoint; **~ head** directeur adjoint, sous-directeur *m*
derail [dɪ'reɪl] *vt*: **to be ~ed** dérailler
deranged [dɪ'reɪndʒd] *adj*: **to be (mentally) ~** avoir le cerveau dérangé
derby ['də:rbɪ] (US) *n* (*bowler hat*) (chapeau *m*) melon *m*
derelict ['dɛrɪlɪkt] *adj* abandonné(e), à l'abandon
derisory [dɪ'raɪsərɪ] *adj* (*sum*) dérisoire; (*smile, person*) moqueur(-euse)
derive [dɪ'raɪv] *vt*: **to ~ sth from** tirer qch de; trouver qch dans ♦ *vi*: **to ~ from** provenir de, dériver de
derogatory [dɪ'rɔgətərɪ] *adj* désobligeant(e); péjoratif(-ive)
descend [dɪ'sɛnd] *vt, vi* descendre; **to ~ from** descendre de, être issu(e) de; **to ~ to (doing) sth** s'abaisser à (faire) qch; **descent** *n* descente *f*; (*origin*) origine *f*
describe [dɪs'kraɪb] *vt* décrire; **description** [dɪs'krɪpʃən] *n* description *f*; (*sort*) sorte *f*, espèce *f*
desecrate ['dɛsɪkreɪt] *vt* profaner
desert [*n* 'dɛzət, *vb* dɪ'zə:t] *n* désert *m* ♦ *vt* déserter, abandonner ♦ *vi* (MIL) déserter; **~s** *npl*: **to get one's just ~s** n'avoir que ce qu'on mérite; **~er** [dɪ'zə:tə^r] *n* déserteur *m*; **~ion** [dɪ'zə:ʃən] *n* (MIL) désertion *f*; (LAW: *of spouse*) abandon *m* du domicile conjugal; **~ island** *n* île déserte
deserve [dɪ'zə:v] *vt* mériter; **deserving** *adj* (*person*) méritant(e); (*action, cause*) méritoire
design [dɪ'zaɪn] *n* (*sketch*) plan *m*, dessin *m*; (*layout, shape*) conception *f*, ligne *f*; (*pattern*) dessin *m*, motif(s) *m(pl)*; (COMM, *art*) design *m*, stylisme *m*; (*in-*

tention) dessein *m* ♦ *vt* dessiner; élaborer; **~er** *n* (*TECH*) concepteur-projeteur *m*; (*ART*) dessinateur(-trice), designer *m*; (*fashion*) styliste *m/f*

desire [dɪ'zaɪəʳ] *n* désir *m* ♦ *vt* désirer

desk [dɛsk] *n* (*in office*) bureau *m*; (*for pupil*) pupitre *m*; (*BRIT*: *in shop, restaurant*) caisse *f*; (*in hotel, at airport*) réception *f*; **~-top publishing** *n* publication assistée par ordinateur, PAO *f*

desolate ['dɛsəlɪt] *adj* désolé(e); (*person*) affligé(e)

despair [dɪs'pɛəʳ] *n* désespoir *m* ♦ *vi*: **to ~ of** désespérer de

despatch [dɪs'pætʃ] *n, vt* = **dispatch**

desperate ['dɛspərɪt] *adj* désespéré(e); (*criminal*) prêt(e) à tout; **to be ~ for sth/to do sth** avoir désespérément besoin de qch/de faire qch; **~ly** *adv* désespérément; (*very*) terriblement, extrêmement; **desperation** [dɛspə'reɪʃən] *n* désespoir *m*; **in (sheer) desperation** en désespoir de cause

despicable [dɪs'pɪkəbl] *adj* méprisable

despise [dɪs'paɪz] *vt* mépriser

despite [dɪs'paɪt] *prep* malgré, en dépit de

despondent [dɪs'pɔndənt] *adj* découragé(e), abattu(e)

dessert [dɪ'zə:t] *n* dessert *m*; **~spoon** *n* cuiller *f* à dessert

destination [dɛstɪ'neɪʃən] *n* destination *f*

destined ['dɛstɪnd] *adj*: **to be ~ to do/for sth** être destiné(e) à faire/à qch

destiny ['dɛstɪnɪ] *n* destinée *f*, destin *m*

destitute ['dɛstɪtju:t] *adj* indigent(e)

destroy [dɪs'trɔɪ] *vt* détruire; (*injured horse*) abattre; (*dog*) faire piquer; **~er** *n* (*NAUT*) contre-torpilleur *m*

destruction [dɪs'trʌkʃən] *n* destruction *f*

detach [dɪ'tætʃ] *vt* détacher; **~ed** *adj* (*attitude, person*) détaché(e); **~ed house** *n* pavillon *m*, maison(nette) (individuelle); **~ment** *n* (*MIL*) détachement *m*; (*fig*) détachement, indifférence *f*

detail ['di:teɪl] *n* détail *m* ♦ *vt* raconter en détail, énumérer; **in ~** en détail; **~ed** *adj* détaillé(e)

detain [dɪ'teɪn] *vt* retenir; (*in captivity*) détenir; (*in hospital*) hospitaliser

detect [dɪ'tɛkt] *vt* déceler, percevoir; (*MED, POLICE*) dépister; (*MIL, RADAR, TECH*) détecter; **~ion** *n* découverte *f*; **~ive** *n* agent *m* de la sûreté, policier *m*; **private ~ive** détective privé; **~ive story** *n* roman policier

detention [dɪ'tɛnʃən] *n* détention *f*; (*SCOL*) retenue *f*, consigne *f*

deter [dɪ'tə:ʳ] *vt* dissuader

detergent [dɪ'tə:dʒənt] *n* détergent *m*, détersif *m*

deteriorate [dɪ'tɪərɪəreɪt] *vi* se détériorer, se dégrader

determine [dɪ'tə:mɪn] *vt* déterminer; **to ~ to do** résoudre de faire, se déterminer à faire; **~d** *adj* (*person*) déterminé(e), décidé(e)

deterrent [dɪ'tɛrənt] *n* effet *m* de dissuasion; force *f* de dissuasion

detest [dɪ'tɛst] *vt* détester, avoir horreur de

detonate ['dɛtəneɪt] *vt* faire détoner *or* exploser

detour ['di:tuəʳ] *n* détour *m*; (*US*: *AUT*: *diversion*) déviation *f*

detract [dɪ'trækt] *vt*: **to ~ from** (*quality, pleasure*) diminuer; (*reputation*) porter atteinte à

detriment ['dɛtrɪmənt] *n*: **to the ~ of** au détriment de, au préjudice de; **~al** [dɛtrɪ'mɛntl] *adj*: **~al to** préjudiciable *or* nuisible à

devaluation [dɪvælju'eɪʃən] *n* dévaluation *f*

devastate ['dɛvəsteɪt] *vt* dévaster; **~d** *adj* (*fig*) anéanti(e); **devastating** *adj* dévastateur(-trice); (*news*) accablant(e)

develop [dɪ'vɛləp] *vt* (*gen*) développer; (*disease*) commencer à souffrir de; (*resources*) mettre en valeur, exploiter ♦ *vi* se développer; (*situation, disease*:

evolve) évoluer; (*facts, symptoms*: *appear*) se manifester, se produire; **~ing country** pays *m* en voie de développement; **the machine has ~ed a fault** un problème s'est manifesté dans cette machine; **~er** [dɪ'vɛləpə^r] *n* (*also:* **property ~er**) promoteur *m*; **~ment** [dɪ'vɛləpmənt] *n* développement *m*; (*of affair, case*) rebondissement *m*, fait(s) nouveau(x)
device [dɪ'vaɪs] *n* (*apparatus*) engin *m*, dispositif *m*
devil ['dɛvl] *n* diable *m*; démon *m*
devious ['di:vɪəs] *adj* (*person*) sournois(e), dissimulé(e)
devise [dɪ'vaɪz] *vt* imaginer, concevoir
devoid [dɪ'vɔɪd] *adj*: **~ of** dépourvu(e) de, dénué(e) de
devolution [di:və'lu:ʃən] *n* (POL) décentralisation *f*
devote [dɪ'vəut] *vt*: **to ~ sth to** consacrer qch à; **~d** [dɪ'vəutɪd] *adj* dévoué(e); **to be ~d to** (*book etc*) être consacré(e) à; (*person*) être très attaché(e) à; **~e** [dɛvəu'ti:] *n* (REL) adepte *m/f*; (MUS, SPORT) fervent(e); **devotion** *n* dévouement *m*, attachement *m*; (REL) dévotion *f*, piété *f*
devour [dɪ'vauə^r] *vt* dévorer
devout [dɪ'vaut] *adj* pieux(-euse), dévot(e)
dew [dju:] *n* rosée *f*
diabetes [daɪə'bi:ti:z] *n* diabète *m*; **diabetic** [daɪə'bɛtɪk] *adj* diabétique ♦ *n* diabétique *m/f*
diabolical [daɪə'bɔlɪkl] (*inf*) *adj* (*weather*) atroce; (*behaviour*) infernal(e)
diagnosis [daɪəg'nəusɪs] (*pl* **diagnoses**) *n* diagnostic *m*
diagonal [daɪ'ægənl] *adj* diagonal(e) ♦ *n* diagonale *f*
diagram ['daɪəgræm] *n* diagramme *m*, schéma *m*
dial ['daɪəl] *n* cadran *m* ♦ *vt* (*number*) faire, composer
dialect ['daɪəlɛkt] *n* dialecte *m*
dialling code (BRIT) *n* indicatif *m* (téléphonique)
dialling tone (BRIT) *n* tonalité *f*
dialogue ['daɪəlɔg] *n* dialogue *m*
dial tone (US) *n* = **dialling tone**
diameter [daɪ'æmɪtə^r] *n* diamètre *m*
diamond ['daɪəmənd] *n* diamant *m*; (*shape*) losange *m*; **~s** *npl* (CARDS) carreau *m*
diaper ['daɪəpə^r] (US) *n* couche *f*
diaphragm ['daɪəfræm] *n* diaphragme *m*
diarrhoea [daɪə'ri:ə] (US **diarrhea**) *n* diarrhée *f*
diary ['daɪərɪ] *n* (*daily account*) journal *m*; (*book*) agenda *m*
dice [daɪs] *n inv* dé *m* ♦ *vt* (CULIN) couper en dés *or* en cubes
dictate [dɪk'teɪt] *vt* dicter; **dictation** *n* dictée *f*
dictator [dɪk'teɪtə^r] *n* dictateur *m*; **~ship** *n* dictature *f*
dictionary ['dɪkʃənrɪ] *n* dictionnaire *m*
did [dɪd] *pt of* **do**; **~n't = did not**
die [daɪ] *vi* mourir; **to be dying for sth** avoir une envie folle de qch; **to be dying to do sth** mourir d'envie de faire qch; **~ away** *vi* s'éteindre; **~ down** *vi* se calmer, s'apaiser; **~ out** *vi* disparaître
diesel ['di:zl] *n* (*vehicle*) diesel *m*; (*also:* **~ oil**) carburant *m* diesel, gas-oil *m*; **~ engine** *n* moteur *m* diesel
diet ['daɪət] *n* alimentation *f*; (*restricted food*) régime *m* ♦ *vi* (*also:* **be on a ~**) suivre un régime
differ ['dɪfə^r] *vi* (*be different*): **to ~ (from)** être différent (de); différer (de); (*disagree*): **to ~ (from sb over sth)** ne pas être d'accord (avec qn au sujet de qch); **~ence** *n* différence *f*; (*quarrel*) différend *m*, désaccord *m*; **~ent** *adj* différent(e); **~entiate** [dɪfə'rɛnʃɪeɪt] *vi*: **to ~entiate (between)** faire une différence (entre)
difficult ['dɪfɪkəlt] *adj* difficile; **~y** *n* difficulté *f*
diffident ['dɪfɪdənt] *adj* qui manque de

confiance *or* d'assurance

dig [dɪg] (*pt, pp* **dug**) *vt* (*hole*) creuser; (*garden*) bêcher ♦ *n* (*prod*) coup *m* de coude; (*fig*) coup de griffe *or* de patte; (*archeological*) fouilles *fpl*; **~ in** *vi* (*MIL*: *also*: **~ o.s. in**) se retrancher; **~ into** *vt fus* (*savings*) puiser dans; **to ~ one's nails into sth** enfoncer ses ongles dans qch; **~ up** *vt* déterrer

digest [*vb* daɪ'dʒɛst, *n* 'daɪdʒɛst] *vt* digérer ♦ *n* sommaire *m*, résumé *m*; **~ion** [dɪ'dʒɛstʃən] *n* digestion *f*

digit ['dɪdʒɪt] *n* (*number*) chiffre *m*; (*finger*) doigt *m*; **~al** *adj* digital(e), à affichage numérique *or* digital; **~al computer** calculateur *m* numérique; **~al TV** *n* télévision *f* numérique; **~al watch** montre *f* à affichage numérique

dignified ['dɪgnɪfaɪd] *adj* digne

dignity ['dɪgnɪtɪ] *n* dignité *f*

digress [daɪ'grɛs] *vi*: **to ~ from** s'écarter de, s'éloigner de

digs [dɪgz] (*BRIT*: *inf*) *npl* piaule *f*, chambre meublée

dilapidated [dɪ'læpɪdeɪtɪd] *adj* délabré(e)

dilemma [daɪ'lɛmə] *n* dilemme *m*

diligent ['dɪlɪdʒənt] *adj* appliqué(e), assidu(e)

dilute [daɪ'luːt] *vt* diluer

dim [dɪm] *adj* (*light*) faible; (*memory, outline*) vague, indécis(e); (*figure*) vague, indistinct(e); (*room*) sombre; (*stupid*) borné(e), obtus(e) ♦ *vt* (*light*) réduire, baisser; (*US*: *AUT*) mettre en code

dime [daɪm] (*US*) *n* = **10 cents**

dimension [daɪ'mɛnʃən] *n* dimension *f*

diminish [dɪ'mɪnɪʃ] *vt, vi* diminuer

diminutive [dɪ'mɪnjutɪv] *adj* minuscule, tout(e) petit(e)

dimmers ['dɪməz] (*US*) *npl* (*AUT*) phares *mpl* code *inv*; feux *mpl* de position

dimple ['dɪmpl] *n* fossette *f*

din [dɪn] *n* vacarme *m*

dine [daɪn] *vi* dîner; **~r** *n* (*person*) dîneur(-euse); (*US*: *restaurant*) petit restaurant

dinghy ['dɪŋgɪ] *n* youyou *m*; (*also*: **rubber ~**) canot *m* pneumatique; (*also*: **sailing ~**) voilier *m*, dériveur *m*

dingy ['dɪndʒɪ] *adj* miteux(-euse), minable

dining car (*BRIT*) *n* wagon-restaurant *m*

dining room *n* salle *f* à manger

dinner ['dɪnə[r]] *n* dîner *m*; (*lunch*) déjeuner *m*; (*public*) banquet *m*; **~ jacket** *n* smoking *m*; **~ party** *n* dîner *m*; **~ time** *n* heure *f* du dîner; (*midday*) heure du déjeuner

dinosaur ['daɪnəsɔː[r]] *n* dinosaure *m*

dip [dɪp] *n* déclivité *f*; (*in sea*) baignade *f*, bain *m*; (*CULIN*) ≃ sauce *f* ♦ *vt* tremper, plonger; (*BRIT*: *AUT*: *lights*) mettre en code, baisser ♦ *vi* plonger

diploma [dɪ'pləumə] *n* diplôme *m*

diplomacy [dɪ'pləuməsɪ] *n* diplomatie *f*

diplomat ['dɪpləmæt] *n* diplomate *m*; **~ic** [dɪplə'mætɪk] *adj* diplomatique

dipstick ['dɪpstɪk] *n* (*AUT*) jauge *f* de niveau d'huile

dipswitch ['dɪpswɪtʃ] (*BRIT*) *n* (*AUT*) interrupteur *m* de lumière réduite

dire [daɪə[r]] *adj* terrible, extrême, affreux(-euse)

direct [daɪ'rɛkt] *adj* direct(e) ♦ *vt* diriger, orienter; (*letter, remark*) adresser; (*film, programme*) réaliser; (*play*) mettre en scène; (*order*): **to ~ sb to do sth** ordonner à qn de faire qch ♦ *adv* directement; **can you ~ me to ...?** pouvez-vous m'indiquer le chemin de ...?; **~ debit** (*BRIT*) *n* prélèvement *m* automatique

direction [dɪ'rɛkʃən] *n* direction *f*; **~s** *npl* (*advice*) indications *fpl*; **sense of ~** sens *m* de l'orientation; **~s for use** mode *m* d'emploi

directly [dɪ'rɛktlɪ] *adv* (*in a straight line*) directement, tout droit; (*at once*) tout de suite, immédiatement

director [dɪ'rɛktə[r]] *n* directeur *m*; (*THEATRE*) metteur *m* en scène; (*CINEMA, TV*) réalisateur(-trice)

directory [dɪ'rɛktərɪ] *n* annuaire *m*; (COMPUT) répertoire *m*; **~ enquiries** (US **directory assistance**) *n* renseignements *mpl*
dirt [də:t] *n* saleté *f*; crasse *f*; (*earth*) terre *f*, boue *f*; **~-cheap** *adj* très bon marché *inv*; **~y** *adj* sale ♦ *vt* salir; **~y trick** coup tordu
disability [dɪsə'bɪlɪtɪ] *n* invalidité *f*, infirmité *f*
disabled [dɪs'eɪbld] *adj* infirme, invalide ♦ *npl*: **the ~** les handicapés
disadvantage [dɪsəd'vɑ:ntɪdʒ] *n* désavantage *m*, inconvénient *m*
disagree [dɪsə'gri:] *vi* (*be different*) ne pas concorder; (*be against, think otherwise*): **to ~ (with)** ne pas être d'accord (avec); **~able** *adj* désagréable; **~ment** *n* désaccord *m*, différend *m*
disallow ['dɪsə'lau] *vt* rejeter
disappear [dɪsə'pɪə^r] *vi* disparaître; **~ance** *n* disparition *f*
disappoint [dɪsə'pɔɪnt] *vt* décevoir; **~ed** *adj* déçu(e); **~ing** *adj* décevant(e); **~ment** *n* déception *f*
disapproval [dɪsə'pru:vəl] *n* désapprobation *f*
disapprove [dɪsə'pru:v] *vi*: **to ~ (of)** désapprouver
disarmament [dɪs'ɑ:məmənt] *n* désarmement *m*
disarray [dɪsə'reɪ] *n*: **in ~** (*army*) en déroute; (*organization*) en désarroi; (*hair, clothes*) en désordre
disaster [dɪ'zɑ:stə^r] *n* catastrophe *f*, désastre *m*; **disastrous** *adj* désastreux(-euse)
disband [dɪs'bænd] *vt* démobiliser; disperser ♦ *vi* se séparer; se disperser
disbelief ['dɪsbə'li:f] *n* incrédulité *f*
disc [dɪsk] *n* disque *m*; (COMPUT) = **disk**
discard [dɪs'kɑ:d] *vt* (*old things*) se débarrasser de; (*fig*) écarter, renoncer à
discern [dɪ'sə:n] *vt* discerner, distinguer; **~ing** *adj* perspicace
discharge [*vb* dɪs'tʃɑ:dʒ, *n* 'dɪstʃɑ:dʒ] *vt* décharger; (*duties*) s'acquitter de; (*patient*) renvoyer (chez lui); (*employee*) congédier, licencier; (*soldier*) rendre à la vie civile, réformer; (*defendant*) relaxer, élargir ♦ *n* décharge *f*; (*dismissal*) renvoi *m*; licenciement *m*; élargissement *m*; (MED) écoulement *m*
discipline ['dɪsɪplɪn] *n* discipline *f*
disc jockey *n* disc-jockey *m*
disclaim [dɪs'kleɪm] *vt* nier
disclose [dɪs'kləuz] *vt* révéler, divulguer; **disclosure** *n* révélation *f*
disco ['dɪskəu] *n abbr* = **discotheque**
discomfort [dɪs'kʌmfət] *n* malaise *m*, gêne *f*; (*lack of comfort*) manque *m* de confort
disconcert [dɪskən'sə:t] *vt* déconcerter
disconnect [dɪskə'nɛkt] *vt* (ELEC, RADIO, *pipe*) débrancher; (TEL, *water*) couper
discontent [dɪskən'tɛnt] *n* mécontentement *m*; **~ed** *adj* mécontent(e)
discontinue [dɪskən'tɪnju:] *vt* cesser, interrompre; **"~d"** (COMM) "fin de série"
discord ['dɪskɔ:d] *n* discorde *f*, dissension *f*; (MUS) dissonance *f*
discotheque ['dɪskəutɛk] *n* discothèque *f*
discount [*n* 'dɪskaunt, *vb* dɪs'kaunt] *n* remise *f*, rabais *m* ♦ *vt* (*sum*) faire une remise de; (*fig*) ne pas tenir compte de
discourage [dɪs'kʌrɪdʒ] *vt* décourager
discover [dɪs'kʌvə^r] *vt* découvrir; **~y** *n* découverte *f*
discredit [dɪs'krɛdɪt] *vt* (*idea*) mettre en doute; (*person*) discréditer
discreet [dɪs'kri:t] *adj* discret(-ète)
discrepancy [dɪs'krɛpənsɪ] *n* divergence *f*, contradiction *f*
discretion [dɪs'krɛʃən] *n* discretion *f*; **use your own ~** à vous de juger
discriminate [dɪs'krɪmɪneɪt] *vi*: **to ~ between** établir une distinction entre, faire la différence entre; **to ~ against** pratiquer une discrimination contre; **discriminating** *adj* qui a du discernement; **discrimination** [dɪskrɪmɪ'neɪʃən] *n* discrimination *f*; (*judgment*)

discernement *m*

discuss [dɪs'kʌs] *vt* discuter de; (*debate*) discuter; **~ion** *n* discussion *f*

disdain [dɪs'deɪn] *n* dédain *m*

disease [dɪ'zi:z] *n* maladie *f*

disembark [dɪsɪm'bɑ:k] *vi* débarquer

disentangle [dɪsɪn'tæŋgl] *vt* (*wool, wire*) démêler, débrouiller; (*from wreckage*) dégager

disfigure [dɪs'fɪgə^r] *vt* défigurer

disgrace [dɪs'greɪs] *n* honte *f*; (*disfavour*) disgrâce *f* ♦ *vt* déshonorer, couvrir de honte; **~ful** *adj* scandaleux(-euse), honteux(-euse)

disgruntled [dɪs'grʌntld] *adj* mécontent(e)

disguise [dɪs'gaɪz] *n* déguisement *m* ♦ *vt* déguiser; **in ~** déguisé(e)

disgust [dɪs'gʌst] *n* dégoût *m*, aversion *f* ♦ *vt* dégoûter, écœurer; **~ing** *adj* dégoûtant(e); révoltant(e)

dish [dɪʃ] *n* plat *m*; **to do** *or* **wash the ~es** faire la vaisselle; **~ out** *vt* servir, distribuer; **~ up** *vt* servir; **~cloth** *n* (*for washing*) lavette *f*

dishearten [dɪs'hɑ:tn] *vt* décourager

dishevelled [dɪ'ʃɛvəld] (*US* **disheveled**) *adj* ébouriffé(e); décoiffé(e); débraillé(e)

dishonest [dɪs'ɔnɪst] *adj* malhonnête

dishonour [dɪs'ɔnə^r] (*US* **dishonor**) *n* déshonneur *m*; **~able** *adj* (*behaviour*) déshonorant(e); (*person*) peu honorable

dishtowel ['dɪʃtauəl] (*US*) *n* torchon *m*

dishwasher ['dɪʃwɔʃə^r] *n* lave-vaisselle *m*

disillusion [dɪsɪ'lu:ʒən] *vt* désabuser, désillusionner

disinfect [dɪsɪn'fɛkt] *vt* désinfecter; **~ant** *n* désinfectant *m*

disintegrate [dɪs'ɪntɪgreɪt] *vi* se désintégrer

disinterested [dɪs'ɪntrəstɪd] *adj* désintéressé(e)

disjointed [dɪs'dʒɔɪntɪd] *adj* décousu(e), incohérent(e)

disk [dɪsk] *n* (*COMPUT*) disque *m*; (: *floppy* ~) disquette *f*; **single-/double-sided ~** disquette simple/double face; **~ drive** *n* lecteur *m* de disquettes; **~ette** [dɪs'kɛt] *n* disquette *f*, disque *m* souple

dislike [dɪs'laɪk] *n* aversion *f*, antipathie *f* ♦ *vt* ne pas aimer

dislocate ['dɪsləkeɪt] *vt* disloquer; déboiter

dislodge [dɪs'lɔdʒ] *vt* déplacer, faire bouger

disloyal [dɪs'lɔɪəl] *adj* déloyal(e)

dismal ['dɪzml] *adj* lugubre, maussade

dismantle [dɪs'mæntl] *vt* démonter

dismay [dɪs'meɪ] *n* consternation *f*

dismiss [dɪs'mɪs] *vt* congédier, renvoyer; (*soldiers*) faire rompre les rangs à; (*idea*) écarter; (*LAW*): **to ~ a case** rendre une fin de non-recevoir; **~al** *n* renvoi *m*

dismount [dɪs'maunt] *vi* mettre pied à terre, descendre

disobedient [dɪsə'bi:dɪənt] *adj* désobéissant(e)

disobey [dɪsə'beɪ] *vt* désobéir à

disorder [dɪs'ɔ:də^r] *n* désordre *m*; (*rioting*) désordres *mpl*; (*MED*) troubles *mpl*; **~ly** *adj* en désordre; désordonné(e)

disorientated [dɪs'ɔ:rɪɛnteɪtɪd] *adj* désorienté(e)

disown [dɪs'əun] *vt* renier

disparaging [dɪs'pærɪdʒɪŋ] *adj* désobligeant(e)

dispassionate [dɪs'pæʃənət] *adj* calme, froid(e); impartial(e), objectif(-ive)

dispatch [dɪs'pætʃ] *vt* expédier, envoyer ♦ *n* envoi *m*, expédition *f*; (*MIL, PRESS*) dépêche *f*

dispel [dɪs'pel] *vt* dissiper, chasser

dispense [dɪs'pɛns] *vt* distribuer, administrer; **~ with** *vt fus* se passer de; **~r** *n* (*machine*) distributeur *m*; **dispensing chemist** (*BRIT*) *n* pharmacie *f*

disperse [dɪs'pə:s] *vt* disperser ♦ *vi* se disperser

dispirited [dɪs'pɪrɪtɪd] *adj* découragé(e), déprimé(e)

displace [dɪs'pleɪs] *vt* déplacer
display [dɪs'pleɪ] *n* étalage *m*; déploiement *m*; affichage *m*; (*screen*) écran *m*, visuel *m*; (*of feeling*) manifestation *f* ♦ *vt* montrer; (*goods*) mettre à l'étalage, exposer; (*results, departure times*) afficher; (*pej*) faire étalage de
displease [dɪs'pli:z] *vt* mécontenter, contrarier; **~d** *adj*: **~d with** mécontent(e) de; **displeasure** [dɪs'plɛʒəʳ] *n* mécontentement *m*
disposable [dɪs'pəuzəbl] *adj* (*pack etc*) jetable, à jeter; (*income*) disponible; **~ nappy** (BRIT) *n* couche *f* à jeter, couche-culotte *f*
disposal [dɪs'pəuzl] *n* (*of goods for sale*) vente *f*; (*of property*) disposition *f*, cession *f*; (*of rubbish*) enlèvement *m*; destruction *f*; **at one's ~** à sa disposition
dispose [dɪs'pəuz] *vt* disposer; **~ of** *vt fus* (*unwanted goods etc*) se débarrasser de, se défaire de; (*problem*) expédier; **~d** *adj*: **to be ~d to do sth** être disposé(e) à faire qch; **disposition** [dɪspə'zɪʃən] *n* disposition *f*; (*temperament*) naturel *m*
disprove [dɪs'pru:v] *vt* réfuter
dispute [dɪs'pju:t] *n* discussion *f*; (*also:* **industrial ~**) conflit *m* ♦ *vt* contester; (*matter*) discuter; (*victory*) disputer
disqualify [dɪs'kwɔlɪfaɪ] *vt* (SPORT) disqualifier; **to ~ sb for sth/from doing** rendre qn inapte à qch/à faire
disquiet [dɪs'kwaɪət] *n* inquiétude *f*, trouble *m*
disregard [dɪsrɪ'gɑ:d] *vt* ne pas tenir compte de
disrepair ['dɪsrɪ'pɛəʳ] *n*: **to fall into ~** (*building*) tomber en ruine
disreputable [dɪs'rɛpjutəbl] *adj* (*person*) de mauvaise réputation; (*behaviour*) déshonorant(e)
disrespectful [dɪsrɪ'spɛktful] *adj* irrespectueux(-euse)
disrupt [dɪs'rʌpt] *vt* (*plans*) déranger; (*conversation*) interrompre
dissatisfied [dɪs'sætɪsfaɪd] *adj*: **~ (with)** insatisfait(e) (de)
dissect [dɪ'sɛkt] *vt* disséquer
dissent [dɪ'sɛnt] *n* dissentiment *m*, différence *f* d'opinion
dissertation [dɪsə'teɪʃən] *n* mémoire *m*
disservice [dɪs'sə:vɪs] *n*: **to do sb a ~** rendre un mauvais service à qn
dissimilar [dɪ'sɪmɪləʳ] *adj*: **~ (to)** dissemblable (à), différent(e) (de)
dissipate ['dɪsɪpeɪt] *vt* dissiper; (*money, efforts*) disperser
dissolute ['dɪsəlu:t] *adj* débauché(e), dissolu(e)
dissolve [dɪ'zɔlv] *vt* dissoudre ♦ *vi* se dissoudre, fondre; **to ~ in(to) tears** fondre en larmes
distance ['dɪstns] *n* distance *f*; **in the ~** au loin
distant ['dɪstnt] *adj* lointain(e), éloigné(e); (*manner*) distant(e), froid(e)
distaste [dɪs'teɪst] *n* dégoût *m*; **~ful** *adj* déplaisant(e), désagréable
distended [dɪs'tɛndɪd] *adj* (*stomach*) dilaté(e)
distil [dɪs'tɪl] (US **distill**) *vt* distiller; **~lery** *n* distillerie *f*
distinct [dɪs'tɪŋkt] *adj* distinct(e); (*clear*) marqué(e); **as ~ from** par opposition à; **~ion** *n* distinction *f*; (*in exam*) mention *f* très bien; **~ive** *adj* distinctif(-ive)
distinguish [dɪs'tɪŋgwɪʃ] *vt* distinguer; **~ed** *adj* (*eminent*) distingué(e); **~ing** *adj* (*feature*) distinctif(-ive), caractéristique
distort [dɪs'tɔ:t] *vt* déformer
distract [dɪs'trækt] *vt* distraire, déranger; **~ed** *adj* distrait(e); (*anxious*) éperdu(e), égaré(e); **~ion** *n* distraction *f*; égarement *m*
distraught [dɪs'trɔ:t] *adj* éperdu(e)
distress [dɪs'trɛs] *n* détresse *f* ♦ *vt* affliger; **~ing** *adj* douloureux(-euse), pénible
distribute [dɪs'trɪbju:t] *vt* distribuer; **distribution** [dɪstrɪ'bju:ʃən] *n* distribu-

tion *f*; **distributor** *n* distributeur *m*

district ['dɪstrɪkt] *n* (*of country*) région *f*; (*of town*) quartier *m*; (ADMIN) district *m*; **~ attorney** (*US*) *n* ≃ procureur *m* de la République; **~ nurse** (*BRIT*) *n* infirmière visiteuse

distrust [dɪs'trʌst] *n* méfiance *f* ♦ *vt* se méfier de

disturb [dɪs'tə:b] *vt* troubler; (*inconvenience*) déranger; **~ance** *n* dérangement *m*; (*violent event, political etc*) troubles *mpl*; **~ed** *adj* (*worried, upset*) agité(e), troublé(e); **to be emotionally ~ed** avoir des problèmes affectifs; **~ing** *adj* troublant(e), inquiétant(e)

disuse [dɪs'ju:s] *n*: **to fall into ~** tomber en désuétude; **~d** [dɪs'ju:zd] *adj* désaffecté(e)

ditch [dɪtʃ] *n* fossé *m*; (*irrigation*) rigole *f* ♦ *vt* (*inf*) abandonner; (*person*) plaquer

dither ['dɪðə^r] *vi* hésiter

ditto ['dɪtəu] *adv* idem

dive [daɪv] *n* plongeon *m*; (*of submarine*) plongée *f* ♦ *vi* plonger; **to ~ into** (*bag, drawer etc*) plonger la main dans; (*shop, car etc*) se précipiter dans; **~r** *n* plongeur *m*

diversion [daɪ'və:ʃən] *n* (*BRIT*: *AUT*) déviation *f*; (*distraction, MIL*) diversion *f*

divert [daɪ'və:t] *vt* (*funds, BRIT*: *traffic*) dévier; (*river, attention*) détourner

divide [dɪ'vaɪd] *vt* diviser; (*separate*) séparer ♦ *vi* se diviser; **~d highway** (*US*) *n* route *f* à quatre voies

dividend ['dɪvɪdɛnd] *n* dividende *m*

divine [dɪ'vaɪn] *adj* divin(e)

diving ['daɪvɪŋ] *n* plongée (sous-marine); **~ board** *n* plongeoir *m*

divinity [dɪ'vɪnɪtɪ] *n* divinité *f*; (*SCOL*) théologie *f*

division [dɪ'vɪʒən] *n* division *f*

divorce [dɪ'vɔ:s] *n* divorce *m* ♦ *vt* divorcer d'avec; (*dissociate*) séparer; **~d** *adj* divorcé(e); **~e** *n* divorcé(e)

D.I.Y. (*BRIT*) *n abbr* = **do-it-yourself**

dizzy ['dɪzɪ] *adj*: **to make sb ~** donner le vertige à qn; **to feel ~** avoir la tête qui tourne

DJ *n abbr* = **disc jockey**

DNA fingerprinting *n* technique *f* des empreintes génétiques

KEYWORD

do [du:] (*pt* **did**, *pp* **done**) *n* (*inf*: *party etc*) soirée *f*, fête *f*

♦ *vb* **1** (*in negative constructions*) *non traduit*; **I don't understand** je ne comprends pas

2 (*to form questions*) *non traduit*; **didn't you know?** vous ne le saviez pas?; **why didn't you come?** pourquoi n'êtes-vous pas venu?

3 (*for emphasis, in polite expressions*): **she does seem rather late** je trouve qu'elle est bien en retard; **do sit down/help yourself** asseyez-vous/servez-vous je vous en prie

4 (*used to avoid repeating vb*): **she swims better than I do** elle nage mieux que moi; **do you agree? - yes, I do/no, I don't** vous êtes d'accord? - oui/non; **she lives in Glasgow - so do I** elle habite Glasgow - moi aussi; **who broke it? - I did** qui l'a cassé? - c'est moi

5 (*in question tags*): **he laughed, didn't he?** il a ri, n'est-ce pas?; **I don't know him, do I?** je ne crois pas le connaître

♦ *vt* (*gen*: *carry out, perform etc*) faire; **what are you doing tonight?** qu'est-ce que vous faites ce soir?; **to do the cooking/washing-up** faire la cuisine/la vaisselle; **to do one's teeth/hair/nails** se brosser les dents/se coiffer/se faire les ongles; **the car was doing 100** ≃ la voiture faisait du 160 (à l'heure)

♦ *vi* **1** (*act, behave*) faire; **do as I do** faites comme moi

2 (*get on, fare*) marcher; **the firm is doing well** l'entreprise marche bien; **how do you do?** comment allez-vous?; (*on being introduced*) enchanté(e)!

3 (*suit*) aller; **will it do?** est-ce que ça ira?
4 (*be sufficient*) suffire, aller; **will £10 do?** est-ce que 10 livres suffiront?; **that'll do** ça suffit, ça ira; **that'll do!** (*in annoyance*) ça va *or* suffit comme ça!; **to make do (with)** se contenter (de)
do away with *vt fus* supprimer
do up *vt* (*laces, dress*) attacher; (*buttons*) boutonner; (*zip*) fermer; (*renovate: room*) refaire; (: *house*) remettre à neuf
do with *vt fus* (*need*): **I could do with a drink/some help** quelque chose à boire/un peu d'aide ne serait pas de refus; (*be connected*): **that has nothing to do with you** cela ne vous concerne pas; **I won't have anything to do with it** je ne veux pas m'en mêler
do without *vi* s'en passer ♦ *vt fus* se passer de

dock [dɔk] *n* dock *m*; (*LAW*) banc *m* des accusés ♦ *vi* se mettre à quai; (*SPACE*) s'arrimer; **~er** *n* docker *m*; **~yard** *n* chantier *m* de construction navale
doctor ['dɔktəʳ] *n* médecin *m*, docteur *m*; (*PhD etc*) docteur ♦ *vt* (*drink*) frelater; **D~ of Philosophy** *n* (*degree*) doctorat *m*; (*person*) Docteur *m* en Droit *or* Lettres *etc*, titulaire *m/f* d'un doctorat
document ['dɔkjumənt] *n* document *m*; **~ary** [dɔkju'mɛntərɪ] *adj* documentaire ♦ *n* documentaire *m*
dodge [dɔdʒ] *n* truc *m*; combine *f* ♦ *vt* esquiver, éviter
dodgems ['dɔdʒəmz] (*BRIT*) *npl* autos tamponneuses
doe [dəu] *n* (*deer*) biche *f*; (*rabbit*) lapine *f*
does [dʌz] *vb see* **do**; **~n't** = **does not**
dog [dɔg] *n* chien(ne) ♦ *vt* suivre de près; poursuivre, harceler; **~ collar** *n* collier *m* de chien; (*fig*) faux-col *m* d'ecclésiastique; **~-eared** *adj* corné(e); **~ged** ['dɔgɪd] *adj* obstiné(e), opiniâtre; **~sbody** *n* bonne *f* à tout faire, tâcheron *m*
doings ['duɪŋz] *npl* activités *fpl*
do-it-yourself ['du:ɪtjɔ:'sɛlf] *n* bricolage *m*
doldrums ['dɔldrəmz] *npl*: **to be in the ~** avoir le cafard; (*business*) être dans le marasme
dole [dəul] *n* (*BRIT: payment*) allocation *f* de chômage; **on the ~** au chômage; **~ out** *vt* donner au compte-goutte
doll [dɔl] *n* poupée *f*
dollar ['dɔləʳ] *n* dollar *m*
dolled up (*inf*) *adj*: **(all) ~** sur son trente et un
dolphin ['dɔlfɪn] *n* dauphin *m*
dome [dəum] *n* dôme *m*
domestic [də'mɛstɪk] *adj* (*task, appliances*) ménager(-ère); (*of country: trade, situation etc*) intérieur(e); (*animal*) domestique; **~ated** *adj* (*animal*) domestiqué(e); (*husband*) pantouflard(e)
dominate ['dɔmɪneɪt] *vt* dominer
domineering [dɔmɪ'nɪərɪŋ] *adj* dominateur(-trice), autoritaire
dominion [də'mɪnɪən] *n* (*territory*) territoire *m*; **to have ~ over** contrôler
domino ['dɔmɪnəu] (*pl* **~es**) *n* domino *m*; **~es** *n* (*game*) dominos *mpl*
don [dɔn] (*BRIT*) *n* professeur *m* d'université
donate [də'neɪt] *vt* faire don de, donner
done [dʌn] *pp of* **do**
donkey ['dɔŋkɪ] *n* âne *m*
donor ['dəunəʳ] *n* (*of blood etc*) donneur(-euse); (*to charity*) donateur(-trice); **~ card** *n* carte *f* de don d'organes
don't [dəunt] *vb* = **do not**
donut ['dəunʌt] (*US*) *n* = **doughnut**
doodle ['du:dl] *vi* griffonner, gribouiller
doom [du:m] *n* destin *m* ♦ *vt*: **to be ~ed (to failure)** être voué(e) à l'échec
door [dɔ:ʳ] *n* porte *f*; (*RAIL, car*) portière *f*; **~bell** *n* sonnette *f*; **~handle** *n* poi-

gnée *f* de la porte; (*car*) poignée de portière; **~man** (*irreg*) *n* (*in hotel*) portier *m*; (*in nightclub etc*) videur *m*; **~mat** *n* paillasson *m*; **~step** *n* pas *m* de (la) porte, seuil *m*; **~way** *n* (embrasure *f* de la) porte *f*

dope [dəup] *n* (*inf: drug*) drogue *f*; (*: person*) andouille *f* ♦ *vt* (*horse etc*) doper

dormant ['dɔːmənt] *adj* assoupi(e)

dormitory ['dɔːmɪtrɪ] *n* dortoir *m*; (*US: building*) résidence *f* universitaire

dormouse ['dɔːmaus] (*pl* **dormice**) *n* loir *m*

DOS [dɔs] *n abbr* (= *disk operating system*) DOS

dose [dəus] *n* dose *f*

dosh [dɔʃ] (*inf*) *n* fric *m*

doss house ['dɔs-] (*BRIT*) *n* asile *m* de nuit

dot [dɔt] *n* point *m*; (*on material*) pois *m* ♦ *vt*: **~ted with** parsemé(e) de; **on the ~** à l'heure tapante *or* pile; **~ted line** *n* pointillé(s) *m(pl)*

double ['dʌbl] *adj* double ♦ *adv* (*twice*): **to cost ~ (sth)** coûter le double (de qch) *or* deux fois plus (que qch) ♦ *n* double *m* ♦ *vt* doubler; (*fold*) plier en deux ♦ *vi* doubler; **~s** *n* (*TENNIS*) double *m*; **on** *or* (*BRIT*) **at the ~** au pas de course; **~ bass** (*BRIT*) *n* contrebasse *f*; **~ bed** *n* grand lit; **~ bend** (*BRIT*) *n* virage *m* en S; **~-breasted** *adj* croisé(e); **~-click** *vi* (*COMPUT*) double-cliquer; **~-cross** *vt* doubler, trahir; **~-decker** *n* autobus *m* à impériale; **~ glazing** (*BRIT*) *n* double vitrage *m*; **~ room** *n* chambre *f* pour deux personnes; **doubly** *adv* doublement, deux fois plus

doubt [daut] *n* doute *m* ♦ *vt* douter de; **to ~ that** douter que; **~ful** *adj* douteux(-euse); (*person*) incertain(e); **~less** *adv* sans doute, sûrement

dough [dəu] *n* pâte *f*; **~nut** (*US* **donut**) *n* beignet *m*

dove [dʌv] *n* colombe *f*

Dover ['dəuvəʳ] *n* Douvres

dovetail ['dʌvteɪl] *vi* (*fig*) concorder

dowdy ['daudɪ] *adj* démodé(e); mal fagoté(e) (*inf*)

down [daun] *n* (*soft feathers*) duvet *m* ♦ *adv* en bas, vers le bas; (*on the ground*) par terre ♦ *prep* en bas de; (*along*) le long de ♦ *vt* (*inf: drink, food*) s'envoyer; **~ with X!** à bas X!; **~-and-out** *n* clochard(e); **~-at-heel** *adj* éculé(e); (*fig*) miteux(-euse); **~cast** *adj* démoralisé(e); **~fall** *n* chute *f*; ruine *f*; **~hearted** *adj* découragé(e); **~hill** *adv*: **to go ~hill** descendre; (*fig*) péricliter; **~ payment** *n* acompte *m*; **~pour** *n* pluie torrentielle, déluge *m*; **~right** *adj* (*lie etc*) effronté(e); (*refusal*) catégorique; **~size** *vt* (*ECON*) réduire ses effectifs

Downing Street

Downing Street *est une rue de Westminster (à Londres) où se trouve la résidence officielle du Premier ministre (numéro 10) et celle du ministre des Finances (numéro 11). Le nom* "**Downing Street**" *est souvent utilisé pour désigner le gouvernement britannique.*

Down's syndrome [daunz-] *n* (*MED*) trisomie *f*

down: ~stairs *adv* au rez-de-chaussée; à l'étage inférieur; **~stream** *adv* en aval; **~-to-earth** *adj* terre à terre *inv*; **~town** *adv* en ville; **~ under** *adv* en Australie/Nouvelle-Zélande; **~ward** *adj, adv* vers le bas; **~wards** *adv* vers le bas

dowry ['daurɪ] *n* dot *f*

doz. *abbr* = **dozen**

doze [dəuz] *vi* sommeiller; **~ off** *vi* s'assoupir

dozen ['dʌzn] *n* douzaine *f*; **a ~ books** une douzaine de livres; **~s of** des centaines de

Dr. *abbr* = **doctor**; **drive**

drab [dræb] *adj* terne, morne

draft [drɑːft] *n* ébauche *f*; (*of letter, essay etc*) brouillon *m*; (*COMM*) traite *f*;

(*US*: *call-up*) conscription *f* ♦ *vt* faire le brouillon *or* un projet de; (*MIL*: *send*) détacher; *see also* **draught**

draftsman ['drɑːftsmən] (*irreg*) (*US*) *n* = **draughtsman**

drag [dræg] *vt* traîner; (*river*) draguer ♦ *vi* traîner ♦ *n* (*inf*) casse-pieds *m/f*; (*women's clothing*): **in ~** (en) travesti; **~ on** *vi* s'éterniser

dragon ['drægn] *n* dragon *m*

dragonfly ['drægənflaɪ] *n* libellule *f*

drain [dreɪn] *n* égout *m*, canalisation *f*; (*on resources*) saignée *f* ♦ *vt* (*land, marshes etc*) drainer, assécher; (*vegetables*) égoutter; (*glass*) vider ♦ *vi* (*water*) s'écouler; **~age** *n* drainage *m*; système *m* d'égouts *or* de canalisations; **~ing board** (*US* **drain board**) *n* égouttoir *m*; **~pipe** *n* tuyau *m* d'écoulement

drama ['drɑːmə] *n* (*art*) théâtre *m*, art *m* dramatique; (*play*) pièce *f* (de théâtre); (*event*) drame *m*; **~tic** [drə'mætɪk] *adj* dramatique; spectaculaire; **~tist** ['dræmətɪst] *n* auteur *m* dramatique; **~tize** ['dræmətaɪz] *vt* (*events*) dramatiser; (*adapt*: *for TV/cinema*) adapter pour la télévision/pour l'écran

drank [dræŋk] *pt of* **drink**

drape [dreɪp] *vt* draper; **~s** (*US*) *npl* rideaux *mpl*

drastic ['dræstɪk] *adj* sévère; énergique; (*change*) radical(e)

draught [drɑːft] (*US* **draft**) *n* courant *m* d'air; (*NAUT*) tirant *m* d'eau; **on ~** (*beer*) à la pression; **~board** (*BRIT*) *n* damier *m*; **~s** (*BRIT*) *n* (jeu *m* de) dames *fpl*

draughtsman ['drɑːftsmən] (*irreg*) *n* dessinateur(-trice) (industriel(le))

draw [drɔː] (*pt* **drew**, *pp* **drawn**) *vt* tirer; (*tooth*) arracher, extraire; (*attract*) attirer; (*picture*) dessiner; (*line, circle*) tracer; (*money*) retirer; (*wages*) toucher ♦ *vi* (*SPORT*) faire match nul ♦ *n* match nul; (*lottery*) tirage *m* au sort; loterie *f*; **to ~ near** s'approcher; approcher; **~ out** *vi* (*lengthen*) s'allonger ♦ *vt* (*money*) retirer; **~ up** *vi* (*stop*) s'arrêter ♦ *vt* (*chair*) approcher; (*document*) établir, dresser; **~back** *n* inconvénient *m*, désavantage *m*; **~bridge** *n* pont-levis *m*

drawer [drɔː^r] *n* tiroir *m*

drawing ['drɔːɪŋ] *n* dessin *m*; **~ board** *n* planche *f* à dessin; **~ pin** (*BRIT*) *n* punaise *f*; **~ room** *n* salon *m*

drawl [drɔːl] *n* accent traînant

drawn [drɔːn] *pp of* **draw**

dread [drɛd] *n* terreur *f*, effroi *m* ♦ *vt* redouter, appréhender; **~ful** *adj* affreux (-euse)

dream [driːm] (*pt, pp* **dreamed** *or* **dreamt**) *n* rêve *m* ♦ *vt, vi* rêver; **~y** *adj* rêveur(-euse); (*music*) langoureux (-euse)

dreary ['drɪərɪ] *adj* morne; monotone

dredge [drɛdʒ] *vt* draguer

dregs [drɛgz] *npl* lie *f*

drench [drɛntʃ] *vt* tremper

dress [drɛs] *n* robe *f*; (*no pl*: *clothing*) habillement *m*, tenue *f* ♦ *vi* s'habiller ♦ *vt* habiller; (*wound*) panser; **to get ~ed** s'habiller; **~ up** *vi* s'habiller; (*in fancy ~*) se déguiser; **~ circle** (*BRIT*) *n* (*THEATRE*) premier balcon; **~er** *n* (*furniture*) vaisselier *m*; (: *US*) coiffeuse *f*, commode *f*; **~ing** *n* (*MED*) pansement *m*; (*CULIN*) sauce *f*, assaisonnement *m*; **~ing gown** (*BRIT*) *n* robe *f* de chambre; **~ing room** *n* (*THEATRE*) loge *f*; (*SPORT*) vestiaire *m*; **~ing table** *n* coiffeuse *f*; **~maker** *n* couturière *f*; **~ rehearsal** *n* (répétition) générale *f*

drew [druː] *pt of* **draw**

dribble ['drɪbl] *vi* (*baby*) baver ♦ *vt* (*ball*) dribbler

dried [draɪd] *adj* (*fruit, beans*) sec (sèche); (*eggs, milk*) en poudre

drier ['draɪə^r] *n* = **dryer**

drift [drɪft] *n* (*of current etc*) force *f*; direction *f*, mouvement *m*; (*of snow*) rafale *f*; (: *on ground*) congère *f*; (*general meaning*) sens (général) ♦ *vi* (*boat*) aller à la dérive, dériver; (*sand, snow*) s'amonceler, s'entasser; **~wood** *n* bois flotté

drill [drɪl] *n* perceuse *f*; (~ *bit*) foret *m*, mèche *f*; (*of dentist*) roulette *f*, fraise *f*; (*MIL*) exercice *m* ♦ *vt* percer; (*troops*) entraîner ♦ *vi* (*for oil*) faire un *or* des forage(s)

drink [drɪŋk] (*pt* **drank**, *pp* **drunk**) *n* boisson *f*; (*alcoholic*) verre *m* ♦ *vt*, *vi* boire; **to have a ~** boire quelque chose, boire un verre; prendre l'apéritif; **a ~ of water** un verre d'eau; **~er** *n* buveur(-euse); **~ing water** *n* eau *f* potable

drip [drɪp] *n* goutte *f*; (*MED*) goutte-à-goutte *m inv*, perfusion *f* ♦ *vi* tomber goutte à goutte; (*tap*) goutter; **~-dry** *adj* (*shirt*) sans repassage; **~ping** *n* graisse *f* (de rôti)

drive [draɪv] (*pt* **drove**, *pp* **driven**) *n* promenade *f or* trajet *m* en voiture; (*also:* **~way**) allée *f*; (*energy*) dynamisme *m*, énergie *f*; (*push*) effort (concerté), campagne *f*; (*also:* **disk ~**) lecteur *m* de disquettes ♦ *vt* conduire; (*push*) chasser, pousser; (*TECH*: *motor, wheel*) faire fonctionner; entraîner; (*nail, stake etc*): **to ~ sth into sth** enfoncer qch dans qch ♦ *vi* (*AUT*: *at controls*) conduire; (: *travel*) aller en voiture; **left-/right-hand ~** conduite *f* à gauche/droite; **to ~ sb mad** rendre qn fou (folle); **to ~ sb home/to the airport** reconduire qn chez lui/conduire qn à l'aéroport; **~-by shooting** *n (tentative d')assassinat par coups de feu tirés d'un voiture*

drivel ['drɪvl] (*inf*) *n* idioties *fpl*

driver ['draɪvə^r] *n* conducteur(-trice); (*of taxi, bus*) chauffeur *m*; **~'s license** (*US*) *n* permis *m* de conduire

driveway ['draɪvweɪ] *n* allée *f*

driving ['draɪvɪŋ] *n* conduite *f*; **~ instructor** *n* moniteur *m* d'auto-école; **~ lesson** *n* leçon *f* de conduite; **~ licence** (*BRIT*) *n* permis *m* de conduire; **~ school** *n* auto-école *f*; **~ test** *n* examen *m* du permis de conduire

drizzle ['drɪzl] *n* bruine *f*, crachin *m*

drool [dru:l] *vi* baver

droop [dru:p] *vi* (*shoulders*) tomber; (*head*) pencher; (*flower*) pencher la tête

drop [drɔp] *n* goutte *f*; (*fall*) baisse *f*; (*also:* **parachute ~**) saut *m* ♦ *vt* laisser tomber; (*voice, eyes, price*) baisser; (*set down from car*) déposer ♦ *vi* tomber; **~s** *npl* (*MED*) gouttes; **~ off** *vi* (*sleep*) s'assoupir ♦ *vt* (*passenger*) déposer; **~ out** *vi* (*withdraw*) se retirer; (*student etc*) abandonner, décrocher; **~out** *n* marginal(e); **~per** *n* compte-gouttes *m inv*; **~pings** *npl* crottes *fpl*

drought [draut] *n* sécheresse *f*

drove [drəuv] *pt of* **drive**

drown [draun] *vt* noyer ♦ *vi* se noyer

drowsy ['drauzɪ] *adj* somnolent(e)

drug [drʌg] *n* médicament *m*; (*narcotic*) drogue *f* ♦ *vt* droguer; **to be on ~s** se droguer; **~ addict** *n* toxicomane *m/f*; **~gist** (*US*) *n* pharmacien(ne)-droguiste; **~store** (*US*) *n* pharmacie-droguerie *f*, drugstore *m*

drum [drʌm] *n* tambour *m*; (*for oil, petrol*) bidon *m*; **~s** *npl* (*kit*) batterie *f*; **~mer** *n* (joueur *m* de) tambour *m*

drunk [drʌŋk] *pp of* **drink** ♦ *adj* ivre, soûl(e) ♦ *n* (*also:* **~ard**) ivrogne *m/f*; **~en** *adj* (*person*) ivre, soûl(e); (*rage, stupor*) ivrogne, d'ivrogne

dry [draɪ] *adj* sec (sèche); (*day*) sans pluie; (*humour*) pince-sans-rire *inv*; (*lake, riverbed, well*) à sec ♦ *vt* sécher; (*clothes*) faire sécher ♦ *vi* sécher; **~ up** *vi* tarir; **~-cleaner's** *n* teinturerie *f*; **~er** *n* séchoir *m*; (*spin-dryer*) essoreuse *f*; **~ness** *n* sécheresse *f*; **~ rot** *n* pourriture sèche (*du bois*)

DSS *n abbr* (= *Department of Social Security*) ≃ Sécurité sociale

DTP *n abbr* (= *desk-top publishing*) PAO *f*

dual ['djuəl] *adj* double; **~ carriageway** (*BRIT*) *n* route *f* à quatre voies *or* à chaussées séparées; **~-purpose** *adj* à double usage

dubbed [dʌbd] *adj* (*CINEMA*) doublé(e)

dubious ['dju:bɪəs] *adj* hésitant(e), incertain(e); (*reputation, company*) douteux(-euse)

duchess ['dʌtʃɪs] *n* duchesse *f*

duck [dʌk] *n* canard *m* ♦ *vi* se baisser vivement, baisser subitement la tête; **~ling** ['dʌklɪŋ] *n* caneton *m*

duct [dʌkt] *n* conduite *f*, canalisation *f*; (*ANAT*) conduit *m*

dud [dʌd] *n* (*object, tool*): **it's a ~** c'est de la camelote, ça ne marche pas ♦ *adj*: **~ cheque** (*BRIT*) chèque sans provision

due [dju:] *adj* dû (due); (*expected*) attendu(e); (*fitting*) qui convient ♦ *n*: **to give sb his** (*or* **her**) **~** être juste envers qn ♦ *adv*: **~ north** droit vers le nord; **~s** *npl* (*for club, union*) cotisation *f*; **in ~ course** en temps utile *or* voulu; finalement; **~ to** dû (due) à; causé(e) par; **he's ~ to finish tomorrow** normalement il doit finir demain

duet [dju:'ɛt] *n* duo *m*

duffel bag ['dʌfl-] *n* sac *m* marin

duffel coat *n* duffel-coat *m*

dug [dʌg] *pt, pp of* **dig**

duke [dju:k] *n* duc *m*

dull [dʌl] *adj* terne, morne; (*boring*) ennuyeux(-euse); (*sound, pain*) sourd(e); (*weather, day*) gris(e), maussade ♦ *vt* (*pain, grief*) atténuer; (*mind, senses*) engourdir

duly ['dju:lɪ] *adv* (*on time*) en temps voulu; (*as expected*) comme il se doit

dumb [dʌm] *adj* muet(te); (*stupid*) bête; **~founded** *adj* sidéré(e)

dummy ['dʌmɪ] *n* (*tailor's model*) mannequin *m*; (*mock-up*) factice *m*, maquette *f*; (*BRIT: for baby*) tétine *f* ♦ *adj* faux (fausse), factice

dump [dʌmp] *n* (*also:* **rubbish ~**) décharge (publique); (*pej*) trou *m* ♦ *vt* (*put down*) déposer; déverser; (*get rid of*) se débarrasser de; (*COMPUT: data*) vider, transférer

dumpling ['dʌmplɪŋ] *n* boulette *f* (de pâte)

dumpy ['dʌmpɪ] *adj* boulot(te)

dunce [dʌns] *n* âne *m*, cancre *m*

dune [dju:n] *n* dune *f*

dung [dʌŋ] *n* fumier *m*

dungarees [dʌŋgə'ri:z] *npl* salopette *f*; bleu(s) *m(pl)*

dungeon ['dʌndʒən] *n* cachot *m*

duplex ['dju:plɛks] (*US*) *n* maison jumelée; (*apartment*) duplex *m*

duplicate [*n* 'dju:plɪkət, *vb* 'dju:plɪkeɪt] *n* double *m* ♦ *vt* faire un double de; (*on machine*) polycopier; photocopier; **in ~** en deux exemplaires

durable ['djuərəbl] *adj* durable; (*clothes, metal*) résistant(e), solide

duration [djuə'reɪʃən] *n* durée *f*

during ['djuərɪŋ] *prep* pendant, au cours de

dusk [dʌsk] *n* crépuscule *m*

dust [dʌst] *n* poussière *f* ♦ *vt* (*furniture*) épousseter, essuyer; (*cake etc*): **to ~ with** saupoudrer de; **~bin** (*BRIT*) *n* poubelle *f*; **~er** *n* chiffon *m*; **~man** (*BRIT*) (*irreg*) *n* boueux *m*, éboueur *m*; **~y** *adj* poussiéreux(-euse)

Dutch [dʌtʃ] *adj* hollandais(e), néerlandais(e) ♦ *n* (*LING*) hollandais *m* ♦ *adv* (*inf*): **to go ~** partager les frais; **the ~** *npl* (*people*) les Hollandais; **~man** (*irreg*) *n* Hollandais; **~woman** (*irreg*) *n* Hollandaise *f*

duty ['dju:tɪ] *n* devoir *m*; (*tax*) droit *m*, taxe *f*; **on ~** de service; (*at night etc*) de garde; **off ~** libre, pas de service *or* de garde; **~-free** *adj* exempté(e) de douane, hors taxe *inv*

duvet ['du:veɪ] (*BRIT*) *n* couette *f*

DVD [di:vi:di:] *n abbr* (= *digital versatile disc*) DVD *m*

dwarf [dwɔ:f] (*pl* **dwarves**) *n* nain(e) ♦ *vt* écraser

dwell [dwɛl] (*pt, pp* **dwelt**) *vi* demeurer; **~ on** *vt fus* s'appesantir sur

dwindle ['dwɪndl] *vi* diminuer

dye [daɪ] *n* teinture *f* ♦ *vt* teindre

dying ['daɪɪŋ] *adj* mourant(e), agonisant(e)

dyke [daɪk] (*BRIT*) *n* digue *f*

dynamic [daɪ'næmɪk] *adj* dynamique

dynamite ['daɪnəmaɪt] *n* dynamite *f*
dynamo ['daɪnəməu] *n* dynamo *f*
dyslexia [dɪs'lɛksɪə] *n* dyslexie *f*

E, e

E [iː] *n* (MUS) mi *m*
each [iːtʃ] *adj* chaque ♦ *pron* chacun(e); **~ other** l'un(e) l'autre; **they hate ~ other** ils se détestent (mutuellement); **you are jealous of ~ other** vous êtes jaloux l'un de l'autre; **they have 2 books ~** ils ont 2 livres chacun
eager ['iːgəʳ] *adj* (*keen*) avide; **to be ~ to do sth** avoir très envie de faire qch; **to be ~ for** désirer vivement, être avide de
eagle ['iːgl] *n* aigle *m*
ear [ɪəʳ] *n* oreille *f*; (*of corn*) épi *m*; **~ache** *n* mal *m* aux oreilles; **~drum** *n* tympan *m*
earl [əːl] (BRIT) *n* comte *m*
earlier ['əːlɪəʳ] *adj* (*date etc*) plus rapproché(e); (*edition, fashion etc*) plus ancien(ne), antérieur(e) ♦ *adv* plus tôt
early ['əːlɪ] *adv* tôt, de bonne heure; (*ahead of time*) en avance; (*near the beginning*) au début ♦ *adj* qui se manifeste (*or* se fait) tôt *or* de bonne heure; (*work*) de jeunesse; (*settler, Christian*) premier(-ère); (*reply*) rapide; (*death*) prématuré(e); **to have an ~ night** se coucher tôt *or* de bonne heure; **in the ~** *or* **~ in the spring/19th century** au début du printemps/19ème siècle; **~ retirement** *n*: **to take ~ retirement** prendre sa retraite anticipée
earmark ['ɪəmɑːk] *vt*: **to ~ sth for** réserver *or* destiner qch à
earn [əːn] *vt* gagner; (COMM: *yield*) rapporter
earnest ['əːnɪst] *adj* sérieux(-euse); **in ~** ♦ *adv* sérieusement
earnings ['əːnɪŋz] *npl* salaire *m*; (*of company*) bénéfices *mpl*
ear: ~phones *npl* écouteurs *mpl*; **~ring** *n* boucle *f* d'oreille; **~shot** *n*: **within ~shot** à portée de voix
earth [əːθ] *n* (*gen, also* BRIT: ELEC) terre *f* ♦ *vt* relier à la terre; **~enware** *n* poterie *f*; faïence *f*; **~quake** *n* tremblement *m* de terre, séisme *m*; **~y** *adj* (*vulgar: humour*) truculent(e)
ease [iːz] *n* facilité *f*, aisance *f*; (*comfort*) bien-être *m* ♦ *vt* (*soothe*) calmer; (*loosen*) relâcher, détendre; **to ~ sth in/out** faire pénétrer/sortir qch délicatement *or* avec douceur; faciliter la pénétration/la sortie de qch; **at ~!** (MIL) repos!; **~ off** *or* **up** *vi* diminuer; (*slow down*) ralentir
easel ['iːzl] *n* chevalet *m*
easily ['iːzɪlɪ] *adv* facilement
east [iːst] *n* est *m* ♦ *adj* (*wind*) d'est; (*side*) est *inv* ♦ *adv* à l'est, vers l'est; **the E~** l'Orient *m*; les pays *mpl* de l'Est
Easter ['iːstəʳ] *n* Pâques *fpl*; **~ egg** *n* œuf *m* de Pâques
east: ~erly ['iːstəlɪ] *adj* (*wind*) d'est; (*direction*) est *inv*; (*point*) à l'est; **~ern** ['iːstən] *adj* de l'est, oriental(e); **~ward(s)** ['iːstwəd(z)] *adv* vers l'est, à l'est
easy ['iːzɪ] *adj* facile; (*manner*) aisé(e) ♦ *adv*: **to take it** *or* **things ~** ne pas se fatiguer; (*not worry*) ne pas (trop) s'en faire; **~ chair** *n* fauteuil *m*; **~-going** *adj* accommodant(e), facile à vivre
eat [iːt] (*pt* **ate**, *pp* **eaten**) *vt, vi* manger; **~ away at, ~ into** *vt fus* ronger, attaquer; (*savings*) entamer
eaves [iːvz] *npl* avant-toit *m*
eavesdrop ['iːvzdrɔp] *vi*: **to ~ (on a conversation)** écouter (une conversation) de façon indiscrète
ebb [ɛb] *n* reflux *m* ♦ *vi* refluer; (*fig: also:* **~ away**) décliner
ebony ['ɛbənɪ] *n* ébène *f*
EC *n abbr* (= *European Community*) C.E. *f*
ECB *n abbr* (= *European Central Bank*) BCE *f*
eccentric [ɪk'sɛntrɪk] *adj* excentrique ♦ *n* excentrique *m/f*
echo ['ɛkəu] (*pl* **~es**) *n* écho *m* ♦ *vt* ré-

péter ♦ *vi* résonner, faire écho
eclipse [ɪ'klɪps] *n* éclipse *f*
ecology [ɪ'kɔlədʒɪ] *n* écologie *f*
e-commerce ['i:kɔmə:s] *n* commerce *m* électronique
economic [i:kə'nɔmɪk] *adj* économique; (*business etc*) rentable; **~al** *adj* économique; (*person*) économe
economics [i:kə'nɔmɪks] *n* économie *f* politique ♦ *npl* (*of project, situation*) aspect *m* financier
economize [ɪ'kɔnəmaɪz] *vi* économiser, faire des économies
economy [ɪ'kɔnəmɪ] *n* économie *f*; **~ class** *n* classe *f* touriste; **~ size** *n* format *m* économique
ecstasy ['ɛkstəsɪ] *n* extase *f* (*drogue aussi*); **ecstatic** [ɛks'tætɪk] *adj* extatique
ECU ['eɪkju:] *n abbr* (= *European Currency Unit*) ECU *m*
eczema ['ɛksɪmə] *n* eczéma *m*
edge [ɛdʒ] *n* bord *m*; (*of knife etc*) tranchant *m*, fil *m* ♦ *vt* border; **on ~** (*fig*) crispé(e), tendu(e); **to ~ away from** s'éloigner furtivement de; **~ways** *adv*: **he couldn't get a word in ~ways** il ne pouvait pas placer un mot
edgy ['ɛdʒɪ] *adj* crispé(e), tendu(e)
edible ['ɛdɪbl] *adj* comestible
Edinburgh ['ɛdɪnbərə] *n* Édimbourg
edit ['ɛdɪt] *vt* (*text, book*) éditer; (*report*) préparer; (*film*) monter; (*broadcast*) réaliser; **~ion** [ɪ'dɪʃən] *n* édition *f*; **~or** *n* (*of column*) rédacteur(-trice); (*of newspaper*) rédacteur(-trice) en chef; (*of sb's work*) éditeur(-trice); **~orial** [ɛdɪ'tɔ:rɪəl] *adj* de la rédaction, éditorial(e) ♦ *n* éditorial *m*
educate ['ɛdjukeɪt] *vt* (*teach*) instruire; (*instruct*) éduquer; **~d** *adj* (*person*) cultivé(e); **education** [ɛdju'keɪʃən] *n* éducation *f*; (*studies*) études *fpl*; (*teaching*) enseignement *m*, instruction *f*; **educational** *adj* (*experience, toy*) pédagogique; (*institution*) scolaire; (*policy*) d'éducation
eel [i:l] *n* anguille *f*
eerie ['ɪərɪ] *adj* inquiétant(e)
effect [ɪ'fɛkt] *n* effet *m* ♦ *vt* effectuer; **to take ~** (*law*) entrer en vigueur, prendre effet; (*drug*) agir, faire son effet; **in ~** en fait; **~ive** [ɪ'fɛktɪv] *adj* efficace; (*actual*) véritable; **~ively** *adv* efficacement; (*in reality*) effectivement; **~iveness** *n* efficacité *f*
effeminate [ɪ'fɛmɪnɪt] *adj* efféminé(e)
effervescent [ɛfə'vɛsnt] *adj* (*drink*) gazeux(-euse)
efficiency [ɪ'fɪʃənsɪ] *n* efficacité *f*; (*of machine*) rendement *m*
efficient [ɪ'fɪʃənt] *adj* efficace; (*machine*) qui a un bon rendement
effort ['ɛfət] *n* effort *m*; **~less** *adj* (*style*) aisé(e); (*achievement*) facile
effusive [ɪ'fju:sɪv] *adj* chaleureux(-euse)
e.g. *adv abbr* (= *exempli gratia*) par exemple, p. ex.
egg [ɛg] *n* œuf *m*; **hard-boiled/soft-boiled ~** œuf dur/à la coque; **~ on** *vt* pousser; **~cup** *n* coquetier *m*; **~plant** *n* (*esp US*) aubergine *f*; **~shell** *n* coquille *f* d'œuf
ego ['i:gəu] *n* (*self-esteem*) amour-propre *m*
egotism ['ɛgəutɪzəm] *n* égotisme *m*
egotist ['ɛgəutɪst] *n* égocentrique *m/f*
Egypt ['i:dʒɪpt] *n* Égypte *f*; **~ian** [ɪ'dʒɪpʃən] *adj* égyptien(ne) ♦ *n* Égyptien(ne)
eiderdown ['aɪdədaun] *n* édredon *m*
Eiffel Tower ['aɪfəl-] *n* tour *f* Eiffel
eight [eɪt] *num* huit; **~een** [eɪ'ti:n] *num* dix-huit; **~h** [eɪtθ] *num* huitième; **~y** ['eɪtɪ] *num* quatre-vingt(s)
Eire ['ɛərə] *n* République *f* d'Irlande
either ['aɪðə^r] *adj* l'un ou l'autre; (*both, each*) chaque ♦ *pron*: **~ (of them)** l'un ou l'autre ♦ *adv* non plus ♦ *conj*: **~ good or bad** ou bon ou mauvais, soit bon soit mauvais; **on ~ side** de chaque côté; **I don't like ~** je n'aime ni l'un ni l'autre; **no, I don't ~** moi non plus
eject [ɪ'dʒɛkt] *vt* (*tenant etc*) expulser;

(*object*) éjecter

elaborate [*adj* ɪ'læbərɪt, *vb* ɪ'læbəreɪt] *adj* compliqué(e), recherché(e) ♦ *vt* élaborer ♦ *vi*: **to ~ (on)** entrer dans les détails (de)

elastic [ɪ'læstɪk] *adj* élastique ♦ *n* élastique *m*; **~ band** *n* élastique *m*

elated [ɪ'leɪtɪd] *adj* transporté(e) de joie

elation [ɪ'leɪʃən] *n* allégresse *f*

elbow ['ɛlbəu] *n* coude *m*

elder ['ɛldə^r] *adj* aîné(e) ♦ *n* (*tree*) sureau *m*; **one's ~s** ses aînés; **~ly** *adj* âgé(e) ♦ *npl*: **the ~ly** les personnes âgées

eldest ['ɛldɪst] *adj, n*: **the ~ (child)** l'aîné(e) (des enfants)

elect [ɪ'lɛkt] *vt* élire ♦ *adj*: **the president ~** le président désigné; **to ~ to do** choisir de faire; **~ion** *n* élection *f*; **~ioneering** [ɪlɛkʃə'nɪərɪŋ] *n* propagande électorale, manœuvres électorales; **~or** *n* électeur(-trice); **~orate** *n* électorat *m*

electric [ɪ'lɛktrɪk] *adj* électrique; **~al** *adj* électrique; **~ blanket** *n* couverture chauffante; **~ fire** (*BRIT*) *n* radiateur *m* électrique; **~ian** [ɪlɛk'trɪʃən] *n* électricien *m*; **~ity** [ɪlɛk'trɪsɪtɪ] *n* électricité *f*;

electrify [ɪ'lɛktrɪfaɪ] *vt* (*RAIL, fence*) électrifier; (*audience*) électriser

electronic [ɪlɛk'trɔnɪk] *adj* électronique; **~ mail** *n* courrier *m* électronique; **~s** *n* électronique *f*

elegant ['ɛlɪgənt] *adj* élégant(e)

element ['ɛlɪmənt] *n* (*gen*) élément *m*; (*of heater, kettle etc*) résistance *f*; **~ary** [ɛlɪ'mɛntərɪ] *adj* élémentaire; (*school, education*) primaire

elephant ['ɛlɪfənt] *n* éléphant *m*

elevation [ɛlɪ'veɪʃən] *n* (*raising, promotion*) avancement *m*, promotion *f*; (*height*) hauteur *f*

elevator ['ɛlɪveɪtə^r] *n* (*in warehouse etc*) élévateur *m*, monte-charge *m inv*; (*US*: *lift*) ascenseur *m*

eleven [ɪ'lɛvn] *num* onze; **~ses** [ɪ'lɛvnzɪz] *npl* ≃ pause-café *f*; **~th** *num* onzième

elicit [ɪ'lɪsɪt] *vt*: **to ~ (from)** obtenir (de), arracher (à)

eligible ['ɛlɪdʒəbl] *adj*: **to be ~ for** remplir les conditions requises pour; **an ~ young man/woman** un beau parti

elm [ɛlm] *n* orme *m*

elongated ['i:lɔŋgeɪtɪd] *adj* allongé(e)

elope [ɪ'ləup] *vi* (*lovers*) s'enfuir (ensemble)

eloquent ['ɛləkwənt] *adj* éloquent(e)

else [ɛls] *adv* d'autre; **something ~** quelque chose d'autre, autre chose; **somewhere ~** ailleurs, autre part; **everywhere ~** partout ailleurs; **nobody ~** personne d'autre; **where ~?** à quel autre endroit?; **little ~** pas grand-chose d'autre; **~where** *adv* ailleurs, autre part

elude [ɪ'lu:d] *vt* échapper à

elusive [ɪ'lu:sɪv] *adj* insaisissable

emaciated [ɪ'meɪsɪeɪtɪd] *adj* émacié(e), décharné(e)

e-mail ['i:meɪl] *n* courrier *m* électronique ♦ *vt* (*person*) envoyer un message électronique à

emancipate [ɪ'mænsɪpeɪt] *vt* émanciper

embankment [ɪm'bæŋkmənt] *n* (*of road, railway*) remblai *m*, talus *m*; (*of river*) berge *f*, quai *m*

embark [ɪm'bɑ:k] *vi* embarquer; **to ~ on** (*journey*) entreprendre; (*fig*) se lancer *or* s'embarquer dans; **~ation** [ɛmbɑ:'keɪʃən] *n* embarquement *m*

embarrass [ɪm'bærəs] *vt* embarrasser, gêner; **~ed** *adj* gêné(e); **~ing** *adj* gênant(e), embarrassant(e); **~ment** *n* embarras *m*, gêne *f*

embassy ['ɛmbəsɪ] *n* ambassade *f*

embedded [ɪm'bɛdɪd] *adj* enfoncé(e)

embellish [ɪm'bɛlɪʃ] *vt* orner, décorer; (*fig*: *account*) enjoliver

embers ['ɛmbəz] *npl* braise *f*

embezzle [ɪm'bɛzl] *vt* détourner; **~ment** *n* détournement *m* de fonds

embitter [ɪm'bɪtə^r] *vt* (*person*) aigrir;

(*relations*) envenimer

embody [ɪm'bɔdɪ] *vt* (*features*) réunir, comprendre; (*ideas*) formuler, exprimer

embossed [ɪm'bɔst] *adj* (*metal*) estampé(e); (*leather*) frappé(e); **~ wallpaper** papier gaufré

embrace [ɪm'breɪs] *vt* embrasser, étreindre; (*include*) embrasser ♦ *vi* s'étreindre, s'embrasser ♦ *n* étreinte *f*

embroider [ɪm'brɔɪdə^r] *vt* broder; **~y** *n* broderie *f*

emerald ['ɛmərəld] *n* émeraude *f*

emerge [ɪ'mə:dʒ] *vi* apparaître; (*from room, car*) surgir; (*from sleep, imprisonment*) sortir

emergency [ɪ'mə:dʒənsɪ] *n* urgence *f*; **in an ~** en cas d'urgence; **~ cord** *n* sonnette *f* d'alarme; **~ exit** *n* sortie *f* de secours; **~ landing** *n* atterrissage forcé; **~ services** *npl*: **the ~ services** (*fire, police, ambulance*) les services *mpl* d'urgence

emery board ['ɛmərɪ-] *n* lime *f* à ongles (*en carton émerisé*)

emigrate ['ɛmɪgreɪt] *vi* émigrer

eminent ['ɛmɪnənt] *adj* éminent(e)

emissions [ɪ'mɪʃənz] *npl* émissions *fpl*

emit [ɪ'mɪt] *vt* émettre

emotion [ɪ'məuʃən] *n* émotion *f*; **~al** *adj* (*person*) émotif(-ive), très sensible; (*needs, exhaustion*) affectif(-ive); (*scene*) émouvant(e); (*tone, speech*) qui fait appel aux sentiments; **emotive** *adj* chargé(e) d'émotion; (*subject*) sensible

emperor ['ɛmpərə^r] *n* empereur *m*

emphasis ['ɛmfəsɪs] (*pl* **-ases**) *n* (*stress*) accent *m*; (*importance*) insistance *f*

emphasize ['ɛmfəsaɪz] *vt* (*syllable, word, point*) appuyer *or* insister sur; (*feature*) souligner, accentuer

emphatic [ɛm'fætɪk] *adj* (*strong*) énergique, vigoureux(-euse); (*unambiguous, clear*) catégorique

empire ['ɛmpaɪə^r] *n* empire *m*

employ [ɪm'plɔɪ] *vt* employer; **~ee** *n* employé(e); **~er** *n* employeur(-euse); **~ment** *n* emploi *m*; **~ment agency** *n* agence *f or* bureau *m* de placement

empower [ɪm'pauə^r] *vt*: **to ~ sb to do** autoriser *or* habiliter qn à faire

empress ['ɛmprɪs] *n* impératrice *f*

emptiness ['ɛmptɪnɪs] *n* (*of area, region*) aspect *m* désertique *m*; (*of life*) vide *m*, vacuité *f*

empty ['ɛmptɪ] *adj* vide; (*threat, promise*) en l'air, vain(e) ♦ *vt* vider ♦ *vi* se vider; (*liquid*) s'écouler; **~-handed** *adj* les mains vides

EMU *n abbr* (= *economic and monetary union*) UME *f*

emulate ['ɛmjuleɪt] *vt* rivaliser avec, imiter

emulsion [ɪ'mʌlʃən] *n* émulsion *f*; (*also:* **~ paint**) peinture mate

enable [ɪ'neɪbl] *vt*: **to ~ sb to do** permettre à qn de faire

enamel [ɪ'næməl] *n* émail *m*; (*also:* **~ paint**) peinture laquée

enchant [ɪn'tʃɑ:nt] *vt* enchanter; **~ing** *adj* ravissant(e), enchanteur(-teresse)

encl. *abbr* = **enclosed**

enclose [ɪn'kləuz] *vt* (*land*) clôturer; (*space, object*) entourer; (*letter etc*): **to ~ (with)** joindre (à); **please find ~d** veuillez trouver ci-joint; **enclosure** *n* enceinte *f*

encompass [ɪn'kʌmpəs] *vt* (*include*) contenir, inclure

encore [ɔŋ'kɔ:^r] *excl* bis ♦ *n* bis *m*

encounter [ɪn'kauntə^r] *n* rencontre *f* ♦ *vt* rencontrer

encourage [ɪn'kʌrɪdʒ] *vt* encourager; **~ment** *n* encouragement *m*

encroach [ɪn'krəutʃ] *vi*: **to ~ (up)on** empiéter sur

encyclop(a)edia [ɛnsaɪkləu'pi:dɪə] *n* encyclopédie *f*

end [ɛnd] *n* (*gen, also*: *aim*) fin *f*; (*of table, street, rope etc*) bout *m*, extrémité *f* ♦ *vt* terminer; (*also:* **bring to an ~, put an ~ to**) mettre fin à ♦ *vi* se terminer, finir; **in the ~** finalement; **on ~** (*object*) debout, dressé(e); **to stand on ~**

(*hair*) se dresser sur la tête; **for hours on ~** pendant des heures et des heures; **~ up** *vi*: **to ~ up in** (*condition*) finir *or* se terminer par; (*place*) finir *or* aboutir à

endanger [ɪn'deɪndʒə^r] *vt* mettre en danger; **an ~ed species** une espèce en voie de disparition

endearing [ɪn'dɪərɪŋ] *adj* attachant(e)

endeavour [ɪn'dɛvə^r] (*US* **endeavor**) *n* tentative *f*, effort *m* ♦ *vi*: **to ~ to do** tenter *or* s'efforcer de faire

ending ['ɛndɪŋ] *n* dénouement *m*, fin *f*; (*LING*) terminaison *f*

endive ['ɛndaɪv] *n* chicorée *f*; (*smooth*) endive *f*

endless ['ɛndlɪs] *adj* sans fin, interminable

endorse [ɪn'dɔːs] *vt* (*cheque*) endosser; (*approve*) appuyer, approuver, sanctionner; **~ment** *n* (*approval*) appui *m*, aval *m*; (*BRIT*: *on driving licence*) *contravention portée au permis de conduire*

endure [ɪn'djuə^r] *vt* supporter, endurer ♦ *vi* durer

enemy ['ɛnəmɪ] *adj, n* ennemi(e)

energetic [ɛnə'dʒɛtɪk] *adj* énergique; (*activity*) qui fait se dépenser (physiquement)

energy ['ɛnədʒɪ] *n* énergie *f*

enforce [ɪn'fɔːs] *vt* (*law*) appliquer, faire respecter

engage [ɪn'geɪdʒ] *vt* engager; (*attention etc*) retenir ♦ *vi* (*TECH*) s'enclencher, s'engrener; **to ~ in** se lancer dans; **~d** *adj* (*BRIT*: *busy, in use*) occupé(e); (*betrothed*) fiancé(e); **to get ~d** se fiancer; **~d tone** *n* (*TEL*) tonalité *f* occupé *inv or* pas libre; **~ment** *n* obligation *f*, engagement *m*; rendez-vous *m inv*; (*to marry*) fiançailles *fpl*; **~ment ring** *n* bague *f* de fiançailles; **engaging** *adj* engageant(e), attirant(e)

engine ['ɛndʒɪn] *n* (*AUT*) moteur *m*; (*RAIL*) locomotive *f*; **~ driver** *n* mécanicien *m*

engineer [ɛndʒɪ'nɪə^r] *n* ingénieur *m*; (*BRIT*: *repairer*) dépanneur *m*; (*NAVY, US RAIL*) mécanicien *m*; **~ing** *n* engineering *m*, ingénierie *f*; (*of bridges, ships*) génie *m*; (*of machine*) mécanique *f*

England ['ɪŋglənd] *n* Angleterre *f*; **English** *adj* anglais(e) ♦ *n* (*LING*) anglais *m*; **the English** *npl* (*people*) les Anglais; **the English Channel** la Manche; **Englishman** (*irreg*) *n* Anglais; **Englishwoman** (*irreg*) *n* Anglaise *f*

engraving [ɪn'greɪvɪŋ] *n* gravure *f*

engrossed [ɪn'grəust] *adj*: **~ in** absorbé(e) par, plongé(e) dans

engulf [ɪn'gʌlf] *vt* engloutir

enhance [ɪn'hɑːns] *vt* rehausser, mettre en valeur

enjoy [ɪn'dʒɔɪ] *vt* aimer, prendre plaisir à; (*have*: *health, fortune*) jouir de; (: *success*) connaître; **to ~ o.s.** s'amuser; **~able** *adj* agréable; **~ment** *n* plaisir *m*

enlarge [ɪn'lɑːdʒ] *vt* accroître; (*PHOT*) agrandir ♦ *vi*: **to ~ on** (*subject*) s'étendre sur; **~ment** [ɪn'lɑːdʒmənt] *n* (*PHOT*) agrandissement *m*

enlighten [ɪn'laɪtn] *vt* éclairer; **~ed** *adj* éclairé(e); **~ment** *n*: **the E~ment** (*HISTORY*) ≃ le Siècle des lumières

enlist [ɪn'lɪst] *vt* recruter; (*support*) s'assurer ♦ *vi* s'engager

enmity ['ɛnmɪtɪ] *n* inimitié *f*

enormous [ɪ'nɔːməs] *adj* énorme

enough [ɪ'nʌf] *adj, pron*: **~ time/books** assez *or* suffisamment de temps/livres ♦ *adv*: **big ~** assez *or* suffisamment grand; **have you got ~?** en avez-vous assez?; **he has not worked ~** il n'a pas assez *or* suffisamment travaillé; **~ to eat** assez à manger; **~!** assez!, ça suffit!; **that's ~, thanks** cela suffit *or* c'est assez, merci; **I've had ~ of him** j'en ai assez de lui; **... which, funnily** *or* **oddly ~** ... qui, chose curieuse

enquire [ɪn'kwaɪə^r] *vt, vi* = **inquire**

enrage [ɪn'reɪdʒ] *vt* mettre en fureur *or* en rage, rendre furieux(-euse)

enrol [ɪn'rəul] (*US* **enroll**) *vt* inscrire ♦ *vi* s'inscrire; **~ment** (*US* **enrollment**) *n* inscription *f*

en suite ['ɔnswi:t] *adj*: **with ~ bathroom** avec salle de bains en attenante

ensure [ɪn'ʃuəʳ] *vt* assurer; garantir; **to ~ that** s'assurer que

entail [ɪn'teɪl] *vt* entraîner, occasionner

entangled [ɪn'tæŋgld] *adj*: **to become ~ (in)** s'empêtrer (dans)

enter ['ɛntəʳ] *vt* (*room*) entrer dans, pénétrer dans; (*club, army*) entrer à; (*competition*) s'inscrire à *or* pour; (*sb for a competition*) (faire) inscrire; (*write down*) inscrire, noter; (COMPUT) entrer, introduire ♦ *vi* entrer; **~ for** *vt fus* s'inscrire à, se présenter pour *or* à; **~ into** *vt fus* (*explanation*) se lancer dans; (*discussion, negotiations*) entamer; (*agreement*) conclure

enterprise ['ɛntəpraɪz] *n* entreprise *f*; (*initiative*) (esprit *m* d')initiative *f*; **free ~** libre entreprise; **private ~** entreprise privée; **enterprising** *adj* entreprenant(e), dynamique; (*scheme*) audacieux(-euse)

entertain [ɛntə'teɪn] *vt* amuser, distraire; (*invite*) recevoir (à dîner); (*idea, plan*) envisager; **~er** *n* artiste *m/f* de variétés; **~ing** *adj* amusant(e), distrayant(e); **~ment** *n* (*amusement*) divertissement *m*, amusement *m*; (*show*) spectacle *m*

enthralled [ɪn'θrɔ:ld] *adj* captivé(e)

enthusiasm [ɪn'θu:zɪæzəm] *n* enthousiasme *m*

enthusiast [ɪn'θu:zɪæst] *n* enthousiaste *m/f*; **~ic** [ɪnθu:zɪ'æstɪk] *adj* enthousiaste; **to be ~ic about** être enthousiasmé(e) par

entire [ɪn'taɪəʳ] *adj* (tout) entier(-ère); **~ly** *adv* entièrement, complètement; **~ty** [ɪn'taɪərətɪ] *n*: **in its ~ty** dans sa totalité

entitle [ɪn'taɪtl] *vt*: **to ~ sb to sth** donner droit à qch à qn; **~d** [ɪn'taɪtld] *adj* (*book*) intitulé(e); **to be ~d to do** avoir le droit de *or* être habilité à faire

entrance [*n* 'ɛntrns, *vb* ɪn'trɑ:ns] *n* entrée *f* ♦ *vt* enchanter, ravir; **to gain ~ to** (*university etc*) être admis à; **~ examination** *n* examen *m* d'entrée; **~ fee** *n* (*to museum etc*) prix *m* d'entrée; (*to join club etc*) droit *m* d'inscription; **~ ramp** (US) *n* (AUT) bretelle *f* d'accès; **entrant** *n* participant(e); concurrent(e); (BRIT: *in exam*) candidat(e)

entrenched [ɛn'trɛntʃt] *adj* retranché(e); (*ideas*) arrêté(e)

entrepreneur ['ɔntrəprə'nə:ʳ] *n* entrepreneur *m*

entrust [ɪn'trʌst] *vt*: **to ~ sth to** confier qch à

entry ['ɛntrɪ] *n* entrée *f*; (*in register*) inscription *f*; **no ~** défense d'entrer, entrée interdite; (AUT) sens interdit; **~ form** *n* feuille *f* d'inscription; **~ phone** (BRIT) *n* interphone *m*

envelop [ɪn'vɛləp] *vt* envelopper

envelope ['ɛnvələup] *n* enveloppe *f*

envious ['ɛnvɪəs] *adj* envieux(-euse)

environment [ɪn'vaɪərnmənt] *n* environnement *m*; (*social, moral*) milieu *m*; **~al** [ɪnvaɪərn'mɛntl] *adj* écologique; du milieu; **~-friendly** *adj* écologique

envisage [ɪn'vɪzɪdʒ] *vt* (*foresee*) prévoir

envoy ['ɛnvɔɪ] *n* (*diplomat*) ministre *m* plénipotentiaire

envy ['ɛnvɪ] *n* envie *f* ♦ *vt* envier; **to ~ sb sth** envier qch à qn

epic ['ɛpɪk] *n* épopée *f* ♦ *adj* épique

epidemic [ɛpɪ'dɛmɪk] *n* épidémie *f*

epilepsy ['ɛpɪlɛpsɪ] *n* épilepsie *f*; **epileptic** *n* épileptique *m/f*

episode ['ɛpɪsəud] *n* épisode *m*

epitome [ɪ'pɪtəmɪ] *n* modèle *m*; **epitomize** *vt* incarner

equal ['i:kwl] *adj* égal(e) ♦ *n* égal(e) ♦ *vt* égaler; **~ to** (*task*) à la hauteur de; **~ity** [i:'kwɔlɪtɪ] *n* égalité *f*; **~ize** *vi* (SPORT) égaliser; **~ly** *adv* également; (*just as*) tout aussi

equanimity [ɛkwə'nɪmɪtɪ] *n* égalité *f* d'humeur

equate [ɪ'kweɪt] *vt*: **to ~ sth with** comparer qch à; assimiler qch à; **equa-**

tion *n* (*MATH*) équation *f*

equator [ɪ'kweɪtə^r^] *n* équateur *m*

equilibrium [iːkwɪ'lɪbrɪəm] *n* équilibre *m*

equip [ɪ'kwɪp] *vt*: **to ~ (with)** équiper (de); **to be well ~ped** être bien équipé(e); **~ment** *n* équipement *m*; (*electrical etc*) appareillage *m*, installation *f*

equities ['ɛkwɪtɪz] (*BRIT*) *npl* (*COMM*) actions cotées en Bourse

equivalent [ɪ'kwɪvələnt] *adj*: **~ (to)** équivalent(e) (à) ♦ *n* équivalent *m*

era ['ɪərə] *n* ère *f*, époque *f*

eradicate [ɪ'rædɪkeɪt] *vt* éliminer

erase [ɪ'reɪz] *vt* effacer; **~r** *n* gomme *f*

erect [ɪ'rɛkt] *adj* droit(e) ♦ *vt* construire; (*monument*) ériger, élever; (*tent etc*) dresser; **~ion** *n* érection *f*

ERM *n abbr* (= *Exchange Rate Mechanism*) MTC *m*

erode [ɪ'rəud] *vt* éroder; (*metal*) ronger

erotic [ɪ'rɔtɪk] *adj* érotique

errand ['ɛrənd] *n* course *f*, commission *f*

erratic [ɪ'rætɪk] *adj* irrégulier(-ère); inconstant(e)

error ['ɛrə^r^] *n* erreur *f*

erupt [ɪ'rʌpt] *vi* entrer en éruption; (*fig*) éclater; **~ion** *n* éruption *f*

escalate ['ɛskəleɪt] *vi* s'intensifier

escalator ['ɛskəleɪtə^r^] *n* escalier roulant

escapade [ɛskə'peɪd] *n* (*misdeed*) fredaine *f*; (*adventure*) équipée *f*

escape [ɪs'keɪp] *n* fuite *f*; (*from prison*) évasion *f* ♦ *vi* s'échapper, fuir; (*from jail*) s'évader; (*fig*) s'en tirer; (*leak*) s'échapper ♦ *vt* échapper à; **to ~ from** (*person*) échapper à; (*place*) s'échapper de; (*fig*) fuir; **escapism** *n* (*fig*) évasion *f*

escort [*n* 'ɛskɔːt, *vb* ɪs'kɔːt] *n* escorte *f* ♦ *vt* escorter

Eskimo ['ɛskɪməu] *n* Esquimau(de)

especially [ɪs'pɛʃlɪ] *adv* (*particularly*) particulièrement; (*above all*) surtout

espionage ['ɛspɪənɑːʒ] *n* espionnage *m*

Esquire [ɪs'kwaɪə^r^] *n*: **J Brown, ~** Monsieur J. Brown

essay ['ɛseɪ] *n* (*SCOL*) dissertation *f*; (*LITERATURE*) essai *m*

essence ['ɛsns] *n* essence *f*

essential [ɪ'sɛnʃl] *adj* essentiel(le); (*basic*) fondamental(e) ♦ *n*: **~s** éléments essentiels; **~ly** *adv* essentiellement

establish [ɪs'tæblɪʃ] *vt* établir; (*business*) fonder, créer; (*one's power etc*) asseoir, affermir; **~ed** *adj* bien établi(e); **~ment** *n* établissement *m*; (*founding*) création *f*

estate [ɪs'teɪt] *n* (*land*) domaine *m*, propriété *f*; (*LAW*) biens *mpl*, succession *f*; (*BRIT*: *also*: **housing ~**) lotissement *m*, cité *f*; **~ agent** *n* agent immobilier; **~ car** (*BRIT*) *n* break *m*

esteem [ɪs'tiːm] *n* estime *f*

esthetic [ɪs'θɛtɪk] (*US*) *adj* = **aesthetic**

estimate [*n* 'ɛstɪmət, *vb* 'ɛstɪmeɪt] *n* estimation *f*; (*COMM*) devis *m* ♦ *vt* estimer; **estimation** [ɛstɪ'meɪʃən] *n* opinion *f*; (*calculation*) estimation *f*

estranged [ɪs'treɪndʒd] *adj* séparé(e); dont on s'est séparé(e)

etc. *abbr* (= *et cetera*) etc

eternal [ɪ'təːnl] *adj* éternel(le)

eternity [ɪ'təːnɪtɪ] *n* éternité *f*

ethical ['ɛθɪkl] *adj* moral(e); **ethics** *n* éthique *f* ♦ *npl* moralité *f*

Ethiopia [iːθɪ'əupɪə] *n* Éthiopie *f*

ethnic ['ɛθnɪk] *adj* ethnique; (*music etc*) folklorique; **~ minority** minorité *f* ethnique

ethos ['iːθɔs] *n* génie *m*

etiquette ['ɛtɪkɛt] *n* convenances *fpl*, étiquette *f*

EU *n abbr* (= *European Union*) UE *f*

euro ['juərəu] *n* (*currency*) euro *m*

Euroland ['juərəulænd] *n* Euroland *m*

Eurocheque ['juərəutʃɛk] *n* eurochèque *m*

Europe ['juərəp] *n* Europe *f*; **~an** [juərə'piːən] *adj* européen(ne) ♦ *n* Européen(ne); **~an Community** Communauté européenne

evacuate [ɪ'vækjueɪt] *vt* évacuer
evade [ɪ'veɪd] *vt* échapper à; (*question etc*) éluder; (*duties*) se dérober à; **to ~ tax** frauder le fisc
evaporate [ɪ'væpəreɪt] *vi* s'évaporer; **~d milk** *n* lait condensé non sucré
evasion [ɪ'veɪʒən] *n* dérobade *f*; **tax ~** fraude fiscale
eve [i:v] *n*: **on the ~ of** à la veille de
even ['i:vn] *adj* (*level, smooth*) régulier(-ère); (*equal*) égal(e); (*number*) pair(e) ♦ *adv* même; **~ if** même si *+indic*; **~ though** alors même que *+cond*; **~ more** encore plus; **~ so** quand même; **not ~** pas même; **to get ~ with sb** prendre sa revanche sur qn
evening ['i:vnɪŋ] *n* soir *m*; (*as duration, event*) soirée *f*; **in the ~** le soir; **~ class** *n* cours *m* du soir; **~ dress** *n* tenue *f* de soirée
event [ɪ'vɛnt] *n* événement *m*; (SPORT) épreuve *f*; **in the ~ of** en cas de; **~ful** *adj* mouvementé(e)
eventual [ɪ'vɛntʃuəl] *adj* final(e); **~ity** [ɪvɛntʃu'ælɪtɪ] *n* possibilité *f*, éventualité *f*; **~ly** *adv* finalement
ever ['ɛvə^r] *adv* jamais; (*at all times*) toujours; **the best ~** le meilleur qu'on ait jamais vu; **have you ~ seen it?** l'as-tu déjà vu?, as-tu eu l'occasion *or* t'est-il arrivé de le voir?; **why ~ not?** mais enfin, pourquoi pas?; **~ since** *adv* depuis ♦ *conj* depuis que; **~green** *n* arbre *m* à feuilles persistantes; **~lasting** *adj* éternel(le)
every ['ɛvrɪ] *adj* chaque; **~ day** tous les jours, chaque jour; **~ other/third day** tous les deux/trois jours; **~ other car** une voiture sur deux; **~ now and then** de temps en temps; **~body** *pron* tout le monde, tous *pl*; **~day** *adj* quotidien(ne), de tous les jours; **~one** *pron* = **everybody**; **~thing** *pron* tout; **~where** *adv* partout
evict [ɪ'vɪkt] *vt* expulser; **~ion** *n* expulsion *f*
evidence ['ɛvɪdns] *n* (*proof*) preuve(s) *f(pl)*; (*of witness*) témoignage *m*; (*sign*): **to show ~ of** présenter des signes de; **to give ~** témoigner, déposer
evident ['ɛvɪdnt] *adj* évident(e); **~ly** *adv* de toute évidence; (*apparently*) apparamment
evil ['i:vl] *adj* mauvais(e) ♦ *n* mal *m*
evoke [ɪ'vəuk] *vt* évoquer
evolution [i:və'lu:ʃən] *n* évolution *f*
evolve [ɪ'vɔlv] *vt* élaborer ♦ *vi* évoluer
ewe [ju:] *n* brebis *f*
ex- [ɛks] *prefix* ex-
exact [ɪg'zækt] *adj* exact(e) ♦ *vt*: **to ~ sth (from)** extorquer qch (à); exiger qch (de); **~ing** *adj* exigeant(e); (*work*) astreignant(e); **~ly** *adv* exactement
exaggerate [ɪg'zædʒəreɪt] *vt, vi* exagérer; **exaggeration** [ɪgzædʒə'reɪʃən] *n* exagération *f*
exalted [ɪg'zɔ:ltɪd] *adj* (*prominent*) élevé(e); (*: person*) haut placé(e)
exam [ɪg'zæm] *n abbr* (SCOL) = **examination**
examination [ɪgzæmɪ'neɪʃən] *n* (SCOL, MED) examen *m*
examine [ɪg'zæmɪn] *vt* (*gen*) examiner; (SCOL: *person*) interroger; **~r** *n* examinateur(-trice)
example [ɪg'zɑ:mpl] *n* exemple *m*; **for ~** par exemple
exasperate [ɪg'zɑ:spəreɪt] *vt* exaspérer; **exasperation** [ɪgzɑ:spə'reɪʃən] *n* exaspération *f*, irritation *f*
excavate ['ɛkskəveɪt] *vt* excaver; **excavation** [ɛkskə'veɪʃən] *n* fouilles *fpl*
exceed [ɪk'si:d] *vt* dépasser; (*one's powers*) outrepasser; **~ingly** *adv* extrêmement
excellent ['ɛksələnt] *adj* excellent(e)
except [ɪk'sɛpt] *prep* (*also:* **~ for, ~ing**) sauf, excepté ♦ *vt* excepter; **~ if/when** sauf si/quand; **~ that** sauf que, si ce n'est que; **~ion** *n* exception *f*; **to take ~ion to** s'offusquer de; **~ional** *adj* exceptionnel(le)
excerpt ['ɛksə:pt] *n* extrait *m*
excess [ɪk'sɛs] *n* excès *m*; **~ baggage**

n excédent *m* de bagages; **~ fare** (*BRIT*) *n* supplément *m*; **~ive** *adj* excessif(-ive)
exchange [ɪks'tʃeɪndʒ] *n* échange *m*; (*also:* **telephone ~**) central *m* ♦ *vt*: **to ~ (for)** échanger (contre); **~ rate** *n* taux *m* de change
Exchequer [ɪks'tʃɛkəʳ] (*BRIT*) *n*: **the ~** l'Échiquier *m*, ≃ le ministère des Finances
excise [*n* 'ɛksaɪz, *vb* ɛk'saɪz] *n* taxe *f* ♦ *vt* exciser
excite [ɪk'saɪt] *vt* exciter; **to get ~d** s'exciter; **~ment** *n* excitation *f*; **exciting** *adj* passionnant(e)
exclaim [ɪks'kleɪm] *vi* s'exclamer; **exclamation** [ɛksklə'meɪʃən] *n* exclamation *f*; **exclamation mark** *n* point *m* d'exclamation
exclude [ɪks'klu:d] *vt* exclure; **exclusion zone** *n* zone interdite; **exclusive** *adj* exclusif(-ive); (*club, district*) sélect(e); (*item of news*) en exclusivité; **exclusive of VAT** TVA non comprise; **mutually exclusive** qui s'excluent l'un(e) l'autre
excruciating [ɪks'kru:ʃieɪtɪŋ] *adj* atroce
excursion [ɪks'kə:ʃən] *n* excursion *f*
excuse [*n* ɪks'kju:s, *vb* ɪks'kju:z] *n* excuse *f* ♦ *vt* excuser; **to ~ sb from** (*activity*) dispenser qn de; **~ me!** excusez-moi!, pardon!; **now if you will ~ me, ...** maintenant, si vous (le) permettez ...
ex-directory ['ɛksdɪ'rɛktərɪ] (*BRIT*) *adj* sur la liste rouge
execute ['ɛksɪkju:t] *vt* exécuter; **execution** *n* exécution *f*
executive [ɪg'zɛkjutɪv] *n* (*COMM*) cadre *m*; (*of organization, political party*) bureau *m* ♦ *adj* exécutif(-ive)
exemplify [ɪg'zɛmplɪfaɪ] *vt* illustrer; (*typify*) incarner
exempt [ɪg'zɛmpt] *adj*: **~ from** exempté(e) *or* dispensé(e) de ♦ *vt*: **to ~ sb from** exempter *or* dispenser qn de
exercise ['ɛksəsaɪz] *n* exercice *m* ♦ *vt* exercer; (*patience etc*) faire preuve de; (*dog*) promener ♦ *vi* prendre de l'exercice; **~ book** *n* cahier *m*
exert [ɪg'zə:t] *vt* exercer, employer; **to ~ o.s.** se dépenser; **~ion** *n* effort *m*
exhale [ɛks'heɪl] *vt* exhaler ♦ *vi* expirer
exhaust [ɪg'zɔ:st] *n* (*also:* **~ fumes**) gaz *mpl* d'échappement; (*also:* **~ pipe**) tuyau *m* d'échappement ♦ *vt* épuiser; **~ed** *adj* épuisé(e); **~ion** *n* épuisement *m*; **nervous ~ion** fatigue nerveuse; surmenage mental; **~ive** *adj* très complet(-ète)
exhibit [ɪg'zɪbɪt] *n* (*ART*) pièce exposée, objet exposé; (*LAW*) pièce à conviction ♦ *vt* exposer; (*courage, skill*) faire preuve de; **~ion** [ɛksɪ'bɪʃən] *n* exposition *f*; (*of ill-temper, talent etc*) démonstration *f*
exhilarating [ɪg'zɪləreɪtɪŋ] *adj* grisant(e); stimulant(e)
ex-husband *n* ex-mari *m*
exile ['ɛksaɪl] *n* exil *m*; (*person*) exilé(e) ♦ *vt* exiler
exist [ɪg'zɪst] *vi* exister; **~ence** *n* existence *f*; **~ing** *adj* actuel(le)
exit ['ɛksɪt] *n* sortie *f* ♦ *vi* (*COMPUT, THEATRE*) sortir; **~ poll** *n* sondage *m* (fait à la sortie de l'isoloir); **~ ramp** *n* (*AUT*) bretelle *f* d'accès
exodus ['ɛksədəs] *n* exode *m*
exonerate [ɪg'zɔnəreɪt] *vt*: **to ~ from** disculper de
exotic [ɪg'zɔtɪk] *adj* exotique
expand [ɪks'pænd] *vt* agrandir; accroître ♦ *vi* (*trade etc*) se développer, s'accroître; (*gas, metal*) se dilater
expanse [ɪks'pæns] *n* étendue *f*
expansion [ɪks'pænʃən] *n* développement *m*, accroissement *m*
expect [ɪks'pɛkt] *vt* (*anticipate*) s'attendre à, s'attendre à ce que *+sub*; (*count on*) compter sur, escompter; (*require*) demander, exiger; (*suppose*) supposer; (*await, also baby*) attendre ♦ *vi*: **to be ~ing** être enceinte; **~ancy** *n* (*anticipation*) attente *f*; **life ~ancy** espérance *f* de vie; **~ant mother** *n* future maman; **~ation** [ɛkspɛk'teɪʃən] *n* attente *f*; espérance(s) *f(pl)*
expedient [ɪks'pi:dɪənt] *adj* indiqué(e),

opportun(e) ♦ *n* expédient *m*
expedition [ɛkspə'dɪʃən] *n* expédition *f*
expel [ɪks'pɛl] *vt* chasser, expulser; (*SCOL*) renvoyer
expend [ɪks'pɛnd] *vt* consacrer; (*money*) dépenser; **~iture** [ɪks'pɛndɪtʃə^r] *n* dépense *f*; dépenses *fpl*
expense [ɪks'pɛns] *n* dépense *f*, frais *mpl*; (*high cost*) coût *m*; **~s** *npl* (*COMM*) frais *mpl*; **at the ~ of** aux dépens de; **~ account** *n* (note *f* de) frais *mpl*; **expensive** *adj* cher (chère), coûteux (-euse); **to be expensive** coûter cher
experience [ɪks'pɪərɪəns] *n* expérience *f* ♦ *vt* connaître, faire l'expérience de; (*feeling*) éprouver; **~d** *adj* expérimenté(e)
experiment [ɪks'pɛrɪmənt] *n* expérience *f* ♦ *vi* faire une expérience; **to ~ with** expérimenter
expert ['ɛkspə:t] *adj* expert(e) ♦ *n* expert *m*; **~ise** [ɛkspə:'ti:z] *n* (grande) compétence
expire [ɪks'paɪə^r] *vi* expirer; **expiry** *n* expiration *f*
explain [ɪks'pleɪn] *vt* expliquer; **explanation** [ɛksplə'neɪʃən] *n* explication *f*; **explanatory** [ɪks'plænətrɪ] *adj* explicatif(-ive)
explicit [ɪks'plɪsɪt] *adj* explicite; (*definite*) formel(le)
explode [ɪks'pləud] *vi* exploser
exploit [*n* 'ɛksplɔɪt, *vb* ɪks'plɔɪt] *n* exploit *m* ♦ *vt* exploiter; **~ation** [ɛksplɔɪ'teɪʃən] *n* exploitation *f*
exploratory [ɪks'plɔrətrɪ] *adj* (*expedition*) d'exploration; (*fig*: *talks*) préliminaire
explore [ɪks'plɔ:^r] *vt* explorer; (*possibilities*) étudier, examiner; **~r** *n* explorateur(-trice)
explosion [ɪks'pləuʒən] *n* explosion *f*; **explosive** *adj* explosif(-ive) ♦ *n* explosif *m*
exponent [ɪks'pəunənt] *n* (*of school of thought etc*) interprète *m*, représentant *m*
export [*vb* ɛks'pɔ:t, *n* 'ɛkspɔ:t] *vt* exporter ♦ *n* exportation *f* ♦ *cpd* d'exportation; **~er** *n* exportateur *m*
expose [ɪks'pəuz] *vt* exposer; (*unmask*) démasquer, dévoiler; **~d** *adj* (*position, house*) exposé(e); **exposure** *n* exposition *f*; (*publicity*) couverture *f*; (*PHOT*) (temps *m* de) pose *f*; (: *shot*) pose; **to die from exposure** (*MED*) mourir de froid; **exposure meter** *n* posemètre *m*
express [ɪks'prɛs] *adj* (*definite*) formel(le), exprès(-esse); (*BRIT*: *letter etc*) exprès *inv* ♦ *n* (*train*) rapide *m*; (*bus*) car *m* express ♦ *vt* exprimer; **~ion** *n* expression *f*; **~ly** *adv* expressément, formellement; **~way** (*US*) *n* (*urban motorway*) voie *f* express (à plusieurs files)
exquisite [ɛks'kwɪzɪt] *adj* exquis(e)
extend [ɪks'tɛnd] *vt* (*visit, street*) prolonger; (*building*) agrandir; (*offer*) présenter, offrir; (*hand, arm*) tendre ♦ *vi* s'étendre; **extension** *n* prolongation *f*; agrandissement *m*; (*building*) annexe *f*; (*to wire, table*) rallonge *f*; (*telephone*: *in offices*) poste *m*; (: *in private house*) téléphone *m* supplémentaire; **extensive** *adj* étendu(e), vaste; (*damage, alterations*) considérable; (*inquiries*) approfondi(e); **extensively** *adv*: **he's travelled extensively** il a beaucoup voyagé
extent [ɪks'tɛnt] *n* étendue *f*; **to some ~** dans une certaine mesure; **to what ~?** dans quelle mesure?, jusqu'à quel point?; **to the ~ of ...** au point de ...; **to such an ~ that ...** à tel point que ...
extenuating [ɪks'tɛnjueɪtɪŋ] *adj*: **~ circumstances** circonstances atténuantes
exterior [ɛks'tɪərɪə^r] *adj* extérieur(e) ♦ *n* extérieur *m*; dehors *m*
external [ɛks'tə:nl] *adj* externe
extinct [ɪks'tɪŋkt] *adj* éteint(e)
extinguish [ɪks'tɪŋgwɪʃ] *vt* éteindre
extort [ɪks'tɔ:t] *vt*: **to ~ sth (from)** extorquer qch (à); **~ionate** *adj* exorbitant(e)
extra ['ɛkstrə] *adj* supplémentaire, de plus ♦ *adv* (*in addition*) en plus ♦ *n* sup-

plément *m*; (*perk*) à-côté *m*; (*THEATRE*) figurant(e) ♦ *prefix* extra...

extract [*vb* ɪks'trækt, *n* 'ɛkstrækt] *vt* extraire; (*tooth*) arracher; (*money, promise*) soutirer ♦ *n* extrait *m*

extracurricular ['ɛkstrəkə'rɪkjulər] *adj* parascolaire

extradite ['ɛkstrədaɪt] *vt* extrader

extra...: **~marital** ['ɛkstrə'mærɪtl] *adj* extra-conjugal(e); **~mural** ['ɛkstrə'mjuərl] *adj* hors faculté *inv*; (*lecture*) public(-que); **~ordinary** [ɪks'trɔːdnrɪ] *adj* extraordinaire

extravagance [ɪks'trævəgəns] *n* prodigalités *fpl*; (*thing bought*) folie *f*, dépense excessive; **extravagant** *adj* extravagant(e); (*in spending: person*) prodigue, dépensier(-ère); (*: tastes*) dispendieux (-euse)

extreme [ɪks'triːm] *adj* extrême ♦ *n* extrême *m*; **~ly** *adv* extrêmement; **extremist** *adj, n* extrémiste *m/f*

extricate ['ɛkstrɪkeɪt] *vt*: **to ~ sth (from)** dégager qch (de)

extrovert ['ɛkstrəvəːt] *n* extraverti(e)

ex-wife *n* ex-femme *f*

eye [aɪ] *n* œil *m* (*pl yeux*); (*of needle*) trou *m*, chas *m* ♦ *vt* examiner; **to keep an ~ on** surveiller; **~brow** *n* sourcil *m*; **~drops** *npl* gouttes *fpl* pour les yeux; **~lash** *n* cil *m*; **~lid** *n* paupière *f*; **~liner** *n* eye-liner *m*; **~-opener** *n* révélation *f*; **~shadow** *n* ombre *f* à paupières; **~sight** *n* vue *f*; **~sore** *n* horreur *f*; **~ witness** *n* témoin *m* oculaire

F, f

F [ɛf] *n* (*MUS*) fa *m*

fable ['feɪbl] *n* fable *f*

fabric ['fæbrɪk] *n* tissu *m*

fabulous ['fæbjuləs] *adj* fabuleux (-euse); (*inf: super*) formidable

face [feɪs] *n* visage *m*, figure *f*; (*expression*) expression *f*; (*of clock*) cadran *m*; (*of cliff*) paroi *f*; (*of mountain*) face *f*; (*of building*) façade *f* ♦ *vt* faire face à; **~ down** (*person*) à plat ventre; (*card*) face en dessous; **to lose/save ~** perdre/sauver la face; **to make** *or* **pull a ~** faire une grimace; **in the ~ of** (*difficulties etc*) face à, devant; **on the ~ of it** à première vue; **~ to ~** face à face; **~ up to** *vt fus* faire face à, affronter; **~ cloth** (*BRIT*) *n* gant *m* de toilette; **~ cream** *n* crème *f* pour le visage; **~ lift** *n* lifting *m*; (*of building etc*) ravalement *m*, retapage *m*; **~ powder** *n* poudre *f* de riz; **~ value** *n* (*of coin*) valeur nominale; **to take sth at ~ value** (*fig*) prendre qch pour argent comptant

facilities [fə'sɪlɪtɪz] *npl* installations *fpl*, équipement *m*; **credit ~** facilités *fpl* de paiement

facing ['feɪsɪŋ] *prep* face à, en face de

facsimile [fæk'sɪmɪlɪ] *n* (*exact replica*) fac-similé *m*; (*fax*) télécopie *f*

fact [fækt] *n* fait *m*; **in ~** en fait

factor ['fæktər] *n* facteur *m*

factory ['fæktərɪ] *n* usine *f*, fabrique *f*

factual ['fæktjuəl] *adj* basé(e) sur les faits

faculty ['fækəltɪ] *n* faculté *f*; (*US: teaching staff*) corps enseignant

fad [fæd] *n* (*craze*) engouement *m*

fade [feɪd] *vi* se décolorer, passer; (*light, sound*) s'affaiblir; (*flower*) se faner

fag [fæg] (*BRIT: inf*) *n* (*cigarette*) sèche *f*

fail [feɪl] *vt* (*exam*) échouer à; (*candidate*) recaler; (*subj: courage, memory*) faire défaut à ♦ *vi* échouer; (*brakes*) lâcher; (*eyesight, health, light*) baisser, s'affaiblir; **to ~ to do sth** (*neglect*) négliger de faire qch; (*be unable*) ne pas arriver *or* parvenir à faire qch; **without ~** à coup sûr; sans faute; **~ing** *n* défaut *m* ♦ *prep* faute de; **~ure** *n* échec *m*; (*person*) raté(e); (*mechanical etc*) défaillance *f*

faint [feɪnt] *adj* faible; (*recollection*) vague; (*mark*) à peine visible ♦ *n* évanouissement *m* ♦ *vi* s'évanouir; **to feel ~** défaillir

fair [fɛəʳ] *adj* équitable, juste, impartial(e); (*hair*) blond(e); (*skin, complexion*) pâle, blanc (blanche); (*weather*) beau (belle); (*good enough*) assez bon(ne); (*sizeable*) considérable ♦ *adv*: **to play ~** jouer franc-jeu ♦ *n* foire *f*; (*BRIT*: *funfair*) fête (foraine); **~ly** *adv* équitablement; (*quite*) assez; **~ness** *n* justice *f*, équité *f*, impartialité *f*

fairy ['fɛərɪ] *n* fée *f*; **~ tale** *n* conte *m* de fées

faith [feɪθ] *n* foi *f*; (*trust*) confiance *f*; (*specific religion*) religion *f*; **~ful** *adj* fidèle; **~fully** *adv* see **yours**

fake [feɪk] *n* (*painting etc*) faux *m*; (*person*) imposteur *m* ♦ *adj* faux (fausse) ♦ *vt* simuler; (*painting*) faire un faux de

falcon ['fɔːlkən] *n* faucon *m*

fall [fɔːl] (*pt* **fell**, *pp* **fallen**) *n* chute *f*; (*US*: *autumn*) automne *m* ♦ *vi* tomber; (*price, temperature, dollar*) baisser; **~s** *npl* (*waterfall*) chute *f* d'eau, cascade *f*; **to ~ flat** (*on one's face*) tomber de tout son long, s'étaler; (*joke*) tomber à plat; (*plan*) échouer; **~ back** *vi* reculer, se retirer; **~ back on** *vt fus* se rabattre sur; **~ behind** *vi* prendre du retard; **~ down** *vi* (*person*) tomber; (*building*) s'effondrer, s'écrouler; **~ for** *vt fus* (*trick, story etc*) se laisser prendre à; (*person*) tomber amoureux de; **~ in** *vi* s'effondrer; (*MIL*) se mettre en rangs; **~ off** *vi* tomber; (*diminish*) baisser, diminuer; **~ out** *vi* (*hair, teeth*) tomber; (*MIL*) rompre les rangs; (*friends etc*) se brouiller; **~ through** *vi* (*plan, project*) tomber à l'eau

fallacy ['fæləsɪ] *n* erreur *f*, illusion *f*

fallout ['fɔːlaut] *n* retombées (radioactives)

fallow ['fæləu] *adj* en jachère; en friche

false [fɔːls] *adj* faux (fausse); **~ alarm** *n* fausse alerte; **~ pretences** *npl*: **under ~ pretences** sous un faux prétexte; **~ teeth** (*BRIT*) *npl* fausses dents

falter ['fɔːltəʳ] *vi* chanceler, vaciller

fame [feɪm] *n* renommée *f*, renom *m*

familiar [fə'mɪlɪəʳ] *adj* familier(-ère); **to be ~ with** (*subject*) connaître

family ['fæmɪlɪ] *n* famille *f* ♦ *cpd* (*business, doctor etc*) de famille; **has he any ~?** (*children*) a-t-il des enfants?

famine ['fæmɪn] *n* famine *f*

famished ['fæmɪʃt] (*inf*) *adj* affamé(e)

famous ['feɪməs] *adj* célèbre; **~ly** *adv* (*get on*) fameusement, à merveille

fan [fæn] *n* (*folding*) éventail *m*; (*ELEC*) ventilateur *m*; (*of person*) fan *m*, admirateur(-trice); (*of team, sport etc*) supporter *m/f* ♦ *vt* éventer; (*fire, quarrel*) attiser

fanatic [fə'nætɪk] *n* fanatique *m/f*

fan belt *n* courroie *f* de ventilateur

fancy ['fænsɪ] *n* fantaisie *f*, envie *f*; imagination *f* ♦ *adj* (de) fantaisie *inv* ♦ *vt* (*feel like, want*) avoir envie de; (*imagine, think*) imaginer; **to take a ~ to** se prendre d'affection pour; s'enticher de; **he fancies her** (*inf*) elle lui plaît; **~ dress** *n* déguisement *m*, travesti *m*; **~-dress ball** *n* bal masqué *or* costumé

fang [fæŋ] *n* croc *m*; (*of snake*) crochet *m*

fantastic [fæn'tæstɪk] *adj* fantastique

fantasy ['fæntəsɪ] *n* imagination *f*, fantaisie *f*; (*dream*) chimère *f*

far [fɑːʳ] *adj* lointain(e), éloigné(e) ♦ *adv* loin; **~ away** *or* **off** au loin, dans le lointain; **at the ~ side/end** à l'autre côté/bout; **~ better** beaucoup mieux; **~ from** loin de; **by ~** de loin, de beaucoup; **go as ~ as the ~m** allez jusqu'à la ferme; **as ~ as I know** pour autant que je sache; **how ~ is it to ...?** combien y a-t-il jusqu'à ...?; **how ~ have you got?** où en êtes-vous?; **~away** ['fɑːrəweɪ] *adj* lointain(e); (*look*) distrait(e)

farce [fɑːs] *n* farce *f*

fare [fɛəʳ] *n* (*on trains, buses*) prix *m* du billet; (*in taxi*) prix de la course; (*food*) table *f*, chère *f*; **half ~** demi-tarif; **full ~** plein tarif

Far East *n* Extrême-Orient *m*

farewell [fɛə'wɛl] *excl* adieu ♦ *n* adieu *m*
farm [fɑːm] *n* ferme *f* ♦ *vt* cultiver; **~er** *n* fermier(-ère); cultivateur(-trice); **~hand** *n* ouvrier(-ère) agricole; **~house** *n* (maison *f* de) ferme *f*; **~ing** *n* agriculture *f*; (*of animals*) élevage *m*; **~land** *n* terres cultivées; **~ worker** *n* = **farmhand**; **~yard** *n* cour *f* de ferme
far-reaching ['fɑː'riːtʃɪŋ] *adj* d'une grande portée
fart [fɑːt] (*inf!*) *vi* péter
farther ['fɑːðəʳ] *adv* plus loin ♦ *adj* plus éloigné(e), plus lointain(e)
farthest ['fɑːðɪst] *superl of* **far**
fascinate ['fæsɪneɪt] *vt* fasciner; **fascinating** *adj* fascinant(e)
fascism ['fæʃɪzəm] *n* fascisme *m*
fashion ['fæʃən] *n* mode *f*; (*manner*) façon *f*, manière *f* ♦ *vt* façonner; **in ~** à la mode; **out of ~** démodé(e); **~able** *adj* à la mode; **~ show** *n* défilé *m* de mannequins *or* de mode
fast [fɑːst] *adj* rapide; (*clock*): **to be ~** avancer; (*dye, colour*) grand *or* bon teint *inv* ♦ *adv* vite, rapidement; (*stuck, held*) solidement ♦ *n* jeûne *m* ♦ *vi* jeûner; **~ asleep** profondément endormi
fasten ['fɑːsn] *vt* attacher, fixer; (*coat*) attacher, fermer ♦ *vi* se fermer, s'attacher; **~er**, **~ing** *n* attache *f*
fast food *n* fast food *m*, restauration *f* rapide
fastidious [fæs'tɪdɪəs] *adj* exigeant(e), difficile
fat [fæt] *adj* gros(se) ♦ *n* graisse *f*; (*on meat*) gras *m*; (*for cooking*) matière grasse
fatal ['feɪtl] *adj* (*injury etc*) mortel(le); (*mistake*) fatal(e); **~ity** [fə'tælɪtɪ] *n* (*road death etc*) victime *f*, décès *m*
fate [feɪt] *n* destin *m*; (*of person*) sort *m*; **~ful** *adj* fatidique
father ['fɑːðəʳ] *n* père *m*; **~-in-law** *n* beau-père *m*; **~ly** *adj* paternel(le)
fathom ['fæðəm] *n* brasse *f* (= 1828 *mm*) ♦ *vt* (*mystery*) sonder, pénétrer
fatigue [fə'tiːg] *n* fatigue *f*
fatten ['fætn] *vt, vi* engraisser
fatty ['fætɪ] *adj* (*food*) gras(se) ♦ *n* (*inf*) gros(se)
fatuous ['fætjuəs] *adj* stupide
faucet ['fɔːsɪt] (*US*) *n* robinet *m*
fault [fɔːlt] *n* faute *f*; (*defect*) défaut *m*; (*GEO*) faille *f* ♦ *vt* trouver des défauts à; **it's my ~** c'est de ma faute; **to find ~ with** trouver à redire *or* à critiquer à; **at ~** fautif(-ive), coupable; **~y** *adj* défectueux(-euse)
fauna ['fɔːnə] *n* faune *f*
favour ['feɪvəʳ] (*US* **favor**) *n* faveur *f*; (*help*) service *m* ♦ *vt* (*proposition*) être en faveur de; (*pupil etc*) favoriser; (*team, horse*) donner gagnant; **to do sb a ~** rendre un service à qn; **to find ~ with** trouver grâce aux yeux de; **in ~ of** en faveur de; **~able** *adj* favorable; **~ite** ['feɪvrɪt] *adj, n* favori(te)
fawn [fɔːn] *n* faon *m* ♦ *adj* (*colour*) fauve ♦ *vi*: **to ~ (up)on** flatter servilement
fax [fæks] *n* (*document*) télécopie *f*; (*machine*) télécopieur *m* ♦ *vt* envoyer par télécopie
FBI *n abbr* (*US*: *Federal Bureau of Investigation*) F.B.I. *m*
fear [fɪəʳ] *n* crainte *f*, peur *f* ♦ *vt* craindre; **for ~ of** de peur que *+sub*, de peur de *+infin*; **~ful** *adj* craintif(-ive); (*sight, noise*) affreux(-euse), épouvantable; **~less** *adj* intrépide
feasible ['fiːzəbl] *adj* faisable, réalisable
feast [fiːst] *n* festin *m*, banquet *m*; (*REL*: *also*: **~ day**) fête *f* ♦ *vi* festoyer
feat [fiːt] *n* exploit *m*, prouesse *f*
feather ['fɛðəʳ] *n* plume *f*
feature ['fiːtʃəʳ] *n* caractéristique *f*; (*article*) chronique *f*, rubrique *f* ♦ *vt* (*subj*: *film*) avoir pour vedette(s) ♦ *vi*: **to ~ in** figurer (en bonne place) dans; (*in film*) jouer dans; **~s** *npl* (*of face*) traits *mpl*; **~ film** *n* long métrage
February ['fɛbruərɪ] *n* février *m*
fed [fɛd] *pt, pp of* **feed**
federal ['fɛdərəl] *adj* fédéral(e); **~ holiday** (*US*) *n jour m* férié

fed up *adj*: **to be ~** en avoir marre, en avoir plein le dos

fee [fi:] *n* rémunération *f*; (*of doctor, lawyer*) honoraires *mpl*; (*for examination*) droits *mpl*; **school ~s** frais *mpl* de scolarité

feeble ['fi:bl] *adj* faible; (*pathetic: attempt, excuse*) pauvre; (: *joke*) piteux (-euse)

feed [fi:d] (*pt, pp* **fed**) *n* (*of animal*) fourrage *m*; pâture *f*; (*on printer*) mécanisme *m* d'alimentation ♦ *vt* (*person*) nourrir; (*BRIT: baby*) allaiter; (: *with bottle*) donner le biberon à; (*horse etc*) donner à manger à; (*machine*) alimenter; (*data, information*): **to ~ sth into** fournir qch à; **~ on** *vt fus* se nourrir de; **~back** *n* feed-back *m inv*

feel [fi:l] (*pt, pp* **felt**) *n* sensation *f*; (*impression*) impression *f* ♦ *vt* toucher; (*explore*) tâter, palper; (*cold, pain*) sentir; (*grief, anger*) ressentir, éprouver; (*think, believe*) trouver; **to ~ hungry/cold** avoir faim/froid; **to ~ lonely/better** se sentir seul/mieux; **I don't ~ well** je ne me sens pas bien; **it ~s soft** c'est doux (douce) au toucher; **to ~ like** (*want*) avoir envie de; **~ about** *vi* fouiller, tâtonner; **~er** *n* (*of insect*) antenne *f*; **~ing** *n* (*physical*) sensation *f*; (*emotional*) sentiment *m*

feet [fi:t] *npl of* **foot**

feign [feɪn] *vt* feindre, simuler

fell [fɛl] *pt of* **fall** ♦ *vt* (*tree, person*) abattre

fellow ['fɛləu] *n* type *m*; (*comrade*) compagnon *m*; (*of learned society*) membre *m* ♦ *cpd*: **their ~ prisoners/students** leurs camarades prisonniers/d'étude; **~ citizen** *n* concitoyen(ne) *m/f*; **~ countryman** (*irreg*) *n* compatriote *m*; **~ men** *npl* semblables *mpl*; **~ship** *n* (*society*) association *f*; (*comradeship*) amitié *f*, camaraderie *f*; (*grant*) sorte de bourse universitaire

felony ['fɛlənɪ] *n* crime *m*, forfait *m*

felt [fɛlt] *pt, pp of* **feel** ♦ *n* feutre *m*; **~-tip pen** *n* stylo-feutre *m*

female ['fi:meɪl] *n* (*ZOOL*) femelle *f*; (*pej: woman*) bonne femme ♦ *adj* (*BIO*) femelle; (*sex, character*) féminin(e); (*vote etc*) des femmes

feminine ['fɛmɪnɪn] *adj* féminin(e)

feminist ['fɛmɪnɪst] *n* féministe *m/f*

fence [fɛns] *n* barrière *f* ♦ *vt* (*also:* **~ in**) clôturer ♦ *vi* faire de l'escrime; **fencing** *n* escrime *m*

fend [fɛnd] *vi*: **to ~ for o.s.** se débrouiller (tout seul); **~ off** *vt* (*attack etc*) parer

fender ['fɛndə^r^] *n* garde-feu *m inv*; (*on boat*) défense *f*; (*US: of car*) aile *f*

ferment [*vb* fə'mɛnt, *n* 'fə:mɛnt] *vi* fermenter ♦ *n* agitation *f*, effervescence *f*

fern [fə:n] *n* fougère *f*

ferocious [fə'rəuʃəs] *adj* féroce

ferret ['fɛrɪt] *n* furet *m*

ferry ['fɛrɪ] *n* (*small*) bac *m*; (*large: also:* **~boat**) ferry(-boat) *m* ♦ *vt* transporter

fertile ['fə:taɪl] *adj* fertile; (*BIO*) fécond(e); **fertilizer** ['fə:tɪlaɪzə^r^] *n* engrais *m*

fester ['fɛstə^r^] *vi* suppurer

festival ['fɛstɪvəl] *n* (*REL*) fête *f*; (*ART, MUS*) festival *m*

festive ['fɛstɪv] *adj* de fête; **the ~ season** (*BRIT: Christmas*) la période des fêtes; **festivities** *npl* réjouissances *fpl*

festoon [fɛs'tu:n] *vt*: **to ~ with** orner de

fetch [fɛtʃ] *vt* aller chercher; (*sell for*) se vendre

fête [feɪt] *n* fête *f*, kermesse *f*

feud [fju:d] *n* dispute *f*, dissension *f*

fever ['fi:və^r^] *n* fièvre *f*; **~ish** *adj* fiévreux(-euse), fébrile

few [fju:] *adj* (*not many*) peu de; **a ~** ♦ *adj* quelques ♦ *pron* quelques-uns (-unes); **~er** ['fju:ə^r^] *adj* moins de; moins (nombreux); **~est** ['fju:ɪst] *adj* le moins (de)

fiancé, e [fɪ'ɑ̃:ŋseɪ] *n* fiancé(e) *m/f*

fib [fɪb] *n* bobard *m*

fibre ['faɪbə^r^] (*US* **fiber**) *n* fibre *f*; **~glass**

['faɪbəglɑːs] (**Fiberglass** ® *US*) *n* fibre de verre

fickle ['fɪkl] *adj* inconstant(e), volage, capricieux(-euse)

fiction ['fɪkʃən] *n* romans *mpl*, littérature *f* romanesque; (*invention*) fiction *f*; **~al** *adj* fictif(-ive)

fictitious *adj* fictif(-ive), imaginaire

fiddle ['fɪdl] *n* (*MUS*) violon *m*; (*cheating*) combine *f*; escroquerie *f* ♦ *vt* (*BRIT*: *accounts*) falsifier, maquiller; **~ with** *vt fus* tripoter

fidget ['fɪdʒɪt] *vi* se trémousser, remuer

field [fiːld] *n* champ *m*; (*fig*) domaine *m*, champ; (*SPORT*: *ground*) terrain *m*; **~work** *n* travaux *mpl* pratiques (sur le terrain)

fiend [fiːnd] *n* démon *m*

fierce [fɪəs] *adj* (*look, animal*) féroce, sauvage; (*wind, attack, person*) (très) violent(e); (*fighting, enemy*) acharné(e)

fiery ['faɪərɪ] *adj* ardent(e), brûlant(e); (*temperament*) fougueux(-euse)

fifteen [fɪf'tiːn] *num* quinze

fifth [fɪfθ] *num* cinquième

fifty ['fɪftɪ] *num* cinquante; **~-fifty** *adj*: **a ~-fifty chance** *etc* une chance *etc* sur deux ♦ *adv* moitié-moitié

fig [fɪg] *n* figue *f*

fight [faɪt] (*pt, pp* **fought**) *n* (*MIL*) combat *m*; (*between persons*) bagarre *f*; (*against cancer etc*) lutte *f* ♦ *vt* se battre contre; (*cancer, alcoholism, emotion*) combattre, lutter contre; (*election*) se présenter à ♦ *vi* se battre; **~er** *n* (*fig*) lutteur *m*; (*plane*) chasseur *m*; **~ing** *n* combats *mpl*; (*brawl*) bagarres *fpl*

figment ['fɪgmənt] *n*: **a ~ of the imagination** une invention

figurative ['fɪgjurətɪv] *adj* figuré(e)

figure ['fɪgə^r^] *n* figure *f*; (*number, cipher*) chiffre *m*; (*body, outline*) silhouette *f*; (*shape*) ligne *f*, formes *fpl* ♦ *vt* (*think*: *esp US*) supposer ♦ *vi* (*appear*) figurer; **~ out** *vt* (*work out*) calculer; **~head** *n* (*NAUT*) figure *f* de proue; (*pej*) prête-nom *m*; **~ of speech** *n* figure *f* de rhétorique

file [faɪl] *n* (*dossier*) dossier *m*; (*folder*) dossier, chemise *f*; (: *with hinges*) classeur *m*; (*COMPUT*) fichier *m*; (*row*) file *f*; (*tool*) lime *f* ♦ *vt* (*nails, wood*) limer; (*papers*) classer; (*LAW*: *claim*) faire enregistrer; déposer ♦ *vi*: **to ~ in/out** entrer/sortir l'un derrière l'autre; **to ~ for divorce** faire une demande en divorce; **filing cabinet** *n* classeur *m* (*meuble*)

fill [fɪl] *vt* remplir; (*need*) répondre à ♦ *n*: **to eat one's ~** manger à sa faim; **to ~ with** remplir de; **~ in** *vt* (*hole*) boucher; (*form*) remplir; **~ up** *vt* remplir; **~ it up, please** (*AUT*) le plein, s'il vous plaît

fillet ['fɪlɪt] *n* filet *m*; **~ steak** *n* filet *m* de bœuf, tournedos *m*

filling ['fɪlɪŋ] *n* (*CULIN*) garniture *f*, farce *f*; (*for tooth*) plombage *m*; **~ station** *n* station-service *f*

film [fɪlm] *n* film *m*; (*PHOT*) pellicule *f*, film; (*of powder, liquid*) couche *f*, pellicule ♦ *vt* (*scene*) filmer ♦ *vi* tourner; **~ star** *n* vedette *f* de cinéma

filter ['fɪltə^r^] *n* filtre *m* ♦ *vt* filtrer; **~ lane** *n* (*AUT*) voie *f* de sortie; **~-tipped** *adj* à bout filtre

filth [fɪlθ] *n* saleté *f*; **~y** *adj* sale, dégoûtant(e); (*language*) ordurier(-ère)

fin [fɪn] *n* (*of fish*) nageoire *f*

final ['faɪnl] *adj* final(e); (*definitive*) définitif(-ive) ♦ *n* (*SPORT*) finale *f*; **~s** *npl* (*SCOL*) examens *mpl* de dernière année; **~e** [fɪ'nɑːlɪ] *n* finale *m*; **~ist** *n* finaliste *m/f*; **~ize** *vt* mettre au point; **~ly** *adv* (*eventually*) enfin, finalement; (*lastly*) en dernier lieu

finance [faɪ'næns] *n* finance *f* ♦ *vt* financer; **~s** *npl* (*financial position*) finances *fpl*; **financial** [faɪ'nænʃəl] *adj* financier(-ère)

find [faɪnd] (*pt, pp* **found**) *vt* trouver; (*lost object*) retrouver ♦ *n* trouvaille *f*, découverte *f*; **to ~ sb guilty** (*LAW*) déclarer qn coupable; **~ out** *vt* (*truth, se-*

cret) découvrir; (*person*) démasquer ♦ *vi*: **to ~ out about** (*make enquiries*) se renseigner; (*by chance*) apprendre; **~ings** *npl* (LAW) conclusions *fpl*, verdict *m*; (*of report*) conclusions

fine [faɪn] *adj* (*excellent*) excellent(e); (*thin, not coarse, subtle*) fin(e); (*weather*) beau (belle) ♦ *adv* (*well*) très bien ♦ *n* (LAW) amende *f*; contravention *f* ♦ *vt* (LAW) condamner à une amende; donner une contravention à; **to be ~** (*person*) aller bien; (*weather*) être beau; **~ arts** *npl* beaux-arts *mpl*; **~ry** *n* parure *f*

finger ['fɪŋgəʳ] *n* doigt *m* ♦ *vt* palper, toucher; **little ~** auriculaire *m*, petit doigt; **index ~** index *m*; **~nail** *n* ongle *m* (de la main); **~print** *n* empreinte digitale; **~tip** *n* bout *m* du doigt

finish ['fɪnɪʃ] *n* fin *f*; (SPORT) arrivée *f*; (*polish etc*) finition *f* ♦ *vt* finir, terminer ♦ *vi* finir, se terminer; **to ~ doing sth** finir de faire qch; **to ~ third** arriver *or* terminer troisième; **~ off** *vt* finir, terminer; (*kill*) achever; **~ up** *vi, vt* finir; **~ing line** *n* ligne *f* d'arrivée

finite ['faɪnaɪt] *adj* fini(e); (*verb*) conjugué(e)

Finland ['fɪnlənd] *n* Finlande *f*; **Finn** [fɪn] *n* Finlandais(e); **Finnish** *adj* finlandais(e) ♦ *n* (LING) finnois *m*

fir [fəːʳ] *n* sapin *m*

fire ['faɪəʳ] *n* feu *m*; (*accidental*) incendie *m*; (*heater*) radiateur *m* ♦ *vt* (*fig*) enflammer, animer; (*inf: dismiss*) mettre à la porte, renvoyer; (*discharge*): **to ~ a gun** tirer un coup de feu ♦ *vi* (*shoot*) tirer, faire feu; **on ~** en feu; **~ alarm** *n* avertisseur *m* d'incendie; **~arm** *n* arme *f* à feu; **~ brigade** *n* (sapeurs-)pompiers *mpl*; **~ department** (US) *n* = **fire brigade**; **~ engine** *n* (*vehicle*) voiture *f* des pompiers; **~ escape** *n* escalier *m* de secours; **~ extinguisher** *n* extincteur *m*; **~man** *n* pompier *m*; **~place** *n* cheminée *f*; **~side** *n* foyer *m*, coin *m* du feu; **~ station** *n* caserne *f* de pompiers; **~wood** *n* bois *m* de chauffage; **~works** *npl* feux *mpl* d'artifice; (*display*) feu(x) d'artifice

firing squad ['faɪərɪŋ-] *n* peloton *m* d'exécution

firm [fəːm] *adj* ferme ♦ *n* compagnie *f*, firme *f*

first [fəːst] *adj* premier(-ère) ♦ *adv* (*before all others*) le premier, la première; (*before all other things*) en premier, d'abord; (*when listing reasons etc*) en premier lieu, premièrement ♦ *n* (*person: in race*) premier(-ère); (BRIT: SCOL) mention *f* très bien; (AUT) première *f*; **at ~** au commencement, au début; **~ of all** tout d'abord, pour commencer; **~ aid** *n* premiers secours *or* soins; **~-aid kit** *n* trousse *f* à pharmacie; **~-class** *adj* de première classe; (*excellent*) excellent(e), exceptionnel(le); **~-hand** *adj* de première main; **~ lady** (US) *n* femme *f* du président; **~ly** *adv* premièrement, en premier lieu; **~ name** *n* prénom *m*; **~-rate** *adj* excellent(e)

fish [fɪʃ] *n inv* poisson *m* ♦ *vt, vi* pêcher; **to go ~ing** aller à la pêche; **~erman** *n* pêcheur *m*; **~ farm** *n* établissement *m* piscicole; **~ fingers** (BRIT) *npl* bâtonnets de poisson (congelés); **~ing boat** *n* barque *f or* bateau *m* de pêche; **~ing line** *n* ligne *f* (de pêche); **~ing rod** *n* canne *f* à pêche; **~ing tackle** *n* attirail *m* de pêche; **~monger's (shop)** *n* poissonnerie *f*; **~ slice** *n* pelle *f* à poisson; **~ sticks** (US) *npl* = **fish fingers**; **~y** (*inf*) *adj* suspect(e), louche

fist [fɪst] *n* poing *m*

fit [fɪt] *adj* (*healthy*) en (bonne) forme; (*proper*) convenable; approprié(e) ♦ *vt* (*subj: clothes*) aller à; (*put in, attach*) installer, poser; adapter; (*equip*) équiper, garnir, munir; (*suit*) convenir à ♦ *vi* (*clothes*) aller; (*parts*) s'adapter; (*in space, gap*) entrer, s'adapter ♦ *n* (MED) accès *m*, crise *f*; (*of anger*) accès; (*of hysterics, jealousy*) crise; **~ to** en état de; **~ for** digne de; apte à; **~ of**

coughing quinte *f* de toux; **a ~ of giggles** le fou rire; **this dress is a good ~** cette robe (me) va très bien; **by ~s and starts** par à-coups; **~ in** *vi* s'accorder; s'adapter; **~ful** *adj* (*sleep*) agité(e); **~ment** *n* meuble encastré, élément *m*; **~ness** *n* (*MED*) forme *f* physique; **~ted carpet** *n* moquette *f*; **~ted kitchen** (*BRIT*) *n* cuisine équipée; **~ter** *n* monteur *m*; **~ting** *adj* approprié(e) ♦ *n* (*of dress*) essayage *m*; (*of piece of equipment*) pose *f*, installation *f*; **~tings** *npl* (*in building*) installations *fpl*; **~ting room** *n* cabine *f* d'essayage

five [faɪv] *num* cinq; **~r** (*inf*) *n* (*BRIT*) billet *m* de cinq livres; (*US*) billet de cinq dollars

fix [fɪks] *vt* (*date, amount etc*) fixer; (*organize*) arranger; (*mend*) réparer; (*meal, drink*) préparer ♦ *n*: **to be in a ~** être dans le pétrin; **~ up** *vt* (*meeting*) arranger; **to ~ sb up with sth** faire avoir qch à qn; **~ation** [fɪk'seɪʃən] *n* (*PSYCH*) fixation *f*; (*fig*) obsession *f*; **~ed** *adj* (*prices etc*) fixe; (*smile*) figé(e); **~ture** *n* installation *f* (fixe); (*SPORT*) rencontre *f* (au programme)

fizzy ['fɪzɪ] *adj* pétillant(e); gazeux (-euse)

flabbergasted ['flæbəgɑːstɪd] *adj* sidéré(e), ahuri(e)

flabby ['flæbɪ] *adj* mou (molle)

flag [flæg] *n* drapeau *m*; (*also:* **~stone**) dalle *f* ♦ *vi* faiblir; fléchir; **~ down** *vt* héler, faire signe (de s'arrêter) à; **~pole** *n* mât *m*; **~ship** *n* vaisseau *m* amiral; (*fig*) produit *m* vedette

flair [flɛə^r] *n* flair *m*

flak [flæk] *n* (*MIL*) tir antiaérien; (*inf*: *criticism*) critiques *fpl*

flake [fleɪk] *n* (*of rust, paint*) écaille *f*; (*of snow, soap powder*) flocon *m* ♦ *vi* (*also:* **~ off**) s'écailler

flamboyant [flæm'bɔɪənt] *adj* flamboyant(e), éclatant(e); (*person*) haut(e) en couleur

flame [fleɪm] *n* flamme *f*

flamingo [flə'mɪŋgəu] *n* flamant *m* (rose)

flammable ['flæməbl] *adj* inflammable

flan [flæn] (*BRIT*) *n* tarte *f*

flank [flæŋk] *n* flanc *m* ♦ *vt* flanquer

flannel ['flænl] *n* (*fabric*) flanelle *f*; (*BRIT*: *also:* **face ~**) gant *m* de toilette

flap [flæp] *n* (*of pocket, envelope*) rabat *m* ♦ *vt* (*wings*) battre (de) ♦ *vi* (*sail, flag*) claquer; (*inf*: *also:* **be in a ~**) paniquer

flare [flɛə^r] *n* (*signal*) signal lumineux; (*in skirt etc*) évasement *m*; **~ up** *vi* s'embraser; (*fig*: *person*) se mettre en colère, s'emporter; (: *revolt etc*) éclater

flash [flæʃ] *n* éclair *m*; (*also:* **news ~**) flash *m* (d'information); (*PHOT*) flash ♦ *vt* (*light*) projeter; (*send*: *message*) câbler; (*look*) jeter; (*smile*) lancer ♦ *vi* (*light*) clignoter; **a ~ of lightning** un éclair; **in a ~** en un clin d'œil; **to ~ one's headlights** faire un appel de phares; **to ~ by** *or* **past** (*person*) passer (devant) comme un éclair; **~bulb** *n* ampoule *f* de flash; **~cube** *n* cube-flash *m*; **~light** *n* lampe *f* de poche; **~y** (*pej*) *adj* tape-à-l'œil *inv*, tapageur(-euse)

flask [flɑːsk] *n* flacon *m*, bouteille *f*; (*also:* **vacuum ~**) thermos ® *m or f*

flat [flæt] *adj* plat(e); (*tyre*) dégonflé(e), à plat; (*beer*) éventé(e); (*denial*) catégorique; (*MUS*) bémol *inv*; (: *voice*) faux (fausse); (*fee, rate*) fixe ♦ *n* (*BRIT*: *apartment*) appartement *m*; (*AUT*) crevaison *f*; (*MUS*) bémol *m*; **to work ~ out** travailler d'arrache-pied; **~ly** *adv* catégoriquement; **~ten** *vt* (*also:* **~ten out**) aplatir; (*crop*) coucher; (*building(s)*) raser

flatter ['flætə^r] *vt* flatter; **~ing** *adj* flatteur(-euse); **~y** *n* flatterie *f*

flaunt [flɔːnt] *vt* faire étalage de

flavour ['fleɪvə^r] (*US* **flavor**) *n* goût *m*, saveur *f*; (*of ice cream etc*) parfum *m* ♦ *vt* parfumer; **vanilla-~ed** à l'arôme de vanille, à la vanille; **~ing** *n* arôme *m*

flaw [flɔː] *n* défaut *m*; **~less** *adj* sans défaut

flax [flæks] *n* lin *m*

flea [fli:] *n* puce *f*

fleck [flɛk] *n* tacheture *f*; moucheture *f*

flee [fli:] (*pt, pp* **fled**) *vt* fuir ♦ *vi* fuir, s'enfuir

fleece [fli:s] *n* toison *f* ♦ *vt* (*inf*) voler, filouter

fleet [fli:t] *n* flotte *f*; (*of lorries etc*) parc *m*, convoi *m*

fleeting ['fli:tɪŋ] *adj* fugace, fugitif (-ive); (*visit*) très bref (brève)

Flemish ['flɛmɪʃ] *adj* flamand(e)

flesh [flɛʃ] *n* chair *f*; **~ wound** *n* blessure superficielle

flew [flu:] *pt of* **fly**

flex [flɛks] *n* fil *m or* câble *m* électrique ♦ *vt* (*knee*) fléchir; (*muscles*) tendre; **~ible** *adj* flexible

flick [flɪk] *n* petite tape; chiquenaude *f*; (*of duster*) petit coup ♦ *vt* donner un petit coup à; (*switch*) appuyer sur; **~ through** *vt fus* feuilleter

flicker ['flɪkəʳ] *vi* (*light*) vaciller; **his eyelids ~ed** il a cillé

flier ['flaɪəʳ] *n* aviateur *m*

flight [flaɪt] *n* vol *m*; (*escape*) fuite *f*; (*also:* **~ of steps**) escalier *m*; **~ attendant** (*US*) *n* steward *m*, hôtesse *f* de l'air; **~ deck** *n* (*AVIAT*) poste *m* de pilotage; (*NAUT*) pont *m* d'envol

flimsy ['flɪmzɪ] *adj* peu solide; (*clothes*) trop léger(-ère); (*excuse*) pauvre, mince

flinch [flɪntʃ] *vi* tressaillir; **to ~ from** se dérober à, reculer devant

fling [flɪŋ] (*pt, pp* **flung**) *vt* jeter, lancer

flint [flɪnt] *n* silex *m*; (*in lighter*) pierre *f* (à briquet)

flip [flɪp] *vt* (*throw*) lancer (d'une chiquenaude); **to ~ sth over** retourner qch

flippant ['flɪpənt] *adj* désinvolte, irrévérencieux(-euse)

flipper ['flɪpəʳ] *n* (*of seal etc*) nageoire *f*; (*for swimming*) palme *f*

flirt [flə:t] *vi* flirter ♦ *n* flirteur(-euse) *m/f*

float [fləut] *n* flotteur *m*; (*in procession*) char *m*; (*money*) réserve *f* ♦ *vi* flotter

flock [flɔk] *n* troupeau *m*; (*of birds*) vol *m*; (*REL*) ouailles *fpl* ♦ *vi*: **to ~ to** se rendre en masse à

flog [flɔg] *vt* fouetter

flood [flʌd] *n* inondation *f*; (*of letters, refugees etc*) flot *m* ♦ *vt* inonder ♦ *vi* (*people*): **to ~ into** envahir; **~ing** *n* inondation *f*; **~light** *n* projecteur *m*

floor [flɔ:ʳ] *n* sol *m*; (*storey*) étage *m*; (*of sea, valley*) fond *m* ♦ *vt* (*subj: question*) décontenancer; (*: blow*) terrasser; **on the ~** par terre; **ground ~**, *(US)* **first ~** rez-de-chaussée *m inv*; **first ~**, *(US)* **second ~** premier étage; **~board** *n* planche *f* (*du plancher*); **~ show** *n* spectacle *m* de variétés

flop [flɔp] *n* fiasco *m* ♦ *vi* être un fiasco; (*fall: into chair*) s'affaler, s'effondrer; **~py** *adj* lâche, flottant(e) ♦ *n* (*COMPUT: also:* **~py disk**) disquette *f*

flora ['flɔ:rə] *n* flore *f*

floral ['flɔ:rl] *adj* (*dress*) à fleurs

florid ['flɔrɪd] *adj* (*complexion*) coloré(e); (*style*) plein(e) de fioritures

florist ['flɔrɪst] *n* fleuriste *m/f*; **~'s (shop)** *n* magasin *m or* boutique *f* de fleuriste

flounder ['flaundəʳ] *vi* patauger ♦ *n* (*ZOOL*) flet *m*

flour ['flauəʳ] *n* farine *f*

flourish ['flʌrɪʃ] *vi* prospérer ♦ *n* (*gesture*) moulinet *m*

flout [flaut] *vt* se moquer de, faire fi de

flow [fləu] *n* (*ELEC, of river*) courant *m*; (*of blood in veins*) circulation *f*; (*of tide*) flux *m*; (*of orders, data*) flot *m* ♦ *vi* couler; (*traffic*) s'écouler; (*robes, hair*) flotter; **the ~ of traffic** l'écoulement *m* de la circulation; **~ chart** *n* organigramme *m*

flower ['flauəʳ] *n* fleur *f* ♦ *vi* fleurir; **~ bed** *n* plate-bande *f*; **~pot** *n* pot *m* (de fleurs); **~y** *adj* fleuri(e)

flown [fləun] *pp of* **fly**

flu [flu:] *n* grippe *f*

fluctuate ['flʌktjueɪt] *vi* varier, fluctuer

fluent ['flu:ənt] *adj* (*speech*) coulant(e), aisé(e); **he speaks ~ French, he's ~ in**

French il parle couramment le français

fluff [flʌf] *n* duvet *m*; (*on jacket, carpet*) peluche *f*; **~y** *adj* duveteux(-euse); (*toy*) en peluche

fluid ['flu:ɪd] *adj* fluide ♦ *n* fluide *m*

fluke [flu:k] (*inf*) *n* (*luck*) coup *m* de veine

flung [flʌŋ] *pt, pp of* **fling**

fluoride ['fluəraɪd] *n* fluorure *f*; **~ toothpaste** dentifrice *m* au fluor

flurry ['flʌrɪ] *n* (*of snow*) rafale *f*, bourrasque *f*; **~ of activity/excitement** affairement *m*/excitation *f* soudain(e)

flush [flʌʃ] *n* (*on face*) rougeur *f*; (*fig: of youth, beauty etc*) éclat *m* ♦ *vt* nettoyer à grande eau ♦ *vi* rougir ♦ *adj*: **~ with** au ras de, de niveau avec; **to ~ the toilet** tirer la chasse (d'eau); **~ed** *adj* (tout(e)) rouge

flustered ['flʌstəd] *adj* énervé(e)

flute [flu:t] *n* flûte *f*

flutter ['flʌtə^r] *n* (*of panic, excitement*) agitation *f*; (*of wings*) battement *m* ♦ *vi* (*bird*) battre des ailes, voleter

flux [flʌks] *n*: **in a state of ~** fluctuant sans cesse

fly [flaɪ] (*pt* **flew**, *pp* **flown**) *n* (*insect*) mouche *f*; (*on trousers: also:* **flies**) braguette *f* ♦ *vt* piloter; (*passengers, cargo*) transporter (par avion); (*distances*) parcourir ♦ *vi* voler; (*passengers*) aller en avion; (*escape*) s'enfuir, fuir; (*flag*) se déployer; **~ away** *vi* (*bird, insect*) s'envoler; **~ off** *vi* = **fly away**; **~-drive** *n* formule *f* avion plus voiture; **~ing** *n* (*activity*) aviation *f*; (*action*) vol *m* ♦ *adj*: **a ~ing visit** une visite éclair; **with ~ing colours** haut la main; **~ing saucer** *n* soucoupe volante; **~ing start** *n*: **to get off to a ~ing start** prendre un excellent départ; **~over** (*BRIT*) *n* (*bridge*) saut-de-mouton *m*; **~sheet** *n* (*for tent*) double toit *m*

foal [fəul] *n* poulain *m*

foam [fəum] *n* écume *f*; (*on beer*) mousse *f*; (*also:* **~ rubber**) caoutchouc mousse *m* ♦ *vi* (*liquid*) écumer; (*soapy water*) mousser

fob [fɔb] *vt*: **to ~ sb off** se débarrasser de qn

focal point ['fəukl-] *n* (*fig*) point central

focus ['fəukəs] (*pl* **~es**) *n* foyer *m*; (*of interest*) centre *m* ♦ *vt* (*field glasses etc*) mettre au point ♦ *vi*: **to ~ (on)** (*with camera*) régler la mise au point (sur); (*person*) fixer son regard (sur); **out of/in ~** (*picture*) flou(e)/net(te); (*camera*) pas au point/au point

fodder ['fɔdə^r] *n* fourrage *m*

foe [fəu] *n* ennemi *m*

fog [fɔg] *n* brouillard *m*; **~gy** *adj*: **it's ~gy** il y a du brouillard; **~ lamp** (*US* **~ light**) *n* (*AUT*) phare *m* antibrouillard

foil [fɔɪl] *vt* déjouer, contrecarrer ♦ *n* feuille *f* de métal; (*kitchen ~*) papier *m* alu(minium); (*complement*) repoussoir *m*

fold [fəuld] *n* (*bend, crease*) pli *m*; (*AGR*) parc *m* à moutons; (*fig*) bercail *m* ♦ *vt* plier; (*arms*) croiser; **~ up** *vi* (*map, table etc*) se plier; (*business*) fermer boutique ♦ *vt* (*map, clothes*) plier; **~er** *n* (*for papers*) chemise *f*; (*: with hinges*) classeur *m*; (*COMPUT*) répertoire *m*; **~ing** *adj* (*chair, bed*) pliant(e)

foliage ['fəulɪɪdʒ] *n* feuillage *m*

folk [fəuk] *npl* gens *mpl* ♦ *cpd* folklorique; **~s** (*inf*) *npl* (*parents*) parents *mpl*; **~lore** ['fəuklɔ:^r] *n* folklore *m*; **~ song** *n* chanson *f* folklorique

follow ['fɔləu] *vt* suivre ♦ *vi* suivre; (*result*) s'ensuivre; **to ~ suit** (*fig*) faire de même; **~ up** *vt* (*letter, offer*) donner suite à; (*case*) suivre; **~er** *n* disciple *m/f*, partisan(e); **~ing** *adj* suivant(e) ♦ *n* partisans *mpl*, disciples *mpl*

folly ['fɔlɪ] *n* inconscience *f*; folie *f*

fond [fɔnd] *adj* (*memory, look*) tendre; (*hopes, dreams*) un peu fou (folle); **to be ~ of** aimer beaucoup

fondle ['fɔndl] *vt* caresser

font [fɔnt] *n* (*in church: for baptism*) fonts baptismaux; (*TYP*) fonte *f*

food [fu:d] *n* nourriture *f*; **~ mixer** *n*

mixer *m*; ~ **poisoning** *n* intoxication *f* alimentaire; ~ **processor** *n* robot *m* de cuisine; ~**stuffs** *npl* denrées *fpl* alimentaires; ~ **technology** *BRIT n* (*SCOL*) technologie *f* des produits alimentaires

fool [fu:l] *n* idiot(e); (*CULIN*) mousse *f* de fruits ♦ *vt* berner, duper ♦ *vi* faire l'idiot *or* l'imbécile; ~**hardy** *adj* téméraire, imprudent(e); ~**ish** *adj* idiot(e), stupide; (*rash*) imprudent(e); insensé(e); ~**proof** *adj* (*plan etc*) infaillible

foot [fut] (*pl* **feet**) *n* pied *m*; (*of animal*) patte *f*; (*measure*) pied (= *30,48 cm; 12 inches*) ♦ *vt* (*bill*) payer; **on** ~ à pied; ~**age** *n* (*CINEMA*: *length*) ≃ métrage *m*; (: *material*) séquences *fpl*; ~**ball** *n* ballon *m* (de football); (*sport*: *BRIT*) football *m*, foot *m*; (: *US*) football américain; ~**ball player** (*BRIT*) *n* (*also:* ~**baller**) joueur *m* de football; ~**bridge** *n* passerelle *f*; ~**hills** *npl* contreforts *mpl*; ~**hold** *n* prise *f* (de pied); ~**ing** *n* (*fig*) position *f*; **to lose one's** ~**ing** perdre pied; ~**lights** *npl* rampe *f*; ~**note** *n* note *f* (en bas de page); ~**path** *n* sentier *m*; (*in street*) trottoir *m*; ~**print** *n* trace *f* (de pas); ~**step** *n* pas *m*; ~**wear** *n* chaussure(s) *f(pl)*

football pools

Les **football pools** *- ou plus familièrement les "***pools***" - consistent à parier sur les résultats des matches de football qui se jouent tous les samedis. L'expression consacrée en anglais est "to do the pools". Les parieurs envoient à l'avance les fiches qu'ils ont complétées à l'organisme qui gère les paris et ils attendent 17 h le samedi que les résultats soient annoncés. Les sommes gagnées se comptent parfois en milliers (ou même en millions) de livres sterling.*

KEYWORD

for [fɔ:ʳ] *prep* **1** (*indicating destination, intention, purpose*) pour; **the train for London** le train pour *or* (à destination) de Londres; **he went for the paper** il est allé chercher le journal; **it's time for lunch** c'est l'heure du déjeuner; **what's it for?** ça sert à quoi?; **what for?** (*why*) pourquoi?

2 (*on behalf of, representing*) pour; **the MP for Hove** le député de Hove; **to work for sb/sth** travailler pour qn/qch; **G for George** G comme Georges

3 (*because of*) pour; **for this reason** pour cette raison; **for fear of being criticized** de peur d'être critiqué

4 (*with regard to*) pour; **it's cold for July** il fait froid pour juillet; **a gift for languages** un don pour les langues

5 (*in exchange for*): **I sold it for £5** je l'ai vendu 5 livres; **to pay 50 pence for a ticket** payer un billet 50 pence

6 (*in favour of*) pour; **are you for or against us?** êtes-vous pour ou contre nous?

7 (*referring to distance*) pendant, sur; **there are roadworks for 5 km** il y a des travaux sur 5 km; **we walked for miles** nous avons marché pendant des kilomètres

8 (*referring to time*) pendant; depuis; pour; **he was away for 2 years** il a été absent pendant 2 ans; **she will be away for a month** elle sera absente (pendant) un mois; **I have known her for years** je la connais depuis des années; **can you do it for tomorrow?** est-ce que tu peux le faire pour demain?

9 (*with infinitive clauses*): **it is not for me to decide** ce n'est pas à moi de décider; **it would be best for you to leave** le mieux serait que vous partiez; **there is still time for you to do it** vous avez encore le temps de le faire; **for this to be possible ...** pour que cela soit possible ...

10 (*in spite of*): **for all his work/**

efforts malgré tout son travail/tous ses efforts; **for all his complaints, he's very fond of her** il a beau se plaindre, il l'aime beaucoup
♦ *conj* (*since, as*: *rather formal*) car

forage ['fɔrɪdʒ] *vi* fourrager
foray ['fɔreɪ] *n* incursion *f*
forbid [fə'bɪd] (*pt* **forbad(e)**, *pp* **forbidden**) *vt* défendre, interdire; **to ~ sb to do** défendre *or* interdire à qn de faire; **~ding** *adj* sévère, sombre
force [fɔːs] *n* force *f* ♦ *vt* forcer; (*push*) pousser (de force); **the F~s** *npl* (MIL) l'armée *f*; **in ~** en vigueur; **~-feed** *vt* nourrir de force; **~ful** *adj* énergique, volontaire; **forcibly** *adv* par la force, de force; (*express*) énergiquement
ford [fɔːd] *n* gué *m*
fore [fɔː[r]] *n*: **to come to the ~** se faire remarquer; **~arm** *n* avant-bras *m inv*; **~boding** *n* pressentiment *m* (néfaste); **~cast** (*irreg*: *like* **cast**) *n* prévision *f* ♦ *vt* prévoir; **~court** *n* (*of garage*) devant *m*; **~finger** *n* index *m*; **~front** *n*: **in the ~front of** au premier rang *or* plan de
foregone ['fɔːgɒn] *adj*: **it's a ~ conclusion** c'est couru d'avance
foreground ['fɔːgraund] *n* premier plan
forehead ['fɔrɪd] *n* front *m*
foreign ['fɔrɪn] *adj* étranger(-ère); (*trade*) extérieur(-e); **~er** *n* étranger (-ère); **~ exchange** *n* change *m*; **F~ Office** (BRIT) *n* ministère *m* des affaires étrangères; **F~ Secretary** (BRIT) *n* ministre *m* des affaires étrangères
fore: **~leg** *n* (*of cat, dog*) patte *f* de devant; (*of horse*) jambe antérieure; **~man** (*irreg*) *n* (*of factory, building site*) contremaître *m*, chef *m* d'équipe; **~most** *adj* le (la) plus en vue; premier(-ère) ♦ *adv*: **first and ~most** avant tout, tout d'abord
forensic [fə'rɛnsɪk] *adj*: **~ medicine** médecine légale; **~ scientist** médecin *m* légiste
fore: **~runner** *n* précurseur *m*; **~see** (*irreg*: *like* **see**) *vt* prévoir; **~seeable** *adj* prévisible; **~shadow** *vt* présager, annoncer, laisser prévoir; **~sight** *n* prévoyance *f*
forest ['fɔrɪst] *n* forêt *f*; **~ry** *n* sylviculture *f*
foretaste ['fɔːteɪst] *n* avant-goût *m*
foretell [fɔː'tɛl] (*irreg*: *like* **tell**) *vt* prédire
forever [fə'rɛvə[r]] *adv* pour toujours; (*fig*) continuellement
foreword ['fɔːwəːd] *n* avant-propos *m inv*
forfeit ['fɔːfɪt] *vt* (*lose*) perdre
forgave [fə'geɪv] *pt of* **forgive**
forge [fɔːdʒ] *n* forge *f* ♦ *vt* (*signature*) contrefaire; (*wrought iron*) forger; **to ~ money** (BRIT) fabriquer de la fausse monnaie; **~ ahead** *vi* pousser de l'avant, prendre de l'avance; **~d** *adj* faux (fausse); **~r** *n* faussaire *m*; **~ry** *n* faux *m*, contrefaçon *f*
forget [fə'gɛt] (*pt* **forgot**, *pp* **forgotten**) *vt, vi* oublier; **~ful** *adj* distrait(e), étourdi(e); **~-me-not** *n* myosotis *m*
forgive [fə'gɪv] (*pt* **forgave**, *pp* **forgiven**) *vt* pardonner; **to ~ sb for sth/for doing sth** pardonner qch à qn/à qn de faire qch; **~ness** *n* pardon *m*
forgo [fɔː'gəu] (*pt* **forwent**, *pp* **forgone**) *vt* renoncer à
fork [fɔːk] *n* (*for eating*) fourchette *f*; (*for gardening*) fourche *f*; (*of roads*) bifurcation *f*; (*of railways*) embranchement *m* ♦ *vi* (*road*) bifurquer; **~ out** *vt* (*inf*) allonger; **~-lift truck** *n* chariot élévateur
forlorn [fə'lɔːn] *adj* (*deserted*) abandonné(e); (*attempt, hope*) désespéré(e)
form [fɔːm] *n* forme *f*; (SCOL) classe *f*; (*questionnaire*) formulaire *m* ♦ *vt* former; (*habit*) contracter; **in top ~** en pleine forme
formal ['fɔːməl] *adj* (*offer, receipt*) en bonne et due forme; (*person*)

cérémonieux(-euse); (*dinner*) officiel(le); (*clothes*) de soirée; (*garden*) à la française; (*education*) à proprement parler; **~ly** *adv* officiellement; cérémonieusement

format ['fɔːmæt] *n* format *m* ♦ *vt* (COMPUT) formater

formation [fɔː'meɪʃən] *n* formation *f*

formative ['fɔːmətɪv] *adj*: **~ years** années *fpl* d'apprentissage *or* de formation

former ['fɔːmə^r] *adj* ancien(ne) (*before n*), précédent(e); **the ~ ... the latter** le premier ... le second, celui-là ... celui-ci; **~ly** *adv* autrefois

formidable ['fɔːmɪdəbl] *adj* redoutable

formula ['fɔːmjulə] (*pl* **~e**) *n* formule *f*

forsake [fə'seɪk] (*pt* **forsook**, *pp* **forsaken**) *vt* abandonner

fort [fɔːt] *n* fort *m*

forte ['fɔːtɪ] *n* (point) fort *m*

forth [fɔːθ] *adv* en avant; **to go back and ~** aller et venir; **and so ~** et ainsi de suite; **~coming** *adj* (*event*) qui va avoir lieu prochainement; (*character*) ouvert(e), communicatif(-ive); (*available*) disponible; **~right** *adj* franc (franche), direct(e); **~with** *adv* sur-le-champ

fortify ['fɔːtɪfaɪ] *vt* fortifier

fortitude ['fɔːtɪtjuːd] *n* courage *m*

fortnight ['fɔːtnaɪt] (BRIT) *n* quinzaine *f*, quinze jours *mpl*; **~ly** (BRIT) *adj* bimensuel(le) ♦ *adv* tous les quinze jours

fortunate ['fɔːtʃənɪt] *adj* heureux (-euse); (*person*) chanceux(-euse); **it is ~ that** c'est une chance que; **~ly** *adv* heureusement

fortune ['fɔːtʃən] *n* chance *f*; (*wealth*) fortune *f*; **~-teller** *n* diseuse *f* de bonne aventure

forty ['fɔːtɪ] *num* quarante

forward ['fɔːwəd] *adj* (*ahead of schedule*) en avance; (*movement, position*) en avant, vers l'avant; (*not shy*) direct(e); effronté(e) ♦ *n* (SPORT) avant *m* ♦ *vt* (*letter*) faire suivre; (*parcel, goods*) expédier; (*fig*) promouvoir, favoriser; **~(s)** *adv* en avant; **to move ~** avancer

fossil ['fɔsl] *n* fossile *m*

foster ['fɔstə^r] *vt* encourager, favoriser; (*child*) élever (*sans obligation d'adopter*); **~ child** *n* enfant adoptif(-ive); **~ mother** *n* mère *f* nourricière *or* adoptive

fought [fɔːt] *pt, pp of* **fight**

foul [faul] *adj* (*weather, smell etc*) infect(e); (*language*) ordurier(-ère) ♦ *n* (SPORT) faute *f* ♦ *vt* (*dirty*) salir, encrasser; **he's got a ~ temper** il a un caractère de chien; **~ play** *n* (LAW) acte criminel

found [faund] *pt, pp of* **find** ♦ *vt* (*establish*) fonder; **~ation** [faun'deɪʃən] *n* (*act*) fondation *f*; (*base*) fondement *m*; (*also:* **~ation cream**) fond *m* de teint; **~ations** *npl* (*of building*) fondations *fpl*

founder ['faundə^r] *n* fondateur *m* ♦ *vi* couler, sombrer

foundry ['faundrɪ] *n* fonderie *f*

fountain ['fauntɪn] *n* fontaine *f*; **~ pen** *n* stylo *m* (à encre)

four [fɔː^r] *num* quatre; **on all ~s** à quatre pattes; **~-poster** *n* (*also:* **~-poster bed**) lit *m* à baldaquin; **~teen** *num* quatorze; **~th** *num* quatrième

fowl [faul] *n* volaille *f*

fox [fɔks] *n* renard *m* ♦ *vt* mystifier

foyer ['fɔɪeɪ] *n* (*hotel*) hall *m*; (THEATRE) foyer *m*

fraction ['frækʃən] *n* fraction *f*

fracture ['fræktʃə^r] *n* fracture *f*

fragile ['frædʒaɪl] *adj* fragile

fragment ['frægmənt] *n* fragment *m*

fragrant ['freɪgrənt] *adj* parfumé(e), odorant(e)

frail [freɪl] *adj* fragile, délicat(e)

frame [freɪm] *n* charpente *f*; (*of picture, bicycle*) cadre *m*; (*of door, window*) encadrement *m*, chambranle *m*; (*of spectacles*: *also:* **~s**) monture *f* ♦ *vt* encadrer; **~ of mind** disposition *f* d'esprit; **~work** *n* structure *f*

France [frɑːns] *n* France *f*

franchise ['fræntʃaɪz] *n* (POL) droit *m* de vote; (COMM) franchise *f*

frank [fræŋk] *adj* franc (franche) ♦ *vt* (*letter*) affranchir; **~ly** *adv* franchement
frantic ['fræntɪk] *adj* (*hectic*) frénétique; (*distraught*) hors de soi
fraternity [frə'tə:nɪtɪ] *n* (*spirit*) fraternité *f*; (*club*) communauté *f*, confrérie *f*
fraud [frɔ:d] *n* supercherie *f*, fraude *f*, tromperie *f*; (*person*) imposteur *m*
fraught [frɔ:t] *adj*: **~ with** chargé(e) de, plein(e) de
fray [freɪ] *vi* s'effilocher
freak [fri:k] *n* (*also cpd*) phénomène *m*, *créature ou événement exceptionnel par sa rareté*
freckle ['frɛkl] *n* tache *f* de rousseur
free [fri:] *adj* libre; (*gratis*) gratuit(e) ♦ *vt* (*prisoner etc*) libérer; (*jammed object or person*) dégager; **~ (of charge), for ~** gratuitement; **~dom** *n* liberté *f*; **F~fone** ® *n* numéro vert; **~-for-all** *n* mêlée générale; **~ gift** *n* prime *f*; **~hold** *n* propriété foncière libre; **~ kick** *n* coup franc; **~lance** *adj* indépendant(e); **~ly** *adv* librement; (*liberally*) libéralement; **F~mason** *n* franc-maçon *m*; **F~post** ® *n* port payé; **~-range** *adj* (*hen, eggs*) de ferme; **~ trade** *n* libre-échange *m*; **~way** (*US*) *n* autoroute *f*; **~ will** *n* libre arbitre *m*; **of one's own ~ will** de son plein gré
freeze [fri:z] (*pt* **froze**, *pp* **frozen**) *vi* geler ♦ *vt* geler; (*food*) congeler; (*prices, salaries*) bloquer, geler ♦ *n* gel *m*; (*fig*) blocage *m*; **~-dried** *adj* lyophilisé(e); **~r** *n* congélateur *m*; **freezing** *adj*: **freezing (cold)** (*weather, water*) glacial(e) ♦ *n*: **3 degrees below freezing** 3 degrés au-dessous de zéro; **freezing point** *n* point *m* de congélation
freight [freɪt] *n* (*goods*) fret *m*, cargaison *f*; (*money charged*) fret, prix *m* du transport; **~ train** *n* train *m* de marchandises
French [frɛntʃ] *adj* français(e) ♦ *n* (*LING*) français *m*; **the ~** *npl* (*people*) les Français; **~ bean** *n* haricot vert; **~ fried (potatoes)** (*US* **~ fries**) *npl* (pommes de terre *fpl*) frites *fpl*; **~ horn** *n* (*MUS*) cor *m* (d'harmonie); **~ kiss** *n* baiser profond; **~ loaf** *n* baguette *f*; **~man** (*irreg*) *n* Français *m*; **~ window** *n* porte-fenêtre *f*; **~woman** (*irreg*) *n* Française *f*
frenzy ['frɛnzɪ] *n* frénésie *f*
frequency ['fri:kwənsɪ] *n* fréquence *f*
frequent [*adj* 'fri:kwənt, *vb* frɪ'kwɛnt] *adj* fréquent(e) ♦ *vt* fréquenter; **~ly** *adv* fréquemment
fresh [frɛʃ] *adj* frais (fraîche); (*new*) nouveau (nouvelle); (*cheeky*) familier(-ère), culotté(e); **~en** *vi* (*wind, air*) fraîchir; **~en up** *vi* faire un brin de toilette; **~er** (*BRIT*: *inf*) *n* (*SCOL*) bizuth *m*, étudiant(e) de 1ère année; **~ly** *adv* nouvellement, récemment; **~man** (*US*) (*irreg*) *n* = **fresher**; **~ness** *n* fraîcheur *f*; **~water** *adj* (*fish*) d'eau douce
fret [frɛt] *vi* s'agiter, se tracasser
friar ['fraɪəʳ] *n* moine *m*, frère *m*
friction ['frɪkʃən] *n* friction *f*
Friday ['fraɪdɪ] *n* vendredi *m*
fridge [frɪdʒ] (*BRIT*) *n* frigo *m*, frigidaire ® *m*
fried [fraɪd] *adj* frit(e); **~ egg** œuf *m* sur le plat
friend [frɛnd] *n* ami(e); **~ly** *adj* amical(e); gentil(le); (*place*) accueillant(e); **they were killed by ~ly fire** ils sont morts sous les tirs de leur propre camp; **~ship** *n* amitié *f*
frieze [fri:z] *n* frise *f*
fright [fraɪt] *n* peur *f*, effroi *m*; **to take ~** prendre peur, s'effrayer; **~en** *vt* effrayer, faire peur à; **~ened** *adj*: **to be ~ened (of)** avoir peur (de); **~ening** *adj* effrayant(e); **~ful** *adj* affreux(-euse)
frigid ['frɪdʒɪd] *adj* frigide
frill [frɪl] *n* (*on dress*) volant *m*; (*on shirt*) jabot *m*
fringe [frɪndʒ] *n* (*BRIT*: *of hair*) frange *f*; (*edge*: *of forest etc*) bordure *f*; **~ benefits** *npl* avantages sociaux *or* en nature
Frisbee ® ['frɪzbɪ] *n* Frisbee ® *m*

frisk [frɪsk] *vt* fouiller
fritter ['frɪtəʳ] *n* beignet *m*; **~ away** *vt* gaspiller
frivolous ['frɪvələs] *adj* frivole
frizzy ['frɪzɪ] *adj* crépu(e)
fro [frəu] *adv*: **to go to and ~** aller et venir
frock [frɔk] *n* robe *f*
frog [frɔg] *n* grenouille *f*; **~man** *n* homme-grenouille *m*
frolic ['frɔlɪk] *vi* folâtrer, batifoler

KEYWORD

from [frɔm] *prep* **1** (*indicating starting place, origin etc*) de; **where do you come from?, where are you from?** d'où venez-vous?; **from London to Paris** de Londres à Paris; **a letter from my sister** une lettre de ma sœur; **to drink from the bottle** boire à (même) la bouteille
2 (*indicating time*) (à partir) de; **from one o'clock to** *or* **until** *or* **till two** d'une heure à deux heures; **from January (on)** à partir de janvier
3 (*indicating distance*) de; **the hotel is one kilometre from the beach** l'hôtel est à un kilomètre de la plage
4 (*indicating price, number etc*) de; **the interest rate was increased from 9% to 10%** le taux d'intérêt est passé de 9 à 10%
5 (*indicating difference*) de; **he can't tell red from green** il ne peut pas distinguer le rouge du vert
6 (*because of, on the basis of*): **from what he says** d'après ce qu'il dit; **weak from hunger** affaibli par la faim

front [frʌnt] *n* (*of house, dress*) devant *m*; (*of coach, train*) avant *m*; (*promenade*: *also:* **sea ~**) bord *m* de mer; (*MIL, METEOROLOGY*) front *m*; (*fig*: *appearances*) contenance *f*, façade *f* ♦ *adj* de devant; (*seat*) avant *inv*; **in ~ (of)** devant; **~age** *n* (*of building*) façade *f*; **~ door** *n* porte *f* d'entrée; (*of car*) portière *f* avant; **~ier** ['frʌntɪəʳ] *n* frontière *f*; **~ page** *n* première page; **~ room** (*BRIT*) *n* pièce *f* de devant, salon *m*; **~-wheel drive** *n* traction *f* avant
frost [frɔst] *n* gel *m*, gelée *f*; (*also:* **hoarfrost**) givre *m*; **~bite** *n* gelures *fpl*; **~ed** *adj* (*glass*) dépoli(e); **~y** *adj* (*weather, welcome*) glacial(e)
froth [frɔθ] *n* mousse *f*; écume *f*
frown [fraun] *vi* froncer les sourcils
froze [frəuz] *pt of* **freeze**
frozen ['frəuzn] *pp of* **freeze**
fruit [fru:t] *n inv* fruit *m*; **~erer** *n* fruitier *m*, marchand(e) de fruits; **~ful** *adj* (*fig*) fructueux(-euse); **~ion** [fru:'ɪʃən] *n*: **to come to ~ion** se réaliser; **~ juice** *n* jus *m* de fruit; **~ machine** (*BRIT*) *n* machine *f* à sous; **~ salad** *n* salade *f* de fruits
frustrate [frʌs'treɪt] *vt* frustrer
fry [fraɪ] (*pt, pp* **fried**) *vt* (faire) frire; *see also* **small**; **~ing pan** *n* poêle *f* (à frire)
ft. *abbr* = **foot**; **feet**
fudge [fʌdʒ] *n* (*CULIN*) caramel *m*
fuel ['fjuəl] *n* (*for heating*) combustible *m*; (*for propelling*) carburant *m*; **~ oil** *n* mazout *m*; **~ tank** *n* (*in vehicle*) réservoir *m*
fugitive ['fju:dʒɪtɪv] *n* fugitif(-ive)
fulfil [ful'fɪl] (*US* **fulfill**) *vt* (*function, condition*) remplir; (*order*) exécuter; (*wish, desire*) satisfaire, réaliser; **~ment** (*US* **fulfillment**) *n* (*of wishes etc*) réalisation *f*; (*feeling*) contentement *m*
full [ful] *adj* plein(e); (*details, information*) complet(-ète); (*skirt*) ample, large ♦ *adv*: **to know ~ well that** savoir fort bien que; **I'm ~ (up)** j'ai bien mangé; **a ~ two hours** deux bonnes heures; **at ~ speed** à toute vitesse; **in ~** (*reproduce, quote*) intégralement; (*write*) en toutes lettres; **~ employment** plein emploi; **to pay in ~** tout payer; **~-length** *adj* (*film*) long métrage; (*portrait, mirror*) en pied; (*coat*) long(ue); **~ moon** *n* pleine lune; **~-scale** *adj* (*attack, war*) complet(-ète), total(e); (*model*) grandeur nature *inv*; **~ stop** *n* point *m*; **~-**

time *adj, adv* (*work*) à plein temps; **~y** *adv* entièrement, complètement; (*at least*) au moins; **~y licensed** (*hotel, restaurant*) autorisé(e) à vendre des boissons alcoolisées; **~y-fledged** *adj* (*barrister etc*) diplômé(e); (*citizen, member*) à part entière

fumble ['fʌmbl] *vi*: **~ with** tripoter

fume [fju:m] *vi* rager; **~s** *npl* vapeurs *fpl*, émanations *fpl*, gaz *mpl*

fun [fʌn] *n* amusement *m*, divertissement *m*; **to have ~** s'amuser; **for ~** pour rire; **to make ~ of** se moquer de

function ['fʌŋkʃən] *n* fonction *f*; (*social occasion*) cérémonie *f*, soirée officielle ♦ *vi* fonctionner; **~al** *adj* fonctionnel(le)

fund [fʌnd] *n* caisse *f*, fonds *m*; (*source, store*) source *f*, mine *f*; **~s** *npl* (*money*) fonds *mpl*

fundamental [fʌndə'mɛntl] *adj* fondamental(e)

funeral ['fju:nərəl] *n* enterrement *m*, obsèques *fpl*; **~ parlour** *n* entreprise *f* de pompes funèbres; **~ service** *n* service *m* funèbre

funfair ['fʌnfɛə^r] (*BRIT*) *n* fête (foraine)

fungi ['fʌŋgaɪ] *npl of* **fungus**

fungus ['fʌŋgəs] (*pl* **fungi**) *n* champignon *m*; (*mould*) moisissure *f*

funnel ['fʌnl] *n* entonnoir *m*; (*of ship*) cheminée *f*

funny ['fʌnɪ] *adj* amusant(e), drôle; (*strange*) curieux(-euse), bizarre

fur [fə:^r] *n* fourrure *f*; (*BRIT*: *in kettle etc*) (dépôt *m* de) tartre *m*

furious ['fjuərɪəs] *adj* furieux(-euse); (*effort*) acharné(e)

furlong ['fə:lɔŋ] *n* = **201,17 m**

furnace ['fə:nɪs] *n* fourneau *m*

furnish ['fə:nɪʃ] *vt* meubler; (*supply*): **to ~ sb with sth** fournir qch à qn; **~ings** *npl* mobilier *m*, ameublement *m*

furniture ['fə:nɪtʃə^r] *n* meubles *mpl*, mobilier *m*; **piece of ~** meuble *m*

furrow ['fʌrəu] *n* sillon *m*

furry ['fə:rɪ] *adj* (*animal*) à fourrure; (*toy*) en peluche

further ['fə:ðə^r] *adj* (*additional*) supplémentaire, autre; nouveau (nouvelle) ♦ *adv* plus loin; (*more*) davantage; (*moreover*) de plus ♦ *vt* faire avancer *or* progresser, promouvoir; **~ education** *n* enseignement *m* postscolaire; **~more** *adv* de plus, en outre

furthest ['fə:ðɪst] *superl of* **far**

fury ['fjuərɪ] *n* fureur *f*

fuse [fju:z] (*US* **fuze**) *n* fusible *m*; (*for bomb etc*) amorce *f*, détonateur *m* ♦ *vt, vi* (*metal*) fondre; **to ~ the lights** (*BRIT*) faire sauter les plombs; **~ box** *n* boîte *f* à fusibles

fuss [fʌs] *n* (*excitement*) agitation *f*; (*complaining*) histoire(s) *f(pl)*; **to make a ~** faire des histoires; **to make a ~ of sb** être aux petits soins pour qn; **~y** *adj* (*person*) tatillon(ne), difficile; (*dress, style*) tarabiscoté(e)

future ['fju:tʃə^r] *adj* futur(e) ♦ *n* avenir *m*; (*LING*) futur *m*; **in ~** à l'avenir

fuze [fju:z] (*US*) *n, vt, vi* = **fuse**

fuzzy ['fʌzɪ] *adj* (*PHOT*) flou(e); (*hair*) crépu(e)

G, g

G [dʒi:] *n* (*MUS*) sol *m*

G7 *n abbr* (= *Group of 7*) le groupe des 7

gabble ['gæbl] *vi* bredouiller

gable ['geɪbl] *n* pignon *m*

gadget ['gædʒɪt] *n* gadget *m*

Gaelic ['geɪlɪk] *adj* gaélique ♦ *n* (*LING*) gaélique *m*

gag [gæg] *n* (*on mouth*) bâillon *m*; (*joke*) gag *m* ♦ *vt* bâillonner

gaiety ['geɪɪtɪ] *n* gaieté *f*

gain [geɪn] *n* (*improvement*) gain *m*; (*profit*) gain, profit *m*; (*increase*): **~ (in)** augmentation *f* (de) ♦ *vt* gagner ♦ *vi* (*watch*) avancer; **to ~ 3 lbs (in weight)** prendre 3 livres; **to ~ on sb** (*catch up*) rattraper qn; **to ~ from/by** gagner de/à

gal. *abbr* = **gallon**

gale ['geɪl] *n* coup *m* de vent
gallant ['gælənt] *adj* vaillant(e), brave; (*towards ladies*) galant
gall bladder ['gɔːl-] *n* vésicule *f* biliaire
gallery ['gæləri] *n* galerie *f*; (*also:* **art ~**) musée *m*; (: *private*) galerie
gallon ['gæln] *n* gallon *m* (BRIT = 4,5 *l*; US = 3,8 *l*)
gallop ['gæləp] *n* galop *m* ♦ *vi* galoper
gallows ['gæləuz] *n* potence *f*
gallstone ['gɔːlstəun] *n* calcul *m* biliaire
galore [gə'lɔːʳ] *adv* en abondance, à gogo
Gambia ['gæmbɪə] *n*: **(The) ~** la Gambie
gambit ['gæmbɪt] *n* (*fig*): **(opening) ~** manœuvre *f* stratégique
gamble ['gæmbl] *n* pari *m*, risque calculé ♦ *vt, vi* jouer; **to ~ on** (*fig*) miser sur; **~r** *n* joueur *m*; **gambling** *n* jeu *m*
game [geɪm] *n* jeu *m*; (*match*) match *m*; (*strategy, scheme*) plan *m*; projet *m*; (HUNTING) gibier *m* ♦ *adj* (*willing*): **to be ~ (for)** être prêt(e) (à *or* pour); **big ~** gros gibier; **~keeper** *n* garde-chasse *m*
gammon ['gæmən] *n* (*bacon*) quartier *m* de lard fumé; (*ham*) jambon fumé
gamut ['gæmət] *n* gamme *f*
gang [gæŋ] *n* bande *f*; (*of workmen*) équipe *f*; **~ up** *vi*: **to ~ up on sb** se liguer contre qn; **~ster** *n* gangster *m*; **~way** ['gæŋweɪ] *n* passerelle *f*; (BRIT: *of bus, plane*) couloir central; (: *in cinema*) allée centrale
gaol [dʒeɪl] (BRIT) *n* = **jail**
gap [gæp] *n* trou *m*; (*in time*) intervalle *m*; (*difference*): **~ between** écart *m* entre
gape [geɪp] *vi* (*person*) être *or* rester bouche bée; (*hole, shirt*) être ouvert(e); **gaping** *adj* (*hole*) béant(e)
garage ['gærɑːʒ] *n* garage *m*
garbage ['gɑːbɪdʒ] *n* (US: *rubbish*) ordures *fpl*, détritus *mpl*; (*inf: nonsense*) foutaises *fpl*; **~ can** (US) *n* poubelle *f*, boîte *f* à ordures
garbled ['gɑːbld] *adj* (*account, message*) embrouillé(e)
garden ['gɑːdn] *n* jardin *m*; **~s** *npl* jardin public; **~er** *n* jardinier *m*; **~ing** *n* jardinage *m*
gargle ['gɑːgl] *vi* se gargariser
garish ['gɛərɪʃ] *adj* criard(e), voyant(e); (*light*) cru(e)
garland ['gɑːlənd] *n* guirlande *f*; couronne *f*
garlic ['gɑːlɪk] *n* ail *m*
garment ['gɑːmənt] *n* vêtement *m*
garrison ['gærɪsn] *n* garnison *f*
garter ['gɑːtəʳ] *n* jarretière *f*; (US) jarretelle *f*
gas [gæs] *n* gaz *m*; (US: *gasoline*) essence *f* ♦ *vt* asphyxier; **~ cooker** (BRIT) *n* cuisinière *f* à gaz; **~ cylinder** *n* bouteille *f* de gaz; **~ fire** (BRIT) *n* radiateur *m* à gaz
gash [gæʃ] *n* entaille *f*; (*on face*) balafre *f*
gasket ['gæskɪt] *n* (AUT) joint *m* de culasse
gas mask *n* masque *m* à gaz
gas meter *n* compteur *m* à gaz
gasoline ['gæsəliːn] (US) *n* essence *f*
gasp [gɑːsp] *vi* haleter
gas: ~ ring *n* brûleur *m*; **~ station** (US) *n* station-service *f*; **~ tap** *n* bouton *m* (de cuisinière à gaz); (*on pipe*) robinet *m* à gaz
gastric ['gæstrɪk] *adj* gastrique; **~ flu** grippe *f* intestinale
gate [geɪt] *n* (*of garden*) portail *m*; (*of field*) barrière *f*; (*of building, at airport*) porte *f*
gateau ['gætəu] *n* (*pl* **~x**) (gros) gâteau à la crème
gatecrash *vt* s'introduire sans invitation dans
gateway *n* porte *f*
gather ['gæðəʳ] *vt* (*flowers, fruit*) cueillir; (*pick up*) ramasser; (*assemble*) rassembler, réunir; recueillir; (*understand*) comprendre; (SEWING) froncer ♦ *vi* (*assemble*) se rassembler; **to ~ speed** prendre de la vitesse; **~ing** *n* rassem-

blement *m*
gaudy ['gɔːdɪ] *adj* voyant(e)
gauge [geɪdʒ] *n* (*instrument*) jauge *f* ♦ *vt* jauger
gaunt [gɔːnt] *adj* (*thin*) décharné(e); (*grim, desolate*) désolé(e)
gauntlet ['gɔːntlɪt] *n* (*glove*) gant *m*
gauze [gɔːz] *n* gaze *f*
gave [geɪv] *pt of* **give**
gay [geɪ] *adj* (*homosexual*) homosexuel(le); (*cheerful*) gai(e), réjoui(e); (*colour etc*) gai, vif (vive)
gaze [geɪz] *n* regard *m* fixe ♦ *vi*: **to ~ at** fixer du regard
gazump [gə'zʌmp] (*BRIT*) *vi revenir sur une promesse de vente (pour accepter une offre plus intéressante)*
GB *abbr* = **Great Britain**
GCE *n abbr* (*BRIT*) = **General Certificate of Education**
GCSE *n abbr* (*BRIT*) = **General Certificate of Secondary Education**
gear [gɪə^r^] *n* matériel *m*, équipement *m*; attirail *m*; (*TECH*) engrenage *m*; (*AUT*) vitesse *f* ♦ *vt* (*fig: adapt*): **to ~ sth to** adapter qch à; **top** *or (US)* **high ~** quatrième (*or* cinquième) vitesse; **low ~** première vitesse; **in ~** en prise; **~ box** *n* boîte *f* de vitesses; **~ lever** (*US* **gear shift**) *n* levier *m* de vitesse
geese [giːs] *npl of* **goose**
gel [dʒɛl] *n* gel *m*
gem [dʒɛm] *n* pierre précieuse
Gemini ['dʒɛmɪnaɪ] *n* les Gémeaux *mpl*
gender ['dʒɛndə^r^] *n* genre *m*
gene [dʒiːn] *n* gène *m*
general ['dʒɛnərl] *n* général *m* ♦ *adj* général(e); **in ~** en général; **~ delivery** *n* poste restante; **~ election** *n* élection(s) législative(s); **~ knowledge** *n* connaissances générales; **~ly** *adv* généralement; **~ practitioner** *n* généraliste *m/f*
generate ['dʒɛnəreɪt] *vt* engendrer; (*electricity etc*) produire; **generation** *n* génération *f*; (*of electricity etc*) production *f*; **generator** *n* générateur *m*
generosity [dʒɛnə'rɔsɪtɪ] *n* générosité *f*
generous ['dʒɛnərəs] *adj* généreux (-euse); (*copious*) copieux(-euse)
genetic [dʒɪ'nɛtɪk] *adj*: **~ engineering** ingéniérie *f* génétique; **~ fingerprinting** système *m* d'empreinte génétique
genetically modified *adj* (*food etc*) génétiquement modifié(e)
genetics [dʒɪ'nɛtɪks] *n* génétique *f*
Geneva [dʒɪ'niːvə] *n* Genève
genial ['dʒiːnɪəl] *adj* cordial(e)
genitals ['dʒɛnɪtlz] *npl* organes génitaux
genius ['dʒiːnɪəs] *n* génie *m*
genteel [dʒɛn'tiːl] *adj* distingué(e)
gentle ['dʒɛntl] *adj* doux (douce)
gentleman ['dʒɛntlmən] *n* monsieur *m*; (*well-bred man*) gentleman *m*
gently ['dʒɛntlɪ] *adv* doucement
gentry ['dʒɛntrɪ] *n inv*: **the ~** la petite noblesse
gents [dʒɛnts] *n* W.-C. *mpl* (pour hommes)
genuine ['dʒɛnjuɪn] *adj* véritable, authentique; (*person*) sincère
geographical [dʒɪə'græfɪkl] *adj* géographique
geography [dʒɪ'ɔgrəfɪ] *n* géographie *f*
geology [dʒɪ'ɔlədʒɪ] *n* géologie *f*
geometric(al) [dʒɪə'mɛtrɪk(l)] *adj* géométrique
geometry [dʒɪ'ɔmətrɪ] *n* géométrie *f*
geranium [dʒɪ'reɪnɪəm] *n* géranium *m*
geriatric [dʒɛrɪ'ætrɪk] *adj* gériatrique
germ [dʒəːm] *n* (*MED*) microbe *m*
German ['dʒəːmən] *adj* allemand(e) ♦ *n* Allemand(e); (*LING*) allemand *m*; **~ measles** (*BRIT*) *n* rubéole *f*
Germany ['dʒəːmənɪ] *n* Allemagne *f*
gesture ['dʒɛstjə^r^] *n* geste *m*

KEYWORD

get [gɛt] (*pt, pp* **got**, *pp* **gotten** (*US*)) *vi* **1** (*become, be*) devenir; **to get old/tired** devenir vieux/fatigué, vieillir/se fatiguer; **to get drunk** s'enivrer; **to get killed** se faire tuer; **when do I get**

paid? quand est-ce que je serai payé?; **it's getting late** il se fait tard
2 (*go*): **to get to/from** aller à/de; **to get home** rentrer chez soi; **how did you get here?** comment es-tu arrivé ici?
3 (*begin*) commencer *or* se mettre à; **I'm getting to like him** je commence à l'apprécier; **let's get going** *or* **started** allons-y
4 (*modal aux vb*): **you've got to do it** il faut que vous le fassiez; **I've got to tell the police** je dois le dire à la police
♦ *vt* **1**: **to get sth done** (*do*) faire qch; (*have done*) faire faire qch; **to get one's hair cut** se faire couper les cheveux; **to get sb to do sth** faire faire qch à qn; **to get sb drunk** enivrer qn
2 (*obtain*: *money, permission, results*) obtenir, avoir; (*find*: *job, flat*) trouver; (*fetch*: *person, doctor, object*) aller chercher; **to get sth for sb** procurer qch à qn; **get me Mr Jones, please** (*on phone*) passez-moi Mr Jones, s'il vous plaît; **can I get you a drink?** est-ce que je peux vous servir à boire?
3 (*receive*: *present, letter*) recevoir, avoir; (*acquire*: *reputation*) avoir; (: *prize*) obtenir; **what did you get for your birthday?** qu'est-ce que tu as eu pour ton anniversaire?
4 (*catch*) prendre, saisir, attraper; (*hit*: *target etc*) atteindre; **to get sb by the arm/throat** prendre *or* saisir *or* attraper qn par le bras/à la gorge; **get him!** arrête-le!
5 (*take, move*) faire parvenir; **do you think we'll get it through the door?** on arrivera à le faire passer par la porte?; **I'll get you there somehow** je me débrouillerai pour t'y emmener
6 (*catch, take*: *plane, bus etc*) prendre
7 (*understand*) comprendre, saisir; (*hear*) entendre; **I've got it!** j'ai compris!, je saisis!; **I didn't get your name** je n'ai pas entendu votre nom
8 (*have, possess*): **to have got** avoir; **how many have you got?** vous en avez combien?
get about *vi* se déplacer; (*news*) se répandre
get along *vi* (*agree*) s'entendre; (*depart*) s'en aller; (*manage*) = **get by**
get at *vt fus* (*attack*) s'en prendre à; (*reach*) attraper, atteindre
get away *vi* partir, s'en aller; (*escape*) s'échapper
get away with *vt fus* en être quitte pour; se faire passer *or* pardonner
get back *vi* (*return*) rentrer ♦ *vt* récupérer, recouvrer
get by *vi* (*pass*) passer; (*manage*) se débrouiller
get down *vi, vt fus* descendre ♦ *vt* descendre; (*depress*) déprimer
get down to *vt fus* (*work*) se mettre à (faire)
get in *vi* rentrer; (*train*) arriver
get into *vt fus* entrer dans; (*car, train etc*) monter dans; (*clothes*) mettre, enfiler, endosser; **to get into bed/a rage** se mettre au lit/en colère
get off *vi* (*from train etc*) descendre; (*depart*: *person, car*) s'en aller; (*escape*) s'en tirer ♦ *vt* (*remove*: *clothes, stain*) enlever ♦ *vt fus* (*train, bus*) descendre de
get on *vi* (*at exam etc*) se débrouiller; (*agree*): **to get on (with)** s'entendre (avec) ♦ *vt fus* monter dans; (*horse*) monter sur
get out *vi* sortir; (*of vehicle*) descendre ♦ *vt* sortir
get out of *vt fus* sortir de; (*duty etc*) échapper à, se soustraire à
get over *vt fus* (*illness*) se remettre de
get round *vt fus* contourner; (*fig*: *person*) entortiller
get through *vi* (*TEL*) avoir la communication; **to get through to sb** atteindre qn
get together *vi* se réunir ♦ *vt* assem-

bler

get up *vi* (*rise*) se lever ♦ *vt fus* monter

get up to *vt fus* (*reach*) arriver à; (*prank etc*) faire

getaway ['gɛtəweɪ] *n* (*escape*) fuite *f*
geyser ['gi:zə^r] *n* (GEO) geyser *m*; (BRIT: *water heater*) chauffe-eau *m inv*
Ghana ['gɑ:nə] *n* Ghana *m*
ghastly ['gɑ:stlɪ] *adj* atroce, horrible; (*pale*) livide, blême
gherkin ['gə:kɪn] *n* cornichon *m*
ghetto blaster ['gɛtəu'blɑ:stə^r] *n* stéréo *f* portable
ghost [gəust] *n* fantôme *m*, revenant *m*
giant ['dʒaɪənt] *n* géant(e) ♦ *adj* géant(e), énorme
gibberish ['dʒɪbərɪʃ] *n* charabia *m*
giblets ['dʒɪblɪts] *npl* abats *mpl*
Gibraltar [dʒɪ'brɔ:ltə^r] *n* Gibraltar
giddy ['gɪdɪ] *adj* (*dizzy*): **to be** *or* **feel ~** avoir le vertige
gift [gɪft] *n* cadeau *m*; (*donation, ability*) don *m*; **~ed** *adj* doué(e); **~ shop** *n* boutique *f* de cadeaux; **~ token** *n* chèque-cadeau *m*
gigantic [dʒaɪ'gæntɪk] *adj* gigantesque
giggle ['gɪgl] *vi* pouffer (de rire), rire sottement
gill [dʒɪl] *n* (*measure*) = *0.25 pints (BRIT = 0.15 l, US = 0.12 l)*
gills [gɪlz] *npl* (*of fish*) ouïes *fpl*, branchies *fpl*
gilt [gɪlt] *adj* doré(e) ♦ *n* dorure *f*; **~-edged** *adj* (COMM) de premier ordre
gimmick ['gɪmɪk] *n* truc *m*
gin [dʒɪn] *n* (*liquor*) gin *m*
ginger ['dʒɪndʒə^r] *n* gingembre *m*; **~ ale, ~ beer** *n boisson gazeuse au gingembre*; **~bread** *n* pain *m* d'épices
gingerly ['dʒɪndʒəlɪ] *adv* avec précaution
gipsy ['dʒɪpsɪ] *n* = **gypsy**
giraffe [dʒɪ'rɑ:f] *n* girafe *f*
girder ['gə:də^r] *n* poutrelle *f*
girl [gə:l] *n* fille *f*, fillette *f*; (*young unmarried woman*) jeune fille; (*daughter*) fille; **an English ~** une jeune Anglaise; **~friend** *n* (*of girl*) amie *f*; (*of boy*) petite amie; **~ish** *adj* de petite *or* de jeune fille; (*for a boy*) efféminé(e)
giro ['dʒaɪrəu] *n* (*bank ~*) virement *m* bancaire; (*post office ~*) mandat *m*; (BRIT: *welfare cheque*) mandat *m* d'allocation chômage
gist [dʒɪst] *n* essentiel *m*
give [gɪv] (*pt* **gave**, *pp* **given**) *vt* donner ♦ *vi* (*break*) céder; (*stretch: fabric*) se prêter; **to ~ sb sth, ~ sth to sb** donner qch à qn; **to ~ a cry/sigh** pousser un cri/un soupir; **~ away** *vt* donner; (*~ free*) faire cadeau de; (*betray*) donner, trahir; (*disclose*) révéler; (*bride*) conduire à l'autel; **~ back** *vt* rendre; **~ in** *vi* céder ♦ *vt* donner; **~ off** *vt* dégager; **~ out** *vt* distribuer; annoncer; **~ up** *vi* renoncer ♦ *vt* renoncer à; **to ~ up smoking** arrêter de fumer; **to ~ o.s. up** se rendre; **~ way** (BRIT) *vi* céder; (AUT) céder la priorité
GLA (BRIT) *n abbr* (= *Greater London Authority*) *conseil municipal de Londres*
glacier ['glæsɪə^r] *n* glacier *m*
glad [glæd] *adj* content(e); **~ly** *adv* volontiers
glamorous ['glæmərəs] *adj* (*person*) séduisant(e); (*job*) prestigieux(-euse)
glamour ['glæmə^r] *n* éclat *m*, prestige *m*
glance [glɑ:ns] *n* coup *m* d'œil ♦ *vi*: **to ~ at** jeter un coup d'œil à; **glancing** *adj* (*blow*) oblique
gland *n* glande *f*
glare [glɛə^r] *n* (*of anger*) regard furieux; (*of light*) lumière éblouissante; (*of publicity*) feux *mpl* ♦ *vi* briller d'un éclat aveuglant; **to ~ at** lancer un regard furieux à; **glaring** *adj* (*mistake*) criant(e), qui saute aux yeux
glass [glɑ:s] *n* verre *m*; **~es** *npl* (*spectacles*) lunettes *fpl*; **~house** (BRIT) *n* (*for plants*) serre *f*; **~ware** *n* verrerie *f*
glaze [gleɪz] *vt* (*door, window*) vitrer;

(*pottery*) vernir ♦ *n* (*on pottery*) vernis *m*; **~d** *adj* (*pottery*) verni(e); (*eyes*) vitreux(-euse)

glazier ['gleɪzɪə^r] *n* vitrier *m*

gleam [gli:m] *vi* luire, briller

glean [gli:n] *vt* (*information*) glaner

glee [gli:] *n* joie *f*

glib [glɪb] *adj* (*person*) qui a du bagou; (*response*) désinvolte, facile

glide [glaɪd] *vi* glisser; (AVIAT, *birds*) planer; **~r** *n* (AVIAT) planeur *m*; **gliding** *n* (SPORT) vol *m* à voile

glimmer ['glɪmə^r] *n* lueur *f*

glimpse [glɪmps] *n* vision passagère, aperçu *m* ♦ *vt* entrevoir, apercevoir

glint [glɪnt] *vi* étinceler

glisten ['glɪsn] *vi* briller, luire

glitter ['glɪtə^r] *vi* scintiller, briller

gloat [gləut] *vi*: **to ~ (over)** jubiler (à propos de)

global ['gləubl] *adj* mondial(e); **~ warming** réchauffement *m* de la planète

globe [gləub] *n* globe *m*

gloom [glu:m] *n* obscurité *f*; (*sadness*) tristesse *f*, mélancolie *f*; **~y** *adj* sombre, triste, lugubre

glorious ['glɔ:rɪəs] *adj* glorieux(-euse); splendide

glory ['glɔ:rɪ] *n* gloire *f*; splendeur *f*

gloss [glɔs] *n* (*shine*) brillant *m*, vernis *m*; **~ over** *vt fus* glisser sur

glossary ['glɔsərɪ] *n* glossaire *m*

glossy ['glɔsɪ] *adj* brillant(e); **~ magazine** magazine *m* de luxe

glove [glʌv] *n* gant *m*; **~ compartment** *n* (AUT) boîte *f* à gants, vide-poches *m inv*

glow [gləu] *vi* rougeoyer; (*face*) rayonner; (*eyes*) briller

glower ['glauə^r] *vi*: **to ~ (at)** lancer des regards mauvais (à)

glucose ['glu:kəus] *n* glucose *m*

glue [glu:] *n* colle *f* ♦ *vt* coller

glum [glʌm] *adj* sombre, morne

glut [glʌt] *n* surabondance *f*

glutton ['glʌtn] *n* glouton(ne); **a ~ for work** un bourreau de travail; **a ~ for punishment** un masochiste (*fig*)

GM *abbr* (= *genetically modified*) génétiquement modifé(e)

gnat [næt] *n* moucheron *m*

gnaw [nɔ:] *vt* ronger

go [gəu] (*pt* **went**, *pp* **gone**, *pl* **~es**) *vi* aller; (*depart*) partir, s'en aller; (*work*) marcher; (*break etc*) céder; (*be sold*): **to ~ for £10** se vendre 10 livres; (*fit, suit*): **to ~ with** aller avec; (*become*): **to ~ pale/mouldy** pâlir/moisir ♦ *n*: **to have a ~ (at)** essayer (de faire); **to be on the ~** être en mouvement; **whose ~ is it?** à qui est-ce de jouer?; **he's ~ing to do** il va faire, il est sur le point de faire; **to ~ for a walk** aller se promener; **to ~ dancing** aller danser; **how did it ~?** comment est-ce que ça s'est passé?; **to ~ round the back/by the shop** passer par derrière/devant le magasin; **~ about** *vi* (*rumour*) se répandre ♦ *vt fus*: **how do I ~ about this?** comment dois-je m'y prendre (pour faire ceci)?; **~ after** *vt fus* (*pursue*) poursuivre, courir après; (*job, record etc*) essayer d'obtenir; **~ ahead** *vi* (*make progress*) avancer; (*get going*) y aller; **~ along** *vi* aller, avancer ♦ *vt fus* longer, parcourir; **~ away** *vi* partir, s'en aller; **~ back** *vi* rentrer; revenir; (*~ again*) retourner; **~ back on** *vt fus* (*promise*) revenir sur; **~ by** *vi* (*years, time*) passer, s'écouler ♦ *vt fus* s'en tenir à; en croire; **~ down** *vi* descendre; (*ship*) couler; (*sun*) se coucher ♦ *vt fus* descendre; **~ for** *vt fus* (*fetch*) aller chercher; (*like*) aimer; (*attack*) s'en prendre à, attaquer; **~ in** *vi* entrer; **~ in for** *vt fus* (*competition*) se présenter à; (*like*) aimer; **~ into** *vt fus* entrer dans; (*investigate*) étudier, examiner; (*embark on*) se lancer dans; **~ off** *vi* partir, s'en aller; (*food*) se gâter; (*explode*) sauter; (*event*) se dérouler ♦ *vt fus* ne plus aimer; **the gun went off** le coup est parti; **~ on** *vi* continuer; (*happen*) se passer; **to ~**

on doing continuer à faire; **~ out** *vi* sortir; (*fire, light*) s'éteindre; **~ over** *vt fus* (*check*) revoir, vérifier; **~ past** *vt fus*: **to ~ past sth** passer devant qch; **~ round** *vi* (*circulate: news, rumour*) circuler; (*revolve*) tourner; (*suffice*) suffire (pour tout le monde); **to ~ round to sb's** (*visit*) passer chez qn; **to ~ round (by)** (*make a detour*) faire un détour (par); **~ through** *vt fus* (*town etc*) traverser; **~ up** *vi* monter; (*price*) augmenter ♦ *vt fus* gravir; **~ with** *vt fus* (*suit*) aller avec; **~ without** *vt fus* se passer de

goad [gəud] *vt* aiguillonner

go-ahead *adj* dynamique, entreprenant(e) ♦ *n* feu vert

goal [gəul] *n* but *m*; **~keeper** *n* gardien *m* de but; **~post** *n* poteau *m* de but

goat [gəut] *n* chèvre *f*

gobble ['gɔbl] *vt* (*also:* **~ down, ~ up**) engloutir

go-between ['gəubıtwi:n] *n* intermédiaire *m/f*

god [gɔd] *n* dieu *m*; **G~** *n* Dieu *m*; **~child** *n* filleul(e); **~daughter** *n* filleule *f*; **~dess** *n* déesse *f*; **~father** *n* parrain *m*; **~-forsaken** *adj* maudit(e); **~mother** *n* marraine *f*; **~send** *n* aubaine *f*; **~son** *n* filleul *m*

goggles ['gɔglz] *npl* (*for skiing etc*) lunettes protectrices

going ['gəuıŋ] *n* (*conditions*) état *m* du terrain ♦ *adj*: **the ~ rate** le tarif (en vigueur)

gold [gəuld] *n* or *m* ♦ *adj* en or; (*reserves*) d'or; **~en** *adj* (*made of gold*) en or; (*gold in colour*) doré(e); **~fish** *n* poisson *m* rouge; **~-plated** *adj* plaqué(e) or *inv*; **~smith** *n* orfèvre *m*

golf [gɔlf] *n* golf *m*; **~ ball** *n* balle *f* de golf; (*on typewriter*) boule *m*; **~ club** *n* club *m* de golf; (*stick*) club *m*, crosse *f* de golf; **~ course** *n* (terrain *m* de) golf *m*; **~er** *n* joueur(-euse) de golf

gone [gɔn] *pp of* **go**

gong [gɔŋ] *n* gong *m*

good [gud] *adj* bon(ne); (*kind*) gentil(le); (*child*) sage ♦ *n* bien *m*; **~s** *npl* (COMM) marchandises *fpl*, articles *mpl*; **~!** bon!, très bien!; **to be ~ at** être bon en; **to be ~ for** être bon pour; **would you be ~ enough to ...?** auriez-vous la bonté *or* l'amabilité de ...?; **a ~ deal (of)** beaucoup (de); **a ~ many** beaucoup (de); **to make ~** *vi* (*succeed*) faire son chemin, réussir ♦ *vt* (*deficit*) combler; (*losses*) compenser; **it's no ~ complaining** cela ne sert à rien de se plaindre; **for ~** pour de bon, une fois pour toutes; **~ morning/afternoon!** bonjour!; **~ evening!** bonsoir!; **~ night!** bonsoir!; (*on going to bed*) bonne nuit!; **~bye** *excl* au revoir!; **G~ Friday** *n* Vendredi saint; **~-looking** *adj* beau (belle), bien *inv*; **~-natured** *adj* (*person*) qui a un bon naturel; **~ness** *n* (*of person*) bonté *f*; **for ~ness sake!** je vous en prie!; **~ness gracious!** mon Dieu!; **~s train** (BRIT) *n* train *m* de marchandises; **~will** *n* bonne volonté

goose [gu:s] (*pl* **geese**) *n* oie *f*

gooseberry ['guzbərı] *n* groseille *f* à maquereau; **to play ~** (BRIT) tenir la chandelle

gooseflesh ['gu:sflɛʃ] *n*, **goose pimples** *npl* chair *f* de poule

gore [gɔ:ʳ] *vt* encorner ♦ *n* sang *m*

gorge [gɔ:dʒ] *n* gorge *f* ♦ *vt*: **to ~ o.s. (on)** se gorger (de)

gorgeous ['gɔ:dʒəs] *adj* splendide, superbe

gorilla [gə'rılə] *n* gorille *m*

gorse [gɔ:s] *n* ajoncs *mpl*

gory ['gɔ:rı] *adj* sanglant(e); (*details*) horrible

go-slow ['gəu'sləu] (BRIT) *n* grève perlée

gospel ['gɔspl] *n* évangile *m*

gossip ['gɔsıp] *n* (*chat*) bavardages *mpl*; commérage *m*, cancans *mpl*; (*person*) commère *f* ♦ *vi* bavarder; (*maliciously*) cancaner, faire des commérages

got [gɔt] *pt, pp of* **get**; **~ten** (US) *pp of*

get

gout [gaut] *n* goutte *f*

govern ['gʌvən] *vt* gouverner; **~ess** *n* gouvernante *f*; **~ment** *n* gouvernement *m*; (*BRIT: ministers*) ministère *m*; **~or** *n* (*of state, bank*) gouverneur *m*; (*of school, hospital*) ≃ membre *m/f* du conseil d'établissement; (*BRIT: of prison*) directeur(-trice)

gown [gaun] *n* robe *f*; (*of teacher, BRIT: of judge*) toge *f*

GP *n abbr* = **general practitioner**

grab [græb] *vt* saisir, empoigner ♦ *vi*: **to ~ at** essayer de saisir

grace [greɪs] *n* grâce *f* ♦ *vt* honorer; (*adorn*) orner; **5 days' ~** cinq jours de répit; **~ful** *adj* gracieux(-euse), élégant(e); **gracious** ['greɪʃəs] *adj* bienveillant(e)

grade [greɪd] *n* (*COMM*) qualité *f*; (*in hierarchy*) catégorie *f*, grade *m*, échelon *m*; (*SCOL*) note *f*; (*US: school class*) classe *f* ♦ *vt* classer; **~ crossing** (*US*) *n* passage *m* à niveau; **~ school** (*US*) *n* école *f* primaire

gradient ['greɪdɪənt] *n* inclinaison *f*, pente *f*

gradual ['grædjuəl] *adj* graduel(le), progressif(-ive); **~ly** *adv* peu à peu, graduellement

graduate [*n* 'grædjuɪt, *vb* 'grædjueɪt] *n* diplômé(e), licencié(e); (*US: of high school*) bachelier(-ère) ♦ *vi* obtenir son diplôme; (*US*) obtenir son baccalauréat; **graduation** [grædju'eɪʃən] *n* (cérémonie *f* de) remise *f* des diplômes

graffiti [grə'fi:tɪ] *npl* graffiti *mpl*

graft [grɑ:ft] *n* (*AGR, MED*) greffe *f*; (*bribery*) corruption *f* ♦ *vt* greffer; **hard ~** (*BRIT: inf*) boulot acharné

grain [greɪn] *n* grain *m*

gram [græm] *n* gramme *m*

grammar ['græmə^r] *n* grammaire *f*; **~ school** (*BRIT*) *n* ≃ lycée *m*; **grammatical** [grə'mætɪkl] *adj* grammatical(e)

gramme [græm] *n* = **gram**

grand [grænd] *adj* magnifique, splendide; (*gesture etc*) noble; **~children** *npl* petits-enfants *mpl*; **~dad** (*inf*) *n* grand-papa *m*; **~daughter** *n* petite-fille *f*; **~father** *n* grand-père *m*; **~ma** (*inf*) *n* grand-maman *f*; **~mother** *n* grand-mère *f*; **~pa** (*inf*) *n* = **granddad**; **~parents** *npl* grands-parents *mpl*; **~ piano** *n* piano *m* à queue; **~son** *n* petit-fils *m*; **~stand** *n* (*SPORT*) tribune *f*

granite ['grænɪt] *n* granit *m*

granny ['grænɪ] (*inf*) *n* grand-maman *f*

grant [grɑ:nt] *vt* accorder; (*a request*) accéder à; (*admit*) concéder ♦ *n* (*SCOL*) bourse *f*; (*ADMIN*) subside *m*, subvention *f*; **to take it for ~ed that** trouver tout naturel que *+sub*; **to take sb for ~ed** considérer qn comme faisant partie du décor

granulated sugar ['grænjuleɪtɪd-] *n* sucre *m* en poudre

grape [greɪp] *n* raisin *m*

grapefruit ['greɪpfru:t] *n* pamplemousse *m*

graph [grɑ:f] *n* graphique *m*; **~ic** ['græfɪk] *adj* graphique; (*account, description*) vivant(e); **~ics** *n* arts *mpl* graphiques; graphisme *m* ♦ *npl* représentations *fpl* graphiques

grapple ['græpl] *vi*: **to ~ with** être aux prises avec

grasp [grɑ:sp] *vt* saisir ♦ *n* (*grip*) prise *f*; (*understanding*) compréhension *f*, connaissance *f*; **~ing** *adj* cupide

grass [grɑ:s] *n* herbe *f*; (*lawn*) gazon *m*; **~hopper** *n* sauterelle *f*; **~-roots** *adj* de la base, du peuple

grate [greɪt] *n* grille *f* de cheminée ♦ *vi* grincer ♦ *vt* (*CULIN*) râper

grateful ['greɪtful] *adj* reconnaissant(e)

grater ['greɪtə^r] *n* râpe *f*

gratifying ['grætɪfaɪɪŋ] *adj* agréable

grating ['greɪtɪŋ] *n* (*iron bars*) grille *f* ♦ *adj* (*noise*) grinçant(e)

gratitude ['grætɪtju:d] *n* gratitude *f*

gratuity [grə'tju:ɪtɪ] *n* pourboire *m*

grave [greɪv] *n* tombe *f* ♦ *adj* grave, sérieux(-euse)

gravel ['grævl] *n* gravier *m*
gravestone ['greɪvstəun] *n* pierre tombale
graveyard ['greɪvjɑ:d] *n* cimetière *m*
gravity ['grævɪtɪ] *n* (*PHYSICS*) gravité *f*; pesanteur *f*; (*seriousness*) gravité
gravy ['greɪvɪ] *n* jus *m* (de viande); sauce *f*
gray [greɪ] (*US*) *adj* = **grey**
graze [greɪz] *vi* paître, brouter ♦ *vt* (*touch lightly*) frôler, effleurer; (*scrape*) écorcher ♦ *n* écorchure *f*
grease [gri:s] *n* (*fat*) graisse *f*; (*lubricant*) lubrifiant *m* ♦ *vt* graisser; lubrifier; **~proof paper** (*BRIT*) *n* papier sulfurisé; **greasy** *adj* gras(se), graisseux(-euse)
great [greɪt] *adj* grand(e); (*inf*) formidable; **G~ Britain** *n* Grande-Bretagne *f*; **~-grandfather** *n* arrière-grand-père *m*; **~-grandmother** *n* arrière-grand-mère *f*; **~ly** *adv* très, grandement; (*with verbs*) beaucoup; **~ness** *n* grandeur *f*
Greece [gri:s] *n* Grèce *f*
greed [gri:d] *n* (*also:* **~iness**) avidité *f*; (*for food*) gourmandise *f*, gloutonnerie *f*; **~y** *adj* avide; gourmand(e), glouton(ne)
Greek [gri:k] *adj* grec (grecque) ♦ *n* Grec (Grecque); (*LING*) grec *m*
green [gri:n] *adj* vert(e); (*inexperienced*) (bien) jeune, naïf (naïve); (*POL*) vert(e), écologiste; (*ecological*) écologique ♦ *n* vert *m*; (*stretch of grass*) pelouse *f*; **~s** *npl* (*vegetables*) légumes verts; (*POL*): **the G~s** les Verts *mpl*; **the G~ Party** (*BRIT: POL*) le parti écologiste; **~ belt** *n* (*round town*) ceinture verte; **~ card** *n* (*AUT*) carte verte; (*US*) permis *m* de travail; **~ery** *n* verdure *f*; **~grocer's** (*BRIT*) *n* marchand *m* de fruits et légumes; **~house** *n* serre *f*; **~house effect** *n* effet *m* de serre; **~house gas** *n* gas *m* à effet de serre; **~ish** *adj* verdâtre
Greenland ['gri:nlənd] *n* Groenland *m*
greet [gri:t] *vt* accueillir; **~ing** *n* salutation *f*; **~ing(s) card** *n* carte *f* de vœux
gregarious [grə'geərɪəs] *adj* (*person*) sociable
grenade [grə'neɪd] *n* grenade *f*
grew [gru:] *pt of* **grow**
grey [greɪ] (*US* **gray**) *adj* gris(e); (*dismal*) sombre; **~-haired** *adj* grisonnant(e); **~hound** *n* lévrier *m*
grid [grɪd] *n* grille *f*; (*ELEC*) réseau *m*; **~lock** *n* (*traffic jam*) embouteillage *m*; **~locked** *adj*: **to be ~locked** (*roads*) être bloqué par un embouteillage; (*talks etc*) être suspendu
grief [gri:f] *n* chagrin *m*, douleur *f*
grievance ['gri:vəns] *n* doléance *f*, grief *m*
grieve [gri:v] *vi* avoir du chagrin; se désoler ♦ *vt* faire de la peine à, affliger; **to ~ for sb** (*dead person*) pleurer qn; **grievous** *adj* (*LAW*): **grievous bodily harm** coups *mpl* et blessures *fpl*
grill [grɪl] *n* (*on cooker*) gril *m*; (*food: also mixed ~*) grillade(s) *f(pl)* ♦ *vt* (*BRIT*) griller; (*inf: question*) cuisiner
grille [grɪl] *n* grille *f*, grillage *m*; (*AUT*) calandre *f*
grim [grɪm] *adj* sinistre, lugubre; (*serious, stern*) sévère
grimace [grɪ'meɪs] *n* grimace *f* ♦ *vi* grimacer, faire une grimace
grime [graɪm] *n* crasse *f*, saleté *f*
grin [grɪn] *n* large sourire *m* ♦ *vi* sourire
grind [graɪnd] (*pt, pp* **ground**) *vt* écraser; (*coffee, pepper etc*) moudre; (*US: meat*) hacher; (*make sharp*) aiguiser ♦ *n* (*work*) corvée *f*
grip [grɪp] *n* (*hold*) prise *f*, étreinte *f*; (*control*) emprise *f*; (*grasp*) connaissance *f*; (*handle*) poignée *f*; (*holdall*) sac *m* de voyage ♦ *vt* saisir, empoigner; **to come to ~s with** en venir aux prises avec; **~ping** *adj* prenant(e), palpitant(e)
grisly ['grɪzlɪ] *adj* sinistre, macabre
gristle ['grɪsl] *n* cartilage *m*
grit [grɪt] *n* gravillon *m*; (*courage*) cran *m* ♦ *vt* (*road*) sabler; **to ~ one's teeth** serrer les dents
groan [grəun] *n* (*of pain*) gémissement

m ♦ *vi* gémir

grocer ['grəusəʳ] *n* épicier *m*; **~ies** *npl* provisions *fpl*; **~'s (shop)** *n* épicerie *f*

groin [grɔɪn] *n* aine *f*

groom [gru:m]ʳ *n* palefrenier *m*; (*also:* **bridegroom**) marié *m* ♦ *vt* (*horse*) panser; (*fig*): **to ~ sb for** former qn pour; **well-~ed** très soigné(e)

groove [gru:v] *n* rainure *f*

grope [grəup] *vi*: **to ~ for** chercher à tâtons

gross [grəus] *adj* grossier(-ère); (COMM) brut(e); **~ly** *adv* (*greatly*) très, grandement

grotto ['grɔtəu] *n* grotte *f*

grotty ['grɔtɪ] (*inf*) *adj* minable, affreux(-euse)

ground [graund] *pt, pp of* **grind** ♦ *n* sol *m*, terre *f*; (*land*) terrain *m*, terres *fpl*; (SPORT) terrain; (US: *also:* **~ wire**) terre; (*reason*: *gen pl*) raison *f* ♦ *vt* (*plane*) empêcher de décoller, retenir au sol; (US: ELEC) équiper d'une prise de terre; **~s** *npl* (*of coffee etc*) marc *m*; (*gardens etc*) parc *m*, domaine *m*; **on the ~, to the ~** par terre; **to gain/lose ~** gagner/perdre du terrain; **~ cloth** (US) *n* = **groundsheet**; **~ing** *n* (*in education*) connaissances *fpl* de base; **~less** *adj* sans fondement; **~sheet** (BRIT) *n* tapis *m* de sol; **~ staff** *n* personnel *m* au sol; **~work** *n* préparation *f*

group [gru:p] *n* groupe *m* ♦ *vt* (*also:* **~ together**) grouper ♦ *vi* se grouper

grouse [graus] *n inv* (*bird*) grouse *f* ♦ *vi* (*complain*) rouspéter, râler

grove [grəuv] *n* bosquet *m*

grovel ['grɔvl] *vi* (*fig*) ramper

grow [grəu] (*pt* **grew**, *pp* **grown**) *vi* pousser, croître; (*person*) grandir; (*increase*) augmenter, se développer; (*become*): **to ~ rich/weak** s'enrichir/s'affaiblir; (*develop*): **he's ~n out of his jacket** sa veste est (devenue) trop petite pour lui ♦ *vt* cultiver, faire pousser; (*beard*) laisser pousser; **he'll ~ out of it!** ça lui passera!; **~ up** *vi* grandir; **~er** *n* producteur *m*; **~ing** *adj* (*fear, amount*) croissant(e), grandissant(e)

growl [graul] *vi* grogner

grown [grəun] *pp of* **grow**; **~-up** *n* adulte *m/f*, grande personne

growth [grəuθ] *n* croissance *f*, développement *m*; (*what has grown*) pousse *f*; poussée *f*; (MED) grosseur *f*, tumeur *f*

grub [grʌb] *n* larve *f*; (*inf*: *food*) bouffe *f*

grubby ['grʌbɪ] *adj* crasseux(-euse)

grudge [grʌdʒ] *n* rancune *f* ♦ *vt*: **to ~ sb sth** (*in giving*) donner qch à qn à contre-cœur; (*resent*) reprocher qch à qn; **to bear sb a ~ (for)** garder rancune *or* en vouloir à qn (de)

gruelling ['gruəlɪŋ] (US **grueling**) *adj* exténuant(e)

gruesome ['gru:səm] *adj* horrible

gruff [grʌf] *adj* bourru(e)

grumble ['grʌmbl] *vi* rouspéter, ronchonner

grumpy ['grʌmpɪ] *adj* grincheux(-euse)

grunt [grʌnt] *vi* grogner

G-string ['dʒi:strɪŋ] *n* (*garment*) cache-sexe *m inv*

guarantee [gærən'ti:] *n* garantie *f* ♦ *vt* garantir

guard [gɑ:d] *n* garde *f*; (*one man*) garde *m*; (BRIT: RAIL) chef *m* de train; (*on machine*) dispositif *m* de sûreté; (*also:* **fireguard**) garde-feu *m* ♦ *vt* garder, surveiller; (*protect*): **to ~ (against** *or* **from)** protéger (contre); **~ against** *vt* (*prevent*) empêcher, se protéger de; **~ed** *adj* (*fig*) prudent(e); **~ian** *n* gardien(ne); (*of minor*) tuteur(-trice); **~'s van** (BRIT) *n* (RAIL) fourgon *m*

guerrilla [gə'rɪlə] *n* guérillero *m*

guess [gɛs] *vt* deviner; (*estimate*) évaluer; (US) croire, penser ♦ *vi* deviner ♦ *n* supposition *f*, hypothèse *f*; **to take** *or* **have a ~** essayer de deviner; **~work** *n* hypothèse *f*

guest [gɛst] *n* invité(e); (*in hotel*) client(e); **~-house** *n* pension *f*; **~ room** *n* chambre *f* d'amis

guffaw [gʌ'fɔ:] *vi* pouffer de rire

guidance ['gaɪdəns] *n* conseils *mpl*
guide [gaɪd] *n* (*person, book etc*) guide *m*; (*BRIT: also:* **girl ~**) guide *f* ♦ *vt* guider; **~book** *n* guide *m*; **~ dog** *n* chien *m* d'aveugle; **~lines** *npl* (*fig*) instructions (générales), conseils *mpl*
guild [gɪld] *n* corporation *f*; cercle *m*, association *f*
guillotine ['gɪləti:n] *n* guillotine *f*
guilt [gɪlt] *n* culpabilité *f*; **~y** *adj* coupable
guinea pig ['gɪnɪ-] *n* cobaye *m*
guise [gaɪz] *n* aspect *m*, apparence *f*
guitar [gɪ'tɑ:ʳ] *n* guitare *f*
gulf [gʌlf] *n* golfe *m*; (*abyss*) gouffre *m*
gull [gʌl] *n* mouette *f*; (*larger*) goéland *m*
gullible ['gʌlɪbl] *adj* crédule
gully ['gʌlɪ] *n* ravin *m*; ravine *f*; couloir *m*
gulp [gʌlp] *vi* avaler sa salive ♦ *vt* (*also:* **~ down**) avaler
gum [gʌm] *n* (*ANAT*) gencive *f*; (*glue*) colle *f*; (*sweet: also ~drop*) boule *f* de gomme; (*also:* **chewing ~**) chewing-gum *m* ♦ *vt* coller; **~boots** (*BRIT*) *npl* bottes *fpl* en caoutchouc
gun [gʌn] *n* (*small*) revolver *m*, pistolet *m*; (*rifle*) fusil *m*, carabine *f*; (*cannon*) canon *m*; **~boat** *n* canonnière *f*; **~fire** *n* fusillade *f*; **~man** *n* bandit armé; **~point** *n*: **at ~point** sous la menace du pistolet (*or* fusil); **~powder** *n* poudre *f* à canon; **~shot** *n* coup *m* de feu
gurgle ['gə:gl] *vi* gargouiller; (*baby*) gazouiller
gush [gʌʃ] *vi* jaillir; (*fig*) se répandre en effusions
gust [gʌst] *n* (*of wind*) rafale *f*; (*of smoke*) bouffée *f*
gusto ['gʌstəu] *n* enthousiasme *m*
gut [gʌt] *n* intestin *m*, boyau *m*; **~s** *npl* (*inf: courage*) cran *m*
gutter ['gʌtəʳ] *n* (*in street*) caniveau *m*; (*of roof*) gouttière *f*
guy [gaɪ] *n* (*inf: man*) type *m*; (*also:* **~rope**) corde *f*; (*BRIT: figure*) effigie de Guy Fawkes (*brûlée en plein air le 5 novembre*)

Guy Fawkes' Night

Guy Fawkes' Night, que l'on appelle également "bonfire night", commémore l'échec du complot (le "Gunpowder Plot") contre James Ist et son parlement le 5 novembre 1605. L'un des conspirateurs, Guy Fawkes, avait été surpris dans les caves du parlement alors qu'il s'apprêtait à y mettre le feu. Chaque année pour le 5 novembre, les enfants préparent à l'avance une effigie de Guy Fawkes et ils demandent aux passants "un penny pour le guy" avec lequel ils pourront s'acheter des fusées de feu d'artifice. Beaucoup de gens font encore un feu dans leur jardin sur lequel ils brûlent le "guy".

guzzle ['gʌzl] *vt* avaler gloutonnement
gym [dʒɪm] *n* (*also:* **~nasium**) gymnase *m*; (*also:* **~nastics**) gym *f*; **~nast** *n* gymnaste *m/f*; **~nastics** [dʒɪm'næstɪks] *n, npl* gymnastique *f*; **~ shoes** *npl* chaussures *fpl* de gym; **~slip** (*BRIT*) *n* tunique *f* (d'écolière)
gynaecologist [gaɪnɪ'kɔlədʒɪst] (*US* **gynecologist**) *n* gynécologue *m/f*
gypsy ['dʒɪpsɪ] *n* gitan(e), bohémien(ne)

H, h

haberdashery [hæbə'dæʃərɪ] (*BRIT*) *n* mercerie *f*
habit ['hæbɪt] *n* habitude *f*; (*REL: costume*) habit *m*; **~ual** *adj* habituel(le); (*drinker, liar*) invétéré(e)
hack [hæk] *vt* hacher, tailler ♦ *n* (*pej: writer*) nègre *m*; **~er** *n* (*COMPUT*) pirate *m* (informatique); (*: enthusiast*) passionné(e) *m/f* des ordinateurs
hackneyed ['hæknɪd] *adj* usé(e), rebat-

tu(e)

had [hæd] *pt, pp of* **have**

haddock ['hædək] (*pl* ~ *or* **~s**) *n* églefin *m*; **smoked ~** haddock *m*

hadn't ['hædnt] = **had not**

haemorrhage ['hɛmərɪdʒ] (*US* **hemorrhage**) *n* hémorragie *f*

haemorrhoids ['hɛmərɔɪdz] (*US* **hemorrhoids**) *npl* hémorroïdes *fpl*

haggle ['hægl] *vi* marchander

Hague [heɪg] *n*: **The ~** La Haye

hail [heɪl] *n* grêle *f* ♦ *vt* (*call*) héler; (*acclaim*) acclamer ♦ *vi* grêler; **~stone** *n* grêlon *m*

hair [hɛəʳ] *n* cheveux *mpl*; (*of animal*) pelage *m*; (*single ~*: *on head*) cheveu *m*; (: *on body; of animal*) poil *m*; **to do one's ~** se coiffer; **~brush** *n* brosse *f* à cheveux; **~cut** *n* coupe *f* (de cheveux); **~do** *n* coiffure *f*; **~dresser** *n* coiffeur (-euse); **~dresser's** *n* salon *m* de coiffure, coiffeur *m*; **~ dryer** *n* sèche-cheveux *m*; **~ gel** *n* gel *m* pour cheveux; **~grip** *n* pince *f* à cheveux; **~net** *n* filet *m* à cheveux; **~piece** *n* perruque *f*; **~pin** *n* épingle *f* à cheveux; **~pin bend** (*US* **hairpin curve**) *n* virage *m* en épingle à cheveux; **~-raising** *adj* à (vous) faire dresser les cheveux sur la tête; **~ removing cream** *n* crème *f* dépilatoire; **~ spray** *n* laque *f* (pour les cheveux); **~style** *n* coiffure *f*; **~y** *adj* poilu(e); (*inf: fig*) effrayant(e)

hake [heɪk] (*pl* ~ *or* **~s**) *n* colin *m*, merlu *m*

half [hɑːf] (*pl* **halves**) *n* moitié *f*; (*of beer: also:* **~ pint**) ≃ demi *m*; (*RAIL, bus: also:* **~ fare**) demi-tarif *m* ♦ *adj* demi(e) ♦ *adv* (à) moitié, à demi; **~ a dozen** une demi-douzaine; **~ a pound** une demi-livre, ≃ 250 g; **two and a ~** deux et demi; **to cut sth in ~** couper qch en deux; **~-caste** ['hɑːfkɑːst] *n* métis(se); **~-hearted** *adj* tiède, sans enthousiasme; **~-hour** *n* demi-heure *f*; **~-mast: at ~-mast** *adv* (*flag*) en berne; **~penny** (*BRIT*) *n* demi-penny *m*; **~-price** *adj, adv*: **(at) ~-price** à moitié prix; **~ term** (*BRIT*) *n* (*SCOL*) congé *m* de demi-trimestre; **~-time** *n* mi-temps *f*; **~way** *adv* à mi-chemin

hall [hɔːl] *n* salle *f*; (*entrance way*) hall *m*, entrée *f*; (*US*) = **corridor**

hallmark ['hɔːlmɑːk] *n* poinçon *m*; (*fig*) marque *f*

hallo [hə'ləu] *excl* = **hello**

hall of residence (*BRIT*) (*pl* **halls of residence**) *n* résidence *f* universitaire

Hallowe'en ['hæləu'iːn] *n* veille *f* de la Toussaint

Hallowe'en

Selon la tradition, **Hallowe'en** *est la nuit des fantômes et des sorcières. En Écosse et aux États-Unis surtout (beaucoup moins en Angleterre) les enfants, pour fêter Hallowe'en, se déguisent ce soir-là et ils vont ainsi de porte en porte en demandant de petits cadeaux (du chocolat, une pomme etc).*

hallucination [həluːsɪ'neɪʃən] *n* hallucination *f*

hallway ['hɔːlweɪ] *n* vestibule *m*

halo ['heɪləu] *n* (*of saint etc*) auréole *f*

halt [hɔːlt] *n* halte *f*, arrêt *m* ♦ *vt* (*progress etc*) interrompre ♦ *vi* faire halte, s'arrêter

halve [hɑːv] *vt* (*apple etc*) partager *or* diviser en deux; (*expense*) réduire de moitié; **~s** *npl of* **half**

ham [hæm] *n* jambon *m*

hamburger ['hæmbəːgəʳ] *n* hamburger *m*

hamlet ['hæmlɪt] *n* hameau *m*

hammer ['hæməʳ] *n* marteau *m* ♦ *vt* (*nail*) enfoncer; (*fig*) démolir ♦ *vi* (*on door*) frapper à coups redoublés; **to ~ an idea into sb** faire entrer de force une idée dans la tête de qn

hammock ['hæmək] *n* hamac *m*

hamper ['hæmpəʳ] *vt* gêner ♦ *n* panier *m* (d'osier)

hamster ['hæmstəʳ] *n* hamster *m*

hand [hænd] *n* main *f*; (*of clock*) aiguille *f*; (*~writing*) écriture *f*; (*worker*) ouvrier(-ère); (*at cards*) jeu *m* ♦ *vt* passer, donner; **to give** *or* **lend sb a ~** donner un coup de main à qn; **at ~** à portée de la main; **in ~** (*time*) à disposition; (*job, situation*) en main; **to be on ~** (*person*) être disponible; (*emergency services*) se tenir prêt(e) (à intervenir); **to ~** (*information etc*) sous la main, à portée de la main; **on the one ~ ..., on the other ~** d'une part ..., d'autre part; **~ in** *vt* remettre; **~ out** *vt* distribuer; **~ over** *vt* transmettre; céder; **~bag** *n* sac *m* à main; **~book** *n* manuel *m*; **~brake** *n* frein *m* à main; **~cuffs** *npl* menottes *fpl*; **~ful** *n* poignée *f*

handicap ['hændıkæp] *n* handicap *m* ♦ *vt* handicaper; **mentally/physically ~ped** handicapé(e) mentalement/physiquement

handicraft ['hændıkrɑ:ft] *n* (travail *m* d')artisanat *m*, technique artisanale; (*object*) objet artisanal

handiwork ['hændıwə:k] *n* ouvrage *m*

handkerchief ['hæŋkətʃıf] *n* mouchoir *m*

handle ['hændl] *n* (*of door etc*) poignée *f*; (*of cup etc*) anse *f*; (*of knife etc*) manche *m*; (*of saucepan*) queue *f*; (*for winding*) manivelle *f* ♦ *vt* toucher, manier; (*deal with*) s'occuper de; (*treat*: *people*) prendre; **"~ with care"** "fragile"; **to fly off the ~** s'énerver; **~bar(s)** *n(pl)* guidon *m*

hand: ~-luggage *n* bagages *mpl* à main; **~made** *adj* fait(e) à la main; **~out** *n* (*from government, parents*) aide *f*, don *m*; (*leaflet*) documentation *f*, prospectus *m*; (*summary of lecture*) polycopié *m*; **~rail** *n* rampe *f*, main courante; **~set** *n* (*TEL*) combiné *m*; **please replace the ~set** raccrochez s'il vous plaît; **~shake** *n* poignée *f* de main

handsome ['hænsəm] *adj* beau (belle); (*profit, return*) considérable

handwriting ['hændraıtıŋ] *n* écriture *f*

handy ['hændı] *adj* (*person*) adroit(e); (*close at hand*) sous la main; (*convenient*) pratique

hang [hæŋ] (*pt, pp* **hung**) *vt* accrocher; (*criminal*: *pt, pp*: *~ed*) pendre ♦ *vi* pendre; (*hair, drapery*) tomber; **to get the ~ of (doing) sth** (*inf*) attraper le coup pour faire qch; **~ about** *vi* traîner; **~ around** *vi* = **hang about**; **~ on** *vi* (*wait*) attendre; **~ up** *vi* (*TEL*): **to ~ up (on sb)** raccrocher (au nez de qn) ♦ *vt* (*coat, painting etc*) accrocher, suspendre

hangar ['hæŋə^r] *n* hangar *m*

hanger ['hæŋə^r] *n* cintre *m*, portemanteau *m*; **~-on** *n* parasite *m*

hang: ~-gliding *n* deltaplane *m*, vol *m* libre; **~over** *n* (*after drinking*) gueule *f* de bois; **~-up** *n* complexe *m*

hanker ['hæŋkə^r] *vi*: **to ~ after** avoir envie de

hankie, hanky ['hæŋkı] *n abbr* = **handkerchief**

haphazard [hæp'hæzəd] *adj* fait(e) au hasard, fait(e) au petit bonheur

happen ['hæpən] *vi* arriver; se passer, se produire; **it so ~s that** il se trouve que; **as it ~s** justement; **~ing** *n* événement *m*

happily ['hæpılı] *adv* heureusement; (*cheerfully*) joyeusement

happiness ['hæpınıs] *n* bonheur *m*

happy ['hæpı] *adj* heureux(-euse); **~ with** (*arrangements etc*) satisfait(e) de; **to be ~ to do** faire volontiers; **~ birthday!** bon anniversaire!; **~-go-lucky** *adj* insouciant(e); **~ hour** *n heure pendant laquelle les consommations sont à prix réduit*

harass ['hærəs] *vt* accabler, tourmenter; **~ment** *n* tracasseries *fpl*

harbour ['hɑ:bə^r] (*US* **harbor**) *n* port *m* ♦ *vt* héberger, abriter; (*hope, fear etc*) entretenir

hard [hɑ:d] *adj* dur(e); (*question, problem*) difficile, dur(e); (*facts, evidence*) concret(-ète) ♦ *adv* (*work*) dur; (*think,* *try*) sérieusement; **to look ~ at** regarder fixement; (*thing*) regarder de près; **no ~ feelings!** sans rancune!; **to be ~ of hearing** être dur(e) d'oreille; **to be ~ done by** être traité(e) injustement; **~back** *n* livre relié; **~ cash** *n* espèces *fpl*; **~ disk** *n* (COMPUT) disque dur; **~en** *vt* durcir; (*fig*) endurcir ♦ *vi* durcir; **~-headed** *adj* réaliste; décidé(e); **~ labour** *n* travaux forcés

hardly ['hɑːdlɪ] *adv* (*scarcely, no sooner*) à peine; **~ anywhere/ever** presque nulle part/jamais

hard: ~ship *n* épreuves *fpl*; **~ shoulder** (BRIT) *n* (AUT) accotement stabilisé; **~ up** (*inf*) *adj* fauché(e); **~ware** *n* quincaillerie *f*; (COMPUT, MIL) matériel *m*; **~ware shop** *n* quincaillerie *f*; **~-wearing** *adj* solide; **~-working** *adj* travailleur(-euse)

hardy ['hɑːdɪ] *adj* robuste; (*plant*) résistant(e) au gel

hare [hɛəʳ] *n* lièvre *m*; **~-brained** *adj* farfelu(e)

harm [hɑːm] *n* mal *m*; (*wrong*) tort *m* ♦ *vt* (*person*) faire du mal *or* du tort à; (*thing*) endommager; **out of ~'s way** à l'abri du danger, en lieu sûr; **~ful** *adj* nuisible; **~less** *adj* inoffensif(-ive); sans méchanceté

harmony ['hɑːmənɪ] *n* harmonie *f*

harness ['hɑːnɪs] *n* harnais *m*; (*safety* ~) harnais de sécurité ♦ *vt* (*horse*) harnacher; (*resources*) exploiter

harp [hɑːp] *n* harpe *f* ♦ *vi*: **to ~ on about** rabâcher

harrowing ['hærəuɪŋ] *adj* déchirant(e), très pénible

harsh [hɑːʃ] *adj* (*hard*) dur(e); (*severe*) sévère; (*unpleasant*: *sound*) discordant(e); (: *light*) cru(e)

harvest ['hɑːvɪst] *n* (*of corn*) moisson *f*; (*of fruit*) récolte *f*; (*of grapes*) vendange *f* ♦ *vt* moissonner; récolter; vendanger

has [hæz] *vb see* **have**

hash [hæʃ] *n* (CULIN) hachis *m*; (*fig*: *mess*) gâchis *m*

hasn't ['hæznt] = **has not**

hassle ['hæsl] *n* (*inf*: *bother*) histoires *fpl*, tracas *mpl*

haste [heɪst] *n* hâte *f*; précipitation *f*; **~n** ['heɪsn] *vt* hâter, accélérer ♦ *vi* se hâter, s'empresser; **hastily** *adv* à la hâte; précipitamment; **hasty** *adj* hâtif(-ive); précipité(e)

hat [hæt] *n* chapeau *m*

hatch [hætʃ] *n* (NAUT: *also*: **~way**) écoutille *f*; (*also*: **service ~**) passe-plats *m inv* ♦ *vi* éclore; **~back** *n* (AUT) modèle *m* avec hayon arrière

hatchet ['hætʃɪt] *n* hachette *f*

hate [heɪt] *vt* haïr, détester ♦ *n* haine *f*; **~ful** *adj* odieux(-euse), détestable; **hatred** ['heɪtrɪd] *n* haine *f*

haughty ['hɔːtɪ] *adj* hautain(e), arrogant(e)

haul [hɔːl] *vt* traîner, tirer ♦ *n* (*of fish*) prise *f*; (*of stolen goods etc*) butin *m*; **~age** *n* transport routier; (*costs*) frais *mpl* de transport; **~ier** ['hɔːlɪəʳ] (US **hauler**) *n* (*company*) transporteur (routier); (*driver*) camionneur *m*

haunch [hɔːntʃ] *n* hanche *f*; (*of meat*) cuissot *m*

haunt [hɔːnt] *vt* (*subj*: *ghost, fear*) hanter; (: *person*) fréquenter ♦ *n* repaire *m*

KEYWORD

have [hæv] (*pt, pp* **had**) *aux vb* **1** (*gen*) avoir; être; **to have arrived/gone** être arrivé(e)/allé(e); **to have eaten/slept** avoir mangé/dormi; **he has been promoted** il a eu une promotion

2 (*in tag questions*): **you've done it, haven't you?** vous l'avez fait, n'est-ce pas?

3 (*in short answers and questions*): **no I haven't/yes we have!** mais non!/mais si!; **so I have!** ah oui!, oui c'est vrai!; **I've been there before, have you?** j'y suis déjà allé, et vous?

♦ *modal aux vb* (*be obliged*): **to have (got) to do sth** devoir faire qch; être obligé(e) de faire qch; **she has (got)**

to do it elle doit le faire, il faut qu'elle le fasse; **you haven't to tell her** vous ne devez pas le lui dire

♦ *vt* **1** (*possess, obtain*) avoir; **he has (got) blue eyes/dark hair** il a les yeux bleus/les cheveux bruns; **may I have your address?** puis-je avoir votre adresse?

2 (*+noun: take, hold etc*): **to have breakfast/a bath/a shower** prendre le petit déjeuner/un bain/une douche; **to have dinner/lunch** dîner/déjeuner; **to have a swim** nager; **to have a meeting** se réunir; **to have a party** organiser une fête

3: to have sth done faire faire qch; **to have one's hair cut** se faire couper les cheveux; **to have sb do sth** faire faire qch à qn

4 (*experience, suffer*) avoir; **to have a cold/flu** avoir un rhume/la grippe; **to have an operation** se faire opérer

5 (*inf: dupe*) avoir; **he's been had** il s'est fait avoir *or* rouler

have out *vt*: **to have it out with sb** (*settle a problem etc*) s'expliquer (franchement) avec qn

haven ['heɪvn] *n* port *m*; (*fig*) havre *m*

haven't ['hævnt] = **have not**

havoc ['hævək] *n* ravages *mpl*

hawk [hɔːk] *n* faucon *m*

hay [heɪ] *n* foin *m*; **~ fever** *n* rhume *m* des foins; **~stack** *n* meule *f* de foin

haywire (*inf*) *adj*: **to go ~** (*machine*) se détraquer; (*plans*) mal tourner

hazard ['hæzəd] *n* (*danger*) danger *m*, risque *m* ♦ *vt* risquer, hasarder; **~ (warning) lights** *npl* (AUT) feux *mpl* de détresse

haze [heɪz] *n* brume *f*

hazelnut ['heɪzlnʌt] *n* noisette *f*

hazy ['heɪzɪ] *adj* brumeux(-euse); (*idea*) vague

he [hiː] *pron* il; **it is ~ who ...** c'est lui qui ...

head [hɛd] *n* tête *f*; (*leader*) chef *m*; (*of school*) directeur(-trice) ♦ *vt* (*list*) être en tête de; (*group*) être à la tête de; **~s (or tails)** pile (ou face); **~ first** la tête la première; **~ over heels in love** follement *or* éperdument amoureux(-euse); **to ~ a ball** faire une tête; **~ for** *vt fus* se diriger vers; **~ache** *n* mal *m* de tête; **~dress** (BRIT) *n* (*of Red Indian etc*) coiffure *f*; **~ing** *n* titre *m*; **~lamp** (BRIT) *n* = **headlight**; **~land** *n* promontoire *m*, cap *m*; **~light** *n* phare *m*; **~line** *n* titre *m*; **~long** *adv* (*fall*) la tête la première; (*rush*) tête baissée; **~master** *n* directeur *m*; **~mistress** *n* directrice *f*; **~ office** *n* bureau central, siège *m*; **~-on** *adj* (*collision*) de plein fouet; (*confrontation*) en face à face; **~phones** *npl* casque *m* (à écouteurs); **~quarters** *npl* bureau *or* siège central; (MIL) quartier général; **~rest** *n* appui-tête *m*; **~room** *n* (*in car*) hauteur *f* de plafond; (*under bridge*) hauteur limite; **~scarf** *n* foulard *m*; **~strong** *adj* têtu(e), entêté(e); **~ teacher** *n* directeur(-trice); (*of secondary school*) proviseur *m*; **~ waiter** *n* maître *m* d'hôtel; **~way** *n*: **to make ~way** avancer, faire des progrès; **~wind** *n* vent *m* contraire; (NAUT) vent debout; **~y** *adj* capiteux(-euse); enivrant(e); (*experience*) grisant(e)

heal [hiːl] *vt, vi* guérir

health [hɛlθ] *n* santé *f*; **~ food** *n* aliment(s) naturel(s); **~ food shop** *n* magasin *m* diététique; **H~ Service** (BRIT) *n*: **the H~ Service** ≃ la Sécurité sociale; **~y** *adj* (*person*) en bonne santé; (*climate, food, attitude etc*) sain(e), bon(ne) pour la santé

heap [hiːp] *n* tas *m* ♦ *vt*: **to ~ (up)** entasser, amonceler; **she ~ed her plate with cakes** elle a chargé son assiette de gâteaux

hear [hɪə*] (*pt, pp* **heard**) *vt* entendre; (*news*) apprendre ♦ *vi* entendre; **to ~ about** entendre parler de; avoir des nouvelles de; **to ~ from sb** recevoir *or* avoir des nouvelles de qn; **~ing** *n*

(*sense*) ouïe *f*; (*of witnesses*) audition *f*; (*of a case*) audience *f*; **~ing aid** *n* appareil *m* acoustique; **~say**: **by ~say** *adv* par ouï-dire *m*
hearse [hə:s] *n* corbillard *m*
heart [hɑ:t] *n* cœur *m*; **~s** *npl* (CARDS) cœur; **to lose/take ~** perdre/prendre courage; **at ~** au fond; **by ~** (*learn, know*) par cœur; **~ attack** *n* crise *f* cardiaque; **~beat** *n* battement *m* du cœur; **~breaking** *adj* déchirant(e), qui fend le cœur; **~broken** *adj*: **to be ~broken** avoir beaucoup de chagrin *or* le cœur brisé; **~burn** *n* brûlures *fpl* d'estomac; **~ failure** *n* arrêt *m* du cœur; **~felt** *adj* sincère
hearth [hɑ:θ] *n* foyer *m*, cheminée *f*
heartily ['hɑ:tɪlɪ] *adv* chaleureusement; (*laugh*) de bon cœur; (*eat*) de bon appétit; **to agree ~** être entièrement d'accord
hearty ['hɑ:tɪ] *adj* chaleureux(-euse); (*appetite*) robuste; (*dislike*) cordial(e)
heat [hi:t] *n* chaleur *f*; (*fig*) feu *m*, agitation *f*; (SPORT: *also:* **qualifying ~**) éliminatoire *f* ♦ *vt* chauffer; **~ up** *vi* (*water*) chauffer; (*room*) se réchauffer ♦ *vt* réchauffer; **~ed** *adj* chauffé(e); (*fig*) passionné(e), échauffé(e); **~er** *n* appareil *m* de chauffage; radiateur *m*; (*in car*) chauffage *m*; (*water heater*) chauffe-eau *m*
heath [hi:θ] (BRIT) *n* lande *f*
heather ['hɛðəʳ] *n* bruyère *f*
heating ['hi:tɪŋ] *n* chauffage *m*
heatstroke ['hi:tstrəuk] *n* (MED) coup *m* de chaleur
heat wave *n* vague *f* de chaleur
heave [hi:v] *vt* soulever (avec effort); (*drag*) traîner ♦ *vi* se soulever; (*retch*) avoir un haut-le-cœur; **to ~ a sigh** pousser un soupir
heaven ['hɛvn] *n* ciel *m*, paradis *m*; (*fig*) paradis; **~ly** *adj* céleste, divin(e)
heavily ['hɛvɪlɪ] *adv* lourdement; (*drink, smoke*) beaucoup; (*sleep, sigh*) profondément
heavy ['hɛvɪ] *adj* lourd(e); (*work, sea, rain, eater*) gros(se); (*snow*) beaucoup de; (*drinker, smoker*) grand(e); (*breathing*) bruyant(e); (*schedule, week*) chargé(e); **~ goods vehicle** *n* poids lourd; **~weight** *n* (SPORT) poids lourd
Hebrew ['hi:bru:] *adj* hébraïque ♦ *n* (LING) hébreu *m*
Hebrides ['hɛbrɪdi:z] *npl*: **the ~** les Hébrides *fpl*
heckle ['hɛkl] *vt* interpeller (*un orateur*)
hectic ['hɛktɪk] *adj* agité(e), trépidant(e)
he'd [hi:d] = **he would**; **he had**
hedge [hɛdʒ] *n* haie *f* ♦ *vi* se dérober; **to ~ one's bets** (*fig*) se couvrir
hedgehog ['hɛdʒhɔg] *n* hérisson *m*
heed [hi:d] *vt* (*also:* **take ~ of**) tenir compte de; **~less** *adj* insouciant(e)
heel [hi:l] *n* talon *m* ♦ *vt* retalonner
hefty ['hɛftɪ] *adj* (*person*) costaud(e); (*parcel*) lourd(e); (*profit*) gros(se)
heifer ['hɛfəʳ] *n* génisse *f*
height [haɪt] *n* (*of person*) taille *f*, grandeur *f*; (*of object*) hauteur *f*; (*of plane, mountain*) altitude *f*; (*high ground*) hauteur, éminence *f*; (*fig: of glory*) sommet *m*; (*: of luxury, stupidity*) comble *m*; **~en** *vt* (*fig*) augmenter
heir [ɛəʳ] *n* héritier *m*; **~ess** *n* héritière *f*; **~loom** *n* héritage *m*, meuble *m* (*or* bijou *m or* tableau *m*) de famille
held [hɛld] *pt, pp of* **hold**
helicopter ['hɛlɪkɔptəʳ] *n* hélicoptère *m*
hell [hɛl] *n* enfer *m*; **~!** (*inf!*) merde!
he'll [hi:l] = **he will**; **he shall**
hellish ['hɛlɪʃ] (*inf*) *adj* infernal(e)
hello [hə'ləu] *excl* bonjour!; (*to attract attention*) hé!; (*surprise*) tiens!
helm [hɛlm] *n* (NAUT) barre *f*
helmet ['hɛlmɪt] *n* casque *m*
help [hɛlp] *n* aide *f*; (*charwoman*) femme *f* de ménage ♦ *vt* aider; **~!** au secours!; **~ yourself** servez-vous; **he can't ~ it** il ne peut pas s'en empêcher; **~er** *n* aide *m/f*, assistant(e); **~ful** *adj* serviable, obligeant(e); (*useful*) utile;

~ing *n* portion *f*; **~less** *adj* impuissant(e); (*defenceless*) faible
hem [hɛm] *n* ourlet *m* ♦ *vt* ourler; **~ in** *vt* cerner
hemorrhage ['hɛmərɪdʒ] (*US*) *n* = **haemorrhage**
hemorrhoids ['hɛmərɔɪdz] (*US*) *npl* = **haemorrhoids**
hen [hɛn] *n* poule *f*
hence [hɛns] *adv* (*therefore*) d'où, de là; **2 years ~** d'ici 2 ans, dans 2 ans; **~forth** *adv* dorénavant
her [həːʳ] *pron* (*direct*) la, l'; (*indirect*) lui; (*stressed, after prep*) elle ♦ *adj* son (sa), ses *pl*; *see also* **me**; **my**
herald ['hɛrəld] *n* héraut *m* ♦ *vt* annoncer; **~ry** *n* (*study*) héraldique *f*; (*coat of arms*) blason *m*
herb [həːb] *n* herbe *f*
herd [həːd] *n* troupeau *m*
here [hɪəʳ] *adv* ici; (*time*) alors ♦ *excl* tiens!, tenez!; **~!** présent!; **~ is, ~ are** voici; **~ he/she is!** le/la voici!; **~after** *adv* après, plus tard; **~by** *adv* (*formal*: *in letter*) par la présente
hereditary [hɪ'rɛdɪtrɪ] *adj* héréditaire
heresy ['hɛrəsɪ] *n* hérésie *f*
heritage ['hɛrɪtɪdʒ] *n* (*of country*) patrimoine *m*
hermit ['həːmɪt] *n* ermite *m*
hernia ['həːnɪə] *n* hernie *f*
hero ['hɪərəu] (*pl* **~es**) *n* héros *m*
heroin ['hɛrəuɪn] *n* héroïne *f*
heroine ['hɛrəuɪn] *n* héroïne *f*
heron ['hɛrən] *n* héron *m*
herring ['hɛrɪŋ] *n* hareng *m*
hers [həːz] *pron* le (la) sien(ne), les siens (siennes); *see also* **mine[1]**
herself [həː'sɛlf] *pron* (*reflexive*) se; (*emphatic*) elle-même; (*after prep*) elle; *see also* **oneself**
he's [hiːz] = **he is; he has**
hesitant ['hɛzɪtənt] *adj* hésitant(e), indécis(e)
hesitate ['hɛzɪteɪt] *vi* hésiter; **hesitation** [hɛzɪ'teɪʃən] *n* hésitation *f*
heterosexual ['hɛtərəu'sɛksjuəl] *adj, n* hétérosexuel(le)
heyday ['heɪdeɪ] *n*: **the ~ of** l'âge *m* d'or de, les beaux jours de
HGV *n abbr* = **heavy goods vehicle**
hi [haɪ] *excl* salut!; (*to attract attention*) hé!
hiatus [haɪ'eɪtəs] *n* (*gap*) lacune *f*; (*interruption*) pause *f*
hibernate ['haɪbəneɪt] *vi* hiberner
hiccough, hiccup ['hɪkʌp] *vi* hoqueter; **~s** *npl* hoquet *m*
hide [haɪd] (*pt* **hid**, *pp* **hidden**) *n* (*skin*) peau *f* ♦ *vt* cacher ♦ *vi*: **to ~ (from sb)** se cacher (de qn); **~-and-seek** *n* cache-cache *m*
hideous ['hɪdɪəs] *adj* hideux(-euse)
hiding ['haɪdɪŋ] *n* (*beating*) correction *f*, volée *f* de coups; **to be in ~** (*concealed*) se tenir caché(e)
hierarchy ['haɪərɑːkɪ] *n* hiérarchie *f*
hi-fi ['haɪfaɪ] *n* hi-fi *f inv* ♦ *adj* hi-fi *inv*
high [haɪ] *adj* haut(e); (*speed, respect, number*) grand(e); (*price*) élevé(e); (*wind*) fort(e), violent(e); (*voice*) aigu (aiguë) ♦ *adv* haut; **20 m ~** haut(e) de 20 m; **~brow** *adj, n* intellectuel(le); **~chair** *n* (*child's*) chaise haute; **~er education** *n* études supérieures; **~-handed** *adj* très autoritaire; très cavalier(-ère); **~-heeled** *adj* à hauts talons; **~ jump** *n* (*SPORT*) saut *m* en hauteur; **~lands** *npl* Highlands *mpl*; **~light** *n* (*fig*: *of event*) point culminant ♦ *vt* faire ressortir, souligner; **~lights** *npl* (*in hair*) reflets *mpl*; **~ly** *adv* très, fort, hautement; **to speak/think ~ly of sb** dire/penser beaucoup de bien de qn; **~ly paid** *adj* très bien payé(e); **~ly strung** *adj* nerveux(-euse), toujours tendu(e); **~ness** *n*: **Her** (*or* **His**) **H~ness** Son Altesse *f*; **~-pitched** *adj* aigu (aiguë); **~-rise** *adj*: **~-rise block, ~-rise flats** tour *f* (d'habitation); **~ school** *n* lycée *m*; (*US*) établissement *m* d'enseignement supérieur; **~ season** (*BRIT*) *n* haute saison; **~ street** (*BRIT*) *n* grand-rue *f*; **~way** *n* route nationale;

H~way Code (BRIT) *n* code *m* de la route

hijack ['haɪdʒæk] *vt* (*plane*) détourner; **~er** *n* pirate *m* de l'air

hike [haɪk] *vi* aller *or* faire des excursions à pied ♦ *n* excursion *f* à pied, randonnée *f*; **~r** *n* promeneur(-euse), excursionniste *m/f*; **hiking** *n* excursions *fpl* à pied

hilarious [hɪ'lɛərɪəs] *adj* (*account, event*) désopilant(e)

hill [hɪl] *n* colline *f*; (*fairly high*) montagne *f*; (*on road*) côte *f*; **~side** *n* (flanc *m* de) coteau *m*; **~-walking** *n* randonnée *f* de basse montagne; **~y** *adj* vallonné(e); montagneux(-euse)

hilt [hɪlt] *n* (*of sword*) garde *f*; **to the ~** (*fig: support*) à fond

him [hɪm] *pron* (*direct*) le, l'; (*stressed, indirect, after prep*) lui; *see also* **me**; **~self** *pron* (*reflexive*) se; (*emphatic*) lui-même; (*after prep*) lui; *see also* **oneself**

hinder ['hɪndə^r] *vt* gêner; (*delay*) retarder; **hindrance** *n* gêne *f*, obstacle *m*

hindsight ['haɪndsaɪt] *n*: **with ~** avec du recul, rétrospectivement

Hindu ['hɪndu:] *adj* hindou(e)

hinge [hɪndʒ] *n* charnière *f* ♦ *vi* (*fig*): **to ~ on** dépendre de

hint [hɪnt] *n* allusion *f*; (*advice*) conseil *m* ♦ *vt*: **to ~ that** insinuer que ♦ *vi*: **to ~ at** faire une allusion à

hip [hɪp] *n* hanche *f*

hippie ['hɪpɪ] *n* hippie *m/f*

hippo ['hɪpəu] (*pl* **~s**), **hippopotamus** [hɪpə'pɔtəməs] (*pl* **~potamuses** *or* **~potami**) *n* hippopotame *m*

hire ['haɪə^r] *vt* (BRIT: *car, equipment*) louer; (*worker*) embaucher, engager ♦ *n* location *f*; **for ~** à louer; (*taxi*) libre; **~(d) car** *n* voiture *f* de location; **~ purchase** (BRIT) *n* achat *m* (*or* vente *f*) à tempérament *or* crédit

his [hɪz] *pron* le (la) sien(ne), les siens (siennes) ♦ *adj* son (sa), ses *pl*; *see also* **my; mine**[1]

hiss [hɪs] *vi* siffler

historic [hɪ'stɔrɪk] *adj* historique; **~al** *adj* historique

history ['hɪstərɪ] *n* histoire *f*

hit [hɪt] (*pt, pp* **hit**) *vt* frapper; (*reach: target*) atteindre, toucher; (*collide with: car*) entrer en collision avec, heurter; (*fig: affect*) toucher ♦ *n* coup *m*; (*success*) succès *m*; (*: song*) tube *m*; **to ~ it off with sb** bien s'entendre avec qn; **~-and-run driver** *n* chauffard *m* (coupable du délit de fuite)

hitch [hɪtʃ] *vt* (*fasten*) accrocher, attacher; (*also:* **~ up**) remonter d'une saccade ♦ *n* (*difficulty*) anicroche *f*, contretemps *m*; **to ~ a lift** faire du stop; **~hike** *vi* faire de l'auto-stop; **~hiker** *n* auto-stoppeur(-euse)

hi-tech ['haɪ'tɛk] *adj* de pointe

hitherto [hɪðə'tu:] *adv* jusqu'ici

hit man *n* tueur *m* à gages

HIV *n*: **~-negative/-positive** *adj* séronégatif(-ive)/-positif(-ive)

hive [haɪv] *n* ruche *f*

HMS *abbr* = **Her/His Majesty's Ship**

hoard [hɔ:d] *n* (*of food*) provisions *fpl*, réserves *fpl*; (*of money*) trésor *m* ♦ *vt* amasser; **~ing** (BRIT) *n* (*for posters*) panneau *m* d'affichage *or* publicitaire

hoarse [hɔ:s] *adj* enroué(e)

hoax [həuks] *n* canular *m*

hob [hɔb] *n* plaque (chauffante)

hobble ['hɔbl] *vi* boitiller

hobby ['hɔbɪ] *n* passe-temps favori

hobo ['həubəu] (US) *n* vagabond *m*

hockey ['hɔkɪ] *n* hockey *m*

hog [hɔg] *n* porc (châtré) ♦ *vt* (*fig*) accaparer; **to go the whole ~** aller jusqu'au bout

hoist [hɔɪst] *n* (*apparatus*) palan *m* ♦ *vt* hisser

hold [həuld] (*pt, pp* **held**) *vt* tenir; (*contain*) contenir; (*believe*) considérer; (*possess*) avoir; (*detain*) détenir ♦ *vi* (*withstand pressure*) tenir (bon); (*be valid*) valoir ♦ *n* (*also fig*) prise *f*; (NAUT) cale *f*; **~ the line!** (TEL) ne quittez pas!; **to ~ one's own** (*fig*) (bien) se défendre; **to catch** *or* **get (a) ~ of** saisir; **to get ~ of** (*fig*) trouver; **~ back** *vt* retenir; (*secret*) taire; **~ down** *vt* (*person*) maintenir à terre; (*job*) occuper; **~ off** *vt* tenir à distance; **~ on** *vi* tenir bon; (*wait*) attendre; **~ on!** (*TEL*) ne quittez pas!; **~ on to** *vt fus* se cramponner à; (*keep*) conserver, garder; **~ out** *vt* offrir ♦ *vi* (*resist*) tenir bon; **~ up** *vt* (*raise*) lever; (*support*) soutenir; (*delay*) retarder; (*rob*) braquer; **~all** (*BRIT*) *n* fourre-tout *m inv*; **~er** *n* (*of ticket, record*) détenteur(-trice); (*of office, title etc*) titulaire *m/f*; (*container*) support *m*; **~ing** *n* (*share*) intérêts *mpl*; (*farm*) ferme *f*; **~-up** *n* (*robbery*) hold-up *m*; (*delay*) retard *m*; (*BRIT*: *in traffic*) bouchon *m*

hole [həul] *n* trou *m*; **~-in-the-wall** *n* (*cash dispenser*) distributeur *m* de billets

holiday ['hɔlɪdeɪ] *n* vacances *fpl*; (*day off*) jour *m* de congé; (*public*) jour férié; **on ~** en congé; **~ camp** *n* (*also:* **~ centre**) camp *m* de vacances; **~-maker** (*BRIT*) *n* vacancier(-ère); **~ resort** *n* centre *m* de villégiature *or* de vacances

Holland ['hɔlənd] *n* Hollande *f*

hollow ['hɔləu] *adj* creux(-euse) ♦ *n* creux *m* ♦ *vt*: **to ~ out** creuser, évider

holly ['hɔlɪ] *n* houx *m*

holocaust ['hɔləkɔ:st] *n* holocauste *m*

holster ['həulstər] *n* étui *m* de revolver

holy ['həulɪ] *adj* saint(e); (*bread, water*) bénit(e); (*ground*) sacré(e); **H~ Ghost** *n* Saint-Esprit *m*

homage ['hɔmɪdʒ] *n* hommage *m*; **to pay ~ to** rendre hommage à

home [həum] *n* foyer *m*, maison *f*; (*country*) pays natal, patrie *f*; (*institution*) maison ♦ *adj* de famille; (*ECON, POL*) national(e), intérieur(e); (*SPORT*: *game*) sur leur (*or* notre) terrain; (*team*) qui reçoit ♦ *adv* chez soi, à la maison; au pays natal; (*right in*: *nail etc*) à fond; **at ~** chez soi, à la maison; **make yourself at ~** faites comme chez vous; **~ address** *n* domicile permanent; **~land** *n* patrie *f*; **~less** *adj* sans foyer; sans abri; **~ly** *adj* (*plain*) simple, sans prétention; **~-made** *adj* fait(e) à la maison; **~ match** *n* match *m* à domicile; **H~ Office** (*BRIT*) *n* ministère *m* de l'Intérieur; **~ page** *n* (*COMPUT*) page *f* d'accueil; **~ rule** *n* autonomie *f*; **H~ Secretary** (*BRIT*) *n* ministre *m* de l'Intérieur; **~sick** *adj*: **to be ~sick** avoir le mal du pays; s'ennuyer de sa famille; **~ town** *n* ville natale; **~ward** *adj* (*journey*) du retour; **~work** *n* devoirs *mpl*

homoeopathic [həumɪəu'pæθɪk] (*US* **homeopathic**) *adj* (*medicine, methods*) homéopathique; (*doctor*) homéopathe

homogeneous [hɔməu'dʒi:nɪəs] *adj* homogène

homosexual [hɔməu'sɛksjuəl] *adj, n* homosexuel(le)

honest ['ɔnɪst] *adj* honnête; (*sincere*) franc (franche); **~ly** *adv* honnêtement; franchement; **~y** *n* honnêteté *f*

honey ['hʌnɪ] *n* miel *m*; **~comb** *n* rayon *m* de miel; **~moon** *n* lune *f* de miel, voyage *m* de noces; **~suckle** (*BOT*) *n* chèvrefeuille *m*

honk [hɔŋk] *vi* (*AUT*) klaxonner

honorary ['ɔnərərɪ] *adj* honoraire; (*duty, title*) honorifique

honour ['ɔnər] (*US* **honor**) *vt* honorer ♦ *n* honneur *m*; **hono(u)rable** *adj* honorable; **hono(u)rs degree** *n* (*SCOL*) *licence avec mention*

hood [hud] *n* capuchon *m*; (*of cooker*) hotte *f*; (*AUT*: *BRIT*) capote *f*; (: *US*) capot *m*

hoof [hu:f] (*pl* **hooves**) *n* sabot *m*

hook [huk] *n* crochet *m*; (*on dress*) agrafe *f*; (*for fishing*) hameçon *m* ♦ *vt* accrocher; (*fish*) prendre

hooligan ['hu:lɪgən] *n* voyou *m*

hoop [hu:p] *n* cerceau *m*

hooray [hu:'reɪ] *excl* hourra

hoot [hu:t] *vi* (*AUT*) klaxonner; (*siren*) mugir; (*owl*) hululer; **~er** *n* (*BRIT*: *AUT*) klaxon *m*; (*NAUT, factory*) sirène *f*

Hoover ® ['hu:vər] (*BRIT*) *n* aspirateur

m ♦ *vt*: **h~** passer l'aspirateur dans *or* sur

hooves [hu:vz] *npl of* **hoof**

hop [hɔp] *vi* (*on one foot*) sauter à cloche-pied; (*bird*) sautiller

hope [həup] *vt, vi* espérer ♦ *n* espoir *m*; **I ~ so** je l'espère; **I ~ not** j'espère que non; **~ful** *adj* (*person*) plein(e) d'espoir; (*situation*) prometteur(-euse), encourageant(e); **~fully** *adv* (*expectantly*) avec espoir, avec optimisme; (*one hopes*) avec un peu de chance; **~less** *adj* désespéré(e); (*useless*) nul(le)

hops [hɔps] *npl* houblon *m*

horizon [hə'raɪzn] *n* horizon *m*; **~tal** [hɔrɪ'zɔntl] *adj* horizontal(e)

horn [hɔ:n] *n* corne *f*; (MUS: *also*: **French ~**) cor *m*; (AUT) klaxon *m*

hornet ['hɔ:nɪt] *n* frelon *m*

horoscope ['hɔrəskəup] *n* horoscope *m*

horrendous [hə'rɛndəs] *adj* horrible, affreux(-euse)

horrible ['hɔrɪbl] *adj* horrible, affreux (-euse)

horrid ['hɔrɪd] *adj* épouvantable

horrify ['hɔrɪfaɪ] *vt* horrifier

horror ['hɔrə^r] *n* horreur *f*; **~ film** *n* film *m* d'épouvante

hors d'oeuvre [ɔ:'də:vrə] *n* (CULIN) hors-d'œuvre *m inv*

horse [hɔ:s] *n* cheval *m*; **~back** *n*: **on ~back** à cheval; **~ chestnut** *n* marron *m* (d'Inde); **~man** (*irreg*) *n* cavalier *m*; **~power** *n* puissance *f* (en chevaux); **~-racing** *n* courses *fpl* de chevaux; **~radish** *n* raifort *m*; **~shoe** *n* fer *m* à cheval

hose [həuz] *n* (*also*: **~pipe**) tuyau *m*; (*also*: **garden ~**) tuyau d'arrosage

hospitable ['hɔspɪtəbl] *adj* hospitalier(-ère)

hospital ['hɔspɪtl] *n* hôpital *m*; **in ~** à l'hôpital

hospitality [hɔspɪ'tælɪtɪ] *n* hospitalité *f*

host [həust] *n* hôte *m*; (TV, RADIO) animateur(-trice); (REL) hostie *f*; (*large number*): **a ~ of** une foule de ♦ *vt* (*conference, games etc*) accueillir

hostage ['hɔstɪdʒ] *n* otage *m*

hostel ['hɔstl] *n* foyer *m*; (*also*: **youth ~**) auberge *f* de jeunesse

hostess ['həustɪs] *n* hôtesse *f*; (TV, RADIO) animatrice *f*

hostile ['hɔstaɪl] *adj* hostile; **hostility** [hɔ'stɪlɪtɪ] *n* hostilité *f*

hot [hɔt] *adj* chaud(e); (*as opposed to only warm*) très chaud; (*spicy*) fort(e); (*contest etc*) acharné(e); (*temper*) passionné(e); **to be ~** (*person*) avoir chaud; (*object*) être (très) chaud; **it is ~** (*weather*) il fait chaud; **~bed** *n* (*fig*) foyer *m*, pépinière *f*; **~ dog** *n* hot-dog *m*

hotel [həu'tɛl] *n* hôtel *m*

hot: **~house** *n* serre (chaude); **~line** *n* (POL) téléphone *m* rouge, ligne directe; **~ly** *adv* passionnément, violemment; **~plate** *n* (*on cooker*) plaque chauffante; **~pot** (BRIT) *n* ragoût *m*; **~-water bottle** *n* bouillotte *f*

hound [haund] *vt* poursuivre avec acharnement ♦ *n* chien courant

hour ['auə^r] *n* heure *f*; **~ly** *adj, adv* toutes les heures; (*rate*) horaire

house [*n* haus, *vb* hauz] *n* maison *f*; (POL) chambre *f*; (THEATRE) salle *f*; auditoire *m* ♦ *vt* (*person*) loger, héberger; (*objects*) abriter; **on the ~** (*fig*) aux frais de la maison; **~ arrest** *n* assignation *f* à résidence; **~boat** *n* bateau *m* (aménagé en habitation); **~bound** *adj* confiné(e) chez soi; **~breaking** *n* cambriolage *m* (avec effraction); **~hold** *n* (*persons*) famille *f*, maisonnée *f*; (ADMIN *etc*) ménage *m*; **~keeper** *n* gouvernante *f*; **~keeping** *n* (*work*) ménage *m*; **~keeping (money)** argent *m* du ménage; **~-warming (party)** *n* pendaison *f* de crémaillère; **~wife** (*irreg*) *n* ménagère *f*; femme *f* au foyer; **~work** *n* (travaux *mpl* du) ménage *m*

housing ['hauzɪŋ] *n* logement *m*; **~ development**, **~ estate** *n* lotissement *m*

hovel ['hɔvl] *n* taudis *m*
hover ['hɔvəʳ] *vi* planer; **~craft** *n* aéroglisseur *m*
how [hau] *adv* comment; **~ are you?** comment allez-vous?; **~ do you do?** bonjour; enchanté(e); **~ far is it to?** combien y a-t-il jusqu'à ...?; **~ long have you been here?** depuis combien de temps êtes-vous là?; **~ lovely!** que *or* comme c'est joli!; **~ many/much?** combien?; **~ many people/much milk?** combien de gens/lait?; **~ old are you?** quel âge avez-vous?
however [hau'ɛvəʳ] *adv* de quelque façon *or* manière que *+subj*; (*+adj*) quelque *or* si ... que *+subj*; (*in questions*) comment ♦ *conj* pourtant, cependant
howl [haul] *vi* hurler
H.P. *abbr* = **hire purchase**
h.p. *abbr* = **horsepower**
HQ *abbr* = **headquarters**
hub [hʌb] *n* (*of wheel*) moyeu *m*; (*fig*) centre *m*, foyer *m*; **~cap** *n* enjoliveur *m*
huddle ['hʌdl] *vi*: **to ~ together** se blottir les uns contre les autres
hue [hju:] *n* teinte *f*, nuance *f*
huff [hʌf] *n*: **in a ~** fâché(e)
hug [hʌg] *vt* serrer dans ses bras; (*shore, kerb*) serrer
huge [hju:dʒ] *adj* énorme, immense
hulk [hʌlk] *n* (*ship*) épave *f*; (*car, building*) carcasse *f*; (*person*) mastodonte *m*
hull [hʌl] *n* coque *f*
hullo [hə'ləu] *excl* = **hello**
hum [hʌm] *vt* (*tune*) fredonner ♦ *vi* fredonner; (*insect*) bourdonner; (*plane, tool*) vrombir
human ['hju:mən] *adj* humain(e) ♦ *n*: **~ being** être humain; **~e** [hju:'meɪn] *adj* humain(e), humanitaire; **~itarian** [hju:mænɪ'tɛərɪən] *adj* humanitaire; **~ity** [hju:'mænɪtɪ] *n* humanité *f*
humble ['hʌmbl] *adj* humble, modeste ♦ *vt* humilier
humdrum ['hʌmdrʌm] *adj* monotone, banal(e)
humid ['hju:mɪd] *adj* humide
humiliate [hju:'mɪlɪeɪt] *vt* humilier; **humiliation** [hju:mɪlɪ'eɪʃən] *n* humiliation *f*
humorous ['hju:mərəs] *adj* humoristique; (*person*) plein(e) d'humour
humour ['hju:məʳ] (*US* **humor**) *n* humour *m*; (*mood*) humeur *f* ♦ *vt* (*person*) faire plaisir à; se prêter aux caprices de
hump [hʌmp] *n* bosse *f*
hunch [hʌntʃ] *n* (*premonition*) intuition *f*; **~back** *n* bossu(e); **~ed** *adj* voûté(e)
hundred ['hʌndrəd] *num* cent; **~s of** des centaines de; **~weight** *n* (*BRIT*) *50.8 kg, 112 lb*; (*US*) *45.3 kg, 100 lb*
hung [hʌŋ] *pt, pp of* **hang**
Hungary ['hʌŋgərɪ] *n* Hongrie *f*
hunger ['hʌŋgəʳ] *n* faim *f* ♦ *vi*: **to ~ for** avoir faim de, désirer ardemment
hungry ['hʌŋgrɪ] *adj* affamé(e); (*keen*): **~ for** avide de; **to be ~** avoir faim
hunk [hʌŋk] *n* (*of bread etc*) gros morceau
hunt [hʌnt] *vt* chasser; (*criminal*) pourchasser ♦ *vi* chasser; (*search*): **to ~ for** chercher (partout) ♦ *n* chasse *f*; **~er** *n* chasseur *m*; **~ing** *n* chasse *f*
hurdle ['hə:dl] *n* (*SPORT*) haie *f*; (*fig*) obstacle *m*
hurl [hə:l] *vt* lancer (avec violence); (*abuse, insults*) lancer
hurrah [hu'rɑ:] *excl* = **hooray**
hurray [hu'reɪ] *excl* = **hooray**
hurricane ['hʌrɪkən] *n* ouragan *m*
hurried ['hʌrɪd] *adj* pressé(e), précipité(e); (*work*) fait(e) à la hâte; **~ly** *adv* précipitamment, à la hâte
hurry ['hʌrɪ] (*vb*: *also*: **~ up**) *n* hâte *f*, précipitation *f* ♦ *vi* se presser, se dépêcher ♦ *vt* (*person*) faire presser, faire se dépêcher; (*work*) presser; **to be in a ~** être pressé(e); **to do sth in a ~** faire qch en vitesse; **to ~ in/out** entrer/sortir précipitamment
hurt [hə:t] (*pt, pp* **hurt**) *vt* (*cause pain to*) faire mal à; (*injure, fig*) blesser ♦ *vi* faire mal ♦ *adj* blessé(e); **~ful** *adj* (*remark*) blessant(e)

hurtle ['hə:tl] *vi*: **to ~ past** passer en trombe; **to ~ down** dégringoler
husband ['hʌzbənd] *n* mari *m*
hush [hʌʃ] *n* calme *m*, silence *m* ♦ *vt* faire taire; **~!** chut!; **~ up** *vt* (*scandal*) étouffer
husk [hʌsk] *n* (*of wheat*) balle *f*; (*of rice, maize*) enveloppe *f*
husky ['hʌskɪ] *adj* rauque ♦ *n* chien *m* esquimau *or* de traîneau
hustle ['hʌsl] *vt* pousser, bousculer ♦ *n*: **~ and bustle** tourbillon *m* (d'activité)
hut [hʌt] *n* hutte *f*; (*shed*) cabane *f*
hutch [hʌtʃ] *n* clapier *m*
hyacinth ['haɪəsɪnθ] *n* jacinthe *f*
hydrant ['haɪdrənt] *n* (*also:* **fire ~**) bouche *f* d'incendie
hydraulic [haɪ'drɔ:lɪk] *adj* hydraulique
hydroelectric ['haɪdrəuɪ'lɛktrɪk] *adj* hydro-électrique
hydrofoil ['haɪdrəfɔɪl] *n* hydrofoil *m*
hydrogen ['haɪdrədʒən] *n* hydrogène *m*
hyena [haɪ'i:nə] *n* hyène *f*
hygiene ['haɪdʒi:n] *n* hygiène *f*; **hygienic** *adj* hygiénique
hymn [hɪm] *n* hymne *m*; cantique *m*
hype [haɪp] (*inf*) *n* battage *m* publicitaire
hypermarket ['haɪpəmɑ:kɪt] (*BRIT*) *n* hypermarché *m*
hypertext ['haɪpətɛkst] *n* (*COMPUT*) hypertexte *m*
hyphen ['haɪfn] *n* trait *m* d'union
hypnotize ['hɪpnətaɪz] *vt* hypnotiser
hypocrisy [hɪ'pɔkrɪsɪ] *n* hypocrisie *f*; **hypocrite** ['hɪpəkrɪt] *n* hypocrite *m/f*; **hypocritical** *adj* hypocrite
hypothesis [haɪ'pɔθɪsɪs] (*pl* **hypotheses**) *n* hypothèse *f*
hysterical [hɪ'stɛrɪkl] *adj* hystérique; (*funny*) hilarant(e); **~ laughter** fou rire *m*
hysterics [hɪ'stɛrɪks] *npl*: **to be in/have ~** (*anger, panic*) avoir une crise de nerfs; (*laughter*) attraper un fou rire

I, i

I [aɪ] *pron* je; (*before vowel*) j'; (*stressed*) moi
ice [aɪs] *n* glace *f*; (*on road*) verglas *m* ♦ *vt* (*cake*) glacer ♦ *vi* (*also:* **~ over, ~ up**) geler; (*window*) se givrer; **~berg** *n* iceberg *m*; **~box** *n* (*US*) réfrigérateur *m*; (*BRIT*) compartiment *m* à glace; (*insulated box*) glacière *f*; **~ cream** *n* glace *f*; **~ cube** *n* glaçon *m*; **~d** *adj* glacé(e); **~ hockey** *n* hockey *m* sur glace; **Iceland** *n* Islande *f*; **~ lolly** *n* (*BRIT*) esquimau *m* (glace); **~ rink** *n* patinoire *f*; **~-skating** *n* patinage *m* (sur glace)
icicle ['aɪsɪkl] *n* glaçon *m* (*naturel*)
icing ['aɪsɪŋ] *n* (*CULIN*) glace *f*; **~ sugar** (*BRIT*) *n* sucre *m* glace
ICT (*BRIT*) *abbr* (*SCOL* = *Information and Communications Technology*) TIC *f*
icy ['aɪsɪ] *adj* glacé(e); (*road*) verglacé(e); (*weather, temperature*) glacial(e)
I'd [aɪd] = **I would**; **I had**
idea [aɪ'dɪə] *n* idée *f*
ideal [aɪ'dɪəl] *n* idéal *m* ♦ *adj* idéal(e)
identical [aɪ'dɛntɪkl] *adj* identique
identification [aɪdɛntɪfɪ'keɪʃən] *n* identification *f*; **means of ~** pièce *f* d'identité
identify [aɪ'dɛntɪfaɪ] *vt* identifier
Identikit picture ® [aɪ'dɛntɪkɪt-] *n* portrait-robot *m*
identity [aɪ'dɛntɪtɪ] *n* identité *f*; **~ card** *n* carte *f* d'identité
ideology [aɪdɪ'ɔlədʒɪ] *n* idéologie *f*
idiom ['ɪdɪəm] *n* expression *f* idiomatique; (*style*) style *m*
idiosyncrasy [ɪdɪəu'sɪŋkrəsɪ] *n* (*of person*) particularité *f*, petite manie
idiot ['ɪdɪət] *n* idiot(e), imbécile *m/f*; **~ic** [ɪdɪ'ɔtɪk] *adj* idiot(e), bête, stupide
idle ['aɪdl] *adj* sans occupation, désœuvré(e); (*lazy*) oisif(-ive), paresseux (-euse); (*unemployed*) au chômage; (*question, pleasures*) vain(e), futile ♦ *vi*

(*engine*) tourner au ralenti; **to lie ~** être arrêté(e), ne pas fonctionner

idol ['aɪdl] *n* idole *f*; **~ize** *vt* idolâtrer, adorer

i.e. *adv abbr* (= *id est*) c'est-à-dire

if [ɪf] *conj* si; **~ so** si c'est le cas; **~ not** sinon; **~ only** si seulement

ignite [ɪg'naɪt] *vt* mettre le feu à, enflammer ♦ *vi* s'enflammer; **ignition** *n* (*AUT*) allumage *m*; **to switch on/off the ignition** mettre/couper le contact; **ignition key** *n* clé *f* de contact

ignorant ['ɪgnərənt] *adj* ignorant(e); **to be ~ of** (*subject*) ne rien connaître à; (*events*) ne pas être au courant de

ignore [ɪg'nɔːʳ] *vt* ne tenir aucun compte de; (*person*) faire semblant de ne pas reconnaître, ignorer; (*fact*) méconnaître

ill [ɪl] *adj* (*sick*) malade; (*bad*) mauvais(e) ♦ *n* mal *m* ♦ *adv*: **to speak/think ~ of** dire/penser du mal de; **~s** *npl* (*misfortunes*) maux *mpl*, malheurs *mpl*; **to be taken ~** tomber malade; **~-advised** *adj* (*decision*) peu judicieux(-euse); (*person*) malavisé(e); **~-at-ease** *adj* mal à l'aise

I'll [aɪl] = **I will; I shall**

illegal [ɪ'liːgl] *adj* illégal(e)

illegible [ɪ'lɛdʒɪbl] *adj* illisible

illegitimate [ɪlɪ'dʒɪtɪmət] *adj* illégitime

ill-fated [ɪl'feɪtɪd] *adj* malheureux (-euse); (*day*) néfaste

ill feeling *n* ressentiment *m*, rancune *f*

illiterate [ɪ'lɪtərət] *adj* illettré(e)

ill: ~-mannered *adj* (*child*) mal élevé(e); **~ness** *n* maladie *f*; **~-treat** *vt* maltraiter

illuminate [ɪ'luːmɪneɪt] *vt* (*room, street*) éclairer; (*for special effect*) illuminer; **illumination** [ɪluːmɪ'neɪʃən] *n* éclairage *m*; illumination *f*

illusion [ɪ'luːʒən] *n* illusion *f*

illustrate ['ɪləstreɪt] *vt* illustrer; **illustration** [ɪlə'streɪʃən] *n* illustration *f*

ill will *n* malveillance *f*

I'm [aɪm] = **I am**

image ['ɪmɪdʒ] *n* image *f*; (*public face*) image de marque; **~ry** *n* images *fpl*

imaginary [ɪ'mædʒɪnərɪ] *adj* imaginaire

imagination [ɪmædʒɪ'neɪʃən] *n* imagination *f*

imaginative [ɪ'mædʒɪnətɪv] *adj* imaginatif(-ive); (*person*) plein(e) d'imagination

imagine [ɪ'mædʒɪn] *vt* imaginer, s'imaginer; (*suppose*) imaginer, supposer

imbalance [ɪm'bæləns] *n* déséquilibre *m*

imitate ['ɪmɪteɪt] *vt* imiter; **imitation** [ɪmɪ'teɪʃən] *n* imitation *f*

immaculate [ɪ'mækjulət] *adj* impeccable; (*REL*) immaculé(e)

immaterial [ɪmə'tɪərɪəl] *adj* sans importance, insignifiant(e)

immature [ɪmə'tjuəʳ] *adj* (*fruit*) (qui n'est) pas mûr(e); (*person*) qui manque de maturité

immediate [ɪ'miːdɪət] *adj* immédiat(e); **~ly** *adv* (*at once*) immédiatement; **~ly next to** juste à côté de

immense [ɪ'mɛns] *adj* immense; énorme

immerse [ɪ'məːs] *vt* immerger, plonger; **immersion heater** (*BRIT*) *n* chauffe-eau *m* électrique

immigrant ['ɪmɪgrənt] *n* immigrant(e); immigré(e); **immigration** [ɪmɪ'greɪʃən] *n* immigration *f*

imminent ['ɪmɪnənt] *adj* imminent(e)

immoral [ɪ'mɔrl] *adj* immoral(e)

immortal [ɪ'mɔːtl] *adj, n* immortel(le)

immune [ɪ'mjuːn] *adj*: **~ (to)** immunisé(e) (contre); (*fig*) à l'abri de; **immunity** *n* immunité *f*

impact ['ɪmpækt] *n* choc *m*, impact *m*; (*fig*) impact

impair [ɪm'pɛəʳ] *vt* détériorer, diminuer

impart [ɪm'pɑːt] *vt* communiquer, transmettre; (*flavour*) donner

impartial [ɪm'pɑːʃl] *adj* impartial(e)

impassable [ɪm'pɑːsəbl] *adj* infranchissable; (*road*) impraticable

impassive [ɪm'pæsɪv] *adj* impassible

impatience [ɪm'peɪʃəns] *n* impatience *f*

impatient [ɪm'peɪʃənt] *adj* impatient(e); **to get** *or* **grow ~** s'impatienter; **~ly** *adv* avec impatience
impeccable [ɪm'pɛkəbl] *adj* impeccable, parfait(e)
impede [ɪm'pi:d] *vt* gêner; **impediment** *n* obstacle *m*; (*also:* **speech impediment**) défaut *m* d'élocution
impending [ɪm'pɛndɪŋ] *adj* imminent(e)
imperative [ɪm'pɛrətɪv] *adj* (*need*) urgent(e), pressant(e); (*tone*) impérieux (-euse) ♦ *n* (LING) impératif *m*
imperfect [ɪm'pə:fɪkt] *adj* imparfait(e); (*goods etc*) défectueux(-euse)
imperial [ɪm'pɪərɪəl] *adj* impérial(e); (*BRIT: measure*) légal(e)
impersonal [ɪm'pə:sənl] *adj* impersonnel(le)
impersonate [ɪm'pə:səneɪt] *vt* se faire passer pour; (THEATRE) imiter
impertinent [ɪm'pə:tɪnənt] *adj* impertinent(e), insolent(e)
impervious [ɪm'pə:vɪəs] *adj* (*fig*): **~ to** insensible à
impetuous [ɪm'pɛtjuəs] *adj* impétueux(-euse), fougueux(-euse)
impetus ['ɪmpətəs] *n* impulsion *f*; (*of runner*) élan *m*
impinge [ɪm'pɪndʒ]: **to ~ on** *vt fus* (*person*) affecter, toucher; (*rights*) empiéter sur
implement [*n* 'ɪmplɪmənt, *vb* 'ɪmplɪmɛnt] *n* outil *m*, instrument *m*; (*for cooking*) ustensile *m* ♦ *vt* exécuter
implicit [ɪm'plɪsɪt] *adj* implicite; (*complete*) absolu(e), sans réserve
imply [ɪm'plaɪ] *vt* suggérer, laisser entendre; indiquer, supposer
impolite [ɪmpə'laɪt] *adj* impoli(e)
import [*vb* ɪm'pɔ:t, *n* 'ɪmpɔ:t] *vt* importer ♦ *n* (COMM) importation *f*
importance [ɪm'pɔ:tns] *n* importance *f*
important [ɪm'pɔ:tənt] *adj* important(e)
importer [ɪm'pɔ:tə^r] *n* importateur (-trice)
impose [ɪm'pəuz] *vt* imposer ♦ *vi*: **to ~ on sb** abuser de la gentillesse de qn; **imposing** *adj* imposant(e), impressionnant(e); **imposition** [ɪmpə'zɪʃən] *n* (*of tax etc*) imposition *f*; **to be an imposition on** (*person*) abuser de la gentillesse *or* la bonté de
impossible [ɪm'pɔsɪbl] *adj* impossible
impotent ['ɪmpətnt] *adj* impuissant(e)
impound [ɪm'paund] *vt* confisquer, saisir
impoverished [ɪm'pɔvərɪʃt] *adj* appauvri(e), pauvre
impractical [ɪm'præktɪkl] *adj* pas pratique; (*person*) qui manque d'esprit pratique
impregnable [ɪm'prɛgnəbl] *adj* (*fortress*) imprenable
impress [ɪm'prɛs] *vt* impressionner, faire impression sur; (*mark*) imprimer, marquer; **to ~ sth on sb** faire bien comprendre qch à qn; **~ed** *adj* impressionné(e)
impression [ɪm'prɛʃən] *n* impression *f*; (*of stamp, seal*) empreinte *f*; (*imitation*) imitation *f*; **to be under the ~ that** avoir l'impression que; **~ist** *n* (ART) impressioniste *m/f*; (*entertainer*) imitateur(-trice) *m/f*
impressive [ɪm'prɛsɪv] *adj* impressionnant(e)
imprint ['ɪmprɪnt] *n* (*outline*) marque *f*, empreinte *f*
imprison [ɪm'prɪzn] *vt* emprisonner, mettre en prison
improbable [ɪm'prɔbəbl] *adj* improbable; (*excuse*) peu plausible
improper [ɪm'prɔpə^r] *adj* (*unsuitable*) déplacé(e), de mauvais goût; indécent(e); (*dishonest*) malhonnête
improve [ɪm'pru:v] *vt* améliorer ♦ *vi* s'améliorer; (*pupil etc*) faire des progrès; **~ment** *n* amélioration *f* (*in* de); progrès *m*
improvise ['ɪmprəvaɪz] *vt, vi* improviser
impudent ['ɪmpjudnt] *adj* impudent(e)
impulse ['ɪmpʌls] *n* impulsion *f*; **on ~**

impulsivement, sur un coup de tête; **impulsive** *adj* impulsif(-ive)

KEYWORD

in [ɪn] *prep* **1** (*indicating place, position*) dans; **in the house/the fridge** dans la maison/le frigo; **in the garden** dans le *or* au jardin; **in town** en ville; **in the country** à la campagne; **in school** à l'école; **in here/there** ici/là

2 (*with place names: of town, region, country*): **in London** à Londres; **in England** en Angleterre; **in Japan** au Japon; **in the United States** aux États-Unis

3 (*indicating time: during*): **in spring** au printemps; **in summer** en été; **in May/1992** en mai/1992; **in the afternoon** (dans) l'après-midi; **at 4 o'clock in the afternoon** à 4 heures de l'après-midi

4 (*indicating time: in the space of*) en; (: *future*) dans; **I did it in 3 hours/days** je l'ai fait en 3 heures/jours; **I'll see you in 2 weeks** *or* **in 2 weeks' time** je te verrai dans 2 semaines

5 (*indicating manner etc*) à; **in a loud/soft voice** à voix haute/basse; **in pencil** au crayon; **in French** en français; **the boy in the blue shirt** le garçon à *or* avec la chemise bleue

6 (*indicating circumstances*): **in the sun** au soleil; **in the shade** à l'ombre; **in the rain** sous la pluie

7 (*indicating mood, state*): **in tears** en larmes; **in anger** sous le coup de la colère; **in despair** au désespoir; **in good condition** en bon état; **to live in luxury** vivre dans le luxe

8 (*with ratios, numbers*): **1 in 10 (households), 1 (household) in 10** 1 (ménage) sur 10; **20 pence in the pound** 20 pence par livre sterling; **they lined up in twos** ils se mirent en rangs (deux) par deux; **in hundreds** par centaines

9 (*referring to people, works*) chez; **the disease is common in children** c'est une maladie courante chez les enfants; **in (the works of) Dickens** chez Dickens, dans (l'œuvre de) Dickens

10 (*indicating profession etc*) dans; **to be in teaching** être dans l'enseignement

11 (*after superlative*) de; **the best pupil in the class** le meilleur élève de la classe

12 (*with present participle*): **in saying this** en disant ceci

♦ *adv*: **to be in** (*person: at home, work*) être là; (*train, ship, plane*) être arrivé(e); (*in fashion*) être à la mode; **to ask sb in** inviter qn à entrer; **to run/limp** *etc* **in** entrer en courant/boitant *etc*

♦ *n*: **the ins and outs (of)** (*of proposal, situation etc*) les tenants et aboutissants (de)

in. *abbr* = **inch**

inability [ɪnə'bɪlɪtɪ] *n* incapacité *f*

inaccurate [ɪn'ækjurət] *adj* inexact(e); (*person*) qui manque de précision

inadequate [ɪn'ædɪkwət] *adj* insuffisant(e), inadéquat(e)

inadvertently [ɪnəd'vəːtntlɪ] *adv* par mégarde

inadvisable [ɪnəd'vaɪzəbl] *adj* (*action*) à déconseiller

inane [ɪ'neɪn] *adj* inepte, stupide

inanimate [ɪn'ænɪmət] *adj* inanimé(e)

inappropriate [ɪnə'prəuprɪət] *adj* inopportun(e), mal à propos; (*word, expression*) impropre

inarticulate [ɪnɑː'tɪkjulət] *adj* (*person*) qui s'exprime mal; (*speech*) indistinct(e)

inasmuch as [ɪnəz'mʌtʃ-] *adv* (*insofar as*) dans la mesure où; (*seeing that*) attendu que

inauguration [ɪnɔːgju'reɪʃən] *n* inauguration *f*; (*of president*) investiture *f*

inborn [ɪn'bɔːn] *adj* (*quality*) inné(e)

inbred [ɪn'brɛd] *adj* inné(e), naturel(le); (*family*) consanguin(e)

Inc. *abbr* = **incorporated**

incapable [ɪn'keɪpəbl] *adj* incapable

incapacitate [ɪnkə'pæsɪteɪt] *vt*: **to ~ sb from doing** rendre qn incapable de faire

incense [*n* 'ɪnsɛns, *vb* ɪn'sɛns] *n* encens *m* ♦ *vt* (*anger*) mettre en colère

incentive [ɪn'sɛntɪv] *n* encouragement *m*, raison *f* de se donner de la peine

incessant [ɪn'sɛsnt] *adj* incessant(e); **~ly** *adv* sans cesse, constamment

inch [ɪntʃ] *n* pouce *m* (= *25 mm; 12 in a foot*); **within an ~ of** à deux doigts de; **he didn't give an ~** (*fig*) il n'a pas voulu céder d'un pouce

incident ['ɪnsɪdnt] *n* incident *m*; **~al** [ɪnsɪ'dɛntl] *adj* (*additional*) accessoire; **~al to** qui accompagne; **~ally** *adv* (*by the way*) à propos

inclination [ɪnklɪ'neɪʃən] *n* (*fig*) inclination *f*

incline [*n* 'ɪnklaɪn, *vb* ɪn'klaɪn] *n* pente *f* ♦ *vt* incliner ♦ *vi* (*surface*) s'incliner; **to be ~d to do** avoir tendance à faire

include [ɪn'klu:d] *vt* inclure, comprendre; **including** *prep* y compris; **inclusive** *adj* inclus(e), compris(e); **inclusive of tax** *etc* taxes *etc* comprises

income ['ɪnkʌm] *n* revenu *m*; **~ tax** *n* impôt *m* sur le revenu

incoming ['ɪnkʌmɪŋ] *adj* qui arrive; (*president*) entrant(e); **~ mail** courrier *m* du jour; **~ tide** marée montante

incompetent [ɪn'kɔmpɪtnt] *adj* incompétent(e), incapable

incomplete [ɪnkəm'pli:t] *adj* incomplet(-ète)

incongruous [ɪn'kɔŋgruəs] *adj* incongru(e)

inconsiderate [ɪnkən'sɪdərət] *adj* (*person*) qui manque d'égards; (*action*) inconsidéré(e)

inconsistency [ɪnkən'sɪstənsɪ] *n* (*of actions etc*) inconséquence *f*; (*of work*) irrégularité *f*; (*of statement etc*) incohérence *f*

inconsistent [ɪnkən'sɪstnt] *adj* inconséquent(e); irrégulier(-ère); peu cohérent(e); **~ with** incompatible avec

inconspicuous [ɪnkən'spɪkjuəs] *adj* qui passe inaperçu(e); (*colour, dress*) discret(-ète)

inconvenience [ɪnkən'vi:njəns] *n* inconvénient *m*; (*trouble*) dérangement *m* ♦ *vt* déranger

inconvenient [ɪnkən'vi:njənt] *adj* (*house*) malcommode; (*time, place*) mal choisi(e), qui ne convient pas; (*visitor*) importun(e)

incorporate [ɪn'kɔ:pəreɪt] *vt* incorporer; (*contain*) contenir; **~d company** (*US*) *n* ≃ société *f* anonyme

incorrect [ɪnkə'rɛkt] *adj* incorrect(e)

increase [*n* 'ɪnkri:s, *vb* ɪn'kri:s] *n* augmentation *f* ♦ *vi, vt* augmenter; **increasing** *adj* (*number*) croissant(e); **increasingly** *adv* de plus en plus

incredible [ɪn'krɛdɪbl] *adj* incroyable

incubator ['ɪnkjubeɪtə[r]] *n* (*for babies*) couveuse *f*

incumbent [ɪn'kʌmbənt] *n* (*president*) président *m* en exercice; (*REL*) titulaire *m/f* ♦ *adj*: **it is ~ on him to ...** il lui incombe *or* appartient de ...

incur [ɪn'kə:[r]] *vt* (*expenses*) encourir; (*anger, risk*) s'exposer à; (*debt*) contracter; (*loss*) subir

indebted [ɪn'dɛtɪd] *adj*: **to be ~ to sb (for)** être redevable à qn (de)

indecent [ɪn'di:snt] *adj* indécent(e), inconvenant(e); **~ assault** (*BRIT*) *n* attentat *m* à la pudeur; **~ exposure** *n* outrage *m* (public) à la pudeur

indecisive [ɪndɪ'saɪsɪv] *adj* (*person*) indécis(e)

indeed [ɪn'di:d] *adv* vraiment; en effet; (*furthermore*) d'ailleurs; **yes ~!** certainement!

indefinitely [ɪn'dɛfɪnɪtlɪ] *adv* (*wait*) indéfiniment

indemnity [ɪn'dɛmnɪtɪ] *n* (*safeguard*) assurance *f*, garantie *f*; (*compensation*) indemnité *f*

independence [ɪndɪ'pɛndns] *n* indépendance *f*

Independence Day

*L'***Independence Day** *est la fête nationale aux États-Unis, le 4 juillet. Il commémore l'adoption de la déclaration d'Indépendance, en 1776, écrite par Thomas Jefferson et proclamant la séparation des 13 colonies américaines de la Grande-Bretagne.*

independent [ɪndɪ'pɛndnt] *adj* indépendant(e); (*school*) privé(e); (*radio*) libre

index ['ɪndɛks] *n* (*pl*: *~es*: *in book*) index *m*; (: *in library etc*) catalogue *m*; (*pl*: *indices*: *ratio, sign*) indice *m*; **~ card** *n* fiche *f*; **~ finger** *n* index *m*; **~-linked** *adj* indexé(e) (sur le coût de la vie *etc*)

India ['ɪndɪə] *n* Inde *f*; **~n** *adj* indien(ne) ♦ *n* Indien(ne); **(American) ~n** Indien(ne) (d'Amérique); **~n Ocean** *n* océan Indien

indicate ['ɪndɪkeɪt] *vt* indiquer; **indication** [ɪndɪ'keɪʃən] *n* indication *f*, signe *m*; **indicative** [ɪn'dɪkətɪv] *adj*: **indicative of** symptomatique de ♦ *n* (LING) indicatif *m*; **indicator** *n* (*sign*) indicateur *m*; (AUT) clignotant *m*

indices ['ɪndɪsi:z] *npl of* **index**

indictment [ɪn'daɪtmənt] *n* accusation *f*

indifferent [ɪn'dɪfrənt] *adj* indifférent(e); (*poor*) médiocre, quelconque

indigenous [ɪn'dɪdʒɪnəs] *adj* indigène

indigestion [ɪndɪ'dʒɛstʃən] *n* indigestion *f*, mauvaise digestion

indignant [ɪn'dɪgnənt] *adj*: **~ (at sth/ with sb)** indigné(e) (de qch/contre qn)

indignity [ɪn'dɪgnɪtɪ] *n* indignité *f*, affront *m*

indirect [ɪndɪ'rɛkt] *adj* indirect(e)

indiscreet [ɪndɪs'kri:t] *adj* indiscret (-ète); (*rash*) imprudent(e)

indiscriminate [ɪndɪs'krɪmɪnət] *adj* (*person*) qui manque de discernement; (*killings*) commis(e) au hasard

indisputable [ɪndɪs'pju:təbl] *adj* incontestable, indiscutable

individual [ɪndɪ'vɪdjuəl] *n* individu *m* ♦ *adj* individuel(le); (*characteristic*) particulier(-ère), original(e)

indoctrination [ɪndɔktrɪ'neɪʃən] *n* endoctrinement *m*

Indonesia [ɪndə'ni:zɪə] *n* Indonésie *f*

indoor ['ɪndɔ:ʳ] *adj* (*plant*) d'appartement; (*swimming pool*) couvert(e); (*sport, games*) pratiqué(e) en salle; **~s** *adv* à l'intérieur

induce [ɪn'dju:s] *vt* (*persuade*) persuader; (*bring about*) provoquer; **~ment** *n* (*incentive*) récompense *f*; (*pej*: *bribe*) pot-de-vin *m*

indulge [ɪn'dʌldʒ] *vt* (*whim*) céder à, satisfaire; (*child*) gâter ♦ *vi*: **to ~ in sth** (*luxury*) se permettre qch; (*fantasies etc*) se livrer à qch; **~nce** *n* fantaisie *f* (que l'on s'offre); (*leniency*) indulgence *f*; **~nt** *adj* indulgent(e)

industrial [ɪn'dʌstrɪəl] *adj* industriel(le); (*injury*) du travail; **~ action** *n* action revendicative; **~ estate** (BRIT) *n* zone industrielle; **~ist** *n* industriel *m*; **~ park** (US) *n* = **industrial estate**

industrious [ɪn'dʌstrɪəs] *adj* travailleur(-euse)

industry ['ɪndəstrɪ] *n* industrie *f*; (*diligence*) zèle *m*, application *f*

inebriated [ɪ'ni:brɪeɪtɪd] *adj* ivre

inedible [ɪn'ɛdɪbl] *adj* immangeable; (*plant etc*) non comestible

ineffective [ɪnɪ'fɛktɪv], **ineffectual** [ɪnɪ'fɛktuəl] *adj* inefficace

inefficient [ɪnɪ'fɪʃənt] *adj* inefficace

inequality [ɪnɪ'kwɔlɪtɪ] *n* inégalité *f*

inescapable [ɪnɪ'skeɪpəbl] *adj* inéluctable, inévitable

inevitable [ɪn'ɛvɪtəbl] *adj* inévitable; **inevitably** *adv* inévitablement

inexpensive [ɪnɪk'spɛnsɪv] *adj* bon marché *inv*

inexperienced [ɪnɪk'spɪərɪənst] *adj* inexpérimenté(e)

infallible [ɪn'fælɪbl] *adj* infaillible

infamous ['ɪnfəməs] *adj* infâme, abominable

infancy ['ɪnfənsɪ] *n* petite enfance, bas âge

infant ['ɪnfənt] *n* (*baby*) nourrisson *m*; (*young child*) petit(e) enfant; **~ school** (*BRIT*) *n* classes *fpl* préparatoires (*entre 5 et 7 ans*)

infatuated [ɪn'fætjueɪtɪd] *adj*: **~ with** entiché(e) de; **infatuation** [ɪnfætju'eɪʃən] *n* engouement *m*

infect [ɪn'fɛkt] *vt* infecter, contaminer; **~ion** *n* infection *f*; (*contagion*) contagion *f*; **~ious** *adj* infectieux(-euse); (*also fig*) contagieux(-euse)

infer [ɪn'fəːʳ] *vt* conclure, déduire

inferior [ɪn'fɪərɪəʳ] *adj* inférieur(e); (*goods*) de qualité inférieure ♦ *n* inférieur(e); (*in rank*) subalterne *m/f*; **~ity** [ɪnfɪərɪ'ɔrətɪ] *n* infériorité *f*

infertile [ɪn'fəːtaɪl] *adj* stérile

infighting ['ɪnfaɪtɪŋ] *n* querelles *fpl* internes

infinite ['ɪnfɪnɪt] *adj* infini(e)

infinitive [ɪn'fɪnɪtɪv] *n* infinitif *m*

infinity [ɪn'fɪnɪtɪ] *n* infinité *f*; (*also MATH*) infini *m*

infirmary [ɪn'fəːmərɪ] *n* (*hospital*) hôpital *m*

inflamed [ɪn'fleɪmd] *adj* enflammé(e)

inflammable [ɪn'flæməbl] (*BRIT*) *adj* inflammable

inflammation [ɪnflə'meɪʃən] *n* inflammation *f*

inflatable [ɪn'fleɪtəbl] *adj* gonflable

inflate [ɪn'fleɪt] *vt* (*tyre, balloon*) gonfler; (*price*) faire monter; **inflation** *n* (*ECON*) inflation *f*; **inflationary** *adj* inflationniste

inflict [ɪn'flɪkt] *vt*: **to ~ on** infliger à

influence ['ɪnfluəns] *n* influence *f* ♦ *vt* influencer; **under the ~ of alcohol** en état d'ébriété; **influential** [ɪnflu'ɛnʃl] *adj* influent(e)

influenza [ɪnflu'ɛnzə] *n* grippe *f*

influx ['ɪnflʌks] *n* afflux *m*

infomercial ['ɪnfəuməːʃl] (*US*) *n* (*for product*) publi-information *f*; (*POL*) *émission où un candidat présente son programme électoral*

inform [ɪn'fɔːm] *vt*: **to ~ sb (of)** informer *or* avertir qn (de) ♦ *vi*: **to ~ on sb** dénoncer qn

informal [ɪn'fɔːml] *adj* (*person, manner, party*) simple; (*visit, discussion*) dénué(e) de formalités; (*announcement, invitation*) non officiel(le); (*colloquial*) familier(-ère); **~ity** [ɪnfɔː'mælɪtɪ] *n* simplicité *f*, absence *f* de cérémonie; caractère non officiel

informant [ɪn'fɔːmənt] *n* informateur(-trice)

information [ɪnfə'meɪʃən] *n* information *f*; renseignements *mpl*; (*knowledge*) connaissances *fpl*; **a piece of ~** un renseignement; **~ desk** *n* accueil *m*; **~ office** *n* bureau *m* de renseignements

informative [ɪn'fɔːmətɪv] *adj* instructif(-ive)

informer [ɪn'fɔːməʳ] *n* (*also:* **police ~**) indicateur(-trice)

infringe [ɪn'frɪndʒ] *vt* enfreindre ♦ *vi*: **to ~ on** empiéter sur; **~ment** *n*: **~ment (of)** infraction *f* (à)

infuriating [ɪn'fjuərɪeɪtɪŋ] *adj* exaspérant(e)

ingenious [ɪn'dʒiːnjəs] *adj* ingénieux(-euse); **ingenuity** [ɪndʒɪ'njuːɪtɪ] *n* ingéniosité *f*

ingenuous [ɪn'dʒɛnjuəs] *adj* naïf (naïve), ingénu(e)

ingot ['ɪŋgət] *n* lingot *m*

ingrained [ɪn'greɪnd] *adj* enraciné(e)

ingratiate [ɪn'greɪʃɪeɪt] *vt*: **to ~ o.s. with** s'insinuer dans les bonnes grâces de, se faire bien voir de

ingredient [ɪn'griːdɪənt] *n* ingrédient *m*; (*fig*) élément *m*

inhabit [ɪn'hæbɪt] *vt* habiter; **~ant** *n* habitant(e)

inhale [ɪn'heɪl] *vt* respirer; (*smoke*) avaler ♦ *vi* aspirer; (*in smoking*) avaler la fumée

inherent [ɪn'hɪərənt] *adj*: **~ (in** *or* **to)** inhérent(e) (à)

inherit [ɪn'hɛrɪt] *vt* hériter (de); **~ance** *n* héritage *m*

inhibit [ɪn'hɪbɪt] *vt* (*PSYCH*) inhiber; (*growth*) freiner; **~ion** [ɪnhɪ'bɪʃən] *n* inhibition *f*

inhuman [ɪn'hju:mən] *adj* inhumain(e)

initial [ɪ'nɪʃl] *adj* initial(e) ♦ *n* initiale *f* ♦ *vt* parafer; **~s** *npl* (*letters*) initiales *fpl*; (*as signature*) parafe *m*; **~ly** *adv* initialement, au début

initiate [ɪ'nɪʃɪeɪt] *vt* (*start*) entreprendre, amorcer; (*entreprise*) lancer; (*person*) initier; **to ~ proceedings against sb** intenter une action à qn; **initiative** *n* initiative *f*

inject [ɪn'dʒɛkt] *vt* injecter; (*person*): **to ~ sb with sth** faire une piqûre de qch à qn; **~ion** *n* injection *f*, piqûre *f*

injure ['ɪndʒə[r]] *vt* blesser; (*reputation etc*) compromettre; **~d** *adj* blessé(e); **injury** *n* blessure *f*; **~ time** *n* (*SPORT*) arrêts *mpl* de jeu

injustice [ɪn'dʒʌstɪs] *n* injustice *f*

ink [ɪŋk] *n* encre *f*

inkling ['ɪŋklɪŋ] *n*: **to have an/no ~ of** avoir une (vague) idée de/n'avoir aucune idée de

inlaid ['ɪnleɪd] *adj* incrusté(e); (*table etc*) marqueté(e)

inland [*adj* 'ɪnlənd, *adv* ɪn'lænd] *adj* intérieur(e) ♦ *adv* à l'intérieur, dans les terres; **Inland Revenue** (*BRIT*) *n* fisc *m*

in-laws ['ɪnlɔ:z] *npl* beaux-parents *mpl*; belle famille

inlet ['ɪnlɛt] *n* (*GEO*) crique *f*

inmate ['ɪnmeɪt] *n* (*in prison*) détenu(e); (*in asylum*) interné(e)

inn [ɪn] *n* auberge *f*

innate [ɪ'neɪt] *adj* inné(e)

inner ['ɪnə[r]] *adj* intérieur(e); **~ city** *n* centre *m* de zone urbaine; **~ tube** *n* (*of tyre*) chambre *f* à air

innings ['ɪnɪŋz] *n* (*CRICKET*) tour *m* de batte

innocent ['ɪnəsnt] *adj* innocent(e)

innocuous [ɪ'nɔkjuəs] *adj* inoffensif (-ive)

innuendo [ɪnju'ɛndəu] (*pl* **~es**) *n* insinuation *f*, allusion (malveillante)

innumerable [ɪ'nju:mrəbl] *adj* innombrable

inpatient ['ɪnpeɪʃənt] *n* malade hospitalisé(e)

input ['ɪnput] *n* (*resources*) ressources *fpl*; (*COMPUT*) entrée *f* (de données); (*: data*) données *fpl*

inquest ['ɪnkwɛst] *n* enquête *f*; **(coroner's) ~** enquête judiciaire

inquire [ɪn'kwaɪə[r]] *vi* demander ♦ *vt* demander; **to ~ about** se renseigner sur; **~ into** *vt fus* faire une enquête sur; **inquiry** *n* demande *f* de renseignements; (*investigation*) enquête *f*, investigation *f*; **inquiries** *npl*: **the inquiries** (*RAIL etc*) les renseignements; **inquiry** *or* **inquiries office** (*BRIT*) *n* bureau *m* des renseignements

inquisitive [ɪn'kwɪzɪtɪv] *adj* curieux (-euse)

ins *abbr* = **inches**

insane [ɪn'seɪn] *adj* fou (folle); (*MED*) aliéné(e); **insanity** [ɪn'sænɪtɪ] *n* folie *f*; (*MED*) aliénation (mentale)

inscription [ɪn'skrɪpʃən] *n* inscription *f*; (*in book*) dédicace *f*

inscrutable [ɪn'skru:təbl] *adj* impénétrable; (*comment*) obscur(e)

insect ['ɪnsɛkt] *n* insecte *m*; **~icide** [ɪn'sɛktɪsaɪd] *n* insecticide *m*; **~ repellent** *n* crème *f* anti-insecte

insecure [ɪnsɪ'kjuə[r]] *adj* peu solide; peu sûr(e); (*person*) anxieux(-euse)

insensitive [ɪn'sɛnsɪtɪv] *adj* insensible

insert [ɪn'sə:t] *vt* insérer; **~ion** *n* insertion *f*

in-service ['ɪn'sə:vɪs] *adj* (*training*) continu(e), en cours d'emploi; (*course*) de perfectionnement; de recyclage

inshore ['ɪn'ʃɔ:[r]] *adj* côtier(-ère) ♦ *adv* près de la côte; (*move*) vers la côte

inside ['ɪn'saɪd] *n* intérieur *m* ♦ *adj* intérieur(e) ♦ *adv* à l'intérieur, dedans ♦ *prep* à l'intérieur de; (*of time*): **~ 10 minutes** en moins de 10 minutes; **~s**

npl (*inf*) intestins *mpl*; **~ information** *n* renseignements obtenus à la source; **~ lane** *n* (*AUT*: *in Britain*) voie *f* de gauche; (: *in US, Europe etc*) voie de droite; **~ out** *adv* à l'envers; (*know*) à fond; **~r dealing**, **~r trading** *n* (*St Ex*) délit *m* d'initié

insight ['ɪnsaɪt] *n* perspicacité *f*; (*glimpse, idea*) aperçu *m*

insignificant [ɪnsɪg'nɪfɪknt] *adj* insignifiant(e)

insincere [ɪnsɪn'sɪə[r]] *adj* hypocrite

insinuate [ɪn'sɪnjueɪt] *vt* insinuer

insist [ɪn'sɪst] *vi* insister; **to ~ on doing** insister pour faire; **to ~ on sth** exiger qch; **to ~ that** insister pour que; (*claim*) maintenir *or* soutenir que; **~ent** *adj* insistant(e), pressant(e); (*noise, action*) ininterrompu(e)

insole ['ɪnsəul] *n* (*removable*) semelle intérieure

insolent ['ɪnsələnt] *adj* insolent(e)

insolvent [ɪn'sɔlvənt] *adj* insolvable

insomnia [ɪn'sɔmnɪə] *n* insomnie *f*

inspect [ɪn'spɛkt] *vt* inspecter; (*ticket*) contrôler; **~ion** *n* inspection *f*; contrôle *m*; **~or** *n* inspecteur(-trice); (*BRIT*: *on buses, trains*) contrôleur(-euse)

inspire [ɪn'spaɪə[r]] *vt* inspirer

install [ɪn'stɔ:l] *vt* installer; **~ation** [ɪnstə'leɪʃən] *n* installation *f*

instalment [ɪn'stɔ:lmənt] (*US* **installment**) *n* acompte *m*, versement partiel; (*of TV serial etc*) épisode *m*; **in ~s** (*pay*) à tempérament; (*receive*) en plusieurs fois

instance ['ɪnstəns] *n* exemple *m*; **for ~** par exemple; **in the first ~** tout d'abord, en premier lieu

instant ['ɪnstənt] *n* instant *m* ♦ *adj* immédiat(e); (*coffee, food*) instantané(e), en poudre; **~ly** *adv* immédiatement, tout de suite

instead [ɪn'stɛd] *adv* au lieu de cela; **~ of** au lieu de; **~ of sb** à la place de qn

instep ['ɪnstɛp] *n* cou-de-pied *m*; (*of shoe*) cambrure *f*

instigate ['ɪnstɪgeɪt] *vt* (*rebellion*) fomenter, provoquer; (*talks etc*) promouvoir

instil [ɪn'stɪl] *vt*: **to ~ (into)** inculquer (à); (*courage*) insuffler (à)

instinct ['ɪnstɪŋkt] *n* instinct *m*

institute ['ɪnstɪtju:t] *n* institut *m* ♦ *vt* instituer, établir; (*inquiry*) ouvrir; (*proceedings*) entamer

institution [ɪnstɪ'tju:ʃən] *n* institution *f*; (*educational*) établissement *m* (scolaire); (*mental home*) établissement (psychiatrique)

instruct [ɪn'strʌkt] *vt*: **to ~ sb in sth** enseigner qch à qn; **to ~ sb to do** charger qn *or* ordonner à qn de faire; **~ion** *n* instruction *f*; **~ions** *npl* (*orders*) directives *fpl*; **~ions (for use)** mode *m* d'emploi; **~or** *n* professeur *m*; (*for skiing, driving*) moniteur *m*

instrument ['ɪnstrumənt] *n* instrument *m*; **~al** [ɪnstru'mɛntl] *adj*: **to be ~al in** contribuer à; **~ panel** *n* tableau *m* de bord

insufficient [ɪnsə'fɪʃənt] *adj* insuffisant(e)

insular ['ɪnsjulə[r]] *adj* (*outlook*) borné(e); (*person*) aux vues étroites

insulate ['ɪnsjuleɪt] *vt* isoler; (*against sound*) insonoriser; **insulation** [ɪnsju'leɪʃən] *n* isolation *f*; insonorisation *f*

insulin ['ɪnsjulɪn] *n* insuline *f*

insult [*n* 'ɪnsʌlt, *vb* ɪn'sʌlt] *n* insulte *f*, affront *m* ♦ *vt* insulter, faire affront à

insurance [ɪn'ʃuərəns] *n* assurance *f*; **fire/life ~** assurance-incendie/-vie; **~ policy** *n* police *f* d'assurance

insure [ɪn'ʃuə[r]] *vt* assurer; **to ~ (o.s.) against** (*fig*) parer à

intact [ɪn'tækt] *adj* intact(e)

intake ['ɪnteɪk] *n* (*of food, oxygen*) consommation *f*; (*BRIT*: *SCOL*): **an ~ of 200 a year** 200 admissions *fpl* par an

integral ['ɪntɪgrəl] *adj* (*part*) intégrant(e)

integrate ['ɪntɪgreɪt] *vt* intégrer ♦ *vi* s'intégrer

intellect ['ɪntəlɛkt] *n* intelligence *f*; **~ual** [ɪntə'lɛktjuəl] *adj, n* intellectuel(le)
intelligence [ɪn'tɛlɪdʒəns] *n* intelligence *f*; (*MIL etc*) informations *fpl*, renseignements *mpl*; **~ service** *n* services secrets; **intelligent** *adj* intelligent(e)
intend [ɪn'tɛnd] *vt* (*gift etc*): **to ~ sth for** destiner qch à; **to ~ to do** avoir l'intention de faire
intense [ɪn'tɛns] *adj* intense; (*person*) véhément(e); **~ly** *adv* intensément; profondément
intensive [ɪn'tɛnsɪv] *adj* intensif(-ive); **~ care unit** *n* service *m* de réanimation
intent [ɪn'tɛnt] *n* intention *f* ♦ *adj* attentif(-ive); **to all ~s and purposes** en fait, pratiquement; **to be ~ on doing sth** être (bien) décidé à faire qch; **~ion** *n* intention *f*; **~ional** *adj* intentionnel(le), délibéré(e); **~ly** *adv* attentivement
interact [ɪntər'ækt] *vi* avoir une action réciproque; (*people*) communiquer; **~ive** *adj* (*COMPUT*) interactif(-ive)
interchange [*n* 'ɪntətʃeɪndʒ, *vb* ɪntə'tʃeɪndʒ] *n* (*exchange*) échange *m*; (*on motorway*) échangeur *m*; **~able** *adj* interchangeable
intercom ['ɪntəkɔm] *n* interphone *m*
intercourse ['ɪntəkɔːs] *n* (*sexual*) rapports *mpl*
interest ['ɪntrɪst] *n* intérêt *m*; (*pastime*): **my main ~** ce qui m'intéresse le plus; (*COMM*) intérêts *mpl* ♦ *vt* intéresser; **to be ~ed in sth** s'intéresser à qch; **I am ~ed in going** ça m'intéresse d'y aller; **~ing** *adj* intéressant(e); **~ rate** *n* taux *m* d'intérêt
interface ['ɪntəfeɪs] *n* (*COMPUT*) interface *f*
interfere [ɪntə'fɪəʳ] *vi*: **to ~ in** (*quarrel*) s'immiscer dans; (*other people's business*) se mêler de; **to ~ with** (*object*) toucher à; (*plans*) contrecarrer; (*duty*) être en conflit avec; **~nce** *n* (*in affairs*) ingérance *f*; (*RADIO, TV*) parasites *mpl*
interim ['ɪntərɪm] *adj* provisoire ♦ *n*: **in the ~** dans l'intérim, entre-temps
interior [ɪn'tɪərɪəʳ] *n* intérieur *m* ♦ *adj* intérieur(e); (*minister, department*) de l'Intérieur; **~ designer** *n* styliste *m/f*, designer *m/f*
interjection [ɪntə'dʒɛkʃən] *n* (*interruption*) interruption *f*; (*LING*) interjection *f*
interlock [ɪntə'lɔk] *vi* s'enclencher
interlude ['ɪntəluːd] *n* intervalle *m*; (*THEATRE*) intermède *m*
intermediate [ɪntə'miːdɪət] *adj* intermédiaire; (*SCOL*) moyen(ne)
intermission [ɪntə'mɪʃən] *n* pause *f*; (*THEATRE, CINEMA*) entracte *m*
intern [*vb* ɪn'təːn, *n* 'ɪntəːn] *vt* interner ♦ *n* (*US*) interne *m/f*
internal [ɪn'təːnl] *adj* interne; (*politics*) intérieur(e); **~ly** *adv*: **"not to be taken ~ly"** "pour usage externe"; **I~ Revenue Service** (*US*) *n* fisc *m*
international [ɪntə'næʃənl] *adj* international(e)
Internet ['ɪntənɛt] *n* Internet *m*; **~ café** cybercafé *m*; **~ service provider** fournisseur *m* d'accès à Internet
interplay ['ɪntəpleɪ] *n* effet *m* réciproque, interaction *f*
interpret [ɪn'təːprɪt] *vt* interpréter ♦ *vi* servir d'interprète; **~er** *n* interprète *m/f*
interrelated [ɪntərɪ'leɪtɪd] *adj* en corrélation, en rapport étroit
interrogate [ɪn'tɛrəugeɪt] *vt* interroger; (*suspect etc*) soumettre à un interrogatoire; **interrogation** [ɪntɛrəu'geɪʃən] *n* interrogation *f*; interrogatoire *m*
interrupt [ɪntə'rʌpt] *vt, vi* interrompre; **~ion** *n* interruption *f*
intersect [ɪntə'sɛkt] *vi* (*roads*) se croiser, se couper; **~ion** *n* (*of roads*) croisement *m*
intersperse [ɪntə'spəːs] *vt*: **to ~ with** parsemer de
intertwine [ɪntə'twaɪn] *vi* s'entrelacer
interval ['ɪntəvl] *n* intervalle *m*; (*BRIT: THEATRE*) entracte *m*; (*: SPORT*) mi-temps

f; **at ~s** par intervalles
intervene [ɪntə'viːn] *vi* (*person*) intervenir; (*event*) survenir; (*time*) s'écouler (entre-temps); **intervention** *n* intervention *f*
interview ['ɪntəvjuː] *n* (RADIO, TV *etc*) interview *f*; (*for job*) entrevue *f* ♦ *vt* interviewer; avoir une entrevue avec; **~er** *n* (RADIO, TV) interviewer *m*
intestine [ɪn'tɛstɪn] *n* intestin *m*
intimacy ['ɪntɪməsɪ] *n* intimité *f*
intimate [*adj* 'ɪntɪmət, *vb* 'ɪntɪmeɪt] *adj* intime; (*friendship*) profond(e); (*knowledge*) approfondi(e) ♦ *vt* (*hint*) suggérer, laisser entendre
into ['ɪntu] *prep* dans; **~ pieces/French** en morceaux/français
intolerant [ɪn'tɔlərnt] *adj*: **~ (of)** intolérant(e) (de)
intoxicated [ɪn'tɔksɪkeɪtɪd] *adj* (*drunk*) ivre
intractable [ɪn'træktəbl] *adj* (*child*) indocile, insoumis(e); (*problem*) insoluble
intranet ['ɪntrənɛt] *n* intranet *m*
intransitive [ɪn'trænsɪtɪv] *adj* intransitif(-ive)
intravenous [ɪntrə'viːnəs] *adj* intraveineux(-euse)
in-tray ['ɪntreɪ] *n* courrier *m* "arrivée"
intricate ['ɪntrɪkət] *adj* complexe, compliqué(e)
intrigue [ɪn'triːg] *n* intrigue *f* ♦ *vt* intriguer; **intriguing** *adj* fascinant(e)
intrinsic [ɪn'trɪnsɪk] *adj* intrinsèque
introduce [ɪntrə'djuːs] *vt* introduire; (TV *show, people to each other*) présenter; **to ~ sb to** (*pastime, technique*) initier qn à; **introduction** *n* introduction *f*; (*of person*) présentation *f*; (*to new experience*) initiation *f*; **introductory** *adj* préliminaire, d'introduction; **introductory offer** *n* (COMM) offre *f* de lancement
intrude [ɪn'truːd] *vi* (*person*) être importun(e); **to ~ on** (*conversation etc*) s'immiscer dans; **~r** *n* intrus(e)
intuition [ɪntjuː'ɪʃən] *n* intuition *f*
inundate ['ɪnʌndeɪt] *vt*: **to ~ with** inonder de
invade [ɪn'veɪd] *vt* envahir
invalid [*n* 'ɪnvəlɪd, *adj* ɪn'vælɪd] *n* malade *m/f*; (*with disability*) invalide *m/f* ♦ *adj* (*not valid*) non valide *or* valable
invaluable [ɪn'væljuəbl] *adj* inestimable, inappréciable
invariably [ɪn'vɛərɪəblɪ] *adv* invariablement; toujours
invent [ɪn'vɛnt] *vt* inventer; **~ion** *n* invention *f*; **~ive** *adj* inventif(-ive); **~or** *n* inventeur(-trice)
inventory ['ɪnvəntrɪ] *n* inventaire *m*
invert [ɪn'vəːt] *vt* intervertir; (*cup, object*) retourner; **~ed commas** (BRIT) *npl* guillemets *mpl*
invest [ɪn'vɛst] *vt* investir ♦ *vi*: **to ~ in sth** placer son argent dans qch; (*fig*) s'offrir qch
investigate [ɪn'vɛstɪgeɪt] *vt* (*crime etc*) faire une enquête sur; **investigation** [ɪnvɛstɪ'geɪʃən] *n* (*of crime*) enquête *f*
investment [ɪn'vɛstmənt] *n* investissement *m*, placement *m*
investor [ɪn'vɛstər] *n* investisseur *m*; actionnaire *m/f*
invigilator [ɪn'vɪdʒɪleɪtər] *n* surveillant(e)
invigorating [ɪn'vɪgəreɪtɪŋ] *adj* vivifiant(e); (*fig*) stimulant(e)
invisible [ɪn'vɪzɪbl] *adj* invisible
invitation [ɪnvɪ'teɪʃən] *n* invitation *f*
invite [ɪn'vaɪt] *vt* inviter; (*opinions etc*) demander; **inviting** *adj* engageant(e), attrayant(e)
invoice ['ɪnvɔɪs] *n* facture *f*
involuntary [ɪn'vɔləntrɪ] *adj* involontaire
involve [ɪn'vɔlv] *vt* (*entail*) entraîner, nécessiter; (*concern*) concerner; (*associate*): **to ~ sb (in)** impliquer qn (dans), mêler qn (à); faire participer qn (à); **~d** *adj* (*complicated*) complexe; **to be ~d in** participer à; **~ment** *n*: **~ment (in)** participation *f* (à); rôle *m* (dans); (*enthusiasm*) enthousiasme *m* (pour)
inward ['ɪnwəd] *adj* (*thought, feeling*)

profond(e), intime; (*movement*) vers l'intérieur; **~(s)** *adv* vers l'intérieur
iodine ['aɪəudiːn] *n* iode *m*
iota [aɪ'əutə] *n* (*fig*) brin *m*, grain *m*
IOU *n abbr* (= *I owe you*) reconnaissance *f* de dette
IQ *n abbr* (= *intelligence quotient*) Q.I. *m*
IRA *n abbr* (= *Irish Republican Army*) IRA *f*
Iran [ɪ'rɑːn] *n* Iran *m*
Iraq [ɪ'rɑːk] *n* Irak *m*
irate [aɪ'reɪt] *adj* courroucé(e)
Ireland ['aɪələnd] *n* Irlande *f*
iris ['aɪrɪs] (*pl* **~es**) *n* iris *m*
Irish ['aɪrɪʃ] *adj* irlandais(e) ♦ *npl*: **the ~** les Irlandais; **~man** (*irreg*) *n* Irlandais *m*; **~ Sea** *n* mer *f* d'Irlande; **~woman** (*irreg*) *n* Irlandaise *f*
iron ['aɪən] *n* fer *m*; (*for clothes*) fer *m* à repasser ♦ *cpd* de *or* en fer; (*fig*) de fer ♦ *vt* (*clothes*) repasser; **~ out** *vt* (*fig*) aplanir; faire disparaître
ironic(al) [aɪ'rɔnɪk(l)] *adj* ironique
ironing ['aɪənɪŋ] *n* repassage *m*; **~ board** *n* planche *f* à repasser
ironmonger's (shop) ['aɪənmʌŋgəz-] *n* quincaillerie *f*
irony ['aɪrənɪ] *n* ironie *f*
irrational [ɪ'ræʃənl] *adj* irrationnel(le)
irregular [ɪ'rɛgjuləʳ] *adj* irrégulier(-ère); (*surface*) inégal(e)
irrelevant [ɪ'rɛləvənt] *adj* sans rapport, hors de propos
irresistible [ɪrɪ'zɪstɪbl] *adj* irrésistible
irrespective [ɪrɪ'spɛktɪv]: **~ of** *prep* sans tenir compte de
irresponsible [ɪrɪ'spɔnsɪbl] *adj* (*act*) irréfléchi(e); (*person*) irresponsable
irrigate ['ɪrɪgeɪt] *vt* irriguer; **irrigation** [ɪrɪ'geɪʃən] *n* irrigation *f*
irritate ['ɪrɪteɪt] *vt* irriter
irritating *adj* irritant(e); **irritation** [ɪrɪ'teɪʃən] *n* irritation *f*
IRS *n abbr* = **Internal Revenue Service**
is [ɪz] *vb see* **be**
Islam ['ɪzlɑːm] *n* Islam *m*; **~ic** *adj* islamique; **~ic fundamentalists** intégristes *mpl* musulmans
island ['aɪlənd] *n* île *f*; **~er** *n* habitant(e) d'une île, insulaire *m/f*
isle [aɪl] *n* île *f*
isn't ['ɪznt] = **is not**
isolate ['aɪsəleɪt] *vt* isoler; **~d** *adj* isolé(e); **isolation** *n* isolation *f*
ISP *n abbr* = **Internet service provider**
Israel ['ɪzreɪl] *n* Israël *m*; **~i** [ɪz'reɪlɪ] *adj* israélien(ne) ♦ *n* Israélien(ne)
issue ['ɪʃjuː] *n* question *f*, problème *m*; (*of book*) publication *f*, parution *f*; (*of banknotes etc*) émission *f*; (*of newspaper etc*) numéro *m* ♦ *vt* (*rations, equipment*) distribuer; (*statement*) publier, faire; (*banknotes etc*) émettre, mettre en circulation; **at ~** en jeu, en cause; **to take ~ with sb (over)** exprimer son désaccord avec qn (sur); **to make an ~ of sth** faire une montagne de qch

KEYWORD

it [ɪt] *pron* **1** (*specific: subject*) il (elle); (*: direct object*) le (la) (l'); (*: indirect object*) lui; **it's on the table** c'est *or* il (*or* elle) est sur la table; **about/from/of it** en; **I spoke to him about it** je lui en ai parlé; **what did you learn from it?** qu'est-ce que vous en avez retiré?; **I'm proud of it** j'en suis fier; **in/to it** y; **put the book in it** mettez-y le livre; **he agreed to it** il y a consenti; **did you go to it?** (*party, concert etc*) est-ce que vous y êtes allé(s)?
2 (*impersonal*) il; ce; **it's raining** il pleut; **it's Friday tomorrow** demain c'est vendredi *or* nous sommes vendredi; **it's 6 o'clock** il est 6 heures; **who is it? - it's me** qui est-ce? - c'est moi

Italian [ɪ'tæljən] *adj* italien(ne) ♦ *n* Italien(ne); (LING) italien *m*
italics [ɪ'tælɪks] *npl* italiques *fpl*
Italy ['ɪtəlɪ] *n* Italie *f*
itch [ɪtʃ] *n* démangeaison *f* ♦ *vi* (*person*) éprouver des démangeaisons; (*part of*

body) démanger; **I'm ~ing to do** l'envie me démange de faire; **~y** *adj* qui démange; **to be ~y** avoir des démangeaisons
it'd ['ɪtd] = **it would; it had**
item ['aɪtəm] *n* article *m*; (*on agenda*) question *f*, point *m*; (*also:* **news ~**) nouvelle *f*; **~ize** *vt* détailler, faire une liste de
itinerary [aɪ'tɪnərərɪ] *n* itinéraire *m*
it'll ['ɪtl] = **it will; it shall**
its [ɪts] *adj* son (sa), ses *pl*
it's [ɪts] = **it is; it has**
itself [ɪt'sɛlf] *pron* (*reflexive*) se; (*emphatic*) lui-même (elle-même)
ITV *n abbr* (BRIT: *Independent Television*) *chaîne privée*
IUD *n abbr* (= *intra-uterine device*) DIU *m*, stérilet *m*
I've [aɪv] = **I have**
ivory ['aɪvərɪ] *n* ivoire *m*
ivy ['aɪvɪ] *n* lierre *m*

J, j

jab [dʒæb] *vt*: **to ~ sth into** enfoncer *or* planter qch dans ♦ *n* (*inf*: *injection*) piqûre *f*
jack [dʒæk] *n* (AUT) cric *m*; (CARDS) valet *m*; **~ up** *vt* soulever (au cric)
jackal ['dʒækl] *n* chacal *m*
jacket ['dʒækɪt] *n* veste *f*, veston *m*; (*of book*) jaquette *f*, couverture *f*; **~ potato** *n* pomme *f* de terre en robe des champs
jack: ~knife *vi*: **the lorry ~knifed** la remorque (du camion) s'est mise en travers; **~ plug** *n* (ELEC) prise jack mâle *f*; **~pot** *n* gros lot
jaded ['dʒeɪdɪd] *adj* éreinté(e), fatigué(e)
jagged ['dʒægɪd] *adj* dentelé(e)
jail [dʒeɪl] *n* prison *f* ♦ *vt* emprisonner, mettre en prison
jam [dʒæm] *n* confiture *f*; (*also:* **traffic ~**) embouteillage *m* ♦ *vt* (*passage etc*) encombrer, obstruer; (*mechanism, drawer etc*) bloquer, coincer; (RADIO) brouiller ♦ *vi* se coincer, se bloquer; (*gun*) s'enrayer; **to be in a ~** (*inf*) être dans le pétrin; **to ~ sth into** entasser qch dans; enfoncer qch dans
Jamaica [dʒə'meɪkə] *n* Jamaïque *f*
jam: ~ jar *n* pot *m* à confiture; **~med** *adj* (*window etc*) coincé(e); **~-packed** *adj*: **~-packed (with)** bourré(e) (de)
jangle ['dʒæŋgl] *vi* cliqueter
janitor ['dʒænɪtə[r]] *n* concierge *m*
January ['dʒænjuərɪ] *n* janvier *m*
Japan [dʒə'pæn] *n* Japon *m*; **~ese** [dʒæpə'ni:z] *adj* japonais(e) ♦ *n inv* Japonais(e); (LING) japonais *m*
jar [dʒɑ:[r]] *n* (*stone, earthenware*) pot *m*; (*glass*) bocal *m* ♦ *vi* (*sound discordant*) produire un son grinçant *or* discordant; (*colours etc*) jurer
jargon ['dʒɑ:gən] *n* jargon *m*
jaundice ['dʒɔ:ndɪs] *n* jaunisse *f*
javelin ['dʒævlɪn] *n* javelot *m*
jaw [dʒɔ:] *n* mâchoire *f*
jay [dʒeɪ] *n* geai *m*; **~walker** *n* piéton indiscipliné
jazz [dʒæz] *n* jazz *m*; **~ up** *vt* animer, égayer
jealous ['dʒɛləs] *adj* jaloux(-ouse); **~y** *n* jalousie *f*
jeans [dʒi:nz] *npl* jean *m*
jeer [dʒɪə[r]] *vi*: **to ~ (at)** se moquer cruellement (de), railler
Jehovah's Witness [dʒɪ'həuvəz-] *n* témoin *m* de Jéhovah
jelly ['dʒɛlɪ] *n* gelée *f*; **~fish** ['dʒɛlɪfɪʃ] *n* méduse *f*
jeopardy ['dʒɛpədɪ] *n*: **to be in ~** être en danger *or* péril
jerk [dʒə:k] *n* secousse *f*; saccade *f*; sursaut *m*, spasme *m*; (*inf*: *idiot*) pauvre type *m* ♦ *vt* (*pull*) tirer brusquement ♦ *vi* (*vehicles*) cahoter
jersey ['dʒə:zɪ] *n* (*pullover*) tricot *m*; (*fabric*) jersey *m*
Jesus ['dʒi:zəs] *n* Jésus
jet [dʒɛt] *n* (*gas, liquid*) jet *m*; (AVIAT)

avion *m* à réaction, jet *m*; **~-black** *adj* (d'un noir) de jais; **~ engine** *n* moteur *m* à réaction; **~ lag** *n* (fatigue due au) décalage *m* horaire

jettison ['dʒɛtɪsn] *vt* jeter par-dessus bord

jetty ['dʒɛtɪ] *n* jetée *f*, digue *f*

Jew [dʒu:] *n* Juif *m*

jewel ['dʒu:əl] *n* bijou *m*, joyau *m*; (*in watch*) rubis *m*; **~ler** (US **jeweler**) *n* bijoutier(-ère), joaillier *m*; **~ler's (shop)** *n* bijouterie *f*, joaillerie *f*; **~lery** (US **jewelry**) *n* bijoux *mpl*

Jewess ['dʒu:ɪs] *n* Juive *f*

Jewish ['dʒu:ɪʃ] *adj* juif (juive)

jibe [dʒaɪb] *n* sarcasme *m*

jiffy ['dʒɪfɪ] (*inf*) *n*: **in a ~** en un clin d'œil

jigsaw ['dʒɪgsɔ:] *n* (*also:* **~ puzzle**) puzzle *m*

jilt [dʒɪlt] *vt* laisser tomber, plaquer

jingle ['dʒɪŋgl] *n* (*for advert*) couplet *m* publicitaire ♦ *vi* cliqueter, tinter

jinx [dʒɪŋks] (*inf*) *n* (mauvais) sort

jitters ['dʒɪtəz] (*inf*) *npl*: **to get the ~** (*inf*) avoir la trouille *or* la frousse

job [dʒɔb] *n* (*chore, task*) travail *m*, tâche *f*; (*employment*) emploi *m*, poste *m*, place *f*; **it's a good ~ that ...** c'est heureux *or* c'est une chance que ...; **just the ~!** (c'est) juste *or* exactement ce qu'il faut!; **~ centre** (BRIT) *n* agence *f* pour l'emploi; **~less** *adj* sans travail, au chômage

jockey ['dʒɔkɪ] *n* jockey *m* ♦ *vi*: **to ~ for position** manœuvrer pour être bien placé

jog [dʒɔg] *vt* secouer ♦ *vi* (SPORT) faire du jogging; **to ~ sb's memory** rafraîchir la mémoire de qn; **~ along** *vi* cheminer; trotter; **~ging** *n* jogging *m*

join [dʒɔɪn] *vt* (*put together*) unir, assembler; (*become member of*) s'inscrire à; (*meet*) rejoindre, retrouver; (*queue*) se joindre à ♦ *vi* (*roads, rivers*) se rejoindre, se rencontrer ♦ *n* raccord *m*; **~ in** *vi* se mettre de la partie, participer ♦ *vt fus* participer à, se mêler à; **~ up** *vi* (*meet*) se rejoindre; (MIL) s'engager

joiner ['dʒɔɪnə[r]] (BRIT) *n* menuisier *m*

joint [dʒɔɪnt] *n* (TECH) jointure *f*, joint *m*; (ANAT) articulation *f*, jointure; (BRIT: CULIN) rôti *m*; (*inf: place*) boîte *f*; (*: of cannabis*) joint *m* ♦ *adj* commun(e); **~ account** *n* (*with bank etc*) compte joint

joke [dʒəuk] *n* plaisanterie *f*; (*also:* **practical ~**) farce *f* ♦ *vi* plaisanter; **to play a ~ on** jouer un tour à, faire une farce à; **~r** *n* (CARDS) joker *m*

jolly ['dʒɔlɪ] *adj* gai(e), enjoué(e); (*enjoyable*) amusant(e), plaisant(e) ♦ *adv* (BRIT: *inf*) rudement, drôlement

jolt [dʒəult] *n* cahot *m*, secousse *f*; (*shock*) choc *m* ♦ *vt* cahoter, secouer

Jordan ['dʒɔ:dən] *n* (*country*) Jordanie *f*

jostle ['dʒɔsl] *vt* bousculer, pousser

jot [dʒɔt] *n*: **not one ~** pas un brin; **~ down** *vt* noter; **~ter** (BRIT) *n* cahier *m* (de brouillon); (*pad*) bloc-notes *m*

journal ['dʒə:nl] *n* journal *m*; **~ism** *n* journalisme *m*; **~ist** *n* journaliste *m/f*

journey ['dʒə:nɪ] *n* voyage *m*; (*distance covered*) trajet *m*

joy [dʒɔɪ] *n* joie *f*; **~ful** *adj* joyeux (-euse); **~rider** *n personne qui fait une virée dans une voiture volée*; **~stick** *n* (AVIAT, COMPUT) manche *m* à balai

JP *n abbr* = **Justice of the Peace**

Jr *abbr* = **junior**

jubilant ['dʒu:bɪlnt] *adj* triomphant(e); réjoui(e)

judge [dʒʌdʒ] *n* juge *m* ♦ *vt* juger; **judg(e)ment** *n* jugement *m*

judicial [dʒu:'dɪʃl] *adj* judiciaire; **judiciary** *n* (pouvoir *m*) judiciaire *m*

judo ['dʒu:dəu] *n* judo *m*

jug [dʒʌg] *n* pot *m*, cruche *f*

juggernaut ['dʒʌgənɔ:t] (BRIT) *n* (*huge truck*) énorme poids lourd

juggle ['dʒʌgl] *vi* jongler; **~r** *n* jongleur *m*

juice [dʒu:s] *n* jus *m*; **juicy** *adj* juteux (-euse)

jukebox ['dʒu:kbɔks] *n* juke-box *m*
July [dʒu:'laɪ] *n* juillet *m*
jumble ['dʒʌmbl] *n* fouillis *m* ♦ *vt* (*also:* **~ up**) mélanger, brouiller; **~ sale** (*BRIT*) *n* vente *f* de charité

jumble sale

Les **jumble sales** *ont lieu dans les églises, salles de fêtes ou halls d'écoles, et l'on y vend des articles de toutes sortes, en général bon marché et surtout d'occasion, pour collecter des fonds pour une œuvre de charité, une école ou encore une église.*

jumbo (jet) ['dʒʌmbəu-] *n* jumbo-jet *m*, gros porteur
jump [dʒʌmp] *vi* sauter, bondir; (*start*) sursauter; (*increase*) monter en flèche ♦ *vt* sauter, franchir ♦ *n* saut *m*, bond *m*; sursaut *m*; **to ~ the queue** (*BRIT*) passer avant son tour
jumper ['dʒʌmpər] *n* (*BRIT*: *pullover*) pull-over *m*; (*US*: *dress*) robe-chasuble *f*
jumper cables (*US*: *BRIT* **jump leads**) *npl* câbles *mpl* de démarrage
jumpy ['dʒʌmpɪ] *adj* nerveux(-euse), agité(e)
Jun. *abbr* = **junior**
junction ['dʒʌŋkʃən] (*BRIT*) *n* (*of roads*) carrefour *m*; (*of rails*) embranchement *m*
juncture ['dʒʌŋktʃər] *n*: **at this ~** à ce moment-là, sur ces entrefaites
June [dʒu:n] *n* juin *m*
jungle ['dʒʌŋgl] *n* jungle *f*
junior ['dʒu:nɪər] *adj*, *n*: **he's ~ to me (by 2 years), he's my ~ (by 2 years)** il est mon cadet (de 2 ans), il est plus jeune que moi (de 2 ans); **he's ~ to me** (*seniority*) il est en dessous de moi (dans la hiérarchie), j'ai plus d'ancienneté que lui; **~ school** (*BRIT*) *n* ≈ école *f* primaire
junk [dʒʌŋk] *n* (*rubbish*) camelote *f*; (*cheap goods*) bric-à-brac *m inv*; **~ food** *n* aliments *mpl* sans grande valeur nutritive; **~ mail** *n* prospectus *mpl* (non sollicités); **~ shop** *n* (boutique *f* de) brocanteur *m*
Junr *abbr* = **junior**
juror ['dʒuərər] *n* juré *m*
jury ['dʒuərɪ] *n* jury *m*
just [dʒʌst] *adj* juste ♦ *adv*: **he's ~ done it/left** il vient de le faire/partir; **~ right/two o'clock** exactement *or* juste ce qu'il faut/deux heures; **she's ~ as clever as you** elle est tout aussi intelligente que vous; **it's ~ as well (that)** ... heureusement que ...; **~ as he was leaving** au moment *or* à l'instant précis où il partait; **~ before/enough/here** juste avant/assez/ici; **it's ~ me/a mistake** ce n'est que moi/(rien) qu'une erreur; **~ missed/caught** manqué/attrapé de justesse; **~ listen to this!** écoutez un peu ça!
justice ['dʒʌstɪs] *n* justice *f*; (*US*: *judge*) juge *m* de la Cour suprême; **J~ of the Peace** *n* juge *m* de paix
justify ['dʒʌstɪfaɪ] *vt* justifier
jut [dʒʌt] *vi* (*also:* **~ out**) dépasser, faire saillie
juvenile ['dʒu:vənaɪl] *adj* juvénile; (*court, books*) pour enfants ♦ *n* adolescent(e)

K, k

K *abbr* (= *one thousand*) K; (= *kilobyte*) Ko
kangaroo [kæŋgə'ru:] *n* kangourou *m*
karate [kə'rɑ:tɪ] *n* karaté *m*
kebab [kə'bæb] *n* kébab *m*
keel [ki:l] *n* quille *f*; **on an even ~** (*fig*) à flot
keen [ki:n] *adj* (*eager*) plein(e) d'enthousiasme; (*interest, desire, competition*) vif (vive); (*eye, intelligence*) pénétrant(e); (*edge*) effilé(e); **to be ~ to do** *or* **on doing sth** désirer vivement faire qch, tenir beaucoup à faire qch; **to be ~ on sth/sb** aimer beaucoup qch/qn

keep [ki:p] (*pt, pp* **kept**) *vt* (*retain, preserve*) garder; (*detain*) retenir; (*shop, accounts, diary, promise*) tenir; (*house*) avoir; (*support*) entretenir; (*chickens, bees etc*) élever ♦ *vi* (*remain*) rester; (*food*) se conserver ♦ *n* (*of castle*) donjon *m*; (*food etc*): **enough for his ~** assez pour (assurer) sa subsistance; (*inf*): **for ~s** pour de bon, pour toujours; **to ~ doing sth** ne pas arrêter de faire qch; **to ~ sb from doing** empêcher qn de faire *or* que qn ne fasse; **to ~ sb happy/a place tidy** faire que qn soit content/qu'un endroit reste propre; **to ~ sth to o.s.** garder qch pour soi, tenir qch secret; **to ~ sth (back) from sb** cacher qch à qn; **to ~ time** (*clock*) être à l'heure, ne pas retarder; **well kept** bien entretenu(e); **~ on** *vi*: **to ~ on doing** continuer à faire; **don't ~ on about it!** arrête (d'en parler)!; **~ out** *vt* empêcher d'entrer; **"~ out"** "défense d'entrer"; **~ up** *vt* continuer, maintenir ♦ *vi*: **to ~ up with sb** (*in race etc*) aller aussi vite que qn; (*in work etc*) se maintenir au niveau de qn; **~er** *n* gardien(ne); **~-fit** *n* gymnastique *f* d'entretien; **~ing** *n* (*care*) garde *f*; **in ~ing with** en accord avec; **~sake** *n* souvenir *m*

kennel ['kɛnl] *n* niche *f*; **~s** *npl* (*boarding ~s*) chenil *m*

kerb [kə:b] (*BRIT*) *n* bordure *f* du trottoir

kernel ['kə:nl] *n* (*of nut*) amande *f*; (*fig*) noyau *m*

kettle ['kɛtl] *n* bouilloire *f*; **~drum** *n* timbale *f*

key [ki:] *n* (*gen* , *MUS*) clé *f*; (*of piano, typewriter*) touche *f* ♦ *cpd* clé ♦ *vt* (*also:* **~ in**) saisir; **~board** *n* clavier *m*; **~ card** *n* (*at hotel etc*) carte *f* magnétique; **~ed up** *adj* (*person*) surexcité(e); **~hole** *n* trou *m* de la serrure; **~hole surgery** *n* chirurgie *f* endoscopique; **~note** *n* (*of speech*) note dominante; (*MUS*) tonique *f*; **~ ring** *n* porte-clés *m*

khaki ['kɑ:kɪ] *n* kaki *m*

kick [kɪk] *vt* donner un coup de pied à ♦ *vi* (*horse*) ruer ♦ *n* coup *m* de pied; (*thrill*): **he does it for ~s** il le fait parce que ça l'excite, il le fait pour le plaisir; **to ~ the habit** (*inf*) arrêter; **~ off** *vi* (*SPORT*) donner le coup d'envoi

kid [kɪd] *n* (*inf: child*) gamin(e), gosse *m/f*; (*animal, leather*) chevreau *m* ♦ *vi* (*inf*) plaisanter, blaguer

kidnap ['kɪdnæp] *vt* enlever, kidnapper; **~per** *n* ravisseur(-euse); **~ping** *n* enlèvement *m*

kidney ['kɪdnɪ] *n* (*ANAT*) rein *m*; (*CULIN*) rognon *m*

kill [kɪl] *vt* tuer ♦ *n* mise *f* à mort; **~er** *n* tueur(-euse); meurtrier(-ère); **~ing** *n* meurtre *m*; (*of group of people*) tuerie *f*, massacre *m*; **to make a ~ing** (*inf*) réussir un beau coup (de filet); **~joy** *n* rabat-joie *m/f*

kiln [kɪln] *n* four *m*

kilo ['ki:ləu] *n* kilo *m*; **~byte** *n* (*COMPUT*) kilo-octet *m*; **~gram(me)** *n* kilogramme *m*; **~metre** (*US* **kilometer**) *n* kilomètre *m*; **~watt** *n* kilowatt *m*

kilt [kɪlt] *n* kilt *m*

kin [kɪn] *n see* **next**

kind [kaɪnd] *adj* gentil(le), aimable ♦ *n* sorte *f*, espèce *f*, genre *m*; **to be two of a ~** se ressembler; **in ~** (*COMM*) en nature

kindergarten ['kɪndəgɑ:tn] *n* jardin *m* d'enfants

kind-hearted [kaɪnd'hɑ:tɪd] *adj* bon (bonne)

kindle ['kɪndl] *vt* allumer, enflammer

kindly ['kaɪndlɪ] *adj* bienveillant(e), plein(e) de gentillesse ♦ *adv* avec bonté; **will you ~ ...!** auriez-vous la bonté *or* l'obligeance de ...?

kindness ['kaɪndnɪs] *n* bonté *f*, gentillesse *f*

king [kɪŋ] *n* roi *m*; **~dom** *n* royaume *m*; **~fisher** *n* martin-pêcheur *m*; **~-size bed** *n* grand lit (*de 1,95 m de large*); **~-size(d)** *adj* format géant *inv*; (*cigarettes*) long (longue)

kiosk ['ki:ɔsk] *n* kiosque *m*; (*BRIT*: *TEL*) cabine *f* (téléphonique)
kipper ['kɪpə^r] *n* hareng fumé et salé
kiss [kɪs] *n* baiser *m* ♦ *vt* embrasser; **to ~ (each other)** s'embrasser; **~ of life** (*BRIT*) *n* bouche à bouche *m*
kit [kɪt] *n* équipement *m*, matériel *m*; (*set of tools etc*) trousse *f*; (*for assembly*) kit *m*
kitchen ['kɪtʃɪn] *n* cuisine *f*; **~ sink** *n* évier *m*
kite [kaɪt] *n* (*toy*) cerf-volant *m*
kitten ['kɪtn] *n* chaton *m*, petit chat
kitty ['kɪtɪ] *n* (*money*) cagnotte *f*
km *abbr* = **kilometre**
knack [næk] *n*: **to have the ~ of doing** avoir le coup pour faire
knapsack ['næpsæk] *n* musette *f*
knead [ni:d] *vt* pétrir
knee [ni:] *n* genou *m*; **~cap** *n* rotule *f*
kneel [ni:l] (*pt, pp* **knelt**) *vi* (*also:* **~ down**) s'agenouiller
knew [nju:] *pt of* **know**
knickers ['nɪkəz] (*BRIT*) *npl* culotte *f* (de femme)
knife [naɪf] (*pl* **knives**) *n* couteau *m* ♦ *vt* poignarder, frapper d'un coup de couteau
knight [naɪt] *n* chevalier *m*; (*CHESS*) cavalier *m*; **~hood** (*BRIT*) *n* (*title*): **to get a ~hood** être fait chevalier
knit [nɪt] *vt* tricoter ♦ *vi* tricoter; (*broken bones*) se ressouder; **to ~ one's brows** froncer les sourcils; **~ting** *n* tricot *m*; **~ting needle** *n* aiguille *f* à tricoter; **~wear** *n* tricots *mpl*, lainages *mpl*
knives [naɪvz] *npl of* **knife**
knob [nɔb] *n* bouton *m*
knock [nɔk] *vt* frapper; (*bump into*) heurter; (*inf*) dénigrer ♦ *vi* (*at door etc*): **to ~ at** *or* **on** frapper à ♦ *n* coup *m*; **~ down** *vt* renverser; **~ off** *vi* (*inf: finish*) s'arrêter (de travailler) ♦ *vt* (*from price*) faire un rabais de; (*inf: steal*) piquer; **~ out** *vt* assommer; (*BOXING*) mettre k.-o.; (*defeat*) éliminer; **~ over** *vt* renverser, faire tomber; **~er** *n* (*on door*) heurtoir *m*; **~out** *n* (*BOXING*) knock-out *m*, K.-O. *m*; **~out competition** compétition *f* avec épreuves éliminatoires
knot [nɔt] *n* (*gen*) nœud *m* ♦ *vt* nouer
know [nəu] (*pt* **knew**, *pp* **known**) *vt* savoir; (*person, place*) connaître; **to ~ how to do** savoir (comment) faire; **to ~ how to swim** savoir nager; **to ~ about** *or* **of sth** être au courant de qch; **to ~ about** *or* **of sb** avoir entendu parler de qn; **~-all** (*pej*) *n* je-sais-tout *m/f*; **~-how** *n* savoir-faire *m*; **~ing** *adj* (*look etc*) entendu(e); **~ingly** *adv* sciemment; (*smile, look*) d'un air entendu
knowledge ['nɔlɪdʒ] *n* connaissance *f*; (*learning*) connaissances, savoir *m*; **~able** *adj* bien informé(e)
knuckle ['nʌkl] *n* articulation *f* (des doigts), jointure *f*
Koran [kɔ'rɑ:n] *n* Coran *m*
Korea [kə'rɪə] *n* Corée *f*
kosher ['kəuʃə^r] *adj* kascher *inv*
Kosovo ['kɔsɔvəu] *n* Kosovo *m*

L, l

L *abbr* (= *lake, large*) L; (= *left*) g; (*BRIT*: *AUT*: *learner*) *signale un conducteur débutant*
lab [læb] *n abbr* (= *laboratory*) labo *m*
label ['leɪbl] *n* étiquette *f* ♦ *vt* étiqueter
labor *etc* ['leɪbə^r] (*US*) = **labour** *etc*
laboratory [lə'bɔrətərɪ] *n* laboratoire *m*
labour ['leɪbə^r] (*US* **labor**) *n* (*work*) travail *m*; (*workforce*) main-d'œuvre *f* ♦ *vi*: **to ~ (at)** travailler dur (à), peiner (sur) ♦ *vt*: **to ~ a point** insister sur un point; **in ~** (*MED*) en travail, en train d'accoucher; **L~, the L~ party** (*BRIT*) le parti travailliste, les travaillistes *mpl*; **~ed** ['leɪbəd] *adj* (*breathing*) pénible, difficile; **~er** *n* manœuvre *m*; **farm ~er** ouvrier *m* agricole
lace [leɪs] *n* dentelle *f*; (*of shoe etc*) lacet *m* ♦ *vt* (*shoe*: *also:* **~ up**) lacer
lack [læk] *n* manque *m* ♦ *vt* manquer

de; **through** *or* **for ~ of** faute de, par manque de; **to be ~ing** manquer, faire défaut; **to be ~ing in** manquer de

lacquer ['lækəʳ] *n* laque *f*

lad [læd] *n* garçon *m*, gars *m*

ladder ['lædəʳ] *n* échelle *f*; (BRIT: *in tights*) maille filée

laden ['leɪdn] *adj*: **~ (with)** chargé(e) (de)

ladle ['leɪdl] *n* louche *f*

lady ['leɪdɪ] *n* dame *f*; (*in address*): **ladies and gentlemen** Mesdames (et) Messieurs; **young ~** jeune fille *f*; (*married*) jeune femme *f*; **the ladies' (room)** les toilettes *fpl* (pour dames); **~bird** (US **ladybug**) *n* coccinelle *f*; **~like** *adj* distingué(e); **~ship** *n*: **your ~ship** Madame la comtesse/la baronne *etc*

lag [læg] *n* retard *m* ♦ *vi* (*also:* **~ behind**) rester en arrière, traîner; (*fig*) rester en traîne ♦ *vt* (*pipes*) calorifuger

lager ['lɑːgəʳ] *n* bière blonde

lagoon [lə'guːn] *n* lagune *f*

laid [leɪd] *pt, pp of* **lay**; **~-back** (*inf*) *adj* relaxe, décontracté(e); **~ up** *adj* alité(e)

lain [leɪn] *pp of* **lie**

lake [leɪk] *n* lac *m*

lamb [læm] *n* agneau *m*; **~ chop** *n* côtelette *f* d'agneau

lame [leɪm] *adj* boiteux(-euse)

lament [lə'mɛnt] *n* lamentation *f* ♦ *vt* pleurer, se lamenter sur

laminated ['læmɪneɪtɪd] *adj* laminé(e); (*windscreen*) (en verre) feuilleté

lamp [læmp] *n* lampe *f*; **~post** (BRIT) *n* réverbère *m*; **~shade** *n* abat-jour *m inv*

lance [lɑːns] *vt* (MED) inciser

land [lænd] *n* (*as opposed to sea*) terre *f* (ferme); (*soil*) terre; terrain *m*; (*estate*) terre(s), domaine(s) *m(pl)*; (*country*) pays *m* ♦ *vi* (AVIAT) atterrir; (*fig*) (re)tomber ♦ *vt* (*passengers, goods*) débarquer; **to ~ sb with sth** (*inf*) coller qch à qn; **~ up** *vi* atterrir, (finir par) se retrouver; **~fill site** *n* décharge *f*; **~ing** *n* (AVIAT) atterrissage *m*; (*of staircase*) palier *m*; (*of troops*) débarquement *m*; **~ing strip** *n* piste *f* d'atterrissage; **~lady** *n* propriétaire *f*, logeuse *f*; (*of pub*) patronne *f*; **~locked** *adj* sans littoral; **~lord** *n* propriétaire *m*, logeur *m*; (*of pub etc*) patron *m*; **~mark** *n* (point *m* de) repère *m*; **to be a ~mark** (*fig*) faire date *or* époque; **~owner** *n* propriétaire foncier *or* terrien; **~scape** *n* paysage *m*; **~scape gardener** *n* jardinier(-ère) paysagiste; **~slide** *n* (GEO) glissement *m* (de terrain); (*fig*: POL) raz-de-marée (électoral)

lane [leɪn] *n* (*in country*) chemin *m*; (AUT) voie *f*; file *f*; (*in race*) couloir *m*; **"get in ~"** (AUT) "mettez-vous dans *or* sur la bonne file"

language ['læŋgwɪdʒ] *n* langue *f*; (*way one speaks*) langage *m*; **bad ~** grossièretés *fpl*, langage grossier; **~ laboratory** *n* laboratoire *m* de langues; **~ school** *n* école *f* de langues

lank [læŋk] *adj* (*hair*) raide et terne

lanky ['læŋkɪ] *adj* grand(e) et maigre, efflanqué(e)

lantern ['læntən] *n* lanterne *f*

lap [læp] *n* (*of track*) tour *m* (de piste); (*of body*): **in** *or* **on one's ~** sur les genoux ♦ *vt* (*also:* **~ up**) laper ♦ *vi* (*waves*) clapoter; **~ up** *vt* (*fig*) avaler, gober

lapel [lə'pɛl] *n* revers *m*

Lapland ['læplænd] *n* Laponie *f*

lapse [læps] *n* défaillance *f*; (*in behaviour*) écart *m* de conduite ♦ *vi* (LAW) cesser d'être en vigueur; (*contract*) expirer; **to ~ into bad habits** prendre de mauvaises habitudes; **~ of time** laps *m* de temps, intervalle *m*

laptop (computer) ['læptɔp(-)] *n* portable *m*

larceny ['lɑːsənɪ] *n* vol *m*

larch [lɑːtʃ] *n* mélèze *m*

lard [lɑːd] *n* saindoux *m*

larder ['lɑːdəʳ] *n* garde-manger *m inv*

large [lɑːdʒ] *adj* grand(e); (*person, animal*) gros(se); **at ~** (*free*) en liberté; (*generally*) en général; *see also* **by**; **~ly**

adv en grande partie; (*principally*) surtout; **~-scale** *adj* (*action*) d'envergure; (*map*) à grande échelle

lark [lɑːk] *n* (*bird*) alouette *f*; (*joke*) blague *f*, farce *f*

laryngitis [lærɪn'dʒaɪtɪs] *n* laryngite *f*

laser ['leɪzəʳ] *n* laser *m*; **~ printer** *n* imprimante *f* laser

lash [læʃ] *n* coup *m* de fouet; (*also:* **eyelash**) cil *m* ♦ *vt* fouetter; (*tie*) attacher; **~ out** *vi*: **to ~ out at** *or* **against** attaquer violemment

lass [læs] (*BRIT*) *n* (jeune) fille *f*

lasso [læ'suː] *n* lasso *m*

last [lɑːst] *adj* dernier(-ère) ♦ *adv* en dernier; (*finally*) finalement ♦ *vi* durer; **~ week** la semaine dernière; **~ night** (*evening*) hier soir; (*night*) la nuit dernière; **at ~** enfin; **~ but one** avant-dernier(-ère); **~-ditch** *adj* (*attempt*) ultime, désespéré(e); **~ing** *adj* durable; **~ly** *adv* en dernier lieu, pour finir; **~-minute** *adj* de dernière minute

latch [lætʃ] *n* loquet *m*

late [leɪt] *adj* (*not on time*) en retard; (*far on in day etc*) tardif(-ive); (*edition, delivery*) dernier(-ère); (*former*) ancien(ne) ♦ *adv* tard; (*behind time, schedule*) en retard; **of ~** dernièrement; **in ~ May** vers la fin (du mois) de mai, fin mai; **the ~ Mr X** feu M. X; **~comer** *n* retardataire *m/f*; **~ly** *adv* récemment; **~r** *adj* (*date etc*) ultérieur(e); (*version etc*) plus récent(e) ♦ *adv* plus tard; **~r on** plus tard; **~st** *adj* tout(e) dernier(-ère); **at the ~st** au plus tard

lathe [leɪð] *n* tour *m*

lather ['lɑːðəʳ] *n* mousse *f* (de savon) ♦ *vt* savonner

Latin ['lætɪn] *n* latin *m* ♦ *adj* latin(e); **~ America** *n* Amérique latine; **~ American** *adj* latino-américain(e)

latitude ['lætɪtjuːd] *n* latitude *f*

latter ['lætəʳ] *adj* deuxième, dernier (-ère) ♦ *n*: **the ~** ce dernier, celui-ci; **~ly** *adv* dernièrement, récemment

laudable ['lɔːdəbl] *adj* louable

laugh [lɑːf] *n* rire *m* ♦ *vi* rire; **~ at** *vt fus* se moquer de; rire de; **~ off** *vt* écarter par une plaisanterie *or* par une boutade; **~able** *adj* risible, ridicule; **~ing stock** *n*: **the ~ing stock of** la risée de; **~ter** *n* rire *m*; rires *mpl*

launch [lɔːntʃ] *n* lancement *m*; (*motorboat*) vedette *f* ♦ *vt* lancer; **~ into** *vt fus* se lancer dans

Launderette ® [lɔːn'drɛt] (*BRIT*), **Laundromat** ® ['lɔːndrəmæt] (*US*) *n* laverie *f* (automatique)

laundry ['lɔːndrɪ] *n* (*clothes*) linge *m*; (*business*) blanchisserie *f*; (*room*) buanderie *f*

laurel ['lɔrl] *n* laurier *m*

lava ['lɑːvə] *n* lave *f*

lavatory ['lævətərɪ] *n* toilettes *fpl*

lavender ['lævəndəʳ] *n* lavande *f*

lavish ['lævɪʃ] *adj* (*amount*) copieux (-euse); (*person*): **~ with** prodigue de ♦ *vt*: **to ~ sth on sb** prodiguer qch à qn; (*money*) dépenser qch sans compter pour qn/qch

law [lɔː] *n* loi *f*; (*science*) droit *m*; **~-abiding** *adj* respectueux(-euse) des lois; **~ and order** *n* l'ordre public; **~ court** *n* tribunal *m*, cour *f* de justice; **~ful** *adj* légal(e); **~less** *adj* (*action*) illégal(e)

lawn [lɔːn] *n* pelouse *f*; **~mower** *n* tondeuse *f* à gazon; **~ tennis** *n* tennis *m*

law school (*US*) *n* faculté *f* de droit

lawsuit ['lɔːsuːt] *n* procès *m*

lawyer ['lɔːjəʳ] *n* (*consultant, with company*) juriste *m*; (*for sales, wills etc*) notaire *m*; (*partner, in court*) avocat *m*

lax [læks] *adj* relâché(e)

laxative ['læksətɪv] *n* laxatif *m*

lay [leɪ] (*pt, pp* **laid**) *pt of* **lie** ♦ *adj* laïque; (*not expert*) profane ♦ *vt* poser, mettre; (*eggs*) pondre; **to ~ the table** mettre la table; **~ aside** *vt* mettre de côté; **~ by** *vt* = **lay aside**; **~ down** *vt* poser; **to ~ down the law** faire la loi; **to ~ down one's life** sacrifier sa vie; **~**

off *vt* (*workers*) licencier; **~ on** *vt* (*provide*) fournir; **~ out** *vt* (*display*) disposer, étaler; **~about** (*inf*) *n* fainéant(e); **~-by** (*BRIT*) *n* aire *f* de stationnement (sur le bas-côté)

layer ['leɪəʳ] *n* couche *f*

layman ['leɪmən] (*irreg*) *n* profane *m*

layout ['leɪaut] *n* disposition *f*, plan *m*, agencement *m*; (*PRESS*) mise *f* en page

laze [leɪz] *vi* (*also:* **~ about**) paresser

lazy ['leɪzɪ] *adj* paresseux(-euse)

lb *abbr* = **pound** *(weight)*

lead[1] [li:d] (*pt, pp* **led**) *n* (*distance, time ahead*) avance *f*; (*clue*) piste *f*; (*THEATRE*) rôle principal; (*ELEC*) fil *m*; (*for dog*) laisse *f* ♦ *vt* mener, conduire; (*be ~er of*) être à la tête de ♦ *vi* (*street etc*) mener, conduire; (*SPORT*) mener, être en tête; **in the ~** en tête; **to ~ the way** montrer le chemin; **~ away** *vt* emmener; **~ back** *vt*: **to ~ back to** ramener à; **~ on** *vt* (*tease*) faire marcher; **~ to** *vt fus* mener à; conduire à; **~ up to** *vt fus* conduire à

lead[2] [lɛd] *n* (*metal*) plomb *m*; (*in pencil*) mine *f*; **~ed petrol** *n* essence *f* au plomb; **~en** *adj* (*sky, sea*) de plomb

leader ['li:dəʳ] *n* chef *m*; dirigeant(e), leader *m*; (*SPORT: in league*) leader; (*: in race*) coureur *m* de tête; **~ship** *n* direction *f*; (*quality*) qualités *fpl* de chef

lead-free ['lɛdfri:] *adj* (*petrol*) sans plomb

leading ['li:dɪŋ] *adj* principal(e); de premier plan; (*in race*) de tête; **~ lady** *n* (*THEATRE*) vedette (féminine); **~ light** *n* (*person*) vedette *f*, sommité *f*; **~ man** (*irreg*) *n* vedette (masculine)

lead singer [li:d-] *n* (*in pop group*) (chanteur *m*) vedette *f*

leaf [li:f] (*pl* **leaves**) *n* feuille *f* ♦ *vi*: **to ~ through** feuilleter; **to turn over a new ~** changer de conduite *or* d'existence

leaflet ['li:flɪt] *n* prospectus *m*, brochure *f*; (*POL, REL*) tract *m*

league [li:g] *n* ligue *f*; (*FOOTBALL*) championnat *m*; **to be in ~ with** avoir partie liée avec, être de mèche avec

leak [li:k] *n* fuite *f* ♦ *vi* (*pipe, liquid etc*) fuir; (*shoes*) prendre l'eau; (*ship*) faire eau ♦ *vt* (*information*) divulguer

lean [li:n] (*pt, pp* **leaned** *or* **leant**) *adj* maigre ♦ *vt*: **to ~ sth on sth** appuyer qch sur qch ♦ *vi* (*slope*) pencher; (*rest*): **to ~ against** s'appuyer contre; être appuyé(e) contre; **to ~ on** s'appuyer sur; **to ~ back/forward** se pencher en arrière/avant; **~ out** *vi* se pencher au dehors; **~ over** *vi* se pencher; **~ing** *n*: **~ing (towards)** tendance *f* (à), penchant *m* (pour); **~t** [lɛnt] *pt, pp of* **lean**

leap [li:p] (*pt, pp* **leaped** *or* **leapt**) *n* bond *m*, saut *m* ♦ *vi* bondir, sauter; **~frog** *n* saute-mouton *m*; **~t** [lɛpt] *pt, pp of* **leap**; **~ year** *n* année *f* bissextile

learn [lə:n] (*pt, pp* **learned** *or* **learnt**) *vt, vi* apprendre; **to ~ to do sth** apprendre à faire qch; **to ~ about** *or* **of sth** (*hear, read*) apprendre qch; **~ed** ['lə:nɪd] *adj* érudit(e), savant(e); **~er** (*BRIT*) *n* (*also:* **~er driver**) (conducteur (-trice)) débutant(e); **~ing** *n* (*knowledge*) savoir *m*; **~t** *pt, pp of* **learn**

lease [li:s] *n* bail *m* ♦ *vt* louer à bail

leash [li:ʃ] *n* laisse *f*

least [li:st] *adj*: **the ~** (*+noun*) le (la) plus petit(e), le (la) moindre; (*: smallest amount of*) le moins de ♦ *adv* (*+verb*) le moins; (*+adj*): **the ~** le (la) moins; **at ~** au moins; (*or rather*) du moins; **not in the ~** pas le moins du monde

leather ['lɛðəʳ] *n* cuir *m*

leave [li:v] (*pt, pp* **left**) *vt* laisser; (*go away from*) quitter; (*forget*) oublier ♦ *vi* partir, s'en aller ♦ *n* (*time off*) congé *m*; (*MIL also: consent*) permission *f*; **to be left** rester; **there's some milk left over** il reste du lait; **on ~** en permission; **~ behind** *vt* (*person, object*) laisser; (*forget*) oublier; **~ out** *vt* oublier, omettre; **~ of absence** *n* congé exceptionnel; (*MIL*) permission spéciale

leaves [li:vz] *npl of* **leaf**

Lebanon ['lɛbənən] *n* Liban *m*
lecherous ['lɛtʃərəs] (*pej*) *adj* lubrique
lecture ['lɛktʃə'] *n* conférence *f*; (*SCOL*) cours *m* ♦ *vi* donner des cours; enseigner ♦ *vt* (*scold*) sermonner, réprimander; **to give a ~ on** faire une conférence sur; donner un cours sur; **~r** (*BRIT*) *n* (*at university*) professeur *m* (d'université)
led [lɛd] *pt, pp of* **lead¹**
ledge [lɛdʒ] *n* (*of window, on wall*) rebord *m*; (*of mountain*) saillie *f*, corniche *f*
ledger ['lɛdʒə'] *n* (*COMM*) registre *m*, grand livre
leech [liːtʃ] *n* (*also fig*) sangsue *f*
leek [liːk] *n* poireau *m*
leer [lɪə'] *vi*: **to ~ at sb** regarder qn d'un air mauvais *or* concupiscent
leeway ['liːweɪ] *n* (*fig*): **to have some ~** avoir une certaine liberté d'action
left [lɛft] *pt, pp of* **leave** ♦ *adj* (*not right*) gauche ♦ *n* gauche *f* ♦ *adv* à gauche; **on the ~, to the ~** à gauche; **the L~** (*POL*) la gauche; **~-handed** *adj* gaucher(-ère); **~-hand side** *n* gauche *f*; **~-luggage locker** *n* (casier *m* à) consigne *f* automatique; **~-luggage (office)** (*BRIT*) *n* consigne *f*; **~overs** *npl* restes *mpl*; **~-wing** *adj* (*POL*) de gauche
leg [lɛg] *n* jambe *f*; (*of animal*) patte *f*; (*of furniture*) pied *m*; (*CULIN*: *of chicken, pork*) cuisse *f*; (: *of lamb*) gigot *m*; (*of journey*) étape *f*; **1st/2nd ~** (*SPORT*) match *m* aller/retour
legacy ['lɛgəsɪ] *n* héritage *m*, legs *m*
legal ['liːgl] *adj* légal(e); **~ holiday** (*US*) *n* jour férié; **~ tender** *n* monnaie légale
legend ['lɛdʒənd] *n* légende *f*
leggings ['lɛgɪŋz] *npl* caleçon *m*
legible ['lɛdʒəbl] *adj* lisible
legislation [lɛdʒɪs'leɪʃən] *n* législation *f*; **legislature** ['lɛdʒɪslətʃə'] *n* (corps *m*) législatif *m*
legitimate [lɪ'dʒɪtɪmət] *adj* légitime
leg-room ['lɛgruːm] *n* place *f* pour les jambes
leisure ['lɛʒə'] *n* loisir *m*, temps *m* libre; loisirs *mpl*; **at ~** (tout) à loisir; à tête reposée; **~ centre** *n* centre *m* de loisirs; **~ly** *adj* tranquille; fait(e) sans se presser
lemon ['lɛmən] *n* citron *m*; **~ade** [lɛmə'neɪd] *n* limonade *f*; **~ tea** *n* thé *m* au citron
lend [lɛnd] (*pt, pp* **lent**) *vt*: **to ~ sth (to sb)** prêter qch (à qn)
length [lɛŋθ] *n* longueur *f*; (*section*: *of road, pipe etc*) morceau *m*, bout *m*; (*of time*) durée *f*; **at ~** (*at last*) enfin, à la fin; (*~ily*) longuement; **~en** *vt* allonger, prolonger ♦ *vi* s'allonger; **~ways** *adv* dans le sens de la longueur, en long; **~y** *adj* (très) long (longue)
lenient ['liːnɪənt] *adj* indulgent(e), clément(e)
lens [lɛnz] *n* lentille *f*; (*of spectacles*) verre *m*; (*of camera*) objectif *m*
Lent [lɛnt] *n* carême *m*
lent [lɛnt] *pt, pp of* **lend**
lentil ['lɛntɪl] *n* lentille *f*
Leo ['liːəu] *n* le Lion
leotard ['liːətɑːd] *n* maillot *m* (*de danseur etc*), collant *m*
leprosy ['lɛprəsɪ] *n* lèpre *f*
lesbian ['lɛzbɪən] *n* lesbienne *f*
less [lɛs] *adj* moins de ♦ *pron, adv* moins ♦ *prep* moins; **~ than that/you** moins que cela/vous; **~ than half** moins de la moitié; **~ than ever** moins que jamais; **~ and ~** de moins en moins; **the ~ he works ...** moins il travaille ...; **~en** *vi* diminuer, s'atténuer ♦ *vt* diminuer, réduire, atténuer; **~er** *adj* moindre; **to a ~er extent** à un degré moindre
lesson ['lɛsn] *n* leçon *f*; **to teach sb a ~** (*fig*) donner une bonne leçon à qn
let [lɛt] (*pt, pp* **let**) *vt* laisser; (*BRIT*: *lease*) louer; **to ~ sb do sth** laisser qn faire qch; **to ~ sb know sth** faire savoir qch à qn, prévenir qn de qch; **~'s go** allons-y; **~ him come** qu'il vienne; **"to ~"** "à louer"; **~ down** *vt* (*tyre*) dégonfler; (*person*) décevoir, faire faux bond à; **~ go** *vi* lâcher prise ♦ *vt* lâcher; **~ in**

vt laisser entrer; (*visitor etc*) faire entrer; **~ off** *vt* (*culprit*) ne pas punir; (*firework etc*) faire partir; **~ on** (*inf*) *vi* dire; **~ out** *vt* laisser sortir; (*scream*) laisser échapper; **~ up** *vi* diminuer; (*cease*) s'arrêter

lethal ['li:θl] *adj* mortel(le), fatal(e)

letter ['lɛtə^r] *n* lettre *f*; **~ bomb** *n* lettre piégée; **~box** (*BRIT*) *n* boîte *f* aux *or* à lettres; **~ing** *n* lettres *fpl*; caractères *mpl*

lettuce ['lɛtɪs] *n* laitue *f*, salade *f*

let-up ['lɛtʌp] *n* répit *m*, arrêt *m*

leukaemia [lu:'ki:mɪə] (*US* **leukemia**) *n* leucémie *f*

level ['lɛvl] *adj* plat(e), plan(e), uni(e); horizontal(e) ♦ *n* niveau *m* ♦ *vt* niveler, aplanir; **to be ~ with** être au même niveau que; **to draw ~ with** (*person, vehicle*) arriver à la hauteur de; **"A" ~s** (*BRIT*) ≃ baccalauréat *m*; **"O" ~s** (*BRIT*) ≃ B.E.P.C.; **on the ~** (*fig: honest*) régulier(-ère); **~ off** *vi* (*prices etc*) se stabiliser; **~ out** *vi* = **level off**; **~ crossing** (*BRIT*) *n* passage *m* à niveau; **~-headed** *adj* équilibré(e)

lever ['li:və^r] *n* levier *m*; **~age** *n*: **~age (on** *or* **with)** prise *f* (sur)

levy ['lɛvɪ] *n* taxe *f*, impôt *m* ♦ *vt* prélever, imposer; percevoir

lewd [lu:d] *adj* obscène, lubrique

liability [laɪə'bɪlətɪ] *n* responsabilité *f*; (*handicap*) handicap *m*; **liabilities** *npl* (*on balance sheet*) passif *m*

liable ['laɪəbl] *adj* (*subject*): **~ to** sujet(te) à; passible de; (*responsible*): **~ (for)** responsable (de); (*likely*): **~ to do** susceptible de faire

liaise [li:'eɪz] *vi*: **to ~ (with)** assurer la liaison avec; **liaison** *n* liaison *f*

liar ['laɪə^r] *n* menteur(-euse)

libel ['laɪbl] *n* diffamation *f*; (*document*) écrit *m* diffamatoire ♦ *vt* diffamer

liberal ['lɪbərl] *adj* libéral(e); (*generous*): **~ with** prodigue de, généreux(-euse) avec; **the L~ Democrats** (*BRIT*) le parti libéral-démocrate

liberation [lɪbə'reɪʃən] *n* libération *f*

liberty ['lɪbətɪ] *n* liberté *f*; **to be at ~ to do** être libre de faire

Libra ['li:brə] *n* la Balance

librarian [laɪ'brɛərɪən] *n* bibliothécaire *m/f*

library ['laɪbrərɪ] *n* bibliothèque *f*

libretto [lɪ'brɛtəu] *n* livret *m*

Libya ['lɪbɪə] *n* Libye *f*

lice [laɪs] *npl of* **louse**

licence ['laɪsns] (*US* **license**) *n* autorisation *f*, permis *m*; (*RADIO, TV*) redevance *f*; **driving ~**, (*US*) **driver's license** permis *m* (de conduire); **~ number** *n* numéro *m* d'immatriculation; **~ plate** *n* plaque *f* minéralogique

license ['laɪsns] *n* (*US*) = **licence** ♦ *vt* donner une licence à; **~d** *adj* (*car*) muni(e) de la vignette; (*to sell alcohol*) patenté(e) pour la vente des spiritueux, qui a une licence de débit de boissons

lick [lɪk] *vt* lécher; (*inf: defeat*) écraser; **to ~ one's lips** (*fig*) se frotter les mains

licorice ['lɪkərɪs] (*US*) *n* = **liquorice**

lid [lɪd] *n* couvercle *m*; (*eyelid*) paupière *f*

lie [laɪ] (*pt* **lay**, *pp* **lain**) *vi* (*rest*) être étendu(e) *or* allongé(e) *or* couché(e); (*in grave*) être enterré(e), reposer; (*be situated*) se trouver, être; (*be untruthful: pt, pp ~d*) mentir ♦ *n* mensonge *m*; **to ~ low** (*fig*) se cacher; **~ about** *vi* traîner; **~ around** *vi* = **lie about**; **~-down** (*BRIT*) *n*: **to have a ~-down** s'allonger, se reposer; **~-in** (*BRIT*) *n*: **to have a ~-in** faire la grasse matinée

lieutenant [lɛf'tɛnənt, (*US*) lu:'tɛnənt] *n* lieutenant *m*

life [laɪf] (*pl* **lives**) *n* vie *f*; **to come to ~** (*fig*) s'animer; **~ assurance** (*BRIT*) *n* = **life insurance**; **~belt** (*BRIT*) *n* bouée *f* de sauvetage; **~boat** *n* canot *m or* chaloupe *f* de sauvetage; **~buoy** *n* bouée *f* de sauvetage; **~guard** *n* surveillant *m* de baignade; **~ insurance** *n* assurance-vie *f*; **~ jacket** *n* gilet *m or* ceinture *f* de sauvetage; **~less** *adj* sans vie, inanimé(e); (*dull*) qui manque de vie *or* de vigueur; **~like** *adj* qui semble vrai(e) *or* vivant(e); (*painting*) réaliste; **~long** *adj* de toute une vie, de toujours; **~ preserver** (*US*) *n* = **lifebelt**; **life jacket**; **~-saving** *n* sauvetage *m*; **~ sentence** *n* condamnation *f* à perpétuité; **~-size(d)** *adj* grandeur nature *inv*; **~ span** *n* (durée *f* de) vie *f*; **~style** *n* style *m or* mode *m* de vie; **~-support system** *n* (*MED*) respirateur artificiel; **~time** *n* vie *f*; **in his ~time** de son vivant

lift [lɪft] *vt* soulever, lever; (*end*) supprimer, lever ♦ *vi* (*fog*) se lever ♦ *n* (*BRIT*: *elevator*) ascenseur *m*; **to give sb a ~** (*BRIT*: *AUT*) emmener *or* prendre qn en voiture; **~-off** *n* décollage *m*

light [laɪt] (*pt, pp* **lit**) *n* lumière *f*; (*lamp*) lampe *f*; (*AUT*: *rear ~*) feu *m*; (: *headlight*) phare *m*; (*for cigarette etc*): **have you got a ~?** avez-vous du feu? ♦ *vt* (*candle, cigarette, fire*) allumer; (*room*) éclairer ♦ *adj* (*room, colour*) clair(e); (*not heavy*) léger(-ère); (*not strenuous*) peu fatigant(e); **~s** *npl* (*AUT*: *traffic ~s*) feux *mpl*; **to come to ~** être dévoilé(e) *or* découvert(e); **~ up** *vi* (*face*) s'éclairer ♦ *vt* (*illuminate*) éclairer, illuminer; **~ bulb** *n* ampoule *f*; **~en** *vt* (*make less heavy*) alléger; **~er** *n* (*also:* **cigarette ~er**) briquet *m*; **~-headed** *adj* étourdi(e); (*excited*) grisé(e); **~-hearted** *adj* gai(e), joyeux(-euse), enjoué(e); **~house** *n* phare *m*; **~ing** *n* (*on road*) éclairage *m*; (*in theatre*) éclairages; **~ly** *adv* légèrement; **to get off ~ly** s'en tirer à bon compte; **~ness** *n* (*in weight*) légèreté *f*

lightning ['laɪtnɪŋ] *n* éclair *m*, foudre *f*; **~ conductor** (*US* **lightning rod**) *n* paratonnerre *m*

light pen *n* crayon *m* optique

lightweight ['laɪtweɪt] *adj* (*suit*) léger(-ère) ♦ *n* (*BOXING*) poids léger

like [laɪk] *vt* aimer (bien) ♦ *prep* comme ♦ *adj* semblable, pareil(le) ♦ *n*: **and the ~** et d'autres du même genre; **his ~s and dislikes** ses goûts *mpl or* préférences *fpl*; **I would ~, I'd ~** je voudrais, j'aimerais; **would you ~ a coffee?** voulez-vous du café?; **to be/look ~ sb/sth** ressembler à qn/qch; **what does it look ~?** de quoi est-ce que ça a l'air?; **what does it taste ~?** quel goût est-ce que ça a?; **that's just ~ him** c'est bien de lui, ça lui ressemble; **do it ~ this** fais-le comme ceci; **it's nothing ~ ...** ce n'est pas du tout comme ...; **~able** *adj* sympathique, agréable

likelihood ['laɪklɪhud] *n* probabilité *f*

likely ['laɪklɪ] *adj* probable; plausible; **he's ~ to leave** il va sûrement partir, il risque fort de partir; **not ~!** (*inf*) pas de danger!

likeness ['laɪknɪs] *n* ressemblance *f*; **that's a good ~** c'est très ressemblant

likewise ['laɪkwaɪz] *adv* de même, pareillement

liking ['laɪkɪŋ] *n* (*for person*) affection *f*; (*for thing*) penchant *m*, goût *m*

lilac ['laɪlək] *n* lilas *m*

lily ['lɪlɪ] *n* lis *m*; **~ of the valley** *n* muguet *m*

limb [lɪm] *n* membre *m*

limber up ['lɪmbəʳ-] *vi* se dégourdir, faire des exercices d'assouplissement

limbo ['lɪmbəu] *n*: **to be in ~** (*fig*) être tombé(e) dans l'oubli

lime [laɪm] *n* (*tree*) tilleul *m*; (*fruit*) lime *f*, citron vert; (*GEO*) chaux *f*

limelight ['laɪmlaɪt] *n*: **in the ~** (*fig*) en vedette, au premier plan

limerick ['lɪmərɪk] *n* poème *m* humoristique (de 5 vers)

limestone ['laɪmstəun] *n* pierre *f* à chaux; (*GEO*) calcaire *m*

limit ['lɪmɪt] *n* limite *f* ♦ *vt* limiter; **~ed** *adj* limité(e), restreint(e); **to be ~ed to** se limiter à, ne concerner que; **~ed (liability) company** (*BRIT*) *n* ≃ société *f* anonyme

limousine ['lɪməziːn] *n* limousine *f*

limp [lɪmp] *n*: **to have a ~** boiter ♦ *vi*

boiter ♦ *adj* mou (molle)
limpet ['lɪmpɪt] *n* patelle *f*
line [laɪn] *n* ligne *f*; (*stroke*) trait *m*; (*wrinkle*) ride *f*; (*rope*) corde *f*; (*wire*) fil *m*; (*of poem*) vers *m*; (*row, series*) rangée *f*; (*of people*) file *f*, queue *f*; (*railway track*) voie *f*; (COMM: *series of goods*) article(s) *m(pl)*; (*work*) métier *m*, type *m* d'activité; (*attitude, policy*) position *f* ♦ *vt* (*subj*: *trees, crowd*) border; **in a ~** aligné(e); **in his ~ of business** dans sa partie, dans son rayon; **in ~ with** en accord avec; **to ~ (with)** (*clothes*) doubler (de); (*box*) garnir *or* tapisser (de); **~ up** *vi* s'aligner, se mettre en rang(s) ♦ *vt* aligner; (*event*) prévoir, préparer; **~d** *adj* (*face*) ridé(e), marqué(e); (*paper*) réglé(e)
linen ['lɪnɪn] *n* linge *m* (de maison); (*cloth*) lin *m*
liner ['laɪnər] *n* paquebot *m* (de ligne); (*for bin*) sac *m* à poubelle
linesman ['laɪnzmən] (*irreg*) *n* juge *m* de touche; (TENNIS) juge *m* de ligne
line-up ['laɪnʌp] *n* (US: *queue*) file *f*; (SPORT) (composition *f* de l')équipe *f*
linger ['lɪŋgər] *vi* s'attarder; traîner; (*smell, tradition*) persister
linguist ['lɪŋgwɪst] *n*: **to be a good ~** être doué(e) par les langues; **~ics** [lɪŋ'gwɪstɪks] *n* linguistique *f*
lining ['laɪnɪŋ] *n* doublure *f*
link [lɪŋk] *n* lien *m*, rapport *m*; (*of a chain*) maillon *m* ♦ *vt* relier, lier, unir; **~s** *npl* (GOLF) (terrain *m* de) golf *m*; **~ up** *vt* relier ♦ *vi* se rejoindre; s'associer
lino ['laɪnəu] *n* = **linoleum**
linoleum [lɪ'nəulɪəm] *n* linoléum *m*
lion ['laɪən] *n* lion *m*; **~ess** *n* lionne *f*
lip [lɪp] *n* lèvre *f*
liposuction ['lɪpəusʌkʃən] *n* liposuccion *f*
lip: ~-read *vi* lire sur les lèvres; **~ salve** *n* pommade *f* rosat *or* pour les lèvres; **~ service** *n*: **to pay ~ service to sth** ne reconnaître le mérite de qch que pour la forme; **~stick** *n* rouge *m* à lèvres
liqueur [lɪ'kjuər] *n* liqueur *f*
liquid ['lɪkwɪd] *adj* liquide ♦ *n* liquide *m*; **~ize** *vt* (CULIN) passer au mixer; **~izer** *n* mixer *m*
liquor ['lɪkər] (US) *n* spiritueux *m*, alcool *m*
liquorice ['lɪkərɪs] (BRIT) *n* réglisse *f*
liquor store (US) *n* magasin *m* de vins et spiritueux
lisp [lɪsp] *vi* zézayer
list [lɪst] *n* liste *f* ♦ *vt* (*write down*) faire une *or* la liste de; (*mention*) énumérer; **~ed building** (BRIT) *n* monument classé
listen ['lɪsn] *vi* écouter; **to ~ to** écouter; **~er** *n* auditeur(-trice)
listless ['lɪstlɪs] *adj* indolent(e), apathique
lit [lɪt] *pt, pp of* **light**
liter ['li:tər] (US) *n* = **litre**
literacy ['lɪtərəsɪ] *n* degré *m* d'alphabétisation, fait *m* de savoir lire et écrire
literal ['lɪtərəl] *adj* littéral(e); **~ly** *adv* littéralement; (*really*) réellement
literary ['lɪtərərɪ] *adj* littéraire
literate ['lɪtərət] *adj* qui sait lire et écrire, instruit(e)
literature ['lɪtrɪtʃər] *n* littérature *f*; (*brochures etc*) documentation *f*
lithe [laɪð] *adj* agile, souple
litigation [lɪtɪ'geɪʃən] *n* litige *m*; contentieux *m*
litre ['li:tər] (US **liter**) *n* litre *m*
litter ['lɪtər] *n* (*rubbish*) détritus *mpl*, ordures *fpl*; (*young animals*) portée *f*; **~ bin** (BRIT) *n* boîte *f* à ordures, poubelle *f*; **~ed** *adj*: **~ed with** jonché(e) de, couvert(e) de
little ['lɪtl] *adj* (*small*) petit(e) ♦ *adv* peu; **~ milk/time** peu de lait/temps; **a ~** un peu (de); **a ~ bit** un peu; **~ by ~** petit à petit, peu à peu
live[1] [laɪv] *adj* (*animal*) vivant(e), en vie; (*wire*) sous tension; (*bullet, bomb*) non explosé(e); (*broadcast*) en direct; (*performance*) en public
live[2] [lɪv] *vi* vivre; (*reside*) vivre, habi-

ter; ~ **down** *vt* faire oublier (avec le temps); ~ **on** *vt fus* (*food, salary*) vivre de; ~ **together** *vi* vivre ensemble, cohabiter; ~ **up to** *vt fus* se montrer à la hauteur de

livelihood ['laɪvlɪhud] *n* moyens *mpl* d'existence

lively ['laɪvlɪ] *adj* vif (vive), plein(e) d'entrain; (*place, book*) vivant(e)

liven up ['laɪvn-] *vt* animer ♦ *vi* s'animer

liver ['lɪvə^r] *n* foie *m*

lives [laɪvz] *npl of* **life**

livestock ['laɪvstɔk] *n* bétail *m*, cheptel *m*

livid ['lɪvɪd] *adj* livide, blafard(e); (*inf: furious*) furieux(-euse), furibond(e)

living ['lɪvɪŋ] *adj* vivant(e), en vie ♦ *n*: **to earn** *or* **make a** ~ gagner sa vie; ~ **conditions** *npl* conditions *fpl* de vie; ~ **room** *n* salle *f* de séjour; ~ **standards** *npl* niveau *m* de vie; ~ **wage** *n* salaire *m* permettant de vivre (décemment)

lizard ['lɪzəd] *n* lézard *m*

load [ləud] *n* (*weight*) poids *m*; (*thing carried*) chargement *m*, charge *f* ♦ *vt* (*also:* ~ **up**): **to** ~ **(with)** charger (de); (*gun, camera*) charger (avec); (COMPUT) charger; **a** ~ **of, ~s of** (*fig*) un *or* des tas de, des masses de; **to talk a** ~ **of rubbish** dire des bêtises; **~ed** *adj* (*question*) insidieux(-euse); (*inf: rich*) bourré(e) de fric

loaf [ləuf] (*pl* **loaves**) *n* pain *m*, miche *f*

loan [ləun] *n* prêt *m* ♦ *vt* prêter; **on** ~ prêté(e), en prêt

loath [ləuθ] *adj*: **to be** ~ **to do** répugner à faire

loathe [ləuð] *vt* détester, avoir en horreur

loaves [ləuvz] *npl of* **loaf**

lobby ['lɔbɪ] *n* hall *m*, entrée *f*; (POL) groupe *m* de pression, lobby *m* ♦ *vt* faire pression sur

lobster ['lɔbstə^r] *n* homard *m*

local ['ləukl] *adj* local(e) ♦ *n* (BRIT: *pub*) pub *m or* café *m* du coin; **the ~s** *npl* (*inhabitants*) les gens *mpl* du pays *or* du coin; ~ **anaesthetic** *n* anesthésie locale; ~ **authority** *n* collectivité locale, municipalité *f*; ~ **call** *n* communication urbaine; ~ **government** *n* administration locale *or* municipale; **~ity** [ləu'kælɪtɪ] *n* région *f*, environs *mpl*; (*position*) lieu *m*

locate [ləu'keɪt] *vt* (*find*) trouver, repérer; (*situate*): **to be ~d in** être situé(e) à *or* en; **location** *n* emplacement *m*; **on location** (CINEMA) en extérieur

loch [lɔx] *n* lac *m*, loch *m*

lock [lɔk] *n* (*of door, box*) serrure *f*; (*of canal*) écluse *f*; (*of hair*) mèche *f*, boucle *f* ♦ *vt* (*with key*) fermer à clé ♦ *vi* (*door etc*) fermer à clé; (*wheels*) se bloquer; ~ **in** *vt* enfermer; ~ **out** *vt* enfermer dehors; (*deliberately*) mettre à la porte; ~ **up** *vt* (*person*) enfermer; (*house*) fermer à clé ♦ *vi* tout fermer (à clé)

locker ['lɔkə^r] *n* casier *m*; (*in station*) consigne *f* automatique

locket ['lɔkɪt] *n* médaillon *m*

locksmith ['lɔksmɪθ] *n* serrurier *m*

lockup ['lɔkʌp] *n* (*prison*) prison *f*

locum ['ləukəm] *n* (MED) suppléant(e) (de médecin)

lodge [lɔdʒ] *n* pavillon *m* (de gardien); (*hunting* ~) pavillon de chasse ♦ *vi* (*person*): **to** ~ **(with)** être logé(e) (chez), être en pension (chez); (*bullet*) se loger ♦ *vt*: **to** ~ **a complaint** porter plainte; **~r** *n* locataire *m/f*; (*with meals*) pensionnaire *m/f*; **lodgings** *npl* chambre *f*; meublé *m*

loft [lɔft] *n* grenier *m*

lofty ['lɔftɪ] *adj* (*noble*) noble, élevé(e); (*haughty*) hautain(e)

log [lɔg] *n* (*of wood*) bûche *f*; (*book*) = **logbook** ♦ *vt* (*record*) noter; **~book** *n* (NAUT) livre *m or* journal *m* de bord; (AVIAT) carnet *m* de vol; (*of car*) ≈ carte grise

loggerheads ['lɔgəhɛdz] *npl*: **at** ~ **(with)** à couteaux tirés (avec)

logic ['lɔdʒɪk] *n* logique *f*; **~al** *adj* logique

loin [lɔɪn] *n* (CULIN) filet *m*, longe *f*

loiter ['lɔɪtəʳ] *vi* traîner

loll [lɔl] *vi* (*also:* **~ about**) se prélasser, fainéanter

lollipop ['lɔlɪpɔp] *n* sucette *f*; **~ man/lady** (*BRIT: irreg*) *n contractuel qui fait traverser la rue aux enfants*

lollipop men/ladies

Les **lollipop men/ladies** *sont employés pour aider les enfants à traverser la rue à proximité des écoles à l'heure où ils entrent en classe et à la sortie. On les repère facilement à cause de leur long ciré blanc et ils portent une pancarte ronde pour faire signe aux automobilistes de s'arrêter. On les appelle ainsi car la forme circulaire de cette pancarte rappelle une sucette.*

lolly ['lɔlɪ] (*inf*) *n* (*lollipop*) sucette *f*; (*money*) fric *m*

London ['lʌndən] *n* Londres *m*; **~er** *n* Londonien(ne)

lone [ləun] *adj* solitaire

loneliness ['ləunlɪnɪs] *n* solitude *f*, isolement *m*

lonely ['ləunlɪ] *adj* seul(e); solitaire, isolé(e)

long [lɔŋ] *adj* long (longue) ♦ *adv* longtemps ♦ *vi*: **to ~ for sth** avoir très envie de qch; attendre qch avec impatience; **so** *or* **as ~ as** pourvu que; **don't be ~!** dépêchez-vous!; **how ~ is this river/course?** quelle est la longueur de ce fleuve/la durée de ce cours?; **6 metres ~** (long) de 6 mètres; **6 months ~** qui dure 6 mois, de 6 mois; **all night ~** toute la nuit; **he no ~er comes** il ne vient plus; **they're no ~er going out together** ils ne sortent plus ensemble; **I can't stand it any ~er** je ne peux plus le supporter; **~ before/after** longtemps avant/après; **before ~** (*+future*) avant peu, dans peu de temps; (*+past*) peu (de temps) après; **at ~ last** enfin; **~-distance** *adj* (*call*) interurbain(e); **~er** ['lɔŋgəʳ] *adv see* **long**; **~hand** *n* écriture normale *or* courante; **~ing** *n* désir *m*, envie *f*, nostalgie *f*

longitude ['lɔŋgɪtju:d] *n* longitude *f*

long: ~ jump *n* saut *m* en longueur; **~-life** *adj* (*batteries etc*) longue durée *inv*; (*milk*) longue conservation; **~-lost** *adj* (*person*) perdu(e) de vue depuis longtemps; **~-range** *adj* à longue portée; **~-sighted** *adj* (MED) presbyte; **~-standing** *adj* de longue date; **~-suffering** *adj* empreint(e) d'une patience résignée; extrêmement patient(e); **~-term** *adj* à long terme; **~ wave** *n* grandes ondes; **~-winded** *adj* intarissable, interminable

loo [lu:] (*BRIT: inf*) *n* W.-C. *mpl*, petit coin

look [luk] *vi* regarder; (*seem*) sembler, paraître, avoir l'air; (*building etc*): **to ~ south/(out) onto the sea** donner au sud/sur la mer ♦ *n* regard *m*; (*appearance*) air *m*, allure *f*, aspect *m*; **~s** *npl* (*good ~s*) physique *m*, beauté *f*; **to have a ~** regarder; **~!** regardez!; **~ (here)!** (*annoyance*) écoutez!; **~ after** *vt fus* (*care for, deal with*) s'occuper de; **~ at** *vt fus* regarder; (*problem etc*) examiner; **~ back** *vi*: **to ~ back on** (*event etc*) évoquer, repenser à; **~ down on** *vt fus* (*fig*) regarder de haut, dédaigner; **~ for** *vt fus* chercher; **~ forward to** *vt fus* attendre avec impatience; **we ~ forward to hearing from you** (*in letter*) dans l'attente de vous lire; **~ into** *vt fus* examiner, étudier; **~ on** *vi* regarder (en spectateur); **~ out** *vi* (*beware*): **to ~ out (for)** prendre garde (à), faire attention (à); **~ out for** *vt fus* être à la recherche de; guetter; **~ round** *vi* regarder derrière soi, se retourner; **~ to** *vt fus* (*rely on*) compter sur; **~ up** *vi* lever les yeux; (*improve*) s'améliorer ♦ *vt* (*word, name*) chercher; **~ up to** *vt fus* avoir du respect pour ♦ *n* poste *m* de guet; (*person*) guetteur *m*; **to be on the ~ out (for)** guetter

loom [lu:m] *vi* (*also:* **~ up**) surgir; (*approach*: *event etc*) être imminent(e); (*threaten*) menacer ♦ *n* (*for weaving*) métier *m* à tisser

loony ['lu:nɪ] (*inf*) *adj, n* timbré(e), cinglé(e)

loop [lu:p] *n* boucle *f*; **~hole** *n* (*fig*) porte *f* de sortie; échappatoire *f*

loose [lu:s] *adj* (*knot, screw*) desserré(e); (*clothes*) ample, lâche; (*hair*) dénoué(e), épars(e); (*not firmly fixed*) pas solide; (*morals, discipline*) relâché(e) ♦ *n*: **on the ~** en liberté; **~ change** *n* petite monnaie; **~ chippings** *npl* (*on road*) gravillons *mpl*; **~ end** *n*: **to be at a ~ end** *or (US)* **at ~ ends** ne pas trop savoir quoi faire; **~ly** *adv* sans serrer; (*imprecisely*) approximativement; **~n** *vt* desserrer

loot [lu:t] *n* (*inf*: *money*) pognon *m*, fric *m* ♦ *vt* piller

lopsided ['lɔp'saɪdɪd] *adj* de travers, asymétrique

lord [lɔ:d] *n* seigneur *m*; **L~ Smith** lord Smith; **the L~** le Seigneur; **good L~!** mon Dieu!; **the (House of) L~s** (*BRIT*) la Chambre des lords; **my L~** = **your Lordship**; **L~ship** *n*: **your L~ship** Monsieur le comte/le baron/le juge; (*to bishop*) Monseigneur

lore [lɔ:ʳ] *n* tradition(s) *f(pl)*

lorry ['lɔrɪ] (*BRIT*) *n* camion *m*; **~ driver** (*BRIT*) *n* camionneur *m*, routier *m*

lose [lu:z] (*pt, pp* **lost**) *vt, vi* perdre; **to ~ (time)** (*clock*) retarder; **to get lost** ♦ *vi* se perdre; **~r** *n* perdant(e)

loss [lɔs] *n* perte *f*; **to be at a ~** être perplexe *or* embarrassé(e)

lost [lɔst] *pt, pp of* **lose** ♦ *adj* perdu(e); **~ and found** (*US*), **~ property** *n* objets trouvés

lot [lɔt] *n* (*set*) lot *m*; **the ~** le tout; **a ~ (of)** beaucoup (de); **~s of** des tas de; **to draw ~s (for sth)** tirer (qch) au sort

lotion ['ləuʃən] *n* lotion *f*

lottery ['lɔtərɪ] *n* loterie *f*

loud [laud] *adj* bruyant(e), sonore; (*voice*) fort(e); (*support, condemnation*) vigoureux(-euse); (*gaudy*) voyant(e), tapageur(-euse) ♦ *adv* (*speak etc*) fort; **out ~** tout haut; **~-hailer** (*BRIT*) *n* porte-voix *m inv*; **~ly** *adv* fort, bruyamment; **~speaker** *n* haut-parleur *m*

lounge [laundʒ] *n* salon *m*; (*at airport*) salle *f*; (*BRIT*: *also:* **~ bar**) (salle de) café *m or* bar *m* ♦ *vi* (*also:* **~ about or around**) se prélasser, paresser; **~ suit** (*BRIT*) *n* complet *m*; (*on invitation*) "tenue de ville"

louse [laus] (*pl* **lice**) *n* pou *m*

lousy ['lauzɪ] (*inf*) *adj* infect(e), moche; **I feel ~** je suis mal fichu(e)

lout [laut] *n* rustre *m*, butor *m*

lovable ['lʌvəbl] *adj* adorable; très sympathique

love [lʌv] *n* amour *m* ♦ *vt* aimer; (*caringly, kindly*) aimer beaucoup; **"~ (from) Anne"** "affectueusement, Anne"; **I ~ chocolate** j'adore le chocolat; **to be/fall in ~ with** être/tomber amoureux (-euse) de; **to make ~** faire l'amour; **"15 ~"** (*TENNIS*) "15 à rien *or* zéro"; **~ affair** *n* liaison (amoureuse); **~ life** *n* vie sentimentale

lovely ['lʌvlɪ] *adj* (très) joli(e), ravissant(e); (*delightful*: *person*) charmant(e); (*holiday etc*) (très) agréable

lover ['lʌvəʳ] *n* amant *m*; (*person in love*) amoureux(-euse); (*amateur*): **a ~ of** un amateur de; un(e) amoureux (-euse) de

loving ['lʌvɪŋ] *adj* affectueux(-euse), tendre

low [ləu] *adj* bas (basse); (*quality*) mauvais(e), inférieur(e); (*person*: *depressed*) déprimé(e); (: *ill*) bas (basse), affaibli(e) ♦ *adv* bas ♦ *n* (*METEOROLOGY*) dépression *f*; **to be ~ on** être à court de; **to feel ~** se sentir déprimé(e); **to reach an all-time ~** être au plus bas; **~-alcohol** *adj* peu alcoolisé(e); **~-calorie** *adj* hypocalorique; **~-cut** *adj* (*dress*) décolleté(e); **~er** *adj* inférieur(e) ♦ *vt* abaisser, baisser; **~er sixth** (*BRIT*) *n* (*SCOL*) première *f*; **~-fat** *adj* maigre; **~lands** *npl* (*GEO*) plaines *fpl*; **~ly** *adj* humble, modeste

loyal ['lɔɪəl] *adj* loyal(e), fidèle; **~ty** *n* loyauté *f*, fidélité *f*; **~ty card** *n* carte *f* de fidélité

lozenge ['lɔzɪndʒ] *n* (*MED*) pastille *f*

LP *n abbr* = **long-playing record**

LPG *n abbr* (*AUT* = *liquefied petroleum gas*) GPL *m*

L-plates ['ɛlpleɪts] (*BRIT*) *npl* plaques *fpl* d'apprenti conducteur

L-plates

Les **L-plates** *sont des carrés blancs portant un "L" rouge que l'on met à l'avant et à l'arrière de sa voiture pour montrer qu'on n'a pas encore son permis de conduire. Jusqu'à l'obtention du permis, l'apprenti conducteur a un permis provisoire et n'a le droit de conduire que si un conducteur qualifié est assis à côté de lui. Il est interdit aux apprentis conducteurs de circuler sur les autoroutes, même s'ils sont accompagnés.*

LRP *n abbr* (*AUT* = *lead replacement petrol*) super *m*

Ltd *abbr* (= *limited*) ≃ S.A.

lubricant ['lu:brɪkənt] *n* lubrifiant *m*

lubricate ['lu:brɪkeɪt] *vt* lubrifier, graisser

luck [lʌk] *n* chance *f*; **bad ~** malchance *f*, malheur *m*; **bad** *or* **hard** *or* **tough ~!** pas de chance!; **good ~!** bonne chance!; **~ily** *adv* heureusement, par bonheur; **~y** *adj* (*person*) qui a de la chance; (*coincidence, event*) heureux(-euse); (*object*) porte-bonheur *inv*

ludicrous ['lu:dɪkrəs] *adj* ridicule, absurde

lug [lʌg] (*inf*) *vt* traîner, tirer

luggage ['lʌgɪdʒ] *n* bagages *mpl*; **~ rack** *n* (*on car*) galerie *f*

lukewarm ['lu:kwɔ:m] *adj* tiède

lull [lʌl] *n* accalmie *f*; (*in conversation*) pause *f* ♦ *vt*: **to ~ sb to sleep** bercer qn pour qu'il s'endorme; **to be ~ed into a false sense of security** s'endormir dans une fausse sécurité

lullaby ['lʌləbaɪ] *n* berceuse *f*

lumbago [lʌm'beɪgəu] *n* lumbago *m*

lumber ['lʌmbə^r] *n* (*wood*) bois *m* de charpente; (*junk*) bric-à-brac *m inv*; **~jack** *n* bûcheron *m*

luminous ['lu:mɪnəs] *adj* lumineux(-euse)

lump [lʌmp] *n* morceau *m*; (*swelling*) grosseur *f* ♦ *vt*: **to ~ together** réunir, mettre en tas; **~ sum** *n* somme globale *or* forfaitaire; **~y** *adj* (*sauce*) avec des grumeaux; (*bed*) défoncé(e), peu confortable

lunar ['lu:nə^r] *adj* lunaire

lunatic ['lu:nətɪk] *adj* fou (folle), cinglé(e) (*inf*)

lunch [lʌntʃ] *n* déjeuner *m*

luncheon ['lʌntʃən] *n* déjeuner *m* (chic); **~ meat** *n sorte de mortadelle*; **~ voucher** (*BRIT*) *n* chèque-repas *m*

lung [lʌŋ] *n* poumon *m*

lunge [lʌndʒ] *vi* (*also:* **~ forward**) faire un mouvement brusque en avant; **to ~ at** envoyer *or* assener un coup à

lurch [lə:tʃ] *vi* vaciller, tituber ♦ *n* écart *m* brusque; **to leave sb in the ~** laisser qn en plan (*inf*)

lure [luə^r] *n* (*attraction*) attrait *m*, charme *m* ♦ *vt* attirer *or* persuader par la ruse

lurid ['luərɪd] *adj* affreux(-euse), atroce; (*pej*: *colour, dress*) criard(e)

lurk [lə:k] *vi* se tapir, se cacher

luscious ['lʌʃəs] *adj* succulent(e); appétissant(e)

lush [lʌʃ] *adj* luxuriant(e)

lust [lʌst] *n* (*sexual*) désir *m*; (*fig*): **~ for** soif *f* de; **~y** *adj* vigoureux(-euse), robuste

Luxembourg ['lʌksəmbə:g] *n* Luxembourg *m*

luxurious [lʌg'zjuərɪəs] *adj* luxueux (-euse)
luxury ['lʌkʃərɪ] *n* luxe *m* ♦ *cpd* de luxe
lying ['laɪɪŋ] *n* mensonge(s) *m(pl)* ♦ *vb see* **lie**
lyrical ['lɪrɪkl] *adj* lyrique
lyrics ['lɪrɪks] *npl* (*of song*) paroles *fpl*

M, m

m. *abbr* = **metre; mile; million**
M.A. *abbr* = **Master of Arts**
mac [mæk] (*BRIT*) *n* imper(méable) *m*
macaroni [mækə'rəunɪ] *n* macaroni *mpl*
machine [mə'ʃi:n] *n* machine *f* ♦ *vt* (*TECH*) façonner à la machine; (*dress etc*) coudre à la machine; **~ gun** *n* mitrailleuse *f*; **~ language** *n* (*COMPUT*) langage-machine *m*; **~ry** *n* machinerie *f*, machines *fpl*; (*fig*) mécanisme(s) *m(pl)*
mackerel ['mækrl] *n inv* maquereau *m*
mackintosh ['mækɪntɔʃ] (*BRIT*) *n* imperméable *m*
mad [mæd] *adj* fou (folle); (*foolish*) insensé(e); (*angry*) furieux(-euse); (*keen*): **to be ~ about** être fou (folle) de
madam ['mædəm] *n* madame *f*
madden ['mædn] *vt* exaspérer
made [meɪd] *pt, pp of* **make**
Madeira [mə'dɪərə] *n* (*GEO*) Madère *f*; (*wine*) madère *m*
made-to-measure ['meɪdtə'mɛʒə^r] (*BRIT*) *adj* fait(e) sur mesure
madly ['mædlɪ] *adv* follement; **~ in love** éperdument amoureux(-euse)
madman ['mædmən] (*irreg*) *n* fou *m*
madness ['mædnɪs] *n* folie *f*
magazine [mægə'zi:n] *n* (*PRESS*) magazine *m*, revue *f*; (*RADIO, TV*: *also*: **~ programme**) magazine
maggot ['mægət] *n* ver *m*, asticot *m*
magic ['mædʒɪk] *n* magie *f* ♦ *adj* magique; **~al** *adj* magique; (*experience, evening*) merveilleux(-euse); **~ian** [mə'dʒɪʃən] *n* magicien(ne)
magistrate ['mædʒɪstreɪt] *n* magistrat *m*; juge *m*
magnet ['mægnɪt] *n* aimant *m*; **~ic** [mæg'nɛtɪk] *adj* magnétique
magnificent [mæg'nɪfɪsnt] *adj* superbe, magnifique; (*splendid*: *robe, building*) somptueux(-euse), magnifique
magnify ['mægnɪfaɪ] *vt* grossir; (*sound*) amplifier; **~ing glass** *n* loupe *f*
magnitude ['mægnɪtju:d] *n* ampleur *f*
magpie ['mægpaɪ] *n* pie *f*
mahogany [mə'hɔgənɪ] *n* acajou *m*
maid [meɪd] *n* bonne *f*
maiden ['meɪdn] *n* jeune fille *f* ♦ *adj* (*aunt etc*) non mariée; (*speech, voyage*) inaugural(e); **~ name** *n* nom *m* de jeune fille
mail [meɪl] *n* poste *f*; (*letters*) courrier *m* ♦ *vt* envoyer (par la poste); **~box** (*US*) *n* boîte *f* aux lettres; **~ing list** *n* liste *f* d'adresses; **~-order** *n* vente *f or* achat *m* par correspondance
maim [meɪm] *vt* mutiler
main [meɪn] *adj* principal(e) ♦ *n*: **the ~(s)** ♦ *n(pl)* (*gas, water*) conduite principale, canalisation *f*; **the ~s** *npl* (*ELEC*) le secteur; **the ~ thing** l'essentiel; **in the ~** dans l'ensemble; **~frame** *n* (*COMPUT*) unité centrale; **~land** *n* continent *m*; **~ly** *adv* principalement, surtout; **~ road** *n* grand-route *f*; **~stay** *n* (*fig*) pilier *m*; **~stream** *n* courant principal
maintain [meɪn'teɪn] *vt* entretenir; (*continue*) maintenir; (*affirm*) soutenir; **maintenance** ['meɪntənəns] *n* entretien *m*; (*alimony*) pension *f* alimentaire
maize [meɪz] *n* maïs *m*
majestic [mə'dʒɛstɪk] *adj* majestueux (-euse)
majesty ['mædʒɪstɪ] *n* majesté *f*
major ['meɪdʒə^r] *n* (*MIL*) commandant *m* ♦ *adj* (*important*) important(e); (*most important*) principal(e); (*MUS*) majeur(e)
Majorca [mə'jɔ:kə] *n* Majorque *f*
majority [mə'dʒɔrɪtɪ] *n* majorité *f*
make [meɪk] (*pt, pp* **made**) *vt* faire; (*manufacture*) faire, fabriquer; (*earn*)

gagner; (*cause to be*): **to ~ sb sad** *etc* rendre qn triste *etc*; (*force*): **to ~ sb do sth** obliger qn à faire qch, faire faire qch à qn; (*equal*): **2 and 2 ~ 4** 2 et 2 font 4 ♦ *n* fabrication *f*; (*brand*) marque *f*; **to ~ a fool of sb** (*ridicule*) ridiculiser qn; (*trick*) avoir *or* duper qn; **to ~ a profit** faire un *or* des bénéfice(s); **to ~ a loss** essuyer une perte; **to ~ it** (*arrive*) arriver; (*achieve sth*) parvenir à qch, réussir; **what time do you ~ it?** quelle heure avez-vous?; **to ~ do with** se contenter de; se débrouiller avec; **~ for** *vt fus* (*place*) se diriger vers; **~ out** *vt* (*write out*: *cheque*) faire; (*decipher*) déchiffrer; (*understand*) comprendre; (*see*) distinguer; **~ up** *vt* (*constitute*) constituer; (*invent*) inventer, imaginer; (*parcel, bed*) faire ♦ *vi* se réconcilier; (*with cosmetics*) se maquiller; **~ up for** *vt fus* compenser; **~-believe** *n*: **it's just ~-believe** (*game*) c'est pour faire semblant; (*invention*) c'est de l'invention pure; **~r** *n* fabricant *m*; **~shift** *adj* provisoire, improvisé(e); **~-up** *n* maquillage *m*

making ['meɪkɪŋ] *n* (*fig*): **in the ~** en formation *or* gestation; **to have the ~s of** (*actor, athlete etc*) avoir l'étoffe de

malaria [mə'lɛərɪə] *n* malaria *f*

Malaysia [mə'leɪzɪə] *n* Malaisie *f*

male [meɪl] *n* (BIO) mâle *m* ♦ *adj* mâle; (*sex, attitude*) masculin(e); (*child etc*) du sexe masculin

malevolent [mə'lɛvələnt] *adj* malveillant(e)

malfunction [mæl'fʌŋkʃən] *n* fonctionnement défectueux

malice ['mælɪs] *n* méchanceté *f*, malveillance *f*; **malicious** [mə'lɪʃəs] *adj* méchant(e), malveillant(e)

malignant [mə'lɪgnənt] *adj* (MED) malin(-igne)

mall [mɔːl] *n* (*also:* **shopping ~**) centre commercial

mallet ['mælɪt] *n* maillet *m*

malpractice [mæl'præktɪs] *n* faute professionnelle; négligence *f*

malt [mɔːlt] *n* malt *m* ♦ *cpd* (*also:* **~ whisky**) pur malt

Malta ['mɔːltə] *n* Malte *f*

mammal ['mæml] *n* mammifère *m*

mammoth ['mæməθ] *n* mammouth *m* ♦ *adj* géant(e), monstre

man [mæn] (*pl* **men**) *n* homme *m* ♦ *vt* (NAUT: *ship*) garnir d'hommes; (MIL: *gun*) servir; (: *post*) être de service à; (*machine*) assurer le fonctionnement de; **an old ~** un vieillard; **~ and wife** mari et femme

manage ['mænɪdʒ] *vi* se débrouiller ♦ *vt* (*be in charge of*) s'occuper de; (: *business etc*) gérer; (*control*: *ship*) manier, manœuvrer; (: *person*) savoir s'y prendre avec; **to ~ to do** réussir à faire; **~able** *adj* (*task*) faisable; (*number*) raisonnable; **~ment** *n* gestion *f*, administration *f*, direction *f*; **~r** *n* directeur *m*; administrateur *m*; (SPORT) manager *m*; (*of artist*) impresario *m*; **~ress** [mænɪdʒə'rɛs] *n* directrice *f*; gérante *f*; **~rial** [mænɪ'dʒɪərɪəl] *adj* directorial(e); (*skills*) de cadre, de gestion; **managing director** *n* directeur général

mandarin ['mændərɪn] *n* (*also:* **~ orange**) mandarine *f*; (*person*) mandarin *m*

mandatory ['mændətərɪ] *adj* obligatoire

mane [meɪn] *n* crinière *f*

maneuver [mə'nuːvə^r] (US) *vt, vi, n* = **manoeuvre**

manfully ['mænfəlɪ] *adv* vaillamment

mangle ['mæŋgl] *vt* déchiqueter; mutiler

mango ['mæŋgəu] (*pl* **~es**) *n* mangue *f*

mangy ['meɪndʒɪ] *adj* galeux(-euse)

man: ~handle *vt* malmener; **~hole** *n* trou *m* d'homme; **~hood** *n* âge *m* d'homme; virilité *f*; **~-hour** *n* heure *f* de main-d'œuvre; **~hunt** *n* (POLICE) chasse *f* à l'homme

mania ['meɪnɪə] *n* manie *f*; **~c** ['meɪnɪæk] *n* maniaque *m/f*; (*fig*) fou (folle) *m/f*; **manic** ['mænɪk] *adj* maniaque

manicure ['mænɪkjuəʳ] *n* manucure *f*

manifest ['mænɪfɛst] *vt* manifester ♦ *adj* manifeste, évident(e); **~o** [mænɪ'fɛstəu] *n* manifeste *m*

manipulate [mə'nɪpjuleɪt] *vt* manipuler; (*system, situation*) exploiter

man: ~kind [mæn'kaɪnd] *n* humanité *f*, genre humain; **~ly** *adj* viril(e); **~-made** *adj* artificiel(le); (*fibre*) synthétique

manner ['mænəʳ] *n* manière *f*, façon *f*; (*behaviour*) attitude *f*, comportement *m*; (*sort*): **all ~ of** toutes sortes de; **~s** *npl* (*behaviour*) manières; **~ism** *n* particularité *f* de langage (*or* de comportement), tic *m*

manoeuvre [mə'nu:vəʳ] (*US* **maneuver**) *vt* (*move*) manœuvrer; (*manipulate: person*) manipuler; (*: situation*) exploiter ♦ *vi* manœuvrer ♦ *n* manœuvre *f*

manor ['mænəʳ] *n* (*also:* **~ house**) manoir *m*

manpower ['mænpauəʳ] *n* main-d'œuvre *f*

mansion ['mænʃən] *n* château *m*, manoir *m*

manslaughter ['mænslɔ:təʳ] *n* homicide *m* involontaire

mantelpiece ['mæntlpi:s] *n* cheminée *f*

manual ['mænjuəl] *adj* manuel(le) ♦ *n* manuel *m*

manufacture [mænju'fæktʃəʳ] *vt* fabriquer ♦ *n* fabrication *f*; **~r** *n* fabricant *m*

manure [mə'njuəʳ] *n* fumier *m*

manuscript ['mænjuskrɪpt] *n* manuscrit *m*

many ['mɛnɪ] *adj* beaucoup de, de nombreux(-euses) ♦ *pron* beaucoup, un grand nombre; **a great ~** un grand nombre (de); **~ a** ... bien des ..., plus d'un(e) ...

map [mæp] *n* carte *f*; (*of town*) plan *m*; **~ out** *vt* tracer; (*task*) planifier

maple ['meɪpl] *n* érable *m*

mar [mɑ:ʳ] *vt* gâcher, gâter

marathon ['mærəθən] *n* marathon *m*

marble ['mɑ:bl] *n* marbre *m*; (*toy*) bille *f*

March [mɑ:tʃ] *n* mars *m*

march [mɑ:tʃ] *vi* marcher au pas; (*fig: protesters*) défiler ♦ *n* marche *f*; (*demonstration*) manifestation *f*

mare [mɛəʳ] *n* jument *f*

margarine [mɑ:dʒə'ri:n] *n* margarine *f*

margin ['mɑ:dʒɪn] *n* marge *f*; **~al (seat)** *n* (*POL*) siège disputé

marigold ['mærɪgəuld] *n* souci *m*

marijuana [mærɪ'wɑ:nə] *n* marijuana *f*

marina [mə'ri:nə] *n* (*harbour*) marina *f*

marine [mə'ri:n] *adj* marin(e) ♦ *n* fusilier marin; (*US*) marine *m*

marital ['mærɪtl] *adj* matrimonial(e); **~ status** situation *f* de famille

marjoram ['mɑ:dʒərəm] *n* marjolaine *f*

mark [mɑ:k] *n* marque *f*; (*of skid etc*) trace *f*; (*BRIT: SCOL*) note *f*; (*currency*) mark *m* ♦ *vt* marquer; (*stain*) tacher; (*BRIT: SCOL*) noter; corriger; **to ~ time** marquer le pas; **~er** *n* (*sign*) jalon *m*; (*bookmark*) signet *m*

market ['mɑ:kɪt] *n* marché *m* ♦ *vt* (*COMM*) commercialiser; **~ garden** (*BRIT*) *n* jardin maraîcher; **~ing** *n* marketing *m*; **~place** *n* place *f* du marché; (*COMM*) marché *m*; **~ research** *n* étude *f* de marché

marksman ['mɑ:ksmən] (*irreg*) *n* tireur *m* d'élite

marmalade ['mɑ:məleɪd] *n* confiture *f* d'oranges

maroon [mə'ru:n] *vt*: **to be ~ed** être abandonné(e); (*fig*) être bloqué(e) ♦ *adj* bordeaux *inv*

marquee [mɑ:'ki:] *n* chapiteau *m*

marriage ['mærɪdʒ] *n* mariage *m*; **~ certificate** *n* extrait *m* d'acte de mariage

married ['mærɪd] *adj* marié(e); (*life, love*) conjugal(e)

marrow ['mærəu] *n* moelle *f*; (*vegetable*) courge *f*

marry ['mærɪ] *vt* épouser, se marier

avec; (*subj*: *father, priest etc*) marier ♦ *vi* (*also:* **get married**) se marier

Mars [mɑːz] *n* (*planet*) Mars *f*

marsh [mɑːʃ] *n* marais *m*, marécage *m*

marshal ['mɑːʃl] *n* maréchal *m*; (*US*: *fire, police*) ≈ capitaine *m*; (*SPORT*) membre *m* du service d'ordre ♦ *vt* rassembler

marshy ['mɑːʃɪ] *adj* marécageux(-euse)

martyr ['mɑːtəʳ] *n* martyr(e); **~dom** *n* martyre *m*

marvel ['mɑːvl] *n* merveille *f* ♦ *vi*: **to ~ (at)** s'émerveiller (de); **~lous** (*US* **marvelous**) *adj* merveilleux(-euse)

Marxist ['mɑːksɪst] *adj* marxiste ♦ *n* marxiste *m/f*

marzipan ['mɑːzɪpæn] *n* pâte *f* d'amandes

mascara [mæs'kɑːrə] *n* mascara *m*

masculine ['mæskjulɪn] *adj* masculin(e)

mash [mæʃ] *vt* écraser, réduire en purée; **~ed potatoes** *npl* purée *f* de pommes de terre

mask [mɑːsk] *n* masque *m* ♦ *vt* masquer

mason ['meɪsn] *n* (*also:* **stonemason**) maçon *m*; (*also:* **freemason**) franc-maçon *m*; **~ry** *n* maçonnerie *f*

masquerade [mæskə'reɪd] *vi*: **to ~ as** se faire passer pour

mass [mæs] *n* multitude *f*, masse *f*; (*PHYSICS*) masse; (*REL*) messe *f* ♦ *cpd* (*communication*) de masse; (*unemployment*) massif(-ive) ♦ *vi* se masser; **the ~es** les masses; **~es of** des tas de

massacre ['mæsəkəʳ] *n* massacre *m*

massage ['mæsɑːʒ] *n* massage *m* ♦ *vt* masser

massive ['mæsɪv] *adj* énorme, massif (-ive)

mass media *n inv* mass-media *mpl*

mass production *n* fabrication *f* en série

mast [mɑːst] *n* mât *m*; (*RADIO*) pylône *m*

master ['mɑːstəʳ] *n* maître *m*; (*in secondary school*) professeur *m*; (*title for boys*): **M~ X** Monsieur X ♦ *vt* maîtriser; (*learn*) apprendre à fond; **~ly** *adj* magistral(e); **~mind** *n* esprit supérieur ♦ *vt* diriger, être le cerveau de; **M~ of Arts/Science** *n* ≈ maîtrise *f* (en lettres/sciences); **~piece** *n* chef-d'œuvre *m*; **~plan** *n* stratégie *f* d'ensemble; **~y** *n* maîtrise *f*; connaissance parfaite

mat [mæt] *n* petit tapis; (*also:* **doormat**) paillasson *m*; (*also:* **tablemat**) napperon *m* ♦ *adj* = **matt**

match [mætʃ] *n* allumette *f*; (*game*) match *m*, partie *f*; (*fig*) égal(e) ♦ *vt* (*also:* **~ up**) assortir; (*go well with*) aller bien avec, s'assortir à; (*equal*) égaler, valoir ♦ *vi* être assorti(e); **to be a good ~** être bien assorti(e); **~box** *n* boîte *f* d'allumettes; **~ing** *adj* assorti(e)

mate [meɪt] *n* (*inf*) copain (copine); (*animal*) partenaire *m/f*, mâle/femelle; (*in merchant navy*) second *m* ♦ *vi* s'accoupler

material [mə'tɪərɪəl] *n* (*substance*) matière *f*, matériau *m*; (*cloth*) tissu *m*, étoffe *f*; (*information, data*) données *fpl* ♦ *adj* matériel(le); (*relevant*: *evidence*) pertinent(e); **~s** *npl* (*equipment*) matériaux *mpl*

maternal [mə'təːnl] *adj* maternel(le)

maternity [mə'təːnɪtɪ] *n* maternité *f*; **~ dress** *n* robe *f* de grossesse; **~ hospital** *n* maternité *f*

mathematical [mæθə'mætɪkl] *adj* mathématique

mathematics [mæθə'mætɪks] *n* mathématiques *fpl*

maths [mæθs] (*US* **math**) *n* math(s) *fpl*

matinée ['mætɪneɪ] *n* matinée *f*

mating call *n* appel *m* du mâle

matrices ['meɪtrɪsiːz] *npl of* **matrix**

matriculation [mətrɪkju'leɪʃən] *n* inscription *f*

matrimonial [mætrɪ'məunɪəl] *adj* matrimonial(e), conjugal(e)

matrimony ['mætrɪmənɪ] *n* mariage *m*

matrix ['meɪtrɪks] (*pl* **matrices**) *n* matrice *f*

matron ['meɪtrən] *n* (*in hospital*) infirmière-chef *f*; (*in school*) infirmière

mat(t) [mæt] *adj* mat(e)

matted ['mætɪd] *adj* emmêlé(e)

matter ['mætər] *n* question *f*; (PHYSICS) matière *f*; (*content*) contenu *m*, fond *m*; (MED: *pus*) pus *m* ♦ *vi* importer; **~s** *npl* (*affairs, situation*) la situation; **it doesn't ~** cela n'a pas d'importance; (*I don't mind*) cela ne fait rien; **what's the ~?** qu'est-ce qu'il y a?, qu'est-ce qui ne va pas?; **no ~ what** quoiqu'il arrive; **as a ~ of course** tout naturellement; **as a ~ of fact** en fait; **~-of-fact** *adj* terre à terre; (*voice*) neutre

mattress ['mætrɪs] *n* matelas *m*

mature [mə'tjuər] *adj* mûr(e); (*cheese*) fait(e); (*wine*) arrivé(e) à maturité ♦ *vi* (*person*) mûrir; (*wine, cheese*) se faire

maul [mɔ:l] *vt* lacérer

mauve [məuv] *adj* mauve

maximum ['mæksɪməm] (*pl* **maxima**) *adj* maximum ♦ *n* maximum *m*

May [meɪ] *n* mai *m*; **~ Day** *n* le Premier Mai; *see also* **mayday**

may [meɪ] (*conditional* **might**) *vi* (*indicating possibility*): **he ~ come** il se peut qu'il vienne; (*be allowed to*): **~ I smoke?** puis-je fumer?; (*wishes*): **~ God bless you!** (que) Dieu vous bénisse!; **you ~ as well go** à votre place, je partirais

maybe ['meɪbi:] *adv* peut-être; **~ he'll** ... peut-être qu'il ...

mayday ['meɪdeɪ] *n* SOS *m*

mayhem ['meɪhɛm] *n* grabuge *m*

mayonnaise [meɪə'neɪz] *n* mayonnaise *f*

mayor [mɛər] *n* maire *m*; **~ess** *n* épouse *f* du maire

maze [meɪz] *n* labyrinthe *m*, dédale *m*

M.D. *n abbr* (= *Doctor of Medicine*) *titre universitaire*; = **managing director**

me [mi:] *pron* me, m' *+vowel*; (*stressed, after prep*) moi; **he heard ~** il m'a entendu(e); **give ~ a book** donnez-moi un livre; **after ~** après moi

meadow ['mɛdəu] *n* prairie *f*, pré *m*

meagre ['mi:gər] (US **meager**) *adj* maigre

meal [mi:l] *n* repas *m*; (*flour*) farine *f*; **~time** *n* l'heure *f* du repas

mean [mi:n] (*pt, pp* **meant**) *adj* (*with money*) avare, radin(e); (*unkind*) méchant(e); (*shabby*) misérable; (*average*) moyen(ne) ♦ *vt* signifier, vouloir dire; (*refer to*) faire allusion à, parler de; (*intend*): **to ~ to do** avoir l'intention de faire ♦ *n* moyenne *f*; **~s** *npl* (*way, money*) moyens *mpl*; **by ~s of** par l'intermédiaire de; au moyen de; **by all ~s!** je vous en prie!; **to be ~t for sb/sth** être destiné(e) à qn/qch; **do you ~ it?** vous êtes sérieux?; **what do you ~?** que voulez-vous dire?

meander [mɪ'ændər] *vi* faire des méandres

meaning ['mi:nɪŋ] *n* signification *f*, sens *m*; **~ful** *adj* significatif(-ive); (*relationship, occasion*) important(e); **~less** *adj* dénué(e) de sens

meanness ['mi:nnɪs] *n* (*with money*) avarice *f*; (*unkindness*) méchanceté *f*; (*shabbiness*) médiocrité *f*

meant [mɛnt] *pt, pp of* **mean**

meantime ['mi:ntaɪm] *adv* (*also:* **in the ~**) pendant ce temps

meanwhile ['mi:nwaɪl] *adv* = **meantime**

measles ['mi:zlz] *n* rougeole *f*

measure ['mɛʒər] *vt, vi* mesurer ♦ *n* mesure *f*; (*ruler*) règle (graduée); **~ments** *npl* mesures *fpl*; **chest/hip ~ment(s)** tour *m* de poitrine/hanches

meat [mi:t] *n* viande *f*; **~ball** *n* boulette *f* de viande

Mecca ['mɛkə] *n* La Mecque

mechanic [mɪ'kænɪk] *n* mécanicien *m*; **~al** *adj* mécanique; **~s** *n* (PHYSICS) mécanique *f* ♦ *npl* (*of reading, government etc*) mécanisme *m*

mechanism ['mɛkənɪzəm] *n* mécanisme *m*

medal ['mɛdl] *n* médaille *f*; **~lion** [mɪ'dælɪən] *n* médaillon *m*; **~list** (*US* **medalist**) *n* (*SPORT*) médaillé(e)

meddle ['mɛdl] *vi*: **to ~ in** se mêler de, s'occuper de; **to ~ with** toucher à

media ['mi:dɪə] *npl* media *mpl*

mediaeval [mɛdɪ'i:vl] *adj* = **medieval**

median ['mi:dɪən] (*US*) *n* (*also:* **~ strip**) bande médiane

mediate ['mi:dɪeɪt] *vi* servir d'intermédiaire

Medicaid ® ['mɛdɪkeɪd] (*US*) *n assistance médicale aux indigents*

medical ['mɛdɪkl] *adj* médical(e) ♦ *n* visite médicale

Medicare ® ['mɛdɪkɛə^r] (*US*) *n assistance médicale aux personnes âgées*

medication [mɛdɪ'keɪʃən] *n* (*drugs*) médicaments *mpl*

medicine ['mɛdsɪn] *n* médecine *f*; (*drug*) médicament *m*

medieval [mɛdɪ'i:vl] *adj* médiéval(e)

mediocre [mi:dɪ'əukə^r] *adj* médiocre

meditate ['mɛdɪteɪt] *vi* méditer

Mediterranean [mɛdɪtə'reɪnɪən] *adj* méditerranéen(ne); **the ~ (Sea)** la (mer) Méditerranée

medium ['mi:dɪəm] (*pl* **media**) *adj* moyen(ne) ♦ *n* (*means*) moyen *m*; (*pl ~s: person*) médium *m*; **the happy ~** le juste milieu; **~-sized** *adj* de taille moyenne; **~ wave** *n* ondes moyennes

medley ['mɛdlɪ] *n* mélange *m*; (*MUS*) pot-pourri *m*

meek [mi:k] *adj* doux (douce), humble

meet [mi:t] (*pt, pp* **met**) *vt* rencontrer; (*by arrangement*) retrouver, rejoindre; (*for the first time*) faire la connaissance de; (*go and fetch*): **I'll ~ you at the station** j'irai te chercher à la gare; (*opponent, danger*) faire face à; (*obligations*) satisfaire à ♦ *vi* (*friends*) se rencontrer, se retrouver; (*in session*) se réunir; (*join: lines, roads*) se rejoindre; **~ with** *vt fus* rencontrer; **~ing** *n* rencontre *f*; (*session: of club etc*) réunion *f*; (*POL*) meeting *m*; **she's at a ~ing** (*COMM*) elle est en conférence

mega ['mɛgə] (*inf*) *adv*: **he's ~ rich** il est hyper-riche; **~byte** *n* (*COMPUT*) méga-octet *m*; **~phone** *n* porte-voix *m inv*

melancholy ['mɛlənkəlɪ] *n* mélancolie *f* ♦ *adj* mélancolique

mellow ['mɛləu] *adj* velouté(e); doux (douce); (*sound*) mélodieux(-euse) ♦ *vi* (*person*) s'adoucir

melody ['mɛlədɪ] *n* mélodie *f*

melon ['mɛlən] *n* melon *m*

melt [mɛlt] *vi* fondre ♦ *vt* faire fondre; (*metal*) fondre; **~ away** *vi* fondre complètement; **~ down** *vt* fondre; **~down** *n* fusion *f* (du cœur d'un réacteur nucléaire); **~ing pot** *n* (*fig*) creuset *m*

member ['mɛmbə^r] *n* membre *m*; **M~ of Parliament** (*BRIT*) député *m*; **M~ of the European Parliament** Eurodéputé *m*; **~ship** *n* adhésion *f*; statut *m* de membre; (*members*) membres *mpl*, adhérents *mpl*; **~ship card** *n* carte *f* de membre

memento [mə'mɛntəu] *n* souvenir *m*

memo ['mɛməu] *n* note *f* (de service)

memoirs ['mɛmwɑ:z] *npl* mémoires *mpl*

memorandum [mɛmə'rændəm] (*pl* **memoranda**) *n* note *f* (de service)

memorial [mɪ'mɔ:rɪəl] *n* mémorial *m* ♦ *adj* commémoratif(-ive)

memorize ['mɛməraɪz] *vt* apprendre par cœur; retenir

memory ['mɛmərɪ] *n* mémoire *f*; (*recollection*) souvenir *m*

men [mɛn] *npl of* **man**

menace ['mɛnɪs] *n* menace *f*; (*nuisance*) plaie *f* ♦ *vt* menacer; **menacing** *adj* menaçant(e)

mend [mɛnd] *vt* réparer; (*darn*) raccommoder, repriser ♦ *n*: **on the ~** en voie de guérison; **to ~ one's ways** s'amender; **~ing** *n* réparation *f*; (*clothes*) raccommodage *m*

menial ['mi:nɪəl] *adj* subalterne

meningitis [mɛnɪn'dʒaɪtɪs] *n* méningite *f*
menopause ['mɛnəupɔ:z] *n* ménopause *f*
menstruation [mɛnstru'eɪʃən] *n* menstruation *f*
mental ['mɛntl] *adj* mental(e); **~ity** [mɛn'tælɪtɪ] *n* mentalité *f*
mention ['mɛnʃən] *n* mention *f* ♦ *vt* mentionner, faire mention de; **don't ~ it!** je vous en prie, il n'y a pas de quoi!
menu ['mɛnju:] *n* (*set ~*, COMPUT) menu *m*; (*list of dishes*) carte *f*
MEP *n abbr* = **Member of the European Parliament**
mercenary ['mə:sɪnərɪ] *adj* intéressé(e), mercenaire ♦ *n* mercenaire *m*
merchandise ['mə:tʃəndaɪz] *n* marchandises *fpl*
merchant ['mə:tʃənt] *n* négociant *m*, marchand *m*; **~ bank** (BRIT) *n* banque *f* d'affaires; **~ navy** (US **merchant marine**) *n* marine marchande
merciful ['mə:sɪful] *adj* miséricordieux(-euse), clément(e); **a ~ release** une délivrance
merciless ['mə:sɪlɪs] *adj* impitoyable, sans pitié
mercury ['mə:kjurɪ] *n* mercure *m*
mercy ['mə:sɪ] *n* pitié *f*, indulgence *f*; (REL) miséricorde *f*; **at the ~ of** à la merci de
mere [mɪə^r] *adj* simple; (*chance*) pur(e); **a ~ two hours** seulement deux heures; **~ly** *adv* simplement, purement
merge [mə:dʒ] *vt* unir ♦ *vi* (*colours, shapes, sounds*) se mêler; (*roads*) se joindre; (COMM) fusionner; **~r** *n* (COMM) fusion *f*
meringue [mə'ræŋ] *n* meringue *f*
merit ['mɛrɪt] *n* mérite *m*, valeur *f*
mermaid ['mə:meɪd] *n* sirène *f*
merry ['mɛrɪ] *adj* gai(e); **M~ Christmas!** Joyeux Noël!; **~-go-round** *n* manège *m*
mesh [mɛʃ] *n* maille *f*
mesmerize ['mɛzməraɪz] *vt* hypnotiser; fasciner
mess [mɛs] *n* désordre *m*, fouillis *m*, pagaille *f*; (*muddle: of situation*) gâchis *m*; (*dirt*) saleté *f*; (MIL) mess *m*, cantine *f*; **~ about** (*inf*) *vi* perdre son temps; **~ about with** (*inf*) *vt fus* tripoter; **~ around** (*inf*) *vi* = **mess about**; **~ around with** *vt fus* = **mess about with**; **~ up** *vt* (*dirty*) salir; (*spoil*) gâcher
message ['mɛsɪdʒ] *n* message *m*;
messenger ['mɛsɪndʒə^r] *n* messager *m*
Messrs ['mɛsəz] *abbr* (*on letters*) MM
messy ['mɛsɪ] *adj* sale; en désordre
met [mɛt] *pt, pp of* **meet**
metal ['mɛtl] *n* métal *m*; **~lic** [mɪ'tælɪk] *adj* métallique
meteorology [mi:tɪə'rɔlədʒɪ] *n* météorologie *f*
meter ['mi:tə^r] *n* (*instrument*) compteur *m*; (*also:* **parking ~**) parcomètre *m*; (US: *unit*) = **metre**
method ['mɛθəd] *n* méthode *f*; **~ical** [mɪ'θɔdɪkl] *adj* méthodique; **M~ist** *n* méthodiste *m/f*
meths [mɛθs] (BRIT), **methylated spirit** ['mɛθɪleɪtɪd-] (BRIT) *n* alcool *m* à brûler
metre ['mi:tə^r] (US **meter**) *n* mètre *m*;
metric ['mɛtrɪk] *adj* métrique
metropolitan [mɛtrə'pɔlɪtn] *adj* métropolitain(e); **the M~ Police** (BRIT) la police londonienne
mettle ['mɛtl] *n*: **to be on one's ~** être d'attaque
mew [mju:] *vi* (*cat*) miauler
mews [mju:z] (BRIT) *n*: **~ cottage** *cottage aménagé dans une ancienne écurie*
Mexico ['mɛksɪkəu] *n* Mexique *m*
miaow [mi:'au] *vi* miauler
mice [maɪs] *npl of* **mouse**
micro ['maɪkrəu] *n* (*also:* **~computer**) micro-ordinateur *m*; **~chip** *n* puce *f*; **~phone** *n* microphone *m*; **~scope** *n* microscope *m*; **~wave** *n* (*also:* **~wave oven**) four *m* à micro-ondes
mid [mɪd] *adj*: **in ~ May** à la mi-mai; **~ afternoon** le milieu de l'après-midi; **in**

~ **air** en plein ciel; **~day** *n* midi *m*

middle ['mɪdl] *n* milieu *m*; (*waist*) taille *f* ♦ *adj* du milieu; (*average*) moyen(ne); **in the ~ of the night** au milieu de la nuit; **~-aged** *adj* d'un certain âge; **M~ Ages** *npl*: **the M~ Ages** le moyen âge; **~-class** *adj* ≃ bourgeois(e); **~ class(es)** *n(pl)*: **the ~ class(es)** ≃ les classes moyennes; **M~ East** *n* Proche-Orient *m*, Moyen-Orient *m*; **~man** (*irreg*) *n* intermédiaire *m*; **~ name** *n* deuxième nom *m*; **~-of-the-road** *adj* (*politician*) modéré(e); (*music*) neutre; **~weight** *n* (BOXING) poids moyen; **middling** *adj* moyen(ne)

midge [mɪdʒ] *n* moucheron *m*

midget ['mɪdʒɪt] *n* nain(e)

Midlands ['mɪdləndz] *npl comtés du centre de l'Angleterre*

midnight ['mɪdnaɪt] *n* minuit *m*

midriff ['mɪdrɪf] *n* estomac *m*, taille *f*

midst [mɪdst] *n*: **in the ~ of** au milieu de

mid [mɪd'-]: **~summer** [mɪd'sʌmə^r] *n* milieu *m* de l'été; **~way** [mɪd'weɪ] *adj, adv*: **~way (between)** à mi-chemin (entre); **~way through ...** au milieu de ..., en plein(e) ...; **~week** [mɪd'wi:k] *adj* au milieu de la semaine

midwife ['mɪdwaɪf] (*pl* **midwives**) *n* sage-femme *f*

might [maɪt] *vb see* **may** ♦ *n* puissance *f*, force *f*; **~y** *adj* puissant(e)

migraine ['mi:greɪn] *n* migraine *f*

migrant ['maɪgrənt] *adj* (*bird*) migrateur(-trice); (*worker*) saisonnier (-ère)

migrate [maɪ'greɪt] *vi* émigrer

mike [maɪk] *n abbr* (= *microphone*) micro *m*

mild [maɪld] *adj* doux (douce); (*reproach, infection*) léger(-ère); (*illness*) bénin(-igne); (*interest*) modéré(e); (*taste*) peu relevé(e) ♦ *n* (*beer*) bière légère; **~ly** *adv* doucement; légèrement; **to put it ~ly** c'est le moins qu'on puisse dire

mile [maɪl] *n* mi(l)le *m* (= *1609 m*); **~age** *n* distance *f* en milles; ≃ kilométrage *m*; **~ometer** [maɪ'lɔmɪtə^r] *n* compteur *m* (kilométrique); **~stone** *n* borne *f*; (*fig*) jalon *m*

militant ['mɪlɪtnt] *adj* militant(e)

military ['mɪlɪtərɪ] *adj* militaire

militia [mɪ'lɪʃə] *n* milice(s) *f(pl)*

milk [mɪlk] *n* lait *m* ♦ *vt* (*cow*) traire; (*fig: person*) dépouiller, plumer; (: *situation*) exploiter à fond; **~ chocolate** *n* chocolat *m* au lait; **~man** (*irreg*) *n* laitier *m*; **~ shake** *n* milk-shake *m*; **~y** *adj* (*drink*) au lait; (*colour*) laiteux(-euse); **M~y Way** *n* voie lactée

mill [mɪl] *n* moulin *m*; (*steel* ~) aciérie *f*; (*spinning* ~) filature *f*; (*flour* ~) minoterie *f* ♦ *vt* moudre, broyer ♦ *vi* (*also:* **~ about**) grouiller; **~er** *n* meunier *m*

millennium bug [mɪ'lɛnɪəm-] *n* bogue *m or* bug *m* de l'an 2000

milligram(me) ['mɪlɪgræm] *n* milligramme *m*

millimetre ['mɪlɪmi:tə^r] (US **millimeter**) *n* millimètre *m*

million ['mɪljən] *n* million *m*; **~aire** *n* millionnaire *m*

milometer [maɪ'lɔmɪtə^r] *n* ≃ compteur *m* kilométrique

mime [maɪm] *n* mime *m* ♦ *vt, vi* mimer; **mimic** ['mɪmɪk] *n* imitateur(-trice) ♦ *vt* imiter, contrefaire

min. *abbr* = **minute(s)**; **minimum**

mince [mɪns] *vt* hacher ♦ *n* (BRIT: CULIN) viande hachée, hachis *m*; **~meat** *n* (*fruit*) *hachis de fruits secs utilisé en pâtisserie*; (US: *meat*) viande hachée, hachis; **~ pie** *n* (*sweet*) *sorte de tarte aux fruits secs*; **~r** *n* hachoir *m*

mind [maɪnd] *n* esprit *m* ♦ *vt* (*attend to, look after*) s'occuper de; (*be careful*) faire attention à; (*object to*): **I don't ~ the noise** le bruit ne me dérange pas; **I don't ~** cela ne me dérange pas; **it is on my ~** cela me préoccupe; **to my ~** à mon avis *or* sens; **to be out of one's ~** ne plus avoir toute sa raison; **to**

keep *or* **bear sth in ~** tenir compte de qch; **to make up one's ~** se décider; **~ you, ...** remarquez ...; **never ~** ça ne fait rien; (*don't worry*) ne vous en faites pas; **"~ the step"** "attention à la marche"; **~er** *n* (*child-minder*) gardienne *f*; (*inf*: *bodyguard*) ange gardien (*fig*); **~ful** *adj*: **~ful of** attentif(-ive) à, soucieux(-euse) de; **~less** *adj* irréfléchi(e); (*boring*: *job*) idiot(e)

mine[1] [maɪn] *pron* le (la) mien(ne), les miens (miennes) ♦ *adj*: **this book is ~** ce livre est à moi

mine[2] [maɪn] *n* mine *f* ♦ *vt* (*coal*) extraire; (*ship, beach*) miner; **~field** *n* champ *m* de mines; (*fig*) situation (très délicate); **~r** *n* mineur *m*

mineral ['mɪnərəl] *adj* minéral(e) ♦ *n* minéral *m*; **~s** *npl* (*BRIT*: *soft drinks*) boissons gazeuses; **~ water** *n* eau minérale

mingle ['mɪŋgl] *vi*: **to ~ with** se mêler à

miniature ['mɪnətʃə^r] *adj* (en) miniature ♦ *n* miniature *f*

minibus ['mɪnɪbʌs] *n* minibus *m*

minimal ['mɪnɪml] *adj* minime

minimize ['mɪnɪmaɪz] *vt* (*reduce*) réduire au minimum; (*play down*) minimiser

minimum ['mɪnɪməm] (*pl* **minima**) *adj, n* minimum *m*

mining ['maɪnɪŋ] *n* exploitation minière

miniskirt ['mɪnɪskə:t] *n* mini-jupe *f*

minister ['mɪnɪstə^r] *n* (*BRIT*: *POL*) ministre *m*; (*REL*) pasteur *m* ♦ *vi*: **to ~ to sb('s needs)** pourvoir aux besoins de qn; **~ial** [mɪnɪs'tɪərɪəl] (*BRIT*) *adj* (*POL*) ministériel(le); **ministry** *n* (*BRIT*: *POL*) ministère *m*; (*REL*): **to go into the ministry** devenir pasteur

mink [mɪŋk] *n* vison *m*

minor ['maɪnə^r] *adj* petit(e), de peu d'importance; (*MUS, poet, problem*) mineur(e) ♦ *n* (*LAW*) mineur(e)

minority [maɪ'nɔrɪtɪ] *n* minorité *f*

mint [mɪnt] *n* (*plant*) menthe *f*; (*sweet*) bonbon *m* à la menthe ♦ *vt* (*coins*) battre; **the (Royal) M~**, (*US*) **the (US) M~** ≃ l'Hôtel *m* de la Monnaie; **in ~ condition** à l'état de neuf

minus ['maɪnəs] *n* (*also:* **~ sign**) signe *m* moins ♦ *prep* moins

minute[1] [maɪ'nju:t] *adj* minuscule; (*detail, search*) minutieux(-euse)

minute[2] ['mɪnɪt] *n* minute *f*; **~s** *npl* (*official record*) procès-verbal, compte rendu

miracle ['mɪrəkl] *n* miracle *m*

mirage ['mɪrɑ:ʒ] *n* mirage *m*

mirror ['mɪrə^r] *n* miroir *m*, glace *f*; (*in car*) rétroviseur *m*

mirth [mə:θ] *n* gaieté *f*

misadventure [mɪsəd'vɛntʃə^r] *n* mésaventure *f*

misapprehension ['mɪsæprɪ'hɛnʃən] *n* malentendu *m*, méprise *f*

misappropriate [mɪsə'prəuprɪeɪt] *vt* détourner

misbehave [mɪsbɪ'heɪv] *vi* mal se conduire

miscalculate [mɪs'kælkjuleɪt] *vt* mal calculer

miscarriage ['mɪskærɪdʒ] *n* (*MED*) fausse couche; **~ of justice** erreur *f* judiciaire

miscellaneous [mɪsɪ'leɪnɪəs] *adj* (*items*) divers(es); (*selection*) varié(e)

mischief ['mɪstʃɪf] *n* (*naughtiness*) sottises *fpl*; (*fun*) farce *f*; (*playfulness*) espièglerie *f*; (*maliciousness*) méchanceté *f*; **mischievous** ['mɪstʃɪvəs] *adj* (*playful, naughty*) coquin(e), espiègle

misconception ['mɪskən'sɛpʃən] *n* idée fausse

misconduct [mɪs'kɔndʌkt] *n* inconduite *f*; **professional ~** faute professionnelle

misdemeanour [mɪsdɪ'mi:nə^r] (*US* **misdemeanor**) *n* écart *m* de conduite; infraction *f*

miser ['maɪzə^r] *n* avare *m/f*

miserable ['mɪzərəbl] *adj* (*person, expression*) malheureux(-euse); (*conditions*) misérable; (*weather*) maussade;

(*offer, donation*) minable; (*failure*) pitoyable
miserly ['maɪzəlɪ] *adj* avare
misery ['mɪzərɪ] *n* (*unhappiness*) tristesse *f*; (*pain*) souffrances *fpl*; (*wretchedness*) misère *f*
misfire [mɪs'faɪə^r] *vi* rater
misfit ['mɪsfɪt] *n* (*person*) inadapté(e)
misfortune [mɪs'fɔːtʃən] *n* malchance *f*, malheur *m*
misgiving [mɪs'gɪvɪŋ] *n* (*apprehension*) craintes *fpl*; **to have ~s about** avoir des doutes quant à
misguided [mɪs'gaɪdɪd] *adj* malavisé(e)
mishandle [mɪs'hændl] *vt* (*mismanage*) mal s'y prendre pour faire *or* résoudre *etc*
mishap ['mɪshæp] *n* mésaventure *f*
misinform [mɪsɪn'fɔːm] *vt* mal renseigner
misinterpret [mɪsɪn'təːprɪt] *vt* mal interpréter
misjudge [mɪs'dʒʌdʒ] *vt* méjuger
mislay [mɪs'leɪ] (*irreg*: *like* **lay**) *vt* égarer
mislead [mɪs'liːd] (*irreg*: *like* **lead**) *vt* induire en erreur; **~ing** *adj* trompeur (-euse)
mismanage [mɪs'mænɪdʒ] *vt* mal gérer
misplace [mɪs'pleɪs] *vt* égarer
misprint ['mɪsprɪnt] *n* faute *f* d'impression
Miss [mɪs] *n* Mademoiselle
miss [mɪs] *vt* (*fail to get, attend, see*) manquer, rater; (*regret absence of*): **I ~ him/it** il/cela me manque ♦ *vi* manquer ♦ *n* (*shot*) coup manqué; **~ out** (BRIT) *vt* oublier
misshapen [mɪs'ʃeɪpən] *adj* difforme
missile ['mɪsaɪl] *n* (MIL) missile *m*; (*object thrown*) projectile *m*
missing ['mɪsɪŋ] *adj* manquant(e); (*after escape, disaster: person*) disparu(e); **to go ~** disparaître; **to be ~** avoir disparu
mission ['mɪʃən] *n* mission *f*; **~ary** ['mɪʃənrɪ] *n* missionnaire *m/f*; **~ statement** *n* déclaration *f* d'intention
mist [mɪst] *n* brume *f* ♦ *vi* (*also*: **~ over**: *eyes*) s'embuer; **~ up** *vi* = **mist over**
mistake [mɪs'teɪk] (*irreg*: *like* **take**) *n* erreur *f*, faute *f* ♦ *vt* (*meaning, remark*) mal comprendre; se méprendre sur; **to make a ~** se tromper, faire une erreur; **by ~** par erreur, par inadvertance; **to ~ for** prendre pour; **~n** *pp of* **mistake** ♦ *adj* (*idea etc*) erroné(e); **to be ~n** faire erreur, se tromper
mister ['mɪstə^r] (*inf*) *n* Monsieur *m*; *see also* **Mr**
mistletoe ['mɪsltəu] *n* gui *m*
mistook [mɪs'tuk] *pt of* **mistake**
mistress ['mɪstrɪs] *n* maîtresse *f*; (BRIT: *in primary school*) institutrice *f*; (: *in secondary school*) professeur *m*
mistrust [mɪs'trʌst] *vt* se méfier de
misty ['mɪstɪ] *adj* brumeux(-euse); (*glasses, window*) embué(e)
misunderstand [mɪsʌndə'stænd] (*irreg*) *vt, vi* mal comprendre; **~ing** *n* méprise *f*, malentendu *m*
misuse [*n* mɪs'juːs, *vb* mɪs'juːz] *n* mauvais emploi; (*of power*) abus *m* ♦ *vt* mal employer; abuser de; **~ of funds** détournement *m* de fonds
mitigate ['mɪtɪgeɪt] *vt* atténuer
mitt(en) ['mɪt(n)] *n* mitaine *f*; moufle *f*
mix [mɪks] *vt* mélanger; (*sauce, drink etc*) préparer ♦ *vi* se mélanger; (*socialize*): **he doesn't ~ well** il est peu sociable ♦ *n* mélange *m*; **to ~ with** (*people*) fréquenter; **~ up** *vt* mélanger; (*confuse*) confondre; **~ed** *adj* (*feelings, reactions*) contradictoire; (*salad*) mélangé(e); (*school, marriage*) mixte; **~ed grill** *n* assortiment *m* de grillades; **~ed-up** *adj* (*confused*) désorienté(e), embrouillé(e); **~er** *n* (*for food*) batteur *m*, mixer *m*; (*person*): **he is a good ~er** il est très liant; **~ture** *n* assortiment *m*, mélange *m*; (MED) préparation *f*; **~-up** *n* confusion *f*
MLA (BRIT) *n abbr* (= *Member of the Legislative Assembly*) député *m*
mm *abbr* (= *millimetre*) mm

moan [məun] *n* gémissement *m* ♦ *vi* gémir; (*inf*: *complain*): **to ~ (about)** se plaindre (de)
moat [məut] *n* fossé *m*, douves *fpl*
mob [mɔb] *n* foule *f*; (*disorderly*) cohue *f* ♦ *vt* assaillir
mobile ['məubaɪl] *adj* mobile ♦ *n* mobile *m*; **~ home** *n* (grande) caravane; **~ phone** *n* téléphone portatif
mock [mɔk] *vt* ridiculiser; (*laugh at*) se moquer de ♦ *adj* faux (fausse); **~ exam** examen blanc; **~ery** *n* moquerie *f*, raillerie *f*; **to make a ~ery of** tourner en dérision; **~-up** *n* maquette *f*
mod [mɔd] *adj see* **convenience**
mode [məud] *n* mode *m*
model ['mɔdl] *n* modèle *m*; (*person*: *for fashion*) mannequin *m*; (: *for artist*) modèle ♦ *vt* (*with clay etc*) modeler ♦ *vi* travailler comme mannequin ♦ *adj* (*railway*: *toy*) modèle réduit *inv*; (*child, factory*) modèle; **to ~ clothes** présenter des vêtements; **to ~ o.s. on** imiter
modem ['məudɛm] (COMPUT) *n* modem *m*
moderate [*adj* 'mɔdərət, *vb* 'mɔdəreɪt] *adj* modéré(e); (*amount, change*) peu important(e) ♦ *vi* se calmer ♦ *vt* modérer
modern ['mɔdən] *adj* moderne; **~ize** *vt* moderniser
modest ['mɔdɪst] *adj* modeste; **~y** *n* modestie *f*
modify ['mɔdɪfaɪ] *vt* modifier
mogul ['məugl] *n* (*fig*) nabab *m*
mohair ['məuhɛə^r] *n* mohair *m*
moist [mɔɪst] *adj* humide, moite; **~en** *vt* humecter, mouiller légèrement; **~ure** *n* humidité *f*; **~urizer** *n* produit hydratant
molar ['məulə^r] *n* molaire *f*
molasses [mə'læsɪz] *n* mélasse *f*
mold [məuld] (US) *n*, *vt* = **mould**
mole [məul] *n* (*animal, fig*: *spy*) taupe *f*; (*spot*) grain *m* de beauté
molest [mə'lɛst] *vt* (*harass*) molester; (LAW: *sexually*) attenter à la pudeur de
mollycoddle ['mɔlɪkɔdl] *vt* chouchouter, couver
molt [məult] (US) *vi* = **moult**
molten ['məultən] *adj* fondu(e); (*rock*) en fusion
mom [mɔm] (US) *n* = **mum**
moment ['məumənt] *n* moment *m*, instant *m*; **at the ~** en ce moment; **at that ~** à ce moment-là; **~ary** *adj* momentané(e), passager(-ère); **~ous** [məu'mɛntəs] *adj* important(e), capital(e)
momentum [məu'mɛntəm] *n* élan *m*, vitesse acquise; (*fig*) dynamique *f*; **to gather ~** prendre de la vitesse
mommy ['mɔmɪ] (US) *n* maman *f*
Monaco ['mɔnəkəu] *n* Monaco *m*
monarch ['mɔnək] *n* monarque *m*; **~y** *n* monarchie *f*
monastery ['mɔnəstərɪ] *n* monastère *m*
Monday ['mʌndɪ] *n* lundi *m*
monetary ['mʌnɪtərɪ] *adj* monétaire
money ['mʌnɪ] *n* argent *m*; **to make ~** gagner de l'argent; **~ belt** *n* ceinture-portefeuille *f*; **~ order** *n* mandat *m*; **~-spinner** (*inf*) *n* mine *f* d'or (*fig*)
mongrel ['mʌŋgrəl] *n* (*dog*) bâtard *m*
monitor ['mɔnɪtə^r] *n* (TV, COMPUT) moniteur *m* ♦ *vt* contrôler; (*broadcast*) être à l'écoute de; (*progress*) suivre (de près)
monk [mʌŋk] *n* moine *m*
monkey ['mʌŋkɪ] *n* singe *m*; **~ nut** (BRIT) *n* cacahuète *f*
monopoly [mə'nɔpəlɪ] *n* monopole *m*
monotone ['mɔnətəun] *n* ton *m* (*or* voix *f*) monocorde; **monotonous** [mə'nɔtənəs] *adj* monotone
monsoon [mɔn'suːn] *n* mousson *f*
monster ['mɔnstə^r] *n* monstre *m*; **monstrous** ['mɔnstrəs] *adj* monstrueux(-euse); (*huge*) gigantesque
month [mʌnθ] *n* mois *m*; **~ly** *adj* mensuel(le) ♦ *adv* mensuellement
monument ['mɔnjumənt] *n* monument *m*
moo [muː] *vi* meugler, beugler

mood [muːd] *n* humeur *f*, disposition *f*; **to be in a good/bad ~** être de bonne/mauvaise humeur; **~y** *adj* (*variable*) d'humeur changeante, lunatique; (*sullen*) morose, maussade

moon [muːn] *n* lune *f*; **~light** *n* clair *m* de lune; **~lighting** *n* travail *m* au noir; **~lit** *adj*: **a ~lit night** une nuit de lune

moor [muəʳ] *n* lande *f* ♦ *vt* (*ship*) amarrer ♦ *vi* mouiller; **~land** *n* lande *f*

moose [muːs] *n inv* élan *m*

mop [mɔp] *n* balai *m* à laver; (*for dishes*) lavette *f* (à vaisselle) ♦ *vt* essuyer; **~ of hair** tignasse *f*; **~ up** *vt* éponger

mope [məup] *vi* avoir le cafard, se morfondre

moped ['məupɛd] *n* cyclomoteur *m*

moral ['mɔrl] *adj* moral(e) ♦ *n* morale *f*; **~s** *npl* (*attitude, behaviour*) moralité *f*

morale [mɔ'rɑːl] *n* moral *m*

morality [mə'rælɪtɪ] *n* moralité *f*

morass [mə'ræs] *n* marais *m*, marécage *m*

KEYWORD

more [mɔːʳ] *adj* **1** (*greater in number etc*) plus (de), davantage; **more people/work (than)** plus de gens/de travail (que)

2 (*additional*) encore (de); **do you want (some) more tea?** voulez-vous encore du thé?; **I have no** *or* **I don't have any more money** je n'ai plus d'argent; **it'll take a few more weeks** ça prendra encore quelques semaines

♦ *pron* plus, davantage; **more than 10** plus de 10; **it cost more than we expected** cela a coûté plus que prévu; **I want more** j'en veux plus *or* davantage; **is there any more?** est-ce qu'il en reste?; **there's no more** il n'y en a plus; **a little more** un peu plus; **many/much more** beaucoup plus, bien davantage

♦ *adv*: **more dangerous/easily (than)** plus dangereux/facilement (que); **more and more expensive** de plus en plus cher; **more or less** plus ou moins; **more than ever** plus que jamais

moreover [mɔː'rəuvəʳ] *adv* de plus

morning ['mɔːnɪŋ] *n* matin *m*; matinée *f* ♦ *cpd* matinal(e); (*paper*) du matin; **in the ~** le matin; **7 o'clock in the ~** 7 heures du matin; **~ sickness** *n* nausées matinales

Morocco [mə'rɔkəu] *n* Maroc *m*

moron ['mɔːrɔn] (*inf*) *n* idiot(e)

Morse [mɔːs] *n*: **~ code** morse *m*

morsel ['mɔːsl] *n* bouchée *f*

mortar ['mɔːtəʳ] *n* mortier *m*

mortgage ['mɔːgɪdʒ] *n* hypothèque *f*; (*loan*) prêt *m* (*or* crédit *m*) hypothécaire ♦ *vt* hypothéquer; **~ company** (*US*) *n* société *f* de crédit immobilier

mortuary ['mɔːtjuərɪ] *n* morgue *f*

mosaic [məu'zeɪɪk] *n* mosaïque *f*

Moscow ['mɔskəu] *n* Moscou

Moslem ['mɔzləm] *adj*, *n* = **Muslim**

mosque [mɔsk] *n* mosquée *f*

mosquito [mɔs'kiːtəu] (*pl* **~es**) *n* moustique *m*

moss [mɔs] *n* mousse *f*

most [məust] *adj* la plupart de; le plus de ♦ *pron* la plupart ♦ *adv* le plus; (*very*) très, extrêmement; **the ~** (*also:* **+ adjective**) le plus; **~ of** la plus grande partie de; **~ of them** la plupart d'entre eux; **I saw (the) ~** j'en ai vu la plupart; c'est moi qui en ai vu le plus; **at the (very) ~** au plus; **to make the ~ of** profiter au maximum de; **~ly** *adv* (*chiefly*) surtout; (*usually*) généralement

MOT *n abbr* (*BRIT*: *Ministry of Transport*): **the MOT (test)** *la visite technique (annuelle) obligatoire des véhicules à moteur*

motel [məu'tɛl] *n* motel *m*

moth [mɔθ] *n* papillon *m* de nuit; (*in clothes*) mite *f*

mother ['mʌðəʳ] *n* mère *f* ♦ *vt* (*act as ~ to*) servir de mère à; (*pamper, protect*) materner; **~ country** mère patrie; **~hood** *n* maternité *f*; **~-in-law** *n* belle-mère *f*; **~ly** *adj* maternel(le); **~-**

of-pearl *n* nacre *f*; **M~'s Day** *n* fête *f* des Mères; **~-to-be** *n* future maman; **~ tongue** *n* langue maternelle

motion ['məuʃən] *n* mouvement *m*; (*gesture*) geste *m*; (*at meeting*) motion *f* ♦ *vt, vi*: **to ~ (to) sb to do** faire signe à qn de faire; **~less** *adj* immobile, sans mouvement; **~ picture** *n* film *m*

motivated ['məutɪveɪtɪd] *adj* motivé(e); **motivation** [məutɪ'veɪʃən] *n* motivation *f*

motive ['məutɪv] *n* motif *m*, mobile *m*

motley ['mɔtlɪ] *adj* hétéroclite

motor ['məutə^r] *n* moteur *m*; (*BRIT*: *inf*: *vehicle*) auto *f* ♦ *cpd* (*industry, vehicle*) automobile; **~bike** *n* moto *f*; **~boat** *n* bateau *m* à moteur; **~car** (*BRIT*) *n* automobile *f*; **~cycle** *n* vélomoteur *m*; **~cycle racing** *n* course *f* de motos; **~cyclist** *n* motocycliste *m/f*; **~ing** (*BRIT*) *n* tourisme *m* automobile; **~ist** *n* automobiliste *m/f*; **~ mechanic** *n* mécanicien *m* garagiste; **~ racing** (*BRIT*) *n* course *f* automobile; **~way** (*BRIT*) *n* autoroute *f*

mottled ['mɔtld] *adj* tacheté(e), marbré(e)

motto ['mɔtəu] (*pl* **~es**) *n* devise *f*

mould [məuld] (*US* **mold**) *n* moule *m*; (*mildew*) moisissure *f* ♦ *vt* mouler, modeler; (*fig*) façonner; **mo(u)ldy** *adj* moisi(e); (*smell*) de moisi

moult [məult] (*US* **molt**) *vi* muer

mound [maund] *n* monticule *m*, tertre *m*; (*heap*) monceau *m*, tas *m*

mount [maunt] *n* mont *m*, montagne *f* ♦ *vt* monter ♦ *vi* (*inflation, tension*) augmenter; (*also*: **~ up**: *problems etc*) s'accumuler; **~ up** *vi* (*bills, costs, savings*) s'accumuler

mountain ['mauntɪn] *n* montagne *f* ♦ *cpd* de montagne; **~ bike** *n* VTT *m*, vélo tout-terrain; **~eer** [mauntɪ'nɪə^r] *n* alpiniste *m/f*; **~eering** *n* alpinisme *m*; **~ous** *adj* montagneux(-euse); **~ rescue team** *n* équipe *f* de secours en montagne; **~side** *n* flanc *m* *or* versant *m* de la montagne

mourn [mɔːn] *vt* pleurer ♦ *vi*: **to ~ (for)** (*person*) pleurer (la mort de); **~er** *n* parent(e) *or* ami(e) du défunt; personne *f* en deuil; **~ing** *n* deuil *m*; **in ~ing** en deuil

mouse [maus] (*pl* **mice**) *n* (*also* *COMPUT*) souris *f*; **~ mat** *n* (*COMPUT*) tapis *m* de souris; **~trap** *n* souricière *f*

mousse [muːs] *n* mousse *f*

moustache [məs'tɑːʃ] (*US* **mustache**) *n* moustache(s) *f(pl)*

mousy ['mausɪ] *adj* (*hair*) d'un châtain terne

mouth [mauθ] (*pl* **~s**) *n* bouche *f*; (*of dog, cat*) gueule *f*; (*of river*) embouchure *f*; (*of hole, cave*) ouverture *f*; **~ful** *n* bouchée *f*; **~ organ** *n* harmonica *m*; **~piece** *n* (*of musical instrument*) embouchure *f*; (*spokesman*) porte-parole *m inv*; **~wash** *n* eau *f* dentifrice; **~-watering** *adj* qui met l'eau à la bouche

movable ['muːvəbl] *adj* mobile

move [muːv] *n* (*~ment*) mouvement *m*; (*in game*) coup *m*; (: *turn to play*) tour *m*; (*change*: *of house*) déménagement *m*; (: *of job*) changement *m* d'emploi ♦ *vt* déplacer, bouger; (*emotionally*) émouvoir; (*POL*: *resolution etc*) proposer; (*in game*) jouer ♦ *vi* (*gen*) bouger, remuer; (*traffic*) circuler; (*also*: **~ house**) déménager; (*situation*) progresser; **that was a good ~** bien joué!; **to get a ~ on** se dépêcher, se remuer; **to ~ sb to do sth** pousser *or* inciter qn à faire qch; **~ about** *vi* (*fidget*) remuer; (*travel*) voyager, se déplacer; (*change residence, job*) ne pas rester au même endroit; **~ along** *vi* se pousser; **~ around** *vi* = **move about**; **~ away** *vi* s'en aller; **~ back** *vi* revenir, retourner; **~ forward** *vi* avancer; **~ in** *vi* (*to a house*) emménager; (*police, soldiers*) intervenir; **~ on** *vi* se remettre en route; **~ out** *vi* (*of house*) déménager; **~ over** *vi* se pousser, se déplacer; **~ up** *vi* (*pupil*) passer dans la classe supérieure; (*employee*) avoir de l'avancement; **~able** *adj* = **movable**

movement ['mu:vmənt] *n* mouvement *m*

movie ['mu:vɪ] *n* film *m*; **the ~s** le cinéma

moving ['mu:vɪŋ] *adj* en mouvement; (*emotional*) émouvant(e)

mow [məu] (*pt* **mowed**, *pp* **mowed** *or* **mown**) *vt* faucher; (*lawn*) tondre; **~ down** *vt* faucher; **~er** *n* (*also:* **lawnmower**) tondeuse *f* à gazon

MP *n abbr* = **Member of Parliament**

mph *abbr* = **miles per hour**

Mr ['mɪstə^r] *n*: **~ Smith** Monsieur Smith, M. Smith

Mrs ['mɪsɪz] *n*: **~ Smith** Madame Smith, Mme Smith

Ms [mɪz] *n* (= *Miss or Mrs*): **~ Smith** Madame Smith, Mme Smith

MSc *abbr* = **Master of Science**

MSP [ɛmɛs'pi:] *n abbr* = **Member of the Scottish Parliament**

much [mʌtʃ] *adj* beaucoup de ♦ *adv, n, pron* beaucoup; **how ~ is it?** combien est-ce que ça coûte?; **too ~** trop (de); **as ~ as** autant de

muck [mʌk] *n* (*dirt*) saleté *f*; **~ about** *or* **around** (*inf*) *vi* faire l'imbécile; **~ up** (*inf*) *vt* (*exam, interview*) se planter à (*fam*); **~y** *adj* (très) sale

mud [mʌd] *n* boue *f*

muddle ['mʌdl] *n* (*mess*) pagaille *f*, désordre *m*; (*mix-up*) confusion *f* ♦ *vt* (*also:* **~ up**) embrouiller; **~ through** *vi* se débrouiller

muddy ['mʌdɪ] *adj* boueux(-euse)

mudguard ['mʌdgɑ:d] *n* garde-boue *m inv*

muesli ['mju:zlɪ] *n* muesli *m*

muffin ['mʌfɪn] *n* muffin *m*

muffle ['mʌfl] *vt* (*sound*) assourdir, étouffer; (*against cold*) emmitoufler; **~d** *adj* (*sound*) étouffé(e); **~r** (*US*) *n* (*AUT*) silencieux *m*

mug [mʌg] *n* (*cup*) grande tasse (*sans soucoupe*); (: *for beer*) chope *f*; (*inf: face*) bouille *f*; (: *fool*) poire *f* ♦ *vt* (*assault*) agresser; **~ger** *n* agresseur *m*; **~ging** *n* agression *f*

muggy ['mʌgɪ] *adj* lourd(e), moite

mule [mju:l] *n* mule *f*

multi-level ['mʌltɪlɛvl] (*US*) *adj* = **multistorey**

multiple ['mʌltɪpl] *adj* multiple ♦ *n* multiple *m*; **~ sclerosis** [-sklɪ'rəusɪs] *n* sclérose *f* en plaques

multiplex cinema ['mʌltɪplɛks-] *n* cinéma *m* multisalles

multiplication [mʌltɪplɪ'keɪʃən] *n* multiplication *f*; **multiply** ['mʌltɪplaɪ] *vt* multiplier ♦ *vi* se multiplier

multistorey ['mʌltɪ'stɔ:rɪ] (*BRIT*) *adj* (*building*) à étages; (*car park*) à étages *or* niveaux multiples ♦ *n* (*car park*) parking *m* à plusieurs étages

mum [mʌm] (*BRIT: inf*) *n* maman *f* ♦ *adj*: **to keep ~** ne pas souffler mot

mumble ['mʌmbl] *vt, vi* marmotter, marmonner

mummy ['mʌmɪ] *n* (*BRIT: mother*) maman *f*; (*embalmed*) momie *f*

mumps [mʌmps] *n* oreillons *mpl*

munch [mʌntʃ] *vt, vi* mâcher

mundane [mʌn'deɪn] *adj* banal(e), terre à terre *inv*

municipal [mju:'nɪsɪpl] *adj* municipal(e)

murder ['mə:də^r] *n* meurtre *m*, assassinat *m* ♦ *vt* assassiner; **~er** *n* meurtrier *m*, assassin *m*; **~ous** ['mə:dərəs] *adj* meurtrier(-ère)

murky ['mə:kɪ] *adj* sombre, ténébreux(-euse); (*water*) trouble

murmur ['mə:mə^r] *n* murmure *m* ♦ *vt, vi* murmurer

muscle ['mʌsl] *n* muscle *m*; (*fig*) force *f*; **~ in** *vi* (*on territory*) envahir; (*on success*) exploiter; **muscular** ['mʌskjulə^r] *adj* musculaire; (*person, arm*) musclé(e)

muse [mju:z] *vi* méditer, songer

museum [mju:'zɪəm] *n* musée *m*

mushroom ['mʌʃrum] *n* champignon *m* ♦ *vi* pousser comme un champignon

music ['mju:zɪk] *n* musique *f*; **~al** *adj* musical(e); (*person*) musicien(ne) ♦ *n* (*show*) comédie musicale; **~al instrument** *n* instrument *m* de musique; **~ centre** *n* chaîne compacte; **~ian** [mju:'zɪʃən] *n* musicien(ne)

Muslim ['mʌzlɪm] *adj, n* musulman(e)

muslin ['mʌzlɪn] *n* mousseline *f*

mussel ['mʌsl] *n* moule *f*

must [mʌst] *aux vb* (*obligation*): **I ~ do it** je dois le faire, il faut que je le fasse; (*probability*): **he ~ be there by now** il doit y être maintenant, il y est probablement maintenant; (*suggestion, invitation*): **you ~ come and see me** il faut que vous veniez me voir; (*indicating sth unwelcome*): **why ~ he behave so badly?** qu'est-ce qui le pousse à se conduire si mal? ♦ *n* nécessité *f*, impératif *m*; **it's a ~** c'est indispensable

mustache ['mʌstæʃ] (*US*) *n* = **moustache**

mustard ['mʌstəd] *n* moutarde *f*

muster ['mʌstə^r] *vt* rassembler

mustn't ['mʌsnt] = **must not**

mute [mju:t] *adj* muet(te); **~d** *adj* (*colour*) sourd(e); (*reaction*) voilé(e)

mutiny ['mju:tɪnɪ] *n* mutinerie *f* ♦ *vi* se mutiner

mutter ['mʌtə^r] *vt, vi* marmonner, marmotter

mutton ['mʌtn] *n* mouton *m*

mutual ['mju:tʃuəl] *adj* mutuel(le), réciproque; (*benefit, interest*) commun(e); **~ly** *adv* mutuellement

muzzle ['mʌzl] *n* museau *m*; (*protective device*) muselière *f*; (*of gun*) gueule *f* ♦ *vt* museler

my [maɪ] *adj* mon (ma), mes *pl*; **~ house/car/gloves** ma maison/mon auto/mes gants; **I've washed ~ hair/cut ~ finger** je me suis lavé les cheveux/coupé le doigt; **~self** [maɪ'sɛlf] *pron* (*reflexive*) me; (*emphatic*) moi-même; (*after prep*) moi; *see also* **oneself**

mysterious [mɪs'tɪərɪəs] *adj* mystérieux(-euse)

mystery ['mɪstərɪ] *n* mystère *m*

mystify ['mɪstɪfaɪ] *vt* mystifier; (*puzzle*) ébahir

myth [mɪθ] *n* mythe *m*; **~ology** [mɪ'θɔlədʒɪ] *n* mythologie *f*

N, n

n/a *abbr* = **not applicable**

naff [næf] (*BRIT*: *inf*) *adj* nul(le)

nag [næg] *vt* (*scold*) être toujours après, reprendre sans arrêt; **~ging** *adj* (*doubt, pain*) persistant(e)

nail [neɪl] *n* (*human*) ongle *m*; (*metal*) clou *m* ♦ *vt* clouer; **to ~ sb down to a date/price** contraindre qn à accepter *or* donner une date/un prix; **~brush** *n* brosse *f* à ongles; **~file** *n* lime *f* à ongles; **~ polish** *n* vernis *m* à ongles; **~ polish remover** *n* dissolvant *m*; **~ scissors** *npl* ciseaux *mpl* à ongles; **~ varnish** (*BRIT*) *n* = **nail polish**

naïve [naɪ'i:v] *adj* naïf(-ïve)

naked ['neɪkɪd] *adj* nu(e)

name [neɪm] *n* nom *m*; (*reputation*) réputation *f* ♦ *vt* nommer; (*identify*: *accomplice etc*) citer; (*price, date*) fixer, donner; **by ~** par son nom; **in the ~ of** au nom de; **what's your ~?** comment vous appelez-vous?; **~less** *adj* sans nom; (*witness, contributor*) anonyme; **~ly** *adv* à savoir; **~sake** *n* homonyme *m*

nanny ['nænɪ] *n* bonne *f* d'enfants

nap [næp] *n* (*sleep*) (petit) somme ♦ *vi*: **to be caught ~ping** être pris à l'improviste *or* en défaut

nape [neɪp] *n*: **~ of the neck** nuque *f*

napkin ['næpkɪn] *n* serviette *f* (de table)

nappy ['næpɪ] (*BRIT*) *n* couche *f* (*gen pl*); **~ rash** *n*: **to have ~ rash** avoir les fesses rouges

narcissus [nɑ:'sɪsəs] (*pl* **narcissi**) *n* narcisse *m*

narcotic [nɑːˈkɔtɪk] *n* (*drug*) stupéfiant *m*; (*MED*) narcotique *m*
narrative [ˈnærətɪv] *n* récit *m*
narrow [ˈnærəu] *adj* étroit(e); (*fig*) restreint(e), limité(e) ♦ *vi* (*road*) devenir plus étroit, se rétrécir; (*gap, difference*) se réduire; **to have a ~ escape** l'échapper belle; **to ~ sth down to** réduire qch à; **~ly** *adv*: **he ~ly missed injury/the tree** il a failli se blesser/rentrer dans l'arbre; **~-minded** *adj* à l'esprit étroit, borné(e); (*attitude*) borné
nasty [ˈnɑːstɪ] *adj* (*person*: *malicious*) méchant(e); (: *rude*) très désagréable; (*smell*) dégoûtant(e); (*wound, situation, disease*) mauvais(e)
nation [ˈneɪʃən] *n* nation *f*
national [ˈnæʃənl] *adj* national(e) ♦ *n* (*abroad*) ressortissant(e); (*when home*) national(e); **~ anthem** *n* hymne national; **~ dress** *n* costume national; **N~ Health Service** (*BRIT*) *n* service national de santé; ≃ Sécurité Sociale; **N~ Insurance** (*BRIT*) *n* ≃ Sécurité Sociale; **~ism** *n* nationalisme *m*; **~ist** *adj* nationaliste ♦ *n* nationaliste *m/f*; **~ity** [næʃəˈnælɪtɪ] *n* nationalité *f*; **~ize** *vt* nationaliser; **~ly** *adv* (*as a nation*) du point de vue national; (*nationwide*) dans le pays entier; **~ park** *n* parc national

National Trust

Le **National Trust** *est un organisme indépendant, à but non lucratif, dont la mission est de protéger et de mettre en valeur les monuments et les sites britanniques en raison de leur intérêt historique ou de leur beauté naturelle.*

nationwide [ˈneɪʃənwaɪd] *adj* s'étendant à l'ensemble du pays; (*problem*) à l'échelle du pays entier ♦ *adv* à travers *or* dans tout le pays
native [ˈneɪtɪv] *n* autochtone *m/f*, habitant(e) du pays ♦ *adj* du pays, indigène; (*country*) natal(e); (*ability*) inné(e); **a ~ of Russia** une personne originaire de Russie; **a ~ speaker of French** une personne de langue maternelle française; **N~ American** *n* Indien(ne) d'Amérique; **~ language** *n* langue maternelle
NATO [ˈneɪtəu] *n abbr* (= *North Atlantic Treaty Organization*) OTAN *f*
natural [ˈnætʃrəl] *adj* naturel(le); **~ gas** *n* gaz naturel; **~ist** *n* naturaliste *m/f*; **~ly** *adv* naturellement
nature [ˈneɪtʃə^r] *n* nature *f*; **by ~** par tempérament, de nature
naught [nɔːt] *n* = **nought**
naughty [ˈnɔːtɪ] *adj* (*child*) vilain(e), pas sage
nausea [ˈnɔːsɪə] *n* nausée *f*
naval [ˈneɪvl] *adj* naval(e); **~ officer** *n* officier *m* de marine
nave [neɪv] *n* nef *f*
navel [ˈneɪvl] *n* nombril *m*
navigate [ˈnævɪgeɪt] *vt* (*steer*) diriger; (*plot course*) naviguer ♦ *vi* naviguer; **navigation** [nævɪˈgeɪʃən] *n* navigation *f*
navvy [ˈnævɪ] (*BRIT*) *n* terrassier *m*
navy [ˈneɪvɪ] *n* marine *f*; **~(-blue)** *adj* bleu marine *inv*
Nazi [ˈnɑːtsɪ] *n* Nazi(e)
NB *abbr* (= *nota bene*) NB
near [nɪə^r] *adj* proche ♦ *adv* près ♦ *prep* (*also*: **~ to**) près de ♦ *vt* approcher de; **~by** [nɪəˈbaɪ] *adj* proche ♦ *adv* tout près, à proximité; **~ly** *adv* presque; **I ~ly fell** j'ai failli tomber; **~ miss** *n* (*AVIAT*) quasi-collision *f*; **that was a ~ miss** (*gen*) il s'en est fallu de peu; (*of shot*) c'est passé très près; **~side** *n* (*AUT*: *in Britain*) côté *m* gauche; (: *in US, Europe etc*) côté droit; **~-sighted** *adj* myope
neat [niːt] *adj* (*person, work*) soigné(e); (*room etc*) bien tenu(e) *or* rangé(e); (*skilful*) habile; (*spirits*) pur(e); **~ly** *adv* avec soin *or* ordre; habilement
necessarily [ˈnɛsɪsrɪlɪ] *adv* nécessairement
necessary [ˈnɛsɪsrɪ] *adj* nécessaire; **ne-**

cessity [nɪ'sɛsɪtɪ] *n* nécessité *f*; (*thing needed*) chose nécessaire *or* essentielle; **necessities** *npl* nécessaire *m*

neck [nɛk] *n* cou *m*; (*of animal, garment*) encolure *f*; (*of bottle*) goulot *m* ♦ *vi* (*inf*) se peloter; **~ and ~** à égalité; **~lace** *n* collier *m*; **~line** *n* encolure *f*; **~tie** *n* cravate *f*

need [ni:d] *n* besoin *m* ♦ *vt* avoir besoin de; **to ~ to do** devoir faire; avoir besoin de faire; **you don't ~ to go** vous n'avez pas besoin *or* vous n'êtes pas obligé de partir

needle ['ni:dl] *n* aiguille *f* ♦ *vt* asticoter, tourmenter

needless ['ni:dlɪs] *adj* inutile

needlework ['ni:dlwə:k] *n* (*activity*) travaux *mpl* d'aiguille; (*object(s)*) ouvrage *m*

needn't ['ni:dnt] = **need not**

needy ['ni:dɪ] *adj* nécessiteux(-euse)

negative ['nɛgətɪv] *n* (PHOT, ELEC) négatif *m*; (LING) terme *m* de négation ♦ *adj* négatif(-ive); **~ equity** *situation dans laquelle la valeur d'une maison est inférieure à celle de l'emprunt-logement contracté pour la payer*

neglect [nɪ'glɛkt] *vt* négliger ♦ *n* le fait de négliger; (*state of ~*) abandon *m*; **~ed** *adj* négligé(e), à l'abandon

negligee ['nɛglɪʒeɪ] *n* déshabillé *m*

negotiate [nɪ'gəuʃɪeɪt] *vi, vt* négocier; **negotiation** [nɪgəuʃɪ'eɪʃən] *n* négociation *f*, pourparlers *mpl*

neigh [neɪ] *vi* hennir

neighbour ['neɪbə^r] (US **neighbor**) *n* voisin(e); **~hood** *n* (*place*) quartier *m*; (*people*) voisinage *m*; **~ing** *adj* voisin(e), avoisinant(e); **~ly** *adj* obligeant(e); (*action etc*) amical(e)

neither ['naɪðə^r] *adj, pron* aucun(e) (des deux), ni l'un(e) ni l'autre ♦ *conj*: **I didn't move and ~ did Claude** je n'ai pas bougé, (et) Claude non plus ♦ *adv*: **~ good nor bad** ni bon ni mauvais; **..., ~ did I refuse ...**, (et *or* mais) je n'ai pas non plus refusé ...

neon ['ni:ɔn] *n* néon *m*; **~ light** *n* lampe *f* au néon

nephew ['nɛvju:] *n* neveu *m*

nerve [nə:v] *n* nerf *m*; (*fig*: *courage*) sang-froid *m*, courage *m*; (: *impudence*) aplomb *m*, toupet *m*; **to have a fit of ~s** avoir le trac; **~-racking** *adj* angoissant(e)

nervous ['nə:vəs] *adj* nerveux(-euse); (*anxious*) inquiet(-ète), plein(e) d'appréhension; (*timid*) intimidé(e); **~ breakdown** *n* dépression nerveuse

nest [nɛst] *n* nid *m* ♦ *vi* (se) nicher, faire son nid; **~ egg** *n* (*fig*) bas *m* de laine, magot *m*

nestle ['nɛsl] *vi* se blottir

net [nɛt] *n* filet *m*; **the N~** (*Internet*) le Net ♦ *adj* net(te) ♦ *vt* (*fish etc*) prendre au filet; (*profit*) rapporter; **~ball** *n* netball *m*

Netherlands ['nɛðələndz] *npl*: **the ~** les Pays-Bas *mpl*

nett [nɛt] *adj* = **net**

netting ['nɛtɪŋ] *n* (*for fence etc*) treillis *m*, grillage *m*

nettle ['nɛtl] *n* ortie *f*

network ['nɛtwə:k] *n* réseau *m*

neurotic [njuə'rɔtɪk] *adj* névrosé(e)

neuter ['nju:tə^r] *adj* neutre ♦ *vt* (*cat etc*) châtrer, couper

neutral ['nju:trəl] *adj* neutre ♦ *n* (AUT) point mort; **~ize** *vt* neutraliser

never ['nɛvə^r] *adv* (ne ...) jamais; **~ again** plus jamais; **~ in my life** jamais de ma vie; *see also* **mind**; **~-ending** *adj* interminable; **~theless** *adv* néanmoins, malgré tout

new [nju:] *adj* nouveau (nouvelle); (*brand ~*) neuf (neuve); **N~ Age** *n* New Age *m*; **~born** *adj* nouveau-né(e); **~comer** *n* nouveau venu/nouvelle venue; **~-fangled** ['nju:'fæŋgld] (*pej*) *adj* ultramoderne (et farfelu(e)); **~-found** *adj* (*enthusiasm*) de fraîche date; (*friend*) nouveau (nouvelle); **~ly** *adv* nouvellement, récemment; **~ly-weds** *npl* jeunes mariés *mpl*

news [nju:z] *n* nouvelle(s) *f(pl)*; (*RADIO, TV*) informations *fpl*, actualités *fpl*; **a piece of ~** une nouvelle; **~ agency** *n* agence *f* de presse; **~agent** (*BRIT*) *n* marchand *m* de journaux; **~caster** *n* présentateur(-trice); **~ flash** *n* flash *m* d'information; **~letter** *n* bulletin *m*; **~paper** *n* journal *m*; **~print** *n* papier *m* (de) journal; **~reader** *n* = **newscaster**; **~reel** *n* actualités (filmées); **~ stand** *n* kiosque *m* à journaux

newt [nju:t] *n* triton *m*

New Year *n* Nouvel An; **~'s Day** *n* le jour de l'An; **~'s Eve** *n* la Saint-Sylvestre

New Zealand [-'zi:lənd] *n* la Nouvelle-Zélande; **~er** *n* Néo-zélandais(e)

next [nɛkst] *adj* (*seat, room*) voisin(e), d'à côté; (*meeting, bus stop*) suivant(e); (*in time*) prochain(e) ♦ *adv* (*place*) à côté; (*time*) la fois suivante, la prochaine fois; (*afterwards*) ensuite; **the ~ day** le lendemain, le jour suivant *or* d'après; **~ year** l'année prochaine; **~ time** la prochaine fois; **~ to** à côté de; **~ to nothing** presque rien; **~, please!** (*at doctor's etc*) au suivant!; **~ door** *adv* à côté ♦ *adj* d'à côté; **~-of-kin** *n* parent *m* le plus proche

NHS *n abbr* = **National Health Service**

nib [nɪb] *n* (bec *m* de) plume *f*

nibble ['nɪbl] *vt* grignoter

nice [naɪs] *adj* (*pleasant, likeable*) agréable; (*pretty*) joli(e); (*kind*) gentil(le); **~ly** *adv* agréablement; joliment; gentiment

niceties ['naɪsɪtɪz] *npl* subtilités *fpl*

nick [nɪk] *n* (*indentation*) encoche *f*; (*wound*) entaille *f* ♦ *vt* (*BRIT*: *inf*) faucher, piquer; **in the ~ of time** juste à temps

nickel ['nɪkl] *n* nickel *m*; (*US*) pièce *f* de 5 cents

nickname ['nɪkneɪm] *n* surnom *m* ♦ *vt* surnommer

nicotine patch ['nɪkəti:n-] *n* timbre *m* anti-tabac, patch *m*

niece [ni:s] *n* nièce *f*

Nigeria [naɪ'dʒɪərɪə] *n* Nigéria *m or f*

niggling ['nɪglɪŋ] *adj* (*person*) tatillon(ne); (*detail*) insignifiant(e); (*doubts, injury*) persistant(e)

night [naɪt] *n* nuit *f*; (*evening*) soir *m*; **at ~** la nuit; **by ~** de nuit; **the ~ before last** avant-hier soir; **~cap** *n boisson prise avant le coucher*; **~ club** *n* boîte *f* de nuit; **~dress** *n* chemise *f* de nuit; **~fall** *n* tombée *f* de la nuit; **~gown** *n*, **~ie** ['naɪtɪ] *n* chemise *f* de nuit; **~ingale** ['naɪtɪŋgeɪl] *n* rossignol *m*; **~life** *n* vie *f* nocturne; **~ly** *adj* de chaque nuit *or* soir; (*by night*) nocturne ♦ *adv* chaque nuit *or* soir; **~mare** *n* cauchemar *m*; **~ porter** *n* gardien *m* de nuit, concierge *m* de service la nuit; **~ school** *n* cours *mpl* du soir; **~ shift** *n* équipe *f* de nuit; **~-time** *n* nuit *f*; **~ watchman** *n* veilleur *m or* gardien *m* de nuit

nil [nɪl] *n* rien *m*; (*BRIT*: *SPORT*) zéro *m*

Nile [naɪl] *n*: **the ~** le Nil

nimble ['nɪmbl] *adj* agile

nine [naɪn] *num* neuf; **to call 999** (*BRIT*) *or* **911** (*US*) appeler les urgences; **~teen** ['naɪn'ti:n] *num* dix-neuf; **~ty** ['naɪntɪ] *num* quatre-vingt-dix; **ninth** [naɪnθ] *num* neuvième

nip [nɪp] *vt* pincer

nipple ['nɪpl] *n* (*ANAT*) mamelon *m*, bout *m* du sein

nitrogen ['naɪtrədʒən] *n* azote *m*

KEYWORD

no [nəu] (*pl* **noes**) *adv* (*opposite of "yes"*) non; **are you coming? - no (I'm not)** est-ce que vous venez? - non; **would you like some more? - no thank you** vous en voulez encore? - non merci

♦ *adj* (*not any*) pas de, aucun(e) (*used with "ne"*); **I have no money/books** je n'ai pas d'argent/de livres; **no student would have done it** aucun étudiant ne l'aurait fait; **"no smoking"** "défense de fumer"; **"no dogs"** "les

chiens ne sont pas admis"
♦ *n* non *m*

nobility [nəu'bılıtı] *n* noblesse *f*
noble ['nəubl] *adj* noble
nobody ['nəubədı] *pron* personne
nod [nɔd] *vi* faire un signe de tête (*affirmatif ou amical*); (*sleep*) somnoler ♦ *vt*: **to ~ one's head** faire un signe de (la) tête; (*in agreement*) faire signe que oui ♦ *n* signe *m* de (la) tête; **~ off** *vi* s'assoupir
noise [nɔız] *n* bruit *m*; **noisy** *adj* bruyant(e)
nominal ['nɔmınl] *adj* symbolique
nominate ['nɔmıneıt] *vt* (*propose*) proposer; (*appoint*) nommer; **nominee** [nɔmı'ni:] *n* candidat agréé; personne nommée
non... [nɔn] *prefix* non-; **~-alcoholic** *adj* non-alcoolisé(e); **~committal** *adj* évasif(-ive); **~descript** *adj* quelconque, indéfinissable
none [nʌn] *pron* aucun(e); **~ of you** aucun d'entre vous, personne parmi vous; **I've ~ left** je n'en ai plus; **he's ~ the worse for it** il ne s'en porte pas plus mal
nonentity [nɔ'nɛntıtı] *n* personne insignifiante
nonetheless ['nʌnðə'lɛs] *adv* néanmoins
non-existent [nɔnıg'zıstənt] *adj* inexistant(e)
non-fiction [nɔn'fıkʃən] *n* littérature *f* non-romanesque
nonplussed [nɔn'plʌst] *adj* perplexe
nonsense ['nɔnsəns] *n* absurdités *fpl*, idioties *fpl*; **~!** ne dites pas d'idioties!
non: ~-smoker *n* non-fumeur *m*; **~-smoking** *adj* non-fumeur; **~-stick** *adj* qui n'attache pas; **~-stop** *adj* direct(e), sans arrêt (*or* escale) ♦ *adv* sans arrêt
noodles ['nu:dlz] *npl* nouilles *fpl*
nook [nuk] *n*: **~s and crannies** recoins *mpl*
noon [nu:n] *n* midi *m*
no one ['nəuwʌn] *pron* = **nobody**
noose [nu:s] *n* nœud coulant; (*hangman's*) corde *f*
nor [nɔ:ʳ] *conj* = **neither** ♦ *adv see* **neither**
norm [nɔ:m] *n* norme *f*
normal *adj* normal(e); **~ly** ['nɔ:məlı] *adv* normalement
Normandy ['nɔ:məndı] *n* Normandie *f*
north [nɔ:θ] *n* nord *m* ♦ *adj* du nord, nord *inv* ♦ *adv* au *or* vers le nord; **N~ America** *n* Amérique *f* du Nord; **~-east** *n* nord-est *m*; **~erly** ['nɔ:ðəlı] *adj* du nord; **~ern** ['nɔ:ðən] *adj* du nord, septentrional(e); **N~ern Ireland** *n* Irlande *f* du Nord; **N~ Pole** *n* pôle *m* Nord; **N~ Sea** *n* mer *f* du Nord; **~ward(s)** *adv* vers le nord; **~-west** *n* nord-ouest *m*
Norway ['nɔ:weı] *n* Norvège *f*; **Norwegian** [nɔ:'wi:dʒən] *adj* norvégien(ne) ♦ *n* Norvégien(ne); (LING) norvégien *m*
nose [nəuz] *n* nez *m*; **~ about, around** *vi* fouiner *or* fureter (partout); **~bleed** *n* saignement *m* du nez; **~-dive** *n* (descente *f* en) piqué *m*; **~y** (*inf*) *adj* = **nosy**
nostalgia [nɔs'tældʒıə] *n* nostalgie *f*
nostril ['nɔstrıl] *n* narine *f*; (*of horse*) naseau *m*
nosy ['nəuzı] (*inf*) *adj* curieux(-euse)
not [nɔt] *adv* (ne ...) pas; **he is ~** *or* **isn't here** il n'est pas ici; **you must ~** *or* **you mustn't do that** tu ne dois pas faire ça; **it's too late, isn't it** *or* **is it ~?** c'est trop tard, n'est-ce pas?; **~ yet/now** pas encore/maintenant; **~ at all** pas du tout; *see also* **all**; **only**
notably ['nəutəblı] *adv* (*particularly*) en particulier; (*markedly*) spécialement
notary ['nəutərı] *n* notaire *m*
notch [nɔtʃ] *n* encoche *f*
note [nəut] *n* note *f*; (*letter*) mot *m*; (*banknote*) billet *m* ♦ *vt* (*also:* **~ down**) noter; (*observe*) constater; **~book** *n* carnet *m*; **~d** *adj* réputé(e); **~pad** *n*

bloc-notes *m*; **~paper** *n* papier *m* à lettres

nothing ['nʌθɪŋ] *n* rien *m*; **he does ~** il ne fait rien; **~ new** rien de nouveau; **for ~** pour rien

notice ['nəutɪs] *n* (*announcement, warning*) avis *m*; (*period of time*) délai *m*; (*resignation*) démission *f*; (*dismissal*) congé *m* ♦ *vt* remarquer, s'apercevoir de; **to take ~ of** prêter attention à; **to bring sth to sb's ~** porter qch à la connaissance de qn; **at short ~** dans un délai très court; **until further ~** jusqu'à nouvel ordre; **to hand in one's ~** donner sa démission, démissionner; **~able** *adj* visible; **~ board** (*BRIT*) *n* panneau *m* d'affichage

notify ['nəutɪfaɪ] *vt*: **to ~ sth to sb** notifier qch à qn; **to ~ sb (of sth)** avertir qn (de qch)

notion ['nəuʃən] *n* idée *f*; (*concept*) notion *f*

notorious [nəu'tɔ:rɪəs] *adj* notoire (*souvent en mal*)

nought [nɔ:t] *n* zéro *m*

noun [naun] *n* nom *m*

nourish ['nʌrɪʃ] *vt* nourrir; **~ing** *adj* nourrissant(e); **~ment** *n* nourriture *f*

novel ['nɔvl] *n* roman *m* ♦ *adj* nouveau (nouvelle), original(e); **~ist** *n* romancier *m*; **~ty** *n* nouveauté *f*

November [nəu'vɛmbə^r] *n* novembre *m*

now [nau] *adv* maintenant ♦ *conj*: **~ (that)** maintenant que; **right ~** tout de suite; **by ~** à l'heure qu'il est; **just ~**: **that's the fashion just ~** c'est la mode en ce moment; **~ and then, ~ and again** de temps en temps; **from ~ on** dorénavant; **~adays** *adv* de nos jours

nowhere ['nəuwɛə^r] *adv* nulle part

nozzle ['nɔzl] *n* (*of hose etc*) ajutage *m*; (*of vacuum cleaner*) suceur *m*

nuclear ['nju:klɪə^r] *adj* nucléaire

nucleus ['nju:klɪəs] (*pl* **nuclei**) *n* noyau *m*

nude [nju:d] *adj* nu(e) ♦ *n* nu *m*; **in the ~** (tout(e)) nu(e)

nudge [nʌdʒ] *vt* donner un (petit) coup de coude à

nudist ['nju:dɪst] *n* nudiste *m/f*

nuisance ['nju:sns] *n*: **it's a ~** c'est (très) embêtant; **he's a ~** il est assommant *or* casse-pieds; **what a ~!** quelle barbe!

null [nʌl] *adj*: **~ and void** nul(le) et non avenu(e)

numb [nʌm] *adj* engourdi(e); (*with fear*) paralysé(e)

number ['nʌmbə^r] *n* nombre *m*; (*numeral*) chiffre *m*; (*of house, bank account etc*) numéro *m* ♦ *vt* numéroter; (*amount to*) compter; **a ~ of** un certain nombre de; **they were seven in ~** ils étaient (au nombre de) sept; **to be ~ed among** compter parmi; **~ plate** *n* (*AUT*) plaque *f* minéralogique *or* d'immatriculation

numeral ['nju:mərəl] *n* chiffre *m*

numerate ['nju:mərɪt] (*BRIT*) *adj*: **to be ~** avoir des notions d'arithmétique

numerical [nju:'mɛrɪkl] *adj* numérique

numerous ['nju:mərəs] *adj* nombreux(-euse)

nun [nʌn] *n* religieuse *f*, sœur *f*

nurse [nə:s] *n* infirmière *f* ♦ *vt* (*patient, cold*) soigner

nursery ['nə:sərɪ] *n* (*room*) nursery *f*; (*institution*) crèche *f*; (*for plants*) pépinière *f*; **~ rhyme** *n* comptine *f*, chansonnette *f* pour enfants; **~ school** *n* école maternelle; **~ slope** *n* (*SKI*) piste *f* pour débutants

nursing ['nə:sɪŋ] *n* (*profession*) profession *f* d'infirmière; (*care*) soins *mpl*; **~ home** *n* clinique *f*; maison *f* de convalescence

nut [nʌt] *n* (*of metal*) écrou *m*; (*fruit*) noix *f*; noisette *f*; cacahuète *f*; **~crackers** *npl* casse-noix *m inv*, casse-noisette(s) *m*

nutmeg ['nʌtmɛg] *n* (noix *f*) muscade *f*

nutritious [nju:'trɪʃəs] *adj* nutritif(-ive),

nourrissant(e)
nuts [nʌts] (*inf*) *adj* dingue
nutshell ['nʌtʃɛl] *n*: **in a ~** en un mot
nutter ['nʌtə^r] (*BRIT*: *inf*) *n*: **he's a complete ~** il est complètement cinglé
nylon ['naɪlɔn] *n* nylon *m* ♦ *adj* de *or* en nylon

O, o

oak [əuk] *n* chêne *m* ♦ *adj* de *or* en (bois de) chêne
OAP (*BRIT*) *n abbr* = **old-age pensioner**
oar [ɔː^r] *n* aviron *m*, rame *f*
oasis [əu'eɪsɪs] (*pl* **oases**) *n* oasis *f*
oath [əuθ] *n* serment *m*; (*swear word*) juron *m*; **under ~, (***BRIT***) on ~** sous serment
oatmeal ['əutmiːl] *n* flocons *mpl* d'avoine
oats [əuts] *n* avoine *f*
obedience [ə'biːdɪəns] *n* obéissance *f*; **obedient** *adj* obéissant(e)
obey [ə'beɪ] *vt* obéir à; (*instructions*) se conformer à
obituary [ə'bɪtjuərɪ] *n* nécrologie *f*
object [*n* 'ɔbdʒɪkt, *vb* əb'dʒɛkt] *n* objet *m*; (*purpose*) but *m*, objet; (*LING*) complément *m* d'objet ♦ *vi*: **to ~ to** (*attitude*) désapprouver; (*proposal*) protester contre; **expense is no ~** l'argent n'est pas un problème; **he ~ed that ...** il a fait valoir *or* a objecté que ...; **I ~!** je proteste!; **~ion** [əb'dʒɛkʃən] *n* objection *f*; **~ionable** *adj* très désagréable; (*language*) choquant(e); **~ive** *n* objectif *m* ♦ *adj* objectif(-ive)
obligation [ɔblɪ'geɪʃən] *n* obligation *f*, devoir *m*; **without ~** sans engagement; **obligatory** [ə'blɪgətərɪ] *adj* obligatoire
oblige [ə'blaɪdʒ] *vt* (*force*): **to ~ sb to do** obliger *or* forcer qn à faire; (*do a favour*) rendre service à, obliger; **to be ~d to sb for sth** être obligé(e) à qn de qch; **obliging** *adj* obligeant(e), serviable
oblique [ə'bliːk] *adj* oblique; (*allusion*) indirect(e)
obliterate [ə'blɪtəreɪt] *vt* effacer
oblivion [ə'blɪvɪən] *n* oubli *m*; **oblivious** *adj*: **oblivious of** oublieux (-euse) de
oblong ['ɔblɔŋ] *adj* oblong (oblongue) ♦ *n* rectangle *m*
obnoxious [əb'nɔkʃəs] *adj* odieux (-euse); (*smell*) nauséabond(e)
oboe ['əubəu] *n* hautbois *m*
obscene [əb'siːn] *adj* obscène
obscure [əb'skjuə^r] *adj* obscur(e) ♦ *vt* obscurcir; (*hide*: *sun*) cacher
observant [əb'zəːvənt] *adj* observateur(-trice)
observation [ɔbzə'veɪʃən] *n* (*remark*) observation *f*; (*watching*) surveillance *f*
observatory [əb'zəːvətrɪ] *n* observatoire *m*
observe [əb'zəːv] *vt* observer; (*remark*) faire observer *or* remarquer; **~r** *n* observateur(-trice)
obsess [əb'sɛs] *vt* obséder; **~ive** *adj* obsédant(e)
obsolete ['ɔbsəliːt] *adj* dépassé(e); démodé(e)
obstacle ['ɔbstəkl] *n* obstacle *m*; **~ race** *n* course *f* d'obstacles
obstinate ['ɔbstɪnɪt] *adj* obstiné(e)
obstruct [əb'strʌkt] *vt* (*block*) boucher, obstruer; (*hinder*) entraver
obtain [əb'teɪn] *vt* obtenir
obvious ['ɔbvɪəs] *adj* évident(e), manifeste; **~ly** *adv* manifestement; **~ly not!** bien sûr que non!
occasion [ə'keɪʒən] *n* occasion *f*; (*event*) événement *m*; **~al** *adj* pris(e) *or* fait(e) *etc* de temps en temps; occasionnel(le); **~ally** *adv* de temps en temps, quelquefois
occupation [ɔkju'peɪʃən] *n* occupation *f*; (*job*) métier *m*, profession *f*; **~al hazard** *n* risque *m* du métier
occupier ['ɔkjupaɪə^r] *n* occupant(e)
occupy ['ɔkjupaɪ] *vt* occuper; **to ~ o.s.**

in *or* **with doing** s'occuper à faire

occur [ə'kəːʳ] *vi* (*event*) se produire; (*phenomenon, error*) se rencontrer; **to ~ to sb** venir à l'esprit de qn; **~rence** *n* (*existence*) présence *f*, existence *f*; (*event*) cas *m*, fait *m*

ocean ['əuʃən] *n* océan *m*

o'clock [ə'klɔk] *adv*: **it is 5 ~** il est 5 heures

OCR *n abbr* = **optical character reader**; **optical character recognition**

October [ɔk'təubəʳ] *n* octobre *m*

octopus ['ɔktəpəs] *n* pieuvre *f*

odd [ɔd] *adj* (*strange*) bizarre, curieux (-euse); (*number*) impair(e); (*not of a set*) dépareillé(e); **60-~** 60 et quelques; **at ~ times** de temps en temps; **the ~ one out** l'exception *f*; **~ity** *n* (*person*) excentrique *m/f*; (*thing*) curiosité *f*; **~-job man** *n* homme *m* à tout faire; **~ jobs** *npl* petits travaux divers; **~ly** *adv* bizarrement, curieusement; **~ments** *npl* (COMM) fins *fpl* de série; **~s** *npl* (*in betting*) cote *f*; **it makes no ~s** cela n'a pas d'importance; **at ~s** en désaccord; **~s and ends** de petites choses

odour ['əudəʳ] (*US* **odor**) *n* odeur *f*

KEYWORD

of [ɔv, əv] *prep* **1** (*gen*) de; **a friend of ours** un de nos amis; **a boy of 10** un garçon de 10 ans; **that was kind of you** c'était gentil de votre part

2 (*expressing quantity, amount, dates etc*) de; **a kilo of flour** un kilo de farine; **how much of this do you need?** combien vous en faut-il?; **there were 3 of them** (*people*) ils étaient 3; (*objects*) il y en avait 3; **3 of us went** 3 d'entre nous y sont allé(e)s; **the 5th of July** le 5 juillet

3 (*from, out of*) en, de; **a statue of marble** une statue de *or* en marbre; **made of wood** (fait) en bois

off [ɔf] *adj, adv* (*engine*) coupé(e); (*tap*) fermé(e); (BRIT: *food*: *bad*) mauvais(e); (: *milk*: *bad*) tourné(e); (*absent*) absent(e); (*cancelled*) annulé(e) ♦ *prep* de; sur; **to be ~** (*to leave*) partir, s'en aller; **to be ~ sick** être absent pour cause de maladie; **a day ~** un jour de congé; **to have an ~ day** n'être pas en forme; **he had his coat ~** il avait enlevé son manteau; **10% ~** (COMM) 10% de rabais; **~ the coast** au large de la côte; **I'm ~ meat** je ne mange plus de viande, je n'aime plus la viande; **on the ~ chance** à tout hasard

offal ['ɔfl] *n* (CULIN) abats *mpl*

off-colour ['ɔf'kʌləʳ] (BRIT) *adj* (*ill*) malade, mal fichu(e)

offence [ə'fɛns] (*US* **offense**) *n* (*crime*) délit *m*, infraction *f*; **to take ~ at** se vexer de, s'offenser de

offend [ə'fɛnd] *vt* (*person*) offenser, blesser; **~er** *n* délinquant(e)

offense [ə'fɛns] (*US*) *n* = **offence**

offensive [ə'fɛnsɪv] *adj* offensant(e), choquant(e); (*smell etc*) très déplaisant(e); (*weapon*) offensif(-ive) ♦ *n* (MIL) offensive *f*

offer ['ɔfəʳ] *n* offre *f*, proposition *f* ♦ *vt* offrir, proposer; **"on ~"** (COMM) "en promotion"; **~ing** *n* offrande *f*

offhand [ɔf'hænd] *adj* désinvolte ♦ *adv* spontanément

office ['ɔfɪs] *n* (*place, room*) bureau *m*; (*position*) charge *f*, fonction *f*; **doctor's ~** (*US*) cabinet (médical); **to take ~** entrer en fonctions; **~ automation** *n* bureautique *f*; **~ block** (*US* **office building**) *n* immeuble *m* de bureaux; **~ hours** *npl* heures *fpl* de bureau; (*US*: MED) heures de consultation

officer ['ɔfɪsəʳ] *n* (MIL *etc*) officier *m*; (*also*: **police ~**) agent *m* (de police); (*of organization*) membre *m* du bureau directeur

office worker *n* employé(e) de bureau

official [ə'fɪʃl] *adj* officiel(le) ♦ *n* officiel *m*; (*civil servant*) fonctionnaire *m/f*; employé(e)

officiate [ə'fɪʃɪeɪt] *vi* (REL) officier; **to ~**

at a marriage célébrer un mariage

officious [ə'fɪʃəs] *adj* trop empressé(e)

offing ['ɔfɪŋ] *n*: **in the ~** (*fig*) en perspective

off: **~-licence** (*BRIT*) *n* (*shop*) débit *m* de vins et de spiritueux; **~-line** *adj, adv* (*COMPUT*) (en mode) autonome; (: *switched off*) non connecté(e); **~-peak** *adj* aux heures creuses; (*electricity, heating, ticket*) au tarif heures creuses; **~-putting** (*BRIT*) *adj* (*remark*) rébarbatif (-ive); (*person*) rebutant(e), peu engageant(e); **~-road vehicle** *n* véhicule *m* tout-terrain; **~-season** *adj, adv* hors-saison *inv*; **~set** (*irreg*) *vt* (*counteract*) contrebalancer, compenser; **~shoot** *n* (*fig*) ramification *f*, antenne *f*; **~shore** *adj* (*breeze*) de terre; (*fishing*) côtier (-ère); **~side** *adj* (*SPORT*) hors jeu; (*AUT*: *in Britain*) de droite; (: *in US, Europe*) de gauche; **~spring** *n inv* progéniture *f*; **~stage** *adv* dans les coulisses; **~-the-peg** (*US* **off-the-rack**) *adv* en prêt-à-porter; **~-white** *adj* blanc cassé *inv*

off-licence

Un **off-licence** *est un magasin où l'on vend de l'alcool (à emporter) aux heures où les pubs sont fermés. On peut également y acheter des boissons non alcoolisées, des cigarettes, des chips, des bonbons, des chocolats etc.*

Oftel ['ɔftɛl] *n organisme qui supervise les télécommunications*

often ['ɔfn] *adv* souvent; **how ~ do you go?** vous y allez tous les combien?; **how ~ have you gone there?** vous y êtes allé combien de fois?

Ofwat ['ɔfwɔt] *n organisme qui surveille les activités des compagnies des eaux*

oh [əu] *excl* ô!, oh!, ah!

oil [ɔɪl] *n* huile *f*; (*petroleum*) pétrole *m*; (*for central heating*) mazout *m* ♦ *vt* (*machine*) graisser; **~can** *n* burette *f* de graissage; (*for storing*) bidon *m* à huile; **~field** *n* gisement *m* de pétrole; **~ filter** *n* (*AUT*) filtre *m* à huile; **~ painting** *n* peinture *f* à l'huile; **~ refinery** *n* raffinerie *f*; **~ rig** *n* derrick *m*; (*at sea*) plate-forme pétrolière; **~ slick** *n* nappe *f* de mazout; **~ tanker** *n* (*ship*) pétrolier *m*; (*truck*) camion-citerne *m*; **~ well** *n* puits *m* de pétrole; **~y** *adj* huileux (-euse); (*food*) gras(se)

ointment ['ɔɪntmənt] *n* onguent *m*

O.K., okay ['əu'keɪ] *excl* d'accord! ♦ *adj* (*average*) pas mal ♦ *vt* approuver; **is it ~?, are you ~?** ça va?

old [əuld] *adj* vieux (vieille); (*person*) vieux, âgé(e); (*former*) ancien(ne), vieux; **how ~ are you?** quel âge avez-vous?; **he's 10 years ~** il a 10 ans, il est âgé de 10 ans; **~er brother/sister** frère/sœur aîné(e); **~ age** *n* vieillesse *f*; **~ age pensioner** (*BRIT*) *n* retraité(e); **~-fashioned** *adj* démodé(e); (*person*) vieux jeu *inv*; **~ people's home** *n* maison *f* de retraite

olive ['ɔlɪv] *n* (*fruit*) olive *f*; (*tree*) olivier *m* ♦ *adj* (*also*: **~-green**) (vert) olive *inv*; **~ oil** *n* huile *f* d'olive

Olympic [əu'lɪmpɪk] *adj* olympique; **the ~ Games, the ~s** les Jeux *mpl* olympiques

omelet(te) ['ɔmlɪt] *n* omelette *f*

omen ['əumən] *n* présage *m*

ominous ['ɔmɪnəs] *adj* menaçant(e), inquiétant(e); (*event*) de mauvais augure

omit [əu'mɪt] *vt* omettre; **to ~ to do** omettre de faire

KEYWORD

on [ɔn] *prep* **1** (*indicating position*) sur; **on the table** sur la table; **on the wall** sur le *or* au mur; **on the left** à gauche

2 (*indicating means, method, condition etc*): **on foot** à pied; **on the train/plane** (*be*) dans le train/l'avion; (*go*) en train/avion; **on the telephone/radio/television** au téléphone/à la radio/à la télévision; **to be on drugs** se droguer;

on holiday en vacances
3 (*referring to time*): **on Friday** vendredi; **on Fridays** le vendredi; **on June 20th** le 20 juin; **a week on Friday** vendredi en huit; **on arrival** à l'arrivée; **on seeing this** en voyant cela
4 (*about, concerning*) sur, de; **a book on Balzac/physics** un livre sur Balzac/de physique
♦ *adv* 1 (*referring to dress, covering*): **to have one's coat on** avoir (mis) son manteau; **to put one's coat on** mettre son manteau; **what's she got on?** qu'est-ce qu'elle porte?; **screw the lid on tightly** vissez bien le couvercle
2 (*further, continuously*): **to walk** *etc* **on** continuer à marcher *etc*; **on and off** de temps à autre
♦ *adj* 1 (*in operation: machine*) en marche; (: *radio, TV, light*) allumé(e); (: *tap, gas*) ouvert(e); (: *brakes*) mis(e); **is the meeting still on?** (*not cancelled*) est-ce que la réunion a bien lieu?; (*in progress*) la réunion dure-t-elle encore?; **when is this film on?** quand passe ce film?
2 (*inf*): **that's not on!** (*not acceptable*) cela ne se fait pas!; (*not possible*) pas question!

once [wʌns] *adv* une fois; (*formerly*) autrefois ♦ *conj* une fois que; **~ he had left/it was done** une fois qu'il fut parti/que ce fut terminé; **at ~** tout de suite, immédiatement; (*simultaneously*) à la fois; **~ a week** une fois par semaine; **~ more** encore une fois; **~ and for all** une fois pour toutes; **~ upon a time** il y avait une fois, il était une fois
oncoming ['ɔnkʌmɪŋ] *adj* (*traffic*) venant en sens inverse

KEYWORD

one [wʌn] *num* un(e); **one hundred and fifty** cent cinquante; **one day** un jour
♦ *adj* 1 (*sole*) seul(e), unique; **the one book which** l'unique *or* le seul livre qui; **the one man who** le seul (homme) qui
2 (*same*) même; **they came in the one car** ils sont venus dans la même voiture
♦ *pron* 1: **this one** celui-ci (celle-ci); **that one** celui-là (celle-là); **I've already got one/a red one** j'en ai déjà un(e)/un(e) rouge; **one by one** un(e) à *or* par un(e)
2: **one another** l'un(e) l'autre; **to look at one another** se regarder
3 (*impersonal*) on; **one never knows** on ne sait jamais; **to cut one's finger** se couper le doigt

one: ~-day excursion (*US*) *n* billet *m* d'aller-retour (valable pour la journée); **~-man** *adj* (*business*) dirigé(e) *etc* par un seul homme; **~-man band** *n* homme-orchestre *m*; **~-off** (*BRIT: inf*) *n* exemplaire *m* unique
oneself [wʌn'sɛlf] *pron* (*reflexive*) se; (*after prep*) soi(-même); (*emphatic*) soi-même; **to hurt ~** se faire mal; **to keep sth for ~** garder qch pour soi; **to talk to ~** se parler à soi-même
one: ~-sided *adj* (*argument*) unilatéral; **~-to-~** *adj* (*relationship*) univoque; **~-way** *adj* (*street, traffic*) à sens unique
ongoing ['ɔngəuɪŋ] *adj* en cours; (*relationship*) suivi(e)
onion ['ʌnjən] *n* oignon *m*
on-line ['ɔnlaɪn] *adj, adv* (*COMPUT*) en ligne; (: *switched on*) connecté(e); **to go ~** se mettre en mode interactif
onlooker ['ɔnlukə^r] *n* spectateur(-trice)
only ['əunlɪ] *adv* seulement ♦ *adj* seul(e), unique ♦ *conj* seulement, mais; **an ~ child** un enfant unique; **not ~ ... but also** non seulement ... mais aussi
onset ['ɔnsɛt] *n* début *m*; (*of winter, old age*) approche *f*
onshore ['ɔnʃɔː^r] *adj* (*wind*) du large
onslaught ['ɔnslɔːt] *n* attaque *f*, assaut *m*
onto ['ɔntu] *prep* = **on to**

onward(s) ['ɔnwəd(z)] *adv* (*move*) en avant; **from that time ~** à partir de ce moment

ooze [u:z] *vi* suinter

opaque [əu'peɪk] *adj* opaque

OPEC ['əupɛk] *n abbr* (= *Organization of Petroleum-Exporting Countries*) O.P.E.P. *f*

open ['əupn] *adj* ouvert(e); (*car*) découvert(e); (*road, view*) dégagé(e); (*meeting*) public(-ique); (*admiration*) manifeste ♦ *vt* ouvrir ♦ *vi* (*flower, eyes, door, debate*) s'ouvrir; (*shop, bank, museum*) ouvrir; (*book etc: commence*) commencer, débuter; **in the ~ (air)** en plein air; **~ on to** *vt fus* (*subj: room, door*) donner sur; **~ up** *vt* ouvrir; (*blocked road*) dégager ♦ *vi* s'ouvrir; **~ing** *n* ouverture *f*; (*opportunity*) occasion *f* ♦ *adj* (*remarks*) préliminaire; **~ing hours** *npl* heures *fpl* d'ouverture; **~ly** *adv* ouvertement; **~-minded** *adj* à l'esprit ouvert; **~-necked** *adj* à col ouvert; **~-plan** *adj* sans cloisons

Open University

*L'***Open University** *a été fondée en 1969. Ce type d'enseignement comprend des cours (certaines plages horaires sont réservées à cet effet à la télévision et à la radio), des devoirs qui sont envoyés par l'étudiant à son directeur ou sa directrice d'études, et un séjour obligatoire en université d'été. Il faut couvrir un certain nombre d'unités de valeur pendant une période de temps déterminée et obtenir la moyenne à un certain nombre d'entre elles pour recevoir le diplôme visé.*

opera ['ɔpərə] *n* opéra *m*; **~ singer** *n* chanteur(-euse) d'opéra

operate ['ɔpəreɪt] *vt* (*machine*) faire marcher, faire fonctionner ♦ *vi* fonctionner; (*MED*): **to ~ (on sb)** opérer (qn)

operatic [ɔpə'rætɪk] *adj* d'opéra

operating table *n* table *f* d'opération

operating theatre *n* salle *f* d'opération

operation [ɔpə'reɪʃən] *n* opération *f*; (*of machine*) fonctionnement *m*; **to be in ~** (*system, law*) être en vigueur; **to have an ~** (*MED*) se faire opérer

operative ['ɔpərətɪv] *adj* (*measure*) en vigueur

operator ['ɔpəreɪtə^r] *n* (*of machine*) opérateur(-trice); (*TEL*) téléphoniste *m/f*

opinion [ə'pɪnjən] *n* opinion *f*, avis *m*; **in my ~** à mon avis; **~ated** *adj* aux idées bien arrêtées; **~ poll** *n* sondage *m* (d'opinion)

opponent [ə'pəunənt] *n* adversaire *m/f*

opportunity [ɔpə'tju:nɪtɪ] *n* occasion *f*; **to take the ~ of doing** profiter de l'occasion pour faire; en profiter pour faire

oppose [ə'pəuz] *vt* s'opposer à; **~d to** opposé(e) à; **as ~d to** par opposition à; **opposing** *adj* (*side*) opposé(e)

opposite ['ɔpəzɪt] *adj* opposé(e); (*house etc*) d'en face ♦ *adv* en face ♦ *prep* en face de ♦ *n* opposé *m*, contraire *m*; **the ~ sex** l'autre sexe, le sexe opposé; **opposition** [ɔpə'zɪʃən] *n* opposition *f*

oppressive [ə'prɛsɪv] *adj* (*political regime*) oppressif(-ive); (*weather*) lourd(e); (*heat*) accablant(e)

opt [ɔpt] *vi*: **to ~ for** opter pour; **to ~ to do** choisir de faire; **~ out** *vi*: **to ~ out of** choisir de ne pas participer à *or* de ne pas faire

optical ['ɔptɪkl] *adj* optique; (*instrument*) d'optique; **~ character recognition/reader** *n* lecture *f*/ lecteur *m* optique

optician [ɔp'tɪʃən] *n* opticien(ne)

optimist ['ɔptɪmɪst] *n* optimiste *m/f*; **~ic** [ɔptɪ'mɪstɪk] *adj* optimiste

option ['ɔpʃən] *n* choix *m*, option *f*; (*SCOL*) matière *f* à option; (*COMM*) option; **~al** *adj* facultatif(-ive); (*COMM*) en option

or [ɔ:^r] *conj* ou; (*with negative*): **he hasn't seen ~ heard anything** il n'a rien vu ni entendu; ~ **else** sinon; ou bien

oral ['ɔːrəl] *adj* oral(e) ♦ *n* oral *m*

orange ['ɔrɪndʒ] *n* (*fruit*) orange *f* ♦ *adj* orange *inv*

orbit ['ɔːbɪt] *n* orbite *f* ♦ *vt* graviter autour de; **~al (motorway)** *n* périphérique *m*

orchard ['ɔːtʃəd] *n* verger *m*

orchestra ['ɔːkɪstrə] *n* orchestre *m*; (*US*: *seating*) (fauteuils *mpl* d')orchestre

orchid ['ɔːkɪd] *n* orchidée *f*

ordain [ɔː'deɪn] *vt* (*REL*) ordonner

ordeal [ɔː'diːl] *n* épreuve *f*

order ['ɔːdə^r] *n* ordre *m*; (*COMM*) commande *f* ♦ *vt* ordonner; (*COMM*) commander; **in ~** en ordre; (*document*) en règle; **in (working) ~** en état de marche; **out of ~** (*not in correct ~*) en désordre; (*not working*) en dérangement; **in ~ to do/that** pour faire/que *+sub*; **on ~** (*COMM*) en commande; **to ~ sb to do** ordonner à qn de faire; **~ form** *n* bon *m* de commande; **~ly** *n* (*MIL*) ordonnance *f*; (*MED*) garçon *m* de salle ♦ *adj* (*room*) en ordre; (*person*) qui a de l'ordre

ordinary ['ɔːdnrɪ] *adj* ordinaire, normal(e); (*pej*) ordinaire, quelconque; **out of the ~** exceptionnel(le)

Ordnance Survey map ['ɔːdnəns-] *n* ≃ carte *f* d'Etat-Major

ore [ɔː^r] *n* minerai *m*

organ ['ɔːgən] *n* organe *m*; (*MUS*) orgue *m*, orgues *fpl*; **~ic** [ɔː'gænɪk] *adj* organique; (*food*) biologique

organization [ɔːgənaɪ'zeɪʃən] *n* organisation *f*

organize ['ɔːgənaɪz] *vt* organiser; **~r** *n* organisateur(-trice)

orgasm ['ɔːgæzəm] *n* orgasme *m*

Orient ['ɔːrɪənt] *n*: **the ~** l'Orient *m*; **o~al** [ɔːrɪ'ɛntl] *adj* oriental(e)

origin ['ɔrɪdʒɪn] *n* origine *f*

original [ə'rɪdʒɪnl] *adj* original(e); (*earliest*) originel(le) ♦ *n* original *m*; **~ly** *adv* (*at first*) à l'origine

originate [ə'rɪdʒɪneɪt] *vi*: **to ~ from** (*person*) être originaire de; (*suggestion*) provenir de; **to ~ in** prendre naissance dans; avoir son origine dans

Orkney ['ɔːknɪ] *n* (*also*: **the ~ Islands**) les Orcades *fpl*

ornament ['ɔːnəmənt] *n* ornement *m*; (*trinket*) bibelot *m*; **~al** [ɔːnə'mɛntl] *adj* décoratif(-ive); (*garden*) d'agrément

ornate [ɔː'neɪt] *adj* très orné(e)

orphan ['ɔːfn] *n* orphelin(e)

orthopaedic [ɔːθə'piːdɪk] (*US* **orthopedic**) *adj* orthopédique

ostensibly [ɔs'tɛnsɪblɪ] *adv* en apparence

ostentatious [ɔstɛn'teɪʃəs] *adj* prétentieux(-euse)

ostracize ['ɔstrəsaɪz] *vt* frapper d'ostracisme

ostrich ['ɔstrɪtʃ] *n* autruche *f*

other ['ʌðə^r] *adj* autre ♦ *pron*: **the ~ (one)** l'autre; **~s** (*~ people*) d'autres; **~ than** autrement que; à part; **~wise** *adv, conj* autrement

otter ['ɔtə^r] *n* loutre *f*

ouch [autʃ] *excl* aïe!

ought [ɔːt] (*pt* **ought**) *aux vb*: **I ~ to do it** je devrais le faire, il faudrait que je le fasse; **this ~ to have been corrected** cela aurait dû être corrigé; **he ~ to win** il devrait gagner

ounce [auns] *n* once *f* (*= 28.35g; 16 in a pound*)

our ['auə^r] *adj* notre, nos *pl*; *see also* **my**; **~s** *pron* le (la) nôtre, les nôtres; *see also* **mine**[1]; **~selves** [auə'sɛlvz] *pron pl* (*reflexive, after preposition*) nous; (*emphatic*) nous-mêmes; *see also* **oneself**

oust [aust] *vt* évincer

out [aut] *adv* dehors; (*published, not at home etc*) sorti(e); (*light, fire*) éteint(e); **~ here** ici; **~ there** là-bas; **he's ~** (*absent*) il est sorti; (*unconscious*) il est sans connaissance; **to be ~ in one's calculations** s'être trompé dans ses calculs; **to run/back** *etc* **~** sortir en courant/en reculant *etc*; **~ loud** à haute voix; **~ of**

(*~side*) en dehors de; (*because of: anger etc*) par; (*from among*): **~ of 10** sur 10; (*without*): **~ of petrol** sans essence, à court d'essence; **~ of order** (*machine*) en panne; (*TEL: line*) en dérangement; **~-and-~** *adj* (*liar, thief etc*) véritable; **~back** *n* (*in Australia*): **the ~back** l'intérieur *m*; **~board** *n* (*also:* **~board motor**) (moteur *m*) hors-bord *m*; **~break** *n* (*of war, disease*) début *m*; (*of violence*) éruption *f*; **~burst** *n* explosion *f*, accès *m*; **~cast** *n* exilé(e); (*socially*) paria *m*; **~come** *n* issue *f*, résultat *m*; **~crop** *n* (*of rock*) affleurement *m*; **~cry** *n* tollé (général); **~dated** *adj* démodé(e); **~do** (*irreg*) *vt* surpasser; **~door** *adj* de *or* en plein air; **~doors** *adv* dehors; au grand air

outer ['autəʳ] *adj* extérieur(e); **~ space** *n* espace *m* cosmique

outfit ['autfɪt] *n* (*clothes*) tenue *f*

out: ~going *adj* (*character*) ouvert(e), extraverti(e); (*departing*) sortant(e); **~goings** (*BRIT*) *npl* (*expenses*) dépenses *fpl*; **~grow** (*irreg*) *vt* (*clothes*) devenir trop grand(e) pour; **~house** *n* appentis *m*, remise *f*

outing ['autɪŋ] *n* sortie *f*; excursion *f*

out: ~law *n* hors-la-loi *m inv* ♦ *vt* mettre hors-la-loi; **~lay** *n* dépenses *fpl*; (*investment*) mise *f* de fonds; **~let** *n* (*for liquid etc*) issue *f*, sortie *f*; (*US: ELEC*) prise *f* de courant; (*also:* **retail ~let**) point *m* de vente; **~line** *n* (*shape*) contour *m*; (*summary*) esquisse *f*, grandes lignes ♦ *vt* (*fig: theory, plan*) exposer à grands traits; **~live** *vt* survivre à; **~look** *n* perspective *f*; **~lying** *adj* écarté(e); **~moded** *adj* démodé(e); dépassé(e); **~number** *vt* surpasser en nombre; **~-of-date** *adj* (*passport*) périmé(e); (*theory etc*) dépassé(e); (*clothes etc*) démodé(e); **~-of-the-way** *adj* (*place*) loin de tout; **~patient** *n* malade *m/f* en consultation externe; **~post** *n* avant-poste *m*; **~put** *n* rendement *m*, production *f*; (*COMPUT*) sortie *f*

outrage ['autreɪdʒ] *n* (*anger*) indignation *f*; (*violent act*) atrocité *f*; (*scandal*) scandale *m* ♦ *vt* outrager; **~ous** [aut'reɪdʒəs] *adj* atroce; scandaleux (-euse)

outright [*adv* aut'raɪt, *adj* 'autraɪt] *adv* complètement; (*deny, refuse*) catégoriquement; (*ask*) carrément; (*kill*) sur le coup ♦ *adj* complet(-ète); catégorique

outset ['autset] *n* début *m*

outside [aut'saɪd] *n* extérieur *m* ♦ *adj* extérieur(e) ♦ *adv* (au) dehors, à l'extérieur ♦ *prep* hors de, à l'extérieur de; **at the ~** (*fig*) au plus *or* maximum; **~ lane** *n* (*AUT: in Britain*) voie *f* de droite; (*: in US, Europe*) voie de gauche; **~ line** *n* (*TEL*) ligne extérieure; **~r** *n* (*stranger*) étranger(-ère)

out: ~size ['autsaɪz] *adj* énorme; (*clothes*) grande taille *inv*; **~skirts** *npl* faubourgs *mpl*; **~spoken** *adj* très franc (franche); **~standing** *adj* remarquable, exceptionnel(le); (*unfinished*) en suspens; (*debt*) impayé(e); (*problem*) non réglé(e); **~stay** *vt*: **to ~stay one's welcome** abuser de l'hospitalité de son hôte; **~stretched** [aut'stretʃt] *adj* (*hand*) tendu(e); **~strip** [aut'strɪp] *vt* (*competitors, demand*) dépasser; **~ tray** *n* courrier *m* "départ"

outward ['autwəd] *adj* (*sign, appearances*) extérieur(e); (*journey*) (d')aller

outweigh [aut'weɪ] *vt* l'emporter sur

outwit [aut'wɪt] *vt* se montrer plus malin que

oval ['əuvl] *adj* ovale ♦ *n* ovale *m*

Oval Office

*L'***Oval Office** *est le bureau personnel du président des États-Unis à la Maison-Blanche, ainsi appelé du fait de sa forme ovale. Par extension, ce terme désigne la présidence elle-même.*

ovary ['əuvərɪ] *n* ovaire *m*

oven ['ʌvn] *n* four *m*; **~proof** *adj* allant au four

over ['əuvəʳ] *adv* (par-)dessus ♦ *adj* (*finished*) fini(e), terminé(e); (*too much*) en plus ♦ *prep* sur; par-dessus; (*above*) au-dessus de; (*on the other side of*) de l'autre côté de; (*more than*) plus de; (*during*) pendant; **~ here** ici; **~ there** là-bas; **all ~** (*everywhere*) partout, fini(e); **~ and ~ (again)** à plusieurs reprises; **~ and above** en plus de; **to ask sb ~** inviter qn (à passer)

overall [*adj, n* 'əuvərɔ:l, *adv* əuvər'ɔ:l] *adj* (*length, cost etc*) total(e); (*study*) d'ensemble ♦ *n* (BRIT) blouse *f* ♦ *adv* dans l'ensemble, en général; **~s** *npl* bleus *mpl* (de travail)

over: ~awe *vt* impressionner; **~balance** *vi* basculer; **~board** *adv* (NAUT) par-dessus bord; **~book** *vt* faire du surbooking; **~cast** *adj* couvert(e)

overcharge [əuvə'tʃɑ:dʒ] *vt*: **to ~ sb for sth** faire payer qch trop cher à qn

overcoat ['əuvəkəut] *n* pardessus *m*

overcome [əuvə'kʌm] (*irreg*) *vt* (*defeat*) triompher de; (*difficulty*) surmonter

over: ~crowded *adj* bondé(e); **~do** (*irreg*) *vt* exagérer; (*overcook*) trop cuire; **to ~do it** (*work etc*) se surmener; **~dose** *n* dose excessive; **~draft** *n* découvert *m*; **~drawn** *adj* (*account*) à découvert; (*person*) dont le compte est à découvert; **~due** *adj* en retard; (*change, reform*) qui tarde; **~estimate** *vt* surestimer

overflow [əuvə'fləu] *vi* déborder ♦ *n* (*also:* **~ pipe**) tuyau *m* d'écoulement, trop-plein *m*

overgrown [əuvə'grəun] *adj* (*garden*) envahi(e) par la végétation

overhaul [*vb* əuvə'hɔ:l, *n* 'əuvəhɔ:l] *vt* réviser ♦ *n* révision *f*

overhead [*adv* əuvə'hɛd, *adj, n* 'əuvəhɛd] *adv* au-dessus ♦ *adj* aérien(ne); (*lighting*) vertical(e) ♦ *n* (US) = **overheads; ~s** *npl* (*expenses*) frais généraux; **~ projector** *n* rétroprojecteur *m*

over: ~hear (*irreg*) *vt* entendre (par hasard); **~heat** *vi* (*engine*) chauffer; **~joyed** *adj*: **~joyed (at)** ravi(e) (de), enchanté(e) (de)

overland ['əuvəlænd] *adj, adv* par voie de terre

overlap [əuvə'læp] *vi* se chevaucher

over: ~leaf *adv* au verso; **~load** *vt* surcharger; **~look** *vt* (*have view of*) donner sur; (*miss: by mistake*) oublier; (*forgive*) fermer les yeux sur

overnight [*adv* əuvə'naɪt, *adj* 'əuvənaɪt] *adv* (*happen*) durant la nuit; (*fig*) soudain ♦ *adj* d'une (*or* de) nuit; **he stayed there ~** il y a passé la nuit

overpass ['əuvəpɑ:s] *n* pont autoroutier

overpower [əuvə'pauəʳ] *vt* vaincre; (*fig*) accabler; **~ing** *adj* (*heat, stench*) suffocant(e)

over: ~rate *vt* surestimer; **~ride** (*irreg: like* **ride**) *vt* (*order, objection*) passer outre à; **~riding** *adj* prépondérant(e); **~rule** *vt* (*decision*) annuler; (*claim*) rejeter; (*person*) rejeter l'avis de; **~run** (*irreg: like* **run**) *vt* (*country*) occuper; (*time limit*) dépasser

overseas [əuvə'si:z] *adv* outre-mer; (*abroad*) à l'étranger ♦ *adj* (*trade*) extérieur(e); (*visitor*) étranger(-ère)

overshadow [əuvə'ʃædəu] *vt* (*fig*) éclipser

oversight ['əuvəsaɪt] *n* omission *f*, oubli *m*

oversleep [əuvə'sli:p] (*irreg*) *vi* se réveiller (trop) tard

overstep [əuvə'stɛp] *vt*: **to ~ the mark** dépasser la mesure

overt [əu'və:t] *adj* non dissimulé(e)

overtake [əuvə'teɪk] (*irreg*) *vt* (AUT) dépasser, doubler

over: ~throw (*irreg*) *vt* (*government*) renverser; **~time** *n* heures *fpl* supplémentaires; **~tone** *n* (*also:* **~tones**) note *f*, sous-entendus *mpl*

overture ['əuvətʃuəʳ] *n* (MUS, *fig*) ouverture *f*

over: ~turn *vt* renverser ♦ *vi* se retourner; **~weight** *adj* (*person*) trop gros(se); **~whelm** *vt* (*subj*: *emotion*) accabler; (*enemy, opponent*) écraser; **~whelming** *adj* (*victory, defeat*) écrasant(e); (*desire*) irrésistible

overwrought [əuvə'rɔːt] *adj* excédé(e)

owe [əu] *vt*: **to ~ sb sth, to ~ sth to sb** devoir qch à qn; **owing to** *prep* à cause de, en raison de

owl [aul] *n* hibou *m*

own [əun] *vt* posséder ♦ *adj* propre; **a room of my ~** une chambre à moi, ma propre chambre; **to get one's ~ back** prendre sa revanche; **on one's ~** tout(e) seul(e); **~ up** *vi* avouer; **~er** *n* propriétaire *m/f*; **~ership** *n* possession *f*

ox [ɔks] (*pl* **~en**) *n* bœuf *m*; **~tail** *n*: **~tail soup** soupe *f* à la queue de bœuf

oxygen ['ɔksɪdʒən] *n* oxygène *m*

oyster ['ɔɪstə^r] *n* huître *f*

oz. *abbr* = **ounce(s)**

ozone ['əuzəun]: **~-friendly** *adj* qui n'attaque pas *or* qui préserve la couche d'ozone; **~ hole** *n* trou *m* d'ozone; **~ layer** *n* couche *f* d'ozone

P, p

p *abbr* = **penny; pence**

PA *n abbr* = **personal assistant; public address system**

pa [pɑː] (*inf*) *n* papa *m*

p.a. *abbr* = **per annum**

pace [peɪs] *n* pas *m*; (*speed*) allure *f*; vitesse *f* ♦ *vi*: **to ~ up and down** faire les cent pas; **to keep ~ with** aller à la même vitesse que; **~maker** *n* (MED) stimulateur *m* cardiaque; (SPORT: *also*: **~setter**) meneur(-euse) de train

Pacific [pə'sɪfɪk] *n*: **the ~ (Ocean)** le Pacifique, l'océan *m* Pacifique

pack [pæk] *n* (*~et*, US: *of cigarettes*) paquet *m*; (*of hounds*) meute *f*; (*of thieves etc*) bande *f*; (*back ~*) sac *m* à dos; (*of cards*) jeu *m* ♦ *vt* (*goods*) empaqueter, emballer; (*box*) remplir; (*cram*) entasser; **to ~ one's suitcase** faire sa valise; **to ~ (one's bags)** faire ses bagages; **to ~ sb off to** expédier qn à; **~ it in!** laisse tomber!, écrase!

package ['pækɪdʒ] *n* paquet *m*; (*also*: **~ deal**) forfait *m*; **~ tour** (BRIT) *n* voyage organisé

packed *adj* (*crowded*) bondé(e); **~ lunch** (BRIT) *n* repas froid

packet ['pækɪt] *n* paquet *m*

packing ['pækɪŋ] *n* emballage *m*; **~ case** *n* caisse *f* (d'emballage)

pact [pækt] *n* pacte *m*; traité *m*

pad [pæd] *n* bloc(-notes) *m*; (*to prevent friction*) tampon *m*; (*inf*: *home*) piaule *f* ♦ *vt* rembourrer; **~ding** *n* rembourrage *m*

paddle ['pædl] *n* (*oar*) pagaie *f*; (US: *for table tennis*) raquette *f* de ping-pong ♦ *vt*: **to ~ a canoe** *etc* pagayer ♦ *vi* barboter, faire trempette; **paddling pool** (BRIT) *n* petit bassin

paddock ['pædək] *n* enclos *m*; (RACING) paddock *m*

padlock ['pædlɔk] *n* cadenas *m*

paediatrics [piːdɪ'ætrɪks] (US **pediatrics**) *n* pédiatrie *f*

pagan ['peɪgən] *adj, n* païen(ne)

page [peɪdʒ] *n* (*of book*) page *f*; (*also*: **~ boy**) groom *m*, chasseur *m*; (*at wedding*) garçon *m* d'honneur ♦ *vt* (*in hotel etc*) (faire) appeler

pageant ['pædʒənt] *n* spectacle *m* historique; **~ry** *n* apparat *m*, pompe *f*

pager ['peɪdʒə^r], **paging device** *n* (TEL) récepteur *m* d'appels

paid [peɪd] *pt, pp of* **pay** ♦ *adj* (*work, official*) rémunéré(e); (*holiday*) payé(e); **to put ~ to** (BRIT) mettre fin à, régler

pail [peɪl] *n* seau *m*

pain [peɪn] *n* douleur *f*; **to be in ~** souffrir, avoir mal; **to take ~s to do** se donner du mal pour faire; **~ed** *adj* peiné(e), chagrin(e); **~ful** *adj* douloureux(-euse); (*fig*) difficile, pénible; **~fully** *adv* (*fig*: *very*) terriblement; **~killer** *n* analgésique *m*; **~less** *adj* indo-

lore; **~staking** ['peɪnzteɪkɪŋ] *adj* (*person*) soigneux(-euse); (*work*) soigné(e)
paint [peɪnt] *n* peinture *f* ♦ *vt* peindre; **to ~ the door blue** peindre la porte en bleu; **~brush** *n* pinceau *m*; **~er** *n* peintre *m*; **~ing** *n* peinture *f*; (*picture*) tableau *m*; **~work** *n* peinture *f*
pair [pɛəʳ] *n* (*of shoes, gloves etc*) paire *f*; (*of people*) couple *m*; **~ of scissors** (paire de) ciseaux *mpl*; **~ of trousers** pantalon *m*
pajamas [pə'dʒɑːməz] (*US*) *npl* pyjama(s) *m(pl)*
Pakistan [pɑːkɪ'stɑːn] *n* Pakistan *m*; **~i** *adj* pakistanais(e) ♦ *n* Pakistanais(e)
pal [pæl] (*inf*) *n* copain (copine)
palace ['pæləs] *n* palais *m*
palatable ['pælɪtəbl] *adj* bon (bonne), agréable au goût
palate ['pælɪt] *n* palais *m* (*ANAT*)
pale [peɪl] *adj* pâle ♦ *n*: **beyond the ~** (*behaviour*) inacceptable; **to grow ~** pâlir
Palestine ['pælɪstaɪn] *n* Palestine *f*; **Palestinian** [pælɪs'tɪnɪən] *adj* palestinien(ne) ♦ *n* Palestinien(ne)
palette ['pælɪt] *n* palette *f*
pall [pɔːl] *n* (*of smoke*) voile *m* ♦ *vi* devenir lassant(e)
pallet ['pælɪt] *n* (*for goods*) palette *f*
pallid ['pælɪd] *adj* blême
palm [pɑːm] *n* (*of hand*) paume *f*; (*also:* **~ tree**) palmier *m* ♦ *vt*: **to ~ sth off on sb** (*inf*) refiler qch à qn; **P~ Sunday** *n* le dimanche des Rameaux
paltry ['pɔːltrɪ] *adj* dérisoire
pamper ['pæmpəʳ] *vt* gâter, dorloter
pamphlet ['pæmflət] *n* brochure *f*
pan [pæn] *n* (*also:* **saucepan**) casserole *f*; (*also:* **frying ~**) poêle *f*; **~cake** *n* crêpe *f*
panda ['pændə] *n* panda *m*
pandemonium [pændɪ'məunɪəm] *n* tohu-bohu *m*
pander ['pændəʳ] *vi*: **to ~ to** flatter bassement; obéir servilement à
pane [peɪn] *n* carreau *m*, vitre *f*
panel ['pænl] *n* (*of wood, cloth etc*) panneau *m*; (*RADIO, TV*) experts *mpl*; (*for interview, exams*) jury *m*; **~ling** (*US* **paneling**) *n* boiseries *fpl*
pang [pæŋ] *n*: **~s of remorse/jealousy** affres *mpl* du remords/de la jalousie; **~s of hunger/conscience** tiraillements *mpl* d'estomac/de la conscience
panic ['pænɪk] *n* panique *f*, affolement *m* ♦ *vi* s'affoler, paniquer; **~ky** *adj* (*person*) qui panique *or* s'affole facilement; **~-stricken** *adj* affolé(e)
pansy ['pænzɪ] *n* (*BOT*) pensée *f*; (*inf: pej*) tapette *f*, pédé *m*
pant [pænt] *vi* haleter
panther ['pænθəʳ] *n* panthère *f*
panties ['pæntɪz] *npl* slip *m*
pantomime ['pæntəmaɪm] (*BRIT*) *n* spectacle *m* de Noël

pantomime

Une **pantomime**, *que l'on appelle également de façon familière "panto", est un genre de farce où le personnage principal est souvent un jeune garçon et où il y a toujours une* **dame**, *c'est-à-dire une vieille femme jouée par un homme, et un méchant. La plupart du temps, l'histoire est basée sur un conte de fées comme Cendrillon ou Le Chat botté, et le public est encouragé à participer en prévenant le héros d'un danger imminent. Ce genre de spectacle, qui s'adresse surtout aux enfants, vise également un public d'adultes au travers des nombreuses plaisanteries faisant allusion à des faits d'actualité.*

pantry ['pæntrɪ] *n* garde-manger *m inv*
pants [pænts] *npl* (*BRIT: woman's*) slip *m*; (*: man's*) slip, caleçon *m*; (*US: trousers*) pantalon *m*
pantyhose ['pæntɪhəuz] (*US*) *npl* collant *m*
paper ['peɪpəʳ] *n* papier *m*; (*also:* **wallpaper**) papier peint; (*also:* **newspaper**)

journal *m*; (*academic essay*) article *m*; (*exam*) épreuve écrite ♦ *adj* en *or* de papier ♦ *vt* tapisser (de papier peint); **~s** *npl* (*also:* **identity ~s**) papiers (d'identité); **~back** *n* livre *m* de poche; livre broché *or* non relié; **~ bag** *n* sac *m* en papier; **~ clip** *n* trombone *m*; **~ hankie** *n* mouchoir *m* en papier; **~weight** *n* presse-papiers *m inv*; **~work** *n* papiers *mpl*; (*pej*) paperasserie *f*

par [pɑːʳ] *n* pair *m*; (GOLF) normale *f* du parcours; **on a ~ with** à égalité avec, au même niveau que

parachute ['pærəʃuːt] *n* parachute *m*

parade [pə'reɪd] *n* défilé *m* ♦ *vt* (*fig*) faire étalage de ♦ *vi* défiler

paradise ['pærədaɪs] *n* paradis *m*

paradox ['pærədɔks] *n* paradoxe *m*; **~ically** [pærə'dɔksɪklɪ] *adv* paradoxalement

paraffin ['pærəfɪn] (BRIT) *n* (*also:* **~ oil**) pétrole (lampant)

paragon ['pærəgən] *n* modèle *m*

paragraph ['pærəgrɑːf] *n* paragraphe *m*

parallel ['pærəlɛl] *adj* parallèle; (*fig*) semblable ♦ *n* (*line*) parallèle *f*; (*fig*, GEO) parallèle *m*

paralyse ['pærəlaɪz] (BRIT) *vt* paralyser; **paralysis** [pə'rælɪsɪs] *n* paralysie *f*; **paralyze** (US) *vt* = **paralyse**

paramount ['pærəmaunt] *adj*: **of ~ importance** de la plus haute *or* grande importance

paranoid ['pærənɔɪd] *adj* (PSYCH) paranoïaque

paraphernalia [pærəfə'neɪlɪə] *n* attirail *m*

parasol ['pærəsɔl] *n* ombrelle *f*; (*over table*) parasol *m*

paratrooper ['pærətruːpəʳ] *n* parachutiste *m* (*soldat*)

parcel ['pɑːsl] *n* paquet *m*, colis *m* ♦ *vt* (*also:* **~ up**) empaqueter

parchment ['pɑːtʃmənt] *n* parchemin *m*

pardon ['pɑːdn] *n* pardon *m*; grâce *f* ♦ *vt* pardonner à; **~ me!, I beg your ~!** pardon!, je suis désolé!; **(I beg your) ~?, (US) ~ me?** pardon?

parent ['pɛərənt] *n* père *m or* mère *f*; **~s** *npl* parents *mpl*

Paris ['pærɪs] *n* Paris

parish ['pærɪʃ] *n* paroisse *f*; (BRIT: *civil*) ≃ commune *f*

Parisian [pə'rɪzɪən] *adj* parisien(ne) ♦ *n* Parisien(ne)

park [pɑːk] *n* parc *m*, jardin public ♦ *vt* garer ♦ *vi* se garer

parking ['pɑːkɪŋ] *n* stationnement *m*; **"no ~"** "stationnement interdit"; **~ lot** (US) *n* parking *m*, parc *m* de stationnement; **~ meter** *n* parcomètre *m*; **~ ticket** *n* P.V. *m*

parliament ['pɑːləmənt] *n* parlement *m*; **~ary** [pɑːlə'mɛntərɪ] *adj* parlementaire

parlour ['pɑːləʳ] (US **parlor**) *n* salon *m*

parochial [pə'rəukɪəl] (*pej*) *adj* à l'esprit de clocher

parole [pə'rəul] *n*: **on ~** en liberté conditionnelle

parrot ['pærət] *n* perroquet *m*

parry ['pærɪ] *vt* (*blow*) esquiver

parsley ['pɑːslɪ] *n* persil *m*

parsnip ['pɑːsnɪp] *n* panais *m*

parson ['pɑːsn] *n* ecclésiastique *m*; (*Church of England*) pasteur *m*

part [pɑːt] *n* partie *f*; (*of machine*) pièce *f*; (THEATRE *etc*) rôle *m*; (*of serial*) épisode *m*; (US: *in hair*) raie *f* ♦ *adv* = **partly** ♦ *vt* séparer ♦ *vi* (*people*) se séparer; (*crowd*) s'ouvrir; **to take ~ in** participer à, prendre part à; **to take sth in good ~** prendre qch du bon côté; **to take sb's ~** prendre le parti de qn, prendre parti pour qn; **for my ~** en ce qui me concerne; **for the most ~** dans la plupart des cas; **~ with** *vt fus* se séparer de; **~ exchange** (BRIT) *n*: **in ~ exchange** en reprise

partial ['pɑːʃl] *adj* (*not complete*) partiel(le); **to be ~ to** avoir un faible pour

participate [pɑː'tɪsɪpeɪt] *vi*: **to ~ (in)**

participer (à), prendre part (à); **participation** [pɑːtɪsɪ'peɪʃən] *n* participation *f*
participle ['pɑːtɪsɪpl] *n* participe *m*
particle ['pɑːtɪkl] *n* particule *f*
particular [pə'tɪkjulə^r] *adj* particulier (-ère); (*special*) spécial(e); (*fussy*) difficile; méticuleux(-euse); **~s** *npl* (*details*) détails *mpl*; (*personal*) *nom, adresse etc*; **in ~** en particulier; **~ly** *adv* particulièrement
parting ['pɑːtɪŋ] *n* séparation *f*; (*BRIT: in hair*) raie *f* ♦ *adj* d'adieu
partisan [pɑːtɪ'zæn] *n* partisan(e) ♦ *adj* partisan(e); de parti
partition [pɑː'tɪʃən] *n* (*wall*) cloison *f*; (*POL*) partition *f*, division *f*
partly ['pɑːtlɪ] *adv* en partie, partiellement
partner ['pɑːtnə^r] *n* partenaire *m/f*; (*in marriage*) conjoint(e); (*boyfriend, girlfriend*) ami(e); (*COMM*) associé(e); (*at dance*) cavalier(-ère); **~ship** *n* association *f*
partridge ['pɑːtrɪdʒ] *n* perdrix *f*
part-time ['pɑːt'taɪm] *adj, adv* à mi-temps, à temps partiel
party ['pɑːtɪ] *n* (*POL*) parti *m*; (*group*) groupe *m*; (*LAW*) partie *f*; (*celebration*) réception *f*; soirée *f*; fête *f* ♦ *cpd* (*POL*) de *or* du parti; **~ dress** *n* robe habillée
pass [pɑːs] *vt* passer; (*place*) passer devant; (*friend*) croiser; (*overtake*) dépasser; (*exam*) être reçu(e) à, réussir; (*approve*) approuver, accepter ♦ *vi* passer; (*SCOL*) être reçu(e) *or* admis(e), réussir ♦ *n* (*permit*) laissez-passer *m inv*; carte *f* d'accès *or* d'abonnement; (*in mountains*) col *m*; (*SPORT*) passe *f*; (*SCOL: also:* **~ mark**): **to get a ~** être reçu(e) (sans mention); **to make a ~ at sb** (*inf*) faire des avances à qn; **~ away** *vi* mourir; **~ by** *vi* passer ♦ *vt* négliger; **~ on** *vt* (*news, object*) transmettre; (*illness*) passer; **~ out** *vi* s'évanouir; **~ up** *vt* (*opportunity*) laisser passer; **~able** *adj* (*road*) praticable; (*work*) acceptable
passage ['pæsɪdʒ] *n* (*also:* **~way**) couloir *m*; (*gen, in book*) passage *m*; (*by boat*) traversée *f*
passbook ['pɑːsbuk] *n* livret *m*
passenger ['pæsɪndʒə^r] *n* passager (-ère)
passer-by [pɑːsə'baɪ] (*pl* **~s-~**) *n* passant(e)
passing ['pɑːsɪŋ] *adj* (*fig*) passager (-ère); **in ~** en passant; **~ place** *n* (*AUT*) aire *f* de croisement
passion ['pæʃən] *n* passion *f*; **~ate** *adj* passionné(e)
passive ['pæsɪv] *adj* (*also LING*) passif (-ive); **~ smoking** *n* tabagisme *m* passif
Passover ['pɑːsəuvə^r] *n* Pâque *f* (*juive*)
passport ['pɑːspɔːt] *n* passeport *m*; **~ control** *n* contrôle *m* des passeports; **~ office** *n* bureau *m* de délivrance des passeports
password ['pɑːswəːd] *n* mot *m* de passe
past [pɑːst] *prep* (*in front of*) devant; (*further than*) au delà de, plus loin que; après; (*later than*) après ♦ *adj* passé(e); (*president etc*) ancien(ne) ♦ *n* passé *m*; **he's ~ forty** il a dépassé la quarantaine, il a plus de *or* passé quarante ans; **for the ~ few/3 days** depuis quelques/3 jours; ces derniers/3 derniers jours; **ten/quarter ~ eight** huit heures dix/un *or* et quart
pasta ['pæstə] *n* pâtes *fpl*
paste [peɪst] *n* pâte *f*; (*meat ~*) pâté *m* (à tartiner); (*tomato ~*) purée *f*, concentré *m*; (*glue*) colle *f* (de pâte) ♦ *vt* coller
pasteurized ['pæstʃəraɪzd] *adj* pasteurisé(e)
pastille ['pæstɪl] *n* pastille *f*
pastime ['pɑːstaɪm] *n* passe-temps *m inv*
pastry ['peɪstrɪ] *n* pâte *f*; (*cake*) pâtisserie *f*
pasture ['pɑːstʃə^r] *n* pâturage *m*
pasty [*n* 'pæstɪ, *adj* 'peɪstɪ] *n* petit pâté (en croûte) ♦ *adj* (*complexion*) terreux (-euse)
pat [pæt] *vt* tapoter; (*dog*) caresser
patch [pætʃ] *n* (*of material*) pièce *f*; (*eye*

~) cache *m*; (*spot*) tache *f*; (*on tyre*) rustine *f* ♦ *vt* (*clothes*) rapiécer; **(to go through) a bad ~** (passer par) une période difficile; **~ up** *vt* réparer (grossièrement); **to ~ up a quarrel** se raccommoder; **~y** *adj* inégal(e); (*incomplete*) fragmentaire

pâté ['pæteɪ] *n* pâté *m*, terrine *f*

patent ['peɪtnt] *n* brevet *m* (d'invention) ♦ *vt* faire breveter ♦ *adj* patent(e), manifeste; **~ leather** *n* cuir verni

paternal [pə'tə:nl] *adj* paternel(le)

path [pɑ:θ] *n* chemin *m*, sentier *m*; (*in garden*) allée *f*; (*trajectory*) trajectoire *f*

pathetic [pə'θɛtɪk] *adj* (*pitiful*) pitoyable; (*very bad*) lamentable, minable

pathological [pæθə'lɔdʒɪkl] *adj* pathologique

pathway ['pɑ:θweɪ] *n* sentier *m*, passage *m*

patience ['peɪʃns] *n* patience *f*; (*BRIT*: *CARDS*) réussite *f*

patient ['peɪʃnt] *n* malade *m/f*; (*of dentist etc*) patient(e) ♦ *adj* patient(e)

patio ['pætɪəu] *n* patio *m*

patriotic [pætrɪ'ɔtɪk] *adj* patriotique; (*person*) patriote

patrol [pə'trəul] *n* patrouille *f* ♦ *vt* patrouiller dans; **~ car** *n* voiture *f* de police; **~man** (*irreg*) (*US*) *n* agent *m* de police

patron ['peɪtrən] *n* (*in shop*) client(e); (*of charity*) patron(ne); **~ of the arts** mécène *m*; **~ize** ['pætrənaɪz] *vt* (*pej*) traiter avec condescendance; (*shop, club*) être (un) client *or* un habitué de

patter ['pætə^r] *n* crépitement *m*, tapotement *m*; (*sales talk*) boniment *m*

pattern ['pætən] *n* (*design*) motif *m*; (*SEWING*) patron *m*

pauper ['pɔ:pə^r] *n* indigent(e)

pause [pɔ:z] *n* pause *f*, arrêt *m* ♦ *vi* faire une pause, s'arrêter

pave [peɪv] *vt* paver, daller; **to ~ the way for** ouvrir la voie à

pavement ['peɪvmənt] (*BRIT*) *n* trottoir *m*

pavilion [pə'vɪlɪən] *n* pavillon *m*; tente *f*

paving ['peɪvɪŋ] *n* (*material*) pavé *m*, dalle *f*; **~ stone** *n* pavé *m*

paw [pɔ:] *n* patte *f*

pawn [pɔ:n] *n* (*CHESS, also fig*) pion *m* ♦ *vt* mettre en gage; **~broker** *n* prêteur *m* sur gages; **~shop** *n* mont-de-piété *m*

pay [peɪ] (*pt, pp* **paid**) *n* salaire *m*; paie *f* ♦ *vt* payer ♦ *vi* payer; (*be profitable*) être rentable; **to ~ attention (to)** prêter attention (à); **to ~ sb a visit** rendre visite à qn; **to ~ one's respects to sb** présenter ses respects à qn; **~ back** *vt* rembourser; **~ for** *vt fus* payer; **~ in** *vt* verser; **~ off** *vt* régler, acquitter; (*person*) rembourser ♦ *vi* (*scheme, decision*) se révéler payant(e); **~ up** *vt* (*money*) payer; **~able** *adj*: **~able to sb** (*cheque*) à l'ordre de qn; **~ee** [peɪ'i:] *n* bénéficiaire *m/f*; **~ envelope** (*US*) *n* = **pay packet**; **~ment** *n* paiement *m*; règlement *m*; **monthly ~ment** mensualité *f*; **~ packet** (*BRIT*) *n* paie *f*; **~ phone** *n* cabine *f* téléphonique, téléphone public; **~roll** *n* registre *m* du personnel; **~ slip** (*BRIT*) *n* bulletin *m* de paie; **~ television** *n* chaînes *fpl* payantes

PC *n abbr* = **personal computer**

p.c. *abbr* = **per cent**

pea [pi:] *n* (petit) pois

peace [pi:s] *n* paix *f*; (*calm*) calme *m*, tranquillité *f*; **~ful** *adj* paisible, calme

peach [pi:tʃ] *n* pêche *f*

peacock ['pi:kɔk] *n* paon *m*

peak [pi:k] *n* (*mountain*) pic *m*, cime *f*; (*of cap*) visière *f*; (*fig: highest level*) maximum *m*; (: *of career, fame*) apogée *m*; **~ hours** *npl* heures *fpl* de pointe

peal [pi:l] *n* (*of bells*) carillon *m*; **~ of laughter** éclat *m* de rire

peanut ['pi:nʌt] *n* arachide *f*, cacahuète *f*; **~ butter** *n* beurre *m* de cacahuète

pear [pɛə^r] *n* poire *f*

pearl [pə:l] *n* perle *f*

peasant ['pɛznt] *n* paysan(ne)
peat [pi:t] *n* tourbe *f*
pebble ['pɛbl] *n* caillou *m*, galet *m*
peck [pɛk] *vt* (*also:* **~ at**) donner un coup de bec à ♦ *n* coup *m* de bec; (*kiss*) bise *f*; **~ing order** *n* ordre *m* des préséances; **~ish** (*BRIT*: *inf*) *adj*: **I feel ~ish** je mangerais bien quelque chose
peculiar [pɪ'kju:lɪər] *adj* étrange, bizarre, curieux(-euse); **~ to** particulier(-ère) à
pedal ['pɛdl] *n* pédale *f* ♦ *vi* pédaler
pedantic [pɪ'dæntɪk] *adj* pédant(e)
peddler ['pɛdlər] *n* (*of drugs*) revendeur(-euse)
pedestal ['pɛdəstl] *n* piédestal *m*
pedestrian [pɪ'dɛstrɪən] *n* piéton *m*; **~ crossing** (*BRIT*) *n* passage clouté; **~ized** *adj*: **a ~ized street** une rue piétonne
pediatrics [pi:dɪ'ætrɪks] (*US*) *n* = **paediatrics**
pedigree ['pɛdɪgri:] *n* ascendance *f*; (*of animal*) pedigree *m* ♦ *cpd* (*animal*) de race
pee [pi:] (*inf*) *vi* faire pipi, pisser
peek [pi:k] *vi* jeter un coup d'œil (furtif)
peel [pi:l] *n* pelure *f*, épluchure *f*; (*of orange, lemon*) écorce *f* ♦ *vt* peler, éplucher ♦ *vi* (*paint etc*) s'écailler; (*wallpaper*) se décoller; (*skin*) peler
peep [pi:p] *n* (*BRIT*: *look*) coup d'œil furtif; (*sound*) pépiement *m* ♦ *vi* (*BRIT*) jeter un coup d'œil (furtif); **~ out** (*BRIT*) *vi* se montrer (furtivement); **~hole** *n* judas *m*
peer [pɪər] *vi*: **to ~ at** regarder attentivement, scruter ♦ *n* (*noble*) pair *m*; (*equal*) pair, égal(e); **~age** ['pɪərɪdʒ] *n* pairie *f*
peeved [pi:vd] *adj* irrité(e), fâché(e)
peg [pɛg] *n* (*for coat etc*) patère *f*; (*BRIT*: *also:* **clothes ~**) pince *f* à linge
Pekin(g)ese [pi:kɪ'ni:z] *n* (*dog*) pékinois *m*
pelican ['pɛlɪkən] *n* pélican *m*; **~ crossing** (*BRIT*) *n* (*AUT*) feu *m* à commande manuelle
pellet ['pɛlɪt] *n* boulette *f*; (*of lead*) plomb *m*
pelt [pɛlt] *vt*: **to ~ sb (with)** bombarder qn (de) ♦ *vi* (*rain*) tomber à seaux; (*inf*: *run*) courir à toutes jambes ♦ *n* peau *f*
pelvis ['pɛlvɪs] *n* bassin *m*
pen [pɛn] *n* (*for writing*) stylo *m*; (*for sheep*) parc *m*
penal ['pi:nl] *adj* pénal(e); (*system, colony*) pénitentiaire; **~ize** ['pi:nəlaɪz] *vt* pénaliser
penalty ['pɛnltɪ] *n* pénalité *f*; sanction *f*; (*fine*) amende *f*; (*SPORT*) pénalisation *f*; (*FOOTBALL*) penalty *m*; (*RUGBY*) pénalité *f*
penance ['pɛnəns] *n* pénitence *f*
pence [pɛns] (*BRIT*) *npl of* **penny**
pencil ['pɛnsl] *n* crayon *m*; **~ case** *n* trousse *f* (d'écolier); **~ sharpener** *n* taille-crayon(s) *m inv*
pendant ['pɛndnt] *n* pendentif *m*
pending ['pɛndɪŋ] *prep* en attendant ♦ *adj* en suspens
pendulum ['pɛndjuləm] *n* (*of clock*) balancier *m*
penetrate ['pɛnɪtreɪt] *vt* pénétrer dans; pénétrer
penfriend ['pɛnfrɛnd] (*BRIT*) *n* correspondant(e)
penguin ['pɛŋgwɪn] *n* pingouin *m*
penicillin [pɛnɪ'sɪlɪn] *n* pénicilline *f*
peninsula [pə'nɪnsjulə] *n* péninsule *f*
penis ['pi:nɪs] *n* pénis *m*, verge *f*
penitentiary [pɛnɪ'tɛnʃərɪ] *n* prison *f*
penknife ['pɛnnaɪf] *n* canif *m*
pen name *n* nom *m* de plume, pseudonyme *m*
penniless ['pɛnɪlɪs] *adj* sans le sou
penny ['pɛnɪ] (*pl* **pennies** *or* (*BRIT*) **pence**) *n* penny *m*
penpal ['pɛnpæl] *n* correspondant(e)
pension ['pɛnʃən] *n* pension *f*; (*from company*) retraite *f*; **~er** (*BRIT*) *n* retraité(e); **~ fund** *n* caisse *f* de pension; **~ plan** *n* plan *m* de retraite

Pentagon

Le **Pentagon** *est le nom donné aux bureaux du ministère de la Défense américain, situés à Arlington en Virginie, à cause de la forme pentagonale du bâtiment dans lequel ils se trouvent. Par extension, ce terme est également utilisé en parlant du ministère lui-même.*

pentathlon [pɛn'tæθlən] *n* pentathlon *m*

Pentecost ['pɛntɪkɔst] *n* Pentecôte *f*

penthouse ['pɛnthaus] *n* appartement *m* (de luxe) (en attique)

pent-up ['pɛntʌp] *adj* (*feelings*) refoulé(e)

penultimate [pɛ'nʌltɪmət] *adj* avant-dernier(-ère)

people ['pi:pl] *npl* gens *mpl*; personnes *fpl*; (*inhabitants*) population *f*; (POL) peuple *m* ♦ *n* (*nation, race*) peuple *m*; **several ~ came** plusieurs personnes sont venues; **~ say that** ... on dit que ...

pep up ['pɛp-] (*inf*) *vt* remonter

pepper ['pɛpə^r] *n* poivre *m*; (*vegetable*) poivron *m* ♦ *vt* (*fig*): **to ~ with** bombarder de; **~ mill** *n* moulin *m* à poivre; **~mint** *n* (*sweet*) pastille *f* de menthe

peptalk ['pɛptɔ:k] (*inf*) *n* (petit) discours d'encouragement

per [pə:^r] *prep* par; **~ hour** (*miles etc*) à l'heure; (*fee*) (de) l'heure; **~ kilo** *etc* le kilo *etc*; **~ annum** par an; **~ capita** par personne, par habitant

perceive [pə'si:v] *vt* percevoir; (*notice*) remarquer, s'apercevoir de

per cent *adv* pour cent; **percentage** *n* pourcentage *m*

perception [pə'sɛpʃən] *n* perception *f*; (*insight*) perspicacité *f*

perceptive [pə'sɛptɪv] *adj* pénétrant(e); (*person*) perspicace

perch [pə:tʃ] *n* (*fish*) perche *f*; (*for bird*) perchoir *m* ♦ *vi*: **to ~ on** se percher sur

percolator ['pə:kəleɪtə^r] *n* cafetière *f* (électrique)

percussion [pə'kʌʃən] *n* percussion *f*

perennial [pə'rɛnɪəl] *adj* perpétuel(le); (BOT) vivace

perfect [*adj, n* 'pə:fɪkt, *vb* pə'fɛkt] *adj* parfait(e) ♦ *n* (*also:* **~ tense**) parfait *m* ♦ *vt* parfaire; mettre au point; **~ly** *adv* parfaitement

perforate ['pə:fəreɪt] *vt* perforer, percer; **perforation** [pə:fə'reɪʃən] *n* perforation *f*

perform [pə'fɔ:m] *vt* (*carry out*) exécuter; (*concert etc*) jouer, donner ♦ *vi* jouer; **~ance** *n* représentation *f*, spectacle *m*; (*of an artist*) interprétation *f*; (SPORT) performance *f*; (*of car, engine*) fonctionnement *m*; (*of company, economy*) résultats *mpl*; **~er** *n* artiste *m/f*, interprète *m/f*

perfume ['pə:fju:m] *n* parfum *m*

perhaps [pə'hæps] *adv* peut-être

peril ['pɛrɪl] *n* péril *m*

perimeter [pə'rɪmɪtə^r] *n* périmètre *m*

period ['pɪərɪəd] *n* période *f*; (*of history*) époque *f*; (SCOL) cours *m*; (*full stop*) point *m*; (MED) règles *fpl* ♦ *adj* (*costume, furniture*) d'époque; **~ic(al)** [pɪərɪ'ɔdɪk(l)] *adj* périodique; **~ical** [pɪərɪ'ɔdɪkl] *n* périodique *m*

peripheral [pə'rɪfərəl] *adj* périphérique ♦ *n* (COMPUT) périphérique *m*

perish ['pɛrɪʃ] *vi* périr; (*decay*) se détériorer; **~able** *adj* périssable

perjury ['pə:dʒərɪ] *n* parjure *m*, faux serment

perk [pə:k] *n* avantage *m* accessoire, à-côté *m*; **~ up** *vi* (*cheer up*) se ragaillardir; **~y** *adj* (*cheerful*) guilleret(te)

perm [pə:m] *n* (*for hair*) permanente *f*

permanent ['pə:mənənt] *adj* permanent(e)

permeate ['pə:mɪeɪt] *vi* s'infiltrer ♦ *vt* s'infiltrer dans; pénétrer

permissible [pə'mɪsɪbl] *adj* permis(e), acceptable

permission [pə'mɪʃən] *n* permission *f*,

autorisation *f*
permissive [pə'mɪsɪv] *adj* tolérant(e), permissif(-ive)
permit [*n* 'pə:mɪt, *vb* pə'mɪt] *n* permis *m* ♦ *vt* permettre
perpendicular [pə:pən'dɪkjuləʳ] *adj* perpendiculaire
perplex [pə'plɛks] *vt* (*person*) rendre perplexe
persecute ['pə:sɪkju:t] *vt* persécuter
persevere [pə:sɪ'vɪəʳ] *vi* persévérer
Persian ['pə:ʃən] *adj* persan(e) ♦ *n* (LING) persan *m*; **the ~ Gulf** le golfe Persique
persist [pə'sɪst] *vi*: **to ~ (in doing)** persister *or* s'obstiner (à faire); **~ent** [pə'sɪstənt] *adj* persistant(e), tenace; **~ent vegetative state** état *m* végétatif persistant
person ['pə:sn] *n* personne *f*; **in ~** en personne; **~al** *adj* personnel(le); **~al assistant** *n* secrétaire privé(e); **~al column** *n* annonces personnelles; **~al computer** *n* ordinateur personnel; **~ality** [pə:sə'nælɪtɪ] *n* personnalité *f*; **~ally** *adv* personnellement; **to take sth ~ally** se sentir visé(e) (par qch); **~al organizer** *n* filofax *m* ®; **~al stereo** *n* Walkman ® *m*, baladeur *m*
personnel [pə:sə'nɛl] *n* personnel *m*
perspective [pə'spɛktɪv] *n* perspective *f*; **to get things into ~** faire la part des choses
Perspex ['pə:spɛks] ® *n* plexiglas ® *m*
perspiration [pə:spɪ'reɪʃən] *n* transpiration *f*
persuade [pə'sweɪd] *vt*: **to ~ sb to do sth** persuader qn de faire qch; **persuasion** [pə'sweɪʒən] *n* persuasion *f*; (*creed*) réligion *f*
perverse [pə'və:s] *adj* pervers(e); (*contrary*) contrariant(e); **pervert** [*n* 'pə:və:t, *vb* pə'və:t] *n* perverti(e) ♦ *vt* pervertir; (*words*) déformer
pessimist ['pɛsɪmɪst] *n* pessimiste *m/f*; **~ic** [pɛsɪ'mɪstɪk] *adj* pessimiste
pest [pɛst] *n* animal *m* (*or* insecte *m*) nuisible; (*fig*) fléau *m*
pester ['pɛstəʳ] *vt* importuner, harceler
pet [pɛt] *n* animal familier ♦ *cpd* (*favourite*) favori(te) ♦ *vt* (*stroke*) caresser, câliner; **teacher's ~** chouchou *m* du professeur; **~ hate** bête noire
petal ['pɛtl] *n* pétale *m*
peter out ['pi:tə-] *vi* (*stream, conversation*) tarir; (*meeting*) tourner court; (*road*) se perdre
petite [pə'ti:t] *adj* menu(e)
petition [pə'tɪʃən] *n* pétition *f*
petrified ['pɛtrɪfaɪd] *adj* (*fig*) mort(e) de peur
petrol ['pɛtrəl] (BRIT) *n* essence *f*; **four-star ~** super *m*; **~ can** *n* bidon *m* à essence
petroleum [pə'trəulɪəm] *n* pétrole *m*
petrol: ~ pump (BRIT) *n* pompe *f* à essence; **~ station** (BRIT) *n* station-service *f*; **~ tank** (BRIT) *n* réservoir *m* d'essence
petticoat ['pɛtɪkəut] *n* combinaison *f*
petty ['pɛtɪ] *adj* (*mean*) mesquin(e); (*unimportant*) insignifiant(e), sans importance; **~ cash** *n* caisse *f* des dépenses courantes; **~ officer** *n* second-maître *m*
petulant ['pɛtjulənt] *adj* boudeur (-euse), irritable
pew [pju:] *n* banc *m* (d'église)
pewter ['pju:təʳ] *n* étain *m*
phantom ['fæntəm] *n* fantôme *m*
pharmacy ['fɑ:məsɪ] *n* pharmacie *f*
phase [feɪz] *n* phase *f* ♦ *vt*: **to ~ sth in/out** introduire/supprimer qch progressivement
PhD *abbr* = **Doctor of Philosophy** ♦ *n abbr* (*title*) ≃ docteur *m* (en droit *or* lettres *etc*), ≃ doctorat *m*; (*person*) titulaire *m/f* d'un doctorat
pheasant ['fɛznt] *n* faisan *m*
phenomenon [fə'nɔmɪnən] (*pl* **phenomena**) *n* phénomène *m*
philosophical [fɪlə'sɔfɪkl] *adj* philosophique
philosophy [fɪ'lɔsəfɪ] *n* philosophie *f*

phobia ['fəubjə] *n* phobie *f*
phone [fəun] *n* téléphone *m* ♦ *vt* téléphoner; **to be on the ~** avoir le téléphone; (*be calling*) être au téléphone; **~ back** *vt, vi* rappeler; **~ up** *vt* téléphoner à ♦ *vi* téléphoner; **~ bill** *n* facture *f* de téléphone; **~ book** *n* annuaire *m*; **~ booth, ~ box** (*BRIT*) *n* cabine *f* téléphonique; **~ call** *n* coup *m* de fil *or* de téléphone; **~card** *n* carte *f* de téléphone; **~-in** (*BRIT*) *n* (*RADIO, TV*) programme *m* à ligne ouverte; **~ number** *n* numéro *m* de téléphone
phonetics [fə'nεtɪks] *n* phonétique *f*
phoney ['fəunɪ] *adj* faux (fausse), factice; (*person*) pas franc (franche), poseur(-euse)
photo ['fəutəu] *n* photo *f*; **~copier** *n* photocopieuse *f*; **~copy** *n* photocopie *f* ♦ *vt* photocopier; **~graph** *n* photographie *f* ♦ *vt* photographier; **~grapher** [fə'tɔgrəfə^r] *n* photographe *m/f*; **~graphy** [fə'tɔgrəfɪ] *n* photographie *f*
phrase [freɪz] *n* expression *f*; (*LING*) locution *f* ♦ *vt* exprimer; **~ book** *n* recueil *m* d'expressions (pour touristes)
physical ['fɪzɪkl] *adj* physique; **~ education** *n* éducation *f* physique; **~ly** *adv* physiquement
physician [fɪ'zɪʃən] *n* médecin *m*
physicist ['fɪzɪsɪst] *n* physicien(ne)
physics ['fɪzɪks] *n* physique *f*
physiotherapist [fɪzɪəu'θεrəpɪst] *n* kinésithérapeute *m/f*
physiotherapy [fɪzɪəu'θεrəpɪ] *n* kinésithérapie *f*
physique [fɪ'zi:k] *n* physique *m*; constitution *f*
pianist ['pi:ənɪst] *n* pianiste *m/f*
piano [pɪ'ænəu] *n* piano *m*
pick [pɪk] *n* (*tool*: *also*: **~axe**) pic *m*, pioche *f* ♦ *vt* choisir; (*fruit etc*) cueillir; (*remove*) prendre; (*lock*) forcer; **take your ~** faites votre choix; **the ~ of** le (la) meilleur(e) de; **to ~ one's nose** se mettre les doigts dans le nez; **to ~ one's teeth** se curer les dents; **to ~ a quarrel with sb** chercher noise à qn; **~ at** *vt fus*: **to ~ at one's food** manger du bout des dents, chipoter; **~ on** *vt fus* (*person*) harceler; **~ out** *vt* choisir; (*distinguish*) distinguer; **~ up** *vi* (*improve*) s'améliorer ♦ *vt* ramasser; (*collect*) passer prendre; (*AUT*: *give lift to*) prendre, emmener; (*learn*) apprendre; (*RADIO*) capter; **to ~ up speed** prendre de la vitesse; **to ~ o.s. up** se relever
picket ['pɪkɪt] *n* (*in strike*) piquet *m* de grève ♦ *vt* mettre un piquet de grève devant
pickle ['pɪkl] *n* (*also*: **~s**: *as condiment*) pickles *mpl*; *petits légumes macérés dans du vinaigre* ♦ *vt* conserver dans du vinaigre *or* dans de la saumure; **to be in a ~** (*mess*) être dans le pétrin
pickpocket ['pɪkpɔkɪt] *n* pickpocket *m*
pick-up ['pɪkʌp] *n* (*small truck*) pick-up *m inv*
picnic ['pɪknɪk] *n* pique-nique *m*
picture ['pɪktʃə^r] *n* image *f*; (*painting*) peinture *f*, tableau *m*; (*etching*) gravure *f*; (*photograph*) photo(graphie) *f*; (*drawing*) dessin *m*; (*film*) film *m*; (*fig*) description *f*; tableau *m* ♦ *vt* se représenter; **the ~s** (*BRIT*: *inf*) le cinéma; **~ book** *n* livre *m* d'images
picturesque [pɪktʃə'rεsk] *adj* pittoresque
pie [paɪ] *n* tourte *f*; (*of fruit*) tarte *f*; (*of meat*) pâté *m* en croûte
piece [pi:s] *n* morceau *m*; (*item*): **a ~ of furniture/advice** un meuble/conseil ♦ *vt*: **to ~ together** rassembler; **to take to ~s** démonter; **~meal** *adv* (*irregularly*) au coup par coup; (*bit by bit*) par bouts; **~work** *n* travail *m* aux pièces
pie chart *n* graphique *m* circulaire, camembert *m*
pier [pɪə^r] *n* jetée *f*
pierce [pɪəs] *vt* percer, transpercer; **~d** *adj* (*ears etc*) percé(e)
pig [pɪg] *n* cochon *m*, porc *m*
pigeon ['pɪdʒən] *n* pigeon *m*; **~hole** *n* casier *m*

piggy bank ['pɪgɪ-] *n* tirelire *f*
pig: **~headed** *adj* entêté(e), têtu(e); **~let** *n* porcelet *m*, petit cochon; **~skin** *n* peau *m* de porc; **~sty** *n* porcherie *f*; **~tail** *n* natte *f*, tresse *f*
pike [paɪk] *n* (*fish*) brochet *m*
pilchard ['pɪltʃəd] *n* pilchard *m* (*sorte de sardine*)
pile [paɪl] *n* (*pillar, of books*) pile *f*; (*heap*) tas *m*; (*of carpet*) poils *mpl* ♦ *vt* (*also:* **~ up**) empiler, entasser ♦ *vi* (*also:* **~ up**) s'entasser, s'accumuler; **to ~ into** (*car*) s'entasser dans; **~s** *npl* hémorroïdes *fpl*; **~-up** *n* (AUT) télescopage *m*, collision *f* en série
pilfering ['pɪlfərɪŋ] *n* chapardage *m*
pilgrim ['pɪlgrɪm] *n* pèlerin *m*
pill [pɪl] *n* pilule *f*
pillage ['pɪlɪdʒ] *vt* piller
pillar ['pɪlə^r] *n* pilier *m*; **~ box** (BRIT) *n* boîte *f* aux lettres (*publique*)
pillion ['pɪljən] *n*: **to ride ~** (*on motorcycle*) monter derrière
pillow ['pɪləu] *n* oreiller *m*; **~case** *n* taie *f* d'oreiller
pilot ['paɪlət] *n* pilote *m* ♦ *cpd* (*scheme etc*) pilote, expérimental(e) ♦ *vt* piloter; **~ light** *n* veilleuse *f*
pimp [pɪmp] *n* souteneur *m*, maquereau *m*
pimple ['pɪmpl] *n* bouton *m*
pin [pɪn] *n* épingle *f*; (TECH) cheville *f* ♦ *vt* épingler; **~s and needles** fourmis *fpl*; **to ~ sb down** (*fig*) obliger qn à répondre; **to ~ sth on sb** (*fig*) mettre qch sur le dos de qn
PIN [pɪn] *n abbr* (= *personal identification number*) numéro *m* d'identification personnel
pinafore ['pɪnəfɔː^r] *n* tablier *m*
pinball ['pɪnbɔːl] *n* flipper *m*
pincers ['pɪnsəz] *npl* tenailles *fpl*; (*of crab etc*) pinces *fpl*
pinch [pɪntʃ] *n* (*of salt etc*) pincée *f* ♦ *vt* pincer; (*inf: steal*) piquer, chiper; **at a ~** à la rigueur
pincushion ['pɪnkuʃən] *n* pelote *f* à épingles
pine [paɪn] *n* (*also:* **~ tree**) pin *m* ♦ *vi*: **to ~ for** s'ennuyer de, désirer ardemment; **~ away** *vi* dépérir
pineapple ['paɪnæpl] *n* ananas *m*
ping [pɪŋ] *n* (*noise*) tintement *m*; **~-pong** ® *n* ping-pong ® *m*
pink [pɪŋk] *adj* rose ♦ *n* (*colour*) rose *m*; (BOT) œillet *m*, mignardise *f*
PIN (number) ['pɪn(-)] *n* code *m* confidentiel
pinpoint ['pɪnpɔɪnt] *vt* indiquer *or* localiser (avec précision); (*problem*) mettre le doigt sur
pint [paɪnt] *n* pinte *f* (BRIT = *0.57l*; US = *0.47l*); (BRIT: *inf*) ≃ demi *m*
pioneer [paɪə'nɪə^r] *n* pionnier *m*
pious ['paɪəs] *adj* pieux(-euse)
pip [pɪp] *n* (*seed*) pépin *m*; **the ~s** *npl* (BRIT: *time signal on radio*) le(s) top(s) sonore(s)
pipe [paɪp] *n* tuyau *m*, conduite *f*; (*for smoking*) pipe *f* ♦ *vt* amener par tuyau; **~s** *npl* (*also:* **bagpipes**) cornemuse *f*; **~ cleaner** *n* cure-pipe *m*; **~ dream** *n* chimère *f*, château *m* en Espagne; **~line** *n* pipe-line *m*; **~r** *n* joueur(-euse) de cornemuse
piping ['paɪpɪŋ] *adv*: **~ hot** très chaud(e)
pique ['piːk] *n* dépit *m*
pirate ['paɪərət] *n* pirate *m*; **~d** *adj* pirate
Pisces ['paɪsiːz] *n* les Poissons *mpl*
piss [pɪs] (*inf!*) *vi* pisser; **~ed** (*inf!*) *adj* (*drunk*) bourré(e)
pistol ['pɪstl] *n* pistolet *m*
piston ['pɪstən] *n* piston *m*
pit [pɪt] *n* trou *m*, fosse *f*; (*also:* **coal ~**) puits *m* de mine; (*quarry*) carrière *f* ♦ *vt*: **to ~ one's wits against sb** se mesurer à qn; **~s** *npl* (AUT) aire *f* de service
pitch [pɪtʃ] *n* (MUS) ton *m*; (BRIT: SPORT) terrain *m*; (*tar*) poix *f*; (*fig*) degré *m*; point *m* ♦ *vt* (*throw*) lancer ♦ *vi* (*fall*) tomber; **to ~ a tent** dresser une tente; **~-black** *adj* noir(e) (comme du cirage);

~**ed battle** *n* bataille rangée
pitfall ['pɪtfɔ:l] *n* piège *m*
pith [pɪθ] *n* (*of orange etc*) intérieur *m* de l'écorce; ~**y** *adj* piquant(e)
pitiful ['pɪtɪful] *adj* (*touching*) pitoyable
pitiless ['pɪtɪlɪs] *adj* impitoyable
pittance ['pɪtns] *n* salaire *m* de misère
pity ['pɪtɪ] *n* pitié *f* ♦ *vt* plaindre; **what a ~!** quel dommage!
pizza ['pi:tsə] *n* pizza *f*
placard ['plækɑ:d] *n* affiche *f*; (*in march*) pancarte *f*
placate [plə'keɪt] *vt* apaiser, calmer
place [pleɪs] *n* endroit *m*, lieu *m*; (*proper position, job, rank, seat*) place *f*; (*home*): **at/to his ~** chez lui ♦ *vt* (*object*) placer, mettre; (*identify*) situer; reconnaître; **to take ~** avoir lieu; **out of ~** (*not suitable*) déplacé(e), inopportun(e); **to change ~s with sb** changer de place avec qn; **in the first ~** d'abord, en premier
plague [pleɪg] *n* fléau *m*; (MED) peste *f* ♦ *vt* (*fig*) tourmenter
plaice [pleɪs] *n inv* carrelet *m*
plaid [plæd] *n* tissu écossais
plain [pleɪn] *adj* (*in one colour*) uni(e); (*simple*) simple; (*clear*) clair(e), évident(e); (*not handsome*) quelconque, ordinaire ♦ *adv* franchement, carrément ♦ *n* plaine *f*; ~ **chocolate** *n* chocolat *m* à croquer; ~ **clothes** *adj* (*police officer*) en civil; ~**ly** *adv* clairement; (*frankly*) carrément, sans détours
plaintiff ['pleɪntɪf] *n* plaignant(e)
plait [plæt] *n* tresse *f*, natte *f*
plan [plæn] *n* plan *m*; (*scheme*) projet *m* ♦ *vt* (*think in advance*) projeter; (*prepare*) organiser; (*house*) dresser les plans de, concevoir ♦ *vi* faire des projets; **to ~ to do** prévoir de faire
plane [pleɪn] *n* (AVIAT) avion *m*; (ART, MATH *etc*) plan *m*; (*fig*) niveau *m*, plan; (*tool*) rabot *m*; (*also:* ~ **tree**) platane *m* ♦ *vt* raboter
planet ['plænɪt] *n* planète *f*
plank [plæŋk] *n* planche *f*
planner ['plænə^r] *n* planificateur(-trice); (*town ~*) urbaniste *m/f*
planning ['plænɪŋ] *n* planification *f*; **family ~** planning familial; ~ **permission** *n* permis *m* de construire
plant [plɑ:nt] *n* plante *f*; (*machinery*) matériel *m*; (*factory*) usine *f* ♦ *vt* planter; (*bomb*) poser; (*microphone, incriminating evidence*) cacher
plaster ['plɑ:stə^r] *n* plâtre *m*; (*also:* ~ **of Paris**) plâtre à mouler; (BRIT: *also:* **sticking ~**) pansement adhésif ♦ *vt* plâtrer; (*cover*): **to ~ with** couvrir de; ~**ed** (*inf*) *adj* soûl(e)
plastic ['plæstɪk] *n* plastique *m* ♦ *adj* (*made of ~*) en plastique; ~ **bag** *n* sac *m* en plastique
Plasticine ® ['plæstɪsi:n] *n* pâte *f* à modeler
plastic surgery *n* chirurgie *f* esthétique
plate [pleɪt] *n* (*dish*) assiette *f*; (*in book*) gravure *f*, planche *f*; (*dental ~*) dentier *m*
plateau ['plætəu] (*pl* ~**s** *or* ~**x**) *n* plateau *m*
plate glass *n* verre *m* (de vitrine)
platform ['plætfɔ:m] *n* plate-forme *f*; (*at meeting*) tribune *f*; (*stage*) estrade *f*; (RAIL) quai *m*
platinum ['plætɪnəm] *n* platine *m*
platter ['plætə^r] *n* plat *m*
plausible ['plɔ:zɪbl] *adj* plausible; (*person*) convaincant(e)
play [pleɪ] *n* (THEATRE) pièce *f* (de théâtre) ♦ *vt* (*game*) jouer à; (*team, opponent*) jouer contre; (*instrument*) jouer de; (*part, piece of music, note*) jouer; (*record etc*) passer ♦ *vi* jouer; **to ~ safe** ne prendre aucun risque; ~ **down** *vt* minimiser; ~ **up** *vi* (*cause trouble*) faire des siennes; ~**boy** *n* playboy *m*; ~**er** *n* joueur(-euse); (THEATRE) acteur(-trice); (MUS) musicien(ne); ~**ful** *adj* enjoué(e); ~**ground** *n* cour *f* de récréation; (*in park*) aire *f* de jeux; ~**group** *n* garderie *f*; ~**ing card** *n* carte *f* à jouer; ~**ing**

field *n* terrain *m* de sport; **~mate** *n* camarade *m/f*, copain (copine); **~-off** *n* (SPORT) belle *f*; **~ park** *n* terrain *m* de jeu; **~pen** *n* parc *m* (pour bébé); **~thing** *n* jouet *m*; **~time** *n* récréation *f*; **~wright** *n* dramaturge *m*
plc *abbr* (= *public limited company*) SARL *f*
plea [pli:] *n* (*request*) appel *m*; (LAW) défense *f*
plead [pli:d] *vt* plaider; (*give as excuse*) invoquer ♦ *vi* (LAW) plaider; (*beg*): **to ~ with sb** implorer qn
pleasant ['plɛznt] *adj* agréable; **~ries** *npl* (*polite remarks*) civilités *fpl*
please [pli:z] *excl* s'il te (*or* vous) plaît ♦ *vt* plaire à ♦ *vi* plaire; (*think fit*): **do as you ~** faites comme il vous plaira; **~ yourself!** à ta (*or* votre) guise!; **~d** *adj*: **~d (with)** content(e) (de); **~d to meet you** enchanté (de faire votre connaissance); **pleasing** *adj* plaisant(e), qui fait plaisir
pleasure ['plɛʒəʳ] *n* plaisir *m*; **"it's a ~"** "je vous en prie"
pleat [pli:t] *n* pli *m*
pledge [plɛdʒ] *n* (*promise*) promesse *f* ♦ *vt* engager; promettre
plentiful ['plɛntɪful] *adj* abondant(e), copieux(-euse)
plenty ['plɛntɪ] *n*: **~ of** beaucoup de; (bien) assez de
pliable ['plaɪəbl] *adj* flexible; (*person*) malléable
pliers ['plaɪəz] *npl* pinces *fpl*
plight [plaɪt] *n* situation *f* critique
plimsolls ['plɪmsəlz] (BRIT) *npl* chaussures *fpl* de tennis, tennis *mpl*
plinth [plɪnθ] *n* (*of statue*) socle *m*
P.L.O. *n abbr* (= *Palestine Liberation Organization*) OLP *f*
plod [plɔd] *vi* avancer péniblement; (*fig*) peiner
plonk [plɔŋk] (*inf*) *n* (BRIT: *wine*) pinard *m*, piquette *f* ♦ *vt*: **to ~ sth down** poser brusquement qch
plot [plɔt] *n* complot *m*, conspiration *f*; (*of story, play*) intrigue *f*; (*of land*) lot *m* de terrain, lopin *m* ♦ *vt* (*sb's downfall*) comploter; (*mark out*) pointer; relever, déterminer ♦ *vi* comploter
plough [plau] (US **plow**) *n* charrue *f* ♦ *vt* (*earth*) labourer; **to ~ money into** investir dans; **~ through** *vt fus* (*snow etc*) avancer péniblement dans; **~man's lunch** (BRIT) *n assiette froide avec du pain, du fromage et des pickles*
ploy [plɔɪ] *n* stratagème *m*
pluck [plʌk] *vt* (*fruit*) cueillir; (*musical instrument*) pincer; (*bird*) plumer; (*eyebrow*) épiler ♦ *n* courage *m*, cran *m*; **to ~ up courage** prendre son courage à deux mains
plug [plʌg] *n* (ELEC) prise *f* de courant; (*stopper*) bouchon *m*, bonde *f*; (AUT: *also:* **spark(ing) ~**) bougie *f* ♦ *vt* (*hole*) boucher; (*inf: advertise*) faire du battage pour; **~ in** *vt* (ELEC) brancher
plum [plʌm] *n* (*fruit*) prune *f* ♦ *cpd*: **~ job** (*inf*) travail *m* en or
plumb [plʌm] *vt*: **to ~ the depths** (*fig*) toucher le fond (du désespoir)
plumber ['plʌməʳ] *n* plombier *m*
plumbing ['plʌmɪŋ] *n* (*trade*) plomberie *f*; (*piping*) tuyauterie *f*
plummet ['plʌmɪt] *vi*: **to ~ (down)** plonger, dégringoler
plump [plʌmp] *adj* rondelet(te), dodu(e), bien en chair ♦ *vi*: **to ~ for** (*inf: choose*) se décider pour
plunder ['plʌndəʳ] *n* pillage *m*; (*loot*) butin *m* ♦ *vt* piller
plunge [plʌndʒ] *n* plongeon *m*; (*fig*) chute *f* ♦ *vt* plonger ♦ *vi* (*dive*) plonger; (*fall*) tomber, dégringoler; **to take the ~** se jeter à l'eau; **plunging** ['plʌndʒɪŋ] *adj*: **plunging neckline** décolleté plongeant
pluperfect [plu:'pə:fɪkt] *n* plus-que-parfait *m*
plural ['pluərl] *adj* pluriel(le) ♦ *n* pluriel *m*
plus [plʌs] *n* (*also:* **~ sign**) signe *m* plus ♦ *prep* plus; **ten/twenty ~** plus de dix/vingt

plush [plʌʃ] *adj* somptueux(-euse)
ply [plaɪ] *vt* (*a trade*) exercer ♦ *vi* (*ship*) faire la navette ♦ *n* (*of wool, rope*) fil *m*, brin *m*; **to ~ sb with drink** donner continuellement à boire à qn; **to ~ sb with questions** presser qn de questions; **~wood** *n* contre-plaqué *m*
PM *abbr* = **Prime Minister**
p.m. *adv abbr* (= *post meridiem*) de l'après-midi
pneumatic drill [nju:'mætɪk-] *n* marteau-piqueur *m*
pneumonia [nju:'məunɪə] *n* pneumonie *f*
poach [pəutʃ] *vt* (*cook*) pocher; (*steal*) pêcher (*or* chasser) sans permis ♦ *vi* braconner; **~ed egg** *n* œuf poché; **~er** *n* braconnier *m*
P.O. box *n abbr* = **post office box**
pocket ['pɔkɪt] *n* poche *f* ♦ *vt* empocher; **to be out of ~** (*BRIT*) en être de sa poche; **~book** (*US*) *n* (*wallet*) portefeuille *m*; **~ calculator** *n* calculette *f*; **~ knife** *n* canif *m*; **~ money** *n* argent *m* de poche
pod [pɔd] *n* cosse *f*
podgy ['pɔdʒɪ] *adj* rondelet(te)
podiatrist [pɔ'di:ətrɪst] (*US*) *n* pédicure *m/f*, podologue *m/f*
poem ['pəuɪm] *n* poème *m*
poet ['pəuɪt] *n* poète *m*; **~ic** [pəu'ɛtɪk] *adj* poétique; **~ry** ['pəuɪtrɪ] *n* poésie *f*
poignant ['pɔɪnjənt] *adj* poignant(e); (*sharp*) vif (vive)
point [pɔɪnt] *n* point *m*; (*tip*) pointe *f*; (*in time*) moment *m*; (*in space*) endroit *m*; (*subject, idea*) point, sujet *m*; (*purpose*) sens *m*; (*ELEC*) prise *f*; (*also:* **decimal ~**): **2 ~ 3 (2.3)** 2 virgule 3 (2,3) ♦ *vt* (*show*) indiquer; (*gun etc*): **to ~ sth at** braquer *or* diriger qch sur ♦ *vi*: **to ~ at** montrer du doigt; **~s** *npl* (*AUT*) vis platinées; (*RAIL*) aiguillage *m*; **to be on the ~ of doing sth** être sur le point de faire qch; **to make a ~ of doing** ne pas manquer de faire; **to get the ~** comprendre, saisir; **to miss the ~** ne pas comprendre; **to come to the ~** en venir au fait; **there's no ~ (in doing)** cela ne sert à rien (de faire); **~ out** *vt* faire remarquer, souligner; **~ to** *vt fus* (*fig*) indiquer; **~-blank** *adv* (*fig*) catégoriquement; (*also:* **at ~-blank range**) à bout portant; **~ed** *adj* (*shape*) pointu(e); (*remark*) plein(e) de sous-entendus; **~er** *n* (*needle*) aiguille *f*; (*piece of advice*) conseil *m*; (*clue*) indice *m*; **~less** *adj* inutile, vain(e); **~ of view** *n* point *m* de vue
poise [pɔɪz] *n* (*composure*) calme *m*
poison ['pɔɪzn] *n* poison *m* ♦ *vt* empoisonner; **~ous** *adj* (*snake*) venimeux(-euse); (*plant*) vénéneux(-euse); (*fumes etc*) toxique
poke [pəuk] *vt* (*fire*) tisonner; (*jab with finger, stick etc*) piquer; pousser du doigt; (*put*): **to ~ sth in(to)** fourrer *or* enfoncer qch dans; **~ about** *vi* fureter; **~r** *n* tisonnier *m*; (*CARDS*) poker *m*
poky ['pəukɪ] *adj* exigu(ë)
Poland ['pəulənd] *n* Pologne *f*
polar ['pəulə^r] *adj* polaire; **~ bear** *n* ours blanc
Pole [pəul] *n* Polonais(e)
pole [pəul] *n* poteau *m*; (*of wood*) mât *m*, perche *f*; (*GEO*) pôle *m*; **~ bean** (*US*) *n* haricot *m* (à rames); **~ vault** *n* saut *m* à la perche
police [pə'li:s] *npl* police *f* ♦ *vt* maintenir l'ordre dans; **~ car** *n* voiture *f* de police; **~man** (*irreg*) *n* agent *m* de police, policier *m*; **~ station** *n* commissariat *m* de police; **~woman** (*irreg*) *n* femme-agent *f*
policy ['pɔlɪsɪ] *n* politique *f*; (*also:* **insurance ~**) police *f* (d'assurance)
polio ['pəulɪəu] *n* polio *f*
Polish ['pəulɪʃ] *adj* polonais(e) ♦ *n* (*LING*) polonais *m*
polish ['pɔlɪʃ] *n* (*for shoes*) cirage *m*; (*for floor*) cire *f*, encaustique *f*; (*shine*) éclat *m*, poli *m*; (*fig: refinement*) raffinement *m* ♦ *vt* (*put ~ on shoes, wood*) cirer; (*make shiny*) astiquer, faire briller; **~**

off (*inf*) *vt* (*food*) liquider; **~ed** *adj* (*fig*) raffiné(e)

polite [pə'laɪt] *adj* poli(e); **in ~ society** dans la bonne société; **~ly** *adv* poliment; **~ness** *n* politesse *f*

political [pə'lɪtɪkl] *adj* politique; **~ly correct** *adj* politiquement correct(e)

politician [pɔlɪ'tɪʃən] *n* homme *m*/femme *f* politique

politics ['pɔlɪtɪks] *npl* politique *f*

poll [pəul] *n* scrutin *m*, vote *m*; (*also:* **opinion ~**) sondage *m* (d'opinion) ♦ *vt* obtenir

pollen ['pɔlən] *n* pollen *m*

polling day ['pəulɪŋ-] (*BRIT*) *n* jour *m* des élections

polling station (*BRIT*) *n* bureau *m* de vote

pollute [pə'lu:t] *vt* polluer; **pollution** *n* pollution *f*

polo ['pəuləu] *n* polo *m*; **~-necked** *adj* à col roulé; **~ shirt** *n* polo *m*

polyester [pɔlɪ'ɛstə^r] *n* polyester *m*

polystyrene [pɔlɪ'staɪri:n] *n* polystyrène *m*

polythene ['pɔlɪθi:n] *n* polyéthylène *m*; **~ bag** *n* sac *m* en plastique

pomegranate ['pɔmɪgrænɪt] *n* grenade *f*

pomp [pɔmp] *n* pompe *f*, faste *f*, apparat *m*; **~ous** *adj* pompeux(-euse)

pond [pɔnd] *n* étang *m*; mare *f*

ponder ['pɔndə^r] *vt* considérer, peser; **~ous** *adj* pesant(e), lourd(e)

pong [pɔŋ] (*BRIT: inf*) *n* puanteur *f*

pony ['pəunɪ] *n* poney *m*; **~tail** *n* queue *f* de cheval; **~ trekking** (*BRIT*) *n* randonnée *f* à cheval

poodle ['pu:dl] *n* caniche *m*

pool [pu:l] *n* (*of rain*) flaque *f*; (*pond*) mare *f*; (*also:* **swimming ~**) piscine *f*; (*billiards*) poule *f* ♦ *vt* mettre en commun; **~s** *npl* (*football ~s*) ≈ loto sportif

poor [puə^r] *adj* pauvre; (*mediocre*) médiocre, faible, mauvais(e) ♦ *npl*: **the ~** les pauvres *mpl*; **~ly** *adj* souffrant(e), malade ♦ *adv* mal; médiocrement

pop [pɔp] *n* (*MUS*) musique *f* pop; (*drink*) boisson gazeuse; (*US: inf: father*) papa *m*; (*noise*) bruit sec ♦ *vt* (*put*) mettre (rapidement) ♦ *vi* éclater; (*cork*) sauter; **~ in** *vi* entrer en passant; **~ out** *vi* sortir (brièvement); **~ up** *vi* apparaître, surgir; **~corn** *n* pop-corn *m*

pope [pəup] *n* pape *m*

poplar ['pɔplə^r] *n* peuplier *m*

popper ['pɔpə^r] (*BRIT: inf*) *n* bouton-pression *m*

poppy ['pɔpɪ] *n* coquelicot *m*; pavot *m*

Popsicle ® ['pɔpsɪkl] (*US*) *n* esquimau *m* (*glace*)

popular ['pɔpjulə^r] *adj* populaire; (*fashionable*) à la mode

population [pɔpju'leɪʃən] *n* population *f*

porcelain ['pɔ:slɪn] *n* porcelaine *f*

porch [pɔ:tʃ] *n* porche *m*; (*US*) véranda *f*

porcupine ['pɔ:kjupaɪn] *n* porc-épic *m*

pore [pɔ:^r] *n* pore *m* ♦ *vi*: **to ~ over** s'absorber dans, être plongé(e) dans

pork [pɔ:k] *n* porc *m*

porn [pɔ:n] (*inf*) *adj, n* porno *m*

pornographic [pɔ:nə'græfɪk] *adj* pornographique

pornography [pɔ:'nɔgrəfɪ] *n* pornographie *f*

porpoise ['pɔ:pəs] *n* marsouin *m*

porridge ['pɔrɪdʒ] *n* porridge *m*

port [pɔ:t] *n* (*harbour*) port *m*; (*NAUT: left side*) bâbord *m*; (*wine*) porto *m*; **~ of call** escale *f*

portable ['pɔ:təbl] *adj* portatif(-ive)

porter ['pɔ:tə^r] *n* (*for luggage*) porteur *m*; (*doorkeeper*) gardien(ne); portier *m*

portfolio [pɔ:t'fəulɪəu] *n* portefeuille *m*; (*of artist*) portfolio *m*

porthole ['pɔ:thəul] *n* hublot *m*

portion ['pɔ:ʃən] *n* portion *f*, part *f*

portrait ['pɔ:treɪt] *n* portrait *m*

portray [pɔ:'treɪ] *vt* faire le portrait de; (*in writing*) dépeindre, représenter; (*subj: actor*) jouer

Portugal ['pɔ:tjugl] *n* Portugal *m*; **Por-**

tuguese [pɔːtjuˈgiːz] *adj* portugais(e) ♦ *n inv* Portugais(e); (*LING*) portugais *m*

pose [pəuz] *n* pose *f* ♦ *vi* (*pretend*): **to ~ as** se poser en ♦ *vt* poser; (*problem*) créer

posh [pɔʃ] (*inf*) *adj* chic *inv*

position [pəˈzɪʃən] *n* position *f*; (*job*) situation *f* ♦ *vt* placer

positive [ˈpɔzɪtɪv] *adj* positif(-ive); (*certain*) sûr(e), certain(e); (*definite*) formel(le), catégorique

possess [pəˈzɛs] *vt* posséder; **~ion** *n* possession *f*

possibility [pɔsɪˈbɪlɪtɪ] *n* possibilité *f*; éventualité *f*

possible [ˈpɔsɪbl] *adj* possible; **as big as ~** aussi gros que possible; **possibly** *adv* (*perhaps*) peut-être; **if you possibly can** si cela vous est possible; **I cannot possibly come** il m'est impossible de venir

post [pəust] *n* poste *f*; (*BRIT*: *letters, delivery*) courrier *m*; (*job, situation, MIL*) poste *m*; (*pole*) poteau *m* ♦ *vt* (*BRIT*: *send by* ~) poster; (: *appoint*): **to ~ to** affecter à; **~age** *n* tarifs *mpl* d'affranchissement; **~al order** *n* mandat(-poste) *m*; **~box** (*BRIT*) *n* boîte *f* aux lettres; **~card** *n* carte postale; **~code** (*BRIT*) *n* code postal

poster [ˈpəustəʳ] *n* affiche *f*

poste restante [pəustˈrɛstɑ̃ːnt] (*BRIT*) *n* poste restante

postgraduate [ˈpəustˈgrædjuət] *n* ≃ étudiant(e) de troisième cycle

posthumous [ˈpɔstjuməs] *adj* posthume

postman [ˈpəustmən] (*irreg*) *n* facteur *m*

postmark [ˈpəustmɑːk] *n* cachet *m* (de la poste)

postmortem [pəustˈmɔːtəm] *n* autopsie *f*

post office *n* (*building*) poste *f*; (*organization*): **the P~ O~** les Postes; **~ ~ box** *n* boîte postale

postpone [pəusˈpəun] *vt* remettre (à plus tard)

posture [ˈpɔstʃəʳ] *n* posture *f*; (*fig*) attitude *f*

postwar [pəustˈwɔːʳ] *adj* d'après-guerre

postwoman *n* factrice *f*

posy [ˈpəuzɪ] *n* petit bouquet

pot [pɔt] *n* pot *m*; (*for cooking*) marmite *f*; casserole *f*; (*teapot*) théière *f*; (*coffeepot*) cafetière *f*; (*inf*: *marijuana*) herbe *f* ♦ *vt* (*plant*) mettre en pot; **to go to ~** (*inf*: *work, performance*) aller à vau-l'eau

potato [pəˈteɪtəu] (*pl* **~es**) *n* pomme *f* de terre; **~ peeler** *n* épluche-légumes *m inv*

potent [ˈpəutnt] *adj* puissant(e); (*drink*) fort(e), très alcoolisé(e); (*man*) viril

potential [pəˈtɛnʃl] *adj* potentiel(le) ♦ *n* potentiel *m*

pothole [ˈpɔthəul] *n* (*in road*) nid *m* de poule; (*BRIT*: *underground*) gouffre *m*, caverne *f*; **potholing** (*BRIT*) *n*: **to go potholing** faire de la spéléologie

potluck [pɔtˈlʌk] *n*: **to take ~** tenter sa chance

pot plant *n* plante *f* d'appartement

potted [ˈpɔtɪd] *adj* (*food*) en conserve; (*plant*) en pot; (*abbreviated*) abrégé(e)

potter [ˈpɔtəʳ] *n* potier *m* ♦ *vi*: **to ~ around, ~ about** (*BRIT*) bricoler; **~y** *n* poterie *f*

potty [ˈpɔtɪ] *adj* (*inf*: *mad*) dingue ♦ *n* (*child's*) pot *m*

pouch [pautʃ] *n* (*ZOOL*) poche *f*; (*for tobacco*) blague *f*; (*for money*) bourse *f*

poultry [ˈpəultrɪ] *n* volaille *f*

pounce [pauns] *vi*: **to ~ (on)** bondir (sur), sauter (sur)

pound [paund] *n* (*unit of money*) livre *f*; (*unit of weight*) livre ♦ *vt* (*beat*) bourrer de coups, marteler; (*crush*) piler, pulvériser ♦ *vi* (*heart*) battre violemment, taper

pour [pɔːʳ] *vt* verser ♦ *vi* couler à flots; **to ~ (with rain)** pleuvoir à verse; **to ~ sb a drink** verser *or* servir à boire à qn; **~ away** *vt* vider; **~ in** *vi* (*people*) affluer, se précipiter; (*news, letters etc*) arriver en masse; **~ off** *vt* = **pour away**; **~ out** *vi* (*people*) sortir en masse ♦ *vt* vider; (*fig*) déverser; (*serve*: *a drink*) verser; **~ing** ['pɔːrɪŋ] *adj*: **~ing rain** pluie torrentielle

pout [paut] *vi* faire la moue

poverty ['pɔvətɪ] *n* pauvreté *f*, misère *f*; **~-stricken** *adj* pauvre, déshérité(e)

powder ['paudəʳ] *n* poudre *f* ♦ *vt*: **to ~ one's face** se poudrer; **~ compact** *n* poudrier *m*; **~ed milk** *n* lait *m* en poudre; **~ room** *n* toilettes *fpl* (pour dames)

power ['pauəʳ] *n* (*strength*) puissance *f*, force *f*; (*ability, authority*) pouvoir *m*; (*of speech, thought*) faculté *f*; (ELEC) courant *m*; **to be in ~** (POL *etc*) être au pouvoir; **~ cut** (BRIT) *n* coupure *f* de courant; **~ed** *adj*: **~ed by** actionné(e) par, fonctionnant à; **~ failure** *n* panne *f* de courant; **~ful** *adj* puissant(e); **~less** *adj* impuissant(e); **~ point** (BRIT) *n* prise *f* de courant; **~ station** *n* centrale *f* électrique; **~ struggle** *n* lutte *f* pour le pouvoir

p.p. *abbr* (= *per procurationem*): **p.p. J. Smith** pour M. J. Smith

PR *n abbr* = **public relations**

practical ['præktɪkl] *adj* pratique; **~ity** [præktɪ'kælɪtɪ] (*no pl*) *n* (*of person*) sens *m* pratique; **~ities** *npl* (*of situation*) aspect *m* pratique; **~ joke** *n* farce *f*; **~ly** *adv* (*almost*) pratiquement

practice ['præktɪs] *n* pratique *f*; (*of profession*) exercice *m*; (*at football etc*) entraînement *m*; (*business*) cabinet *m* ♦ *vt, vi* (US) = **practise**; **in ~** (*in reality*) en pratique; **out of ~** rouillé(e)

practise ['præktɪs] (US **practice**) *vt* (*musical instrument*) travailler; (*train for*: *sport*) s'entraîner à; (*a sport, religion*) pratiquer; (*profession*) exercer ♦ *vi* s'exercer, travailler; (*train*) s'entraîner; (*lawyer, doctor*) exercer; **practising** *adj* (*Christian etc*) pratiquant(e); (*lawyer*) en exercice

practitioner [præk'tɪʃənəʳ] *n* praticien(ne)

prairie ['prɛərɪ] *n* steppe *f*, prairie *f*

praise [preɪz] *n* éloge(s) *m(pl)*, louange(s) *f(pl)* ♦ *vt* louer, faire l'éloge de; **~worthy** *adj* digne d'éloges

pram [præm] (BRIT) *n* landau *m*, voiture *f* d'enfant

prance [prɑːns] *vi* (*also*: **~ about**: *person*) se pavaner

prank [præŋk] *n* farce *f*

prawn [prɔːn] *n* crevette *f* (rose); **~ cocktail** *n* cocktail *m* de crevettes

pray [preɪ] *vi* prier; **~er** [prɛəʳ] *n* prière *f*

preach [priːtʃ] *vt, vi* prêcher

precaution [prɪ'kɔːʃən] *n* précaution *f*

precede [prɪ'siːd] *vt* précéder

precedent ['prɛsɪdənt] *n* précédent *m*

preceding *adj* qui précède/précédait *etc*

precinct ['priːsɪŋkt] *n* (US) circonscription *f*, arrondissement *m*; **~s** *npl* (*neighbourhood*) alentours *mpl*, environs *mpl*; **pedestrian ~** (BRIT) zone piétonnière *or* piétonne; **shopping ~** (BRIT) centre commercial

precious ['prɛʃəs] *adj* précieux(-euse)

precipitate [prɪ'sɪpɪteɪt] *vt* précipiter

precise [prɪ'saɪs] *adj* précis(e); **~ly** *adv* précisément

precocious [prɪ'kəuʃəs] *adj* précoce

precondition ['priːkən'dɪʃən] *n* condition *f* nécessaire

predecessor ['priːdɪsɛsəʳ] *n* prédécesseur *m*

predicament [prɪ'dɪkəmənt] *n* situation *f* difficile

predict [prɪ'dɪkt] *vt* prédire; **~able** *adj* prévisible

predominantly [prɪ'dɔmɪnəntlɪ] *adv* en majeure partie; surtout

pre-empt [priː'ɛmt] *vt* anticiper, devancer

preen [priːn] *vt*: **to ~ itself** (*bird*) se lisser les plumes; **to ~ o.s.** s'admirer

prefab ['priːfæb] *n* bâtiment préfabriqué

preface ['prɛfəs] *n* préface *f*

prefect ['pri:fɛkt] (BRIT) *n* (*in school*) élève chargé(e) de certaines fonctions de discipline

prefer [prɪ'fə:ʳ] *vt* préférer; **~ably** ['prɛfrəblɪ] *adv* de préférence; **~ence** ['prɛfrəns] *n* préférence *f*; **~ential** [prɛfə'rɛnʃəl] *adj*: **~ential treatment** traitement *m* de faveur *or* préférentiel

prefix ['pri:fɪks] *n* préfixe *m*

pregnancy ['prɛgnənsɪ] *n* grossesse *f*

pregnant ['prɛgnənt] *adj* enceinte; (*animal*) pleine

prehistoric ['pri:hɪs'tɔrɪk] *adj* préhistorique

prejudice ['prɛdʒudɪs] *n* préjugé *m*; **~d** *adj* (*person*) plein(e) de préjugés; (*in a matter*) partial(e)

premarital ['pri:'mærɪtl] *adj* avant le mariage

premature ['prɛmətʃuəʳ] *adj* prématuré(e)

premenstrual syndrome [pri:'mɛnstruəl-] *n* syndrome prémenstruel

premier ['prɛmɪəʳ] *adj* premier(-ère), principal(e) ♦ *n* (POL) Premier ministre

première ['prɛmɪɛəʳ] *n* première *f*

Premier League *n* première division

premise ['prɛmɪs] *n* prémisse *f*; **~s** *npl* (*building*) locaux *mpl*; **on the ~s** sur les lieux; sur place

premium ['pri:mɪəm] *n* prime *f*; **to be at a ~** faire prime; **~ bond** (BRIT) *n* bon *m* à lot, obligation *f* à prime

premonition [prɛmə'nɪʃən] *n* prémonition *f*

preoccupied [pri:'ɔkjupaɪd] *adj* préoccupé(e)

prep [prɛp] *n* (SCOL) étude *f*

prepaid [pri:'peɪd] *adj* payé(e) d'avance

preparation [prɛpə'reɪʃən] *n* préparation *f*; **~s** *npl* (*for trip, war*) préparatifs *mpl*

preparatory [prɪ'pærətərɪ] *adj* préliminaire; **~ school** (BRIT) *n* école primaire privée

prepare [prɪ'pɛəʳ] *vt* préparer ♦ *vi*: **to ~ for** se préparer à; **~d to** prêt(e) à

preposition [prɛpə'zɪʃən] *n* préposition *f*

preposterous [prɪ'pɔstərəs] *adj* absurde

prep school *n* = **preparatory school**

prerequisite [pri:'rɛkwɪzɪt] *n* condition *f* préalable

Presbyterian [prɛzbɪ'tɪərɪən] *adj, n* presbytérien(ne) *m/f*

prescribe [prɪ'skraɪb] *vt* prescrire; **prescription** [prɪ'skrɪpʃən] *n* (MED) ordonnance *f*; (: *medicine*) médicament (obtenu sur ordonnance)

presence ['prɛzns] *n* présence *f*; **~ of mind** présence d'esprit

present [*adj, n* 'prɛznt, *vb* prɪ'zɛnt] *adj* présent(e) ♦ *n* (*gift*) cadeau *m*; (*actuality*) présent *m* ♦ *vt* présenter; (*prize, medal*) remettre; (*give*): **to ~ sb with sth** *or* **sth to sb** offrir qch à qn; **to give sb a ~** offrir un cadeau à qn; **at ~** en ce moment; **~ation** [prɛzn'teɪʃən] *n* présentation *f*; (*ceremony*) remise *f* du cadeau (*or* de la médaille *etc*); **~-day** *adj* contemporain(e), actuel(le); **~er** *n* (RADIO, TV) présentateur(-trice); **~ly** *adv* (*with verb in past*) peu après; (*soon*) tout à l'heure, bientôt; (*at present*) en ce moment

preservative [prɪ'zə:vətɪv] *n* agent *m* de conservation

preserve [prɪ'zə:v] *vt* (*keep safe*) préserver, protéger; (*maintain*) conserver, garder; (*food*) mettre en conserve ♦ *n* (*often pl*: *jam*) confiture *f*

president ['prɛzɪdənt] *n* président(e); **~ial** [prɛzɪ'dɛnʃl] *adj* présidentiel(le)

press [prɛs] *n* presse *f*; (*for wine*) pressoir *m* ♦ *vt* (*squeeze*) presser, serrer; (*push*) appuyer sur; (*clothes*: *iron*) repasser; (*put ~ure on*) faire pression sur; (*insist*): **to ~ sth on sb** presser qn d'accepter qch ♦ *vi* appuyer, peser; **to ~ for sth** faire pression pour obtenir qch; **we are ~ed for time/money** le temps/l'argent nous manque; **~ on** *vi* continuer; **~ conference** *n* conférence *f* de presse; **~ing** *adj* urgent(e), pressant(e); **~ stud** (*BRIT*) *n* bouton-pression *m*; **~-up** (*BRIT*) *n* traction *f*

pressure ['prɛʃəʳ] *n* pression *f*; (*stress*) tension *f*; **to put ~ on sb (to do)** faire pression sur qn (pour qu'il/elle fasse); **~ cooker** *n* cocotte-minute *f*; **~ gauge** *n* manomètre *m*; **~ group** *n* groupe *m* de pression

prestige [prɛs'ti:ʒ] *n* prestige *m*; **prestigious** [prɛs'tɪdʒəs] *adj* prestigieux(-euse)

presumably [prɪ'zju:məblɪ] *adv* vraisemblablement

presume [prɪ'zju:m] *vt* présumer, supposer

pretence [prɪ'tɛns] (*US* **pretense**) *n* (*claim*) prétention *f*; **under false ~s** sous des prétextes fallacieux

pretend [prɪ'tɛnd] *vt* (*feign*) feindre, simuler ♦ *vi* faire semblant

pretext ['pri:tɛkst] *n* prétexte *m*

pretty ['prɪtɪ] *adj* joli(e) ♦ *adv* assez

prevail [prɪ'veɪl] *vi* (*be usual*) avoir cours; (*win*) l'emporter, prévaloir; **~ing** *adj* dominant(e); **prevalent** ['prɛvələnt] *adj* répandu(e), courant(e)

prevent [prɪ'vɛnt] *vt*: **to ~ (from doing)** empêcher (de faire); **~ative** [prɪ'vɛntətɪv], **~ive** [prɪ'vɛntɪv] *adj* préventif(-ive)

preview ['pri:vju:] *n* (*of film etc*) avant-première *f*

previous ['pri:vɪəs] *adj* précédent(e); antérieur(e); **~ly** *adv* précédemment, auparavant

prewar [pri:'wɔ:ʳ] *adj* d'avant-guerre

prey [preɪ] *n* proie *f* ♦ *vi*: **to ~ on** s'attaquer à; **it was ~ing on his mind** cela le travaillait

price [praɪs] *n* prix *m* ♦ *vt* (*goods*) fixer le prix de; **~less** *adj* sans prix, inestimable; **~ list** *n* liste *f* des prix, tarif *m*

prick [prɪk] *n* piqûre *f* ♦ *vt* piquer; **to ~ up one's ears** dresser *or* tendre l'oreille

prickle ['prɪkl] *n* (*of plant*) épine *f*; (*sensation*) picotement *m*; **prickly** *adj* piquant(e), épineux(-euse); **prickly heat** *n* fièvre *f* miliaire

pride [praɪd] *n* orgueil *m*; fierté *f* ♦ *vt*: **to ~ o.s. on** se flatter de; s'enorgueillir de

priest [pri:st] *n* prêtre *m*; **~hood** *n* prêtrise *f*, sacerdoce *m*

prim [prɪm] *adj* collet monté *inv*, guindé(e)

primarily ['praɪmərɪlɪ] *adv* principalement, essentiellement

primary ['praɪmərɪ] *adj* (*first in importance*) premier(-ère), primordial(e), principal(e) ♦ *n* (*US*: *election*) (élection *f*) primaire *f*; **~ school** (*BRIT*) *n* école primaire *f*

prime [praɪm] *adj* primordial(e), fondamental(e); (*excellent*) excellent(e) ♦ *n*: **in the ~ of life** dans la fleur de l'âge ♦ *vt* (*wood*) apprêter; (*fig*) mettre au courant; **P~ Minister** *n* Premier ministre *m*

primeval *adj* primitif(-ive); **~ forest** forêt *f* vierge

primitive ['prɪmɪtɪv] *adj* primitif(-ive)

primrose ['prɪmrəuz] *n* primevère *f*

primus (stove) ® ['praɪməs-] (*BRIT*) *n* réchaud *m* de camping

prince [prɪns] *n* prince *m*

princess [prɪn'sɛs] *n* princesse *f*

principal ['prɪnsɪpl] *adj* principal(e) ♦ *n* (*headmaster*) directeur(-trice), principal *m*

principle ['prɪnsɪpl] *n* principe *m*; **in/on ~** en/par principe

print [prɪnt] *n* (*mark*) empreinte *f*; (*letters*) caractères *mpl*; (*ART*) gravure *f*, estampe *f*; (: *photograph*) photo *f* ♦ *vt* imprimer; (*publish*) publier; (*write in block letters*) écrire en caractères d'imprimerie; **out of ~** épuisé(e); **~ed matter** *n* imprimé(s) *m(pl)*; **~er** *n* imprimeur *m*; (*machine*) imprimante *f*; **~ing** *n* impression *f*; **~-out** *n* copie *f* papier

prior ['praɪəʳ] *adj* antérieur(e), précédent(e); (*more important*) prioritaire ♦ *adv*: ~ **to doing** avant de faire; **~ity** [praɪ'ɔrɪtɪ] *n* priorité *f*

prise [praɪz] *vt*: **to ~ open** forcer

prison ['prɪzn] *n* prison *f* ♦ *cpd* pénitentiaire; **~er** *n* prisonnier(-ère)

pristine ['prɪsti:n] *adj* parfait(e)

privacy ['prɪvəsɪ] *n* intimité *f*, solitude *f*

private ['praɪvɪt] *adj* privé(e); (*personal*) personnel(le); (*house, lesson*) particulier(-ère); (*quiet*: *place*) tranquille; (*reserved*: *person*) secret(-ète) ♦ *n* soldat *m* de deuxième classe; **"~"** (*on envelope*) "personnelle"; **in ~** en privé; **~ detective** *n* détective privé; **~ enterprise** *n* l'entreprise privée; **~ property** *n* propriété privée; **privatize** *vt* privatiser

privet ['prɪvɪt] *n* troène *m*

privilege ['prɪvɪlɪdʒ] *n* privilège *m*

privy ['prɪvɪ] *adj*: **to be ~ to** être au courant de

prize [praɪz] *n* prix *m* ♦ *adj* (*example, idiot*) parfait(e); (*bull, novel*) primé(e) ♦ *vt* priser, faire grand cas de; **~-giving** *n* distribution *f* des prix; **~winner** *n* gagnant(e)

pro [prəu] *n* (SPORT) professionnel(le); **the ~s and cons** le pour et le contre

probability [prɔbə'bɪlɪtɪ] *n* probabilité *f*

probable ['prɔbəbl] *adj* probable; **probably** *adv* probablement

probation [prə'beɪʃən] *n*: **on ~** (LAW) en liberté surveillée, en sursis; (*employee*) à l'essai

probe [prəub] *n* (MED, SPACE) sonde *f*; (*enquiry*) enquête *f*, investigation *f* ♦ *vt* sonder, explorer

problem ['prɔbləm] *n* problème *m*

procedure [prə'si:dʒə^r] *n* (ADMIN, LAW) procédure *f*; (*method*) marche *f* à suivre, façon *f* de procéder

proceed [prə'si:d] *vi* continuer; (*go forward*) avancer; **to ~ (with)** continuer, poursuivre; **to ~ to do** se mettre à faire; **~ings** *npl* (LAW) poursuites *fpl*; (*meeting*) réunion *f*, séance *f*; **~s** ['prəusi:dz] *npl* produit *m*, recette *f*

process ['prəusɛs] *n* processus *m*; (*method*) procédé *m* ♦ *vt* traiter; **~ing** *n* (PHOT) développement *m*; **~ion** [prə'sɛʃən] *n* défilé *m*, cortège *m*; (REL) procession *f*; **funeral ~ion** (*on foot*) cortège *m* funèbre; (*in cars*) convoi *m* mortuaire

proclaim [prə'kleɪm] *vt* déclarer, proclamer

procrastinate [prəu'kræstɪneɪt] *vi* faire traîner les choses, vouloir tout remettre au lendemain

procure [prə'kjuə^r] *vt* obtenir

prod [prɔd] *vt* pousser

prodigal ['prɔdɪgl] *adj* prodigue

prodigy ['prɔdɪdʒɪ] *n* prodige *m*

produce [*n* 'prɔdju:s, *vb* prə'dju:s] *n* (AGR) produits *mpl* ♦ *vt* produire; (*to show*) présenter; (*cause*) provoquer, causer; (THEATRE) monter, mettre en scène; **~r** *n* producteur *m*; (THEATRE) metteur *m* en scène

product ['prɔdʌkt] *n* produit *m*

production [prə'dʌkʃən] *n* production *f*; (THEATRE) mise *f* en scène; **~ line** *n* chaîne *f* (de fabrication)

productivity [prɔdʌk'tɪvɪtɪ] *n* productivité *f*

profession [prə'fɛʃən] *n* profession *f*; **~al** *n* professionnel(le) ♦ *adj* professionnel(le); (*work*) de professionnel; **~ally** *adv* professionnellement; (SPORT: *play*) en professionnel; **she sings ~ally** c'est une chanteuse professionnelle; **I only know him ~ally** je n'ai avec lui que des relations de travail

professor [prə'fɛsə^r] *n* professeur *m* (*titulaire d'une chaire*)

proficiency [prə'fɪʃənsɪ] *n* compétence *f*, aptitude *f*

profile ['prəufaɪl] *n* profil *m*

profit ['prɔfɪt] *n* bénéfice *m*; profit *m* ♦ *vi*: **to ~ (by** *or* **from)** profiter (de); **~able** *adj* lucratif(-ive), rentable

profound [prə'faund] *adj* profond(e)

profusely [prə'fju:slɪ] *adv* abondamment; avec effusion

prognosis [prɔg'nəusɪs] (*pl* **prognoses**) *n* pronostic *m*

programme ['prəugræm] (*US* **program**) *n* programme *m*; (*RADIO, TV*) émission *f* ♦ *vt* programmer; **~r** (*US* **programer**) *n* programmeur(-euse); **programming** (*US* **programing**) *n* programmation *f*

progress [*n* 'prəugrɛs, *vb* prə'grɛs] *n* progrès *m(pl)* ♦ *vi* progresser, avancer; **in ~** en cours; **~ive** [prə'grɛsɪv] *adj* progressif(-ive); (*person*) progressiste

prohibit [prə'hɪbɪt] *vt* interdire, défendre

project [*n* 'prɔdʒɛkt, *vb* prə'dʒɛkt] *n* (*plan*) projet *m*, plan *m*; (*venture*) opération *f*, entreprise *f*; (*research*) étude *f*, dossier *m* ♦ *vt* projeter ♦ *vi* faire saillie, s'avancer; **~ion** *n* projection *f*; (*overhang*) saillie *f*; **~or** *n* projecteur *m*

prolong [prə'lɔŋ] *vt* prolonger

prom [prɔm] *n abbr* = **promenade**; (*US: ball*) bal *m* d'étudiants

promenade [prɔmə'nɑːd] *n* (*by sea*) esplanade *f*, promenade *f*; **~ concert** (*BRIT*) *n* concert *m* populaire (de musique classique)

promenade concert

En Grande-Bretagne, un **promenade concert** *(ou* **prom***) est un concert de musique classique, ainsi appelé car, à l'origine, le public restait debout et se promenait au lieu de rester assis. De nos jours, une partie du public reste debout, mais il y a également des places assises (plus chères). Les Proms les plus connus sont les Proms londoniens. La dernière séance (the Last Night of the Proms) est un grand événement médiatique où se jouent des airs traditionnels et patriotiques. Aux États-Unis et au Canada, le* **prom** *ou* **promenade** *est un bal organisé par le lycée.*

prominent ['prɔmɪnənt] *adj* (*standing out*) proéminent(e); (*important*) important(e)

promiscuous [prə'mɪskjuəs] *adj* (*sexually*) de mœurs légères

promise ['prɔmɪs] *n* promesse *f* ♦ *vt, vi* promettre; **promising** *adj* prometteur(-euse)

promote [prə'məut] *vt* promouvoir; (*new product*) faire la promotion de; **~r** *n* (*of event*) organisateur(-trice); (*of cause, idea*) promoteur(-trice); **promotion** *n* promotion *f*

prompt [prɔmpt] *adj* rapide ♦ *adv* (*punctually*) à l'heure ♦ *n* (*COMPUT*) message *m* (de guidage) ♦ *vt* provoquer; (*person*) inciter, pousser; (*THEATRE*) souffler (son rôle *or* ses répliques) à; **~ly** *adv* rapidement, sans délai; ponctuellement

prone [prəun] *adj* (*lying*) couché(e) (face contre terre); **~ to** enclin(e) à

prong [prɔŋ] *n* (*of fork*) dent *f*

pronoun ['prəunaun] *n* pronom *m*

pronounce [prə'nauns] *vt* prononcer; **pronunciation** [prənʌnsɪ'eɪʃən] *n* prononciation *f*

proof [pruːf] *n* preuve *f*; (*TYP*) épreuve *f* ♦ *adj*: **~ against** à l'épreuve de

prop [prɔp] *n* support *m*, étai *m*; (*fig*) soutien *m* ♦ *vt* (*also:* **~ up**) étayer, soutenir; (*lean*): **to ~ sth against** appuyer qch contre *or* à

propaganda [prɔpə'gændə] *n* propagande *f*

propel [prə'pɛl] *vt* propulser, faire avancer; **~ler** *n* hélice *f*

propensity [prə'pɛnsɪtɪ] *n*: **a ~ for** *or* **to/to do** une propension à/à faire

proper ['prɔpə[r]] *adj* (*suited, right*) approprié(e), bon (bonne); (*seemly*) correct(e), convenable; (*authentic*) vrai(e), véritable; (*referring to place*): **the village ~** le village proprement dit; **~ly** *adv* correctement, convenablement; **~ noun** *n* nom *m* propre

property ['prɔpətɪ] *n* propriété *f*;

(*things owned*) biens *mpl*; propriété(s) *f(pl)*; (*land*) terres *fpl*
prophecy ['prɔfɪsɪ] *n* prophétie *f*
prophesy ['prɔfɪsaɪ] *vt* prédire
prophet ['prɔfɪt] *n* prophète *m*
proportion [prə'pɔːʃən] *n* proportion *f*; (*share*) part *f*; partie *f*; **~al, ~ate** *adj* proportionnel(le)
proposal [prə'pəuzl] *n* proposition *f*, offre *f*; (*plan*) projet *m*; (*of marriage*) demande *f* en mariage
propose [prə'pəuz] *vt* proposer, suggérer ♦ *vi* faire sa demande en mariage; **to ~ to do** avoir l'intention de faire; **proposition** [prɔpə'zɪʃən] *n* proposition *f*
proprietor [prə'praɪətə^r] *n* propriétaire *m/f*
propriety [prə'praɪətɪ] *n* (*seemliness*) bienséance *f*, convenance *f*
prose [prəuz] *n* (*not poetry*) prose *f*
prosecute ['prɔsɪkjuːt] *vt* poursuivre; **prosecution** [prɔsɪ'kjuːʃən] *n* poursuites *fpl* judiciaires; (*accusing side*) partie plaignante; **prosecutor** *n* (*US*: *plaintiff*) plaignant(e); (*also*: **public prosecutor**) procureur *m*, ministère public
prospect [*n* 'prɔspɛkt, *vb* prə'spɛkt] *n* perspective *f* ♦ *vt, vi* prospecter; **~s** *npl* (*for work etc*) possibilités *fpl* d'avenir, débouchés *mpl*; **~ing** *n* (*for gold, oil etc*) prospection *f*; **~ive** *adj* (*possible*) éventuel(le); (*future*) futur(e)
prospectus [prə'spɛktəs] *n* prospectus *m*
prosperity [prɔ'spɛrɪtɪ] *n* prospérité *f*
prostitute ['prɔstɪtjuːt] *n* prostitué(e)
protect [prə'tɛkt] *vt* protéger; **~ion** *n* protection *f*; **~ive** *adj* protecteur(-trice); (*clothing*) de protection
protein ['prəutiːn] *n* protéine *f*
protest [*n* 'prəutɛst, *vb* prə'tɛst] *n* protestation *f* ♦ *vi, vt*: **to ~ (that)** protester (que)
Protestant ['prɔtɪstənt] *adj, n* protestant(e)
protester [prə'tɛstə^r] *n* manifestant(e)
protracted [prə'træktɪd] *adj* prolongé(e)
protrude [prə'truːd] *vi* avancer, dépasser
proud [praud] *adj* fier(-ère); (*pej*) orgueilleux(-euse)
prove [pruːv] *vt* prouver, démontrer ♦ *vi*: **to ~ (to be) correct** *etc* s'avérer juste *etc*; **to ~ o.s.** montrer ce dont on est capable
proverb ['prɔvəːb] *n* proverbe *m*
provide [prə'vaɪd] *vt* fournir; **to ~ sb with sth** fournir qch à qn; **~ for** *vt fus* (*person*) subvenir aux besoins de; (*future event*) prévoir; **~d (that)** *conj* à condition que *+sub*; **providing** *conj*: **providing (that)** à condition que *+sub*
province ['prɔvɪns] *n* province *f*; (*fig*) domaine *m*; **provincial** [prə'vɪnʃəl] *adj* provincial(e)
provision [prə'vɪʒən] *n* (*supplying*) fourniture *f*; approvisionnement *m*; (*stipulation*) disposition *f*; **~s** *npl* (*food*) provisions *fpl*; **~al** *adj* provisoire
proviso [prə'vaɪzəu] *n* condition *f*
provocative [prə'vɔkətɪv] *adj* provocateur(-trice), provocant(e)
provoke [prə'vəuk] *vt* provoquer
prowess ['prauɪs] *n* prouesse *f*
prowl [praul] *vi* (*also*: **~ about, ~ around**) rôder ♦ *n*: **on the ~** à l'affût; **~er** *n* rôdeur(-euse)
proxy ['prɔksɪ] *n* procuration *f*
prudent ['pruːdnt] *adj* prudent(e)
prune [pruːn] *n* pruneau *m* ♦ *vt* élaguer
pry [praɪ] *vi*: **to ~ into** fourrer son nez dans
PS *n abbr* (= *postscript*) p.s.
psalm [sɑːm] *n* psaume *m*
pseudonym ['sjuːdənɪm] *n* pseudonyme *m*
psyche ['saɪkɪ] *n* psychisme *m*
psychiatrist [saɪ'kaɪətrɪst] *n* psychiatre *m/f*
psychic ['saɪkɪk] *adj* (*also*: **~al**) (méta)psychique; (*person*) doué(e) d'un sixième sens

psychoanalyst [saɪkəu'ænəlɪst] *n* psychanalyste *m/f*
psychological [saɪkə'lɔdʒɪkl] *adj* psychologique
psychologist [saɪ'kɔlədʒɪst] *n* psychologue *m/f*
psychology [saɪ'kɔlədʒɪ] *n* psychologie *f*
PTO *abbr (= please turn over)* T.S.V.P.
pub [pʌb] *n (public house)* pub *m*

pub

Un **pub** *comprend en général deux salles: l'une ("the lounge") est plutôt confortable, avec des fauteuils et des bancs capitonnés, tandis que l'autre ("the public bar") est simplement un bar où les consommations sont en général moins chères. Cette dernière est souvent aussi une salle de jeux, les jeux les plus courants étant les fléchettes, les dominos et le billard. Il y a parfois aussi une petite arrière-salle douillette appelée "the snug". Beaucoup de pubs servent maintenant des repas, surtout à l'heure du déjeuner, et c'est alors le seul moment où les enfants sont acceptés, à condition d'être accompagnés. Les pubs sont en général ouverts de 11 h à 23 h, mais cela peut varier selon leur licence; certains pubs ferment l'après-midi.*

public ['pʌblɪk] *adj* public(-ique) ♦ *n* public *m*; **in ~** en public; **to make ~** rendre public; **~ address system** *n* (système *m* de) sonorisation *f*; hauts-parleurs *mpl*
publican ['pʌblɪkən] *n* patron *m* de pub
public: ~ company *n* société *f* anonyme (*cotée en Bourse*); **~ convenience** (*BRIT*) *n* toilettes *fpl*; **~ holiday** *n* jour férié; **~ house** (*BRIT*) *n* pub *m*
publicity [pʌb'lɪsɪtɪ] *n* publicité *f*
publicize ['pʌblɪsaɪz] *vt* faire connaître, rendre public(-ique)
public: ~ opinion *n* opinion publique; **~ relations** *n* relations publiques; **~ school** *n* (*BRIT*) école (secondaire) privée; (*US*) école publique; **~-spirited** *adj* qui fait preuve de civisme; **~ transport** *n* transports *mpl* en commun
publish ['pʌblɪʃ] *vt* publier; **~er** *n* éditeur *m*; **~ing** *n* édition *f*
pub lunch *n* repas *m* de bistrot
pucker ['pʌkə^r] *vt* plisser
pudding ['pudɪŋ] *n* pudding *m*; (*BRIT: sweet*) dessert *m*, entremets *m*; **black ~**, (*US*) **blood ~** boudin (noir)
puddle ['pʌdl] *n* flaque *f* (d'eau)
puff [pʌf] *n* bouffée *f* ♦ *vt*: **to ~ one's pipe** tirer sur sa pipe ♦ *vi* (*pant*) haleter; **~ out** *vt* (*fill with air*) gonfler; **~ pastry** (*US* **puff paste**) *n* pâte feuilletée; **~y** *adj* bouffi(e), boursouflé(e)
pull [pul] *n* (*tug*): **to give sth a ~** tirer sur qch ♦ *vt* tirer; (*trigger*) presser ♦ *vi* tirer; **to ~ to pieces** mettre en morceaux; **to ~ one's punches** ménager son adversaire; **to ~ one's weight** faire sa part (du travail); **to ~ o.s. together** se ressaisir; **to ~ sb's leg** (*fig*) faire marcher qn; **~ apart** *vt* (*break*) mettre en pièces, démantibuler; **~ down** *vt* (*house*) démolir; **~ in** *vi* (*AUT*) entrer; (*RAIL*) entrer en gare; **~ off** *vt* enlever, ôter; (*deal etc*) mener à bien, conclure; **~ out** *vi* démarrer, partir ♦ *vt* sortir; arracher; **~ over** *vi* (*AUT*) se ranger; **~ through** *vi* s'en sortir; **~ up** *vi* (*stop*) s'arrêter ♦ *vt* remonter; (*uproot*) déraciner, arracher
pulley ['pulɪ] *n* poulie *f*
pullover ['puləuvə^r] *n* pull(-over) *m*, tricot *m*
pulp [pʌlp] *n* (*of fruit*) pulpe *f*
pulpit ['pulpɪt] *n* chaire *f*
pulsate [pʌl'seɪt] *vi* battre, palpiter; (*music*) vibrer
pulse [pʌls] *n* (*of blood*) pouls *m*; (*of heart*) battement *m*; (*of music, engine*) vibrations *fpl*; (*BOT, CULIN*) légume sec
pump [pʌmp] *n* pompe *f*; (*shoe*) escar-

pin *m* ♦ *vt* pomper; **~ up** *vt* gonfler

pumpkin ['pʌmpkɪn] *n* potiron *m*, citrouille *f*

pun [pʌn] *n* jeu *m* de mots, calembour *m*

punch [pʌntʃ] *n* (*blow*) coup *m* de poing; (*tool*) poinçon *m*; (*drink*) punch *m* ♦ *vt* (*hit*): **to ~ sb/sth** donner un coup de poing à qn/sur qch; **~line** *n* (*of joke*) conclusion *f*; **~-up** (*BRIT*: *inf*) *n* bagarre *f*

punctual ['pʌŋktjuəl] *adj* ponctuel(le)

punctuation [pʌŋktju'eɪʃən] *n* ponctuation *f*

puncture ['pʌŋktʃə^r] *n* crevaison *f*

pundit ['pʌndɪt] *n* individu *m* qui pontifie, pontife *m*

pungent ['pʌndʒənt] *adj* piquant(e), âcre

punish ['pʌnɪʃ] *vt* punir; **~ment** *n* punition *f*, châtiment *m*

punk [pʌŋk] *n* (*also*: **~ rocker**) punk *m/f*; (*also*: **~ rock**) le punk rock; (*US*: *inf*: *hoodlum*) voyou *m*

punt [pʌnt] *n* (*boat*) bachot *m*

punter ['pʌntə^r] (*BRIT*) *n* (*gambler*) parieur(-euse); (*inf*): **the ~s** le public

puny ['pju:nɪ] *adj* chétif(-ive); (*effort*) piteux(-euse)

pup [pʌp] *n* chiot *m*

pupil ['pju:pl] *n* (*SCOL*) élève *m/f*; (*of eye*) pupille *f*

puppet ['pʌpɪt] *n* marionnette *f*, pantin *m*

puppy ['pʌpɪ] *n* chiot *m*, jeune chien(ne)

purchase ['pə:tʃɪs] *n* achat *m* ♦ *vt* acheter; **~r** *n* acheteur(-euse)

pure [pjuə^r] *adj* pur(e); **~ly** *adv* purement

purge [pə:dʒ] *n* purge *f* ♦ *vt* purger

purple ['pə:pl] *adj* violet(te); (*face*) cramoisi(e)

purpose ['pə:pəs] *n* intention *f*, but *m*; **on ~** exprès; **~ful** *adj* déterminé(e), résolu(e)

purr [pə:^r] *vi* ronronner

purse [pə:s] *n* (*BRIT*: *for money*) porte-monnaie *m inv*; (*US*: *handbag*) sac *m* à main ♦ *vt* serrer, pincer

purser *n* (*NAUT*) commissaire *m* du bord

pursue [pə'sju:] *vt* poursuivre; **pursuit** [pə'sju:t] *n* poursuite *f*; (*occupation*) occupation *f*, activité *f*

push [puʃ] *n* poussée *f* ♦ *vt* pousser; (*button*) appuyer sur; (*product*) faire de la publicité pour; (*thrust*): **to ~ sth (into)** enfoncer qch (dans) ♦ *vi* pousser; (*demand*): **to ~ for** exiger, demander avec insistance; **~ aside** *vt* écarter; **~ off** (*inf*) *vi* filer, ficher le camp; **~ on** *vi* (*continue*) continuer; **~ through** *vi* se frayer un chemin ♦ *vt* (*measure*) faire accepter; **~ up** *vt* (*total, prices*) faire monter; **~chair** (*BRIT*) *n* poussette *f*; **~er** *n* (*drug pusher*) revendeur(-euse) (de drogue), ravitailleur(-euse) (en drogue); **~over** (*inf*) *n*: **it's a ~over** c'est un jeu d'enfant; **~-up** (*US*) *n* traction *f*; **~y** (*pej*) *adj* arriviste

puss [pus], **pussy (cat)** ['pusɪ(kæt)] (*inf*) *n* minet *m*

put [put] (*pt, pp* **put**) *vt* mettre, poser, placer; (*say*) dire, exprimer; (*a question*) poser; (*case, view*) exposer, présenter; (*estimate*) estimer; **~ about** *vt* (*rumour*) faire courir; **~ across** *vt* (*ideas etc*) communiquer; **~ away** *vt* (*store*) ranger; **~ back** *vt* (*replace*) remettre, replacer; (*postpone*) remettre; (*delay*) retarder; **~ by** *vt* (*money*) mettre de côté, économiser; **~ down** *vt* (*parcel etc*) poser, déposer; (*in writing*) mettre par écrit, inscrire; (*suppress*: *revolt etc*) réprimer, faire cesser; (*animal*) abattre; (*dog, cat*) faire piquer; (*attribute*) attribuer; **~ forward** *vt* (*ideas*) avancer; **~ in** *vt* (*gas, electricity*) installer; (*application, complaint*) soumettre; (*time, effort*) consacrer; **~ off** *vt* (*light etc*) éteindre; (*postpone*) remettre à plus tard, ajourner; (*discourage*) dissuader; **~ on** *vt* (*clothes, lipstick, record*) mettre; (*light etc*) allumer; (*play etc*) monter; (*food*:

cook) mettre à cuire *or* à chauffer; (*gain*): **to ~ on weight** prendre du poids, grossir; **to ~ the brakes on** freiner; **to ~ the kettle on** mettre l'eau à chauffer; **~ out** *vt* (*take out*) mettre dehors; (*one's hand*) tendre; (*light etc*) éteindre; (*person*: *inconvenience*) déranger, gêner; **~ through** *vt* (TEL: *call*) passer; (: *person*) mettre en communication; (*plan*) faire accepter; **~ up** *vt* (*raise*) lever, relever, remonter; (*pin up*) afficher; (*hang*) accrocher; (*build*) construire, ériger; (*tent*) monter; (*umbrella*) ouvrir; (*increase*) augmenter; (*accommodate*) loger; **~ up with** *vt fus* supporter

putt [pʌt] *n* coup roulé; **~ing green** *n* green *m*

putty ['pʌtɪ] *n* mastic *m*

put-up ['putʌp] (BRIT) *adj*: **~-~ job** coup monté

puzzle ['pʌzl] *n* énigme *f*, mystère *m*; (*jigsaw*) puzzle *m* ♦ *vt* intriguer, rendre perplexe ♦ *vi* se creuser la tête; **~d** *adj* perplexe; **puzzling** *adj* déconcertant(e)

pyjamas [pə'dʒɑːməz] (BRIT) *npl* pyjama(s) *m(pl)*

pylon ['paɪlən] *n* pylône *m*

pyramid ['pɪrəmɪd] *n* pyramide *f*

Pyrenees [pɪrə'niːz] *npl*: **the ~** les Pyrénées *fpl*

Q, q

quack [kwæk] *n* (*of duck*) coin-coin *m inv*; (*pej*: *doctor*) charlatan *m*

quad [kwɔd] *n abbr* = **quadrangle**; **quadruplet**

quadrangle ['kwɔdræŋgl] *n* (*courtyard*) cour *f*

quadruple [kwɔ'druːpl] *vt, vi* quadrupler; **~ts** *npl* quadruplés

quail [kweɪl] *n* (ZOOL) caille *f* ♦ *vi*: **to ~ at** *or* **before** reculer devant

quaint [kweɪnt] *adj* bizarre; (*house, village*) au charme vieillot, pittoresque

quake [kweɪk] *vi* trembler

qualification [kwɔlɪfɪ'keɪʃən] *n* (*often pl*: *degree etc*) diplôme *m*; (*training*) qualification(s) *f(pl)*, expérience *f*; (*ability*) compétence(s) *f(pl)*; (*limitation*) réserve *f*, restriction *f*

qualified ['kwɔlɪfaɪd] *adj* (*trained*) qualifié(e); (*professionally*) diplômé(e); (*fit, competent*) compétent(e), qualifié(e); (*limited*) conditionnel(le)

qualify ['kwɔlɪfaɪ] *vt* qualifier; (*modify*) atténuer, nuancer ♦ *vi*: **to ~ (as)** obtenir son diplôme (de); **to ~ (for)** remplir les conditions requises (pour); (SPORT) se qualifier (pour)

quality ['kwɔlɪtɪ] *n* qualité *f*; **~ time** *n* moments privilégiés

quality (news)papers

Les **quality (news)papers** *(ou la* **quality press***) englobent les journaux sérieux, quotidiens ou hebdomadaires, par opposition aux journaux populaires (***tabloid press***). Ces journaux visent un public qui souhaite des informations détaillées sur un évantail très vaste de sujets et qui est prêt à consacrer beaucoup de temps à leur lecture. Les quality newspapers sont en général de grand format.*

qualm [kwɑːm] *n* doute *m*; scrupule *m*

quandary ['kwɔndrɪ] *n*: **in a ~** devant un dilemme, dans l'embarras

quantity ['kwɔntɪtɪ] *n* quantité *f*; **~ surveyor** *n* métreur *m* vérificateur

quarantine ['kwɔrntiːn] *n* quarantaine *f*

quarrel ['kwɔrl] *n* querelle *f*, dispute *f* ♦ *vi* se disputer, se quereller

quarry ['kwɔrɪ] *n* (*for stone*) carrière *f*; (*animal*) proie *f*, gibier *m*

quart [kwɔːt] *n* ≃ litre *m*

quarter ['kwɔːtə[r]] *n* quart *m*; (US: *coin*: *25 cents*) quart de dollar; (*of year*) trimestre *m*; (*district*) quartier *m* ♦ *vt* (*divide*) partager en quartiers *or* en quatre;

~s *npl* (*living ~*) logement *m*; (MIL) quartiers *mpl*, cantonnement *m*; **a ~ of an hour** un quart d'heure; **~ final** *n* quart *m* de finale; **~ly** *adj* trimestriel(le) ♦ *adv* tous les trois mois

quartet(te) [kwɔː'tɛt] *n* quatuor *m*; (*jazz players*) quartette *m*

quartz [kwɔːts] *n* quartz *m*

quash [kwɔʃ] *vt* (*verdict*) annuler

quaver ['kweɪvəʳ] *vi* trembler

quay [kiː] *n* (*also:* **~side**) quai *m*

queasy ['kwiːzɪ] *adj*: **to feel ~** avoir mal au cœur

queen [kwiːn] *n* reine *f*; (CARDS *etc*) dame *f*; **~ mother** *n* reine mère *f*

queer [kwɪəʳ] *adj* étrange, curieux (-euse); (*suspicious*) louche ♦ *n* (*inf!*) homosexuel *m*

quell [kwɛl] *vt* réprimer, étouffer

quench [kwɛntʃ] *vt*: **to ~ one's thirst** se désaltérer

query ['kwɪərɪ] *n* question *f* ♦ *vt* remettre en question, mettre en doute

quest [kwɛst] *n* recherche *f*, quête *f*

question ['kwɛstʃən] *n* question *f* ♦ *vt* (*person*) interroger; (*plan, idea*) remettre en question, mettre en doute; **beyond ~** sans aucun doute; **out of the ~** hors de question; **~able** *adj* discutable; **~ mark** *n* point *m* d'interrogation; **~naire** [kwɛstʃə'nɛəʳ] *n* questionnaire *m*

queue [kjuː] (BRIT) *n* queue *f*, file *f* ♦ *vi* (*also:* **~ up**) faire la queue

quibble ['kwɪbl] *vi*: **~ (about)** *or* **(over)** *or* **(with sth)** ergoter (sur qch)

quick [kwɪk] *adj* rapide; (*agile*) agile, vif (vive) ♦ *n*: **cut to the ~** (*fig*) touché(e) au vif; **be ~!** dépêche-toi!; **~en** *vt* accélérer, presser ♦ *vi* s'accélérer, devenir plus rapide; **~ly** *adv* vite, rapidement; **~sand** *n* sables mouvants; **~-witted** *adj* à l'esprit vif

quid [kwɪd] (BRIT: *inf*) *n, pl inv* livre *f*

quiet ['kwaɪət] *adj* tranquille, calme; (*voice*) bas(se); (*ceremony, colour*) discret(-ète) ♦ *n* tranquillité *f*, calme *m*; (*silence*) silence *m* ♦ *vt, vi* (US) = **quieten**; **keep ~!** tais-toi!; **~en** *vi* (*also:* **~en down**) se calmer, s'apaiser ♦ *vt* calmer, apaiser; **~ly** *adv* tranquillement, calmement; (*silently*) silencieusement; **~ness** *n* tranquillité *f*, calme *m*; (*silence*) silence *m*

quilt [kwɪlt] *n* édredon *m*; (*continental ~*) couette *f*

quin [kwɪn] *n abbr* = **quintuplet**

quintuplets [kwɪn'tjuːplɪts] *npl* quintuplé(e)s

quip [kwɪp] *n* remarque piquante *or* spirituelle, pointe *f*

quirk [kwəːk] *n* bizarrerie *f*

quit [kwɪt] (*pt, pp* **quit** *or* **quitted**) *vt* quitter; (*smoking, grumbling*) arrêter de ♦ *vi* (*give up*) abandonner, renoncer; (*resign*) démissionner

quite [kwaɪt] *adv* (*rather*) assez, plutôt; (*entirely*) complètement, tout à fait; (*following a negative = almost*): **that's not ~ big enough** ce n'est pas tout à fait assez grand; **I ~ understand** je comprends très bien; **~ a few of them** un assez grand nombre d'entre eux; **~ (so)!** exactement!

quits [kwɪts] *adj*: **~ (with)** quitte (envers); **let's call it ~** restons-en là

quiver ['kwɪvəʳ] *vi* trembler, frémir

quiz [kwɪz] *n* (*game*) jeu-concours *m* ♦ *vt* interroger; **~zical** *adj* narquois(e)

quota ['kwəutə] *n* quota *m*

quotation [kwəu'teɪʃən] *n* citation *f*; (*estimate*) devis *m*; **~ marks** *npl* guillemets *mpl*

quote [kwəut] *n* citation *f*; (*estimate*) devis *m* ♦ *vt* citer; (*price*) indiquer; **~s** *npl* guillemets *mpl*

R, r

rabbi ['ræbaɪ] *n* rabbin *m*
rabbit ['ræbɪt] *n* lapin *m*; **~ hutch** *n* clapier *m*
rabble ['ræbl] (*pej*) *n* populace *f*
rabies ['reɪbi:z] *n* rage *f*
RAC *n abbr* (*BRIT*) = *Royal Automobile Club*
rac(c)oon [rə'ku:n] *n* raton laveur
race [reɪs] *n* (*species*) race *f*; (*competition, rush*) course *f* ♦ *vt* (*horse*) faire courir ♦ *vi* (*compete*) faire la course, courir; (*hurry*) aller à toute vitesse, courir; (*engine*) s'emballer; (*pulse*) augmenter; **~ car** (*US*) *n* = **racing car**; **~ car driver** *n* (*US*) = **racing driver**; **~course** *n* champ *m* de courses; **~horse** *n* cheval *m* de course; **~r** *n* (*bike*) vélo *m* de course; **~track** *n* piste *f*
racial ['reɪʃl] *adj* racial(e)
racing ['reɪsɪŋ] *n* courses *fpl*; **~ car** (*BRIT*) *n* voiture *f* de course; **~ driver** (*BRIT*) *n* pilote *m* de course
racism ['reɪsɪzəm] *n* racisme *m*; **racist** *adj* raciste ♦ *n* raciste *m/f*
rack [ræk] *n* (*for guns, tools*) râtelier *m*; (*also*: **luggage ~**) porte-bagages *m inv*, filet *m* à bagages; (*also*: **roof ~**) galerie *f*; (*dish ~*) égouttoir *m* ♦ *vt* tourmenter; **to ~ one's brains** se creuser la cervelle
racket ['rækɪt] *n* (*for tennis*) raquette *f*; (*noise*) tapage *m*; vacarme *m*; (*swindle*) escroquerie *f*
racquet ['rækɪt] *n* raquette *f*
racy ['reɪsɪ] *adj* plein(e) de verve; (*slightly indecent*) osé(e)
radar ['reɪdɑ:ʳ] *n* radar *m*
radial ['reɪdɪəl] *adj* (*also*: **~-ply**) à carcasse radiale
radiant ['reɪdɪənt] *adj* rayonnant(e)
radiate ['reɪdɪeɪt] *vt* (*heat*) émettre, dégager; (*emotion*) rayonner de ♦ *vi* (*lines*) rayonner; **radiation** [reɪdɪ'eɪʃən] *n* rayonnement *m*; (*radioactive*) radiation *f*; **radiator** ['reɪdɪeɪtəʳ] *n* radiateur *m*
radical ['rædɪkl] *adj* radical(e)
radii ['reɪdɪaɪ] *npl of* **radius**
radio ['reɪdɪəu] *n* radio *f* ♦ *vt* appeler par radio; **on the ~** à la radio; **~active** ['reɪdɪəu'æktɪv] *adj* radioactif(-ive); **~ cassette** *n* radiocassette *m*; **~-controlled** *adj* téléguidé(e); **~ station** *n* station *f* de radio
radish ['rædɪʃ] *n* radis *m*
radius ['reɪdɪəs] (*pl* **radii**) *n* rayon *m*
RAF *n abbr* = **Royal Air Force**
raffle ['ræfl] *n* tombola *f*
raft [rɑ:ft] *n* (*craft; also*: *life ~*) radeau *m*
rafter ['rɑ:ftəʳ] *n* chevron *m*
rag [ræg] *n* chiffon *m*; (*pej*: *newspaper*) feuille *f* de chou, torchon *m*; (*student ~*) *attractions organisées au profit d'œuvres de charité*; **~s** *npl* (*torn clothes etc*) haillons *mpl*; **~ doll** *n* poupée *f* de chiffon
rage [reɪdʒ] *n* (*fury*) rage *f*, fureur *f* ♦ *vi* (*person*) être fou (folle) de rage; (*storm*) faire rage, être déchaîné(e); **it's all the ~** cela fait fureur
ragged ['rægɪd] *adj* (*edge*) inégal(e); (*clothes*) en loques; (*appearance*) déguenillé(e)
raid [reɪd] *n* (*attack, also*: *MIL*) raid *m*; (*criminal*) hold-up *m inv*; (*by police*) descente *f*, rafle *f* ♦ *vt* faire un raid sur *or* un hold-up *or* une descente dans
rail [reɪl] *n* (*on stairs*) rampe *f*; (*on bridge, balcony*) balustrade *f*; (*of ship*) bastingage *m*; **~s** *npl* (*track*) rails *mpl*, voie ferrée; **by ~** par chemin de fer, en train; **~ing(s)** *n(pl)* grille *f*; **~road** (*US*), **~way** (*BRIT*) *n* (*track*) voie ferrée; (*company*) chemin *m* de fer; **~way line** (*BRIT*) *n* ligne *f* de chemin de fer; **~wayman** (*BRIT*) (*irreg*) *n* cheminot *m*; **~way station** (*BRIT*) *n* gare *f*
rain [reɪn] *n* pluie *f* ♦ *vi* pleuvoir; **in the ~** sous la pluie; **it's ~ing** il pleut; **~bow** *n* arc-en-ciel *m*; **~coat** *n* imperméable *m*; **~drop** *n* goutte *f* de pluie; **~fall** *n* chute *f* de pluie; (*measurement*)

hauteur *f* des précipitations; **~forest** *n* forêt *f* tropicale humide; **~y** *adj* pluvieux(-euse)

raise [reɪz] *n* augmentation *f* ♦ *vt* (*lift*) lever; hausser; (*increase*) augmenter; (*morale*) remonter; (*standards*) améliorer; (*question, doubt*) provoquer, soulever; (*cattle, family*) élever; (*crop*) faire pousser; (*funds*) rassembler; (*loan*) obtenir; (*army*) lever; **to ~ one's voice** élever la voix

raisin ['reɪzn] *n* raisin sec

rake [reɪk] *n* (*tool*) râteau *m* ♦ *vt* (*garden, leaves*) ratisser

rally ['rælɪ] *n* (POL *etc*) meeting *m*, rassemblement *m*; (AUT) rallye *m*; (TENNIS) échange *m* ♦ *vt* (*support*) gagner ♦ *vi* (*sick person*) aller mieux; (*Stock Exchange*) reprendre; **~ round** *vt fus* venir en aide à

RAM [ræm] *n abbr* (= *random access memory*) mémoire vive

ram [ræm] *n* bélier *m* ♦ *vt* enfoncer; (*crash into*) emboutir; percuter

ramble ['ræmbl] *n* randonnée *f* ♦ *vi* (*walk*) se promener, faire une randonnée; (*talk: also:* **~ on**) discourir, pérorer; **~r** *n* promeneur(-euse), randonneur (-euse); (BOT) rosier grimpant; **rambling** *adj* (*speech*) décousu(e); (*house*) plein(e) de coins et de recoins; (BOT) grimpant(e)

ramp [ræmp] *n* (*incline*) rampe *f*; dénivellation *f*; **on ~, off ~** (US: AUT) bretelle *f* d'accès

rampage [ræm'peɪdʒ] *n*: **to be on the ~** se déchaîner

rampant ['ræmpənt] *adj* (*disease etc*) qui sévit

ram raiding [-reɪdɪŋ] *n pillage d'un magasin en enfonçant la vitrine avec une voiture*

ramshackle ['ræmʃækl] *adj* (*house*) délabré(e); (*car etc*) déglingué(e)

ran [ræn] *pt of* **run**

ranch [rɑːntʃ] *n* ranch *m*; **~er** *n* propriétaire *m* de ranch

rancid ['rænsɪd] *adj* rance

rancour ['ræŋkəʳ] (US **rancor**) *n* rancune *f*

random ['rændəm] *adj* fait(e) *or* établi(e) au hasard; (MATH) aléatoire ♦ *n*: **at ~** au hasard; **~ access** *n* (COMPUT) accès sélectif

randy ['rændɪ] (BRIT: *inf*) *adj* excité(e); lubrique

rang [ræŋ] *pt of* **ring**

range [reɪndʒ] *n* (*of mountains*) chaîne *f*; (*of missile, voice*) portée *f*; (*of products*) choix *m*, gamme *f*; (MIL: *also:* **shooting ~**) champ *m* de tir; (*indoor*) stand *m* de tir; (*also:* **kitchen ~**) fourneau *m* (de cuisine) ♦ *vt* (*place in a line*) mettre en rang, ranger ♦ *vi*: **to ~ over** (*extend*) couvrir; **to ~ from ... to** aller de ... à; **a ~ of** (*series: of proposals etc*) divers(e)

ranger ['reɪndʒəʳ] *n* garde forestier

rank [ræŋk] *n* rang *m*; (MIL) grade *m*; (BRIT: *also:* **taxi ~**) station *f* de taxis ♦ *vi*: **to ~ among** compter *or* se classer parmi ♦ *adj* (*stinking*) fétide, puant(e); **the ~ and file** (*fig*) la masse, la base

ransack ['rænsæk] *vt* fouiller (à fond); (*plunder*) piller

ransom ['rænsəm] *n* rançon *f*; **to hold to ~** (*fig*) exercer un chantage sur

rant [rænt] *vi* fulminer

rap [ræp] *vt* frapper sur *or* à; taper sur ♦ *n*: **~ music** rap *m*

rape [reɪp] *n* viol *m*; (BOT) colza *m* ♦ *vt* violer; **~(seed) oil** *n* huile *f* de colza

rapid ['ræpɪd] *adj* rapide; **~s** *npl* (GEO) rapides *mpl*

rapist ['reɪpɪst] *n* violeur *m*

rapport [ræ'pɔːʳ] *n* entente *f*

rapturous ['ræptʃərəs] *adj* enthousiaste, frénétique

rare [rɛəʳ] *adj* rare; (CULIN: *steak*) saignant(e)

raring ['rɛərɪŋ] *adj*: **~ to go** (*inf*) très impatient(e) de commencer

rascal ['rɑːskl] *n* vaurien *m*

rash [ræʃ] *adj* imprudent(e), irréfléchi(e)

♦ *n* (*MED*) rougeur *f*, éruption *f*; (*spate*: *of events*) série (noire)

rasher ['ræʃəʳ] *n* fine tranche (de lard)

raspberry ['rɑːzbərɪ] *n* framboise *f*; **~ bush** *n* framboisier *m*

rasping ['rɑːspɪŋ] *adj*: **~ noise** grincement *m*

rat [ræt] *n* rat *m*

rate [reɪt] *n* taux *m*; (*speed*) vitesse *f*, rythme *m*; (*price*) tarif *m* ♦ *vt* classer; évaluer; **~s** *npl* (*BRIT*: *tax*) impôts locaux; (*fees*) tarifs *mpl*; **to ~ sb/sth as** considérer qn/qch comme; **~able value** (*BRIT*) *n* valeur locative imposable; **~payer** ['reɪtpeɪəʳ] (*BRIT*) *n* contribuable *m/f* (*payant les impôts locaux*)

rather ['rɑːðəʳ] *adv* plutôt; **it's ~ expensive** c'est assez cher; (*too much*) c'est un peu cher; **there's ~ a lot** il y en a beaucoup; **I would** *or* **I'd ~ go** j'aimerais mieux *or* je préférerais partir

rating ['reɪtɪŋ] *n* (*assessment*) évaluation *f*; (*score*) classement *m*; **~s** *npl* (*RADIO, TV*) indice *m* d'écoute

ratio ['reɪʃɪəu] *n* proportion *f*

ration ['ræʃən] *n* (*gen pl*) ration(s) *f(pl)*

rational ['ræʃənl] *adj* raisonnable, sensé(e); (*solution, reasoning*) logique; **~e** [ræʃə'nɑːl] *n* raisonnement *m*; **~ize** *vt* rationaliser; (*conduct*) essayer d'expliquer *or* de motiver

rat race *n* foire *f* d'empoigne

rattle ['rætl] *n* (*of door, window*) battement *m*; (*of coins, chain*) cliquetis *m*; (*of train, engine*) bruit *m* de ferraille; (*object*: *for baby*) hochet *m* ♦ *vi* cliqueter; (*car, bus*): **to ~ along** rouler dans un bruit de ferraille ♦ *vt* agiter (bruyamment); (*unnerve*) décontenancer; **~snake** *n* serpent *m* à sonnettes

raucous ['rɔːkəs] *adj* rauque; (*noisy*) bruyant(e), tapageur(-euse)

rave [reɪv] *vi* (*in anger*) s'emporter; (*with enthusiasm*) s'extasier; (*MED*) délirer ♦ *n* (*BRIT*: *inf*: *party*) rave *f*, soirée *f* techno

raven ['reɪvən] *n* corbeau *m*

ravenous ['rævənəs] *adj* affamé(e)

ravine [rə'viːn] *n* ravin *m*

raving ['reɪvɪŋ] *adj*: **~ lunatic** ♦ *n* fou (folle) furieux(-euse)

ravishing ['rævɪʃɪŋ] *adj* enchanteur(-eresse)

raw [rɔː] *adj* (*uncooked*) cru(e); (*not processed*) brut(e); (*sore*) à vif, irrité(e); (*inexperienced*) inexpérimenté(e); (*weather, day*) froid(e) et humide; **~ deal** (*inf*) *n* sale coup *m*; **~ material** *n* matière première

ray [reɪ] *n* rayon *m*; **~ of hope** lueur *f* d'espoir

raze [reɪz] *vt* (*also:* **~ to the ground**) raser, détruire

razor *n* rasoir *m*; **~ blade** *n* lame *f* de rasoir

Rd *abbr* = **road**

RE *n abbr* = **religious education**

re [riː] *prep* concernant

reach [riːtʃ] *n* portée *f*, atteinte *f*; (*of river etc*) étendue *f* ♦ *vt* atteindre; (*conclusion, decision*) parvenir à ♦ *vi* s'étendre, étendre le bras; **out of/within ~** hors de/à portée; **within ~ of the shops** pas trop loin des *or* à proximité des magasins; **~ out** *vt* tendre ♦ *vi*: **to ~ out (for)** allonger le bras (pour prendre)

react [riː'ækt] *vi* réagir; **~ion** *n* réaction *f*

reactor [riː'æktəʳ] *n* réacteur *m*

read [riːd, *pt, pp* rɛd] (*pt, pp* **read**) *vi* lire ♦ *vt* lire; (*understand*) comprendre, interpréter; (*study*) étudier; (*meter*) relever; **~ out** *vt* lire à haute voix; **~able** *adj* facile *or* agréable à lire; (*writing*) lisible; **~er** *n* lecteur(-trice); (*BRIT*: *at university*) chargé(e) d'enseignement; **~ership** *n* (*of paper etc*) (nombre *m* de) lecteurs *mpl*

readily ['rɛdɪlɪ] *adv* volontiers, avec empressement; (*easily*) facilement

readiness ['rɛdɪnɪs] *n* empressement *m*; **in ~** (*prepared*) prêt(e)

reading ['riːdɪŋ] *n* lecture *f*; (*under-

standing) interprétation *f*; (*on instrument*) indications *fpl*

ready ['rɛdɪ] *adj* prêt(e); (*willing*) prêt, disposé(e); (*available*) disponible ♦ *n*: **at the ~** (MIL) prêt à faire feu; **to get ~** se préparer ♦ *vt* préparer; **~-made** *adj* tout(e) fait(e); **~-to-wear** *adj* prêt(e) à porter

real [rɪəl] *adj* véritable; réel(le); **in ~ terms** dans la réalité; **~ estate** *n* biens fonciers *or* immobiliers; **~istic** [rɪə'lɪstɪk] *adj* réaliste; **~ity** [riː'ælɪtɪ] *n* réalité *f*

realization [rɪəlaɪ'zeɪʃən] *n* (*awareness*) prise *f* de conscience; (*fulfilment; also: of asset*) réalisation *f*

realize ['rɪəlaɪz] *vt* (*understand*) se rendre compte de; (*a project*, COMM: *asset*) réaliser

really ['rɪəlɪ] *adv* vraiment; **~?** vraiment?, c'est vrai?

realm [rɛlm] *n* royaume *m*; (*fig*) domaine *m*

realtor ® ['rɪəltɔːʳ] (*US*) *n* agent immobilier

reap [riːp] *vt* moissonner; (*fig*) récolter

reappear [riːə'pɪəʳ] *vi* réapparaître, reparaître

rear [rɪəʳ] *adj* de derrière, arrière *inv*; (*AUT*: *wheel etc*) arrière ♦ *n* arrière *m* ♦ *vt* (*cattle, family*) élever ♦ *vi* (*also:* **~ up**: *animal*) se cabrer; **~guard** *n* (MIL) arrière-garde *f*; **~-view mirror** *n* (AUT) rétroviseur *m*

reason ['riːzn] *n* raison *f* ♦ *vi*: **to ~ with sb** raisonner qn, faire entendre raison à qn; **to have ~ to think** avoir lieu de penser; **it stands to ~ that** il va sans dire que; **~able** *adj* raisonnable; (*not bad*) acceptable; **~ably** *adv* raisonnablement; **~ing** *n* raisonnement *m*

reassurance [riːə'ʃuərəns] *n* réconfort *m*; (*factual*) assurance *f*, garantie *f*

reassure [riːə'ʃuəʳ] *vt* rassurer

rebate ['riːbeɪt] *n* (*on tax etc*) dégrèvement *m*

rebel [*n* 'rɛbl, *vb* rɪ'bɛl] *n* rebelle *m/f* ♦ *vi* se rebeller, se révolter; **~lious** [rɪ'bɛljəs] *adj* rebelle

rebound [*vb* rɪ'baund, *n* 'riːbaund] *vi* (*ball*) rebondir ♦ *n* rebond *m*; **to marry on the ~** se marier immédiatement après une déception amoureuse

rebuff [rɪ'bʌf] *n* rebuffade *f*

rebuke [rɪ'bjuːk] *vt* réprimander

rebut [rɪ'bʌt] *vt* réfuter

recall [*vb* rɪ'kɔːl, *n* 'riːkɔl] *vt* rappeler; (*remember*) se rappeler, se souvenir de ♦ *n* rappel *m*; (*ability to remember*) mémoire *f*

recant [rɪ'kænt] *vi* se rétracter; (REL) abjurer

recap ['riːkæp], **recapitulate** [riːkə'pɪtjuleɪt] *vt, vi* récapituler

rec'd *abbr* = **received**

recede [rɪ'siːd] *vi* (*tide*) descendre; (*disappear*) disparaître peu à peu; (*memory, hope*) s'estomper; **receding** *adj* (*chin*) fuyant(e); **receding hairline** front dégarni

receipt [rɪ'siːt] *n* (*document*) reçu *m*; (*for parcel etc*) accusé *m* de réception; (*act of receiving*) réception *f*; **~s** *npl* (COMM) recettes *fpl*

receive [rɪ'siːv] *vt* recevoir; **~r** *n* (TEL) récepteur *m*, combiné *m*; (RADIO) récepteur *m*; (*of stolen goods*) receleur *m*; (LAW) administrateur *m* judiciaire

recent ['riːsnt] *adj* récent(e); **~ly** *adv* récemment

receptacle [rɪ'sɛptɪkl] *n* récipient *m*

reception [rɪ'sɛpʃən] *n* réception *f*; (*welcome*) accueil *m*, réception; **~ desk** *n* réception *f*; **~ist** *n* réceptionniste *m/f*

recess [rɪ'sɛs] *n* (*in room*) renfoncement *m*, alcôve *f*; (*secret place*) recoin *m*; (POL *etc*: *holiday*) vacances *fpl*

recession [rɪ'sɛʃən] *n* récession *f*

recipe ['rɛsɪpɪ] *n* recette *f*

recipient [rɪ'sɪpɪənt] *n* (*of payment*) bénéficiaire *m/f*; (*of letter*) destinataire *m/f*

recital [rɪ'saɪtl] *n* récital *m*

recite [rɪ'saɪt] *vt* (*poem*) réciter

reckless ['rɛkləs] *adj* (*driver etc*) imprudent(e)

reckon ['rɛkən] *vt* (*count*) calculer, compter; (*think*): **I ~ that ...** je pense que ...; **~ on** *vt fus* compter sur, s'attendre à; **~ing** *n* compte *m*, calcul *m*; estimation *f*

reclaim [rɪ'kleɪm] *vt* (*demand back*) réclamer (le remboursement *or* la restitution de); (*land: from sea*) assécher; (*waste materials*) récupérer

recline [rɪ'klaɪn] *vi* être allongé(e) *or* étendu(e); **reclining** *adj* (*seat*) à dossier réglable

recluse [rɪ'klu:s] *n* reclus(e), ermite *m*

recognition [rɛkəg'nɪʃən] *n* reconnaissance *f*; **to gain ~** être reconnu(e); **transformed beyond ~** méconnaissable

recognizable ['rɛkəgnaɪzəbl] *adj*: **~ (by)** reconnaissable (à)

recognize ['rɛkəgnaɪz] *vt*: **to ~ (by/as)** reconnaître (à/comme étant)

recoil [*vb* rɪ'kɔɪl, *n* 'ri:kɔɪl] *vi* (*person*): **to ~ (from sth/doing sth)** reculer (devant qch/l'idée de faire qch) ♦ *n* (*of gun*) recul *m*

recollect [rɛkə'lɛkt] *vt* se rappeler, se souvenir de; **~ion** *n* souvenir *m*

recommend [rɛkə'mɛnd] *vt* recommander

reconcile ['rɛkənsaɪl] *vt* (*two people*) réconcilier; (*two facts*) concilier, accorder; **to ~ o.s. to** se résigner à

recondition [ri:kən'dɪʃən] *vt* remettre à neuf; réviser entièrement

reconnoitre [rɛkə'nɔɪtə^r] (*US* **reconnoiter**) *vt* (*MIL*) reconnaître

reconsider [ri:kən'sɪdə^r] *vt* reconsidérer

reconstruct [ri:kən'strʌkt] *vt* (*building*) reconstruire; (*crime, policy, system*) reconstituer

record [*n* 'rɛkɔ:d, *vb* rɪ'kɔ:d] *n* rapport *m*, récit *m*; (*of meeting etc*) procès-verbal *m*; (*register*) registre *m*; (*file*) dossier *m*; (*also:* **criminal ~**) casier *m* judiciaire; (*MUS: disc*) disque *m*; (*SPORT*) record *m*; (*COMPUT*) article *m* ♦ *vt* (*set down*) noter; (*MUS: song etc*) enregistrer; **in ~ time** en un temps record *inv*; **off the ~** ♦ *adj* officieux(-euse) ♦ *adv* officieusement; **~ card** *n* (*in file*) fiche *f*; **~ed delivery** *n* (*BRIT: POST*): **~ed delivery letter** *etc* lettre *etc* recommandée; **~er** *n* (*MUS*) flûte *f* à bec; **~ holder** *n* (*SPORT*) détenteur(-trice) du record; **~ing** *n* (*MUS*) enregistrement *m*; **~ player** *n* tourne-disque *m*

recount [rɪ'kaunt] *vt* raconter

re-count ['ri:kaunt] *n* (*POL: of votes*) deuxième compte *m*

recoup [rɪ'ku:p] *vt*: **to ~ one's losses** récupérer ce qu'on a perdu, se refaire

recourse [rɪ'kɔ:s] *n*: **to have ~ to** avoir recours à

recover [rɪ'kʌvə^r] *vt* récupérer ♦ *vi*: **to ~ (from)** (*illness*) se rétablir (de); (*from shock*) se remettre (de); **~y** *n* récupération *f*; rétablissement *m*; (*ECON*) redressement *m*

recreation [rɛkrɪ'eɪʃən] *n* récréation *f*, détente *f*; **~al** *adj* pour la détente, récréatif(-ive)

recruit [rɪ'kru:t] *n* recrue *f* ♦ *vt* recruter

rectangle ['rɛktæŋgl] *n* rectangle *m*; **rectangular** [rɛk'tæŋgjulə^r] *adj* rectangulaire

rectify ['rɛktɪfaɪ] *vt* (*error*) rectifier, corriger

rector ['rɛktə^r] *n* (*REL*) pasteur *m*

recuperate [rɪ'kju:pəreɪt] *vi* récupérer; (*from illness*) se rétablir

recur [rɪ'kə:^r] *vi* se reproduire; (*symptoms*) réapparaître; **~rence** *n* répétition *f*; réapparition *f*; **~rent** *adj* périodique, fréquent(e)

recycle [ri:'saɪkl] *vt* recycler; **recycling** *n* recyclage *m*

red [rɛd] *n* rouge *m*; (*POL: pej*) rouge *m/f* ♦ *adj* rouge; (*hair*) roux (rousse); **in the ~** (*account*) à découvert; (*business*) en déficit; **~ carpet treatment** *n* réception *f* en grande pompe; **R~ Cross** *n*

Croix-Rouge *f*; **~currant** *n* groseille *f* (rouge); **~den** *vt, vi* rougir

redecorate [riː'dɛkəreɪt] *vi* (*with wallpaper*) retapisser; (*with paint*) refaire les peintures

redeem [rɪ'diːm] *vt* (*debt*) rembourser; (*sth in pawn*) dégager; (*fig, also* REL) racheter; **~ing** *adj* (*feature*) qui sauve, qui rachète (le reste)

redeploy [riːdɪ'plɔɪ] *vt* (*resources*) réorganiser

red: ~-haired *adj* roux (rousse); **~-handed** *adj*: **to be caught ~-handed** être pris(e) en flagrant délit *or* la main dans le sac; **~head** *n* roux (rousse); **~ herring** *n* (*fig*) diversion *f*, fausse piste; **~-hot** *adj* chauffé(e) au rouge, brûlant(e)

redirect [riːdaɪ'rɛkt] *vt* (*mail*) faire suivre

red light *n*: **to go through a ~** (AUT) brûler un feu rouge; **red-light district** *n* quartier *m* des prostituées

redo [riː'duː] (*irreg*) *vt* refaire

redress [rɪ'drɛs] *n* réparation *f* ♦ *vt* redresser

red: R~ Sea *n* mer Rouge *f*; **~skin** *n* Peau-Rouge *m/f*; **~ tape** *n* (*fig*) paperasserie (administrative)

reduce [rɪ'djuːs] *vt* réduire; (*lower*) abaisser; **"~ speed now"** (AUT) "ralentir"; **reduction** [rɪ'dʌkʃən] *n* réduction *f*; (*discount*) rabais *m*

redundancy [rɪ'dʌndənsɪ] (BRIT) *n* licenciement *m*, mise *f* au chômage

redundant [rɪ'dʌndnt] *adj* (BRIT: *worker*) mis(e) au chômage, licencié(e); (*detail, object*) superflu(e); **to be made ~** être licencié(e), être mis(e) au chômage

reed [riːd] *n* (BOT) roseau *m*; (MUS: *of clarinet etc*) hanche *f*

reef [riːf] *n* (*at sea*) récif *m*, écueil *m*

reek [riːk] *vi*: **to ~ (of)** puer, empester

reel [riːl] *n* bobine *f*; (FISHING) moulinet *m*; (CINEMA) bande *f*; (*dance*) quadrille écossais ♦ *vi* (*sway*) chanceler; **~ in** *vt* (*fish, line*) ramener

ref [rɛf] (*inf*) *n abbr* (= *referee*) arbitre *m*

refectory [rɪ'fɛktərɪ] *n* réfectoire *m*

refer [rɪ'fəː^r] *vt*: **to ~ sb to** (*inquirer: for information, patient: to specialist*) adresser qn à; (*reader: to text*) renvoyer qn à; (*dispute, decision*): **to ~ sth to** soumettre qch à ♦ *vi*: **~ to** (*allude to*) parler de, faire allusion à; (*consult*) se reporter à

referee [rɛfə'riː] *n* arbitre *m*; (BRIT: *for job application*) répondant(e)

reference ['rɛfrəns] *n* référence *f*, renvoi *m*; (*mention*) allusion *f*, mention *f*; (*for job application: letter*) références, lettre *f* de recommandation; **with ~ to** (COMM: *in letter*) me référant à, suite à; **~ book** *n* ouvrage *m* de référence

refill [*vb* riː'fɪl, *n* 'riːfɪl] *vt* remplir à nouveau; (*pen, lighter etc*) recharger ♦ *n* (*for pen etc*) recharge *f*

refine [rɪ'faɪn] *vt* (*sugar, oil*) raffiner; (*taste*) affiner; (*theory, idea*) fignoler (*inf*); **~d** *adj* (*person, taste*) raffiné(e); **~ry** *n* raffinerie *f*

reflect [rɪ'flɛkt] *vt* (*light, image*) réfléchir, refléter; (*fig*) refléter ♦ *vi* (*think*) réfléchir, méditer; **it ~s badly on him** cela le discrédite; **it ~s well on him** c'est tout à son honneur; **~ion** *n* réflexion *f*; (*image*) reflet *m*; (*criticism*): **~ion on** critique *f* de; atteinte *f* à; **on ~ion** réflexion faite

reflex ['riːflɛks] *adj* réflexe ♦ *n* réflexe *m*; **~ive** [rɪ'flɛksɪv] *adj* (LING) réfléchi(e)

reform [rɪ'fɔːm] *n* réforme *f* ♦ *vt* réformer; **~atory** [rɪ'fɔːmətərɪ] (US) *n* ≃ centre *m* d'éducation surveillée

refrain [rɪ'freɪn] *vi*: **to ~ from doing** s'abstenir de faire ♦ *n* refrain *m*

refresh [rɪ'frɛʃ] *vt* rafraîchir; (*subj: sleep*) reposer; **~er course** (BRIT) *n* cours *m* de recyclage; **~ing** *adj* (*drink*) rafraîchissant(e); (*sleep*) réparateur(-trice); **~ments** *npl* rafraîchissements *mpl*

refrigerator [rɪ'frɪdʒəreɪtə^r] *n* réfrigérateur *m*, frigidaire ® *m*

refuel [riː'fjuəl] *vi* se ravitailler en carburant

refuge ['rɛfjuːdʒ] *n* refuge *m*; **to take ~ in** se réfugier dans; **~e** [rɛfju'dʒiː] *n* réfugié(e)

refund [*n* 'riːfʌnd, *vb* rɪ'fʌnd] *n* remboursement *m* ♦ *vt* rembourser

refurbish [riː'fəːbɪʃ] *vt* remettre à neuf

refusal [rɪ'fjuːzəl] *n* refus *m*; **to have first ~ on** avoir droit de préemption sur

refuse¹ [rɪ'fjuːz] *vt, vi* refuser

refuse² ['rɛfjuːs] *n* ordures *fpl*, détritus *mpl*; **~ collection** *n* ramassage *m* d'ordures

regain [rɪ'geɪn] *vt* regagner; retrouver

regal ['riːgl] *adj* royal(e)

regard [rɪ'gɑːd] *n* respect *m*, estime *f*, considération *f* ♦ *vt* considérer; **to give one's ~s to** faire ses amitiés à; **"with kindest ~s"** "bien amicalement"; **as ~s, with ~ to = regarding**; **~ing** *prep* en ce qui concerne; **~less** *adv* quand même; **~less of** sans se soucier de

régime [reɪ'ʒiːm] *n* régime *m*

regiment ['rɛdʒɪmənt] *n* régiment *m*; **~al** [rɛdʒɪ'mɛntl] *adj* d'un *or* du régiment

region ['riːdʒən] *n* région *f*; **in the ~ of** (*fig*) aux alentours de; **~al** *adj* régional(e)

register ['rɛdʒɪstə^r] *n* registre *m*; (*also:* **electoral ~**) liste électorale ♦ *vt* enregistrer; (*birth, death*) déclarer; (*vehicle*) immatriculer; (*POST: letter*) envoyer en recommandé; (*subj: instrument*) marquer ♦ *vi* s'inscrire; (*at hotel*) signer le registre; (*make impression*) être (bien) compris(e); **~ed** *adj* (*letter, parcel*) recommandé(e); **~ed trademark** *n* marque déposée; **registrar** ['rɛdʒɪstrɑː^r] *n* officier *m* de l'état civil; **registration** [rɛdʒɪs'treɪʃən] *n* enregistrement *m*; (*BRIT: AUT: also:* **registration number**) numéro *m* d'immatriculation

registry ['rɛdʒɪstrɪ] *n* bureau *m* de l'enregistrement; **~ office** (*BRIT*) *n* bureau *m* de l'état civil; **to get married in a ~ office** ≃ se marier à la mairie

regret [rɪ'grɛt] *n* regret *m* ♦ *vt* regretter; **~fully** *adv* à *or* avec regret

regular ['rɛgjulə^r] *adj* régulier(-ère); (*usual*) habituel(le); (*soldier*) de métier ♦ *n* (*client etc*) habitué(e); **~ly** *adv* régulièrement

regulate ['rɛgjuleɪt] *vt* régler; **regulation** [rɛgju'leɪʃən] *n* (*rule*) règlement *m*; (*adjustment*) réglage *m*

rehabilitation ['riːəbɪlɪ'teɪʃən] *n* (*of offender*) réinsertion *f*; (*of addict*) réadaptation *f*

rehearsal [rɪ'həːsəl] *n* répétition *f*

rehearse [rɪ'həːs] *vt* répéter

reign [reɪn] *n* règne *m* ♦ *vi* régner

reimburse [riːɪm'bəːs] *vt* rembourser

rein [reɪn] *n* (*for horse*) rêne *f*

reindeer ['reɪndɪə^r] *n, pl inv* renne *m*

reinforce [riːɪn'fɔːs] *vt* renforcer; **~d concrete** *n* béton armé; **~ments** *npl* (*MIL*) renfort(s) *m(pl)*

reinstate [riːɪn'steɪt] *vt* rétablir, réintégrer

reject [*n* 'riːdʒɛkt, *vb* rɪ'dʒɛkt] *n* (*COMM*) article *m* de rebut ♦ *vt* refuser; (*idea*) rejeter; **~ion** *n* rejet *m*, refus *m*

rejoice [rɪ'dʒɔɪs] *vi*: **to ~ (at** *or* **over)** se réjouir (de)

rejuvenate [rɪ'dʒuːvəneɪt] *vt* rajeunir

relapse [rɪ'læps] *n* (*MED*) rechute *f*

relate [rɪ'leɪt] *vt* (*tell*) raconter; (*connect*) établir un rapport entre ♦ *vi*: **this ~s to** cela se rapporte à; **to ~ to sb** entretenir des rapports avec qn; **~d** *adj* apparenté(e); **relating to** *prep* concernant

relation [rɪ'leɪʃən] *n* (*person*) parent(e); (*link*) rapport *m*, lien *m*; **~ship** *n* rapport *m*, lien *m*; (*personal ties*) relations *fpl*, rapports; (*also:* **family ~ship**) lien de parenté

relative ['rɛlətɪv] *n* parent(e) ♦ *adj* relatif(-ive); **all her ~s** toute sa famille; **~ly** *adv* relativement

relax [rɪ'læks] *vi* (*muscle*) se relâcher;

(*person*: *unwind*) se détendre ♦ *vt* relâcher; (*mind, person*) détendre; **~ation** [ri:læk'seɪʃən] *n* relâchement *m*; (*of mind*) détente *f*, relaxation *f*; (*recreation*) détente, délassement *m*; **~ed** *adj* détendu(e); **~ing** *adj* délassant(e)

relay [*n* 'ri:leɪ, *vb* rɪ'leɪ] *n* (SPORT) course *f* de relais ♦ *vt* (*message*) retransmettre, relayer

release [rɪ'li:s] *n* (*from prison, obligation*) libération *f*; (*of gas etc*) émission *f*; (*of film etc*) sortie *f*; (*new recording*) disque *m* ♦ *vt* (*prisoner*) libérer; (*gas etc*) émettre, dégager; (*free*: *from wreckage etc*) dégager; (TECH: *catch, spring etc*) faire jouer; (*book, film*) sortir; (*report, news*) rendre public, publier

relegate ['rɛləgeɪt] *vt* reléguer; (BRIT: SPORT): **to be ~d** descendre dans une division inférieure

relent [rɪ'lɛnt] *vi* se laisser fléchir; **~less** *adj* implacable; (*unceasing*) continuel(le)

relevant ['rɛləvənt] *adj* (*question*) pertinent(e); (*fact*) significatif(-ive); (*information*) utile; **~ to** ayant rapport à, approprié à

reliable [rɪ'laɪəbl] *adj* (*person, firm*) sérieux(-euse), fiable; (*method, machine*) fiable; (*news, information*) sûr(e); **reliably** *adv*: **to be reliably informed** savoir de source sûre

reliance [rɪ'laɪəns] *n*: **~ (on)** (*person*) confiance *f* (en); (*drugs, promises*) besoin *m* (de), dépendance *f* (de)

relic ['rɛlɪk] *n* (REL) relique *f*; (*of the past*) vestige *m*

relief [rɪ'li:f] *n* (*from pain, anxiety etc*) soulagement *m*; (*help, supplies*) secours *m(pl)*; (ART, GEO) relief *m*

relieve [rɪ'li:v] *vt* (*pain, patient*) soulager; (*fear, worry*) dissiper; (*bring help*) secourir; (*take over from*: *gen*) relayer; (: *guard*) relever; **to ~ sb of sth** débarrasser qn de qch; **to ~ o.s.** se soulager

religion [rɪ'lɪdʒən] *n* religion *f*; **religious** *adj* religieux(-euse); (*book*) de piété

relinquish [rɪ'lɪŋkwɪʃ] *vt* abandonner; (*plan, habit*) renoncer à

relish ['rɛlɪʃ] *n* (CULIN) condiment *m*; (*enjoyment*) délectation *f* ♦ *vt* (*food etc*) savourer; **to ~ doing** se délecter à faire

relocate [ri:ləu'keɪt] *vt* installer ailleurs ♦ *vi* déménager, s'installer ailleurs

reluctance [rɪ'lʌktəns] *n* répugnance *f*

reluctant [rɪ'lʌktənt] *adj* peu disposé(e), qui hésite; **~ly** *adv* à contrecœur

rely on [rɪ'laɪ-] *vt fus* (*be dependent*) dépendre de; (*trust*) compter sur

remain [rɪ'meɪn] *vi* rester; **~der** *n* reste *m*; **~ing** *adj* qui reste; **~s** *npl* restes *mpl*

remake ['ri:meɪk] *n* (CINEMA) remake *m*

remand [rɪ'mɑ:nd] *n*: **on ~** en détention préventive ♦ *vt*: **to be ~ed in custody** être placé(e) en détention préventive

remark [rɪ'mɑ:k] *n* remarque *f*, observation *f* ♦ *vt* (faire) remarquer, dire; **~able** *adj* remarquable; **~ably** *adv* remarquablement

remarry [ri:'mærɪ] *vi* se remarier

remedial [rɪ'mi:dɪəl] *adj* (*tuition, classes*) de rattrapage; **~ exercises** gymnastique corrective

remedy ['rɛmədɪ] *n*: **~ (for)** remède *m* (contre *or* à) ♦ *vt* remédier à

remember [rɪ'mɛmbə^r^] *vt* se rappeler, se souvenir de; (*send greetings*): **~ me to him** saluez-le de ma part; **remembrance** *n* souvenir *m*; mémoire *f*; **Remembrance Day** *n* le jour de l'Armistice

Remembrance Sunday

Remembrance Sunday *ou* **Remembrance Day** *est le dimanche le plus proche du 11 novembre, jour où la Première Guerre mondiale a officiellement pris fin, et rend hommage aux victimes des deux guerres mondiales. À cette occasion, un silence de deux minutes est observé à 11 h, heure de la signature de l'armistice avec l'Alle-*

magne en 1918; certains membres de la famille royale et du gouvernement déposent des gerbes de coquelicots au cénotaphe de Whitehall, et des couronnes sont placées sur les monuments aux morts dans toute la Grande-Bretagne; par ailleurs, les gens portent des coquelicots artificiels fabriqués et vendus par des membres de la légion britannique blessés au combat, au profit des blessés de guerre et de leur famille.

remind [rɪ'maɪnd] *vt*: **to ~ sb of** rappeler à qn; **to ~ sb to do** faire penser à qn à faire, rappeler à qn qu'il doit faire; **~er** *n* (*souvenir*) souvenir *m*; (*letter*) rappel *m*

reminisce [rɛmɪ'nɪs] *vi*: **to ~ (about)** évoquer ses souvenirs (de); **~nt** *adj*: **to be ~nt of** rappeler, faire penser à

remiss [rɪ'mɪs] *adj* négligent(e); **~ion** *n* (*of illness, sins*) rémission *f*; (*of debt, prison sentence*) remise *f*

remit [rɪ'mɪt] *vt* (*send*: *money*) envoyer; **~tance** *n* paiement *m*

remnant ['rɛmnənt] *n* reste *m*, restant *m*; (*of cloth*) coupon *m*; **~s** *npl* (COMM) fins *fpl* de série

remorse [rɪ'mɔːs] *n* remords *m*; **~ful** *adj* plein(e) de remords; **~less** *adj* (*fig*) impitoyable

remote [rɪ'məut] *adj* éloigné(e), lointain(e); (*person*) distant(e); (*possibility*) vague; **~ control** *n* télécommande *f*; **~ly** *adv* au loin; (*slightly*) très vaguement

remould ['riːməuld] (BRIT) *n* (*tyre*) pneu rechapé

removable [rɪ'muːvəbl] *adj* (*detachable*) amovible

removal [rɪ'muːvəl] *n* (*taking away*) enlèvement *m*; suppression *f*; (BRIT: *from house*) déménagement *m*; (*from office*: *dismissal*) renvoi *m*; (*of stain*) nettoyage *m*; (MED) ablation *f*; **~ van** (BRIT) *n* camion *m* de déménagement

remove [rɪ'muːv] *vt* enlever, retirer; (*employee*) renvoyer; (*stain*) faire partir; (*abuse*) supprimer; (*doubt*) chasser

render ['rɛndə^r] *vt* rendre; **~ing** *n* (MUS *etc*) interprétation *f*

rendezvous ['rɔndɪvuː] *n* rendez-vous *m inv*

renew [rɪ'njuː] *vt* renouveler; (*negotiations*) reprendre; (*acquaintance*) renouer; **~able** *adj* (*energy*) renouvelable; **~al** *n* renouvellement *m*; reprise *f*

renounce [rɪ'nauns] *vt* renoncer à

renovate ['rɛnəveɪt] *vt* rénover; (*art work*) restaurer

renown [rɪ'naun] *n* renommée *f*; **~ed** *adj* renommé(e)

rent [rɛnt] *n* loyer *m* ♦ *vt* louer; **~al** *n* (*for television, car*) (prix *m* de) location *f*

reorganize [riː'ɔːgənaɪz] *vt* réorganiser

rep [rɛp] *n abbr* = **representative**; **repertory**

repair [rɪ'pɛə^r] *n* réparation *f* ♦ *vt* réparer; **in good/bad ~** en bon/mauvais état; **~ kit** *n* trousse *f* de réparation

repatriate [riː'pætrɪeɪt] *vt* rapatrier

repay [riː'peɪ] (*irreg*) *vt* (*money, creditor*) rembourser; (*sb's efforts*) récompenser; **~ment** *n* remboursement *m*

repeal [rɪ'piːl] *n* (*of law*) abrogation *f* ♦ *vt* (*law*) abroger

repeat [rɪ'piːt] *n* (RADIO, TV) reprise *f* ♦ *vt* répéter; (COMM: *order*) renouveler; (SCOL: *a class*) redoubler ♦ *vi* répéter; **~edly** *adv* souvent, à plusieurs reprises

repel [rɪ'pɛl] *vt* repousser; **~lent** *adj* repoussant(e) ♦ *n*: **insect ~lent** insectifuge *m*

repent [rɪ'pɛnt] *vi*: **to ~ (of)** se repentir (de); **~ance** *n* repentir *m*

repertory ['rɛpətərɪ] *n* (*also*: **~ theatre**) théâtre *m* de répertoire

repetition [rɛpɪ'tɪʃən] *n* répétition *f*

repetitive [rɪ'pɛtɪtɪv] *adj* (*movement, work*) répétitif(-ive); (*speech*) plein(e) de redites

replace [rɪ'pleɪs] *vt* (*put back*) remettre, replacer; (*take the place of*) remplacer;

~ment *n* (*substitution*) remplacement *m*; (*person*) remplaçant(e)
replay ['ri:pleɪ] *n* (*of match*) match rejoué; (*of tape, film*) répétition *f*
replenish [rɪ'plɛnɪʃ] *vt* (*glass*) remplir (de nouveau); (*stock etc*) réapprovisionner
replica ['rɛplɪkə] *n* réplique *f*, copie exacte
reply [rɪ'plaɪ] *n* réponse *f* ♦ *vi* répondre
report [rɪ'pɔ:t] *n* rapport *m*; (*PRESS etc*) reportage *m*; (*BRIT*: *also*: **school ~**) bulletin *m* (scolaire); (*of gun*) détonation *f* ♦ *vt* rapporter, faire un compte rendu de; (*PRESS etc*) faire un reportage sur; (*bring to notice*: *occurrence*) signaler ♦ *vi* (*make a ~*) faire un rapport (*or* un reportage); (*present o.s.*): **to ~ (to sb)** se présenter (chez qn); (*be responsible to*): **to ~ to sb** être sous les ordres de qn; **~ card** (*US, SCOTTISH*) *n* bulletin *m* scolaire; **~edly** *adv*: **she is ~edly living in ...** elle habiterait ...; **he ~edly told them to ...** il leur aurait ordonné de ...; **~er** *n* reporter *m*
repose [rɪ'pəuz] *n*: **in ~** en *or* au repos
represent [rɛprɪ'zɛnt] *vt* représenter; (*view, belief*) présenter, expliquer; (*describe*): **to ~ sth as** présenter *or* décrire qch comme; **~ation** [rɛprɪzɛn'teɪʃən] *n* représentation *f*; **~ations** *npl* (*protest*) démarche *f*; **~ative** [rɛprɪ'zɛntətɪv] *n* représentant(e); (*US*: *POL*) député *m* ♦ *adj* représentatif(-ive), caractéristique
repress [rɪ'prɛs] *vt* réprimer; **~ion** *n* répression *f*
reprieve [rɪ'pri:v] *n* (*LAW*) grâce *f*; (*fig*) sursis *m*, délai *m*
reprisal [rɪ'praɪzl] *n*: **~s** ♦ *npl* représailles *fpl*
reproach [rɪ'prəutʃ] *vt*: **to ~ sb with sth** reprocher qch à qn; **~ful** *adj* de reproche
reproduce [ri:prə'dju:s] *vt* reproduire ♦ *vi* se reproduire; **reproduction** [ri:prə'dʌkʃən] *n* reproduction *f*
reproof [rɪ'pru:f] *n* reproche *m*
reptile ['rɛptaɪl] *n* reptile *m*
republic [rɪ'pʌblɪk] *n* république *f*; **~an** *adj* républicain(e)
repudiate [rɪ'pju:dɪeɪt] *vt* répudier, rejeter
repulsive [rɪ'pʌlsɪv] *adj* repoussant(e), répulsif(-ive)
reputable ['rɛpjutəbl] *adj* de bonne réputation; (*occupation*) honorable
reputation [rɛpju'teɪʃən] *n* réputation *f*
reputed [rɪ'pju:tɪd] *adj* (*supposed*) supposé(e); **~ly** *adv* d'après ce qu'on dit
request [rɪ'kwɛst] *n* demande *f*; (*formal*) requête *f* ♦ *vt*: **to ~ (of** *or* **from sb)** demander (à qn); **~ stop** (*BRIT*) *n* (*for bus*) arrêt facultatif
require [rɪ'kwaɪə^r] *vt* (*need*: *subj*: *person*) avoir besoin de; (: *thing, situation*) demander; (*want*) exiger; (*order*): **to ~ sb to do sth/sth of sb** exiger que qn fasse qch/qch de qn; **~ment** *n* exigence *f*; besoin *m*; condition requise
requisition [rɛkwɪ'zɪʃən] *n*: **~ (for)** demande *f* (de) ♦ *vt* (*MIL*) réquisitionner
rescue ['rɛskju:] *n* (*from accident*) sauvetage *m*; (*help*) secours *mpl* ♦ *vt* sauver; **~ party** *n* équipe *f* de sauvetage; **~r** *n* sauveteur *m*
research [rɪ'sə:tʃ] *n* recherche(s) *f(pl)* ♦ *vt* faire des recherches sur
resemblance [rɪ'zɛmbləns] *n* ressemblance *f*
resemble [rɪ'zɛmbl] *vt* ressembler à
resent [rɪ'zɛnt] *vt* être contrarié(e) par; **~ful** *adj* irrité(e), plein(e) de ressentiment; **~ment** *n* ressentiment *m*
reservation [rɛzə'veɪʃən] *n* (*booking*) réservation *f*; (*doubt*) réserve *f*; (*for tribe*) réserve; **to make a ~ (in a hotel/a restaurant/on a plane)** réserver *or* retenir une chambre/une table/une place
reserve [rɪ'zə:v] *n* réserve *f*; (*SPORT*) remplaçant(e) ♦ *vt* (*seats etc*) réserver, retenir; **~s** *npl* (*MIL*) réservistes *mpl*; **in ~** en réserve; **~d** *adj* réservé(e)

reshuffle [riːˈʃʌfl] *n*: **Cabinet ~** (*POL*) remaniement ministériel

residence [ˈrɛzɪdəns] *n* résidence *f*; **~ permit** (*BRIT*) *n* permis *m* de séjour

resident [ˈrɛzɪdənt] *n* résident(e) ♦ *adj* résidant(e); **~ial** [rɛzɪˈdɛnʃəl] *adj* résidentiel(le); (*course*) avec hébergement sur place; **~ial school** *n* internat *m*

residue [ˈrɛzɪdjuː] *n* reste *m*; (*CHEM, PHYSICS*) résidu *m*

resign [rɪˈzaɪn] *vt* (*one's post*) démissionner de ♦ *vi* démissionner; **to ~ o.s. to** se résigner à; **~ation** [rɛzɪgˈneɪʃən] *n* (*of post*) démission *f*; (*state of mind*) résignation *f*; **~ed** *adj* résigné(e)

resilient [rɪˈzɪlɪənt] *adj* (*material*) élastique; (*person*) qui réagit, qui a du ressort

resist [rɪˈzɪst] *vt* résister à; **~ance** *n* résistance *f*

resit [riːˈsɪt] *vt* (*exam*) repasser ♦ *n* deuxième session *f* (*d'un examen*)

resolution [rɛzəˈluːʃən] *n* résolution *f*

resolve [rɪˈzɔlv] *n* résolution *f* ♦ *vt* (*problem*) résoudre ♦ *vi*: **to ~ to do** résoudre *or* décider de faire

resort [rɪˈzɔːt] *n* (*seaside town*) station *f* balnéaire; (*ski ~*) station de ski; (*recourse*) recours *m* ♦ *vi*: **to ~ to** avoir recours à; **in the last ~** en dernier ressort

resounding [rɪˈzaundɪŋ] *adj* retentissant(e)

resource [rɪˈsɔːs] *n* ressource *f*; **~s** *npl* (*supplies, wealth etc*) ressources; **~ful** *adj* ingénieux(-euse), débrouillard(e)

respect [rɪsˈpɛkt] *n* respect *m* ♦ *vt* respecter; **~s** *npl* (*compliments*) respects, hommages *mpl*; **with ~ to** en ce qui concerne; **in this ~** à cet égard; **~able** *adj* respectable; **~ful** *adj* respectueux (-euse); **~ively** *adv* respectivement

respite [ˈrɛspaɪt] *n* répit *m*

respond [rɪsˈpɔnd] *vi* répondre; (*react*) réagir; **response** *n* réponse *f*; réaction *f*

responsibility [rɪspɔnsɪˈbɪlɪtɪ] *n* responsabilité *f*

responsible [rɪsˈpɔnsɪbl] *adj* (*liable*): **~ (for)** responsable (de); (*person*) digne de confiance; (*job*) qui comporte des responsabilités

responsive [rɪsˈpɔnsɪv] *adj* qui réagit; (*person*) qui n'est pas réservé(e) *or* indifférent(e)

rest [rɛst] *n* repos *m*; (*stop*) arrêt *m*, pause *f*; (*MUS*) silence *m*; (*support*) support *m*, appui *m*; (*remainder*) reste *m*, restant *m* ♦ *vi* se reposer; (*be supported*): **to ~ on** appuyer *or* reposer sur; (*remain*) rester ♦ *vt* (*lean*): **to ~ sth on/against** appuyer qch sur/contre; **the ~ of them** les autres; **it ~s with him to ...** c'est à lui de ...

restaurant [ˈrɛstərɔŋ] *n* restaurant *m*; **~ car** (*BRIT*) *n* wagon-restaurant *m*

restful [ˈrɛstful] *adj* reposant(e)

restive [ˈrɛstɪv] *adj* agité(e), impatient(e); (*horse*) rétif(-ive)

restless [ˈrɛstlɪs] *adj* agité(e)

restoration [rɛstəˈreɪʃən] *n* restauration *f*; restitution *f*; rétablissement *m*

restore [rɪˈstɔː[r]] *vt* (*building*) restaurer; (*sth stolen*) restituer; (*peace, health*) rétablir; **to ~ to** (*former state*) ramener à

restrain [rɪsˈtreɪn] *vt* contenir; (*person*): **to ~ (from doing)** retenir (de faire); **~ed** *adj* (*style*) sobre; (*manner*) mesuré(e); **~t** *n* (*restriction*) contrainte *f*; (*moderation*) retenue *f*

restrict [rɪsˈtrɪkt] *vt* restreindre, limiter; **~ion** *n* restriction *f*, limitation *f*

rest room (*US*) *n* toilettes *fpl*

result [rɪˈzʌlt] *n* résultat *m* ♦ *vi*: **to ~ in** aboutir à, se terminer par; **as a ~ of** à la suite de

resume [rɪˈzjuːm] *vt, vi* (*work, journey*) reprendre

résumé [ˈreɪzjuːmeɪ] *n* résumé *m*; (*US*) curriculum vitae *m*

resumption [rɪˈzʌmpʃən] *n* reprise *f*

resurgence [rɪˈsəːdʒəns] *n* (*of energy, activity*) regain *m*

resurrection [rɛzəˈrɛkʃən] *n* résurrection *f*

resuscitate [rɪ'sʌsɪteɪt] *vt* (*MED*) réanimer

retail ['ri:teɪl] *adj* de *or* au détail ♦ *adv* au détail; **~er** *n* détaillant(e); **~ price** *n* prix *m* de détail

retain [rɪ'teɪn] *vt* (*keep*) garder, conserver; **~er** *n* (*fee*) acompte *m*, provision *f*

retaliate [rɪ'tælɪeɪt] *vi*: **to ~ (against)** se venger (de); **retaliation** [rɪtælɪ'eɪʃən] *n* représailles *fpl*, vengeance *f*

retarded [rɪ'tɑ:dɪd] *adj* retardé(e)

retch [rɛtʃ] *vi* avoir des haut-le-cœur

retentive [rɪ'tɛntɪv] *adj*: **~ memory** excellente mémoire

retina ['rɛtɪnə] *n* rétine *f*

retire [rɪ'taɪə[r]] *vi* (*give up work*) prendre sa retraite; (*withdraw*) se retirer, partir; (*go to bed*) (aller) se coucher; **~d** *adj* (*person*) retraité(e); **~ment** *n* retraite *f*; **retiring** *adj* (*shy*) réservé(e); (*leaving*) sortant(e)

retort [rɪ'tɔ:t] *vi* riposter

retrace [ri:'treɪs] *vt*: **to ~ one's steps** revenir sur ses pas

retract [rɪ'trækt] *vt* (*statement, claws*) rétracter; (*undercarriage, aerial*) rentrer, escamoter

retrain [ri:'treɪn] *vt* (*worker*) recycler

retread ['ri:trɛd] *n* (*tyre*) pneu rechapé

retreat [rɪ'tri:t] *n* retraite *f* ♦ *vi* battre en retraite

retribution [rɛtrɪ'bju:ʃən] *n* châtiment *m*

retrieval [rɪ'tri:vəl] *n* (*see vb*) récupération *f*; réparation *f*

retrieve [rɪ'tri:v] *vt* (*sth lost*) récupérer; (*situation, honour*) sauver; (*error, loss*) réparer; **~r** *n* chien *m* d'arrêt

retrospect ['rɛtrəspɛkt] *n*: **in ~** rétrospectivement, après coup; **~ive** [rɛtrə'spɛktɪv] *adj* rétrospectif(-ive); (*law*) rétroactif(-ive)

return [rɪ'tə:n] *n* (*going or coming back*) retour *m*; (*of sth stolen etc*) restitution *f*; (*FINANCE: from land, shares*) rendement *m*, rapport *m* ♦ *cpd* (*journey*) de retour; (*BRIT: ticket*) aller et retour; (*match*) retour ♦ *vi* (*come back*) revenir; (*go back*) retourner ♦ *vt* rendre; (*bring back*) rapporter; (*send back; also: ball*) renvoyer; (*put back*) remettre; (*POL: candidate*) élire; **~s** *npl* (*COMM*) recettes *fpl*; (*FINANCE*) bénéfices *mpl*; **in ~ (for)** en échange (de); **by ~ (of post)** par retour (du courrier); **many happy ~s (of the day)!** bon anniversaire!

reunion [ri:'ju:nɪən] *n* réunion *f*

reunite [ri:ju:'naɪt] *vt* réunir

reuse [ri:'ju:z] *vt* réutiliser

rev [rɛv] *n abbr* (*AUT: = revolution*) tour *m* ♦ *vt* (*also:* **rev up**) emballer

revamp [ri:'væmp] *vt* (*firm, system etc*) réorganiser

reveal [rɪ'vi:l] *vt* (*make known*) révéler; (*display*) laisser voir; **~ing** *adj* révélateur(-trice); (*dress*) au décolleté généreux *or* suggestif

revel ['rɛvl] *vi*: **to ~ in sth/in doing** se délecter de qch/à faire

revenge [rɪ'vɛndʒ] *n* vengeance *f*; **to take ~ on** (*enemy*) se venger sur

revenue ['rɛvənju:] *n* revenu *m*

reverberate [rɪ'və:bəreɪt] *vi* (*sound*) retentir, se répercuter; (*fig: shock etc*) se propager

reverence ['rɛvərəns] *n* vénération *f*, révérence *f*

Reverend ['rɛvərənd] *adj* (*in titles*): **the ~ John Smith** (*Anglican*) le révérend John Smith; (*Catholic*) l'abbé (John) Smith; (*Protestant*) le pasteur (John) Smith

reversal [rɪ'və:sl] *n* (*of opinion*) revirement *m*; (*of order*) renversement *m*; (*of direction*) changement *m*

reverse [rɪ'və:s] *n* contraire *m*, opposé *m*; (*back*) dos *m*, envers *m*; (*of paper*) verso *m*; (*of coin; also: setback*) revers *m*; (*AUT: also:* **~ gear**) marche *f* arrière ♦ *adj* (*order, direction*) opposé(e), inverse ♦ *vt* (*order, position*) changer, inverser; (*direction, policy*) changer complètement de; (*decision*) annuler; (*roles*) renverser; (*car*) faire marche arrière avec ♦ *vi* (*BRIT: AUT*) faire marche arrière; **he ~d (the car) into a wall** il a embouti un mur en marche arrière; **~d charge call** (*BRIT*) *n* (*TEL*) communication *f* en PCV; **reversing lights** (*BRIT*) *npl* (*AUT*) feux *mpl* de marche arrière *or* de recul

revert [rɪ'vəːt] *vi*: **to ~ to** revenir à, retourner à

review [rɪ'vjuː] *n* revue *f*; (*of book, film*) critique *f*, compte rendu; (*of situation, policy*) examen *m*, bilan *m* ♦ *vt* passer en revue; faire la critique de; examiner; **~er** *n* critique *m*

revise [rɪ'vaɪz] *vt* réviser, modifier; (*manuscript*) revoir, corriger ♦ *vi* (*study*) réviser; **revision** [rɪ'vɪʒən] *n* révision *f*

revival [rɪ'vaɪvəl] *n* reprise *f*; (*recovery*) rétablissement *m*; (*of faith*) renouveau *m*

revive [rɪ'vaɪv] *vt* (*person*) ranimer; (*custom*) rétablir; (*economy*) relancer; (*hope, courage*) raviver, faire renaître; (*play*) reprendre ♦ *vi* (*person*) reprendre connaissance; (: *from ill health*) se rétablir; (*hope etc*) renaître; (*activity*) reprendre

revoke [rɪ'vəuk] *vt* révoquer; (*law*) abroger

revolt [rɪ'vəult] *n* révolte *f* ♦ *vi* se révolter, se rebeller ♦ *vt* révolter, dégoûter; **~ing** *adj* dégoûtant(e)

revolution [rɛvə'luːʃən] *n* révolution *f*; (*of wheel etc*) tour *m*, révolution; **~ary** *adj* révolutionnaire ♦ *n* révolutionnaire *m/f*

revolve [rɪ'vɔlv] *vi* tourner

revolver [rɪ'vɔlvə^r^] *n* revolver *m*

revolving [rɪ'vɔlvɪŋ] *adj* tournant(e); (*chair*) pivotant(e); **~ door** *n* (porte *f* à) tambour *m*

revulsion [rɪ'vʌlʃən] *n* dégoût *m*, répugnance *f*

reward [rɪ'wɔːd] *n* récompense *f* ♦ *vt*: **to ~ (for)** récompenser (de); **~ing** *adj* (*fig*) qui (en) vaut la peine, gratifiant(e)

rewind [riː'waɪnd] (*irreg*) *vt* (*tape*) rembobiner

rewire [riː'waɪə^r^] *vt* (*house*) refaire l'installation électrique de

rheumatism ['ruːmətɪzəm] *n* rhumatisme *m*

Rhine [raɪn] *n* Rhin *m*

rhinoceros [raɪ'nɔsərəs] *n* rhinocéros *m*

Rhone [rəun] *n* Rhône *m*

rhubarb ['ruːbɑːb] *n* rhubarbe *f*

rhyme [raɪm] *n* rime *f*; (*verse*) vers *mpl*

rhythm ['rɪðm] *n* rythme *m*

rib [rɪb] *n* (*ANAT*) côte *f*

ribbon ['rɪbən] *n* ruban *m*; **in ~s** (*torn*) en lambeaux

rice [raɪs] *n* riz *m*; **~ pudding** *n* riz au lait

rich [rɪtʃ] *adj* riche; (*gift, clothes*) somptueux(-euse) ♦ *npl*: **the ~** les riches *mpl*; **~es** *npl* richesses *fpl*; **~ly** *adv* richement; (*deserved, earned*) largement

rickets ['rɪkɪts] *n* rachitisme *m*

rid [rɪd] (*pt, pp* **rid**) *vt*: **to ~ sb of** débarrasser qn de; **to get ~ of** se débarrasser de

riddle ['rɪdl] *n* (*puzzle*) énigme *f* ♦ *vt*: **to be ~d with** être criblé(e) de; (*fig: guilt, corruption, doubts*) être en proie à

ride [raɪd] (*pt* **rode**, *pp* **ridden**) *n* promenade *f*, tour *m*; (*distance covered*) trajet *m* ♦ *vi* (*as sport*) monter (à cheval), faire du cheval; (*go somewhere: on horse, bicycle*) aller (à cheval *or* bicyclette *etc*); (*journey: on bicycle, motorcycle, bus*) rouler ♦ *vt* (*a certain horse*) monter; (*distance*) parcourir, faire; **to take sb for a ~** (*fig*) faire marcher qn; **to ~ a horse/bicycle** monter à cheval/à bicyclette; **~r** *n* cavalier(-ère); (*in race*) jockey *m*; (*on bicycle*) cycliste *m/f*; (*on motorcycle*) motocycliste *m/f*

ridge [rɪdʒ] *n* (*of roof, mountain*) arête *f*; (*of hill*) faîte *m*; (*on object*) strie *f*

ridicule ['rɪdɪkjuːl] *n* ridicule *m*; dérision *f*

ridiculous [rɪ'dɪkjuləs] *adj* ridicule

riding ['raɪdɪŋ] *n* équitation *f*; **~**

school *n* manège *m*, école *f* d'équitation

rife [raɪf] *adj* répandu(e); ~ **with** abondant(e) en, plein(e) de

riffraff ['rɪfræf] *n* racaille *f*

rifle ['raɪfl] *n* fusil *m* (à canon rayé) ♦ *vt* vider, dévaliser; ~ **through** *vt* (*belongings*) fouiller; (*papers*) feuilleter; ~ **range** *n* champ *m* de tir; (*at fair*) stand *m* de tir

rift [rɪft] *n* fente *f*, fissure *f*; (*fig*: *disagreement*) désaccord *m*

rig [rɪg] *n* (*also:* **oil** ~: *at sea*) plateforme pétrolière ♦ *vt* (*election etc*) truquer; ~ **out** (BRIT) *vt*: **to** ~ **out as/in** habiller en/de; ~ **up** *vt* arranger, faire avec des moyens de fortune; **~ging** *n* (NAUT) gréement *m*

right [raɪt] *adj* (*correctly chosen*: *answer, road etc*) bon (bonne); (*true*) juste, exact(e); (*suitable*) approprié(e), convenable; (*just*) juste, équitable; (*morally good*) bien *inv*; (*not left*) droit(e) ♦ *n* (*what is morally* ~) bien *m*; (*title, claim*) droit *m*; (*not left*) droite *f* ♦ *adv* (*answer*) correctement, juste; (*treat*) bien, comme il faut; (*not on the left*) à droite ♦ *vt* redresser ♦ *excl* bon!; **to be** ~ (*person*) avoir raison; (*answer*) être juste *or* correct(e); (*clock*) à l'heure (juste); **by ~s** en toute justice; **on the** ~ à droite; **to be in the** ~ avoir raison; ~ **now** en ce moment même; tout de suite; ~ **in the middle** en plein milieu; ~ **away** immédiatement; ~ **angle** *n* (MATH) angle droit; **~eous** ['raɪtʃəs] *adj* droit(e), vertueux(-euse); (*anger*) justifié(e); **~ful** *adj* légitime; **~-handed** *adj* (*person*) droitier(-ère); **~-hand man** *n* bras droit (*fig*); **~-hand side** *n* la droite; **~ly** *adv* (*with reason*) à juste titre; ~ **of way** *n* droit *m* de passage; (AUT) priorité *f*; **~-wing** *adj* (POL) de droite

rigid ['rɪdʒɪd] *adj* rigide; (*principle, control*) strict(e)

rigmarole ['rɪgmərəul] *n* comédie *f*

rigorous ['rɪgərəs] *adj* rigoureux(-euse)

rile [raɪl] *vt* agacer

rim [rɪm] *n* bord *m*; (*of spectacles*) monture *f*; (*of wheel*) jante *f*

rind [raɪnd] *n* (*of bacon*) couenne *f*; (*of lemon etc*) écorce *f*, zeste *m*; (*of cheese*) croûte *f*

ring [rɪŋ] (*pt* **rang**, *pp* **rung**) *n* anneau *m*; (*on finger*) bague *f*; (*also:* **wedding** ~) alliance *f*; (*of people, objects*) cercle *m*; (*of spies*) réseau *m*; (*of smoke etc*) rond *m*; (*arena*) piste *f*, arène *f*; (*for boxing*) ring *m*; (*sound of bell*) sonnerie *f* ♦ *vi* (*telephone, bell*) sonner; (*person*: *by telephone*) téléphoner; (*also:* ~ **out**: *voice, words*) retentir; (*ears*) bourdonner ♦ *vt* (BRIT: TEL: *also:* ~ **up**) téléphoner à, appeler; (*bell*) faire sonner; **to** ~ **the bell** sonner; **to give sb a** ~ (BRIT: TEL) appeler qn; ~ **back** (BRIT) *vt, vi* (TEL) rappeler; ~ **off** (BRIT) *vi* (TEL) raccrocher; ~ **up** (BRIT) *vt* (TEL) appeler; ~ **binder** *n* classeur *m* à anneaux; **~ing** ['rɪŋɪŋ] *n* (*of telephone*) sonnerie *f*; (*of bell*) tintement *m*; (*in ears*) bourdonnement *m*; **~ing tone** (BRIT) *n* (TEL) sonnerie *f*; **~leader** *n* (*of gang*) chef *m*, meneur *m*; **~lets** *npl* anglaises *fpl*; ~ **road** (BRIT) *n* route *f* de ceinture; (*motorway*) périphérique *m*

rink [rɪŋk] *n* (*also:* **ice** ~) patinoire *f*

rinse [rɪns] *vt* rincer

riot ['raɪət] *n* émeute *f*; (*of flowers, colour*) profusion *f* ♦ *vi* faire une émeute, manifester avec violence; **to run** ~ se déchaîner; **~ous** *adj* (*mob, assembly*) séditieux(-euse), déchaîné(e); (*living, behaviour*) débauché(e); (*party*) très animé(e); (*welcome*) délirant(e)

rip [rɪp] *n* déchirure *f* ♦ *vt* déchirer ♦ *vi* se déchirer; **~cord** *n* poignée *f* d'ouverture

ripe [raɪp] *adj* (*fruit*) mûr(e); (*cheese*) fait(e); **~n** *vt* mûrir ♦ *vi* mûrir

rip-off (*inf*) *n*: **it's a ~-~!** c'est de l'arnaque!

ripple ['rɪpl] *n* ondulation *f*; (*of applause, laughter*) cascade *f* ♦ *vi* onduler

rise [raɪz] (*pt* **rose**, *pp* **risen**) *n* (*slope*) côte *f*, pente *f*; (*hill*) hauteur *f*; (*increase*: *in wages*: BRIT) augmentation *f*; (: *in prices, temperature*) hausse *f*, augmentation; (*fig*: *to power etc*) ascension *f* ♦ *vi* s'élever, monter; (*prices, numbers*) augmenter; (*waters*) monter; (*sun; person*: *from chair, bed*) se lever; (*also*: **~ up**: *tower, building*) s'élever; (: *rebel*) se révolter; se rebeller; (*in rank*) s'élever; **to give ~ to** donner lieu à; **to ~ to the occasion** se montrer à la hauteur; **~r** *n*: **to be an early ~r** être matinal(e); **rising** *adj* (*number, prices*) en hausse; (*tide*) montant(e); (*sun, moon*) levant(e)

risk [rɪsk] *n* risque *m* ♦ *vt* risquer; **at ~** en danger; **at one's own ~** à ses risques et périls; **~y** *adj* risqué(e)

rissole ['rɪsəul] *n* croquette *f*

rite [raɪt] *n* rite *m*; **last ~s** derniers sacrements

ritual ['rɪtjuəl] *adj* rituel(le) ♦ *n* rituel *m*

rival ['raɪvl] *adj, n* rival(e); (*in business*) concurrent(e) ♦ *vt* (*match*) égaler; **~ry** ['raɪvlrɪ] *n* rivalité *f*, concurrence *f*

river ['rɪvə[r]] *n* rivière *f*; (*major, also fig*) fleuve *m* ♦ *cpd* (*port, traffic*) fluvial(e); **up/down ~** en amont/aval; **~bank** *n* rive *f*, berge *f*; **~bed** *n* lit *m* (de rivière *or* de fleuve)

rivet ['rɪvɪt] *n* rivet *m* ♦ *vt* (*fig*) river, fixer

Riviera [rɪvɪ'ɛərə] *n*: **the (French) ~** la Côte d'Azur; **the Italian ~** la Riviera (italienne)

road [rəud] *n* route *f*; (*in town*) rue *f*; (*fig*) chemin, voie *f*; **major/minor ~** route principale *or* à priorité/voie secondaire; **~ accident** *n* accident *m* de la circulation; **~block** *n* barrage routier; **~hog** *n* chauffard *m*; **~ map** *n* carte routière; **~ rage** *n comportement très agressif de certains usagers de la route*; **~ safety** *n* sécurité routière; **~side** *n* bord *m* de la route, bas-côté *m*; **~ sign** *n* panneau *m* de signalisation; **~way** *n* chaussée *f*; **~ works** *npl* travaux *mpl* (de réfection des routes); **~worthy** *adj* en bon état de marche

roam [rəum] *vi* errer, vagabonder

roar [rɔː[r]] *n* rugissement *m*; (*of crowd*) hurlements *mpl*; (*of vehicle, thunder, storm*) grondement *m* ♦ *vi* rugir; hurler; gronder; **to ~ with laughter** éclater de rire; **to do a ~ing trade** faire des affaires d'or

roast [rəust] *n* rôti *m* ♦ *vt* (faire) rôtir; (*coffee*) griller, torréfier; **~ beef** *n* rôti *m* de bœuf, rosbif *m*

rob [rɔb] *vt* (*person*) voler; (*bank*) dévaliser; **to ~ sb of sth** voler *or* dérober qch à qn; (*fig*: *deprive*) priver qn de qch; **~ber** *n* bandit *m*, voleur *m*; **~bery** *n* vol *m*

robe [rəub] *n* (*for ceremony etc*) robe *f*; (*also*: **bathrobe**) peignoir *m*; (US) couverture *f*

robin ['rɔbɪn] *n* rouge-gorge *m*

robot ['rəubɔt] *n* robot *m*

robust [rəu'bʌst] *adj* robuste; (*material, appetite*) solide

rock [rɔk] *n* (*substance*) roche *f*, roc *m*; (*boulder*) rocher *m*; (US: *small stone*) caillou *m*; (BRIT: *sweet*) ≃ sucre *m* d'orge ♦ *vt* (*swing gently*: *cradle*) balancer; (: *child*) bercer; (*shake*) ébranler, secouer ♦ *vi* (se) balancer; être ébranlé(e) *or* secoué(e); **on the ~s** (*drink*) avec des glaçons; (*marriage etc*) en train de craquer; **~ and roll** *n* rock (and roll) *m*, rock'n'roll *m*; **~-bottom** *adj* (*fig*: *prices*) sacrifié(e); **~ery** *n* (jardin *m* de) rocaille *f*

rocket ['rɔkɪt] *n* fusée *f*; (MIL) fusée, roquette *f*; (CULIN) roquette *f*

rocking chair *n* fauteuil *m* à bascule

rocking horse *n* cheval *m* à bascule

rocky ['rɔkɪ] *adj* (*hill*) rocheux(-euse); (*path*) rocailleux(-euse)

rod [rɔd] *n* (*wooden*) baguette *f*; (*metallic*) tringle *f*; (TECH) tige *f*; (*also*: **fishing ~**) canne *f* à pêche

rode [rəud] *pt of* **ride**

rodent ['rəudnt] *n* rongeur *m*

rodeo ['rəudɪəu] (*US*) *n* rodéo *m*

roe [rəu] *n* (*species*: *also:* **~ deer**) chevreuil *m*; (*of fish*: *also:* **hard ~**) œufs *mpl* de poisson; **soft ~** laitance *f*

rogue [rəug] *n* coquin(e)

role [rəul] *n* rôle *m*; **~ play** *n* jeu *m* de rôle

roll [rəul] *n* rouleau *m*; (*of banknotes*) liasse *f*; (*also:* **bread ~**) petit pain; (*register*) liste *f*; (*sound*: *of drums etc*) roulement *m* ♦ *vt* rouler; (*also:* **~ up**: *string*) enrouler; (: *sleeves*) retrousser; (*also:* **~ out**: *pastry*) étendre au rouleau, abaisser ♦ *vi* rouler; **~ about** *vi* rouler ça et là; (*person*) se rouler par terre; **~ around** *vi* = **roll about**; **~ by** *vi* (*time*) s'écouler, passer; **~ over** *vi* se retourner; **~ up** *vi* (*inf*: *arrive*) arriver, s'amener ♦ *vt* rouler; **~ call** *n* appel *m*; **~er** *n* rouleau *m*; (*wheel*) roulette *f*; (*for road*) rouleau compresseur; **~er blade** *n* patin *m* en ligne; **~er coaster** *n* montagnes *fpl* russes; **~er skates** *npl* patins *mpl* à roulettes; **~er skating** *n* patin *m* à roulettes; **~ing** *adj* (*landscape*) onduleux(-euse); **~ing pin** *n* rouleau *m* à pâtisserie; **~ing stock** *n* (*RAIL*) matériel roulant

ROM [rɔm] *n abbr* (= *read only memory*) mémoire morte

Roman ['rəumən] *adj* romain(e); **~ Catholic** *adj, n* catholique *m/f*

romance [rə'mæns] *n* (*love affair*) idylle *f*; (*charm*) poésie *f*; (*novel*) roman *m* à l'eau de rose

Romania [rəu'meɪnɪə] *n* Roumanie *f*; **~n** *adj* roumain(e) ♦ *n* Roumain(e); (*LING*) roumain *m*

Roman numeral *n* chiffre romain

romantic [rə'mæntɪk] *adj* romantique; sentimental(e)

Rome [rəum] *n* Rome

romp [rɔmp] *n* jeux bruyants ♦ *vi* (*also:* **~ about**) s'ébattre, jouer bruyamment; **~ers** *npl* barboteuse *f*

roof [ru:f] (*pl* **~s**) *n* toit *m* ♦ *vt* couvrir (d'un toit); **the ~ of the mouth** la voûte du palais; **~ing** *n* toiture *f*; **~ rack** *n* (*AUT*) galerie *f*

rook [ruk] *n* (*bird*) freux *m*; (*CHESS*) tour *f*

room [ru:m] *n* (*in house*) pièce *f*; (*also: bedroom*) chambre *f* (à coucher); (*in school etc*) salle *f*; (*space*) place *f*; **~s** *npl* (*lodging*) meublé *m*; **"~s to let"** (*BRIT*) *or* **"~s for rent"** (*US*) "chambres à louer"; **single/double ~** chambre pour une personne/deux personnes; **there is ~ for improvement** cela laisse à désirer; **~ing house** (*US*) *n* maison *f or* immeuble *m* de rapport; **~mate** *n* camarade *m/f* de chambre; **~ service** *n* service *m* des chambres (*dans un hôtel*); **~y** *adj* spacieux(-euse); (*garment*) ample

roost [ru:st] *vi* se jucher

rooster ['ru:stə[r]] *n* (*esp US*) coq *m*

root [ru:t] *n* (*BOT, MATH*) racine *f*; (*fig*: *of problem*) origine *f*, fond *m* ♦ *vi* (*plant*) s'enraciner; **~ about** *vi* (*fig*) fouiller; **~ for** *vt fus* encourager, applaudir; **~ out** *vt* (*find*) dénicher

rope [rəup] *n* corde *f*; (*NAUT*) cordage *m* ♦ *vt* (*tie up or together*) attacher; (*climbers*: *also:* **~ together**) encorder; (*area*: **~ off**) interdire l'accès de; (: *divide off*) séparer; **to know the ~s** (*fig*) être au courant, connaître les ficelles; **~ in** *vt* (*fig*: *person*) embringuer

rosary ['rəuzərɪ] *n* chapelet *m*

rose [rəuz] *pt of* **rise** ♦ *n* rose *f*; (*also:* **~bush**) rosier *m*; (*on watering can*) pomme *f*

rosé ['rəuzeɪ] *n* rosé *m*

rosebud ['rəuzbʌd] *n* bouton *m* de rose

rosemary ['rəuzmərɪ] *n* romarin *m*

roster ['rɔstə[r]] *n*: **duty ~** tableau *m* de service

rostrum ['rɔstrəm] *n* tribune *f* (*pour un orateur etc*)

rosy ['rəuzɪ] *adj* rose; **a ~ future** un bel avenir

rot [rɔt] *n* (*decay*) pourriture *f*; (*fig*: *pej*)

idioties *fpl* ♦ *vt, vi* pourrir

rota ['rəutə] *n* liste *f*, tableau *m* de service; **on a ~ basis** par roulement

rotary ['rəutərɪ] *adj* rotatif(-ive)

rotate [rəu'teɪt] *vt* (*revolve*) faire tourner; (*change round*: *jobs*) faire à tour de rôle ♦ *vi* (*revolve*) tourner; **rotating** *adj* (*movement*) tournant(e)

rotten ['rɔtn] *adj* (*decayed*) pourri(e); (*dishonest*) corrompu(e); (*inf*: *bad*) mauvais(e), moche; **to feel ~** (*ill*) être mal fichu(e)

rotund [rəu'tʌnd] *adj* (*person*) rondelet(te)

rough [rʌf] *adj* (*cloth, skin*) rêche, rugueux(-euse); (*terrain*) accidenté(e); (*path*) rocailleux(-euse); (*voice*) rauque, rude; (*person, manner*: *coarse*) rude, fruste; (: *violent*) brutal(e); (*district, weather*) mauvais(e); (*sea*) houleux(-euse); (*plan etc*) ébauché(e); (*guess*) approximatif(-ive) ♦ *n* (GOLF) rough *m* ♦ *vt*: **to ~ it** vivre à la dure; **to sleep ~** (BRIT) coucher à la dure; **~age** *n* fibres *fpl* alimentaires; **~-and-ready** *adj* rudimentaire; **~ copy**, **~ draft** *n* brouillon *m*; **~ly** *adv* (*handle*) rudement, brutalement; (*speak*) avec brusquerie; (*make*) grossièrement; (*approximately*) à peu près, en gros

roulette [ru:'lɛt] *n* roulette *f*

Roumania [ru:'meɪnɪə] *n* = **Romania**

round [raund] *adj* rond(e) ♦ *n* (BRIT: *of toast*) tranche *f*; (*duty*: *of policeman, milkman etc*) tournée *f*; (: *of doctor*) visites *fpl*; (*game*: *of cards, in competition*) partie *f*; (BOXING) round *m*; (*of talks*) série *f* ♦ *vt* (*corner*) tourner ♦ *prep* autour de ♦ *adv*: **all ~** tout autour; **the long way ~** (par) le chemin le plus long; **all the year ~** toute l'année; **it's just ~ the corner** (*fig*) c'est tout près; **~ the clock** 24 heures sur 24; **to go ~ to sb's (house)** aller chez qn; **go ~ the back** passez par derrière; **enough to go ~** assez pour tout le monde; **~ of ammunition** cartouche *f*; **~ of applause** ban *m*, applaudissements *mpl*; **~ of drinks** tournée *f*; **~ of sandwiches** sandwich *m*; **~ off** *vt* (*speech etc*) terminer; **~ up** *vt* rassembler; (*criminals*) effectuer une rafle de; (*price, figure*) arrondir (au chiffre supérieur); **~about** *n* (BRIT: AUT) rond-point *m* (à sens giratoire); (: *at fair*) manège *m* (de chevaux de bois) ♦ *adj* (*route, means*) détourné(e); **~ers** *n* (*game*) *sorte de baseball*; **~ly** *adv* (*fig*) tout net, carrément; **~ trip** *n* (voyage *m*) aller et retour *m*; **~up** *n* rassemblement *m*; (*of criminals*) rafle *f*

rouse [rauz] *vt* (*wake up*) réveiller; (*stir up*) susciter; provoquer; éveiller; **rousing** *adj* (*welcome*) enthousiaste

route [ru:t] *n* itinéraire *m*; (*of bus*) parcours *m*; (*of trade, shipping*) route *f*

routine [ru:'ti:n] *adj* (*work*) ordinaire, courant(e); (*procedure*) d'usage ♦ *n* (*habits*) habitudes *fpl*; (*pej*) train-train *m*; (THEATRE) numéro *m*

rove [rəuv] *vt* (*area, streets*) errer dans

row¹ [rəu] *n* (*line*) rangée *f*; (*of people, seats,* KNITTING) rang *m*; (*behind one another*: *of cars, people*) file *f* ♦ *vi* (*in boat*) ramer; (*as sport*) faire de l'aviron ♦ *vt* (*boat*) faire aller à la rame *or* à l'aviron; **in a ~** (*fig*) d'affilée

row² [rau] *n* (*noise*) vacarme *m*; (*dispute*) dispute *f*, querelle *f*; (*scolding*) réprimande *f*, savon *m* ♦ *vi* se disputer, se quereller

rowboat ['rəubəut] (US) *n* canot *m* (à rames)

rowdy ['raudɪ] *adj* chahuteur(-euse); (*occasion*) tapageur(-euse)

rowing ['rəuɪŋ] *n* canotage *m*; (*as sport*) aviron *m*; **~ boat** (BRIT) *n* canot *m* (à rames)

royal ['rɔɪəl] *adj* royal(e); **R~ Air Force** (BRIT) *n armée de l'air britannique*; **~ty** *n* (*royal persons*) (membres *mpl* de la) famille royale; (*payment*: *to author*) droits *mpl* d'auteur; (: *to inventor*) royalties *fpl*

rpm *abbr* (AUT) (= *revolutions per minute*)

tr/mn

RSVP *abbr* (= *répondez s'il vous plaît*) R.S.V.P.

Rt Hon. *abbr* (*BRIT*: *Right Honourable*) *titre donné aux députés de la Chambre des communes*

rub [rʌb] *vt* frotter; frictionner; (*hands*) se frotter ♦ *n* (*with cloth*) coup *m* chiffon *or* de torchon; **to give sth a ~** donner un coup de chiffon *or* de torchon à; **to ~ sb up** *(BRIT) or* **to ~ sb** *(US)* **the wrong way** prendre qn à rebrousse-poil; **~ off** *vi* partir; **~ off on** *vt fus* déteindre sur; **~ out** *vt* effacer

rubber ['rʌbəʳ] *n* caoutchouc *m*; (*BRIT*: *eraser*) gomme *f* (à effacer); **~ band** *n* élastique *m*; **~ plant** *n* caoutchouc *m* (*plante verte*)

rubbish ['rʌbɪʃ] *n* (*from household*) ordures *fpl*; (*fig*: *pej*) camelote *f*; (: *nonsense*) bêtises *fpl*, idioties *fpl*; **~ bin** (*BRIT*) *n* poubelle *f*; **~ dump** *n* décharge publique, dépotoir *m*

rubble ['rʌbl] *n* décombres *mpl*; (*smaller*) gravats *mpl*; (*CONSTR*) blocage *m*

ruby ['ru:bɪ] *n* rubis *m*

rucksack ['rʌksæk] *n* sac *m* à dos

rudder ['rʌdəʳ] *n* gouvernail *m*

ruddy ['rʌdɪ] *adj* (*face*) coloré(e); (*inf*: *damned*) sacré(e), fichu(e)

rude [ru:d] *adj* (*impolite*) impoli(e); (*coarse*) grossier(-ère); (*shocking*) indécent(e), inconvenant(e)

ruffle ['rʌfl] *vt* (*hair*) ébouriffer; (*clothes*) chiffonner; (*fig*: *person*): **to get ~d** s'énerver

rug [rʌg] *n* petit tapis; (*BRIT*: *blanket*) couverture *f*

rugby ['rʌgbɪ] *n* (*also*: **~ football**) rugby *m*

rugged ['rʌgɪd] *adj* (*landscape*) accidenté(e); (*features, character*) rude

ruin ['ru:ɪn] *n* ruine *f* ♦ *vt* ruiner; (*spoil, clothes*) abîmer; (*event*) gâcher; **~s** *npl* (*of building*) ruine(s)

rule [ru:l] *n* règle *f*; (*regulation*) règlement *m*; (*government*) autorité *f*, gouvernement *m* ♦ *vt* (*country*) gouverner; (*person*) dominer ♦ *vi* commander; (*LAW*) statuer; **as a ~** normalement, en règle générale; **~ out** *vt* exclure; **~d** *adj* (*paper*) réglé(e); **~r** *n* (*sovereign*) souverain(e); (*for measuring*) règle *f*; **ruling** *adj* (*party*) au pouvoir; (*class*) dirigeant(e) ♦ *n* (*LAW*) décision *f*

rum [rʌm] *n* rhum *m*

Rumania [ru:'meɪnɪə] *n* = **Romania**

rumble ['rʌmbl] *vi* gronder; (*stomach, pipe*) gargouiller

rummage ['rʌmɪdʒ] *vi* fouiller

rumour ['ru:məʳ] (*US* **rumor**) *n* rumeur *f*, bruit *m* (qui court) ♦ *vt*: **it is ~ed that** le bruit court que

rump [rʌmp] *n* (*of animal*) croupe *f*; (*inf*: *of person*) postérieur *m*; **~ steak** *n* rumsteck *m*

rumpus ['rʌmpəs] (*inf*) *n* tapage *m*, chahut *m*

run [rʌn] (*pt* **ran**, *pp* **run**) *n* (*fast pace*) (pas *m* de) course *f*; (*outing*) tour *m or* promenade *f* (en voiture); (*distance travelled*) parcours *m*, trajet *m*; (*series*) suite *f*, série *f*; (*THEATRE*) série de représentations; (*SKI*) piste *f*; (*CRICKET, BASEBALL*) point *m*; (*in tights, stockings*) maille filée, échelle *f* ♦ *vt* (*operate*: *business*) diriger; (: *competition, course*) organiser; (: *hotel, house*) tenir; (*race*) participer à; (*COMPUT*) exécuter; (*to pass*: *hand, finger*) passer; (*water, bath*) faire couler; (*PRESS*: *feature*) publier ♦ *vi* courir; (*flee*) s'enfuir; (*work*: *machine, factory*) marcher; (*bus, train*) circuler; (*continue*: *play*) se jouer; (: *contract*) être valide; (*flow*: *river, bath; nose*) couler; (*colours, washing*) déteindre; (*in election*) être candidat, se présenter; **to go for a ~** faire un peu de course à pied; **there was a ~ on ...** (*meat, tickets*) les gens se sont rués sur ...; **in the long ~** à longue échéance; à la longue; en fin de compte; **on the ~** en fuite; **I'll ~ you to the station** je vais vous emmener *or* conduire à la gare; **to ~ a risk** courir un risque; ~ **about** *vi* (*children*) courir çà et là; ~ **across** *vt fus* (*find*) trouver par hasard; ~ **around** *vi* = **run about**; ~ **away** *vi* s'enfuir; ~ **down** *vt* (*production*) réduire progressivement; (*factory*) réduire progressivement la production de; (*AUT*) renverser; (*criticize*) critiquer, dénigrer; **to be ~ down** (*person*: *tired*) être fatigué(e) *or* à plat; ~ **in** (*BRIT*) *vt* (*car*) roder; ~ **into** *vt fus* (*meet*: *person*) rencontrer par hasard; (*trouble*) se heurter à; (*collide with*) heurter; ~ **off** *vi* s'enfuir ♦ *vt* (*water*) laisser s'écouler; (*copies*) tirer; ~ **out** *vi* (*person*) sortir en courant; (*liquid*) couler; (*lease*) expirer; (*money*) être épuisé(e); ~ **out of** *vt fus* se trouver à court de; ~ **over** *vt* (*AUT*) écraser ♦ *vt fus* (*revise*) revoir, reprendre; ~ **through** *vt fus* (*recapitulate*) reprendre; (*play*) répéter; ~ **up** *vt*: **to ~ up against** (*difficulties*) se heurter à; **to ~ up a debt** s'endetter; **~away** *adj* (*horse*) emballé(e); (*truck*) fou (folle); (*person*) fugitif(-ive); (*teenager*) fugeur(-euse)

rung [rʌŋ] *pp of* **ring** ♦ *n* (*of ladder*) barreau *m*

runner ['rʌnə^r] *n* (*in race*: *person*) coureur(-euse); (: *horse*) partant *m*; (*on sledge*) patin *m*; (*for drawer etc*) coulisseau *m*; ~ **bean** (*BRIT*) *n* haricot *m* (à rames); **~-up** *n* second(e)

running ['rʌnɪŋ] *n* course *f*; (*of business, organization*) gestion *f*, direction *f* ♦ *adj* (*water*) courant(e); **to be in/out of the ~ for sth** être/ne pas être sur les rangs pour qch; **6 days ~** 6 jours de suite; ~ **commentary** *n* commentaire détaillé; ~ **costs** *npl* frais *mpl* d'exploitation

runny ['rʌnɪ] *adj* qui coule

run-of-the-mill ['rʌnəvðə'mɪl] *adj* ordinaire, banal(e)

runt [rʌnt] *n* avorton *m*

run-up ['rʌnʌp] *n*: **~-~ to sth** (*election etc*) période *f* précédant qch

runway ['rʌnweɪ] *n* (*AVIAT*) piste *f*

rupture ['rʌptʃə^r] *n* (*MED*) hernie *f*

rural ['ruərl] *adj* rural(e)

rush [rʌʃ] *n* (*hurry*) hâte *f*, précipitation *f*; (*of crowd, COMM*: *sudden demand*) ruée *f*; (*current*) flot *m*; (*of emotion*) vague *f*; (*BOT*) jonc *m* ♦ *vt* (*hurry*) transporter *or* envoyer d'urgence ♦ *vi* se précipiter; ~ **hour** *n* heures *fpl* de pointe

rusk [rʌsk] *n* biscotte *f*

Russia ['rʌʃə] *n* Russie *f*; **~n** *adj* russe ♦ *n* Russe *m/f*; (*LING*) russe *m*

rust [rʌst] *n* rouille *f* ♦ *vi* rouiller

rustic ['rʌstɪk] *adj* rustique

rustle ['rʌsl] *vi* bruire, produire un bruissement ♦ *vt* froisser

rustproof ['rʌstpru:f] *adj* inoxydable

rusty ['rʌstɪ] *adj* rouillé(e)

rut [rʌt] *n* ornière *f*; (*ZOOL*) rut *m*; **to be in a ~** suivre l'ornière, s'encroûter

ruthless ['ru:θlɪs] *adj* sans pitié, impitoyable

rye [raɪ] *n* seigle *m*

S, s

Sabbath ['sæbəθ] *n* (*Jewish*) sabbat *m*; (*Christian*) dimanche *m*

sabotage ['sæbətɑ:ʒ] *n* sabotage *m* ♦ *vt* saboter

saccharin(e) ['sækərɪn] *n* saccharine *f*

sachet ['sæʃeɪ] *n* sachet *m*

sack [sæk] *n* (*bag*) sac *m* ♦ *vt* (*dismiss*) renvoyer, mettre à la porte; (*plunder*) piller, mettre à sac; **to get the ~** être renvoyé(e), être mis(e) à la porte; **~ing** *n* (*material*) toile *f* à sac; (*dismissal*) renvoi *m*

sacrament ['sækrəmənt] *n* sacrement *m*

sacred ['seɪkrɪd] *adj* sacré(e)

sacrifice ['sækrɪfaɪs] *n* sacrifice *m* ♦ *vt* sacrifier

sad [sæd] *adj* triste; (*deplorable*) triste, fâcheux(-euse)

saddle ['sædl] *n* selle *f* ♦ *vt* (*horse*) seller; **to be ~d with sth** (*inf*) avoir qch

sur les bras; **~bag** *n* sacoche *f*
sadistic [sə'dɪstɪk] *adj* sadique
sadly ['sædlɪ] *adv* tristement; (*unfortunately*) malheureusement; (*seriously*) fort
sadness ['sædnɪs] *n* tristesse *f*
s.a.e. *n abbr* = **stamped addressed envelope**
safe [seɪf] *adj* (*out of danger*) hors de danger, en sécurité; (*not dangerous*) sans danger; (*cautious*) prudent(e); (*sure*: *bet etc*) assuré(e) ♦ *n* coffre-fort *m*; **~ from** à l'abri de; **~ and sound** sain(e) et sauf (sauve); **(just) to be on the ~ side** pour plus de sûreté, par précaution; **~ journey!** bon voyage!; **~-conduct** *n* sauf-conduit *m*; **~-deposit** *n* (*vault*) dépôt *m* de coffres-forts; (*box*) coffre-fort *m*; **~guard** *n* sauvegarde *f*, protection *f* ♦ *vt* sauvegarder, protéger; **~keeping** *n* bonne garde; **~ly** *adv* (*assume, say*) sans risque d'erreur; (*drive, arrive*) sans accident; **~ sex** *n* rapports *mpl* sexuels sans risque
safety ['seɪftɪ] *n* sécurité *f*; **~ belt** *n* ceinture *f* de sécurité; **~ pin** *n* épingle *f* de sûreté *or* de nourrice; **~ valve** *n* soupape *f* de sûreté
sag [sæg] *vi* s'affaisser; (*hem, breasts*) pendre
sage [seɪdʒ] *n* (*herb*) sauge *f*; (*person*) sage *m*
Sagittarius [sædʒɪ'tɛərɪəs] *n* le Sagittaire
Sahara [sə'hɑːrə] *n*: **the ~ (Desert)** le (désert du) Sahara
said [sɛd] *pt, pp of* **say**
sail [seɪl] *n* (*on boat*) voile *f*; (*trip*): **to go for a ~** faire un tour en bateau ♦ *vt* (*boat*) manœuvrer, piloter ♦ *vi* (*travel*: *ship*) avancer, naviguer; (*set off*) partir, prendre la mer; (*SPORT*) faire de la voile; **they ~ed into Le Havre** ils sont entrés dans le port du Havre; **~ through** *vi, vt fus* (*fig*) réussir haut la main; **~boat** (*US*) *n* bateau *m* à voiles, voilier *m*; **~ing** *n* (*SPORT*) voile *f*; **to go ~ing** faire de la voile; **~ing boat** *n* bateau *m* à voiles, voilier *m*; **~ing ship** *n* grand voilier; **~or** *n* marin *m*, matelot *m*
saint [seɪnt] *n* saint(e)
sake [seɪk] *n*: **for the ~ of** pour (l'amour de), dans l'intérêt de; par égard pour
salad ['sæləd] *n* salade *f*; **~ bowl** *n* saladier *m*; **~ cream** (*BRIT*) *n* (sorte *f* de) mayonnaise *f*; **~ dressing** *n* vinaigrette *f*
salami [sə'lɑːmɪ] *n* salami *m*
salary ['sælərɪ] *n* salaire *m*
sale [seɪl] *n* vente *f*; (*at reduced prices*) soldes *mpl*; **"for ~"** "à vendre"; **on ~** en vente; **on ~ or return** vendu(e) avec faculté de retour; **~room** *n* salle *f* des ventes; **~s assistant** (*US* **sales clerk**) *n* vendeur(-euse); **~sman** (*irreg*) *n* vendeur *m*; (*representative*) représentant *m*; **~s rep** *n* (*COMM*) représentant(e) *m/f*; **~swoman** (*irreg*) *n* vendeuse *f*; (*representative*) représentante *f*
salmon ['sæmən] *n inv* saumon *m*
salon ['sælɔn] *n* salon *m*
saloon [sə'luːn] *n* (*US*) bar *m*; (*BRIT*: *AUT*) berline *f*; (*ship's lounge*) salon *m*
salt [sɔːlt] *n* sel *m* ♦ *vt* saler; **~ cellar** *n* salière *f*; **~water** *adj* de mer; **~y** *adj* salé(e)
salute [sə'luːt] *n* salut *m* ♦ *vt* saluer
salvage ['sælvɪdʒ] *n* (*saving*) sauvetage *m*; (*things saved*) biens sauvés *or* récupérés ♦ *vt* sauver, récupérer
salvation [sæl'veɪʃən] *n* salut *m*; **S~ Army** *n* armée *f* du Salut
same [seɪm] *adj* même ♦ *pron*: **the ~** le (la) même, les mêmes; **the ~ book as** le même livre que; **at the ~ time** en même temps; **all** *or* **just the ~** tout de même, quand même; **to do the ~** faire de même, en faire autant; **to do the ~ as sb** faire comme qn; **the ~ to you!** à vous de même!; (*after insult*) toi-même!
sample ['sɑːmpl] *n* échantillon *m*; (*blood*) prélèvement *m* ♦ *vt* (*food, wine*)

goûter

sanction ['sæŋkʃən] *n* approbation *f*, sanction *f*

sanctity ['sæŋktɪtɪ] *n* sainteté *f*, caractère sacré

sanctuary ['sæŋktjuərɪ] *n* (*holy place*) sanctuaire *m*; (*refuge*) asile *m*; (*for wild life*) réserve *f*

sand [sænd] *n* sable *m* ♦ *vt* (*furniture*: *also:* ~ **down**) poncer

sandal ['sændl] *n* sandale *f*

sand: **~box** (*US*) *n* tas *m* de sable; **~castle** *n* château *m* de sable; **~paper** *n* papier *m* de verre; **~pit** (*BRIT*) *n* (*for children*) tas *m* de sable; **~stone** *n* grès *m*

sandwich ['sændwɪtʃ] *n* sandwich *m*; **cheese/ham ~** sandwich au fromage/jambon; **~ course** (*BRIT*) *n* cours *m* de formation professionnelle

sandy ['sændɪ] *adj* sablonneux(-euse); (*colour*) sable *inv*, blond roux *inv*

sane [seɪn] *adj* (*person*) sain(e) d'esprit; (*outlook*) sensé(e), sain(e)

sang [sæŋ] *pt of* **sing**

sanitary ['sænɪtərɪ] *adj* (*system, arrangements*) sanitaire; (*clean*) hygiénique; **~ towel** (*US* **sanitary napkin**) *n* serviette *f* hygiénique

sanitation [sænɪ'teɪʃən] *n* (*in house*) installations *fpl* sanitaires; (*in town*) système *m* sanitaire; **~ department** (*US*) *n* service *m* de voirie

sanity ['sænɪtɪ] *n* santé mentale; (*common sense*) bon sens

sank [sæŋk] *pt of* **sink**

Santa Claus [sæntə'klɔːz] *n* le père Noël

sap [sæp] *n* (*of plants*) sève *f* ♦ *vt* (*strength*) saper, miner

sapling ['sæplɪŋ] *n* jeune arbre *m*

sapphire ['sæfaɪə^r] *n* saphir *m*

sarcasm ['sɑːkæzm] *n* sarcasme *m*, raillerie *f*; **sarcastic** [sɑː'kæstɪk] *adj* sarcastique

sardine [sɑː'diːn] *n* sardine *f*

Sardinia [sɑː'dɪnɪə] *n* Sardaigne *f*

sash [sæʃ] *n* écharpe *f*

sat [sæt] *pt, pp of* **sit**

satchel ['sætʃl] *n* cartable *m*

satellite ['sætəlaɪt] *n* satellite *m*; **~ dish** *n* antenne *f* parabolique; **~ television** *n* télévision *f* par câble

satin ['sætɪn] *n* satin *m* ♦ *adj* en *or* de satin, satiné(e)

satire ['sætaɪə^r] *n* satire *f*

satisfaction [sætɪs'fækʃən] *n* satisfaction *f*

satisfactory [sætɪs'fæktərɪ] *adj* satisfaisant(e)

satisfied ['sætɪsfaɪd] *adj* satisfait(e)

satisfy ['sætɪsfaɪ] *vt* satisfaire, contenter; (*convince*) convaincre, persuader; **~ing** *adj* satisfaisant(e)

Saturday ['sætədɪ] *n* samedi *m*

sauce [sɔːs] *n* sauce *f*; **~pan** *n* casserole *f*

saucer ['sɔːsə^r] *n* soucoupe *f*

Saudi ['saudi-]: **~ Arabia** *n* Arabie Saoudite; **~ (Arabian)** *adj* saoudien(ne)

sauna ['sɔːnə] *n* sauna *m*

saunter ['sɔːntə^r] *vi*: **to ~ along/in/out** *etc* marcher/entrer/sortir *etc* d'un pas nonchalant

sausage ['sɔsɪdʒ] *n* saucisse *f*; (*cold meat*) saucisson *m*; **~ roll** *n* ≃ friand *m*

savage ['sævɪdʒ] *adj* (*cruel, fierce*) brutal(e), féroce; (*primitive*) primitif(-ive), sauvage ♦ *n* sauvage *m/f*

save [seɪv] *vt* (*person, belongings*) sauver; (*money*) mettre de côté, économiser; (*time*) (faire) gagner; (*keep*) garder; (*COMPUT*) sauvegarder; (*SPORT*: *stop*) arrêter; (*avoid*: *trouble*) éviter ♦ *vi* (*also:* **~ up**) mettre de l'argent de côté ♦ *n* (*SPORT*) arrêt *m* (du ballon) ♦ *prep* sauf, à l'exception de

saving ['seɪvɪŋ] *n* économie *f* ♦ *adj*: **the ~ grace of sth** ce qui rachète qch; **~s** *npl* (*money saved*) économies *fpl*; **~s account** *n* compte *m* d'épargne; **~s bank** *n* caisse *f* d'épargne

saviour ['seɪvjə^r] (*US* **savior**) *n* sauveur *m*

savour ['seɪvəʳ] (*US* **savor**) *vt* savourer; **~y** (*US* **savory**) *adj* (*dish: not sweet*) salé(e)

saw [sɔː] (*pt* **sawed**, *pp* **sawed** *or* **sawn**) *vt* scier ♦ *n* (*tool*) scie *f* ♦ *pt of* **see**; **~dust** *n* sciure *f*; **~mill** *n* scierie *f*; **~n-off** *adj*: **~n-off shotgun** carabine *f* à canon scié

sax [sæks] (*inf*) *n* saxo *m*

saxophone ['sæksəfəun] *n* saxophone *m*

say [seɪ] (*pt, pp* **said**) *n*: **to have one's ~** dire ce qu'on a à dire ♦ *vt* dire; **to have a** *or* **some ~ in sth** avoir voix au chapitre; **could you ~ that again?** pourriez-vous répéter ce que vous venez de dire?; **that goes without ~ing** cela va sans dire, cela va de soi; **~ing** *n* dicton *m*, proverbe *m*

scab [skæb] *n* croûte *f*; (*pej*) jaune *m*

scaffold ['skæfəld] *n* échafaud *m*; **~ing** *n* échafaudage *m*

scald [skɔːld] *n* brûlure *f* ♦ *vt* ébouillanter

scale [skeɪl] *n* (*of fish*) écaille *f*; (*MUS*) gamme *f*; (*of ruler, thermometer etc*) graduation *f*, échelle (graduée); (*of salaries, fees etc*) barème *m*; (*of map, also size, extent*) échelle ♦ *vt* (*mountain*) escalader; **~s** *npl* (*for weighing*) balance *f*; (*also:* **bathroom ~**) pèse-personne *m inv*; **on a large ~** sur une grande échelle, en grand; **~ of charges** tableau *m* des tarifs; **~ down** *vt* réduire

scallop ['skɔləp] *n* coquille *f* Saint-Jacques; (*SEWING*) feston *m*

scalp [skælp] *n* cuir chevelu ♦ *vt* scalper

scampi ['skæmpɪ] *npl* langoustines (frites), scampi *mpl*

scan [skæn] *vt* scruter, examiner; (*glance at quickly*) parcourir; (*TV, RADAR*) balayer ♦ *n* (*MED*) scanographie *f*

scandal ['skændl] *n* scandale *m*; (*gossip*) ragots *mpl*

Scandinavia [skændɪ'neɪvɪə] *n* Scandinavie *f*; **~n** *adj* scandinave

scant [skænt] *adj* insuffisant(e); **~y** ['skæntɪ] *adj* peu abondant(e), insuffisant(e); (*underwear*) minuscule

scapegoat ['skeɪpgəut] *n* bouc *m* émissaire

scar [skɑː] *n* cicatrice *f* ♦ *vt* marquer (d'une cicatrice)

scarce [skɛəs] *adj* rare, peu abondant(e); **to make o.s. ~** (*inf*) se sauver; **~ly** *adv* à peine; **scarcity** *n* manque *m*, pénurie *f*

scare [skɛəʳ] *n* peur *f*, panique *f* ♦ *vt* effrayer, faire peur à; **to ~ sb stiff** faire une peur bleue à qn; **bomb ~** alerte *f* à la bombe; **~ away** *vt* faire fuir; **~ off** *vt* = **scare away**; **~crow** *n* épouvantail *m*; **~d** *adj*: **to be ~d** avoir peur

scarf [skɑːf] (*pl* **~s** *or* **scarves**) *n* (*long*) écharpe *f*; (*square*) foulard *m*

scarlet ['skɑːlɪt] *adj* écarlate; **~ fever** *n* scarlatine *f*

scary ['skɛərɪ] (*inf*) *adj* effrayant(e)

scathing ['skeɪðɪŋ] *adj* cinglant(e), acerbe

scatter ['skætəʳ] *vt* éparpiller, répandre; (*crowd*) disperser ♦ *vi* se disperser; **~brained** *adj* écervelé(e), étourdi(e)

scavenger ['skævəndʒəʳ] *n* (*person: in bins etc*) pilleur *m* de poubelles

scene [siːn] *n* scène *f*; (*of crime, accident*) lieu(x) *m(pl)*; (*sight, view*) spectacle *m*, vue *f*; **~ry** ['siːnərɪ] *n* (*THEATRE*) décor(s) *m(pl)*; (*landscape*) paysage *m*; **scenic** *adj* (*picturesque*) offrant de beaux paysages *or* panoramas

scent [sɛnt] *n* parfum *m*, odeur *f*; (*track*) piste *f*

sceptical ['skɛptɪkl] (*US* **skeptical**) *adj* sceptique

schedule ['ʃɛdjuːl, (*US*) 'skɛdjuːl] *n* programme *m*, plan *m*; (*of trains*) horaire *m*; (*of prices etc*) barème *m*, tarif *m* ♦ *vt* prévoir; **on ~** à l'heure (prévue); à la date prévue; **to be ahead of/behind ~** avoir de l'avance/du retard; **~d flight** *n* vol régulier

scheme [skiːm] *n* plan *m*, projet *m*;

(*dishonest plan, plot*) complot *m*, combine *f*; (*arrangement*) arrangement *m*, classification *f*; (*pension ~ etc*) régime *m* ♦ *vi* comploter, manigancer; **scheming** *adj* rusé(e), intrigant(e) ♦ *n* manigances *fpl*, intrigues *fpl*

scholar ['skɔlə^r] *n* érudit(e); (*pupil*) boursier(-ère); **~ship** *n* (*knowledge*) érudition *f*; (*grant*) bourse *f* (d'études)

school [sku:l] *n* école *f*; (*secondary ~*) collège *m*, lycée *m*; (*US: university*) université *f*; (*in university*) faculté *f* ♦ *cpd* scolaire; **~book** *n* livre *m* scolaire *or* de classe; **~boy** *n* écolier *m*; collégien *m*, lycéen *m*; **~children** *npl* écoliers *mpl*; collégiens *mpl*, lycéens *mpl*; **~girl** *n* écolière *f*; collégienne *f*, lycéenne *f*; **~ing** *n* instruction *f*, études *fpl*; **~master** *n* professeur *m*; **~mistress** *n* professeur *m*; **~teacher** *n* instituteur(-trice); professeur *m*

science ['saɪəns] *n* science *f*; **~ fiction** *n* science-fiction *f*; **scientific** [saɪən'tɪfɪk] *adj* scientifique; **scientist** *n* scientifique *m/f*; (*eminent*) savant *m*

scissors ['sɪzəz] *npl* ciseaux *mpl*

scoff [skɔf] *vt* (*BRIT: inf: eat*) avaler, bouffer ♦ *vi*: **to ~ (at)** (*mock*) se moquer (de)

scold [skəuld] *vt* gronder

scone [skɔn] *n sorte de petit pain rond au lait*

scoop [sku:p] *n* pelle *f* (à main); (*for ice cream*) boule *f* à glace; (*PRESS*) scoop *m*; **~ out** *vt* évider, creuser; **~ up** *vt* ramasser

scooter ['sku:tə^r] *n* (*also: **motor ~***) scooter *m*; (*toy*) trottinette *f*

scope [skəup] *n* (*capacity: of plan, undertaking*) portée *f*, envergure *f*; (*: of person*) compétence *f*, capacités *fpl*; (*opportunity*) possibilités *fpl*; **within the ~ of** dans les limites de

scorch [skɔ:tʃ] *vt* (*clothes*) brûler (légèrement), roussir; (*earth, grass*) dessécher, brûler

score [skɔ:^r] *n* score *m*, décompte *m* des points; (*MUS*) partition *f*; (*twenty*) vingt ♦ *vt* (*goal, point*) marquer; (*success*) remporter ♦ *vi* marquer des points; (*FOOTBALL*) marquer un but; (*keep ~*) compter les points; **~s of** (*very many*) beaucoup de, un tas de (*fam*); **on that ~** sur ce chapitre, à cet égard; **to ~ 6 out of 10** obtenir 6 sur 10; **~ out** *vt* rayer, barrer, biffer; **~board** *n* tableau *m*

scorn [skɔ:n] *n* mépris *m*, dédain *m*

Scorpio ['skɔ:pɪəu] *n* le Scorpion

Scot [skɔt] *n* Écossais(e)

Scotch [skɔtʃ] *n* whisky *m*, scotch *m*

scot-free ['skɔt'fri:] *adv*: **to get off ~-~** s'en tirer sans être puni(e)

Scotland ['skɔtlənd] *n* Écosse *f*; **Scots** *adj* écossais(e); **Scotsman** (*irreg*) *n* Écossais; **Scotswoman** (*irreg*) *n* Écossaise *f*; **Scottish** *adj* écossais(e); **Scottish Parliament** *n* Parlement *m* écossais

scoundrel ['skaundrl] *n* vaurien *m*

scour ['skauə^r] *vt* (*search*) battre, parcourir

scout [skaut] *n* (*MIL*) éclaireur *m*; (*also: **boy ~***) scout *m*; **girl ~** (*US*) guide *f*; **~ around** *vi* explorer, chercher

scowl [skaul] *vi* avoir l'air maussade; **to ~ at** regarder de travers

scrabble ['skræbl] *vi* (*also: **~ around**: search*) chercher à tâtons; (*claw*): **to ~ (at)** gratter ♦ *n*: **S~** ® Scrabble ® *m*

scram [skræm] (*inf*) *vi* ficher le camp

scramble ['skræmbl] *n* (*rush*) bousculade *f*, ruée *f* ♦ *vi*: **to ~ up/down** grimper/descendre tant bien que mal; **to ~ out** sortir *or* descendre à toute vitesse; **to ~ through** se frayer un passage (à travers); **to ~ for** se bousculer *or* se disputer pour (avoir); **~d eggs** *npl* œufs brouillés

scrap [skræp] *n* bout *m*, morceau *m*; (*fight*) bagarre *f*; (*also: **~ iron***) ferraille *f* ♦ *vt* jeter, mettre au rebut; (*fig*) abandonner, laisser tomber ♦ *vi* (*fight*) se bagarrer; **~s** *npl* (*waste*) déchets *mpl*;

~book *n* album *m*; **~ dealer** *n* marchand *m* de ferraille

scrape [skreɪp] *vt, vi* gratter, racler ♦ *n*: **to get into a ~** s'attirer des ennuis; **to ~ through** réussir de justesse; **~ together** *vt* (*money*) racler ses fonds de tiroir pour réunir

scrap: ~ heap *n*: **on the ~ heap** (*fig*) au rancart *or* rebut; **~ merchant** (BRIT) *n* marchand *m* de ferraille; **~ paper** *n* papier *m* brouillon

scratch [skrætʃ] *n* égratignure *f*, rayure *f*; éraflure *f*; (*from claw*) coup *m* de griffe ♦ *cpd*: **~ team** équipe de fortune *or* improvisée ♦ *vt* (*rub*) (se) gratter; (*record*) rayer; (*paint etc*) érafler; (*with claw, nail*) griffer ♦ *vi* (se) gratter; **to start from ~** partir de zéro; **to be up to ~** être à la hauteur

scrawl [skrɔːl] *vi* gribouiller

scrawny ['skrɔːnɪ] *adj* décharné(e)

scream [skriːm] *n* cri perçant, hurlement *m* ♦ *vi* crier, hurler

screech [skriːtʃ] *vi* hurler; (*tyres*) crisser; (*brakes*) grincer

screen [skriːn] *n* écran *m*; (*in room*) paravent *m*; (*fig*) écran, rideau *m* ♦ *vt* (*conceal*) masquer, cacher; (*from the wind etc*) abriter, protéger; (*film*) projeter; (*candidates etc*) filtrer; **~ing** *n* (MED) test *m* (*or* tests) de dépistage; **~play** *n* scénario *m*; **~ saver** *n* (COMPUT) économiseur *m* d'écran

screw [skruː] *n* vis *f* ♦ *vt* (*also:* **~ in**) visser; **~ up** *vt* (*paper etc*) froisser; **to ~ up one's eyes** plisser les yeux; **~driver** *n* tournevis *m*

scribble ['skrɪbl] *vt, vi* gribouiller, griffonner

script [skrɪpt] *n* (CINEMA *etc*) scénario *m*, texte *m*; (*writing*) (écriture *f*) script *m*

Scripture(s) ['skrɪptʃəʳ(-əz)] *n(pl)* (*Christian*) Écriture sainte; (*other religions*) écritures saintes

scroll [skrəul] *n* rouleau *m*

scrounge [skraundʒ] (*inf*) *vt*: **to ~ sth off** *or* **from sb** taper qn de qch; **~r** (*inf*) *n* parasite *m*

scrub [skrʌb] *n* (*land*) broussailles *fpl* ♦ *vt* (*floor*) nettoyer à la brosse; (*pan*) récurer; (*washing*) frotter; (*inf: cancel*) annuler

scruff [skrʌf] *n*: **by the ~ of the neck** par la peau du cou

scruffy ['skrʌfɪ] *adj* débraillé(e)

scrum(mage) ['skrʌm(ɪdʒ)] *n* (RUGBY) mêlée *f*

scruple ['skruːpl] *n* scrupule *m*

scrutiny ['skruːtɪnɪ] *n* examen minutieux

scuff [skʌf] *vt* érafler

scuffle ['skʌfl] *n* échauffourée *f*, rixe *f*

sculptor ['skʌlptəʳ] *n* sculpteur *m*

sculpture ['skʌlptʃəʳ] *n* sculpture *f*

scum [skʌm] *n* écume *f*, mousse *f*; (*pej: people*) rebut *m*, lie *f*

scurry ['skʌrɪ] *vi* filer à toute allure; **to ~ off** détaler, se sauver

scuttle ['skʌtl] *n* (*also:* **coal ~**) seau *m* (à charbon) ♦ *vt* (*ship*) saborder ♦ *vi* (*scamper*): **to ~ away** *or* **off** détaler

scythe [saɪð] *n* faux *f*

SDP *n abbr* (= *Social Democratic Party*)

sea [siː] *n* mer *f* ♦ *cpd* marin(e), de (la) mer; **by ~** (*travel*) par mer, en bateau; **on the ~** (*boat*) en mer; (*town*) au bord de la mer; **to be all at ~** (*fig*) nager complètement; **out to ~** au large; **(out) at ~** en mer; **~board** *n* côte *f*; **~food** *n* fruits *mpl* de mer; **~front** *n* bord *m* de mer; **~going** *adj* (*ship*) de mer; **~gull** *n* mouette *f*

seal [siːl] *n* (*animal*) phoque *m*; (*stamp*) sceau *m*, cachet *m* ♦ *vt* sceller; (*envelope*) coller; (: *with* ~) cacheter; **~ off** *vt* (*forbid entry to*) interdire l'accès de

sea level *n* niveau *m* de la mer

sea lion *n* otarie *f*

seam [siːm] *n* couture *f*; (*of coal*) veine *f*, filon *m*

seaman ['siːmən] (*irreg*) *n* marin *m*

seance ['seɪɔns] *n* séance *f* de spiritisme

seaplane ['si:pleɪn] *n* hydravion *m*

search [sə:tʃ] *n* (*for person, thing,* COMPUT) recherche(s) *f(pl)*; (LAW: *at sb's home*) perquisition *f* ♦ *vt* fouiller; (*examine*) examiner minutieusement; scruter ♦ *vi*: **to ~ for** chercher; **in ~ of** à la recherche de; **~ through** *vt fus* fouiller; **~ing** *adj* pénétrant(e); **~light** *n* projecteur *m*; **~ party** *n* expédition *f* de secours; **~ warrant** *n* mandat *m* de perquisition

sea: ~shore *n* rivage *m*, plage *f*, bord *m* de (la) mer; **~sick** *adj*: **to be ~sick** avoir le mal de mer; **~side** *n* bord *m* de la mer; **~side resort** *n* station *f* balnéaire

season ['si:zn] *n* saison *f* ♦ *vt* assaisonner, relever; **to be in/out of ~** être/ne pas être de saison; **~al** *adj* (*work*) saisonnier(-ère); **~ed** *adj* (*fig*) expérimenté(e); **~ ticket** *n* carte *f* d'abonnement

seat [si:t] *n* siège *m*; (*in bus, train: place*) place *f*; (*buttocks*) postérieur *m*; (*of trousers*) fond *m* ♦ *vt* faire asseoir, placer; (*have room for*) avoir des places assises pour, pouvoir accueillir; **~ belt** *n* ceinture *f* de sécurité

sea: ~ water *n* eau *f* de mer; **~weed** *n* algues *fpl*; **~worthy** *adj* en état de naviguer

sec. *abbr* = **second(s)**

secluded [sɪ'klu:dɪd] *adj* retiré(e), à l'écart

seclusion [sɪ'klu:ʒən] *n* solitude *f*

second¹ [sɪ'kɔnd] (BRIT) *vt* (*employee*) affecter provisoirement

second² ['sɛkənd] *adj* deuxième, second(e) ♦ *adv* (*in race etc*) en seconde position ♦ *n* (*unit of time*) seconde *f*; (AUT: *~ gear*) seconde; (COMM: *imperfect*) article *m* de second choix; (BRIT: UNIV) licence *f* avec mention ♦ *vt* (*motion*) appuyer; **~ary** *adj* secondaire; **~ary school** *n* collège *m*, lycée *m*; **~-class** *adj* de deuxième classe; (RAIL) de seconde (classe); (POST) au tarif réduit; (*pej*) de qualité inférieure ♦ *adv* (RAIL) en seconde; (POST) au tarif réduit; **~hand** *adj* d'occasion; de seconde main; **~ hand** *n* (*on clock*) trotteuse *f*; **~ly** *adv* deuxièmement; **~ment** [sɪ'kɔndmənt] (BRIT) *n* détachement *m*; **~-rate** *adj* de deuxième ordre, de qualité inférieure; **~ thoughts** *npl* doutes *mpl*; **on ~ thoughts** *or (US)* **thought** à la réflexion

secrecy ['si:krəsɪ] *n* secret *m*

secret ['si:krɪt] *adj* secret(-ète) ♦ *n* secret *m*; **in ~** en secret, secrètement, en cachette

secretary ['sɛkrətərɪ] *n* secrétaire *m/f*; (COMM) secrétaire général; **S~ of State (for)** (BRIT: POL) ministre *m* (de)

secretive ['si:krətɪv] *adj* dissimulé(e)

secretly ['si:krɪtlɪ] *adv* en secret, secrètement

sectarian [sɛk'tɛərɪən] *adj* sectaire

section ['sɛkʃən] *n* section *f*; (*of document*) section, article *m*, paragraphe *m*; (*cut*) coupe *f*

sector ['sɛktə^r] *n* secteur *m*

secular ['sɛkjulə^r] *adj* profane; laïque; séculier(-ère)

secure [sɪ'kjuə^r] *adj* (*free from anxiety*) sans inquiétude, sécurisé(e); (*firmly fixed*) solide, bien attaché(e) (*or* fermé(e) *etc*); (*in safe place*) en lieu sûr, en sûreté ♦ *vt* (*fix*) fixer, attacher; (*get*) obtenir, se procurer

security [sɪ'kjuərɪtɪ] *n* sécurité *f*, mesures *fpl* de sécurité; (*for loan*) caution *f*, garantie *f*; **~ guard** *n* garde chargé de la securité; (*when transporting money*) convoyeur *m* de fonds

sedate [sɪ'deɪt] *adj* calme; posé(e) ♦ *vt* (MED) donner des sédatifs à

sedative ['sɛdɪtɪv] *n* calmant *m*, sédatif *m*

seduce [sɪ'dju:s] *vt* séduire; **seduction** [sɪ'dʌkʃən] *n* séduction *f*; **seductive** *adj* séduisant(e); (*smile*) séducteur (-trice); (*fig: offer*) alléchant(e)

see [si:] (*pt* **saw**, *pp* **seen**) *vt* voir; (*accompany*): **to ~ sb to the door** reconduire *or* raccompagner qn jusqu'à la porte ♦ *vi* voir ♦ *n* évêché *m*; **to ~ that** (*ensure*) veiller à ce que *+sub*, faire en sorte que *+sub*, s'assurer que; **~ you soon!** à bientôt!; **~ about** *vt fus* s'occuper de; **~ off** *vt* accompagner (à la gare *or* à l'aéroport *etc*); **~ through** *vt* mener à bonne fin ♦ *vt fus* voir clair dans; **~ to** *vt fus* s'occuper de, se charger de

seed [siːd] *n* graine *f*; (*sperm*) semence *f*; (*fig*) germe *m*; (TENNIS *etc*) tête *f* de série; **to go to ~** monter en graine; (*fig*) se laisser aller; **~ling** *n* jeune plant *m*, semis *m*; **~y** *adj* (*shabby*) minable, miteux(-euse)

seeing ['siːɪŋ] *conj*: **~ (that)** vu que, étant donné que

seek [siːk] (*pt, pp* **sought**) *vt* chercher, rechercher

seem [siːm] *vi* sembler, paraître; **there ~s to be ...** il semble qu'il y a ...; on dirait qu'il y a ...; **~ingly** *adv* apparemment

seen [siːn] *pp of* **see**

seep [siːp] *vi* suinter, filtrer

seesaw ['siːsɔː] *n* (jeu *m* de) bascule *f*

seethe [siːð] *vi* être en effervescence; **to ~ with anger** bouillir de colère

see-through ['siːθruː] *adj* transparent(e)

segment ['sɛgmənt] *n* segment *m*; (*of orange*) quartier *m*

segregate ['sɛgrɪgeɪt] *vt* séparer, isoler

seize [siːz] *vt* saisir, attraper; (*take possession of*) s'emparer de; (*opportunity*) saisir; **~ up** *vi* (TECH) se gripper; **~ (up)on** *vt fus* saisir, sauter sur

seizure ['siːʒə^r] *n* (MED) crise *f*, attaque *f*; (*of power*) prise *f*

seldom ['sɛldəm] *adv* rarement

select [sɪ'lɛkt] *adj* choisi(e), d'élite ♦ *vt* sélectionner, choisir; **~ion** *n* sélection *f*, choix *m*

self [sɛlf] (*pl* **selves**) *n*: **the ~** le moi *inv* ♦ *prefix* auto-; **~-assured** *adj* sûr(e) de soi; **~-catering** (BRIT) *adj* avec cuisine, où l'on peut faire sa cuisine; **~-centred** (US **self-centered**) *adj* égocentrique; **~-confidence** *n* confiance *f* en soi; **~-conscious** *adj* timide, qui manque d'assurance; **~-contained** (BRIT) *adj* (*flat*) avec entrée particulière, indépendant(e); **~-control** *n* maîtrise *f* de soi; **~-defence** (US **self-defense**) *n* autodéfense *f*; (LAW) légitime défense *f*; **~-discipline** *n* discipline personnelle; **~-employed** *adj* qui travaille à son compte; **~-evident** *adj*: **to be ~-evident** être évident(e), aller de soi; **~-governing** *adj* autonome; **~-indulgent** *adj* qui ne se refuse rien; **~-interest** *n* intérêt personnel; **~ish** *adj* égoïste; **~ishness** *n* égoïsme *m*; **~less** *adj* désintéressé(e); **~-pity** *n* apitoiement *m* sur soi-même; **~-possessed** *adj* assuré(e); **~-preservation** *n* instinct *m* de conservation; **~-respect** *n* respect *m* de soi, amour-propre *m*; **~-righteous** *adj* suffisant(e); **~-sacrifice** *n* abnégation *f*; **~-satisfied** *adj* content(e) de soi, suffisant(e); **~-service** *adj* libre-service, self-service; **~-sufficient** *adj* autosuffisant(e); (*person*: *independent*) indépendant(e); **~-taught** *adj* (*artist, pianist*) qui a appris par lui-même

sell [sɛl] (*pt, pp* **sold**) *vt* vendre ♦ *vi* se vendre; **to ~ at** *or* **for 10 F** se vendre 10 F; **~ off** *vt* liquider; **~ out** *vi*: **to ~ out (of sth)** (*use up stock*) vendre tout son stock (de qch); **the tickets are all sold out** il ne reste plus de billets; **~-by date** *n* date *f* limite de vente; **~er** *n* vendeur(-euse), marchand(e); **~ing price** *n* prix *m* de vente

Sellotape ® ['sɛləuteɪp] (BRIT) *n* papier *m* collant, scotch ® *m*

selves [sɛlvz] *npl of* **self**

semblance ['sɛmbl̩ns] *n* semblant *m*

semen ['siːmən] *n* sperme *m*

semester [sɪ'mɛstə^r] (*esp* US) *n* semestre *m*

semi ['sɛmɪ] *prefix* semi-, demi-; à demi,

à moitié; **~circle** *n* demi-cercle *m*; **~colon** *n* point-virgule *m*; **~detached (house)** (*BRIT*) *n* maison jumelée *or* jumelle; **~final** *n* demi-finale *f*
seminar ['sɛmɪnɑːʳ] *n* séminaire *m*; **~y** *n* (*REL*: *for priests*) séminaire *m*
semiskilled [sɛmɪ'skɪld] *adj*: **~ worker** ouvrier(-ère) spécialisé(e)
semi-skimmed milk [sɛmɪ'skɪmd-] *n* lait *m* demi-écrémé
senate ['sɛnɪt] *n* sénat *m*; **senator** *n* sénateur *m*
send [sɛnd] (*pt, pp* **sent**) *vt* envoyer; **~ away** *vt* (*letter, goods*) envoyer, expédier; (*unwelcome visitor*) renvoyer; **~ away for** *vt fus* commander par correspondance, se faire envoyer; **~ back** *vt* renvoyer; **~ for** *vt fus* envoyer chercher; faire venir; **~ off** *vt* (*goods*) envoyer, expédier; (*BRIT*: *SPORT*: *player*) expulser *or* renvoyer du terrain; **~ out** *vt* (*invitation*) envoyer (par la poste); (*light, heat, signal*) émettre; **~ up** *vt* faire monter; (*BRIT*: *parody*) mettre en boîte, parodier; **~er** *n* expéditeur (-trice); **~-off** *n*: **a good ~-off** des adieux chaleureux
senior ['siːnɪəʳ] *adj* (*high-ranking*) de haut niveau; (*of higher rank*): **to be ~ to sb** être le supérieur de qn ♦ *n* (*older*): **she is 15 years his ~** elle est son aînée de 15 ans, elle est plus âgée que lui de 15 ans; **~ citizen** *n* personne âgée; **~ity** [siːnɪ'ɔrɪtɪ] *n* (*in service*) ancienneté *f*
sensation [sɛn'seɪʃən] *n* sensation *f*; **~al** *adj* qui fait sensation; (*marvellous*) sensationnel(le)
sense [sɛns] *n* sens *m*; (*feeling*) sentiment *m*; (*meaning*) sens, signification *f*; (*wisdom*) bon sens ♦ *vt* sentir, pressentir; **it makes ~** c'est logique; **~less** *adj* insensé(e), stupide; (*unconscious*) sans connaissance
sensible ['sɛnsɪbl] *adj* sensé(e), raisonnable; sage
sensitive ['sɛnsɪtɪv] *adj* sensible
sensual ['sɛnsjuəl] *adj* sensuel(le)
sensuous ['sɛnsjuəs] *adj* voluptueux (-euse), sensuel(le)
sent [sɛnt] *pt, pp of* **send**
sentence ['sɛntns] *n* (*LING*) phrase *f*; (*LAW*: *judgment*) condamnation *f*, sentence *f*; (: *punishment*) peine *f* ♦ *vt*: **to ~ sb to death/to 5 years in prison** condamner qn à mort/à 5 ans de prison
sentiment ['sɛntɪmənt] *n* sentiment *m*; (*opinion*) opinion *f*, avis *m*; **~al** [sɛntɪ'mɛntl] *adj* sentimental(e)
sentry ['sɛntrɪ] *n* sentinelle *f*
separate [*adj* 'sɛprɪt, *vb* 'sɛpəreɪt] *adj* séparé(e), indépendant(e), différent(e) ♦ *vt* séparer; (*make a distinction between*) distinguer ♦ *vi* se séparer; **~ly** *adv* séparément; **~s** *npl* (*clothes*) coordonnés *mpl*; **separation** [sɛpə'reɪʃən] *n* séparation *f*
September [sɛp'tɛmbəʳ] *n* septembre *m*
septic ['sɛptɪk] *adj* (*wound*) infecté(e); **~ tank** *n* fosse *f* septique
sequel ['siːkwl] *n* conséquence *f*; séquelles *fpl*; (*of story*) suite *f*
sequence ['siːkwəns] *n* ordre *m*, suite *f*; (*film ~*) séquence *f*; (*dance ~*) numéro *m*
sequin ['siːkwɪn] *n* paillette *f*
Serbia ['səːbɪə] *n* Serbie *f*
serene [sɪ'riːn] *adj* serein(e), calme, paisible
sergeant ['sɑːdʒənt] *n* sergent *m*; (*POLICE*) brigadier *m*
serial ['sɪərɪəl] *n* feuilleton *m*; **~ killer** *n* meurtrier *m* tuant en série; **~ number** *n* numéro *m* de série
series ['sɪərɪz] *n inv* série *f*; (*PUBLISHING*) collection *f*
serious ['sɪərɪəs] *adj* sérieux(-euse); (*illness*) grave; **~ly** *adv* sérieusement; (*hurt*) gravement
sermon ['səːmən] *n* sermon *m*
serrated [sɪ'reɪtɪd] *adj* en dents de scie
servant ['səːvənt] *n* domestique *m/f*;

(*fig*) serviteur/servante

serve [sə:v] *vt* (*employer etc*) servir, être au service de; (*purpose*) servir à; (*customer, food, meal*) servir; (*subj*: *train*) desservir; (*apprenticeship*) faire, accomplir; (*prison term*) purger ♦ *vi* servir; (*be useful*): **to ~ as/for/to do** servir de/à/à faire ♦ *n* (*TENNIS*) service *m*; **it ~s him right** c'est bien fait pour lui; **~ out, ~ up** *vt* (*food*) servir

service ['sə:vɪs] *n* service *m*; (*AUT*: *maintenance*) révision *f* ♦ *vt* (*car, washing machine*) réviser; **the S~s** les forces armées; **to be of ~ to sb** rendre service à qn; **15% ~ included** service 15% compris; **~ not included** service non compris; **~able** *adj* pratique, commode; **~ area** *n* (*on motorway*) aire *f* de services; **~ charge** (*BRIT*) *n* service *m*; **~man** (*irreg*) *n* militaire *m*; **~ station** *n* station-service *f*

serviette [sə:vɪ'ɛt] (*BRIT*) *n* serviette *f* (de table)

session ['sɛʃən] *n* séance *f*

set [sɛt] (*pt, pp* **set**) *n* série *f*, assortiment *m*; (*of tools etc*) jeu *m*; (*RADIO, TV*) poste *m*; (*TENNIS*) set *m*; (*group of people*) cercle *m*, milieu *m*; (*THEATRE*: *stage*) scène *f*; (: *scenery*) décor *m*; (*MATH*) ensemble *m*; (*HAIRDRESSING*) mise *f* en plis ♦ *adj* (*fixed*) fixe, déterminé(e); (*ready*) prêt(e) ♦ *vt* (*place*) poser, placer; (*fix, establish*) fixer; (: *record*) établir; (*adjust*) régler; (*decide*: *rules etc*) fixer, choisir; (*task*) donner; (*exam*) composer ♦ *vi* (*sun*) se coucher; (*jam, jelly, concrete*) prendre; (*bone*) se ressouder; **to be ~ on doing** être résolu à faire; **to ~ the table** mettre la table; **to ~ (to music)** mettre en musique; **to ~ on fire** mettre le feu à; **to ~ free** libérer; **to ~ sth going** déclencher qch; **to ~ sail** prendre la mer; **~ about** *vt fus* (*task*) entreprendre, se mettre à; **~ aside** *vt* mettre de côté; (*time*) garder; **~ back** *vt* (*in time*): **to ~ back (by)** retarder (de); (*cost*): **to ~ sb back £5** coûter 5 livres à qn; **~ off** *vi* se mettre en route, partir ♦ *vt* (*bomb*) faire exploser; (*cause to start*) déclencher; (*show up well*) mettre en valeur, faire valoir; **~ out** *vi* se mettre en route, partir ♦ *vt* (*arrange*) disposer; (*arguments*) présenter, exposer; **to ~ out to do** entreprendre de faire, avoir pour but *or* intention de faire; **~ up** *vt* (*organization*) fonder, créer; **~back** *n* (*hitch*) revers *m*, contretemps *m*; **~ menu** *n* menu *m*

settee [sɛ'ti:] *n* canapé *m*

setting ['sɛtɪŋ] *n* cadre *m*; (*of jewel*) monture *f*; (*position*: *of controls*) réglage *m*

settle ['sɛtl] *vt* (*argument, matter, account*) régler; (*problem*) résoudre; (*MED*: *calm*) calmer ♦ *vi* (*bird, dust etc*) se poser; (*also*: **~ down**) s'installer, se fixer; (*calm down*) se calmer; **to ~ for sth** accepter qch, se contenter de qch; **to ~ on sth** opter *or* se décider pour qch; **~ in** *vi* s'installer; **~ up** *vi*: **to ~ up with sb** régler (ce que l'on doit à) qn; **~ment** *n* (*payment*) règlement *m*; (*agreement*) accord *m*; (*village etc*) établissement *m*; hameau *m*; **~r** *n* colon *m*

setup ['sɛtʌp] *n* (*arrangement*) manière *f* dont les choses sont organisées; (*situation*) situation *f*

seven ['sɛvn] *num* sept; **~teen** *num* dix-sept; **~th** *num* septième; **~ty** *num* soixante-dix

sever ['sɛvə^r] *vt* couper, trancher; (*relations*) rompre

several ['sɛvərl] *adj, pron* plusieurs *m/fpl*; **~ of us** plusieurs d'entre nous

severance ['sɛvərəns] *n* (*of relations*) rupture *f*; **~ pay** *n* indemnité *f* de licenciement

severe [sɪ'vɪə^r] *adj* (*stern*) sévère, strict(e); (*serious*) grave, sérieux(-euse); (*plain*) sévère, austère; **severity** [sɪ'vɛrɪtɪ] *n* sévérité *f*; gravité *f*; rigueur *f*

sew [səu] (*pt* **sewed**, *pp* **sewn**) *vt, vi* coudre; **~ up** *vt* (re)coudre

sewage ['suːɪdʒ] *n* vidange(s) *f(pl)*
sewer ['suːə^r] *n* égout *m*
sewing ['səuɪŋ] *n* couture *f*; (*item(s)*) ouvrage *m*; **~ machine** *n* machine *f* à coudre
sewn [səun] *pp of* **sew**
sex [sɛks] *n* sexe *m*; **to have ~ with** avoir des rapports (sexuels) avec; **~ism** *n* sexisme *m*; **~ist** *adj* sexiste; **~ual** ['sɛksjuəl] *adj* sexuel(le); **~uality** [sɛksju'ælɪtɪ] *n* sexualité *f*; **~y** *adj* sexy *inv*
shabby ['ʃæbɪ] *adj* miteux(-euse); (*behaviour*) mesquin(e), méprisable
shack [ʃæk] *n* cabane *f*, hutte *f*
shackles ['ʃæklz] *npl* chaînes *fpl*, entraves *fpl*
shade [ʃeɪd] *n* ombre *f*; (*for lamp*) abat-jour *m inv*; (*of colour*) nuance *f*, ton *m* ♦ *vt* abriter du soleil, ombrager; **in the ~** à l'ombre; **a ~ too large/more** un tout petit peu trop grand(e)/plus
shadow ['ʃædəu] *n* ombre *f* ♦ *vt* (*follow*) filer; **~ cabinet** (BRIT) *n* (POL) *cabinet parallèle formé par l'Opposition*; **~y** *adj* ombragé(e); (*dim*) vague, indistinct(e)
shady ['ʃeɪdɪ] *adj* ombragé(e); (*fig: dishonest*) louche, véreux(-euse)
shaft [ʃɑːft] *n* (*of arrow, spear*) hampe *f*; (AUT, TECH) arbre *m*; (*of mine*) puits *m*; (*of lift*) cage *f*; (*of light*) rayon *m*, trait *m*
shaggy ['ʃægɪ] *adj* hirsute; en broussaille
shake [ʃeɪk] (*pt* **shook**, *pp* **shaken**) *vt* secouer; (*bottle, cocktail*) agiter; (*house, confidence*) ébranler ♦ *vi* trembler; **to ~ one's head** (*in refusal*) dire *or* faire non de la tête; (*in dismay*) secouer la tête; **to ~ hands with sb** serrer la main à qn; **~ off** *vt* secouer; (*pursuer*) se débarrasser de; **~ up** *vt* secouer; **~n** *pp of* **shake**; **shaky** *adj* (*hand, voice*) tremblant(e); (*building*) branlant(e), peu solide
shall [ʃæl] *aux vb*: **I ~ go** j'irai; **~ I open the door?** j'ouvre la porte?; **I'll get the coffee, ~ I?** je vais chercher le café, d'accord?
shallow ['ʃæləu] *adj* peu profond(e); (*fig*) superficiel(le)
sham [ʃæm] *n* frime *f* ♦ *vt* simuler
shambles ['ʃæmblz] *n* (*muddle*) confusion *f*, pagaïe *f*, fouillis *m*
shame [ʃeɪm] *n* honte *f* ♦ *vt* faire honte à; **it is a ~ (that/to do)** c'est dommage (que *+sub*/de faire); **what a ~!** quel dommage!; **~ful** *adj* honteux(-euse), scandaleux(-euse); **~less** *adj* éhonté(e), effronté(e)
shampoo [ʃæm'puː] *n* shampooing *m* ♦ *vt* faire un shampooing à; **~ and set** *n* shampooing *m* (et) mise *f* en plis
shamrock ['ʃæmrɔk] *n* trèfle *m* (*emblème de l'Irlande*)
shandy ['ʃændɪ] *n* bière panachée
shan't [ʃɑːnt] = **shall not**
shanty town ['ʃæntɪ-] *n* bidonville *m*
shape [ʃeɪp] *n* forme *f* ♦ *vt* façonner, modeler; (*sb's ideas*) former; (*sb's life*) déterminer ♦ *vi* (*also:* **~ up**: *events*) prendre tournure; (: *person*) faire des progrès, s'en sortir; **to take ~** prendre forme *or* tournure; **-~d** *suffix*: **heart-~d** en forme de cœur; **~less** *adj* informe, sans forme; **~ly** *adj* bien proportionné(e), beau (belle)
share [ʃɛə^r] *n* part *f*; (COMM) action *f* ♦ *vt* partager; (*have in common*) avoir en commun; **~ out** *vi* partager; **~holder** *n* actionnaire *m/f*
shark [ʃɑːk] *n* requin *m*
sharp [ʃɑːp] *adj* (*razor, knife*) tranchant(e), bien aiguisé(e); (*point, voice*) aigu(-guë); (*nose, chin*) pointu(e); (*outline, increase*) net(te); (*cold, pain*) vif (vive); (*taste*) piquant(e), âcre; (MUS) dièse; (*person: quick-witted*) vif (vive), éveillé(e); (: *unscrupulous*) malhonnête ♦ *n* (MUS) dièse *m* ♦ *adv* (*precisely*): **at 2 o'clock ~** à 2 heures pile *or* précises; **~en** *vt* aiguiser; (*pencil*) tailler; **~ener** *n* (*also:* **pencil ~ener**) taille-crayon(s) *m inv*; **~-eyed** *adj* à qui rien n'échappe;

~ly *adv* (*turn, stop*) brusquement; (*stand out*) nettement; (*criticize, retort*) sèchement, vertement

shatter ['ʃætəʳ] *vt* briser; (*fig: upset*) bouleverser; (*: ruin*) briser, ruiner ♦ *vi* voler en éclats, se briser

shave [ʃeɪv] *vt* raser ♦ *vi* se raser ♦ *n*: **to have a ~** se raser; **~r** *n* (*also:* **electric ~r**) rasoir *m* électrique

shaving ['ʃeɪvɪŋ] (*action*) rasage *m*; **~s** *npl* (*of wood etc*) copeaux *mpl*; **~ brush** *n* blaireau *m*; **~ cream** *n* crème *f* à raser; **~ foam** *n* mousse *f* à raser

shawl [ʃɔ:l] *n* châle *m*

she [ʃi:] *pron* elle ♦ *prefix*: **~-cat** chatte *f*; **~-elephant** éléphant *m* femelle

sheaf [ʃi:f] (*pl* **sheaves**) *n* gerbe *f*; (*of papers*) liasse *f*

shear [ʃɪəʳ] (*pt* **sheared**, *pp* **shorn**) *vt* (*sheep*) tondre; **~s** *npl* (*for hedge*) cisaille(s) *f(pl)*

sheath [ʃi:θ] *n* gaine *f*, fourreau *m*, étui *m*; (*contraceptive*) préservatif *m*

shed [ʃɛd] (*pt, pp* **shed**) *n* remise *f*, resserre *f* ♦ *vt* perdre; (*tears*) verser, répandre; (*workers*) congédier

she'd [ʃi:d] = **she had; she would**

sheen [ʃi:n] *n* lustre *m*

sheep [ʃi:p] *n inv* mouton *m*; **~dog** *n* chien *m* de berger; **~skin** *n* peau *f* de mouton

sheer [ʃɪəʳ] *adj* (*utter*) pur(e), pur et simple; (*steep*) à pic, abrupt(e); (*almost transparent*) extrêmement fin(e) ♦ *adv* à pic, abruptement

sheet [ʃi:t] *n* (*on bed*) drap *m*; (*of paper*) feuille *f*; (*of glass, metal etc*) feuille, plaque *f*

sheik(h) [ʃeɪk] *n* cheik *m*

shelf [ʃɛlf] (*pl* **shelves**) *n* étagère *f*, rayon *m*

shell [ʃɛl] *n* (*on beach*) coquillage *m*; (*of egg, nut etc*) coquille *f*; (*explosive*) obus *m*; (*of building*) carcasse *f* ♦ *vt* (*peas*) écosser; (MIL) bombarder (d'obus)

she'll [ʃi:l] = **she will; she shall**

shellfish ['ʃɛlfɪʃ] *n inv* (*crab etc*) crustacé *m*; (*scallop etc*) coquillage *m* ♦ *npl* (*as food*) fruits *mpl* de mer

shell suit *n* survêtement *m* (*en synthétique froissé*)

shelter ['ʃɛltəʳ] *n* abri *m*, refuge *m* ♦ *vt* abriter, protéger; (*give lodging to*) donner asile à ♦ *vi* s'abriter, se mettre à l'abri; **~ed housing** *n* foyers *mpl* (*pour personnes âgées ou handicapées*)

shelve [ʃɛlv] *vt* (*fig*) mettre en suspens *or* en sommeil; **~s** *npl of* **shelf**

shepherd ['ʃɛpəd] *n* berger *m* ♦ *vt* (*guide*) guider, escorter; **~'s pie** (BRIT) *n* ≃ hachis *m* Parmentier

sheriff ['ʃɛrɪf] (US) *n* shérif *m*

sherry ['ʃɛrɪ] *n* xérès *m*, sherry *m*

she's [ʃi:z] = **she is; she has**

Shetland ['ʃɛtlənd] *n* (*also:* **the ~ Islands**) les îles *fpl* Shetland

shield [ʃi:ld] *n* bouclier *m*; (*protection*) écran *m* de protection ♦ *vt*: **to ~ (from)** protéger (de *or* contre)

shift [ʃɪft] *n* (*change*) changement *m*; (*work period*) période *f* de travail; (*of workers*) équipe *f*, poste *m* ♦ *vt* déplacer, changer de place; (*remove*) enlever ♦ *vi* changer de place, bouger; **~ work** *n* travail *m* en équipe *or* par relais *or* par roulement; **~y** *adj* sournois(e); (*eyes*) fuyant(e)

shimmer ['ʃɪməʳ] *vi* miroiter, chatoyer

shin [ʃɪn] *n* tibia *m*

shine [ʃaɪn] (*pt, pp* **shone**) *n* éclat *m*, brillant *m* ♦ *vi* briller ♦ *vt* (*torch etc*): **to ~ on** braquer sur; (*polish: pt, pp ~d*) faire briller *or* reluire

shingle ['ʃɪŋgl] *n* (*on beach*) galets *mpl*; **~s** *n* (MED) zona *m*

shiny ['ʃaɪnɪ] *adj* brillant(e)

ship [ʃɪp] *n* bateau *m*; (*large*) navire *m* ♦ *vt* transporter (par mer); (*send*) expédier (par mer); **~building** *n* construction navale; **~ment** *n* cargaison *f*; **~ping** *n* (*ships*) navires *mpl*; (*the industry*) industrie navale; (*transport*) transport *m*; **~wreck** *n* (*ship*) épave *f*; (*event*) naufrage *m* ♦ *vt*: **to be**

~wrecked faire naufrage; **~yard** *n* chantier naval

shire [ˈʃaɪəʳ] (*BRIT*) *n* comté *m*

shirt [ʃəːt] *n* (*man's*) chemise *f*; (*woman's*) chemisier *m*; **in (one's) ~ sleeves** en bras de chemise

shit [ʃɪt] (*inf!*) *n, excl* merde *f* (*!*)

shiver [ˈʃɪvəʳ] *n* frisson *m* ♦ *vi* frissonner

shoal [ʃəul] *n* (*of fish*) banc *m*; (*fig: also:* **~s**) masse *f*, foule *f*

shock [ʃɔk] *n* choc *m*; (*ELEC*) secousse *f*; (*MED*) commotion *f*, choc ♦ *vt* (*offend*) choquer, scandaliser; (*upset*) bouleverser; **~ absorber** *n* amortisseur *m*; **~ing** *adj* (*scandalizing*) choquant(e), scandaleux(-euse); (*appalling*) épouvantable

shoddy [ˈʃɔdɪ] *adj* de mauvaise qualité, mal fait(e)

shoe [ʃuː] (*pt, pp* **shod**) *n* chaussure *f*, soulier *m*; (*also:* **horseshoe**) fer *m* à cheval ♦ *vt* (*horse*) ferrer; **~lace** *n* lacet *m* (de soulier); **~ polish** *n* cirage *m*; **~ shop** *n* magasin *m* de chaussures; **~string** *n* (*fig*): **on a ~string** avec un budget dérisoire

shone [ʃɔn] *pt, pp of* **shine**

shook [ʃuk] *pt of* **shake**

shoot [ʃuːt] (*pt, pp* **shot**) *n* (*on branch, seedling*) pousse *f* ♦ *vt* (*game*) chasser; tirer; abattre; (*person*) blesser (*or* tuer) d'un coup de fusil (*or* de revolver); (*execute*) fusiller; (*arrow*) tirer; (*gun*) tirer un coup de; (*film*) tourner ♦ *vi* (*with gun, bow*): **to ~ (at)** tirer (sur); (*FOOTBALL*) shooter, tirer; **~ down** *vt* (*plane*) abattre; **~ in** *vi* entrer comme une flèche; **~ out** *vi* sortir comme une flèche; **~ up** *vi* (*fig*) monter en flèche; **~ing** *n* (*shots*) coups *mpl* de feu, fusillade *f*; (*HUNTING*) chasse *f*; **~ing star** *n* étoile filante

shop [ʃɔp] *n* magasin *m*; (*workshop*) atelier *m* ♦ *vi* (*also:* **go ~ping**) faire ses courses *or* ses achats; **~ assistant** (*BRIT*) *n* vendeur(-euse); **~ floor** (*BRIT*) *n* (*INDUSTRY: fig*) ouvriers *mpl*; **~keeper** *n* commerçant(e); **~lifting** *n* vol *m* à l'étalage; **~per** *n* personne *f* qui fait ses courses, acheteur(-euse); **~ping** *n* (*goods*) achats *mpl*, provisions *fpl*; **~ping bag** *n* sac *m* (à provisions); **~ping centre** (*US* **shopping center**) *n* centre commercial; **~-soiled** *adj* défraîchi(e), qui a fait la vitrine; **~ steward** (*BRIT*) *n* (*INDUSTRY*) délégué(e) syndical(e); **~ window** *n* vitrine *f*

shore [ʃɔːʳ] *n* (*of sea, lake*) rivage *m*, rive *f* ♦ *vt*: **to ~ (up)** étayer; **on ~** à terre

shorn [ʃɔːn] *pp of* **shear**

short [ʃɔːt] *adj* (*not long*) court(e); (*soon finished*) court, bref (brève); (*person, step*) petit(e); (*curt*) brusque, sec (sèche); (*insufficient*) insuffisant(e); **to be/run ~ of sth** être à court de *or* manquer de qch; **in ~** bref; en bref; **~ of doing ...** à moins de faire ...; **everything ~ of** tout sauf; **it is ~ for** c'est l'abréviation *or* le diminutif de; **to cut ~** (*speech, visit*) abréger, écourter; **to fall ~ of** ne pas être à la hauteur de; **to run ~ of** arriver à court de, venir à manquer de; **to stop ~** s'arrêter net; **to stop ~ of** ne pas aller jusqu'à; **~age** *n* manque *m*, pénurie *f*; **~bread** *n* ≃ sablé *m*; **~-change** *vt* ne pas rendre assez à; **~-circuit** *n* court-circuit *m*; **~coming** *n* défaut *m*; **~(crust) pastry** (*BRIT*) *n* pâte brisée; **~cut** *n* raccourci *m*; **~en** *vt* raccourcir; (*text, visit*) abréger; **~fall** *n* déficit *m*; **~hand** (*BRIT*) *n* sténo(graphie) *f*; **~hand typist** (*BRIT*) *n* sténodactylo *m/f*; **~list** (*BRIT*) *n* (*for job*) liste *f* des candidats sélectionnés; **~ly** *adv* bientôt, sous peu; **~ notice** *n*: **at ~ notice** au dernier moment; **~s** *npl*: **(a pair of) ~s** un short; **~-sighted** *adj* (*BRIT*) myope; (*fig*) qui manque de clairvoyance; **~-staffed** *adj* à court de personnel; **~-stay** *adj* (*car park*) de courte durée; **~ story** *n* nouvelle *f*; **~-tempered** *adj* qui s'emporte facilement; **~-term** *adj* (*effect*) à court terme; **~ wave** *n* (*RADIO*) ondes courtes

shot [ʃɔt] *pt, pp of* **shoot** ♦ *n* coup *m* (de feu); (*try*) coup, essai *m*; (*injection*) piqûre *f*; (*PHOT*) photo *f*; **he's a good/ poor ~** il tire bien/mal; **like a ~** comme une flèche; (*very readily*) sans hésiter; **~gun** *n* fusil *m* de chasse

should [ʃud] *aux vb*: **I ~ go now** je devrais partir maintenant; **he ~ be there now** il devrait être arrivé maintenant; **I ~ go if I were you** si j'étais vous, j'irais; **I ~ like to** j'aimerais bien, volontiers

shoulder [ˈʃəuldəʳ] *n* épaule *f* ♦ *vt* (*fig*) endosser, se charger de; **~ bag** *n* sac *m* à bandoulière; **~ blade** *n* omoplate *f*

shouldn't [ˈʃudnt] = **should not**

shout [ʃaut] *n* cri *m* ♦ *vt* crier ♦ *vi* (*also:* **~ out**) crier, pousser des cris; **~ down** *vt* huer; **~ing** *n* cris *mpl*

shove [ʃʌv] *vt* pousser; (*inf*: *put*): **to ~ sth in** fourrer *or* ficher qch dans; **~ off** (*inf*) *vi* ficher le camp

shovel [ˈʃʌvl] *n* pelle *f*

show [ʃəu] (*pt* **showed**, *pp* **shown**) *n* (*of emotion*) manifestation *f*, démonstration *f*; (*semblance*) semblant *m*, apparence *f*; (*exhibition*) exposition *f*, salon *m*; (*THEATRE, TV*) spectacle *m* ♦ *vt* montrer; (*film*) donner; (*courage etc*) faire preuve de, manifester; (*exhibit*) exposer ♦ *vi* se voir, être visible; **for ~** pour l'effet; **on ~** (*exhibits etc*) exposé(e); **~ in** *vt* (*person*) faire entrer; **~ off** *vi* (*pej*) crâner ♦ *vt* (*display*) faire valoir; **~ out** *vt* (*person*) reconduire (jusqu'à la porte); **~ up** *vi* (*stand out*) ressortir; (*inf*: *turn up*) se montrer ♦ *vt* (*flaw*) faire ressortir; **~ business** *n* le monde du spectacle; **~down** *n* épreuve *f* de force

shower [ˈʃauəʳ] *n* (*rain*) averse *f*; (*of stones etc*) pluie *f*, grêle *f*; (*~bath*) douche *f* ♦ *vi* prendre une douche, se doucher ♦ *vt*: **to ~ sb with** (*gifts etc*) combler qn de; **to have** *or* **take a ~** prendre une douche; **~ gel** *n* gel *m* douche; **~proof** *adj* imperméabilisé(e)

showing [ˈʃəuɪŋ] *n* (*of film*) projection *f*

show jumping *n* concours *m* hippique

shown [ʃəun] *pp of* **show**

show: ~-off (*inf*) *n* (*person*) crâneur (-euse), m'as-tu-vu(e); **~piece** *n* (*of exhibition*) trésor *m*; **~room** *n* magasin *m* *or* salle *f* d'exposition

shrank [ʃræŋk] *pt of* **shrink**

shrapnel [ˈʃræpnl] *n* éclats *mpl* d'obus

shred [ʃrɛd] *n* (*gen pl*) lambeau *m*, petit morceau ♦ *vt* mettre en lambeaux, déchirer; (*CULIN*: *grate*) râper; (: *lettuce etc*) couper en lanières; **~der** *n* (*for vegetables*) râpeur *m*; (*for documents*) déchiqueteuse *f*

shrewd [ʃru:d] *adj* astucieux(-euse), perspicace; (*businessman*) habile

shriek [ʃri:k] *vi* hurler, crier

shrill [ʃrɪl] *adj* perçant(e), aigu(-guë), strident(e)

shrimp [ʃrɪmp] *n* crevette *f*

shrine [ʃraɪn] *n* (*place*) lieu *m* de pèlerinage

shrink [ʃrɪŋk] (*pt* **shrank**, *pp* **shrunk**) *vi* rétrécir; (*fig*) se réduire, diminuer; (*move*: *also:* **~ away**) reculer ♦ *vt* (*wool*) (faire) rétrécir ♦ *n* (*inf*: *pej*) psychiatre *m/f*, psy *m/f*; **to ~ from (doing) sth** reculer devant (la pensée de faire) qch; **~wrap** *vt* emballer sous film plastique

shrivel [ˈʃrɪvl] *vt* (*also:* **~ up**) ratatiner, flétrir ♦ *vi* se ratatiner, se flétrir

shroud [ʃraud] *n* linceul *m* ♦ *vt*: **~ed in mystery** enveloppé(e) de mystère

Shrove Tuesday [ˈʃrəuv-] *n* (le) Mardi gras

shrub *n* arbuste *m*; **~bery** *n* massif *m* d'arbustes

shrug [ʃrʌg] *vt, vi*: **to ~ (one's shoulders)** hausser les épaules; **~ off** *vt* faire fi de

shrunk [ʃrʌŋk] *pp of* **shrink**

shudder [ˈʃʌdəʳ] *vi* frissonner, frémir

shuffle [ˈʃʌfl] *vt* (*cards*) battre; **to ~ (one's feet)** traîner les pieds

shun [ʃʌn] *vt* éviter, fuir

shunt [ʃʌnt] *vt* (*RAIL*) aiguiller

shut [ʃʌt] (*pt, pp* **shut**) *vt* fermer ♦ *vi*

(se) fermer; **~ down** *vt, vi* fermer définitivement; **~ off** *vt* couper, arrêter; **~ up** *vi* (*inf: keep quiet*) se taire ♦ *vt* (*close*) fermer; (*silence*) faire taire; **~ter** *n* volet *m*; (PHOT) obturateur *m*

shuttle ['ʃʌtl] *n* navette *f*; (*also:* **~ service**) (service *m* de) navette *f*; **~cock** *n* volant *m* (*de badminton*); **~ diplomacy** *n* navettes *fpl* diplomatiques

shy [ʃaɪ] *adj* timide

Siberia [saɪ'bɪərɪə] *n* Sibérie *f*

Sicily ['sɪsɪlɪ] *n* Sicile *f*

sick [sɪk] *adj* (*ill*) malade; (*vomiting*): **to be ~** vomir; (*humour*) noir(e), macabre; **to feel ~** avoir envie de vomir, avoir mal au cœur; **to be ~ of** (*fig*) en avoir assez de; **~ bay** *n* infirmerie *f*; **~en** *vt* écœurer; **~ening** *adj* (*fig*) écœurant(e), dégoûtant(e)

sickle ['sɪkl] *n* faucille *f*

sick: ~ leave *n* congé *m* de maladie; **~ly** *adj* maladif(-ive), souffreteux(-euse); (*causing nausea*) écœurant(e); **~ness** *n* maladie *f*; (*vomiting*) vomissement(s) *m(pl)*; **~ note** *n* (*from parents*) mot *m* d'absence; (*from doctor*) certificat médical; **~ pay** *n* indemnité *f* de maladie

side [saɪd] *n* côté *m*; (*of lake, road*) bord *m*; (*team*) camp *m*, équipe *f* ♦ *adj* (*door, entrance*) latéral(e) ♦ *vi*: **to ~ with sb** prendre le parti de qn, se ranger du côté de qn; **by the ~ of** au bord de; **~ by ~** côte à côte; **from ~ to ~** d'un côté à l'autre; **to take ~s (with)** prendre parti (pour); **~board** *n* buffet *m*; **~boards** (BRIT), **~burns** *npl* (*whiskers*) pattes *fpl*; **~ drum** *n* tambour plat; **~ effect** *n* effet *m* secondaire; **~light** *n* (AUT) veilleuse *f*; **~line** *n* (SPORT) (ligne *f* de) touche *f*; (*fig*) travail *m* secondaire; **~long** *adj* oblique; **~show** *n* attraction *f*; **~step** *vt* (*fig*) éluder; éviter; **~ street** *n* (petite) rue transversale; **~track** *vt* (*fig*) faire dévier de son sujet; **~walk** (US) *n* trottoir *m*; **~ways** *adv* de côté

siding ['saɪdɪŋ] *n* (RAIL) voie *f* de garage

siege [siːdʒ] *n* siège *m*

sieve [sɪv] *n* tamis *m*, passoire *f*

sift [sɪft] *vt* (*fig: also:* **~ through**) passer en revue; (*lit: flour etc*) passer au tamis

sigh [saɪ] *n* soupir *m* ♦ *vi* soupirer, pousser un soupir

sight [saɪt] *n* (*faculty*) vue *f*; (*spectacle*) spectacle *m*; (*on gun*) mire *f* ♦ *vt* apercevoir; **in ~** visible; **out of ~** hors de vue; **~seeing** *n* tourisme *m*; **to go ~seeing** faire du tourisme

sign [saɪn] *n* signe *m*; (*with hand etc*) signe, geste *m*; (*notice*) panneau *m*, écriteau *m* ♦ *vt* signer; **~ on** *vi* (*as unemployed*) s'inscrire au chômage; (*for course*) s'inscrire ♦ *vt* (*employee*) embaucher; **~ over** *vt*: **to ~ sth over to sb** céder qch par écrit à qn; **~ up** *vt* engager ♦ *vi* (MIL) s'engager; (*for course*) s'inscrire

signal ['sɪgnl] *n* signal *m* ♦ *vi* (AUT) mettre son clignotant ♦ *vt* (*person*) faire signe à; (*message*) communiquer par signaux; **~man** (*irreg*) *n* (RAIL) aiguilleur *m*

signature ['sɪgnətʃə^r] *n* signature *f*; **~ tune** *n* indicatif musical

signet ring ['sɪgnət-] *n* chevalière *f*

significance [sɪg'nɪfɪkəns] *n* signification *f*; importance *f*

significant [sɪg'nɪfɪkənt] *adj* significatif(-ive); (*important*) important(e), considérable

sign language *n* langage *m* per signes

signpost *n* poteau indicateur

silence ['saɪləns] *n* silence *m* ♦ *vt* faire taire, réduire au silence; **~r** *n* (*on gun*, BRIT: AUT) silencieux *m*

silent ['saɪlənt] *adj* silencieux(-euse); (*film*) muet(te); **to remain ~** garder le silence, ne rien dire; **~ partner** *n* (COMM) bailleur *m* de fonds, commanditaire *m*

silhouette [sɪluː'ɛt] *n* silhouette *f*

silicon chip ['sɪlɪkən-] *n* puce *f* électronique

silk [sɪlk] *n* soie *f* ♦ *cpd* de *or* en soie; **~y**

adj soyeux(-euse)
silly ['sɪlɪ] *adj* stupide, sot(te), bête
silt [sɪlt] *n* vase *f*; limon *m*
silver ['sɪlvə^r] *n* argent *m*; (*money*) monnaie *f* (en pièces d'argent); (*also:* **~ware**) argenterie *f* ♦ *adj* d'argent, en argent; **~ paper** (*BRIT*) *n* papier *m* d'argent *or* d'étain; **~-plated** *adj* plaqué(e) argent *inv*; **~smith** *n* orfèvre *m/f*; **~y** *adj* argenté(e)
similar ['sɪmɪlə^r] *adj*: **~ (to)** semblable (à); **~ly** *adv* de la même façon, de même
simmer ['sɪmə^r] *vi* cuire à feu doux, mijoter
simple ['sɪmpl] *adj* simple; **simplicity** [sɪm'plɪsɪtɪ] *n* simplicité *f*; **simply** *adv* (*without fuss*) avec simplicité
simultaneous [sɪməl'teɪnɪəs] *adj* simultané(e)
sin [sɪn] *n* péché *m* ♦ *vi* pécher
since [sɪns] *adv, prep* depuis ♦ *conj* (*time*) depuis que; (*because*) puisque, étant donné que, comme; **~ then, ever ~** depuis ce moment-là
sincere [sɪn'sɪə^r] *adj* sincère; **~ly** *adv see* **yours**; **sincerity** [sɪn'sɛrɪtɪ] *n* sincérité *f*
sinew ['sɪnju:] *n* tendon *m*
sing [sɪŋ] (*pt* **sang**, *pp* **sung**) *vt, vi* chanter
Singapore [sɪŋgə'pɔ:^r] *n* Singapour *m*
singe [sɪndʒ] *vt* brûler légèrement; (*clothes*) roussir
singer ['sɪŋə^r] *n* chanteur(-euse)
singing ['sɪŋɪŋ] *n* chant *m*
single ['sɪŋgl] *adj* seul(e), unique; (*unmarried*) célibataire; (*not double*) simple ♦ *n* (*BRIT: also:* **~ ticket**) aller *m* (simple); (*record*) 45 tours *m*; **~ out** *vt* choisir; (*distinguish*) distinguer; **~ bed** *n* lit *m* d'une personne; **~-breasted** *adj* droit(e); **~ file** *n*: **in ~ file** en file indienne; **~-handed** *adv* tout(e) seul(e), sans (aucune) aide; **~-minded** *adj* résolu(e), tenace; **~ parent** *n* parent *m* unique; **~ room** *n* chambre *f* à un lit *or* pour une personne; **~s** *n* (*TENNIS*) simple *m*; **~-track road** *n* route *f* à voie unique; **singly** *adv* séparément
singular ['sɪŋgjulə^r] *adj* singulier(-ère), étrange; (*outstanding*) remarquable; (*LING*) (au) singulier, du singulier ♦ *n* singulier *m*
sinister ['sɪnɪstə^r] *adj* sinistre
sink [sɪŋk] (*pt* **sank**, *pp* **sunk**) *n* évier *m* ♦ *vt* (*ship*) (faire) couler, faire sombrer; (*foundations*) creuser ♦ *vi* couler, sombrer; (*ground etc*) s'affaisser; (*also:* **~ back, ~ down**) s'affaisser, se laisser retomber; **to ~ sth into** enfoncer qch dans; **my heart sank** j'ai complètement perdu courage; **~ in** *vi* (*fig*) pénétrer, être compris(e)
sinner ['sɪnə^r] *n* pécheur(-eresse)
sinus ['saɪnəs] *n* sinus *m inv*
sip [sɪp] *n* gorgée *f* ♦ *vt* boire à petites gorgées
siphon ['saɪfən] *n* siphon *m*; **~ off** *vt* siphonner; (*money: illegally*) détourner
sir [sə^r] *n* monsieur *m*; **S~ John Smith** sir John Smith; **yes ~** oui, Monsieur
siren ['saɪərn] *n* sirène *f*
sirloin ['sə:lɔɪn] *n* (*also:* **~ steak**) aloyau *m*
sissy ['sɪsɪ] (*inf*) *n* (*coward*) poule mouillée
sister ['sɪstə^r] *n* sœur *f*; (*nun*) religieuse *f*, sœur; (*BRIT: nurse*) infirmière *f* en chef; **~-in-law** *n* belle-sœur *f*
sit [sɪt] (*pt, pp* **sat**) *vi* s'asseoir; (*be ~ting*) être assis(e); (*assembly*) être en séance, siéger; (*for painter*) poser ♦ *vt* (*exam*) passer, se présenter à; **~ down** *vi* s'asseoir; **~ in on** *vt fus* assister à; **~ up** *vi* s'asseoir; (*straight*) se redresser; (*not go to bed*) rester debout, ne pas se coucher
sitcom ['sɪtkɔm] *n abbr* (= *situation comedy*) comédie *f* de situation
site [saɪt] *n* emplacement *m*, site *m*; (*also:* **building ~**) chantier *m* ♦ *vt* placer
sit-in ['sɪtɪn] *n* (*demonstration*) sit-in *m inv*, occupation *f* (de locaux)

sitting ['sɪtɪŋ] *n* (*of assembly etc*) séance *f*; (*in canteen*) service *m*; **~ room** *n* salon *m*
situated ['sɪtjueɪtɪd] *adj* situé(e)
situation [sɪtju'eɪʃən] *n* situation *f*; **"~s vacant"** (*BRIT*) "offres d'emploi"
six [sɪks] *num* six; **~teen** *num* seize; **~th** *num* sixième; **~ty** *num* soixante
size [saɪz] *n* taille *f*; dimensions *fpl*; (*of clothing*) taille; (*of shoes*) pointure *f*; (*fig*) ampleur *f*; (*glue*) colle *f*; **~ up** *vt* juger, jauger; **~able** *adj* assez grand(e); assez important(e)
sizzle ['sɪzl] *vi* grésiller
skate [skeɪt] *n* patin *m*; (*fish*: *pl inv*) raie *f* ♦ *vi* patiner; **~board** *n* skateboard *m*, planche *f* à roulettes; **~boarding** *n* skateboard *m*; **~r** *n* patineur(-euse); **skating** *n* patinage *m*; **skating rink** *n* patinoire *f*
skeleton ['skɛlɪtn] *n* squelette *m*; (*outline*) schéma *m*; **~ staff** *n* effectifs réduits
skeptical ['skɛptɪkl] (*US*) *adj* = **sceptical**
sketch [skɛtʃ] *n* (*drawing*) croquis *m*, esquisse *f*; (*THEATRE*) sketch *m*, saynète *f* ♦ *vt* esquisser, faire un croquis *or* une esquisse de; **~ book** *n* carnet *m* à dessin; **~y** *adj* incomplet(-ète), fragmentaire
skewer ['skjuːəʳ] *n* brochette *f*
ski [skiː] *n* ski *m* ♦ *vi* skier, faire du ski; **~ boot** *n* chaussure *f* de ski
skid [skɪd] *vi* déraper
ski: ~er *n* skieur(-euse); **~ing** *n* ski *m*; **~ jump** *n* saut *m* à skis
skilful ['skɪlful] (*US* **skillful**) *adj* habile, adroit(e)
ski lift *n* remonte-pente *m inv*
skill [skɪl] *n* habileté *f*, adresse *f*, talent *m*; (*requiring training*: *gen pl*) compétences *fpl*; **~ed** *adj* habile, adroit(e); (*worker*) qualifié(e)
skim [skɪm] *vt* (*milk*) écrémer; (*glide over*) raser, effleurer ♦ *vi*: **to ~ through** (*fig*) parcourir; **~med milk** *n* lait écrémé
skimp [skɪmp] *vt* (*also*: **~ on**: *work*) bâcler, faire à la va-vite; (: *cloth etc*) lésiner sur; **~y** *adj* (*skirt*) étriqué(e)
skin [skɪn] *n* peau *f* ♦ *vt* (*fruit etc*) éplucher; (*animal*) écorcher; **~ cancer** *n* cancer *m* de la peau; **~-deep** *adj* superficiel(le); **~-diving** *n* plongée sous-marine; **~head** *n* skinhead *m/f*; **~ny** *adj* maigre, maigrichon(ne); **~tight** *adj* (*jeans etc*) moulant(e), ajusté(e)
skip [skɪp] *n* petit bond *or* saut; (*BRIT*: *container*) benne *f* ♦ *vi* gambader, sautiller; (*with rope*) sauter à la corde ♦ *vt* sauter
ski pass *n* forfait-skieur(s) *m*
ski pole *n* bâton *m* de ski
skipper ['skɪpəʳ] *n* capitaine *m*; (*in race*) skipper *m*
skipping rope ['skɪpɪŋ-] (*BRIT*) *n* corde *f* à sauter
skirmish ['skəːmɪʃ] *n* escarmouche *f*, accrochage *m*
skirt [skəːt] *n* jupe *f* ♦ *vt* longer, contourner; **~ing board** (*BRIT*) *n* plinthe *f*
ski: ~ slope *n* piste *f* de ski; **~ suit** *n* combinaison *f* (de ski); **~ tow** *n* remonte-pente *m inv*
skittle ['skɪtl] *n* quille *f*; **~s** *n* (*game*) (jeu *m* de) quilles *fpl*
skive [skaɪv] (*BRIT*: *inf*) *vi* tirer au flanc
skull [skʌl] *n* crâne *m*
skunk [skʌŋk] *n* mouffette *f*
sky [skaɪ] *n* ciel *m*; **~light** *n* lucarne *f*; **~scraper** *n* gratte-ciel *m inv*
slab [slæb] *n* (*of stone*) dalle *f*; (*of food*) grosse tranche
slack [slæk] *adj* (*loose*) lâche, desserré(e); (*slow*) stagnant(e); (*careless*) négligent(e), peu sérieux(-euse) *or* consciencieux(-euse); **~s** *npl* (*trousers*) pantalon *m*; **~en** *vi* ralentir, diminuer ♦ *vt* (*speed*) réduire; (*grip*) relâcher; (*clothing*) desserrer
slag heap [slæg-] *n* crassier *m*
slag off (*BRIT*: *inf*) *vt* dire du mal de

slam [slæm] *vt* (*door*) (faire) claquer; (*throw*) jeter violemment, flanquer (*fam*); (*criticize*) démolir ♦ *vi* claquer

slander ['slɑːndəʳ] *n* calomnie *f*; diffamation *f*

slang [slæŋ] *n* argot *m*

slant [slɑːnt] *n* inclinaison *f*; (*fig*) angle *m*, point *m* de vue; **~ed** *adj* = **slanting**; **~ing** *adj* en pente, incliné(e); **~ing eyes** yeux bridés

slap [slæp] *n* claque *f*, gifle *f*; tape *f* ♦ *vt* donner une claque *or* une gifle *or* une tape à; (*paint*) appliquer rapidement ♦ *adv* (*directly*) tout droit, en plein; **~dash** *adj* fait(e) sans soin *or* à la va-vite; (*person*) insouciant(e), négligent(e); **~stick** *n* (*comedy*) grosse farce, style *m* tarte à la crème; **~-up** (BRIT) *adj*: **a ~-up meal** un repas extra *or* fameux

slash [slæʃ] *vt* entailler, taillader; (*fig: prices*) casser

slat [slæt] *n* latte *f*, lame *f*

slate [sleɪt] *n* ardoise *f* ♦ *vt* (*fig: criticize*) éreinter, démolir

slaughter ['slɔːtəʳ] *n* carnage *m*, massacre *m* ♦ *vt* (*animal*) abattre; (*people*) massacrer; **~house** *n* abattoir *m*

slave [sleɪv] *n* esclave *m/f* ♦ *vi* (*also:* **~ away**) trimer, travailler comme un forçat; **~ry** *n* esclavage *m*

slay [sleɪ] (*pt* **slew**, *pp* **slain**) *vt* tuer

sleazy ['sliːzɪ] *adj* miteux(-euse), minable

sledge [slɛdʒ] *n* luge *f* ♦ *vi*: **to go sledging** faire de la luge

sledgehammer *n* marteau *m* de forgeron

sleek [sliːk] *adj* (*hair, fur etc*) brillant(e), lisse; (*car, boat etc*) aux lignes pures *or* élégantes

sleep [sliːp] (*pt, pp* **slept**) *n* sommeil *m* ♦ *vi* dormir; (*spend night*) dormir, coucher; **to go to ~** s'endormir; **~ around** *vi* coucher à droite et à gauche; **~ in** *vi* (*oversleep*) se réveiller trop tard; **~er** (BRIT) *n* (RAIL: *train*) train-couchettes *m*; (: *berth*) couchette *f*; **~ing bag** *n* sac *m* de couchage; **~ing car** *n* (RAIL) wagon-lit *m*, voiture-lit *f*; **~ing partner** (BRIT) *n* = **silent partner**; **~ing pill** *n* somnifère *m*; **~less** *adj*: **a ~less night** une nuit blanche; **~walker** *n* somnambule *m/f*; **~y** *adj* qui a sommeil; (*fig*) endormi(e)

sleet [sliːt] *n* neige fondue

sleeve [sliːv] *n* manche *f*; (*of record*) pochette *f*

sleigh [sleɪ] *n* traîneau *m*

sleight [slaɪt] *n*: **~ of hand** tour *m* de passe-passe

slender ['slɛndəʳ] *adj* svelte, mince; (*fig*) faible, ténu(e)

slept [slɛpt] *pt, pp of* **sleep**

slew [sluː] *vi* (*also:* **~ around**) virer, pivoter ♦ *pt of* **slay**

slice [slaɪs] *n* tranche *f*; (*round*) rondelle *f*; (*utensil*) spatule *f*, truelle *f* ♦ *vt* couper en tranches (*or* en rondelles)

slick [slɪk] *adj* (*skilful*) brillant(e) (en apparence); (*salesman*) qui a du bagout ♦ *n* (*also:* **oil ~**) nappe *f* de pétrole, marée noire

slide [slaɪd] (*pt, pp* **slid**) *n* (*in playground*) toboggan *m*; (PHOT) diapositive *f*; (BRIT: *also:* **hair ~**) barrette *f*; (*in prices*) chute *f*, baisse *f* ♦ *vt* (faire) glisser ♦ *vi* glisser; **sliding** *adj* (*door*) coulissant(e); **sliding scale** *n* échelle *f* mobile

slight [slaɪt] *adj* (*slim*) mince, menu(e); (*frail*) frêle; (*trivial*) faible, insignifiant(e); (*small*) petit(e), léger(-ère) (*before n*) ♦ *n* offense *f*, affront *m*; **not in the ~est** pas le moins du monde, pas du tout; **~ly** *adv* légèrement, un peu

slim [slɪm] *adj* mince ♦ *vi* maigrir; (*diet*) suivre un régime amaigrissant

slime [slaɪm] *n* (*mud*) vase *f*; (*other substance*) substance visqueuse

slimming ['slɪmɪŋ] *adj* (*diet, pills*) amaigrissant(e); (*foodstuff*) qui ne fait pas grossir

sling [slɪŋ] (*pt, pp* **slung**) *n* (MED) écharpe *f*; (*for baby*) porte-bébé *m*; (*weapon*) fronde *f*, lance-pierre *m* ♦ *vt* lancer, jeter

slip [slɪp] *n* faux pas; (*mistake*) erreur *f*; étourderie *f*; bévue *f*; (*underskirt*) combinaison *f*; (*of paper*) petite feuille, fiche *f* ♦ *vt* (*slide*) glisser ♦ *vi* glisser; (*decline*) baisser; (*move smoothly*): **to ~ into/out of** se glisser *or* se faufiler dans/hors de; **to ~ sth on/off** enfiler/enlever qch; **to give sb the ~** fausser compagnie à qn; **a ~ of the tongue** un lapsus; **~ away** *vi* s'esquiver; **~ in** *vt* glisser ♦ *vi* (*errors*) s'y glisser; **~ out** *vi* sortir; **~ up** *vi* faire une erreur, gaffer; **~ped disc** *n* déplacement *m* de vertèbre

slipper ['slɪpəʳ] *n* pantoufle *f*

slippery ['slɪpərɪ] *adj* glissant(e)

slip: ~ road (BRIT) *n* (*to motorway*) bretelle *f* d'accès; **~-up** *n* bévue *f*; **~way** *n* cale *f* (de construction *or* de lancement)

slit [slɪt] (*pt, pp* **slit**) *n* fente *f*; (*cut*) incision *f* ♦ *vt* fendre; couper; inciser

slither ['slɪðəʳ] *vi* glisser; (*snake*) onduler

sliver ['slɪvəʳ] *n* (*of glass, wood*) éclat *m*; (*of cheese etc*) petit morceau, fine tranche

slob [slɔb] (*inf*) *n* rustaud(e)

slog [slɔg] (BRIT) *vi* travailler très dur ♦ *n* gros effort; tâche fastidieuse

slogan ['sləugən] *n* slogan *m*

slope [sləup] *n* pente *f*, côte *f*; (*side of mountain*) versant *m*; (*slant*) inclinaison *f* ♦ *vi*: **to ~ down** être *or* descendre en pente; **to ~ up** monter; **sloping** *adj* en pente; (*writing*) penché(e)

sloppy ['slɔpɪ] *adj* (*work*) peu soigné(e), bâclé(e); (*appearance*) négligé(e), débraillé(e)

slot [slɔt] *n* fente *f* ♦ *vt*: **to ~ sth into** encastrer *or* insérer qch dans

sloth [sləuθ] *n* (*laziness*) paresse *f*

slouch [slautʃ] *vi* avoir le dos rond, être voûté(e)

slovenly ['slʌvənlɪ] *adj* sale, débraillé(e); (*work*) négligé(e)

slow [sləu] *adj* lent(e); (*watch*): **to be ~** retarder ♦ *adv* lentement ♦ *vt, vi* (*also:* **~ down, ~ up**) ralentir; **"~"** (*road sign*) "ralentir"; **~ly** *adv* lentement; **~ motion** *n*: **in ~ motion** au ralenti

sludge [slʌdʒ] *n* boue *f*

slug [slʌg] *n* limace *f*; (*bullet*) balle *f*

sluggish ['slʌgɪʃ] *adj* (*person*) mou (molle), lent(e); (*stream, engine, trading*) lent

sluice [slu:s] *n* (*also:* **~ gate**) vanne *f*

slum [slʌm] *n* (*house*) taudis *m*

slump [slʌmp] *n* baisse soudaine, effondrement *m*; (ECON) crise *f* ♦ *vi* s'effondrer, s'affaisser

slung [slʌŋ] *pt, pp of* **sling**

slur [slə:ʳ] *n* (*fig*: *smear*): **~ (on)** atteinte *f* (à); insinuation *f* (contre) ♦ *vt* mal articuler

slush [slʌʃ] *n* neige fondue

slut [slʌt] (*pej*) *n* souillon *f*

sly [slaɪ] *adj* (*person*) rusé(e); (*smile, expression, remark*) sournois(e)

smack [smæk] *n* (*slap*) tape *f*; (*on face*) gifle *f* ♦ *vt* donner une tape à; (*on face*) gifler; (*on bottom*) donner la fessée à ♦ *vi*: **to ~ of** avoir des relents de, sentir

small [smɔ:l] *adj* petit(e); **~ ads** (BRIT) *npl* petites annonces; **~ change** *n* petite *or* menue monnaie; **~holder** (BRIT) *n* petit cultivateur; **~ hours** *npl*: **in the ~ hours** au petit matin; **~pox** *n* variole *f*; **~ talk** *n* menus propos

smart [smɑ:t] *adj* (*neat, fashionable*) élégant(e), chic *inv*; (*clever*) intelligent(e), astucieux(-euse), futé(e); (*quick*) rapide, vif (vive), prompt(e) ♦ *vi* faire mal, brûler; (*fig*) être piqué(e) au vif; **~ card** *n* carte *f* à puce; **~en up** *vi* devenir plus élégant(e), se faire beau (belle) ♦ *vt* rendre plus élégant(e)

smash [smæʃ] *n* (*also:* **~-up**) collision *f*, accident *m*; (*also:* **~ hit**) succès foudroyant ♦ *vt* casser, briser, fracasser; (*opponent*) écraser; (SPORT: *record*) pulvériser ♦ *vi* se briser, se fracasser; s'écraser; **~ing** (*inf*) *adj* formidable

smattering ['smætərɪŋ] *n*: **a ~ of** quelques notions de

smear [smɪəʳ] *n* tache *f*, salissure *f*; trace *f*; (*MED*) frottis *m* ♦ *vt* enduire; (*make dirty*) salir; **~ campaign** *n* campagne *f* de diffamation

smell [smɛl] (*pt, pp* **smelt** *or* **smelled**) *n* odeur *f*; (*sense*) odorat *m* ♦ *vt* sentir ♦ *vi* (*food etc*): **to ~ (of)** sentir (de); (*pej*) sentir mauvais; **~y** *adj* qui sent mauvais, malodorant(e)

smile [smaɪl] *n* sourire *m* ♦ *vi* sourire

smirk [smə:k] *n* petit sourire suffisant *or* affecté

smock [smɔk] *n* blouse *f*

smog [smɔg] *n* brouillard mêlé de fumée, smog *m*

smoke [sməuk] *n* fumée *f* ♦ *vt, vi* fumer; **~d** *adj* (*bacon, glass*) fumé(e); **~r** *n* (*person*) fumeur(-euse); (*RAIL*) wagon *m* fumeurs; **~ screen** *n* rideau *m* *or* écran *m* de fumée; (*fig*) paravent *m*; **smoking** *n* tabagisme *m*; **"no smoking"** (*sign*) "défense de fumer"; **to give up smoking** arrêter de fumer; **smoking compartment** (*US* **smoking car**) *n* wagon *m* fumeurs; **smoky** *adj* enfumé(e); (*taste*) fumé(e)

smolder ['sməuldəʳ] (*US*) *vi* = **smoulder**

smooth [smu:ð] *adj* lisse; (*sauce*) onctueux(-euse); (*flavour, whisky*) moelleux(-euse); (*movement*) régulier (-ère), sans à-coups *or* heurts; (*pej*: *person*) doucereux(-euse), mielleux(-euse) ♦ *vt* (*also:* **~ out**: *skirt, paper*) lisser, défroisser; (: *creases, difficulties*) faire disparaître

smother ['smʌðəʳ] *vt* étouffer

smoulder ['sməuldəʳ] (*US* **smolder**) *vi* couver

smudge [smʌdʒ] *n* tache *f*, bavure *f* ♦ *vt* salir, maculer

smug [smʌg] *adj* suffisant(e)

smuggle ['smʌgl] *vt* passer en contrebande *or* en fraude; **~r** *n* contrebandier(-ère); **smuggling** *n* contrebande *f*

smutty ['smʌtɪ] *adj* (*fig*) grossier(-ère), obscène

snack [snæk] *n* casse-croûte *m inv*; **~ bar** *n* snack(-bar) *m*

snag [snæg] *n* inconvénient *m*, difficulté *f*

snail [sneɪl] *n* escargot *m*

snake [sneɪk] *n* serpent *m*

snap [snæp] *n* (*sound*) claquement *m*, bruit sec; (*photograph*) photo *f*, instantané *m* ♦ *adj* subit(e); fait(e) sans réfléchir ♦ *vt* (*break*) casser net; (*fingers*) faire claquer ♦ *vi* se casser net *or* avec un bruit sec; (*speak sharply*) parler d'un ton brusque; **to ~ shut** se refermer brusquement; **~ at** *vt fus* (*subj*: *dog*) essayer de mordre; **~ off** *vi* (*break*) casser net; **~ up** *vt* sauter sur, saisir; **~py** (*inf*) *adj* prompt(e); (*slogan*) qui a du punch; **make it ~py!** grouille-toi!, et que ça saute!; **~shot** *n* photo *f*, instantané *m*

snare [snɛəʳ] *n* piège *m*

snarl [snɑ:l] *vi* gronder

snatch [snætʃ] *n* (*small amount*): **~es of** des fragments *mpl* *or* bribes *fpl* de ♦ *vt* saisir (*d'un geste vif*); (*steal*) voler

sneak [sni:k] *vi*: **to ~ in/out** entrer/sortir furtivement *or* à la dérobée ♦ *n* (*inf*: *pej*: *informer*) faux jeton; **to ~ up on sb** s'approcher de qn sans faire de bruit; **~ers** *npl* tennis *mpl*, baskets *mpl*

sneer [snɪəʳ] *vi* ricaner; **to ~ at** traiter avec mépris

sneeze [sni:z] *vi* éternuer

sniff [snɪf] *vi* renifler ♦ *vt* renifler, flairer; (*glue, drugs*) sniffer, respirer

snigger ['snɪgəʳ] *vi* ricaner; pouffer de rire

snip [snɪp] *n* (*cut*) petit coup; (*BRIT*: *inf*: *bargain*) (bonne) occasion *or* affaire ♦ *vt* couper

sniper ['snaɪpəʳ] *n* tireur embusqué

snippet ['snɪpɪt] *n* bribe(s) *f(pl)*

snob [snɔb] *n* snob *m/f*; **~bish** *adj* snob *inv*

snooker ['snu:kəʳ] *n sorte de jeu de billard*

snoop [snu:p] *vi*: **to ~ about** fureter

snooze [snu:z] *n* petit somme ♦ *vi* faire un petit somme

snore [snɔ:ʳ] *vi* ronfler

snorkel ['snɔ:kl] *n* (*of swimmer*) tuba *m*

snort [snɔ:t] *vi* grogner; (*horse*) renâcler

snout [snaut] *n* museau *m*

snow [snəu] *n* neige *f* ♦ *vi* neiger; **~ball** *n* boule *f* de neige; **~bound** *adj* enneigé(e), bloqué(e) par la neige; **~drift** *n* congère *f*; **~drop** *n* perce-neige *m or f*; **~fall** *n* chute *f* de neige; **~flake** *n* flocon *m* de neige; **~man** (*irreg*) *n* bonhomme *m* de neige; **~plough** (US **snowplow**) *n* chasse-neige *m inv*; **~shoe** *n* raquette *f* (*pour la neige*); **~storm** *n* tempête *f* de neige

snub [snʌb] *vt* repousser, snober ♦ *n* rebuffade *f*; **~-nosed** *adj* au nez retroussé

snuff [snʌf] *n* tabac *m* à priser

snug [snʌg] *adj* douillet(te), confortable; (*person*) bien au chaud

snuggle ['snʌgl] *vi*: **to ~ up to sb** se serrer *or* se blottir contre qn

KEYWORD

so [səu] *adv* **1** (*thus, likewise*) ainsi; **if so** si oui; **so do** *or* **have I** moi aussi; **it's 5 o'clock – so it is!** il est 5 heures – en effet! *or* c'est vrai!; **I hope/think so** je l'espère/le crois; **so far** jusqu'ici, jusqu'à maintenant; (*in past*) jusque-là

2 (*in comparisons etc: to such a degree*) si, tellement; **so big (that)** si *or* tellement grand (que); **she's not so clever as her brother** elle n'est pas aussi intelligente que son frère

3: so much

♦ *adj, adv* tant (de); **I've got so much work** j'ai tant de travail; **I love you so much** je vous aime tant; **so many** tant (de)

4 (*phrases*): **10 or so** à peu près *or* environ 10; **so long!** (*inf: goodbye*) au revoir!, à un de ces jours!

♦ *conj* **1** (*expressing purpose*): **so as to do** pour faire, afin de faire; **so (that)** pour que *or* afin que *+sub*

2 (*expressing result*) donc, par conséquent; **so that** si bien que, de (telle) sorte que

soak [səuk] *vt* faire tremper; (*drench*) tremper ♦ *vi* tremper; **~ in** *vi* être absorbé(e); **~ up** *vt* absorber; **~ing** *adj* trempé(e)

soap [səup] *n* savon *m*; **~flakes** *npl* paillettes *fpl* de savon; **~ opera** *n* feuilleton télévisé; **~ powder** *n* lessive *f*; **~y** *adj* savonneux(-euse)

soar [sɔ:ʳ] *vi* monter (en flèche), s'élancer; (*building*) s'élancer

sob [sɔb] *n* sanglot *m* ♦ *vi* sangloter

sober ['səubəʳ] *adj* qui n'est pas (*or* plus) ivre; (*serious*) sérieux(-euse), sensé(e); (*colour, style*) sobre, discret(-ète); **~ up** *vt* dessoûler (*inf*) ♦ *vi* dessoûler (*inf*)

so-called ['səu'kɔ:ld] *adj* soi-disant *inv*

soccer ['sɔkəʳ] *n* football *m*

social ['səuʃl] *adj* social(e); (*sociable*) sociable ♦ *n* (petite) fête; **~ club** *n* amicale *f*, foyer *m*; **~ism** *n* socialisme *m*; **~ist** *adj* socialiste ♦ *n* socialiste *m/f*; **~ize** *vi*: **to ~ize (with)** lier connaissance (avec); parler (avec); **~ security** (BRIT) *n* aide sociale; **~ work** *n* assistance sociale, travail social; **~ worker** *n* assistant(e) social(e)

society [sə'saɪətɪ] *n* société *f*; (*club*) société, association *f*; (*also*: **high ~**) (haute) société, grand monde

sociology [səusɪ'ɔlədʒɪ] *n* sociologie *f*

sock [sɔk] *n* chaussette *f*

socket ['sɔkɪt] *n* cavité *f*; (BRIT: ELEC: *also*: **wall ~**) prise *f* de courant

sod [sɔd] *n* (*of earth*) motte *f*; (BRIT: *inf!*) con *m* (*!*); salaud *m* (*!*)

soda ['səudə] *n* (CHEM) soude *f*; (*also*: **~ water**) eau *f* de Seltz; (US: *also*: **~ pop**) soda *m*

sofa ['səufə] *n* sofa *m*, canapé *m*

soft [sɔft] *adj* (*not rough*) doux (douce); (*not hard*) doux; mou (molle); (*not loud*) doux, léger(-ère); (*kind*) doux, gentil(le); **~ drink** *n* boisson non alcoolisée; **~en** *vt* (r)amollir; (*fig*) adoucir; atténuer ♦ *vi* se ramollir; s'adoucir; s'atténuer; **~ly** *adv* doucement; gentiment; **~ness** *n* douceur *f*; **~ware** *n* (COMPUT) logiciel *m*, software *m*

soggy ['sɔgɪ] *adj* trempé(e); détrempé(e)

soil [sɔɪl] *n* (*earth*) sol *m*, terre *f* ♦ *vt* salir; (*fig*) souiller

solar ['səulə^r] *adj* solaire; **~ panel** *n* panneau *m* solaire; **~ power** *n* énergie solaire

sold [səuld] *pt, pp of* **sell**

solder ['səuldə^r] *vt* souder (*au fil à souder*) ♦ *n* soudure *f*

soldier ['səuldʒə^r] *n* soldat *m*, militaire *m*

sole [səul] *n* (*of foot*) plante *f*; (*of shoe*) semelle *f*; (*fish*: *pl inv*) sole *f* ♦ *adj* seul(e), unique

solemn ['sɔləm] *adj* solennel(le); (*person*) sérieux(-euse), grave

sole trader *n* (COMM) chef *m* d'entreprise individuelle

solicit [sə'lɪsɪt] *vt* (*request*) solliciter ♦ *vi* (*prostitute*) racoler

solicitor [sə'lɪsɪtə^r] *n* (*for wills etc*) ≃ notaire *m*; (*in court*) ≃ avocat *m*

solid ['sɔlɪd] *adj* solide; (*not hollow*) plein(e), compact(e), massif(-ive); (*entire*): **3 ~ hours** 3 heures entières ♦ *n* solide *m*

solidarity [sɔlɪ'dærɪtɪ] *n* solidarité *f*

solitary ['sɔlɪtərɪ] *adj* solitaire; **~ confinement** *n* (LAW) isolement *m*

solo ['səuləu] *n* solo *m* ♦ *adv* (*fly*) en solitaire; **~ist** *n* soliste *m/f*

soluble ['sɔljubl] *adj* soluble

solution [sə'lu:ʃən] *n* solution *f*

solve [sɔlv] *vt* résoudre

solvent ['sɔlvənt] *adj* (COMM) solvable ♦ *n* (CHEM) (dis)solvant *m*

KEYWORD

some [sʌm] *adj* **1** (*a certain amount or number of*): **some tea/water/ice cream** du thé/de l'eau/de la glace; **some children/apples** des enfants/pommes

2 (*certain*: *in contrasts*): **some people say that ...** il y a des gens qui disent que ...; **some films were excellent, but most ...** certains films étaient excellents, mais la plupart ...

3 (*unspecified*): **some woman was asking for you** il y avait une dame qui vous demandait; **he was asking for some book (or other)** il demandait un livre quelconque; **some day** un de ces jours; **some day next week** un jour la semaine prochaine

♦ *pron* **1** (*a certain number*) quelques-un(e)s, certain(e)s; **I've got some** (*books etc*) j'en ai (quelques-uns); **some (of them) have been sold** certains ont été vendus

2 (*a certain amount*) un peu; **I've got some** (*money, milk*) j'en ai (un peu)

♦ *adv*: **some 10 people** quelque 10 personnes, 10 personnes environ

some: ~body ['sʌmbədɪ] *pron* = **someone**; **~how** *adv* d'une façon ou d'une autre; (*for some reason*) pour une raison ou une autre; **~one** *pron* quelqu'un; **~place** (US) *adv* = **somewhere**

somersault ['sʌməsɔ:lt] *n* culbute *f*, saut périlleux ♦ *vi* faire la culbute *or* un saut périlleux; (*car*) faire un tonneau

some: ~thing *pron* quelque chose; **~thing interesting** quelque chose d'intéressant; **~time** *adv* (*in future*) un de ces jours, un jour ou l'autre; (*in past*): **~time last month** au cours du mois dernier; **~times** *adv* quelquefois, parfois; **~what** *adv* quelque peu, un peu; **~where** *adv* quelque part

son [sʌn] *n* fils *m*

song [sɔŋ] *n* chanson *f*; (*of bird*) chant

m

son-in-law *n* gendre *m*, beau-fils *m*

soon [su:n] *adv* bientôt; (*early*) tôt; **~ afterwards** peu après; *see also* **as**; **~er** *adv* (*time*) plus tôt; (*preference*): **I would ~er do** j'aimerais autant *or* je préférerais faire; **~er or later** tôt ou tard

soot [sut] *n* suie *f*

soothe [su:ð] *vt* calmer, apaiser

sophisticated [sə'fɪstɪkeɪtɪd] *adj* raffiné(e); sophistiqué(e); (*machinery*) hautement perfectionné(e), très complexe

sophomore ['sɔfəmɔ:ʳ] (*US*) *n* étudiant(e) de seconde année

sopping ['sɔpɪŋ] *adj* (*also:* **~ wet**) complètement trempé(e)

soppy ['sɔpɪ] (*pej*) *adj* sentimental(e)

soprano [sə'prɑ:nəu] *n* (*singer*) soprano *m/f*

sorcerer ['sɔ:sərəʳ] *n* sorcier *m*

sore [sɔ:ʳ] *adj* (*painful*) douloureux (-euse), sensible ♦ *n* plaie *f*; **~ly** ['sɔ:lɪ] *adv* (*tempted*) fortement

sorrow ['sɔrəu] *n* peine *f*, chagrin *m*

sorry ['sɔrɪ] *adj* désolé(e); (*condition, excuse*) triste, déplorable; **~!** pardon!, excusez-moi!; **~?** pardon?; **to feel ~ for sb** plaindre qn

sort [sɔ:t] *n* genre *m*, espèce *f*, sorte *f* ♦ *vt* (*also:* **~ out**) trier; classer; ranger; (: *problems*) résoudre, régler; **~ing office** ['sɔ:tɪŋ-] *n* bureau *m* de tri

SOS *n* S.O.S. *m*

so-so ['səusəu] *adv* comme ci comme ça

sought [sɔ:t] *pt, pp of* **seek**

soul [səul] *n* âme *f*; **~ful** ['səulful] *adj* sentimental(e); (*eyes*) expressif(-ive)

sound [saund] *adj* (*healthy*) en bonne santé, sain(e); (*safe, not damaged*) solide, en bon état; (*reliable, not superficial*) sérieux(-euse), solide; (*sensible*) sensé(e) ♦ *adv*: **~ asleep** profondément endormi(e) ♦ *n* son *m*; bruit *m*; (*GEO*) détroit *m*, bras *m* de mer ♦ *vt* (*alarm*) sonner ♦ *vi* sonner, retentir; (*fig*: *seem*) sembler (être); **to ~ like** ressembler à; **~ out** *vt* sonder; **~ barrier** *n* mur *m* du son; **~ bite** *n* phrase *f* toute faite (*pour être citée dans les médias*); **~ effects** *npl* bruitage *m*; **~ly** *adv* (*sleep*) profondément; (*beat*) complètement, à plate couture; **~proof** *adj* insonorisé(e); **~track** *n* (*of film*) bande *f* sonore

soup [su:p] *n* soupe *f*, potage *m*; **~ plate** *n* assiette creuse *or* à soupe; **~spoon** *n* cuiller *f* à soupe

sour ['sauəʳ] *adj* aigre; **it's ~ grapes** (*fig*) c'est du dépit

source [sɔ:s] *n* source *f*

south [sauθ] *n* sud *m* ♦ *adj* sud *inv*, du sud ♦ *adv* au sud, vers le sud; **S~ Africa** *n* Afrique *f* du Sud; **S~ African** *adj* sud-africain(e) ♦ *n* Sud-Africain(e); **S~ America** *n* Amérique *f* du Sud; **S~ American** *adj* sud-américain(e) ♦ *n* Sud-Américain(e); **~-east** *n* sud-est *m*; **~erly** ['sʌðəlɪ] *adj* du sud; au sud; **~ern** ['sʌðən] *adj* (du) sud; méridional(e); **S~ Pole** *n* Pôle *m* Sud; **S~ Wales** *n* sud *m* du Pays de Galles; **~ward(s)** *adv* vers le sud; **~-west** *n* sud-ouest *m*

souvenir [su:və'nɪəʳ] *n* (*objet*) souvenir *m*

sovereign ['sɔvrɪn] *n* souverain(e)

soviet ['səuvɪət] *adj* soviétique; **the S~ Union** l'Union *f* soviétique

sow¹ [sau] *n* truie *f*

sow² [səu] (*pt* **sowed**, *pp* **sown**) *vt* semer

sown [səun] *pp of* **sow²**

soya ['sɔɪə] (*US* **soy**) *n*: **~ bean** graine *f* de soja; **soy(a) sauce** sauce *f* au soja

spa [spɑ:] *n* (*town*) station thermale; (*US*: *also:* **health ~**) établissement *m* de cure de rajeunissement *etc*

space [speɪs] *n* espace *m*; (*room*) place *f*; espace; (*length of time*) laps *m* de temps ♦ *cpd* spatial(e) ♦ *vt* (*also:* **~ out**) espacer; **~craft** *n* engin spatial; **~man** (*irreg*) *n* astronaute *m*, cosmonaute *m*; **~ship** *n* = **spacecraft**; **spacing** *n* es-

pacement *m;* **spacious** ['speɪʃəs] *adj* spacieux(-euse), grand(e)
spade [speɪd] *n* (*tool*) bêche *f*, pelle *f*; (*child's*) pelle; **~s** *npl* (*CARDS*) pique *m*
Spain [speɪn] *n* Espagne *f*
span [spæn] *n* (*of bird, plane*) envergure *f*; (*of arch*) portée *f*; (*in time*) espace *m* de temps, durée *f* ♦ *vt* enjamber, franchir; (*fig*) couvrir, embrasser
Spaniard ['spænjəd] *n* Espagnol(e)
spaniel ['spænjəl] *n* épagneul *m*
Spanish ['spænɪʃ] *adj* espagnol(e) ♦ *n* (*LING*) espagnol *m;* **the ~** *npl* les Espagnols *mpl*
spank [spæŋk] *vt* donner une fessée à
spanner ['spænə^r^] (*BRIT*) *n* clé *f* (de mécanicien)
spare [speə^r^] *adj* de réserve, de rechange; (*surplus*) de *or* en trop, de reste ♦ *n* (*part*) pièce *f* de rechange, pièce détachée ♦ *vt* (*do without*) se passer de; (*afford to give*) donner, accorder; (*refrain from hurting*) épargner; **to ~** (*surplus*) en surplus, de trop; **~ part** *n* pièce *f* de rechange, pièce détachée; **~ time** *n* moments *mpl* de loisir, temps *m* libre; **~ wheel** *n* (*AUT*) roue *f* de secours; **sparingly** *adv* avec modération
spark [spɑːk] *n* étincelle *f*; **~(ing) plug** *n* bougie *f*
sparkle ['spɑːkl] *n* scintillement *m*, éclat *m* ♦ *vi* étinceler, scintiller; **sparkling** *adj* (*wine*) mousseux(-euse), pétillant(e); (*water*) pétillant(e); (*fig: conversation, performance*) étincelant(e), pétillant(e)
sparrow ['spærəu] *n* moineau *m*
sparse [spɑːs] *adj* clairsemé(e)
spartan ['spɑːtən] *adj* (*fig*) spartiate
spasm ['spæzəm] *n* (*MED*) spasme *m;* **~odic** [spæz'mɔdɪk] *adj* (*fig*) intermittent(e)
spastic ['spæstɪk] *n* handicapé(e) moteur
spat [spæt] *pt, pp of* **spit**
spate [speɪt] *n* (*fig*): **a ~ of** une avalanche *or* un torrent de
spawn [spɔːn] *vi* frayer ♦ *n* frai *m*
speak [spiːk] (*pt* **spoke**, *pp* **spoken**) *vt* parler; (*truth*) dire ♦ *vi* parler; (*make a speech*) prendre la parole; **to ~ to sb/of** *or* **about sth** parler à qn/de qch; **~ up!** parle plus fort!; **~er** *n* (*in public*) orateur *m;* (*also:* **loudspeaker**) haut-parleur *m;* **the S~er** (*BRIT: POL*) *le président de la chambre des Communes;* (*US: POL*) *le président de la chambre des Représentants*
spear [spɪə^r^] *n* lance *f* ♦ *vt* transpercer; **~head** *vt* (*attack etc*) mener
spec [spɛk] (*inf*) *n*: **on ~** à tout hasard
special ['spɛʃl] *adj* spécial(e); **~ist** *n* spécialiste *m/f*; **~ity** [spɛʃɪ'ælɪtɪ] *n* spécialité *f*; **~ize** *vi*: **to ~ize (in)** se spécialiser (dans); **~ly** *adv* spécialement, particulièrement; **~ty** (*esp US*) *n* = **speciality**
species ['spiːʃiːz] *n inv* espèce *f*
specific [spə'sɪfɪk] *adj* précis(e); particulier(-ère); (*BOT, CHEM etc*) spécifique; **~ally** *adv* expressément, explicitement; **~ation** [spɛsɪfɪ'keɪʃən] *n* (*TECH*) spécification *f*; (*requirement*) stipulation *f*
specimen ['spɛsɪmən] *n* spécimen *m*, échantillon *m;* (*of blood*) prélèvement *m*
speck [spɛk] *n* petite tache, petit point; (*particle*) grain *m*
speckled ['spɛkld] *adj* tacheté(e), moucheté(e)
specs [spɛks] (*inf*) *npl* lunettes *fpl*
spectacle ['spɛktəkl] *n* spectacle *m;* **~s** *npl* (*glasses*) lunettes *fpl;* **spectacular** [spɛk'tækjulə^r^] *adj* spectaculaire
spectator [spɛk'teɪtə^r^] *n* spectateur (-trice)
spectrum ['spɛktrəm] (*pl* **spectra**) *n* spectre *m*
speculation [spɛkju'leɪʃən] *n* spéculation *f*
speech [spiːtʃ] *n* (*faculty*) parole *f*; (*talk*) discours *m*, allocution *f*; (*manner of speaking*) façon *f* de parler, langage *m;* (*enunciation*) élocution *f*; **~less** *adj*

muet(te)

speed [spiːd] *n* vitesse *f*; (*promptness*) rapidité *f* ♦ *vi*: **to ~ along/past** *etc* aller/passer *etc* à toute vitesse *or* allure; **at full** *or* **top ~** à toute vitesse *or* allure; **~ up** *vi* aller plus vite, accélérer ♦ *vt* accélérer; **~boat** *n* vedette *f*, hors-bord *m inv*; **~ily** *adv* rapidement, promptement; **~ing** *n* (*AUT*) excès *m* de vitesse; **~ limit** *n* limitation *f* de vitesse, vitesse maximale permise; **~ometer** [spɪ'dɔmɪtəʳ] *n* compteur *m* (de vitesse); **~way** *n* (*SPORT*: *also:* **~way racing**) épreuve(s) *f(pl)* de vitesse de motos; **~y** *adj* rapide, prompt(e)

spell [spɛl] (*pt, pp* **spelt** *or* **spelled**) *n* (*also:* **magic ~**) sortilège *m*, charme *m*; (*period of time*) (courte) période ♦ *vt* (*in writing*) écrire, orthographier; (*aloud*) épeler; (*fig*) signifier; **to cast a ~ on sb** jeter un sort à qn; **he can't ~** il fait des fautes d'orthographe; **~bound** *adj* envoûté(e), subjugué(e); **~ing** *n* orthographe *f*

spend [spɛnd] (*pt, pp* **spent**) *vt* (*money*) dépenser; (*time, life*) passer; consacrer; **~thrift** *n* dépensier(-ère)

sperm [spəːm] *n* sperme *m*

sphere [sfɪəʳ] *n* sphère *f*

spice [spaɪs] *n* épice *f*; **spicy** *adj* épicé(e), relevé(e); (*fig*) piquant(e)

spider ['spaɪdəʳ] *n* araignée *f*

spike [spaɪk] *n* pointe *f*; (*BOT*) épi *m*

spill [spɪl] (*pt, pp* **spilt** *or* **spilled**) *vt* renverser; répandre ♦ *vi* se répandre; **~ over** *vi* déborder

spin [spɪn] (*pt* **spun** *or* **span**, *pp* **spun**) *n* (*revolution of wheel*) tour *m*; (*AVIAT*) (chute *f* en) vrille *f*; (*trip in car*) petit tour, balade *f* ♦ *vt* (*wool etc*) filer; (*wheel*) faire tourner ♦ *vi* filer; (*turn*) tourner, tournoyer

spinach ['spɪnɪtʃ] *n* épinard *m*; (*as food*) épinards

spinal ['spaɪnl] *adj* vertébral(e), spinal(e); **~ cord** *n* moelle épinière

spin doctor *n personne employée pour présenter un parti politique sous un jour favorable*

spin-dryer [spɪn'draɪəʳ] (*BRIT*) *n* essoreuse *f*

spine [spaɪn] *n* colonne vertébrale; (*thorn*) épine *f*; **~less** *adj* (*fig*) mou (molle)

spinning ['spɪnɪŋ] *n* (*of thread*) filature *f*; **~ top** *n* toupie *f*

spin-off ['spɪnɔf] *n* avantage inattendu; sous-produit *m*

spinster ['spɪnstəʳ] *n* célibataire *f*; vieille fille (*péj*)

spiral ['spaɪərl] *n* spirale *f* ♦ *vi* (*fig*) monter en flèche; **~ staircase** *n* escalier *m* en colimaçon

spire ['spaɪəʳ] *n* flèche *f*, aiguille *f*

spirit ['spɪrɪt] *n* esprit *m*; (*mood*) état *m* d'esprit; (*courage*) courage *m*, énergie *f*; **~s** *npl* (*drink*) spiritueux *mpl*, alcool *m*; **in good ~s** de bonne humeur; **~ed** *adj* vif (vive), fougueux(-euse), plein(e) d'allant; **~ual** *adj* spirituel(le); (*religious*) religieux(-euse)

spit [spɪt] (*pt, pp* **spat**) *n* (*for roasting*) broche *f*; (*saliva*) salive *f* ♦ *vi* cracher; (*sound*) crépiter

spite [spaɪt] *n* rancune *f*, dépit *m* ♦ *vt* contrarier, vexer; **in ~ of** en dépit de, malgré; **~ful** *adj* méchant(e), malveillant(e)

spittle ['spɪtl] *n* salive *f*; (*of animal*) bave *f*; (*spat out*) crachat *m*

splash [splæʃ] *n* (*sound*) plouf *m*; (*of colour*) tache *f* ♦ *vt* éclabousser ♦ *vi* (*also:* **~ about**) barboter, patauger

spleen [spliːn] *n* (*ANAT*) rate *f*

splendid ['splɛndɪd] *adj* splendide, superbe, magnifique

splint [splɪnt] *n* attelle *f*, éclisse *f*

splinter ['splɪntəʳ] *n* (*wood*) écharde *f*; (*glass*) éclat *m* ♦ *vi* se briser, se fendre

split [splɪt] (*pt, pp* **split**) *n* fente *f*, déchirure *f*; (*fig*: *POL*) scission *f* ♦ *vt* diviser; (*work, profits*) partager, répartir ♦ *vi* (*divide*) se diviser; **~ up** *vi* (*couple*) se séparer, rompre; (*meeting*) se disperser

spoil [spɔɪl] (*pt, pp* **spoilt** *or* **spoiled**) *vt* (*damage*) abîmer; (*mar*) gâcher; (*child*) gâter; **~s** *npl* butin *m*; (*fig*: *profits*) bénéfices *npl*; **~sport** *n* trouble-fête *m*, rabat-joie *m*

spoke [spəuk] *pt of* **speak** ♦ *n* (*of wheel*) rayon *m*

spoken ['spəukn] *pp of* **speak**

spokesman ['spəuksmən], **spokeswoman** ['spəukswumən] (*irreg*) *n* porte-parole *m inv*

sponge [spʌndʒ] *n* éponge *f*; (*also:* **~ cake**) ≃ biscuit *m* de Savoie ♦ *vt* éponger ♦ *vi*: **to ~ off** *or* **on** vivre aux crochets de; **~ bag** (*BRIT*) *n* trousse *f* de toilette

sponsor ['spɔnsə^r] *n* (*RADIO, TV, SPORT*) sponsor *m*; (*for application*) parrain *m*, marraine *f*; (*BRIT*: *for fund-raising event*) donateur(-trice) ♦ *vt* sponsoriser; parrainer; faire un don à; **~ship** *n* sponsoring *m*; parrainage *m*; dons *mpl*

spontaneous [spɔn'teɪnɪəs] *adj* spontané(e)

spooky ['spu:kɪ] (*inf*) *adj* qui donne la chair de poule

spool [spu:l] *n* bobine *f*

spoon [spu:n] *n* cuiller *f*; **~-feed** *vt* nourrir à la cuiller; (*fig*) mâcher le travail à; **~ful** *n* cuillerée *f*

sport [spɔ:t] *n* sport *m*; (*person*) chic type (*fille*) ♦ *vt* arborer; **~ing** *adj* sportif(-ive); **to give sb a ~ing chance** donner sa chance à qn; **~ jacket** (*US*) *n* = **sports jacket**; **~s car** *n* voiture *f* de sport; **~s jacket** (*BRIT*) *n* veste *f* de sport; **~sman** (*irreg*) *n* sportif *m*; **~smanship** *n* esprit sportif, sportivité *f*; **~swear** *n* vêtements *mpl* de sport; **~swoman** (*irreg*) *n* sportive *f*; **~y** *adj* sportif(-ive)

spot [spɔt] *n* tache *f*; (*dot*: *on pattern*) pois *m*; (*pimple*) bouton *m*; (*place*) endroit *m*, coin *m*; (*RADIO, TV*: *in programme*: *for person*) numéro *m*; (: *for activity*) rubrique *f*; (*small amount*): **a ~ of** un peu de ♦ *vt* (*notice*) apercevoir, repérer; **on the ~** sur place, sur les lieux; (*immediately*) sur-le-champ; (*in difficulty*) dans l'embarras; **~ check** *n* sondage *m*, vérification ponctuelle; **~less** *adj* immaculé(e); **~light** *n* projecteur *m*; **~ted** *adj* (*fabric*) à pois; **~ty** *adj* (*face, person*) boutonneux(-euse)

spouse [spaus] *n* époux (épouse)

spout [spaut] *n* (*of jug*) bec *m*; (*of pipe*) orifice *m* ♦ *vi* jaillir

sprain [spreɪn] *n* entorse *f*, foulure *f* ♦ *vt*: **to ~ one's ankle** *etc* se fouler *or* se tordre la cheville *etc*

sprang [spræŋ] *pt of* **spring**

sprawl [sprɔ:l] *vi* s'étaler

spray [spreɪ] *n* jet *m* (en fines gouttelettes); (*from sea*) embruns *mpl*, vaporisateur *m*; (*for garden*) pulvérisateur *m*; (*aerosol*) bombe *f*; (*of flowers*) petit bouquet ♦ *vt* vaporiser, pulvériser; (*crops*) traiter

spread [sprɛd] (*pt, pp* **spread**) *n* (*distribution*) répartition *f*; (*CULIN*) pâte *f* à tartiner; (*inf*: *meal*) festin *m* ♦ *vt* étendre, étaler; répandre; (*wealth, workload*) distribuer ♦ *vi* (*disease, news*) se propager; (*also:* **~ out**: *stain*) s'étaler; **~ out** *vi* (*people*) se disperser; **~-eagled** *adj* étendu(e) bras et jambes écartés; **~sheet** *n* (*COMPUT*) tableur *m*

spree [spri:] *n*: **to go on a ~** faire la fête

sprightly ['spraɪtlɪ] *adj* alerte

spring [sprɪŋ] (*pt* **sprang**, *pp* **sprung**) *n* (*leap*) bond *m*, saut *m*; (*coiled metal*) ressort *m*; (*season*) printemps *m*; (*of water*) source *f* ♦ *vi* (*leap*) bondir, sauter; **in ~** au printemps; **to ~ from** provenir de; **~ up** *vi* (*problem*) se présenter, surgir; (*plant, buildings*) surgir de terre; **~board** *n* tremplin *m*; **~-clean(ing)** *n* grand nettoyage de printemps; **~time** *n* printemps *m*

sprinkle ['sprɪŋkl] *vt*: **to ~ water** *etc* **on, ~ with water** *etc* asperger d'eau *etc*; **to ~ sugar** *etc* **on, ~ with sugar** *etc* saupoudrer de sucre *etc*; **~r** *n* (*for* *lawn*) arroseur *m*; (*to put out fire*) diffuseur *m* d'extincteur automatique d'incendie

sprint [sprɪnt] *n* sprint *m* ♦ *vi* courir à toute vitesse; (SPORT) sprinter; **~er** *n* sprinteur(-euse)

sprout [spraut] *vi* germer, pousser; **~s** *npl* (*also:* **Brussels ~s**) choux *mpl* de Bruxelles

spruce [spru:s] *n inv* épicéa *m* ♦ *adj* net(te), pimpant(e)

sprung [sprʌŋ] *pp of* **spring**

spun [spʌn] *pt, pp of* **spin**

spur [spə:ʳ] *n* éperon *m*; (*fig*) aiguillon *m* ♦ *vt* (*also:* **~ on**) éperonner; aiguillonner; **on the ~ of the moment** sous l'impulsion du moment

spurious ['spjuərɪəs] *adj* faux (fausse)

spurn [spə:n] *vt* repousser avec mépris

spurt [spə:t] *n* (*of blood*) jaillissement *m*; (*of energy*) regain *m*, sursaut *m* ♦ *vi* jaillir, gicler

spy [spaɪ] *n* espion(ne) ♦ *vi*: **to ~ on** espionner, épier; (*see*) apercevoir; **~ing** *n* espionnage *m*

sq. *abbr* = **square**

squabble ['skwɔbl] *vi* se chamailler

squad [skwɔd] *n* (MIL, POLICE) escouade *f*, groupe *m*; (FOOTBALL) contingent *m*

squadron ['skwɔdrn] *n* (MIL) escadron *m*; (AVIAT, NAUT) escadrille *f*

squalid ['skwɔlɪd] *adj* sordide

squall [skwɔ:l] *n* rafale *f*, bourrasque *f*

squalor ['skwɔləʳ] *n* conditions *fpl* sordides

squander ['skwɔndəʳ] *vt* gaspiller, dilapider

square [skwɛəʳ] *n* carré *m*; (*in town*) place *f* ♦ *adj* carré(e); (*inf: ideas, tastes*) vieux jeu *inv* ♦ *vt* (*arrange*) régler; arranger; (MATH) élever au carré ♦ *vi* (*reconcile*) concilier; **all ~** quitte; à égalité; **a ~ meal** un repas convenable; **2 metres ~** (de) 2 mètres sur 2; **2 ~ metres** 2 mètres carrés; **~ly** *adv* carrément

squash [skwɔʃ] *n* (BRIT: *drink*): **lemon/orange ~** citronnade *f*/orangeade *f*; (US: *marrow*) courge *f*; (SPORT) squash *m* ♦ *vt* écraser

squat [skwɔt] *adj* petit(e) et épais(se), ramassé(e) ♦ *vi* (*also:* **~ down**) s'accroupir; **~ter** *n* squatter *m*

squeak [skwi:k] *vi* grincer, crier; (*mouse*) pousser un petit cri

squeal [skwi:l] *vi* pousser un *or* des cri(s) aigu(s) *or* perçant(s); (*brakes*) grincer

squeamish ['skwi:mɪʃ] *adj* facilement dégoûté(e)

squeeze [skwi:z] *n* pression *f*; (ECON) restrictions *fpl* de crédit ♦ *vt* presser; (*hand, arm*) serrer; **~ out** *vt* exprimer

squelch [skwɛltʃ] *vi* faire un bruit de succion

squid [skwɪd] *n* calmar *m*

squiggle ['skwɪgl] *n* gribouillis *m*

squint [skwɪnt] *vi* loucher ♦ *n*: **he has a ~** il louche, il souffre de strabisme

squirm [skwə:m] *vi* se tortiller

squirrel ['skwɪrəl] *n* écureuil *m*

squirt [skwə:t] *vi* jaillir, gicler

Sr *abbr* = **senior**

St *abbr* = **saint**; **street**

stab [stæb] *n* (*with knife etc*) coup *m* (de couteau *etc*); (*of pain*) lancée *f*; (*inf: try*): **to have a ~ at (doing) sth** s'essayer à (faire) qch ♦ *vt* poignarder

stable ['steɪbl] *n* écurie *f* ♦ *adj* stable

stack [stæk] *n* tas *m*, pile *f* ♦ *vt* (*also:* **~ up**) empiler, entasser

stadium ['steɪdɪəm] (*pl* **stadia** *or* **~s**) *n* stade *m*

staff [stɑ:f] *n* (*workforce*) personnel *m*; (BRIT: SCOL) professeurs *mpl* ♦ *vt* pourvoir en personnel

stag [stæg] *n* cerf *m*

stage [steɪdʒ] *n* scène *f*; (*platform*) estrade *f* ♦ *n* (*point*) étape *f*, stade *m*; (*profession*): **the ~** le théâtre ♦ *vt* (*play*) monter, mettre en scène; (*demonstration*) organiser; **in ~s** par étapes, par degrés; **~coach** *n* diligence *f*; **~ manager** *n* régisseur *m*

stagger ['stægəʳ] *vi* chanceler, tituber ♦ *vt* (*person*: *amaze*) stupéfier; (*hours, holidays*) étaler, échelonner; **~ing** *adj* (*amazing*) stupéfiant(e), renversant(e)
stagnate [stæg'neɪt] *vi* stagner, croupir
stag party *n* enterrement *m* de vie de garçon
staid [steɪd] *adj* posé(e), rassis(e)
stain [steɪn] *n* tache *f*; (*colouring*) colorant *m* ♦ *vt* tacher; (*wood*) teindre; **~ed glass window** *n* vitrail *m*; **~less steel** *n* acier *m* inoxydable, inox *m*; **~ remover** *n* détachant *m*
stair [stɛəʳ] *n* (*step*) marche *f*; **~s** *npl* (*flight of steps*) escalier *m*; **~case, ~way** *n* escalier *m*
stake [steɪk] *n* pieu *m*, poteau *m*; (BETTING) enjeu *m*; (COMM: *interest*) intérêts *mpl* ♦ *vt* risquer, jouer; **to be at ~** être en jeu; **to ~ one's claim (to)** revendiquer
stale [steɪl] *adj* (*bread*) rassis(e); (*food*) pas frais (fraîche); (*beer*) éventé(e); (*smell*) de renfermé; (*air*) confiné(e)
stalemate ['steɪlmeɪt] *n* (CHESS) pat *m*; (*fig*) impasse *f*
stalk [stɔːk] *n* tige *f* ♦ *vt* traquer ♦ *vi*: **to ~ out/off** sortir/partir d'un air digne
stall [stɔːl] *n* (BRIT: *in street, market etc*) éventaire *m*, étal *m*; (*in stable*) stalle *f* ♦ *vt* (AUT) caler; (*delay*) retarder ♦ *vi* (AUT) caler; (*fig*) essayer de gagner du temps; **~s** *npl* (BRIT: *in cinema, theatre*) orchestre *m*
stallion ['stæljən] *n* étalon *m* (*cheval*)
stamina ['stæmɪnə] *n* résistance *f*, endurance *f*
stammer ['stæməʳ] *n* bégaiement *m* ♦ *vi* bégayer
stamp [stæmp] *n* timbre *m*; (*rubber ~*) tampon *m*; (*mark, also fig*) empreinte *f* ♦ *vi* (*also:* **~ one's foot**) taper du pied ♦ *vt* (*letter*) timbrer; (*with rubber ~*) tamponner; **~ album** *n* album *m* de timbres(-poste); **~ collecting** *n* philatélie *f*
stampede [stæm'piːd] *n* ruée *f*
stance [stæns] *n* position *f*
stand [stænd] (*pt, pp* **stood**) *n* (*position*) position *f*; (*for taxis*) station *f* (de taxis); (*music ~*) pupitre *m* à musique; (COMM) étalage *m*, stand *m*; (SPORT: *also:* **~s**) tribune *f* ♦ *vi* être *or* se tenir (debout); (*rise*) se lever, se mettre debout; (*be placed*) se trouver; (*remain*: *offer etc*) rester valable; (BRIT: *in election*) être candidat(e), se présenter ♦ *vt* (*place*) mettre, poser; (*tolerate, withstand*) supporter; (*treat, invite to*) offrir, payer; **to make** *or* **take a ~** prendre position; **to ~ at** (*score, value etc*) être de; **to ~ for parliament** (BRIT) se présenter aux élections législatives; **~ by** *vi* (*be ready*) se tenir prêt(e) ♦ *vt fus* (*opinion*) s'en tenir à; (*person*) ne pas abandonner, soutenir; **~ down** *vi* (*withdraw*) se retirer; **~ for** *vt fus* (*signify*) représenter, signifier; (*tolerate*) supporter, tolérer; **~ in for** *vt fus* remplacer; **~ out** *vi* (*be prominent*) ressortir; **~ up** *vi* (*rise*) se lever, se mettre debout; **~ up for** *vt fus* défendre; **~ up to** *vt fus* tenir tête à, résister à
standard ['stændəd] *n* (*level*) niveau (voulu); (*norm*) norme *f*, étalon *m*; (*criterion*) critère *m*; (*flag*) étendard *m* ♦ *adj* (*size etc*) ordinaire, normal(e); courant(e); (*text*) de base; **~s** *npl* (*morals*) morale *f*, principes *mpl*; **~ lamp** (BRIT) *n* lampadaire *m*; **~ of living** *n* niveau *m* de vie
stand-by ['stændbaɪ] *n* remplaçant(e); **to be on ~-~** se tenir prêt(e) (à intervenir); être de garde; **~-~ ticket** *n* (AVIAT) billet *m* stand-by
stand-in ['stændɪn] *n* remplaçant(e)
standing ['stændɪŋ] *adj* debout *inv*; (*permanent*) permanent(e) ♦ *n* réputation *f*, rang *m*, standing *m*; **of many years' ~** qui dure *or* existe depuis longtemps; **~ joke** *n* vieux sujet de plaisanterie; **~ order** (BRIT) *n* (*at bank*) virement *m* automatique, prélèvement *m* bancaire; **~ room** *n* places *fpl* debout

standpoint ['stændpɔɪnt] *n* point *m* de vue

standstill ['stændstɪl] *n*: **at a ~** paralysé(e); **to come to a ~** s'immobiliser, s'arrêter

stank [stæŋk] *pt of* **stink**

staple ['steɪpl] *n* (*for papers*) agrafe *f* ♦ *adj* (*food etc*) de base ♦ *vt* agrafer; **~r** *n* agrafeuse *f*

star [stɑːʳ] *n* étoile *f*; (*celebrity*) vedette *f* ♦ *vi*: **to ~ (in)** être la vedette (de) ♦ *vt* (CINEMA *etc*) avoir pour vedette; **the ~s** *npl* l'horoscope *m*

starboard ['stɑːbɔːd] *n* tribord *m*

starch [stɑːtʃ] *n* amidon *m*; (*in food*) fécule *f*

stardom ['stɑːdəm] *n* célébrité *f*

stare [steəʳ] *n* regard *m* fixe ♦ *vi*: **to ~ at** regarder fixement

starfish ['stɑːfɪʃ] *n* étoile *f* de mer

stark [stɑːk] *adj* (*bleak*) désolé(e), morne ♦ *adv*: **~ naked** complètement nu(e)

starling ['stɑːlɪŋ] *n* étourneau *m*

starry ['stɑːrɪ] *adj* étoilé(e); **~-eyed** *adj* (*innocent*) ingénu(e)

start [stɑːt] *n* commencement *m*, début *m*; (*of race*) départ *m*; (*sudden movement*) sursaut *m*; (*advantage*) avance *f*, avantage *m* ♦ *vt* commencer; (*found*) créer; (*engine*) mettre en marche ♦ *vi* partir, se mettre en route; (*jump*) sursauter; **to ~ doing** *or* **to do sth** se mettre à faire qch; **~ off** *vi* commencer; (*leave*) partir; **~ up** *vi* commencer; (*car*) démarrer ♦ *vt* (*business*) créer; (*car*) mettre en marche; **~er** *n* (AUT) démarreur *m*; (SPORT: *official*) starter *m*; (BRIT: CULIN) entrée *f*; **~ing point** *n* point *m* de départ

startle ['stɑːtl] *vt* faire sursauter; donner un choc à; **startling** *adj* (*news*) surprenant(e)

starvation [stɑː'veɪʃən] *n* faim *f*, famine *f*

starve [stɑːv] *vi* mourir de faim; être affamé(e) ♦ *vt* affamer

state [steɪt] *n* état *m*; (POL) État ♦ *vt* déclarer, affirmer; **the S~s** *npl* (*America*) les États-Unis *mpl*; **to be in a ~** être dans tous ses états; **~ly** *adj* majestueux(-euse), imposant(e); **~ly home** *n* château *m*; **~ment** *n* déclaration *f*; **~sman** (*irreg*) *n* homme *m* d'État

static ['stætɪk] *n* (RADIO, TV) parasites *mpl* ♦ *adj* statique

station ['steɪʃən] *n* gare *f*; (*police ~*) poste *m* de police ♦ *vt* placer, poster

stationary ['steɪʃnərɪ] *adj* à l'arrêt, immobile

stationer ['steɪʃənəʳ] *n* papetier(-ère); **~'s (shop)** *n* papeterie *f*; **~y** *n* papier *m* à lettres, petit matériel de bureau

stationmaster ['steɪʃənmɑːstəʳ] *n* (RAIL) chef *m* de gare

station wagon (US) *n* break *m*

statistic *n* statistique *f*; **~s** [stə'tɪstɪks] *n* (*science*) statistique *f*

statue ['stætjuː] *n* statue *f*

status ['steɪtəs] *n* position *f*, situation *f*; (*official*) statut *m*; (*prestige*) prestige *m*; **~ symbol** *n* signe extérieur de richesse

statute ['stætjuːt] *n* loi *f*, statut *m*; **statutory** *adj* statutaire, prévu(e) par un article de loi

staunch [stɔːntʃ] *adj* sûr(e), loyal(e)

stay [steɪ] *n* (*period of time*) séjour *m* ♦ *vi* rester; (*reside*) loger; (*spend some time*) séjourner; **to ~ put** ne pas bouger; **to ~ with friends** loger chez des amis; **to ~ the night** passer la nuit; **~ behind** *vi* rester en arrière; **~ in** *vi* (*at home*) rester à la maison; **~ on** *vi* rester; **~ out** *vi* (*of house*) ne pas rentrer; **~ up** *vi* (*at night*) ne pas se coucher; **~ing power** *n* endurance *f*

stead [stɛd] *n*: **in sb's ~** à la place de qn; **to stand sb in good ~** être très utile à qn

steadfast ['stɛdfɑːst] *adj* ferme, résolu(e)

steadily ['stɛdɪlɪ] *adv* (*regularly*) progressivement; (*firmly*) fermement; (: *walk*) d'un pas ferme; (*fixedly*: *look*) sans détourner les yeux

steady ['stɛdɪ] *adj* stable, solide, ferme; (*regular*) constant(e), régulier(-ère); (*person*) calme, pondéré(e) ♦ *vt* stabiliser; (*nerves*) calmer; **a ~ boyfriend** un petit ami

steak [steɪk] *n* (*beef*) bifteck *m*, steak *m*; (*fish, pork*) tranche *f*

steal [sti:l] (*pt* **stole**, *pp* **stolen**) *vt* voler ♦ *vi* voler; (*move secretly*) se faufiler, se déplacer furtivement

stealth [stɛlθ] *n*: **by ~** furtivement

steam [sti:m] *n* vapeur *f* ♦ *vt* (CULIN) cuire à la vapeur ♦ *vi* fumer; **~ engine** *n* locomotive *f* à vapeur; **~er** *n* (bateau *m* à) vapeur *m*; **~ship** *n* = **steamer**; **~y** *adj* embué(e), humide

steel [sti:l] *n* acier *m* ♦ *adj* d'acier; **~works** *n* aciérie *f*

steep [sti:p] *adj* raide, escarpé(e); (*price*) excessif(-ive)

steeple ['sti:pl] *n* clocher *m*

steer [stɪə^r] *vt* diriger; (*boat*) gouverner; (*person*) guider, conduire ♦ *vi* tenir le gouvernail; **~ing** *n* (AUT) conduite *f*; **~ing wheel** *n* volant *m*

stem [stɛm] *n* (*of plant*) tige *f*; (*of glass*) pied *m* ♦ *vt* contenir, arrêter, juguler; **~ from** *vt fus* provenir de, découler de

stench [stɛntʃ] *n* puanteur *f*

stencil ['stɛnsl] *n* stencil *m*; (*pattern used*) pochoir *m* ♦ *vt* polycopier

stenographer [stɛ'nɔgrəfə^r] (US) *n* sténographe *m/f*

step [stɛp] *n* pas *m*; (*stair*) marche *f*; (*action*) mesure *f*, disposition *f* ♦ *vi*: **to ~ forward/back** faire un pas en avant/arrière, avancer/reculer; **~s** *npl* (BRIT) = **stepladder**; **to be in/out of ~ (with)** (*fig*) aller dans le sens (de)/être déphasé(e) (par rapport à); **~ down** *vi* (*fig*) se retirer, se désister; **~ up** *vt* augmenter; intensifier; **~brother** *n* demi-frère *m*; **~daughter** *n* belle-fille *f*; **~father** *n* beau-père *m*; **~ladder** (BRIT) *n* escabeau *m*; **~mother** *n* belle-mère *f*; **~ping stone** *n* pierre *f* de gué; (*fig*) tremplin *m*; **~sister** *n* demi-sœur *f*; **~son** *n* beau-fils *m*

stereo ['stɛrɪəu] *n* (*sound*) stéréo *f*; (*hi-fi*) chaîne *f* stéréo *inv* ♦ *adj* (*also:* **~phonic**) stéréo(phonique)

sterile ['stɛraɪl] *adj* stérile; **sterilize** ['stɛrɪlaɪz] *vt* stériliser

sterling ['stə:lɪŋ] *adj* (*silver*) de bon aloi, fin(e) ♦ *n* (ECON) livres *fpl* sterling *inv*; **a pound ~** une livre sterling

stern [stə:n] *adj* sévère ♦ *n* (NAUT) arrière *m*, poupe *f*

stew [stju:] *n* ragoût *m* ♦ *vt, vi* cuire (à la casserole)

steward ['stju:əd] *n* (*on ship, plane, train*) steward *m*; **~ess** *n* hôtesse *f* (de l'air)

stick [stɪk] (*pt, pp* **stuck**) *n* bâton *m*; (*walking ~*) canne *f* ♦ *vt* (*glue*) coller; (*inf: put*) mettre, fourrer; (*: tolerate*) supporter; (*thrust*): **to ~ sth into** planter *or* enfoncer qch dans ♦ *vi* (*become attached*) rester collé(e) *or* fixé(e); (*be unmoveable: wheels etc*) se bloquer; (*remain*) rester; **~ out** *vi* dépasser, sortir; **~ up** *vi* = **stick out**; **~ up for** *vt fus* défendre; **~er** *n* auto-collant *m*; **~ing plaster** *n* sparadrap *m*, pansement adhésif

stick-up ['stɪkʌp] (*inf*) *n* braquage *m*, hold-up *m inv*

sticky ['stɪkɪ] *adj* poisseux(-euse); (*label*) adhésif(-ive); (*situation*) délicat(e)

stiff [stɪf] *adj* raide; rigide; dur(e); (*difficult*) difficile, ardu(e); (*cold*) froid(e), distant(e); (*strong, high*) fort(e), élevé(e) ♦ *adv*: **to be bored/scared/frozen ~** s'ennuyer à mort/être mort(e) de peur/froid; **~en** *vi* se raidir; **~ neck** *n* torticolis *m*

stifle ['staɪfl] *vt* étouffer, réprimer

stigma ['stɪgmə] *n* stigmate *m*

stile [staɪl] *n* échalier *m*

stiletto [stɪ'lɛtəu] (BRIT) *n* (*also:* **~ heel**) talon *m* aiguille

still [stɪl] *adj* immobile ♦ *adv* (*up to this time*) encore, toujours; (*even*) encore; (*nonetheless*) quand même, tout de même; **~born** *adj* mort-né(e); **~ life** *n* nature morte

stilt [stɪlt] *n* (*for walking on*) échasse *f*; (*pile*) pilotis *m*

stilted ['stɪltɪd] *adj* guindé(e), emprunté(e)

stimulate ['stɪmjuleɪt] *vt* stimuler

stimuli ['stɪmjulaɪ] *npl of* **stimulus**

stimulus ['stɪmjuləs] (*pl* **stimuli**) *n* stimulant *m*; (*BIOL, PSYCH*) stimulus *m*

sting [stɪŋ] (*pt, pp* **stung**) *n* piqûre *f*; (*organ*) dard *m* ♦ *vt, vi* piquer

stingy ['stɪndʒɪ] *adj* avare, pingre

stink [stɪŋk] (*pt* **stank**, *pp* **stunk**) *n* puanteur *f* ♦ *vi* puer, empester; **~ing** (*inf*) *adj* (*fig*) infect(e), vache; **a ~ing ...** un(e) foutu(e) ...

stint [stɪnt] *n* part *f* de travail ♦ *vi*: **to ~ on** lésiner sur, être chiche de

stir [stəːʳ] *n* agitation *f*, sensation *f* ♦ *vt* remuer ♦ *vi* remuer, bouger; **~ up** *vt* (*trouble*) fomenter, provoquer

stirrup ['stɪrəp] *n* étrier *m*

stitch [stɪtʃ] *n* (*SEWING*) point *m*; (*KNITTING*) maille *f*; (*MED*) point de suture; (*pain*) point de côté ♦ *vt* coudre, piquer; (*MED*) suturer

stoat [stəut] *n* hermine *f* (*avec son pelage d'été*)

stock [stɔk] *n* réserve *f*, provision *f*; (*COMM*) stock *m*; (*AGR*) cheptel *m*, bétail *m*; (*CULIN*) bouillon *m*; (*descent, origin*) souche *f*; (*FINANCE*) valeurs *fpl*, titres *mpl* ♦ *adj* (*fig: reply etc*) classique ♦ *vt* (*have in ~*) avoir, vendre; **~s and shares** valeurs (mobilières), titres; **in/out of ~** en stock *or* en magasin/épuisé(e); **to take ~ of** (*fig*) faire le point de; **~ up** *vi*: **to ~ up (with)** s'approvisionner (en); **~broker** *n* agent *m* de change; **~ cube** *n* bouillon-cube *m*; **~ exchange** *n* Bourse *f*

stocking ['stɔkɪŋ] *n* bas *m*

stock: ~ market *n* Bourse *f*, marché financier; **~pile** *n* stock *m*, réserve *f* ♦ *vt* stocker, accumuler; **~taking** (*BRIT*) *n* (*COMM*) inventaire *m*

stocky ['stɔkɪ] *adj* trapu(e), râblé(e)

stodgy ['stɔdʒɪ] *adj* bourratif(-ive), lourd(e)

stoke [stəuk] *vt* (*fire*) garnir, entretenir; (*boiler*) chauffer

stole [stəul] *pt of* **steal** ♦ *n* étole *f*

stolen ['stəuln] *pp of* **steal**

stomach ['stʌmək] *n* estomac *m*; (*abdomen*) ventre *m* ♦ *vt* digérer, supporter; **~ache** *n* mal *m* à l'estomac *or* au ventre

stone [stəun] *n* pierre *f*; (*pebble*) caillou *m*, galet *m*; (*in fruit*) noyau *m*; (*MED*) calcul *m*; (*BRIT: weight*) 6,348 *kg* ♦ *adj* de *or* en pierre ♦ *vt* (*person*) lancer des pierres sur, lapider; **~-cold** *adj* complètement froid(e); **~-deaf** *adj* sourd(e) comme un pot; **~work** *n* maçonnerie *f*

stood [stud] *pt, pp of* **stand**

stool [stuːl] *n* tabouret *m*

stoop [stuːp] *vi* (*also:* **have a ~**) être voûté(e); (*also:* **~ down**: *bend*) se baisser

stop [stɔp] *n* arrêt *m*; halte *f*; (*in punctuation: also:* **full ~**) point *m* ♦ *vt* arrêter, bloquer; (*break off*) interrompre; (*also:* **put a ~ to**) mettre fin à ♦ *vi* s'arrêter; (*rain, noise etc*) cesser, s'arrêter; **to ~ doing sth** cesser *or* arrêter de faire qch; **~ dead** *vi* s'arrêter net; **~ off** *vi* faire une courte halte; **~ up** *vt* (*hole*) boucher; **~gap** *n* (*person*) bouche-trou *m*; (*measure*) mesure *f* intérimaire; **~over** *n* halte *f*; (*AVIAT*) escale *f*; **~page** *n* (*strike*) arrêt de travail; (*blockage*) obstruction *f*; **~per** *n* bouchon *m*; **~ press** *n* nouvelles *fpl* de dernière heure; **~watch** *n* chronomètre *m*

storage ['stɔːrɪdʒ] *n* entreposage *m*; **~ heater** *n* radiateur *m* électrique par accumulation

store [stɔːʳ] *n* (*stock*) provision *f*, réserve *f*; (*depot*) entrepôt *m*; (*BRIT: large shop*) grand magasin; (*US*) magasin *m* ♦ *vt* emmagasiner; (*information*) enregistrer; **~s** *npl* (*food*) provisions; **in ~** en réserve; **~ up** *vt* mettre en réserve; accumuler; **~room** *n* réserve *f*, magasin *m*

storey ['stɔːrɪ] (*US* **story**) *n* étage *m*

stork [stɔːk] *n* cigogne *f*

storm [stɔːm] *n* tempête *f*; (*thunderstorm*) orage *m* ♦ *vi* (*fig*) fulminer ♦ *vt* prendre d'assaut; **~y** *adj* orageux(-euse)

story ['stɔːrɪ] *n* histoire *f*; récit *m*; (*US*) = **storey**; **~book** *n* livre *m* d'histoires *or* de contes

stout [staut] *adj* solide; (*fat*) gros(se), corpulent(e) ♦ *n* bière brune

stove [stəuv] *n* (*for cooking*) fourneau *m*; (*: small*) réchaud *m*; (*for heating*) poêle *m*

stow [stəu] *vt* (*also:* **~ away**) ranger; **~away** *n* passager(-ère) clandestin(e)

straddle ['strædl] *vt* enjamber, être à cheval sur

straggle ['strægl] *vi* être (*or* marcher) en désordre

straight [streɪt] *adj* droit(e); (*hair*) raide; (*frank*) honnête, franc (franche); (*simple*) simple ♦ *adv* (tout) droit; (*drink*) sec, sans eau; **to put** *or* **get ~** (*fig*) mettre au clair; **~ away, ~ off** (*at once*) tout de suite; **~en** *vt* ajuster; (*bed*) arranger; **~en out** *vt* (*fig*) débrouiller; **~-faced** *adj* impassible; **~forward** *adj* simple; (*honest*) honnête, direct(e)

strain [streɪn] *n* tension *f*; pression *f*; (*physical*) effort *m*; (*mental*) tension (nerveuse); (*breed*) race *f* ♦ *vt* (*stretch: resources etc*) mettre à rude épreuve, grever; (*hurt: back etc*) se faire mal à; (*vegetables*) égoutter; **~s** *npl* (*MUS*) accords *mpl*, accents *mpl*; **back ~** tour *m* de rein; **~ed** *adj* (*muscle*) froissé(e); (*laugh etc*) forcé(e), contraint(e); (*relations*) tendu(e); **~er** *n* passoire *f*

strait [streɪt] *n* (*GEO*) détroit *m*; **~s** *npl*: **to be in dire ~s** avoir de sérieux ennuis (d'argent); **~jacket** *n* camisole *f* de force; **~-laced** *adj* collet monté *inv*

strand [strænd] *n* (*of thread*) fil *m*, brin *m*; (*of rope*) toron *m*; (*of hair*) mèche *f*; **~ed** *adj* en rade, en plan

strange [streɪndʒ] *adj* (*not known*) inconnu(e); (*odd*) étrange, bizarre; **~ly** *adv* étrangement, bizarrement; *see also* **enough**; **~r** *n* inconnu(e); (*from another area*) étranger(-ère)

strangle ['stræŋgl] *vt* étrangler; **~hold** *n* (*fig*) emprise totale, mainmise *f*

strap [stræp] *n* lanière *f*, courroie *f*, sangle *f*; (*of slip, dress*) bretelle *f*; **~py** *adj* (*dress*) à bretelles; (*sandals*) à lanières

strategy ['strætɪdʒɪ] *n* stratégie *f*

straw [strɔː] *n* paille *f*; **that's the last ~!** ça, c'est le comble!

strawberry ['strɔːbərɪ] *n* fraise *f*

stray [streɪ] *adj* (*animal*) perdu(e), errant(e); (*scattered*) isolé(e) ♦ *vi* s'égarer; **~ bullet** *n* balle perdue

streak [striːk] *n* bande *f*, filet *m*; (*in hair*) raie *f* ♦ *vt* zébrer, strier ♦ *vi*: **to ~ past** passer à toute allure

stream [striːm] *n* (*brook*) ruisseau *m*; (*current*) courant *m*, flot *m*; (*of people*) défilé ininterrompu, flot ♦ *vt* (*SCOL*) répartir par niveau ♦ *vi* ruisseler; **to ~ in/out** entrer/sortir à flots

streamer ['striːmə^r^] *n* serpentin *m*; (*banner*) banderole *f*

streamlined ['striːmlaɪnd] *adj* aérodynamique; (*fig*) rationalisé(e)

street [striːt] *n* rue *f*; **~car** (*US*) *n* tramway *m*; **~ lamp** *n* réverbère *m*; **~ plan** *n* plan *m* (des rues); **~wise** (*inf*) *adj* futé(e), réaliste

strength [streŋθ] *n* force *f*; (*of girder, knot etc*) solidité *f*; **~en** *vt* (*muscle etc*) fortifier; (*nation, case etc*) renforcer; (*building, ECON*) consolider

strenuous ['strenjuəs] *adj* vigoureux(-euse), énergique

stress [stres] *n* (*force, pressure*) pression *f*; (*mental strain*) tension (nerveuse), stress *m*; (*accent*) accent *m* ♦ *vt* insister sur, souligner

stretch [stretʃ] *n* (*of sand etc*) étendue *f* ♦ *vi* s'étirer; (*extend*): **to ~ to** *or* **as far**

as s'étendre jusqu'à ♦ *vt* tendre, étirer; (*fig*) pousser (au maximum); **~ out** *vi* s'étendre ♦ *vt* (*arm etc*) allonger, tendre; (*spread*) étendre

stretcher ['stretʃəʳ] *n* brancard *m*, civière *f*

stretchy ['stretʃi] *adj* élastique

strewn [stru:n] *adj*: **~ with** jonché(e) de

stricken ['strɪkən] *adj* (*person*) très éprouvé(e); (*city, industry etc*) dévasté(e); **~ with** (*disease etc*) frappé(e) *or* atteint(e) de

strict [strɪkt] *adj* strict(e)

stride [straɪd] (*pt* **strode**, *pp* **stridden**) *n* grand pas, enjambée *fretar* ♦ *vi* marcher à grands pas

strife [straɪf] *n* conflit *m*, dissensions *fpl*

strike [straɪk] (*pt, pp* **struck**) *n* grève *f*; (*of oil etc*) découverte *f*; (*attack*) raid *m* ♦ *vt* frapper; (*oil etc*) trouver, découvrir; (*deal*) conclure ♦ *vi* faire grève; (*attack*) attaquer; (*clock*) sonner; **on ~** (*workers*) en grève; **to ~ a match** frotter une allumette; **~ down** *vt* terrasser; **~ up** *vt* (MUS) se mettre à jouer; **to ~ up a friendship with** se lier d'amitié avec; **to ~ up a conversation (with)** engager une conversation (avec); **~r** *n* gréviste *m/f*; (SPORT) buteur *m*; **striking** *adj* frappant(e), saisissant(e); (*attractive*) éblouissant(e)

string [strɪŋ] (*pt, pp* **strung**) *n* ficelle *f*; (*row: of beads*) rang *m*; (*: of onions*) chapelet *m*; (MUS) corde *f* ♦ *vt*: **to ~ out** échelonner; **the ~s** *npl* (MUS) les instruments *mpl* à cordes; **to ~ together** enchaîner; **to pull ~s** (*fig*) faire jouer le piston; **~(ed) instrument** *n* (MUS) instrument *m* à cordes

stringent ['strɪndʒənt] *adj* rigoureux (-euse)

strip [strɪp] *n* bande *f* ♦ *vt* (*undress*) déshabiller; (*paint*) décaper; (*also:* **~ down**: *machine*) démonter ♦ *vi* se déshabiller; **~ cartoon** *n* bande dessinée

stripe [straɪp] *n* raie *f*, rayure *f*; (MIL) galon *m*; **~d** *adj* rayé(e), à rayures

strip: **~ lighting** (BRIT) *n* éclairage *m* au néon *or* fluorescent; **~per** *n* strip-teaseur(-euse) *f*; **~ search** *n* fouille corporelle (*en faisant se déshabiller la personne*) ♦ *vt*: **he was ~ searched** on l'a fait se déshabiller et soumis à une fouille corporelle

stripy ['straɪpɪ] *adj* rayé(e)

strive [straɪv] (*pt* **strove**, *pp* **striven**) *vi*: **to ~ to do/for sth** s'efforcer de faire/d'obtenir qch

strode [strəud] *pt of* **stride**

stroke [strəuk] *n* coup *m*; (SWIMMING) nage *f*; (MED) attaque *f* ♦ *vt* caresser; **at a ~** d'un (seul) coup

stroll [strəul] *n* petite promenade ♦ *vi* flâner, se promener nonchalamment; **~er** (US) *n* (*pushchair*) poussette *f*

strong [strɔŋ] *adj* fort(e); vigoureux (-euse); (*heart, nerves*) solide; **they are 50 ~** ils sont au nombre de 50; **~hold** *n* bastion *m*; **~ly** *adv* fortement, avec force; vigoureusement; solidement; **~room** *n* chambre forte

strove [strəuv] *pt of* **strive**

struck [strʌk] *pt, pp of* **strike**

structural ['strʌktʃrəl] *adj* structural(e); (CONSTR: *defect*) de construction; (*damage*) affectant les parties portantes

structure ['strʌktʃəʳ] *n* structure *f*; (*building*) construction *f*

struggle ['strʌgl] *n* lutte *f* ♦ *vi* lutter, se battre

strum [strʌm] *vt* (*guitar*) jouer (en sourdine) de

strung [strʌŋ] *pt, pp of* **string**

strut [strʌt] *n* étai *m*, support *m* ♦ *vi* se pavaner

stub [stʌb] *n* (*of cigarette*) bout *m*, mégot *m*; (*of cheque etc*) talon *m* ♦ *vt*: **to ~ one's toe** se cogner le doigt de pied; **~ out** *vt* écraser

stubble ['stʌbl] *n* chaume *m*; (*on chin*) barbe *f* de plusieurs jours

stubborn ['stʌbən] *adj* têtu(e), obstiné(e), opiniâtre

stuck [stʌk] *pt, pp of* **stick** ♦ *adj* (*jammed*) bloqué(e), coincé(e); **~-up** (*inf*) *adj* prétentieux(-euse)

stud [stʌd] *n* (*on boots etc*) clou *m*; (*on collar*) bouton *m* de col; (*earring*) petite boucle d'oreille; (*of horses*: *also:* **~ farm**) écurie *f*, haras *m*; (*also:* **~ horse**) étalon *m* ♦ *vt* (*fig*): **~ded with** parsemé(e) *or* criblé(e) de

student ['stju:dənt] *n* étudiant(e) ♦ *adj* estudiantin(e); d'étudiant; **~ driver** (*US*) *n* (conducteur(-trice)) débutant(e)

studio ['stju:dɪəu] *n* studio *m*, atelier *m*; (*TV etc*) studio

studious ['stju:dɪəs] *adj* studieux (-euse), appliqué(e); (*attention*) soutenu(e); **~ly** *adv* (*carefully*) soigneusement

study ['stʌdɪ] *n* étude *f*; (*room*) bureau *m* ♦ *vt* étudier; (*examine*) examiner ♦ *vi* étudier, faire ses études

stuff [stʌf] *n* chose(s) *f(pl)*; affaires *fpl*, trucs *mpl*; (*substance*) substance *f* ♦ *vt* rembourrer; (*CULIN*) farcir; (*inf*: *push*) fourrer; **~ing** *n* bourre *f*, rembourrage *m*; (*CULIN*) farce *f*; **~y** *adj* (*room*) mal ventilé(e) *or* aéré(e); (*ideas*) vieux jeu *inv*

stumble ['stʌmbl] *vi* trébucher; **to ~ across** *or* **on** (*fig*) tomber sur; **stumbling block** *n* pierre *f* d'achoppement

stump [stʌmp] *n* souche *f*; (*of limb*) moignon *m* ♦ *vt*: **to be ~ed** sécher, ne pas savoir que répondre

stun [stʌn] *vt* étourdir; (*fig*) abasourdir

stung [stʌŋ] *pt, pp of* **sting**

stunk [stʌŋk] *pp of* **stink**

stunned [stʌnd] *adj* sidéré(e)

stunning ['stʌnɪŋ] *adj* (*news etc*) stupéfiant(e); (*girl etc*) éblouissant(e)

stunt [stʌnt] *n* (*in film*) cascade *f*, acrobatie *f*; (*publicity* ~) truc *m* publicitaire ♦ *vt* retarder, arrêter; **~man** ['stʌntmæn] (*irreg*) *n* cascadeur *m*

stupendous [stju:'pɛndəs] *adj* prodigieux(-euse), fantastique

stupid ['stju:pɪd] *adj* stupide, bête; **~ity** [stju:'pɪdɪtɪ] *n* stupidité *f*, bêtise *f*

sturdy ['stə:dɪ] *adj* robuste; solide

stutter ['stʌtə^r] *vi* bégayer

sty [staɪ] *n* (*for pigs*) porcherie *f*

stye [staɪ] *n* (*MED*) orgelet *m*

style [staɪl] *n* style *m*; (*distinction*) allure *f*, cachet *m*, style; **stylish** *adj* élégant(e), chic *inv*

stylus ['staɪləs] (*pl* **styli** *or* **~es**) *n* (*of record player*) pointe *f* de lecture

suave [swɑ:v] *adj* doucereux(-euse), onctueux(-euse)

sub... [sʌb] *prefix* sub..., sous-; **~conscious** *adj* subconscient(e); **~contract** *vt* sous-traiter

subdue [səb'dju:] *vt* subjuguer, soumettre; **~d** *adj* (*light*) tamisé(e); (*person*) qui a perdu de son entrain

subject [*n* 'sʌbdʒɪkt, *vb* səb'dʒɛkt] *n* sujet *m*; (*SCOL*) matière *f* ♦ *vt*: **to ~ to** soumettre à; exposer à; **to be ~ to** (*law*) être soumis(e) à; (*disease*) être sujet(te) à; **~ive** [səb'dʒɛktɪv] *adj* subjectif(-ive); **~ matter** *n* (*content*) contenu *m*

sublet [sʌb'lɛt] *vt* sous-louer

submarine [sʌbmə'ri:n] *n* sous-marin *m*

submerge [səb'mə:dʒ] *vt* submerger ♦ *vi* plonger

submission [səb'mɪʃən] *n* soumission *f*; **submissive** *adj* soumis(e)

submit [səb'mɪt] *vt* soumettre ♦ *vi* se soumettre

subnormal [sʌb'nɔ:ml] *adj* au-dessous de la normale

subordinate [sə'bɔ:dɪnət] *adj* subalterne ♦ *n* subordonné(e)

subpoena [səb'pi:nə] *n* (*LAW*) citation *f*, assignation *f*

subscribe [səb'skraɪb] *vi* cotiser; **to ~ to** (*opinion, fund*) souscrire à; (*newspaper*) s'abonner à; être abonné(e) à; **~r** *n* (*to periodical, telephone*) abonné(e); **subscription** [səb'skrɪpʃən] *n* (*to magazine etc*) abonnement *m*

subsequent ['sʌbsɪkwənt] *adj* ultérieur(e), suivant(e); consécutif(-ive); **~ly**

adv par la suite
subside [səb'saɪd] *vi* (*flood*) baisser; (*wind, feelings*) tomber; **~nce** [səb'saɪdns] *n* affaissement *m*
subsidiary [səb'sɪdɪərɪ] *adj* subsidiaire; accessoire ♦ *n* filiale *f*
subsidize ['sʌbsɪdaɪz] *vt* subventionner;
subsidy ['sʌbsɪdɪ] *n* subvention *f*
substance ['sʌbstəns] *n* substance *f*
substantial [səb'stænʃl] *adj* substantiel(le); (*fig*) important(e); **~ly** *adv* considérablement; (*in essence*) en grande partie
substantiate [səb'stænʃɪeɪt] *vt* étayer, fournir des preuves à l'appui de
substitute ['sʌbstɪtju:t] *n* (*person*) remplaçant(e); (*thing*) succédané *m* ♦ *vt*: **to ~ sth/sb for** substituer qch/qn à, remplacer par qch/qn
subterranean [sʌbtə'reɪnɪən] *adj* souterrain(e)
subtitle ['sʌbtaɪtl] *n* (CINEMA, TV) sous-titre *m*; **~d** *adj* sous-titré(e)
subtle ['sʌtl] *adj* subtil(e)
subtotal [sʌb'təutl] *n* total partiel
subtract [səb'trækt] *vt* soustraire, retrancher; **~ion** *n* soustraction *f*
suburb ['sʌbə:b] *n* faubourg *m*; **the ~s** *npl* la banlieue; **~an** [sə'bə:bən] *adj* de banlieue, suburbain(e); **~ia** [sə'bə:bɪə] *n* la banlieue
subway ['sʌbweɪ] *n* (US: *railway*) métro *m*; (BRIT: *underpass*) passage souterrain
succeed [sək'si:d] *vi* réussir ♦ *vt* succéder à; **to ~ in doing** réussir à faire; **~ing** *adj* (*following*) suivant(e)
success [sək'sɛs] *n* succès *m*; réussite *f*; **~ful** *adj* (*venture*) couronné(e) de succès; **to be ~ful (in doing)** réussir (à faire); **~fully** *adv* avec succès
succession [sək'sɛʃən] *n* succession *f*; **3 days in ~** 3 jours de suite
successive [sək'sɛsɪv] *adj* successif (-ive); consécutif(-ive)
such [sʌtʃ] *adj* tel (telle); (*of that kind*): **~ a book** un livre de ce genre, un livre pareil, un tel livre; (*so much*): **~ courage** un tel courage ♦ *adv* si; **~ books** des livres de ce genre, des livres pareils, de tels livres; **~ a long trip** un si long voyage; **~ a lot of** tellement *or* tant de; **~ as** (*like*) tel que, comme; **as ~** en tant que tel, à proprement parler; **~-and-~** *adj* tel ou tel
suck [sʌk] *vt* sucer; (*breast, bottle*) téter; **~er** *n* ventouse *f*; (*inf*) poire *f*
suction ['sʌkʃən] *n* succion *f*
sudden ['sʌdn] *adj* soudain(e), subit(e); **all of a ~** soudain, tout à coup; **~ly** *adv* brusquement, tout à coup, soudain
suds [sʌdz] *npl* eau savonneuse
sue [su:] *vt* poursuivre en justice, intenter un procès à
suede [sweɪd] *n* daim *m*
suet ['suɪt] *n* graisse *f* de rognon
suffer ['sʌfə[r]] *vt* souffrir, subir; (*bear*) tolérer, supporter ♦ *vi* souffrir; **~er** *n* (MED) malade *m/f*; **~ing** *n* souffrance(s) *f(pl)*
sufficient [sə'fɪʃənt] *adj* suffisant(e); **~ money** suffisamment d'argent; **~ly** *adv* suffisamment, assez
suffocate ['sʌfəkeɪt] *vi* suffoquer; étouffer
sugar ['ʃugə[r]] *n* sucre *m* ♦ *vt* sucrer; **~ beet** *n* betterave sucrière; **~ cane** *n* canne *f* à sucre
suggest [sə'dʒɛst] *vt* suggérer, proposer; (*indicate*) dénoter; **~ion** *n* suggestion *f*
suicide ['suɪsaɪd] *n* suicide *m*; *see also* **commit**
suit [su:t] *n* (*man's*) costume *m*, complet *m*; (*woman's*) tailleur *m*, ensemble *m*; (LAW) poursuite(s) *f(pl)*, procès *m*; (CARDS) couleur *f* ♦ *vt* aller à; convenir à; (*adapt*): **to ~ sth to** adapter *or* approprier qch à; **well ~ed** (*well matched*) faits l'un pour l'autre, très bien assortis; **~able** *adj* qui convient; approprié(e); **~ably** *adv* comme il se doit (*or* se devait *etc*), convenablement
suitcase ['su:tkeɪs] *n* valise *f*
suite [swi:t] *n* (*of rooms, also* MUS) suite

f; (*furniture*): **bedroom/dining room ~** (ensemble *m* de) chambre *f* à coucher/ salle *f* à manger
suitor ['su:tə^r] *n* soupirant *m*, prétendant *m*
sulfur ['sʌlfə^r] (*US*) *n* = **sulphur**
sulk [sʌlk] *vi* bouder; **~y** *adj* boudeur (-euse), maussade
sullen ['sʌlən] *adj* renfrogné(e), maussade
sulphur ['sʌlfə^r] (*US* **sulfur**) *n* soufre *m*
sultana [sʌl'tɑ:nə] *n* (*CULIN*) raisin (sec) de Smyrne
sultry ['sʌltrɪ] *adj* étouffant(e)
sum [sʌm] *n* somme *f*; (*SCOL etc*) calcul *m*; **~ up** *vt, vi* résumer
summarize ['sʌməraɪz] *vt* résumer
summary ['sʌmərɪ] *n* résumé *m*
summer ['sʌmə^r] *n* été *m* ♦ *adj* d'été, estival(e); **~house** *n* (*in garden*) pavillon *m*; **~time** *n* été *m*; **~ time** *n* (*by clock*) heure *f* d'été
summit ['sʌmɪt] *n* sommet *m*
summon ['sʌmən] *vt* appeler, convoquer; **~ up** *vt* rassembler, faire appel à; **~s** *n* citation *f*, assignation *f*
sun [sʌn] *n* soleil *m*; **in the ~** au soleil; **~bathe** *vi* prendre un bain de soleil; **~block** *n* écran *m* total; **~burn** *n* coup *m* de soleil; **~burned**, **~burnt** *adj* (*tanned*) bronzé(e)
Sunday ['sʌndɪ] *n* dimanche *m*; **~ school** *n* ≃ catéchisme *m*
sundial ['sʌndaɪəl] *n* cadran *m* solaire
sundown ['sʌndaun] *n* coucher *m* du (*or* de) soleil
sundries ['sʌndrɪz] *npl* articles divers
sundry ['sʌndrɪ] *adj* divers(e), différent(e) ♦ *n*: **all and ~** tout le monde, n'importe qui
sunflower ['sʌnflauə^r] *n* tournesol *m*
sung [sʌŋ] *pp of* **sing**
sunglasses ['sʌnglɑ:sɪz] *npl* lunettes *fpl* de soleil
sunk [sʌŋk] *pp of* **sink**
sun: ~light *n* (lumière *f* du) soleil *m*; **~lit** *adj* ensoleillé(e); **~ny** *adj* ensoleillé(e); **~rise** *n* lever *m* du (*or* de) soleil; **~ roof** *n* (*AUT*) toit ouvrant; **~screen** *n* crème *f* solaire; **~set** *n* coucher *m* du (*or* de) soleil; **~shade** *n* (*over table*) parasol *m*; **~shine** *n* (lumière *f* du) soleil *m*; **~stroke** *n* insolation *f*; **~tan** *n* bronzage *m*; **~tan lotion** *n* lotion *f or* lait *m* solaire; **~tan oil** *n* huile *f* solaire
super ['su:pə^r] (*inf*) *adj* formidable
superannuation [su:pərænju'eɪʃən] *n* (*contribution*) cotisations *fpl* pour la pension
superb [su:'pə:b] *adj* superbe, magnifique
supercilious [su:pə'sɪlɪəs] *adj* hautain(e), dédaigneux(-euse)
superficial [su:pə'fɪʃəl] *adj* superficiel(le)
superimpose ['su:pərɪm'pəuz] *vt* superposer
superintendent [su:pərɪn'tɛndənt] *n* directeur(-trice); (*POLICE*) ≃ commissaire *m*
superior [su'pɪərɪə^r] *adj, n* supérieur(e); **~ity** [supɪərɪ'ɔrɪtɪ] *n* supériorité *f*
superlative [su'pə:lətɪv] *n* (*LING*) superlatif *m*
superman ['su:pəmæn] (*irreg*) *n* surhomme *m*
supermarket ['su:pəmɑ:kɪt] *n* supermarché *m*
supernatural [su:pə'nætʃərəl] *adj* surnaturel(le)
superpower ['su:pəpauə^r] *n* (*POL*) superpuissance *f*
supersede [su:pə'si:d] *vt* remplacer, supplanter
superstitious [su:pə'stɪʃəs] *adj* superstitieux(-euse)
supervise ['su:pəvaɪz] *vt* surveiller; diriger; **supervision** [su:pə'vɪʒən] *n* surveillance *f*; contrôle *m*; **supervisor** *n* surveillant(e); (*in shop*) chef *m* de rayon
supper ['sʌpə^r] *n* dîner *m*; (*late*) souper *m*
supple ['sʌpl] *adj* souple
supplement [*n* 'sʌplɪmənt, *vb*

sʌplɪ'mɛnt] *n* supplément *m* ♦ *vt* compléter; **~ary** [sʌplɪ'mɛntərɪ] *adj* supplémentaire; **~ary benefit** (*BRIT*) *n* allocation *f* (supplémentaire) d'aide sociale

supplier [sə'plaɪər] *n* fournisseur *m*

supply [sə'plaɪ] *vt* (*provide*) fournir; (*equip*): **to ~ (with)** approvisionner *or* ravitailler (en); fournir (en) ♦ *n* provision *f*, réserve *f*; (*~ing*) approvisionnement *m*; **supplies** *npl* (*food*) vivres *mpl*; (*MIL*) subsistances *fpl*; **~ teacher** (*BRIT*) *n* suppléant(e)

support [sə'pɔ:t] *n* (*moral, financial etc*) soutien *m*, appui *m*; (*TECH*) support *m*, soutien ♦ *vt* soutenir, supporter; (*financially*) subvenir aux besoins de; (*uphold*) être pour, être partisan de, appuyer; **~er** *n* (*POL etc*) partisan(e); (*SPORT*) supporter *m*

suppose [sə'pəuz] *vt* supposer; imaginer; **to be ~d to do** être censé(e) faire; **~dly** [sə'pəuzɪdlɪ] *adv* soi-disant; **supposing** *conj* si, à supposer que *+sub*

suppress [sə'prɛs] *vt* (*revolt*) réprimer; (*information*) supprimer; (*yawn*) étouffer; (*feelings*) refouler

supreme [su'pri:m] *adj* suprême

surcharge ['sə:tʃɑ:dʒ] *n* surcharge *f*

sure [ʃuər] *adj* sûr(e); (*definite, convinced*) sûr, certain(e); **~!** (*of course*) bien sûr!; **~ enough** effectivement; **to make ~ of sth** s'assurer de *or* vérifier qch; **to make ~ that** s'assurer *or* vérifier que; **~ly** *adv* sûrement; certainement

surf [sə:f] *n* (*waves*) ressac *m*

surface ['sə:fɪs] *n* surface *f* ♦ *vt* (*road*) poser un revêtement sur ♦ *vi* remonter à la surface; faire surface; **~ mail** *n* courrier *m* par voie de terre (*or* maritime)

surfboard ['sə:fbɔ:d] *n* planche *f* de surf

surfeit ['sə:fɪt] *n*: **a ~ of** un excès de; une indigestion de

surfing ['sə:fɪŋ] *n* surf *m*

surge [sə:dʒ] *n* vague *f*, montée *f* ♦ *vi* déferler

surgeon ['sə:dʒən] *n* chirurgien *m*

surgery ['sə:dʒərɪ] *n* chirurgie *f*; (*BRIT*: *room*) cabinet *m* (de consultation); (: *also*: **~ hours**) heures *fpl* de consultation

surgical ['sə:dʒɪkl] *adj* chirurgical(e); **~ spirit** (*BRIT*) *n* alcool *m* à 90°

surname ['sə:neɪm] *n* nom *m* de famille

surplus ['sə:pləs] *n* surplus *m*, excédent *m* ♦ *adj* en surplus, de trop; (*COMM*) excédentaire

surprise [sə'praɪz] *n* surprise *f*; (*astonishment*) étonnement *m* ♦ *vt* surprendre; (*astonish*) étonner; **surprising** *adj* surprenant(e), étonnant(e); **surprisingly** *adv* (*easy, helpful*) étonnamment

surrender [sə'rɛndər] *n* reddition *f*, capitulation *f* ♦ *vi* se rendre, capituler

surreptitious [sʌrəp'tɪʃəs] *adj* subreptice, furtif(-ive)

surrogate ['sʌrəgɪt] *n* substitut *m*; **~ mother** *n* mère porteuse *or* de substitution

surround [sə'raund] *vt* entourer; (*MIL etc*) encercler; **~ing** *adj* environnant(e); **~ings** *npl* environs *mpl*, alentours *mpl*

surveillance [sə:'veɪləns] *n* surveillance *f*

survey [*n* 'sə:veɪ, *vb* sə:'veɪ] *n* enquête *f*, étude *f*; (*in housebuying etc*) inspection *f*, (rapport *m* d')expertise *f*; (*of land*) levé *m* ♦ *vt* enquêter sur; inspecter; (*look at*) embrasser du regard; **~or** *n* (*of house*) expert *m*; (*of land*) (arpenteur *m*) géomètre *m*

survival [sə'vaɪvl] *n* survie *f*; (*relic*) vestige *m*

survive [sə'vaɪv] *vi* survivre; (*custom etc*) subsister ♦ *vt* survivre à; **survivor** *n* survivant(e); (*fig*) battant(e)

susceptible [sə'sɛptəbl] *adj*: **~ (to)** sensible (à); (*disease*) prédisposé(e) (à)

suspect [*adj, n* 'sʌspɛkt, *vb* səs'pɛkt] *adj, n* suspect(e) ♦ *vt* soupçonner, suspecter

suspend [sə'pɛnd] *vt* suspendre; **~ed sentence** *n* condamnation *f* avec sursis; **~er belt** *n* porte-jarretelles *m inv*; **~ers** *npl* (*BRIT*) jarretelles *fpl*; (*US*) bretelles *fpl*

suspense [səs'pɛns] *n* attente *f*, incertitude *f*; (*in film etc*) suspense *m*

suspension [səs'pɛnʃən] *n* suspension *f*; (*of driving licence*) retrait *m* provisoire; **~ bridge** *n* pont suspendu

suspicion [səs'pɪʃən] *n* soupçon(s) *m(pl)*; **suspicious** *adj* (*suspecting*) soupçonneux(-euse), méfiant(e); (*causing suspicion*) suspect(e)

sustain [səs'teɪn] *vt* soutenir; (*food etc*) nourrir, donner des forces à; (*suffer*) subir; recevoir; **~able** *adj* (*development, growth etc*) viable; **~ed** *adj* (*effort*) soutenu(e), prolongé(e); **sustenance** ['sʌstɪnəns] *n* nourriture *f*; (*money*) moyens *mpl* de subsistance

swab [swɔb] *n* (*MED*) tampon *m*

swagger ['swægə^r] *vi* plastronner

swallow ['swɔləu] *n* (*bird*) hirondelle *f* ♦ *vt* avaler; **~ up** *vt* engloutir

swam [swæm] *pt of* **swim**

swamp [swɔmp] *n* marais *m*, marécage *m* ♦ *vt* submerger

swan [swɔn] *n* cygne *m*

swap [swɔp] *vt*: **to ~ (for)** échanger (contre), troquer (contre)

swarm [swɔ:m] *n* essaim *m* ♦ *vi* fourmiller, grouiller

swastika ['swɔstɪkə] *n* croix gammée

swat [swɔt] *vt* écraser

sway [sweɪ] *vi* se balancer, osciller ♦ *vt* (*influence*) influencer

swear [swɛə^r] (*pt* **swore**, *pp* **sworn**) *vt, vi* jurer; **~word** *n* juron *m*, gros mot

sweat [swɛt] *n* sueur *f*, transpiration *f* ♦ *vi* suer

sweater ['swɛtə^r] *n* tricot *m*, pull *m*

sweaty ['swɛtɪ] *adj* en sueur, moite *or* mouillé(e) de sueur

Swede [swi:d] *n* Suédois(e)

swede [swi:d] (*BRIT*) *n* rutabaga *m*

Sweden ['swi:dn] *n* Suède *f*; **Swedish** *adj* suédois(e) ♦ *n* (*LING*) suédois *m*

sweep [swi:p] (*pt, pp* **swept**) *n* (*also:* **chimney ~**) ramoneur *m* ♦ *vt* balayer; (*subj: current*) emporter; **~ away** *vt* balayer; entraîner; emporter; **~ past** *vi* passer majestueusement *or* rapidement; **~ up** *vt, vi* balayer; **~ing** *adj* (*gesture*) large; circulaire; **a ~ing statement** une généralisation hâtive

sweet [swi:t] *n* (*candy*) bonbon *m*; (*BRIT: pudding*) dessert *m* ♦ *adj* doux (douce); (*not savoury*) sucré(e); (*fig: kind*) gentil(le); (*baby*) mignon(ne); **~corn** ['swi:tkɔ:n] *n* maïs *m*; **~en** *vt* adoucir; (*with sugar*) sucrer; **~heart** *n* amoureux(-euse); **~ness** *n* goût sucré; douceur *f*; **~ pea** *n* pois *m* de senteur

swell [swɛl] (*pt* **swelled**, *pp* **swollen** *or* **swelled**) *n* (*of sea*) houle *f* ♦ *adj* (*US: inf: excellent*) chouette ♦ *vi* grossir, augmenter; (*sound*) s'enfler; (*MED*) enfler; **~ing** *n* (*MED*) enflure *f*; (*lump*) grosseur *f*

sweltering ['swɛltərɪŋ] *adj* étouffant(e), oppressant(e)

swept [swɛpt] *pt, pp of* **sweep**

swerve [swə:v] *vi* faire une embardée *or* un écart; dévier

swift [swɪft] *n* (*bird*) martinet *m* ♦ *adj* rapide, prompt(e)

swig [swɪg] (*inf*) *n* (*drink*) lampée *f*

swill [swɪl] *vt* (*also:* **~ out, ~ down**) laver à grande eau

swim [swɪm] (*pt* **swam**, *pp* **swum**) *n*: **to go for a ~** aller nager *or* se baigner ♦ *vi* nager; (*SPORT*) faire de la natation; (*head, room*) tourner ♦ *vt* traverser (à la nage); (*a length*) faire (à la nage); **~mer** *n* nageur(-euse); **~ming** *n* natation *f*; **~ming cap** *n* bonnet *m* de bain; **~ming costume** (*BRIT*) *n* maillot *m* (de bain); **~ming pool** *n* piscine *f*; **~ming trunks** *npl* caleçon *m or* slip *m* de bain; **~suit** *n* maillot *m* (de bain)

swindle ['swɪndl] *n* escroquerie *f*

swine [swaɪn] (*inf!*) *n inv* salaud *m* (*!*)

swing [swɪŋ] (*pt, pp* **swung**) *n* balançoire *f*; (*movement*) balancement *m*, oscillations *fpl*; (*change*: *in opinion etc*) revirement *m* ♦ *vt* balancer, faire osciller; (*also:* ~ **round**) tourner, faire virer ♦ *vi* se balancer, osciller; (*also:* ~ **round**) virer, tourner; **to be in full** ~ battre son plein; ~ **bridge** *n* pont tournant; ~ **door** (*US* **swinging door**) *n* porte battante

swingeing ['swɪndʒɪŋ] (*BRIT*) *adj* écrasant(e); (*cuts etc*) considérable

swipe [swaɪp] (*inf*) *vt* (*steal*) piquer

swirl [swəːl] *vi* tourbillonner, tournoyer

Swiss [swɪs] *adj* suisse ♦ *n inv* Suisse *m/f*

switch [swɪtʃ] *n* (*for light, radio etc*) bouton *m*; (*change*) changement *m*, revirement *m* ♦ *vt* changer; ~ **off** *vt* éteindre; (*engine*) arrêter; ~ **on** *vt* allumer; (*engine, machine*) mettre en marche; ~**board** *n* (*TEL*) standard *m*

Switzerland ['swɪtsələnd] *n* Suisse *f*

swivel ['swɪvl] *vi* (*also:* ~ **round**) pivoter, tourner

swollen ['swəulən] *pp of* **swell**

swoon [swuːn] *vi* se pâmer

swoop [swuːp] *n* (*by police*) descente *f* ♦ *vi* (*also:* ~ **down**) descendre en piqué, piquer

swop [swɔp] *vt* = **swap**

sword [sɔːd] *n* épée *f*; ~**fish** *n* espadon *m*

swore [swɔːʳ] *pt of* **swear**

sworn [swɔːn] *pp of* **swear** ♦ *adj* (*statement, evidence*) donné(e) sous serment

swot [swɔt] *vi* bûcher, potasser

swum [swʌm] *pp of* **swim**

swung [swʌŋ] *pt, pp of* **swing**

syllable ['sɪləbl] *n* syllabe *f*

syllabus ['sɪləbəs] *n* programme *m*

symbol ['sɪmbl] *n* symbole *m*

symmetry ['sɪmɪtrɪ] *n* symétrie *f*

sympathetic [sɪmpə'θɛtɪk] *adj* compatissant(e); bienveillant(e), compréhensif(-ive); (*likeable*) sympathique; ~ **towards** bien disposé(e) envers

sympathize ['sɪmpəθaɪz] *vi*: **to** ~ **with sb** plaindre qn; (*in grief*) s'associer à la douleur de qn; **to** ~ **with sth** comprendre qch; ~**r** *n* (*POL*) sympathisant(e)

sympathy ['sɪmpəθɪ] *n* (*pity*) compassion *f*; **sympathies** *npl* (*support*) soutien *m*; **left-wing** *etc* **sympathies** penchants *mpl* à gauche *etc*; **in** ~ **with** (*strike*) en *or* par solidarité avec; **with our deepest** ~ en vous priant d'accepter nos sincères condoléances

symphony ['sɪmfənɪ] *n* symphonie *f*

symptom ['sɪmptəm] *n* symptôme *m*; indice *m*

syndicate ['sɪndɪkɪt] *n* syndicat *m*, coopérative *f*

synopsis [sɪ'nɔpsɪs] (*pl* **synopses**) *n* résumé *m*

synthetic [sɪn'θɛtɪk] *adj* synthétique

syphon ['saɪfən] *n, vb* = **siphon**

Syria ['sɪrɪə] *n* Syrie *f*

syringe [sɪ'rɪndʒ] *n* seringue *f*

syrup ['sɪrəp] *n* sirop *m*; (*also:* **golden** ~) mélasse raffinée

system ['sɪstəm] *n* système *m*; (*ANAT*) organisme *m*; ~**atic** [sɪstə'mætɪk] *adj* systématique; méthodique; ~ **disk** *n* (*COMPUT*) disque *m* système; ~**s analyst** *n* analyste fonctionnel(le)

T, t

ta [tɑː] (*BRIT*: *inf*) *excl* merci!

tab [tæb] *n* (*label*) étiquette *f*; (*on drinks can etc*) languette *f*; **to keep** ~**s on** (*fig*) surveiller

tabby ['tæbɪ] *n* (*also:* ~ **cat**) chat(te) tigré(e)

table ['teɪbl] *n* table *f* ♦ *vt* (*BRIT*: *motion etc*) présenter; **to lay** *or* **set the** ~ mettre le couvert *or* la table; ~**cloth** *n* nappe *f*; ~ **d'hôte** [tɑːbl'dəut] *adj* (*meal*) à prix fixe; ~ **lamp** *n* lampe *f* de table; ~**mat** *n* (*for plate*) napperon *m*, set *m*; (*for hot dish*) dessous-de-plat *m inv*; ~ **of contents** *n* table *f* des matières; ~**spoon** *n* cuiller *f* de service;

(*also:* **~spoonful**: *as measurement*) cuillerée *f* à soupe
tablet ['tæblɪt] *n* (MED) comprimé *m*
table tennis *n* ping-pong ® *m*, tennis *m* de table
table wine *n* vin *m* de table
tabloid ['tæblɔɪd] *n* quotidien *m* populaire

tabloid press

Le terme **tabloid press** *désigne les journaux populaires de demi-format où l'on trouve beaucoup de photos et qui adoptent un style très concis. Ce type de journaux vise des lecteurs s'intéressant aux faits divers ayant un parfum de scandale; voir* **quality (news)papers.**

tack [tæk] *n* (*nail*) petit clou ♦ *vt* clouer; (*fig*) direction *f*; (BRIT: *stitch*) faufiler ♦ *vi* tirer un *or* des bord(s)
tackle ['tækl] *n* matériel *m*, équipement *m*; (*for lifting*) appareil *m* de levage; (RUGBY) plaquage *m* ♦ *vt* (*difficulty, animal, burglar etc*) s'attaquer à; (*person: challenge*) s'expliquer avec; (RUGBY) plaquer
tacky ['tækɪ] *adj* collant(e); (*pej: of poor quality*) miteux(-euse)
tact [tækt] *n* tact *m*; **~ful** *adj* plein(e) de tact
tactical ['tæktɪkl] *adj* tactique
tactics ['tæktɪks] *npl* tactique *f*
tactless ['tæktlɪs] *adj* qui manque de tact
tadpole ['tædpəul] *n* têtard *m*
tag [tæg] *n* étiquette *f*; **~ along** *vi* suivre
tail [teɪl] *n* queue *f*; (*of shirt*) pan *m* ♦ *vt* (*follow*) suivre, filer; **~s** *npl* habit *m*; **~ away, ~ off** *vi* (*in size, quality etc*) baisser peu à peu; **~back** (BRIT) *n* (AUT) bouchon *m*; **~ end** *n* bout *m*, fin *f*; **~gate** *n* (AUT) hayon *m* arrière
tailor ['teɪləʳ] *n* tailleur *m*; **~ing** *n* (*cut*) coupe *f*; **~-made** *adj* fait(e) sur mesure; (*fig*) conçu(e) spécialement
tailwind ['teɪlwɪnd] *n* vent *m* arrière *inv*
tainted ['teɪntɪd] *adj* (*food*) gâté(e); (*water, air*) infecté(e); (*fig*) souillé(e)
take [teɪk] (*pt* **took**, *pp* **taken**) *vt* prendre; (*gain: prize*) remporter; (*require: effort, courage*) demander; (*tolerate*) accepter, supporter; (*hold: passengers etc*) contenir; (*accompany*) emmener, accompagner; (*bring, carry*) apporter, emporter; (*exam*) passer, se présenter à; **to ~ sth from** (*drawer etc*) prendre qch dans; (*person*) prendre qch à; **I ~ it that ...** je suppose que ...; **~ after** *vt fus* ressembler à; **~ apart** *vt* démonter; **~ away** *vt* enlever; (*carry off*) emporter; **~ back** *vt* (*return*) rendre, rapporter; (*one's words*) retirer; **~ down** *vt* (*building*) démolir; (*letter etc*) prendre, écrire; **~ in** *vt* (*deceive*) tromper, rouler; (*understand*) comprendre, saisir; (*include*) comprendre, inclure; (*lodger*) prendre; **~ off** *vi* (AVIAT) décoller ♦ *vt* (*go away*) s'en aller; (*remove*) enlever; **~ on** *vt* (*work*) accepter, se charger de; (*employee*) prendre, embaucher; (*opponent*) accepter de se battre contre; **~ out** *vt* (*invite*) emmener, sortir; (*remove*) enlever; **to ~ sth out of sth** (*drawer, pocket etc*) prendre qch dans qch; **~ over** *vt* (*business*) reprendre ♦ *vi*: **to ~ over from sb** prendre la relève de qn; **~ to** *vt fus* (*person*) se prendre d'amitié pour; (*thing*) prendre goût à; **~ up** *vt* (*activity*) se mettre à; (*dress*) raccourcir; (*occupy: time, space*) prendre, occuper; **to ~ sb up on an offer** accepter la proposition de qn; **~away** (BRIT) *adj* (*food*) à emporter ♦ *n* (*shop, restaurant*) café *m* qui vend de plats à emporter; **~off** *n* (AVIAT) décollage *m*; **~over** *n* (COMM) rachat *m*; **takings** *npl* (COMM) recette *f*
talc [tælk] *n* (*also:* **~um powder**) talc *m*
tale [teɪl] *n* (*story*) conte *m*, histoire *f*; (*account*) récit *m*; **to tell ~s** (*fig*) rapporter
talent ['tælnt] *n* talent *m*, don *m*; **~ed**

adj doué(e), plein(e) de talent
talk [tɔːk] *n* (*a speech*) causerie *f*, exposé *m*; (*conversation*) discussion *f*, entretien *m*; (*gossip*) racontars *mpl* ♦ *vi* parler; **~s** *npl* (*POL etc*) entretiens *mpl*; **to ~ about** parler de; **to ~ sb into/out of doing** persuader qn de faire/ne pas faire; **to ~ shop** parler métier *or* affaires; **~ over** *vt* discuter (de); **~ative** *adj* bavard(e); **~ show** *n* causerie (télévisée *or* radiodiffusée)
tall [tɔːl] *adj* (*person*) grand(e); (*building, tree*) haut(e); **to be 6 feet ~** ≃ mesurer 1 mètre 80; **~ story** *n* histoire *f* invraisemblable
tally ['tælɪ] *n* compte *m* ♦ *vi*: **to ~ (with)** correspondre (à)
talon ['tælən] *n* griffe *f*; (*of eagle*) serre *f*
tame [teɪm] *adj* apprivoisé(e); (*fig*: *story, style*) insipide
tamper ['tæmpə[r]] *vi*: **to ~ with** toucher à
tampon ['tæmpɔn] *n* tampon *m* (hygiénique *or* périodique)
tan [tæn] *n* (*also:* **suntan**) bronzage *m* ♦ *vt, vi* bronzer ♦ *adj* (*colour*) brun clair
tang [tæŋ] *n* odeur (*or* saveur) piquante
tangent ['tændʒənt] *n* (*MATH*) tangente *f*; **to go off at a ~** (*fig*) changer de sujet
tangerine [tændʒə'riːn] *n* mandarine *f*
tangle ['tæŋgl] *n* enchevêtrement *m*; **to get in(to) a ~** s'embrouiller
tank [tæŋk] *n* (*water ~*) réservoir *m*; (*for fish*) aquarium *m*; (*MIL*) char *m* d'assaut
tanker ['tæŋkə[r]] *n* (*ship*) pétrolier *m*, tanker *m*; (*truck*) camion-citerne *m*
tantalizing ['tæntəlaɪzɪŋ] *adj* (*smell*) extrêmement appétissant(e); (*offer*) terriblement tentant(e)
tantamount ['tæntəmaunt] *adj*: **~ to** qui équivaut à
tantrum ['tæntrəm] *n* accès *m* de colère
Taoiseach ['tiːʃəx] *n* Premier ministre *m* irlandais
tap [tæp] *n* (*on sink etc*) robinet *m*; (*gentle blow*) petite tape ♦ *vt* frapper *or* taper légèrement; (*resources*) exploiter, utiliser; (*telephone*) mettre sur écoute; **on ~** (*fig*: *resources*) disponible; **~-dancing** *n* claquettes *fpl*
tape [teɪp] *n* ruban *m*; (*also:* **magnetic ~**) bande *f* (magnétique); (*cassette*) cassette *f*; (*sticky*) scotch *m* ♦ *vt* (*record*) enregistrer; (*stick with ~*) coller avec du scotch; **~ deck** *n* platine *f* d'enregistrement; **~ measure** *n* mètre *m* à ruban
taper ['teɪpə[r]] *vi* s'effiler
tape recorder *n* magnétophone *m*
tapestry ['tæpɪstrɪ] *n* tapisserie *f*
tar [tɑː] *n* goudron *m*
target ['tɑːgɪt] *n* cible *f*; (*fig*) objectif *m*
tariff ['tærɪf] *n* (*COMM*) tarif *m*; (*taxes*) tarif douanier
tarmac ['tɑːmæk] *n* (*BRIT*: *on road*) macadam *m*; (*AVIAT*) piste *f*
tarnish ['tɑːnɪʃ] *vt* ternir
tarpaulin [tɑː'pɔːlɪn] *n* bâche (goudronnée)
tarragon ['tærəgən] *n* estragon *m*
tart [tɑːt] *n* (*CULIN*) tarte *f*; (*BRIT*: *inf*: *prostitute*) putain *f* ♦ *adj* (*flavour*) âpre, aigrelet(te); **~ up** (*BRIT*: *inf*) *vt* (*object*) retaper; **to ~ o.s. up** se faire beau (belle), s'attifer (*pej*)
tartan ['tɑːtn] *n* tartan *m* ♦ *adj* écossais(e)
tartar ['tɑːtə[r]] *n* (*on teeth*) tartre *m*; **~(e) sauce** *n* sauce *f* tartare
task [tɑːsk] *n* tâche *f*; **to take sb to ~** prendre qn à partie; **~ force** *n* (*MIL, POLICE*) détachement spécial
tassel ['tæsl] *n* gland *m*; pompon *m*
taste [teɪst] *n* goût *m*; (*fig*: *glimpse, idea*) idée *f*, aperçu *m* ♦ *vt* goûter ♦ *vi*: **to ~ of** *or* **like** (*fish etc*) avoir le *or* un goût de; **you can ~ the garlic (in it)** on sent bien l'ail; **can I have a ~ of this wine?** puis-je goûter un peu de ce vin?; **in good/bad ~** de bon/mauvais goût; **~ful** *adj* de bon goût; **~less** *adj* (*food*) fade; (*remark*) de mauvais goût;

tasty *adj* savoureux(-euse), délicieux (-euse)
tatters ['tætəz] *npl*: **in ~** en lambeaux
tattoo [tə'tu:] *n* tatouage *m*; (*spectacle*) parade *f* militaire ♦ *vt* tatouer
tatty ['tætɪ] (*BRIT*: *inf*) *adj* (*clothes*) frippé(e); (*shop, area*) délabré(e)
taught [tɔ:t] *pt, pp of* **teach**
taunt [tɔ:nt] *n* raillerie *f* ♦ *vt* railler
Taurus ['tɔ:rəs] *n* le Taureau
taut [tɔ:t] *adj* tendu(e)
tax [tæks] *n* (*on goods etc*) taxe *f*; (*on income*) impôts *mpl*, contributions *fpl* ♦ *vt* taxer; imposer; (*fig*: *patience etc*) mettre à l'épreuve; **~able** *adj* (*income*) imposable; **~ation** [tæk'seɪʃən] *n* taxation *f*; impôts *mpl*, contributions *fpl*; **~ avoidance** *n* dégrèvement fiscal; **~ disc** (*BRIT*) *n* (*AUT*) vignette *f* (automobile); **~ evasion** *n* fraude fiscale; **~-free** *adj* exempt(e) d'impôts
taxi ['tæksɪ] *n* taxi *m* ♦ *vi* (*AVIAT*) rouler (lentement) au sol; **~ driver** *n* chauffeur *m* de taxi; **~ rank** (*BRIT*) *n* station *f* de taxis; **~ stand** *n* = **taxi rank**
tax: ~ payer *n* contribuable *m/f*; **~ relief** *n* dégrèvement fiscal; **~ return** *n* déclaration *f* d'impôts *or* de revenus
TB *n abbr* = **tuberculosis**
tea [ti:] *n* thé *m*; (*BRIT*: *snack*: *for children*) goûter *m*; **high ~** *collation combinant goûter et dîner*; **~ bag** *n* sachet *m* de thé; **~ break** (*BRIT*) *n* pause-thé *f*
teach [ti:tʃ] (*pt, pp* **taught**) *vt*: **to ~ sb sth, ~ sth to sb** apprendre qch à qn; (*in school etc*) enseigner qch à qn ♦ *vi* enseigner; **~er** *n* (*in secondary school*) professeur *m*; (*in primary school*) instituteur(-trice); **~ing** *n* enseignement *m*
tea: ~ cloth *n* torchon *m*; **~ cosy** *n* cloche *f* à thé; **~cup** *n* tasse *f* à thé
teak [ti:k] *n* teck *m*
tea leaves *npl* feuilles *fpl* de thé
team [ti:m] *n* équipe *f*; (*of animals*) attelage *m*; **~work** *n* travail *m* d'équipe
teapot ['ti:pɔt] *n* théière *f*
tear[1] [tɛə^r] (*pt* **tore**, *pp* **torn**) *n* déchirure *f* ♦ *vt* déchirer ♦ *vi* se déchirer; **~ along** *vi* (*rush*) aller à toute vitesse; **~ up** *vt* (*sheet of paper etc*) déchirer, mettre en morceaux *or* pièces
tear[2] [tɪə^r] *n* larme *f*; **in ~s** en larmes; **~ful** *adj* larmoyant(e); **~ gas** *n* gaz *m* lacrymogène
tearoom ['ti:ru:m] *n* salon *m* de thé
tease [ti:z] *vt* taquiner; (*unkindly*) tourmenter
tea set *n* service *m* à thé
teaspoon ['ti:spu:n] *n* petite cuiller; (*also*: **~ful**: *as measurement*) ≃ cuillerée *f* à café
teat [ti:t] *n* tétine *f*
teatime ['ti:taɪm] *n* l'heure *f* du thé
tea towel (*BRIT*) *n* torchon *m* (à vaisselle)
technical ['tɛknɪkl] *adj* technique; **~ity** [tɛknɪ'kælɪtɪ] *n* (*detail*) détail *m* technique; (*point of law*) vice *m* de forme; **~ly** *adv* techniquement; (*strictly speaking*) en théorie
technician [tɛk'nɪʃən] *n* technicien(ne)
technique [tɛk'ni:k] *n* technique *f*
techno ['tɛknəu] *n* (*music*) techno *f*
technological [tɛknə'lɔdʒɪkl] *adj* technologique
technology [tɛk'nɔlədʒɪ] *n* technologie *f*
teddy (bear) ['tɛdɪ(-)] *n* ours *m* en peluche
tedious ['ti:dɪəs] *adj* fastidieux(-euse)
tee [ti:] *n* (*GOLF*) tee *m*
teem [ti:m] *vi*: **to ~ (with)** grouiller (de); **it is ~ing (with rain)** il pleut à torrents
teenage ['ti:neɪdʒ] *adj* (*fashions etc*) pour jeunes, pour adolescents; (*children*) adolescent(e); **~r** *n* adolescent(e)
teens [ti:nz] *npl*: **to be in one's ~** être adolescent(e)
tee-shirt ['ti:ʃə:t] *n* = **T-shirt**
teeter ['ti:tə^r] *vi* chanceler, vaciller
teeth [ti:θ] *npl of* **tooth**
teethe [ti:ð] *vi* percer ses dents

teething troubles *npl* (*fig*) difficultés initiales
teetotal ['ti:'təutl] *adj* (*person*) qui ne boit jamais d'alcool
tele: ~communications *npl* télécommunications *fpl*; **~conferencing** *n* téléconférence(s) *f(pl)*; **~gram** *n* télégramme *m*; **~graph** *n* télégraphe *m*; **~graph pole** *n* poteau *m* télégraphique
telephone ['tɛlɪfəun] *n* téléphone *m* ♦ *vt* (*person*) téléphoner à; (*message*) téléphoner; **on the ~** au téléphone; **to be on the ~** (*BRIT*: *have a ~*) avoir le téléphone; **~ booth**, **~ box** (*BRIT*) *n* cabine *f* téléphonique; **~ call** *n* coup *m* de téléphone, appel *m* téléphonique; **~ directory** *n* annuaire *m* (du téléphone); **~ number** *n* numéro *m* de téléphone; **telephonist** [tə'lɛfənɪst] (*BRIT*) *n* téléphoniste *m/f*
telesales ['tɛlɪseɪlz] *n* télévente *f*
telescope ['tɛlɪskəup] *n* télescope *m*
television ['tɛlɪvɪʒən] *n* télévision *f*; **on ~** à la télévision; **~ set** *n* (poste *f* de) télévision *m*
telex ['tɛlɛks] *n* télex *m*
tell [tɛl] (*pt, pp* **told**) *vt* dire; (*relate*: *story*) raconter; (*distinguish*): **to ~ sth from** distinguer qch de ♦ *vi* (*talk*): **to ~ (of)** parler (de); (*have effect*) se faire sentir, se voir; **to ~ sb to do** dire à qn de faire; **~ off** *vt* réprimander, gronder; **~er** *n* (*in bank*) caissier(-ère); **~ing** *adj* (*remark, detail*) révélateur(-trice); **~tale** *adj* (*sign*) éloquent(e), révélateur(-trice)
telly ['tɛlɪ] (*BRIT*: *inf*) *n abbr* (= *television*) télé *f*
temp [tɛmp] *n abbr* (= *temporary*) (secrétaire *f*) intérimaire *f*
temper ['tɛmpə^r] *n* (*nature*) caractère *m*; (*mood*) humeur *f*; (*fit of anger*) colère *f* ♦ *vt* (*moderate*) tempérer, adoucir; **to be in a ~** être en colère; **to lose one's ~** se mettre en colère
temperament ['tɛmprəmənt] *n* (*nature*) tempérament *m*; **~al** [tɛmprə'mɛntl] *adj* capricieux(-euse)
temperate ['tɛmprət] *adj* (*climate, country*) tempéré(e)
temperature ['tɛmprətʃə^r] *n* température *f*; **to have** *or* **run a ~** avoir de la fièvre
temple ['tɛmpl] *n* (*building*) temple *m*; (*ANAT*) tempe *f*
temporary ['tɛmpərərɪ] *adj* temporaire, provisoire; (*job, worker*) temporaire
tempt [tɛmpt] *vt* tenter; **to ~ sb into doing** persuader qn de faire; **~ation** [tɛmp'teɪʃən] *n* tentation *f*; **~ing** *adj* tentant(e)
ten [tɛn] *num* dix
tenacity [tə'næsɪtɪ] *n* ténacité *f*
tenancy ['tɛnənsɪ] *n* location *f*; état *m* de locataire
tenant ['tɛnənt] *n* locataire *m/f*
tend [tɛnd] *vt* s'occuper de ♦ *vi*: **to ~ to do** avoir tendance à faire; **~ency** ['tɛndənsɪ] *n* tendance *f*
tender ['tɛndə^r] *adj* tendre; (*delicate*) délicat(e); (*sore*) sensible ♦ *n* (*COMM*: *offer*) soumission *f* ♦ *vt* offrir
tenement ['tɛnəmənt] *n* immeuble *m*
tennis ['tɛnɪs] *n* tennis *m*; **~ ball** *n* balle *f* de tennis; **~ court** *n* (court *m* de) tennis; **~ player** *n* joueur(-euse) de tennis; **~ racket** *n* raquette *f* de tennis; **~ shoes** *npl* (chaussures *fpl* de) tennis *mpl*
tenor ['tɛnə^r] *n* (*MUS*) ténor *m*
tenpin bowling ['tɛnpɪn-] (*BRIT*) *n* bowling *m* (à dix quilles)
tense [tɛns] *adj* tendu(e) ♦ *n* (*LING*) temps *m*
tension ['tɛnʃən] *n* tension *f*
tent [tɛnt] *n* tente *f*
tentative ['tɛntətɪv] *adj* timide, hésitant(e); (*conclusion*) provisoire
tenterhooks ['tɛntəhuks] *npl*: **on ~** sur des charbons ardents
tenth [tɛnθ] *num* dixième
tent peg *n* piquet *m* de tente
tent pole *n* montant *m* de tente
tenuous ['tɛnjuəs] *adj* ténu(e)
tenure ['tɛnjuə^r] *n* (*of property*) bail *m*;

(*of job*) période *f* de jouissance

tepid ['tɛpɪd] *adj* tiède

term [tə:m] *n* terme *m*; (*SCOL*) trimestre *m* ♦ *vt* appeler; **~s** *npl* (*conditions*) conditions *fpl*; (*COMM*) tarif *m*; **in the short/long ~** à court/long terme; **to come to ~s with** (*problem*) faire face à

terminal ['tə:mɪnl] *adj* (*disease*) dans sa phase terminale; (*patient*) incurable ♦ *n* (*ELEC*) borne *f*; (*for oil, ore etc, COMPUT*) terminal *m*; (*also:* **air ~**) aérogare *f*; (*BRIT: also:* **coach ~**) gare routière; **~ly** *adv*: **to be ~ly ill** être condamné(e)

terminate ['tə:mɪneɪt] *vt* mettre fin à; (*pregnancy*) interrompre

terminus ['tə:mɪnəs] (*pl* **termini**) *n* terminus *m inv*

terrace ['tɛrəs] *n* terrasse *f*; (*BRIT: row of houses*) rangée *f* de maisons (*attenantes*); **the ~s** *npl* (*BRIT: SPORT*) les gradins *mpl*; **~d** *adj* (*garden*) en terrasses

terracotta ['tɛrə'kɔtə] *n* terre cuite

terrain [tɛ'reɪn] *n* terrain *m* (*sol*)

terrible ['tɛrɪbl] *adj* terrible, atroce; (*weather, conditions*) affreux(-euse), épouvantable; **terribly** *adv* terriblement; (*very badly*) affreusement mal

terrier ['tɛrɪə^r] *n* terrier *m* (*chien*)

terrific [tə'rɪfɪk] *adj* fantastique, incroyable, terrible; (*wonderful*) formidable, sensationnel(le)

terrify ['tɛrɪfaɪ] *vt* terrifier

territory ['tɛrɪtərɪ] *n* territoire *m*

terror ['tɛrə^r] *n* terreur *f*; **~ism** *n* terrorisme *m*; **~ist** *n* terroriste *m/f*

test [tɛst] *n* (*trial, check*) essai *m*; (*of courage etc*) épreuve *f*; (*MED*) examen *m*; (*CHEM*) analyse *f*; (*SCOL*) interrogation *f*; (*also:* **driving ~**) (examen du) permis *m* de conduire ♦ *vt* essayer; mettre à l'épreuve; examiner; analyser; faire subir une interrogation à

testament ['tɛstəmənt] *n* testament *m*; **the Old/New T~** l'Ancien/le Nouveau Testament

testicle ['tɛstɪkl] *n* testicule *m*

testify ['tɛstɪfaɪ] *vi* (*LAW*) témoigner, déposer; **to ~ to sth** attester qch

testimony ['tɛstɪmənɪ] *n* témoignage *m*; (*clear proof*): **to be (a) ~ to** être la preuve de

test match *n* (*CRICKET, RUGBY*) match international

test tube *n* éprouvette *f*

tetanus ['tɛtənəs] *n* tétanos *m*

tether ['tɛðə^r] *vt* attacher ♦ *n*: **at the end of one's ~** à bout (de patience)

text [tɛkst] *n* texte *m* ♦ *vt* envoyer un texto à; **~book** *n* manuel *m*; **~ message** *n* texto *m*

textile ['tɛkstaɪl] *n* textile *m*

texture ['tɛkstʃə^r] *n* texture *f*; (*of skin, paper etc*) grain *m*

Thailand ['taɪlænd] *n* Thaïlande *f*

Thames [tɛmz] *n*: **the ~** la Tamise

than [ðæn, ðən] *conj* que; (*with numerals*): **more ~ 10/once** plus de 10/d'une fois; **I have more/less ~ you** j'en ai plus/moins que toi; **she has more apples ~ pears** elle a plus de pommes que de poires

thank [θæŋk] *vt* remercier, dire merci à; **~s** *npl* (*gratitude*) remerciements *mpl* ♦ *excl* merci!; **~ you (very much)** merci (beaucoup); **~s to** grâce à; **~ God!** Dieu merci!; **~ful** *adj*: **~ful (for)** reconnaissant(e) (de); **~less** *adj* ingrat(e); **T~sgiving (Day)** *n* jour *m* d'action de grâce (*fête américaine*)

Thanksgiving Day

Thanksgiving Day *est un jour de congé aux États-Unis, le quatrième jeudi du mois de novembre, commémorant la bonne récolte que les Pèlerins venus de Grande-Bretagne ont eue en 1621; traditionnellement, c'est un jour où l'on remerciait Dieu et où l'on organisait un grand festin. Une fête semblable a lieu au Canada le deuxième lundi d'octobre.*

KEYWORD

that [ðæt] *adj* (*demonstrative*: *pl those*) ce, cet *+vowel or h mute*, cette *f*; **that man/woman/book** cet homme/cette femme/ce livre; (*not "this"*) cet homme-là/cette femme-là/ce livre-là; **that one** celui-là (celle-là)

♦ *pron* **1** (*demonstrative*: *pl those*) ce; (*not "this one"*) cela, ça; **who's that?** qui est-ce?; **what's that?** qu'est-ce que c'est?; **is that you?** c'est toi?; **I prefer this to that** je préfère ceci à cela *or* ça; **that's what he said** c'est *or* voilà ce qu'il a dit; **that is (to say)** c'est-à-dire, à savoir

2 (*relative*: *subject*) qui; (: *object*) que; (: *indirect*) lequel (laquelle), lesquels (lesquelles) *pl*; **the book that I read** le livre que j'ai lu; **the books that are in the library** les livres qui sont dans la bibliothèque; **all that I have** tout ce que j'ai; **the box that I put it in** la boîte dans laquelle je l'ai mis; **the people that I spoke to** les gens auxquels *or* à qui j'ai parlé

3 (*relative*: *of time*) où; **the day that he came** le jour où il est venu

♦ *conj* que; **he thought that I was ill** il pensait que j'étais malade

♦ *adv* (*demonstrative*): **I can't work that much** je ne peux pas travailler autant que cela; **I didn't know it was that bad** je ne savais pas que c'était si *or* aussi mauvais; **it's about that high** c'est à peu près de cette hauteur

thatched [θætʃt] *adj* (*roof*) de chaume; **~ cottage** chaumière *f*

thaw [θɔː] *n* dégel *m* ♦ *vi* (*ice*) fondre; (*food*) dégeler ♦ *vt* (*food*: *also*: **~ out**) (faire) dégeler

KEYWORD

the [ðiː, ðə] *def art* **1** (*gen*) le, la *f*, l' *+vowel or h mute*, les *pl*; **the boy/girl/ink** le garçon/la fille/l'encre; **the children** les enfants; **the history of the world** l'histoire du monde; **give it to the postman** donne-le au facteur; **to play the piano/flute** jouer du piano/de la flûte; **the rich and the poor** les riches et les pauvres

2 (*in titles*): **Elizabeth the First** Elisabeth première; **Peter the Great** Pierre le Grand

3 (*in comparisons*): **the more he works, the more he earns** plus il travaille, plus il gagne de l'argent

theatre ['θɪətə^r] *n* théâtre *m*; (*also*: **lecture ~**) amphi(théâtre) *m*; (*MED*: *also*: **operating ~**) salle *f* d'opération; **~-goer** *n* habitué(e) du théâtre; **theatrical** [θɪ'ætrɪkl] *adj* théâtral(e)

theft [θɛft] *n* vol *m* (*larcin*)

their [ðɛə^r] *adj* leur; (*pl*) leurs; *see also* **my**; **~s** *pron* le (la) leur; (*pl*) les leurs; *see also* **mine**[1]

them [ðɛm, ðəm] *pron* (*direct*) les; (*indirect*) leur; (*stressed, after prep*) eux (elles); *see also* **me**

theme [θiːm] *n* thème *m*; **~ park** *n* parc *m* (d'attraction) à thème; **~ song** *n* chanson principale

themselves [ðəm'sɛlvz] *pl pron* (*reflexive*) se; (*emphatic, after prep*) eux-mêmes (elles-mêmes); *see also* **oneself**

then [ðɛn] *adv* (*at that time*) alors, à ce moment-là; (*next*) puis, ensuite; (*and also*) et puis ♦ *conj* (*therefore*) alors, dans ce cas ♦ *adj*: **the ~ president** le président d'alors *or* de l'époque; **by ~** (*past*) à ce moment-là; (*future*) d'ici là; **from ~ on** dès lors

theology [θɪ'ɔlədʒɪ] *n* théologie *f*

theoretical [θɪə'rɛtɪkl] *adj* théorique

theory ['θɪərɪ] *n* théorie *f*

therapy ['θɛrəpɪ] *n* thérapie *f*

KEYWORD

there [ðɛə^r] *adv* **1**: **there is, there are** il y a; **there are 3 of them** (*people, things*) il y en a 3; **there has been an**

accident il y a eu un accident
2 (*referring to place*) là, là-bas; **it's there** c'est là(-bas); **in/on/up/down there** là-dedans/là-dessus/là-haut/en bas; **he went there on Friday** il y est allé vendredi; **I want that book there** je veux ce livre-là; **there he is!** le voilà!
3: **there, there** (*esp to child*) allons, allons!

there: ~abouts *adv* (*place*) par là, près de là; (*amount*) environ, à peu près; **~after** *adv* par la suite; **~by** *adv* ainsi; **~fore** *adv* donc, par conséquent; **~'s** = **there is; there has**

thermal ['θə:ml] *adj* (*springs*) thermal(e); (*underwear*) en thermolactyl ®; (COMPUT: *paper*) thermosensible; (: *printer*) thermique

thermometer [θə'mɔmɪtə^r] *n* thermomètre *m*

Thermos ® ['θə:məs] *n* (*also:* **~ flask**) thermos ® *m or f inv*

thermostat ['θə:məustæt] *n* thermostat *m*

thesaurus [θɪ'sɔ:rəs] *n* dictionnaire *m* des synonymes

these [ði:z] *pl adj* ces; (*not "those"*): **~ books** ces livres-ci ♦ *pl pron* ceux-ci (celles-ci)

thesis ['θi:sɪs] (*pl* **theses**) *n* thèse *f*

they [ðeɪ] *pl pron* ils (elles); (*stressed*) eux (elles); **~ say that ...** (*it is said that*) on dit que ...; **~'d** = **they had; they would; ~'ll** = **they shall; they will; ~'re** = **they are; ~'ve** = **they have**

thick [θɪk] *adj* épais(se); (*stupid*) bête, borné(e) ♦ *n*: **in the ~ of** au beau milieu de, en plein cœur de; **it's 20 cm ~** il/elle a 20 cm d'épaisseur; **~en** *vi* s'épaissir ♦ *vt* (*sauce etc*) épaissir; **~ness** *n* épaisseur *f*; **~set** *adj* trapu(e), costaud(e)

thief [θi:f] (*pl* **thieves**) *n* voleur(-euse)

thigh [θaɪ] *n* cuisse *f*

thimble ['θɪmbl] *n* dé *m* (à coudre)

thin [θɪn] *adj* mince; (*skinny*) maigre; (*soup, sauce*) peu épais(se), clair(e); (*hair, crowd*) clairsemé(e) ♦ *vt*: **to ~ (down)** (*sauce, paint*) délayer

thing [θɪŋ] *n* chose *f*; (*object*) objet *m*; (*contraption*) truc *m*; (*mania*): **to have a ~ about** être obsédé(e) par; **~s** *npl* (*belongings*) affaires *fpl*; **poor ~!** le (la) pauvre!; **the best ~ would be to** le mieux serait de; **how are ~s?** comment ça va?

think [θɪŋk] (*pt, pp* **thought**) *vi* penser, réfléchir; (*believe*) penser ♦ *vt* (*imagine*) imaginer; **what did you ~ of them?** qu'avez-vous pensé d'eux?; **to ~ about sth/sb** penser à qch/qn; **I'll ~ about it** je vais y réfléchir; **to ~ of doing** avoir l'idée de faire; **I ~ so/not** je crois *or* pense que oui/non; **to ~ well of** avoir une haute opinion de; **~ over** *vt* bien réfléchir à; **~ up** *vt* inventer, trouver; **~ tank** *n* groupe *m* de réflexion

thinly ['θɪnlɪ] *adv* (*cut*) en fines tranches; (*spread*) en une couche mince

third [θə:d] *num* troisième ♦ *n* (*fraction*) tiers *m*; (AUT) troisième (vitesse) *f*; (BRIT: SCOL: *degree*) ≃ licence *f* sans mention; **~ly** *adv* troisièmement; **~ party insurance** (BRIT) *n* assurance *f* au tiers; **~-rate** *adj* de qualité médiocre; **the T~ World** *n* le tiers monde

thirst [θə:st] *n* soif *f*; **~y** *adj* (*person*) qui a soif, assoiffé(e); (*work*) qui donne soif; **to be ~y** avoir soif

thirteen [θə:'ti:n] *num* treize

thirty ['θə:tɪ] *num* trente

KEYWORD

this [ðɪs] *adj* (*demonstrative*: *pl these*) ce, cet *+vowel or h mute*, cette *f*; **this man/woman/book** cet homme/cette femme/ce livre; (*not "that"*) cet homme-ci/cette femme-ci/ce livre-ci; **this one** celui-ci (celle-ci)
♦ *pron* (*demonstrative*: *pl these*) ce; (*not "that one"*) celui-ci (celle-ci), ceci; **who's this?** qui est-ce?; **what's this?** qu'est-ce que c'est?; **I prefer this to**

that je préfère ceci à cela; **this is what he said** voici ce qu'il a dit; **this is Mr Brown** (*in introductions*) je vous présente Mr Brown; (*in photo*) c'est Mr Brown; (*on telephone*) ici Mr Brown ♦ *adv* (*demonstrative*): **it was about this big** c'était à peu près de cette grandeur *or* grand comme ça; **I didn't know it was this bad** je ne savais pas que c'était si *or* aussi mauvais

thistle ['θɪsl] *n* chardon *m*
thorn [θɔːn] *n* épine *f*
thorough ['θʌrə] *adj* (*search*) minutieux(-euse); (*knowledge, research*) approfondi(e); (*work, person*) consciencieux(-euse); (*cleaning*) à fond; **~bred** *n* (*horse*) pur-sang *m inv*; **~fare** *n* route *f*; **"no ~fare"** "passage interdit"; **~ly** *adv* minutieusement; en profondeur; à fond; (*very*) tout à fait
those [ðəuz] *pl adj* ces; (*not "these"*): **~ books** ces livres-là ♦ *pl pron* ceux-là (celles-là)
though [ðəu] *conj* bien que *+sub*, quoique *+sub* ♦ *adv* pourtant
thought [θɔːt] *pt, pp of* **think** ♦ *n* pensée *f*; (*idea*) idée *f*; (*opinion*) avis *m*; **~ful** *adj* (*deep in thought*) pensif(-ive); (*serious*) réfléchi(e); (*considerate*) prévenant(e); **~less** *adj* étourdi(e); qui manque de considération
thousand ['θauzənd] *num* mille; **two ~** deux mille; **~s of** des milliers de; **~th** *num* millième
thrash [θræʃ] *vt* rouer de coups; donner une correction à; (*defeat*) battre à plate couture; **~ about**, **~ around** *vi* se débattre; **~ out** *vt* débattre de
thread [θrɛd] *n* fil *m*; (*TECH*) pas *m*, filetage *m* ♦ *vt* (*needle*) enfiler; **~bare** *adj* râpé(e), élimé(e)
threat [θrɛt] *n* menace *f*; **~en** *vi* menacer ♦ *vt*: **to ~en sb with sth/to do** menacer qn de qch/de faire
three [θriː] *num* trois; **~-dimensional** *adj* à trois dimensions; **~-piece suit** *n* complet *m* (avec gilet); **~-piece suite** *n* salon *m* comprenant un canapé et deux fauteuils assortis; **~-ply** *adj* (*wool*) trois fils *inv*
threshold ['θrɛʃhəuld] *n* seuil *m*
threw [θruː] *pt of* **throw**
thrifty ['θrɪftɪ] *adj* économe
thrill [θrɪl] *n* (*excitement*) émotion *f*, sensation forte; (*shudder*) frisson *m* ♦ *vt* (*audience*) électriser; **to be ~ed** (*with gift etc*) être ravi(e); **~er** *n* film *m* (*or* roman *m or* pièce *f*) à suspense; **~ing** *adj* saisissant(e), palpitant(e)
thrive [θraɪv] (*pt, pp* **thrived**) *vi* pousser, se développer; (*business*) prospérer; **he ~s on it** cela lui réussit; **thriving** *adj* (*business, community*) prospère
throat [θrəut] *n* gorge *f*; **to have a sore ~** avoir mal à la gorge
throb [θrɔb] *vi* (*heart*) palpiter; (*engine*) vibrer; **my head is ~bing** j'ai des élancements dans la tête
throes [θrəuz] *npl*: **in the ~ of** au beau milieu de
throne [θrəun] *n* trône *m*
throng ['θrɔŋ] *n* foule *f* ♦ *vt* se presser dans
throttle ['θrɔtl] *n* (*AUT*) accélérateur *m* ♦ *vt* étrangler
through [θruː] *prep* à travers; (*time*) pendant, durant; (*by means of*) par, par l'intermédiaire de; (*owing to*) à cause de ♦ *adj* (*ticket, train, passage*) direct(e) ♦ *adv* à travers; **to put sb ~ to sb** (*BRIT*: *TEL*) passer qn à qn; **to be ~** (*BRIT*: *TEL*) avoir la communication; (*esp US*: *have finished*) avoir fini; **to be ~ with sb** (*relationship*) avoir rompu avec qn; **"no ~ road"** (*BRIT*) "impasse"; **~out** *prep* (*place*) partout dans; (*time*) durant tout(e) le (la) ♦ *adv* partout
throw [θrəu] (*pt* **threw**, *pp* **thrown**) *n* jet *m*; (*SPORT*) lancer *m* ♦ *vt* lancer, jeter; (*SPORT*) lancer; (*rider*) désarçonner; (*fig*) décontenancer; **to ~ a party** donner une réception; **~ away** *vt* jeter; **~ off** *vt* se débarrasser de; **~ out** *vt* jeter; (*re-*

ject) rejeter; (*person*) mettre à la porte; **~ up** *vi* vomir; **~away** *adj* à jeter; (*remark*) fait(e) en passant; **~-in** *n* (SPORT) remise *f* en jeu

thru [θruː] (US) = **through**

thrush [θrʌʃ] *n* (*bird*) grive *f*

thrust [θrʌst] (*pt, pp* **thrust**) *n* (TECH) poussée *f* ♦ *vt* pousser brusquement; (*push in*) enfoncer

thud [θʌd] *n* bruit sourd

thug [θʌg] *n* voyou *m*

thumb [θʌm] *n* (ANAT) pouce *m* ♦ *vt*: **to ~ a lift** faire de l'auto-stop, arrêter une voiture; **~ through** *vt* (*book*) feuilleter; **~tack** (US) *n* punaise *f* (*clou*)

thump [θʌmp] *n* grand coup; (*sound*) bruit sourd ♦ *vt* cogner sur ♦ *vi* cogner, battre fort

thunder [ˈθʌndəʳ] *n* tonnerre *m* ♦ *vi* tonner; (*train etc*): **to ~ past** passer dans un grondement *or* un bruit de tonnerre; **~bolt** *n* foudre *f*; **~clap** *n* coup *m* de tonnerre; **~storm** *n* orage *m*; **~y** *adj* orageux(-euse)

Thursday [ˈθəːzdɪ] *n* jeudi *m*

thus [ðʌs] *adv* ainsi

thwart [θwɔːt] *vt* contrecarrer

thyme [taɪm] *n* thym *m*

tiara [tɪˈɑːrə] *n* diadème *m*

tick [tɪk] *n* (*sound*: *of clock*) tic-tac *m*; (*mark*) coche *f*; (ZOOL) tique *f*; (BRIT: *inf*): **in a ~** dans une seconde ♦ *vi* faire tic-tac ♦ *vt* (*item on list*) cocher; **~ off** *vt* (*item on list*) cocher; (*person*) réprimander, attraper; **~ over** *vi* (*engine*) tourner au ralenti; (*fig*) aller *or* marcher doucettement

ticket [ˈtɪkɪt] *n* billet *m*; (*for bus, tube*) ticket *m*; (*in shop*: *on goods*) étiquette *f*; (*for library*) carte *f*; (*parking ~*) papillon *m*, p.-v. *m*; **~ collector**, **~ inspector** *n* contrôleur(-euse); **~ office** *n* guichet *m*, bureau *m* de vente des billets

tickle [ˈtɪkl] *vt, vi* chatouiller; **ticklish** *adj* (*person*) chatouilleux(-euse); (*problem*) épineux(-euse)

tidal [ˈtaɪdl] *adj* (*force*) de la marée; (*estuary*) à marée; **~ wave** *n* raz-de-marée *m inv*

tidbit [ˈtɪdbɪt] (US) *n* = **titbit**

tiddlywinks [ˈtɪdlɪwɪŋks] *n* jeu *m* de puce

tide [taɪd] *n* marée *f*; (*fig*: *of events*) cours *m* ♦ *vt*: **to ~ sb over** dépanner qn; **high/low ~** marée haute/basse

tidy [ˈtaɪdɪ] *adj* (*room*) bien rangé(e); (*dress, work*) net(te), soigné(e); (*person*) ordonné(e), qui a de l'ordre ♦ *vt* (*also*: **~ up**) ranger

tie [taɪ] *n* (*string etc*) cordon *m*; (BRIT: *also*: **necktie**) cravate *f*; (*fig*: *link*) lien *m*; (SPORT: *draw*) égalité *f* de points; match nul ♦ *vt* (*parcel*) attacher; (*ribbon, shoelaces*) nouer ♦ *vi* (SPORT) faire match nul; finir à égalité de points; **to ~ sth in a bow** faire un nœud à *or* avec qch; **to ~ a knot in sth** faire un nœud à qch; **~ down** *vt* (*fig*): **to ~ sb down (to)** contraindre qn (à accepter); **to be ~d down** (*by relationship*) se fixer; **~ up** *vt* (*parcel*) ficeler; (*dog, boat*) attacher; (*prisoner*) ligoter; (*arrangements*) conclure; **to be ~d up** (*busy*) être pris(e) *or* occupé(e)

tier [tɪəʳ] *n* gradin *m*; (*of cake*) étage *m*

tiger [ˈtaɪgəʳ] *n* tigre *m*

tight [taɪt] *adj* (*rope*) tendu(e), raide; (*clothes*) étroit(e), très juste; (*budget, programme, bend*) serré(e); (*control*) strict(e), sévère; (*inf*: *drunk*) ivre, rond(e) ♦ *adv* (*squeeze*) très fort; (*shut*) hermétiquement, bien; **~en** *vt* (*rope*) tendre; (*screw*) resserrer; (*control*) renforcer ♦ *vi* se tendre, se resserrer; **~fisted** *adj* avare; **~ly** *adv* (*grasp*) bien, très fort; **~rope** *n* corde *f* raide; **~s** (BRIT) *npl* collant *m*

tile [taɪl] *n* (*on roof*) tuile *f*; (*on wall or floor*) carreau *m*; **~d** *adj* en tuiles; carrelé(e)

till [tɪl] *n* caisse (enregistreuse) ♦ *vt* (*land*) cultiver ♦ *prep, conj* = **until**

tiller [ˈtɪləʳ] *n* (NAUT) barre *f* (du gouvernail)

tilt [tɪlt] *vt* pencher, incliner ♦ *vi* pencher, être incliné(e)

timber ['tɪmbəʳ] *n* (*material*) bois *m* (de construction); (*trees*) arbres *mpl*

time [taɪm] *n* temps *m*; (*epoch*: *often pl*) époque *f*, temps; (*by clock*) heure *f*; (*moment*) moment *m*; (*occasion, also* MATH) fois *f*; (MUS) mesure *f* ♦ *vt* (*race*) chronométrer; (*programme*) minuter; (*visit*) fixer; (*remark etc*) choisir le moment de; **a long ~** un long moment, longtemps; **for the ~ being** pour le moment; **4 at a ~** 4 à la fois; **from ~ to ~** de temps en temps; **at ~s** parfois; **in ~** (*soon enough*) à temps; (*after some* ~) avec le temps, à la longue; (MUS) en mesure; **in a week's ~** dans une semaine; **in no ~** en un rien de temps; **any ~** n'importe quand; **on ~** à l'heure; **5 ~s 5** 5 fois 5; **what ~ is it?** quelle heure est-il?; **to have a good ~** bien s'amuser; **~ bomb** *n* bombe *f* à retardement; **~ lag** (BRIT) *n* décalage *m*; (*in travel*) décalage horaire; **~less** *adj* éternel(le); **~ly** *adj* opportun(e); **~ off** *n* temps *m* libre; **~r** *n* (TECH) minuteur *m*; (*in kitchen*) compte-minutes *m inv*; **~scale** *n* délais *mpl*; **~-share** *n* maison *f*/appartement *m* en multipropriété; **~ switch** (BRIT) *n* minuteur *m*; (*for lighting*) minuterie *f*; **~table** *n* (RAIL) (indicateur *m*) horaire *m*; (SCOL) emploi *m* du temps; **~ zone** *n* fuseau *m* horaire

timid ['tɪmɪd] *adj* timide; (*easily scared*) peureux(-euse)

timing ['taɪmɪŋ] *n* minutage *m*; chronométrage *m*; **the ~ of his resignation** le moment choisi pour sa démission

timpani ['tɪmpənɪ] *npl* timbales *fpl*

tin [tɪn] *n* étain *m*; (*also*: **~ plate**) fer-blanc *m*; (BRIT: *can*) boîte *f* (de conserve); (*for storage*) boîte *f*; **~foil** *n* papier *m* d'étain *or* aluminium

tinge [tɪndʒ] *n* nuance *f* ♦ *vt*: **~d with** teinté(e) de

tingle ['tɪŋgl] *vi* picoter; (*person*) avoir des picotements

tinker ['tɪŋkəʳ] *n* (*gipsy*) romanichel *m*; **~ with** *vt fus* bricoler, rafistoler

tinkle ['tɪŋkl] *vi* tinter

tinned [tɪnd] (BRIT) *adj* (*food*) en boîte, en conserve

tin opener (BRIT) *n* ouvre-boîte(s) *m*

tinsel ['tɪnsl] *n* guirlandes *fpl* de Noël (*argentées*)

tint [tɪnt] *n* teinte *f*; (*for hair*) shampooing colorant; **~ed** *adj* (*hair*) teint(e); (*spectacles, glass*) teinté(e)

tiny ['taɪnɪ] *adj* minuscule

tip [tɪp] *n* (*end*) bout *m*; (*gratuity*) pourboire *m*; (BRIT: *for rubbish*) décharge *f*; (*advice*) tuyau *m* ♦ *vt* (*waiter*) donner un pourboire à; (*tilt*) incliner; (*overturn*: *also*: **~ over**) renverser; (*empty*: ~ *out*) déverser; **~-off** *n* (*hint*) tuyau *m*; **~ped** (BRIT) *adj* (*cigarette*) (à bout) filtre *inv*

tipsy ['tɪpsɪ] (*inf*) *adj* un peu ivre, éméché(e)

tiptoe ['tɪptəu] *n*: **on ~** sur la pointe des pieds

tiptop [tɪp'tɔp] *adj*: **in ~ condition** en excellent état

tire ['taɪəʳ] *n* (US) = **tyre** ♦ *vt* fatiguer ♦ *vi* se fatiguer; **~d** *adj* fatigué(e); **to be ~d of** en avoir assez de, être las (lasse) de; **~less** *adj* (*person*) infatigable; (*efforts*) inlassable; **~some** *adj* ennuyeux(-euse); **tiring** *adj* fatigant(e)

tissue ['tɪʃuː] *n* tissu *m*; (*paper handkerchief*) mouchoir *m* en papier, kleenex ® *m*; **~ paper** *n* papier *m* de soie

tit [tɪt] *n* (*bird*) mésange *f*; **to give ~ for tat** rendre la pareille

titbit ['tɪtbɪt] *n* (*food*) friandise *f*; (*news*) potin *m*

title ['taɪtl] *n* titre *m*; **~ deed** *n* (LAW) titre (constitutif) de propriété; **~ role** *n* rôle principal

TM *abbr* = **trademark**

KEYWORD

to [tuː, tə] *prep* **1** (*direction*) à; **to go to**

France/Portugal/London/school aller en France/au Portugal/à Londres/à l'école; **to go to Claude's/the doctor's** aller chez Claude/le docteur; **the road to Edinburgh** la route d'Édimbourg
2 (*as far as*) (jusqu')à; **to count to 10** compter jusqu'à 10; **from 40 to 50 people** de 40 à 50 personnes
3 (*with expressions of time*): **a quarter to 5** 5 heures moins le quart; **it's twenty to 3** il est 3 heures moins vingt
4 (*for, of*) de; **the key to the front door** la clé de la porte d'entrée; **a letter to his wife** une lettre (adressée) à sa femme
5 (*expressing indirect object*) à; **to give sth to sb** donner qch à qn; **to talk to sb** parler à qn
6 (*in relation to*) à; **3 goals to 2** 3 (buts) à 2; **30 miles to the gallon** 9,4 litres aux cent (km)
7 (*purpose, result*): **to come to sb's aid** venir au secours de qn, porter secours à qn; **to sentence sb to death** condamner qn à mort; **to my surprise** à ma grande surprise
♦ *with vb* **1** (*simple infinitive*): **to go/eat** aller/manger
2 (*following another vb*): **to want/try/start to do** vouloir/essayer de/commencer à faire
3 (*with vb omitted*): **I don't want to** je ne veux pas
4 (*purpose, result*) pour; **I did it to help you** je l'ai fait pour vous aider
5 (*equivalent to relative clause*): **I have things to do** j'ai des choses à faire; **the main thing is to try** l'important est d'essayer
6 (*after adjective etc*): **ready to go** prêt(e) à partir; **too old/young to ...** trop vieux/jeune pour ...
♦ *adv*: **push/pull the door to** tirez/poussez la porte

toad [təud] *n* crapaud *m*
toadstool ['təudstu:l] *n* champignon (vénéneux)
toast [təust] *n* (CULIN) pain grillé, toast *m*; (*drink, speech*) toast ♦ *vt* (CULIN) faire griller; (*drink to*) porter un toast à; **~er** *n* grille-pain *m inv*
tobacco [tə'bækəu] *n* tabac *m*; **~nist** *n* marchand(e) de tabac; **~nist's (shop)** *n* (bureau *m* de) tabac *m*
toboggan [tə'bɔgən] *n* toboggan *m*; (*child's*) luge *f* ♦ *vi*: **to go ~ing** faire de la luge
today [tə'deɪ] *adv* (*also fig*) aujourd'hui ♦ *n* aujourd'hui *m*
toddler ['tɔdlə^r] *n* enfant *m/f* qui commence à marcher, bambin *m*
toe [təu] *n* doigt *m* de pied, orteil *m*; (*of shoe*) bout *m* ♦ *vt*: **to ~ the line** (*fig*) obéir, se conformer; **~nail** *n* ongle *m* du pied
toffee ['tɔfɪ] *n* caramel *m*; **~ apple** (BRIT) *n* pomme caramélisée
together [tə'gɛðə^r] *adv* ensemble; (*at same time*) en même temps; **~ with** avec
toil [tɔɪl] *n* dur travail, labeur *m* ♦ *vi* peiner
toilet ['tɔɪlət] *n* (BRIT: *lavatory*) toilettes *fpl* ♦ *cpd* (*accessories etc*) de toilette; **~ bag** *n* nécessaire *m* de toilette; **~ paper** *n* papier *m* hygiénique; **~ries** *npl* articles *mpl* de toilette; **~ roll** *n* rouleau *m* de papier hygiénique
token ['təukən] *n* (*sign*) marque *f*, témoignage *m*; (*metal disc*) jeton *m* ♦ *adj* (*strike, payment etc*) symbolique; **book/record ~** (BRIT) chèque-livre/-disque *m*; **gift ~** bon-cadeau *m*
told [təuld] *pt, pp of* **tell**
tolerable ['tɔlərəbl] *adj* (*bearable*) tolérable; (*fairly good*) passable
tolerant ['tɔlərnt] *adj*: **~ (of)** tolérant(e) (à l'égard de)
tolerate ['tɔləreɪt] *vt* supporter, tolérer
toll [təul] *n* (*tax, charge*) péage *m* ♦ *vi* (*bell*) sonner; **the accident ~ on the**

roads le nombre des victimes de la route

tomato [tə'mɑːtəu] (*pl* **~es**) *n* tomate *f*

tomb [tuːm] *n* tombe *f*

tomboy ['tɔmbɔɪ] *n* garçon manqué

tombstone ['tuːmstəun] *n* pierre tombale

tomcat ['tɔmkæt] *n* matou *m*

tomorrow [tə'mɔrəu] *adv* (*also fig*) demain ♦ *n* demain *m*; **the day after ~** après-demain; **~ morning** demain matin

ton [tʌn] *n* tonne *f* (*BRIT* = *1016kg; US* = *907kg*); (*metric*) tonne (= *1000 kg*); **~s of** (*inf*) des tas de

tone [təun] *n* ton *m* ♦ *vi* (*also:* **~ in**) s'harmoniser; **~ down** *vt* (*colour, criticism*) adoucir; (*sound*) baisser; **~ up** *vt* (*muscles*) tonifier; **~-deaf** *adj* qui n'a pas d'oreille

tongs [tɔŋz] *npl* (*for coal*) pincettes *fpl*; (*for hair*) fer *m* à friser

tongue [tʌŋ] *n* langue *f*; **~ in cheek** ironiquement; **~-tied** *adj* (*fig*) muet(te); **~ twister** *n* phrase *f* très difficile à prononcer

tonic ['tɔnɪk] *n* (*MED*) tonique *m*; (*also:* **~ water**) tonic *m*, Schweppes ® *m*

tonight [tə'naɪt] *adv, n* cette nuit; (*this evening*) ce soir

tonsil ['tɔnsl] *n* amygdale *f*; **~litis** [tɔnsɪ'laɪtɪs] *n* angine *f*

too [tuː] *adv* (*excessively*) trop; (*also*) aussi; **~ much** *adv* trop ♦ *adj* trop de; **~ many** trop de; **~ bad!** tant pis!

took [tuk] *pt of* **take**

tool [tuːl] *n* outil *m*; **~ box** *n* boîte *f* à outils

toot [tuːt] *n* (*of car horn*) coup *m* de klaxon; (*of whistle*) coup de sifflet ♦ *vi* (*with car horn*) klaxonner

tooth [tuːθ] (*pl* **teeth**) *n* (*ANAT, TECH*) dent *f*; **~ache** *n* mal *m* de dents; **~brush** *n* brosse *f* à dents; **~paste** *n* (pâte *f*) dentifrice *m*; **~pick** *n* cure-dent *m*

top [tɔp] *n* (*of mountain, head*) sommet *m*; (*of page, ladder, garment*) haut *m*; (*of box, cupboard, table*) dessus *m*; (*lid: of box, jar*) couvercle *m*; (: *of bottle*) bouchon *m*; (*toy*) toupie *f* ♦ *adj* du haut; (*in rank*) premier(-ère); (*best*) meilleur(e) ♦ *vt* (*exceed*) dépasser; (*be first in*) être en tête de; **on ~ of** sur; (*in addition to*) en plus de; **from ~ to bottom** de fond en comble; **~ up** (*US* **~ off**) *vt* (*bottle*) remplir; (*salary*) compléter; **~ floor** *n* dernier étage; **~ hat** *n* haut-de-forme *m*; **~-heavy** *adj* (*object*) trop lourd(e) du haut

topic ['tɔpɪk] *n* sujet *m*, thème *m*; **~al** *adj* d'actualité

top: ~less *adj* (*bather etc*) aux seins nus; **~-level** *adj* (*talks*) au plus haut niveau; **~most** *adj* le (la) plus haut(e)

topple ['tɔpl] *vt* renverser, faire tomber ♦ *vi* basculer; tomber

top-secret ['tɔp'siːkrɪt] *adj* top secret (-ète)

topsy-turvy ['tɔpsɪ'təːvɪ] *adj, adv* sens dessus dessous

torch [tɔːtʃ] *n* torche *f*; (*BRIT: electric*) lampe *f* de poche

tore [tɔːʳ] *pt of* **tear**[1]

torment [*n* 'tɔːmɛnt, *vb* tɔː'mɛnt] *n* tourment *m* ♦ *vt* tourmenter; (*fig: annoy*) harceler

torn [tɔːn] *pp of* **tear**[1]

tornado [tɔː'neɪdəu] (*pl* **~es**) *n* tornade *f*

torpedo [tɔː'piːdəu] (*pl* **~es**) *n* torpille *f*

torrent ['tɔrnt] *n* torrent *m*; **~ial** [tɔ'rɛnʃl] *adj* torrentiel(le)

tortoise ['tɔːtəs] *n* tortue *f*; **~shell** *adj* en écaille

torture ['tɔːtʃəʳ] *n* torture *f* ♦ *vt* torturer

Tory ['tɔːrɪ] (*BRIT: POL*) *adj, n* tory (*m/f*), conservateur(-trice)

toss [tɔs] *vt* lancer, jeter; (*pancake*) faire sauter; (*head*) rejeter en arrière; **to ~ a coin** jouer à pile ou face; **to ~ up for sth** jouer qch à pile ou face; **to ~ and turn** (*in bed*) se tourner et se retourner

tot [tɔt] *n* (*BRIT: drink*) petit verre; (*child*)

bambin *m*

total ['təutl] *adj* total(e) ♦ *n* total *m* ♦ *vt* (*add up*) faire le total de, additionner; (*amount to*) s'élever à; **~ly** *adv* totalement

totter ['tɔtəʳ] *vi* chanceler

touch [tʌtʃ] *n* contact *m*, toucher *m*; (*sense, also skill*: *of pianist etc*) toucher ♦ *vt* toucher; (*tamper with*) toucher à; **a ~ of** (*fig*) un petit peu de; une touche de; **to get in ~ with** prendre contact avec; **to lose ~** (*friends*) se perdre de vue; **~ on** *vt fus* (*topic*) effleurer, aborder; **~ up** *vt* (*paint*) retoucher; **~-and-go** *adj* incertain(e); **~down** *n* atterrissage *m*; (*on sea*) amerrissage *m*; (*US*: FOOTBALL) touché-en-but *m*; **~ed** *adj* (*moved*) touché(e); **~ing** *adj* touchant(e), attendrissant(e); **~line** *n* (SPORT) (ligne *f* de) touche *f*; **~y** *adj* (*person*) susceptible

tough [tʌf] *adj* dur(e); (*resistant*) résistant(e), solide; (*meat*) dur, coriace; (*firm*) inflexible; (*task*) dur, pénible; **~en** *vt* (*character*) endurcir; (*glass etc*) renforcer

toupee ['tu:peɪ] *n* postiche *m*

tour ['tuəʳ] *n* voyage *m*; (*also*: **package ~**) voyage organisé; (*of town, museum*) tour *m*, visite *f*; (*by artist*) tournée *f* ♦ *vt* visiter; **~ guide** *n* (*person*) guide *m/f*

tourism ['tuərɪzm] *n* tourisme *m*

tourist ['tuərɪst] *n* touriste *m/f* ♦ *cpd* touristique; **~ office** *n* syndicat *m* d'initiative

tournament ['tuənəmənt] *n* tournoi *m*

tousled ['tauzld] *adj* (*hair*) ébouriffé(e)

tout [taut] *vi*: **to ~ for** essayer de raccrocher, racoler ♦ *n* (*also*: **ticket ~**) revendeur *m* de billets

tow [təu] *vt* remorquer; (*caravan, trailer*) tracter; **"on ~"** (*BRIT*) *or* **"in ~"** (*US*) (AUT) "véhicule en remorque"

toward(s) [tə'wɔ:d(z)] *prep* vers; (*of attitude*) envers, à l'égard de; (*of purpose*) pour

towel ['tauəl] *n* serviette *f* (de toilette); **~ling** *n* (*fabric*) tissu éponge *m*; **~ rail** (*US* **towel rack**) *n* porte-serviettes *m inv*

tower ['tauəʳ] *n* tour *f*; **~ block** (BRIT) *n* tour *f* (d'habitation); **~ing** *adj* très haut(e), imposant(e)

town [taun] *n* ville *f*; **to go to ~** aller en ville; (*fig*) y mettre le paquet; **~ centre** *n* centre *m* de la ville, centre-ville *m*; **~ council** *n* conseil municipal; **~ hall** *n* ≃ mairie *f*; **~ plan** *n* plan *m* de ville; **~ planning** *n* urbanisme *m*

towrope ['təurəup] *n* (câble *m* de) remorque *f*

tow truck (*US*) *n* dépanneuse *f*

toy [tɔɪ] *n* jouet *m*; **~ with** *vt fus* jouer avec; (*idea*) caresser

trace [treɪs] *n* trace *f* ♦ *vt* (*draw*) tracer, dessiner; (*follow*) suivre la trace de; (*locate*) retrouver; **tracing paper** *n* papier-calque *m*

track [træk] *n* (*mark*) trace *f*; (*path*: *gen*) chemin *m*, piste *f*; (: *of bullet etc*) trajectoire *f*; (: *of suspect, animal*) piste; (RAIL) voie ferrée, rails *mpl*; (*on tape*, SPORT) piste; (*on record*) plage *f* ♦ *vt* suivre la trace *or* la piste de; **to keep ~ of** suivre; **~ down** *vt* (*prey*) trouver et capturer; (*sth lost*) finir par retrouver; **~suit** *n* survêtement *m*

tract [trækt] *n* (*of land*) étendue *f*

traction ['trækʃən] *n* traction *f*; (MED): **in ~** en extension

tractor ['træktəʳ] *n* tracteur *m*

trade [treɪd] *n* commerce *m*; (*skill, job*) métier *m* ♦ *vi* faire du commerce ♦ *vt* (*exchange*): **to ~ sth (for sth)** échanger qch (contre qch); **~ in** *vt* (*old car etc*) faire reprendre; **~ fair** *n* foire(-exposition) commerciale; **~-in price** *n* prix *m* à la reprise; **~mark** *n* marque *f* de fabrique; **~ name** *n* nom *m* de marque; **~r** *n* commerçant(e), négociant(e); **~sman** (*irreg*) *n* (*shopkeeper*) commerçant; **~ union** *n* syndicat *m*; **~ unionist** *n* syndicaliste *m/f*

tradition [trə'dɪʃən] *n* tradition *f*; **~al** *adj* traditionnel(le)

traffic ['træfɪk] *n* trafic *m*; (*cars*) circulation *f* ♦ *vi*: **to ~ in** (*pej*: *liquor, drugs*) faire le trafic de; **~ calming** *n* ralentissement *m* de la circulation; **~ circle** (*US*) *n* rond-point *m*; **~ jam** *n* embouteillage *m*; **~ lights** *npl* feux *mpl* (de signalisation); **~ warden** *n* contractuel(le)

tragedy ['trædʒədɪ] *n* tragédie *f*

tragic ['trædʒɪk] *adj* tragique

trail [treɪl] *n* (*tracks*) trace *f*, piste *f*; (*path*) chemin *m*, piste; (*of smoke etc*) traînée *f* ♦ *vt* traîner, tirer; (*follow*) suivre ♦ *vi* traîner; (*in game, contest*) être en retard; **~ behind** *vi* traîner, être à la traîne; **~er** *n* (*AUT*) remorque *f*; (*US*) caravane *f*; (*CINEMA*) bande-annonce *f*; **~er truck** (*US*) *n* (camion *m*) semi-remorque *m*

train [treɪn] *n* train *m*; (*in underground*) rame *f*; (*of dress*) traîne *f* ♦ *vt* (*apprentice, doctor etc*) former; (*sportsman*) entraîner; (*dog*) dresser; (*memory*) exercer; (*point*: *gun etc*): **to ~ sth on** braquer qch sur ♦ *vi* suivre une formation; (*SPORT*) s'entraîner; **one's ~ of thought** le fil de sa pensée; **~ed** *adj* qualifié(e), qui a reçu une formation; (*animal*) dressé(e); **~ee** [treɪ'ni:] *n* stagiaire *m/f*; (*in trade*) apprenti(e); **~er** *n* (*SPORT*: *coach*) entraîneur(-euse); (: *shoe*) chaussure *f* de sport; (*of dogs etc*) dresseur (-euse); **~ing** *n* formation *f*; entraînement *m*; **in ~ing** (*SPORT*) à l'entraînement; (*fit*) en forme; **~ing college** *n* école professionnelle; (*for teachers*) ≈ école normale; **~ing shoes** *npl* chaussures *fpl* de sport

trait [treɪt] *n* trait *m* (de caractère)

traitor ['treɪtə^r] *n* traître *m*

tram [træm] (*BRIT*) *n* (*also*: **~car**) tram(way) *m*

tramp [træmp] *n* (*person*) vagabond(e), clochard(e); (*inf*: *pej*: *woman*): **to be a ~** être coureuse ♦ *vi* marcher d'un pas lourd

trample ['træmpl] *vt*: **to ~ (underfoot)** piétiner

trampoline ['træmpəli:n] *n* trampoline *m*

tranquil ['træŋkwɪl] *adj* tranquille; **~lizer** (*US* **tranquilizer**) *n* (*MED*) tranquillisant *m*

transact [træn'zækt] *vt* (*business*) traiter; **~ion** *n* transaction *f*

transatlantic ['trænzət'læntɪk] *adj* transatlantique

transfer [*n* 'trænsfə^r, *vb* træns'fə:^r] *n* (*gen, also SPORT*) transfert *m*; (*POL*: *of power*) passation *f*; (*picture, design*) décalcomanie *f*; (: *stick-on*) autocollant *m* ♦ *vt* transférer; passer; **to ~ the charges** (*BRIT*: *TEL*) téléphoner en P.C.V.; **~ desk** *n* (*AVIAT*) guichet *m* de transit

transform [træns'fɔ:m] *vt* transformer

transfusion [træns'fju:ʒən] *n* transfusion *f*

transient ['trænzɪənt] *adj* transitoire, éphémère

transistor [træn'zɪstə^r] *n* (*~ radio*) transistor *m*

transit ['trænzɪt] *n*: **in ~** en transit

transitive ['trænzɪtɪv] *adj* (*LING*) transitif(-ive)

transit lounge *n* salle *f* de transit

translate [trænz'leɪt] *vt* traduire; **translation** *n* traduction *f*; **translator** *n* traducteur(-trice)

transmission [trænz'mɪʃən] *n* transmission *f*

transmit [trænz'mɪt] *vt* transmettre; (*RADIO, TV*) émettre

transparency [træns'pɛərnsɪ] *n* (*of glass etc*) transparence *f*; (*BRIT*: *PHOT*) diapositive *f*

transparent [træns'pærnt] *adj* transparent(e)

transpire [træns'paɪə^r] *vi* (*turn out*): **it ~d that ...** on a appris que ...; (*happen*) arriver

transplant [*vb* træns'plɑ:nt, *n* 'trænsplɑ:nt] *vt* transplanter; (*seedlings*) repiquer ♦ *n* (*MED*) transplantation *f*

transport [*n* 'trænspɔ:t, *vb* træns'pɔ:t]

n transport *m*; (*car*) moyen *m* de transport, voiture *f* ♦ *vt* transporter; **~ation** ['trænspɔː'teɪʃən] *n* transport *m*; (*means of transportation*) moyen *m* de transport; **~ café** (*BRIT*) *n* ≃ restaurant *m* de routiers

trap [træp] *n* (*snare, trick*) piège *m*; (*carriage*) cabriolet *m* ♦ *vt* prendre au piège; (*confine*) coincer; **~ door** *n* trappe *f*

trapeze [trə'piːz] *n* trapèze *m*

trappings ['træpɪŋz] *npl* ornements *mpl*; attributs *mpl*

trash [træʃ] (*pej*) *n* (*goods*) camelote *f*; (*nonsense*) sottises *fpl*; **~ can** (*US*) *n* poubelle *f*; **~y** (*inf*) *adj* de camelote; (*novel*) de quatre sous

trauma ['trɔːmə] *n* traumatisme *m*; **~tic** [trɔː'mætɪk] *adj* traumatisant(e)

travel ['trævl] *n* voyage(s) *m(pl)* ♦ *vi* voyager; (*news, sound*) circuler, se propager ♦ *vt* (*distance*) parcourir; **~ agency** *n* agence *f* de voyages; **~ agent** *n* agent *m* de voyages; **~ler** (*US* **traveler**) *n* voyageur(-euse); **~ler's cheque** (*US* **traveler's check**) *n* chèque *m* de voyage; **~ling** (*US* **traveling**) *n* voyage(s) *m(pl)*; **~ sickness** *n* mal *m* de la route (*or* de mer *or* de l'air)

trawler ['trɔːlə^r] *n* chalutier *m*

tray [treɪ] *n* (*for carrying*) plateau *m*; (*on desk*) corbeille *f*

treacherous ['trɛtʃərəs] *adj* (*person, look*) traître(-esse); (*ground, tide*) dont il faut se méfier

treacle ['triːkl] *n* mélasse *f*

tread [trɛd] (*pt* **trod**, *pp* **trodden**) *n* pas *m*; (*sound*) bruit *m* de pas; (*of tyre*) chape *f*, bande *f* de roulement ♦ *vi* marcher; **~ on** *vt fus* marcher sur

treason ['triːzn] *n* trahison *f*

treasure ['trɛʒə^r] *n* trésor *m* ♦ *vt* (*value*) tenir beaucoup à; **~r** *n* trésorier(-ère); **treasury** *n*: **the Treasury,** (*US*) **the Treasury Department** le ministère des Finances

treat [triːt] *n* petit cadeau, petite surprise ♦ *vt* traiter; **to ~ sb to sth** offrir qch à qn

treatment *n* traitement *m*

treaty ['triːtɪ] *n* traité *m*

treble ['trɛbl] *adj* triple ♦ *vt, vi* tripler; **~ clef** *n* (*MUS*) clé *f* de sol

tree [triː] *n* arbre *m*

trek [trɛk] *n* (*long*) voyage; (*on foot*) (longue) marche, tirée *f*

tremble ['trɛmbl] *vi* trembler

tremendous [trɪ'mɛndəs] *adj* (*enormous*) énorme, fantastique; (*excellent*) formidable

tremor ['trɛmə^r] *n* tremblement *m*; (*also:* **earth ~**) secousse *f* sismique

trench [trɛntʃ] *n* tranchée *f*

trend [trɛnd] *n* (*tendency*) tendance *f*; (*of events*) cours *m*; (*fashion*) mode *f*; **~y** *adj* (*idea, person*) dans le vent; (*clothes*) dernier cri *inv*

trespass ['trɛspəs] *vi*: **to ~ on** s'introduire sans permission dans; **"no ~ing"** "propriété privée", "défense d'entrer"

trestle ['trɛsl] *n* tréteau *m*

trial ['traɪəl] *n* (*LAW*) procès *m*, jugement *m*; (*test*: *of machine etc*) essai *m*; **~s** *npl* (*unpleasant experiences*) épreuves *fpl*; **to be on ~** (*LAW*) passer en jugement; **by ~ and error** par tâtonnements; **~ period** *n* période *f* d'essai

triangle ['traɪæŋgl] *n* (*MATH, MUS*) triangle *m*; **triangular** [traɪ'æŋgjulə^r] *adj* triangulaire

tribe [traɪb] *n* tribu *f*; **~sman** (*irreg*) *n* membre *m* d'une tribu

tribunal [traɪ'bjuːnl] *n* tribunal *m*

tributary ['trɪbjutərɪ] *n* (*river*) affluent *m*

tribute ['trɪbjuːt] *n* tribut *m*, hommage *m*; **to pay ~ to** rendre hommage à

trick [trɪk] *n* (*magic ~*) tour *m*; (*joke, prank*) tour, farce *f*; (*skill, knack*) astuce *f*, truc *m*; (*CARDS*) levée *f* ♦ *vt* attraper, rouler; **to play a ~ on sb** jouer un tour à qn; **that should do the ~** ça devrait faire l'affaire; **~ery** *n* ruse *f*

trickle ['trɪkl] *n* (*of water etc*) filet *m*

♦ *vi* couler en un filet *or* goutte à goutte

tricky ['trɪkɪ] *adj* difficile, délicat(e)

tricycle ['traɪsɪkl] *n* tricycle *m*

trifle ['traɪfl] *n* bagatelle *f*; (*CULIN*) ≃ diplomate *m* ♦ *adv*: **a ~ long** un peu long; **trifling** *adj* insignifiant(e)

trigger ['trɪgəʳ] *n* (*of gun*) gâchette *f*; **~ off** *vt* déclencher

trim [trɪm] *adj* (*house, garden*) bien tenu(e); (*figure*) svelte ♦ *n* (*haircut etc*) légère coupe; (*on car*) garnitures *fpl* ♦ *vt* (*cut*) couper légèrement; (*NAUT*: *a sail*) gréer; (*decorate*): **to ~ (with)** décorer (de); **~mings** *npl* (*CULIN*) garniture *f*

trinket ['trɪŋkɪt] *n* bibelot *m*; (*piece of jewellery*) colifichet *m*

trip [trɪp] *n* voyage *m*; (*excursion*) excursion *f*; (*stumble*) faux pas ♦ *vi* faire un faux pas, trébucher; **on a ~** en voyage; **~ up** *vi* trébucher ♦ *vt* faire un croc-en-jambe à

tripe [traɪp] *n* (*CULIN*) tripes *fpl*; (*pej*: *rubbish*) idioties *fpl*

triple ['trɪpl] *adj* triple; **~ts** *npl* triplés (-ées); **triplicate** ['trɪplɪkət] *n*: **in triplicate** en trois exemplaires

tripod ['traɪpɔd] *n* trépied *m*

trite [traɪt] (*pej*) *adj* banal(e)

triumph ['traɪʌmf] *n* triomphe *m* ♦ *vi*: **to ~ (over)** triompher (de)

trivia ['trɪvɪə] (*pej*) *npl* futilités *fpl*; **~l** *adj* insignifiant(e); (*commonplace*) banal(e)

trod [trɔd] *pt of* **tread**; **~den** *pp of* **tread**

trolley ['trɔlɪ] *n* chariot *m*

trombone [trɔm'bəun] *n* trombone *m*

troop [tru:p] *n* bande *f*, groupe *m* ♦ *vi*: **~ in/out** entrer/sortir en groupe; **~s** *npl* (*MIL*) troupes *fpl*; (: *men*) hommes *mpl*, soldats *mpl*; **~ing the colour** (*BRIT*) *n* (*ceremony*) le salut au drapeau

trophy ['trəufɪ] *n* trophée *m*

tropic ['trɔpɪk] *n* tropique *m*; **~al** *adj* tropical(e)

trot [trɔt] *n* trot *m* ♦ *vi* trotter; **on the ~** (*BRIT*: *fig*) d'affilée

trouble ['trʌbl] *n* difficulté(s) *f(pl)*, problème(s) *m(pl)*; (*worry*) ennuis *mpl*, soucis *mpl*; (*bother, effort*) peine *f*; (*POL*) troubles *mpl*; (*MED*): **stomach** *etc* **~** troubles gastriques *etc* ♦ *vt* (*disturb*) déranger, gêner; (*worry*) inquiéter ♦ *vi*: **to ~ to do** prendre la peine de faire; **~s** *npl* (*POL etc*) troubles *mpl*; (*personal*) ennuis, soucis; **to be in ~** avoir des ennuis; (*ship, climber etc*) être en difficulté; **what's the ~?** qu'est-ce qui ne va pas?; **~d** *adj* (*person*) inquiet(-ète); (*epoch, life*) agité(e); **~maker** *n* élément perturbateur, fauteur *m* de troubles; **~shooter** *n* (*in conflict*) médiateur *m*; **~some** *adj* (*child*) fatigant(e), difficile; (*cough etc*) gênant(e)

trough [trɔf] *n* (*also*: **drinking ~**) abreuvoir *m*; (*also*: **feeding ~**) auge *f*; (*depression*) creux *m*

trousers ['trauzəz] *npl* pantalon *m*; **short ~** culottes courtes

trout [traut] *n inv* truite *f*

trowel ['trauəl] *n* truelle *f*; (*garden tool*) déplantoir *m*

truant ['truənt] (*BRIT*) *n*: **to play ~** faire l'école buissonnière

truce [tru:s] *n* trêve *f*

truck [trʌk] *n* camion *m*; (*RAIL*) wagon *m* à plate-forme; **~ driver** *n* camionneur *m*; **~ farm** (*US*) *n* jardin maraîcher

true [tru:] *adj* vrai(e); (*accurate*) exact(e); (*genuine*) vrai, véritable; (*faithful*) fidèle; **to come ~** se réaliser

truffle ['trʌfl] *n* truffe *f*

truly ['tru:lɪ] *adv* vraiment, réellement; (*truthfully*) sans mentir; *see also* **yours**

trump [trʌmp] *n* (*also*: **~ card**) atout *m*

trumpet ['trʌmpɪt] *n* trompette *f*

truncheon ['trʌntʃən] (*BRIT*) *n* bâton *m* (d'agent de police); matraque *f*

trundle ['trʌndl] *vt, vi*: **to ~ along** rouler lentement (et bruyamment)

trunk [trʌŋk] *n* (*of tree, person*) tronc *m*; (*of elephant*) trompe *f*; (*case*) malle *f*; (*US*: *AUT*) coffre *m*; **~s** *npl* (*also*: **swimming ~s**) maillot *m or* slip *m* de bain

truss [trʌs] *vt*: **to ~ (up)** ligoter
trust [trʌst] *n* confiance *f*; (*responsibility*) charge *f*; (*LAW*) fidéicommis *m* ♦ *vt* (*rely on*) avoir confiance en; (*hope*) espérer; (*entrust*): **to ~ sth to sb** confier qch à qn; **to take sth on ~** accepter qch les yeux fermés; **~ed** *adj* en qui l'on a confiance; **~ee** [trʌs'ti:] *n* (*LAW*) fidéicommissaire *m/f*; (*of school etc*) administrateur(-trice); **~ful**, **~ing** *adj* confiant(e); **~worthy** *adj* digne de confiance
truth [tru:θ] *n* vérité *f*; **~ful** *adj* (*person*) qui dit la vérité; (*answer*) sincère
try [traɪ] *n* essai *m*, tentative *f*; (*RUGBY*) essai ♦ *vt* (*attempt*) essayer, tenter; (*test*: *sth new*: *also*: *~ out*) essayer, tester; (*LAW*: *person*) juger; (*strain*) éprouver ♦ *vi* essayer; **to have a ~** essayer; **to ~ to do** essayer de faire; (*seek*) chercher à faire; **~ on** *vt* (*clothes*) essayer; **~ing** *adj* pénible
T-shirt ['ti:ʃə:t] *n* tee-shirt *m*
T-square ['ti:skwɛə^r] *n* équerre *f* en T, té *m*
tub [tʌb] *n* cuve *f*; (*for washing clothes*) baquet *m*; (*bath*) baignoire *f*
tubby ['tʌbɪ] *adj* rondelet(te)
tube [tju:b] *n* tube *m*; (*BRIT*: *underground*) métro *m*; (*for tyre*) chambre *f* à air
tuberculosis [tjubə:kju'ləusɪs] *n* tuberculose *f*
TUC *n abbr* (*BRIT*: *Trades Union Congress*) *confédération des syndicats britanniques*
tuck [tʌk] *vt* (*put*) mettre; **~ away** *vt* cacher, ranger; **~ in** *vt* rentrer; (*child*) border ♦ *vi* (*eat*) manger (de bon appétit); **~ up** *vt* (*child*) border; **~ shop** (*BRIT*) *n* boutique *f* à provisions (*dans une école*)
Tuesday ['tju:zdɪ] *n* mardi *m*
tuft [tʌft] *n* touffe *f*
tug [tʌg] *n* (*ship*) remorqueur *m* ♦ *vt* tirer (sur); **~-of-war** *n* lutte *f* à la corde; (*fig*) lutte acharnée
tuition [tju:'ɪʃən] *n* (*BRIT*) leçons *fpl*; (: *private ~*) cours particuliers; (*US*: *school fees*) frais *mpl* de scolarité
tulip ['tju:lɪp] *n* tulipe *f*
tumble ['tʌmbl] *n* (*fall*) chute *f*, culbute *f* ♦ *vi* tomber, dégringoler; **to ~ to sth** (*inf*) réaliser qch; **~down** *adj* délabré(e); **~ dryer** (*BRIT*) *n* séchoir *m* à air chaud
tumbler ['tʌmblə^r] *n* (*glass*) verre (droit), gobelet *m*
tummy ['tʌmɪ] (*inf*) *n* ventre *m*; **~ upset** *n* maux *mpl* de ventre
tumour ['tju:mə^r] (*US* **tumor**) *n* tumeur *f*
tuna ['tju:nə] *n inv* (*also*: **~ fish**) thon *m*
tune [tju:n] *n* (*melody*) air *m* ♦ *vt* (*MUS*) accorder; (*RADIO, TV, AUT*) régler; **to be in/out of ~** (*instrument*) être accordé/désaccordé; (*singer*) chanter juste/faux; **to be in/out of ~ with** (*fig*) être en accord/désaccord avec; **~ in** *vi* (*RADIO, TV*): **to ~ in (to)** se mettre à l'écoute (de); **~ up** *vi* (*musician*) accorder son instrument; **~ful** *adj* mélodieux(-euse); **~r** *n*: **piano ~r** accordeur *m* (de pianos)
tunic ['tju:nɪk] *n* tunique *f*
Tunisia [tju:'nɪzɪə] *n* Tunisie *f*
tunnel ['tʌnl] *n* tunnel *m*; (*in mine*) galerie *f* ♦ *vi* percer un tunnel
turbulence ['tə:bjuləns] *n* (*AVIAT*) turbulence *f*
tureen [tə'ri:n] *n* (*for soup*) soupière *f*; (*for vegetables*) légumier *m*
turf [tə:f] *n* gazon *m*; (*clod*) motte *f* (de gazon) ♦ *vt* gazonner; **~ out** (*inf*) *vt* (*person*) jeter dehors
Turk [tə:k] *n* Turc (Turque)
Turkey ['tə:kɪ] *n* Turquie *f*
turkey ['tə:kɪ] *n* dindon *m*, dinde *f*
Turkish ['tə:kɪʃ] *adj* turc (turque) ♦ *n* (*LING*) turc *m*
turmoil ['tə:mɔɪl] *n* trouble *m*, bouleversement *m*; **in ~** en émoi, en effervescence
turn [tə:n] *n* tour *m*; (*in road*) tournant *m*; (*of mind, events*) tournure *f*; (*performance*) numéro *m*; (*MED*) crise *f*, atta-

que *f* ♦ *vt* tourner; (*collar, steak*) retourner; (*change*): **to ~ sth into** changer qch en ♦ *vi* (*object, wind, milk*) tourner; (*person: look back*) se (re)tourner; (*reverse direction*) faire demi-tour; (*become*) devenir; (*age*) atteindre; **to ~ into** se changer en; **a good ~** un service; **it gave me quite a ~** ça m'a fait un coup; **"no left ~"** (*AUT*) "défense de tourner à gauche"; **it's your ~** c'est (à) votre tour; **in ~** à son tour; à tour de rôle; **to take ~s (at)** se relayer (pour *or* à); **~ away** *vi* se détourner ♦ *vt* (*applicants*) refuser; **~ back** *vi* revenir, faire demi-tour ♦ *vt* (*person, vehicle*) faire faire demi-tour à; (*clock*) reculer; **~ down** *vt* (*refuse*) rejeter, refuser; (*reduce*) baisser; (*fold*) rabattre; **~ in** *vi* (*inf: go to bed*) aller se coucher ♦ *vt* (*fold*) rentrer; **~ off** *vi* (*from road*) tourner ♦ *vt* (*light, radio etc*) éteindre; (*tap*) fermer; (*engine*) arrêter; **~ on** *vt* (*light, radio etc*) allumer; (*tap*) ouvrir; (*engine*) mettre en marche; **~ out** *vt* (*light, gas*) éteindre; (*produce*) produire ♦ *vi* (*voters, troops etc*) se présenter; **to ~ out to be ...** s'avérer ..., se révéler ...; **~ over** *vi* (*person*) se retourner ♦ *vt* (*object*) retourner; (*page*) tourner; **~ round** *vi* faire demi-tour; (*rotate*) tourner; **~ up** *vi* (*person*) arriver, se pointer (*inf*); (*lost object*) être retrouvé(e) ♦ *vt* (*collar*) remonter; (*radio, heater*) mettre plus fort; **~ing** *n* (*in road*) tournant *m*; **~ing point** *n* (*fig*) tournant *m*, moment décisif

turnip ['tə:nɪp] *n* navet *m*

turn: ~out *n* (*of voters*) taux *m* de participation; **~over** *n* (*COMM: amount of money*) chiffre *m* d'affaires; (*: of goods*) roulement *m*; (*of staff*) renouvellement *m*, changement *m*; **~pike** (*US*) *n* autoroute *f* à péage; **~stile** *n* tourniquet *m* (*d'entrée*); **~table** *n* (*on record player*) platine *f*; **~-up** (*BRIT*) *n* (*on trousers*) revers *m*

turpentine ['tə:pəntaɪn] *n* (*also:* **turps**) (essence *f* de) térébenthine *f*

turquoise ['tə:kwɔɪz] *n* (*stone*) turquoise *f* ♦ *adj* turquoise *inv*

turret ['tʌrɪt] *n* tourelle *f*

turtle ['tə:tl] *n* tortue marine *or* d'eau douce; **~neck (sweater)** *n* (*BRIT*) pullover *m* à col montant; (*US*) pullover à col roulé

tusk [tʌsk] *n* défense *f*

tutor ['tju:tə[r]] *n* (*in college*) directeur (-trice) d'études; (*private teacher*) précepteur(-trice); **~ial** [tju:'tɔ:rɪəl] *n* (*SCOL*) (séance *f* de) travaux *mpl* pratiques

tuxedo [tʌk'si:dəu] (*US*) *n* smoking *m*

TV *n abbr* (= *television*) télé *f*

twang [twæŋ] *n* (*of instrument*) son vibrant; (*of voice*) ton nasillard

tweed [twi:d] *n* tweed *m*

tweezers ['twi:zəz] *npl* pince *f* à épiler

twelfth [twɛlfθ] *num* douzième

twelve [twɛlv] *num* douze; **at ~ (o'clock)** à midi; (*midnight*) à minuit

twentieth ['twɛntɪɪθ] *num* vingtième

twenty ['twɛntɪ] *num* vingt

twice [twaɪs] *adv* deux fois; **~ as much** deux fois plus

twiddle ['twɪdl] *vt, vi*: **to ~ (with) sth** tripoter qch; **to ~ one's thumbs** (*fig*) se tourner les pouces

twig [twɪg] *n* brindille *f* ♦ *vi* (*inf*) piger

twilight ['twaɪlaɪt] *n* crépuscule *m*

twin [twɪn] *adj, n* jumeau(-elle) ♦ *vt* jumeler; **~(-bedded) room** *n* chambre *f* à deux lits; **~ beds** *npl* lits jumeaux

twine [twaɪn] *n* ficelle *f* ♦ *vi* (*plant*) s'enrouler

twinge [twɪndʒ] *n* (*of pain*) élancement *m*; **a ~ of conscience** un certain remords; **a ~ of regret** un pincement au cœur

twinkle ['twɪŋkl] *vi* scintiller; (*eyes*) pétiller

twirl [twə:l] *vt* faire tournoyer ♦ *vi* tournoyer

twist [twɪst] *n* torsion *f*, tour *m*; (*in road*) virage *m*; (*in wire, flex*) tortillon m; (*in story*) coup *m* de théâtre ♦ *vt* tordre; (*weave*) entortiller; (*roll around*) enrouler; (*fig*) déformer ♦ *vi* (*road, river*) serpenter

twit [twɪt] (*inf*) *n* crétin(e)

twitch [twɪtʃ] *n* (*pull*) coup sec, saccade *f*; (*nervous*) tic *m* ♦ *vi* se convulser; avoir un tic

two [tu:] *num* deux; **to put ~ and ~ together** (*fig*) faire le rapprochement; **~-door** *adj* (AUT) à deux portes; **~-faced** (*pej*) *adj* (*person*) faux (fausse); **~fold** *adv*: **to increase ~fold** doubler; **~-piece (suit)** *n* (*man's*) costume *m* (deux-pièces); (*woman's*) (tailleur *m*) deux-pièces *m inv*; **~-piece (swimsuit)** *n* (maillot *m* de bain) deux-pièces *m inv*; **~some** *n* (*people*) couple *m*; **~-way** *adj* (*traffic*) dans les deux sens

tycoon [taɪ'ku:n] *n*: **(business) ~** gros homme d'affaires

type [taɪp] *n* (*category*) type *m*, genre *m*, espèce *f*; (*model, example*) type *m*, modèle *m*; (TYP) type, caractère *m* ♦ *vt* (*letter etc*) taper (à la machine); **~-cast** *adj* (*actor*) condamné(e) à toujours jouer le même rôle; **~face** *n* (TYP) œil *m* de caractère; **~script** *n* texte dactylographié; **~writer** *n* machine *f* à écrire; **~written** *adj* dactylographié(e)

typhoid ['taɪfɔɪd] *n* typhoïde *f*

typical ['tɪpɪkl] *adj* typique, caractéristique

typing ['taɪpɪŋ] *n* dactylo(graphie) *f*

typist ['taɪpɪst] *n* dactylo *m/f*

tyrant ['taɪərnt] *n* tyran *m*

tyre ['taɪə^r] (US **tire**) *n* pneu *m*; **~ pressure** *n* pression *f* (de gonflage)

U, u

U-bend ['ju:bɛnd] *n* (*in pipe*) coude *m*

ubiquitous [ju:'bɪkwɪtəs] *adj* omniprésent(e)

udder ['ʌdə^r] *n* pis *m*, mamelle *f*

UFO ['ju:fəu] *n abbr* (= *unidentified flying object*) OVNI *m*

Uganda [ju:'gændə] *n* Ouganda *m*

ugh [ə:h] *excl* pouah!

ugly ['ʌglɪ] *adj* laid(e), vilain(e); (*situation*) inquiétant(e)

UHT *abbr* (= *ultra heat treated*): **UHT milk** lait *m* UHT *or* longue conservation

UK *n abbr* = **United Kingdom**

ulcer ['ʌlsə^r] *n* ulcère *m*; (*also:* **mouth ~**) aphte *f*

Ulster ['ʌlstə^r] *n* Ulster *m*; (*inf: Northern Ireland*) Irlande *f* du Nord

ulterior [ʌl'tɪərɪə^r] *adj*: **~ motive** arrière-pensée *f*

ultimate ['ʌltɪmət] *adj* ultime, final(e); (*authority*) suprême; **~ly** *adv* (*at last*) en fin de compte; (*fundamentally*) finalement

ultrasound ['ʌltrəsaund] *n* ultrason *m*

umbilical cord [ʌm'bɪlɪkl-] *n* cordon ombilical

umbrella [ʌm'brɛlə] *n* parapluie *m*; (*for sun*) parasol *m*

umpire ['ʌmpaɪə^r] *n* arbitre *m*

umpteen [ʌmp'ti:n] *adj* je ne sais combien de; **~th** *adj*: **for the ~th time** pour la nième fois

UN *n abbr* = **United Nations**

unable [ʌn'eɪbl] *adj*: **to be ~ to** ne pas pouvoir, être dans l'impossibilité de; (*incapable*) être incapable de

unacceptable [ʌnək'sɛptəbl] *adj* (*behaviour*) inadmissible; (*price, proposal*) inacceptable

unaccompanied [ʌnə'kʌmpənɪd] *adj* (*child, lady*) non accompagné(e); (*song*) sans accompagnement

unaccustomed [ʌnə'kʌstəmd] *adj*: **to be ~ to sth** ne pas avoir l'habitude de qch

unanimous [ju:'nænɪməs] *adj* unanime; **~ly** *adv* à l'unanimité

unarmed [ʌn'ɑ:md] *adj* (*without a weapon*) non armé(e); (*combat*) sans armes

unattached [ʌnə'tætʃt] *adj* libre, sans attaches; (*part*) non attaché(e), indépendant(e)

unattended [ʌnə'tɛndɪd] *adj* (*car, child, luggage*) sans surveillance

unattractive [ʌnə'træktɪv] *adj* peu attrayant(e); (*character*) peu sympathique

unauthorized [ʌn'ɔ:θəraɪzd] *adj* non autorisé(e), sans autorisation

unavoidable [ʌnə'vɔɪdəbl] *adj* inévitable

unaware [ʌnə'wɛəʳ] *adj*: **to be ~ of** ignorer, être inconscient(e) de; **~s** *adv* à l'improviste, au dépourvu

unbalanced [ʌn'bælənst] *adj* déséquilibré(e); (*report*) peu objectif(-ive)

unbearable [ʌn'bɛərəbl] *adj* insupportable

unbeatable [ʌn'bi:təbl] *adj* imbattable

unbeknown(st) [ʌnbɪ'nəun(st)] *adv*: **~ to me/Peter** à mon insu/l'insu de Peter

unbelievable [ʌnbɪ'li:vəbl] *adj* incroyable

unbend [ʌn'bɛnd] (*irreg*) *vi* se détendre ♦ *vt* (*wire*) redresser, détordre

unbiased [ʌn'baɪəst] *adj* impartial(e)

unborn [ʌn'bɔ:n] *adj* à naître, qui n'est pas encore né(e)

unbreakable [ʌn'breɪkəbl] *adj* incassable

unbroken [ʌn'brəukən] *adj* intact(e); (*fig*) continu(e), ininterrompu(e)

unbutton [ʌn'bʌtn] *vt* déboutonner

uncalled-for [ʌn'kɔ:ldfɔ:ʳ] *adj* déplacé(e), injustifié(e)

uncanny [ʌn'kænɪ] *adj* étrange, troublant(e)

unceremonious [ʌnsɛrɪ'məunɪəs] *adj* (*abrupt, rude*) brusque

uncertain [ʌn'sə:tn] *adj* incertain(e); (*hesitant*) hésitant(e); **in no ~ terms** sans équivoque possible; **~ty** *n* incertitude *f*, doute(s) *m(pl)*

uncivilized [ʌn'sɪvɪlaɪzd] *adj* (*gen*) non civilisé(e); (*fig: behaviour etc*) barbare; (*hour*) indu(e)

uncle ['ʌŋkl] *n* oncle *m*

uncomfortable [ʌn'kʌmfətəbl] *adj* inconfortable, peu confortable; (*uneasy*) mal à l'aise, gêné(e); (*situation*) désagréable

uncommon [ʌn'kɔmən] *adj* rare, singulier(-ère), peu commun(e)

uncompromising [ʌn'kɔmprəmaɪzɪŋ] *adj* intransigeant(e), inflexible

unconcerned [ʌnkən'sə:nd] *adj*: **to be ~ (about)** ne pas s'inquiéter (de)

unconditional [ʌnkən'dɪʃənl] *adj* sans conditions

unconscious [ʌn'kɔnʃəs] *adj* sans connaissance, évanoui(e); (*unaware*): **~ of** inconscient(e) de ♦ *n*: **the ~** l'inconscient *m*; **~ly** *adv* inconsciemment

uncontrollable [ʌnkən'trəuləbl] *adj* indiscipliné(e); (*temper, laughter*) irrépressible

unconventional [ʌnkən'vɛnʃənl] *adj* peu conventionnel(le)

uncouth [ʌn'ku:θ] *adj* grossier(-ère), fruste

uncover [ʌn'kʌvəʳ] *vt* découvrir

undecided [ʌndɪ'saɪdɪd] *adj* indécis(e), irrésolu(e)

under ['ʌndəʳ] *prep* sous; (*less than*) (de) moins de; au-dessous de; (*according to*) selon, en vertu de ♦ *adv* au-dessous; en dessous; **~ there** là-dessous; **~ repair** en (cours de) réparation; **~age** *adj* (*person*) qui n'a pas l'âge réglementaire; **~carriage** *n* (AVIAT) train *m* d'atterrissage; **~charge** *vt* ne pas faire payer assez à; **~coat** *n* (*paint*) couche *f* de fond; **~cover** *adj* secret(-ète), clandestin(e); **~current** *n* courant *or* sentiment sous-jacent; **~cut** (*irreg*) *vt* vendre moins cher que; **~dog** *n* opprimé *m*; **~done** *adj* (CULIN) saignant(e); (*pej*) pas assez cuit(e); **~estimate** *vt* sous-estimer; **~fed** *adj* sous-alimenté(e); **~foot** *adv* sous les pieds; **~go** (*irreg*) *vt* subir; (*treatment*) suivre; **~graduate** *n* étudiant(e) (qui prépare la licence); **~ground** *n* (BRIT: *railway*) métro *m*; (POL) clandestinité *f* ♦ *adj* souterrain(e); (*fig*) clandestin(e) ♦ *adv* dans la clandestinité, clandestinement; **~growth** *n* broussailles *fpl*, sous-bois *m*; **~hand(ed)** *adj* (*fig*: *behaviour, method etc*) en dessous; **~lie** (*irreg*) *vt* être à la base de; **~line** *vt* souligner; **~mine** *vt* saper, miner; **~neath** *adv* (en) dessous ♦ *prep* sous, au-dessous de; **~paid** *adj* sous-payé(e); **~pants** *npl* caleçon *m*, slip *m*; **~pass** (*BRIT*) *n* passage souterrain; (*on motorway*) passage inférieur; **~privileged** *adj* défavorisé(e), économiquement faible; **~rate** *vt* sous-estimer; **~shirt** (*US*) *n* tricot *m* de corps; **~shorts** (*US*) *npl* caleçon *m*, slip *m*; **~side** *n* dessous *m*; **~skirt** (*BRIT*) *n* jupon *m*

understand [ʌndəˈstænd] (*irreg*: *like* **stand**) *vt, vi* comprendre; **I ~ that ...** je me suis laissé dire que ...; je crois comprendre que ...; **~able** *adj* compréhensible; **~ing** *adj* compréhensif(-ive) ♦ *n* compréhension *f*; (*agreement*) accord *m*

understatement [ˈʌndəsteɪtmənt] *n*: **that's an ~** c'est (bien) peu dire, le terme est faible

understood [ʌndəˈstud] *pt, pp of* **understand** ♦ *adj* entendu(e); (*implied*) sous-entendu(e)

understudy [ˈʌndəstʌdɪ] *n* doublure *f*

undertake [ʌndəˈteɪk] (*irreg*) *vt* entreprendre; se charger de; **to ~ to do sth** s'engager à faire qch

undertaker [ˈʌndəteɪkəʳ] *n* entrepreneur *m* des pompes funèbres, croque-mort *m*

undertaking [ˈʌndəteɪkɪŋ] *n* entreprise *f*; (*promise*) promesse *f*

under: ~tone *n*: **in an ~tone** à mi-voix; **~water** *adv* sous l'eau ♦ *adj* sous-marin(e); **~wear** *n* sous-vêtements *mpl*; (*women's only*) dessous *mpl*; **~world** *n* (*of crime*) milieu *m*, pègre *f*; **~write** *n* (*INSURANCE*) assureur *m*

undies [ˈʌndɪz] (*inf*) *npl* dessous *mpl*, lingerie *f*

undiplomatic [ˈʌndɪpləˈmætɪk] *adj* peu diplomatique

undo [ʌnˈduː] (*irreg*) *vt* défaire; **~ing** *n* ruine *f*, perte *f*

undoubted [ʌnˈdautɪd] *adj* indubitable, certain(e); **~ly** *adv* sans aucun doute

undress [ʌnˈdrɛs] *vi* se déshabiller

undue [ʌnˈdjuː] *adj* indu(e), excessif (-ive)

undulating [ˈʌndjuleɪtɪŋ] *adj* ondoyant(e), onduleux(-euse)

unduly [ʌnˈdjuːlɪ] *adv* trop, excessivement

unearth [ʌnˈəːθ] *vt* déterrer; (*fig*) dénicher

unearthly [ʌnˈəːθlɪ] *adj* (*hour*) indu(e), impossible

uneasy [ʌnˈiːzɪ] *adj* mal à l'aise, gêné(e); (*worried*) inquiet(-ète); (*feeling*) désagréable; (*peace, truce*) fragile

uneconomic(al) [ˈʌniːkəˈnɔmɪk(l)] *adj* peu économique

uneducated [ʌnˈɛdjukeɪtɪd] *adj* (*person*) sans instruction

unemployed [ʌnɪmˈplɔɪd] *adj* sans travail, en *or* au chômage ♦ *n*: **the ~** les chômeurs *mpl*; **unemployment** *n* chômage *m*

unending [ʌnˈɛndɪŋ] *adj* interminable, sans fin

unerring [ʌnˈəːrɪŋ] *adj* infaillible, sûr(e)

uneven [ʌnˈiːvn] *adj* inégal(e); (*quality, work*) irrégulier(-ère)

unexpected [ʌnɪksˈpɛktɪd] *adj* inattendu(e), imprévu(e); **~ly** [ʌnɪksˈpɛktɪdlɪ] *adv* (*arrive*) à l'improviste; (*succeed*) contre toute attente

unfailing [ʌnˈfeɪlɪŋ] *adj* inépuisable; (*remedy*) infaillible

unfair [ʌnˈfɛəʳ] *adj*: **~ (to)** injuste (envers)

unfaithful [ʌnˈfeɪθful] *adj* infidèle

unfamiliar [ʌnfəˈmɪlɪəʳ] *adj* étrange, inconnu(e); **to be ~ with** mal connaître

unfashionable [ʌnˈfæʃnəbl] *adj*

(*clothes*) démodé(e); (*place*) peu chic *inv*
unfasten [ʌn'fɑːsn] *vt* défaire; détacher; (*open*) ouvrir
unfavourable [ʌn'feɪvrəbl] (*US* **unfavorable**) *adj* défavorable
unfeeling [ʌn'fiːlɪŋ] *adj* insensible, dur(e)
unfinished [ʌn'fɪnɪʃt] *adj* inachevé(e)
unfit [ʌn'fɪt] *adj* en mauvaise santé; pas en forme; (*incompetent*): ~ **(for)** impropre (à); (*work, service*) inapte (à)
unfold [ʌn'fəuld] *vt* déplier ♦ *vi* se dérouler
unforeseen ['ʌnfɔː'siːn] *adj* imprévu(e)
unforgettable [ʌnfə'getəbl] *adj* inoubliable
unfortunate [ʌn'fɔːtʃənət] *adj* malheureux(-euse); (*event, remark*) malencontreux(-euse); **~ly** *adv* malheureusement
unfounded [ʌn'faundɪd] *adj* sans fondement
unfriendly [ʌn'frɛndlɪ] *adj* inamical(e), peu aimable
ungainly [ʌn'geɪnlɪ] *adj* gauche, dégingandé(e)
ungodly [ʌn'gɔdlɪ] *adj* (*hour*) indu(e)
ungrateful [ʌn'greɪtful] *adj* ingrat(e)
unhappiness [ʌn'hæpɪnɪs] *n* tristesse *f*, peine *f*
unhappy [ʌn'hæpɪ] *adj* triste, malheureux(-euse); ~ **about** *or* **with** (*arrangements etc*) mécontent(e) de, peu satisfait(e) de
unharmed [ʌn'hɑːmd] *adj* indemne, sain(e) et sauf (sauve)
UNHCR *n abbr* (= *United Nations High Commission for refugees*) HCR *m*
unhealthy [ʌn'hɛlθɪ] *adj* malsain(e); (*person*) maladif(-ive)
unheard-of [ʌn'həːdɔv] *adj* inouï(e), sans précédent
unhurt [ʌn'həːt] *adj* indemne
unidentified [ʌnaɪ'dɛntɪfaɪd] *adj* non identifié(e); *see also* **UFO**
uniform ['juːnɪfɔːm] *n* uniforme *m* ♦ *adj* uniforme
uninhabited [ʌnɪn'hæbɪtɪd] *adj* inhabité(e)
unintentional [ʌnɪn'tɛnʃənəl] *adj* involontaire
union ['juːnjən] *n* union *f*; (*also:* **trade** ~) syndicat *m* ♦ *cpd* du syndicat, syndical(e); **U~ Jack** *n drapeau du Royaume-Uni*
unique [juː'niːk] *adj* unique
UNISON ['juːnɪsn] *n grand syndicat des services publics en Grande-Bretagne*
unison ['juːnɪsn] *n*: **in** ~ (*sing*) à l'unisson; (*say*) en chœur
unit ['juːnɪt] *n* unité *f*; (*section: of furniture etc*) élément *m*, bloc *m*; **kitchen** ~ élément de cuisine
unite [juː'naɪt] *vt* unir ♦ *vi* s'unir; **~d** *adj* uni(e); unifié(e); (*effort*) conjugué(e); **U~d Kingdom** *n* Royaume-Uni *m*; **U~d Nations (Organization)** *n* (Organisation *f* des) Nations unies; **U~d States (of America)** *n* États-Unis *mpl*
unit trust (*BRIT*) *n* fonds commun de placement
unity ['juːnɪtɪ] *n* unité *f*
universal [juːnɪ'vəːsl] *adj* universel(le)
universe ['juːnɪvəːs] *n* univers *m*
university [juːnɪ'vəːsɪtɪ] *n* université *f*
unjust [ʌn'dʒʌst] *adj* injuste
unkempt [ʌn'kɛmpt] *adj* négligé(e), débraillé(e); (*hair*) mal peigné(e)
unkind [ʌn'kaɪnd] *adj* peu gentil(le), méchant(e)
unknown [ʌn'nəun] *adj* inconnu(e)
unlawful [ʌn'lɔːful] *adj* illégal(e)
unleaded ['ʌn'lɛdɪd] *adj* (*petrol, fuel*) sans plomb
unleash [ʌn'liːʃ] *vt* (*fig*) déchaîner, déclencher
unless [ʌn'lɛs] *conj*: ~ **he leaves** à moins qu'il ne parte
unlike [ʌn'laɪk] *adj* dissemblable, différent(e) ♦ *prep* contrairement à
unlikely [ʌn'laɪklɪ] *adj* (*happening*) improbable; (*explanation*) invraisemblable
unlimited [ʌn'lɪmɪtɪd] *adj* illimité(e)
unlisted ['ʌn'lɪstɪd] (*US*) *adj* (*TEL*) sur la

liste rouge

unload [ʌn'ləud] *vt* décharger

unlock [ʌn'lɔk] *vt* ouvrir

unlucky [ʌn'lʌkɪ] *adj* (*person*) malchanceux(-euse); (*object, number*) qui porte malheur; **to be ~** (*person*) ne pas avoir de chance

unmarried [ʌn'mærɪd] *adj* célibataire

unmistak(e)able [ʌnmɪs'teɪkəbl] *adj* indubitable; qu'on ne peut pas ne pas reconnaître

unmitigated [ʌn'mɪtɪgeɪtɪd] *adj* non mitigé(e), absolu(e), pur(e)

unnatural [ʌn'nætʃrəl] *adj* non naturel(le); (*habit*) contre nature

unnecessary [ʌn'nɛsəsərɪ] *adj* inutile, superflu(e)

unnoticed [ʌn'nəutɪst] *adj*: **(to go** *or* **pass) ~** (passer) inaperçu(e)

UNO *n abbr* = **United Nations Organization**

unobtainable [ʌnəb'teɪnəbl] *adj* impossible à obtenir

unobtrusive [ʌnəb'tru:sɪv] *adj* discret(-ète)

unofficial [ʌnə'fɪʃl] *adj* (*news*) officieux(-euse); (*strike*) sauvage

unorthodox [ʌn'ɔ:θədɔks] *adj* peu orthodoxe; (REL) hétérodoxe

unpack [ʌn'pæk] *vi* défaire sa valise ♦ *vt* (*suitcase*) défaire; (*belongings*) déballer

unpalatable [ʌn'pælətəbl] *adj* (*meal*) mauvais(e); (*truth*) désagréable (à entendre)

unparalleled [ʌn'pærəlɛld] *adj* incomparable, sans égal

unpleasant [ʌn'plɛznt] *adj* déplaisant(e), désagréable

unplug [ʌn'plʌg] *vt* débrancher

unpopular [ʌn'pɔpjulə^r] *adj* impopulaire

unprecedented [ʌn'prɛsɪdɛntɪd] *adj* sans précédent

unpredictable [ʌnprɪ'dɪktəbl] *adj* imprévisible

unprofessional [ʌnprə'fɛʃənl] *adj*: **~ conduct** manquement *m* aux devoirs de la profession

UNPROFOR *n abbr* (= *United Nations Protection Force*) FORPRONU *f*

unqualified [ʌn'kwɔlɪfaɪd] *adj* (*teacher*) non diplômé(e), sans titres; (*success, disaster*) sans réserve, total(e)

unquestionably [ʌn'kwɛstʃənəblɪ] *adv* incontestablement

unravel [ʌn'rævl] *vt* démêler

unreal [ʌn'rɪəl] *adj* irréel(le); (*extraordinary*) incroyable

unrealistic ['ʌnrɪə'lɪstɪk] *adj* irréaliste; peu réaliste

unreasonable [ʌn'ri:znəbl] *adj* qui n'est pas raisonnable

unrelated [ʌnrɪ'leɪtɪd] *adj* sans rapport; sans lien de parenté

unreliable [ʌnrɪ'laɪəbl] *adj* sur qui (*or* quoi) on ne peut pas compter, peu fiable

unremitting [ʌnrɪ'mɪtɪŋ] *adj* inlassable, infatigable, acharné(e)

unreservedly [ʌnrɪ'zə:vɪdlɪ] *adv* sans réserve

unrest [ʌn'rɛst] *n* agitation *f*, troubles *mpl*

unroll [ʌn'rəul] *vt* dérouler

unruly [ʌn'ru:lɪ] *adj* indiscipliné(e)

unsafe [ʌn'seɪf] *adj* (*in danger*) en danger; (*journey, car*) dangereux(-euse)

unsaid [ʌn'sɛd] *adj*: **to leave sth ~** passer qch sous silence

unsatisfactory ['ʌnsætɪs'fæktərɪ] *adj* peu satisfaisant(e)

unsavoury [ʌn'seɪvərɪ] (US **unsavory**) *adj* (*fig*) peu recommandable

unscathed [ʌn'skeɪðd] *adj* indemne

unscrew [ʌn'skru:] *vt* dévisser

unscrupulous [ʌn'skru:pjuləs] *adj* sans scrupules

unsettled [ʌn'sɛtld] *adj* perturbé(e); instable

unshaven [ʌn'ʃeɪvn] *adj* non *or* mal rasé(e)

unsightly [ʌn'saɪtlɪ] *adj* disgracieux (-euse), laid(e)

unskilled [ʌn'skɪld] *adj*: **~ worker** manœuvre *m*
unspeakable [ʌn'spi:kəbl] *adj* indicible; (*awful*) innommable
unstable [ʌn'steɪbl] *adj* instable
unsteady [ʌn'stɛdɪ] *adj* mal assuré(e), chancelant(e), instable
unstuck [ʌn'stʌk] *adj*: **to come ~** se décoller; (*plan*) tomber à l'eau
unsuccessful [ʌnsək'sɛsful] *adj* (*attempt*) infructueux(-euse), vain(e); (*writer, proposal*) qui n'a pas de succès; **to be ~** (*in attempting sth*) ne pas réussir; ne pas avoir de succès; (*application*) ne pas être retenu(e)
unsuitable [ʌn'su:təbl] *adj* qui ne convient pas, peu approprié(e); inopportun(e)
unsure [ʌn'ʃuəʳ] *adj* pas sûr(e); **to be ~ of o.s.** manquer de confiance en soi
unsuspecting [ʌnsəs'pɛktɪŋ] *adj* qui ne se doute de rien
unsympathetic ['ʌnsɪmpə'θɛtɪk] *adj* (*person*) antipathique; (*attitude*) peu compatissant(e)
untapped [ʌn'tæpt] *adj* (*resources*) inexploité(e)
unthinkable [ʌn'θɪŋkəbl] *adj* impensable, inconcevable
untidy [ʌn'taɪdɪ] *adj* (*room*) en désordre; (*appearance, person*) débraillé(e); (*person: in character*) sans ordre, désordonné
untie [ʌn'taɪ] *vt* (*knot, parcel*) défaire; (*prisoner, dog*) détacher
until [ən'tɪl] *prep* jusqu'à; (*after negative*) avant ♦ *conj* jusqu'à ce que *+sub*; (*in past, after negative*) avant que *+sub*; **~ he comes** jusqu'à ce qu'il vienne, jusqu'à son arrivée; **~ now** jusqu'à présent, jusqu'ici; **~ then** jusque-là
untimely [ʌn'taɪmlɪ] *adj* inopportun(e); (*death*) prématuré(e)
untold [ʌn'təuld] *adj* (*story*) jamais raconté(e); (*wealth*) incalculable; (*joy, suffering*) indescriptible
untoward [ʌntə'wɔ:d] *adj* fâcheux (-euse), malencontreux(-euse)
unused¹ [ʌn'ju:zd] *adj* (*clothes*) neuf (neuve)
unused² [ʌn'ju:st] *adj*: **to be ~ to sth/to doing sth** ne pas avoir l'habitude de qch/de faire qch
unusual [ʌn'ju:ʒuəl] *adj* insolite, exceptionnel(le), rare
unveil [ʌn'veɪl] *vt* dévoiler
unwanted [ʌn'wɔntɪd] *adj* (*child, pregnancy*) non désiré(e); (*clothes etc*) à donner
unwelcome [ʌn'wɛlkəm] *adj* importun(e); (*news*) fâcheux(-euse)
unwell [ʌn'wɛl] *adj* souffrant(e); **to feel ~** ne pas se sentir bien
unwieldy [ʌn'wi:ldɪ] *adj* (*object*) difficile à manier; (*system*) lourd(e)
unwilling [ʌn'wɪlɪŋ] *adj*: **to be ~ to do** ne pas vouloir faire; **~ly** *adv* à contrecœur, contre son gré
unwind [ʌn'waɪnd] (*irreg*) *vt* dérouler ♦ *vi* (*relax*) se détendre
unwise [ʌn'waɪz] *adj* irréfléchi(e), imprudent(e)
unwitting [ʌn'wɪtɪŋ] *adj* involontaire
unworkable [ʌn'wə:kəbl] *adj* (*plan*) impraticable
unworthy [ʌn'wə:ðɪ] *adj* indigne
unwrap [ʌn'ræp] *vt* défaire; ouvrir
unwritten [ʌn'rɪtn] *adj* (*agreement*) tacite

KEYWORD

up [ʌp] *prep*: **he went up the stairs/the hill** il a monté l'escalier/la colline; **the cat was up a tree** le chat était dans un arbre; **they live further up the street** ils habitent plus haut dans la rue
♦ *adv* **1** (*upwards, higher*): **up in the sky/the mountains** (là-haut) dans le ciel/les montagnes; **put it a bit higher up** mettez-le un peu plus haut; **up there** là-haut; **up above** au-dessus
2: **to be up** (*out of bed*) être levé(e); (*prices*) avoir augmenté *or* monté

3: **up to** (*as far as*) jusqu'à; **up to now** jusqu'à présent
4: **to be up to** (*depending on*): **it's up to you** c'est à vous de décider; (*equal to*): **he's not up to it** (*job, task etc*) il n'en est pas capable; (*inf: be doing*): **what is he up to?** qu'est-ce qu'il peut bien faire?
♦ *n*: **ups and downs** hauts et bas *mpl*

up-and-coming [ʌpənd'kʌmɪŋ] *adj* plein(e) d'avenir *or* de promesses
upbringing ['ʌpbrɪŋɪŋ] *n* éducation *f*
update [ʌp'deɪt] *vt* mettre à jour
upgrade [ʌp'greɪd] *vt* (*house*) moderniser; (*job*) revaloriser; (*employee*) promouvoir
upheaval [ʌp'hiːvl] *n* bouleversement *m*; branle-bas *m*
uphill ['ʌp'hɪl] *adj* qui monte; (*fig: task*) difficile, pénible ♦ *adv* (*face, look*) en amont; **to go ~** monter
uphold [ʌp'həuld] (*irreg*) *vt* (*law, decision*) maintenir
upholstery [ʌp'həulstərɪ] *n* rembourrage *m*; (*cover*) tissu *m* d'ameublement; (*of car*) garniture *f*
upkeep ['ʌpkiːp] *n* entretien *m*
upon [ə'pɔn] *prep* sur
upper ['ʌpə^r] *adj* supérieur(e); du dessus ♦ *n* (*of shoe*) empeigne *f*; **~-class** *adj* de la haute société, aristocratique; **~ hand** *n*: **to have the ~ hand** avoir le dessus; **~most** *adj* le (la) plus haut(e); **what was ~most in my mind** ce à quoi je pensais surtout; **~ sixth** *n* terminale *f*
upright ['ʌpraɪt] *adj* droit(e); vertical(e); (*fig*) droit, honnête
uprising ['ʌpraɪzɪŋ] *n* soulèvement *m*, insurrection *f*
uproar ['ʌprɔː^r] *n* tumulte *m*; (*protests*) tempête *f* de protestations
uproot [ʌp'ruːt] *vt* déraciner
upset [*n* 'ʌpsɛt, *vb, adj* ʌp'sɛt] (*irreg: like* **set**) *n* bouleversement *m*; (*stomach ~*) indigestion *f* ♦ *vt* (*glass etc*) renverser; (*plan*) déranger; (*person: offend*) contrarier; (*: grieve*) faire de la peine à; bouleverser ♦ *adj* contrarié(e); peiné(e); (*stomach*) dérangé(e)
upshot ['ʌpʃɔt] *n* résultat *m*
upside-down [ʌpsaɪd'daun] *adv* à l'envers; **to turn ~ ~** mettre sens dessus dessous
upstairs [ʌp'stɛəz] *adv* en haut ♦ *adj* (*room*) du dessus, d'en haut ♦ *n*: **the ~** l'étage *m*
upstart ['ʌpstɑːt] (*pej*) *n* parvenu(e)
upstream [ʌp'striːm] *adv* en amont
uptake ['ʌpteɪk] *n*: **to be quick/slow on the ~** comprendre vite/être lent à comprendre
uptight [ʌp'taɪt] (*inf*) *adj* très tendu(e), crispé(e)
up-to-date ['ʌptə'deɪt] *adj* moderne; (*information*) très récent(e)
upturn ['ʌptəːn] *n* (*in luck*) retournement *m*; (COMM: *in market*) hausse *f*
upward ['ʌpwəd] *adj* ascendant(e); vers le haut; **~(s)** *adv* vers le haut; **~(s) of 200** 200 et plus
urban ['əːbən] *adj* urbain(e); **~ clearway** *n* rue *f* à stationnement einterdit
urbane [əː'beɪn] *adj* urbain(e), courtois(e)
urchin ['əːtʃɪn] *n* polisson *m*
urge [əːdʒ] *n* besoin *m*; envie *f*; forte envie, désir *m* ♦ *vt*: **to ~ sb to do** exhorter qn à faire, pousser qn à faire; recommander vivement à qn de faire
urgency ['əːdʒənsɪ] *n* urgence *f*; (*of tone*) insistance *f*
urgent ['əːdʒənt] *adj* urgent(e); (*tone*) insistant(e), pressant(e)
urinal ['juərɪnl] *n* urinoir *m*
urine ['juərɪn] *n* urine *f*
urn [əːn] *n* urne *f*; (*also:* **tea ~**) fontalne *f* à thé
US *n abbr* = **United States**
us [ʌs] *pron* nous; *see also* **me**
USA *n abbr* = **United States of America**
use [*n* juːs, *vb* juːz] *n* emploi *m*, utilisa-

tion *f*; usage *m*; (*~fulness*) utilité *f* ♦ *vt* se servir de, utiliser, employer; **in ~** en usage; **out of ~** hors d'usage; **to be of ~** servir, être utile; **it's no ~** ça ne sert à rien; **she ~d to do it** elle le faisait (autrefois), elle avait coutume de le faire; **~d to**: **to be ~d to** avoir l'habitude de, être habitué(e) à; **~ up** *vt* finir, épuiser; consommer; **~d** [ju:zd] *adj* (*car*) d'occasion; **~ful** ['ju:sful] *adj* utile; **~fulness** *n* utilité *f*; **~less** ['ju:slɪs] *adj* inutile; (*person*: *hopeless*) nul(le); **~r** ['ju:zəʳ] *n* utilisateur(-trice), usager *m*; **~r-friendly** *adj* (*computer*) convivial(e), facile d'emploi

usher ['ʌʃəʳ] *n* (*at wedding ceremony*) placeur *m*; **~ette** [ʌʃə'rɛt] *n* (*in cinema*) ouvreuse *f*

usual ['ju:ʒuəl] *adj* habituel(le); **as ~** comme d'habitude; **~ly** ['ju:ʒuəlɪ] *adv* d'habitude, d'ordinaire

utensil [ju:'tɛnsl] *n* ustensile *m*

uterus ['ju:tərəs] *n* utérus *m*

utility [ju:'tɪlɪtɪ] *n* utilité *f*; (*also*: **public ~**) service public; **~ room** *n* buanderie *f*

utmost ['ʌtməust] *adj* extrême, le (la) plus grand(e) ♦ *n*: **to do one's ~** faire tout son possible

utter ['ʌtəʳ] *adj* total(e), complet(-ète) ♦ *vt* (*words*) prononcer, proférer; (*sounds*) émettre; **~ance** *n* paroles *fpl*; **~ly** *adv* complètement, totalement

U-turn ['ju:'tə:n] *n* demi-tour *m*

V, v

v. *abbr* = **verse**; **versus**; **volt**; (= *vide*) voir

vacancy ['veɪkənsɪ] *n* (*BRIT*: *job*) poste vacant; (*room*) chambre *f* disponible; **"no vacancies"** "complet"

vacant ['veɪkənt] *adj* (*seat etc*) libre, disponible; (*expression*) distrait(e)

vacate [və'keɪt] *vt* quitter

vacation [və'keɪʃən] *n* vacances *fpl*

vaccinate ['væksɪneɪt] *vt* vacciner

vacuum ['vækjum] *n* vide *m*; **~ cleaner** *n* aspirateur *m*; **~-packed** *adj* emballé(e) sous vide

vagina [və'dʒaɪnə] *n* vagin *m*

vagrant ['veɪgrənt] *n* vagabond(e)

vague [veɪg] *adj* vague, imprécis(e); (*blurred*: *photo, outline*) flou(e); **~ly** *adv* vaguement

vain [veɪn] *adj* (*useless*) vain(e); (*conceited*) vaniteux(-euse); **in ~** en vain

valentine ['væləntaɪn] *n* (*also*: **~ card**) carte *f* de la Saint-Valentin; (*person*) bien-aimé(e) (*le jour de la Saint-Valentin*); **V~'s day** *n* Saint-Valentin *f*

valiant ['vælɪənt] *adj* vaillant(e)

valid ['vælɪd] *adj* valable; (*document*) valable, valide

valley ['vælɪ] *n* vallée *f*

valour ['væləʳ] (*US* **valor**) *n* courage *m*

valuable ['væljuəbl] *adj* (*jewel*) de valeur; (*time, help*) précieux(-euse); **~s** *npl* objets *mpl* de valeur

valuation [vælju'eɪʃən] *n* (*price*) estimation *f*; (*quality*) appréciation *f*

value ['vælju:] *n* valeur *f* ♦ *vt* (*fix price*) évaluer, expertiser; (*appreciate*) apprécier; **~ added tax** (*BRIT*) *n* taxe *f* à la valeur ajoutée; **~d** *adj* (*person*) estimé(e); (*advice*) précieux(-euse)

valve [vælv] *n* (*in machine*) soupape *f*, valve *f*; (*MED*) valve, valvule *f*

van [væn] *n* (*AUT*) camionnette *f*

vandal ['vændl] *n* vandale *m/f*; **~ism** *n* vandalisme *m*; **~ize** *vt* saccager

vanguard ['vængɑ:d] *n* (*fig*): **in the ~ of** à l'avant-garde de

vanilla [və'nɪlə] *n* vanille *f*

vanish ['vænɪʃ] *vi* disparaître

vanity ['vænɪtɪ] *n* vanité *f*

vantage point ['vɑ:ntɪdʒ-] *n* bonne position

vapour ['veɪpəʳ] (*US* **vapor**) *n* vapeur *f*; (*on window*) buée *f*

variable ['vɛərɪəbl] *adj* variable; (*mood*) changeant(e)

variance ['vɛərɪəns] *n*: **to be at ~**

(with) être en désaccord (avec); (*facts*) être en contradiction (avec)
varicose ['værɪkəus] *adj*: **~ veins** varices *fpl*
varied ['vɛərɪd] *adj* varié(e), divers(e)
variety [və'raɪətɪ] *n* variété *f*; (*quantity*) nombre *m*, quantité *f*; **~ show** *n* (spectacle *m* de) variétés *fpl*
various ['vɛərɪəs] *adj* divers(e), différent(e); (*several*) divers, plusieurs
varnish ['vɑːnɪʃ] *n* vernis *m* ♦ *vt* vernir
vary ['vɛərɪ] *vt, vi* varier, changer
vase [vɑːz] *n* vase *m*
Vaseline ® ['væsɪliːn] *n* vaseline *f*
vast [vɑːst] *adj* vaste, immense; (*amount, success*) énorme
VAT [væt] *n abbr* (= *value added tax*) TVA *f*
vat [væt] *n* cuve *f*
vault [vɔːlt] *n* (*of roof*) voûte *f*; (*tomb*) caveau *m*; (*in bank*) salle *f* des coffres; chambre forte ♦ *vt* (*also:* **~ over**) sauter (d'un bond)
vaunted ['vɔːntɪd] *adj*: **much-~** tant vanté(e)
VCR *n abbr* = **video cassette recorder**
VD *n abbr* = **venereal disease**
VDU *n abbr* = **visual display unit**
veal [viːl] *n* veau *m*
veer [vɪəʳ] *vi* tourner; virer
vegan ['viːgən] *n* végétalien(ne)
vegeburger ['vɛdʒɪbəːgəʳ] *n* burger végétarien
vegetable ['vɛdʒtəbl] *n* légume *m* ♦ *adj* végétal(e)
vegetarian [vɛdʒɪ'tɛərɪən] *adj, n* végétarien(ne)
vehement ['viːɪmənt] *adj* violent(e), impétueux(-euse); (*impassioned*) ardent(e)
vehicle ['viːɪkl] *n* véhicule *m*
veil [veɪl] *n* voile *m*
vein [veɪn] *n* veine *f*; (*on leaf*) nervure *f*
velocity [vɪ'lɔsɪtɪ] *n* vitesse *f*
velvet ['vɛlvɪt] *n* velours *m*
vending machine ['vɛndɪŋ-] *n* distributeur *m* automatique
veneer [və'nɪəʳ] *n* (*on furniture*) placage *m*; (*fig*) vernis *m*
venereal [vɪ'nɪərɪəl] *adj*: **~ disease** maladie vénérienne
Venetian blind [vɪ'niːʃən-] *n* store vénitien
vengeance ['vɛndʒəns] *n* vengeance *f*; **with a ~** (*fig*) vraiment, pour de bon
venison ['vɛnɪsn] *n* venaison *f*
venom ['vɛnəm] *n* venin *m*
vent [vɛnt] *n* conduit *m* d'aération; (*in dress, jacket*) fente *f* ♦ *vt* (*fig: one's feelings*) donner libre cours à
ventilator ['vɛntɪleɪtəʳ] *n* ventilateur *m*
ventriloquist [vɛn'trɪləkwɪst] *n* ventriloque *m/f*
venture ['vɛntʃəʳ] *n* entreprise *f* ♦ *vt* risquer, hasarder ♦ *vi* s'aventurer, se risquer
venue ['vɛnjuː] *n* lieu *m*
verb [vəːb] *n* verbe *m*; **~al** *adj* verbal(e); (*translation*) littéral(e)
verbatim [vəː'beɪtɪm] *adj, adv* mot pour mot
verdict ['vəːdɪkt] *n* verdict *m*
verge [vəːdʒ] *n* (BRIT) bord *m*, bas-côté *m*; **"soft ~s"** (BRIT: AUT) "accotement non stabilisé"; **on the ~ of doing** sur le point de faire; **~ on** *vt fus* approcher de
verify ['vɛrɪfaɪ] *vt* vérifier; (*confirm*) confirmer
vermin ['vəːmɪn] *npl* animaux *mpl* nuisibles; (*insects*) vermine *f*
vermouth ['vəːməθ] *n* vermouth *m*
versatile ['vəːsətaɪl] *adj* polyvalent(e)
verse [vəːs] *n* (*poetry*) vers *mpl*; (*stanza*) strophe *f*; (*in Bible*) verset *m*
version ['vəːʃən] *n* version *f*
versus ['vəːsəs] *prep* contre
vertical ['vəːtɪkl] *adj* vertical(e) ♦ *n* verticale *f*
vertigo ['vəːtɪgəu] *n* vertige *m*
verve [vəːv] *n* brio *m*, enthousiasme *m*
very ['vɛrɪ] *adv* très ♦ *adj*: **the ~ book which** le livre même que; **the ~ last** le tout dernier; **at the ~ least** tout au

moins; ~ **much** beaucoup
vessel ['vɛsl] *n* (*ANAT, NAUT*) vaisseau *m*; (*container*) récipient *m*
vest [vɛst] *n* (*BRIT*) tricot *m* de corps; (*US*: *waistcoat*) gilet *m*
vested interest *n* (*COMM*) droits acquis
vet [vɛt] *n abbr* (*BRIT*: *veterinary surgeon*) vétérinaire *m/f* ♦ *vt* examiner soigneusement
veteran ['vɛtərn] *n* vétéran *m*; (*also*: **war** ~) ancien combattant
veterinary surgeon ['vɛtrɪnərɪ-] (*BRIT*), **veterinarian** [vɛtrɪ'nɛərɪən] (*US*) *n* vétérinaire *m/f*
veto ['vi:təu] (*pl* **~es**) *n* veto *m* ♦ *vt* opposer son veto à
vex [vɛks] *vt* fâcher, contrarier; **~ed** *adj* (*question*) controversé(e)
via ['vaɪə] *prep* par, via
viable ['vaɪəbl] *adj* viable
vibrate [vaɪ'breɪt] *vi* vibrer
vicar ['vɪkə^r] *n* pasteur *m* (*de l'Église anglicane*); **~age** *n* presbytère *m*
vicarious [vɪ'kɛərɪəs] *adj* indirect(e)
vice [vaɪs] *n* (*evil*) vice *m*; (*TECH*) étau *m*
vice- [vaɪs] *prefix* vice-
vice squad *n* ≃ brigade mondaine
vice versa ['vaɪsɪ'və:sə] *adv* vice versa
vicinity [vɪ'sɪnɪtɪ] *n* environs *mpl*, alentours *mpl*
vicious ['vɪʃəs] *adj* (*remark*) cruel(le), méchant(e); (*blow*) brutal(e); (*dog*) méchant(e), dangereux(-euse); (*horse*) vicieux(-euse); ~ **circle** *n* cercle vicieux
victim ['vɪktɪm] *n* victime *f*
victor ['vɪktə^r] *n* vainqueur *m*
Victorian [vɪk'tɔ:rɪən] *adj* victorien(ne)
victory ['vɪktərɪ] *n* victoire *f*
video ['vɪdɪəu] *cpd* vidéo *inv* ♦ *n* (~ *film*) vidéo *f*; (*also*: ~ **cassette**) vidéocassette *f*; (*also*: ~ **cassette recorder**) magnétoscope *m*; ~ **tape** *n* bande *f* vidéo *inv*; (*cassette*) vidéocassette *f*; ~ **wall** *n* mur *m* d'images vidéo
vie [vaɪ] *vi*: **to ~ with** rivaliser avec
Vienna [vɪ'ɛnə] *n* Vienne
Vietnam ['vjɛt'næm] *n* Viêt-Nam *m*, Vietnam *m*; **~ese** [vjɛtnə'mi:z] *adj* vietnamien(ne) ♦ *n inv* Vietnamien(ne); (*LING*) vietnamien *m*
view [vju:] *n* vue *f*; (*opinion*) avis *m*, vue ♦ *vt* voir, regarder; (*situation*) considérer; (*house*) visiter; **in full ~ of** sous les yeux de; **in ~ of the weather/the fact that** étant donné le temps/que; **in my ~** à mon avis; **~er** *n* (*TV*) téléspectateur(-trice); **~finder** *n* viseur *m*; **~point** *n* point *m* de vue
vigorous ['vɪgərəs] *adj* vigoureux (-euse)
vile [vaɪl] *adj* (*action*) vil(e); (*smell, food*) abominable; (*temper*) massacrant(e)
villa ['vɪlə] *n* villa *f*
village ['vɪlɪdʒ] *n* village *m*; **~r** *n* villageois(e)
villain ['vɪlən] *n* (*scoundrel*) scélérat *m*; (*BRIT*: *criminal*) bandit *m*; (*in novel etc*) traître *m*
vindicate ['vɪndɪkeɪt] *vt* (*person*) innocenter; (*action*) justifier
vindictive [vɪn'dɪktɪv] *adj* vindicatif (-ive), rancunier(-ère)
vine [vaɪn] *n* vigne *f*; (*climbing plant*) plante grimpante
vinegar ['vɪnɪgə^r] *n* vinaigre *m*
vineyard ['vɪnjɑ:d] *n* vignoble *m*
vintage ['vɪntɪdʒ] *n* (*year*) année *f*, millésime *m*; ~ **car** *n* voiture *f* d'époque; ~ **wine** *n* vin *m* de grand cru
viola [vɪ'əulə] *n* (*MUS*) alto *m*
violate ['vaɪəleɪt] *vt* violer
violence ['vaɪələns] *n* violence *f*
violent ['vaɪələnt] *adj* violent(e)
violet ['vaɪələt] *adj* violet(te) ♦ *n* (*colour*) violet *m*; (*plant*) violette *f*
violin [vaɪə'lɪn] *n* violon *m*; **~ist** [vaɪə'lɪnɪst] *n* violoniste *m/f*
VIP *n abbr* (= *very important person*) V.I.P. *m*
virgin ['və:dʒɪn] *n* vierge *f* ♦ *adj* vierge
Virgo ['və:gəu] *n* la Vierge
virile ['vɪraɪl] *adj* viril(e)
virtually ['və:tjuəlɪ] *adv* (*almost*) pratiquement

virtual reality ['vəːtjuəl-] *n* (COMPUT) réalité virtuelle
virtue ['vəːtjuː] *n* vertu *f*; (*advantage*) mérite *m*, avantage *m*; **by ~ of** en vertu *or* en raison de; **virtuous** *adj* vertueux(-euse)
virus ['vaɪərəs] *n* (COMPUT) virus *m*
visa ['viːzə] *n* visa *m*
visibility [vɪzɪ'bɪlɪtɪ] *n* visibilité *f*
visible ['vɪzəbl] *adj* visible
vision ['vɪʒən] *n* (*sight*) vue *f*, vision *f*; (*foresight, in dream*) vision
visit ['vɪzɪt] *n* visite *f*; (*stay*) séjour *m* ♦ *vt* (*person*) rendre visite à; (*place*) visiter; **~ing hours** *npl* (*in hospital etc*) heures *fpl* de visite; **~or** *n* visiteur(-euse); (*to one's house*) visite *f*, invité(e); **~or centre** *n* hall *m or* centre *m* d'accueil
visor ['vaɪzə^r] *n* visière *f*
vista ['vɪstə] *n* vue *f*
visual ['vɪzjuəl] *adj* visuel(le); **~ aid** *n* support visuel; **~ display unit** *n* console *f* de visualisation, visuel *m*; **~ize** *vt* se représenter, s'imaginer; **~ly-impaired** *adj* malvoyant(e)
vital ['vaɪtl] *adj* vital(e); (*person*) plein(e) d'entrain; **~ly** *adv* (*important*) absolument; **~ statistics** *npl* (*fig*) mensurations *fpl*
vitamin ['vɪtəmɪn] *n* vitamine *f*
vivacious [vɪ'veɪʃəs] *adj* animé(e), qui a de la vivacité
vivid ['vɪvɪd] *adj* (*account*) vivant(e); (*light, imagination*) vif (vive); **~ly** *adv* (*describe*) d'une manière vivante; (*remember*) de façon précise
V-neck ['viːnɛk] *n* décolleté *m* en V
vocabulary [vəu'kæbjulərɪ] *n* vocabulaire *m*
vocal ['vəukl] *adj* vocal(e); (*articulate*) qui sait s'exprimer; **~ cords** *npl* cordes vocales
vocation [vəu'keɪʃən] *n* vocation *f*; **~al** *adj* professionnel(le)
vociferous [və'sɪfərəs] *adj* bruyant(e)
vodka ['vɔdkə] *n* vodka *f*
vogue [vəug] *n*: **in ~** en vogue *f*
voice [vɔɪs] *n* voix *f* ♦ *vt* (*opinion*) exprimer, formuler; **~ mail** *n* (*system*) messagerie *f* vocale; (*device*) boîte *f* vocale
void [vɔɪd] *n* vide *m* ♦ *adj* nul(le); **~ of** vide de, dépourvu(e) de
volatile ['vɔlətaɪl] *adj* volatil(e); (*person*) versatile; (*situation*) explosif(-ive)
volcano [vɔl'keɪnəu] (*pl* **~es**) *n* volcan *m*
volition [və'lɪʃən] *n*: **of one's own ~** de son propre gré
volley ['vɔlɪ] *n* (*of gunfire*) salve *f*; (*of stones etc*) grêle *f*, volée *f*; (*of questions*) multitude *f*, série *f*; (TENNIS *etc*) volée *f*; **~ball** *n* volley(-ball) *m*
volt [vəult] *n* volt *m*; **~age** *n* tension *f*, voltage *m*
volume ['vɔljuːm] *n* volume *m*
voluntarily ['vɔləntrɪlɪ] *adv* volontairement
voluntary ['vɔləntərɪ] *adj* volontaire; (*unpaid*) bénévole
volunteer [vɔlən'tɪə^r] *n* volontaire *m/f* ♦ *vi* (MIL) s'engager comme volontaire; **to ~ to do** se proposer pour faire
vomit ['vɔmɪt] *vt, vi* vomir
vote [vəut] *n* vote *m*, suffrage *m*; (*cast*) voix *f*, vote; (*franchise*) droit *m* de vote ♦ *vt* (*elect*): **to be ~d chairman** *etc* être élu président *etc*; (*propose*): **to ~ that** proposer que ♦ *vi* voter; **~ of thanks** discours *m* de remerciement; **~r** *n* électeur(-trice); **voting** *n* scrutin *m*, vote *m*
voucher ['vautʃə^r] *n* (*for meal, petrol, gift*) bon *m*
vouch for ['vautʃ-] *vt fus* se porter garant de
vow [vau] *n* vœu *m*, serment *m* ♦ *vi* jurer
vowel ['vauəl] *n* voyelle *f*
voyage ['vɔɪɪdʒ] *n* voyage *m* par mer, traversée *f*; (*by spacecraft*) voyage
vulgar ['vʌlgə^r] *adj* vulgaire
vulnerable ['vʌlnərəbl] *adj* vulnérable
vulture ['vʌltʃə^r] *n* vautour *m*

W, w

wad [wɔd] *n* (*of cotton wool, paper*) tampon *m*; (*of banknotes etc*) liasse *f*
waddle ['wɔdl] *vi* se dandiner
wade [weɪd] *vi*: **to ~ through** marcher dans, patauger dans; (*fig*: *book*) s'evertuer à lire
wafer ['weɪfəʳ] *n* (CULIN) gaufrette *f*
waffle ['wɔfl] *n* (CULIN) gaufre *f*; (*inf*) verbiage *m*, remplissage *m* ♦ *vi* parler pour ne rien dire, faire du remplissage
waft [wɔft] *vt* porter ♦ *vi* flotter
wag [wæg] *vt* agiter, remuer ♦ *vi* remuer
wage [weɪdʒ] *n* (*also:* **~s**) salaire *m*, paye *f* ♦ *vt*: **to ~ war** faire la guerre; **~ earner** *n* salarié(e); **~ packet** *n* (enveloppe *f* de) paye *f*
wager ['weɪdʒəʳ] *n* pari *m*
wag(g)on ['wægən] *n* (*horse-drawn*) chariot *m*; (BRIT: RAIL) wagon *m* (de marchandises)
wail [weɪl] *vi* gémir; (*siren*) hurler
waist [weɪst] *n* taille *f*; **~coat** (BRIT) *n* gilet *m*; **~line** *n* (tour *m* de) taille *f*
wait [weɪt] *n* attente *f* ♦ *vi* attendre; **to keep sb ~ing** faire attendre qn; **to ~ for** attendre; **I can't ~ to ...** (*fig*) je meurs d'envie de ...; **~ behind** *vi* rester (à attendre); **~ on** *vt fus* servir; **~er** *n* garçon *m* (de café), serveur *m*; **~ing** *n*: **"no ~ing"** (BRIT: AUT) "stationnement interdit"; **~ing list** *n* liste *f* d'attente; **~ing room** *n* salle *f* d'attente; **~ress** *n* serveuse *f*
waive [weɪv] *vt* renoncer à, abandonner
wake [weɪk] (*pt* **woke, waked**, *pp* **woken, waked**) *vt* (*also:* **~ up**) réveiller ♦ *vi* (*also:* **~ up**) se réveiller ♦ *n* (*for dead person*) veillée *f* mortuaire; (NAUT) sillage *m*
Wales [weɪlz] *n* pays *m* de Galles; **the Prince of ~** le prince de Galles
walk [wɔːk] *n* promenade *f*; (*short*) petit tour; (*gait*) démarche *f*; (*path*) chemin *m*; (*in park etc*) allée *f* ♦ *vi* marcher; (*for pleasure, exercise*) se promener ♦ *vt* (*distance*) faire à pied; (*dog*) promener; **10 minutes' ~ from** à 10 minutes à pied de; **from all ~s of life** de toutes conditions sociales; **~ out** *vi* (*audience*) sortir, quitter la salle; (*workers*) se mettre en grève; **~ out on** (*inf*) *vt fus* quitter, plaquer; **~er** *n* (*person*) marcheur (-euse); **~ie-talkie** *n* talkie-walkie *m*; **~ing** *n* marche *f* à pied; **~ing shoes** *npl* chaussures *fpl* de marche; **~ing stick** *n* canne *f*; **W~man** ® *n* Walkman ® *m*; **~out** *n* (*of workers*) grève-surprise *f*; **~over** (*inf*) *n* victoire *f or* examen *m etc* facile; **~way** *n* promenade *f*
wall [wɔːl] *n* mur *m*; (*of tunnel, cave etc*) paroi *m*; **~ed** *adj* (*city*) fortifié(e); (*garden*) entouré(e) d'un mur, clos(e)
wallet ['wɔlɪt] *n* portefeuille *m*
wallflower ['wɔːlflauəʳ] *n* giroflée *f*; **to be a ~** (*fig*) faire tapisserie
wallow ['wɔləu] *vi* se vautrer
wallpaper ['wɔːlpeɪpəʳ] *n* papier peint ♦ *vt* tapisser
walnut ['wɔːlnʌt] *n* noix *f*; (*tree, wood*) noyer *m*
walrus ['wɔːlrəs] (*pl* **~** *or* **~es**) *n* morse *m*
waltz [wɔːlts] *n* valse *f* ♦ *vi* valser
wand [wɔnd] *n* (*also:* **magic ~**) baguette *f* (magique)
wander ['wɔndəʳ] *vi* (*person*) errer; (*thoughts*) vagabonder, errer ♦ *vt* errer dans
wane [weɪn] *vi* (*moon*) décroître; (*reputation*) décliner
wangle ['wæŋgl] (BRIT: *inf*) *vt* se débrouiller pour avoir; carotter
want [wɔnt] *vt* vouloir; (*need*) avoir besoin de ♦ *n*: **for ~ of** par manque de, faute de; **~s** *npl* (*needs*) besoins *mpl*; **to ~ to do** vouloir faire; **to ~ sb to do** vouloir que qn fasse; **~ed** *adj* (*criminal*)

recherché(e) par la police; **"cook ~ed"** "on recherche un cuisinier"; **~ing** *adj*: **to be found ~ing** ne pas être à la hauteur

war [wɔːʳ] *n* guerre *f*; **to make ~ (on)** faire la guerre (à)

ward [wɔːd] *n* (*in hospital*) salle *f*; (*POL*) canton *m*; (*LAW*: *child*) pupille *m/f*; **~ off** *vt* (*attack, enemy*) repousser, éviter

warden ['wɔːdn] *n* gardien(ne); (*BRIT*: *of institution*) directeur(-trice); (: *also*: **traffic ~**) contractuel(le); (*of youth hostel*) père *m or* mère *f* aubergiste

warder ['wɔːdəʳ] (*BRIT*) *n* gardien *m* de prison

wardrobe ['wɔːdrəub] *n* (*cupboard*) armoire *f*; (*clothes*) garde-robe *f*; (*THEATRE*) costumes *mpl*

warehouse ['wɛəhaus] *n* entrepôt *m*

wares [wɛəz] *npl* marchandises *fpl*

warfare ['wɔːfɛəʳ] *n* guerre *f*

warhead ['wɔːhɛd] *n* (*MIL*) ogive *f*

warily ['wɛərɪlɪ] *adv* avec prudence

warm [wɔːm] *adj* chaud(e); (*thanks, welcome, applause, person*) chaleureux(-euse); **it's ~** il fait chaud; **I'm ~** j'ai chaud; **~ up** *vi* (*person, room*) se réchauffer; (*water*) chauffer; (*athlete*) s'échauffer ♦ *vt* (*food*) (faire) réchauffer, (faire) chauffer; (*engine*) faire chauffer; **~-hearted** *adj* affectueux(-euse); **~ly** *adv* chaudement; chaleureusement; **~th** *n* chaleur *f*

warn [wɔːn] *vt* avertir, prévenir; **to ~ sb (not) to do** conseiller à qn de (ne pas) faire; **~ing** *n* avertissement *m*; (*notice*) avis *m*; (*signal*) avertisseur *m*; **~ing light** *n* avertisseur lumineux; **~ing triangle** *n* (*AUT*) triangle *m* de présignalisation

warp [wɔːp] *vi* (*wood*) travailler, se déformer ♦ *vt* (*fig*: *character*) pervertir

warrant ['wɔrnt] *n* (*guarantee*) garantie *f*; (*LAW*: *to arrest*) mandat *m* d'arrêt; (: *to search*) mandat de perquisition; **~y** *n* garantie *f*

warren ['wɔrən] *n* (*of rabbits*) terrier *m*; (*fig*: *of streets etc*) dédale *m*

warrior ['wɔrɪəʳ] *n* guerrier(-ère)

Warsaw ['wɔːsɔː] *n* Varsovie

warship ['wɔːʃɪp] *n* navire *m* de guerre

wart [wɔːt] *n* verrue *f*

wartime ['wɔːtaɪm] *n*: **in ~** en temps de guerre

wary ['wɛərɪ] *adj* prudent(e)

was [wɔz] *pt of* **be**

wash [wɔʃ] *vt* laver ♦ *vi* se laver; (*sea*): **to ~ over/against sth** inonder/baigner qch ♦ *n* (*clothes*) lessive *f*; (*~ing programme*) lavage *m*; (*of ship*) sillage *m*; **to have a ~** se laver, faire sa toilette; **to give sth a ~** laver qch; **~ away** *vt* (*stain*) enlever au lavage; (*subj*: *river etc*) emporter; **~ off** *vi* partir au lavage; **~ up** *vi* (*BRIT*) faire la vaisselle; (*US*) se débarbouiller; **~able** *adj* lavable; **~basin** (*US* **washbowl**) *n* lavabo *m*; **~cloth** (*US*) *n* gant *m* de toilette; **~er** *n* (*TECH*) rondelle *f*, joint *m*; **~ing** *n* (*dirty*) linge *m*; (*clean*) lessive *f*; **~ing machine** *n* machine *f* à laver; **~ing powder** (*BRIT*) *n* lessive *f* (en poudre); **~ing-up** *n* vaisselle *f*; **~ing-up liquid** *n* produit *m* pour la vaisselle; **~-out** (*inf*) *n* désastre *m*; **~room** (*US*) *n* toilettes *fpl*

wasn't ['wɔznt] = **was not**

wasp [wɔsp] *n* guêpe *f*

wastage ['weɪstɪdʒ] *n* gaspillage *m*; (*in manufacturing, transport etc*) pertes *fpl*, déchets *mpl*; **natural ~** départs naturels

waste [weɪst] *n* gaspillage *m*; (*of time*) perte *f*; (*rubbish*) déchets *mpl*; (*also*: **household ~**) ordures *fpl* ♦ *adj* (*land, ground*: *in city*) à l'abandon; (*leftover*): **~ material** déchets *mpl* ♦ *vt* gaspiller; (*time, opportunity*) perdre; **~s** *npl* (*area*) étendue *f* désertique; **~ away** *vi* dépérir; **~ disposal unit** (*BRIT*) *n* broyeur *m* d'ordures; **~ful** *adj* gaspilleur(-euse); (*process*) peu économique; **~ ground** (*BRIT*) *n* terrain *m* vague; **~paper basket** *n* corbeille *f* à papier

watch [wɔtʃ] *n* montre *f*; (*act of ~ing*)

surveillance *f*; guet *m*; (MIL: *guards*) garde *f*; (NAUT: *guards, spell of duty*) quart *m* ♦ *vt* (*look at*) observer; (: *match, programme, TV*) regarder; (*spy on, guard*) surveiller; (*be careful of*) faire attention à ♦ *vi* regarder; (*keep guard*) monter la garde; **~ out** *vi* faire attention; **~dog** *n* chien *m* de garde; (*fig*) gardien(ne); **~ful** *adj* attentif(-ive), vigilant(e); **~maker** *n* horloger(-ère); **~man** (*irreg*) *n* see **night**; **~strap** *n* bracelet *m* de montre

water ['wɔːtəʳ] *n* eau *f* ♦ *vt* (*plant, garden*) arroser ♦ *vi* (*eyes*) larmoyer; (*mouth*): **it makes my mouth ~** j'en ai l'eau à la bouche; **in British ~s** dans les eaux territoriales britanniques; **~ down** *vt* (*milk*) couper d'eau; (*fig*: *story*) édulcorer; **~colour** (US **watercolor**) *n* aquarelle *f*; **~cress** *n* cresson *m* (de fontaine); **~fall** *n* chute *f* d'eau; **~ heater** *n* chauffe-eau *m*; **~ing can** *n* arrosoir *m*; **~ lily** *n* nénuphar *m*; **~line** *n* (NAUT) ligne *f* de flottaison; **~logged** *adj* (*ground*) détrempé(e); **~ main** *n* canalisation *f* d'eau; **~melon** *n* pastèque *f*; **~proof** *adj* imperméable; **~shed** *n* (GEO) ligne *f* de partage des eaux; (*fig*) moment *m* critique, point décisif; **~-skiing** *n* ski *m* nautique; **~tight** *adj* étanche; **~works** *n* (*building*) station *f* hydraulique; **~y** *adj* (*coffee, soup*) trop faible; (*eyes*) humide, larmoyant(e)

watt [wɔt] *n* watt *m*

wave [weɪv] *n* vague *f*; (*of hand*) geste *m*, signe *m*; (RADIO) onde *f*; (*in hair*) ondulation *f* ♦ *vi* faire signe de la main; (*flag*) flotter au vent; (*grass*) ondoyer ♦ *vt* (*handkerchief*) agiter; (*stick*) brandir; **~length** *n* longueur *f* d'ondes

waver ['weɪvəʳ] *vi* vaciller; (*voice*) trembler; (*person*) hésiter

wavy ['weɪvɪ] *adj* (*hair, surface*) ondulé(e); (*line*) onduleux(-euse)

wax [wæks] *n* cire *f*; (*for skis*) fart *m* ♦ *vt* cirer; (*car*) lustrer; (*skis*) farter ♦ *vi* (*moon*) croître; **~works** *npl* personnages *mpl* de cire ♦ *n* musée *m* de cire

way [weɪ] *n* chemin *m*, voie *f*; (*distance*) distance *f*; (*direction*) chemin, direction *f*; (*manner*) façon *f*, manière *f*; (*habit*) habitude *f*, façon; **which ~? - this ~** par où? - par ici; **on the ~** (*en route*) en route; **to be on one's ~** être en route; **to go out of one's ~ to do** (*fig*) se donner du mal pour faire; **to be in the ~** bloquer le passage; (*fig*) gêner; **to lose one's ~** perdre son chemin; **under ~** en cours; **in a ~** dans un sens; **in some ~s** à certains égards; **no ~!** (*inf*) pas question!; **by the ~ ...** à propos ...; **"~ in"** (BRIT) "entrée"; **"~ out"** (BRIT) "sortie"; **the ~ back** le chemin du retour; **"give ~"** (BRIT: AUT) "cédez le passage"; **~lay** (*irreg*) *vt* attaquer

wayward ['weɪwəd] *adj* capricieux (-euse), entêté(e)

W.C. *n abbr* w.c. *mpl*, waters *mpl*

we [wiː] *pl pron* nous

weak [wiːk] *adj* faible; (*health*) fragile; (*beam etc*) peu solide; **~en** *vi* faiblir, décliner ♦ *vt* affaiblir; **~ling** *n* (*physically*) gringalet *m*; (*morally etc*) faible *m/f*; **~ness** *n* faiblesse *f*; (*fault*) point *m* faible; **to have a ~ness for** avoir un faible pour

wealth [wɛlθ] *n* (*money, resources*) richesse(s) *f(pl)*; (*of details*) profusion *f*; **~y** *adj* riche

wean [wiːn] *vt* sevrer

weapon ['wɛpən] *n* arme *f*

wear [wɛəʳ] (*pt* **wore**, *pp* **worn**) *n* (*use*) usage *m*; (*deterioration through use*) usure *f*; (*clothing*): **sports/babywear** vêtements *mpl* de sport/pour bébés ♦ *vt* (*clothes*) porter; (*put on*) mettre; (*damage*: *through use*) user ♦ *vi* (*last*) faire de l'usage; (*rub etc through*) s'user; **town/evening ~** tenue *f* de ville/soirée; **~ away** *vt* user, ronger ♦ *vi* (*inscription*) s'effacer; **~ down** *vt* user; (*strength, person*) épuiser; **~ off** *vi* disparaître; **~ out** *vt* user; (*person, strength*) épuiser; **~ and tear** *n* usure *f*

weary ['wɪərɪ] *adj* (*tired*) épuisé(e); (*dispirited*) las (lasse), abattu(e) ♦ *vi*: **to ~ of** se lasser de
weasel ['wi:zl] *n* (ZOOL) belette *f*
weather ['wɛðə^r] *n* temps *m* ♦ *vt* (*tempest, crisis*) essuyer, réchapper à, survivre à; **under the ~** (*fig*: *ill*) mal fichu(e); **~-beaten** *adj* (*person*) hâlé(e); (*building*) dégradé(e) par les intempéries; **~cock** *n* girouette *f*; **~ forecast** *n* prévisions *fpl* météorologiques, météo *f*; **~ man** (*irreg*) (*inf*) *n* météorologue *m*; **~ vane** *n* = **weathercock**
weave [wi:v] (*pt* **wove**, *pp* **woven**) *vt* (*cloth*) tisser; (*basket*) tresser; **~r** *n* tisserand(e)
web [wɛb] *n* (*of spider*) toile *f*; (*on foot*) palmure *f*; (*fabric, also fig*) tissu *m*; **the (World Wide) W~** le Web
website ['wɛbsaɪt] *n* (COMPUT) site *m* Web
wed [wɛd] (*pt, pp* **wedded**) *vt* épouser ♦ *vi* se marier
we'd [wi:d] = **we had**; **we would**
wedding [wɛdɪŋ] *n* mariage *m*; **silver/golden ~ (anniversary)** noces *fpl* d'argent/d'or; **~ day** *n* jour *m* du mariage; **~ dress** *n* robe *f* de mariée; **~ ring** *n* alliance *f*
wedge [wɛdʒ] *n* (*of wood etc*) coin *m*, cale *f*; (*of cake*) part *f* ♦ *vt* (*fix*) caler; (*pack tightly*) enfoncer
Wednesday ['wɛdnzdɪ] *n* mercredi *m*
wee [wi:] (SCOTTISH) *adj* (tout(e)) petit(e)
weed [wi:d] *n* mauvaise herbe ♦ *vt* désherber; **~killer** *n* désherbant *m*; **~y** *adj* (*man*) gringalet
week [wi:k] *n* semaine *f*; **a ~ today/on Friday** aujourd'hui/vendredi en huit; **~day** *n* jour *m* de semaine; (COMM) jour ouvrable; **~end** *n* week-end *m*; **~ly** *adv* une fois par semaine, chaque semaine ♦ *adj* hebdomadaire
weep [wi:p] (*pt, pp* **wept**) *vi* (*person*) pleurer; **~ing willow** *n* saule pleureur
weigh [weɪ] *vt, vi* peser; **to ~ anchor** lever l'ancre; **~ down** *vt* (*person, animal*) écraser; (*fig*: *with worry*) accabler; **~ up** *vt* examiner
weight [weɪt] *n* poids *m*; **to lose/put on ~** maigrir/grossir; **~ing** *n* (*allowance*) indemnité *f*, allocation *f*; **~lifter** *n* haltérophile *m*; **~lifting** *n* haltérophilie *f*; **~y** *adj* lourd(e); (*important*) de poids, important(e)
weir [wɪə^r] *n* barrage *m*
weird [wɪəd] *adj* bizarre
welcome ['wɛlkəm] *adj* bienvenu(e) ♦ *n* accueil *m* ♦ *vt* accueillir; (*also*: **bid ~**) souhaiter la bienvenue à; (*be glad of*) se réjouir de; **thank you - you're ~!** merci - de rien *or* il n'y a pas de quoi!
welder [wɛldə^r] *n* soudeur(-euse)
welfare ['wɛlfɛə^r] *n* (*wellbeing*) bien-être *m*; (*social aid*) assistance sociale; **~ state** *n* État-providence *m*
well [wɛl] *n* puits *m* ♦ *adv* bien ♦ *adj*: **to be ~** aller bien ♦ *excl* eh bien!; (*relief also*) bon!; (*resignation*) enfin!; **as ~** aussi, également; **as ~ as** en plus de; **~ done!** bravo!; **get ~ soon** remets-toi vite!; **to do ~** bien réussir; (*business*) prospérer; **~ up** *vi* monter
we'll [wi:l] = **we will**; **we shall**
well: ~-behaved *adj* sage, obéissant(e); **~-being** *n* bien-être *m*; **~-built** *adj* (*person*) bien bâti(e); **~-deserved** *adj* (bien) mérité(e); **~-dressed** *adj* bien habillé(e); **~-heeled** (*inf*) *adj* (*wealthy*) nanti(e)
wellingtons ['wɛlɪŋtənz] *npl* (*also*: **wellington boots**) bottes *fpl* de caoutchouc
well: ~-known *adj* (*person*) bien connu(e); **~-mannered** *adj* bien élevé(e); **~-meaning** *adj* bien intentionné(e); **~-off** *adj* aisé(e); **~-read** *adj* cultivé(e); **~-to-do** *adj* aisé(e); **~-wishers** *npl* amis *mpl* et admirateurs *mpl*; (*friends*) amis *mpl*
Welsh [wɛlʃ] *adj* gallois(e) ♦ *n* (LING) gallois *m*; **the ~** *npl* (*people*) les Gallois *mpl*; **~ Assembly** *n* Parlement *m* gallois; **~man** (*irreg*) *n* Gallois *m*;

~woman (*irreg*) *n* Galloise *f*
went [wɛnt] *pt of* **go**
wept [wɛpt] *pt, pp of* **weep**
were [wəːʳ] *pt of* **be**
we're [wɪəʳ] = **we are**
weren't [wəːnt] = **were not**
west [wɛst] *n* ouest *m* ♦ *adj* ouest *inv*, de *or* à l'ouest ♦ *adv* à *or* vers l'ouest; **the W~** l'Occident *m*, l'Ouest; **the W~ Country** (*BRIT*) ♦ *n* le sud-ouest de l'Angleterre; **~erly** *adj* (*wind*) d'ouest; (*point*) à l'ouest; **~ern** *adj* occidental(e), de *or* à l'ouest ♦ *n* (*CINEMA*) western *m*; **W~ Indian** *adj* antillais(e) ♦ *n* Antillais(e); **W~ Indies** *npl* Antilles *fpl*; **~ward(s)** *adv* vers l'ouest
wet [wɛt] *adj* mouillé(e); (*damp*) humide; (*soaked*) trempé(e); (*rainy*) pluvieux(-euse) ♦ *n* (*BRIT: POL*) modéré *m* du parti conservateur; **to get ~** se mouiller; **"~ paint"** "attention peinture fraîche"; **~ suit** *n* combinaison *f* de plongée
we've [wiːv] = **we have**
whack [wæk] *vt* donner un grand coup à
whale [weɪl] *n* (*ZOOL*) baleine *f*
wharf [wɔːf] (*pl* **wharves**) *n* quai *m*

KEYWORD

what [wɔt] *adj* quel(le); **what size is he?** quelle taille fait-il?; **what colour is it?** de quelle couleur est-ce?; **what books do you need?** quels livres vous faut-il?; **what a mess!** quel désordre!
♦ *pron* **1** (*interrogative*) que, *prep* +quoi; **what are you doing?** que faites-vous?, qu'est-ce que vous faites?; **what is happening?** qu'est-ce qui se passe?, que se passe-t-il?; **what are you talking about?** de quoi parlez-vous?; **what is it called?** comment est-ce que ça s'appelle?; **what about me?** et moi?; **what about doing ...?** et si on faisait ...?
2 (*relative: subject*) ce qui; (*: direct object*) ce que; (*: indirect object*) ce +*prep* +quoi, ce dont; **I saw what you did/was on the table** j'ai vu ce que vous avez fait/ce qui était sur la table; **tell me what you remember** dites-moi ce dont vous vous souvenez
♦ *excl* (*disbelieving*) quoi!, comment!

whatever [wɔt'ɛvəʳ] *adj*: **~ book** quel que soit le livre que (*or* qui) +*sub*; n'importe quel livre ♦ *pron*: **do ~ is necessary** faites (tout) ce qui est nécessaire; **~ happens** quoi qu'il arrive; **no reason ~** pas la moindre raison; **nothing ~** rien du tout
whatsoever [wɔtsəu'ɛvəʳ] *adj* = **whatever**
wheat [wiːt] *n* blé *m*, froment *m*
wheedle ['wiːdl] *vt*: **to ~ sb into doing sth** cajoler *or* enjôler qn pour qu'il fasse qch; **to ~ sth out of sb** obtenir qch de qn par des cajoleries
wheel [wiːl] *n* roue *f*; (*also:* **steering ~**) volant *m*; (*NAUT*) gouvernail *m* ♦ *vt* (*pram etc*) pousser ♦ *vi* (*birds*) tournoyer; (*also:* **~ round**: *person*) virevolter; **~barrow** *n* brouette *f*; **~chair** *n* fauteuil roulant; **~ clamp** *n* (*AUT*) sabot *m* (de Denver)
wheeze [wiːz] *vi* respirer bruyamment

KEYWORD

when [wɛn] *adv* quand; **when did he go?** quand est-ce qu'il est parti?
♦ *conj* **1** (*at, during, after the time that*) quand, lorsque; **she was reading when I came in** elle lisait quand *or* lorsque je suis entré
2 (*on, at which*): **on the day when I met him** le jour où je l'ai rencontré
3 (*whereas*) alors que; **I thought I was wrong when in fact I was right** j'ai cru que j'avais tort alors qu'en fait j'avais raison

whenever [wɛn'ɛvəʳ] *adv* quand donc ♦ *conj* quand; (*every time that*) chaque fois que

where [wɛəʳ] *adv, conj* où; **this is ~** c'est là que; **~abouts** ['wɛərəbauts] *adv* où donc ♦ *n*: **nobody knows his ~abouts** personne ne sait où il se trouve; **~as** [wɛər'æz] *conj* alors que; **~by** *adv* par lequel (*or* laquelle *etc*); **~ver** [wɛər'ɛvəʳ] *adv* où donc ♦ *conj* où que *+sub*; **~withal** ['wɛəwɪðɔːl] *n* moyens *mpl*

whether ['wɛðəʳ] *conj* si; **I don't know ~ to accept or not** je ne sais pas si je dois accepter ou non; **it's doubtful ~** il est peu probable que *+sub*; **~ you go or not** que vous y alliez ou non

KEYWORD

which [wɪtʃ] *adj* (*interrogative*: *direct, indirect*) quel(le); **which picture do you want?** quel tableau voulez-vous?; **which one?** lequel (laquelle)?; **in which case** auquel cas

♦ *pron* **1** (*interrogative*) lequel (laquelle), lesquels (lesquelles) *pl*; **I don't mind which** peu importe lequel; **which (of these) are yours?** lesquels sont à vous?; **tell me which you want** dites-moi lesquels *or* ceux que vous voulez

2 (*relative*: *subject*) qui; (: *object*) que, *prep* +lequel (laquelle); **the apple which you ate/which is on the table** la pomme que vous avez mangée/qui est sur la table; **the chair on which you are sitting** la chaise sur laquelle vous êtes assis; **the book of which you spoke** le livre dont vous avez parlé; **he knew, which is true/I feared** il le savait, ce qui est vrai/ce que je craignais; **after which** après quoi

whichever [wɪtʃ'ɛvəʳ] *adj*: **take ~ book you prefer** prenez le livre que vous préférez, peu importe lequel; **~ book you take** quel que soit le livre que vous preniez

while [waɪl] *n* moment *m* ♦ *conj* pendant que; (*as long as*) tant que; (*whereas*) alors que; bien que *+sub*; **for a ~** pendant quelque temps; **~ away** *vt* (*time*) (faire) passer

whim [wɪm] *n* caprice *m*

whimper ['wɪmpəʳ] *vi* geindre

whimsical ['wɪmzɪkəl] *adj* (*person*) capricieux(-euse); (*look, story*) étrange

whine [waɪn] *vi* gémir, geindre

whip [wɪp] *n* fouet *m*; (*for riding*) cravache *f*; (*POL*: *person*) *chef de file assurant la discipline dans son groupe parlementaire* ♦ *vt* fouetter; (*eggs*) battre; **~ped cream** *n* crème fouettée; **~-round** (*BRIT*) *n* collecte *f*

whirl [wəːl] *vi* tourbillonner; (*dancers*) tournoyer ♦ *vt* faire tourbillonner; faire tournoyer; **~pool** *n* tourbillon *m*; **~wind** *n* tornade *f*

whirr [wəːʳ] *vi* (*motor etc*) ronronner; (: *louder*) vrombir

whisk [wɪsk] *n* (*CULIN*) fouet *m* ♦ *vt* fouetter; (*eggs*) battre; **to ~ sb away** *or* **off** emmener qn rapidement

whiskers ['wɪskəz] *npl* (*of animal*) moustaches *fpl*; (*of man*) favoris *mpl*

whisky ['wɪskɪ] (*IRELAND, US* **whiskey**) *n* whisky *m*

whisper ['wɪspəʳ] *vt, vi* chuchoter

whistle ['wɪsl] *n* (*sound*) sifflement *m*; (*object*) sifflet *m* ♦ *vi* siffler

white [waɪt] *adj* blanc (blanche); (*with fear*) blême ♦ *n* blanc *m*; (*person*) blanc (blanche); **~ coffee** (*BRIT*) *n* café *m* au lait, (café) crème *m*; **~-collar worker** *n* employé(e) de bureau; **~ elephant** *n* (*fig*) objet dispendieux et superflu; **~ lie** *n* pieux mensonge; **W~ Pages** (*US*) *npl* (*TEL*) pages *fpl* blanches; **~ paper** *n* (*POL*) livre blanc; **~wash** *vt* blanchir à la chaux; (*fig*) blanchir ♦ *n* (*paint*) blanc *m* de chaux

whiting ['waɪtɪŋ] *n inv* (*fish*) merlan *m*

Whitsun ['wɪtsn] *n* la Pentecôte

whizz [wɪz] *vi*: **to ~ past** *or* **by** passer à toute vitesse; **~ kid** (*inf*) *n* petit prodige

who [huː] *pron* qui; **~dunit** [huː'dʌnɪt] (*inf*) *n* roman policier

whoever [huːˈɛvəʳ] *pron*: **~ finds it** celui (celle) qui le trouve(, qui que ce soit), quiconque le trouve; **ask ~ you like** demandez à qui vous voulez; **~ he marries** quelle que soit la personne qu'il épouse; **~ told you that?** qui a bien pu vous dire ça?

whole [həul] *adj* (*complete*) entier(-ère), tout(e); (*not broken*) intact(e), complet(-ète) ♦ *n* (*all*): **the ~ of** la totalité de, tout(e) le (la); (*entire unit*) tout *m*; **the ~ of the town** la ville tout entière; **on the ~, as a ~** dans l'ensemble; **~food(s)** *n(pl)* aliments complets; **~hearted** *adj* sans réserve(s); **~meal** (*BRIT*) *adj* (*bread, flour*) complet(-ète); **~sale** *n* (vente *f* en) gros *m* ♦ *adj* (*price*) de gros; (*destruction*) systématique ♦ *adv* en gros; **~saler** *n* grossiste *m/f*; **~some** *adj* sain(e); **~wheat** *adj* = **wholemeal**; **wholly** [ˈhəulɪ] *adv* entièrement, tout à fait

KEYWORD

whom [huːm] *pron* **1** (*interrogative*) qui; **whom did you see?** qui avez-vous vu?; **to whom did you give it?** à qui l'avez-vous donné?

2 (*relative*) que, *prep* +qui; **the man whom I saw/to whom I spoke** l'homme que j'ai vu/à qui j'ai parlé

whooping cough [ˈhuːpɪŋ-] *n* coqueluche *f*

whore [hɔːʳ] (*inf: pej*) *n* putain *f*

KEYWORD

whose [huːz] *adj* **1** (*possessive: interrogative*): **whose book is this?** à qui est ce livre?; **whose pencil have you taken?** à qui est le crayon que vous avez pris?, c'est le crayon de qui que vous avez pris?; **whose daughter are you?** de qui êtes-vous la fille?

2 (*possessive: relative*): **the man whose son you rescued** l'homme dont *or* de qui vous avez sauvé le fils; **the girl whose sister you were speaking to** la fille à la sœur de qui *or* de laquelle vous parliez; **the woman whose car was stolen** la femme dont la voiture a été volée

♦ *pron* à qui; **whose is this?** à qui est ceci?; **I know whose it is** je sais à qui c'est

why [waɪ] *adv* pourquoi ♦ *excl* eh bien!, tiens!; **the reason ~** la raison pour laquelle; **tell me ~** dites-moi pourquoi; **~ not?** pourquoi pas?

wicked [ˈwɪkɪd] *adj* mauvais(e), méchant(e); (*crime*) pervers(e); (*mischievous*) malicieux(-euse)

wicket [ˈwɪkɪt] *n* (*CRICKET*) guichet *m*; terrain *m* (*entre les deux guichets*)

wide [waɪd] *adj* large; (*area, knowledge*) vaste, très étendu(e); (*choice*) grand(e) ♦ *adv*: **to open ~** ouvrir tout grand; **to shoot ~** tirer à côté; **~-awake** *adj* bien éveillé(e); **~ly** *adv* (*differing*) radicalement; (*spaced*) sur une grande étendue; (*believed*) généralement; (*travel*) beaucoup; **~n** *vt* élargir ♦ *vi* s'élargir; **~ open** *adj* grand(e) ouvert(e); **~spread** *adj* (*belief etc*) très répandu(e)

widow [ˈwɪdəu] *n* veuve *f*; **~ed** *adj* veuf (veuve); **~er** *n* veuf *m*

width [wɪdθ] *n* largeur *f*

wield [wiːld] *vt* (*power*) exercer

wife [waɪf] (*pl* **wives**) *n* femme *f*, épouse *f*

wig [wɪg] *n* perruque *f*

wiggle [ˈwɪgl] *vt* agiter, remuer

wild [waɪld] *adj* sauvage; (*sea*) déchaîné(e); (*idea, life*) fou (folle); (*behaviour*) extravagant(e), déchaîné(e); **to make a ~ guess** émettre une hypothèse à tout hasard; **~card** *n* (*COMPUT*) (caractère *m*) joker *m*; **~erness** [ˈwɪldənɪs] *n* désert *m*, région *f* sauvage; **~life** *n* (*animals*) faune *f*; **~ly** *adv* (*behave*) de manière déchaînée; (*applaud*) frénétiquement; (*hit, guess*) au hasard; (*happy*) follement; **~s** *npl* (*re-*

mote area) régions *fpl* sauvages

wilful ['wɪlful] (*US* **willful**) *adj* (*person*) obstiné(e); (*action*) délibéré(e)

KEYWORD

will [wɪl] (*vt: pt, pp* **willed**) *aux vb* **1** (*forming future tense*): **I will finish it tomorrow** je le finirai demain; **I will have finished it by tomorrow** je l'aurai fini d'ici demain; **will you do it? - yes I will/no I won't** le ferez-vous? - oui/non

2 (*in conjectures, predictions*): **he will** *or* **he'll be there by now** il doit être arrivé à l'heure qu'il est; **that will be the postman** ça doit être le facteur

3 (*in commands, requests, offers*): **will you be quiet!** voulez-vous bien vous taire!; **will you help me?** est-ce que vous pouvez m'aider?; **will you have a cup of tea?** voulez-vous une tasse de thé?; **I won't put up with it!** je ne le tolérerai pas!

♦ *vt*: **to will sb to do** souhaiter ardemment que qn fasse; **he willed himself to go on** par un suprême effort de volonté, il continua

♦ *n* volonté *f*; testament *m*

willing ['wɪlɪŋ] *adj* de bonne volonté, serviable; **he's ~ to do it** il est disposé à le faire, il veut bien le faire; **~ly** *adv* volontiers; **~ness** *n* bonne volonté

willow ['wɪləu] *n* saule *m*

willpower ['wɪl'pauəʳ] *n* volonté *f*

willy-nilly ['wɪlɪ'nɪlɪ] *adv* bon gré mal gré

wilt [wɪlt] *vi* dépérir; (*flower*) se faner

win [wɪn] (*pt, pp* **won**) *n* (*in sports etc*) victoire *f* ♦ *vt* gagner; (*prize*) remporter; (*popularity*) acquérir ♦ *vi* gagner; **~ over** *vt* convaincre; **~ round** (*BRIT*) *vt* = **win over**

wince [wɪns] *vi* tressaillir

winch [wɪntʃ] *n* treuil *m*

wind¹ [wɪnd] *n* (*also MED*) vent *m*; (*breath*) souffle *m* ♦ *vt* (*take breath*) couper le souffle à

wind² [waɪnd] (*pt, pp* **wound**) *vt* enrouler; (*wrap*) envelopper; (*clock, toy*) remonter ♦ *vi* (*road, river*) serpenter; **~ up** *vt* (*clock*) remonter; (*debate*) terminer, clôturer

windfall ['wɪndfɔːl] *n* coup *m* de chance

winding ['waɪndɪŋ] *adj* (*road*) sinueux(-euse); (*staircase*) tournant(e)

wind instrument ['wɪnd-] *n* (*MUS*) instrument *m* à vent

windmill ['wɪndmɪl] *n* moulin *m* à vent

window ['wɪndəu] *n* fenêtre *f*; (*in car, train, also*: *~ pane*) vitre *f*; (*in shop etc*) vitrine *f*; **~ box** *n* jardinière *f*; **~ cleaner** *n* (*person*) laveur(-euse) de vitres; **~ ledge** *n* rebord *m* de la fenêtre; **~ pane** *n* vitre *f*, carreau *m*; **~-shopping** *n*: **to go ~-shopping** faire du lèche-vitrines; **~sill** ['wɪndəusɪl] *n* (*inside*) appui *m* de la fenêtre; (*outside*) rebord *m* de la fenêtre

windpipe ['wɪndpaɪp] *n* trachée *f*

wind power ['wɪnd-] *n* énergie éolienne

windscreen ['wɪndskriːn] *n* pare-brise *m inv*; **~ washer** *n* lave-glace *m inv*; **~ wiper** *n* essuie-glace *m inv*

windshield ['wɪndʃiːld] (*US*) *n* = **windscreen**

windswept ['wɪndswɛpt] *adj* balayé(e) par le vent; (*person*) ébouriffé(e)

windy ['wɪndɪ] *adj* venteux(-euse); **it's ~** il y a du vent

wine [waɪn] *n* vin *m*; **~ bar** *n* bar *m* à vin; **~ cellar** *n* cave *f* à vin; **~ glass** *n* verre *m* à vin; **~ list** *n* carte *f* des vins; **~ waiter** *n* sommelier *m*

wing [wɪŋ] *n* aile *f*; **~s** *npl* (*THEATRE*) coulisses *fpl*; **~er** *n* (*SPORT*) ailier *m*

wink [wɪŋk] *n* clin *m* d'œil ♦ *vi* faire un clin d'œil; (*blink*) cligner des yeux

winner ['wɪnəʳ] *n* gagnant(e)

winning ['wɪnɪŋ] *adj* (*team*) gagnant(e); (*goal*) décisif(-ive); **~s** *npl* gains *mpl*

winter ['wɪntəʳ] *n* hiver *m*; **in ~** en hiver; **~ sports** *npl* sports *mpl* d'hiver; **wintry** *adj* hivernal(e)

wipe [waɪp] *n*: **to give sth a ~** donner un coup de torchon/de chiffon/d'éponge à qch ♦ *vt* essuyer; (*erase*: *tape*) effacer; **~ off** *vt* enlever; **~ out** *vt* (*debt*) éteindre, amortir; (*memory*) effacer; (*destroy*) anéantir; **~ up** *vt* essuyer

wire ['waɪəʳ] *n* fil *m* (de fer); (ELEC) fil électrique; (TEL) télégramme *m* ♦ *vt* (*house*) faire l'installation électrique de; (*also*: **~ up**) brancher; (*person*: *send telegram to*) télégraphier à; **~less** (BRIT) *n* poste *m* de radio; **wiring** *n* installation *f* électrique; **wiry** *adj* noueux(-euse), nerveux(-euse); (*hair*) dru(e)

wisdom ['wɪzdəm] *n* sagesse *f*; (*of action*) prudence *f*; **~ tooth** *n* dent *f* de sagesse

wise [waɪz] *adj* sage, prudent(e); (*remark*) judicieux(-euse) ♦ *suffix*: **...wise**: **timewise** *etc* en ce qui concerne le temps *etc*

wish [wɪʃ] *n* (*desire*) désir *m*; (*specific desire*) souhait *m*, vœu *m* ♦ *vt* souhaiter, désirer, vouloir; **best ~es** (*on birthday etc*) meilleurs vœux; **with best ~es** (*in letter*) bien amicalement; **to ~ sb goodbye** dire au revoir à qn; **he ~ed me well** il m'a souhaité bonne chance; **to ~ to do/sb to do** désirer *or* vouloir faire/que qn fasse; **to ~ for** souhaiter; **~ful** *adj*: **it's ~ful thinking** c'est prendre ses désirs pour des réalités

wistful ['wɪstful] *adj* mélancolique

wit [wɪt] *n* (*gen pl*) intelligence *f*, esprit *m*; (*presence of mind*) présence *f* d'esprit; (*wittiness*) esprit; (*person*) homme/femme d'esprit

witch [wɪtʃ] *n* sorcière *f*; **~craft** *n* sorcellerie *f*

KEYWORD

with [wɪð, wɪθ] *prep* **1** (*in the company of*) avec; (*at the home of*) chez; **we stayed with friends** nous avons logé chez des amis; **I'll be with you in a minute** je suis à vous dans un instant

2 (*descriptive*): **a room with a view** une chambre avec vue; **the man with the grey hat/blue eyes** l'homme au chapeau gris/aux yeux bleus

3 (*indicating manner, means, cause*): **with tears in her eyes** les larmes aux yeux; **to walk with a stick** marcher avec une canne; **red with anger** rouge de colère; **to shake with fear** trembler de peur; **to fill sth with water** remplir qch d'eau

4: **I'm with you** (*I understand*) je vous suis; **to be with it** (*inf*: *up-to-date*) être dans le vent

withdraw [wɪθ'drɔː] (*irreg*) *vt* retirer ♦ *vi* se retirer; **~al** *n* retrait *m*; **~al symptoms** *npl* (MED): **to have ~al symptoms** être en état de manque; **~n** *adj* (*person*) renfermé(e)

wither ['wɪðəʳ] *vi* (*plant*) se faner

withhold [wɪθ'həuld] (*irreg*) *vt* (*money*) retenir; **to ~ (from)** (*information*) cacher (à); (*permission*) refuser (à)

within [wɪð'ɪn] *prep* à l'intérieur de ♦ *adv* à l'intérieur; **~ his reach** à sa portée; **~ sight of** en vue de; **~ a kilometre of** à moins d'un kilomètre de; **~ the week** avant la fin de la semaine

without [wɪð'aut] *prep* sans; **~ a coat** sans manteau; **~ speaking** sans parler; **to go ~ sth** se passer de qch

withstand [wɪθ'stænd] (*irreg*) *vt* résister à

witness ['wɪtnɪs] *n* (*person*) témoin *m* ♦ *vt* (*event*) être témoin de; (*document*) attester l'authenticité de; **to bear ~ (to)** (*fig*) attester; **~ box** (US **witness stand**) *n* barre *f* des témoins

witty ['wɪtɪ] *adj* spirituel(le), plein(e) d'esprit

wives [waɪvz] *npl of* **wife**

wizard ['wɪzəd] *n* magicien *m*

wk *abbr* = **week**

wobble ['wɔbl] *vi* trembler; (*chair*)

branler

woe [wəu] *n* malheur *m*

woke [wəuk] *pt of* **wake**; **~n** *pp of* **wake**

wolf [wulf] (*pl* **wolves**) *n* loup *m*

woman ['wumən] (*pl* **women**) *n* femme *f*; **~ doctor** *n* femme *f* médecin; **~ly** *adj* féminin(e)

womb [wu:m] *n* (ANAT) utérus *m*

women ['wɪmɪn] *npl of* **woman**; **~'s lib** (*inf*) *n* MLF *m*; **W~'s (Liberation) Movement** *n* mouvement *m* de libération de la femme

won [wʌn] *pt, pp of* **win**

wonder ['wʌndə[r]] *n* merveille *f*, miracle *m*; (*feeling*) émerveillement *m* ♦ *vi*: **to ~ whether/why** se demander si/pourquoi; **to ~ at** (*marvel*) s'émerveiller de; **to ~ about** songer à; **it's no ~ (that)** il n'est pas étonnant (que +*sub*); **~ful** *adj* merveilleux(-euse)

won't [wəunt] = **will not**

wood [wud] *n* (*timber, forest*) bois *m*; **~ed** *adj* boisé(e); **~en** *adj* en bois; (*fig*) raide; inexpressif(-ive); **~pecker** *n* pic *m* (*oiseau*); **~wind** *n* (MUS): **the ~wind** les bois *mpl*; **~work** *n* menuiserie *f*; **~worm** *n* ver *m* du bois

wool [wul] *n* laine *f*; **to pull the ~ over sb's eyes** (*fig*) en faire accroire à qn; **~len** (US **woolen**) *adj* de *or* en laine; (*industry*) lainier(-ère); **~lens** *npl* (*clothes*) lainages *mpl*; **~ly** (US **wooly**) *adj* laineux(-euse); (*fig*: *ideas*) confus(e)

word [wə:d] *n* mot *m*; (*promise*) parole *f*; (*news*) nouvelles *fpl* ♦ *vt* rédiger, formuler; **in other ~s** en d'autres termes; **to break/keep one's ~** manquer à sa parole/tenir parole; **~ing** *n* termes *mpl*; libellé *m*; **~ processing** *n* traitement *m* de texte; **~ processor** *n* machine *f* de traitement de texte

wore [wɔ:[r]] *pt of* **wear**

work [wə:k] *n* travail *m*; (ART, LITERATURE) œuvre *f* ♦ *vi* travailler; (*mechanism*) marcher, fonctionner; (*plan etc*) marcher; (*medicine*) agir ♦ *vt* (*clay, wood etc*) travailler; (*mine etc*) exploiter; (*machine*) faire marcher *or* fonctionner; (*miracles, wonders etc*) faire; **to be out of ~** être sans emploi; **to ~ loose** se défaire, se desserrer; **~ on** *vt fus* travailler à; (*influence*) (essayer d')influencer; **~ out** *vi* (*plans etc*) marcher ♦ *vt* (*problem*) résoudre; (*plan*) élaborer; **it ~s out at £100** ça fait 100 livres; **~ up** *vt*: **to get ~ed up** se mettre dans tous ses états; **~able** *adj* (*solution*) réalisable; **~aholic** [wə:kə'hɔlɪk] *n* bourreau *m* de travail; **~er** *n* travailleur(-euse), ouvrier(-ère); **~ experience** *n* stage *m*; **~force** *n* main-d'œuvre *f*; **~ing class** *n* classe ouvrière; **~ing-class** *adj* ouvrier(-ère); **~ing order** *n*: **in ~ing order** en état de marche; **~man** (*irreg*) *n* ouvrier *m*; **~manship** (*skill*) *n* métier *m*, habileté *f*; **~s** *n* (BRIT: *factory*) usine *f* ♦ *npl* (*of clock, machine*) mécanisme *m*; **~ sheet** *n* (*for pupil*) fiche *f* d'exercices; (COMPUT) feuille *f* de programmation; **~shop** *n* atelier *m*; **~ station** *n* poste *m* de travail; **~-to-rule** (BRIT) *n* grève *f* du zèle

world [wə:ld] *n* monde *m* ♦ *cpd* (*champion*) du monde; (*power, war*) mondial(e); **to think the ~ of sb** (*fig*) ne jurer que par qn; **~ly** *adj* de ce monde; (*knowledgeable*) qui a l'expérience du monde; **~wide** *adj* universel(le); **W~-Wide Web** *n* Web *m*

worm [wə:m] *n* ver *m*

worn [wɔ:n] *pp of* **wear** ♦ *adj* usé(e); **~-out** *adj* (*object*) complètement usé(e); (*person*) épuisé(e)

worried ['wʌrɪd] *adj* inquiet(-ète)

worry ['wʌrɪ] *n* souci *m* ♦ *vt* inquiéter ♦ *vi* s'inquiéter, se faire du souci

worse [wə:s] *adj* pire, plus mauvais(e) ♦ *adv* plus mal ♦ *n* pire *m*; **a change for the ~** une détérioration; **~n** *vt, vi* empirer; **~ off** *adj* moins à l'aise financièrement; (*fig*): **you'll be ~ off this way** ça ira moins bien de cette façon

worship ['wə:ʃɪp] *n* culte *m* ♦ *vt* (*God*)

rendre un culte à; (*person*) adorer; **Your W~** (*BRIT: to mayor*) Monsieur le maire; (: *to judge*) Monsieur le juge

worst [wə:st] *adj* le (la) pire, le (la) plus mauvais(e) ♦ *adv* le plus mal ♦ *n* pire *m*; **at ~** au pis aller

worth [wə:θ] *n* valeur *f* ♦ *adj*: **to be ~** valoir; **it's ~ it** cela en vaut la peine, ça vaut la peine; **it is ~ one's while (to do)** on gagne (à faire); **~less** *adj* qui ne vaut rien; **~while** *adj* (*activity, cause*) utile, louable

worthy [wə:ðɪ] *adj* (*person*) digne; (*motive*) louable; **~ of** digne de

KEYWORD

would [wud] *aux vb* **1** (*conditional tense*): **if you asked him he would do it** si vous le lui demandiez, il le ferait; **if you had asked him he would have done it** si vous le lui aviez demandé, il l'aurait fait

2 (*in offers, invitations, requests*): **would you like a biscuit?** voulez-vous un biscuit?; **would you close the door please?** voulez-vous fermer la porte, s'il vous plaît?

3 (*in indirect speech*): **I said I would do it** j'ai dit que je le ferais

4 (*emphatic*): **it WOULD have to snow today!** naturellement il neige aujourd'hui! *or* il fallait qu'il neige aujourd'hui!

5 (*insistence*): **she wouldn't do it** elle n'a pas voulu *or* elle a refusé de le faire

6 (*conjecture*): **it would have been midnight** il devait être minuit

7 (*indicating habit*): **he would go there on Mondays** il y allait le lundi

would-be ['wudbi:] (*pej*) *adj* soi-disant

wouldn't ['wudnt] = **would not**

wound[1] [wu:nd] *n* blessure *f* ♦ *vt* blesser

wound[2] [waund] *pt, pp of* **wind**[2]

wove [wəuv] *pt of* **weave**; **~n** *pp of* **weave**

wrap [ræp] *vt* (*also:* **~ up**) envelopper, emballer; (*wind*) enrouler; **~per** *n* (*BRIT: of book*) couverture *f*; (*on chocolate*) emballage *m*, papier *m*; **~ping paper** *n* papier *m* d'emballage; (*for gift*) papier cadeau

wreak [ri:k] *vt*: **to ~ havoc (on)** avoir un effet désastreux (sur)

wreath [ri:θ] (*pl* **~s**) *n* couronne *f*

wreck [rɛk] *n* (*ship*) épave *f*; (*vehicle*) véhicule accidenté; (*pej: person*) loque humaine ♦ *vt* démolir; (*fig*) briser, ruiner; **~age** *n* débris *mpl*; (*of building*) décombres *mpl*; (*of ship*) épave *f*

wren [rɛn] *n* (*ZOOL*) roitelet *m*

wrench [rɛntʃ] *n* (*TECH*) clé *f* (à écrous); (*tug*) violent mouvement de torsion; (*fig*) déchirement *m* ♦ *vt* tirer violemment sur, tordre; **to ~ sth from** arracher qch à *or* de

wrestle ['rɛsl] *vi*: **to ~ (with sb)** lutter (avec qn); **~r** *n* lutteur(-euse); **wrestling** *n* lutte *f*; (*also:* **all-in wrestling**) catch *m*, lutte *f* libre

wretched ['rɛtʃɪd] *adj* misérable; (*inf*) maudit(e)

wriggle ['rɪgl] *vi* (*also:* **~ about**) se tortiller

wring [rɪŋ] (*pt, pp* **wrung**) *vt* tordre; (*wet clothes*) essorer; (*fig*): **to ~ sth out of sb** arracher qch à qn

wrinkle ['rɪŋkl] *n* (*on skin*) ride *f*; (*on paper etc*) pli *m* ♦ *vt* plisser ♦ *vi* se plisser; **~d** *adj* (*skin, face*) ridé(e)

wrist [rɪst] *n* poignet *m*; **~watch** *n* montre-bracelet *f*

writ [rɪt] *n* acte *m* judiciaire

write [raɪt] (*pt* **wrote**, *pp* **written**) *vt, vi* écrire; (*prescription*) rédiger; **~ down** *vt* noter; (*put in writing*) mettre par écrit; **~ off** *vt* (*debt*) passer aux profits et pertes; (*project*) mettre une croix sur; **~ out** *vt* écrire; **~ up** *vt* rédiger; **~-off** *n* perte totale; **~r** *n* auteur *m*, écrivain *m*

writhe [raɪð] *vi* se tordre

writing ['raɪtɪŋ] *n* écriture *f*; (*of author*) œuvres *fpl*; **in ~** par écrit; **~ paper** *n* papier *m* à lettres

wrong [rɔŋ] *adj* (*incorrect*) faux (fausse); (*morally*) mauvais(e); (*wicked*) mal; (*unfair*) injuste ♦ *adv* mal ♦ *n* tort *m* ♦ *vt* faire du tort à, léser; **you are ~ to do it** tu as tort de le faire; **you are ~ about that, you've got it ~** tu te trompes; **what's ~?** qu'est-ce qui ne va pas?; **you've got the ~ number** vous vous êtes trompé de numéro; **to go ~** (*person*) se tromper; (*plan*) mal tourner; (*machine*) tomber en panne; **to be in the ~** avoir tort; **~ful** *adj* injustifié(e); **~ly** *adv* mal, incorrectement; **~ side** *n* (*of material*) envers *m*

wrote [rəut] *pt of* **write**

wrought iron [rɔ:t] *n* fer forgé

wrung [rʌŋ] *pt, pp of* **wring**

wt. *abbr* = **weight**

WWW *n abbr* (= *World Wide Web*): **the ~** le Web

X, x

Xmas ['ɛksməs] *n abbr* = **Christmas**

X-ray ['ɛksreɪ] *n* (*ray*) rayon *m* X; (*photo*) radio(graphie) *f*

xylophone ['zaɪləfəun] *n* xylophone *m*

Y, y

Y2K *abbr* (= *year 2000*) l'an *m* 2000

yacht [jɔt] *n* yacht *m*; voilier *m*; **~ing** *n* yachting *m*, navigation *f* de plaisance; **~sman** (*irreg*) *n* plaisancier *m*

Yank [jæŋk], **Yankee** ['jæŋkɪ] (*pej*) *n* Amerloque *m/f*

yap [jæp] *vi* (*dog*) japper

yard [jɑ:d] *n* (*of house etc*) cour *f*; (*measure*) yard *m* (= *91,4 cm*); **~stick** *n* (*fig*) mesure *f*, critères *mpl*

yarn [jɑ:n] *n* fil *m*; (*tale*) longue histoire

yawn [jɔ:n] *n* bâillement *m* ♦ *vi* bâiller; **~ing** *adj* (*gap*) béant(e)

yd. *abbr* = **yard(s)**

yeah [jɛə] (*inf*) *adv* ouais

year [jɪə[r]] *n* an *m*, année *f*; **to be 8 ~s old** avoir 8 ans; **an eight-~-old child** un enfant de huit ans; **~ly** *adj* annuel(le) ♦ *adv* annuellement

yearn [jə:n] *vi*: **to ~ for sth** aspirer à qch, languir après qch

yeast [ji:st] *n* levure *f*

yell [jɛl] *vi* hurler

yellow ['jɛləu] *adj* jaune; **Y~ Pages ®** (*BRIT*) *npl* (*TEL*) pages *fpl* jaunes

yelp [jɛlp] *vi* japper; glapir

yes [jɛs] *adv* oui; (*answering negative question*) si ♦ *n* oui *m*; **to say/answer ~** dire/répondre oui

yesterday ['jɛstədɪ] *adv* hier ♦ *n* hier *m*; **~ morning/evening** hier matin/soir; **all day ~** toute la journée d'hier

yet [jɛt] *adv* encore; déjà ♦ *conj* pourtant, néanmoins; **it is not finished ~** ce n'est pas encore fini *or* toujours pas fini; **the best ~** le meilleur jusqu'ici *or* jusque-là; **as ~** jusqu'ici, encore

yew [ju:] *n* if *m*

yield [ji:ld] *n* production *f*, rendement *m*; rapport *m* ♦ *vt* produire, rendre, rapporter; (*surrender*) céder ♦ *vi* céder; (*US: AUT*) céder la priorité

YMCA *n abbr* (= *Young Men's Christian Association*) YMCA *m*

yob [jɔb] (*BRIT: inf*) *n* loubar(d) *m*

yog(h)urt ['jəugət] *n* yaourt *m*

yoke [jəuk] *n* joug *m*

yolk [jəuk] *n* jaune *m* (d'œuf)

KEYWORD

you [ju:] *pron* **1** (*subject*) tu; (*polite form*) vous; (*plural*) vous; **you French enjoy your food** vous autres Français, vous aimez bien manger; **you and I will go** toi et moi *or* vous et moi, nous irons

2 (*object: direct, indirect*) te, t' *+vowel*, vous; **I know you** je te *or* vous connais; **I gave it to you** je vous l'ai donné, je te l'ai donné

3 (*stressed*) toi; vous; **I told YOU to do it** c'est à toi *or* vous que j'ai dit de le faire

4 (*after prep, in comparisons*) toi; vous; **it's for you** c'est pour toi *or* vous; **she's younger than you** elle est plus jeune que toi *or* vous
5 (*impersonal: one*) on; **fresh air does you good** l'air frais fait du bien; **you never know** on ne sait jamais

you'd [ju:d] = **you had**; **you would**
you'll [ju:l] = **you will**; **you shall**
young [jʌŋ] *adj* jeune ♦ *npl* (*of animal*) petits *mpl*; (*people*): **the ~** les jeunes, la jeunesse; **~er** [jʌŋgə^r] *adj* (*brother etc*) cadet(te); **~ster** *n* jeune *m* (garçon *m*); (*child*) enfant *m/f*
your [jɔ:^r] *adj* ton (ta), tes *pl*; (*polite form, pl*) votre, vos *pl*; *see also* **my**
you're [juə^r] = **you are**
yours [jɔ:z] *pron* le (la) tien(ne), les tiens (tiennes); (*polite form, pl*) le (la) vôtre, les vôtres; **~ sincerely/faithfully/truly** veuillez agréer l'expression de mes sentiments les meilleurs; *see also* **mine**[1]
yourself [jɔ:'sɛlf] *pron* (*reflexive*) te; (: *polite form*) vous; (*after prep*) toi; vous; (*emphatic*) toi-même; vous-même; *see also* **oneself**; **yourselves** *pl pron* vous; (*emphatic*) vous-mêmes
youth [ju:θ] *n* jeunesse *f*; (*young man: pl ~s*) jeune homme *m*; **~ club** *n* centre *m* de jeunes; **~ful** *adj* jeune; (*enthusiasm*) de jeunesse, juvénile; **~ hostel** *n* auberge *f* de jeunesse
you've [ju:v] = **you have**
YTS *n abbr* (*BRIT: Youth Training Scheme*) ≃ TUC *m*
Yugoslav ['ju:gəusla:v] *adj* yougoslave ♦ *n* Yougoslave *m/f*
Yugoslavia ['ju:gəu'sla:vɪə] *n* Yougoslavie *f*
yuppie ['jʌpɪ] (*inf*) *n* yuppie *m/f*
YWCA *n abbr* (= *Young Women's Christian Association*) YWCA *m*

Z, z

zany ['zeɪnɪ] *adj* farfelu(e), loufoque
zap [zæp] *vt* (*COMPUT*) effacer
zeal [zi:l] *n* zèle *m*, ferveur *f*; empressement *m*
zebra ['zi:brə] *n* zèbre *m*; **~ crossing** (*BRIT*) *n* passage clouté *or* pour piétons
zero ['zɪərəu] *n* zéro *m*
zest [zɛst] *n* entrain *m*, élan *m*; (*of orange*) zeste *m*
zigzag ['zɪgzæg] *n* zigzag *m*
Zimbabwe [zɪm'ba:bwɪ] *n* Zimbabwe *m*
Zimmer frame ['zɪmə-] *n* déambulateur *m*
zinc [zɪŋk] *n* zinc *m*
zip [zɪp] *n* fermeture *f* éclair ® ♦ *vt* (*also:* **~ up**) fermer avec une fermeture éclair ®; **~ code** (*US*) *n* code postal; **~per** (*US*) *n* = **zip**
zit [zɪt] (*inf*) *n* bouton *m*
zodiac ['zəudɪæk] *n* zodiaque *m*
zone [zəun] *n* zone *f*
zoo [zu:] *n* zoo *m*
zoom [zu:m] *vi*: **to ~ past** passer en trombe; **~ lens** *n* zoom *m*
zucchini [zu:'ki:nɪ] (*US*) *n(pl)* courgette(s) *f(pl)*

FRENCH VERB TABLES

Contents

VERBS

▸ How to Form a Regular Verb

Simple tenses are one-word tenses which are formed by adding endings to a verb stem. The endings show the number and person of the subject of the verb. The stem and endings of regular verbs are totally predictable.

There are three regular verb patterns (called conjugations), each identifiable by the ending of the infinitive.

- First conjugation verbs end in **-er** e.g. **aimer** to love (*see* p. 4).

TENSE	STEM	EXAMPLE
Present Imperfect Present Subjunctive	infinitive minus **-er**	**aim-**
Future Conditional	infinitive	**aimer-**

- Second conjugation verbs end in **-ir** e.g. **finir** to finish (*see* p. 7).

TENSE	STEM	EXAMPLE
Present Imperfect Present Subjunctive	infinitive minus **-ir**	**fin-**
Future Conditional	infinitive	**finir-**

- Third conjugation verbs end in **-re** e.g. **attendre** to wait (*see* p. 8).

TENSE	STEM	EXAMPLE
Present Imperfect Present Subjunctive	infinitive minus **-re**	**attend-**
Future Conditional	infinitive minus **-e**	**attendr-**

aimer to love

PRESENT

j'	aime
tu	aim**es**
il	aime
nous	aim**ons**
vous	aim**ez**
ils	aim**ent**

IMPERFECT

j'	aim**ais**
tu	aim**ais**
il	aim**ait**
nous	aim**ions**
vous	aim**iez**
ils	aim**aient**

PERFECT

j'	**ai** aimé
tu	**as** aimé
il	**a** aimé
nous	**avons** aimé
vous	**avez** aimé
ils	**ont** aimé

FUTURE

j'	aimer**ai**
tu	aimer**as**
il	aimer**a**
nous	aimer**ons**
vous	aimer**ez**
ils	aimer**ont**

PRESENT SUBJUNCTIVE

j'	aime
tu	aim**es**
il	aime
nous	aim**ions**
vous	aim**iez**
ils	aim**ent**

CONDITIONAL

j'	aimer**ais**
tu	aimer**ais**
il	aimer**ait**
nous	aimer**ions**
vous	aimer**iez**
ils	aimer**aient**

PRESENT PARTICIPLE

aimant

PAST PARTICIPLE

aimé

IMPERATIVE

aime aimons aimez

▸ First Conjugation Spelling Irregularities

Before certain endings, the stems of some '**-er**' verbs may change slightly.

Verbs ending:	**-cer**
Change:	**c** becomes **ç** before **a** or **o** to retain its soft [s] pronunciation
Tenses affected:	Present, Imperfect, Present Participle
Example:	**lancer** *to throw* → je lan**c**e <u>but</u> nous lan**ç**ons
Verbs ending:	**-ger**
Change:	**g** becomes **ge** before **a** or **o** to retain its soft [ʒ] pronunciation
Tenses affected:	Present, Imperfect, Present Participle
Example:	**manger** *to eat* → nous man**g**ions <u>but</u> ils man**ge**aient
Verbs ending:	**-eler**
Change:	**-l** doubles before **-e**, **-es**, **-ent** and throughout the Future and Conditional tenses
Tenses affected:	Present, Present Subjunctive, Future, Conditional
Example:	**appeler** *to call* → nous appe**l**ons <u>but</u> j'appe**ll**e

• EXCEPTIONS: **geler** *to freeze*, **peler** *to peel* — like **mener** (*see following page*)

VERBS

Verbs ending: **-eter**
Change: **-t** doubles before **-e**, **-es**, **-ent** and throughout the Future and Conditional tenses
Tenses affected: Present, Present Subjunctive, Future, Conditional
Example: **jeter** *to throw* → nous je**t**ons but je je**tt**e

- EXCEPTIONS: **acheter** *to buy*, **haleter** *to pant* } like **mener** (*see below*)

Verbs ending **-yer**
Change: **y** changes to **i** before **-e**, **-es**, **-ent** and throughout the Future and Conditional tenses
Tenses affected: Present, Present Subjunctive, Future, Conditional
Example: **essuyer** *to wipe* → vous essu**y**ez but il essu**i**e

- The change described is optional for verbs ending in **-ayer** e.g. **payer** *to pay*, **essayer** *to try*.

Verbs like: **mener**, **peser**, **lever** etc
Change: **e** changes to **è**, for **-e**, **-es**, and **-ent** endings and throughout the Future and Conditional tenses
Tenses affected: Present, Present Subjunctive, Future, Conditional
Example: **mener** *to lead* → nous m**e**nons but je m**è**ne

Verbs like: **céder**, **régler**, **espérer** etc
Change: **é** changes to **è** for **-e**, **-es**, and **-ent** endings
Tenses affected: Present, Present Subjunctive
Example: **espérer** *to hope* → nous esp**é**rons but j'esp**è**re

PRESENT	
je	fin**is**
tu	fin**is**
il	fin**it**
nous	fin**issons**
vous	fin**issez**
ils	fin**issent**

IMPERFECT	
je	fin**issais**
tu	fin**issais**
il	fin**issait**
nous	fin**issions**
vous	fin**issiez**
ils	fin**issaient**

PERFECT	
j'	**ai** fini
tu	**as** fini
il	**a** fini
nous	**avons** fini
vous	**avez** fini
ils	**ont** fini

FUTURE	
je	finir**ai**
tu	finir**as**
il	finir**a**
nous	finir**ons**
vous	finir**ez**
ils	finir**ont**

PRESENT SUBJUNCTIVE	
je	fin**isse**
tu	fin**isses**
il	fin**isse**
nous	fin**issions**
vous	fin**issiez**
ils	fin**issent**

CONDITIONAL	
je	finir**ais**
tu	finir**ais**
il	finir**ait**
nous	finir**ions**
vous	finir**iez**
ils	finir**aient**

PRESENT PARTICIPLE

finissant

PAST PARTICIPLE

fini

IMPERATIVE

finis finissons finissez

attendre to wait

PRESENT

j' attend**s**
tu attend**s**
il attend
nous attend**ons**
vous attend**ez**
ils attend**ent**

PERFECT

j' **ai** attend**u**
tu **as** attend**u**
il **a** attend**u**
nous **avons** attend**u**
vous **avez** attend**u**
ils **ont** attend**u**

PRESENT SUBJUNCTIVE

j' attend**e**
tu attend**es**
il attend**e**
nous attend**ions**
vous attend**iez**
ils attend**ent**

PRESENT PARTICIPLE

attendant

IMPERFECT

j' attend**ais**
tu attend**ais**
il attend**ait**
nous attend**ions**
vous attend**iez**
ils attend**aient**

FUTURE

j' attendr**ai**
tu attendr**as**
il attendr**a**
nous attendr**ons**
vous attendr**ez**
ils attendr**ont**

CONDITIONAL

j' attendr**ais**
tu attendr**ais**
il attendr**ait**
nous attendr**ions**
vous attendr**iez**
ils attendr**aient**

PAST PARTICIPLE

attendu

IMPERATIVE

attends attendons attendez

▸ Reflexive Verbs

A reflexive verb is one accompanied by a reflexive pronoun, e.g. **se laver** *to wash (oneself)*. The pronouns are:

se laver – PRESENT TENSE

PERSON	SINGULAR	PLURAL
1st	je **me** lave	nous **nous** lavons
2nd	tu **te** laves	vous **vous** lavez
3rd	il/elle **se** lave	ils/elles **se** lavent

Before a vowel, an **h** 'mute' or the pronoun **y**, **me** becomes **m'**, **te** becomes **t'** and **se** becomes **s'**:

Je **m'**appelle ... *I am called ...*
Tu **t'**habilles? *Are you getting dressed?*
On **s'**y intéresse *We 're interested in it*

- In positive commands, **te** changes to **toi**:

Assieds-**toi** *Sit down*
Tais-**toi** *Be quiet*

- In constructions other than the imperative affirmative the pronoun comes before the verb:

Je **me** couche tôt *I go to bed early*
Il ne **s'**est pas rasé *He hasn't shaved*
Comment **vous** appelez-vous? *What is your name?*
Ne **t'**asseois pas là *Don't sit down there*

- In the imperative affirmative, the pronoun follows the verb and is attached to it by a hyphen:

Renseignons-**nous** *Let's find out*
Asseyez-**vous** *Sit down*

- Compound tenses of reflexive verbs are formed with the auxiliary **être**:

se laver – PERFECT TENSE

PERSON	SINGULAR	PLURAL
1st	je me **suis** lavé(e)	nous nous **sommes** lavé(e)s
2nd	tu t'**es** lavé(e)	vous vous **êtes** lavé(e)(s)
3rd	il/elle s'**est** lavé(e)	ils/elles se **sont** lavé(e)s

⚠ NOTE that the past participle (e.g. **lavé**) agrees in number and gender with a direct object which *precedes* the verb (usually, but not always, the reflexive pronoun).

The past participle does not change if the direct object follows the verb:

Elle s'est **lavé** les cheveux *She (has) washed her hair*

▸ The Imperative

The imperative is the form of the verb used to give commands or orders. It can be used politely, as in English 'Shut the door, please'.

The imperative is the same as the present tense **tu**, **vous** and **nous** forms without the subject pronouns:

donner	→	**donne***	→	**donnons**	→	**donnez**
to give		give		let's give		give
finir	→	**finis**	→	**finissons**	→	**finissez**
to finish		finish		let's finish		finish
attendre	→	**attends**	→	**attendons**	→	**attendez**
to wait		wait		let's wait		wait

The final 's' of the present of the first conjugation verbs is dropped, except before* **y *and* **en**.

Position of Object Pronouns

In POSITIVE commands, they follow the verb and are attached to it by hyphens:

Excusez-moi	**Rends-la-lui**	**Expliquez-le-moi**
Excuse me	Give it back to him/her	Explain it to me

In NEGATIVE commands, they precede the verb and are not attached to it:

Ne me dérange pas	**Ne la lui rends pas**
Don't disturb me	Don't give it back to him/her

For reflexive verbs – e.g. **se lever** *to get up* – the object pronoun is the reflexive pronoun:

Lève-toi	**Ne te lève pas**
Get up	Don't get up
Dépêchons-nous	**Ne nous affolons pas**
Let's hurry	Let's not panic

The imperative of irregular verbs is given in the verb tables.

▸ Compound Tenses: Formation

Compound tenses consist of the past participle of the verb together with an auxiliary verb. Most verbs take the auxiliary **avoir**, but some take **être** (*see below*).

Compound tenses are formed in exactly the same way for both regular and irregular verbs, the only difference being that irregular verbs may have an irregular past participle. The past participle of irregular verbs is given for each verb in the verb tables.

▸ The Past Participle

For all compound tenses you need to know how to form the past participle of the verb. For regular verbs this is as follows:

- 1st conjugation: replace the **-er** of the infinitive by **-é**

aimer → **aimé**
to love → loved

- 2nd conjugation: replace the **-ir** of the infinitive by **-i**

finir → **fini**
to finish → finished

- 3rd conjugation: replace the **-re** of the infinitive by **-u**

attendre → **attendu**
to wait → waited

▸ Verbs which take the auxiliary *être*

- Reflexive verbs (*see* pp 9 and 10)
- The following intransitive verbs (i.e. verbs which cannot take a direct object), largely expressing motion or a change of state:

aller *to go*
arriver *to arrive; to happen*

descendre	*to go/come down*
devenir	*to become*
entrer	*to go/come in*
monter	*to go/come up*
mourir	*to die*
naître	*to be born*
partir	*to leave*
passer	*to pass*
rentrer	*to go back/in*
rester	*to stay*
retourner	*to go back*
revenir	*to come back*
sortir	*to go/come out*
tomber	*to fall*
venir	*to come*

- Of these, the following are conjugated with **avoir** when used transitively (i.e. with a direct object):

descendre	*to bring/take down*
entrer	*to bring/take in*
monter	*to bring/take up*
passer	*to pass; to spend*
rentrer	*to bring/take in*
retourner	*to turn over*
sortir	*to bring/take out*

⚠ NOTE that the past participle must show an agreement in number and gender whenever the auxiliary is **être** EXCEPT FOR REFLEXIVE VERBS WHERE THE REFLEXIVE PRONOUN IS THE INDIRECT OBJECT (*see* p 10).

avoir to have

PRESENT

j' **ai**
tu **as**
il **a**
nous **avons**
vous **avez**
ils **ont**

IMPERFECT

j' **avais**
tu **avais**
il **avait**
nous **avions**
vous **aviez**
ils **avaient**

PERFECT

j' **ai eu**
tu **as eu**
il **a eu**
nous **avons eu**
vous **avez eu**
ils **ont eu**

FUTURE

j' **aurai**
tu **auras**
il **aura**
nous **aurons**
vous **aurez**
ils **auront**

PRESENT SUBJUNCTIVE

j' **aie**
tu **aies**
il **ait**
nous **ayons**
vous **ayez**
ils **aient**

CONDITIONAL

j' **aurais**
tu **aurais**
il **aurait**
nous **aurions**
vous **auriez**
ils **auraient**

PRESENT PARTICIPLE

ayant

PAST PARTICIPLE

eu

IMPERATIVE

aie ayons ayez

PRESENT		IMPERFECT	
je	**suis**	*j'*	**étais**
tu	**es**	*tu*	**étais**
il	**est**	*il*	**était**
nous	**sommes**	*nous*	**étions**
vous	**êtes**	*vous*	**étiez**
ils	**sont**	*ils*	**étaient**

PERFECT		FUTURE	
j'	**ai été**	*je*	**serai**
tu	**as été**	*tu*	**seras**
il	**a été**	*il*	**sera**
nous	**avons été**	*nous*	**serons**
vous	**avez été**	*vous*	**serez**
ils	**ont été**	*ils*	**seront**

PRESENT SUBJUNCTIVE		CONDITIONAL	
je	**sois**	*je*	**serais**
tu	**sois**	*tu*	**serais**
il	**soit**	*il*	**serait**
nous	**soyons**	*nous*	**serions**
vous	**soyez**	*vous*	**seriez**
ils	**soient**	*ils*	**seraient**

PRESENT PARTICIPLE	PAST PARTICIPLE
étant	**été**

IMPERATIVE

sois soyons soyez

aller to go

PRESENT

je	**vais**
tu	**vas**
il	**va**
nous	allons
vous	allez
ils	**vont**

IMPERFECT

j'	allais
tu	allais
il	allait
nous	allions
vous	alliez
ils	allaient

PERFECT

je	suis allé
tu	es allé
il	est allé
nous	sommes allés
vous	êtes allé(s)
ils	sont allés

FUTURE

j'	**irai**
tu	**iras**
il	**ira**
nous	**irons**
vous	**irez**
ils	**iront**

PRESENT SUBJUNCTIVE

j'	**aille**
tu	**ailles**
il	**aille**
nous	allions
vous	alliez
ils	**aillent**

CONDITIONAL

j'	**irais**
tu	**irais**
il	**irait**
nous	**irions**
vous	**iriez**
ils	**iraient**

PRESENT PARTICIPLE

allant

PAST PARTICIPLE

allé

IMPERATIVE

va allons allez

falloir to be necessary

PRESENT	IMPERFECT
il **faut**	*il* **fallait**
PERFECT	**FUTURE**
il **a fallu**	*il* **faudra**
PRESENT SUBJUNCTIVE	**CONDITIONAL**
il **faille**	*il* **faudrait**
PRESENT PARTICIPLE	**PAST PARTICIPLE**
not used	**fallu**

IMPERATIVE

not used

pleuvoir to rain

PRESENT	IMPERFECT
il **pleut**	*il* **pleuvait**
PERFECT	**FUTURE**
il **a plu**	*il* **pleuvra**
PRESENT SUBJUNCTIVE	**CONDITIONAL**
il **pleuve**	*il* **pleuvrait**
PRESENT PARTICIPLE	**PAST PARTICIPLE**
pleuvant	**plu**

IMPERATIVE

not used

acquérir to acquire

+ *other verbs ending in -quérir*

PRESENT		IMPERFECT	
j'	**acquiers**	*j'*	**acquérais**
tu	**acquiers**	*tu*	**acquérais**
il	**acquiert**	*il*	**acquérait**
nous	**acquérons**	*nous*	**acquérions**
vous	**acquérez**	*vous*	**acquériez**
ils	**acquièrent**	*ils*	**acquéraient**

PERFECT		FUTURE	
j'	**ai acquis**	*j'*	**acquerrai**
tu	**as acquis**	*tu*	**acquerras**
il	**a acquis**	*il*	**acquerra**
nous	**avons acquis**	*nous*	**acquerrons**
vous	**avez acquis**	*vous*	**acquerrez**
ils	**ont acquis**	*ils*	**acquerront**

PRESENT SUBJUNCTIVE		CONDITIONAL	
j'	**acquière**	*j'*	**acquerrais**
tu	**acquières**	*tu*	**acquerrais**
il	**acquière**	*il*	**acquerrait**
nous	**acquérions**	*nous*	**acquerrions**
vous	**acquériez**	*vous*	**acquerriez**
ils	**acquièrent**	*ils*	**acquerraient**

PRESENT PARTICIPLE

acquérant

PAST PARTICIPLE

acquis

IMPERATIVE

acquiers acquérons acquérez

s'asseoir to sit down

PRESENT

je **m'assieds**
tu **t'assieds**
il **s'assied**
nous **nous asseyons**
vous **vous asseyez**
ils **s'asseyent**

IMPERFECT

je **m'asseyais**
tu **t'asseyais**
il **s'asseyait**
nous **nous asseyions**
vous **vous asseyiez**
ils **s'asseyaient**

PERFECT

je **me suis assis**
tu **t'es assis**
il **s'est assis**
nous **nous sommes assis**
vous **vous êtes assis**
ils **se sont assis**

FUTURE

je **m'assiérai**
tu **t'assiéras**
il **s'assiéra**
nous **nous assiérons**
vous **vous assiérez**
ils **s'assiéront**

PRESENT SUBJUNCTIVE

je **m'asseye**
tu **t'asseyes**
il **s'asseye**
nous **nous asseyions**
vous **vous asseyiez**
ils **s'asseyent**

CONDITIONAL

je **m'assiérais**
tu **t'assiérais**
il **s'assiérait**
nous **nous assiérions**
vous **vous assiériez**
ils **s'assiéraient**

PRESENT PARTICIPLE

s'asseyant

PAST PARTICIPLE

assis

IMPERATIVE

assieds-toi **asseyons-nous** **asseyez-vous**

battre to beat

➕ *other verbs ending in* **-battre**

PRESENT		IMPERFECT	
je	**bats**	*je*	battais
tu	**bats**	*tu*	battais
il	**bat**	*il*	battait
nous	battons	*nous*	battions
vous	battez	*vous*	battiez
ils	battent	*ils*	battaient

PERFECT		FUTURE	
j'	ai battu	*je*	battrai
tu	as battu	*tu*	battras
il	a battu	*il*	battra
nous	avons battu	*nous*	battrons
vous	avez battu	*vous*	battrez
ils	ont battu	*ils*	battront

PRESENT SUBJUNCTIVE		CONDITIONAL	
je	batte	*je*	battrais
tu	battes	*tu*	battrais
il	batte	*il*	battrait
nous	battions	*nous*	battrions
vous	battiez	*vous*	battriez
ils	battent	*ils*	battraient

PRESENT PARTICIPLE	PAST PARTICIPLE
battant	battu

IMPERATIVE

bats battons battez

PRESENT

je bois
tu bois
il boit
nous **buvons**
vous **buvez**
ils **boivent**

IMPERFECT

je **buvais**
tu **buvais**
il **buvait**
nous **buvions**
vous **buviez**
ils **buvaient**

PERFECT

j' **ai bu**
tu **as bu**
il **a bu**
nous **avons bu**
vous **avez bu**
ils **ont bu**

FUTURE

je boirai
tu boiras
il boira
nous boirons
vous boirez
ils boiront

PRESENT SUBJUNCTIVE

je **boive**
tu **boives**
il **boive**
nous **buvions**
vous **buviez**
ils **boivent**

CONDITIONAL

je boirais
tu boirais
il boirait
nous boirions
vous boiriez
ils boiraient

PRESENT PARTICIPLE

buvant

PAST PARTICIPLE

bu

IMPERATIVE

bois **buvons** **buvez**

bouillir to boil

PRESENT

je	**bous**
tu	**bous**
il	**bout**
nous	**bouillons**
vous	**bouillez**
ils	**bouillent**

IMPERFECT

je	**bouillais**
tu	**bouillais**
il	**bouillait**
nous	**bouillions**
vous	**bouilliez**
ils	**bouillaient**

PERFECT

j'	ai bouilli
tu	as bouilli
il	a bouilli
nous	avons bouilli
vous	avez bouilli
ils	ont bouilli

FUTURE

je	bouillirai
tu	bouilliras
il	bouillira
nous	bouillirons
vous	bouillirez
ils	bouilliront

PRESENT SUBJUNCTIVE

je	**bouille**
tu	**bouilles**
il	**bouille**
nous	**bouillions**
vous	**bouilliez**
ils	**bouillent**

CONDITIONAL

je	bouillirais
tu	bouillirais
il	bouillirait
nous	bouillirions
vous	bouilliriez
ils	bouilliraient

PRESENT PARTICIPLE

bouillant

PAST PARTICIPLE

bouilli

IMPERATIVE

bous **bouillons** **bouillez**

connaître to know

➕ *other verbs ending in* **-aître**

PRESENT

je **connais**
tu **connais**
il connaît
nous **connaissons**
vous **connaissez**
ils **connaissent**

IMPERFECT

je **connaissais**
tu **connaissais**
il **connaissait**
nous **connaissions**
vous **connaissiez**
ils **connaissaient**

PERFECT

j' **ai connu**
tu **as connu**
il **a connu**
nous **avons connu**
vous **avez connu**
ils **ont connu**

FUTURE

je connaîtrai
tu connaîtras
il connaîtra
nous connaîtrons
vous connaîtrez
ils connaîtront

PRESENT SUBJUNCTIVE

je **connaisse**
tu **connaisses**
il **connaisse**
nous **connaissions**
vous **connaissiez**
ils **connaissent**

CONDITIONAL

je connaîtrais
tu connaîtrais
il connaîtrait
nous connaîtrions
vous connaîtriez
ils connaîtraient

PRESENT PARTICIPLE

connaissant

PAST PARTICIPLE

connu

IMPERATIVE

connais **connaissons** **connaissez**

coudre to sew

PRESENT

je couds
tu couds
il coud
nous **cousons**
vous **cousez**
ils **cousent**

IMPERFECT

je **cousais**
tu **cousais**
il **cousait**
nous **cousions**
vous **cousiez**
ils **cousaient**

PERFECT

j' **ai cousu**
tu **as cousu**
il **a cousu**
nous **avons cousu**
vous **avez cousu**
ils **ont cousu**

FUTURE

je coudrai
tu coudras
il coudra
nous coudrons
vous coudrez
ils coudront

PRESENT SUBJUNCTIVE

je **couse**
tu **couses**
il **couse**
nous **cousions**
vous **cousiez**
ils **cousent**

CONDITIONAL

je coudrais
tu coudrais
il coudrait
nous coudrions
vous coudriez
ils coudraient

PRESENT PARTICIPLE

cousant

PAST PARTICIPLE

cousu

IMPERATIVE

couds **cousons** **cousez**

courir to run

⊞ *other verbs ending in* **-courir**

PRESENT

je	**cours**
tu	**cours**
il	**court**
nous	**courons**
vous	**courez**
ils	**courent**

IMPERFECT

je	**courais**
tu	**courais**
il	**courait**
nous	**courions**
vous	**couriez**
ils	**couraient**

PERFECT

j'	**ai couru**
tu	**as couru**
il	**a couru**
nous	**avons couru**
vous	**avez couru**
ils	**ont couru**

FUTURE

je	**courrai**
tu	**courras**
il	**courra**
nous	**courrons**
vous	**courrez**
ils	**courront**

PRESENT SUBJUNCTIVE

je	**coure**
tu	**coures**
il	**coure**
nous	**courions**
vous	**couriez**
ils	**courent**

CONDITIONAL

je	**courrais**
tu	**courrais**
il	**courrait**
nous	**courrions**
vous	**courriez**
ils	**courraient**

PRESENT PARTICIPLE

courant

PAST PARTICIPLE

couru

IMPERATIVE

cours **courons** **courez**

26 craindre to fear

+ *other verbs ending in* **-aindre**

PRESENT

je	**crains**
tu	**crains**
il	**craint**
nous	**craignons**
vous	**craignez**
ils	**craignent**

IMPERFECT

je	**craignais**
tu	**craignais**
il	**craignait**
nous	**craignions**
vous	**craigniez**
ils	**craignaient**

PERFECT

j'	**ai craint**
tu	**as craint**
il	**a craint**
nous	**avons craint**
vous	**avez craint**
ils	**ont craint**

FUTURE

je	craindrai
tu	craindras
il	craindra
nous	craindrons
vous	craindrez
ils	craindront

PRESENT SUBJUNCTIVE

je	**craigne**
tu	**craignes**
il	**craigne**
nous	**craignions**
vous	**craigniez**
ils	**craignent**

CONDITIONAL

je	craindrais
tu	craindrais
il	craindrait
nous	craindrions
vous	craindriez
ils	craindraient

PRESENT PARTICIPLE

craignant

PAST PARTICIPLE

craint

IMPERATIVE

crains craignons craignez

croire to believe

PRESENT		IMPERFECT	
je	crois	*je*	**croyais**
tu	crois	*tu*	**croyais**
il	**croit**	*il*	**croyait**
nous	**croyons**	*nous*	**croyions**
vous	**croyez**	*vous*	**croyiez**
ils	croient	*ils*	**croyaient**

PERFECT		FUTURE	
j'	**ai cru**	*je*	croirai
tu	**as cru**	*tu*	croiras
il	**a cru**	*il*	croira
nous	**avons cru**	*nous*	croirons
vous	**avez cru**	*vous*	croirez
ils	**ont cru**	*ils*	croiront

PRESENT SUBJUNCTIVE		CONDITIONAL	
je	croie	*je*	croirais
tu	croies	*tu*	croirais
il	croie	*il*	croirait
nous	**croyions**	*nous*	croirions
vous	**croyiez**	*vous*	croiriez
ils	croient	*ils*	croiraient

PRESENT PARTICIPLE	PAST PARTICIPLE
croyant	**cru**

IMPERATIVE

crois **croyons** **croyez**

croître to grow

+ *other verbs ending in -croître*

PRESENT

je	**croîs**
tu	**croîs**
il	croît
nous	**croissons**
vous	**croissez**
ils	**croissent**

IMPERFECT

je	**croissais**
tu	**croissais**
il	**croissait**
nous	**croissions**
vous	**croissiez**
ils	**croissaient**

PERFECT

j'	**ai crû**
tu	**as crû**
il	**a crû**
nous	**avons crû**
vous	**avez crû**
ils	**ont crû**

FUTURE

je	croîtrai
tu	croîtras
il	croîtra
nous	croîtrons
vous	croîtrez
ils	croîtront

PRESENT SUBJUNCTIVE

je	**croisse**
tu	**croisses**
il	**croisse**
nous	**croissions**
vous	**croissiez**
ils	**croissent**

CONDITIONAL

je	croîtrais
tu	croîtrais
il	croîtrait
nous	croîtrions
vous	croîtriez
ils	croîtraient

PRESENT PARTICIPLE

croissant

PAST PARTICIPLE

crû (NB: **crue, crus, crues**)

IMPERATIVE

croîs **croissons** **croissez**

➕ *other verbs ending in* **-cueillir**

PRESENT		IMPERFECT	
je	**cueille**	*je*	**cueillais**
tu	**cueilles**	*tu*	**cueillais**
il	**cueille**	*il*	**cueillait**
nous	**cueillons**	*nous*	**cueillions**
vous	**cueillez**	*vous*	**cueilliez**
ils	**cueillent**	*ils*	**cueillaient**

PERFECT		FUTURE	
j'	ai cueilli	*je*	**cueillerai**
tu	as cueilli	*tu*	**cueilleras**
il	a cueilli	*il*	**cueillera**
nous	avons cueilli	*nous*	**cueillerons**
vous	avez cueilli	*vous*	**cueillerez**
ils	ont cueilli	*ils*	**cueilleront**

PRESENT SUBJUNCTIVE		CONDITIONAL	
je	**cueille**	*je*	**cueillerais**
tu	**cueilles**	*tu*	**cueillerais**
il	**cueille**	*il*	**cueillerait**
nous	**cueillions**	*nous*	**cueillerions**
vous	**cueilliez**	*vous*	**cueilleriez**
ils	**cueillent**	*ils*	**cueilleraient**

PRESENT PARTICIPLE	PAST PARTICIPLE
cueillant	cueilli

IMPERATIVE

cueille **cueillons** **cueillez**

cuire to cook

other verbs ending in **-uire**

PRESENT		IMPERFECT	
je	cuis	*je*	**cuisais**
tu	cuis	*tu*	**cuisais**
il	**cuit**	*il*	**cuisait**
nous	**cuisons**	*nous*	**cuisions**
vous	**cuisez**	*vous*	**cuisiez**
ils	**cuisent**	*ils*	**cuisaient**

PERFECT		FUTURE	
j'	**ai cuit**	*je*	cuirai
tu	**as cuit**	*tu*	cuiras
il	**a cuit**	*il*	cuira
nous	**avons cuit**	*nous*	cuirons
vous	**avez cuit**	*vous*	cuirez
ils	**ont cuit**	*ils*	cuiront

PRESENT SUBJUNCTIVE		CONDITIONAL	
je	**cuise**	*je*	cuirais
tu	**cuises**	*tu*	cuirais
il	**cuise**	*il*	cuirait
nous	**cuisions**	*nous*	cuirions
vous	**cuisiez**	*vous*	cuiriez
ils	**cuisent**	*ils*	cuiraient

PRESENT PARTICIPLE	PAST PARTICIPLE
cuisant	**cuit**

IMPERATIVE

cuis **cuisons** **cuisez**

devoir to have to; to owe

PRESENT		IMPERFECT	
je	**dois**	*je*	**devais**
tu	**dois**	*tu*	**devais**
il	**doit**	*il*	**devait**
nous	**devons**	*nous*	**devions**
vous	**devez**	*vous*	**deviez**
ils	**doivent**	*ils*	**devaient**

PERFECT		FUTURE	
j'	**ai dû**	*je*	**devrai**
tu	**as dû**	*tu*	**devras**
il	**a dû**	*il*	**devra**
nous	**avons dû**	*nous*	**devrons**
vous	**avez dû**	*vous*	**devrez**
ils	**ont dû**	*ils*	**devront**

PRESENT SUBJUNCTIVE		CONDITIONAL	
je	**doive**	*je*	**devrais**
tu	**doives**	*tu*	**devrais**
il	**doive**	*il*	**devrait**
nous	**devions**	*nous*	**devrions**
vous	**deviez**	*vous*	**devriez**
ils	**doivent**	*ils*	**devraient**

PRESENT PARTICIPLE	PAST PARTICIPLE
devant	**dû** (NB: **due, dus, dues**)

IMPERATIVE

dois devons devez

dire to say

+ *other verbs ending in -dire*

PRESENT

je	dis
tu	dis
il	**dit**
nous	**disons**
vous	**dites**
ils	**disent**

IMPERFECT

je	**disais**
tu	**disais**
il	**disait**
nous	**disions**
vous	**disiez**
ils	**disaient**

PERFECT

j'	**ai dit**
tu	**as dit**
il	**a dit**
nous	**avons dit**
vous	**avez dit**
ils	**ont dit**

FUTURE

je	dirai
tu	diras
il	dira
nous	dirons
vous	direz
ils	diront

PRESENT SUBJUNCTIVE

je	**dise**
tu	**dises**
il	**dise**
nous	**disions**
vous	**disiez**
ils	**disent**

CONDITIONAL

je	dirais
tu	dirais
il	dirait
nous	dirions
vous	diriez
ils	diraient

PRESENT PARTICIPLE

disant

PAST PARTICIPLE

dit

IMPERATIVE

dis **disons** **dites**

+ *s'endormir*

PRESENT		IMPERFECT	
je	**dors**	*je*	**dormais**
tu	**dors**	*tu*	**dormais**
il	**dort**	*il*	**dormait**
nous	**dormons**	*nous*	**dormions**
vous	**dormez**	*vous*	**dormiez**
ils	**dorment**	*ils*	**dormaient**

PERFECT		FUTURE	
j'	ai dormi	*je*	dormirai
tu	as dormi	*tu*	dormiras
il	a dormi	*il*	dormira
nous	avons dormi	*nous*	dormirons
vous	avez dormi	*vous*	dormirez
ils	ont dormi	*ils*	dormiront

PRESENT SUBJUNCTIVE		CONDITIONAL	
je	**dorme**	*je*	dormirais
tu	**dormes**	*tu*	dormirais
il	**dorme**	*il*	dormirait
nous	**dormions**	*nous*	dormirions
vous	**dormiez**	*vous*	dormiriez
ils	**dorment**	*ils*	dormiraient

PRESENT PARTICIPLE	PAST PARTICIPLE
dormant	dormi

IMPERATIVE

dors dormons dormez

écrire to write

➕ *other verbs ending in -crire*

PRESENT

j'	écris
tu	écris
il	**écrit**
nous	**écrivons**
vous	**écrivez**
ils	**écrivent**

IMPERFECT

j'	**écrivais**
tu	**écrivais**
il	**écrivait**
nous	**écrivions**
vous	**écriviez**
ils	**écrivaient**

PERFECT

j'	**ai écrit**
tu	**as écrit**
il	**a écrit**
nous	**avons écrit**
vous	**avez écrit**
ils	**ont écrit**

FUTURE

j'	écrirai
tu	écriras
il	écrira
nous	écrirons
vous	écrirez
ils	écriront

PRESENT SUBJUNCTIVE

j'	**écrive**
tu	**écrives**
il	**écrive**
nous	**écrivions**
vous	**écriviez**
ils	**écrivent**

CONDITIONAL

j'	écrirais
tu	écrirais
il	écrirait
nous	écririons
vous	écririez
ils	écriraient

PRESENT PARTICIPLE

écrivant

PAST PARTICIPLE

écrit

IMPERATIVE

écris **écrivons** **écrivez**

+ *renvoyer*

PRESENT		IMPERFECT	
j'	envoie	*j'*	envoyais
tu	envoies	*tu*	envoyais
il	envoie	*il*	envoyait
nous	envoyons	*nous*	envoyions
vous	envoyez	*vous*	envoyiez
ils	envoient	*ils*	envoyaient

PERFECT		FUTURE	
j'	ai envoyé	*j'*	**enverrai**
tu	as envoyé	*tu*	**enverras**
il	a envoyé	*il*	**enverra**
nous	avons envoyé	*nous*	**enverrons**
vous	avez envoyé	*vous*	**enverrez**
ils	ont envoyé	*ils*	**enverront**

PRESENT SUBJUNCTIVE		CONDITIONAL	
j'	envoie	*j'*	**enverrais**
tu	envoies	*tu*	**enverrais**
il	envoie	*il*	**enverrait**
nous	envoyions	*nous*	**enverrions**
vous	envoyiez	*vous*	**enverriez**
ils	envoient	*ils*	**enverraient**

PRESENT PARTICIPLE	PAST PARTICIPLE
envoyant	envoyé

IMPERATIVE

envoie envoyons envoyez

faire to do; to make

+ *other verbs ending in* **-faire**

PRESENT		IMPERFECT	
je	fais	*je*	**faisais**
tu	fais	*tu*	**faisais**
il	**fait**	*il*	**faisait**
nous	**faisons**	*nous*	**faisions**
vous	**faites**	*vous*	**faisiez**
ils	**font**	*ils*	**faisaient**

PERFECT		FUTURE	
j'	**ai fait**	*je*	**ferai**
tu	**as fait**	*tu*	**feras**
il	**a fait**	*il*	**fera**
nous	**avons fait**	*nous*	**ferons**
vous	**avez fait**	*vous*	**ferez**
ils	**ont fait**	*ils*	**feront**

PRESENT SUBJUNCTIVE		CONDITIONAL	
je	**fasse**	*je*	**ferais**
tu	**fasses**	*tu*	**ferais**
il	**fasse**	*il*	**ferait**
nous	**fassions**	*nous*	**ferions**
vous	**fassiez**	*vous*	**feriez**
ils	**fassent**	*ils*	**feraient**

PRESENT PARTICIPLE	PAST PARTICIPLE
faisant	**fait**

IMPERATIVE

fais **faisons** **faites**

fuir to flee

■ *s'enfuir*

PRESENT

je fuis
tu fuis
il fuit
nous **fuyons**
vous **fuyez**
ils **fuient**

IMPERFECT

je **fuyais**
tu **fuyais**
il **fuyait**
nous **fuyions**
vous **fuyiez**
ils **fuyaient**

PERFECT

j' ai fui
tu as fui
il a fui
nous avons fui
vous avez fui
ils ont fui

FUTURE

je fuirai
tu fuiras
il fuira
nous fuirons
vous fuirez
ils fuiront

PRESENT SUBJUNCTIVE

je **fuie**
tu **fuies**
il **fuie**
nous **fuyions**
vous **fuyiez**
ils **fuient**

CONDITIONAL

je fuirais
tu fuirais
il fuirait
nous fuirions
vous fuiriez
ils fuiraient

PRESENT PARTICIPLE

fuyant

PAST PARTICIPLE

fui

IMPERATIVE

fuis **fuyons** **fuyez**

haïr to hate

PRESENT

je	**hais**
tu	**hais**
il	**hait**
nous	haïssons
vous	haïssez
ils	haïssent

IMPERFECT

je	haïssais
tu	haïssais
il	haïssait
nous	haïssions
vous	haïssiez
ils	haïssaient

PERFECT

j'	ai haï
tu	as haï
il	a haï
nous	avons haï
vous	avez haï
ils	ont haï

FUTURE

je	haïrai
tu	haïras
il	haïra
nous	haïrons
vous	haïrez
ils	haïront

PRESENT SUBJUNCTIVE

je	haïsse
tu	haïsses
il	haïsse
nous	haïssions
vous	haïssiez
ils	haïssent

CONDITIONAL

je	haïrais
tu	haïrais
il	haïrait
nous	haïrions
vous	haïriez
ils	haïraient

PRESENT PARTICIPLE

haïssant

PAST PARTICIPLE

haï

IMPERATIVE

hais haïssons haïssez

■ *other verbs ending in* **-lire**

PRESENT		IMPERFECT	
je	lis	*je*	**lisais**
tu	lis	*tu*	**lisais**
il	**lit**	*il*	**lisait**
nous	**lisons**	*nous*	**lisions**
vous	**lisez**	*vous*	**lisiez**
ils	**lisent**	*ils*	**lisaient**

PERFECT		FUTURE	
j'	**ai lu**	*je*	lirai
tu	**as lu**	*tu*	liras
il	**a lu**	*il*	lira
nous	**avons lu**	*nous*	lirons
vous	**avez lu**	*vous*	lirez
ils	**ont lu**	*ils*	liront

PRESENT SUBJUNCTIVE		CONDITIONAL	
je	**lise**	*je*	lirais
tu	**lises**	*tu*	lirais
il	**lise**	*il*	lirait
nous	**lisions**	*nous*	lirions
vous	**lisiez**	*vous*	liriez
ils	**lisent**	*ils*	liraient

PRESENT PARTICIPLE	PAST PARTICIPLE
lisant	**lu**

IMPERATIVE

lis **lisons** **lisez**

mettre to put

■ *other verbs ending in* **-mettre**

PRESENT		IMPERFECT	
je	**mets**	*je*	mettais
tu	**mets**	*tu*	mettais
il	**met**	*il*	mettait
nous	mettons	*nous*	mettions
vous	mettez	*vous*	mettiez
ils	mettent	*ils*	mettaient

PERFECT		FUTURE	
j'	**ai mis**	*je*	mettrai
tu	**as mis**	*tu*	mettras
il	**a mis**	*il*	mettra
nous	**avons mis**	*nous*	mettrons
vous	**avez mis**	*vous*	mettrez
ils	**ont mis**	*ils*	mettront

PRESENT SUBJUNCTIVE		CONDITIONAL	
je	mette	*je*	mettrais
tu	mettes	*tu*	mettrais
il	mette	*il*	mettrait
nous	mettions	*nous*	mettrions
vous	mettiez	*vous*	mettriez
ils	mettent	*ils*	mettraient

PRESENT PARTICIPLE	PAST PARTICIPLE
mettant	**mis**

IMPERATIVE

mets mettons mettez

PRESENT		IMPERFECT	
je	**meurs**	*je*	**mourais**
tu	**meurs**	*tu*	**mourais**
il	**meurt**	*il*	**mourait**
nous	**mourons**	*nous*	**mourions**
vous	**mourez**	*vous*	**mouriez**
ils	**meurent**	*ils*	**mouraient**

PERFECT		FUTURE	
je	**suis mort**	*je*	**mourrai**
tu	**es mort**	*tu*	**mourras**
il	**est mort**	*il*	**mourra**
nous	**sommes morts**	*nous*	**mourrons**
vous	**êtes mort(s)**	*vous*	**mourrez**
ils	**sont morts**	*ils*	**mourront**

PRESENT SUBJUNCTIVE		CONDITIONAL	
je	**meure**	*je*	**mourrais**
tu	**meures**	*tu*	**mourrais**
il	**meure**	*il*	**mourrait**
nous	**mourions**	*nous*	**mourrions**
vous	**mouriez**	*vous*	**mourriez**
ils	**meurent**	*ils*	**mourraient**

PRESENT PARTICIPLE	PAST PARTICIPLE
mourant	**mort**

IMPERATIVE

meurs **mourons** **mourez**

naître to be born

PRESENT		IMPERFECT	
je	**nais**	*je*	**naissais**
tu	**nais**	*tu*	**naissais**
il	naît	*il*	**naissait**
nous	**naissons**	*nous*	**naissions**
vous	**naissez**	*vous*	**naissiez**
ils	**naissent**	*ils*	**naissaient**

PERFECT		FUTURE	
je	**suis né**	*je*	naîtrai
tu	**es né**	*tu*	naîtras
il	**est né**	*il*	naîtra
nous	**sommes nés**	*nous*	naîtrons
vous	**êtes né(s)**	*vous*	naîtrez
ils	**sont nés**	*ils*	naîtront

PRESENT SUBJUNCTIVE		CONDITIONAL	
je	**naisse**	*je*	naîtrais
tu	**naisses**	*tu*	naîtrais
il	**naisse**	*il*	naîtrait
nous	**naissions**	*nous*	naîtrions
vous	**naissiez**	*vous*	naîtriez
ils	**naissent**	*ils*	naîtraient

PRESENT PARTICIPLE	PAST PARTICIPLE
naissant	**né**

IMPERATIVE

nais **naissons** **naissez**

ouvrir to open

other verbs ending in **-vrir, -frir**

PRESENT		IMPERFECT	
j'	**ouvre**	*j'*	**ouvrais**
tu	**ouvres**	*tu*	**ouvrais**
il	**ouvre**	*il*	**ouvrait**
nous	**ouvrons**	*nous*	**ouvrions**
vous	**ouvrez**	*vous*	**ouvriez**
ils	**ouvrent**	*ils*	**ouvraient**

PERFECT		FUTURE	
j'	**ai ouvert**	*j'*	ouvrirai
tu	**as ouvert**	*tu*	ouvriras
il	**a ouvert**	*il*	ouvrira
nous	**avons ouvert**	*nous*	ouvrirons
vous	**avez ouvert**	*vous*	ouvrirez
ils	**ont ouvert**	*ils*	ouvriront

PRESENT SUBJUNCTIVE		CONDITIONAL	
j'	**ouvre**	*j'*	ouvrirais
tu	**ouvres**	*tu*	ouvrirais
il	**ouvre**	*il*	ouvrirait
nous	**ouvrions**	*nous*	ouvririons
vous	**ouvriez**	*vous*	ouvririez
ils	**ouvrent**	*ils*	ouvriraient

PRESENT PARTICIPLE

ouvrant

PAST PARTICIPLE

ouvert

IMPERATIVE

ouvre ouvrons ouvrez

paraître to appear

➕ *other verbs ending in* **-aître**

PRESENT		IMPERFECT	
je	**parais**	*je*	**paraissais**
tu	**parais**	*tu*	**paraissais**
il	paraît	*il*	**paraissait**
nous	**paraissons**	*nous*	**paraissions**
vous	**paraissez**	*vous*	**paraissiez**
ils	**paraissent**	*ils*	**paraissaient**

PERFECT		FUTURE	
j'	**ai paru**	*je*	paraîtrai
tu	**as paru**	*tu*	paraîtras
il	**a paru**	*il*	paraîtra
nous	**avons paru**	*nous*	paraîtrons
vous	**avez paru**	*vous*	paraîtrez
ils	**ont paru**	*ils*	paraîtront

PRESENT SUBJUNCTIVE		CONDITIONAL	
je	**paraisse**	*je*	paraîtrais
tu	**paraisses**	*tu*	paraîtrais
il	**paraisse**	*il*	paraîtrait
nous	**paraissions**	*nous*	paraîtrions
vous	**paraissiez**	*vous*	paraîtriez
ils	**paraissent**	*ils*	paraîtraient

PRESENT PARTICIPLE	PAST PARTICIPLE
paraissant	**paru**

IMPERATIVE

parais **paraissons** **paraissez**

⊞ *other verbs ending in* **-partir**

PRESENT		IMPERFECT	
je	**pars**	*je*	**partais**
tu	**pars**	*tu*	**partais**
il	**part**	*il*	**partait**
nous	**partons**	*nous*	**partions**
vous	**partez**	*vous*	**partiez**
ils	**partent**	*ils*	**partaient**

PERFECT		FUTURE	
je	suis parti	*je*	partirai
tu	es parti	*tu*	partiras
il	est parti	*il*	partira
nous	sommes partis	*nous*	partirons
vous	êtes parti(s)	*vous*	partirez
ils	sont partis	*ils*	partiront

PRESENT SUBJUNCTIVE		CONDITIONAL	
je	**parte**	*je*	partirais
tu	**partes**	*tu*	partirais
il	**parte**	*il*	partirait
nous	**partions**	*nous*	partirions
vous	**partiez**	*vous*	partiriez
ils	**partent**	*ils*	partiraient

PRESENT PARTICIPLE	PAST PARTICIPLE
partant	parti

IMPERATIVE

pars partons partez

plaire to please

+ *other verbs ending in* **-plaire**

PRESENT		IMPERFECT	
je	plais	*je*	**plaisais**
tu	plais	*tu*	**plaisais**
il	**plaît**	*il*	**plaisait**
nous	**plaisons**	*nous*	**plaisions**
vous	**plaisez**	*vous*	**plaisiez**
ils	**plaisent**	*ils*	**plaisaient**

PERFECT		FUTURE	
j'	**ai plu**	*je*	plairai
tu	**as plu**	*tu*	plairas
il	**a plu**	*il*	plaira
nous	**avons plu**	*nous*	plairons
vous	**avez plu**	*vous*	plairez
ils	**ont plu**	*ils*	plairont

PRESENT SUBJUNCTIVE		CONDITIONAL	
je	**plaise**	*je*	plairais
tu	**plaises**	*tu*	plairais
il	**plaise**	*il*	plairait
nous	**plaisions**	*nous*	plairions
vous	**plaisiez**	*vous*	plairiez
ils	**plaisent**	*ils*	plairaient

PRESENT PARTICIPLE	PAST PARTICIPLE
plaisant	**plu**

IMPERATIVE

plais **plaisons** **plaisez**

PRESENT

je **peux***
tu **peux**
il **peut**
nous **pouvons**
vous **pouvez**
ils **peuvent**

IMPERFECT

je **pouvais**
tu **pouvais**
il **pouvait**
nous **pouvions**
vous **pouviez**
ils **pouvaient**

PERFECT

j' **ai pu**
tu **as pu**
il **a pu**
nous **avons pu**
vous **avez pu**
ils **ont pu**

FUTURE

je **pourrai**
tu **pourras**
il **pourra**
nous **pourrons**
vous **pourrez**
ils **pourront**

PRESENT SUBJUNCTIVE

je **puisse**
tu **puisses**
il **puisse**
nous **puissions**
vous **puissiez**
ils **puissent**

CONDITIONAL

je **pourrais**
tu **pourrais**
il **pourrait**
nous **pourrions**
vous **pourriez**
ils **pourraient**

PRESENT PARTICIPLE

pouvant

PAST PARTICIPLE

pu

IMPERATIVE

not used

* In questions: **puis-*je*?**

prendre to take

⊞ *other verbs ending in* **-prendre**

PRESENT

je prends
tu prends
il prend
nous **prenons**
vous **prenez**
ils **prennent**

IMPERFECT

je **prenais**
tu **prenais**
il **prenait**
nous **prenions**
vous **preniez**
ils **prenaient**

PERFECT

j' **ai pris**
tu **as pris**
il **a pris**
nous **avons pris**
vous **avez pris**
ils **ont pris**

FUTURE

je prendrai
tu prendras
il prendra
nous prendrons
vous prendrez
ils prendront

PRESENT SUBJUNCTIVE

je **prenne**
tu **prennes**
il **prenne**
nous **prenions**
vous **preniez**
ils **prennent**

CONDITIONAL

je prendrais
tu prendrais
il prendrait
nous prendrions
vous prendriez
ils prendraient

PRESENT PARTICIPLE

prenant

PAST PARTICIPLE

pris

IMPERATIVE

prends **prenons** **prenez**

other verbs ending in **-cevoir**

PRESENT		IMPERFECT	
je	**reçois**	*je*	**recevais**
tu	**reçois**	*tu*	**recevais**
il	**reçoit**	*il*	**recevait**
nous	**recevons**	*nous*	**recevions**
vous	**recevez**	*vous*	**receviez**
ils	**reçoivent**	*ils*	**recevaient**

PERFECT		FUTURE	
j'	**ai reçu**	*je*	**recevrai**
tu	**as reçu**	*tu*	**recevras**
il	**a reçu**	*il*	**recevra**
nous	**avons reçu**	*nous*	**recevrons**
vous	**avez reçu**	*vous*	**recevrez**
ils	**ont reçu**	*ils*	**recevront**

PRESENT SUBJUNCTIVE		CONDITIONAL	
je	**reçoive**	*je*	**recevrais**
tu	**reçoives**	*tu*	**recevrais**
il	**reçoive**	*il*	**recevrait**
nous	**recevions**	*nous*	**recevrions**
vous	**receviez**	*vous*	**recevriez**
ils	**reçoivent**	*ils*	**recevraient**

PRESENT PARTICIPLE	PAST PARTICIPLE
recevant	**reçu**

IMPERATIVE

reçois recevons recevez

résoudre to solve

+ *other verbs ending in -soudre*

PRESENT

je **résous**
tu **résous**
il **résout**
nous **résolvons**
vous **résolvez**
ils **résolvent**

IMPERFECT

je **résolvais**
tu **résolvais**
il **résolvait**
nous **résolvions**
vous **résolviez**
ils **résolvaient**

PERFECT

j' **ai résolu**
tu **as résolu**
il **a résolu**
nous **avons résolu**
vous **avez résolu**
ils **ont résolu**

FUTURE

je résoudrai
tu résoudras
il résoudra
nous résoudrons
vous résoudrez
ils résoudront

PRESENT SUBJUNCTIVE

je **résolve**
tu **résolves**
il **résolve**
nous **résolvions**
vous **résolviez**
ils **résolvent**

CONDITIONAL

je résoudrais
tu résoudrais
il résoudrait
nous résoudrions
vous résoudriez
ils résoudraient

PRESENT PARTICIPLE

résolvant

PAST PARTICIPLE

résolu

IMPERATIVE

résous résolvons résolvez

rire to laugh

+ *sourire*

PRESENT		IMPERFECT	
je	ris	*je*	riais
tu	ris	*tu*	riais
il	**rit**	*il*	riait
nous	rions	*nous*	riions
vous	riez	*vous*	riiez
ils	rient	*ils*	riaient

PERFECT		FUTURE	
j'	**ai ri**	*je*	rirai
tu	**as ri**	*tu*	riras
il	**a ri**	*il*	rira
nous	**avons ri**	*nous*	rirons
vous	**avez ri**	*vous*	rirez
ils	**ont ri**	*ils*	riront

PRESENT SUBJUNCTIVE		CONDITIONAL	
je	rie	*je*	rirais
tu	ries	*tu*	rirais
il	rie	*il*	rirait
nous	riions	*nous*	ririons
vous	riiez	*vous*	ririez
ils	rient	*ils*	riraient

PRESENT PARTICIPLE

riant

PAST PARTICIPLE

ri

IMPERATIVE

ris rions riez

rompre to break

■ *other verbs ending in* **-rompre**

PRESENT

je romps
tu romps
il **rompt**
nous rompons
vous rompez
ils rompent

IMPERFECT

je rompais
tu rompais
il rompait
nous rompions
vous rompiez
ils rompaient

PERFECT

j' ai rompu
tu as rompu
il a rompu
nous avons rompu
vous avez rompu
ils ont rompu

FUTURE

je romprai
tu rompras
il rompra
nous romprons
vous romprez
ils rompront

PRESENT SUBJUNCTIVE

je rompe
tu rompes
il rompe
nous rompions
vous rompiez
ils rompent

CONDITIONAL

je romprais
tu romprais
il romprait
nous romprions
vous rompriez
ils rompraient

PRESENT PARTICIPLE

rompant

PAST PARTICIPLE

rompu

IMPERATIVE

romps rompons rompez

PRESENT		IMPERFECT	
je	**sais**	*je*	**savais**
tu	**sais**	*tu*	**savais**
il	**sait**	*il*	**savait**
nous	**savons**	*nous*	**savions**
vous	**savez**	*vous*	**saviez**
ils	**savent**	*ils*	**savaient**

PERFECT		FUTURE	
j'	**ai su**	*je*	**saurai**
tu	**as su**	*tu*	**sauras**
il	**a su**	*il*	**saura**
nous	**avons su**	*nous*	**saurons**
vous	**avez su**	*vous*	**saurez**
ils	**ont su**	*ils*	**sauront**

PRESENT SUBJUNCTIVE		CONDITIONAL	
je	**sache**	*je*	**saurais**
tu	**saches**	*tu*	**saurais**
il	**sache**	*il*	**saurait**
nous	**sachions**	*nous*	**saurions**
vous	**sachiez**	*vous*	**sauriez**
ils	**sachent**	*ils*	**sauraient**

PRESENT PARTICIPLE	PAST PARTICIPLE
sachant	**su**

IMPERATIVE

sache sachons sachez

54 **sentir** to smell; to feel

other verbs ending in **-entir**

PRESENT		IMPERFECT	
je	**sens**	*je*	**sentais**
tu	**sens**	*tu*	**sentais**
il	**sent**	*il*	**sentait**
nous	**sentons**	*nous*	**sentions**
vous	**sentez**	*vous*	**sentiez**
ils	**sentent**	*ils*	**sentaient**

PERFECT		FUTURE	
j'	ai senti	*je*	sentirai
tu	as senti	*tu*	sentiras
il	a senti	*il*	sentira
nous	avons senti	*nous*	sentirons
vous	avez senti	*vous*	sentirez
ils	ont senti	*ils*	sentiront

PRESENT SUBJUNCTIVE		CONDITIONAL	
je	**sente**	*je*	sentirais
tu	**sentes**	*tu*	sentirais
il	**sente**	*il*	sentirait
nous	**sentions**	*nous*	sentirions
vous	**sentiez**	*vous*	sentiriez
ils	**sentent**	*ils*	sentiraient

PRESENT PARTICIPLE	PAST PARTICIPLE
sentant	senti

IMPERATIVE

sens sentons sentez

other verbs ending in **-servir**

PRESENT		IMPERFECT	
je	**sers**	*je*	**servais**
tu	**sers**	*tu*	**servais**
il	**sert**	*il*	**servait**
nous	**servons**	*nous*	**servions**
vous	**servez**	*vous*	**serviez**
ils	**servent**	*ils*	**servaient**

PERFECT		FUTURE	
j'	ai servi	*je*	servirai
tu	as servi	*tu*	serviras
il	a servi	*il*	servira
nous	avons servi	*nous*	servirons
vous	avez servi	*vous*	servirez
ils	ont servi	*ils*	serviront

PRESENT SUBJUNCTIVE		CONDITIONAL	
je	**serve**	*je*	servirais
tu	**serves**	*tu*	servirais
il	**serve**	*il*	servirait
nous	**servions**	*nous*	servirions
vous	**serviez**	*vous*	serviriez
ils	**servent**	*ils*	serviraient

PRESENT PARTICIPLE	PAST PARTICIPLE
servant	servi

IMPERATIVE

sers servons servez

sortir to go out

+ ressortir

PRESENT

je **sors**
tu **sors**
il **sort**
nous **sortons**
vous **sortez**
ils **sortent**

IMPERFECT

je **sortais**
tu **sortais**
il **sortait**
nous **sortions**
vous **sortiez**
ils **sortaient**

PERFECT

je suis sorti
tu es sorti
il est sorti
nous sommes sortis
vous êtes sorti(s)
ils sont sortis

FUTURE

je sortirai
tu sortiras
il sortira
nous sortirons
vous sortirez
ils sortiront

PRESENT SUBJUNCTIVE

je sorte
tu sortes
il sorte
nous sortions
vous sortiez
ils sortent

CONDITIONAL

je sortirais
tu sortirais
il sortirait
nous sortirions
vous sortiriez
ils sortiraient

PRESENT PARTICIPLE

sortant

PAST PARTICIPLE

sorti

IMPERATIVE

sors sortons sortez

PRESENT		IMPERFECT	
je	suffis	*je*	**suffisais**
tu	suffis	*tu*	**suffisais**
il	suffit	*il*	**suffisait**
nous	**suffisons**	*nous*	**suffisions**
vous	**suffisez**	*vous*	**suffisiez**
ils	**suffisent**	*ils*	**suffisaient**

PERFECT		FUTURE	
j'	**ai suffi**	*je*	suffirai
tu	**as suffi**	*tu*	suffiras
il	**a suffi**	*il*	suffira
nous	**avons suffi**	*nous*	suffirons
vous	**avez suffi**	*vous*	suffirez
ils	**ont suffi**	*ils*	suffiront

PRESENT SUBJUNCTIVE		CONDITIONAL	
je	**suffise**	*je*	suffirais
tu	**suffises**	*tu*	suffirais
il	**suffise**	*il*	suffirait
nous	**suffisions**	*nous*	suffirions
vous	**suffisiez**	*vous*	suffiriez
ils	**suffisent**	*ils*	suffiraient

PRESENT PARTICIPLE	PAST PARTICIPLE
suffisant	**suffi**

IMPERATIVE

suffis **suffisons** **suffisez**

suivre to follow

other verbs ending in **-suivre**

PRESENT		IMPERFECT	
je	**suis**	*je*	suivais
tu	**suis**	*tu*	suivais
il	**suit**	*il*	suivait
nous	suivons	*nous*	suivions
vous	suivez	*vous*	suiviez
ils	suivent	*ils*	suivaient

PERFECT		FUTURE	
j'	**ai suivi**	*je*	suivrai
tu	**as suivi**	*tu*	suivras
il	**a suivi**	*il*	suivra
nous	**avons suivi**	*nous*	suivrons
vous	**avez suivi**	*vous*	suivrez
ils	**ont suivi**	*ils*	suivront

PRESENT SUBJUNCTIVE		CONDITIONAL	
je	suive	*je*	suivrais
tu	suives	*tu*	suivrais
il	suive	*il*	suivrait
nous	suivions	*nous*	suivrions
vous	suiviez	*vous*	suivriez
ils	suivent	*ils*	suivraient

PRESENT PARTICIPLE	PAST PARTICIPLE
suivant	**suivi**

IMPERATIVE

suis suivons suivez

PRESENT		IMPERFECT	
je	me tais	*je*	**me taisais**
tu	te tais	*tu*	**te taisais**
il	se tait	*il*	**se taisait**
nous	**nous taisons**	*nous*	**nous taisions**
vous	**vous taisez**	*vous*	**vous taisiez**
ils	**se taisent**	*ils*	**se taisaient**

PERFECT		FUTURE	
je	**me suis tu**	*je*	me tairai
tu	**t'es tu**	*tu*	te tairas
il	**s'est tu**	*il*	se taira
nous	**nous sommes tus**	*nous*	nous tairons
vous	**vous êtes tu(s)**	*vous*	vous tairez
ils	**se sont tus**	*ils*	se tairont

PRESENT SUBJUNCTIVE		CONDITIONAL	
je	**me taise**	*je*	me tairais
tu	**te taises**	*tu*	te tairais
il	**se taise**	*il*	se tairait
nous	**nous taisions**	*nous*	nous tairions
vous	**vous taisiez**	*vous*	vous tairiez
ils	**se taisent**	*ils*	se tairaient

PRESENT PARTICIPLE	PAST PARTICIPLE
se taisant	**tu**

IMPERATIVE

tais-toi **taisons-nous** **taisez-vous**

tenir to hold

other verbs ending in **-enir**

PRESENT		IMPERFECT	
je	**tiens**	*je*	**tenais**
tu	**tiens**	*tu*	**tenais**
il	**tient**	*il*	**tenait**
nous	**tenons**	*nous*	**tenions**
vous	**tenez**	*vous*	**teniez**
ils	**tiennent**	*ils*	**tenaient**

PERFECT		FUTURE	
j'	**ai tenu**	*je*	**tiendrai**
tu	**as tenu**	*tu*	**tiendras**
il	**a tenu**	*il*	**tiendra**
nous	**avons tenu**	*nous*	**tiendrons**
vous	**avez tenu**	*vous*	**tiendrez**
ils	**ont tenu**	*ils*	**tiendront**

PRESENT SUBJUNCTIVE		CONDITIONAL	
je	**tienne**	*je*	**tiendrais**
tu	**tiennes**	*tu*	**tiendrais**
il	**tienne**	*il*	**tiendrait**
nous	**tenions**	*nous*	**tiendrions**
vous	**teniez**	*vous*	**tiendriez**
ils	**tiennent**	*ils*	**tiendraient**

PRESENT PARTICIPLE	PAST PARTICIPLE
tenant	**tenu**

IMPERATIVE

tiens tenons tenez

vainere to defeat

+ *convaincre*

PRESENT		IMPERFECT	
je	vaincs	*je*	**vainquais**
tu	vaincs	*tu*	**vainquais**
il	vainc	*il*	**vainquait**
nous	**vainquons**	*nous*	**vainquions**
vous	**vainquez**	*vous*	**vainquiez**
ils	**vainquent**	*ils*	**vainquaient**

PERFECT		FUTURE	
j'	ai vaincu	*je*	vaincrai
tu	as vaincu	*tu*	vaincras
il	a vaincu	*il*	vaincra
nous	avons vaincu	*nous*	vaincrons
vous	avez vaincu	*vous*	vaincrez
ils	ont vaincu	*ils*	vaincront

PRESENT SUBJUNCTIVE		CONDITIONAL	
je	**vainque**	*je*	vaincrais
tu	**vainques**	*tu*	vaincrais
il	**vainque**	*il*	vaincrait
nous	**vainquions**	*nous*	vaincrions
vous	**vainquiez**	*vous*	vaincriez
ils	**vainquent**	*ils*	vaincraient

PRESENT PARTICIPLE	PAST PARTICIPLE
vainquant	vaincu

IMPERATIVE

vaincs **vainquons** **vainquez**

valoir to be worth

⊞ *other verbs ending in -valoir*

PRESENT		IMPERFECT	
je	**vaux**	*je*	**valais**
tu	**vaux**	*tu*	**valais**
il	**vaut**	*il*	**valait**
nous	**valons**	*nous*	**valions**
vous	**valez**	*vous*	**valiez**
ils	**valent**	*ils*	**valaient**

PERFECT		FUTURE	
j'	**ai valu**	*je*	**vaudrai**
tu	**as valu**	*tu*	**vaudras**
il	**a valu**	*il*	**vaudra**
nous	**avons valu**	*nous*	**vaudrons**
vous	**avez valu**	*vous*	**vaudrez**
ils	**ont valu**	*ils*	**vaudront**

PRESENT SUBJUNCTIVE		CONDITIONAL	
je	**vaille**	*je*	**vaudrais**
tu	**vailles**	*tu*	**vaudrais**
il	**vaille**	*il*	**vaudrait**
nous	**valions**	*nous*	**vaudrions**
vous	**valiez**	*vous*	**vaudriez**
ils	**vaillent**	*ils*	**vaudraient**

PRESENT PARTICIPLE	PAST PARTICIPLE
valant	**valu**

IMPERATIVE

vaux valons valez

+ *other verbs ending in* **-enir**

PRESENT		IMPERFECT	
je	**viens**	*je*	**venais**
tu	**viens**	*tu*	**venais**
il	**vient**	*il*	**venait**
nous	**venons**	*nous*	**venions**
vous	**venez**	*vous*	**veniez**
ils	**viennent**	*ils*	**venaient**

PERFECT		FUTURE	
je	**suis venu**	*je*	**viendrai**
tu	**es venu**	*tu*	**viendras**
il	**est venu**	*il*	**viendra**
nous	**sommes venus**	*nous*	**viendrons**
vous	**êtes venu(s)**	*vous*	**viendrez**
ils	**sont venus**	*ils*	**viendront**

PRESENT SUBJUNCTIVE		CONDITIONAL	
je	**vienne**	*je*	**viendrais**
tu	**viennes**	*tu*	**viendrais**
il	**vienne**	*il*	**viendrait**
nous	**venions**	*nous*	**viendrions**
vous	**veniez**	*vous*	**viendriez**
ils	**viennent**	*ils*	**viendraient**

PRESENT PARTICIPLE	PAST PARTICIPLE
venant	**venu**

IMPERATIVE

viens venons venez

vêtir to dress

+ *other verbs ending in -vêtir*

PRESENT		IMPERFECT	
je	**vêts**	*je*	**vêtais**
tu	**vêts**	*tu*	**vêtais**
il	**vêt**	*il*	**vêtait**
nous	**vêtons**	*nous*	**vêtions**
vous	**vêtez**	*vous*	**vêtiez**
ils	**vêtent**	*ils*	**vêtaient**

PERFECT		FUTURE	
j'	**ai vêtu**	*je*	vêtirai
tu	**as vêtu**	*tu*	vêtiras
il	**a vêtu**	*il*	vêtira
nous	**avons vêtu**	*nous*	vêtirons
vous	**avez vêtu**	*vous*	vêtirez
ils	**ont vêtu**	*ils*	vêtiront

PRESENT SUBJUNCTIVE		CONDITIONAL	
je	**vête**	*je*	vêtirais
tu	**vêtes**	*tu*	vêtirais
il	**vête**	*il*	vêtirait
nous	**vêtions**	*nous*	vêtirions
vous	**vêtiez**	*vous*	vêtiriez
ils	**vêtent**	*ils*	vêtiraient

PRESENT PARTICIPLE	PAST PARTICIPLE
vêtant	**vêtu**

IMPERATIVE

vêts vêtons vêtez

⊞ *other verbs ending in* **-vivre**

PRESENT

je **vis**
tu **vis**
il **vit**
nous vivons
vous vivez
ils vivent

IMPERFECT

je vivais
tu vivais
il vivait
nous vivions
vous viviez
ils vivaient

PERFECT

j' **ai vécu**
tu **as vécu**
il **a vécu**
nous **avons vécu**
vous **avez vécu**
ils **ont vécu**

FUTURE

je vivrai
tu vivras
il vivra
nous vivrons
vous vivrez
ils vivront

PRESENT SUBJUNCTIVE

je vive
tu vives
il vive
nous vivions
vous viviez
ils vivent

CONDITIONAL

je vivrais
tu vivrais
il vivrait
nous vivrions
vous vivriez
ils vivraient

PRESENT PARTICIPLE

vivant

PAST PARTICIPLE

vécu

IMPERATIVE

vis vivons vivez

voir to see

other verbs ending in *-voir*

PRESENT		IMPERFECT	
je	**vois**	*je*	**voyais**
tu	**vois**	*tu*	**voyais**
il	**voit**	*il*	**voyait**
nous	**voyons**	*nous*	**voyions**
vous	**voyez**	*vous*	**voyiez**
ils	**voient**	*ils*	**voyaient**

PERFECT		FUTURE	
j'	**ai vu**	*je*	**verrai**
tu	**as vu**	*tu*	**verras**
il	**a vu**	*il*	**verra**
nous	**avons vu**	*nous*	**verrons**
vous	**avez vu**	*vous*	**verrez**
ils	**ont vu**	*ils*	**verront**

PRESENT SUBJUNCTIVE		CONDITIONAL	
je	**voie**	*je*	**verrais**
tu	**voies**	*tu*	**verrais**
il	**voie**	*il*	**verrait**
nous	**voyions**	*nous*	**verrions**
vous	**voyiez**	*vous*	**verriez**
ils	**voient**	*ils*	**verraient**

PRESENT PARTICIPLE	PAST PARTICIPLE
voyant	**vu**

IMPERATIVE

vois voyons voyez

PRESENT		IMPERFECT	
je	**veux**	*je*	**voulais**
tu	**veux**	*tu*	**voulais**
il	**veut**	*il*	**voulait**
nous	**voulons**	*nous*	**voulions**
vous	**voulez**	*vous*	**vouliez**
ils	**veulent**	*ils*	**voulaient**

PERFECT		FUTURE	
j'	**ai voulu**	*je*	**voudrai**
tu	**as voulu**	*tu*	**voudras**
il	**a voulu**	*il*	**voudra**
nous	**avons voulu**	*nous*	**voudrons**
vous	**avez voulu**	*vous*	**voudrez**
ils	**ont voulu**	*ils*	**voudront**

PRESENT SUBJUNCTIVE		CONDITIONAL	
je	**veuille**	*je*	**voudrais**
tu	**veuilles**	*tu*	**voudrais**
il	**veuille**	*il*	**voudrait**
nous	**voulions**	*nous*	**voudrions**
vous	**vouliez**	*vous*	**voudriez**
ils	**veuillent**	*ils*	**voudraient**

PRESENT PARTICIPLE	PAST PARTICIPLE
voulant	**voulu**

IMPERATIVE

veuille **veuillons** **veuillez**